T0222946

Lecture Notes in Artificial Intelligence   10619

Subseries of Lecture Notes in Computer Science

More information about this series at http://www.springer.com/series/1244

Xuanjing Huang · Jing Jiang
Dongyan Zhao · Yansong Feng
Yu Hong (Eds.)

Natural Language Processing and Chinese Computing

6th CCF International Conference, NLPCC 2017
Dalian, China, November 8–12, 2017
Proceedings

 Springer

Editors
Xuanjing Huang
Fudan University
Shanghai
China

Jing Jiang
Singapore Management University
Singapore
Singapore

Dongyan Zhao
Peking University
Beijing
China

Yansong Feng
Peking University
Beijing
China

Yu Hong
Soochow University
Suzhou
China

ISSN 0302-9743 ISSN 1611-3349 (electronic)
Lecture Notes in Artificial Intelligence
ISBN 978-3-319-73617-4 ISBN 978-3-319-73618-1 (eBook)
https://doi.org/10.1007/978-3-319-73618-1

Library of Congress Control Number: 2017963756

LNCS Sublibrary: SL7 – Artificial Intelligence

Printed on acid-free paper

This Springer imprint is published by Springer Nature
The registered company is Springer International Publishing AG
The registered company address is: Gewerbestrasse 11, 6330 Cham, Switzerland

Preface

We are very pleased to present the proceedings of the NLPCC 2017, the 6th International Conference on Natural Language Processing and Chinese Computing. NLPCC is the annual conference of CCF-TCCI (Technical Committee of Chinese Information, China Computer Federation). The previous five NLPCC conferences were successfully held in Beijing in 2012, Chongqing in 2013, Shenzhen in 2014, Nanchang in 2015, and Kunming in 2016. This year was the fourth year since NLPCC became an international conference. As a leading conference in the field of NLP and Chinese Computing, NLPCC has been the main forum for researchers and practitioners in NLP from academia, industry, and government to share their ideas, research results, and experiences, and to promote the research and technical innovations in these fields.

We received 252 submissions this year, covering a wide range of topics including NLP fundamentals, NLP applications, text mining, machine translation, machine learning, knowledge graph, information extraction, question answering, information retrieval and search, and social networks. Among the submissions, 31 manuscripts were written in Chinese and 221 in English. All submissions underwent a double-blind review by at least three reviewers. The final decisions were made at a meeting attended by Program Committee (PC) chairs and area chairs. Finally, 53 (21.0%) were accepted as long papers (six in Chinese and 47 in English) and 42 (16.7%) as posters (three in Chinese and 39 in English). Six papers were nominated for the best paper award by the area chairs. The final selection of the best papers was made by an independent Best Paper Committee. The proceedings includes the accepted English papers only, while the accepted Chinese papers are published in *ACTA Scientiarum Naturalium Universitatis Pekinensis*.

We sincerely thank our four distinguished keynote speakers: Mirella Lapata (School of Informatics at the University of Edinburgh), Jianfeng Gao (Microsoft AI & Research), Noah Smith (Paul G. Allen School of Computer Science and Engineering at the University of Washington), and Hua Wu (Baidu).

We would also like to thank all the people who have contributed to NLPCC 2017. First of all, we would like to thank the area chairs for their hard work in recruiting reviewers, monitoring the review and discussion processes, and carefully rating and recommending submissions. We would like to thank all 168 reviewers for their time and effort to review the submissions. We are very grateful to Min Zhang, Vincent Ng, Yue Zhang, and Zhiyuan Liu for their participation in the Best Paper Committee. We are also grateful for the help and support from the general chairs, Tiejun Zhao and Hans Uszkoreit, and from the Organizing Committee chairs, Dongyan Zhao and Hongfei Lin. Special thanks go to Yansong Feng and Yu Hong, the publication chairs, for their great help. We appreciate all your help very much!

Finally, we would like to thank all the authors who submitted their work to the conference, and thank our sponsors for their contributions to the conference.

December 2017

Xuanjing Huang
Jing Jiang

Organization

NLPCC 2017 was organized by the Technical Committee of Chinese Information of CCF, Dalian University of Technology, and the State Key Lab of Digital Publishing Technology.

Organizing Committee

General Chairs

Tiejun Zhao	Harbin Institute of Technology, China
Hans Uszkoreit	German Research Center for Artificial Intelligence (DFKI), Germany

Program Co-chairs

Xuanjing Huang	Fudan University, China
Jing Jiang	Singapore Management University, Singapore

Area Chairs

NLP Fundamentals

Wei Lu	Singapore University of Technology and Design, Singapore
Hai Zhao	Shanghai Jiao Tong University, China

NLP Applications

Fei Liu	University of Central Florida, USA
Shoushan Li	Soochow University, China

Text Mining

Vincent Ng	University of Texas at Dallas, America
Qi Zhang	Fudan University, China

Machine Translation

Jiajun Zhang	Institute of Automation, Chinese Academy of Sciences, China
Haitao Mi	IBM Research, USA

Machine Learning

Zhiyuan Liu	Tsinghua University, China
Yangqiu Song	Hong Kong University for Science and Technology, SAR China

Knowledge Graph/IE/QA

Kang Liu	Institute of Automation, Chinese Academy of Sciences, China
Fangtao Li	Google, USA

IR/Conversational Bot

Xin Zhao   Renmin University, China
Bonan Min   Raytheon BBN Technologies, USA

NLP for Social Network

Huawei Shen   Institute of Computing Technology, Chinese Academy
                                  of Sciences, China
Hanghang Tong   Arizona State University, USA

Organization Co-chairs

Dongyan Zhao   Peking University, China
Hongfei Lin   Dalian University of Technology, China

ADL/Tutorial Chairs

Ruifeng Xu   Shenzhen Graduate School, HIT, China
Kang Liu   Institute of Automation, Chinese Academy of Sciences,
                                  China

Student Workshop Chairs

Deyi Xiong   Soochow University, China
Xu Sun   Peking University, China

Sponsorship Co-chairs

Ming Zhou   Microsoft Research Asia, China
Kam-Fai Wong   The Chinese University of Hong Kong, China

Publication Chairs

Yansong Feng   Peking University, China
Yu Hong   Soochow University China

Finance Chair

Lin Ma   Secretary of China Computer Federation, China

Publicity Chairs

William Wang   University of California at Santa Barbara, USA
Zhihao Yang   Dalian University of Technology, China

Evaluation Chairs

Xiaojun Wan   Peking University, China
Jie Tang   Tsinghua University, China

Program Committee

Deng Cai	Xiamen University, China
Hailong Cao	Harbin Institute of Technology, China
Kai Cao	New York University, USA
Shaosheng Cao	Ant Financial Services Group AI Department, China
Yee Seng Chan	Raytheon BBN Technologies, USA
Wanxiang Che	Harbin Institute of Technology, China
Boxing Chen	National Research Council, Canada
Chen Chen	Arizona State University, USA
Danqi Chen	Stanford University, USA
Hongsehn Chen	Institute of Computing, Chinese Academy of Sciences, China
Huajun Chen	Zhejiang University, China
Jiajun Chen	Nanjing University, China
Nancy Chen	Institute for Infocomm Research, Singapore
Weizheng Chen	Peking University, China
Wenliang Chen	Soochow University, China
Xu Chen	Tsinghua University, China
Yidong Chen	Xiamen University, China
Yubo Chen	Institute of Automation, Chinese Academy of Sciences, China
Hai Leong Chieu	DSO National Laboratories, Singapore
Thilini Cooray	Singapore University of Technology and Design, Singapore
Lei Cui	Microsoft Research Asia, China
Peng Cui	Tsinghua University, China
Daniel Dahlmeier	SAP Research, Singapore
Zhicheng Dou	Renmin University of China, China
Jinhua Du	Dublin City University, Ireland
Xiangyu Duan	Soochow University, China
Miao Fan	Tsinghua University, China
Yuan Fang	Institute for Infocomm Research, Singapore
Geli Fei	University of Illinois at Chicago, USA
Minwei Feng	IBM Research, China
Yang Feng	Tsinghua University, China
Yansong Feng	Peking University, China
Wei Gao	Qatar Computing Research Institute, Qatar
Tao Ge	Peking University, China
Jiang Guo	Harbin Institute of Technology, China
Weiwei Guo	LinkedIn, USA
Zhijiang Guo	Singapore University of Technology and Design, Singapore
Jialong Han	Nanyang Technological University, China
Tianyong Hao	Guangdong University of Foreign Studies, China
Ruidan He	National University of Singapore, Singapore

Shizhu He   Institute of Automation, Chinese Academy of Sciences,
                                China
Wei He   Baidu Inc., China
Yanqing He   Institute of Scientific and Technical Information
                                of China, China
Yifan He   New York University, USA
Zhongjun He   Baidu Inc., China
Yu Hong   Soochow University, China
Xia (Ben) Hu   Texas A&M University, USA
Lifu Huang   Rensselaer Polytechnic Institute, USA
Shujian Huang   Nanjing University, China
Zhongqiang Huang   Raytheon BBN Technologies, USA
Wenbin Jiang   Institute of Computing Technology, CAS, China
Zhanming Jie   Singapore University of Technology and Design,
                                Singapore
Fang Kong   Soochow University, China
Jun Lang   Alibaba Inc., China
Yoong Keok Lee   IBM Thomas J. Watson Research Center, USA
Binyang Li   University of International Relations, China
Chenliang Li   Wuhan University, China
Fangtao Li   Google, USA
Hao Li   Singapore University of Technology and Design,
                                Singapore
Junhui Li   Soochow University, China
Liangyue Li   Arizona State University, USA
Maoxi Li   Jiangxi Normal University, China
Peng Li   Tencent, China
Sheng Li   Northeastern University, China
Xiang Li   Cambia Health Solutions, USA
Xiaoqing Li   Alibaba, China
Yaliang Li   University at Buffalo, USA
Zhenghua Li   Soochow University, China
Xiangwen Liao   Fuzhou University, China
Lemao Liu   Tencent AI Lab, China
Qun Liu   Dublin City University, Ireland
Shenghua Liu   Institute of Computing Technology, CAS, China
Tao Liu   Renmin University of China, China
Yang Liu   Tsinghua University, China
Zhanyi Liu   Baidu Inc., China
Zhunchen Luo   China Defense Science and Technology Information
                                Center, China
Linyuan Lv   Hangzhou Normal University, China
Qiang Ma   Yahoo!, China
Zongyang Ma   The University of New South Wales, Australia
Cunli Mao   Kunming University of Science and Technology, China
Xian-Ling Mao   Beijing Institute of Technology, China

Aldrian Obaja Muis	Singapore University of Technology and Design, Singapore
Wentao Ouyang	Institute of Computing Technology, CAS, China
Haoruo Peng	University of Illinois Urbana-Champaign, USA
Peter Phandi	Singapore University of Technology and Design, Singapore
Roozbeh Sanaei	Singapore University of Technology and Design, Singapore
Lei Shi	Institute of Software, CAS, China
Xiaodong Shi	Xiamen University, China
Guojie Song	Peking University, China
Yangqiu Song	Hong Kong University of Science and Technology, SAR China
Jinsong Su	Xiamen University, China
Xing Su	City University of New York, USA
Yu Su	University of California, Santa Barbara, USA
Xu Sun	Peking University, China
Raymond Hendy Susanto	Singapore University of Technology and Design, Singapore
Jian Tang	University of Michigan, USA
Jia Tao	Southwest Jiaotong University, China
Ming-Feng Tsai	National Chengchi University, Taipei, Taiwan
Mei Tu	Samsung Research China, China
Zhaopeng Tu	Tencent AI Lab, China
Chuan-Ju Wang	Academia Sinica, Taipei, Taiwan
Li Wang	Tai Yuan University of Technology, China
Rui Wang	Shanghai Jiaotong University, China
Xuancong Wang	Institute for Infocomm Research, Singapore
Zhi Wang	Tsinghua University, China
Zhiguo Wang	IBM Research, USA
Yuanbin Wu	East China Normal University, China
Rui Xia	Nanjing University of Science and Technology, China
Tong Xiao	Northeastern University, China
Yanghua Xiao	Fudan University, China
Xin Xin	Beijing Institute of Technology, China
Tong Xiong	Northest University, China
Jinan Xu	Beijing Jiaotong University, China
Jingwei Xu	Nanjing University, China
Ruifeng Xu	Harbin Institute of Technology, China
Xiaoke Xu	Dalian Nationalities University, China
Junchi Yan	IBM Research, China
Bishan Yang	Carnegie Mellon University, USA
Tao Yang	Baidu Research, China
Yang Yang	Zhejiang University, China
Wenlin Yao	Texas A&M University, USA
Yuan Yao	Nanjing University, China

Jun Yin	Peking University, China
Yichun Yin	Peking University, China
Dianhai Yu	Baidu Inc., China
Dong Yu	Beijing Language and Culture University, China
Daojian Zeng	Changsha University of Science and Technology, China
Feifei Zhai	Sogou, China
Dakun Zhang	Systran, China
Dongdong Zhang	Microsoft Research Asia, China
Fuzheng Zhang	Microsoft Research, China
Jing Zhang	Renmin University of China, China
Meishan Zhang	Heilongjiang University, China
Peng Zhang	Tianjin University, China
Qi Zhang	Fudan University, China
Wei Zhang	Alibaba Inc., China
Weinan Zhang	Harbin Institute of Technology, China
Yan Zhang	Singapore University of Technology and Design, Singapore
Yongfeng Zhang	University of Massachusetts Amherst, USA
Sendong Zhao	Harbin Institute of Technology, China
Tiejun Zhao	Harbin Institute of Technology, China
Vincent Zheng	Advanced Digital Sciences Center, Singapore
Chuan Zhou	Institute of Information Engineering, CAS, China
Dong Zhou	Hunan University of Science and Technology, China
Junsheng Zhou	Nanjing Normal University, China
Hengshu Zhu	Baidu Inc., China
Jingbo Zhu	Northest University, China
Muhua Zhu	Tencent AI Lab, China
Yanyan Zou	Singapore University of Technology and Design, Singapore

Organizers

Organized by

China Computer Federation, China

Supported by

Asian Federation of Natural Language Processing

Hosted by

Dalian University of Technology

State Key Lab of Digital Publishing Technology

In Cooperation with

Lecture Notes in Computer Science

 Springer

Springer

ACTA Scientiarum Naturalium Universitatis Pekinensis

Sponsoring Institutions

Diamond Sponsors

Global Tone Communication Technology   WeChat

Platinum Sponsors

Microsoft   Baidu

Vpark   Gridsum

Toutiao   Sogou

Naturali   XINHUAZHIYUN

Golden Sponsors

Intel Corporation   NiuTrans

Lenovo

Contents

Machine Learning

Machine Translation

NLP Applications

NLP Fundamentals

Short Papers

IR/Search/Bot

Jointly Modeling Intent Identification and Slot Filling with Contextual and Hierarchical Information

Liyun Wen[1(✉)], Xiaojie Wang[1], Zhenjiang Dong[2], and Hong Chen[2]

[1] Beijing University of Posts and Telecommunications, Beijing, China
{wenliyun,xjwang}@bupt.edu.cn
[2] ZTE Corporation, Nanjing, China
dongzhenjiangvip@163.com, chen.hong3@zte.com.cn

Abstract. Intent classification and slot filling are two critical subtasks of natural language understanding (NLU) in task-oriented dialogue systems. Previous work has made use of either hierarchical or contextual information when jointly modeling intent classification and slot filling, proving that either of them is helpful for joint models. This paper proposes a cluster of joint models to encode both types of information at the same time. Experimental results on different datasets show that the proposed models outperform joint models without either hierarchical or contextual information. Besides, finding the balance between two loss functions of two subtasks is important to achieve best overall performances.

Keywords: Joint models · Contextual and hierarchical information
Natural language understanding

1 Introduction

Natural Language Understanding (NLU), which refers to the targeted understanding of human language directed at machines [1], is a critical component in dialogue systems. An NLU system typically consists of three subtasks, namely domain identification, intent classification and slot filling [2].

Conventionally, the subtasks are processed in a pipeline framework; firstly the domain of an input is detected, secondly the intent is classified and finally the semantic slots are extracted. Lots of work has been done for each subtask, respectively. For example, Haffner et al. [3] built a Support Vector Machines (SVM) based classifier to classify intent (call) labels. Yao et al. [4] investigated Long Short-Term Memory (LSTM) methods for slot filling. Pipeline systems not only suffer from the problem of error accumulation, but also cannot model the interaction between different subtasks.

Recent work has shown the advantages of jointly modeling NLU subtasks. The ability of featuring the correlations between subtasks helps joint models achieve competitive performances. Shi et al. [5] proposed a Recurrent Neural

© Springer International Publishing AG 2018
X. Huang et al. (Eds.): NLPCC 2017, LNAI 10619, pp. 3–15, 2018.
https://doi.org/10.1007/978-3-319-73618-1_1

Network (RNN) model to jointly optimize domain identification, intent classification and slot filling, which obtained state-of-the-art results on ATIS dataset. Hakkani et al. [6] presented a method for simultaneously modeling domain recognition, intent classification and slot filling by introducing an extra token <EOS> for sentence-level labels in an LSTM-based slot sequential labeling model.

Apart from correlative information, hierarchical structure is considered as another useful information for joint modeling. Zhou et al. [7] proposed a hierarchical Long Short-Term Memory (HLSTM) model to implement intent identification in the lower layer and slot filling in the higher layer. They demonstrated joint models with hierarchical structure outperformed non-hierarchical joint methods. But contextual information was not used in their model. Previous work on single subtask has proved that contextual information is an effective feature for NLU subtasks. Yao et al. [8] presented a window-based RNN model to capture contextual features in NLU. Mesnil et al. [9] applied bidirectional Elman and Jordan RNN to encode the future and past information in inputs during slot filling.

We think that contextual and hierarchical information help NLU subtasks in different dimensions. Hierarchy could characterize the nature order among different tasks: as pointed in [10], primary tasks are better kept at the lower layers in a deep network. While contextual idiosyncrasies could bring the richness of representation by observing features from preceding and following positions in its vicinity, which could facilitate a morpheme/word unit based recognition task like slot filling. It is therefore possible to improve performances by combining both of them. Zhang and Wang [11] proposed a two-layer hierarchical joint model, with a lower RNN tackling slot filling and an upper max-pooling handling intent recognition. Liu and Lane [12] presented an attention-based RNN model with both contextual and hierarchical information captured, which obtained better results on ATIS dataset.

In order to encode the two kinds of information and detail the specific effects of them, this paper proposes a cluster of contextual hierarchical joint (CHJ) models to jointly model intent classification and slot filling. The models have a two-layer-LSTM structure, where intent classification and slot filling are dealt by different layers. Distinguished from HLSTM, our proposed models take bidirectional or backward order to utilize contextual information. All parameters are learned simultaneously to minimize a joint loss function, i.e. the weighted sum of two losses. Experiments show that on different NLU datasets CHJ models outperform non-hierarchical or non-contextual models, respectively.

The rest of the paper is structured as follows. Section 2 demonstrates our proposed models in detail; Sect. 3 presents the tasks and experimental results; and finally, conclusions are drawn in Sect. 4.

2 Models

LSTM is the basic unit in all CHJ models. We therefore introduce LSTM first, and then propose our models.

2.1   LSTM

LSTM [13], a variant of RNN, consists of one or more memory cells and three nonlinear summation units, i.e. the input, output and forget gate. Detailed introduction and equations about LSTMs can be found in [14]. At time t, the calculating process of hidden state vector $\boldsymbol{h}_t$ is abbreviated as follows:

$$\boldsymbol{h}_t = LSTM(\boldsymbol{W}_x \boldsymbol{x}_t + \boldsymbol{W}_h \boldsymbol{h}_{t-1}) \tag{1}$$

where $LSTM$ is the recurrent neural function that calculates the current hidden state vector $\boldsymbol{h}_t$ given the previous one $\boldsymbol{h}_{t-1}$ and the current input $\boldsymbol{x}_t$. $\boldsymbol{W}_x$ and $\boldsymbol{W}_h$ are the associated weight matrices.

    According to the processing order, LSTMs can be classified to different categories: forward LSTMs, backward LSTMs and bi-directional LSTMs. Forward LSTMs take the standard forward order when reading sequences, and symmetrically backward LSTMs read the sequence in a reversed way. Bi-directional LSTMs (bi-LSTMs) [15] present each sequence forwards and backwards to two separate LSTM hidden layers and concatenate both to the same output layer [14].

2.2   Contextual Hierarchical Joint (CHJ) Models

Given an input utterance $w_{(1:T)} = (w_1, w_2, ..., w_T)$, NLU is to predict an intent class for current utterance and to label slot tags among all words. Let $Y = \{Y_1, Y_2, ..., Y_M\}$ denote the intent label set and $S = \{S_1, S_2, ..., S_N\}$ denote the slot set. Slot filling is implemented via sequence labeling methods. All slot classes are transformed into semantic tags according to the IOB annotated method [16]; each slot class S_i can generate two semantic tags: $B - S_i$ and $I - S_i$, as well as the label O representing the out-of-slot tag. The corresponding semantic tags set can be denoted as $Z = \{Z_1, Z_2, ..., Z_{2N+1}\}$. Thus the process is to map $w_{(1:T)} = (w_1, w_2, ..., w_T)$ to a predicted intent label y and a set of semantic tags $z_{(1:T)} = (z_1, z_2, ..., z_T)$.

    A hierarchical LSTM is built to model the mapping at first. The structure of the model is shown in Fig. 1(a). It is a two-layer LSTM, where a forward LSTM is stacked on the top of a bi-LSTM. The overall flow of information is from the lower to the upper, namely the upper layer takes the hidden state vector of the lower layer directly as input, and inputs of the lower bi-LSTM are the embedding vectors of words in the current sentence. Intent classification is tackled by the lower layer: the final output of the bi-LSTM is fed to a softmax classifier to get an intent label of the sentence. Slot filling is dealt by the upper: the output of each LSTM unit is fed to a softmax classifier to get a slot label of the corresponding word.

    This structure tries to utilize both hierarchical and contextual information in jointly modeling intent identification and slot filling. The hierarchical structure is used to capture internal relations, like order or dependency, of two subtasks. The bi-LSTM is used to capture contextual idiosyncrasies from past and future positions of a certain word during the current sentence.

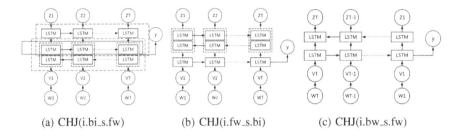

(a) CHJ(i.bi_s.fw)   (b) CHJ(i.fw_s.bi)   (c) CHJ(i.bw_s.fw)

Fig. 1. Some structures of the cluster of CHJ models

For an input sentence, each word $w_t(t = 1, 2, ..., T)$ is first mapped into its embedding vector $v_t(t = 1, 2, ..., T)$. Bi-directionally taking the embedding representations as input, according to (1), the lower layer calculates two sets of hidden state vectors and concatenate them into one: $h^1_{(1:T)} = (h^1_1, ..., h^1_T)$. The last hidden state vector h^1_T is fed into a softmax classifier. The probability distribution of all intent labels y is obtained by softmax.

$$y = softmax(W^1 h^1_T), \tag{2}$$

where W^1 is the softmax weight matrix of the lower LSTM. A predicted intent tag can be calculated by getting argmax of y.

The upper layer takes the hidden state vector of the lower layer as input directly.

$$x^2_t = h^1_t, t = 1, 2, ..., T \tag{3}$$

where x^2_t denote the upper layer inputs.

Following (1) and (3), we get the set of hidden state vectors of the upper layer $h^2_{(1:T)} = (h^2_1, ..., h^2_T)$. Every hidden state vector is fed into a softmax to obtain corresponding probabilities z_t.

$$z_t = softmax(W^2 h^2_t), t = 1, 2, ..., T \tag{4}$$

where W^2 is the softmax weight matrix of the upper LSTM. Argmax can be used on z_t to get predicted slot tags.

The parameter set of the whole network is $\theta = \{W_x, W_h, W^1, W^2\}$. All parameters of two tasks are learned simultaneously to minimize a joint objective function $J(\theta)$, which is represented as the weighted sum of two losses, together with an l_2-norm term:

$$J(\theta) = \alpha L_I + (1 - \alpha)L_S + \frac{\lambda}{2}||\theta||^2_2, 0 \leq \alpha \leq 1, \tag{5}$$

where L_S represents the slot filling loss and L_I represents the intent identification loss. Let D be the whole training set and $L(\cdot)$ be the cross-entropy operation. Suppose $\hat{y}^{(i)}$ and $\hat{z}^{(i)}_{(1:T)}$ are the true intent label and semantic tags of the ith training sample. The two losses are calculated as follows:

$$L_S = \frac{1}{|\mathcal{D}|} \sum_i^{|\mathcal{D}|} \frac{1}{T} \sum_{t=1}^{T} L(z_t^{(i)}, \hat{z}_t^{(i)}), \tag{6}$$

$$L_I = \frac{1}{|\mathcal{D}|} \sum_i^{|\mathcal{D}|} L(\boldsymbol{y}^{(i)}, \hat{\boldsymbol{y}}^{(i)}), \tag{7}$$

The tradeoff between two objectives relies on the hyper-parameter α. When α is bigger than 0.5, the total joint loss function pays more attention to the intent identification. On the contrary, when α is smaller than 0.5, the slot loss plays a more important role in supervised learning.

The model can be thought as an extension of several previous models by combing contextual or hierarchical information. If an intent-relevant tag is attached before or after each sentence, sentence-level intent identification and word-level slot filling can be jointly modeled in a single sequence labeling model. The forward LSTM in the red solid frame in Fig. 1(a) is one kind of these sequence labeling models by feeding each unit's output to a softmax classifier, as proposed in [6] (forward Hakkani's Model, denoted as Fw-Hakkani's Model afterwards). It is a flap style of joint models, only correlative information between two subtasks is taken into consideration in this joint model. Based on the flap structure, two improvements can be made. One is shown in the red dotted frame, in which contextual information is included by using bi-LSTM (denoted as Bi-Hakkani's Model). The other is highlighted by the blue dotted frame, where the flap structure was improved to become a hierarchical structure as Zhou et al. proposed [7] (denoted as Zhou's Model). A two-layer LSTM (not bi-LSTM) was used in Zhou's model, where the upper layer is for slot filling and the lower layer is for intent identification. It is obvious that structures in red dotted frame and blue dotted frame extend Fw-Hakkani's Model in two different dimensions. Our model combines both of them.

The proposed model can have several different variants by changing the way of combining contextual and hierarchical information. We consider two different ways to include contextual information for slot filling. One is to use bi-LSTM for slot filling no matter the subtask is modeled in the lower layer or the upper; another way is to tackle slot filling by an LSTM in the upper layer, and an LSTM with the inversed direction is employed in the lower layer for intent identification. By using two inversed LSTMs instead of one LSTM and one bi-LSTM, the model can be simplified. We also consider two possible hierarchies: one is putting intent identification in the lower and slot filling in the upper, the other is an interchange of layers in the precious one.

For convenience, the model illustrated in Fig. 1(a) is denoted by CHJ(i.bi_s.fw): i.bi before the underscore describes the lower layer structure, representing a bi-LSTM model for intent identification; s.fw after the underscore describes the upper layer structure, denoting a forward LSTM structure for slot filling. By using these denotation, we elucidate several variants of model CHJ(i.bi_s.fw) in Table 1.

Table 1. Several variants of model CHJ(i.bi_s.fw)

Denotation	Description
CHJ(i.fw_s.bi)	A forward LSTM for intent classification in the lower layer; the upper layer tackles slot filling by a bi-LSTM (Fig. 1(b))
CHJ(i.bw_s.fw)	A backward LSTM for intent classification in the lower layer; a forward LSTM for slot filling in the upper layer (Fig. 1(c))
CHJ(i.fw_s.bw)	A forward LSTM for intent classification in the lower layer; a backward LSTM for slot filling in the upper layer
CHJ(s.bi_i.fw)	The lower layer deals with slot filling by a bi-LSTM; while the upper layer solves intent classification forwards

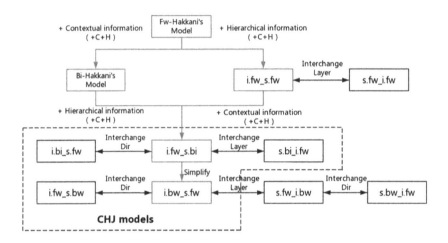

Fig. 2. The cluster of proposed CHJ models and their transformation relationship

The transformative relations between these models are illustrated in Fig. 2, where "Simplify" represents the operation that utilizes reversed directions to replace bi-LSTM, as we pointed before; "InterchangeLayer" denotes the operation that totally interchanges the two layers, such as the operation between i.fw_s.bi and s.bi_i.fw; "InterchangeDir" represents the operation that remains the tasks order unchanged and interchanges the directions of two layers.

In Fig. 2, from Fw-Hakkani's Model, there are two paths to add hierarchical and contextual information. One is to add contextual information first and then the hierarchical one, as shown in the left path; the other is an inverse order, which is listed in the right path. Both paths lead to the same destination i.fw_s.bi, which can be simplified into i.bw_s.fw. Based on i.fw_s.bi and i.bw_s.fw, certain operations can be implemented to generate some other CHJ models. All models in the dotted frame are CHJ models. We should note that s.fw_i.bw and s.bw_i.fw are not CHJ models. Both of them condition slot filling in the lower layer; no matter how they change the lower direction (forwards or backwards), slot filling cannot simultaneously take both past and future context into consideration. More precisely, simplified versions of contextually modeling slot filling, viewed as substitutes for bi-LSTMs, need slot filling to be tackled by the upper layer.

3 Experiments

First, the datasets and the experimental setup are illustrated. Second, our results and related benchmarks are compared. Then the tradeoff between multi-tasks is discussed in detail. Finally, the case study is presented.

3.1 Datasets and Settings

The experiments are implemented in three different corpora: the DSTC2[1] [17], DSTC5[2] [18] and our Chinese meeting room reservation corpus collected from a Chinese meeting-room reservation system (CMRS). Basic information about these three corpora is listed in Table 2.

Table 2. The number of sentences in each corpus

Dataset	Train	Dev	Test
DSTC2	4,790	1,579	4,485
DSTC5	27,528	3,441	3,447
CMRS	2,901	969	967

In DSTC2, each user utterance with only one intent (act) label is used. The number of intent labels is 13, the number of different slots is 4, and thus the total number of semantic tags is 9 ($2 * 4 + 1$; each slot can generate two semantic tags: $B - slot$ and $I - slot$, as well as the label O).

In DSTC5, each user utterance with only one intent (act) label is used. The number of intent labels is 84, the number of different fine-grained slots is 266, and thus the total number of semantic tags is 533. In order to exclude the influence of cross-language problem, only English sentences are used.

As for CMRS, the number of intent labels is 5, the number of different slots is 5, and thus the total number of semantic tags is 11.

We choose commonly used configurations for experimental settings. For each group of tasks, we use AdaGrad [19] with mini-batches [20] to minimize the objective function. Derivatives are calculated from standard back-propagation. The model achieving the best performance on the development set is used as the final model to be evaluated. Statistical significance tests are implemented by 5-fold cross validation and Student's t-test, with the significance level set to 0.05.

---

[1] http://camdial.org/~mh521/dstc/.
[2] http://workshop.colips.org/dstc5/.

3.2   Comparisons with Recent Work

Tables 3, 4 and 5 exhibit the experimental results on DSTC2, DSTC5 and CMRS, respectively. Performances are computed in terms of slot F1-measure (at the slot level)[3], intent F1-measure (at the label level) and the average of both, as a measure of overall performance.

From the three tables, we have some general conclusions. (1) The model that gets best overall performance is always among the CHJ models on all three datasets, proving the effectiveness of combining hierarchical and contextual information in joint modeling of NLU. (2) Once hierarchical information is included,

Table 3. Results on DSTC2 corpus

Information (C/H)	Model	Slot(F1)%	Intent(F1)%	Avg(F1)%
None	Fw-Hakkani's model	96.22	99.22	97.72
+C	Bi-Hakkani's model	98.92	99.18	99.05
+H	i.fw_s.fw	96.67	99.23	97.95
	s.fw_i.fw	96.64	99.46	98.05
	s.fw_i.bw	96.62	99.39	98.01
	s.bw_i.fw	97.96	99.48	98.72
+C+H (CHJ models)	s.bi_i.fw	98.96	99.45	99.21
	i.fw_s.bi	98.81	99.33	99.07
	i.bi_s.fw	98.93	99.37	99.15
	i.bw_s.fw	**99.01**	**99.48**	**99.25**
	i.fw_s.bw	98.91	99.34	99.13

Table 4. Results on DSTC5 corpus

Information (C/H)	Model	Slot(F1)%	Intent(F1)%	Avg(F1)%
None	Fw-Hakkani's model	36.22	53.02	44.62
+C	Bi-Hakkani's model	45.17	52.54	48.86
+H	i.fw_s.fw	23.45	49.15	36.30
	s.fw_i.fw	33.45	**53.48**	43.47
	s.fw_i.bw	35.99	52.89	44.44
	s.bw_i.fw	38.81	53.27	46.04
+C+H (CHJ models)	s.bi_i.fw	**45.51**	53.35	**49.43**
	i.fw_s.bi	40.29	51.84	46.07
	i.bi_s.fw	39.36	50.84	45.10
	i.bw_s.fw	42.85	51.38	47.12
	i.fw_s.bw	35.68	49.65	42.67

---

[3] http://www.cnts.ua.ac.be/conll2000/chunking/conlleval.txt.

Table 5. Results on CMRS corpus

Information (C/H)	Model	Slot(F1)%	Intent(F1)%	Avg(F1)%
None	Fw-Hakkani's model	61.16	92.61	76.89
+C	Bi-Hakkani's model	82.91	92.69	87.80
+H	i.fw_s.fw	61.83	**92.84**	77.34
	s.fw_i.fw	61.15	92.58	76.87
	s.fw_i.bw	61.72	92.72	77.22
	s.bw_i.fw	67.61	92.44	80.03
+C+H (CHJ models)	s.bi_i.fw	81.68	92.41	87.05
	i.fw_s.bi	84.14	92.76	88.45
	i.bi_s.fw	84.93	92.53	88.73
	i.bw_s.fw	**85.80**	92.60	**89.20**
	i.fw_s.bw	83.91	92.75	88.34

an improvement on intent identification is achieved, which suggests that hierarchical information is helpful, especially for intent classification. (The improvements are statistical significant; from None to +H: 4.0836 > 2.7764; from +C to +C+H: 5.9496 > 2.7764) (3) If we introduce contextual information into models, the slot performance gets a considerable boost; this phenomenon indicates that contextual information could benefit slot filling to a great extent. (The improvements are statistical significant; from None to +C: 41.8951 > 2.7764; from +H to +C+H: 12.5448 > 2.7764) (4) Among the four +H models, s.bw_i.fw performs better than any other one does in slot filling task, indicating that backward encoding is more helpful than forward encoding. We notice that slot values often consist of phrases in the form of pre-modifications + head words; in this structure, the posteriori head words play a vital role in slot recognition. Backward networks could previously see the posteriori center words and therefore perform better than forward networks which have troubles in labeling those pre-modifiers without the information of head words. For structures in the form of head word + post-modification, forward networks could perform better. Transparently, contextual (such as bi-directional) networks do the best. (5) All corpora support that i.bw_s.fw gets higher performances than i.bi_s.fw does. As we pointed in Sect. 2.2, i.bw_s.fw is a simplified version of i.bi_s.fw. They combine contextual and hierarchical information in similar ways, but i.bw_s.fw has a more concise structure, which conduces to better performances.

3.3 Tradeoff Between Multi-tasks

α is the parameter used to leverage the loss functions of two tasks in CHJ models. When α is bigger than 0.5, the total joint loss function pays more attention to the intent loss. On the contrary, when α is smaller than 0.5, the slot loss plays a more important role in supervision.

Figure 3 shows the α-performances curves of model CHJ(s.bi_i.fw) on different datasets. By summarizing the universality, we can draw several points. (1)

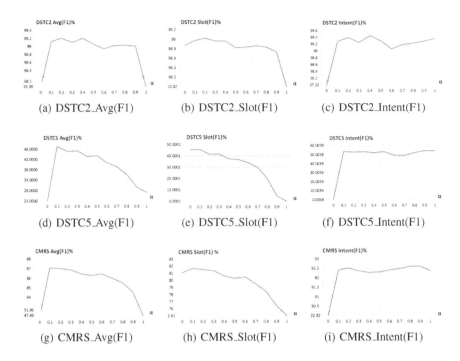

Fig. 3. α-performances curves on three datasets

Slot filling, intent classification and overall performance all get best results when $\alpha \neq 0$ and $\alpha \neq 1$, supporting that the interaction of two tasks can be beneficial if they are properly combined. (2) More specifically, a smaller non-zero α could help achieve more competitive overall performance. $\alpha = 0.1$ or $\alpha = 0.2$ seems to be a good choice. (3) It is clear that for slot filling, a small α has absolute advantages compared with a larger one. (4) For intent classification, small α and large α bring comparable results. It can be referred that two losses are equally important for intent recognition in joint modeling of NLU.

3.4   Case Study

An example in CMRS corpus is listed in Table 6, where "30 号" (thirty date) is a Chinese time expression. "30" can be used in both time-relevant and number-relevant slots. In this case, contextual information is demanded for disambiguating. It can be seen that models with only hierarchical (+H) information mislabel "30". While, models with only contextual information label "30" correctly, but misjudge the intent label. In fact, a time slot is a strong hint for intent identification. It seems hierarchical structures can make better use of this hint. CHJ models, which combine the two kinds of information, do a correct work on both subtasks.

Although CHJ models have taken considerable results, there are still some places to be improved. Table 7 shows two transcripts in which CHJ models mis-

Table 6. A positive example in CMRS corpus. The original utterance is "30 号", representing the 30th of a certain month.

Input	30	号	
	Semantic tags		Intent label
Gold	B-time	I-time	inf
+H models	B-pernum	I-time	inf
+C models	B-time	I-time	other
+C+H (CHJ) models	B-time	I-time	inf

Table 7. Some negative results transcripts of CHJ models. "budget" and "pernum" are different slot names, representing the budget-relevant and person-number-relevant slots respectively.

Input	100		
	Semantic tags		Intent label
Gold	B-pernum		inf
+C+H (CHJ) models	B-budget		inf
Input	3000	People	
	Semantic tags		Intent label
Gold	B-pernum	I-pernum	inf
+C+H (CHJ) models	B-budget	I-pernum	inf

judge slot filling or intent classification. In the first example, the input utterance only comprises one number. In fact, the user was providing the attendance (pernum). Without the information of history utterances, it seems unlikely to label correctly. In the second example, "B-budget" is followed by "I-pernum", which is illegal. CHJ models misjudge slot filling for lack of tag dependency. These defects provide a direction for our future work.

4   Conclusion

We have presented a cluster of CHJ models to jointly optimize slot filling and intent classification in NLU. The models are able to capture both contextual and hierarchical information in one joint structure. The combination of both kinds of information has been proved effective by comparison to other recent work. Finding the balance of two task losses is a great key to achieve best overall performances. We believe that CHJ models provide a novel hint for jointly learning subtasks of NLU.

There are several problems waiting for future work. For now, the lower supervision cannot affect the upper LSTM. In future work, we plan to figure out a more reasonable way for joint models that two losses could transmit supervision information equitably. Besides, we also want to incorporate tag dependency relations and history utterance information in our future work.

Acknowledgments. This paper is supported by 111 Project (No. B08004), NSFC (No. 61273365), Beijing Advanced Innovation Center for Imaging Technology, Engineering Research Center of Information Networks of MOE, and ZTE.

References

1. Tur, G., De Mori, R.: Spoken Language Understanding: Systems for Extracting Semantic Information from Speech. Wiley, Hoboken (2011)
2. De Mori, R., Bechet, F., Hakkani-Tur, D., et al.: Spoken language understanding. IEEE Sig. Process. Mag. **25**(3), 50–58 (2008)
3. Haffner, P., Tur, G., Wright, J.H.: Optimizing SVMs for complex call classification. In: Proceedings of 2003 IEEE International Conference on Acoustics, Speech, and Signal Processing (ICASSP 2003), vol. 1, p. 1. IEEE (2003)
4. Yao, K., Peng, B., Zhang, Y., et al.: Spoken language understanding using long short-term memory neural networks. In: Spoken Language Technology Workshop (SLT), pp. 189–194. IEEE (2014)
5. Shi, Y., Yao, K., Chen, H., et al.: Contextual spoken language understanding using recurrent neural networks. In: 2015 IEEE International Conference on Acoustics, Speech and Signal Processing (ICASSP), pp. 5271–5275. IEEE (2015)
6. Hakkani-Tür, D., Tur, G., Celikyilmaz, A., et al.: Multi-domain joint semantic frame parsing using bi-directional RNN-LSTM. In: The, Meeting of the International Speech Communication Association (2016)
7. Zhou, Q., Wen, L., Wang, X., Ma, L., Wang, Y.: A hierarchical LSTM model for joint tasks. In: Sun, M., Huang, X., Lin, H., Liu, Z., Liu, Y. (eds.) CCL/NLP-NABD-2016. LNCS (LNAI), vol. 10035, pp. 324–335. Springer, Cham (2016). https://doi.org/10.1007/978-3-319-47674-2_27
8. Yao, K., Zweig, G., Hwang, M.Y., et al.: Recurrent neural networks for language understanding. In: INTERSPEECH, pp. 2524–2528 (2013)
9. Mesnil, G., Dauphin, Y., Yao, K., et al.: Using recurrent neural networks for slot filling in spoken language understanding. IEEE/ACM Trans. Audio Speech Lang. Process. (TASLP) **23**(3), 530–539 (2015)
10. Søgaard, A., Goldberg, Y.: Deep multi-task learning with low level tasks supervised at lower layers. In: Proceedings of the 54th Annual Meeting of the Association for Computational Linguistics, vol. 2, pp. 231–235. Association for Computational Linguistics (2016)
11. Zhang, X., Wang, H.: A joint model of intent determination and slot filling for spoken language understanding. In: IJCAI (2016)
12. Liu, B., Lane, I.: Attention-based recurrent neural network models for joint intent detection and slot filling. arXiv preprint arXiv:1609.01454 (2016)
13. Hochreiter, S., Schmidhuber, J.: Long short-term memory. Neural Comput. **9**(8), 1735–1780 (1997)
14. Graves, A.: Supervised sequence labelling. In: Graves, A. (ed.) Supervised Sequence Labelling with Recurrent Neural Networks, vol. 385, pp. 5–13. Springer, Heidelberg (2012). https://doi.org/10.1007/978-3-642-24797-2_2
15. Graves, A., Schmidhuber, J.: Framewise phoneme classification with bidirectional LSTM networks. In: Proceedings of 2005 IEEE International Joint Conference on Neural Networks, IJCNN 2005, vol. 4, pp. 2047–2052. IEEE (2005)

16. Ramshaw, L.A., Marcus, M.P.: Text chunking using transformation-based learning. In: Armstrong, S., Church, K., Isabelle, P., Manzi, S., Tzoukermann, E., Yarowsky, D. (eds.) Natural Language Processing Using Very Large Corpora, vol. 11, pp. 157–176. Springer, Dordrecht (1999). https://doi.org/10.1007/978-94-017-2390-9_10

17. Williams, J., Raux, A., Ramachandran, D., et al.: The dialog state tracking challenge. In: Proceedings of the SIGDIAL 2013 Conference, pp. 404–413 (2013)

18. Kim, S., D'Haro, L.F., Banchs, R.E., Williams, J.D., Henderson, M.: The fourth dialog state tracking challenge. In: Jokinen, K., Wilcock, G. (eds.) Dialogues with Social Robots. LNEE, vol. 999, pp. 435–449. Springer, Singapore (2017). https://doi.org/10.1007/978-981-10-2585-3_36

19. Duchi, J., Hazan, E., Singer, Y.: Adaptive subgradient methods for online learning and stochastic optimization. J. Mach. Learn. Res. **12**(Jul), 2121–2159 (2011)

20. Cotter, A., Shamir, O., Srebro, N., et al.: Better mini-batch algorithms via accelerated gradient methods. In: Advances in Neural Information Processing Systems, pp. 1647–1655 (2011)

Augmenting Neural Sentence Summarization Through Extractive Summarization

Junnan Zhu[1], Long Zhou[1], Haoran Li[1], Jiajun Zhang[1], Yu Zhou[1],
and Chengqing Zong[1,2(✉)]

[1] National Laboratory of Pattern Recognition, CASIA,
University of Chinese Academy of Sciences, Beijing, China
{junnan.zhu,jjzhang,yzhou,cqzong}@nlpr.ia.ac.cn
[2] CAS Center for Excellence in Brain Science and Intelligence Technology,
Beijing, China

Abstract. Neural sequence-to-sequence model has achieved great success in abstractive summarization task. However, due to the limit of input length, most of previous works can only utilize lead sentences as the input to generate the abstractive summarization, which ignores crucial information of the document. To alleviate this problem, we propose a novel approach to improve neural sentence summarization by using extractive summarization, which aims at taking full advantage of the document information as much as possible. Furthermore, we present both of streamline strategy and system combination strategy to achieve the fusion of the contents in different views, which can be easily adapted to other domains. Experimental results on CNN/Daily Mail dataset demonstrate both our proposed strategies can significantly improve the performance of neural sentence summarization.

1 Introduction

Text summarization is a task to condense a piece of text to a shorter version that preserves its meaning. There are two broad approaches for summarization: extractive summarization [6,10] and abstractive summarization [3,7]. Extractive methods extract parts of a document (usually whole sentences) to form a summary in two steps: sentence ranking and sentence selection. While abstractive methods generate and paraphrase sentences not featured in the source text – as a human-written summary usually does.

Due to the difficulty of abstractive summarization [3,7], great majority of previous works focus on extractive summarization [6,10]. Recently, sequence-to-sequence (seq2seq) models [19] provide an effective new way for abstractive summarization [11,15]. These works all use lead (first) sentence-headline pairs to train seq2seq sentence summarization model. However, previous works take no account of the fact that lead sentences can not offer sufficient information for summarization. Alfonseca et al. [1] also indicate that the most important information is usually distributed in multiple sentences in a document.

© Springer International Publishing AG 2018
X. Huang et al. (Eds.): NLPCC 2017, LNAI 10619, pp. 16–28, 2018.
https://doi.org/10.1007/978-3-319-73618-1_2

To address this problem, we propose in this paper a new approach to boost neural sentence summarization by using extractive summarization that can extract most important sentences of document. We further present two strategies to fuse the extracted contents in different views, which aims at leveraging the document information as much as possible. On one hand, streamline strategy is designed to concatenate and compress each summary of several extractive methods to get an intermediate summary. Then we can obtain the final summary by a seq2seq model. On the other hand, we propose a neural system combination strategy for sentence summarization, which is adapted from neural system combination for machine translation [23]. It employs a hierarchical attention mechanism to utilize document information.

Specifically, we make the following contributions in this paper:

- We present a simple but effective streamline strategy to leverage the content information provided by extractive methods for neural sentence summarization.
- We propose a neural system combination strategy for sentence summarization, which takes the summaries of several extractive systems as input and produces the final summary.
- Experiments on CNN/DailyMail corpus show that two proposed strategies achieve substantial improvements over strong baselines.

2   Neural Sentence Summarization

Rush et al. [15] were the first to apply the seq2seq framework to abstractive sentence summarization, which provides an effective new way for text generation. Rush et al. [15] assume that the first sentence contains the most important information, therefore they train a seq2seq neural network on first sentences and headlines. In this section we briefly introduce the seq2seq model and its encoder-decoder framework.

2.1   Sequence-to-Sequence Model

Seq2seq model consists of two Recurrent neural networks (RNN) [4]: an encoder that processes a input sequence $X = (x_1, x_2, ..., x_m)$ and maps it to a sequence of vector representation $h = (h_1, h_2, ..., h_m)$, and a decoder that generates the output sequence of symbols $Y = (y_1, y_2, ..., y_n)$ from the vector representation. Specifically, the encoder maps a variable-length source sequence to a fixed-length vector, and the decoder maps the vector representation back to a variable-length target sequence of symbol. The two networks are trained jointly to maximize the conditional probability of target sequence given a source sequence:

$$P(Y|X; \theta) = \prod_{j=1}^{N} P(y_j | \{y_1, y_2, ..., y_{j-1}\}, h; \theta) \qquad (1)$$

2.2   Encoder

The role of the encoder is to read the input sequence and map it to hidden representation. The output sequence is depended not only on the previous predicted word but also on the previous hidden representation. In this paper, we use a bidirectional Gated Recurrent Units (BiGRU) [4].

The BiGRU consists of a forward GRU and a backward GRU. The forward GRU reads the input from left to right, while the backward reads the input reversely. Then forward hidden representation will be concatenated to the backward hidden representation to get the basic sentence representation.

2.3   Decoder

The decoder reads the previous predicted word and the previous context vector to predict next word. We use GRU with attention as the decoder to produce the output sequence. Attention mechanism [2] can make the decoder focus on the different positions of the input. In this paper, we compute the context vector c_j for current time step j by the concatenate attention mechanism [9], which matches the current decoder state s_j with each encoder hidden state h_i to get an importance score. The score is then normalized to get the current context vector by the weighted sum:

$$e_{j,i} = v_a^T tanh(W_a \tilde{s}_{j-1} + U_a h_i) \tag{2}$$

$$\alpha_{t,i} = \frac{\exp(e_{j,i})}{\sum_{k=1}^{m} \exp(e_{j,k})} \tag{3}$$

$$c_j = \sum_{i=1}^{m} \alpha_{j,i} h_i \tag{4}$$

The decoder then combines current context vector, previous predicted word embedding, and decoder state to predict current word.

3   Our Models

A document is too long to be the input to the seq2seq model. Recent works tend to limit the length of a document to a fixed length such as 100 or 200 words. However, it will destroy the consistency of the document. Since not all sentences in the source document are important. Therefore we apply extractive summarization method to filter out some less important sentences to improve the performance of sentence summarization.

We propose two strategies to alleviate this problem. The first method is similar to the idea of pipeline, we use three different extractive methods to obtain the most important sentences to form three different summaries. Then we merge the summaries to an intermediate summary under the limit of a fixed length. Lastly, the summary is fed to the seq2seq model to generate the final result. The second one uses different summaries from the perspective of neural system combination. Each summary is encoded independently followed by a unified decoding with a hierarchical attention mechanism.

Our baseline model is similar to Nallapati et al. [11]. Our model consists of a sentence encoder using a BiGRU [4] and an decoder using GRU. First, the bidirectional encoder reads an input sequence $x = (x_1, x_2, ..., x_m)$ and encodes it into a sequence of hidden representations $h = (h_1, h_2, ..., h_m)$. Then the GRU decoder predicts a target sequence $y = (y_1, y_2, ..., y_n)$ with attention to the tailored representation. Each word y_j is predicted based on a recurrent hidden state s_j, a previous predicted word y_{j-1} and a context vector c_j. c_j is calculated by the weighted sum of the annotations h_i.

3.1   Extractive Summarization

We conduct extractive methods to select the most salient sentences from the input document. The advantage of extractive methods is the guarantee of correctness of grammar. Extractive methods have also been studied for a long time. We employ three typical extractive methods to produce the summaries of input documents. The length limit of summaries is set to 50 words. The extractive summarization methods are:

Submodular: Submodular method performs summarization by maximizing submodular functions under a budget constraint. The submodularity of the coverage, diversity and non-redundancy can be reflected by a series of submodular functions. We use the same two submodular functions as [22] for extractive summarization.

LexRank: LexRank [6] is inspired by PageRank [13] algorithm. A graph is constructed by creating vertices representing sentences in the document. Edges between sentences are obtained based on cosine similarity of TF-IDF vectors. It computes sentence score based on the concept of eigenvector centrality in the graph representation.

LSA: LSA [18] uses Singular Value Decomposition (SVD) to acquire the semantic meaning of sentences. It can generate concept dimensions which are orthogonal to each other, and then picks the most salient sentences from each dimensions.

3.2   Fusion of Extractive Summaries

In order to construct text of limited length as input to seq2seq model but also to ensure the consistency of the text, we first use extractive summarization methods to extract the most important sentences. Each summarization method represents a different view. Submodular method treats summarization as an optimization problem. Lexrank uses graph models to tackle this problem. LSA tries to improve the summarization from the perspective of matrix decomposition. There are two benefits for using three different methods. First, this can increase the diversity of the input. Second, different methods bring us different views of information so that it can be attractive to fuse these information. We then propose two strategies to achieve fusion of three extractive summaries.

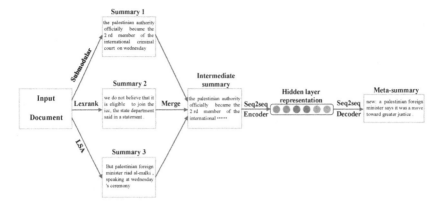

Fig. 1. The framework of our streamline strategy

Streamline Strategy. As depicted in Fig. 1, the input text is summarized to three different summaries by three extractive summarization methods. Then we propose two ways to merge these summaries to intermediate summary. One is simply concatenating these summaries; the other employs Round-robin (RR) scheme to compress the summaries. RR scheme picks the first sentence from the first summary and then the second and so no until the summary length is reached. We apply this scheme due to its efficiency and low cost of time. Lastly, the intermediate summary is fed into seq2seq model to generate the meta-summary.

Neural System Combination Strategy. In addition to fusion of various summaries in the source, we can also fuse these extractive summaries in the multi-source seq2seq model. Inspired by neural system combination for machine translation [23], which aims at combining the advantages of different machine translation systems through a multi-source model, we propose a neural system combination strategy for sentence summarization.

As depicted in Fig. 2, each encoder encodes summary independently to hidden vector representation. However, decoder must be adapted to three inputs with a hierarchical attention mechanism.

We illustrate encoder-decoder for neural system combination in Fig. 3. The network can take as input the results of extractive summarization or abstractive summarization. Extractive summaries have good readability, while abstractive methods such as neural network can generate fluent sentences. It is very attractive to combine both of these advantages. Therefore we attempt to use neural system combination to fuse different summaries to achieve complementary effects. Here, we use summarization results to detail the model.

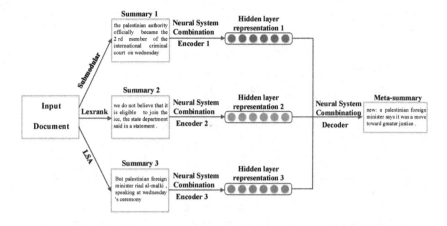

Fig. 2. Encoder-decoder for neural system combination strategy

At time j, the state s_{j-1} meets the previous prediction y_{j-1} to transfer to an intermediate state $\tilde{s}_{j-1}$, which can be calculated as follows:

$$s_j = GRU(\tilde{s}_{j-1}, c_j) \tag{5}$$

$$\tilde{s}_{j-1} = GRU(s_{j-1}, y_{j-1}) \tag{6}$$

where y_{j-1} represents the word embeddings of the previous word. c_{ja}, c_{jb}, and c_{jc} represent the context vectors of different encoders, attention weight α_{ji} is computed as described in (4). The attention model calculates c_j as weighted sum of three summarization context vectors, as described in the red box in Fig. 3:

$$c_j = \sum_{k=1}^{K} \beta_{jk} c_{jk} \tag{7}$$

where k is the number of summarization systems, and β_{jk} is calculated as follows:

$$\beta_{jk} = \frac{exp(s_j c_{jk})}{\sum_{\tilde{k}} exp(s_j c_{j\tilde{k}})} \tag{8}$$

In order to keep consistency in training and testing, we use the similar training data simulation strategy as [23] when train the single seq2seq system. We select most of the training data, such as two-thirds of data, to train the seq2seq model. And the trained model is used to transform the rest of training data to the summaries. Then re-divide the training data and repeat the above steps until all the training data is summarized. Since extractive methods we use are all unsupervised, there is no need to do this step for extractive summarization.

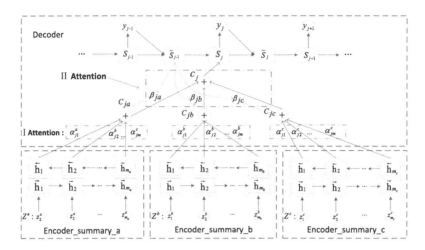

Fig. 3. The framework of our neural system combination strategy (Color figure online)

4 Experiment

4.1 Dataset

We use the CNN/Daily Mail dataset[1] [8,11], which contains online news articles (781 tokens on average) paired with multi-sentence highlight as summaries (3.75 sentences or 56 tokens on average). We use open-source scripts supplied by See et al. [16] to obtain the same non-anonymized version of the data. After filtering out data that article text is missing, we obtain 287,113 training pairs, 13,368 validation pairs and 11,490 test pairs. We use the first highlight as our gold label.

4.2 Implementation

The articles and the summaries in the dataset we obtained are all lowercased and tokenized by Stanford Corenlp toolkit[2]. We replace all the digit characters with # similar to Rush et al. [15]. We illustrate different methods as follows:

(1) Baseline

ABS. Rush et al. [15] use an attentive Convolutional Neural Network (CNN) encoder and a Neural Network Language Model (NNLM) decoder to do this task. We trained this baseline with its released code[3].
Seq2seq+attn. We implement a sequence-to-sequence model with attention based on the latest implementation of attention-based NMT[4].

---

[1] http://cs.nyu.edu/~kcho/DMQA/.
[2] https://stanfordnlp.github.io/CoreNLP/.
[3] https://github.com/facebook/NAMAS.
[4] https://github.com/nyu-dl/dl4mt-tutorial.

abstractive model. Nallapati et al. [11] used both RNN as encoder and decoder, and added some features such as POS, named-entities and TF-IDF, into encoder.

(2) **Extractive**

In order to compare with extractive methods, we also directly use three extractive methods to obtain the summaries. The reference summaries have 14.89 tokens on average in test set. We limit the length of output to 20 tokens in order to prevent zero output due to too short length limit.

(3) **Streamline**

Sub+seq2seq. We use the summary which is summarized by Submodular method as the input to the seq2seq model above. The length limit of all extractive summaries are all set to 50 words and so do Lex+seq2seq and LSA+seq2seq.
Sub+Lex+LSA. We simply concatenate these three summaries. Since the length of each summary is less than 50 words, the length of the intermediate summary does not exceed 150 words.
Sub+Lex+LSA+RR. We merge the summaries of the three extractive method by the Round-robin [20] scheme. We deduplicate the sentences in this step. To fully fuse all the important information, we set the length limit of the intermediate summary to 100 words. If the length limit is too short, the intermediate summaries usually come from the first two summaries so as not to achieve the fusion.

(4) **Neural System Combination**

Sub+Lex+LSA. We employ the Neural System Combination (NSC) to map the three inputs to the output.
Neural+Sub+Lex. We use the seq2seq+attn model as a single system to the NSC. And the other two inputs use the summaries of Submodular and LexRank, so do Neural+Sub+LSA and Neural+Lex+LSA.

4.3 Training Details

The hyper-parameters used in our model are described as follows. For all experiments, we use a vocabulary of 50K words for source and 30K words for target. We set word embedding size to 128 and all GRU hidden state sizes to 256. We use dropout [17] with the probability of 0.5. We do not pretrain the word embeddings, they are learned from scratch during training. We use Adadelta [21] with learning rate 0.0001 to update parameters in the network. We also apply gradient clipping [14] with range [−1, 1] during training. We use mini-batch size 64 to both speed up the training and converge quickly. We employ beam search to generate multiple summary candidates to get better results. The beam size is set to 10. We use a single NVIDIA TITAN X to train our models. We trained all our models for about 30 epochs. All the models can be trained in 24 h. And single seq2seq model using one input source can be trained in 12 h.

Table 1. Summarization results (ROUGE F1 score) for different sentence summarization strategies or neural system combination methods. Sub, Lex, and LSA denote Submodular, Lexrank and LSA respectively. **Best** results per category are highlighted.

	Model	ROUGE-1	ROUGE-2	ROUGE-L
Baseline	ABS [15]	13.85	4.13	12.64
	Seq2seq+attn	15.66	4.38	14.30
	Abstractive model [11]	**17.58**	**5.45**	**16.22**
Extractive	Sub	**18.86**	**6.77**	**16.56**
	Lex	14.98	3.93	12.92
	LSA	13.12	3.06	11.32
Streamline	Sub+seq2seq	17.18	5.25	15.82
	Lex+seq2seq	10.70	1.94	9.74
	LSA+seq2seq	9.25	1.37	8.47
	Sub+Lex+LSA	20.46	7.39	18.61
	Sub+Lex+LSA+RR	**23.06**	**9.29**	**21.08**
Neural system combination	Sub+Lex+LSA	17.24	5.28	15.82
	Neural+Sub+Lex	**21.55**	**8.16**	**19.90**
	Neural+Sub+LSA	20.44	7.55	18.89
	Neural+Lex+LSA	19.81	7.19	18.38

4.4   Experimental Results

We evaluate our models with the standard ROUGE metric, reporting the F1 scores for ROUGE-1, ROUGE-2 and ROUGE-L (which measure unigram-overlap, bigram-overlap, and longest common sequence between the reference summary and summary to be evaluated respectively). We use the files2rouge package[5] to obtain our ROUGE scores. Our results are given in Table 1.

It is clear from Table 1 that seq2seq model with summary summarized by Submodular method as input achieves higher than the other single seq2seq model. Compare extractive methods with streamline strategy, we have noticed that it is difficult to improve the performance by simply making the extractive summaries as the input to the seq2seq model. See et al. [16] find that their lead-3 baseline outperforms all other methods in their experiment. They attribute it to the reason that news articles tend to be structured with the most important information at the start. This is consistent with Rush's [15] assumption. We conduct an experiment on test data to analyze the position of the extractive summary sentences statistically.

As shown in Table 2, Submodular summaries cover more lead sentences than the others. The former average position locates, the higher performance of seq2seq model achieves. However, it is not to say that non-lead sentences

---

[5] https://github.com/pltrdy/files2rouge.

Table 2. Statistics of the position of the three extractive summaries. Position denotes the average position of summary sentences and 1 denotes the first sentence of the article. Lead (%) denotes the percentage of lead sentences (first three sentences) of summary sentences.

Metric	Submodular	Lexrank	LSA
Position	9.67	15.93	17.64
Lead (%)	49.04	13.99	10.96

are useless. The score of Sub+Lex+LSA (Streamline) shows these different sentences can still benefit this task. Although the length of input becomes longer, it does not mean that input contains more valuable information. The input of Sub+Lex+LSA (Streamline) contains the input in Sub+Lex+LSA+RR (Streamline), but the latter scores higher. It illustrates that filtering out some redundant information can improve the performance of our model.

From the experimental results of neural system combination, we find that the fusion of the three extractive summaries achieves the lowest score. It may be due to the redundancy of multiple extractive summaries. Extractive summarization selects contents from source text in sentence level, it can meet the diversity requirements of system combination. Therefore the performance of the neural system combination is proportional to the amount of information in summaries. From the analysis above, Submodular summaries contain the most informative content, then Lexrank, and finally LSA. Therefore Neural+Sub+Lex (NSC) achieves the highest score among all the methods under NSC strategy.

The same is fusion of several system results, Sub+Lex+LSA+RR (Streamline) outperforms all the methods under NSC strategy. Since we have deduplicated the sentences in Round-robin step and all sentences come from a single

---

Lead: -lrb- cnn -rrb- the palestinian authority officially became the ###rd member of the international criminal court on wednesday , a step that gives the court jurisdiction over alleged crimes in palestinian territories .
Submodular: -lrb- cnn -rrb- the palestinian authority officially became the ###rd member of the international criminal court on wednesday , a step that gives the court jurisdiction over alleged crimes in palestinian territories . as members of the court , palestinians may be subject to counter-charges as well .
LexRank: rights group human rights watch welcomed the development . as we have said repeatedly , we do not believe that palestine is a state and therefore we do not believe that it is eligible to join the icc , " the state department said in a statement .
LSA: but palestinian foreign minister riad al-malki , speaking at wednesday 's ceremony , said it was a move toward greater justice . it urged the warring sides to resolve their differences through direct negotiations . the inquiry will include alleged war crimes committed since june .

Gold: membership gives the icc jurisdiction over alleged crimes committed in palestinian territories since last june .
Seq2seq+attn: new : `` we 're going to be a UNK , " spokesman says .
Sub+seq2seq: UNK UNK , ## , was sentenced to ## years in prison .
Sub+Lex+Lsa+RR: new : a palestinian foreign minister says it was a move toward greater justice .
Neural+Sub+Lex(NCS): the court of the international criminal court is being held in the united states .

Fig. 4. Summaries generated by extractive methods and our model. Lead denotes the lead sentence in the source document. Gold denotes our gold summary. The last four are the most representative methods in our experiments. Some of the important information in the source is shown in red. (Color figure online)

document, there does not exist residual redundancy information. This further demonstrates the importance of removing redundant information. From the comparison of Sub+Lex+LSA (Streamline) and Sub+Lex+LSA (NSC), our conclusion is that Streamline strategy is more effective than NSC strategy. And the Streamline strategy requires much less time to train the network since there is only a single seq2seq model. Some of examples are given in Fig. 4.

As shown in Fig. 4, the single seq2seq models result in poor output though the inputs contain some contents which match the output. We can also see that the summaries generated by our two strategies actually leverage the information from three extractive summaries, and are more fluent. There are less UNKs in the summaries in the last two summaries. This is consistent with observation in Zhou et al. [23]. It also further illustrates the effectiveness of our model.

5   Related Work

Human-written summaries are highly abstracted and seldom consist of reproduction of original sentences from the document. Previous work [3,7] which focused on abstractive summarization has employed sentence fusion to construct a sentence whose fragments come from different source sentences.

With the emergence of deep learning, researchers have considered the framework as a fully data-driven alternative to abstractive summarization. Rush et al. [15] firstly apply neural network to abstractive sentence summarization. They propose leveraging news data in Gigaword [12] corpus to construct large scale parallel corpus for sentence summarizaiton task. Their model consists of an attentive Convolutional Neural Network encoder and an neural network language model decoder, producing state-of-the-art results on Gigaword and DUC datasets. In an extension to this work, Chopra et al. [5] used a similar CNN encoder, but replaced the decoder with an Recurrent Neural Network decoder, producing further improvement on both dataset.

However, their models all take lead sentences as input with assumption that lead sentences carry the most information. This causes most of the information to be lost at the input. It is difficult for neural network to take whole document as input. We propose two strategies that can filter out some less important contents in the text so that it can be processed by neural network and we can leverage most information in the source text indirectly. And the greatest advantage of our approach is that we do not need to make any assumptions about the corpus. In other words, it is general to be adapted to other domains.

6   Conclusion

In this paper, we propose a novel approach to enhance neural sentence summarization by utilizing extractive summarization, which aims at taking full advantage of the document information, instead of lead sentences in conventional neural sentence summarization. Furthermore, we present streamline strategy and system combination strategy to achieve the fusion of the contents in different views. To show the effectiveness of our proposed approaches, we conduct experiments on CNN/DailyMail corpus. Experimental results demonstrate that our strategies achieve significant improvements over strong baselines.

Acknowledgments. The research work has been funded by the Natural Science Foundation of China under Grant No. 61673380, No. 61402478 and No. 61403379.

References

1. Alfonseca, E., Pighin, D., Garrido, G.: HEADY: news headline abstraction through event pattern clustering. In: Proceedings of ACL (2013)
2. Bahdanau, D., Cho, K., Bengio, Y.: Neural machine translation by jointly learning to align and translate. In: Proceedings of ICLR (2015)
3. Barzilay, R., McKeown, K.R.: Sentence fusion for multidocument news summarization. Comput. Linguist. **31**(3), 297–328 (2005)
4. Cho, K., van Merrienboer, B., Gulcehre, C., Bahdanau, D., Bougares, F., Schwenk, H., Bengio, Y.: Learning phrase representations using RNN encoder-decoder for statistical machine translation. In: Proceedings of EMNLP (2014)
5. Chopra, S., Auli, M., Rush., A.M.: Abstractive sentence summarization with attentive recurrent neural networks. In: North American Chapter of the Association for Computational Linguistics (2016)
6. Erkan, G., Radev, D.R.: LexRank: graph-based lexical centrality as salience in text summarization. J. Qiqihar Junior Teach. Coll. **22** (2011)
7. Filippova, K., Strube, M.: Sentence fusion via dependency graph compression. In: Proceedings of EMNLP (2008)
8. Hermann, K.M., Kocisky, T., Grefenstette, E., Espeholt, L., Kay, W., Suleyman, M., Blunsom, P.: Teaching machines to read and comprehend. In: Proceedings of NIPS (2015)
9. Luong, T., Pham, H., Manning, C.D.: Effective approaches to attention-based neural machine translation. In: Proceedings of EMNLP (2015)
10. Nallapati, R., Zhai, F., Zhou, B.: SummaRuNNer: a recurrent neural network based sequence model for extractive summarization of documents. In: Proceedings of AAAI (2017)
11. Nallapati, R., Zhou, B., glar Gulcehre, C.: Abstractive text summarization using sequence-to-sequence RNNs and beyond. In: Proceedings of the 20th SIGNLL Conference on Computational Natural Language Learning (2016)
12. Napoles, C., Gormley, M., Durme, B.V.: Annotated gigaword. In: Proceedings of the Joint Workshop on Automatic Knowledge Base Construction and Web-Scale Knowledge Extraction (2012)
13. Page, L., Brin, S., Motwani, R., Winograd, T.: The PageRank Citation Ranking: Bringing Order to the Web (1999)
14. Pascanu, R., Mikolov, T., Bengio, Y.: On the difficulty of training recurrent neural networks. In: Proceedings of ICML (2013)
15. Rush, A.M., Chopra, S., Weston, J.: A neural attention model for abstractive sentence summarization. In: Proceedings of EMNLP (2015)
16. See, A., Liu, P.J., Manning, C.D.: Get to the point: summarization with pointer-generator networks. In: Proceedings of ACL (2017)
17. Srivastava, N., Hinton, G.E., Krizhevsky, A., Sutskever, I., Salakhutdinov, R.: Dropout: a simple way to prevent neural networks from overfitting. J. Mach. Learn. **15**(1), 1929–1958 (2014)

18. Steinberger, J., Ježek, K.: Text summarization and singular value decomposition. In: Yakhno, T. (ed.) ADVIS 2004. LNCS, vol. 3261, pp. 245–254. Springer, Heidelberg (2004). https://doi.org/10.1007/978-3-540-30198-1_25
19. Sutskever, I., Vinyals, O., Le, Q.V.: Sequence to sequence learning with neural networks. In: Proceedings of Neural Information Processing Systems (2014)
20. Wang, D., Li, T.: Weighted consensus multi-document summarization. Inf. Process. Manag. **48**(3), 513–523 (2012)
21. Zeiler, M.D.: ADADELTA: an adaptive learning rate method. CoRR (2012)
22. Zhang, J., Wang, T., Wan, X.: PKUSUMSUM: a Java platform for multilingual document summarization. In: Proceedings of COLING (2016)
23. Zhou, L., Hu, W., Zhang, J., Zong, C.: Neural system combination for machine translation. In: Proceedings of ACL (2017)

Cascaded LSTMs Based Deep Reinforcement Learning for Goal-Driven Dialogue

Yue Ma[1(✉)], Xiaojie Wang[1], Zhenjiang Dong[2], and Hong Chen[2]

[1] Beijing University of Posts and Telecommunications, Beijing, China
{myue,xjwang}@bupt.edu.cn
[2] ZTE Corporation, Nanjing, China
dongzhenjiangvip@163.com, chen.hong3@zte.com.cn

Abstract. This paper proposes a deep neural network model for jointly modeling Natural Language Understanding and Dialogue Management in goal-driven dialogue systems. There are three parts in this model. A Long Short-Term Memory (LSTM) at the bottom of the network encodes utterances in each dialogue turn into a turn embedding. Dialogue embeddings are learned by a LSTM at the middle of the network, and updated by the feeding of all turn embeddings. The top part is a forward Deep Neural Network which converts dialogue embeddings into the Q-values of different dialogue actions. The cascaded LSTMs based reinforcement learning network is jointly optimized by making use of the rewards received at each dialogue turn as the only supervision information. There is no explicit NLU and dialogue states in the network. Experimental results show that our model outperforms both traditional Markov Decision Process (MDP) model and single LSTM with Deep Q-Network on meeting room booking tasks. Visualization of dialogue embeddings illustrates that the model can learn the representation of dialogue states.

Keywords: Cascaded LSTMs · Deep reinforcement learning
Goal-driven dialogue

1 Introduction

A goal-driven dialogue system usually has three components [1]: Natural Language Understanding (NLU), Dialogue Management (DM), Natural Language Generation (NLG). Each component includes several subtasks. For example, DM has dialogue state tracking (ST) and action selection (AS). The subtasks are traditionally modeled independently and concatenated in a pipeline way.

There are some important limitations exist in the traditional pipeline system [2]. First, the information cannot be shared between different subtasks due to the separated training methods, for example, the error in the DM could not pass to the NLU. Second, different modules are trained in different ways because they usually use different models, when one of them, for example, NLU is updated

© Springer International Publishing AG 2018
X. Huang et al. (Eds.): NLPCC 2017, LNAI 10619, pp. 29–41, 2018.
https://doi.org/10.1007/978-3-319-73618-1_3

with more data, the other modules will fail to adapt to the new parameters in NLU. Third, it is necessary to explicitly define the dialogue states and actions. As the number of slots increases in dialogue tasks, state and action spaces will increase exponentially, this requires significant human efforts.

In order to break these limitations, many researchers have proposed models to deal with the subtasks mentioned above jointly. Some of them jointly modeled subtasks in NLU [3,4], some of them jointly modeled subtasks from NLU to ST [5]. Although there are few successful cases on jointly modeling NLU, ST and AS, similar ideas are already applied in computer games. Mnih et al. [6,7] proposed a deep reinforcement learning (DRL) model for implementing a video game playing agent. By utilizing Deep Q-Network (DQN), screen understanding and game operation selection are blended into an end-to-end model.

Understanding the screen images and text descriptions is similar to NLU, game action selection is similar to AS. The goal of game agent is to achieve maximum long-term rewards [8] during gameplay, this principle is similarly analogy to the goal in the goal-driven dialogue. Although there are several similarities between a game and a dialogue, a DRL model for game control cannot be simply applied to dialogue control. Different from a game controller, a dialogue agent for goal-driven tasks should not only learn dialogue policies but also track and update a series of explainable dialogue states by merging current utterances with dialogue history.

There are few works on jointly modeling from text input to action selection for goal-driven dialogue in a DRL framework. Narasimhan et al. [9] proposed a LSTM based DQN (LSTM-DQN) model for playing text-based games. There are two differences between their model and ours. First, the text provided to the player in the game is the description of its current state. Differently, in goal-driven dialogue, the agent does not have complete information about the environment and the states in dialogues should have been tracked and updated by the agent itself. A single LSTM structure cannot be applied to dialogue domain easily, but the cascaded LSTMs structure in our model can deal with the variable-length dialogues more flexibly and efficiently. Zhao and Eskenazi [2] proposed a framework which is similar to above LSTM-DQN for jointly modeling both state tracking and dialogue policy. The LSTM in their model received a current turn embedding and a history vector as the inputs at each time, while our model employs a shared LSTM to encode both the user utterances and the agent utterances into a turn embedding at each turn, and then use another LSTM to encode all turn embeddings into a dialogue embedding.

Inspired by the proposed ideas about DRL [6,7,9], this paper proposes a cascaded LSTMs based deep reinforcement learning network for building a dialogue agent which jointly models all subtasks through NLU to AS. To the best of our knowledge, it is the first cascaded LSTMs reinforcement learning model. The major contributions of the work are: (1) A cascaded LSTMs structure is designed for firstly encoding user and agent utterances at each dialogue turn into a turn embedding, and then merging turn embeddings into dialogue embedding. Although we do not define any internal delexicalized dialogue states, experimental results showed that dialogue embeddings correlate with some explainable dialogue states well. (2) A deep neural network (DNN) maps dialogue embeddings to the Q-values of different actions. The parameters of cascaded LSTMs and DNN are learned jointly using only the rewards of dialogues. Experimental results showed that our model outperforms a MDP model with fully correct NLU and state tracking and it also outperforms some previous models.

The rest of this paper is organized as follows. The proposed network and its learning algorithm are described in Sect. 2. Section 3 gives experimental results and analysis. Some conclusions are drawn in Sect. 4.

2 Model

This section is organized as follows. Section 2.1 gives an overview of our model. Details of turn embedding and dialogue embedding are described in Sect. 2.2. The learning method is presented at Sect. 2.3.

2.1 Overview

By using all historical information and observations at each moment, our model uses the cascaded LSTMs to model the internal dialogue states without using probabilistic method. The main concepts in our framework are detailed as follows:

1. Let $D = \{D^1, D^2, ..., D^T\}$ be the set of user input utterances, where $D^t = d_1^t d_2^t ... d_n^t$ is user input at time t (or t-th turn), d_i^t is the i-th word of D^t.
2. Let $M = \{M^1, M^2, ..., M^T\}$ be the set of agent outputs, where $M^t = m_1^t m_2^t ... m_k^t$ is the agent output at time t (or t-th turn), m_i^t is the i-th word of M^t.
3. Let S be the set of states, s_t be the dialogue state at time t.
4. Let A be the set of agent's actions. a_t is the action at time t.
5. Let R be the set of rewards, r_t is the reward at time t. A small negative reward is assigned for each turn. The last turn of a successful dialogue receives a positive reward.

The goal of the dialogue agent is to find an action a_t belonging to A according to state s_t at time t, which maximizes the expected long-term discounted reward of a dialogue, i.e., to find an optimal policy $\pi : s_t \to a_t$ satisfying Formula (1).

$$Q^*(s, a) = \max_{\pi} E\{\sum_{t=0}^{\infty} \gamma^t r_t | s_t = s, a_t = a, \pi\} \tag{1}$$

where $\gamma \in (0, 1)$ is the discount factor that controls how much the agent prioritizes long-term or short-term rewards, Q^* represents the maximum sum of rewards r_t discounted by factor γ at each time step. Dialogue state s_t should be estimated and tracked before action selection.

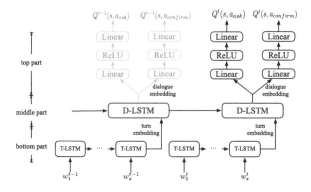

Fig. 1. The model structure

The model we propose here jointly models NLU, ST and AS three subtasks. As shown in Fig. 1, there are three parts in the network. At the bottom, it is a turn embedding generator which encodes sentences at each turn into a turn embedding. The middle part is dialogue embedding generator which receives previous turn embeddings up to current time and encodes them into a current dialogue embedding. The top part is an action scorer based on DNN which maps dialogue embeddings to the Q-value of each action. All these three parts are cascaded and trained jointly.

2.2   Turn Embedding and Dialogue Embedding

We utilize LSTM [10] networks as generators of turn embeddings and dialogue embeddings. LSTM is a recurrent network with the ability to connect and recognize long-range patterns between words in text.

At each turn, the same LSTM (named T-LSTM) is used to encode both agent and user utterances into a turn embedding. The input of T-LSTM is a concatenation of agent utterances and user utterances. For t-th turn, let $I^t = w_1^t w_2^t ... w_k^t w_{k+1}^t w_{k+2}^t \cdots w_{z-1}^t w_z^t = m_1^t m_2^t \cdots m_k^t \# d_1^t d_2^t \cdots d_n^t @$ denote the input of T-LSTM, where a symbol "#" is appended to agent word sequence and a "@" is appended to user word sequence in order to distinguish user and agent utterances. $z = n + k + 2$. w_i^t denotes m_i^t for $1 \leq i \leq k$, and w_i^t denotes d_{i-k-1}^t for $k + 2 \leq i \leq z - 1$. Let $h^t = [h_1^t h_2^t \cdots h_z^t]$ denotes the hidden states of T-LSTM, $c^t = [c_1^t c_2^t \cdots c_z^t]$ is the output of T-LSTM cells. Formulas 2 give details of the network computing.

$$h_z^t, c_z^t = T - LSTM(h_{z-1}^t, w_z) \tag{2}$$

The final output c_z^t is turn embedding of I^t and then passed to dialogue embedding generator.

A LSTM (named D-LSTM) is used to track dialogue states and generate dialogue embeddings. When a dialogue goes to T-th turn, D-LSTM takes T turn embeddings $[c_z^1 c_z^2 \cdots c_z^T]$ as input and encodes them into a dialogue embedding of T turns. For simplicity, we use $[c_1 c_2 \cdots c_T]$ to denote $[c_z^1 c_z^2 \cdots c_z^T]$. The output of D-LSTM is $[h_1' h_2' \cdots h_T']$ and its cell output is $[c_1' c_2' \cdots c_T']$. Formulas 3 calculate the output of D-LSTM.

$$h_T', c_T' = D - LSTM(h_{T-1}', c_T) \tag{3}$$

Finally, the top part includes several DNNs. All DNNs share the same dialogue embeddings as network inputs and share the same DNN structure. The number of the DNNs is determined by how many actions it has in dialogue task. For example, if there are actions "request" and "confirm" in the dialogue, two DNNs should be used in the top part. One DNN stands for one action. The number of output nodes of each DNN is the slot number of the action plus one (used for no act). The outputs of DNN are Q-values of the actions on each slot. Supposing action "request" can be followed by 5 slots, then the number of output nodes for its DNN is 6. If the first node is for time slot, then the output of this node is the Q-value of action "request time slot". Each DNN selects a slot (or no act) with maximum Q-value separately at each turn. For example, if "request" DNN selects time slot and "confirm" DNN selects location slot, then a final action "ask time slot and confirm location slot" is selected.

By using these three cascaded parts from bottom T-LSTM to top DNNs, the network maps text inputs to dialogue actions end-to-end. At the meantime, dialogue states are kept and updated as dialogue embedding by D-LSTM.

2.3 Learning Method

Let Θ be parameters of the model. Double Q-learning [11] is applied to the proposed network to alleviate the problem of over-estimation. The model keeps two separate networks: a behavior network θ and a target network θ^-. These two networks have the same network structure. After every L updates, the new parameters of θ are copied over to θ^-. At the j-th update process, the difference between predicted Q-value $Q(s_t, a_t; \theta_j)$ from the behavior network and the target value y from the target network is used as the error for back-propagation. The target value y is the sum of the reward of taking action a_t at state s_t and the expected Q-value at s_{t+1} which is calculated by $\max_a Q(s_{t+1}, a; \theta^-)$. The detail is shown in Formulas (4.1) and (4.2). Formula (5) gives the gradient of the error.

$$\mathcal{L}(\theta_j) = E[(y - Q(s_t, a_t; \theta_j))^2] \tag{4.1}$$

$$y = r_t + \gamma \max_{a_{t+1}} Q(s_{t+1}, a_{t+1}; \theta^-) \tag{4.2}$$

$$\frac{\partial \mathcal{L}(\theta_j)}{\partial \theta} = E[2\left(r_t + \gamma \max_{a_{t+1}} Q(s_{t+1}, a_{t+1}; \theta^-) - Q(s_t, a_t; \theta_j)\right) \frac{Q(s_t, a_t; \theta_j)}{\theta}] \tag{5}$$

A replay memory pool X is maintained during the training process. Mini-batch transitions are sampled from X at each iteration. Rank-based sampling [12] method is used as our selection strategy of transition. The probability of sampling transition X is defined as $P(x) = \frac{p_x^\alpha}{\sum_l p_l^\alpha}$, where $p_x = \frac{1}{rank(x)}$ is the priority of transition x. $rank(x)$ is the ranking of transition x in replay memory X which is determined by the deviations. The exponent α determines how much prioritization is used, with $\alpha = 0$ back to the uniform case. At the beginning of the training, the agent interacts with a user simulator by using random action to generate some transitions, and these transitions will be used to initialize the replay memory. After each mini-batch updated, the model will use new transitions to update replay memory following the rank-based strategy.

3   Experiments

3.1   Experimental Settings

The model is applied to build several dialogue agents. A meeting room booking task is used to test the proposed model. The agent communicates with users and gathers required information to book a meeting room for users. To book a meeting room successfully, the agent should gather values for five required slots in the real-world online system. In order to evaluate the model's performance comprehensively, four tasks with different number of slots are used. They are listed in Table 1. As the number of slots increases, the task becomes more difficult.

Table 1. Four tasks with different slots

Slot number	Name of slots
2	Start time, location
3	Start time, location, lasting time
4	Start time, location, lasting time number of participants
5	Start time, location, lasting time number of participants, budget

The inputs of the model are raw utterances come from the agents and user. To train the DRL algorithm, a real-time environment is necessary. The agents built for gameplay are trained by using a game simulator. For dialogue task, it is infeasible to train the agent by communicating with a human in real-time. A user simulator should be used for simulating human behavior and generating user utterances.

According to the data collected in the online system and the basic mode of construction proposed in Li et al. [13], several simulators have been built to evaluate the model. Some of the details of the user simulators are as follows: (1) For each slot, there are 25 different slot values and 25 alias values. The alias values are used for simulating errors in Named Entity Recognition (NER), which is named NER-Error. For example, the meeting place which passed to the agent at the first time can be Research Building 09 (the correct one is Research Building 809) (Supplementary A gives an example dialogue). (2) Before giving the right slot value, user simulator first gives an alias value according to the rate of NER-Error. When agents confirm an alias value, the simulator has two choices, one is to reject the confirm action by using general reject templates with a probability of 0.75, and then it waits agents to ask again, the other one is to answer the agents with the true slot value directly. (3) Specified templates are designed for answering questions and for confirming slot values for each slot. Moreover, all slots also share a set of general confirm templates and a set of general reject templates. The simulator can use specified templates for replying agent's questions with a probability of 0.4, or use a general pattern with a probability of 0.6. In order to make the utterances generated by the simulators more complex and make the simulators behave like humans, we collected utterances from the DSTC5 Corpus[1] as a supplement. Utterances which are tagged with *RES(POSITIVE)* and *FOL(ACK)* in corpus (453 expressions) are used to extend confirm templates. Utterances which are tagged with *RES(NEGATIVE)* in corpus (37 expressions) are used to extend reject templates.

The simulators do not set the order of slot filling. It brings more combinations of actions to dialogue, and adds extra complexity to our model to get the optimal policy. In Bordes and Weston [14], the variety of dialogue states is reduced because they have set the order of slot filling.

The agents collect information by asking and confirming slot values. So, two DNNs are employed for action "ask" and "confirm" respectively. We considered 36 possible command combinations of 6 ask actions and 6 confirm actions. The hyper-parameters of the neural network model are as follows: the word embedding size is 64; the size of turn embedding and dialogue embedding is 64; the size of LSTMs is 128; each DNN has two hidden layers, with 128 nodes in the first layer and the 64 nodes in second layer. Adam optimizer is used for training. The behavior network was updated every 4 steps and the interval between each target network update is 1000 steps. The discount factor γ is 0.98. The mini-batch size is 32 and the learning rate is 0.00008.

At each turn, the agent receives a reward of -0.01 if its action is logically acceptable, -1 if not. We do not set a priority level for those acceptable actions. The reward for a successful dialogue is $+1$ and for an unfinished dialogue is -1. A dialogue ends successfully if an agent get all required slot values from the user simulator within a given number of turns (10 turns, each turn includes no more than 40 words), otherwise, it is unfinished or failed.

We implement the model with Tensorflow. The codes of experiments are available in https://github.com/Damcy/cascadeLSTMDRL. As described in Sect. 2.3, a replay memory pool is used. By comparing different replay memory sizes, we found a correlation between the agent's performance and the replay memory size. The replay memory size which is too large or too small is unfavorable to the model performance. We finally employed a replay memory size of 20000 in all experiments.

We first show some comparisons between the model and some previous models, then give some analysis on the model.

---

[1] http://workshop.colips.org/dstc5/data.html.

3.2   Model Comparison

We compared our model with a traditional pipeline agent and LSTM-DQN [9] on 2, 3 slot tasks as described in above section. The pipeline agent is built with perfect NLU and ST modules, its dialogue state in each turn is fully observable. A tabular Q-learning for MDP is used for action selection. The same $\epsilon - greedy$ strategy is used for MDP method.

For building pipeline agents for tasks with different slot numbers, different sets of states and actions should be explicitly predefined separately. 9 states and 9 actions for 2 slots, 27 states and 16 actions for 3 slots are defined for building 2 slots and 3 slots tasks respectively. For bigger number of slots, the sets of states and actions will increase exponentially. More human efforts will be needed. As for our model, the only necessary change is the number of nodes in DNN's output layer when the model is applied to those tasks with different number of slots.

Table 2. Results of task with 2 slots and 3 slots

	2 slots		3 slots	
	Avg. reward	Avg. length	Avg. reward	Avg. length
MDP	0.902	4.735	0.826	5.984
LSTM-DQN	0.960	4.142	0.557	6.437
Our model	**0.961**	**4.138**	**0.882**	**5.622**
Our model*	0.943	4.32	0.855	5.782

Because LSTM cannot deal with long sentences (concatenated each turn utterance in the dialogue, the max input length would be 400), the input of LSTM-DQN could not be the word embeddings. Our model trains the network parameters and word embeddings while LSTM-DQN trains its network parameters and sentence embeddings. Besides the comparison with other models, human evaluation was also carried for our model. Ten graduate students were invited to test the model. Each student completed five dialogues on 2 slots and 3 slots tasks (we showed them all the valid slot values at the beginning). Average length and average total rewards in human evaluation were also reported in evaluation results. Average dialogue length and average total rewards are calculated on 1000 dialogue steps for three models respectively. And for human evaluation, the averages are obtained from the total number of dialogues.

Table 2 show experimental results on 2 and 3 slots tasks respectively, where "Avg. reward" is the average of total reward and "Avg. length" is the average number of turns for each dialogue. "our model*" is the result by human evaluation. It can be seen that our model achieved consistent higher average total rewards and lower average lengths than those in LSTM-DQN agent and MDP method in all tasks. In 2 slot task, LSTM-DQN and our model have similar performance. In 3 slots task, our model outperforms LSTM-DQN significantly. Average total reward of LSTM-DQN falls by 40.3% from 2 slots to 3 slots, while our model falls by 7.9%, this shows the robustness of our model. In human evaluation, our model also achieves good performance. Compared with dialogues with simulators, the average total rewards of dialogues with human descends less than 3% in both 2 and 3 slots tasks.

3.3   Hyper-Parameter Analysis

Our model is data-driven. Besides the advantage of reducing human efforts, it is with capabilities of error-toleration and robustness, which will be investigated in this subsection by checking the influence of some parameters.

We give some experimental results on the influence of two parameters. They are the number of slots and NER-Error. Several statistics are used for evaluating the influence. One is the Success Rate of Dialogue (SRD). It is defined in Formula (6).

$$SRD = \frac{\#successful\ dialogues}{\#total\ dialogues\ in\ test} \tag{6}$$

where a successful dialogue represents that the agent gets all necessary slot values within a given number of turns (The number is set as 10 in all experiments).

The others are No Error Rate (NoER), One Error Rate (OER) and Two Error Rate (TER). NoER is defined in Formula (7). OER is the successful dialogue rate with one action selection error (ASE), TER is the successful dialogue rate with two ASE.

$$NoER = \frac{\#successful\ dialogues\ without\ ASE}{\#successful\ dialogues} \tag{7}$$

where an ASE means the agent selects a wrong action. If the agent can find correct response in every turn, then the $NoER = 1$. If the agent can finish a dialogue successfully even with one or more ASEs in it ($NoER < 1$), it means the agent can recover from the errors.

Number of Slots: Number of slots is a task-related parameter. As the number of slots increases, the task becomes more complex. Four models are trained for dialogue tasks with 2, 3, 4 and 5 slots. Table 3 shows the SRD and other statistics in different tasks. Our model achieves 100%, 100%, 89.06% and 79.73% SRD on 2, 3, 4 and 5 slots respectively. The model is sensitive to the complexity of tasks.

Results in Table 3 also show that our agents can successfully recover from one ASE, and even have chance to recover from two ASEs. For example, in 3 slots task, 91.35% successful dialogues have no ASE, 8.65% successful dialogues are recovered from one ASE. In 4 slots task, 6.25% of successful dialogues include one ASE, and 1.56% of successful dialogues are recovered from two ASEs. With the increasing of the complexity of tasks, it might be unavoidable for the agent to make mistakes. The more important thing is to recover from mistakes. Figure 2 gives the reward curves for these tasks. More epochs of training will bring bigger rewards in all tasks. Improvements on dialogues with 4 and 5 slots are needed. In another way, we can split a 5 slots task into one 2 slots subtask and one 3

Table 3. Statistics on different slot number and NER-error

Slot number & NER-error	SRD	NoER	OER	TER
2 slots (15%)	100%	95.52%	4.48%	0%
3 slots (15%)	100%	91.35%	8.65%	0%
4 slots (15%)	89.06%	81.25%	6.25%	1.56%
5 slots (15%)	79.37%	71.43%	6.35%	1.59%
2 slots (25%)	100%	94.81%	5.19%	0%
2 slots (35%)	100%	91.30%	8.70%	0%

slots subtask according to the independence assumption of slots, the result for SRD was 100% as well.

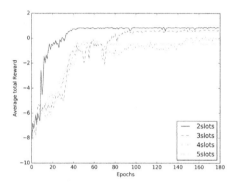

Fig. 2. Reward curves for different tasks

NER-Error: Our model not only can recover from its action selection error, but also can deal with errors in NLU. Table 3 also shows the experimental results on 2 slots task when different levels of NER-Error are introduced in user simulator. Our model keeps achieving 100% success rate even when the NER-Error rate is raised from 15% to 35%. But it increases the difficulty for leaning the optimal policy. Higher NER-error in training data causes more vibrations and converge slowly (Supplementary B). More NER-error causes higher ASE. The increaseing of OER in Table 3 shows our model deals with more ASE with the increaseing of NER-error.

3.4   Dialogue Embedding Analysis

As mentioned before, the dialogue embedding at T-th turn merges all information from previous T turns. PCA projection is used to visualize dialogue embeddings. By using PCA projection, we can see the relation between dialogue embeddings. For 2 slot tasks, let 0_0 denotes the dialogue state when a dialogue begins with all slot values unknown, 1_0 denotes the dialogue state when the first slot is given, 2_0 denotes the dialogue state when the first slot is confirmed, so does the second slot. A subset of dialogue embeddings in test dialogues is collected. The embeddings are then labeled with its state, such as 0_0, 1_0 etc. We cluster the embeddings and visualized them in Fig. 3.

From Fig. 3, we can find that dialogue embeddings in different dialogues are clustered well. For example, embeddings labeled with 1_0 in different dialogues are clustered at the bottom of Fig. 3, while 2_1s are clustered at the top right. The number of 1_1s is small because the agent tends to combine ask action and confirm action at one turn in most of dialogues. This method is better than the one that just confirm the slot what it just asked (it causes the dialogue state transfer from 1_0 to 2_0) and then ask a new slot (the dialogue state transfers from 2_0 to 2_1), because the latter method needs two turns to achieve the same goal. The agent learns the better strategy by itself through interaction with the user simulator. The agent also find two equivalent ways from 1_0 to 2_1. One is from 1_0 to 1_1 and then to 2_1, another way is from 1_0 to 2_0 and then to 2_1. Being well clustered of different dialogue embeddings shows the ability of the model that it can automatically organize context information in different dialogues and implicitly learn the same dialogue states in different dialogues.

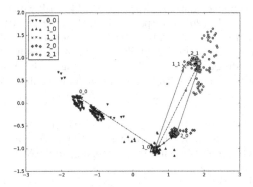

Fig. 3. Visualization of dialogue embeddings, big symbols are for cluster center points

The above properties of dialogue embeddings gives an efficient way to identify and explain the dialogue state represented by it. For a dialogue embedding in a dialogue, by identifying which cluster the dialogue embedding belongs to, we can identify which state current dialogue is at. In this way, we explain dialogue embeddings explicity.

4   Conclusion

This paper proposes a deep reinforcement learning model for training end-to-end goal-driven dialogue agents. This model uses cascaded LSTMs and DNN structure to model NLU, ST and AS in a single network. The network maps raw utterances to agent actions directly. Experimental results on meeting room booking tasks show our model outperforms previous models. Visualization of dialogue embeddings illustrates they keep the information of dialogue states. For dialogue tasks with more slots, the model cannot converge well. More efficient training methods should be explored in the future.

Acknowledgments. This paper is supported by 111 Project (No. B08004), NSFC (No. 61273365), Beijing Advanced Innovation Center for Imaging Technology, Engineering Research Center of Information Networks of MOE, and ZTE.

References

1. Jurafsky, D., Martin, J.H.: Speech and Language Processing: An Introduction to Natural Language Processing, Computational Linguistics, and Speech Recognition (2000)
2. Zhao, T., Eskenazi, M.: Towards end-to-end learning for dialog state tracking and management using deep reinforcement learning. In: Proceedings of the 17th Annual Meeting of the Special Interest Group on Discourse and Dialogue (2016). https://doi.org/10.18653/v1/w16-3601
3. Guo, D., Tur, G., Yih, W., Zweig, G.: Joint semantic utterance classification and slot filling with recursive neural networks. In: 2014 IEEE Spoken Language Technology Workshop (SLT) (2014). https://doi.org/10.1109/slt.2014.7078634
4. Lee, C., Ko, Y., Seo, J.: A simultaneous recognition framework for the spoken language understanding module of intelligent personal assistant software on smart phones. In: Proceedings of the 53rd Annual Meeting of the Association for Computational Linguistics and the 7th International Joint Conference on Natural Language Processing (vol. 2: Short Papers) (2015). https://doi.org/10.3115/v1/p15-2134
5. Henderson, M., Thomson, B., Young, S.: Word-based dialog state tracking with recurrent neural networks. In: Proceedings of the 15th Annual Meeting of the Special Interest Group on Discourse and Dialogue (SIGDIAL) (2014). https://doi.org/10.3115/v1/w14-4340
6. Mnih, V., Kavukcuoglu, K., Silver, D., Graves, A., Antonoglou, I., Wierstra, D., Riedmiller, M.: Playing atari with deep reinforcement learning. arXiv preprint arXiv:1312.5602 (2013)
7. Mnih, V., Kavukcuoglu, K., Silver, D., Rusu, A.A., Veness, J., Bellemare, M.G., Hassabis, D.: Human-level control through deep reinforcement learning. Nature **518**(7540), 529–533 (2015). https://doi.org/10.1038/nature14236
8. Sutton, R.S., Barto, A.G.: Introduction to Reinforcement Learning, vol. 135. MIT Press, Cambridge (1998)
9. Narasimhan, K., Kulkarni, T., Barzilay, R.: Language understanding for text-based games using deep reinforcement learning. In: Proceedings of the 2015 Conference on Empirical Methods in Natural Language Processing (2015). https://doi.org/10.18653/v1/d15-1001
10. Hochreiter, S., Schmidhuber, J.: Long short-term memory. Neural Comput. **9**(8), 1735–1780 (1997). https://doi.org/10.1162/neco.1997.9.8.1735
11. Van Hasselt, H., Guez, A., Silver, D.: Deep reinforcement learning with double q-learning. In: AAAI, pp. 2094–2100, February 2016

12. Schaul, T., Quan, J., Antonoglou, I., Silver, D.: Prioritized experience replay. arXiv preprint arXiv:1511.05952 (2015)
13. Li, X., Lipton, Z.C., Dhingra, B., Li, L., Gao, J., Chen, Y.N.: A user simulator for task-completion dialogues. arXiv preprint arXiv:1612.05688 (2016)
14. Bordes, A., Boureau, Y., Weston, J.: Learning end-to-end goal-oriented dialog. In: Proceedings of the 5th International Conference on Learning Representations (ICLR) (2017)

Dialogue Intent Classification with Long Short-Term Memory Networks

Lian Meng[✉] and Minlie Huang

State Key Laboratory of Intelligent Technology and Systems,
Tsinghua National Laboratory for Information Science and Technology,
Department of Computer Science and Technology, Tsinghua University,
Beijing 100084, People's Republic of China
mengl15@foxmail.com, aihuang@tsinghua.edu.cn

Abstract. Dialogue intent analysis plays an important role for dialogue systems. In this paper, we present a deep hierarchical LSTM model to classify the intent of a dialogue utterance. The model is able to recognize and classify user's dialogue intent in an efficient way. Moreover, we introduce a memory module to the hierarchical LSTM model, so that our model can utilize more context information to perform classification. We evaluate the two proposed models on a real-world conversational dataset from a Chinese famous e-commerce service. The experimental results show that our proposed model outperforms the baselines.

1 Introduction

Dialogue intent analysis is an important task that dialogue systems need to perform in order to understand the user's utterance in the dialogue. The intention of a speaker delivered in dialogue is called a dialogue act (DA) [1]. In real-world applications, understanding user's utterances is crucial for downstream processes such as dialogue management, knowledge base search, and language generation.

In open-domain conversations, context information (one or a few previous utterances) is particularly important to language understanding [2]. The real spoken dialogue scenario always have multiple turns, and the number of back and forth between both sides increases as the complexity of the scenarios grows. The accurate understanding of next dialogue sentence often requires reasoning from its previous conversational history, to which we refer as context. Failing to consider the contextual information may result in incorrect interpretation of the user's intent.

In order to perform dialogue intent analysis, various classification models have been proposed to deal with natural language understanding tasks. However, models that use original lexical features without any modifications always encounter the problem of data sparseness, and constructing sufficient training data to overcome this problem is labor-intensive, time-consuming, and expensive.

In recent studies, the method of deep learning is widely used in Natural Language Processing (NLP) tasks. Inspired by the performance of recent studies utilizing deep learning in NLP, various RNN structures have been proposed.

© Springer International Publishing AG 2018
X. Huang et al. (Eds.): NLPCC 2017, LNAI 10619, pp. 42–50, 2018.
https://doi.org/10.1007/978-3-319-73618-1_4

RNN is now the most popular method in text or sentence classification [3] which is also a typical NLP task. While neural network based techniques have been extensively applied to most of the dialogue problems in recent years, they have not been fully explored for contextual understanding.

In this paper, we propose neural networks for classifying the intent of online service conversations. We present a hierarchical long short-term memory (HLSTM) network for dialogue intent classification, where a word-level LSTM is used to model a utterance and a sentence-level LSTM to model the contextual dependence between sentences. Further, we propose a memory module in this network to enhance the capability of context modeling. Results show these attempts improve the basic LSTM model.

2   Related Work

2.1   Dialogue Act Classification

Previous work in dialogue act classification mainly focused on domain-specific classification for goal-oriented dialogue systems [4] and researchers in linguistics, computational linguistics, and natural language processing had conducted these previous research. Those work has showed that the dialogue act recognition performance was dependent on the classification systems and the methods used.

Previous work on dialogue act recognition has mainly focused on supervised learning method. Almost all standard approaches to classification have been applied in DA classification, from Support Vector Machines (SVM) and Hidden Markov Models (HMM) [5] to Decision Trees (DT) [6], Bayesian Networks (BN) [7] and rule-based approaches [8].

The above studies do not consider context information from the whole session level. The main disadvantage of previous methods is their heavy dependency on the size of the training dataset for recognizing multiple contexts within the same user utterance and correctly identifying the user's intention in ambiguous expressions. Recently, approaches based on deep learning methods were used to build contextual information model in dialogue. Since a dialogue session is naturally a sequence-to-sequence process at the utterance level, recurrent neural network (RNN) is proposed to model the process [9] and deep RNN was used to classify dialogue acts [10].

2.2   Memory Network

The Memory network architecture, introduced by [11], consists of two main components:supporting memories and final answer prediction. It is trained end-to-end, and hence requires significantly less supervision during training, making it more generally applicable in realistic settings. Supporting memories are in turn comprised of a set of input and output memory representations with memory cells.

Memory networks can extend the state representation of RNN with an external memory, which can represent more information and offer a more flexible way for context modeling [12]. [13] showed a neural network with an explicit memory and a recurrent attention mechanism, in their language modeling tasks, it slightly outperforms tuned RNNs and LSTMs of comparable complexity. [14] introduced a dynamic memory network (DMN) to do NLP applications including sequence modeling, classification and question answering.

Classical neural network memory models such as associative memory networks aim to provide content-addressable memory, given a key vector to output a value vector and references therein.

3   Proposed Model

3.1   Overview

Recurrent Neural Networks (RNN) [15] are increasingly used to do classify task. For sequence modeling task such as intent classification, capturing long distance information is a key issue. Figure 1 illustrates a typical structure of an RNN, where x_t is the input at time step t and h_t is the hidden state. As can be seen, information from previous layers h_{t-1}, is contributed to the succeeding layer's computations that generate h_t.

$$h_t = f(W_x x_t + W_h h_{t-1} + b_n) \tag{1}$$

Theoretically, RNN is able to capture dependence of arbitrary length, it tends to suffer from the gradient vanishing and exploding problems which limit the length of reachable context. In addition, an additive function of the previous hidden layer and the current input is too simple to describe the complex interactions within a sequence.

We care about remembering some information that is crucial for the final result and it is important to have some information omitted during the operation of the network, as not everything affects positively the network performance. Considering the aforementioned problems with RNNs, we use Long Short Term Memory (LSTM), which is a variation of RNNs that is tuned to preserve long-distance dependencies as their default specificity. It adopted a gating mechanism. Another reason for using LSTM is that it uses a forget gate layer to distill trivial weights, which belong to unimportant words from the cell state. There are many variants of LSTM unit, here we adopt one widely used architecture where inputs are d dimensional vectors, i_t is the input gate, f_t is the forget gate, o_t is the output gate, c_t is the memory cell, h_t is the hidden state, t denotes time step and $\odot$ represents element-wise multiplication.

$$i_t = \sigma(W^{(i)} X_t + U^{(i)} h_{t-1} + b^{(i)}) \tag{2}$$

$$f_t = \sigma(W^{(f)} X_t + U^{(f)} h_{t-1} + b^{(f)}) \tag{3}$$

$$o_t = \sigma(W^{(o)} X_t + U^{(o)} h_{t-1} + b^{(o)}) \tag{4}$$

$$u_t = \tanh(W^{(u)} X_t + U^{(u)} h_{t-1} + b^{(u)}) \tag{5}$$

$$c_t = i_t \odot u_t + f_t \odot c_{t-1} \qquad (6)$$

$$h_t = o_t \odot \tanh(c_t) \qquad (7)$$

In LSTMs, the gates in each cell that decide dynamically which signals are allowed to pass through the whole chain. LSTMs are able to view information over multiple time scales due to the fact that gating variables are assigned different values for each vector element. Deep LSTM structure had been used to classifying dialogue acts [10].

3.2 Hierarchical LSTM

The basic LSTM model is used to encode the information from the input word sequence into a fixed-length vector representation. The dialogue is a hierarchical sequence of data: each sentence is a sequence of words, and each session is a list of sentences. To model the whole context, compared to the basic LSTM model, we introduce the power of context into a standard LSTM model and propose the Hierarchical LSTM (HLSTM) model. The initial of this model is to represent the diolague session more completely. Given a dialogue (n sentences) $d = [s_1, s_2, ..., s_n]$. We first use a LSTM (LSTM$_1$) to model all the sentences in each session independently. The hidden states of sentence s_i obtained at this step are used to generate a sentence vector v_i using another LSTM (LSTM$_2$) for each sentence s_i in the dialogue. These sentence vectors can be used as features for dialogue act analysis in next step.

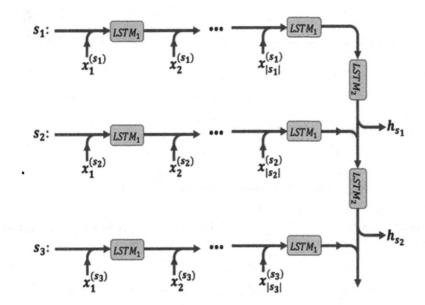

Fig. 1. The hierarchical LSTM model

The hierarchical LSTM model connect the relationship between sentences and context information more closely, so it can combinate the dialogue session context to make the sentence intent classification more effectively. The output sentence vector of LSTM$_2$ is two dimension Matrix, we do dropout operation at a certain ratio. After dropout, we reshape the Matrix based sentence number rows and there is a softmax layer over output vectors.

$$P_\theta(y_j|h_{s_i}) = softmax(h_{s_i}w + b) \tag{8}$$

$$Y_{pred} = argmaxP_\theta \tag{9}$$

The final prediction is the label with the highest probability P_θ.

3.3   Memory Augmented Hierarchial LSTM

To further enhance the modeling of complex dialogues context information, we add a memory component to the HLSTM model. This component is placed on the output of LSTM$_2$, which will memorize and provide useful context information when calculate the sentence vector. The saved vectors in memory will be updated after each read (Fig. 2).

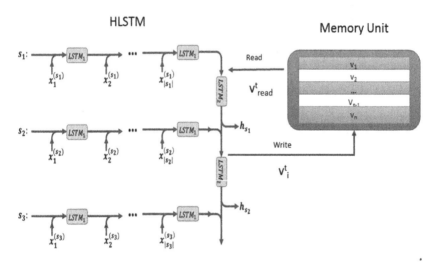

Fig. 2. The memory-augmented HLSTM.

We use $v = [v_1, v_2...v_n]$ to represent the vectors we set in the memory, the read and write procedure of the memory can be formulated:

$$a_i = softmax(h_{s_{t-1}}v_i^{t-1}) \tag{10}$$

where the softmax is normalized over all memory units.

$$v_{read}^t = \sum_{i=1}^{N} a_i v_i^{t-1} \tag{11}$$

We use $h_{s_{t-1}}$ to represent the prior hidden vector given by LSTM$_2$, s_t is sentence vector given by LSTM$_1$, the c_t and h_{s_t} can be updated by:

$$c_t, h_{s_t} = LSTM(c_{t-1}, h_{s_{t-1}}, s_t, v_{read}^t) \tag{12}$$

The write process of memory is formulated as:

$$v_i^t = tanh(W_v v_i^{t-1} + W_{s_t} s_t + b) \tag{13}$$

The weight of the memory units will be updated after the calculation of LSTM$_2$'s hidden vector.

3.4 Model Training

We formulate the DA classification as a mutiple classification task. The training criterion is a cross-entropy loss [16] for a session example, which is annotated by true lables predefined. To train our network, we use mini-batch stochastic gradient descent (SGD) with adaptive learning rate computed by Adadelta, which shows better performance and convergence property. We update model parameters after every mini batch, check validation accuracy and save model after every 10 batches. After each optimization epoch, we monitor the performance of the model. When the performance stops increasing for several iterations, we terminate the training and select the best-performing model.

4 Experiments

The domain of the dialogue dataset we use focus on the scenario of buy cellphone online. According to our daily experience of shopping online, we usually ask some questions about the cellphone we about to buy. For example, the property of cellphone is our most concern aspect. We need to know clearly about its price, performance, express delivery and other aspects we care about. To accurately identify the intent of every sentence, the related team in this e-commerce company had done some significant and effective work. They build a shopping online ontology system based on several different interactive scenario, including purchase, commodity, after sale and so on. Under each ontology, they also classified more detailed intent as the second level. According to the actual transaction scenario, every ontology has two or three level subordinate intent. The dialogue intent label mainly focus on the third level.

4.1 Data and Setup

We perform experiments on the real dialogue dataset provided by one e-commerce company. The dataset includes about 1504 real online dialogue annotated sessions from the cellphone domain, contains 24760 sentences and 108 labels. The average length of each session is 16. The dataset is randomly split into training set (80%), validation set (10%) and test set (10%) (Table 1).

Table 1. The size of used dataset

Sessions	Sentences	Labels	Avg number of sentences per session
1504	24760	108	16.4

We used this dataset to tune all hyperparameters of model. The sessions in the training set were preprocessed, so the LSTM parameters can be trained though a reasonable number of epochs. Each time we tuned one parameter value and measured the accuracy on the test set, if the accuracy on the development set did not change for 10 epochs, we stop training.

Our implementation of HLSTM is based on open source library Theano. We use word2vec vectors [17] which were trained on 400 billion words from Weibo corpus as word embedding. The vectors' dimensionality is 100 and those words not in the vectors are set randomly. We update model parameters after every mini-batch, we run 50 epochs in total, and the model with highest test accuracy is treated as the optimal model.

4.2   Results

We evaluated the performance of DA classification on the basic LSTM single sentence modle, HLSTM model and HLSTM+Mem model. Results are shown in Table 2. The average accuracy of the baseline LSTM model on this dataset is 74.5%, while the average accuracy of the HLSTM model is 76.3%. The HLSTM model has an improvement of 1.8% over the basic single sentence model.

Table 2. Accuracy of the three models.

Model	Accuracy (%)
Basic LSTM	74.5
HLSTM	76.3
HLSTM+Mem	76.7

Because the dialogue act of each sentence is labeled by predefined rules, which conducted by the specific programs. In the real data, there is a certain proportion of sentences can not match the existing labelling ontology system, these sentences were labeled by 'N/A'. To eliminate the impact of these sentences on contextual information of each session. We sort the labels based on their statistics and chose the top 20 label to do the classification task. Results are shown in Table 3. As we can see, the overall performance of 20 classification task was higher than before.

Compare the above two experimental results, we can find out the HLSTM model achieved better results in comparison to basic LSTM. After add the memory unit, performance had been further improved, the number of intent label which used to classify and the proportion of sentences under the same label are important factors which determine the model's performance.

Table 3. 20 classification accuracy.

Model (20 label)	Accuracy (%)
Basic LSTM	79.7
HLSTM	81.6
HLSTM+Mem	83.9

4.3 Error Analysis

Based on the experimental results and analysis of the existing data, we summarized some characteristics and difficulties in the data.

The data contains different kinds of emojis, URL addresses, photograph links and other non-literal symbols. All these symbols have its own unique meaning, they also represent a dialogue intent of user utterance. So identifying and translating these symbols is very important for us to get contextual information.

Since the data based on true conversation, the task of labelling spoken, conversational data is clearly complex. Some categories in the ontology system are difficult for humans and machines to separate. The existing labelling mechanism is not enough to deal with all possible situations.

5   Conclusion

In this study, we proposed deep hierarchical LSTM models for classifying dialogue intents in an e-commerce domain. The two models include an HLSTM and an memory-augmented HLSTM. Experiment results show that our proposed models efficiently utilize dialogue context information for intent classification. The adoption of the memory component can further improve the model's performance.

In the future, we would like to further improve our model and apply to other classification problems in the dialogue system.

References

1. Austin, J.L., Gu, Y.: How to Do Things With Words. Clarendon Press, Oxford (2012)
2. Liu, C., Xu, P., Sarikaya, R.: Deep Contextual Language Understanding in Spoken Dialogue Systems (2015)
3. Shen, L., Zhang, J.: Empirical Evaluation of RNN Architectures on Sentence Classification Task (2016)
4. Bub, T., Schwinn, J.: VERBMOBIL: The Evolution of a Complex Large Speech-to-Speech Translation System, vol. 4, pp. 2371–2374, October 1996
5. Surendran, D., Levow, G.A.: Dialog act tagging with support vector machines and hidden Markov models. In: Proceedings of INTERSPEECH/ICSLP, pp. 1–28 (2006)

6. Ali, S.A., Sulaiman, N., Mustapha, A., Mustapha, N.: Improving accuracy of intention-based response classification using decision tree. Inf. Technol. J. **8**(6), 923–928 (2009)
7. Keizer, S.: Dialogue Act Modelling Using Bayesian Networks (2001)
8. Niimi, Y., Oku, T., Nishimoto, T., Araki, M.: A rule based approach to extraction of topics and dialog acts in a spoken dialog system. In: EUROSPEECH 2001 Scandinavia, European Conference on Speech Communication and Technology, INTERSPEECH Event, Aalborg, Denmark, September, pp. 2185–2188 (2001)
9. Henderson, M., Thomson, B., Young, S.: Word-based dialog state tracking with recurrent neural networks. In: Meeting of the Special Interest Group on Discourse and Dialogue, pp. 292–299 (2014)
10. Khanpour, H., Guntakandla, N., Nielsen, R.: Dialogue act classification in domain-independent conversations using a deep recurrent neural network. In: COLING (2016)
11. Weston, J., Chopra, S., Bordes, A.: Memory networks. Eprint Arxiv (2014)
12. Peng, B., Yao, K., Jing, L., Wong, K.-F.: Recurrent neural networks with external memory for spoken language understanding. In: Li, J., Ji, H., Zhao, D., Feng, Y. (eds.) NLPCC 2015. LNCS (LNAI), vol. 9362, pp. 25–35. Springer, Cham (2015). https://doi.org/10.1007/978-3-319-25207-0_3
13. Sukhbaatar, S., Szlam, A., Weston, J., Fergus, R.: End-to-end memory networks. Comput. Sci. (2015)
14. Kumar, A., Irsoy, O., Ondruska, P., Iyyer, M., Bradbury, J., Gulrajani, I., Zhong, V., Paulus, R., Socher, R.: Ask me anything: dynamic memory networks for natural language processing. Comput. Sci. 1378–1387 (2015)
15. Mikolov, T., Karafiát, M., Burget, L., Cernocký, J., Khudanpur, S.: Recurrent neural network based language model. In: INTERSPEECH 2010, Conference of the International Speech Communication Association, Makuhari, Chiba, Japan, September, pp. 1045–1048 (2010)
16. Deng, L.Y.: The cross-entropy method: a unified approach to combinatorial optimization, Monte-Carlo simulation, and machine learning. Technometrics **48**(1), 147–148 (2006)
17. Mikolov, T., Chen, K., Corrado, G., Dean, J.: Efficient estimation of word representations in vector space. Comput. Sci. (2013)

An Ensemble Approach to Conversation Generation

Yimeng Zhuang[1]([✉]), Xianliang Wang[1], Han Zhang[2], Jinghui Xie[1],
and Xuan Zhu[1]

[1] Samsung R&D Institute (SRC-BJ), Beijing, China
ym.zhuang@samsung.com, xl0126.wang@samsung.com, jh.xie@samsung.com,
xuan.zhu@samsung.com
[2] School of Software and Microelectronics, Peking University, Beijing, China
zhanghanss@pku.edu.cn

Abstract. As an important step of human-computer interaction, conversion generation has attracted much attention and has a rising tendency in recent years. This paper gives a detailed description about an ensemble system for short text conversation generation. The proposed system consists of four subsystems, a quick response candidates selecting module, an information retrieval system, a generation-based system and an ensemble module. An advantage of this system is that multiple versions of generated responses are taken into account resulting a more reliable output. In the NLPCC 2017 shared task "Emotional Conversation Generation Challenge", the ensemble system generates appropriate responses for Chinese SNS posts and ranks at the top of participant list.

1 Introduction

Dialogue system plays an important role in human life, and its application field is very extensive, such as train routing [1], intelligent tutoring [2]. Contrary to domain-specific dialog system, open-domain tasks are more fascinating and challenging, since it requires the system to adapt to more diverse user needs. Therefore, traditional rule-based [3] or template-based [4] approaches may be not enough. Nowadays, two promising methods are retrieval-based system [5,6] and generation-based system [7,8].

Retrieval system deals with user's query by searching for a most related utterance in a database. This data-oriented method highly depends on the coverage of a database, if the ideal response does not exist in the database, the returned response may seriously degrade user experience. On the other hand, generation-based system always gives brand new response by synthesizing utterances. A weakness of generation-based system is that the generated response tends to be short, universal and meaningless, and sometimes has incorrect grammar. In [9], a novel ensemble of retrieval-based and generation-based dialog system is proposed and achieves good performance.

The objective of this paper is to give a detailed description about our submitted conversation generation system in the NLPCC 2017 shared task "Emotional

© Springer International Publishing AG 2018
X. Huang et al. (Eds.): NLPCC 2017, LNAI 10619, pp. 51–62, 2018.
https://doi.org/10.1007/978-3-319-73618-1_5

Conversation Generation Challenge". Our system ensembles the retrieval system's results and a seq2seq generation system's results, and achieves promising performance. This paper is just a system description for NLPCC 2017 shared task and does not propose any brand new techniques, most techniques used in this system are derived from [9,12,15], etc. Section 2 details on our system's overall architecture, as well as the works on data processing. Section 3 gives the evaluation results for the system, and various aspects of the system are analyzed by case study. Section 4 concludes the whole paper.

2   System Architecture

In the NLPCC Emotional Conversation Generation Challenge [10], the participants are asked to build an one-round dialogue system to generate response in natural language, given a Chinese post and the target user-specified emotion category. The possible emotions include anger, disgust, happiness, like, sadness and other.

2.1   Overview

Due to the posts are sentences collected from Weibo[1], in most cases the length of the post is not exceed 20 words, the task can be seem as a short text conversation problem enhanced by the user-specified emotion category requirement.

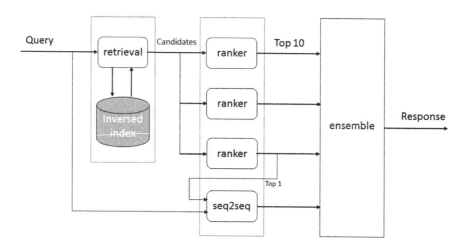

Fig. 1. The overall framework of the proposed method.

Figure 1 indicates the overall framework of our proposed short text conversation generation system. The system are mainly composed of four steps: a quick response candidates selecting module, an information retrieval system, a generation system and an ensemble module.

---

[1] http://weibo.com.

– At beginning, for a given query post q, there are tens of thousands possible post-response pairs $<p, r>$ in the database but only a few post-response pairs have related semantics with the query q. The computational complexity is unacceptable high, if we compare query q to each post-response pair $<p, r>$. The function of the quick response candidates selecting module is to retrieve coarse-grained response candidates efficiently, so as to perform the following complex semantic comparisons only within a small number of candidates.

– Multi-step learn-to-rank neural network models are used to rank the candidates by semantic similarity between the query q and candidate r. Only the top N candidates are remained as the candidate replies. Since there are multiple ranker models, we can obtain different versions of ranking results about the same candidate set that makes the following ensemble result more reliable.

– Seq2seq model based natural language generation is a hot academic topic in recent years, though this technique is still not mature enough as business applications. In our system, we try to implement a seq2seq system as an optional component, which takes the query q and a retrieved candidate response r as input and generates a new utterance as another response candidate.

– Given the response candidates produced by the retrieval and generation approaches, ensemble module re-ranks those responses and outputs the top 1 candidate as the final reply.

2.2   Data Preprocessing

The training data and the testing data provided by the NLPCC 2017 are the only data that we used in our system. The training data set consists of about 1.1 million SNS post-response pairs crawled from Weibo, we split it into three parts, a training set for tuning model, a development set for crossing validation, and a small development set for training ensemble module.

After an arbitrary split, an imperfect ranking model described in Sect. 2.5 can be trained on this data set, and the original training data will be evaluated using this model for data filter. The semantics similarity between each post-response pair is calculated through model, and filter out those post-response pairs that either get score lower than a threshold or the length of any sentence in the post-response pair is less than 3 words. The split result is depicted in Table 1.

For the test data, we just remove some insignificant words from the posts, such as '转帖' (repost), '网友制作' (net friend making), etc. As well as, convert full-width alphabet to half-width alphabet.

2.3   Candidates Selecting

The candidates selecting module is accomplished by an inverse indexing. Here, the data is split into six conversation classes according to the emotion label of the response r in conversation $<p, r>$. For each conversation class, a mapping

Table 1. Data statistics. Small dev set will be filtered manually as described in Sect. 2.7.

-	First split	Second split
Training set	1100000	259150
Dev set	10000	2049
Small dev set	9207	-

between words and conversations is built, that is, if a word w exists in either the post p or the response r of a conversation $c = <p, r>$ then word w and conversation c are connected. The mapping is many-to-many, which means different words may correspond to diverse number of conversations, and the number of connected conversations reflects the discrimination capacity of a word. Like the Inverse Document Frequency (IDF), the less the number is, the more unique a word is.

Candidates are selected as following. First, the words in a query post q are sorted in ascending order by the number of connected conversations in the target emotion corresponding inverse indexing. Second, the responses of each word's connected conversations are selected as candidates in the sorted word order until N_{inv} candidates are obtained. In this paper, $N_{inv} = 1000$ is adopted.

In practice, the above co-occurred keyword based approach sometimes may miss appropriate responses particularly when target response emotion is required. Therefore, to relieve this problem, a fixed number of special responses are selected artificially from each emotion class and added as candidates as a supplement. Those special responses have clear sentiment and are general to answer most queries.

2.4 Embedding Pre-training

Word embeddings are obtained by unsupervised learning algorithm for constructing vector representations for words. In a good embedding space, word embeddings map semantic meaning into a geometric space and the distance between any two vectors captures the semantic relationship between that two associated words.

In order to achieve a better training result, the lexicon is well-designed in the proposed system. Instead of using word-level embedding or character-level embedding simply, high-frequency words and Chinese characters together constitute the lexicon. In the system, two sets of lexicon are generated for training different ranking models, one contains 3532 entities formed by words appeared more than 2000 times in the training data and Chinese characters with frequency larger than 120 and all other characters are forced to be mapped to UNK. Another set of lexicon contains 10179 entities consisted of high-frequency words appeared more than 100 times in the training data and Chinese characters with frequency larger than 120 and an UNK label corresponding to other low-frequency characters. The motivation is straightforward, but in practice this is an effective measure for training better models.

Word embeddings are computed via word2vec toolkit [11], which applies a shadow neural network to discover the co-occurence statistics between words in a corpus of text. The detailed configurations and parameters are shown as follows,

./word2vec -train train.data -output skipgram.txt -size 100 -window 8 - sample 1e-4 -negative 5 -hs 1 -binary 0 -cbow 0 -iter 15 -min-count 1 -nthread 12

Here, the file 'train.data' is a preprocessed training corpus, in which words and characters have been mapped into lexicon entities as mentioned previously.

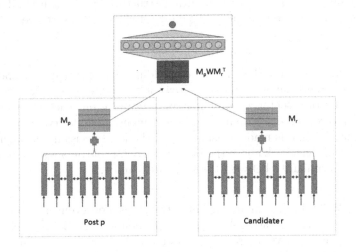

Fig. 2. The structure of the ranking model.

2.5   Learn-to-Rank Model

Model Structure. In this paper, learn-to-rank models are used to rank those candidates by the semantic similarity. The overall structure of our model for semantics ranking is depicted in Fig. 2.

The model consists of two part, one is the sentence embedding extractor corresponding to the green dashed rectangle part in the figure, another is the semantics similarity computing structure corresponding to the red dashed rectangle part in the figure.

In the sentence embedding extractor, we use same bidirectional LSTM and attention mechanism for the input query and response candidate, which means the parameters of this part model are shared. The input of this part model are the word embeddings, which are pre-trained as described in Sect. 2.4 and fixed in the training process. Here, a structured self-attentive sentence embedding [12] is adopted. In this approach, sentence's semantics is represented by a 2-dimensional matrix rather than the widely used vector representation, an advantage of this approach is that the embedding matrix attends on different parts of the sentence. Formally, the weight matrix A produced by the attention mechanism is,

$$A = softmax(W_{s2}tanh(W_{s1}H^T)) \qquad (1)$$

where H is the biLSTM hidden states, W_{s1} and W_{s2} are two trainable parameter matrices. The row number of W_{s2} reflects the number of different parts to be extracted from the input sentence. In this paper, the row number of W_{s2} is 20 and the dimension of hidden state vector is 300. Therefore, the resulting sentence embedding matrix is,

$$M = AH \qquad (2)$$

In the semantics similarity computing structure, a 2-dimensional bilinear model firstly makes the local decisions on different parts of sentence p and sentence r by

$$match(p, r) = M_p W M_r^T \qquad (3)$$

where M_q and M_r denote the sentence embedding matrix of p and r respectively, W is a parameter matrix. Since each row of the sentence embedding matrix attends a part of a sentence, after matrix multiplications each element of the resulting matrix $match(p, r)$ reflects a local semantics similarity.

The final decision is made considering all the local decisions through a fully connected neural network above the bilinear model. It outputs a score represents the semantics similarity between the sentence p and r.

Training. We train the ranking model in two steps. For a conversation $<p, r^+>$ in the training set, we firstly select 10 other responses from the N_{inv} candidates of the post p as negative samples by random. So there will be 10 times training cases than the original training set. Each training case consists of a post, a correct response and an incorrect response, which can be denote as a triple $<p, r^+, r^->$. In the first step, the parameters of a ranking model are tuned on those data. After having the first well-tuned ranking model, the candidates of each post in training set are ranked by this model, and re-sample 10 negative samples only from the top 100 candidates of each post. In the second step, another ranking model is trained from scratch on these new training cases. The reason is that randomly selected negative samples may have less semantics relation with the post while the correct response always has a strong semantics similarity with the post, which leads to an easy case for the ranking model to differentiate and makes limited contribution for model learning. By re-sampling negative samples, the ranking model can learning more information from confusion data.

In training process, for a particular mini-batch of training cases, the max-margin loss function is optimized,

$$loss = \frac{1}{N} \sum_{i=1}^{N} max(0, margin - (score_i^+ - score_i^-)) + P \qquad (4)$$

where N is the size of a mini-batch, $score_i^+$ and $scpre_i^-$ are represent the semantics similarities of the correct response and the negative sample respectively, $margin$ is a hyper-parameter. In our paper, $N = 256$ and $margin = 0.10$. P is the penalization term for self-attention mechanism proposed in [12].

In order to do an more elaborate re-sampling and data filter, we add a regular term on the loss function when training the first ranking model to make the scores concentrate around zero.

$$R = \frac{1}{N} \sum_{i=1}^{N} \beta \left| score_i^+ \right| \tag{5}$$

where β is a hyper-parameter.

2.6 Generation-Based Method

In recent years, there has been a rising tendency to the research of the generation-based method. The generation-based method usually builds an end-to end trainable system using neural networks and it can generate variable utterances.

The generation-based method used in the system is built on the *biseq2seq* utterance generator proposed in [9]. According to [9], it is the first work to combine retrieval and generative models for open-domain conversation. Two main differences between [9] and ours are that: (1) Diverse Beam Search algorithm is adopted in our generative model. (2) Instead of using retrieval-based dialogue system for post-reranking, generated and retrieval utterances are fed to a linear ensemble model in our system.

The overall architecture of the generation-based method is depicted in Fig. 3. Two contributive mechanisms are integrated in the architecture: (1) In the encoding phase, the retrieve model is ensembled to get retrieved query. And the embeddings of the original query and retrieved query are concatenated; (2) After the decoding, Diverse Beam Search algorithm [13] is adopted to decode a list of diverse outputs.

Given an user query sequential object $X = [x_1, ..., x_{Lx}]$, the vocabulary is embedded by looking up the pre-trained embedding table which is trained using word2vec tool [11]. Then an encoding GRU transforms the vector sequence into an encoded representation E_1. In the meanwhile, retrieval-based system is utilized to retrieve the analogous query sequential object $Y = [y_1, ..., y_{Ly}]$ from the data base. The retrieved query is also encoded into a retrieved representation E_2. The two vectors are concatenated, and an decoder GRU is modelled to generate the target sequence $O = [o_1, ..., o_{Lo}]$.

In the results, the dimension of the word embedding was 100. The utterances with out-of-vocabulary are removed in the training to get better models. Single-layer GRU was used and the dimension of the hidden layer was 220.

After the decoding, Diverse Beam Search algorithm is used to decode a list of diverse output by optimizing for a diversity-augmented objective [13]. It divides the beam budget into groups and enforcing diversity between groups of beams. The Diverse Beam Search is a doubly greedy approximate inference algorithm

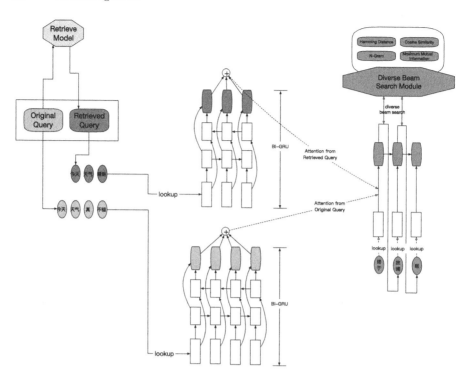

Fig. 3. The overall architecture of the generation-based method

which greedily optimizes the diversity-augmented model score along both time and groups. Results show the algorithm can produce more diverse reply than the traditional Beam Search Algorithm.

The ranker is then used to select the most matched reply from the diverse list. Hamming Distance, Cosine Similarity, N-Gram and Maximum Mutual Information are used in the ranker.

2.7   Ensemble

In the system, a set of 2-step ranking models, a set of 3-step ranking models, and a seq2seq model are trained, therefore, for a query there will be at most 60 unique responses generated from those six models. The small dev set mentioned in Sect. 2.2 is used for tuning the ensemble model. For each post in the small dev set, 20 to 60 unique responses are firstly generated by the six models, and then these responses are labeled as suitable or unsuitable manually. We finish this by crowd-sourcing, and 1922 posts are labeled in total. These labeled cases constitute the training set for ensemble model.

The ensemble model used in this system is a linear ranking model based on xgboost [14] with pairwise ranking objective using linear booster. The input features for ranking responses include five semantics similarity scores from the five ranking models, the emotion labels, the source (generated by which model), the length of sentence, a language model score, and the five simply matching features proposed in [15]. When training ensemble model using xgboost, each post's responses form a group and responses labeled as suitable rank in front of responses labeled as unsuitable. In runtime, given a query and its responses produced by ranking and seq2seq models, extract input features firstly, and then the ensemble model ranks these responses and returns only the top 1 response as the system's final result.

3 Experiments

3.1 Experimental Setup

The test data contains more than 5000 Weibo posts, participants are required to generate one response per emotion for each post. But due to it is a huge effort for manually assessing, only 200 posts are selected and checked by human. Which post will be selected is unknown for the participants for fair comparison. It is guaranteed that the selected data has clear emotion and is fluent.

The evaluation for submitted responses considers three metrics including content coherence, fluency and emotion consistency. If a response is appropriate in terms of both logic and content and is fluent in grammar, it can get 1 point and will check whether the emotion of this response is the same as the pre-specified emotion, if the emotion is consistent too, then the response will get another point. The final performance is evaluated by the sum and average score of all the test cases. Manual assessing is finished by voting among three evaluators.

Table 2. Overall score and the performance of each emotion class.

Submission/Emotion	0 point	1 point	2 points	Count	Total score	Average score
samsung_1_EGG	267	82	247	596	576	0.966
samsung_2_EGG	272	93	231	596	555	0.961
Like	50	16	67	133	150	1.128
Sad	56	15	48	119	111	0.933
Disgust	88	24	32	144	88	0.611
Angry	37	5	29	71	63	0.887
Happy	36	22	71	129	164	1.271

3.2 Results

Table 2 shows the final performance of our systems, samsung_1_EGG and samsung_2_EGG are our two submissions whose only difference is the lexicon, samsung_1_EGG has 3532 entities while samsung_2_EGG has 10179 entities as described in Sect. 2.4.

As shown in the table, the ensemble approach achieves fairly good performance. samsung_1_EGG is slightly better than samsung_2_EGG indicates that introducing appropriate amount of high-frequency words into lexicon may help improve the overall performance. The last five lines give the statistics of samsung_1_EGG on every emotion. It is clear that the performances on positive emotions are much better than negative emotions.

Table 3. An randomly selected example of generated responses.

Query	你要狠狠喜欢自己，才会有人很很喜欢你！
Emotion	Generated responses
Like	好吧，我也是，我喜欢你，我也喜欢你喜欢的人
	真的很喜欢你，我喜欢的人，我也会喜欢的，我也爱你
	其实我也会觉得很好的人，我也爱你，我也会喜欢的
	爱你的人都会爱我的，我也会爱你的。
	也会很好。但人也很好的，我也会喜欢的人。
Disgust	是啊，我也不知道你是男人，你也不喜欢你，我也不喜欢你
	其实我也不知道你是男人，你也不喜欢你的人。
	说得对！我也不喜欢你，你也不知道你的意思！
	没人说的，我也不知道你是男人，你也不知道你的意思。
	我们都是这样的，但我也不喜欢你的人。你也不知道你的意思。

Table 4. The effectiveness of ensemble module.

Query		最大的快乐莫过于平凡.			
Emotion	Labels	Candidate responses		Ranker	Ensemble
Sadness	Suitable	可是我不快乐		14	1
	Suitable	不快乐，我悲催		2	2
	Suitable	不快乐，日子太无聊了		5	3
	Suitable	原本快乐多过痛苦，现在痛苦多过欢乐		24	4
	Suitable	那就不快乐了，一起痛苦吧。		11	5
Happiness	Suitable	的确。最开心的是莫过于此		1	1
	Suitable	最开心的事莫过于此.		2	2
	Suitable	哈哈因为我们很平凡		28	3
	Suitable	最开心的莫过于你们说的满意俩字了！		12	4
	Unsuitable	高一是最开心的!		3	5

3.3 Case Study of the Seq2seq Results

Case study is an intuitive way to get a better understanding of the effectiveness of the proposed system. Table 3 illustrates the results of the seq2seq model through several examples. The examples show that the generated responses tend to be general, and include many repeated patterns. For example, in this table, "也喜欢" (also like) appears so many times, though it does not affect expression, it makes the sentence weird.

3.4   Analysis of the Ensemble Module

The ensemble module is one of the most important components in our system, Table 4 illustrates the changes after the introduction of ensemble module. From the table, we can clearly see that more appropriate responses are ranked higher by the ensemble module, while unsuitable responses are degraded. More specifically, the sentence "可是我不快乐" (But I'm not happy.) looks more like a response replied by human, because of the transitional word "可是" (but).

4   Conclusions

In this paper, we give a detailed description about an ensemble system for short text conversation generation. The system filters out most unrelated utterances by a quick candidates selecting module, and then several rankers take the candidates as input and output the top 10 best responses. The system also uses a generation-based method as a supplement to increase the diversity of response. At last, responses produced by rankers and generation are ranked by the ensemble module, and system returns final response. Although the experiments are conducted on an emotion conversation generation task, the results is fairly good. Besides, a few case studies are conducted in this paper.

References

1. Sikorski, T., Allen, J.F.: A task-based evaluation of the TRAINS-95 dialogue system. In: Maier, E., Mast, M., LuperFoy, S. (eds.) DPSLS 1996. LNCS, vol. 1236, pp. 207–220. Springer, Heidelberg (1997). https://doi.org/10.1007/3-540-63175-5_48
2. Litman, D.J., Silliman, S.: ITSPOKE: an intelligent tutoring spoken dialogue system. In: Demonstration Papers at HLT-NAACL 2004. Association for Computational Linguistics (2004)
3. Clancey, W.J.: Tutoring rules for guiding a case method dialogue. Int. J. Man Mach. Stud. **11**(1), 25–49 (1979)
4. Levin, E., Pieraccini, R., Eckert, W.: Using Markov decision process for learning dialogue strategies. In: Proceedings of the 1998 IEEE International Conference on Acoustics, Speech and Signal Processing, vol. 1. IEEE (1998)
5. Huang, C., et al.: LODESTAR: a mandarin spoken dialogue system for travel information retrieval. In: Sixth European Conference on Speech Communication and Technology (1999)
6. Eric, M., Manning, C.D.: Key-value retrieval networks for task-oriented dialogue. arXiv preprint arXiv:1705.05414 (2017)
7. Serban, I.V., et al.: Building end-to-end dialogue systems using generative hierarchical neural network models. In: AAAI (2016)
8. Li, J., et al.: Deep reinforcement learning for dialogue generation. arXiv preprint arXiv:1606.01541 (2016)
9. Song, Y., et al.: Two are better than one: an ensemble of retrieval-and generation-based dialog systems. arXiv preprint arXiv:1610.07149 (2016)
10. Zhou, H., Huang, M., Zhu, X., Liu, B.: Emotional chatting machine: emotional conversation generation with internal and external memory. arXiv:1704.01074 (2017)

11. http://code.google.com/p/word2vec/
12. Lin, Z., et al.: A structured self-attentive sentence embedding. arXiv preprint arXiv:1703.03130 (2017)
13. Vijayakumar, A.K., Cogswell, M., Selvaraju, R.R., et al.: Diverse Beam Search: Decoding Diverse Solutions from Neural Sequence Models (2016)
14. https://github.com/dmlc/xgboost
15. Ji, Z., Lu, Z., Li, H.: An information retrieval approach to short text conversation. arXiv:1408.6988 (2014)

First Place Solution for NLPCC 2017 Shared Task Social Media User Modeling

Lingfei Qian, Anran Wang, Yan Wang, Yuhang Huang,
Jian Wang[(✉)], and Hongfei Lin

Dalian University of Technology, Dalian 116023, Liaoning, China
wangjian@dlut.edu.cn

Abstract. With the popularity of mobile Internet, many social networking applications provide users with the function to share their personal information. It is of high commercial value to leverage the users' personal information such as tweets, preferences and locations for user profiling. There are two subtasks working in user profiling. Subtask one is to predict the Point-of-Interest (POI) a user will check in at. We adopted a combination of multiple approach results, including user-based collaborative filtering (CF) and social-based CF to predict the locations. Subtask two is to predict the users' gender. We divided the users into two groups, depending on whether the user has posted or not. We treat this task subtask as a classification task. Our results achieved first place in both subtasks.

Keywords: Location prediction · Gender prediction · User modeling
Collaborative filtering · Classification algorithm

1 Introduction

User modeling on social media is critical both in recommendation system and precise advertisement to get the target users [1]. With the rapid development of mobile devices and popularity of social applications, users also like to share their location by logging their point-of-interests (POIs) while posting both text and photos. The (POIs) previously logged are used to recommend and predict new places users may be interested in. Meanwhile, people are really active posting blogs on social media and user profiling is getting more attention as precise advertisement is now very essential. Therefore it's possible and necessary to extract information from social media to build user profiles.

This shared task contains two subtasks. Subtask one is check-in location prediction for users, which can be considered as a point-of-interest (POI) recommendation problem in location-based social networks (LBSNs). Subtask two is user's attributes prediction, which can be considered as a classification problem. We will introduce the two subtasks respectively in the following sections.

1.1 Subtask One

There are some common approaches for POI recommendation. The classic approach to the recommendation problem is collaborative filtering (CF) [2], which is comprised of

© Springer International Publishing AG 2018
X. Huang et al. (Eds.): NLPCC 2017, LNAI 10619, pp. 63–72, 2018.
https://doi.org/10.1007/978-3-319-73618-1_6

two main methods, memory-based CF and model-based CF [3]. The former includes user-based CF [4] and item-based CF [5] or both of them together [6], the latter is mainly based on Matrix Factorization (MF) [7].

Similar to traditional recommendation systems, users' location check-in data can be processed by CF approaches to calculate the similarities of one user to candidate POIs (items) in POI recommendation. Ye et al. [3] adopted user-based CF to obtain POI interest score for a user according the user's most similar neighbors. As for the MF method, by mapping users and POIs to a lower dimensionality joint latent factor space, the algorithm learns the interest score for POIs the users haven't visit [8].

On the other hand, POI recommendation has some unique characteristics compared to other recommendation systems. The first is a geographical clustering phenomenon [9]. Users prefer and are more likely to visit POIs nearby. Several studies show that the geographical information can contribute to the POI recommendation result. Ye et al. [3] quantified the geographical influence by applying a power-law distribution to model the relationship between distance and the possibility of user's visiting. Lian [10] proposed a method called GeoMF, which combines geographic information with MF by augmenting the activity areas matrix into users' latent feature matrix and influence area matrix into POIs'. The second characteristic is social relationship influence. Experiment result shows that adding friend-based CF [3, 11] or integrating social influence with probabilistic matrix factorization [11] can improve the POI recommendation quality.

For subtask one, we proposed a fusion method on memory-based CF methods and rules to realize users' POI prediction. There are three parts in our method, we will elaborate in the next section.

1.2 Subtask Two

There are many works in the area of gender prediction with textual information and other data from social media. Some work has been done to analysis the writing style and preference of words of authors to infer the latent attributes of authors such as gender [12]. Some work paid attention to the POS (part of speech) of words and select features to improve the accuracy of gender classification [13].

Other works take author's affective factors into consideration [14]. However, these works tend to focus on collections of lengthy text posts and extract features from text. There are also works that focus on short text, combining textual features with other information. Burger et al. [15] extract n-gram features from users' microblog, users' personal description and user names. They combined the improved balance Windows algorithm [16] to do the gender prediction. Some researchers have proved that social networks can also be united with logistic regression to improve the accuracy rate of user region [17]. Another related work has taken social tags of users into consideration to build user model and proves this is a helpful approach [18]. Ma et al. [19] have used factorization of matrix by analyzing locations and interaction records of users to classify the users.

For subtask two, we divided the users into two groups based on whether the user has post information or not. We propose different feature combinations for the two groups. These combinations will be described in the following sections.

2 Method

2.1 Subtask One

User-Based CF
The key to get the POI interest score by the user-based CF approach is to find users similar to the target user. In this subtask, we adopted check-in data to build the similarity between users. The user set denoted as $U = \{u_1, u_2, \cdots, u_M, \}$, and location (POI) set denoted as $L = \{l_1, l_2, \cdots, l_N, \}$. We also built user-location check-in matrix $C \in \mathcal{R}^{M \times N}$, and each element $c_{i,j} = 1$ or 0 depends on if the user i has visited location j. To simplify the calculations, we utilized matrix multiplication to get the user similarity matrix M_{user_user} after L2 normalized matrix C by each line.

$$M_{user\_user} = \text{Norm}(C) \cdot \text{Norm}(C)^T \tag{1}$$

where, $M_{user\_user} \in \mathcal{R}^{M \times M}$ and each element $a_{i,k}$ represents the similarity between user i and user k. With the user similarity, we can gain the score of new POIS for each user using another matrix multiplication as follow:

$$P^{user\_cf} = M_{user\_user} \cdot C - C \tag{2}$$

where, $P^{user\_cf} \in \mathcal{R}^{M \times N}$ and each element $p_{i,j}^{user\_cf}$ represents the score for user i and location j.

Social Friend (SF) Based CF
Similar to user-based CF, we gained user similarity matrix through social networks check-in data. The friend set denoted as $F = \{f_1, f_2, \cdots, f_Z, \}$ and the social network Matrix $S \in \mathcal{R}^{M \times F}$, where $S_{i,j} = 1$ or 0 depends on if the user i has followed user j. Same steps as user-based CF, finally we can get the score matrix $P^{sf\_cf} \in \mathcal{R}^{M \times N}$, where each element $p_{i,j}^{sf\_cf}$ represents the score for user i to location j.

Social Location (SL) Based CF
Using social networks to measure user similarity is helpful, but the problem is some people might be irrelevant when they just follow popular people like stars. Therefore, we adopted another way to get the similarity $b_{i,k}$ between users by their POI coincidence instead of friend coincidence. We adopted the Jaccard similarity coefficient to measure the similarity between a user and his friends as follows:

$$b_{i,k} = \frac{|L_i \cap L_k|}{|L_i \cup L_k|} \tag{3}$$

where L_i and L_k denote the location set for user i and user k who is watched by user i. And the score for SL-Based CF is:

$$p_{i,j}^{sl\_cf} = \sum_{k \in F_i} (b_{i,k} \cdot c_{k,j}) \tag{4}$$

where $c_{k,j}$ means if user k has gone to location j.

Social Location-Item (SLI) Based CF

In the consideration of the large set of POIs, item-based CFs have a great amount of computing cost. Therefore, we chose the POIs that occur in close friends' check-in history. The close friends for user i, are those who have $b_{i,k} > 0$, and their POI list will be the mini-candidate POIs for user i, except the POIs user i has already gone to. First we measure the new POI score by using item-based CF on the mini-candidate POI set as follows:

$$p_{i,j}^{item\_cf} = \frac{\sum_{q \in L_i} w_{j,q}}{\sum_{q \in L_i} c_{i,q}} \tag{5}$$

where $w_{j,q}$ denotes the similarity between location j and location q, which is also calculated in the Jaccard similarity coefficient as follow:

$$w_{j,q} = \frac{|U_j \cap U_q|}{|U_j \cup U_q|} \tag{6}$$

Then we combine the item-CF on the mini-candidate POI set with SL-CF as follows, to rearrange the candidate POIs after item-based CF by how many friends of user i have been to location j.

$$p_{i,j}^{sl\_item\_cf} = p_{i,j}^{item\_cf} \cdot p_{i,j}^{sl\_cf} \tag{7}$$

In the end, we integrated the ranking lists we discussed above. Let P denotes the results set $P = \{P^{user\_cf}, P^{sf\_cf}, P^{sli\_cf}\}$ and $S_{i,j}$ denotes the fused score for or user i to location j. We fused our results in linearly with hyper-parameter α for each result as follow:

$$S_{i,j} = \sum_{p \in P} \alpha_p \cdot p'_{i,j} \tag{8}$$

where α_p represent the hyper-parameter for result p and $\sum_{p \in P} \alpha_p = 1$, $p'_{i,j}$ is the normalized score for each ranking set. The normalization method is shown as follows:

$$p'_{i,j} = \frac{p_{i,j} - min}{max - min} \tag{9}$$

where max or min is the max or min in $\{p_{i,j}\}_{j \in L_i}$. We get the top 10 POIs for each user as our POI prediction results.

2.2   Subtask Two

Subtask two is user profiling, here we just have to do the gender prediction. Gender prediction can be seen as a binary classification. With data of users' tweets, tags, social connections, and names of the places users had visited, predicting users' gender.

In this paper, we screen the users with tweet information and divide these as a group. Then all of the users are treated as a training set to predict the gender of users without tweet information. As is shown in Fig. 1, we extract textual information from users' tweets and this textual information is trained to predict genders of users with tweet information. On the other hand, almost all of the users have data about their social connections, tags, and names of check-in locations. These features are utilized to predict the genders of users without tweet information.

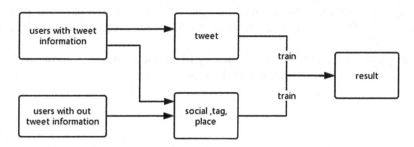

Fig. 1. The workflow for subtask two

Textual Information

In this paper, all the tweets of the same user were connected together to get the user's textual information. Then TF-IDF was used to generate a sparse matrix, for every word in each user's document, first to calculate the TF (Term Frequency), and then to get the IDF (Inverse Document Frequency) of the word. TF represents the frequency of the word in this exact user's document. IDF counts how many documents contain this word, and take the reciprocal of it. TF then is multiplied by IDF to get the vector of the user. We use different models for comparison in the further experiments.

Social, Tag, Place Information

Social and tag information is made up of a serious of numbers, but the size of the number is meaningless, so we treat numbers as characters. We cut the names of the place into words. Then we extract statistical features of users' social network and tags to get the vector representation respectively. As for location information, we treat them as textual information. We also try different models with these features.

3 Experiments and Results Analysis

3.1 Subtask One

Dataset and Evaluation

We used check-in data and social network data for subtask one. We split check in data to form an offline training set and test set by POI groups. For each POI, split out 0.75% of the check-in data (rounded up) to get the training set, so that all the POIs already appear in training set. Then we filter out the users who don't exist in the training set from the rest of check-in data to become test data. Our offline training set has 7,017,632 check-in actions with 276,442 users and 620,195 POIs, and 1,699,732 check-in actions with 119,765 users and 173,397 POIs for the test set. Also in the test set, we found that less than half the users have more than 10 POIs recorded and those users' check-in data makeup 89% of all the data gathered. We removed the users who have less than 10 POIs record to form another test set, which contains 58,058 users which can be considered active users.

The quality of subtask one is evaluated by $F1@K$ ($K = 10$), and we also list $P@K$ $R@K$ for analysis. The calculation formula is as follows:

$$P_i@K = \frac{|H_i|}{K} \tag{10}$$

$$R_i@K = \frac{|H_i|}{|V_i|} \tag{11}$$

$$F1_i@K = \frac{2 \times P_i@K \times R_i@K}{P_i@K + R_i@K} \tag{12}$$

$$P@K = \frac{1}{N} \sum_{i=1}^{N} P_i@K \tag{13}$$

$$R@K = \frac{1}{N} \sum_{i=1}^{N} R_i@K \tag{14}$$

$$F1@K = \frac{1}{N} \sum_{i=1}^{N} F1_i@K \tag{15}$$

where $|H_i|$ is the correctly predicted locations for user i's top K prediction, $|V_i|$ is the correct locations for user i. $P_i@K$, $R_i@K$, and $F1_i@K$ is the precision, recall and F1 for a user i. N is the user count.

Experimental Results and Analysis

We evaluate our method in both a normal test named test set 1, and a test with more than 10 POIs record for each user, named test set 2. First we evaluate every single method on both test sets and the results are shown in Table 1. Then we integrate the results by different combination and the results are shown in Table 2.

Table 1. The results of each CF method

Method	Test set 1			Test set 2		
	F1@K	P@K	R@K	F1@K	P@K	R@K
User-based CF	1.250%	1.683%	1.422%	1.661%	2.762%	1.291%
SF-based CF	1.999%	3.099%	1.932%	3.221%	5.682%	2.433%
SL-based CF	0.147%	0.188%	0.229%	0.163%	0.287%	0.126%
SLI-based CF	0.208%	0.267%	0.300%	0.243%	0.415%	0.188%

Table 2. The results of fusion work

Method	α_U	α_{SF}	α_{SLI}	Test set 1			Test set 2		
				F1@K	P@K	R@K	F1@K	P@K	R@K
U + SF	0.2	0.8	0	2.120%	3.227%	2.098%	3.334%	5.839%	2.528%
U + SLI	0.4	0	0.6	1.291%	1.727%	1.507%	1.695%	2.820%	1.317%
SF + SLI	0	0.7	0.3	2.018%	3.111%	1.965%	3.230%	5.684%	2.444%
U + SF + SLI	0.1	0.6	0.3	2.122%	3.232%	2.078%	3.348%	5.862%	2.539%

Based on the results in Table 1, we find that the SF-based CF has the best performance. This demonstrates that social network information is effective in POI recommendation compared to the normal user-based CF method. However, the performance of SL-based CF and its related methods are much worse than other CF methods. We believe the reason is that only 3.6% of friends in social networks have check-in data, this makes it hard to utilize users' check-in coincidence to measure user similarity. Also adding item-based CF and SL-based CF can achieve a slight improvement.

In the Table 2, we list out the fusion result and the best hyper-parameters. Based on the table, we find that fusion work did improve the final result especially for user-based CF and SF-based CF. We adopted the U + SLI method in the shared task, but the result shows SF-based CF is much more effective in this task. Also the α parameters indicate the significance of social network information.

3.2   Subtask Two

Dataset and Evaluation

In this task, there are several data sets given, including users' check-in information, users' tag information, user's social information, users' tweets and users' gender and their picture information. The check-in information includes POI, different categories of location, latitude, longitude, and names of the places. There are about 300,000 users in total, and about 75,000 users have tweet information. The quality of the User Profiling subtask is evaluated by accuracy, where δ is the indicator function where Label$_i$ and Predict$_i$ is the same.

$$\text{Accuracy} = \frac{1}{N} \sum_{i=1}^{N} \delta(\text{Label}_i, \text{Predict}_i) \tag{16}$$

Experimental Results and Analysis

Some results from the experiments which use Logistic Regression (LR [20]) to train different features are shown in Table 3. Different models were used to train the tweet features and the features combination of tag, place and social. The results are displayed in Table 4. We attempted on LR, NB (Naïve Bayes), RF (Radom Forest) [21], XGBoost (eXtreme Gradient Boosting) [22]. We used two LR model where the penalty item parameter penalty of LR1 is L1 normalization, penalty of LR2 is L2 normalization.

Table 3. The results of different features combination trained by LR

Feature combination	Accuracy
tweet	94.08%
tweet + place	93.45%
tweet + tag	93.97%
tweet + social	94.62%
tag	76.09%
place	73.27%
social	74.20%
tag + social + place	82.34%

Table 4. The performance of various models

Model	Accuracy (tweet)	Accuracy (tag + place + social)
LR1	93.07%	81.78%
NB	81.12%	70.89%
RF	80.24%	72.65%
XGBoost	94.16%	82.15%
LR2	94.08%	82.34%
LR1 + XGBoost + LR2	94.08%	82.54%

As we can see from the table, the place and tag information did not help to improve the performance, but social connection does improve the results. However place and tag are useful without tweet. Naïve Bayes did not perform well in this dataset, probably because the attributes are not totally independent of each other. Tree models were not suitable for the dataset, probably due to over fitting. We use simple voting to combine the results of LR1, LR2 and XGBoost. The voting algorithm doesn't work because the differences between these models are not large enough. We use tweet features for users who have posted tweets, and tag, place, social for users without tweets, and both of them are trained by LR2. The accuracy of offline tests was 85.25%, and the final result was 85.64%.

4 Conclusion and Future Work

In this paper, we elaborate our methods and ideas on user modeling shared tasks. For subtask one, we take it as a recommendation problem and adopted a memory-based collaborative filtering method. Our online submission results are based on user-based CF and SLI-based CF result. However, we found that SF-based CF is much more effective than SL-based CF in this subtask. We believe the reason for the undesirable performance for SL-based CF is due to the lack of check-in data for social networks. In the future, we are going to study how to utilize the geographical information and categories of locations in this subtask.

For subtask two, we treat the task as a classification problem. We focused more on data analysis and the combination of features. Our online submission divided the users into two groups and construct features respectively. However we found some features from other groups can also help to improve the result. In the future, ensemble learning should be investigated deeply. Also the information of categories for locations was not used in our method, this data could contribute to the results.

Acknowledgments. This research is supported by the National Key Research Development Program of China (No. 2016YFB1001103) and Natural Science Foundation of China (No. 61572098, 61572102).

References

1. Farseev, A., Nie, L., Akbari, M., et al.: Harvesting multiple sources for user profile learning: a big data study. In: Proceedings of the 5th ACM on International Conference on Multimedia Retrieval, pp. 235–242. ACM (2015)
2. Goldberg, D., Nichols, D., Oki, B.M., et al.: Using collaborative filtering to weave an information tapestry. Commun. ACM **35**, 61–70 (1992)
3. Ye, M., Yin, P., Lee, W.-C., et al.: Exploiting geographical influence for collaborative point-of-interest recommendation. In: Proceedings of the 34th International ACM SIGIR Conference on Research and Development in Information Retrieval, pp. 325–334. ACM (2011)
4. Breese, J.S., Heckerman, D., Kadie, C.: Empirical analysis of predictive algorithms for collaborative filtering. In: Proceedings of the Fourteenth Conference on Uncertainty in Artificial Intelligence, pp. 43–52. Morgan Kaufmann Publishers Inc. (1998)
5. Sarwar, B., Karypis, G., Konstan, J., et al.: Item-based collaborative filtering recommendation algorithms. In: Proceedings of the 10th International Conference on World Wide Web, pp. 285–295. ACM (2001)
6. Wang, J., De Vries, A.P., Reinders, M.J.: Unifying user-based and item-based collaborative filtering approaches by similarity fusion. In: Proceedings of the 29th Annual International ACM SIGIR Conference on Research and Development in Information Retrieval, pp. 501–508. ACM (2006)
7. Koren, Y., Bell, R., Volinsky, C.: Matrix factorization techniques for recommender systems. Computer **42**(8), 30–37 (2009)
8. Berjani, B., Strufe, T.: A recommendation system for spots in location-based online social networks. In: Proceedings of the 4th Workshop on Social Network Systems, p. 4. ACM (2011)

9. Cao, X., Cong, G., Jensen, C.S.: Mining significant semantic locations from GPS data. Proc. VLDB Endow. **3**, 1009–1020 (2010)

10. Lian, D., Zhao, C., Xie, X., et al.: GeoMF: joint geographical modeling and matrix factorization for point-of-interest recommendation. In: Proceedings of the 20th ACM SIGKDD International Conference on Knowledge Discovery and Data Mining, pp. 831–840. ACM (2014)

11. Ye, M., Yin, P., Lee, W.-C.: Location recommendation for location-based social networks. In: Proceedings of the 18th SIGSPATIAL International Conference on Advances in Geographic Information Systems, pp. 458–461. ACM (2010)

12. Schler, J., Koppel, M., Argamon, S., et al.: Effects of age and gender on blogging. In: AAAI Spring Symposium: Computational Approaches to Analyzing Weblogs, pp. 199–205 (2006)

13. Mukherjee, A., Liu, B.: Improving gender classification of blog authors. In: Proceedings of the 2010 Conference on Empirical Methods in Natural Language Processing, pp. 207–217. Association for Computational Linguistics (2010)

14. Rangel, F., Rosso, P.: On the impact of emotions on author profiling. Inf. Process. Manag. **52**, 73–92 (2016)

15. Burger, J.D., Henderson, J., Kim, G., et al.: Discriminating gender on Twitter. In: Proceedings of the Conference on Empirical Methods in Natural Language Processing, pp. 1301–1309. Association for Computational Linguistics (2011)

16. Littlestone, N.: Learning quickly when irrelevant attributes abound: a new linear-threshold algorithm. Mach. Learn. **2**, 285–318 (1988)

17. Rahimi, A., Vu, D., Cohn, T., et al.: Exploiting text and network context for geolocation of social media users. arXiv preprint arXiv:1506.04803 (2015)

18. Carmagnola, F., Cena, F., Cortassa, O., Gena, C., Torre, I.: Towards a tag-based user model: how can user model benefit from tags? In: Conati, C., McCoy, K., Paliouras, G. (eds.) UM 2007. LNCS (LNAI), vol. 4511, pp. 445–449. Springer, Heidelberg (2007). https://doi.org/10.1007/978-3-540-73078-1_62

19. Ma, H., Cao, H., Yang, Q., et al.: A habit mining approach for discovering similar mobile users. In: Proceedings of the 21st International Conference on World Wide Web, pp. 231–240. ACM (2012)

20. Kurt, I., Ture, M., Kurum, A.T.: Comparing performances of logistic regression, classification and regression tree, and neural networks for predicting coronary artery disease. Expert Syst. Appl. **34**, 366–374 (2008)

21. Breiman, L.: Random forests. Mach. Learn. **45**, 5–32 (2001)

22. Chen, T., Guestrin, C.: XGBoost: a scalable tree boosting system. In: Proceedings of the 22nd ACM SIGKDD International Conference on Knowledge Discovery and Data Mining, pp. 785–794. ACM (2016)

Knowledge Graph/IE/QA

Large-Scale Simple Question Generation
by Template-Based Seq2seq Learning

Tianyu Liu[✉], Bingzhen Wei, Baobao Chang, and Zhifang Sui

Key Laboratory of Computational Linguistics, Ministry of Education,
School of Electronics Engineering and Computer Science, Peking University,
No. 5 Yiheyuan Road, Haidian District, Beijing 100871, China
{tianyu0421,weibz,chbb,szf}@pku.edu.cn

Abstract. Numerous machine learning tasks achieved substantial advances with the help of large-scale supervised learning corpora over past decade. However, there's no large-scale question-answer corpora available for Chinese question answering over knowledge bases. In this paper, we present a 28M Chinese Q&A corpora based on the Chinese knowledge base provided by NLPCC2017 KBQA challenge. We propose a novel neural network architecture which combines template-based method and seq2seq learning to generate highly fluent and diverse questions. Both automatic and human evaluation results show that our model achieves outstanding performance (76.8 BLEU and 43.1 ROUGE). We also propose a new statistical metric called DIVERSE to measure the linguistic diversity of generated questions and prove that our model can generate much more diverse questions compared with other baselines.

Keywords: Question generation · Template-based seq2seq
Linguistic diversity

1 Introduction

Question Answering (QA) over knowledge bases (KBs) aims at providing accurate answers formulated in natural language, with factual retrieval and inference in the knowledge bases. One of the major obstacles for training QA systems is the lack of high quality labeled data. The performances of question answering over knowledge bases (KBQA) systems highly depend on the data scale and quality because answer selection in KBQA always involves complex inference over relevant relationships between entities in the knowledge graph, which demands large-scale dataset in the training stage. Furthermore, even more labeled question-answer pairs are required in neural network-based QA systems.

Automatic question generation (QG) [4,6,15] has become a popular task for solving the data insufficient problems in QA systems. Most KB-based question generation methods have focused on constructing questions by utilizing multiple related facts in the KB. However, the simpler question-answering that involves only one single fact, which is called *Simple Question Answering* [4], is still far

© Springer International Publishing AG 2018
X. Huang et al. (Eds.): NLPCC 2017, LNAI 10619, pp. 75–87, 2018.
https://doi.org/10.1007/978-3-319-73618-1_7

from solved. Besides, simple QA itself can cover a wide range of practical usage if the referring KB is well-organized. For instances, all of questions in the training set of NLPCC2017 KBQA challenge can be answered by simple QA reasoning. Hence, as shown in Fig. 1, we focus on generating simple questions which are only related to single facts in this paper.

Fact #1	全球通史			装帧			软装
Fact #2	商务星健身管理软件			经营范围			健身俱乐部管理软件
Fact #3	倭叉角羚			纲			哺乳纲
Fact #4	焖子			主要食材			地瓜淀粉 精瘦肉
Fact #5	真相			译者			陈睿 杨通

Fact	Gold	Pure Template	Seq2seq	Tseq2seq
#1	全球通史的装帧是什么样子的?	**全球通史这本书共多少页?**	全球通史的装帧是什么?	全球通史是怎样装帧的?
#2	商务星健身管理软件的经营范围是什么?	**商务星健身管理软件主要做什么生意?**	商务星健身管理软件的经营范围是什么?	商务星健身管理软件经营范围包括哪些?
#3	你知道倭叉角羚这种动物是什么纲的吗?	谁能告诉我倭叉角羚属于什么纲?	谁知道*倭叉角羚*是哪个纲的?	倭叉角羚属于什么纲?
#4	我想知道做焖子都需要什么食材?	焖子主要食材有什么?	*伙子*的主要食材是什么?	做焖子需要用什么材料?
#5	我想知道真相这本书是谁翻译的呀?	谁翻译了真相?	真相的译者是谁?	请问真相是谁翻译的?

Fig. 1. Simple questions generated by pure **Template-based Method**, vanilla **seq2seq** framework and **Template-based seq2seq** learning (Tseq2seq). Misleading questions generated by pure template-based method are marked in red. Questions that generates wrong subjects entities of the corresponding facts are marked in green. (Color figure online)

Previous rule-based approaches [5,13,14] mainly relied on hand-crafted rules and heuristics to synthesize artificial QA corpora. The performances of these approaches hinges critically on the well-designed templates or rules. Although template-based methods are capable of generating reasonable questions in most cases, the generated questions still suffer from lack of diversity and fluency due to the limits of pre-defined templates or rules. As shown in Fig. 1, the two red-marked questions generated by pure template-based method are misleading ones compared with the target gold questions.

Motivated by recent development of end-to-end neural generation models for machine translation [2,12], image captioning [7,10,17] and dialogue generation [16,18]. We propose a neural generation baseline based on Encoder-decoder architecture. Seq2seq learning with attention mechanism achieves competitive performances in QG. However, vanilla seq2seq model still suffers from generating irrelevant or improper topic entities. Improper topic entities can cause severe damage to the quality of generated questions because factual inference and retrieval over KB are based on the recognized topic words or phrases while answering the questions. As shown in Fig. 1, the topic words of the green-marked questions are generated improperly as ‘偃叉角羚’ and ‘仗子’ while the true topic words are ‘倭叉角羚’ and ‘焖子’.

In this paper, we propose the following three models for generating simple questions based on Chinese KB: (1) Pure template-based method which utilizes the templates extracted from the training set to generate new questions for corresponding facts in the testing set, (2) Vanilla seq2seq architecture for neural question generation, (3) An integration of pure template-based method and vanilla seq2seq structure — Template-based seq2seq learning for generating highly accurate and linguistically diverse questions. The main contributions of our work can be summarized as follows:

- We propose a new Template-based seq2seq neural question generation architecture to tackle the improper-topic-words problem in vanilla seq2seq generation as well as the lack of linguistic diversity and misleading generation problems in pure template-based method.
- Our proposed template-based seq2seq question generation achieve outstanding performance in both human (92.5% in accuracy) and automatic evaluation (76.8 BLEU and 43.1 ROUGE).
- We propose a new statistical metric based on the sentence similarity called **DIVERSE** to measure the linguistic diversity of generated questions and prove that template-based method can generate more diverse questions than vanilla seq2seq structure and pure template-based method.
- To the best of our knowledge, we first proposed a large-scale QA corpus (28M) for Chinese KBQA.

2 Task Definition

In this section, we describe the knowledge base used in this paper and the probabilistic framework for question generation.

2.1 Knowledge Bases

A knowledge base (KB) is a highly structured multi-relational database, which consists of entities and corresponding relationships. The relationships in the KBs are directed and always connect exactly two entities. For example, in Freebase [3], two entities *Barack Obama* and *Honolulu* are connected by the relation *place of birth* which represents the birthplace of Barack Obama is Honolulu. The two entities with a particular relationship that connects them consist a *factual triple* of the KB. The knowledge base we used in this paper is the Chinese knowledge base provided by the NLPCC2017 KBQA challenge[1]. Table 1 lists the number of entities, relations and facts in the NLPCC2017 Chinese Knowledge base.

[1] http://tcci.ccf.org.cn/conference/2017/cfp.php.

Table 1. Statistics of the NLPCC2017 Chinese knowledge base used in this paper. The two versions of **Freebase**, **FB2M** and **FB5M** are provided for comparison.

	FB2M	FB5M	NLPCC2017
Entities	2,150,604	4,904,397	6,502,738
Relationships	6,701	7,523	548,225
Facts	14,180,937	22,441,880	43,063,796

2.2   Generating Questions from Triples

We intend to generate questions from given factual triples. Given a single factual triple $F = (Subject, Relationship, Object)$, we aims to produce a question which is concerned with the subject and the relationship of the fact and can be properly answered by corresponding object. The question generation procedure can be modeled in a probabilistic framework:

$$P(Q|F) = \prod_{i=1}^{N} P(w_i|w_{<i}, F) \tag{1}$$

where $Q = (w_1, w_2, \cdots, w_N)$ represents the generated question which consists of tokens $w_1, w_2, \cdots, w_N$. In most cases, the last generated token w_N is '?'.

3   Pure Template-Based Method

Template-based method is an automatic question generation baseline which utilizes templates extracted from training set and then generates questions by filling the particular templates with certain topic entities. Given a question Q and its corresponding factual triple (T, R, O) in which T represents *topic entity*, P represents *relationship*, O represents *object*. As shown in Fig. 2, template-based question generation framework consists of two phases: **Template Collection** and **Selective Generation**.

In template collection phase, we extract question templates from training set and produce a template pool P for each relation. Firstly, a question template is produced by replacing the topic entity T in the question with a special token *(SUB)*, and then we regard the question template as an instance of the template pool for corresponding relationship R. As show in Fig. 2, each relationship R has a template pool which consists of one or more templates.

In selective generation phase, given a triple $H = (t, r, o)$ from KB and template pool P generated in template collection phase, we randomly select a template Q whose corresponding relationship is r from template pool P. Then, we replace the special token *(SUB)* in the template Q with topic entity t in triple H to get specific generated question.

Template-based method can generate understandable questions for most triples and achieve competitive performance in automatic and human evaluation. However, as described in Sect. 1 and Fig. 1, the questions generated by

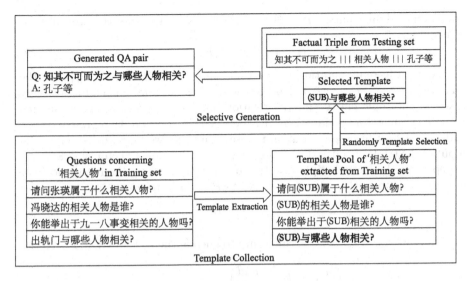

Fig. 2. Framework for template-based question generation method. The *topic entities* are marked in red while the *selected template* is marked in green. In **Template Collection** module, question templates are extracted from questions in the training set to form a *template pool* for certain relationship. In **Selective Generation** module, the randomly selected templates from *template pool* and the corresponding factual triples are used to generate target QA pairs. (Color figure online)

pure template-based method could be misleading or lack linguistic diversity due to the limits of templates.

4   Template-Based Neural Generation

In this section, we describe the architecture of proposed template-based neural generation by seq2seq learning. Seq2seq model is an effective structure in modeling sequence-to-sequence translation. Our templated-based seq2seq can be viewed as a translation from structured data (factual triples in the KB) to simple questions that can be answered by single triples. The model can be divided into triple encoder and template decoder. The procedure of template-based seq2seq question generation is introduced in the final part of this section.

4.1   Triple Encoder

Given a factual triple $F = (t, r, o)$, in which topic entity $t = \{T_1, T_2, \cdots, T_m\}$ and relationship $r = \{R_1, R_2, \cdots, R_n\}$, where m, n represent the length of topic entity t and relationship r respectively. One-hot vectors $T_i, R_j \in \mathbb{R}^{|V|}$, where $|V|$ is the size of vocabulary, represent one single token (including a Chinese character, a punctuation and a letter) respectively in the topic entity and corresponding relationship. We get the word embeddings t_i, r_j of T_i, R_j by looking up the embedding matrix $E \in \mathbb{R}^{|V| \times K}$, where K represents the size of word embedding:

$$t_i = E \cdot T_i; r_j = E \cdot R_j \tag{2}$$

We get the representation of the topic entity $\mathbf{t} = \{t_1, t_2, \cdots, t_m\}$ and the relationship $\mathbf{r} = \{r_1, r_2, \cdots, r_n\}$ by concatenating the word embedding of every token in the topic entity and the relationship. To represent the given factual triple F, we insert a special token SEP between the topic entity representation $\mathbf{t}$ and the relationship representation $\mathbf{r}$ to separate the two parts in the sequential input of the triple encoder. To be more specific, we exploit a vector $\mathbf{w} \in \mathbb{R}^{m+n+1}$ to represent the factual triple $F = (t, r, o)$ by concatenating the representations of the topic entity, the separation token SEP and the relationship:

$$\mathbf{w} = [t_1, t_2, \cdots, t_m, SEP, r_1, r_2, \cdots, r_n] \tag{3}$$

Then, we use the LSTM architecture to encode the factual triple F:

$$\begin{pmatrix} i_t \\ f_t \\ o_t \\ \hat{c}_t \end{pmatrix} = \begin{pmatrix} sigmoid \\ sigmoid \\ sigmoid \\ tanh \end{pmatrix} W_{4n,2n} \begin{pmatrix} w_t \\ h_{t-1} \end{pmatrix} \tag{4}$$

$$c_t = f_t \odot c_{t-1} + i_t \odot \hat{c}_t \tag{5}$$

$$h_t = o_t \odot tanh(c_t) \tag{6}$$

where h_t is the hidden state at time step t, n is the size of hidden layer, $i_t, f_t, o_t \in \mathbb{R}_n$ are input, forget, output gate of each LSTM unit respectively, $\hat{c}_t$ and c_t are proposed cell value and true cell state at time t, $W_{4n,2n}$ is the model parameter to be learned.

4.2   Template Decoder

To exploit the alignment information between factual triples and generated questions, we use LSTM architecture with attention mechanism as our neural generator. As defined in the Eq. 1, the generated token y_t at time t in the decoder is predicated based on all the previously generated tokens $y_{<t}$ before y_t and the hidden states $H = \{h_t\}_{t=1}^{L}$ of the triple encoder. To be more specific:

$$P(y_t|H, y_{<t}) = softmax(W_s \odot tanh(W_t[s_t, a_t])) \tag{7}$$

$$s_t = LSTM(y_{t-1}, s_{t-1}) \tag{8}$$

s_t is the t-th hidden state of the decoder calculated by the LSTM unit in which the computational details can be referred in Eqs. 4, 5 and 11. a_t is the attention vector which is represented by the weighted sum of encoder hidden states.

$$a_t = \sum_{i=1}^{L} \alpha_{t_i} h_i; \alpha_{t_i} = \frac{e^{g(s_t, h_i)}}{\sum_{j=1}^{N} e^{g(s_t, h_j)}} \tag{9}$$

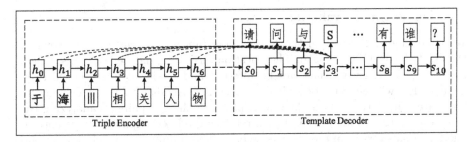

Fig. 3. An example for template-based seq2seq learning. Given an certain factual triple (t, r, o), the topic entity t (marked in red), *SEP* token ('|||') and corresponding relationship r are feed sequentially into the **Triple Encoder** as described in Sect. 4.1. Then the **Template Decoder** elaborated in Sect. 4.2 generates a question template in which topic entity is replaced by a specific token *SUB* (red-marked 'S'). Finally, the generated question template is transformed into the complete question by changing the *SUB* token into the topic entity t. (Color figure online)

where $g(s_t, h_i)$ is a relevant score between decoder hidden state s_t and encoder hidden state h_i. There are many different ways to calculate the relevant scores, in our paper, we use the following dot product to measure the similarity between $s_{t'}$ and h_i. W_s, W_t, W_p, W_q are all parameters that can be learnt in the model.

$$g(s_t, h_i) = tanh(W_p h_i) \odot tanh(W_q s_t) \tag{10}$$

4.3 Template-Based Seq2seq

As explained in Sect. 1, vanilla seq2seq baseline has a quite severe problem: improper topic words. To alleviate the improper-topic-words problem, we propose template-based seq2seq framework. As shown in Fig. 3, after feeding the triple representation **w** in Eq. 3 into the triple encoder, we intend to generate a *question template* for that triple rather than the complete question.

In the neural generated *question template*, the topic entity is replaced by a specific token *SUB*. To get the complete question, we change the *SUB* token back to the specific topic entity. In the training procedure, the topic entities of target gold questions are also replaced by *SUB*. We use cross-entropy loss function between the replaced target questions and generated questions while training.

5 Experiments

In this section, we first evaluate the correctness of generated questions in the three proposed models by human and automatic evaluation. After that, we prove that template-based seq2seq model can generate more diverse questions than the other two baselines by the **DIVERSE** metric defined in Sect. 5.4.

5.1   Dataset and Evaluation Metrics

We conduct experiments on the *Simple Question Answering* dataset provided by NLPCC KBQA Challenge. The question-answering dataset contains 24,479 questions with answers that can be inferred and retrieved from the NLPCC Chinese Knowledge Base described in Sect. 2.1. As shown in the Table 2, we integrated the corresponding factual triples into the QA pairs by analyzing the given questions and answers and then retrieving related triples by topic entities and target answers from the knowledge base. The training set, validation set and testing set contains 11687/2922/9870 QA pairs respectively.

We measure the performance of our models by both automatic and human evaluation. To evaluate the correctness of the generated questions, we use **BLEU** (BLEU-4), **ROUGE** (ROUGE-4 F measure) evaluation and human evaluation. For human evaluation, We randomly select 200 instances from the generated questions and manually determine whether a specific question is proper or not. The human evaluation results are the ratio of proper questions. To measure the diversity of generated question, we propose a **DIVERSE** evaluation (described in Sect. 5.4) which is based on the sentence similarities within a cluster of questions.

Table 2. An instance of (question, triple, answer) tuples used in the experiments.

Question	有人知道鸡黍之交的相关人物都有谁吗？
Factual Triple	鸡黍之交 ||| 相关人物 ||| 范式与张劭
Answer	范式与张劭

5.2   Experiment Setup

We use character-by-character input in the seq2seq learning, the triple inputs for the encoder and the question inputs for the decoder are all split into characters, including Chinese characters, letters and punctuations. All the word embeddings of these characters are initialized with the 400-dimensional vectors without pre-training. We build the vocabulary dictionary, which contains 3652 unique tokens, by including all the characters in the training set. Long Short Term Memory Unit (LSTM) [9] is chosen for our models and the hidden size of LSTM unit is set to 200. All the variables used in the network are initialized by Xavier initializer [8]. We use Adam optimizer [11] for optimization with a first momentum coefficient of 0.9 and a second momentum coefficient of 0.999. The initial learning rate is 5e−4 and the batch size in the training stage is 32 determined by a grid search over combinations of initial learning rate [1e−4, 5e−4, 1e−3, 5e−3] and batch sizes [16, 32, 64, 128]. We get the best configuration of parameters based on performance on the validation set, and only evaluate that specific configuration on the testing set. All the implementations of our models are based on the TensorFlow [1] framework.

5.3 Quality Analysis

In order to analyze the correctness and quality of generated questions by our models. We use both automatic and human evaluation to analyze the performance of proposed template-based neural generation model as well as template-based method and vanilla seq2seq generation model. Table 3 shows the performances of three models that we proposed. We have following observations:

(1) **Pure Template-Based Method** achieves competitive results in both automatic and human evaluation, especially in the BLEU metric. We assume the underlying reasons for this condition are the homogeneity between training and testing dataset and the limited size of testing set. The templates extracted from training set suit the factual triples in the testing set well because of similar sentence patterns in both training and testing set. Furthermore, the size of testing set are comparatively small so that the several extracted templates are able to cover most of questions in the testing set.

(2) **Vanilla Seq2seq** model achieves a little better performance in ROUGE metric than template-based method because of the strong ability of the encoder-decoder architecture in language generation. However, its results for both ROUGE and human evaluation can't rival those of template-based method because vanilla seq2seq generation might produce wrong topic entities, especially for long and complex entities, which greatly hurt the quality of generated questions.

(3) **Template-Based Seq2seq** model gets the best performance among all three proposed models. Template-based seq2seq model combines the advantages of template-based baseline and seq2seq learning. Compared with vanilla seq2seq model, template-based seq2seq model deal with the improper-topic-entity problem by incorporating template mechanism so that it outperforms the vanilla seq2seq model by approximately 5 ROUGE and 2 BLEU. Additionally, template-based model outperform the pure template-based method by 0.5 BLEU on the condition that training set and testing set are highly homogeneous.

Table 3. Automatic and human evaluation performance of proposed models.

Models	ROUGE	BLEU	Human
Template-based baseline	37.84	76.33	87.0
Seq2seq	38.41	74.86	83.5
Template-based seq2seq	**43.11**	**76.84**	**92.5**

5.4   Study on Diversity

In the question generation task, the capability of generating linguistically diverse questions is another key point apart from the semantic correctness of the questions. So we make a comparison over the linguistic diversity of all the generated questions among the three proposed models.

To measure the linguistic diversity of generated questions, we propose a new statistical metric called **DIVERSE** which is based on the TF-IDF similarities of n generated questions $Q = (q_1, q_2, \cdots, q_n)$ that share the same relationship in the factual triples $Fs = ([S_1, S_2, \cdots, S_n], R, [O_1, O_2, \cdots, O_n])$. We call these triples Fs *triple clusters*. The TF-IDF question similarity $Tfidf_{sim}$ is a statistical measurement base on the frequencies of words within the questions generated by the *triple clusters*. We use *gensim*[2] to calculate the TF-IDF similarities between questions. To determine the aggregated similarity among all the questions in the cluster, the DIVERSE metric is defined as the average TF-I DF similarity of all possible permutations in the *Cartesian Product* of (Q, Q):

$$\mathbf{DIVERSE} = \frac{1}{C_n^2} \sum_{i=1}^{n} \sum_{j=1}^{n} 1(i \neq j) \times Tfidf_{sim}(q_i, q_j) \tag{11}$$

where C_n^2 is a combination number, $1(x)$ is a conditional expression whose value is 1 if boolean expression x is True, otherwise 0. DIVERSE of certain question cluster generated by a particular *triple cluster* reflects the aggregated similarity of questions within that cluster. Since generated questions within the same cluster share the same relationship, we believe those clusters in which the aggregated sentence similarities are smaller are more linguistically diverse. In other words, **the smaller DIVERSE is, the more linguistically diverse the generated questions are.**

Table 4 shows the DIVERSE in different experimental configurations. To avoid the negative influence of relationships which are included only in one or two triples. We chose 505 relationships from the testing set which are included in more than two triples. The number of relationships which are included in exactly 3, 4, 5, 6 and more than 6 facts are 6/400/4/81 and 14 respectively. $N = [3, 4]$ means the DIVERSE of relationships which are included in 3 and 4 facts while $N = [5, \sim]$ means the DIVERSE of relationships which are included in more than

Table 4. Results of **DIVERSE** in different configurations. As explained in Sect. 5.4, the smaller DIVERSE is, the more linguistically diverse the generated questions are.

Models	N = [3,4]	N = [5,~]	Aggregate
Template-based baseline	12.30	9.33	11.97
Seq2seq	10.35	7.23	9.74
Template-based seq2seq	**4.98**	**3.63**	**4.65**

---

[2] http://radimrehurek.com/gensim/.

4 facts. As demonstrated in Table 4, we can see that template-based seq2seq have smallest DIVERSE in all configurations which means template-based neural generation model can create more diverse questions than the other two proposed models.

5.5 Proposed KBQA Corpus

To make full use of the proposed template-based neural generation model, we create a large-scale Chinese simple question-answering dataset[3]. Firstly, we retrieve all the triples whose relationships are contained in the training set of NLPCC2017 KBQA Challenge dataset and then generate raw questions according to corresponding triples under the best configuration of proposed model. After that, we utilize the following filtering approaches to reprocess the raw questions to get the filtered questions: (1) filtering out the questions which contain *UNK* token. (2) To make sure the neural generated questions are readable and understandable, we also filter questions which doesn't end with '?' or whose length is longer than 50 to avoid meaningless repetitive questions.

The details of the proposed corpus are listed in Table 5. From the table, we can find out that our dataset has much larger scale than the famous Simple-Question dataset [4]. We hope the given dataset might be useful while conducting further researches in the field of Chinese KBQA.

Table 5. Statistics of proposed QA corpus for Chinese KBQA. We compare our propose corpus with the famous SimpleQuestion [4] dataset.

	SimpleQuestion	Proposed corpus
Entities	131,684	5,997,954
Relationships	1,837	4,222
Questions	108,442	28,133,837

6 Conclusion

We propose a Template-based Seq2seq Neural Generation model for generating simple Chinese questions for question-answering over knowledge bases. The proposed template-based seq2seq model achieves outstanding performance in both human and automatic evaluations. Furthermore, we propose a new statistical metric **DIVERSE** to measure the linguistic diversity of the generated questions and prove that the template-based seq2seq model can also generate more diverse questions than vanilla seq2seq model and pure template-based method. We also utilize the template-based seq2seq model and several filtering approaches to create a large-scale dataset for Chinese KBQA.

---

[3] We will release the dataset in the future.

Acknowledgments. We thank the anonymous reviewers for their valuable comments. This work is supported by the National Key Basic Research Program of China (No. 2014CB340504) and the National Natural Science Foundation of China (No. 61375074, 61273318). The contact authors are Zhifang Sui and Baobao Chang.

References

1. Abadi, M., Agarwal, A., Barham, P., Brevdo, E., Chen, Z., Citro, C., Corrado, G., Davis, A., Dean, J., Devin, M., et al.: TensorFlow: large-scale machine learning on heterogeneous distributed systems (2016)
2. Bahdanau, D., Cho, K., Bengio, Y.: Neural machine translation by jointly learning to align and translate. arXiv preprint arXiv:1409.0473 (2014)
3. Bollacker, K.D., Evans, C., Paritosh, P., Sturge, T., Taylor, J.: Freebase: a collaboratively created graph database for structuring human knowledge, pp. 1247–1250 (2008)
4. Bordes, A., Usunier, N., Chopra, S., Weston, J.: Large-scale simple question answering with memory networks. arXiv preprint arXiv:1506.02075 (2015)
5. Bordes, A., Weston, J., Usunier, N.: Open question answering with weakly supervised embedding models. In: Calders, T., Esposito, F., Hüllermeier, E., Meo, R. (eds.) ECML PKDD 2014. LNCS (LNAI), vol. 8724, pp. 165–180. Springer, Heidelberg (2014). https://doi.org/10.1007/978-3-662-44848-9_11
6. Du, X., Shao, J., Cardie, C.: Learning to ask: neural question generation for reading comprehension. arXiv preprint arXiv:1705.00106 (2017)
7. Fang, H., Gupta, S., Iandola, F., Srivastava, R.K., Deng, L., Dollár, P., Gao, J., He, X., Mitchell, M., Platt, J.C., et al.: From captions to visual concepts and back. In: Proceedings of the IEEE Conference on Computer Vision and Pattern Recognition, pp. 1473–1482 (2015)
8. Glorot, X., Bengio, Y.: Understanding the difficulty of training deep feedforward neural networks. J. Mach. Learn. Res. 249–256 (2010)
9. Hochreiter, S., Schmidhuber, J.: Long short-term memory. Neural Comput. **9**(8), 1735 (1997)
10. Karpathy, A., Fei-Fei, L.: Deep visual-semantic alignments for generating image descriptions. In: Proceedings of the IEEE Conference on Computer Vision and Pattern Recognition, pp. 3128–3137 (2015)
11. Kingma, D.P., Ba, J.: Adam: a method for stochastic optimization. Comput. Sci. (2014)
12. Luong, M.-T., Sutskever, I., Le, Q.V., Vinyals, O., Zaremba, W.: Addressing the rare word problem in neural machine translation. arXiv preprint arXiv:1410.8206 (2014)
13. Mitkov, R., Ha, L.A.: Computer-aided generation of multiple-choice tests. In: Proceedings of the HLT-NAACL 2003 Workshop on Building Educational Applications Using Natural Language Processing, vol. 2, pp. 17–22. Association for Computational Linguistics (2003)
14. Rus, V., Wyse, B., Piwek, P., Lintean, M., Stoyanchev, S., Moldovan, C.: The first question generation shared task evaluation challenge. In: Proceedings of the 6th International Natural Language Generation Conference, pp. 251–257. Association for Computational Linguistics (2010)
15. Serban, I.V., García-Durán, A., Gulcehre, C., Ahn, S., Chandar, S., Courville, A., Bengio, Y.: Generating factoid questions with recurrent neural networks: the 30m factoid question-answer corpus. arXiv preprint arXiv:1603.06807 (2016)

16. Shang, L., Lu, Z., Li, H.: Neural responding machine for short-text conversation. arXiv preprint arXiv:1503.02364 (2015)
17. Vinyals, O., Toshev, A., Bengio, S., Erhan, D.: Show and tell: a neural image caption generator. In: Proceedings of the IEEE Conference on Computer Vision and Pattern Recognition, pp. 3156–3164 (2015)
18. Wen, T.-H., Gasic, M., Mrksic, N., Su, P.-H., Vandyke, D., Young, S.: Semantically conditioned LSTM-based natural language generation for spoken dialogue systems. arXiv preprint arXiv:1508.01745 (2015)

A Dual Attentive Neural Network Framework with Community Metadata for Answer Selection

Zhiqiang Liu[1,2(✉)], Mengzhang Li[2], Tianyu Bai[2], Rui Yan[1], and Yan Zhang[1]

[1] School of Electronics Engineering and Computer Science,
Peking University, Beijing, China
{lucien,ruiyan,zhyzhy001}@pku.edu.cn
[2] Academy for Advanced Interdisciplinary Studies, Peking University, Beijing, China
{mcmong,tybai}@pku.edu.cn

Abstract. Nowadays the community-based question answering (cQA) sites become popular Web service, which have accumulated millions of questions and their associated answers over time. Thus, the answer selection component plays an important role in a cQA system, which ranks the relevant answers to the given question. With the development of this area, problems of noise prevalence and data sparsity become more tough. In our paper, we consider the task of answer selection from two aspects including deep semantic matching and user community metadata representation. We propose a novel dual attentive neural network framework (DANN) to embed question topics and user network structures for answer selection. The representation of questions and answers are first learned by convolutional neural networks (CNNs). Then the DANN learns interactions of questions and answers, which is guided via user network structures and semantic matching of question topics with double attention. We evaluate the performance of our method on the well-known question answering site Stack exchange. The experiments show that our framework outperforms other state-of-the-art solutions to the problem.

1 Introduction

Community-based question answering (cQA) is an Internet-based web service which enables users to post their questions on a cQA website, which might be answered by other users later. Some cQA sites are popular such as Yahoo! Answers[1] and Quora[2], which have accumulated millions of questions and answers pairs over time [2]. However, there are some challenges needing to be overcome in cQA field. One is the problems of redundancy and noise prevalent which were usually ignored by previous research. The other is the bottleneck of data sparsity: previous research relies on the content similarity between questions and answers, therefore it suffers from the sparsity of cQA data.

Most of the existing works consider cQA problem as a text matching task. In recent years, many researchers have proposed various deep learning methods

---

[1] https://answers.yahoo.com.
[2] https://www.quora.com.

© Springer International Publishing AG 2018
X. Huang et al. (Eds.): NLPCC 2017, LNAI 10619, pp. 88–100, 2018.
https://doi.org/10.1007/978-3-319-73618-1_8

that automatically select answers. These methods usually learn representations of two pieces of texts using neural networks, e.g. convolutional neural networks (CNNs) [12] or recurrent neural networks (RNNs) [17]. Based on the representations, a function is given to calculate the matching score. Instead of learning a global representation of the texts, some researchers have proposed models that learn the interaction information of the representations and have achieved better results [5]. Although previous question answering methods have achieved promising performance, they mainly focus on the deep semantic matching models of the problem, which is not suitable for redundant and noisy text and ignores the importance of user community metadata in cQA sites.

On the other hand, with the prevalence of online social networks in cQA sites [2], some researchers adopt a random walk method to exploit the rich social information from heterogeneous social networks, aiming to solve the problem of sparsity in cQA tasks. They combine it with a deep recurrent neural network which excellently models the textual contents of questions and answers. However, this method is still complicated during integrating community network information and text information. Its effect is limited as a result that additional social network data is necessary in an effective way [20].

In this paper, we formulate the problem of community-based question answering from two aspects including deep semantic relevance of question-answer pairs with question topic attention and the user expertise authority with community metadata attention in order to solve the problems of the data sparsity and noise prevalent. The major contribution of this paper is listed below:

- Different from previous studies, we formulate the problem of answer selection from two aspects to solve the problems of the data sparsity and noise prevalent. That is, we learn the ranking function based on both the deep semantic matching and user community metadata in cQA sites.
- We propose a novel dual attentive neural network framework named as DANN, which yields better performance than other state-of-the-art methods. This framework can also be used in other tasks.

2   Related Work

2.1   Deep Semantic Matching

Recently, some works are proposed on applications of deep neural networks of cQA tasks, aiming to solve a general sentence matching problem. In detail, these methods usually learn representations of two pieces of texts using neural networks, e.g. convolutional neural networks (CNNs) or recurrent neural networks (RNNs). In [14], the authors calculate a similarity matrix for each pair of questions and answers to contain the lexical and sequential information and then use a deep convolutional neural network (CNN) to estimate the suitable answer probability. Different from the classical convolutional neural network used in [14], some researchers [12] introduce a dynamic convolutional neural network [8] to encode the sentences of questions and answers in semantic space and model their interactions with tensors on the top layer. Besides the CNNs, another kind of neural networks has been successfully applied in textual content analysis. In [9], recurrent neural network is employed to represent each sentence or document by a dense vector which is trained to predict words in the document and in [15], a multi-layer RNN is used to map the input sentence into a fixed dimensional vector.

2.2 Network Representation Learning

On the other hand, aiming to improve the quality of QA tasks, additional information is introduced by some methods. In [6], a recursive neural network with sentence dependency-tree is utilized for simulating question answering tasks. In [21], the authors propose a concept base of world knowledge of Wikipeida and then change these semantic relations to optimize the question retrieval task. Recently, network representation learning has been proposed as a critical technique for community network analysis tasks. For example, DeepWalk [11] performs random walks over networks to learn network embeddings. LINE [16] optimizes the joint and conditional probabilities of edges in large-scale networks to learn vertex representations. Node2vec [3] modifies the random walk strategy in DeepWalk into biased random walks to explore the network structure more efficiently.

With the prevalence of online social networks in cQA sites, some researchers adopt the Network Representation Learning (NRL) methods to exploit the rich social information from heterogeneous social networks to solve the sparsity problem in cQA tasks and combine it with a deep neural network. Some works are proposed on exploiting the social information for QA tasks. In [2], the authors develop a graph-regularized matrix completion algorithm for inferring the user model and thus improve the performance of expert finding in cQA systems. The cross-domain social information integration is considered in [7]. They represent a social network as a star-structured hybrid graph centered on a social domain and propose a hybrid random walk method which incorporates cross-domain social information to predict user-item links in a target domain. We think these methods does make sense.

2.3 Attention Mechanism

Attention-based deep learning systems are studied in NLP after its success in computer vision and speech recognition, and mainly rely on recurrent neural network for end-to-end encoder-decoder system for tasks such as machine translation [1] and text reconstruction [13]. In [18], they take the lead in exploring attention mechanism in CNN for NLP tasks and propose multi-level attention convolutional neural network for modeling sentence pairs. After that, some researchers adopt attention mechanism to measure the importance of each segment and combine the interactions to obtain fixed-length representations for questions and answers [19]. Similar to the spirit of these studies, we propose this dual attentive neural network framework with community metadata to solve answer selection in cQA sites.

3   Model

In this section, we introduce a dual attentive neural network model. Firstly, we consider the problem of community-based question answering as a high-quality answer selecting task, which is based on the question-answer pairs according to deep semantic relevance with the question topics and user community metadata. Then we implement this model and experiments on our dataset from a real world cQA site Stack exchange show that the model indeed achieves better performance than other cQA methods.

3.1   The Problem

Before presenting the problem, we first introduce some basic notions and terminologies. Since the questions and answers in cQA sites are sentences, which are the sequential data with variant length, we then encode their contents into fixed length feature vectors for abstractive representation. Different from [5], which use convolution to learn interaction directly, we split the process of representation learning and interaction learning. In our work, we use GoogleNews[3] corpus to pre-train representations.

3.2   User Community Metadata

An overview of the cQA heterogeneous network is illustrated in Fig. 1. The heterogeneous network is composed of three parts, i.e. **User** $U = \{u_1, u_2, ..., u_k\}$ consisting answerer and asker information such as user badges, user reputations, **Question** $Q = \{q_1, q_2, ..., q_n\}$ and **Answer** $A = \{a_1, a_2, ..., a_m\}$. Among them, the relationship between users can be either following relation or user badges relation.

In our work, we denote the user network by $G = (V, E)$, where the set of nodes is Users **U**, the set of edges is user relations including *Asker-Question, Answerer-Answer, Question-Answer and User-User* in cQA sites. We define that there is an edge between two users in G if there are more than λ common *badges* between them. Then our method learn network embeddings of users via *DeepWalk* [11]. In this way, user badges are contained at the users set as **community metadata** in the cQA system, which will guide deep semantic learning of question-answer pairs in DANN. It is also applicable to create user networks in other ways. In this paper, we aim to propose a framework, which make the most of user information to guide deep semantic learning with attention. The reason why we created the network in this way is the experiment's conclusion. In our opinion, users with similar badges have similar characteristics and can be referred in the selection of answers. An overview of the user network is illustrated in Fig. 2, where the value of λ is 2 in order to show it intuitively.

---

[3] https://code.google.com/archive/p/word2vec.

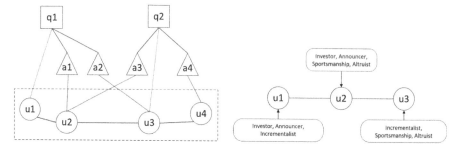

Fig. 1. The heterogeneous cQA network. The network contains three types of nodes: User, Question and Answer. And the edges include Asker-Question, Answerer-Answer, Question-Answer and User-User.

Fig. 2. The user network. The network nodes are users and the $\lambda = 2$ in this instance. (Red and blue fonts represent the common badges of the users.) (Color figure online)

3.3 Model Illustration

We now introduce our model that is based on CNN model. It consists of two weight-sharing CNNs, one to process question sentences and the other to process answer sentences. In the semantic matching process, we introduce the double attention mechanism including word level attention and sentence level attention (Fig. 3). We refer to this architecture as DANN. There are four layers in DANN: input layer with attention, convolution layer with attention, pooling layer and output layer.

Input Layer with Attention: The two input sentences have no more than n words, respectively in it. Each word is represented as a d-dimensional precomputed *word2vec* [9,10] embedding, $d = 300$. As a result, each sentence is represented as a feature map of dimension $d \times s$.

In detail, the DANN method employs an attention feature matrix $A^{(1)}$ to influence convolution as the first attention. Attention features are intended to weight those units of s^q more highly in convolution that are relevant to a unit of s^a, and weight those units of s^a more highly in convolution that are relevant to a unit of s^q. In addition, they are relevant to the topics of question. Each column is the representation of a word. We first describe the attention feature matrix $A^{(1)}$ informally. $A^{(1)}$ is generated by matching words of the question representation feature map with words of the answer representation feature map such that the attention values of row i in $A^{(1)}$ denote the attention distribution of the i-th word of s^q with respect to s^a, and the attention values of column j in $A^{(1)}$ denote the attention distribution of the j-th word of s^a with respect to s^q. $A^{(1)}$ can be viewed as a new feature map of s^q in row direction because each row is a new feature vector of a word in s^q. Thus, it is reasonable to combine this new feature map with the representation of feature maps and use both as input to the convolution operation. We achieve this by transforming $A^{(1)}$ into the two matrices that have the same format as the representation of feature

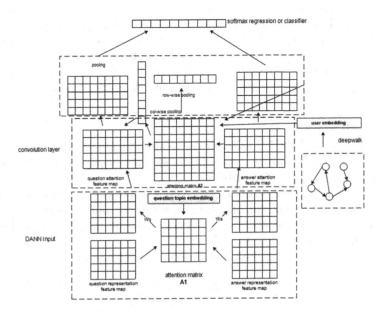

Fig. 3. The structure of DANN framework.

maps in Fig. 3. As a result, the new input of convolution has two feature maps for each sentence. Our motivation is that the attention feature map will guide the convolution to learn sentence representations with question topics.

More formally, let $q = \{e_i^q | i \in [1, s_q]\}$ and $a = \{e_i^a | i \in [1, s_a]\}$ be the representation feature map of question sentences and answer sentences. And let $t = \{e_i^t | i \in [1, s_t]\}$ be the embeddings of question topics. Then we define the attention matrix $A^{(1)} \in R^{s \times s}$ as follows:

$$A_{i,j}^{(1)} = kernel(e_i^q, e_i^a, e_i^t) \tag{1}$$

The function kernel can be defined:

$$max\{\frac{1}{1 + |e_i^q - e_j^a|}, \frac{1}{1 + |e_i^q - e_i^t|}, \frac{1}{1 + |e_j^a - e_i^t|}\} \tag{2}$$

where $|\cdot|$ is distance function. This kernel function can measure the matching scores in the words level of questions and answers based on the topics of the questions. As a result, given attention matrix $\mathbf{A}^{(1)}$, we generate the attention feature map E for s_i as follows:

$$E^q = W^q \cdot A^T \tag{3}$$

$$E^a = W^a \cdot A \tag{4}$$

The weight matrices $W^q \in R^{d \times s}$, $W^a \in R^{d \times s}$ are parameters of the model to be learned in training.

Convolution Layer with Attention: Let $\{e_1, e_2, ..., e_s\}$ be the words of a sentence and $c_i \in R^{w \cdot d_0}$, $0 < i < s + w$, the concatenated embeddings of $e_{i-w+1}, e_{i-w}, ..., e_i$ where embeddings for e_i (where $i < 1$ and $i > s$), are set to zero. We then generate the representation $h_i \in R^{d_1}$ for the phrase $e_{i-w+1}, e_{i-w}, ..., e_i$ using the convolution weights $\mathbf{W} \in R^{d_1 \times w d_0}$ as follows:

$$h_i = tanh(\mathbf{W} \cdot c_i + b) \tag{5}$$

where $b \in R^{d_1}$ is the bias. We use wide convolution by applying the convolution weights W to words e_i (where $i < 1$ and $i > s$). This ensures that each word v_i can be detected by all weights in W.

The second level attention of DANN computes attention weights on the output of convolution with the aim of re-weighting this convolution output. In addition, we define asker embedding as u^q and answerer embedding as u^a, which are learnt via the user network in Fig. 2.

Let A be the attention matrix and α is defined as follows, where $f(a, b) = a^T b$:

$$\alpha_i^q = \frac{exp(f(A[i, :], u^q))}{\sum_k exp(f(A[k, :], u^q))} \tag{6}$$

$$\alpha_j^a = \frac{exp(f(A[:, j], u^a))}{\sum_k exp(f(A[:, k], u^a))} \tag{7}$$

Attention Pooling Layer: The pooling layer, including min pooling, max pooling and average pooling, is commonly used to extract robust features from convolution. In this paper, we use attention pooling. According to α^q and α^a, we can obtain attention pooling result R, which will be the representation of question-answer pairs. In detail, R is defined as follows:

$$r_i^q = \sum_{k=i:i+w} \alpha_k^q \cdot h_k^q (i = 1, ..., s_q) \tag{8}$$

$$r_j^a = \sum_{k=j:j+w} \alpha_k^a \cdot h_k^a (j = 1, ..., s_a) \tag{9}$$

$$R = [r_{avg}^q, r_{avg}^a] \tag{10}$$

Output Layer: The last layer is an output layer, chosen according to the task; e.g., for binary classification tasks, this layer is logistic regression (see Fig. 3). The simplest way to train the model is to use a Softmax classifier with cross entropy as the loss function.

$$score(q, a) = softmax(W^T \cdot R + b) \tag{11}$$

3.4   Attention Calculation

In our model, two distinctive attentive methods are introduced. Question topic embedding attention matrix $A^{(1)}$ and user embedding attention matrix $A^{(2)}$. In actual Q&A forum such as Stack Overflow and Quora, many segments are redundant. Then refine the essence and discard the waste. By introducing prevalent attention mechanism at neural network, we aim to calculate the importance of each text segment. The numerical value of attention model is trained together with the whole neural network. Five kinds of information are computed the attention, including segment representation, word representation of pairwise question and answer as interaction with other segment, question topic and user community metadata, and what's more, we introduced the network representation by *DeepWalk*. Basically, the second-level attention α_j^q and α_j^a of each segment in a question or answer is calculated as Formulas 6 and 7. We aim to propose this dual attentive framework and you can define other styles using different additional information based on our framework.

4   Experiment

4.1   Dataset

We evaluate DANN on Stack exchange dataset. This dataset consists of real data from the community-created Stack Exchange forums. The whole dataset consists and over 133 question answering forums and the Stack Overflow is the most popular forum among them. In our experiment, we choose two forums history data to validate our framework against some baselines. The themes of these two forums are "English", "Academia" and the "English" forum is a smaller dataset and the "Academia" forum is a larger dataset. We present the detail of these two forums data in Table 1. There are three parts: user, question and answer. Given a question from a certain topic, the participant systems rank the comments according to their relevance associated with the question. Each answer has its own score and is labeled with one of two labels "Good" or "Not good". Table 1 demonstrates statistics of the datasets.

Table 1. Statistics of the stack exchange dataset

Forums	English	Academia
Question	5000	12052
Answer	13461	31046
User	6472	5875
Avg len of ques.	65.87	84.33
Avg len of ans.	255.54	326.75

As we can see, questions in two forums received distinct proportion of answers, and the average length of questions and answers vary from each other, which can demonstrate the versatility of our model. In addition, we choose CQADupstack[4] [4] scripts to process these datasets. We then split the datasets into training set, validation set and testing set without overlapping in our experiments. We fix the validation set as 10% of the total data to tune the hyper parameters and the size of testing set is 30%.

4.2 Baselines

We compare our model with other methods of answer selection in cQA sites. For example *AvgWord* method utilizes average word embedding to achieve text vectors for every question and answer. Then they are predicted by some method such as random forest and svm. It is reasonable that DANN is more useful than those traditional methods for its network representation and the attention mechanism. We divide our model into two related methods DANN with and without the attention mechanism. Then they are compared with other baseline methods.

- **AvgWord + Random Forest:** This method first achieves the sum of every text word embeddings and divide number of words. The results can be considered as representation of sentences. Then some regression methods are utilized such as random forests and svm to compare related sentence representations of questions and answers.
- **BOW:** Bag-of-words (BOW) is a classical representation for natural language processing tasks. In our experiments, we represent the questions and answers by BOW feature vectors and then calculate the relevant score to rank the candidate answers for each question.
- **BM25:** Okapi BM25 (BM stands for Best Matching) is a ranking function used by search engines to rank matching documents according to their relevance to a given search query.
- **CNTN** [12]: This method introduces a convolutional neural tensor network to integrate sentence modeling and semantic matching information, which can hardly be captured by convolutional and pooling layers.
- **LSTM + Multi-Layer-Perceptron:** It learns the sentence pairs embedding via LSTM and use MLP predict the matching score of question-answer pairs.
- **AI-CNN** [19]: This model distinguishes different text segments differently and designs an attentive interactive neural network (AI-NN) to focus on those text segments useful to answer selection. The representations of questions and answers are first learned by convolutional neural networks (CNNs). No user network structure is considered.

4.3 Evaluation Criteria

Two ranking metrics are used for evaluation, mean reciprocal rank (MRR) and mean average precision (MAP). The definitions are given below and we utilize them as evaluation metrics.

---

[4] http://nlp.cis.unimelb.edu.au/resources/CQAdupstack/.

$$MRR = \frac{1}{|Q|} \sum_{i=1}^{|Q|} \frac{1}{rank_i} \tag{12}$$

$|Q|$ denotes the total number of questions in the evaluation set. $rank_i$ denotes the position of the first correct answer in the generated answer set C_i for the ith question Q_i. If C_i doesn't overlap with the golden answers A_i for Q_i, $\frac{1}{rank_i}$ is set to 0.

$$MAP = \frac{1}{|Q|} \sum_{i=1}^{|Q|} AveP(C_i, A_i) \tag{13}$$

$AveP(C_i, A_i) = \frac{\sum_{k=1}^{n} (P(k) \cdot rel(k))}{min(m,n)}$ denotes the average precision. k is the rank in the sequence of retrieved answer sentences. m is the number of correct answer sentences. n is the number of retrieved answer sentences. If $min(m, n)$ is 0, $AveP(C, A)$ is set to 0. $P(k)$ is the precision at cut-off k in the list. $rel(k)$ is an indictor function equaling 1 if the item at rank k is an answer sentence, and 0 otherwise.

4.4   Experimental Settings

The questions and answers in English are tokenized and lemmatized using NLTK[5]. In addition, we do some pre-processing. We remove stop words, delete identical questions and put the question titles and bodies into one single text string. The GoogleNews corpus is utilized to pre-train word embeddings in out experiment. Adagrad is used to update parameters. During the model training, we try to compare our model by varying value of window size and parameter λ in Fig. 4. Finally, we observe that our method achieves the best performance when the value of window size is set to 4 and the value of parameter λ is set to 10. The dimension of question topics, words and user embeddings is 300 and initial learning rate is 0.01. The details are known in Table 2.

Table 2. Experiment parameters setting

Papameters	Value
λ	10
Learning rate	0.01
Window size	4
Batch size	64
Vector dimension	300
User embedding method	Deepwalk
Word2vec	GoogleNews

---

[5] http://www.nltk.org.

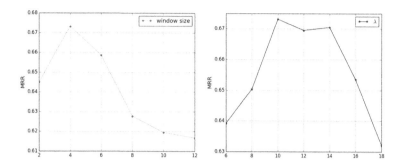

Fig. 4. Effect of parameter window size, λ on MRR using the English cQA forum.

Table 3. Experiment results on English forum

Method	MAP	MRR
AvgWord + RF	0.4812	0.5240
BOW	0.5157	0.5361
BM25	0.5676	0.5742
LSTM + MLP	0.5907	0.6163
CNTN [12]	0.6369	0.6403
AI-CNN [19]	0.6425	0.6591
DANN(w/o attention)	0.6322	0.6584
DANN	**0.6557**	**0.6732**

Table 4. Experiment results on Academia forum

Method	MAP	MRR
AvgWord + RF	0.5106	0.5311
BOW	0.5425	0.5507
BM25	0.5899	0.6102
LSTM + MLP	0.6692	0.6920
CNTN [12]	0.7411	0.7667
AI-CNN [19]	0.7795	0.7931
DANN(w/o attention)	0.7524	0.7652
DANN	**0.7856**	**0.8095**

4.5   Experimental Results

Tables 3 and 4 present the results of our model and the baseline methods. The experiments show that our framework can outperform other state-of-the-art solutions to the problem. We can see that DANN outperforms DANN(w/o attention), demonstrating that the multi-level attention is helpful for answer selection in cQA cites. And the CNTN and AI-CNN model behave better than other baselines. Compared with these method, our model can obtain best result. Particularly, the model in the larger Academia forum dataset can shows a greater advantage than other baselines because fewer users and more edges can learning effective embeddings in user network.

5   Conclusion and Future Work

In this paper, we construct a novel dual attentive neural network framework (DANN) to achieve answer selection in the cQA field. The DANN with community metadata learns network structures of users and uses it to guide interaction learning of texts by the attention mechanism which can avoid redundant and noisy text. This double attention mechanism measure segments to select answers. The extensive experiments demonstrate that our method can achieve better performance than several state-of-the-art solutions to the problem. In the future, we will explore the following directions:

- We will extend this model to other fields such as question retrieval, expert finding in cQA sites.
- It is of interest to explore other QA or user additional information and such data can be used to enhance the performance.

Acknowledgment. This work is supported by NSFC under Grant No. 61532001 and No. 61370054. We thank the three anonymous reviewers for their valuable comments.

References

1. Bahdanau, D., Cho, K., Bengio, Y.: Neural machine translation by jointly learning to align and translate. arXiv preprint arXiv:1409.0473 (2014)
2. Fang, H., Wu, F., Zhao, Z., Duan, X., Zhuang, Y., Ester, M.: Community-based question answering via heterogeneous social network learning. In: Thirtieth AAAI Conference on Artificial Intelligence (2016)
3. Grover, A., Leskovec, J.: Node2vec: scalable feature learning for networks. In: Proceedings of the 22nd ACM SIGKDD International Conference on Knowledge Discovery and Data Mining, pp. 855–864. ACM (2016)
4. Hoogeveen, D., Verspoor, K.M., Baldwin, T.: CQADupStack: a benchmark data set for community question-answering research. In: Proceedings of the 20th Australasian Document Computing Symposium, p. 3. ACM (2015)
5. Hu, B., Lu, Z., Li, H., Chen, Q.: Convolutional neural network architectures for matching natural language sentences. In: Advances in Neural Information Processing Systems, pp. 2042–2050 (2014)
6. Iyyer, M., Boyd-Graber, J.L., Claudino, L.M.B., Socher, R., Daumé III, H.: A neural network for factoid question answering over paragraphs. In: EMNLP, pp. 633–644 (2014)
7. Jiang, M., Cui, P., Chen, X., Wang, F., Zhu, W., Yang, S.: Social recommendation with cross-domain transferable knowledge. IEEE Trans. Knowl. Data Eng. **27**(11), 3084–3097 (2015)
8. Kalchbrenner, N., Grefenstette, E., Blunsom, P.: A convolutional neural network for modelling sentences. arXiv preprint arXiv:1404.2188 (2014)
9. Le, Q., Mikolov, T.: Distributed representations of sentences and documents. In: Proceedings of the 31st International Conference on Machine Learning (ICML 2014), pp. 1188–1196 (2014)
10. Mikolov, T., Sutskever, I., Chen, K., Corrado, G.S., Dean, J.: Distributed representations of words and phrases and their compositionality. In: Advances in Neural Information Processing Systems, pp. 3111–3119 (2013)
11. Perozzi, B., Al-Rfou, R., Skiena, S.: DeepWalk: online learning of social representations. In: Proceedings of the 20th ACM SIGKDD International Conference on Knowledge Discovery and Data Mining, pp. 701–710. ACM (2014)
12. Qiu, X., Huang, X.: Convolutional neural tensor network architecture for community-based question answering. In: IJCAI, pp. 1305–1311 (2015)
13. Rush, A.M., Chopra, S., Weston, J.: A neural attention model for abstractive sentence summarization. arXiv preprint arXiv:1509.00685 (2015)

14. Shen, Y., Rong, W., Sun, Z., Ouyang, Y., Xiong, Z.: Question/answer matching for CQA system via combining lexical and sequential information. In: AAAI, pp. 275–281 (2015)
15. Sutskever, I., Vinyals, O., Le, Q.V.: Sequence to sequence learning with neural networks. In: Advances in Neural Information Processing Systems, pp. 3104–3112 (2014)
16. Tang, J., Qu, M., Wang, M., Zhang, M., Yan, J., Mei, Q.: LINE: large-scale information network embedding. In: Proceedings of the 24th International Conference on World Wide Web, pp. 1067–1077. International World Wide Web Conferences Steering Committee (2015)
17. Wang, D., Nyberg, E.: A long short-term memory model for answer sentence selection in question answering. In: ACL, vol. 2, pp. 707–712 (2015)
18. Yin, W., Schütze, H., Xiang, B., Zhou, B.: ABCNN: attention-based convolutional neural network for modeling sentence pairs. arXiv preprint arXiv:1512.05193 (2015)
19. Zhang, X., Li, S., Sha, L., Wang, H.: Attentive interactive neural networks for answer selection in community question answering. In: Thirty-First AAAI Conference on Artificial Intelligence (2017)
20. Zhao, Z., Lu, H., Zheng, V.W., Cai, D., He, X., Zhuang, Y.: Community-based question answering via asymmetric multi-faceted ranking network learning. In: AAAI, pp. 3532–3539 (2017)
21. Zhou, G., Liu, Y., Liu, F., Zeng, D., Zhao, J.: Improving question retrieval in community question answering using world knowledge. In: IJCAI, vol. 13, pp. 2239–2245 (2013)

Geography Gaokao-Oriented Knowledge Acquisition for Comparative Sentences Based on Logic Programming

Xuelian Li[1,2], Qian Liu[3], Man Zhu[3], Feifei Xu[2], Yunxiu Yu[1,2], Shang Zhang[1,2], Zhaoxi Ni[1,2], and Zhiqiang Gao[1,2(✉)]

[1] Key Lab of Computer Network and Information Integration (Southeast University), Ministry of Education, Nanjing, China
[2] School of Computer Science and Engineering, Southeast University, Nanjing, China
{lixuelian,zqgao}@seu.edu.cn
[3] School of Computer Science and Technology, Nanjing University of Posts and Telecommunications, Nanjing, China
{qianliu,mzhu}@njupt.edu.cn

Abstract. Multiple-choice questions of comparing one entity with another in a university's entrance examination like Gaokao in China are very common but require high knowledge skill. As a preliminary attempt to address this problem, we build a geography Gaokao-oriented knowledge acquisition system for comparative sentences based on logic programming to help solve real geography examinations. Our work consists of two consecutive tasks: identify comparative sentences from geographical texts and extract comparative elements from the identified comparative sentences. Specifically, for the former task, logic programming is employed to filter out non-comparative sentences, and for the latter task, the information of dependency grammar and heuristic position is adopted to represent the relations among comparative elements. The experimental results show that our system achieves outstanding performance for practical use.

Keywords: Knowledge acquisition · Comparative sentences
Logic programming · Answer set programming

1 Introduction

The grand challenge of an AI robot, to pass entrance examinations at different levels of education has been approached. Much research has been devoted to AI robots on the education, such as the NII's Todai Robot Project [1] and the Allen Institute for Artificial Intelligence's Project Aristo [2]. Recently, China shared a similar motivation with them and has launched a similar project that would enable the computer to "learn" from textbooks and Web resources, and then pass the National Higher Education Entrance Examination (commonly known as Gaokao). This project is dedicated to four out of nine subjects in Gaokao, namely,

© Springer International Publishing AG 2018
X. Huang et al. (Eds.): NLPCC 2017, LNAI 10619, pp. 101–113, 2018.
https://doi.org/10.1007/978-3-319-73618-1_9

Chinese, mathematics, geography and history. Cheng et al. [3] develop a three-stage approach including retrieving, ranking, and filtering concept and quote pages to automatically answer multiple-choice questions of history in Gaokao, which is a general solution to the question. Because of the diversity of questions in Gaokao, for example, some questions required to be more profound understanding and more fine-grained analysis, their approach may be not suitable for such questions. Therefore, answering complex multiple-choice questions of comparing one entity with another in Gaokao such as in Fig. 1 requires specialized knowledge and is still far from being solved.

The 30th Summer Olympic Games are to be held in London, the United Kingdom from July 27 to August 12, 2012. Please read Figure and answer Q1.

Q1: In July and August, _____ in London than in Beijing.

A. the temperature is higher and covers a wider daily range   B. it is less windy but more foggy and rainy

C. the sun rises later, days get shorter but nights longer   D. the noontime altitude of the sun is smaller

---

Fig. 1. A multiple-choice item on the geographical subtest of the 2012 Gaokao held in Beijing, consisting of a stem and four possible options.

As a preliminary attempt to deal with this problem, we aim at building a geography Gaokao-oriented knowledge acquisition system for comparative sentences to solve real geography examinations. This problem consists of two challenging tasks. The former refers to a sentence classification problem while the latter refers to an information extraction problem.

Task 1. Identify candidate comparative sentences from a given collection of geographical texts like textbooks, reference books and relevant geographical web pages and then filter out non-comparative sentences.

Task 2. Extract comparative elements from the identified comparative sentences. For example, the sentence "伦敦的气温比北京高。(The temperature in London is higher than that in Beijing.)" is a comparative sentence, the word "伦敦 (London)" is the subject entity (SE), the word "北京 (Beijing)" is the object entity (OE), the word "气温 (temperature)" is the comparative aspect (CA), and the word "高 (higher)" is the comparative result (CR).

In recent years, the aforementioned tasks have been studied extensively. There are two main approaches: *machine learning approach* and *rule-based approach*. Some existing work [4] has shown that the rule-based approach is more appropriate because of the structural uniqueness of comparative sentences. The key idea of the rule-based approach is that it can describe the explicit domain information of comparative elements in a declarative way. Due to the fact that Logic Programming can offer detail-giving, natural-language explanations for its answers, it is more suitable for answering comparative questions in geographical domain. Specially, the non-monotonicity and scalability of answer set programming (ASP) - a variant of Logic Programming, provide an intuitively appealing way to address these issues.

For the first task, we present an approach that integrates ASP and keyword-based method to implement comparative sentence identification by constructing a linguistic-based comparative keyword lexicon which takes into account the comparative keyword collocation principles.

For the second task, we propose to employ ASP to implement comparative element extraction by adopting dependency grammar and heuristic position to represent the relations among comparative elements.

Moreover, we manually construct a geographical dataset of comparative sentences to answer multiple-choice questions of comparing one entity with another. It achieves good results on a set of real multiple-choice questions collected from recent geography examinations. Also, this dataset, which covers more comparative relations of physical and human geographical topics, has been combined with linked data for the geographical domain, such as Clinga[1], GeoNames[2] and GeoLink[3] to help realize real artificial intellegence, enabling the computer to pass the geography exams in Gaokao.

2   Related Work

Linguistic researchers have studied the syntax and semantics of comparative constructs from the beginning of modern Chinese linguistic research [5,6]. However, our focus is mainly on computational methods.

The most related works are comparative opinion mining [4,7]. There are two main approaches: *machine learning approach* and *rule-based approach*. The former is mainly based on some of the most popular approaches such as conditional random fields (CRF) [8,9] and support vector machine (SVM) [10], while the latter is mainly based on the combination between machine learning methods and rules [11–13].

Wang et al. [9,10] build a SVM model for comparative sentence extraction and use CRF for comparative element extraction. Jindal and Liu [11,12] apply Class Sequential Rules (CSR) and Label Sequential Rules (LSR) to extract comparative sentences and relations from English text documents. Varathan [4] gives a good survey of existing methods of comparative opinion mining. And it is shown that the pattern-based approach or rule-based approach are suitable for comparative opinion mining because comparative sentences follow a specific pattern or rule. In this paper, we show that our method obtains a better performance than these approaches for our tasks in geographical domain.

Our work is also related to information retrieval. Specifically, the most relevant work is by Cheng et al. [3] on multiple-choice questions in Gaokao. They propose a three-stage framework for answering multiple-choice questions in history tests. As their method is based on a set of Wikipedia pages, it is a general solution to the problem, thereby, it is not suitable for some questions required to be

---

[1] http://w3id.org/clinga.

[2] http://www.geonames.org/ontology.

[3] http://www.geolink.org.

more profound understanding and more fine-grained analysis, such as questions about comparative sentence identification and comparative element extraction.

3   System Architecture

Answer Set Programming originates from non-monotonic logic and logic programming. It is a logic programming paradigm based on the answer set semantics [14], which offers an elegant declarative semantics to the negation as failure operator in Prolog. An ASP program consists of *rules* of the form:

$$l_0 :\text{-} l_1, \ldots, l_m, \text{ not } l_{m+1}, \ldots, \text{ not } l_n.$$

where each l_i for $i \in [0..n]$ is a literal of some signature, i.e., expressions of the form $p(t)$ or $\neg p(t)$ where p is a predicate and t is a term, and *not* is called *negation as failure* or *default negation*. A rule without body is called a *fact*.

An ASP based system architecture of knowledge acquisition for comparative sentences consists of the following steps:

(1) Extract relevant parts of the knowledge base and represent the POS tags of words and collocation relations with comparative keywords as ASP facts;
(2) Extract relevant parts from comparative sentences and represent the POS tags, dependency relations of words and heuristic position relations with comparative keywords as ASP facts;
(3) Identify non-comparative sentence filtering rules and comparative element extraction rules, respectively, and represent them by ASP rules;
(4) Compute the answer set of the logic program resulted from the first and the third steps to perform the first task, and then from the second and the third steps to perform the second task using an ASP solver like clingo[4]. Finally the non-comparative sentences and comparative elements are extracted respectively from the answer set.

We now give an introduction on dependency grammar as it is useful to our proposed approach. Dependency grammar is adopted to describe the syntactic structure of a sentence by using a dependency tree to establish dependency relation between sentence components. The dependency relations among comparative elements contain *SBV* (subject-verb), *ATT* (attribute), *ADV* (adverbial), *POB* (preposition-object), *COO* (coordinate), *RAD* (right adjunct) and *HED* (head). Since we need part-of-speech (POS) tags throughout the paper, let us show the important POS tags of Language Technology Platform (LTP)[5]. n: general noun, nd: direction noun, nh: person name, ni: organization name, nl: location noun, ns: geographical name, nz: other proper noun, a: adjective, d: adverb, p: preposition, u: auxiliary, v: verb, c: conjunction, r: pronoun.

---

[4] https://potassco.org/.
[5] http://www.ltp-cloud.com/demo/.

4   Identifying Comparative Sentences from Geographical Texts

In this section, we first introduce how to use keyword-based method to identify all candidate comparative sentences and then discuss in detail how to filter out non-comparative sentences using ASP.

4.1   Identifying Candidate Comparative Sentences

According to the category of comparative questions in geographical tests, comparative sentences can be divided into two broad comparative types: gradable comparison such as "伦敦的气温比北京高。" and superlative comparison such as "中国是世界最大的稻米生产国。".

As comparative keywords are an important symbol for comparative sentences, both the keyword-based method [13] and CSR-based method [11] use them to identify comparative sentences but show a relatively low precision. This is mainly because lexicon can not perfectly express the meaning or structure of the Chinese comparative sentences. Furthermore, some complicated comparative sentences tend to be more flexible in forms, comparative keywords need to pair with the words such as predicate verb, adjective and preposition to identify comparative sentences. Therefore, this paper makes some improvement and proposes an approach combining ASP with keyword-based method to recognize comparative sentences. Firstly, our strategy is to manually construct a linguistic-based comparative keyword lexicon containing a total of 202 common comparative keywords and their synonyms. The comparative keyword lexicon (CK) consists of a gradable keyword lexicon (CK_1) and a superlative keyword lexicon (CK_2). Subsequently, the lexicon CK is used for scanning the geographical corpus to identify all candidate comparative sentences S. Once the candidate comparative sentences are recognized, the next step is to filter out non-comparative ones using ASP.

4.2   Filtering Out Non-comparative Sentences

To efficiently filter out these non-comparative sentences T from the identified candidate comparative sentences S, the collocation relations between pairs of words can be manually constructed, and the information about the POS tag of every word in S can be directly captured by LTP. We first represent them as ASP facts such as the form $keyword$ (CK) representing that CK is a comparative keyword. Subsequently, the rules of filtering out non-comparative sentences are denoted by ASP rules.

For example, one filter-out rule of non-gradable comparisons could be "*if a word W has the direct collocation relation in the sentence T with CK_1, such as "于", a preposition after W, and there is no reason to believe that W is an adjective, then the sentence T is a non-gradable comparison*", which can be formulated by the following rule r_1:

non-gradableComparison (T):- collocation (lb, W, CK_1, T), keyword (CK_1), pos
$$(CK_1, p), \text{ not pos } (W, a).$$

where *not* is used to exclude the fact that the POS of W is an adjective, *collocation* (lb, W, CK_1, T) means W and CK_1 have a collocation relation *lb*, namely, W is located on the left of CK_1 in the sentence T. For example, given the sentence, "南京位于江苏。(Nanjing is located in Jiangsu.)", we can identify it as a non-comparative sentence using this rule.

To filter out non-comparative sentences, we group collocation rules (or filtering rules) $\mathcal{R}$ into two types ($\mathcal{R}^1$, $\mathcal{R}^2$) based on the classification of comparative sentences as below:

Type 1 rules ($\mathcal{R}^1$): Using gradable comparative keywords to filter out non-gradable comparisons (based on some collocation relations between them), e.g., rule r_1. A gradable keyword lexicon CK_1 including the gradable comparative keywords and their POS tags is given a priori.

Type 2 rules ($\mathcal{R}^2$): Using superlative comparative keywords to filter out non-superlative comparisons (based on some collocation rules between them). A set of superlative keyword lexicon CK_2 including the superlative keywords and their POS tags are the known seeds. The following is an example of such rules:

non-superlativeComparison (T):- collocation (la, W, CK_2, T), keyword (CK_2),
$$\text{pos } (CK_2, d), \text{ pos } (W, v).$$

where *collocation* (la, W, CK_2, T) means W and CK_2 have a collocation relation *la*, namely, W is located on the right of CK_2 in the sentence T.

As shown in Algorithm 1, by repeatedly implementing $\mathcal{R}$ based on the identified candidate comparative sentences $\mathcal{S}$ and comparative keyword lexicon $\mathcal{CK}$, a set of non-comparative sentences $\mathcal{T}$ are identified.

5   Extracting Comparative Elements from the Identified Sentences

In our work, a gradable comparison can be defined as a quadruple $\langle SE, OE, CA, CR \rangle$ and a superlative comparison can also be expressed as a quadruple $\langle SE, CS, CA, CR \rangle$. For example, given the comparative sentence "伦敦的气温比北京高。", our objective is to extract the following comparative elements (CE):

$$\langle 伦敦(London), 北京(Beijing), 气温(temperature), 高(higher) \rangle$$

To achieve the goal, a comparative keyword lexicon CK is given a priori. And a converted lexicon of comparative keywords CK' is manually constructed to address comparative sentences with the same meaning but different structures, for example, "伦敦的气温比北京高。" and "北京的气温不及伦敦高。". They are represented as facts *convertKeyword* (CK') denoting that CK' needs to be converted to accomplish the change from a negative keyword "不及 (lower than)" to

---

Algorithm 1. Non-Comparison($\mathcal{S}$, $\mathcal{R}$, $\mathcal{CK}$)

Input: Candidate comparative sentences $\mathcal{S}$, pre-defined filtering rules $\mathcal{R}$ ($\mathcal{R}^1$, $\mathcal{R}^2$), comparative keyword lexicon $\mathcal{CK}$ ($\mathcal{CK}_1$, $\mathcal{CK}_2$).

Output: A non-comparative sentence set $\mathcal{T}$.

```
 1: T ← {};    // initialize an empty non-comparative sentence set T
 2: for each sentence s ∈ S do
 3:    if CK₁ in s then
 4:       implement R¹;
 5:       if s is a non-gradable comparison then
 6:          insert s into T;
 7:       end if
 8:    else if CK₂ in s then
 9:       implement R²;
10:       if s is a non-superlative comparison then
11:          insert s into T;
12:       end if
13:    end if
14: end for
15: Output T as the final non-comparative sentence set.
```

---

a positive keyword "比 (higher than)". The information about the POS of words and dependency relations that connect pairs of words or phrases in our corpus are automatically generated by LTP. The knowledge about heuristic position relations is generated according to the location between comparative elements and CK. According to the structure of comparative sentences in our corpus, the gradable comparisons are divided into five types and the superlative comparisons are divided into three types. We identify 35 extraction rules from gradable comparative sentences and 15 extraction rules from superlative comparative sentences. In the following, we will present some examples of the ASP based extraction rules for comparative elements.

$R1_1$: Rule $R1_1$ means "if a word CR, whose POS is an adjective, is located on the right of the comparative keyword CK_1, and directly depends on *Root* through dependency relation HED-Dep (namely, CR is the head of a comparative sentence), then CR is a gradable comparative result." This rule can be represented as follows:

result (CR):- depends (HED-Dep, Root, CR),
         location (la, CR, CK₁),
         keyword (CK₁), pos (CR, a).

$R2_1$: Rule $R2_1$ means "if a word CA, whose POS is a noun, directly depends on a gradable comparative result CR through dependency relation SVB-Dep, and it can be depended by a subject entity SE through dependency relation ATT-Dep, then CA is a gradable comparative aspect." It is represented as follows:

```
aspect (CA):- depends (SVB-Dep, CA, CR),
              depends (ATT-Dep, SE, CA),
              pos (CA, n).
```

$R3_1$: Rule $R3_1$ means "if a word SE, whose POS is a noun, is located on the left of the comparative keyword CK_1, and directly depends on a gradable comparative aspect CA through dependency relation $ATT\text{-}Dep$, then SE is a subject entity of gradable comparative sentence." This rule can be represented as follows:

```
subject (SE):- depends (ATT-Dep, SE, CA),
               location (lb, SE, CK₁),
               keyword (CK₁), pos (SE, n).
```

$R4_1$: Rule $R4_1$ means "if a word OE, whose POS is a noun, is located on the right of the comparative keyword CK_1, and directly depends on a gradable comparative aspect CA through dependency relation $ATT\text{-}Dep$, then OE is an object entity of gradable comparative sentence." This rule can be represented as follows:

```
object (OE):- depends (ATT-Dep, OE, CA),
              location (la, OE, CK₁),
              keyword (CK₁), pos (OE, n).
```

$R5_1$: Rule $R5_1$ outputs gradable comparative template of comparative elements. This rule can be represented as follows:

```
gradableTem (SE, OE, CA, CR):- subject (SE), object (OE),
                               aspect (CA), result (CR),
                               not convertKeyword (CK′).
```

where *not* is used to exclude the comparative keywords that need to be converted. For example, the comparative keyword "比" in "伦敦的气温比北京高", is a positive keyword with no exceptions.

$R5_2$: Rule $R5_2$ outputs gradable comparative template of comparative elements. It is represented as follows:

```
gradableTem (OE, SE, CA, CR):- object (OE), subject (SE),
                               aspect (CA), result (CR),
                               convertKeyword (CK′).
```

where CK' belongs to the converted lexicon, thereby, it needs to be converted to accomplish the change from a negative keyword to a positive keyword.

The proposed algorithm of comparative element extraction is called CE-Extraction, short for comparative element extraction. As shown in Algorithm 2, given the identified comparative sentence set S, the extraction rules for comparative elements R, a comparative keyword lexicon CK, and a converted lexicon of comparative keywords CK', we apply extraction rules R to extract all possible comparative elements according to the type of comparative keywords existing in each sentence s. Finally the comparative element set CE is generated.

Algorithm 2. CE-Extraction($\mathcal{S}$, $\mathcal{R}$, $\mathcal{CK}$, $\mathcal{CK}'$)

Input: Comparative sentences $\mathcal{S}$, pre-defined extraction rules $\mathcal{R}$, comparative keyword lexicon $\mathcal{CK}$, converted lexicon of comparative keywords $\mathcal{CK}'$.
Output: A comparative element set $\mathcal{CE}$.
1: $\mathcal{CE} \leftarrow \{\}$;   // initialize an empty comparative element set $\mathcal{CE}$
2: **for** each sentence $s \in \mathcal{S}$ **do**
3:     **if** $\mathcal{CK}$ in s **then**
4:         implement $\mathcal{R}1$ - $\mathcal{R}4$ and $\mathcal{R}5_1$;
5:         insert results of $\mathcal{R}5_1$ into $\mathcal{CE}$;
6:     **end if**
7:     **if** $\mathcal{CK}'$ in s **then**
8:         implement $\mathcal{R}1$ - $\mathcal{R}4$ and $\mathcal{R}5_2$;
9:         insert results of $\mathcal{R}5_2$ into $\mathcal{CE}$;
10:     **end if**
11: **end for**
12: Output $\mathcal{CE}$ as the final comparative element set.

---

6 Experiment

6.1 Datasets

For the identifying task of comparative sentences, 2500 comparative sentences were collected from geographical texts like textbooks, reference books and relevant geographical web pages such as Baidu Baike[6], the largest collaboratively-built Chinese wiki encyclopedia, to represent different types of data. For the extracting task of comparative elements, 500 comparative sentences (Gradable: 400, Superlative: 100) are randomly selected from a population of 2500 comparative sentences as the development dataset to identify extraction rules and the remaining 2000 comparative sentences (Gradable: 1600, Superlative: 400) are used for evaluating the effectiveness of the proposed approach as the testing dataset, in which multiple-word comparative elements are very common. The related resources are partially available[7] for research purposes.

6.2 Labeling

The datasets were all annotated manually. Word segmentation and POS tagging were firstly conducted by using LTP and then double-checked by human labelers to guarantee the quality. IOB tags used in text chunking [16] and named entity recognition [17] tasks were employed for annotating the comparative elements in the 2500 comparative sentences with the corresponding CE labels by four trained human annotators. The sentence below has been labeled with IOB tags corresponding to phrases that should be extracted as comparative elements. Table 1 lists the process of representing comparative elements by using IOB tags.

---

[6] http://baike.baidu.com.
[7] http://www.corpora.com.cn/GaoKaoGeographyComSen/.

Our work was double-checked by one another, and any disagreement between two annotators was resolved by discussion among the four annotators before reaching an agreement.

Table 1. Feature examples for labeling.

Original sentence	"伦敦的气温比北京高。" (The temperature in London is higher than that in Beijing.)					
After word segmentation	伦敦　的　气温　比　北京　高。					
After POS	伦敦/ns	的/u	气温/n	比/p	北京/ns	高/a 。/wp
After IOB tags	伦敦/ns B-SE	的/u O	气温/n B-aspect	比/p keyword	北京/ns B-OE	高/a 。/wp B-result

6.3 Identifying Comparative Sentences

In the experiments for Task 1, we compare our approach with other representative approaches: the CSR-based approach [11,15] and the keyword-based approach [13] for performance evaluation on comparative sentence identification. The comparison results are presented in Table 2, showing that our approach based on the combination of ASP and keywords achieves a higher precision. The keyword-based approach shows that these comparative keywords are good indicators, but the precision is low, which indicates that many sentences that contain comparative keywords are not comparative sentences. However, our method can properly deal with this issue and filter out those non-comparative sentences correctly. Although the results of the CSR-based approach are competitive to our approach, we can employ some collocation relation to filter out non-comparative sentences that the CSR-based approach can not address. Moreover, we also analyzed the incorrectly identified comparative sentences, and found that there are inherently ambiguity, which conforms to Huang et al.'s [15] analysis.

Table 2. Final results in comparative sentence identification (%).

Systems	Gradable			Superlative		
	P	R	F_1	P	R	F_1
Keyword	90.8	97.9	88.1	91.7	97.3	90.4
CSR	93.4	97.2	92.3	95.3	96.8	94.2
Keyword + ASP	96.2	97.4	94.8	97.9	97.2	96.4

6.4 Extracting Comparative Elements

In order to demonstrate whether our proposed logic programming approach is effective, we first evaluate our approach with different number of comparative sentences and then compare our approach to conditional random fields (CRF). Tables 3 and 4 show comparisons of precision, recall and F-score results of our approach and CRF in gradable and superlative sentences separately. For CRF, the POS tags, dependency relations of words and heuristic position relations with comparative keywords were used as features for the element extraction, and the ratio of the training set and test set in both gradable and superlative comparative sentences was 2:1. Obviously, with all of the four sets of different number of comparative sentences, our method still reaches good performance and outperforms CRF.

Table 3. Precision, recall and F_1-score of our method with different number of gradable sentences and CRF (%).

	SE			OE			CA			CR		
	P	R	F_1	P	R	F_1	P	R	F_1	P	R	F_1
400	98.67	82.36	87.97	92.11	75.81	83.17	95.23	79.46	88.56	97.81	95.71	96.75
800	98.58	82.25	87.89	92.02	75.69	83.03	95.04	79.23	88.43	97.70	95.54	96.61
1200	98.43	81.16	87.73	91.99	75.54	82.94	95.97	79.12	88.32	97.58	95.41	96.45
1600	98.31	80.99	87.54	91.67	75.42	82.87	95.84	79.01	88.16	97.40	95.32	96.25
CRF	82.41	80.18	81.28	69.81	66.67	68.20	74.55	67.21	70.69	97.20	93.69	95.41

Table 4. Precision, recall and F_1-score of our method with different number of superlative sentences and CRF (%).

	SE			CS			CA			CR		
	P	R	F_1	P	R	F_1	P	R	F_1	P	R	F_1
100	92.59	83.33	87.72	87.50	70.00	77.78	71.74	66.67	68.56	98.89	97.74	98.68
200	92.38	83.16	87.69	87.46	70.09	77.53	70.04	66.23	68.43	98.70	97.57	98.64
300	92.33	82.99	87.63	87.23	69.94	77.34	69.87	66.09	68.37	98.56	97.46	98.58
400	92.31	82.87	87.59	87.17	69.85	77.27	69.84	66.02	68.19	97.99	97.39	98.51
CRF	91.30	70.01	79.25	83.33	50.03	62.58	63.16	40.56	48.98	96.26	92.79	94.51

For SE, our approach gave a precision of more than 98% for different number of gradable comparative sentences and a precision of more than 92% for different number of superlative comparative sentences, because subject entities have nice characteristics, e.g., a noun or noun phrase, occurring at the start of a sentence, before a comparative keyword. For CR, our approach gave a precision of more than 97% for different number of both gradable and superlative comparative sentences, because comparative results also have nice characteristics, e.g., an adjective, occurring at the end of a sentence, after a comparative keyword. For CA, it could appear after a subject entity or an object entity in gradable sentences, as long as it is extracted once, we think it is successfully extracted, therefore, it has a relatively higher precision. However, our approach showed bad performance on CA in superlative sentences, because they are omitted frequently and quite fuzzy, sometimes it is not easy for human to identify them. Moreover, a number of omitted comparative scopes and the high multiple-word portion in comparative scopes caused relatively lower recall in superlative sentences.

7 Conclusion

This paper has studied a Chinese knowledge acquisition system for comparative sentences in geographical domain, including two important tasks, namely, comparative sentence identification and comparative element extraction. For the first task, both final precision and F_1-score rates are over 94%, and higher than the baseline, indicating the proposed method is effective and performs well in identifying comparative sentences. For the second task, we compare our approach with the state-of-the-art statistical method CRF. The proposed approach is much more effective in extracting comparative elements. These results demonstrated that Answer Set Programming could be used effectively and concisely in practical applications. Since multiple-choice questions of comparing one entity with another in Gaokao are very common, our study can contribute greatly to Chinese geographical data. In future work, we will investigate more extraction rules and increase the amount of geographical data to help answer a question correctly in Gaokao.

Acknowledgement. This work is partially funded by the 863 Program under Grant 2015AA015406 and the National Natural Science Foundation of China under Grant 61702279, 61170165, 61602260, 61502095.

References

1. Fujita, A., Kameda, A., Kawazoe, A., Miyao, Y.: Overview of Todai robot project and evaluation framework of its NLP-based problem solving. In: Proceedings of the 9th International Conference on Language Resources and Evaluation (2014)
2. Clark, P.: Elementary school science and math tests as a driver for AI: take the Aristo challenge!. In: AAAI, pp. 4019–4021 (2015)
3. Cheng, G., Zhu, W., Wang, Z., Chen, J., Qu, Y.: Taking up the Gaokao challenge: an information retrieval approach. In: IJCAI, pp. 2479–2485 (2016)
4. Varathan, K.D., Giachanou, A., Crestani, F.: Comparative opinion mining: a review. J. Assoc. Inf. Sci. Technol. **68**(4), 811–829 (2016)
5. Ma, J.: Mashi Wentong. The Commercial Press, Shanghai (1898)
6. Chen, J., Zhou, X.B.: The selection and arrangement of grammatical items concerning comparative sentences. Lang. Teach. Linguist. Stud. (2), 22–33 (2005)

7. Liu, B.: Sentiment Analysis: Mining Opinions, Sentiments, and Emotions. Cambridge University Press, Cambridge (2015)
8. Liu, C., Xu, R., Liu, J., Qu, P., Wang, H., Zou C.: Comparative opinion sentences identification and elements extraction. In: Proceedings of the ICMLC, IEEE (2013)
9. Wang, W., Zhao, T.J., Xin, G.D., Xu, Y.D.: Extraction of comparative elements using conditional random fields. Acta Autom. Sin. **41**(8), 1385–1393 (2015)
10. Wang, W., Zhao, T.J., Xin, G.D., Xu, Y.D.: Exploiting machine learning for comparative sentences extraction. Int. J. Hybrid Inf. Technol. **8**(3), 347–354 (2015)
11. Jindal, N., Liu, B.: Identifying comparative sentences in text documents. In: Proceedings of SIGIR 2006, pp. 244–251 (2006)
12. Jindal, N., Liu, B.: Mining comparative sentences and relations. In: AAAI (2006)
13. Yang, S., Ko, Y.: Extracting comparative entities and predicates from texts using comparative type classification. In: Proceedings of HLT 2011, pp. 1636–1644 (2011)
14. Gelfond, M., Lifschitz, V.: The stable model semantics for logic programming. In: Proceedings of the Fifth International Conference on Logic Programming (ICLP), pp. 1070–1080 (1988)
15. Huang, X., Wan, X., Yang, J., Xiao, J.: Learning to identify Chinese comparative sentences. J. Chin. Inf. Process. **22**(5), 30–38 (2008)
16. Zhai, F., Potdar, S., Xiang, B., Zhou, B.: Neural models for sequence chunking. In: AAAI, pp. 3365–3371 (2017)
17. Jie, Z., Muis, A.O., Lu, W.: Efficient dependency-guided named entity recognition. In: AAAI, pp. 3457–3465 (2017)

Chinese Question Classification Based on Semantic Joint Features

Xia Li[1,2(✉)], HanFeng Liu[2], and ShengYi Jiang[1,2]

[1] Key Laboratory of Language Engineering and Computing,
Guangdong University of Foreign Studies, Guangzhou, China
shelly_lx@126.com
[2] School of Information Science and Technology, School of Cyber Security,
Guangdong University of Foreign Studies, Guangzhou, China
hanfeng_liu@126.com, jiangshengyi@163.com

Abstract. Question classification is an important research content in automatic question-answering system. Chinese question sentences are different from long texts and those short texts like comments on product. They generally contain interrogative words such as who, which, where or how to specify the information required, and include complete grammatical components in the sentence. Based on these characteristics, we propose a more effective feature extraction method for Chinese question classification in this paper. We first extract the head verb of the sentence and its dependency words combined with interrogative words of the sentence as our base features. And then we use latent semantic analysis to help remove semantic noises from the base features. In the end, we expand those features to be semantic representation features by our weighted word-embedding method. Several experimental results show that our semantic joint feature extraction method outperforms classical syntactic based or content vector based method and superior to convolutional neural network based sentence classification method.

Keywords: Question classification · Semantic joint feature · Feature extraction

1 Introduction

Automatic question-answering system includes question analysis, information retrieval and answer extraction [1]. Question classification is to automatically analyze and figure out the corresponding categories of questions under predefined question systems, such as human, location and time categories etc.

The classification of Chinese questions is more specific than that of long Chinese text. This is because the length of the question is much shorter and there are some special components in Chinese questions, such as interrogative words, abbreviations, colloquial words, new words, and relatively complete grammatical components. For example, the average length of a Chinese question is about 6–15 words, which can result in sparse of large text by classical feature extraction and representation method. According to these specific problems, Chinese question classification mainly focuses on surface lexical features and semantic extension methods to seek better classification

© Springer International Publishing AG 2018
X. Huang et al. (Eds.): NLPCC 2017, LNAI 10619, pp. 114–123, 2018.
https://doi.org/10.1007/978-3-319-73618-1_10

results. Some of prior works on semantic extension are based on ontology knowledge or thesaurus like WordNet or Chinese thesaurus to improve the similarities of the sentences. These methods can not solve the problem of semantic noises when faced with large-scale data well. In recent years, convolutional neural network models have subsequently been shown to be effective for sentence classification [2]. Convolutional neural network models can automatically learn the features of the sentence and improve accuracy of the classification. But convolutional neural network models need more training time and do not have good interpretability.

In this paper, we try to extract more interpretative and effective semantic joint features based on the specific characteristics of Chinese question sentences. We first extract syntactic features of the question as base features, and then remove some semantic noises using latent semantic analysis. In the end, we use weighted word-embedding vector learned from open corpus to expand the semantic of sentence features. The results of our several experiments in two datasets show that our semantic joint feature extraction method has a certain improvement compared with existing methods including convolutional neural network based sentence classification.

2   Related Work

Chinese question classification methods mainly include ontology based methods for specific domain and semantic extension based methods for open domain. Works on ontology based use ontology knowledge in the specific filed of question classification to improve the results. Zhang et al. [3] think that the categories of questions are small and the types of the categories are not enough. For example, people usually not only ask "who is so-and-so?" but also ask "what happened in 9.11?" or "what are the great inventions of ancient China?". According to these problems, they present a method based on ontology and conceptual model to improve accuracy of the questions classification. Zhang and Chen [4] first extract Uni-grams and Bi-grams as base features of the questions, and then expand these base features as extended features based on ontology knowledge in the field of hospital. Their experimental results show that the extended features have an improvement of classification accuracy. Pan [5] also use ontology knowledge database in the field of the university to improve the accuracy of the question classification.

Works for open domain are mainly focus on surface lexical features and semantic extension of the questions. Li et al. [6] extract surface lexical features of the sentence and dependency syntactic features, and then use chi-square statistic to expand the semantic features of those surface features from WordNet. The accuracy on SVM classifier is 91.6%. Lin et al. [7] use semantic dependency relationship as semantic features of the sentence to improve the result. The experimental result shows that the best classification accuracy is 84.31%. By using the shallow syntax analysis and extracting the question sentence trunk, question words and their subsidiary components as the classification characteristics, Ji et al. [8] shows the average classification accuracy is 89.66% and 84.13% respectively in the classification data of restricted domain problems. Wen et al. [9] use syntactic analysis to extract the question trunk, question word and its related features as a supplementary feature of classification and use

Bayesian classifier for classification. The experimental results show that the method can reduce some noise and the accuracy on large categories and small categories is 86.62% and 71.92% respectively. Ye et al. [10] transform the problem of short text into long text to reduce the noise of semantic. They first get long texts from search engine by inputting and returning. And then they extract topic words using topic model from those long texts. By calculating similarities of the topic words and feature words of class specific, the category of the question can be get. The average F value is 71.3%. Duan et al. [11] use interrogative words, sense words, name entity and noun words as features of the sentence, the accuracy is 92.82% in the test set of given datasets in the paper.

Prior works on Chinese question classification mostly extract the syntactic and grammatical features of the question sentences, and extend semantic features from WordNet or synonyms. However, there are various possible vocabularies, such as acronyms, new words, ambiguous words, which lead to the expansion of semantics through ordinary synonyms or WordNet can't adequately extracts the latent semantic information of partial word features. Although there are some deep learning based methods like convolutional neural network models (CNN) [2] have effective results on sentence classification, but the difficulties in tuning parameters and interpretability for the models promotes us to compare if our classical machine learning methods based on rich features can outperform CNN methods.

3 Chinese Question Classification with Semantic Joint Features

3.1 Surface Word Features

Term frequency and inverse document frequency (abbreviate as TFIDF) is used to evaluate the importance of a word for a document in corpus, and it is widely used as weight measure in information retrieval [12, 13]. In this paper, we use TFIDF as weight of the word to obtain the importance of different words in the feature set.

For a word w_i in the question d_j, term frequency $tf_{i,j}$ and inverse document frequency idf_i are calculated as below:

$$tf_{i,j} = \frac{n_{i,j}}{\sum_k n_{k,j}} \quad idfi = \log \frac{1 + |D|}{1 + |\{j : t_i \in d_j\}|}$$

$n_{i,j}$ is the number of word w_i appears in the sentence d_j, $|D|$ is the total number of questions in the dataset.

3.2 Syntactic Trunk Features

Chinese sentence usually has the subject, predicate and object compositions, and other modifying words like adjective and adverbs. As for Chinese question classification, we need to know the core information about the question type which can help us to find the category of the question. We find that head verbs and interrogative words can represent most of the core information of the question. Here the head verb means that the head verb in the sentence is the center of the other components, and itself is not subject to any other ingredients, all the dominant elements are subordinate to their dominators in a certain dependent relationship. We extract the head verbs, words dominated by head verbs, interrogative words and words dominated by interrogative words as our syntactic features called syntactic trunk features in this paper.

A worked example of our syntactic trunk features extraction method is shown as Fig. 1. For a question "著名的长城位于哪个城市? (Which city is the famous Great Wall located in?)". We can get the dependency syntactic tree from LTP (Language Technology Platform Cloud, LTP) [14] shown in Fig. 1. We first extract the head word "位于 (lives in)" and it's syntactic dependency words "长城 (Great Wall)" and "城市 (city)" as one of our trunk features. And then we extract the interrogative words "哪个 (which)" and it's syntactic dependency words "城市 (city)" as our another syntactic trunk features. Then, the end of our trunk features for the sentence are ["长城 (Great Wall)", "位于 (lives in)", "哪个 (which)", "城市 (city)"]. From the extracted syntactic trunk features, we can see some of key and core information for the question and some of unwanted noise components in the question are removed from the extracted features.

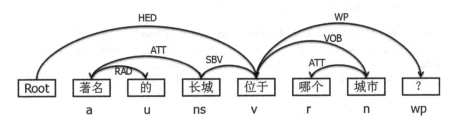

Fig. 1. An example of dependency parsing results using LTP

3.3 Weighed Word-Embedding Semantic Extension

Word2vec uses distributed representation to stand for a vector of a word. It maps each word into a k-dimensional real vector by training on large public corpus data, and the semantic similarities are determined by the distance between words. In this paper, we use the skip-gram model proposed by Mikolov [15] to train word embedding model quickly and efficiently. The main idea of this model is to predict the context based on current word. Suppose there is a series of word, the target of the skip-gram model is to maximize the probability P, P is show as:

$$P = \frac{1}{N}\sum_{n=1}^{N}\sum_{-c \le i \le c, i \neq 0} \log p(w_{n+i}|w_n)$$

Here c is the number of context words centered on the current word which also called window length. The structure of skip-gram model includes three layers: input layer, projection layer and output layer. The input is the word embedding of the current word, and the output is the word embedding of their neighbor word.

We find that the interrogative words can be more important in predicting the category of the question than that of other trunk features. So, we take a weighted semantic expansion method when using word-embedding as extension of semantic to the question trunk features. If we get a trunk features $F = [F1, F2, F3]$, $F1$ includes interrogative words, $F2$ includes interrogative word's dependency words, $F3$ includes head verbs and their dependency words. We get the extension of semantic from weighted word-embedding as $F' = \sum (\alpha F1 + \beta F2 + \gamma F3)$ meaning that we can apply different semantic weight to interrogative words features than that of other trunk features.

3.4   Semantic Joint Features

On the basis of fully considering the characteristics of Chinese questions, a semantic joint features method is proposed to represent the semantic of the questions more accurately by combining semantic expansion features and those base trunk features. Firstly, surface lexical features and syntactic trunk features are extracted from the Chinese questions. Through latent semantic analysis, some semantic noise in trunk features and surface features is reduced. Finally, the weighted word-embedding is used to expand the semantic of the question features. Our method of semantic joint feature extraction method is described as Algorithm 1.

Algorithm 1: Semantic Joint Features Extraction Method

Input: Question sentences $S = \{s_1, s_2, ..., s_n\}$, pre-trained word-embedding vector model M, latent semantic analysis parameter k, parameter α, β, γ;

Output: Matrix representation after semantic expansion

1:   *For s_i in $\{s_1, s_2, ..., s_n\}$:*

2:      Get words list of the sentence $w = \{w_1, w_2, ..., w_n\}$;

3:      Extract trunk features of the sentence $F = [F1, F2, F3]$, $F1$ includes interrogative words, $F2$ includes interrogative word's dependency words, $F3$ includes head verbs and their dependency words;

4:      Calculate each word's *TF-IDF* in the trunk features F as a vector v_i;

5:   *End For*

6:   $M1 = \{v_1, v_2, ..., v_n\}$

7:   Decomposed M1 using SVD and get $M2$;

8:   Calculate matrix M2 by weighted word-embedding semantic expansion as
     $F' = \sum (\alpha F1 + \beta F2 + \gamma F3)$

9:   Output the matrix $M2$ represented with semantic joint features.

---

4   Experimental Setup and Results

4.1   Data Description

In our experiment, three types are used as standard of Chinese question classification system, they are the type of answer based [16], question semantic information based [17] and mixed information based [18]. Most of the existing question-answering systems use a classification system based on the type of answer. The international authority of the classification system is UIUC question classification system [19] which is corresponding to the English question classification system. In UIUC system, questions are divided into six categories and 50 sub-categories. For Chinese question classification, HIR system is introduced by social computing and information retrieval research center of Harbin institute of technology. HIR system is widely used in Chinese question classification. According to the characteristics of Chinese, HIR system includes seven major categories and 60 small classes. The seven major categories include HUMAN, LOCATION, NUMBER, TIME, OBJECT, DESCRIPTION, and UNKNOWN. The details are shown in Table 1. In order to better compare our experimental results with baseline methods, we select HUMAN, LOCTION, NUMBER and TIME as four major categories, and the OBJECT and DESCRIPTION are merged into OTHER category.

Table 1. HIR question categories description

Major categories	Sub-categories
HUMAN	Specific characters, group institutions, description of characters, characters enumerated, other people
LOCATION	Planets, cities, continents, countries, provinces, rivers, lakes, mountains, oceans, islands, places, addresses, places
NUMBER	Number, quantity, price, percentage, distance, weight, temperature, age, area, frequency, speed, range, order, number, number of other things
TIME	Year, month, day, time, time range, time enumeration, time other
OBJECT	Animals, plants, food, colors, money, language, materials, machinery, transportation, religion, entertainment, entities, other entities
DESCRIPTION	Abbreviation, meaning, method, reason, definition, description of others
UNKNOWN	unknown

We use two datasets in our experiments. The first data is published by the Research Center for Social Computing and Information Retrieval (HIR), which has a total of 6295 questions. The details of the data are showed in Table 2. We find that there is slight unbalance distribution in HIR dataset. For example, the number of questions in HUMAN category is 511, and the number of questions in TIME category is more than 1300. In order to get more widely results, we construct about 5093 Chinese questions in the same categories by artificial. The details of our artificial dataset are also showed in Table 2. As Table 2 shown, we can see that artificial data is more balanced than that of HIR data.

Table 2. Details of the datasets

Data set	HUMAN	LOCATION	TIME	NUMBER	OTHER	TOTAL
HIR	511	1326	1320	751	2387	6295
Artificial	1052	785	779	956	1522	5093

4.2   Experimental Setup

We use the average accuracy of five folds cross validation as our experimental result. In each fold, we randomly select 80% as training data, and the rest of 20% as test data. In our experiment, scikit-learn [20] machine learning kit is used as auxiliary tool for surface and LSA procession. LTP [14] is used for word tagging and extraction the trunk features. We use support vector machine as classifier in our experiment.

In our experiments, the word2vec file used in our semantic joint features extraction method, non-static CNN method and static CNN method is 200 dimensions and about 2.6G file size. The latent semantic analysis parameter k is 400. Parameters α, β, γ used in weighted word-embedding semantic expansion is 1.2, 1 and 1 respectively.

4.3   Experimental Results

We do several experiments on HIR and artificial datasets. We first just use the surface word features as representation of the question (we called it TFIDF method), and we get accuracy of 90.58% in HIR and 95.82% in artificial data respectively. We then use LSA method helping to remove some semantic noise from surface features (we called it TFIDF + LSA), and we get the accuracy of 91.76% in HIR and 96.19% in artificial data respectively which means that latent semantic analysis method certainly removes some semantic noises and improve some accuracy compared with surface features representation.

We also use syntactic trunk features exclusively as representation for questions (we called it trunk method), we can get accuracy of 90.68% in HIR and 95.15% in artificial data. Similarly, we add LSA into the trunk features representation (we called it trunk + LSA method), the results all show slight improvements in the two datasets. If we just use word2vec as representation of questions (we called it word2vec method), we get the lowest accuracy in all the methods which is 86.32% in HIR and 92.91% in artificial data.

When we use the semantic joint features proposed in this paper (we call it semantic joint features method), we can see the results are the best in the all methods in two datasets. We can get the accuracy of 93.87% in HIR and 96.88% in artificial data (Table 3).

Table 3. Results of different methods on HIR

Feature extraction method	Accuracy (%)
TFIDF	90.58
TFIDF + LSA	91.76
Word2vec	86.32
Trunk	90.68
Trunk + LSA	90.87
Semantic joint features	**93.87**
Wen et al. [9]	91.63
Non-static CNN [2]	**92.58**
Static CNN [2]	**93.51**

In order to better compare the performance of our method with deep learning based methods and classical features based method, we take Wen et al. [9] and convolutional neural network model in sentence classification [2] as our two baseline methods. From the experimental results, we can see that static CNN method also has good accuracy which is 93.51% in HIR and 96.28% in artificial data. But non-static CNN is not very well in HIR which is 92.58%. And our semantic joint features method gets the best performance in the two datasets (Table 4).

Table 4. Results of different methods on artificial data

Feature extraction method	Accuracy (%)
TFIDF	95.82
TFIDF + LSA	96.19
Word2vec	92.91
Trunk	95.15
Trunk + LSA	95.78
Semantic joint features	**96.88**
Wen et al. [9]	95.36
Non-static CNN [2]	**96.27**
Static CNN [2]	**96.28**

Compared with the traditional feature extraction algorithms, our semantic joint feature extraction method has the highest classification accuracy in all two datasets. Compared with convolutional neural network model based sentence classification [2], our method still outperforms static-CNN and non-static CNN method in the two datasets. That means for Chinese question classification, if we can extract more about core and important sentence trunk features and expand them into full semantic representation, we can get good results based on classical machine learning classifier algorithms.

In addition, in order to compare the cost time of each method, we get the runtime by different methods on the two datasets. The results are show in Table 5. From the result we can see that although the performance of convolutional neural network method like static CNN or non-static CNN [2] is good, but the runtime of the method is much

Table 5. The comparison of runtime (seconds) in each method

Feature extraction method	HIR	Artificial data
TFIDF	324.54	276.15
TFIDF + LSA	112.33	108.87
Word2Vec	40.35	39.99
Trunk	311.63	266.33
Trunk + LSA	101.77	97.57
Semantic joint features	**112.69**	**107.56**
Wen et al. [9]	289.74	253.18
Non-static CNN [2]	**2732.72**	**2585.33**
Static CNN [2]	**1325.68**	**1201.14**

longer than that of our method. For example, on HIR dataset, our semantic joint features method costs 112.69 s and non-static CNN method costs 2732.72 s and static CNN method costs 1325.68 s.

5 Conclusion

Based on the problems of the existing feature selection method, this paper presents a Chinese question classification method based on semantic joint feature extraction. Compared with the previous Chinese question classification methods, our method combines the features of question trunk and fully expanded into semantic representation by our weighted word-embedding semantic expansion method. The experimental results show that our method is effective and have improvements in classification accuracy compared with prior methods. And the features extracted by our method is interpretative than that of deep learning methods.

In the future, we will continue try to find a more effective method of parameter setting in the side of weighted semantic expansion to obtain better results.

Acknowledgment. This work is supported by the National Science Foundation of China (61402119, 61572145).

References

1. Mao, X.L., Li, X.M.: A survey on question and answering systems. J. Front. Comput. Sci. Technol. **6**(3), 193–207 (2012)
2. Kim, Y.: Convolutional neural networks for sentence classification. arXiv preprint arXiv: 1408.5882 (2014)
3. Zhang, L., Huang, H.Y., Hu, C.L.: On question classification in an ontology-based Chinese question-answering System. J. Libr. Sci. China **2**(02), 60–65 (2006)
4. Zhang, W., Chen, J.J.: Method of information entropy and its application in Chinese question classification. Comput. Eng. Appl. **49**(10), 129–131 (2013)
5. Pan, Z.A.: Research on ontology based problem feature model in Chinese problem classification. Taiyuan University of Technology (2010)
6. Li, X., Du, Y., Huang, X., Wu, L.: Problem classification based on syntactic information and semantic information. In: National Conference on Information Retrieval and Content Security (2004)
7. Lin, X.D., Sun, A.D., Lin, P.P., Liu, H.X.: Chinese question classification using SVM based on dependency relations. J. Zhengzhou Univ. **41**(1), 69–73 (2009)
8. Ji, Y., Wang, R.B., Chen, Z.Q.: Question classification in restricted domain using syntactic parsing-based quadratic-Bayesian model. J. Comput. Appl. **32**(6), 1685–1687 (2012)
9. Wen, X., Zhang, Y., Liu, T., Ma, J.S.: Syntactic structure parsing based Chinese question classification. J. Chin. Inf. Process. **20**(2), 33–39 (2006)
10. Ye, Z.L., Yang, Y., Jiang, Z., Ying, H.F.: Short question classification based on semantic extensions. J. Comput. Appl. **35**(3), 792–796 (2015)
11. Duan, L., Chen, J., Niu, Y.: Study on question classification approach mixing multiple semantics characteristics. J. Taiyuan Univ. Technol. **42**(5), 494–498 (2011)

12. Li, X., Roth, D.: Learning question classifiers: the role of semantic information. J. Natl. Lang. Eng. **12**(3), 229–250 (2006)
13. Zhang, D., Lee, W.: Question classification using support vector machines. In: Proceedings of the 26th Annual International ACM SIGIR Conference On Research and Development in Information Retrieval, pp. 26–32. ACM Press, New York (2003)
14. Liu, T., Che, W., Li, Z.: Language technology platform. J. Chin. Inf. Process. **25**(6), 53–62 (2011)
15. Mikolov, T., Sutskever, I., Chen, K.: Distributed representations of words and phrases and their compositionality. In: Advances in Neural Information Processing Systems, pp. 3111–3119 (2013)
16. Prager, J., Radev, D., Brown, E., Coden, A.: The use of predictive annotation for question answering in TREC8. In: The Eighth Text Retrieval Conference (TREC 8), pp. 500–246. NIST Special Publication (1999)
17. Hull, D.: Xerox TREC-8 question answering track report. TREC (1999)
18. Li, X., Roth, D.: Learning question classifiers: the role of semantic information. Nat. Lang. Eng. **12**(3), 229–249 (2006)
19. Li, B., Liu, Y., Ram, A.: Exploring question subjectivity prediction in community QA. In: Proceedings of the 31st Annual International ACM SIGIR Conference on Research and Development in Information Retrieval ACM, pp. 735–736 (2008)
20. Abraham, A., Pedregosa, F., Eickenberg, M.: Machine learning for neuroimaging with scikit-learn. arXiv preprint arXiv:1412.3919 (2014)

A Chinese Question Answering System for Single-Relation Factoid Questions

Yuxuan Lai[(⊠)], Yanyan Jia, Yang Lin, Yansong Feng, and Dongyan Zhao

Institute of Computer Science & Technology, Peking University, Beijing, China
{erutan,jiayanyan,linyang,fengyansong,zhaody}@pku.edu.cn

Abstract. Aiming at the task of open domain question answering based on knowledge base in NLPCC 2017, we build a question answering system which can automatically find the promised entities and predicates for single-relation questions. After a features based entity linking component and a word vector based candidate predicates generation component, deep convolutional neural networks are used to rerank the entity-predicate pairs, and all intermediary scores are used to choose the final predicted answers. Our approach achieved the F1-score of 47.23% on test data which obtained the first place in the contest of NLPCC 2017 Shared Task 5 (KBQA sub-task). Furthermore, there are also a series of experiments which can help other developers understand the contribution of every part of our system.

Keywords: Natural language question answering · Knowledge base
Information extraction · Deep convolutional neural network

1 Introduction

Open-domain question answering is an important and yet challenging problem that remains largely unsolved. In recent years, with the development of large-scale knowledge bases, such as DBPedia [12] and Freebase [13], many studies focus on generating precise and reliable answers for open-domain questions from knowledge bases. In this paper, we introduce a system that can answer single-relation factoid questions in Chinese, which is the main component of the NLPCC KBQA evaluation task. We proposed a novel method based on deep CNNs to rerank the entity-predicate pairs which generated by approaches based on shallow features. Our system achieved the F1-score of 47.23% on test data which obtained the first place in the evaluation task.

In the rest of the paper, we first review related works in Sect. 2, and in Sect. 3, we introduce the architecture of our method in detail. Experimental setup, results and implementation tricks are discussed in Sect. 4. We conclude the whole paper and look forward to the future research in Sect. 5.

© Springer International Publishing AG 2018
X. Huang et al. (Eds.): NLPCC 2017, LNAI 10619, pp. 124–135, 2018.
https://doi.org/10.1007/978-3-319-73618-1_11

2   Related Work

Open domain question answering is a perennial problem in the field of natural language processing, which is known as an AI-complete problem. Answering open domain questions over knowledge bases can generate more precise and reliable answers. Many traditional KBQA technologies are based on information retrieval [7,8] and semantic parsing [9–11]. Recently, some works use representation learning to determine similarity between entity mentions and knowledge base entities [1], question patterns and knowledge base predicates [1] or knowledge base subgraphs [2]. They proved that neural network approaches can handle high-level semantic similarity better. When dealing with complicated natural language tasks such as question answering, it is rewarding to combine neural networks with traditional shallow features [2–4]. Following their ideas, we also combine traditional shallow features with CNNs features in our system.

Deep convolution neural networks have emerged great power in field of computer vision. Recently, a few works try to use deep architectures in NLP tasks such as text classification [5] and machine translation [6]. They followed the design of VGG [14] and ResNet [15], using narrow filters and residual connections to reduce parameters and make the deep architecture easier to train. We also attempt to achieve a deep CNNs in our system but followed the GoogLeNet [16] architecture, using multi-perspective filters with residual connections.

NLPCC have organized Chinese KBQA evaluation task for three years. The Ye's system [18], which achieved the best performance in NLPCC 2015 Chinese KBQA task, combined a subject predicate extraction algorithm with web knowledge retrieval. Lai [19] used word vector based features to search best subject-predicate pair and achieved the best performance in NLPCC 2016 KBQA task. Yang [20] combined features based entity linking, Naive Bayes based answers selection, and CNNs based reranking and achieved the second place in 2016. Our system is mainly inspired by their works [19,20], but we achieved a novel CNN architecture and combined advantages of their system appropriately. We also ameliorate the word vector based predicates selection algorithm in [19] and our entity linking approach is slightly different from [20]. Furthermore, an exquisite generative adversarial like negative sampling approach are adopted to deal with the data unbalance of CNN training.

3   Architecture

The architecture of our system is shown in Fig. 1. Enlightened from previous works [19], several hand-written rules are adopted to correct spider error such as unexpected special symbols in knowledge base and extract core expressions from questions. Then, a feature based approach is used to select promised entity mentions followed by an unsupervised word vector based predicates scoring method. After candidate entity-predicate pairs are generated, deep CNNs models are used to rerank them. All intermediary scores are used to choose the final predicted answers.

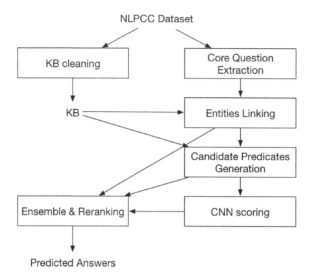

Fig. 1. Architecture of our KBQA system

The rules used to pretreat NLPCC dataset are almost the same as the pervious work (See Appendix in [19]). But when dealing with the knowledge base, delete rules are ignored. If the core expression of a question is an entity, we will add the word "introduce" so that our system will attempt to give an introduction of this entity. Anyway, only 26 of the 7631 questions are influenced by this introduction trick.

3.1 Entity Linking

A KB entity "Li Na (Diving Athlete)" is consist of the entity name "Li Na" and the entity explanation "Diving Athlete" (sometimes absence). Topic entities of questions are the core entities of the corresponding KB queries and entity mentions are substrings of question which entails topic entities. An entity mention entails a topic entity if and only if the mention is the same as the topic entity, or just the name of, or the correspondence are mentioned in the provided file "nlpcc-iccpol-2016.kbqa.kb.mention2id". Enlightened from previous works [20], a features based GBDT (gradient boost decision tree) are trained to select promised entity mentions from all possible substrings of questions.

In order to train supervised entity linking models, golden mentions labeling is a prerequisite. A golden mention must entail a KB entity with an object same as the golden answer. To ensure the precision of the golden labeling, several rules considering coverage between mentions, mention lengths and positions are adopted and every question has at most one golden mention. The statistical results are demonstrated in Table 1. Inspected manually, most of the excluded mention candidates are defective.

Table 1. Statistics of golden entity labeling

Dataset	#All questions	#Have candidates	#Labeled golden
16-train	14609	14323	14306
16-test	9870	9493	9482
17-test	7631	4833	4829

All features adopted in entity linking model are demonstrated below, which is similar to the pervious work [20]. But no part-of-speech information is considered and most of the features have several perspectives. Since our mentions are substrings, not continuous words but Chinese characters, FMM (forward maximum matching) is used to find the next word and RMM (reverse maximum matching) is used to find the last word. A GBDT model is trained on questions which have gloden mention based on these features. Settings and results are shown in Sect. 4.

- **Position and Length.** The absolute and relative position of the head, the middle, and the tail of the mention. The absolute and relative length of the mention. Whether the mention is a single Chinese character.
- **IDF Score.** IDF Score of the mentioned string in all questions. We use 4 methods to compute the IDF score according to wikipedia[1].
- **Post- and Pre-word Possibility.** The possibility of the preword and postword to appear before or after a golden mention. OOV will set to 0.05.
- **Other Features.** Whether there is any Chinese in the mention, whether the mention equals to the entity name, whether the mention is covered by other mentions.

3.2 Candidate Predicates Generation

We use the same method as [19] to evaluate whether semantic of the question pattern can cover the predicate (see Eq. 1), but most of tricks such as question classification and high frequency entities filtering are deleted. A variant (see Eq. 2) is used to evaluate whether semantic of the predicate can cover the question pattern, where ave_q is the average vector of words in all questions, which is designed to match the stop words. The word segmentation method in this section is the same as that in [19]. Therefore, all possible words in questions and predicates will take into account. The detailed explanation of this word vector based evaluation method and discussions of the chosen word segmentation method can be found in Sect. 3.2 of [19].

$$S_p = \frac{\sum_i (lp_i * \max_j Cos(wp_i, wq_j))}{\sum_i lp_i} \tag{1}$$

---

[1] https://en.wikipedia.org/wiki/Tf-idf.

$$S_q = \frac{\sum\limits_{j}(lq_j * \max\limits_{wp_i \in p \cup \{ave_q\}} Cos(wp_i, wq_j))}{\sum\limits_{j} lq_j} \tag{2}$$

In order to limit the amount of candidate entity-predicate pairs in reranking procedure, we used a linear combination of these feature (see Eq. 3) to filter out the unlikely candidates which is similar to the previous work [19]. Where l_{men} represents the length of the mention, and l_{pre} represents the length of the predicate. If an entity mention entails more than one KB entities which have the same predicate, only the predicate of the first entity (ordered by appearance in KB file) will be considered, so that no duplicate entity-predicate pair will be generated.

$$S_f = (S_p + S_q * 0.8)/1.8 * 1.4 + 0.1 * l_{men} + 0.00001 * l_{pre} \tag{3}$$

3.3 Deep CNNs Architecture

Deep convolutional neural networks are adopted to rerank the candidate entity-predicate pairs. The detailed architecture of our deep CNNs model used in submission version are illustrated in Fig. 2. This model evaluates the similairty between a prediate and a question pattern, that is the question without the entity mention. Pretrained word vectors are used to represent inputs, followed by several convolutional blocks (2 convolutional blocks in Fig. 2) to generate high level features. Then, after max-pooling layers, element-wise multiplication are adopted to combine features from questions and predicates. Finally, a MLP (multilayer perceptron) with dropout is used to evaluate the final similarity. The parameters of convolutional layers are shared between the processing of predicates and questions.

Inspire by GoogLeNet [16], there are multiple filter widths in each convolutional block (in Fig. 2, 256 filters with width 1, 512 filters with width 2, and 256 filters with width 3). Following ResNet [15], there are residual connections between neighbouring blocks. Limited by the pool improvement brought by deeper model and computing capability, the submission version has only 2 blocks.

3.4 Ranking

A linear combination of all intermediary scores is adopted to generate the final ranking of candidate answers. Since the high accuracy of entity linking (Sect. 3.1) and the good performance of the single feature produced by deep CNNs (Sect. 3.3) or word vector based approach (Sect. 3.2), the combination equation is very rough without finely adjusting (see Eq. 4). Where S_{men}, S_f, and S_{cnn} are score of entity mentions, entity-predicate pairs evaluated by word vectors based approach, and predicates evaluated by CNNs respectively.

$$S_{final} = S_{men} + S_f + S_{cnn} * 2 \tag{4}$$

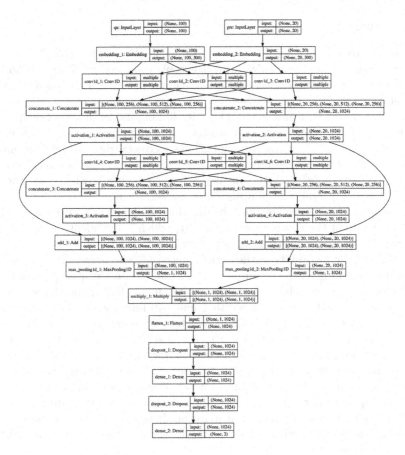

Fig. 2. Architecture of our deep CNN model

4 Experiment

4.1 Dataset

The dataset is published by NLPCC 2017 evaluation task including a knowledge base and question-answer pairs for training and testing. There are about 43M SPO pairs in the knowledge, where about 6M subjects, 0.6M predicates and 16M objects are involved. The 2017-training set contains 14,609 2016-training question-answer pairs and 9,870 2016-testing question-answer pairs. The 2017-testing set contains 7,631 question-answer pairs. The answers are labeled by human and most questions can be answer by a KB object.

4.2 Settings

All word vectors in our system are the same as the word vector list in the pervious work [19], which uses word2vector tools produced by Tomas Mikolov[2] and CBOW [17] model trained on Baidubaike corpus. Word list used in word segmentation consists of all words in the word vectors list.

The parameters used in the GBDT entity linking model are: max depth $= 8$, eta $= 0.1$, objective $=$ reg:logistic, nrounds $= 100$. When training the CNN models, the batch size is 64, the loss function is binary crossentropy, and the optimizer is adadelta [23]. The submission version have trained for 21 epoches, but the best f1-score with the same settings appeared when 7 epoches finished and reached 47.35%. The CNN models are implemented by keras[3].

In entity linking procedure, only the mentions rank in top 3 with score higher than 0.01 times of the top mention's will left, which is our mentions filter rule. Only top 20 candidate entity-predicate pairs will be used in CNNs.

Because of the instability of the performance of CNNs over training epoches, an ensemble learning method is implemented. The S_{cnn} is the average of outputs of 8 CNNs. Four of them have the same architecture as Fig. 2, and the others are similar but have 384 filters with width 1 and 640 filters with width 2 in every convolutional blocks. All of the CNN models have different seeds in initialization.

Although most of the negative entity-predicate pairs have been filtered out in candidate predicates generation before training CNN models, the amount of positive and negative samples is still unbalance. So a dynamic negative sampling approach is adopted. The possibility of a negative entity-predicate pair P_{ep_i} is shown in Eq. 5, where $rank_{ep_i}$ is the rank of this entity-predicate pair in its question scored by the end of the last iteration. It is just like a simple generative adversarial mechanism, where the generative model is the last iteration of the discriminative model.

$$P_{ep_i} = min(1.0, \ \frac{16.0}{rank_{ep_i}^2}) \tag{5}$$

4.3 Results

Entity Linking. The results of our entity linking model are shown in Table 2. We use 5-fold cross-validation to test our model on 2016 and 2017 training datasets as well as each test datasets with the corresponding training data. Rec_filter is the recall of our mentions filter rule. Compared with the previous work [20], on 2016 training data, the accuracy of our model (98.75%) is a little lower than the f1-score of theirs (99.04%). But they just labeled 14033 questions while we labeled 14306 and every question in our data has only one golden mention. So it is not obvious that which model is better.

---

[2] https://code.google.com/archive/p/word2vec.
[3] https://keras.io.

Table 2. Entity linking results

Dataset&Settings	Acc@1	Acc@3	Acc@10	#questions	Rec_filter
5f-cv 2016 train	98.75%	99.89%	—	14306	99.82%
2016 test	98.57%	99.81%	99.94%	9482	99.75%
5f-cv all trn	98.74%	99.89%	99.97%	23788	99.84%
2017 test	92.23%	98.41%	99.86%	4829	97.58%

Candidate Predicates Generation. Some detailed information is demonstrated in Table 3, including number of questions, number of candidate mentions per question, and number of candidate KB triples per question. Since the top-1 accuracy of entity linking on 2017 testing data gets lower, the entity filter holds more entity mentions per question automatically.

Table 3. Detailed information in candidate predicates generation

Dataset	#questions	#men_ave	#triple_ave
2016-train	9870	1.499	32.28
2016-test	14609	1.473	35.68
2017-test	7631	1.893	62.93

Furthermore, results of the word vector based approach with different settings on 2016 testing set are shown in Table 4. Baseline is the best system in NLPCC 2016 KBQA task [19]. But for impartial comparison with our approaches, only one object will be answered for the same entity-predicate pair, so that the top-n precision (n > 1) will be lower than reported. Baseline-rules is the baseline system without the tricks such as question classification and pattern based training, which is the actual baseline of our system. We think these rules should be summarized by CNNs automatically. Full system using entity linking filter and the reverse word vector based similarity S_q. From Table 4, it is obvious that both the entity linking and the reverse similarity can improve the performance, and the limitation of candidate entities can largely elevate pre@20, which is an important indicator for CNN reranking.

Table 4. Performance of candidate predicates generation on 2016 test-set

System	Pre@1	Pre@2	Pre@5	Pre@20
Baseline [19]	82.41%	87.06%	89.84%	91.02%
Baseline-rules	81.76%	86.75%	89.70%	90.95%
Full-S_q	82.17%	87.18%	90.24%	92.01%
Full	82.97%	87.50%	90.44%	92.02%

CNN Reranking. The results on 2017 testing set of our CNN models with different depth are listed in Table 5. $+s_f \& s_{men}$ stands for the combination of ensemble CNNs and previous features. Each block has 1024 filters same as Fig. 2. It seems that going deeper can bring an unsteady improvement. Limited by computing capability, we could not finely tune the parameters such as filter numbers and block structures. So there is still large potential for deep architectures. The best pre@1 of our submission architecture is 47.35%, which contains 8 2-block models. The word vector based feature s_f can achieve 43.10% on 2017 testing set. Combine pervious features with CNNs gains prominent improvement.

Table 5. Pre@1 of CNNs with different depth on 2017 test-set

#blocks	1	2	3	5	All
Single model	43.57%	43.82%	43.85%	42.13%	—
*4 ensemble	44.32%	44.45%	44.16%	43.28%	44.62%
$+s_f \& s_{men}$	47.32%	47.31%	47.23%	46.44%	47.45%

The detailed results of our submission architecture are demonstrated in Table 6. CNN models are trained for 17 epoches on 2016 dataset and 7 epoches on 2017 dataset. Accoraging to [19], if the performance is judged by finding the correct entity-predicate pair, the accuracy of baseline system will be up to 85.61% on 2016 testing set while that of our system will be 89.65%.

Table 6. Full system performance

	2016 testing set			2017 testing set		
	Pre@1	Pre@2	Pre@5	Pre@1	Pre@2	Pre@5
Baseline [19]	82.41%	87.06%	89.84%			
s_f only	82.97%	87.50%	90.36%	42.94%	48.67%	54.75%
CNN single	84.55%	88.63%	91.03%	43.63%	49.98%	55.59%
CNN ensemble	85.40%	89.01%	91.17%	44.31%	50.18%	56.05%
name_system (full)	86.60%	89.67%	91.38%	47.35%	52.47%	56.74%

The submission results of NLPCC2017 evaluation task are shown in Table 7 (the top 5 results of 14 submissions in total). Our system achieves the best performance among all teams.

4.4 Upper Bound Analysis

However, our system can only label golden KB triples on 63.28% of 2017 testing questions, witch is the upper bound of our system. About 22% of answers in 2017

Table 7. Evaluation results in this evaluation task

Team	F1 Score
PKU.name_system (ours)	**47.23**%
NEU	41.96%
PKU.ICL	40.68%
ZJU.TeamTCM	40.08%
CCNU.NLP-Blaze	38.63%

testing dataset are not KB objects and about 14% of them whose topic entity mentions are aliases of KB entities and are not mentioned in file "nlpcc-iccpol-2016.kbqa.kb.mention2id" so that our entity liking method becomes invalid with them. So, aliases linking is also very important and more imformation besides the given KB is also in demand.

4.5 Further Experiments

We also do experiments on a subset of qald dataset[4]. Since training data in qald are not large enough for deep CNN models, the s_f only setting are used, which is an unsupervised method. 78 single relation factoid questions in English are selected from the training set of qald-6 task 1 (Multilingual question answering over RDF data, which contains 350 questions) and 82% (64/78) of them can be answered correctly by our system, which demonstrates that language is not a restriction of our system.

5 Conclusion

In this paper, we present a complicated KBQA system consists of features based entity liking, word vector based candidate predicate generation, and deep CNNs based reranking approach, which can answer simple-relation Chinese questions. For the unbalance of CNNs inputs, we present a generative adversarial like negative sampling approach. Our system obtained the first place in the contest of NLPCC 2017 Shared Task 5 (KBQA sub-task). Detailed experimental results are demonstrated, which can be helpful for other developers to understand the contributions of our components. In the future, we would like to extend our system to answer multi-relation questions and try to combine information from object of KB triples.

Acknowledgement. We would like to thank members in our NLP group and the anonymous reviewers for their helpful feedback. This work was supported by National High Technology R&D Program of China (Grant No. 2015AA015403), Natural Science Foundation of China (Grant No. 61672057, 61672058).

---

[4] https://qald.sebastianwalter.org.

References

1. Yih, W., He, X., Meek, C.: Semantic parsing for single-relation question answering. In: Meeting of the association for computational linguistics (2014)
2. Yih, W., Chang, M.-W., He, X., Gao, J.: Semantic parsing via staged query graph generation: question answering with knowledge base. In: Proceedings of ACL (2015)
3. Yu, L., Hermann, K.M., Blunsom, P., Pulman, S.: Deep learning for answer sentence selection. Computer Science (2014)
4. Yang, Y., Yih, W., Meek, C.: WikiQA: a challenge dataset for open-domain question answering. In: Proceedings of EMNLP (2015)
5. Conneau, A., Schwenk, H., Le Cun, Y., Barrault, L.: Very deep convolutional networks for text classification. In: Proceedings of EACL (2017)
6. Gehring, J., Auli, M., Grangier, D., Yarats, D., Dauphin, Y.N.: Convolutional sequence to sequence learning. arXiv preprint arXiv: 1705.03122v2 (2017)
7. Yao, X., Van Durme, B.: Information extraction over structured data: question answering with freebase. In: Proceedings of ACL (2014)
8. Fader, A., Zettlemoyer, L., Etzioni, O: Open question answering over curated and extracted knowledge bases. In: ACM SIGKDD International Conference on Knowledge Discovery and Data Mining ACM (2014)
9. Berant, J., Chou, A., Frostig, R., Liang, P.: Semantic parsing on freebase from question-answer Pairs. In: Proceedings of EMNLP (2013)
10. Berant, J., Liang, P.: Semantic parsing via paraphrasing. In: Proceedings of ACL (2014)
11. Liang, P., Jordan, M., Klein, D.: Learning dependency-based compositional semantics. In: Proceedings of ACL (2011)
12. Auer, S., Bizer, C., Kobilarov, G., Lehmann, J., Cyganiak, R., Ives, Z.: DBpedia: a nucleus for a web of open data. In: Aberer, K., et al. (eds.) ASWC/ISWC-2007. LNCS, vol. 4825, pp. 722–735. Springer, Heidelberg (2007). https://doi.org/10.1007/978-3-540-76298-0_52
13. Bollacker, K., Evans, C., Paritosh, P., Sturge, T., Taylor, J.: Freebase: a collaboratively created graph database for structuring human knowledge. In: Proceedings of the 2008 ACM SIGMOD International Conference on Management of Data, SIGMOD 2008, pp. 1247–1250 (2008)
14. Simonyan, K., Zisserman, A.: Very deep convolutional networks for large-scale image recognition. Computer Science (2014)
15. He, K., Zhang, X., Ren, S., Sun, J.: Deep residual learning for image recognition. In: Proceedings of Computer Vision and Pattern Recognition (2015)
16. Szegedy, C., Ioffe, S., Vanhoucke, V., Alemi, A.: Inception-v4, Inception-ResNet and the impact of residual connections on learning. In: AAAI Conference on Artificial Intelligence (2017)
17. Mikolov, T., Sutskever, I., Chen, K., Corrado, G., Dean, J.: Distributed representations of words and phrases and their compositionality. In: Proceedings of NIPS (2013)
18. Ye, Z., Jia, Z., Yang, Y., Huang, J., Yin, H.: Research on open domain question answering system. In: Proceedings of NLPCC (2015)
19. Lai, Y., Lin, Y., Chen, J., Feng, Y., Zhao, D.: Open domain question answering system based on knowledge base. In: Lin, C.-Y., Xue, N., Zhao, D., Huang, X., Feng, Y. (eds.) ICCPOL/NLPCC-2016. LNCS (LNAI), vol. 10102, pp. 722–733. Springer, Cham (2016). https://doi.org/10.1007/978-3-319-50496-4_65

20. Yang, F., Gan, L., Li, A., Huang, D., Chou, X., Liu, H.: Combining deep learning with information retrieval for question answering. In: Proceedings of NLPCC (2016)
21. Xie, Z., Zeng, Z., Zhou, G., He, T.: Knowledge base question answering based on deep learning models. In: Lin, C.-Y., Xue, N., Zhao, D., Huang, X., Feng, Y. (eds.) ICCPOL/NLPCC-2016. LNCS (LNAI), vol. 10102, pp. 300–311. Springer, Cham (2016). https://doi.org/10.1007/978-3-319-50496-4_25
22. Wang, L., Zhang, Y., Liu, T.: A deep learning approach for question answering over knowledge base. In: Lin, C.-Y., Xue, N., Zhao, D., Huang, X., Feng, Y. (eds.) ICCPOL/NLPCC-2016. LNCS (LNAI), vol. 10102, pp. 885–892. Springer, Cham (2016). https://doi.org/10.1007/978-3-319-50496-4_82
23. Zeiler, M.D.: ADADELTA: an adaptive learning rate method. Computer Science (2012)

Enhancing Document-Based Question Answering via Interaction Between Question Words and POS Tags

Zhipeng Xie[✉]

School of Computer Science, Fudan University, Shanghai, China
xiezp@fudan.edu.cn

Abstract. The document-based question answering is to select the answer from a set of candidate sentence for a given question. Most Existing works focus on the sentence-pair modeling, but ignore the peculiars of question-answer pairs. This paper proposes to model the interaction between question words and POS tags, as a special kind of information that is peculiar to question-answer pairs. Such information is integrated into a neural model for answer selection. Experimental results on DBQA Task have shown that our model has achieved better results, compared with several state-of-the-art systems. In addition, it also achieves the best result on NLPCC 2017 Shared Task on DBQA.

Keywords: Question answering · Deep learning · Question words
Part-of-speech tags

1 Introduction

In document-based question answering, one important subtask is to identify sentences as answers from a given document with respect to a question, which is also called *answer selection*. The main problem is how to extract informative features in order to decide whether a candidate sentence contains the semantic and/or syntactic information required by the question. Traditional work on answer selection usually used human-crafted feature engineering that may exploit linguistic tools or external linguistic knowledge resources [12].

Recently, with the upsurge of deep learning, a variety of neural approaches have been proposed to solve the answer selection problem, which have achieved substantial out-performance compared with the traditional methods. These neural approaches usually work by firstly generating the representations of questions and candidates, and then ranking their semantic similarities. Like traditional methods, these neural approaches also assume that an appropriate answer should have high semantic similarity with the question, and they make their judgement mainly based on this assumption.

In some neural approaches, the representations of questions and answers are generated separately. For example, Yu et al. [14] proposed two simple models,

© Springer International Publishing AG 2018
X. Huang et al. (Eds.): NLPCC 2017, LNAI 10619, pp. 136–147, 2018.
https://doi.org/10.1007/978-3-319-73618-1_12

bag-of-words model and bigram model, where bag-of-words model generated the vector representation of a sentence as the centroid of the embeddings of all words in the sentence, and bigram model used one convolutional layer and one average-pooling layer to generate the vector representation of a sentence. Severyn and Moschitti [6] and Feng et al. [1] presented convolutional neural network architectures for reranking pairs of questions and answers. They used convolutional network to generate intermediate representations of input sentences, and then learned how to calculate their similarities.

Some recent neural approaches introduced attention mechanisms and produced conditional representations of answers and questions, taking interdependence between questions and answers into consideration. Tan et al. [8] proposed an attentive Bi-LSTM reader to leverage a simple one-way attention model that emphasizes a certain part of answer based on the question embedding. Yin et al. [13] and dos Santos et al. [5] used two-way attention mechanisms tailored to convolutional neural network.

Although these existing works have achieved good performance in answer selection, most of them treat the answer selection problem as the sentence-pair modeling, and do not take the information peculiar to question-answer pairs into consideration. However, intuitively, the question words that are peculiar to questions often play important roles in answer selection. For example:

- The question word "when" often requires that the answer sentence should contain a time noun;
- the question word "where" requires that the answer sentence should contain a location noun.

Based on this observation, this paper proposes to make use of a special kind of such information, i.e. the interaction between question words and POS tags, and integrates it into a neural model. We evaluate the neural model on the DBQA Shared Task of NLPCC2017 and report the results.

2   The Proposed Model

The document-based question answering task is described as follows. Each question $\mathbf{q}^i \in \mathcal{Q}$ is associcated with a set of candidate sentences, $\mathcal{D}^i = \{\mathbf{d}_1^i, \mathbf{d}_2^i, \ldots, \mathbf{d}_{|\mathcal{D}^i|}^i\}$, where $|\mathbf{d}_j^i|$ is the j-th candidate sentence for the question $\mathbf{q}$. Each candidate sentence $\mathbf{d}_j^i$ is associated with a class label y_j^i, whose value is 1 if the candidate $\mathbf{d}_j^i$ is an appropriate answer to the question $\mathbf{q}^i$, and 0 otherwise. The goal is to train a binary classifier: $f(\mathbf{q}^i, \mathbf{d}_j^i) \to y_j^i$, where f maps a question-candidate pair to its class labels.

For each pair of question $\mathbf{q}$ and candidate $\mathbf{d}$, assume that $\mathbf{q}$ is a sequence of m words, $q_1 q_2 \ldots q_m$, and $\mathbf{d}$ is a sequence of n words, $d_1 d_2 \ldots d_n$.

We use $\mathbf{f}_{\mathbf{d}|\mathbf{q}}^{wo} = f_{\mathbf{d}|\mathbf{q},1}^{wo} f_{\mathbf{d}|\mathbf{q},2}^{wo} \cdots f_{\mathbf{d}|\mathbf{q},n}^{wo}$ to denote the sequence of word-overlap features for $\mathbf{d}$, where j-th element $f_{\mathbf{d}|\mathbf{q},j}^{wo}$ equals 1 if the j-th word d_j in $\mathbf{d}$ appears in the question $\mathbf{q}$, and 0 otherwise. In addition, $\mathbf{f}_{\mathbf{q}|\mathbf{d}}^{wo} = f_{\mathbf{q}|\mathbf{d},1}^{wo} f_{\mathbf{q}|\mathbf{d},2}^{wo} \cdots f_{\mathbf{q}|\mathbf{d},m}^{wo}$ denotes the sequence of word-overlap features for $\mathbf{q}$, in a similar way.

We hypothesize that a candidate sentence **d** that is qualified to be an answer to the question **q** must satisfy at least the following conditions:

– (Semantic matching) **d** is semantically related to **q**; or in other words, the feature vector of **q** should share high similarity with the feature vector of **d**, in some perspectives;
– (Interaction between question words and POS tags) **d** contains a word whose part-of-speech tag is closely related to the question word of **q**, and the word does not occur in **q**. For example, if the question word *"when"* appears in the question, it is expected that there is a temporal noun in the answer; if the question word *"where"* appears in the question, a sentence that contains a location noun or geographical name is more likely to serve as the answer; if there is the question phrase *"how many"* in the question, the answer will have a large probability to include a number or quantity.

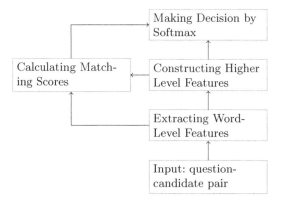

Fig. 1. The architecture of our neural model.

To materialize our hypothesis, we propose a neural model in this paper, with the modular architecture shown in Fig. 1. The details are described in the remaining part of this section:

– Section 2.1 will describe the word level features and how to extract them;
– Section 2.2 will introduce how the convolutional and pooling module is used to construct higher-level features (called the intermediate representations) from the lower word-level features;
– Section 2.3 will present four different matching scores and their calculation;
– Section 2.4 will use a hidden layer and a softmax layer to make the decision based on the calculated matching scores and the intermediate representations of the question and the candidate sentence.

2.1 Word-Level Feature Extraction

Before we delve into the details of the neural network, let us first have a look at the word-level features to be used, which include word embeddings, word-overlap feature embeddings, question-word embeddings, POS tag embeddings, and the IDF features. These features are then concatenated to form the vector representations for the words in the question $\mathbf{q}$ and the candidate sentence $\mathbf{d}$.

Word Embeddings. Each word w, no matter in the question $\mathbf{q}$ or in the candidate sentence $\mathbf{d}$, can be transformed into a d_{word}-dimensional vector $\mathbf{e}_{word}(w)$ by looking up a word embedding matrix $\mathbf{M}_{word} \in \mathbb{R}^{d_{word} \times |\mathbf{\Sigma}|}$, where $|\mathbf{\Sigma}_{word}|$ denote the size of the word dictionary $\mathbf{\Sigma}_{word}$.

We obtain the word embedding matrix $\mathbf{M}_{word}$ by training the skip-gram neural language model (provided in Word2Vec[1] [4]) on a large unsupervised text corpus of size about 20GB, crawled from Internet. We choose the dimensionality of word embeddings to be 300, window size to be 3, negative sampling to be 5, and number of epochs to be 5. The pretrained word embeddings are kept fixed during the training process.

Word-Overlap Feature Embeddings. Let f_j^{wo} denote the word-overlap feature of the j-th word in the candidate sentence $\mathbf{d}$. It can be transformed into a d_{wo}-dimensional vector $\mathbf{e}_{wo}(f_j^{wo})$ by looking up an embedding matrix $\mathbf{M}_{wo}$ of size $2 \times d_{wo}$. Similar to $\mathbf{M}_{qw}$ and $\mathbf{M}_{tag}$, the matrix $\mathbf{M}_{wo}$ is also randomly initialized, and gets tuned in the training process.

To model the interactions between the question words and POS tags, we have to identify all the interested question words from the question $\mathbf{q}$ and the POS tags from the candidate sentence $\mathbf{d}$.

- Firstly, we manually construct a dictionary of question words, denoted by Σ_{qw}. For a given question $\mathbf{q}$, we use $\gamma(\mathbf{q})$ to denote the set of all its words that belong to the question word dictionary $\mathbf{\Sigma}_{qw}$.
- Secondly, we make use of the part-of-speech tagger provided in PyLTP[2] to predict the POS tags for the words in a given candidate sentence $\mathbf{d}$. The POS tag dictionary is the POS tag set used by PyLTP, which contains 28 different POS tags as described at http://www.ltp-cloud.com/intro/#pos_how.

Question-Words and Their Embeddings. In a given question $\mathbf{q}$, each question word $q \in \gamma(\mathbf{q})$ is mapped to a d_{qw}-dimensional vector $\mathbf{e}_{qw}(q)$ by looking-up an embedding matrix $\mathbf{M}_{qw}$ of size $|\mathbf{\Sigma}_{qw}| \times d_{qw}$.

---

[1] http://code.google.com/archive/p/word2vec.
[2] https://github.com/HIT-SCIR/pyltp.

POS Tags and Their Embeddings. Let t_j denote the part-of-speech (POS) tag of the j-th word in the candidate sentence **d**. The POS-tag sequence of **d** is then $t_1 t_2 \ldots t_n$. Each POS tag t_i ($1 \leq i \leq n$) is mapped to a d_{tag}-dimensional vector $\mathbf{e}_{tag}(t_i)$ by looking-up an embedding matrix $\mathbf{M}_{tag}$ of size $|\mathbf{\Sigma}_{tag}| \times d_{tag}$.

Both the two embedding matrices $\mathbf{M}_{qw}$ and $\mathbf{M}_{tag}$ are initialized randomly, and get tuned during the training process.

Inverse Document Frequency (IDF). To measure the importance of words, we make use of their inverse document frequencies. We collect all the questions in the training data, and treat each question as a document.

$$idf(w) = \log \frac{|\mathcal{Q}|}{count(w, \mathcal{Q})} \tag{1}$$

where $count(w, \mathcal{Q})$ denotes the number of documents in $\mathcal{Q}$ that contain the word w. It is evident that $idf(w) > 0$ for all words w. The less frequently a word appears in the documents, the higher its IDF value is and the more important the word is.

As to the answer selection task, it is expected that a word in the question with high IDF value has a good match with a word in the answer. Thus, we calculate the IDF value of all the words in the question and feed them into the neural model.

Word-Level Vector Representations. Based on the word-level features described above, we can not construct the word-level vector representations for the words in the question **q** or the candidate sentence **d**.

Each word q_i in the question **q** is represented as a vector $\mathbf{e}(q_i)$ by concatenating its word embedding, word-overlap feature embedding, question-word embedding, and IDF feature:

$$\mathbf{e}(q_i) = [\mathbf{e}_{word}(q_i); \mathbf{e}_{wo}(q_i); \mathbf{e}_{qw}(q_i); idf(q_i)] \tag{2}$$

The dimensionality of $\mathbf{e}(q_i)$ is $d_{w\_in\_q} = d_{word} + d_{wo} + d_{qw} + 1$.

Each word d_i in the candidate sentence **d** is represented as a vector $\mathbf{e}(d_i)$ by concatenating its word embedding, its word-overlap feature embedding, and its POS-tag embedding:

$$\mathbf{e}(d_i) = [\mathbf{e}_{word}(d_i); \mathbf{e}_{wo}(d_i); \mathbf{e}_{tag}(d_i)] \tag{3}$$

Thus, the dimensionality of $\mathbf{e}(d_i)$ is $d_{w\_in\_d} = d_{word} + d_{wo} + d_{tag}$.

2.2   Convolutional and Pooling Module

After each word token has been represented as a vector, the convolutional layer can be applied to compose them in order to extract features at a higher level, and the pooling layer can be used to aggregate the information and reduce the representation.

Convolution Layer. The aim of the convolutional layer is to extract informative higher-level features by composing lower-level ones. Given an input sentence matrix $\mathbf{S} \in \mathbb{R}^{d \times s}$ where s is the length of the sentence and d is the dimensionality of the vector representation of the words, a convolution filter with size f is a matrix of weights: $\mathbf{F} \in \mathbb{R}^{d \times f}$. The convolution operator between $\mathbf{S}$ and $\mathbf{F}$ will result in a vector $\mathbf{c} \in \mathbb{R}^{s+f-1}$, where each component is calculated as follows:

$$\mathbf{c}_i = \sum_{j=1}^{d} \sum_{k=1}^{f} \mathbf{S}[j, i - k + 1] \cdot \mathbf{F}[j, f - k + 1] \tag{4}$$

Note that in real implementation, each $\mathbf{c}_i$ is added with a bias and then passed through a tanh nonlinear transformation. If there are d_f filters in the convolutional layer, then the output will be a matrix $\mathbf{C} \in \mathbb{R}^{d_f \times (s+f-1)}$.

Pooling. The output from the convolutional layer are passed to the pooling layer, which can aggregate the information and represent a variable-length sentence (question or candidate) as a fixed-sized vector. There are two common choices for pooling functions: max-pooling and average-pooling. We choose to use global max-pooling in the model. It takes maximum value along the temporal dimension of the output matrix $\mathbf{C}$ from the convolutional layer, and results in a vector $\mathbf{v}_{pool} \in \mathbb{R}^{d_f}$ whose i-th component is calculated as:

$$\mathbf{v}_{pool}[i] = \max_{1 \le j \le (s+f-1)} \mathbf{C}[i, j] \tag{5}$$

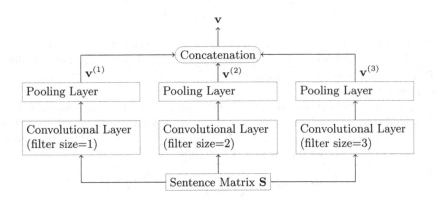

Fig. 2. The convolutional and pooling module

In our model, we use two convolutional and pooling modules, one for questions and the other for candidate sentences. Both the modules share the same architecture, but have different parameters. As illustrated in Fig. 2, the module have three convolutional layers whose filter sizes are 1, 2 and 3 respectively.

Each convolutional layer is fed directly with a sentence matrix $\mathbf{S}$ and followed by a global max-pooling layer. The output vectors of the three pooling layers are denoted as $\mathbf{v}^{(1)}$, $\mathbf{v}^{(2)}$ and $\mathbf{v}^{(3)}$ respectively, which are concatenated into the output vector of the module, $\mathbf{v} = \left[\mathbf{v}^{(1)}; \mathbf{v}^{(2)}; \mathbf{v}^{(3)}\right] \in \mathbb{R}^{3 \times d_f}$.

For a given question $\mathbf{q}$, we use $\mathbf{x}_q$ to denote the output vector of the convolutional and pooling module for questions; while for candidate sentence $\mathbf{d}$, we use annotation $\mathbf{x}_d$. We call $\mathbf{x}_q$ and $\mathbf{x}_d$ the intermediate representations of the question $\mathbf{q}$ and the candidate sentence $\mathbf{d}$ respectively.

2.3   Matching Scores Between Questions and Candidate Sentences

Based on the question-candidate pairs, the word-level features and the output from the convolutional and pooling module, we can calculate four matching scores between questions and candidate sentences:

- The first matching score is used to measure the interaction between question words in $\mathbf{q}$ and the POS tags in $\mathbf{d}$;
- The second matching score is used to measure the semantic similarity between $\mathbf{q}$ and $\mathbf{d}$ according to their outputs from the convolutional and pooling modules;
- The last two matching score is the simplest, which measures the word-overlapping and the weighted word-overlapping degrees between $\mathbf{q}$ and $\mathbf{d}$.

Interaction between Question Words and POS Tags. Given a question-candidate pair $(\mathbf{q}, \mathbf{d})$, the interaction score between a question word $q \in \gamma(\mathbf{q})$ and a POS tag t_i is defined as follows:

$$IScore(q, t_i) = \mathbf{e}_{qw}(q)^T \cdot \mathbf{e}_{tag}(t_i) \cdot (1 - f_i^{wo}) \tag{6}$$

A POS tag t_i has a large interaction score with a question word $q \in \gamma(\mathbf{q})$ only if it satisfies two conditions: (1) the tag embedding of t_i has a large inner product with the question-word embedding of q, and (2) the word d_i does not appear in the question $\mathbf{q}$.

For a candidate sentence $\mathbf{d}$ to be an appropriate answer to the question $\mathbf{q}$, it is expected that, for each question word $q \in \gamma(\mathbf{q})$, there exists a word t_i in $\mathbf{d}$ that best match it, i.e., the word t_i has a large interaction score with q. Therefore, the interaction score between $\mathbf{q}$ and $\mathbf{d}$ is defined as:

$$Score_{int}(\mathbf{q}, \mathbf{d}) = \min_{q \in \gamma(\mathbf{q})} \max_{1 \leq i \leq n} IScore(q, t_i) \tag{7}$$

Semantic Matching between Question and Candidate Sentence. Let $\mathbf{x}_q$ and $\mathbf{x}_d$ denote the resulting vector representations produced by the convolutional and pooling modules, on the question $\mathbf{q}$ and the candidate sentence $\mathbf{d}$ respectively. We define the semantic matching score between $\mathbf{q}$ and $\mathbf{d}$ as follow:

$$Score_{sem}(\mathbf{q}, \mathbf{d}) = \mathbf{x}_q^T \mathbf{M}_{match} \mathbf{x}_d \tag{8}$$

where $\mathbf{M}_{match} \in \mathbb{R}^{d_{sent} \times d_{sent}}$ is a similarity matrix (d_{sent} is the dimensionality of $\mathbf{x}_q$ and $\mathbf{x}_d$. The matrix $\mathbf{M}_{match}$ is initialized randomly and gets optimized during the training process.

Word Overlap Score. Intuitively, the candidate sentence that has more overlapped words with the question is more likely to be topic-related or semantically-related.

$$Score_{wo}(\mathbf{q}, \mathbf{d}) = \sum_{q \in \mathbf{q}} \mathbb{1}_{\mathbf{d}}(q) \tag{9}$$

where the symbol $\mathbb{1}$ denotes an indicator function, that is:

$$\mathbb{1}_{\mathbf{d}}(q) = \begin{cases} 1, \text{ if } q \in \mathbf{d} \\ 0, \text{ otherwise} \end{cases} \tag{10}$$

In addition, we also calculate the IDF-weighted word overlap score:

$$Score_{idf}(\mathbf{q}, \mathbf{d}) = \sum_{q \in \mathbf{q}} \mathbb{1}_{\mathbf{d}}(q) \cdot idf(q) \tag{11}$$

where $idf(\cdot)$ is calculated according to Eq. (1).

2.4 Softmax Output Module

Given a question-candidate pair $(\mathbf{q}, \mathbf{d})$, it is now represented, by concatenating their intermediate representations ($\mathbf{x}_q$ and $\mathbf{x}_d$) and the four matching scores between them, as a vector $\mathbf{x}_{pair}$ of dimensionality $d_{pair} = 6 \times d_f + 4$, called the final pair representation.

The softmax output module consists of a hidden layer followed by a softmax layer. The hidden layer with d_{hid} hidden units does the following transformation:

$$\mathbf{x}_{hid} = \tanh(\mathbf{W}_{hid} \cdot \mathbf{x}_{pair} + \mathbf{b}_{hid}) \tag{12}$$

where $\mathbf{W}_{hid}$ is a weight matrix of size $d_{hid} \times d_{pair}$, and $\mathbf{b}_{hid}$ is a bias vector of size d_{hid}.

In turn, the vector $\mathbf{x}_{hid}$ is fed to the softmax layer. It first calculate a 2-dimensional score vector $\mathbf{x}_{output} = [x_0, x_1]$:

$$\mathbf{x}_{output} = \mathbf{W}_{output} \cdot \mathbf{x}_{hid} + \mathbf{b}_{output} \tag{13}$$

where $\mathbf{W}_{output} \in \mathbb{R}^{2 \times d_{hid}}$ is a weight matrix, and $\mathbf{b}_{output} \in \mathbb{R}^2$ is a bias vector. Next, the softmax layer applies softmax transformation on the score vector, resulting in a probability distribution $\mathbf{o} = [o_0, o_1]$ whose component o_i ($i \in 0, 1$) is:

$$o_i = \frac{\exp x_i}{\sum_{j \in \{0,1\}} \exp x_j} \tag{14}$$

2.5   Cross-Entropy Loss Function

Since the answer selection task is formulated as a binary classification problem, we train the model to minimize the cross-entropy loss function defined as follows:

$$L = -\frac{1}{N} \sum_{i=1}^{N} t_i \log o_{i,t_i} \tag{15}$$

where t_i is the golden class label for the i-th pair of question and candidate, and o_{i,t_i} denotes the predicted probability that the i-th pair has the class label t_i.

The parameters are optimized to minimize the cross entropy loss function in Eq. (15) by using the Adam algorithm [3], where the learning rate is set to 0.001, beta1 is set to 0.9, and beta2 is set to 0.999.

2.6   Dropout

Dropout is an effective technique to regularize neural networks by randomly drop units during training. It has achieved a great success when working with feed-forward networks [7], convolutional networks, or even recurrent neural networks [15].

In our model, dropout is applied to both the input and the output of the convolutional and pooling modules, with dropout probabilities being 0.4 and 0.7 respectively.

3   Experiments

We evaluate our model on DBQA Shared Task of NLPCC2017. The characteristics of the dataset is described in Table 1.

Table 1. Dataset of NLPCC 2017 Shared Task on DBQA

Dataset	Questions	QA-pairs
Train	8772	181882
Validation	5997	122532

The quality of our DBQA system is evaluated by mean reciprocal rank (**MRR**) and mean average precision (**MAP**) defined as:

– Mean Reciprocal Rank (MRR):

$$MRR = \frac{1}{|\mathcal{Q}|} \sum_{i=1}^{|\mathcal{Q}|} \frac{1}{rank_i} \tag{16}$$

where $|\mathcal{Q}|$ is the total number of questions in the evaluation set, $rank_i$ denotes the position of the first correct answer in the set of candidate sentences for the i-th question.

– Mean Average Precision (MAP):

$$MAP = \frac{1}{|\mathcal{Q}|} \sum_{i=1}^{|\mathcal{Q}|} AveP(C_i, A_i) \qquad (17)$$

Here, $AveP(C, A) = \frac{\sum_{k=1}^{n}(P(k) \cdot rel(k))}{min(m,n)}$ denotes the average precision, where k is the rank in the sequence of retrieved candidate sentences, m is the number of correct answer sentences, n is the number of retrieved answer sentences, $P(k)$ is the precision at cut-off k in the list, and $rel(k)$ is an indicator function equaling 1 if the item at rank k is an answer sentence (0 otherwise).

3.1 Performance on the Validation Dataset

The experimental results of our model are listed in Table 2. It is compared with several state-of-the-art systems that participate in the DBQA task of previous year (NLPCC2016).

Table 2. Experimental results on the validation dataset for NLPCC2017 DBQA Task

Model	MRR	MAP
Fu et al. [2]	0.8592	0.8586
Wu et al. [11]	0.8120	0.8111
Wang et al. [9]	0.8008	0.8005
Our model	0.8768	0.8763

In Table 2, the model proposed by Fu et al. [2] learns to map the input sentence pairs to vectors, and then to compute their similarity, which achieved the highest MRR and MAP on the DBQA task of NLPCC2016. Wu et al. [11] proposed a hybrid approach to select answer sentences by combining existing model via the rank SVM model, which achieved the third place on the DBQA task of NLPCC2016. Wang and Nyberg [10] integrated count-based features and embedding-based features together, which also achieved a good performance.

3.2 Performance on the Test Dataset

In addition to the train dataset and the validation dataset, the DBQA task of NLPCC2017 also releases a test dataset where the golden answer annotations are not provided. We obtain our submission result file as follows:

– A larger training dataset is obtained by merging the training and validation datasets.
– On the larger training dataset, our model is trained for 20 epochs, and the model at the final epoch is chosen to make predictions for the test dataset.

The result file by our model has achieved the highest MRR and MAP scores, as listed in Table 3, among all the submitted result files.

Table 3. Experimental results on the open test data for NLPCC2017 DBQA Task

	MRR	MAP
Our model	0.7202	0.7166

4   Conclusion

In this paper, we propose to model the interaction between question words and POS tags, as a special kind of information peculiar to question-answer pairs. Such information gets integrated into a neural model to measure the matching degree between questions and answer candidates. Experimental results on NLPCC2017 DBQA task have shown that this neural model has achieve better performance when compared with several state-of-the-art systems.

Acknowledgments. This work is partially supported by National High-Tech R&D Program of China (863 Program) (No. 2015AA015404), and Science and Technology Commission of Shanghai Municipality (No. 14511106802). We are grateful to the anonymous reviewers for their valuable comments.

References

1. Feng, M., Xiang, B., Glass, M.R., Wang, L., Zhou, B.: Applying deep learning to answer selection: a study and an open task. In: 2015 IEEE Workshop on Automatic Speech Recognition and Understanding (ASRU), pp. 813–820. IEEE (2015)
2. Fu, J., Qiu, X., Huang, X.: Convolutional deep neural networks for document-based question answering. In: Lin, C.-Y., Xue, N., Zhao, D., Huang, X., Feng, Y. (eds.) ICCPOL/NLPCC -2016. LNCS (LNAI), vol. 10102, pp. 790–797. Springer, Cham (2016). https://doi.org/10.1007/978-3-319-50496-4_71
3. Kingma, D., Ba, J.: Adam: a method for stochastic optimization. arXiv preprint arXiv:1412.6980 (2014)
4. Mikolov, T., Sutskever, I., Chen, K., Corrado, G.S., Dean, J.: Distributed representations of words and phrases and their compositionality. In: Advances in Neural Information Processing Systems (NIPS), pp. 3111–3119 (2013)
5. dos Santos, C.N., Tan, M., Xiang, B., Zhou, B.: Attentive pooling networks. CoRR, abs/1602.03609 (2016)
6. Severyn, A., Moschitti, A.: Learning to rank short text pairs with convolutional deep neural networks. In: Proceedings of the 38th International ACM SIGIR Conference on Research and Development in Information Retrieval, pp. 373–382 (2015)
7. Srivastava, N.: Improving neural networks with dropout. Ph.D. thesis, University of Toronto (2013)
8. Tan, M., Santos, C.D., Xiang, B., Zhou, B.: LSTM-based deep learning models for non-factoid answer selection. arXiv preprint arXiv:1511.04108 (2015)
9. Wang, B., Niu, J., Ma, L., Zhang, Y., Zhang, L., Li, J., Zhang, P., Song, D.: A chinese question answering approach integrating count-based and embedding-based features. In: Lin, C.-Y., Xue, N., Zhao, D., Huang, X., Feng, Y. (eds.) ICCPOL/NLPCC -2016. LNCS (LNAI), vol. 10102, pp. 934–941. Springer, Cham (2016). https://doi.org/10.1007/978-3-319-50496-4_88

10. Wang, D., Nyberg, E.: A long short-term memory model for answer sentence selection in question answering. In: ACL, vol. 2, pp. 707–712 (2015)
11. Wu, F., Yang, M., Zhao, T., Han, Z., Zheng, D., Zhao, S.: A hybrid approach to DBQA. In: Lin, C.-Y., Xue, N., Zhao, D., Huang, X., Feng, Y. (eds.) ICCPOL/NLPCC -2016. LNCS (LNAI), vol. 10102, pp. 926–933. Springer, Cham (2016). https://doi.org/10.1007/978-3-319-50496-4_87
12. Yih, W., Chang, M., Meek, C., Pastusiak, A.: Question answering using enhanced lexical semantic models. In: Proceedings of the 51st Annual Meeting of the Association for Computational Linguistics, Long Papers, vol. 1, pp. 1744–1753 (2013)
13. Yin, W., Schütze, H., Xiang, B., Zhou, B.: ABCNN: attention-based convolutional neural network for modeling sentence pairs. arXiv preprint arXiv:1512.05193 (2015)
14. Yu, L., Hermann, K.M., Blunsom, P., Pulman, S.: Deep learning for answer sentence selection. In: NIPS Deep Learning Workshop, December 2014. http://arxiv.org/abs/1412.1632
15. Zaremba, W., Sutskever, I., Vinyals, O.: Recurrent neural network regularization. arXiv preprint arXiv:1409.2329 (2014)

Machine Learning

A Deep Learning Way for Disease Name Representation and Normalization

Hongwei Liu and Yun Xu[✉]

University of Science and Technology of China, Hefei, China
xuyun@ustc.edu.cn

Abstract. Disease name normalization aims at mapping various disease names to standardized disease vocabulary entries. Disease names have such a wide variation that dictionary lookup method couldn't get a high accuracy on this task. Dnorm is the first machine learning approach for this task. It is not robust enough due to strong dependence on training dataset. In this article, we propose a deep learning way for disease name representation and normalization. Representations of composing words can be learned from large unlabelled literature corpus. Rich semantic and syntactic properties of disease names are encoded in the representations during the process. With the new way of representations for disease names, a higher accuracy is achieved in the normalization task.

Keywords: Disease name representation · Disease name normalization

1 Introduction

There is a rapid growth in biological research recently which results in an exponential growth of biomedical literature [1]. Extracting useful information for better use of biological literature becomes important but difficult. During tasks in biomedical text mining, disease name recognition and normalization is a fundamental task which can be further used for tasks like disease-gene [2], disease-drug [3] relation extraction. Generally, there are two steps to find disease concepts showing in literatures. The first step is to extract mentions of disease names from literatures which can be done by tools like BANNER [4]. The next important step is the normalization of various disease mentions to standardized disease vocabulary entries. An entry in standardized disease vocabulary represents a disease concept. A disease concept is uniquely identified by a disease identifier. However, a disease concept may have multiple different disease names because a disease concept can be named by its anatomical locations, symptoms, treatment, causative agent and so on. This wide variation in disease names makes the normalization task difficult.

Dictionary lookup and pattern matching algorithms were often used in early years in the task of disease name normalization. Doğan and Lu proposed an inference method [5] for disease name normalization which was mainly based on

© Springer International Publishing AG 2018
X. Huang et al. (Eds.): NLPCC 2017, LNAI 10619, pp. 151–157, 2018.
https://doi.org/10.1007/978-3-319-73618-1_13

dictionary lookup and pattern matching. A string similarity is calculated during the process. A disease concept is assigned to a disease mention if their names are very similar in spelling. But with a rich variation, some disease mentions are hardly mapped to the correct disease concepts. After that, a rule-based method was proposed by Kang et al. [6]. They focused on some obvious mistakes made by dictionary lookup method and designed several rules to correct the mistakes. Since the rules were designed by human, they could only deal with mistakes in limited circumstances. Recently, Leaman and Doğan implemented a disease normalization tool called Dnorm [7]. It is based on a machine learning method called pairwise learning to rank (pLTR) [8]. The method learns the semantic correlation between words from training dataset and calculates a similarity score between a disease mention and a disease concept. Disease concept with the highest similarity score will be assigned to the disease mention. There are two main shortcomings of this method: (1) It is not robust enough since it is strongly dependent on the training dataset. (2) The method ignores syntactic properties which play important roles in measuring the similarity between phrases.

In this article, we propose a deep learning way for disease name representation and normalization. Word2vec [9,10] is used to generate a distributed representation for each word of disease names. Large unlabeled literature corpus can be used to train the representation. TreeLSTM [11] is used to integrate words' representations into a representation for a disease name. Finally, a simple perceptron is used to calculate a similarity score between a disease mention and a disease concept. High robustness can be achieved since the method doesn't have strong dependence on training dataset. Also, rich semantic and syntactic properties of disease names can be captured during the process. In this paper, the details of the method will be first described in the following. The results of several experiments are shown after that. Finally, a conclusion is given to summarize the main ideas in this paper.

2   Methods

2.1   Processing Pipeline

Our processing pipeline is summarized as Fig. 1. For each disease name, a distributed representation is generated using Word2Vec and TreeLSTM. A similarity score is calculated between a disease mention and each disease concept name using a simple perceptron. Finally, the disease concept whose name has the highest similarity score is assigned to the disease mention. Following is the details of the pipeline.

2.2   Word2vec and TreeLSTM for Distributed Representation

Usually, a disease name is a phrase composed of several words. And these words are organized based on syntax and grammar to construct the disease name. In order to fully represent a disease name, we need to utilize both the meaning

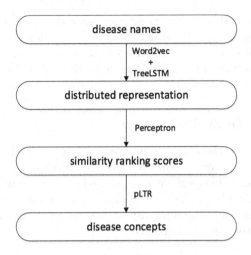

Fig. 1. Processing pipeline

of composing words and the syntactic properties of the disease name. First, a distributed representation is generated for each word with the help of Word2vec. Word2Vec is a tool that learns to represent each word as a fixed-length vector in an unsupervised way. With enough training corpus, the distributed representation can reflect the meaning of words. And then, each disease name is analyzed by a dependency parser to generate a structured tree which reflects syntactic properties of that disease name. In the end, we integrate words' representations into a phrase representation based on that structured tree. Given a tree, let $C(j)$ denote the set of children of node j. Following is the concrete integrating equations from representations of children nodes to representation of their parent node:

$$\widetilde{h}_j = \sum_{k \in C(j)} h_k \tag{1}$$

$$i_j = \sigma \left(W^{(i)} x_j + U^{(i)} \widetilde{h}_j + b^{(i)} \right) \tag{2}$$

$$f_{jk} = \sigma \left(W^{(f)} x_j + U^{(f)} h_k + b^{(f)} \right) \tag{3}$$

$$o_j = \sigma \left(W^{(o)} x_j + U^{(o)} \widetilde{h}_j + b^{(o)} \right) \tag{4}$$

$$u_j = tanh \left(W^{(u)} x_j + U^{(u)} \widetilde{h}_j + b^{(u)} \right) \tag{5}$$

$$c_j = i_j \odot u_j + \sum_{k \in C(j)} f_{jk} \odot c_k \tag{6}$$

$$h_j = o_j \odot tanh \left(c_j \right) \tag{7}$$

Recursively calculating the representations of nodes from tree's left to right, from bottom to up, we can get a final representation for the tree's root. The representation of the tree's root captures both meanings of composing words and syntactic properties of the disease name so that it can be used as the representation for the disease name.

2.3   Perceptron for Similarity Score

For each pair $<m, n>$ where m is a disease mention extracted from corpus and n is a disease concept name in the controlled vocabulary, a score is needed to measure the similarity between them. A simple perceptron is used here which can be trained with other parts of the neural network. Distance and angle are two key points to measure the similarity of two vectors. Here, the inner product and distance are inputs to the perceptron:

$$h_p = h_L \odot h_R \tag{8}$$

$$h_s = |h_L - h_R| \tag{9}$$

$$h_d = \sigma \left(W^{(p)} h_p + W^{(s)} h_s + b^{(h)} \right) \tag{10}$$

$$\hat{p}_\theta = softmax \left(W^{(p)} h_d + b^{(p)} \right) \tag{11}$$

$$score = r^T \hat{p}_\theta \tag{12}$$

h_L and h_R are distributed representations for a disease mention and a disease concept name. The final score is a real number in interval $[0, 1]$ where higher similarity results in a higher score. $\hat{p}_\theta$ represents the distribution of different score. r is a static vector that equals to $[0, 1]$.

2.4   PLTR for Concept Assignment

To simplify the problem, let M represent a set of disease mentions, D represent a set of disease identifiers and N represent a set of disease concept names. Several disease concept names $n \in N$ may correspond to one identifier $d \in D$ but one disease name $n \in N$ corresponds to only one disease identifier $d \in D$ in standardized disease vocabulary. Then we can describe the normalization task as follows: for each disease mention $m \in M$, we need to assign a unique identifier $d \in D$ by comparing disease mention m and the set of disease names N. For a disease mention m, d^+ is a notation for a right identifier while d^- is a notation for a wrong identifier. Following is the process of pLTR. Given a disease mention m and a pair of identifier (d^+, d^-) in training set, we learns to give a higher similarity score for $\langle m, d^+ \rangle$ than $\langle m, d^- \rangle$. Given a new disease mention, identifier with the highest similarity score is chosen.

2.5   Training Details

There are two training tasks in training process: training for words' representations and training for similarity scores. We crawl more than 8 million abstracts from PubMed website with search keywords "disease or disorder or syndrome or deficiency or dysfunction or cancer or tumor" for words' embedding training. When training parameters in TreeLSTM and perceptron, there are more incorrect names than correct names for a disease mention. We randomly sample 200 incorrect concept names and select an incorrect concept name with the highest similarity score as n^-. Then the output score of perceptron is made to be 1 for $\langle m, n^+ \rangle$ and 0 for $\langle m, n^- \rangle$. We test different values for model's hyper parameters and optimal values among test ones are chosen based on model's performance on the development set. The length of word embedding is set to be 300; the length of hidden embedding (including TreeLSTM's internal nodes and root node) is set to be 300; we use stochastic gradient descent with a learning rate of 0.01 as the optimization algorithm; cost function is the KL-divergence between the distribution of manually assigned score and the distribution of perceptron output score; library Theano [12] is used to build the TreeLSTM and the perceptron.

3   Datasets and Results

3.1   Datasets

Medical Subject Headings (MeSH) [13] and Online Mendelian Inheritance in Man (OMIM) [14] are two main terminologies for disease concepts. In 2012, a disease lexicon, namely MEDIC [15], merged OMIM into the disease branch of MeSH which makes it a deep and broad vocabulary for disease names. And a dataset called NCBI [16] disease corpus was created with MEDIC as the lexicon to help researchers develop powerful and highly effective tools for disease name recognition and normalization task. NCBI disease corpus consists of 793 PubMed [17] abstracts which are split into three subsets. We train our model with the help of training and development subset and evaluate our model on test subset. And another dataset created for Biocreative V CDR [18] task is used to test the robustness of our method.

3.2   Results

Several methods including Lucene, cosine similarity and pLTR + weight matrix are listed as a comparison. Manually-marking mentions with MeSH or OMIM identifiers which can be seen as a gold standard are fed into normalization tools. Accuracy is calculated based on result (Table 1).

With Word2vec and TreeLSTM, we get richer semantic and syntactic properties of disease names. For example, "autosomal dominant disease" is correctly mapped into "genetic disease" in our method which can't be done by others. Our system successfully learns the relationship between "autosomal" and "genetic" and gives a high similarity score when comparing those two disease phrases.

Table 1. Accuracy on gold-standard mentions (train and test on NCBI)

Method	Right number	Total number	Accuracy
Lucene	674	960	0.702
Cosine similarity	687		0.716
pLTR + weight matrix (DNorm)	789		0.822
pLTR + TreeLSTM (Ours)	819		0.853

Also, different syntactic structures with the same meaning can be captured by our method. For example, "inherited disorder" can be correctly mapped into "Disease, Hereditary".

To evaluate the robustness of two machine learning methods, we did an experiment on another dataset (BC5CDR). This time we train both our method and Dnorm on NCBI training subset only. And we evaluate two methods on BC5DR dataset which is a totally new dataset for both methods (Table 2).

Table 2. Accuracy on gold-standard mentions (train on NCBI, test on BC5CDR)

Method	Right number	Total number	Accuracy
pLTR + weight matrix (DNorm)	3060	4424	0.715
pLTR + TreeLSTM (Ours)	3339		0.765

Though accuracy goes down for both methods, our method shows higher robustness.

4   Conclusion

In this article, we introduce a deep learning way for the disease normalization task. A distributed representation of disease name is generated with the help of Word2vec and TreeLSTM. The similarity between a disease mention and a disease concept is measured based on that distributed representation using a simple perceptron. Compared with pLTR, higher robustness is achieved since word embedding can be learned with a large unlabeled corpus. Rich semantic and syntactic properties are captured with the distributed representation in the process. And we get better results than DNorm in disease name normalization task on different datasets.

References

1. Lu, Z.: PubMed and beyond: a survey of web tools for searching biomedical literature. Database **2011**, baq036 (2011)
2. Garcia-Albornoz, M., Nielsen, J.: Finding directionality and gene-disease predictions in disease associations. BMC Syst. Biol. **9**(1), 35 (2015)
3. Yu, L., Huang, J., Ma, Z., et al.: Inferring drug-disease associations based on known protein complexes. BMC Med. Genomics **8**(2), S2 (2015)
4. Leaman, R., Gonzalez, G.: BANNER: an executable survey of advances in biomedical named entity recognition. In: Pacific Symposium on Biocomputing, vol. 13, pp. 652–663 (2008)
5. Doğan, R.I., Lu, Z.: An inference method for disease name normalization. In: AAAI Fall Symposium Series (2012)
6. Kang, N., Singh, B., Afzal, Z., et al.: Using rule-based natural language processing to improve disease normalization in biomedical text. J. Am. Med. Inform. Assoc. **20**(5), 876–881 (2013)
7. Leaman, R., Doğan, R.I., Lu, Z.: DNorm: disease name normalization with pairwise learning to rank. Bioinformatics **29**(22), 2909–2917 (2013)
8. Cao, Z., Qin, T., Liu, T.Y., et al.: Learning to rank: from pairwise approach to listwise approach. In: Proceedings of the 24th International Conference on Machine learning, pp. 129–136. ACM (2007)
9. Mikolov, T., Chen, K., Corrado, G., et al.: Efficient estimation of word representations in vector space. In: ICLR Workshop (2013)
10. Mikolov, T., Sutskever, I., Chen, K., et al.: Distributed representations of words and phrases and their compositionality. In: Advances in Neural Information Processing Systems, pp. 3111–3119 (2013)
11. Tai, K.S., Socher, R., Manning, C.D.: Improved semantic representations from tree-structured long short-term memory networks. In: Proceedings of the 53rd Annual Meeting of the Association for Computational Linguistics and the 7th International Joint Conference on Natural Language Processing, pp. 1556–1566 (2015)
12. Al-Rfou, R., et al.: Theano: A Python framework for fast computation of mathematical expressions. arXiv preprint (2016)
13. Medical Subject Headings. https://www.nlm.nih.gov/mesh
14. An Online Catalog of Human Genes and Genetic Disorders. https://www.omim.org
15. Davis, A.P., Wiegers, T.C., Rosenstein, M.C., et al.: MEDIC: a practical disease vocabulary used at the comparative toxicogenomics database. Database **2012**, bar065 (2012)
16. Doğan, R.I., Leaman, R., Lu, Z.: NCBI disease corpus: a resource for disease name recognition and concept normalization. J. Biomed. Inform. **47**, 1–10 (2014)
17. US National Labrary of Medicine. https://www.ncbi.nlm.nih.gov/pubmed
18. Li, J., Sun, Y., Johnson, R.J., et al.: BioCreative V CDR task corpus: a resource for chemical disease relation extraction. Database **2016**, baw068 (2016)

Externally Controllable RNN for Implicit Discourse Relation Classification

Xihan Yue, Luoyi Fu, and Xinbing Wang[✉]

Department of Computer Science and Engineering,
Shanghai Jiao Tong University, Shanghai, China
{yuexihan,yiluofu,xwang8}@sjtu.edu.cn

Abstract. Without discourse connectives, recognizing implicit discourse relations is a great challenge and a bottleneck for discourse parsing. The key factor lies in proper representing the two discourse arguments as well as modeling their interactions. This paper proposes two novel neural networks, i.e., externally controllable LSTM (ECLSTM) and attention-augmented GRU (AAGRU), which can be stacked to incorporate arguments' interactions into their representing process. The two networks are variants of Recurrent Neural Network (RNN) but equipped with externally controllable cells that their working processes can be dynamically regulated. ECLSTM is relatively conservative and easily comprehensible while AAGRU works better for small datasets. Multi-level RNN with smaller hidden state allows critical information to be gradually exploited, and thus enables our model to fit deeper structures with slightly increased complexity. Experiments on the Penn Discourse Treebank (PDTB) benchmark show that our method achieves significant performance gain over vanilla LSTM/CNN models and competitive with previous state-of-the-art models.

Keywords: Implicit discourse relation classification
Recurrent neural network · Sequence pair modeling

1 Introduction

A text span may connect to another span when there is a causal relation between them or when they contrast each other. Such semantic relations are termed rhetorical or discourse relations [5]. Discourse parsing, the process of which is to understand the internal structure of a text and identify the discourse relations in between its segments, is a fundamental task in Natural Language Processing (NLP) since it benefits a lot of downstream applications such as information retrieval, question answering and automatic summarization [11].

Discourse connectives (e.g. *and, because,* etc.) are considered as one of the most critical linguistic cues for discourse relations. Depending on whether there are connectives in between text arguments, discourse relations can be categorized into implicit and explicit ones. According to Pitler [3], an over 90% of accuracy

© Springer International Publishing AG 2018
X. Huang et al. (Eds.): NLPCC 2017, LNAI 10619, pp. 158–169, 2018.
https://doi.org/10.1007/978-3-319-73618-1_14

rate can be achieved in classifying the explicit relations, so that the bottleneck of discourse parsing lies in recognizing implicit relations.

Conventional methods using one-hot representations [4,7] and recent neural network (NN) models [13,15] using dense real-value representations, despite their differences in feature representations, all follow a strategy that decomposes the process to two independent steps, modeling the two discourse arguments and then modeling their interactions. Intuitively, these methods simulate the single-pass reading process [19]. However, a large number of irrelevant components in texts make crucial information easily concealed. **Without specific learning aims and guidances, single-pass reading is heavily affected by data sparsity while still inadequate to capture comprehensive representations of the text arguments.**

In order to solve the dilemma, we leverage the intuition that critical information could be dynamically exploited through several passes of reading [19]. Specifically, we use previously obtained argument representations as guidance and reread the texts to gradually get deeper and preciser understandings. Now, let us check one real example to elaborate the new strategy.

[*Arg1*]: The World Psychiatric Association voted at an Athens parley to conditionally readmit the Soviet Union.

[*Arg2*]: Moscow could be suspended if the misuse of psychiatry against dissenters is discovered during a review within a year.

[*Implicit Connective*]: However

[*Discourse relation*]: Contrast

In the above example, each argument is composed of multiple phrases containing different meanings that without information from the other one we can only allocate identical attentions to them. In the second stage of reading, we have guidance and can retain only the most relevant parts, reaching the conclusion that there exists a relation rather than no relation. In order to discriminate different relation types, we further move to the third stage of reading where we term the process of gradually capturing the most relevant information for classification as mutually guided sequence pairs modeling. Here, we use "sequence pairs" rather than "argument pairs" to emphasize that the guidance mechanism acts upon the sequential processing of words and our method can be generally adopted on sequences-interaction related tasks.

We note that the key to implement the repeated reading strategy is finding a proper model for the process of guided regenerating. Since Recurrent Neural Network (RNN) is the most natural way to model sequence, we customize it by equipping its internal computational unit with externally controllable gates. Gated RNNs such as Long Short-Term Memory (LSTM) are not suitable for naive stacking. Usually, outputs of lower-level LSTM are weighted and summed and feed as input to higher-level LSTM to model the hierarchical structure of articles [17]. Here, we take several layers of RNNs with their inputs directly connected to the original text arguments and use lower layer's outputs as higher layer's guidance to integrate them into a multilevel structure. In this paper, we propose two novel recurrent neural networks to implement the strategy of mutually guided modeling. One is Externally Controllable Long Short Term Memory (ECLSTM), whose internal gates can be controlled by externally supplied vector. The other is Attention-Augmented Gated Recurrent Unit (AAGRU), which uses attention mechanism to augment traditional GRU. The difference between ECLSTM and AAGRU lies in that AAGRU renders supplied vector stronger controlling power and bears a simpler structure. In summary, this paper makes the following contributions:

1. We propose stacked RNN to implement the repeated reading strategy and prove its practicability in experiments.
2. We design ECLSTM as a conservative extension of LSTM and AAGRU as a strengthened version. Their efficiencies are both empirically verified in experiments and AAGRU exhibits better performance in small datasets.

2 Related Work

The first formal study of implicit discourse classification dates back to Marcu and Echihabi [1], which proposes a method for cheap acquisition of training data. However, their idea, which deletes connectives in unambiguous explicit patterns and treats the remaining spans as belonging to implicit relations, has been proven to be inadequate to generate realistic examples [4]. The interest in implicit discourse parsing surges since the release of PDTB [2], a resource of annotated discourse relations including implicit ones.

Conventional methods for implicit relations classification use hand-crafted linguistic features [4,7]. Those methods, which make heavy use of word pairs, suffer from data sparsity problems. Recently, unsupervised dense real-value word representations are demonstrated to outperform previous one-hot representations [12,21], and neural network models, which alleviate the need for traditional extensive feature engineering, can achieve even better performance [13,15].

Incorporating arguments' interactions into their modeling processes is not a new concept since the use of word pairs naively implements the strategy. Chen [15] extends the naive methods by utilizing dense representations and contextual information, which augments word vectors with contextual information through a bidirectional LSTM neural network and generates pair-wise representations with those newly calculated vectors. Liu and Li [19] proposes neural networks, which consist of one bidirectional LSTM layer and multiple attention layers, to mimic the repeated reading strategy. Rather than simply adding attention layers, we merge attention mechanism in RNN units that enables our model to fit deeper structures with little increased complexity.

Another notable line aims at building multi-model approaches and using external resources to help improve accuracy. Multi-task neural network model, which share partial architecture for implicit discourse classification tasks of different corpora, is proposed to alleviate the shortage of labeled data [16,18]. Qin [20] proposes an adversarial network, which leverages implicit connectives manually added in PDTB, as an regularization mechanism to adaptively regularize parameters. Those approaches can be seen as integrated frameworks, and our methods can be used as replacement parts.

3   Methods

The strategy proposed in this paper is to incorporate arguments' interactions into their modeling process to dynamically exploit critical information. Firstly, each arguments are independently processed to get a general sense, then we reprocess the argument pairs under the guidance of the general understanding to get more relevant representations to the recognition task. The newly acquired representations are then used as guidance for further processing. In practice, we limit the upper bound of total guiding and reprocessing times to 2.

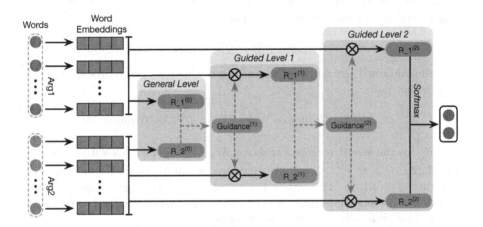

Fig. 1. Architecture of the model.

3.1   Model Architecture

The overall architecture of our model is illustrated in Fig. 1. Let us take $(Args, y)$ as a pair of input and output, where $Args = (Arg_1, Arg_2)$ is the argument pair and y is the golden standard relation. The two arguments contain different amounts of words:

$$Arg_1 = [w_{1,1}, w_{1,2}, \ldots, w_{1,L_1}], \quad Arg_2 = [w_{2,1}, w_{2,2}, \ldots, w_{2,L_2}]$$

Initially, we associate each lemma in lemma vocabulary with a vector representation $e_l \in R^{D_l}$ and each part of speech (POS) tag in POS vocabulary with a vector representation $e_p \in R^{D_p}$. Firstly, words in arguments are converted to word embeddings by concatenating their corresponding lemma vectors and pos vectors:

$$x_{i,j} = e_{L(w_{i,j})} \oplus e_{P(w_{i,j})}$$

where $x_{i,j} \in R^{D_e}$ is word embedding vector of $w_{i,j}$. L denotes the operation of lemmatization, P represents the operation of POS tagging and $D_e = D_l + D_p$ is the dimension of word embedding.

Let $E(Arg_i)$ denote the process of transforming Arg_i's words to their vector representations, we have:

$$X_1 = E(Arg_1) = [x_{1,1}, x_{1,2}, \ldots, x_{1,L_1}], \quad X_2 = E(Arg_2) = [x_{2,1}, x_{2,2}, \ldots, x_{2,L_2}]$$

Then we calculate the general-level representations of arguments as:

$$R_1^{(0)} = g^{(0)}(X_1), \quad R_2^{(0)} = g^{(0)}(X_2)$$

In implementing $g^{(0)}$, we separately adopt one-dimensional CNN and bi-LSTM with attention to compare their effects. Now we can obtain the level-1 guidance vector by concatenating $R_1^{(0)}$ and $R_2^{(0)}$:

$$Guidance^{(1)} = R_1^{(0)} \oplus R_2^{(0)}$$

Having obtained the guidance vector, we re-calculate the representations of the argument pairs:

$$R_1^{(1)} = g_1^{(1)}(X_1, Guidance^{(1)}), \quad R_2^{(1)} = g_2^{(1)}(X_2, Guidance^{(1)})$$

where $R_i^{(1)}$ is the level-1 representation for Arg_i. We adopt RNN with externally controllable cells as $g_i^{(1)}$ to enable guidance vector to control the sequential processing of words in Arg_i. After K-th repeating of the guided level, we use the newest representations derived from the top level to recognize the discourse relation through a fully connected softmax layer:

$$P = softmax(W_p(R_1^{(K)} \oplus R_2^{(K)}) + b_p)$$

3.2   General Sequence Pairs Modeling

The operations of general modeling the two arguments will be the same since it conforms to common sense and reduces parameters. So we treat X_1 and X_2 obtained from the embedding-lookup layer as a unified form $X = [x_1, x_2, \ldots, x_L]$.

Here we briefly introduce two methods, which are one-dimensional CNN with max pooling and bi-LSTM with attention.

One-Dimensional Convolutional Neural Network has been broadly used for modeling sequences. Filter matrices $[W_1, W_2, \ldots, W_k]$ with variable sizes $[l_1, l_2, \ldots, l_k]$ are utilized to perform convolutional operations. The argument embeddings will be transformed to sequences C_j:

$$C_j = [\ldots, \tanh(W_j X_{[i:i+l_j-1]} + b_j), \ldots], \quad j \in [1, k]$$

where $X_{[i:i+l_j-1]} = [x_i, x_i+1, \ldots, x_i+l_j-1]$ is the convolutional window with l_j words. After convolution, argument vector is obtained by concatenating maximal value of each sequence:

$$s_j = \max(C_j), \quad R^{(0)} = [s_1, s_2, \ldots, s_k]$$

Long-Short Term Memory Recurrent Neural Network is a variant of RNN and broadly used for modeling sequences. The mechanism in LSTM is showed as follows:

$$i_t = \sigma(W_i x_t + U_i c_{t-1} + b_i), \quad f_t = \sigma(W_f x_t + U_f c_{t-1} + b_f),$$
$$c_t = f_t \circ c_{t-1} + i_t \circ \tanh(W_c x_t + U_c c_{t-1} + b_c),$$
$$o_t = \sigma(W_o x_t + U_o c_t + b_o), \quad h_t = o_t \circ c_t$$

where i_t, f_t and o_t are called input gate, forget gate and output gate. c_t is the cell-state vector that is used to store long-term information. h_t is the output vector.

We get annotations of words by using bidirectional LSTM to summarize information from both directions:

$$\overrightarrow{h_t} = \overrightarrow{LSTM}(x_t), \quad \overleftarrow{h_t} = \overleftarrow{LSTM}(x_t), \quad h_t = \overrightarrow{h_t} \oplus \overleftarrow{h_t}, \quad t \in [1, L]$$

Argument vector is then obtained through an attention layer:

$$\alpha_t = \frac{\exp(h_t^T u)}{\sum \exp(h_t^T u)}, \quad R^{(0)} = \sum \alpha_t h_t$$

3.3 Mutually Guided Sequence Pairs Modeling

Once guidance vector $Guidance^{(k-1)} \in R^{4D_{k-1}}$ is obtained, we can use it to re-calculate argument vectors. Here, we propose two novel RNN networks with externally controllable cells to implement the strategy of mutually guided modeling. Since the same guidance vector is used for both arguments, the operations for re-calculating new vector representations of the two arguments can not be exactly the same. However, we can share most of parameters among them.

Externally Controllable LSTM (ECLSTM) is derived from LSTM by adding mechanism to enable guidance vector to influence internal gates. In order to maintain conciseness, we omit the (k) and $(k-1)$ superscripts and only take Arg_1 for example.

$$i_t^1 = \sigma(W_i x_{1,t} + U_i c_{1,t-1} + V_i^1 Guidance + b_i)$$
$$f_t^1 = \sigma(W_f x_{1,t} + U_f c_{1,t-1} + V_f^1 Guidance + b_f)$$
$$o_t^1 = \sigma(W_o x_{1,t} + U_o c_{1,t-1} + V_o^1 Guidance + b_o)$$
$$c_{1,t} = f_t^1 \circ c_{1,t-1} + i_t^1 \circ \tanh(W_c x_{1,t} + U_c c_{1,t-1} + b_c)$$
$$h_{1,t} = o_t^1 \circ c_{1,t}$$

where $W_i, W_f, W_o \in R^{D_k \times D_e}$, $U_i, U_f, U_o \in R^{D_k \times D_k}$, $V_i^1, V_f^1, V_o^1 \in R^{D_k \times 4D_{k-1}}$ and $b_i, b_f, b_o \in R^{D_k}$. The parameters without superscript 1 are shared between processing of Arg_1 and Arg_2. The parameters not shared between two arguments are those directly multiplied with guidance vector. So, V_i^1, V_f^1 and V_o^1 are used exclusively in processing of Arg_1 and V_i^2, V_f^2 and V_o^2 are used exclusively in processing of Arg_2.

ECLSTM slightly differs from the original LSTM to retain most advantages of LSTM. However, since guidance vector has to interact with inputs and hidden states to generate gates' values, the active mechanism of guidance vector's influence is quit unclear.

Attention-Augmented Gated Recurrent Unit (AAGRU) is proposed because the influence of guidance vector to the gates in ECLSTM is quit limited. We strengthen the dominance of guidance vector by incorporating attention mechanism into GRU that we can reduce parameters in one single layer and stack more guided layers without increasing complexity. Specifically, we sequentially process each word in Arg_i as below:

$$u_i = \tanh(V_u^i Guidance + b_u)$$
$$r_t^i = \sigma(W_r x_{i,t} + U_r c_{i,t-1} + b_r)$$
$$\tilde{c}_{i,t} = \tanh(W_c x_{i,t} + U_c(r_t^i \circ c_{i,t-1}) + b_h)$$
$$a_t^i = \sigma(\tilde{c}_{i,t}^T u_i)$$
$$c_{i,t} = (1 - a_t^i) \circ c_{i,t-1} + a_t^i \circ \tilde{c}_{i,t}$$
$$h_{i,t} = a_t^i \circ c_{i,t}$$

Here, we still omit the (k) and $(k-1)$ superscripts to maintain conciseness and superscript i and subscript i have the same meaning that the variable is exclusive for $Arg_i, i \in \{1, 2\}$. In AAGRU, the original update gate of GRU is replaced by the attention gate a_t^i. We first generate attention vector u_i for Arg_i, then u_i is used to perform inner product with temporal cell-state vector $\tilde{c}_{i,t}$ to calculate attention gate's value. Obtaining output $h_{i,t}$ by multiplying cell-state vector $c_{i,t}$ with attention gate a_t^i is to alleviate imbalance introduced by the fierce mechanism.

To get the new annotations of words, we summarize information from both sides as conducted in bi-LSTM:

$$\overrightarrow{h_{i,t}} = \overrightarrow{g_i}(x_{i,t}), \quad \overleftarrow{h_{i,t}} = \overleftarrow{g_i}(x_{i,t}), \quad h_{i,t} = \overrightarrow{h_{i,t}} \oplus \overleftarrow{h_{i,t}}, \quad t \in [1, L_i]$$

Here g_i represents $ECLSTM_i$ and $AAGRU_i$. Then we get argument vectors by simply summing word vectors:

$$R_i = \frac{1}{L_i} \sum_t h_{i,t}, \quad R_i \in R^{2D_k}.$$

3.4   Model Training

After the hierarchical architecture of our model is detailed and implemented, we train our model to minimize the cross-entropy error between y the golden standard relations and P the outputs of the softmax layer as well as the L2 regularization of arguments:

$$L(\theta) = \frac{1}{m} \sum_{k=1}^{m} \left(- \sum_{j} y_{kj} \log P_{kj} \right) + \frac{\lambda}{2} \theta^T \theta$$

Dropout operations are applied between each layers and the keeping ratio is set to be 0.5. The model is trained end to end through standard back-propagation. We adopt AdamOptimizer [14] with initial learning rate of 0.001 for optimization process.

4   Experiments

4.1   Settings

Penn Discourse Treebank (PDTB) is a manually annotated corpus. We evaluate our model on this corpus. The classification granularity of PDTB has three levels and the first level contains four kinds of relations, namely Comparison, Contingency, Expansion and Temporal. To compare with prior works, we follow traditions that formulate the implicit discourse classification tasks as four one-versus-other binary classification problems. Data is divided into three sets, respectively training set (sections 2–20), validation set (sections 0–1) and testing set (sections 21–22). Since positive samples in Temporal are quit limited, we augment training data of Temporal by exchanging the positions of Arg_1 and Arg_2 in it.

We use Stanford NLP Toolkit [9] to conduct tokenization, lemmatization and part-of-speech tagging. The embedding vectors of lemmas are initialized with pre-trained vectors provide by Glove [10]. To prevent from overfitting, in model training, we do not update lemma embedding vectors in the first ten epochs and then use validation set to conduct early stopping.

The dimensions of lemma embeddings and POS embeddings are 300 and 50 respectively. When using CNN as the general feature extractor, we utilize three groups of filters with window sizes of (2, 4, 8) and their filter numbers are all set to 256. So the dimension of general level's output is 768. When using LSTM as the general modeling method, D_0 the dimension of each unidirectional LSTM is set to 50 that the dimension of general level's output is 100. The dimensions of next two guided levels' outputs are set to 100, which means D_k the output size of the unidirectional RNN variants is 50.

4.2   Results

We set our model with different stacked layers and components and their performances are compared in Table 1.

The basic CNN and LSTM models perform the worst. By stacking guided layers, we get significant performance gains. We also witness that stacking more ECLSTM degenerates performance. It may be because ECLSTM contains a lot

Table 1. Models with variable layers measured by F_1 scores (%).

	Comparison	Contingency	Expansion	Temporal
CNN only	33.05	50.92	63.51	28.42
CNN+ECLSTM	39.33	54.71	69.51	**33.44**
CNN+AAGRU	38.23	52.41	65.07	29.05
CNN+ECLSTM+ECLSTM	38.47	52.65	66.99	28.59
CNN+AAGRU+AAGRU	38.69	55.47	69.41	32.40
LSTM only	36.11	53.04	67.23	27.74
LSTM+ECLSTM	39.08	53.97	68.33	32.49
LSTM+AAGRU	38.77	53.35	66.81	30.14
LSTM+ECLSTM+ECLSTM	37.39	54.08	67.89	27.42
LSTM+AAGRU+AAGRU	**40.03**	**56.38**	**70.10**	32.85

of parameters that it begin to overfit. AAGRU with reinforced controlling power and less parameters can continually improve performance by stacking more layers. In our experiments, we find that the model with LSTM as general level and two stacked AAGRU as guided levels achieves the best over-all performance.

Table 2. Comparisons of different models measured by F_1 scores (%).

	Comparison	Contingency	Expansion	Temporal
Zhou et al. 2010	31.79	47.16	70.11	20.30
Park and Cardie 2012	31.32	49.82	-	26.57
Rutherford and Xue 2014	39.70	54.42	70.23	28.69
Braud and Denis 2015	36.36	55.76	67.42	29.3
Zhang et al. 2015	34.22	52.04	69.59	30.54
Wu et al. 2016	37.07	42.37	66.84	23.81
Liu et al. 2016	37.91	55.88	69.97	**37.17**
Qin et al. 2017	**40.87**	54.56	**72.38**	36.20
CNN+ECLSTM	39.33	54.71	69.51	33.44
LSTM+AAGRU+AAGRU	40.03	**56.38**	70.10	32.85

We compare our models with previously state-of-the-art models and the results are listed in Table 2. The main ideas of those baselines are introduced as follows:

– Zhou et al. [6] inserts discourse connectives between arguments with the use of a language model and use these predicted implicit connectives as additional features in a supervised model.

- Park and Cardie [7] provides a systematic study of linguistic features and identifies new feature combinations that optimize F1-score.
- Rutherford and Xue [8] employs Brown cluster pairs and coreference patterns as features and trains a maximum entropy classifier.
- Braud and Denis [12] uses low-dimensional representations based on Brown clusters and word embeddings and other hand-crafted features to identify implicit discourse relations.
- Zhang et al. [13] proposes a shallow convolutional neural network, which contains only one hidden layer and captures max, min and average information.
- Wu et al. [16] incorporates data from corpus with different languages via a multi-task neural network model to alleviate the shortage of labeled data.
- Liu et al. [18] proposes a convolutional neural network embedded multi-task learning system to combine different discourse corpora.
- Qin et al. [20] proposes an adversarial network, which leverages implicit connectives manually added in PDTB, as an regularization mechanism to adaptively regularize parameters.

From the comparison results, we can conclude that our model is better in recognizing Comparison and Contingency and comparative with the best models in classifying Expansion and Temporal.

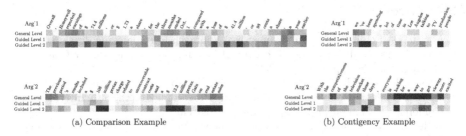

(a) Comparison Example   (b) Contigency Example

Fig. 2. Visualization of intermediate weights. (a) is an example of the Comparison relation and (b) is an example of Contingency. Each one contains two figures for its two arguments respectively. Each figure illustrate three layers of weights that correspond to the attention weights of general level and the values of attention gates in the next two AAGRU layers. (Color figure online)

4.3 Discussion

We have quantitatively analyzed the attention weights in the general level and the values of attention gates in the guided levels of the LSTM+AAGRU+AAGRU model. Some examples are visualized in Fig. 2. More blue the grid means the word is paid less attention than average, while more red means more attention is paid. We find that general level focuses on proper nouns, terminologies and time-related phrases, which are generally most informative components for getting the general sense of a text. The first guided level tends to focus on components which are neglected by general level and can be seen as a complement of general level. The second guided level, which is also the final level to generate argument representations, is relatively similar to general level. It is more accurate and comprehensive than the general level that it can be seen as a refinement of general level. It discards components which are paid attention by general level but inessential for classifying the relation and allocates extra attention to those verbs and adjectives which are neglected but important.

5   Conclusion

We incorporate arguments' interactions into their modeling process to dynamically exploit critical information for implicit discourse classification. We designed ECLSTM and AAGRU, two variants of recurrent neural network units with externally controllable gating mechanism, to regenerate argument representations under the guidance of previous obtained argument vectors. Our experiments demonstrate that performance can be greatly promoted by applying the guided regenerating strategy. Due to the shortage of labeled data, we stacked only two AAGRU layers to get the best performance. Through visualization we show that relevant information are gradually complemented and refined layer by layer.

References

1. Marcu, D., Echihabi, A.: An unsupervised approach to recognizing discourse relations. In: Proceedings of the 40th Annual Meeting on Association for Computational Linguistics, pp. 368–375 (2002)
2. Prasad, R., Dinesh, N., Lee, A., Miltsakaki, E., Robaldo, L., Joshi, A., Webber, B.: The Penn Discourse Treebank 2.0. In: Proceedings of the 6th International Conference on Language Resources and Evaluation (2008)
3. Pitler, E., Raghupathy, M., Mehta, H., Nenkova, A., Lee, A., Joshi, A.: Easily identifiable discourse relations. In: Proceedings of the 22nd International Conference on Computational Linguistics (2008)
4. Pitler, E., Louis, A., Nenkova, A.: Automatic sense prediction for implicit discourse relations in text. In: Proceedings of the Joint Conference of the 47th Annual Meeting of the ACL and the 4th International Joint Conference on Natural Language Processing of the AFNLP, pp. 683–691 (2009)
5. Lin, Z., Ng, H.T., Kan, M.Y.: PDTB-styled end-to-end discourse parser. Technical report, School of Computing, National University of Singapore (2010)
6. Zhou, Z., Lan, M., Xu, Y., Niu, Z., Su, J., Tan, C.L.: Predicting discourse connectives for implicit discourse relation recognition. In: Proceedings of the 23rd International Conference on Computational Linguistics, pp. 1507–1514 (2010)
7. Park, J., Cardie, C.: Improving implicit discourse relation recognition through feature set optimization. In: Proceedings of the 13th Annual Meeting of the Special Interest Group on Discourse and Dialogue, pp. 108–112 (2012)
8. Rutherford, A.T., Xue, N.: Discovering implicit discourse relations through brown cluster pair representation and coreference patterns. In: Proceedings of the 14th Conference of the European Chapter of the Association for Computational Linguistics, pp. 645–654 (2014)

9. Manning, C.D., Surdeanu, M., Bauer, J., Finkel, J., Bethard, S.J., McClosky, D.: The Stanford CoreNLP natural language processing toolkit. In: Proceedings of the 52nd Annual Meeting of the Association for Computational Linguistics: System Demonstrations, pp. 55–60 (2014)
10. Pennington, J., Socher, R., Manning, C.D.: GloVe: Global vectors for word representation. In: Proceedings of the 2014 Conference Empiricial Methods in Natural Language Processing (2014)
11. Wang, J., Lan, M.: A refined end-to-end discourse parser. In: Proceedings of the Nineteenth Conference on Computational Natural Language Learning: Shared Task, pp. 17–24 (2015)
12. Braud, C., Denis, P.: Comparing word representations for implicit discourse relation classification. In: Proceedings of the 2015 Conference on Empirical Methods in Natural Language Processing, pp. 2201–2211 (2015)
13. Zhang, B., Su, J., Xiong, D., Lu, Y., Duan, H., Yao, J.: Shallow convolutional neural network for implicit discourse relation recognition. In: Proceedings of the 2015 Conference on Empirical Methods in Natural Language Processing, pp. 2230–2235 (2015)
14. Kingma, D.P., Adam, J.B.: A method for stochastic optimization. In: Proceedings of the 3rd International Conference for Learning Representations (2015)
15. Chen, J., Zhang, Q., Liu, P., Qiu, X., Huang, X.: Implicit discourse relation detection via a deep architecture with gated relevance network. In: Proceedings of the 54th Annual Meeting of the Association for Computational Linguistics, pp. 1726–1735 (2016)
16. Wu, C., Shi, X., Cheng, Y., Huang, Y., Su, J.: Bilingually-constrained synthetic data for implicit discourse relation recognition. In: Proceedings of the 2016 Conference on Empirical Methods in Natural Language Processing, pp. 2306–2312 (2016)
17. Yang, Z., Yang, D., Dyer, C., He, X., Smola, A., Hovy, E.: Hierarchical attention networks for document classification. In: Proceedings of NAACL Conference (2016)
18. Liu, Y., Li, S., Zhang, X., Sui, Z.: Implicit discourse relation classification via multi-task neural networks. In: Proceedings of the Thirtieth AAAI Conference on Artificial Intelligence, pp. 2750–2756 (2016)
19. Liu, Y., Li, S.: Recognizing implicit discourse relations via repeated reading: neural networks with multi-level attention. In: Proceedings of the 2016 Conference on Empirical Methods in Natural Language Processing, pp. 1224–1233 (2016)
20. Qin, L., Zhang, Z., Zhao, H., Hu, Z., Xing, E.P.: Adversarial connective-exploiting networks for implicit discourse relation classification. In: Proceedings of ACL Conference (2017)
21. Li, H., Zhang, J., Zong, C.: Implicit discourse relation recognition for english and Chinese with multiview modeling and effective representation learning. ACM Trans. Asian Low-Resour. Lang. Inf. Process. **16**, 19 (2017)

Random Projections with Bayesian Priors

Keegan Kang$^{(\boxtimes)}$

Singapore University of Technology and Design, Singapore 487372, Singapore
keegan_kang@sutd.edu.sg

Abstract. The technique of random projection is one of dimension reduction, where high dimensional vectors in $\mathbb{R}^D$ are projected down to a smaller subspace in $\mathbb{R}^k$. Certain forms of distances or distance kernels such as Euclidean distances, inner products [10], and l_p distances [12] between high dimensional vectors are approximately preserved in this smaller dimensional subspace. Word vectors which are represented in a bag of words model can thus be projected down to a smaller subspace via random projections, and their relative similarity computed via distance metrics. We propose using marginal information and Bayesian probability to improve the estimates of the inner product between pairs of vectors, and demonstrate our results on actual datasets.

1 Introduction

Suppose we have N documents and D words in our language. One popular model used to represent these words is the bag of words model. Every document could be represented as a binary vector $\mathbf{x}_i \in \mathbb{R}^D$, where the ith element in the vector represents whether the word is present or not. Instead of using binary vectors, term weighting could also occur where the ith element is some measure of frequency of the ith word appearing in the document, such as square root weighting, log weighting etc.

Having represented such documents as vectors in $\mathbb{R}^D$, appropriate distance metrics could be used to cluster such documents such as the inner product between each pair of vectors. Classification of these documents could also take place via kernels [15] representing higher dimensional features, with the kernel output fed into algorithms like support vector machines (SVMs).

For N documents, computing their pairwise distance under some distance metric would take $O(N^2 D)$, which can be computationally intensive when D is large. With a bigram model or trigram model, the dimension of the word vector and eventual resultant computational cost would increase exponentially.

Random projections become a solution to this problem. Suppose the matrix $X_{n \times D}$ represents the matrix of word vectors, where each row is a document vector. Suppose we generate a random matrix $R_{D \times k}$, where each entry r_{ij} is i.i.d. Normal $N(0, 1)$, and compute the matrix product $V = XR$. If we consider the row vectors

X. Huang et al. (Eds.): NLPCC 2017, LNAI 10619, pp. 170–182, 2018.
https://doi.org/10.1007/978-3-319-73618-1_15

$$\mathbf{x}_i := (x_{i1}, x_{i2}, \ldots, x_{iD}) \tag{1}$$

$$\mathbf{x}_j := (x_{j1}, x_{j2}, \ldots, x_{jD}) \tag{2}$$

$$\mathbf{v}_i := (v_{i1}, v_{i2}, \ldots, v_{ik}) \tag{3}$$

$$\mathbf{v}_j := (v_{j1}, v_{j2}, \ldots, v_{jk}) \tag{4}$$

we note that

$$\mathbb{E}[v_{i1}v_{j1}] = \mathbb{E}\left[\left(\sum_{s=1}^{D} x_{is}r_{s1}\right)\left(\sum_{s=1}^{D} y_{is}r_{s1}\right)\right]$$

$$= \mathbb{E}\left[\sum_{s=1}^{D} x_{is}y_{is}r_{s1}^2 + \sum_{s \neq t} x_{is}y_{jt}r_{s1}r_{t1}\right] = \langle \mathbf{x}_i, \mathbf{y}_i \rangle \tag{5}$$

Therefore, by the Law of Large Numbers we have that

$$\frac{\langle \mathbf{v}_i, \mathbf{v}_j \rangle}{k} \approx \langle \mathbf{x}_i, \mathbf{x}_j \rangle \tag{6}$$

and sharp probability bounds [18] on the error can be given, which we give here without proof

$$\mathbb{P}\left[(1-\epsilon)\langle \mathbf{x}_i, \mathbf{x}_j \rangle \leq \frac{\langle \mathbf{v}_i, \mathbf{v}_j \rangle}{k} \leq (1+\epsilon)\langle \mathbf{x}_i, \mathbf{x}_j \rangle\right] \leq 1 - 4\exp\left\{-(\epsilon^2 - \epsilon^3)k/4\right\} \tag{7}$$

This bound can therefore be used to choose a value of k, such that the error in the estimate is no more than $(1 + \epsilon)$ away from the true value, which is independent of D, the original dimensions of the data.

Furthermore, random projections can also be used with other distance metrics such as the l_p distance (for even p) [12], or even with kernels such as the polynomial kernel [15] to get close estimates as well.

The time taken under random projections is $O(NDk + N^2k)$, where $O(NDk)$ of time is taken to do the matrix multiplication XR, and N^2k to compute the respective distances between vectors. When $k \ll D$, the time saving is substantial.

Random projection can therefore be seen as a method to effectively deal with large vectors [2]. In natural language processing (NLP) which is computationally intensive, other concerns such as *accuracy, speed,* and *storage* arise.

Speeding up the computation of the vectors $\mathbf{v} \in \mathbb{R}^k$ has been done in the last decade, by changing the structure of the random projection matrices. The r_{ij} in the random projection matrix R could come from i.i.d. distributions (binary random projections [1], very sparse random projections [11]), or correlated r_{ij} (fast Johnson Lindenstrauss transform [3], subsampled randomized Hadamard transform [5]).

Reducing the storage of the vectors $\mathbf{v} \in \mathbb{R}^k$ has also been done with sign random projections [10]. The output matrix V would consist only of 1 s and 0s, where each entry takes up 1 bit of space. Otherwise, storing the entries in $\mathbf{v}$ as doubles would take up 64 bits of space per entry.

The accuracy of the random projection estimates is not just limited to computing the probability bounds of the estimates. Statistical theory can also help to sharpen these probability bounds, and hence get better estimates. For example, previous work by Li [10] used marginal information about the data, while our previous work [8] used variance reduction techniques in Monte Carlo methods.

Our method proposes using a Bayesian estimator of the inner product by assuming a prior distribution on the data. We show how to compute this estimator, and also demonstrate its effectiveness.

2   Related Work

Consider the row vectors $\mathbf{v}_i$, $\mathbf{v}_j$ in (3) and (4). Without loss of generality, suppose we normalize our word vectors $\mathbf{x}_i$ where $\|\mathbf{x}_i\|_2^2 = 1$, and we let $\{(v_1, v_2)\}_{s=1}^k$ denote the tuples (v_{is}, v_{js}). Then each tuple can be represented as

$$\begin{pmatrix} v_1 \\ v_2 \end{pmatrix} \sim N\left(\begin{pmatrix} 0 \\ 0 \end{pmatrix}, \begin{pmatrix} 1 & a \\ a & 1 \end{pmatrix} \right) \tag{8}$$

where a denotes the true inner product $\langle \mathbf{x}_i, \mathbf{x}_j \rangle$. Here, the tuple is seen as being drawn from a bivariate normal. In statistical theory, this can be seen as estimating an unknown correlation of a bivariate normal when both variances are known [6].

In Li [10] used a maximum likelihood estimator to improve the estimate of the inner product. Given observations of k tuples $(v_1, v_2)^{(1)}$, $(v_1, v_2)^{(2)}, \ldots, (v_1, v_2)^{(k)}$, Li derived the likelihood equation in terms of the inner product a, and found the value of $\hat{a}$ which maximized the likelihood.

More recently, our previous work [8] used control variates to improve the estimate of quadratic forms, one of which consisted the inner product. By using random variables where the true mean θ was known, we used a control variate correction to reduce the error of the estimate of the inner product.

Both our work and Li achieved the same improvement of the estimate of the inner product. With normalized data, the ordinary inner product estimate (6) had a variance

$$\mathrm{Var}[a] = 1 + a^2 \tag{9}$$

but under our estimate and Li's estimate, the reduced variance was

$$\mathrm{Var}[a] = \frac{(1 - a^2)^2}{1 + a^2} \tag{10}$$

We use the variance of the inner product here instead of probability bounds, since the derivation of the bounds make use of the variance, and the variance can be used as a proxy to how tight the probability bounds are.

Figure 1 shows the relationship between the original variance, our variance, and Li's variance. We see that substantial variance reduction occurs when vector pairs are correlated with $|a|$ near 1, but otherwise little variance reduction when a is near 0.

3 Inherent Challenges with High Dimensional Word Vectors

Geometry theory [4] states that as the dimension p increases, any two randomly drawn vectors are with high probability almost mutually orthogonal. While word vectors (and data in general) usually have some structure and are not seen as randomly drawn, most pairwise inner products a tend to be small in magnitude but non-zero in extremely high dimensions.

Based on Fig. 1, both our technique and Li's technique would work well on datasets where a high proportion of vector pairs $\mathbf{x}_i, \mathbf{x}_j$ are heavily correlated. Otherwise, there would be no advantage is using their techniques.

For example, consider the following four high dimensional datasets, two of which are document-word datasets (*Kos blogposts* [13], *NIPS conference papers* [17]), and two non document-word datasets (*Arcene* [7], *MNIST* [9]). We use log term weighting for the *Kos blogposts* and *NIPS conference papers* datasets.

Figure 2 shows the distribution of true pairwise inner products for these datasets. The document-word datasets have a significantly higher proportion of pairwise inner products near 0 compared to the non document-word datasets, hence our algorithm and Li's algorithm would not be useful at all. Relying on basic principal component analysis (PCA) to reduce the dimension of data would also not be of much help. We show the following scree plots of the same four datasets.

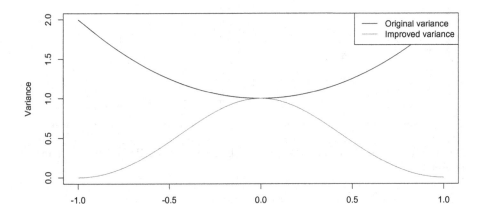

Fig. 1. Comparison of original variance and improved variance under both our estimate and Li's estimate. Both our estimate and Li's estimate have the same variance (in blue). Recall that if the inner product between two vectors is 1, they are in the same direction. If the inner product is −1, there are in opposite directions. If the inner product is 0, they are orthogonal. (Color figure online)

Plot of inner product distribution of datasets

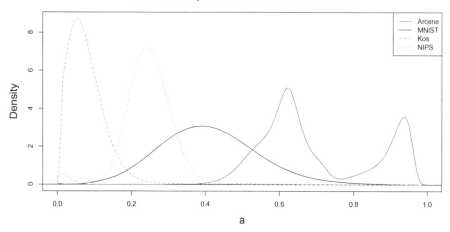

Fig. 2. Distribution of pairwise inner products for Arcene, MNIST, Kos blog posts, NIPS conference papers datasets.

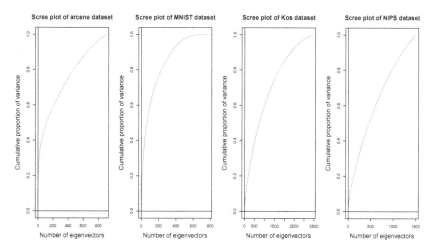

Fig. 3. Scree plots of arcene, MNIST, Kos blogposts, and NIPS conference papers datasets.

We can see from Fig. 3 that the first few principal components of *arcene* and *MNIST* account for a significant proportion of the variance. However, the proportion of variance for the *Kos blogposts, NIPS conferences* datasets increases linearly with the number of principal components. Therefore, it is difficult to adopt a strategy similar to our previous work (using a control variate of a known quantity) or Li (using marginal information) with knowledge of the first few eigenvectors. Even if PCA produces good results (several principal components accounting for most of the variance), there is usually a loss of actual distance information.

We therefore proceed in an orthogonal direction to PCA as well as our method and Li's method and look at Bayes Rule for inspiration.

4   Our Contributions

In this paper, we propose a method which estimates the inner product of vector word pairs which has lower variance than either Li's method and our previous method. We analyze the time taken for our method. We also evaluate and demonstrate our method on actual datasets.

4.1   Bayes Rule and Information Updating

Theorem 1. *Bayes Rule*
Let A, B be any two events, and $\mathbb{P}[B] = 0$. Then

$$\mathbb{P}[A|B] = \frac{\mathbb{P}[B|A]\mathbb{P}[A]}{\mathbb{P}[B]} \tag{11}$$

Intuitively, suppose we had some prior belief about A, which we encode as $\mathbb{P}[A]$. In our NLP framework, this can be how we believe the (true) inner product a between pairs of vectors are distributed. Then for some observations B which we see, we can update our initial belief via $\mathbb{P}[B|A]$. Similarly, our observations B in this context would be our tuples $\{(v_1, v_2)\}_{s=1}^{k}$. The posterior $\mathbb{P}[A|B]$ describes our final belief, based on our observations. We want this to be our inner product estimate $\hat{a}$.

4.2   Our Proposed Algorithm

Using Bayes Rule, our estimate for the inner product a can be written as

$$\mathbb{E}[a \mid \{(v_1, v_2)\}_{s=1}^{k}] = \frac{1}{K} \int_0^1 a \, p(a) \, L(a) \, da \tag{12}$$

where

$$p(a) = \text{prior belief of how inner product is distributed} \tag{13}$$

$$L(a) = \text{likelihood based on observations} \{(v_1, v_2)\}_{s=1}^{k} \tag{14}$$

$$\frac{1}{K} = \text{the normalizing constant to make} \int_0^1 \frac{p(a)L(a)}{K} \, da$$

$$\text{be a probability density function (pdf) and integrate to 1} \tag{15}$$

We can express the likelihood function of the bivariate normal as

$$
L(a) \propto \left(1 - a^2\right)^{-k/2} \exp\left\{ -\sum_{s=1}^{k} \frac{(v_{1s}\ v_{2s}) \begin{pmatrix} 1 & -a \\ -a & 1 \end{pmatrix} \begin{pmatrix} v_{1s} \\ v_{2s} \end{pmatrix}}{2(1 - a^2)} \right\} \tag{16}
$$

$$
\propto \left(1 - a^2\right)^{-k/2} \exp\left\{ -\frac{\sum_{s=1}^{k} v_{1s}^2 + v_{2s}^2 - 2a v_{1s} v_{2s}}{2(1 - a^2)} \right\} \tag{17}
$$

We do not need the exact form of $L(a)$, since the constant can be part of $\frac{1}{K}$. We now consider the prior distribution $p(a)$.

4.3   Computing the Integral $\int_0^1 a\, p(a)\, L(a)\, da$

If we treat the distribution of pairwise inner products (Fig. 2) as a probability distribution $p(a)$, statistical theory tells us that we can get a good idea of the distribution by sampling from it. In this paper, we recommend sampling $\left\lfloor \sqrt{\frac{N(N-1)}{2}} \right\rfloor$ pairwise inner products out of $\frac{N(N-1)}{2}$ total pairwise inner products to get convergence to a good prior.

We do not place any assumptions on $p(a)$ being a commonly known distribution like the beta distribution (Kos blog posts, NIPS conference papers datasets), or a bivariate mixture model distribution (Arcene dataset). Rather, we use kernel density estimators [16] such as the Nadaraya Watson estimator to evaluate $p(a)$ at several equally spaced points from the interval $[0, 1]$.

The motivation for doing so is that we only pass the value of $p(a)$ into a numerical integration algorithm to compute $\int_0^1 a\, p(a)\, L(a)\, da$. However, numerical integration algorithms work by evaluating the integral at equally spaced points. Therefore, we do not need a closed form expression of $p(a)$, and the evaluation of $p(a)$ at these equally spaced points suffices.

We give the following example using Simpson's Rule as our numerical integration algorithm. Suppose we consider the interval $[0, 1]$ with equally spaced points $a_0 := 0, a_1, a_2, \ldots, a_{2s} := 1$. Suppose we let α denote the length of the interval $[a_i, a_{i+1}]$. Further suppose we use the Nadaraya Watson estimator to evaluate $p(a)$ at the points $a_0, a_1, \ldots, a_{2s}$. Using Simpson's Rule gives

$$
\int_0^1 a\, p(a)\, L(a)\, da = \int_0^{a_2} a\, p(a)\, L(a)\, da + \int_{a_2}^{a_4} a\, p(a)\, L(a)\, da
$$

$$
+ \ldots + \int_{a_{2s-2}}^1 a\, p(a)\, L(a)\, da = \frac{2\alpha}{6} \left[f(0) + 4f(a_1) + f(a_2) \right]
$$

$$
+ \ldots + \frac{2\alpha}{6} \left[f(a_{2s-2}) + 4f(a_{2s-1}) + f(1) \right]
$$

$$
= \frac{2\alpha}{6} \sum_{t=1}^{s} \left[f(a_{2t-2}) + 4f(a_{2t-1}) + f(a_{2t}) \right] \tag{18}
$$

and do likewise for $\int_0^1 p(a)\, L(a)\, da$.

The only other assumption we make is that the distribution of inner products is relatively smooth, so we need a small number of equally spaced points.

Theorem 2. *The expected variance of the inner product estimate given by our algorithm in (12) is smaller than the original variance of the inner product estimate.*

Proof. From the law of total variance, we have

$$\text{Var}[a] = \mathbb{E}\left[\text{Var}[a \mid \{(v_1, v_2)\}_{s=1}^k]\right] + \text{Var}\left[\mathbb{E}[a \mid \{(v_1, v_2)\}_{s=1}^k]\right] \qquad (19)$$

and rearranging this, we have

$$\text{Var}\left[\mathbb{E}[a \mid \{(v_1, v_2)\}_{s=1}^k]\right] = \text{Var}[a] - \mathbb{E}\left[\text{Var}[a \mid \{(v_1, v_2)\}_{s=1}^k]\right] \qquad (20)$$

$$\Rightarrow \text{Var}\left[\mathbb{E}[a \mid \{(v_1, v_2)\}_{s=1}^k]\right] < \text{Var}[a] \qquad (21)$$

This does not imply that the actual variance of our inner product estimate is always lower than the variance of the original estimate, but in practice this is usually the case if we sample enough inner products.

4.4   Numerical Analysis of Algorithm and Time Taken

To compute our improved estimate of the inner product, this is equivalent to computing the quotient of two integrals

$$\frac{\int_0^1 a\, p(a)\, L(a)\, da}{\int_0^1 p(a)\, L(a)\, da} \qquad (22)$$

where the denominator is the normalizing constant K. We need to use numerical integration tools like Simpson's Rule or Gauss-Hermite Quadrature as shown in the previous subsection.

The time taken for this algorithm thus depends on the number of inner products sampled, as well as the number of equally spaced points to compute the kernel density estimates.

We first consider the pre-processing period. Sampling $\left\lfloor \sqrt{\frac{N(N-1)}{2}} \right\rfloor$ inner products is of order $O(ND)$. Evaluating $p(a)$ at s equally spaced points is of order $O(Ns)$. Computing the matrix product $V = XR$ is of order $O(NDk)$. The overall pre-processing cost is therefore $O(NDk + ND + Ns)$.

We need to do numerical integration to compute the inner product estimate after random projection. For each inner product pair, it takes $O(k)$ time (and $O(1)$ space) to compute and store the constant terms in (17). We then take $O(s)$ time to compute the integral for our estimate, as in (17). The total time taken for all pairwise estimates is therefore $O(N^2(k + s))$.

The overall time taken for our algorithm is $O(NDk + ND + Ns + N^2(k + s)) = O(NDk + N^2(k + s))$. Ordinary random projections, Li's method, and Kang's method all take $O(NDk + N^2k)$, and are therefore faster.

However, we will show in our experiments that while our algorithm takes an extra $O(N^2 s)$ time, the tradeoff in accuracy is worth the decrease in speed.

We further note that our algorithm does not necessarily need to be used for estimating the inner product. We can also estimate other distances such as l_p distances, but modify $p(a), L(a)$ respectively.

5   Our Experiments

We look at three word datasets for our experiments. They are the *Kos blogposts* [13] ($N = 3,430$, $D = 6,906$, $\tilde{p} = 5,880,735$), *NIPS conference papers* [13] ($N = 1,500$, $D = 12,419$, $\tilde{p} = 1,124,250$), and the *MSN web crawl* dataset [11] ($N = 2,702$, $D = 65,536$, $\tilde{p} = 3,649,051$), where $\tilde{p}$ is the number of pairwise inner products. We use log term weighting for our data, before normalizing each word vector to have norm 1.

For each dataset, we compute the average root mean square error (RMSE) of the inner product estimates over all pairs for 1000 iterations. We project down from D dimensions to $k = \{10, 20, \ldots, 100\}$ with our random projection matrix. For each iteration, we randomly sample an increasing number of pairwise inner products up to the nearest power of 2 greater than $\sqrt{\tilde{p}}$ to show how this affects our kernel density estimate of $p(a)$ and hence our inner product estimate. We evaluate our integral at 101 equally spaced points. We compare the estimates of our RMSE against ordinary random projections, Li's method, and our control variate method, and compute error bounds of 3 standard deviations for each RMSE estimate.

Since we normalize our data to have norm of 1, the RMSE becomes a number between 0 and 1. If the RMSE is near 0, it means that most estimates of pairwise inner products are close to the truth. Otherwise, if the RMSE is near 1, it means that most estimates of the inner product are far from the truth.

The code for our experiments can be found at https://github.com/erwin4d/research_projects/.

Figures 4, 5, and 6 show the results of our experiments. The left plots in these figures shows the average RMSE as the number of columns k increases. The right plots in these figures shows the average RMSE at $k = 100$, but with increasing number of inner products sampled to compute the kernel density estimate $p(a)$ as a proportion of $\lfloor \sqrt{\tilde{p}} \rfloor$. Note that the scale on the x-axis is logarithmic. The horizontal dotted lines and the crosses represent 3 standard deviations around the RMSE. The red vertical dotted line represents $\lfloor \log \tilde{p} \rfloor$ and the blue vertical dotted line represents $\lfloor \sqrt{\tilde{p}} \rfloor$.

From our results, we can see that Li's method and our previous control variate method performs similarly to ordinary random projections, our Bayesian prior method has a significantly lower RMSE as k increases. This is not surprising, as the proportion of highly correlated pairwise inner products in these datasets is small compared to the proportion of weakly correlated pairwise inner products.

Furthermore, we see that sampling $\lfloor \sqrt{\tilde{p}} \rfloor$ inner products for the kernel density estimate of our prior $p(a)$ can be too conservative, as there is "convergence"

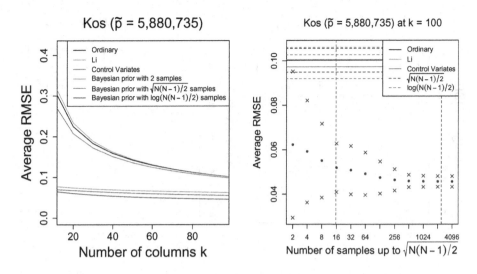

Fig. 4. The plots show the average RMSE of the inner product estimates over all 5,880,735 pairs for the Kos blogposts dataset. (Color figure online)

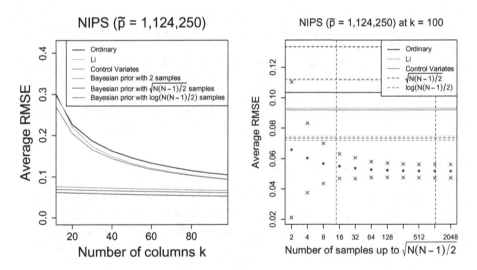

Fig. 5. The plots show the average RMSE of the inner product estimates over all 1,124,250 pairs for the NIPS conference papers dataset. (Color figure online)

in the average pairwise RMSE for much fewer samples. Even before this "convergence", taking $\lfloor \log \tilde{p} \rfloor$ samples gives a significantly lower RMSE with smaller standard deviations than ordinary random projections, Li's method, and the control variate method. Nevertheless, we keep the number of samples fixed at

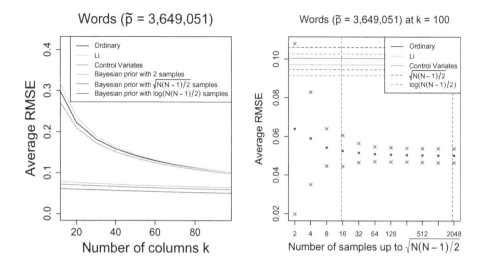

Fig. 6. The plots show the average RMSE of the inner product estimates over all 3,649,051 pairs for the words dataset. (Color figure online)

$\lfloor \sqrt{\tilde{p}} \rfloor$ as a rule of thumb just to be safe, as other datasets might not have a smooth distribution of inner products.

Intuitively the performance of our algorithm on these datasets can be seen as an updating process based on the observation of the tuples (v_{is}, v_{js}), using Bayes' Rule. Thus, we end up updating our beliefs based on our observations, hence we get more accurate estimates and lower RMSE provided we started with the right beliefs.

6   Conclusion and Future Work

NLP deals with extremely high dimensional sparse data which can be computationally intensive. Dimension reduction techniques are essential, but current dimension reduction techniques may not work well for word vectors. Figures 1 and 2 show how random projection techniques may not work well for word vectors due to the distribution of inner products. Figure 3 also shows why PCA may also not be useful in reducing the number of dimensions with certain word datasets.

We have demonstrated an algorithm using Bayes Rule which performs well in estimating the inner product between all pairwise word vectors rather than "good correlated pairs" for small K, provided we have some notion of the underlying distribution of the inner product. While our algorithm takes $O(N^2(k + s))$ time in estimating all pairwise inner products compared to $O(N^2 k)$ time, the average RMSE is significantly lower for the same value of k. In fact, if we picked some k for ordinary random projections, we can set $\hat{k} = k - s$ for our Bayesian prior algorithm to keep to the same runtime, and yet get smaller error. From our results, using $k = 10$ for our Bayesian prior algorithm still yields a much lower RMSE than $k = 100$ for Li's algorithm, our control variate algorithm, or ordinary random projection estimates.

We have also given a recipe on how to use our algorithm with different estimates of distances, not just the inner product. The likelihood function $L(a)$ necessarily needs to change based on the distance estimate.

We believe that there is potential synthesis of this random projection algorithm together with existing and future NLP works, such as [2,14], leading to better and more accurate results.

Acknowledgements. We thank the reviewers who provided us with many helpful comments. We hope we have addressed most of these comments in this version of the paper where possible. This research was supported by the SUTD Faculty Fellow Award.

References

1. Achlioptas, D.: Database-friendly random projections: Johnson-Lindenstrauss with binary coins. J. Comput. Syst. Sci. **66**(4), 671–687 (2003). https://doi.org/10.1016/S0022-0000(03)00025-4

2. Agustí, P., Traver, V.J., Pla, F.: Bag-of-words with aggregated temporal pair-wise word co-occurrence for human action recognition. Pattern Recogn. Lett. **49**(C), 224–230 (2014). https://doi.org/10.1016/j.patrec.2014.07.014

3. Ailon, N., Chazelle, B.: The fast Johnson-Lindenstrauss transform and approximate nearest neighbors. SIAM J. Comput. **39**(1), 302–322 (2009). https://doi.org/10.1137/060673096

4. Ball, K.: An elementary introduction to modern convex geometry. Flavors Geom. **31**, 1–58 (1997). http://library.msri.org/books/Book31/files/ball.pdf

5. Boutsidis, C., Gittens, A.: Improved matrix algorithms via the subsampled randomized hadamard transform. CoRR abs/1204.0062 (2012). http://arxiv.org/abs/1204.0062

6. Fosdick, B.K., Raftery, A.E.: Estimating the correlation in bivariate normal data with known variances and small sample sizes. Am. Stat. **66**(1), 34–41 (2012). http://EconPapers.repec.org/RePEc:taf:amstat:v:66:y:2012:i:1:p:34--41

7. Guyon, I., Gunn, S., Ben-Hur, A., Dror, G.: Result analysis of the NIPS 2003 feature selection challenge. In: Saul, L.K., Weiss, Y., Bottou, L. (eds.) Advances in Neural Information Processing Systems, vol. 17, pp. 545–552. MIT Press (2005). http://papers.nips.cc/paper/2728-result-analysis-of-the-nips-2003-feature-selection-challenge.pdf

8. Kang, K., Hooker, G.: Random projections with control variates. In: Proceedings of the 6th International Conference on Pattern Recognition Applications and Methods: ICPRAM, vol. 1, pp. 138–147. INSTICC, ScitePress (2017)

9. Lecun, Y., Bottou, L., Bengio, Y., Haffner, P.: Gradient-based learning applied to document recognition. In: Proceedings of the IEEE, pp. 2278–2324 (1998)

10. Li, P., Hastie, T.J., Church, K.W.: Improving random projections using marginal information. In: Lugosi, G., Simon, H.U. (eds.) COLT 2006. LNCS (LNAI), vol. 4005, pp. 635–649. Springer, Heidelberg (2006). https://doi.org/10.1007/11776420_46

11. Li, P., Hastie, T.J., Church, K.W.: Very sparse random projections. In: Proceedings of the 12th ACM SIGKDD International Conference on Knowledge Discovery and Data Mining, KDD 2006, pp. 287–296. ACM, New York (2006). http://doi.acm.org/10.1145/1150402.1150436

12. Li, P., Mahoney, M.W., She, Y.: Approximating higher-order distances using random projections. CoRR abs/1203.3492 (2012). http://arxiv.org/abs/1203.3492

13. Lichman, M.: UCI machine learning repository (2013). http://archive.ics.uci.edu/ml

14. Maqueda, A.I., Ruano, A., del Blanco, C.R., Carballeira, P., Jaureguizar, F., García, N.: Novel multi-feature bag-of-words descriptor via subspace random projection for efficient human-action recognition. In: 2015 12th IEEE International Conference on Advanced Video and Signal Based Surveillance (AVSS), pp. 1–6, August 2015

15. Murphy, K.P.: Machine Learning: A Probabilistic Perspective. MIT Press, Cambridge (2012)

16. Nadaraya, E.A.: On estimating regression. Theory Probab. Appl. **9**(1), 141–142 (1964)

17. Perrone, V., Jenkins, P.A., Spano, D., Teh, Y.W.: Poisson random fields for dynamic feature models (2016). arXiv e-prints: arXiv:1611.07460

18. Vempala, S.S.: The Random Projection Method, DIMACS Series in Discrete Mathematics and Theoretical Computer Science, vol. 65. American Mathematical Society, Providence, R.I. (2004). Appendice pp. 101–105. http://opac.inria.fr/record=b1101689

A Convolutional Attention Model for Text Classification

Jiachen Du[1,2], Lin Gui[1], Ruifeng Xu[1,3(✉)], and Yulan He[4]

[1] Laboratory of Network Oriented Intelligent Computation,
Shenzhen Graduate School, Harbin Institute of Technology, Shenzhen, China
dujiachen@stmail.hitsz.edu.cn, guilin.nlp@gmail.com, xuruifeng@hit.edu.cn
[2] Department of Computing, The Hong Kong Polytechnic University,
Hung Hom, Hong Kong
[3] Guangdong Provincial Engineering Technology Research Center for Data Science,
Guangzhou, China
[4] School of Engineering and Applied Science, Aston University, Birmingham, UK
y.he9@aston.ac.uk

Abstract. Neural network models with attention mechanism have shown their efficiencies on various tasks. However, there is little research work on attention mechanism for text classification and existing attention model for text classification lacks of cognitive intuition and mathematical explanation. In this paper, we propose a new architecture of neural network based on the attention model for text classification. In particular, we show that the convolutional neural network (CNN) is a reasonable model for extracting attentions from text sequences in mathematics. We then propose a novel attention model base on CNN and introduce a new network architecture which combines recurrent neural network with our CNN-based attention model. Experimental results on five datasets show that our proposed models can accurately capture the salient parts of sentences to improve the performance of text classification.

1 Introduction

In recent years, there is no doubt that deep learning has ushered in amazing technological advances on natural language processing (NLP) researches. Much of the work with deep learning involves learning word vector representations through natural language models [15] and composition over word vectors for various tasks like text classification [4], machine translation [9], document summarization [2] and so on.

In this paper, we focus on the text classification problem. Traditional approaches to text classification firstly represent text sequences with sparse features, such as n-grams [3], topic-based representation [26] and kernel methods [8]. Recently deep-learning models have shown their big success in text classification, such as convolutional neural networks [12] and recurrent neural networks based on long short-term memory [7].

Applying convolutional neural network (CNN) to NLP including text classification has drawn many interests in recent years. It has been shown that CNNs

X. Huang et al. (Eds.): NLPCC 2017, LNAI 10619, pp. 183–195, 2018.
https://doi.org/10.1007/978-3-319-73618-1_16

can be directly applied to embeddings of words [11]. Unlike word level models, [27] proposed a character-level CNN for text classification which achieved competitive results. Although CNN has been proven efficient on text classification, it usually ignores important long-distance sequential information which greatly impacts the classification performance, especially in sentences which have negation and semantic transition. Recurrent neural network (RNN) is another important model in NLP. [22] used gated recurrent neural network to model documents and applied this model to sentiment classification. [21] explored the structure of a sentence and used a tree-structured recurrent neural network with long-short term memory (LSTM) for text classification. The advantage of RNN is its ability to better capture the contextual information, especially the semantics of long texts. However RNN model cannot pay attention to the salient parts of text. This limitation reduces the effectiveness of RNN when applied to text classification.

Recently, based on the aforementioned architectures, a new direction of neural networks has emerged. It learns to focus "attention" to specific parts of text as the simulation of human's attention while reading. However, the researches on neural network with attention mechanism only show promising results on a sequence-to-sequence (seq2seq) tasks in NLP, including machine translation [1], caption generation [24] and text summarization [18]. It's not appropriate to use the same alignment mechanism for classification. For example, [25] applies the attention model used in seq2seq tasks to document-level classification. The attention is modeled by a one hidden layer perceptron with RNN hidden unit as input. Compare with non-attention methods, the improvement is limited in the reported result. The reason is that, in the seq2seq problem, each word has a corresponding label, such as the word in another language (for machine translation tasks), or a Part-Of-Speech label (for POS tagging tasks). In text classification, there are no target labels for each word to indicate the word is category-relevant or not. So, there is no evidence showing why the perceptron with one hidden layer attention is efficient for text classification.

Motivated by the cognitive and neuroscience research, we propose a novel attention model. The basic idea is to first use the convolution operation to capture attention signals, each of which stands for the local information of a word in its context; then use RNN to model text with attention signals. A word with higher attention weight, which carries more valuable information, will be more important in text modeling. Our main contributions in this paper is three-fold:

- This is the first time a convolutional neural network model is presented to stimulate human's reading attention based on cognitive and neuroscience research, and a detailed mathematical deduction of this model is given in this work.
- Moreover, a novel attention extraction method based on this model has been proposed that can be used in several tasks.
- Finally, we propose a new architecture based on convolutional attention extraction model, and this neural network shows competitive results compared with state-of-the-art models in text classification.

The rest of our paper is structured as follows, Sect. 2 explores a novel attention model based on convolutional neural networks and gives detailed reduction of this model. Section 3 gives a description of the Convolutional Recurrent Attention Network (CRAN) for text classification. Section 4 presents some experiments to justify the effectiveness of CRAN on text classification. Section 5 concludes the paper and outlines the future work.

2   A CNN-Based Attention Model

It is commonly known that we can pay attention to only small amount of information presented in visual scenes and only concentrate on the information related to a specific task at hand. Cognitive and neuroscience researches have confirmed this hypothesis, and a lot of experiments have shown that humans depict in brains a visual representation or "search template" of certain task and try to only pay attention to the information which can match the "task-oriented template" [5]. Psycholinguistics has proven that template-matching process also helps us emphasize the important content while our brain is processing texts. Although this mechanism of attention has been thoroughly studied in neuroscience and psychology, there is few research on how to introduce it to computational linguistic and natural language processing. Motivated by that, we propose a novel model introducing the aforementioned attention mechanism to natural language processing, especially to text classification.

Based on in-depth investigation, we found that Convolutional Neural Network (CNN) is a natural model to stimulate human being's reading attention mechanism, since the convolution operation as the core component of CNN is similar to the process of template matching. For textual data, CNN always applies one-dimensional convolution to the concatenate of vector representation of each words. Our first goal is to show that one-dimension convolution of CNN is precisely the process of calculating the similarity between snippets of text and the "attention searching templates". In neural-network based models, a text sequence of length T (padded where necessary) is often represented as

$$x_{0:T-1} = x_0 \oplus x_1 \oplus \ldots \oplus x_{T-1} \tag{1}$$

where $x_t \in \mathcal{R}^d$ ($t = \{0, 1, \ldots, T-1\}$) corresponds to the d-dimensional vector representation of the t-th word in the text sequence, and $\oplus$ is the vector concatenation operator. Convolution operation applies a filter $w = w_0 \oplus w_1 \oplus \ldots \oplus w_{l-1}$ to a window of l words in the original sequence to get a convolutional similarity c_t, where each column of the filter $w_t \in \mathcal{R}^d$ ($t = \{0, 1, \ldots, l-1\}$) is a vector of the same length of word embeddings. The convolution operation apply the following transformation to each continuous subsequence of length l in $[x_0, x_1, \ldots, x_{T-1}]$. Suppose the current subsequence is $x_{t:t+l-1} = x_t \oplus x_{t+1} \oplus \ldots \oplus x_{t+l-1}$:

$$
\begin{aligned}
c_t &= f\left(<w, x_{t:t+l-1}> + b \right) \\
&= f\left(||w|| \times ||x_{t:t+l-1}|| \times \frac{<w, x_{t:t+l-1}>}{||w|| \times ||x_{t:t+l-1}||} + b \right)
\end{aligned}
\tag{2}
$$

In Eq. 2, $< \cdot, \cdot >$ is dot product of two vectors as $< a, b >= a^T b$, $|| \cdot ||$ is the $\mathcal{L}^2$ norm of vectors. f is the non-linear function such as hyperbolic tangent, sigmoid and rectified linear function. Notice that w and $x_{t:t+l-1}$ are $l \times d$-dimensional vector, assuming that each dimension has its own distribution. According to Chebyshev Law, there exists M, for any w and any $x_{t:t+l-1}$, if $l \times d$ is large enough (usually larger than 25), it is true that for any $\varepsilon > 0$, $P(|M - ||w|| \times ||x_{t:t+l-1}||| < \varepsilon) = 1$. since $l \times d$, namely the shape of convolution filters is always larger than 25, we can replace $||w|| \times ||x_{t:t+l-1}||$ by M in this equation, and define a function $F(x) = f(Mx)$ to replace the original function f, let $b' = b/M$, we will obtain:

$$c_t = F(\cos(w, x_{t:t+l-1}) + b') \tag{3}$$

In Eq. 3 we notice that F is only a compression function that satisfies $F'(x) > 0$. Then we can consider the convolutional filter w be the "search template" mentioned before in human's attention while reading. And c_t can be treated as the cosine similarity between the search template and the part of text which is processed currently. b' in Eq. 3 is the threshold of this similarity. When the similarity is greater than b', the textual part being processed is considered task-relevant; otherwise it is task-irrelevant.

The output of each convolutional filter is an attention signal from the original text. In order to reduce the noise in the attention signals, we choose multiple convolutional filters applied to the vector representation of original text and average the results of these filters to obtain a smooth attention signal. Suppose the number of convolutional filters is m, these filter is denoted by $[w^1, w^2, \ldots, w^m]$, and the corresponding attention similarity is $[c^1, c^2, \ldots, c^m]$. After averaging the attention similarities along the filter-axis, we will obtain the smooth attention signal $c \in \mathcal{R}^T$ of which each element represents the importance of the corresponding word.

$$c = \sum_{i=1}^{m} c^i \tag{4}$$

The whole CNN-based attention model is shown in Fig. 1.

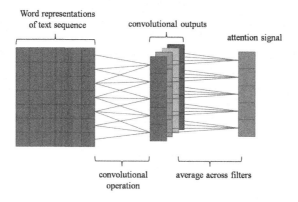

Fig. 1. CNN-based model of attention extraction.

3 Convolutional-Recurrent Attention Neural Networks

Based on the attention model we described in Sect. 2, we propose a model named Convolutional-Recurrent Attention Network (CRAN) that combines recurrent neural network (RNN) and the convolutional attention model in Sect. 2. The reason why we use RNN as a part of our model rather than directly using the traditional CNN architecture is that traditional CNN uses a pooling layer over the whole sentence which results in a single vector being extracted as the representation of the sequence. It makes CNN difficult to capture the long-distance dependencies in sequences like negation and transition. However RNN with long short-term memory (LSTM) is designed for handling the long-distance dependency problem. We speculate that combining RNN with our proposed CNN-based attention model will give better performance compared with using a pure CNN model, and the experimental results which will be presented in Sect. 4 confirm our hypothesis.

The overall architecture of the Convolutional Attention Neural Network (CRAN) is shown in Fig. 2. It consists of two main parts: a recurrent neural network (RNN) as the text encoder and a convolutional neural network (CNN) as the attention extractor. We describe the details of these two parts in the following subsections.

3.1 RNN-Based Sequence Encoder

An RNN [6] is a kind of neural network that processes sequences of arbitrary length by recursively applying a function to its hidden state vector $h_t \in \mathcal{R}^d$

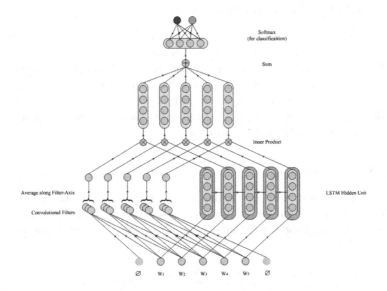

Fig. 2. Architecture of convolutional attention network

of each element in the input sequences. The hidden state vector at time-step depends on the input symbol x_t and the hidden state vector at last time-step h_{t-1} is:

$$h_t = \begin{cases} 0 & t = 0 \\ g(g_{t-1}, x_t) & \text{otherwise} \end{cases} \tag{5}$$

A fundamental problem in traditional RNN is that gradients propagated over many steps tend to either vanish or explode. It makes RNN difficult to learn long-dependency correlations in a sequence. Long short-term memory network (LSTM) was proposed by [7] to alleviate this problem. LSTM has three gates: an input gate i_t, a forget gate f_t, an output gate o_t and a memory cell c_t. They are all vectors in $\mathcal{R}^d$. The LSTM transition equations are:

$$\begin{aligned} i_t &= \sigma(W_i x_t + U_i h_{t-1} + V_i c_{t-1}), \\ f_t &= \sigma(W_f x_t + U_f h_{t-1} + V_f c_{t-1}), \\ o_t &= \sigma(W_o x_t + U_o h_{t-1} + V_o c_{t-1}), \\ \tilde{c}_t &= \tanh(W_c x_t + U_c h_{t-1}), \\ c_t &= f_t \odot c_{t-1} + i_t \odot \tilde{c}_t, \\ h_t &= o_t \odot \tanh(c_t) \end{aligned} \tag{6}$$

where x_t is the input at the current time step, σ is the sigmoid function and $\odot$ is the elementwise multiplication operation. In our model, we use the hidden-state vector of each time step as the representation of corresponding word in the sentence.

3.2   CNN-Based Attention Extraction

As discussed in Sect. 2, we use a CNN-based network to model the attention signal in sentences. Suppose the input text sequence is $[x_0, x_1, \ldots, x_{T-1}]$, where $x_t \in \mathcal{R}^d$ ($t = 0, 1, \ldots, T-1$), m convolutional filters of length l are denoted as $[w^1, w^2, \ldots, w^m]$, the corresponding convolution results are $[c^1, c^2, \ldots, c^m]$, where $c^i \in \mathcal{R}^T$ ($t = 1, 2, \ldots, m$) represents the attention distributed on the sequence of length T. We average the m filters to get the stable attention signal c witch is a vector of length T as described in Sect. 2.

3.3   Text Classification

We use the product of attention signal c_t and the corresponding hidden state vector of RNN h_t to represent the word t in a sequence with attention signal. The representation of the whole sequence can be obtained by averaging the word representations:

$$s = \frac{1}{T} \sum_{t=0}^{T-1} c_t h_t \tag{7}$$

where $s \in \mathcal{R}^d$ is the vector representation of the text sequence and it can be used as features for text classification:

$$p = \mathrm{softmax}(W_c s + b_c) \qquad (8)$$

where p is the predicted label for text sequence s, W_c and b_c are parameters of the classification layer.

4 Experiments

In this section, we investigate the empirical performance of our proposed CRAN on various datasets and compare it with state-of-the-art models for text classification.

4.1 Datasets

We choose five different text classification datasets and test our model on various benchmarks. We briefly summarize these datasets as follows:

- **MR**: Movie reviews with one sentence per review. Classification involves binary categories of reviews (positive and negative)[1] [17].
- **SST-1**: An extension of MR but with train/dev/test splits provided and fine-grinned labels (negative, somewhat negative, neutral, somewhat positive, positive)[2] [20].
- **SST-2**: Same as SST-1 but with neural reviews removed and only containing binary labels (positive and negative).
- **Subj**: Subjectivity dataset where task is to classify a sentence as objective or subjective [16].
- **IMDB**: A document-level text classification dataset containing 100,000 movie reviews with binary labels[3] [14].

Table 1. Summary statistics of the five datasets.

Dataset	Class	Average length	Vocabulary size	Text size	Test size
MR	2	20	18K	10662	CV
SST-1	5	19	18K	11855	2210
SST-2	2	18	15K	9613	1821
Subj	2	21	21K	10000	CV
IMDB	2	294	392K	50000	25000

---

[1] http://www.cs.cornell.edu/people/pabo/movie-review-data/.
[2] http://ai.stanford.edu/sentiment/.
[3] http://ai.stanford.edu/~amaas/data/sentiment/.

The first four datasets are for sentence-level classification and the last one is for document-level classification. We conduct experiments on the standard test sets on SST-1,SST-2 and IMDB. For datasets without standard train/test split, we use 10-fold cross validation instead. The summary statistics of the datasets are listed in Table 1.

4.2   Model Training and Hyper-parameters

We train our proposed convolutional attention model with two different initialization strategies:

– **CRAN_rand:** The convolutional attention layer is randomly initialized.
– **CRAN_pretrain:** The convolutional attention layer is pre-trained by a standard standard convolutional neural network which is connected to a fully-connected layer to the final labels as a classifier.

The model can be trained in an end-to-end way by back-propagation, where the objective function is cross-entropy of error loss. Training is done through gradient descent with the Adadelta update rule. In all of these experiments, the word embeddings are initialized with the publicly available word2vec vectors that were trained on 100 billion words from Google News (Mikolov et al. [15]). Other parameters are set as follows. The number of hidden units of LSTM and convolution filters in CNN is 100, the length of convolution filter is 3, dropout rate is 0.5 and mini-batch size is 16. These hyper-parameters are chosen via a grid search on the SST-2 development set.

4.3   Baselines

To illustrate the performance boost of our proposed attention model, we compare our model with some baseline methods. Since we use RNN as component of our model, we implement an RNN with LSTM memory unit as a baseline. We also compare our model with LSTM with the attention model proposed by [25].

– **LSTM:** LSTM for text classification.
– **LSTM + RNN attention:** The attention-based LSTM model proposed by [25]. Since most datasets used in our experiments are for sentence-level classification, we implement a flatten variant of this model without aggregating the attention signals from sentences to form the document-level attention signal.

We also compare our model with the following state-of-the-art models:

– **NBOW:** The NBOW sums the word vectors within the sentence and applies a softmax classifier.
– **MV-RNN:** Matrix-Vector Recursive Neural Network with parse trees [19].
– **F-Dropout:** Fast Dropout from [23].
– **DCNN:** Convolutional Neural Network with dynamic k-max pooling [10].

- **CNN:** Convolutional neural networks with max pooling [11].
- **Tree-LSTM:** Tree-Structured Long Short-Term Memory Networks [21].
- **Multi-task:** Shared-layer multi-task learning model trained on four different datasets [13].

4.4 Results and Analysis

The experimental results on all datasets are shown in Table 2. Firstly we notice that LSTM performs the worst among all the models since the sequential features extracted by RNN models is not suitable for text classification. But we find that our proposed CRAN can combine the merits of CNN and RNN to improve the performance. Results show that CRAN improves the performance significantly compared with the LSTM by 3.0% on average. For the two variations of CRAN, we can see that CRAN_rand model performs slightly better than CRAN_pretrain model except on the IMDB dataset. This is because CRAN_pretrain uses a different architecture to pre-train the convolutional attention layer. Both CRAN variants perform better than the LSTM with RNN attention. This shows that our proposed attention modelling method can capture more accurate attention information from text.

Compared with the state-of-the-art models in text classification, CRAN gives the best performance on three out of five datasets. Although CRAN uses a similar CNN network as its attention extractor, CRAN improves upon CNN by 0.9% on average. This is because combining RNN helps our model capture the long-distance semantic dependencies in sentences which cannot be dealt with by traditional CNNs. Tree-LSTM outperforms our model on SST-1 by 0.6%. However it needs an external parser to derive the tree-structure of each sentence, and the performance listed in Table 2 is reported on the exact parsing results of

Table 2. Results of our proposed CRAN against baselines. Results marked * are models that need external tools or resources.

Model	MR	SST-1	SST-2	Subj	IMDB
CRAN_rand	**82.8**	50.0	87.7	**94.1**	92.0
CRAN_pretrain	82.0	48.1	86.9	94.0	**92.1**
LSTM	80.1	46.2	85.2	91.2	88.5
LSTM + RNN attention	82.0	48.0	86.1	93.2	90.6
NBOW	77.1	42.1	79.0	90.8	80.7
MV-RNN (Socher et al. [19])	79.0	44.4	82.9	-	-
F-Dropout (Wang and Manning [23])	79.1	-	-	93.6	91.1
DCNN (Kalchbrenner et al. [10])	-	48.5	86.8		
CNN ([11])	81.5	48.0	**88.1**	93.4	-
Tree-LSTM (Tai et al. [21])*	-	**50.6**	86.9	-	-
Multi-Task (Liu et al. [13])*	-	49.6	87.9	**94.1**	91.3

sentences labelled by annotators. It is worth noting that our models are comparable with the recurrent neural network with multi-task learning proposed by (Liu et al. [13]). This model is an extremely strong baseline which was trained jointly on four datasets (SST-1, SST-2, Subj and IMDB).

4.5   Case Study

In order to validate that our model is able to select salient parts in a text sequence, we visualize the attention layers in Fig. 3 for several sentences from the MR dataset in which our model predicted the class labels correctly. Each line in the figure is a heatmap of the attention signals extracted by our model. The attention signal is normalized in the range of $[-1,1]$, and the actual label of each sentence is shown to the left of each heatmap. The red color in the heatmap means a high attention for the positive label and the blue color means a high attention for the negative label, while the white color means neural.

Figure 3 shows that our model can not only select words carrying strong sentiments like *repelling, annoyance, dull, et al.*, but also deal with transitions of sentiments in sentences. For example, in the second sentence, our model assigns a high positive attention to the first half of the sentence before the word *but*, and it also finds the second half of this sentence is highly related to the negative sentiment. Also, the negative attention value is greater than the positive attention value in this sentence, which makes the final predicted label to be negative.

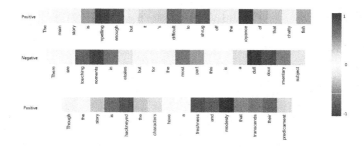

Fig. 3. Visualization of attention signals in sample sentences in the MR dataset. (Color figure online)

We also analyze the sentences from which our model failed to extract attention signals properly. We show an attention visualization in Fig. 4 which is extracted from a sentence in the MR dataset:

Imagine the James Woods character from video drome making a home movie of audrey rose and showing it to the kid from the sixth sense and youve imagined the ring.

The label of this sentence is negative, but our model predicts its labels positive. We can see that this is a complex sentence with some metaphors. To understand the real meaning of this sentence, readers must have the background knowledge of the movies mentioned in this sentence. For people who are unfamiliar with the movies, James Woods and Sixth Sense, they will not know these are all horror movies and hence would have a difficulty in understanding the metaphoric meaning of these terms.

We can obverse that, for this sentence, the attention signals extracted by our model is somewhat randomized and do not reflect the actual sentiment expressed in the sentence. It seems that our model can only extract the attention signals from the literal meanings of words. Nevertheless, understanding complicated linguistic phenomena such as analogy, metaphor and irony is a huge challenge commonly faced by many NLP tasks, not just in text classification.

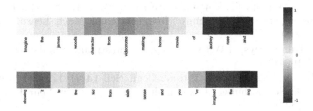

Fig. 4. Visualization of wrongly classified sentence in the MR dataset.

5   Conclusion

In this paper, we have shown that the convolutional neural network is a reasonable model for extracting attentions from text sequences. Based on this finding, we have proposed a novel attention extraction model based on the convolutional neural network. Utilizing this CNN-based attention model, we have introduced a new neural network architecture which combines RNN with our CNN-based attention model. We have conducted extensive experiments on five datasets. The experimental results show that (1) our model is capable of extracting salient parts from sentences; (2) our model can combine the merits of CNN and RNN to improve the sentence classification performance. Finally, the visualization of some attentions extracted by our model shows the impressive capability of our model to process the sentiment transitions in sentences. We have also presented an attentional visualization result of a sentence whose class label was wrongly predicted by our model. This shows that our model has a difficulty in dealing with more subtle meanings embedded in sentences, a huge challenge commonly faced by many NLP tasks. In future works, we will mainly focus on extending our CNN-based attention model to other tasks like text generation and sequence to sequence learning.

Acknowledgements. This work was supported by the National Natural Science Foundation of China 61370165, U1636103, 61632011, 61528302, Shenzhen Foundational

Research Funding JCYJ20150625142543470, Guangdong Provincial Engineering Technology Research Center for Data Science 2016KF09 and grant from the Hong Kong Polytechnic University (G-YBJP).

References

1. Bahdanau, D., Cho, K., Bengio, Y.: Neural machine translation by jointly learning to align and translate. arXiv preprint arXiv:1409.0473 (2014)
2. Cao, Z., Wei, F., Dong, L., Li, S., Zhou, M.: Ranking with recursive neural networks and its application to multi-document summarization. In: AAAI, pp. 2153–2159 (2015)
3. Cavnar, W.B., Trenkle, J.M.: N-gram-based text categorization. Ann Arbor MI **48113**(2), 161–175 (1994)
4. Collobert, R., Weston, J., Bottou, L., Karlen, M., Kavukcuoglu, K., Kuksa, P.: Natural language processing (almost) from scratch. J. Mach. Learn. Res. **12**(Aug), 2493–2537 (2011)
5. Duncan, J., Humphreys, G.W.: Visual search and stimulus similarity. Psychol. Rev. **96**(3), 433 (1989)
6. Elman, J.L.: Finding structure in time. Cogn. Sci. **14**(2), 179–211 (1990)
7. Hochreiter, S., Schmidhuber, J.: Long short-term memory. Neural Comput. **9**(8), 1735–1780 (1997)
8. Joachims, T.: Text categorization with support vector machines: learning with many relevant features. In: Nédellec, C., Rouveirol, C. (eds.) ECML 1998. LNCS, vol. 1398, pp. 137–142. Springer, Heidelberg (1998). https://doi.org/10.1007/BFb0026683
9. Kalchbrenner, N., Blunsom, P.: Recurrent continuous translation models. In: EMNLP, vol. 3, p. 413 (2013)
10. Kalchbrenner, N., Grefenstette, E., Blunsom, P.: A convolutional neural network for modelling sentences. arXiv preprint arXiv:1404.2188 (2014)
11. Kim, Y.: Convolutional neural networks for sentence classification. arXiv preprint arXiv:1408.5882 (2014)
12. LeCun, Y., Bottou, L., Bengio, Y., Haffner, P.: Gradient-based learning applied to document recognition. Proc. IEEE **86**(11), 2278–2324 (1998)
13. Liu, P., Qiu, X., Huang, X.: Recurrent neural network for text classification with multi-task learning. arXiv preprint arXiv:1605.05101 (2016)
14. Maas, A.L., Daly, R.E., Pham, P.T., Huang, D., Ng, A.Y., Potts, C.: Learning word vectors for sentiment analysis. In: Proceedings of the 49th Annual Meeting of the Association for Computational Linguistics: Human Language Technologies, vol. 1, pp. 142–150. Association for Computational Linguistics (2011)
15. Mikolov, T., Sutskever, I., Chen, K., Corrado, G.S., Dean, J.: Distributed representations of words and phrases and their compositionality. In: Advances in Neural Information Processing Systems, pp. 3111–3119 (2013)
16. Pang, B., Lee, L.: A sentimental education: sentiment analysis using subjectivity summarization based on minimum cuts. In: Proceedings of the 42nd Annual Meeting on Association for Computational Linguistics, p. 271. Association for Computational Linguistics (2004)
17. Pang, B., Lee, L.: Seeing stars: exploiting class relationships for sentiment categorization with respect to rating scales. In: Proceedings of the 43rd Annual Meeting on Association for Computational Linguistics, pp. 115–124. Association for Computational Linguistics (2005)

18. Rush, A.M., Chopra, S., Weston, J.: A neural attention model for abstractive sentence summarization. arXiv preprint arXiv:1509.00685 (2015)
19. Socher, R., Huval, B., Manning, C.D., Ng, A.Y.: Semantic compositionality through recursive matrix-vector spaces. In: Proceedings of the 2012 Joint Conference on Empirical Methods in Natural Language Processing and Computational Natural Language Learning, pp. 1201–1211. Association for Computational Linguistics (2012)
20. Socher, R., Perelygin, A., Wu, J.Y., Chuang, J., Manning, C.D., Ng, A.Y., Potts, C.: Recursive deep models for semantic compositionality over a sentiment treebank. In: Proceedings of the Conference on Empirical Methods in Natural Language Processing (EMNLP), vol. 1631, p. 1642. Citeseer (2013)
21. Tai, K.S., Socher, R., Manning, C.D.: Improved semantic representations from tree-structured long short-term memory networks. arXiv preprint arXiv:1503.00075 (2015)
22. Tang, D., Qin, B., Liu, T.: Document modeling with gated recurrent neural network for sentiment classification. In: Proceedings of the 2015 Conference on Empirical Methods in Natural Language Processing, pp. 1422–1432 (2015)
23. Wang, S.I., Manning, C.D.: Fast dropout training. In: ICML, no. 2, pp. 118–126 (2013)
24. Xu, K., Ba, J., Kiros, R., Cho, K., Courville, A., Salakhutdinov, R., Zemel, R.S., Bengio, Y.: Show, attend and tell: neural image caption generation with visual attention. arXiv preprint arXiv:1502.03044 2(3), 5 (2015)
25. Yang, Z., Yang, D., Dyer, C., He, X., Smola, A., Hovy, E.: Hierarchical attention networks for document classification. In: Proceedings of the 2016 Conference of the North American Chapter of the Association for Computational Linguistics: Human Language Technologies (2016)
26. Zelikovitz, S., Hirsh, H.: Using LSI for text classification in the presence of background text. In: Proceedings of the Tenth International Conference on Information and Knowledge Management, pp. 113–118. ACM (2001)
27. Zhang, X., Zhao, J., LeCun, Y.: Character-level convolutional networks for text classification. In: Advances in Neural Information Processing Systems, pp. 649–657 (2015)

Shortcut Sequence Tagging

Huijia Wu[1,3]($\boxtimes$), Jiajun Zhang[1,2], and Chengqing Zong[1,2,3]

[1] National Laboratory of Pattern Recognition, Institute of Automation,
CAS, Beijing, China
{huijia.wu,jjzhang,cqzong}@nlpr.ia.ac.cn
[2] CAS Center for Excellence in Brain Science and Intelligence Technology,
Beijing, China
[3] University of Chinese Academy of Sciences, Beijing, China

Abstract. Deep stacked RNNs are usually hard to train. Recent studies have shown that shortcut connections across different RNN layers bring substantially faster convergence. However, shortcuts increase the computational complexity of the recurrent computations. To reduce the complexity, we propose the shortcut block, which is a refinement of the shortcut LSTM blocks. Our approach is to replace the self-connected parts (c_t^l) with shortcuts (h_t^{l-2}) in the internal states. We present extensive empirical experiments showing that this design performs better than the original shortcuts. We evaluate our method on CCG supertagging task, obtaining a 8% relatively improvement over current state-of-the-art results.

1 Introduction

In natural language processing, sequence tagging mainly refers to the tasks of assigning discrete labels to each token in a sequence. Typical examples include Part-of-Speech (POS) tagging and Combinatory Category Grammar (CCG) supertagging. A regular feature of sequence tagging is that the input tokens in a sequence cannot be assumed to be independent since the same token in different contexts can be assigned to different tags. Therefore, the classifier should have memories to remember the contexts to make a correct prediction.

Bidirectional Long Short-Term Memory (Bi-LSTM) [5] become dominant in sequence tagging problems due to the superior performance [13,25]. The horizontal hierarchy of LSTMs with bidirectional processing can remember the long-range dependencies without affecting the short-term storage. Although the models have a deep horizontal hierarchy (the depth refers to sequence length), the vertical hierarchy is often shallow, which may not be efficient at representing each token. Stacked LSTMs are deep in both dimensions, but become harder to train due to the feed-forward structure of stacked layers.

Shortcut connections (shortcuts, or skip connections) enable unimpeded information flow by adding direct connections across different layers [4,7]. Recent works have shown the effectiveness of using shortcuts in deep stacked models

X. Huang et al. (Eds.): NLPCC 2017, LNAI 10619, pp. 196–207, 2018.
https://doi.org/10.1007/978-3-319-73618-1_17

[6,21,27]. These works share a common way of adding shortcuts as increments to the original network.

In this paper, we focus on the refinement of shortcut stacked models to reduce the computational cost. Concretely, we replace the self-connected parts in LSTM cells with the gated shortcuts to simplify the updates, while preserving the recurrent information flow through cell outputs. We also investigate deterministic or stochastic gates to find the preferable way to control the shortcut connections.

We present extensive experiments on the Combinatory Category Grammar (CCG) supertagging task to compare shortcut block varieties, gating functions, and combinations of the blocks. Our model obtains the state-of-the-art results on CCG supertagging.

2   Recurrent Neural Networks for Sequence Tagging

Given a sequence $x = (x_1, \ldots, x_T)$, a recurrent neural network (RNN) computes the hidden states $h = (h_1, \ldots, h_T)$ and the outputs $y = (y_1, \ldots, y_T)$ by iterating the following equations:

$$h_t = f(x_t, h_{t-1}; \theta_h) \tag{1}$$

$$y_t = g(h_t; \theta_o) \tag{2}$$

where the recurrent information h_{t-1} and the inputs x_t are processed through the iteration function $f(\cdot, \cdot)$ to compute h_t.

There are many iteration functions to pass the information through the sequence. Long Short-Term Memory (LSTM) is one kind of function that preserves the hidden activations h_t for a long time. The computation of the recurrent flow in LSTM is:

$$c_t = c_{t-1} + \Delta \tag{3}$$

where c_t are the cells' internal states that used to iterate the recurrent information. Δ refer to the increments to the cells. Adding such increments through time make the gradient of the internal states more stable. Therefore, the short-term memory can be kept for a long time under this construction.

Another advantage of LSTM is the gating mechanism, which is used to avoid weight update conflicts. The activation of the gates decides when to keep or override information in the controlled units.

We use a negative log-likelihood cost to evaluate the performance, which can be written as:

$$\mathcal{C} = -\frac{1}{N} \sum_{n=1}^{N} \log y_{t^n} \tag{4}$$

where $t^n \in \mathbb{N}$ is the true target for sample n, and y_{t^n} is the t-th output in the *softmax* layer given the inputs x^n.

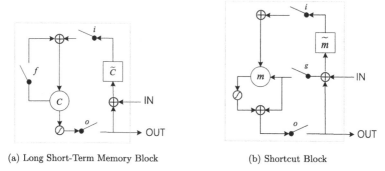

(a) Long Short-Term Memory Block   (b) Shortcut Block

Fig. 1. Illustration of (a) LSTM block and (b) shortcut block. (a) i, f and o represent input, forget and output gate, respectively. $\tilde{C}$ denotes the increments to the cell, and C denotes the cell's internal state. (b) g is the shortcut gate, $\tilde{m}$ denotes the cell inputs, and m denotes the internal state of the cell. Notice that (b) replaces the self-connected links (through f gate) in (a) with shortcut connections (through g gate).

3 Exploration of Shortcuts

3.1 Shortcut Blocks

The hidden units in stacked LSTMs can be divided into two parts: One is the hidden units within the same layer $\{h_t^l, t \in 1, \ldots, T\}$, which are connected through an LSTM. The other is the hidden units at the same time step $\{h_t^l, l \in 1, \ldots, L\}$, which are connected through a feed-forward network. LSTM keep the short-term memory for a long time. Thus the error signals can be easily passed through $\{1, \ldots, T\}$. However, when the number of stacked layers is large, the feed-forward network will suffer from gradient vanishing/exploding problems, which make the gradients hard to pass through $\{1, \ldots, L\}$.

Shortcut connections make training much easier by adding a direct link between different layers. An intuitive explanation is that such links can make the error signal passing jump the layers, not just one by one. This behavior may lead to faster convergence and better generalization.

LSTM block [8] composes memory cells sharing the same input and output gate. He et al. [6] create a residual block which adds shortcut connections across different CNN layers. All these inspired us to build a shortcut block across different LSTM layers. Our shortcut block is mainly based on Wu et al. [27]. We start our construction from a special case of shortcuts: adding shortcuts to both c_t and h_t.

$$\begin{pmatrix} i \\ f \\ o \\ s \end{pmatrix} = \begin{pmatrix} \text{sigm} \\ \text{sigm} \\ \text{sigm} \\ \text{tanh} \end{pmatrix} W^l \begin{pmatrix} h_t^{l-1} \\ h_{t-1}^l \end{pmatrix} \tag{5}$$

$$g = \text{sigm}(U^l h_t^{l-1} + V^l h_t^{l-2}) \tag{6}$$

$$c_t = f \odot c_{t-1} + i \odot s_t^l + g \odot h_t^{l-2} \tag{7}$$

$$h_t^l = o \odot \tanh(c_t) + g \odot h_t^{l-2} \tag{8}$$

We want to simplify the computation of the cell updates. Notice that the internal states contain three parts (Eq. 7): the self-connected parts c_{t-1}, the original cell inputs s_t^l, and the shortcuts h_t^{l-2}. We observe that there exists two kinds of recurrent information flow in the internal states: one is the recurrent flow along the horizontal direction, controlled by self-connected parts, the other is along the vertical direction, controlled by shortcuts.

We find that omit the self-connected parts $f_t \odot c_{t-1}$ in Eq. (7) is helpful to bring faster convergence and improve the performance. An intuitive explanation is that the input sequence and the output sequence are exactly matched in sequence tagging. Specifically, the input token $x_i, i \in \{1, \ldots, n\}$ in a sequence provides the most relevant information to predict y_i. We want to enhance the information flow in the vertical direction through shortcuts, while decreasing the horizontal flow controlled by the self-connected units. Based on the observations, we get the following construction:

$$\begin{pmatrix} i \\ o \\ s \end{pmatrix} = \begin{pmatrix} \text{sigm} \\ \text{sigm} \\ \text{tanh} \end{pmatrix} W^l \begin{pmatrix} h_t^{l-1} \\ h_{t-1}^l \end{pmatrix} \tag{9}$$

$$g = \text{sigm}(U^l h_t^{l-1} + V^l h_t^{l-2})$$

$$m = i \odot s_t^l + g \odot h_t^{l-2} \tag{10}$$

$$h_t^l = o \odot \tanh(m) + g \odot h_t^{l-2}$$

where h_t^{l-2} are the outputs from layer $l-2$. g is the gate which is used to access the shortcut connections h_t^{l-2} or block it (See Fig. 1b).

Comparison with Wu et al. [27]. Wu et al. [27] introduced gated shortcuts connecting to cell outputs:

$$c_t^l = i \odot s_t^l + f \odot c_{t-1}^l$$

$$h_t^l = o \odot \tanh(c_t) + g \odot h_t^{l-2} \tag{11}$$

Comparison of (10) and (11) we can see the difference: Eq. (10) replaces the self-connected parts $f \odot c_{t-1}^l$ with shortcuts $g \odot h_t^{l-2}$ in the computation of the internal states.

Although the difference is tiny, our refinement is much easier to compute, since we do not need extra space to preserve the cell's internal state. Similarly, this behavior arises in the construction of Gated Recurrent Units (GRUs):

$$\tilde{h}_t^l = \tanh(W^l h_t^{l-1} + U^l(r_t \odot h_{t-1}^l))$$

$$h_t^l = (1 - z_t) \odot h_{t-1}^l + z_t \odot \tilde{h}_t^l \tag{12}$$

But the recurrent iterations in GRUs are very different from us. Our construction is built on the stacked LSTMs.

Comparison with LSTMs. LSTMs introduce a memory cell with a fixed self-connection to make the constant error flow (Fig. 1a). LSTM compute the following increment to the self-connected cell at each time step:

$$c_t = c_{t-1} + s_t \tag{13}$$

Here we remove the multiplicative gates to simplify the explanation. The self-connected cells c_t can keep the recurrent information for a long time. s_t are the cell inputs.

In the shortcut block, we use the shortcuts to replace the self-connected parts. Our cell states become:

$$m = h_t^{l-2} + s_t \tag{14}$$

Although we ignore the self-connected parts in LSTM cells, it does not mean we throw away the recurrent information. As shown in Fig. 1b, the connections from cell outputs to inputs preserve the recurrent information flow.

3.2   Gates Computation

Shortcut gates are used to make the skipped path deterministic [21] or stochastic [10]. We explore many ways to compute the shortcut gates (denoted by g_t^l). The simplest case is to use g_t^l as a linear operator. In this case, g_t^l is a weight matrix, and the element-wise product $g_t^l \odot h_t^{-l}$ in (10) becomes a matrix-vector multiplication:

$$g_t^l \odot h_t^{-l} := W^l h_t^{-l} \tag{15}$$

We can also get g_t^l under a non-linear mapping, which is similar to the computation of gates in LSTM:

$$g_t^l = \sigma(W^l h_t^{l-1}) \tag{16}$$

Here we use the output of layer $l-1$ to control the shortcuts. Notice that this non-linear mapping is not unique, we just show the simplest case.

Furthermore, inspired by the dropout [20] strategy, we can sample from a Bernoulli stochastic variable to get g_t^l. In this case, the gate is stochastic:

$$g_t^l \sim \text{Bernoulli}(p) \tag{17}$$

where g_t^l is a vector of independent Bernoulli random variables each of which has probability p of being 1. We can either fix p with a specific value or learn it with a non-linear mapping. For example, we can learn p by:

$$p = \sigma(H^l h_t^{l-1}) \tag{18}$$

At test time, h_t^{-l} is multiplied by p.

Discussion. The gates of LSTMs are essential parts to avoid weight update conflicts, which are also invoked by the shortcuts. In experiments, we find that using deterministic gates is better than the stochastic gates. We recommend using the logistic gates to compute g_t^l.

4   Neural Architecture for Sequence Tagging

Sequence tagging can be formulated as $P(t|w; \theta)$, where $w = [w_1, \ldots, w_T]$ indicates the T words in a sentence, and $t = [t_1, \ldots, t_T]$ indicates the corresponding T tags. In this section we introduce an neural architecture for $P(\cdot)$, which includes an input layer, a stacked hidden layers and an output layer. Since the stacked hidden layers have already been introduced in the previous section, we only introduce the input and the output layer here.

4.1   Network Inputs

The inputs of the network are the distributed representation of each token in a sequence. Following Wu et al. [27], we use a local window approach together with a concatenation of word representations, character representations, and capitalization representations:

$$f_{w_t} = [L_w(w_t); L_a(a_t); L_c(c_w)] \tag{19}$$

where w_t, a_t represent the current word and its capitalization. $c_w :=$ $[c_1, c_2, \ldots, c_{T_w}]$, where T_w is the length of the word and $c_i, i \in \{1, \ldots, T_w\}$ is the i-th character for the particular word. $L_w(\cdot) \in \mathbb{R}^{|V_w| \times n}$, $L_a(\cdot) \in \mathbb{R}^{|V_a| \times m}$ and $L_c(\cdot) \in \mathbb{R}^{|V_c| \times r}$ are the look-up tables for the words, capitalization and characters, respectively. f_{w_t} represents the distributed feature of w_t. A context window of size d surrounding the current word is used as an input:

$$x_t = [f_{w_{t-\lfloor d/2 \rfloor}}; \ldots; f_{w_{t+\lfloor d/2 \rfloor}}] \tag{20}$$

where x_t is a concatenation of the context features.

4.2   Network Outputs

For sequence tagging, we use a *softmax* activation function $g(\cdot)$ in the output layer:

$$y_t = g(W^{hy}[\overrightarrow{h_t}; \overleftarrow{h_t}]) \tag{21}$$

where y_t is a probability distribution over all possible tags. $y_k(t) = \frac{\exp(h_k)}{\sum_{k'} \exp(h_{k'})}$ is the k-th dimension of y_t, which corresponds to the k-th tag in the tag set. W^{hy} is the hidden-to-output weight.

5 Experiments

5.1 Combinatory Category Grammar Supertagging

We evaluate our method on Combinatory Category Grammar (CCG) supertagging task, which is a sequence tagging problem in natural language processing. The task is to assign supertags to each word in a sentence. In CCG the supertags stand for the lexical categories, which are composed of the basic categories such as N, NP and PP, and complex categories, which are the combination of the basic categories based on a set of rules. Detailed explanations of CCG refer to [22,23].

Dataset and Pre-processing. Our experiments are performed on CCGBank [9], which is a translation from Penn Treebank [16] to CCG with a coverage 99.4%. We follow the standard splits, using sections 02–21 for training, section 00 for development and section 23 for the test. We use a full category set containing 1285 tags. All digits are mapped into the same digit '9', and all words are lowercased.

Network Configuration

Initialization. There are two types of weights in our experiments: recurrent and non-recurrent weights. For non-recurrent weights, we initialize word embeddings with the pre-trained 100-dimensional GolVe vectors [17]. Other weights are initialized with the Gaussian distribution $\mathcal{N}(0, \frac{1}{\sqrt{\text{fan-in}}})$ scaled by a factor of 0.1, where *fan-in* is the number of units in the input layer. For recurrent weight matrices, following [18] we initialize with random orthogonal matrices through SVD to avoid unstable gradients. All bias terms are initialized with zero vectors.

Hyperparameters. Our context window size is set to 3. The dimension of character embedding and capitalization embeddings are 5. The number of cells of the stacked bidirectional LSTM is also set to 465 for orthogonal initialization. All stacked hidden layers have the same number of cells. The output layer has 1286 neurons, which equals to the number of tags in the training set with a RARE symbol.

Training. We use stochastic gradient descent (SGD) algorithm with an initial learning rate 0.02 for training. The learning rate is then scaled by 0.5 when the following condition satisfied:

$$\frac{|e_p - e_c|}{e_p} <= 0.005 \text{ and } lr >= 0.0005$$

where e_p is the error rate on the validation set on the previous epoch. e_c is the error rate on the current epoch. An intuitive explanation of the rule is when the growth of the performance become lower, we need to use a smaller learning rate to adjust the weights. We use on-line learning in our experiments.

We use dropout to avoid overfitting. We add a binary dropout mask to the local context windows with a drop rate p of 0.25. We also apply dropout to the output of the first hidden layer and the last hidden layer, with a 0.5 drop rate. At test time, weights are scaled with a factor $1 - p$.

Comparison with Other Systems. We compare our methods with other systems. The comparison does not include any externally labeled data or POS tags. We present experiments trained on the training set and evaluated on the test set using the highest 1-best supertagging accuracy on the development set.

Table 1 shows deep stacked models perform better than other non-stacked models. Specically, our shortcut block achieves state-of-the-art results (95.12% on test set). Notice that 9 is the number of stacked Bi-LSTM layers. The total layer of the networks contains 11 (9 + 1 input-to-hidden layer + 1 hidden-to-output layer) layers. We find the 9 or 11 stacked depth are the proper choices for the task.

Table 1. 1-best supertagging accuracy on CCGbank. The "mixed block" indicates adding shortcut connections to both c_t^l and h_t^l, as shown in Eq. (7).

Model	Dev	Test
Clark and Curran [2]	91.5	92.0
MLP (Lewis and Steedman [15])	91.3	91.6
Bi-LSTM (Lewis et al. [14])	94.1	94.3
Elman-RNN (Xu et al. [28])	93.1	93.0
Bi-RNN (Xu et al. [29])	93.49	93.52
Bi-LSTM (Vaswani et al. [24])	94.24	94.5
9-stacked Bi-LSTM (Wu et al. [27])	94.55	94.69
9-stacked: mixed block (ours)	94.72	95.08
9-stacked: shortcut block (ours)	**94.93**	**95.12**

Exploration of Shortcuts. To get a better understanding of the shortcuts proposed in Eq. (10), we experiment with its variants to compare the performance. Our analysis mainly focuses on three parts: the variants of shortcut blocks, gating functions. The comparisons are summarized as follows:

Shortcut Variants. Table 2 presents the shortcut variants. In the variants of mixed block (Eq. 7), the shortcuts for both c_t^l and h_t^l obtains the highest accuracy (95.08%) on the test set, but with high computational cost. In the variants of shortcut block, the "no gate in m" case performs better than the others.

Table 2. Comparsion of shortcut variants. We use $\tilde{h}_t^l$ to represent the original cell output of LSTM block, which equals $o \odot \tanh(c_t^l)$, similar to $\tilde{c}_t^l := i \odot s_t^l + f \odot c_{t-1}$.

Case	Variant	Dev	Test
h_t^l updated [27]	with gate: $h_t^l = \tilde{h}_t^l + g \odot h_t^{l-2}$	94.51	94.67
mixed block (Eq.7)	no gate: $c_t^l = \tilde{c}_t^l + h_t^{l-2}, h_t^l = \tilde{h}_t^l + h_t^l$	93.84	93.84
	highway gate: $\begin{array}{l} c_t^l = (1-g) \odot \tilde{c}_t^l + g \odot h_t^{l-2} \\ h_t^l = (1-g) \odot \tilde{h}_t^l + g \odot h_t^{l-2} \end{array}$	94.49	94.62
	shortcuts for both c_t^l and h_t^l: $\begin{array}{l} c_t^l = \tilde{c}_t^l + g_c \odot c_t^{l-2} \\ h_t^l = \tilde{h}_t^l + g_h \odot h_t^{l-2} \end{array}$	94.72	94.98
shortcut block (Eq.10)	no gate in h_t^l: $h_t^l = o \odot \tanh(m) + h_t^{l-2}$	94.15	94.29
	no gate in m: $m = i \odot s_t^l + h_t^{l-2}$	94.77	94.97
	no shortcut in internal: $h_t^l = o \odot \tanh(i_t \odot s_t) + g \odot h_t^{l-2}$	93.83	94.01
	no shortcut in cell output: $h_t^l = o \odot \tanh(m)$	93.58	93.82

Gating Functions. Table 3 presents the comparison of several gating functions proposed in Sect. 3.2. We use the tanh function in the previous outputs to break the identity link. The result is 94.81% (Table 3), which is poorer than the identity function. We can infer that the identity function is more suitable than other scaled functions such as sigmoid or tanh to transmit information.

We find the deterministic gates performs better than the stochastic gates. Further, non-linear mapping $g_t^l = \sigma(W^l h_t^{l-1})$ achieves the best test accuracy (Table 3, 94.79%), while other types such as linear or stochastic gates are not generalize well.

Table 3. Comparsion of gating functions.

Case	Variant	Dev	Test
Scaled mapping	replace h_t^{l-2} with $\tanh(h_t^{l-2})$	94.60	94.81
Linear mapping	$g_t^l \odot h_t^{-l} = w^l \odot h_t^{-l}$	92.07	92.15
Non-linear mapping	$g_t^l = \sigma(W^l h_t^{l-1})$	**94.79**	**94.91**
	$g_t^l = \sigma(U^l h_{t-1}^l)$	94.21	94.56
	$g_t^l = \sigma(V^l h_t^{l-2})$	94.60	94.78
Stochastic sampling	$g_t^l \sim \text{Bernoulli}(p), p = 0.5$	91.12	91.47
	$g_t^l \sim \text{Bernoulli}(p), p = \sigma(H^l h_t^{l-1})$	93.90	94.06

Comparison of Hyper-parameters. As described in Sect. 4.1, we use a complex input encoding for our model. Concretely, we use a context window approach, together with character-level information to get a better representation for the raw input. We give comparisons for the system with/without this approaches while keeping the hidden and the output parts unchanged.

Table 4 shows the effects of the hyper-parameters on the task. We find that the model does not perform well (94.06%) without using local context windows.

Although LSTMs can memorize recent inputs for a long time, it is still necessary to use a convolution-like operator to convolve the input tokens to get a better representation. Character-level information also plays an important role for this task (13% relatively improvement), but the performance would be heavily damaged if using characters only.

Table 4. Comparsion of hyper-parameters.

Case	Variant	Dev	Test
Window size	$k = 0$	93.96	94.06
	$k = 5$	94.27	94.81
	$k = 7$	94.52	94.71
Character-level	$l_w = 0$	93.59	93.71
	$l_w = 3$	94.21	94.41
	$l_w = 7$	94.43	94.75
Character only	-	92.17	93.0

6 Related Work

Skip connections have been widely used for training deep neural networks. For recurrent neural networks, Schmidhuber [19]; El Hihi and Bengio [3] introduce deep RNNs by stacking hidden layers on top of each other. Graves [4]; Hermans and Schrauwen [7] propose the use of skip connections in stacked RNNs. However, the researchers have paid less attention to the analysis of various kinds of skip connections, which is our focus in this paper.

Recently, deep stacked networks have been widely used for applications. Srivastava et al. [21] and He et al. [6] mainly focus on feed-forward neural network, using well-designed skip connections across different layers to make the information pass more easily. The Grid LSTM proposed by Kalchbrenner et al. [11] extends the one dimensional LSTMs to many dimensional LSTMs, which provides a more general framework to construct deep LSTMs.

Zhang et al. [30] proposed highway LSTMs by introducing gated direct connections between internal states in adjacent layers. Zilly et al. [31] introduced recurrent highway networks (RHNs) which use a single recurrent layer to make RNN deep in a vertical direction. These works do not use skip connections, and the hierarchical structure is reflected in the LSTM internal states or cell outputs. Wu et al. [26,27] proposed a similar architecture for the shortcuts in stacked Bi-LSTMs, we make a improvement to their design.

There are also some works using stochastic gates to transmit the information. Zoneout [12] provides a stochastic link between the previous hidden states and the current states, forcing the current states to maintain their previous values during the recurrent step. Chung et al. [1] proposes a stochastic boundary state to update the internal states and cell outputs. These stochastic connections are connected between adjacent layers, while our constructions of the shortcuts are mostly cross-layered. Also, the updating mechanisms of LSTM blocks are different.

7   Conclusions

In this paper, we propose the shortcut block as a basic architecture for constructing deep stacked models. We compare several gating functions and find that the non-linear deterministic gate performs the best. These explorations can help us to train deep stacked Bi-LSTMs successfully. Based on this shortcuts structure, we achieve the state-of-the-art results on CCG supertagging. Our explorations could easily be applied to other sequence processing problems, which can be modeled with RNN architectures.

References

1. Chung, J., Ahn, S., Bengio, Y.: Hierarchical multiscale recurrent neural networks. arXiv preprint arXiv:1609.01704 (2016)
2. Clark, S., Curran, J.R.: Wide-coverage efficient statistical parsing with CCG and log-linear models. Comput. Linguist. **33**(4), 493–552 (2007)
3. El Hihi, S., Bengio, Y.: Hierarchical recurrent neural networks for long-term dependencies. In: NIPS. vol. 400, p. 409. Citeseer (1995)
4. Graves, A.: Generating sequences with recurrent neural networks. arXiv preprint arXiv:1308.0850 (2013)
5. Graves, A., Schmidhuber, J.: Framewise phoneme classification with bidirectional lstm and other neural network architectures. Neural Netw. **18**(5), 602–610 (2005)
6. He, K., Zhang, X., Ren, S., Sun, J.: Deep residual learning for image recognition. arXiv preprint arXiv:1512.03385 (2015)
7. Hermans, M., Schrauwen, B.: Training and analysing deep recurrent neural networks. In: Advances in Neural Information Processing Systems, pp. 190–198 (2013)
8. Hochreiter, S., Schmidhuber, J.: LSTM can solve hard long time lag problems. In: Advances in Neural Information Processing Systems, pp. 473–479 (1997)
9. Hockenmaier, J., Steedman, M.: CCGbank: a corpus of CCG derivations and dependency structures extracted from the penn treebank. Comput. Linguist. **33**(3), 355–396 (2007)
10. Huang, G., Sun, Y., Liu, Z., Sedra, D., Weinberger, K.: Deep networks with stochastic depth. arXiv preprint arXiv:1603.09382 (2016)
11. Kalchbrenner, N., Danihelka, I., Graves, A.: Grid long short-term memory. arXiv preprint arXiv:1507.01526 (2015)
12. Krueger, D., Maharaj, T., Kramár, J., Pezeshki, M., Ballas, N., Ke, N.R., Goyal, A., Bengio, Y., Larochelle, H., Courville, A., et al.: Zoneout: Regularizing RNNs by randomly preserving hidden activations. arXiv preprint arXiv:1606.01305 (2016)
13. Lample, G., Ballesteros, M., Subramanian, S., Kawakami, K., Dyer, C.: Neural architectures for named entity recognition. arXiv preprint arXiv:1603.01360 (2016)
14. Lewis, M., Lee, K., Zettlemoyer, L.: LSTM CCG parsing. In: Proceedings of the 15th Annual Conference of the North American Chapter of the Association for Computational Linguistics (2016)

15. Lewis, M., Steedman, M.: Improved CCG parsing with semi-supervised supertagging. Trans. Assoc. Comput. Linguist. **2**, 327–338 (2014)
16. Marcus, M.P., Marcinkiewicz, M.A., Santorini, B.: Building a large annotated corpus of english: the penn treebank. Comput. Linguist. **19**(2), 313–330 (1993)
17. Pennington, J., Socher, R., Manning, C.D.: Glove: global vectors for word representation. In: EMNLP, vol. 14, pp. 1532–1543 (2014)
18. Saxe, A.M., McClelland, J.L., Ganguli, S.: Exact solutions to the nonlinear dynamics of learning in deep linear neural networks. arXiv preprint arXiv:1312.6120 (2013)
19. Schmidhuber, J.: Learning complex, extended sequences using the principle of history compression. Neural Comput. **4**(2), 234–242 (1992)
20. Srivastava, N., Hinton, G., Krizhevsky, A., Sutskever, I., Salakhutdinov, R.: Dropout: a simple way to prevent neural networks from overfitting. J. Mach. Learn. Res. **15**(1), 1929–1958 (2014)
21. Srivastava, R.K., Greff, K., Schmidhuber, J.: Highway networks. arXiv preprint arXiv:1505.00387 (2015)
22. Steedman, M.: The Syntactic Process, vol. 24. MIT Press, Cambridge (2000)
23. Steedman, M., Baldridge, J.: Combinatory categorial grammar. In: Non-Transformational Syntax: Formal and Explicit Models of Grammar. Wiley, Hoboken (2011)
24. Vaswani, A., Bisk, Y., Sagae, K., Musa, R.: Supertagging with LSTMs. In: Proceedings of the Human Language Technology Conference of the NAACL (2016)
25. Wang, P., Qian, Y., Soong, F.K., He, L., Zhao, H.: Part-of-speech tagging with bidirectional long short-term memory recurrent neural network. arXiv preprint arXiv:1510.06168 (2015)
26. Wu, H., Zhang, J., Zong, C.: A dynamic window neural network for CCG supertagging. In: National Conference on Artificial Intelligence, pp. 3337–3343 (2016)
27. Wu, H., Zhang, J., Zong, C.: An empirical exploration of skip connections for sequential tagging. In: International Conference on Computational Linguistics, pp. 203–212 (2016)
28. Xu, W., Auli, M., Clark, S.: CCG supertagging with a recurrent neural network. Volume 2: Short Papers, p. 250 (2015)
29. Xu, W., Auli, M., Clark, S.: Expected f-measure training for shift-reduce parsing with recurrent neural networks. In: Proceedings of NAACL-HLT, pp. 210–220 (2016)
30. Zhang, Y., Chen, G., Yu, D., Yaco, K., Khudanpur, S., Glass, J.: Highway long short-term memory RNNs for distant speech recognition. In: 2016 IEEE International Conference on Acoustics, Speech and Signal Processing (ICASSP), pp. 5755–5759. IEEE (2016)
31. Zilly, J.G., Srivastava, R.K., Koutník, J., Schmidhuber, J.: Recurrent highway networks. arXiv preprint arXiv:1607.03474 (2016)

Machine Translation

Look-Ahead Attention for Generation in Neural Machine Translation

Long Zhou[1], Jiajun Zhang[1], and Chengqing Zong[1,2(✉)]

[1] National Laboratory of Pattern Recognition, CASIA,
University of Chinese Academy of Sciences, Beijing, China
{long.zhou,jjzhang,cqzong}@nlpr.ia.ac.cn
[2] CAS Center for Excellence in Brain Science and Intelligence Technology,
Beijing, China

Abstract. The attention model has become a standard component in neural machine translation (NMT) and it guides translation process by selectively focusing on parts of the source sentence when predicting each target word. However, we find that the generation of a target word does not only depend on the source sentence, but also rely heavily on the previous generated target words, especially the distant words which are difficult to model by using recurrent neural networks. To solve this problem, we propose in this paper a novel look-ahead attention mechanism for generation in NMT, which aims at directly capturing the dependency relationship between target words. We further design three patterns to integrate our look-ahead attention into the conventional attention model. Experiments on NIST Chinese-to-English and WMT English-to-German translation tasks show that our proposed look-ahead attention mechanism achieves substantial improvements over state-of-the-art baselines.

1 Introduction

Neural machine translation (NMT) has significantly improved the quality of machine translation in recent several years [1,9,10,26], in which the attention model increasingly plays an important role. Unlike traditional statistical machine translation (SMT) [4,13,32] which contains multiple separately tuned components, NMT builds upon a single and large neural network to directly map source sentence to associated target sentence.

Typically, NMT adopts the encoder-decoder architecture which consists of two recurrent neural networks. The encoder network models the semantics of the source sentence and transforms the source sentence into context vector representation, from which the decoder network generates the target translation word by word. Attention mechanism has become an indispensable component in NMT, which enables the model to dynamically compose source representation for each timestep during decoding, instead of a single and static representation. Specifically, the attention model shows which source words the model should focus on in order to predict the next target word.

However, previous attention models are mainly designed to predict the alignment of a target word with respect to source words, which take no account of the

X. Huang et al. (Eds.): NLPCC 2017, LNAI 10619, pp. 211–223, 2018.
https://doi.org/10.1007/978-3-319-73618-1_18

fact that the generation of a target word may have a stronger correlation with the previous generated target words. Recurrent neural networks, such as gated recurrent units (GRU) [5] and long short term memory (LSTM) [8], still suffer from long-distance dependency problems, according to pioneering studies [1,12] that the performance of NMT is getting worse as source sentences get longer. Figure 1 illustrates an example of Chinese-English translation. The dependency relationship of target sentence determines whether the predicate of the sentence should be singular (is) or plural (are). While the conventional attention model does not have a specific mechanism to learn the dependency relationship between target words.

To address this problem, we propose in this paper a novel look-ahead attention mechanism for generation in NMT, which can directly model the long-distance dependency relationship between target words. The look-ahead attention model does not only align to source words, but also refer to the previous generated target words when generating a target word. Furthermore, we present and investigate three patterns for the look-ahead attention, which can be integrated into any attention-based NMT. To show the effectiveness of our look-ahead attention, we have conducted experiments on NIST Chinese-to-English translation tasks and WMT14 English-to-German translation tasks. Experiments show that our proposed model obtains significant BLEU score improvements over strong SMT baselines and a state-of-the-art NMT baseline.

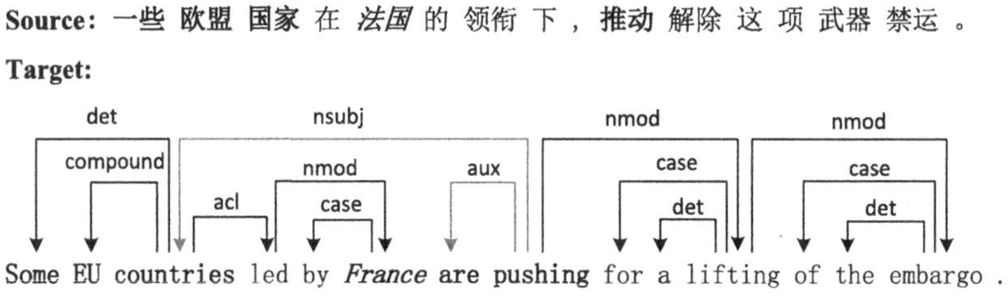

Source: 一些 欧盟 国家 在 *法国* 的 领衔 下 ， 推动 解除 这 项 武器 禁运 。

Target:

Some EU countries led by *France* are pushing for a lifting of the embargo .

Fig. 1. An example of Chinese-English translation. The English sentence is analyzed using Stanford online parser (http://nlp.stanford.edu:8080/parser/index.jsp.). Although the predicate *"are pushing"* is close to the word *"France"*, it has a stronger dependency on the word *"countries"* instead of *"France"*.

2 Neural Machine Translation

Our framework integrating the look-ahead attention mechanism into NMT can be applied in any conventional attention model. Without loss of generality, we use the improved attention-based NMT proposed by Luong et al. [16], which utilizes stacked LSTM layers for both encoder and decoder as illustrated in Fig. 2.

The NMT first encodes the source sentence $X = (x_1, x_2, ..., x_m)$ into a sequence of context vector representation $C = (h_1, h_2, ..., h_m)$ whose size varies with respect to the source sentence length. Then, the NMT decodes from the context vector representation C and generates target translation $Y = (y_1, y_2, ..., y_n)$ one word each time by maximizing the probability of $p(y_j|y_{<j}, C)$. Next, we briefly review the encoder introducing how to obtain C and the decoder addressing how to calculate $p(y_j|y_{<j}, C)$.

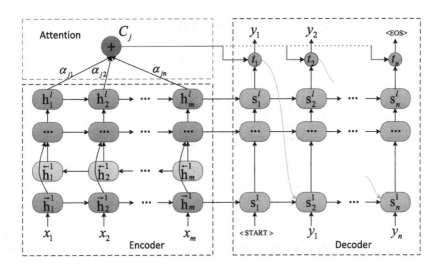

Fig. 2. The architecture of neural machine translation model.

Encoder: The context vector representation $C = (h_1^l, h_2^l, ..., h_m^l)$ are generated by the encoder using l stacked LSTM layers. Bi-directional connections are used for the bottom encoder layer, and h_i^1 is a concatenation of a left-to-right $\overrightarrow{h}_i^1$ and a right-to-left $\overleftarrow{h}_i^1$,

$$h_i^1 = \begin{bmatrix} \overrightarrow{h}_i^1 \\ \overleftarrow{h}_i^1 \end{bmatrix} = \begin{bmatrix} LSTM(\overrightarrow{h}_{i-1}^1, x_i) \\ LSTM(\overleftarrow{h}_{i-1}^1, x_i) \end{bmatrix} \tag{1}$$

All other encoder layers are unidirectional, and h_i^k is calculated as follows:

$$h_i^k = LSTM(h_{i-1}^k, h_i^{k-1}) \tag{2}$$

Decoder: The conditional probability $p(y_j|y_{<j}, C)$ is formulated as

$$p(y_j|Y_{<j}, C) = p(y_j|Y_{<j}, c_j) = softmax(W_s t_j) \tag{3}$$

Specifically, we employ a simple concatenation layer to produce an attentional hidden state t_j:

$$t_j = tanh(W_c[s_j^l; c_j] + b) = tanh(W_c^1 s_j^l + W_c^2 c_j + b) \tag{4}$$

where s_j^l denotes the target hidden state at the top layer of a stacking LSTM. The attention model calculates c_j as the weighted sum of the source-side context vector representation, just as illustrated in the upper left corner of Fig. 2.

$$c_j = \sum_{i=1}^{m} ATT(s_j^l, h_i^l) \cdot h_i^l = \sum_{i=1}^{m} \alpha_{ji} h_i^l \tag{5}$$

where α_{ji} is a normalized item calculated as follows:

$$\alpha_{ji} = \frac{exp(h_i^l \cdot s_j^l)}{\sum_{i'} exp(h_{i'}^l \cdot s_j^l)} \tag{6}$$

s_j^k is computed by using the following formula:

$$s_j^k = LSTM(s_{j-1}^k, s_j^{k-1}) \tag{7}$$

If $k = 1$, s_j^1 will be calculated by combining t_{j-1} as feed input [16]:

$$s_j^1 = LSTM(s_{j-1}^1, y_{j-1}, t_{j-1}) \tag{8}$$

Given the bilingual training data $D = \{(X^{(z)}, Y^{(z)})\}_{z=1}^{Z}$, all parameters of the attention-based NMT are optimized to maximize the following conditional log-likelihood:

$$L(\theta) = \frac{1}{Z} \sum_{z=1}^{Z} \sum_{j=1}^{n} log p(y_j^{(z)} | y_{<j}^{(z)}, X^{(z)}, \theta) \tag{9}$$

3   Model Description

Learning long-distance dependencies is a key challenge in machine translation. Although the attention model introduced above has shown its effectiveness in NMT, it takes no account of the dependency relationship between target words. Hence, in order to relieve the burden of LSTM or GRU to carry on the target-side long-distance dependencies, we design a novel look-ahead attention mechanism, which directly establishes a connection between the current target word and the previous generated target words. In this section, we will elaborate on three proposed approaches about integrating the look-ahead attention into the generation of attention-based NMT.

3.1   Concatenation Pattern

Figure 3(b) illustrates concatenation pattern of the look-ahead attention mechanism. We not only compute the attention between current target hidden state and source hidden states, but also calculate the attention between current target hidden state and previous target hidden states. The look-ahead attention output at timestep j is computed as:

$$c_j^d = \sum_{i=1}^{j-1} ATT(s_j^l, s_i^l) \cdot s_i^l \qquad (10)$$

where $ATT(s_j^l, s_i^l)$ is a normalized item.

Specifically, given the target hidden state s_j^l, the source-side context vector representation c_j, and the target-side context vector representation c_j^d, we employ a concatenation layer to combine the information to produce an attentional hidden state as follows:

$$t_j^{final} = tanh(W_c[s_j^l; c_j; c_j^d] + b) \qquad (11)$$

After getting the attentional hidden state t_j^{final}, we can calculate the conditional probability $p(y_j|y_{<j}, C)$ as formulated in Eq. 3.

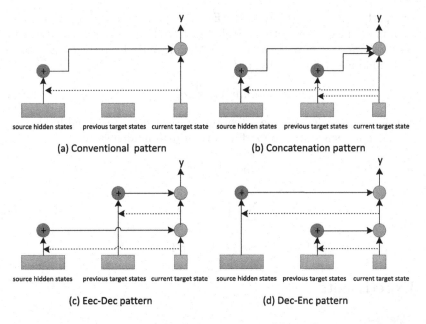

Fig. 3. Different architectures of look-ahead attention. (a) is the conventional attention pattern as introduced in Eq. 4 of Sect. 2. (b), (c) and (d) are our three approaches which integrate look-ahead attention mechanism into attention-based NMT.

3.2   Enc-Dec Pattern

Concatenation pattern is a simple method to achieve look-ahead attention, which regards source-side context vector representation and target-side context vector representation as the same importance. Different from concatenation pattern, Enc-Dec pattern utilizes a hierarchical architecture to integrate look-ahead attention as shown in Fig. 3(c).

Once we get the attentional hidden state of conventional attention-based NMT, we can employ look-ahead attention mechanism to update the previous attentional hidden state. In detail, the model first computes the attentional hidden state t_j^e of conventional attention-based NMT as Eq. 4. Second, the model calculates the attention between the attentional hidden state t_j^e and previous target hidden states:

$$c_j^d = \sum_{i=1}^{j-1} ATT(t_j^e, s_i^l) \cdot s_i^l \tag{12}$$

Then, the final attentional hidden state is calculated as followed:

$$t_j^{final} = tanh(W_{c2}[t_j^e; c_j^d] + b_2) \tag{13}$$

3.3 Dec-Enc Pattern

Dec-Enc pattern is the opposite of the Enc-Dec pattern, and it uses look-ahead attention mechanism to help the model align to source words. Figure 3(d) shows this pattern. We compute look-ahead attention output firstly as Eq. 10, and attentional hidden state is computed by:

$$t_j^d = tanh(W_{c1}[s_j^l; c_j^d] + b) \tag{14}$$

Finally, we can calculate the attention between the attentional hidden state t_j^d and source hidden states to get final attentional hidden state:

$$t_j^{final} = tanh(W_{c2}[t_j^d; c_j^e] + b_2) \tag{15}$$

$$c_j^e = \sum_{i=1}^{m} ATT(t_j^d, h_i^l) \cdot h_i^l \tag{16}$$

where h_i^l is source-side hidden state at the top layer.

4 Experiments

4.1 Dataset

We perform our experiments on the NIST Chinese-English translation tasks and WMT14 English-German translation tasks. The evaluation metric is BLEU [21] as calculated by the `multi-blue.perl` script.

For Chinese-English, our training data consists of 630K sentence pairs extracted from LDC corpus[1]. We use NIST 2003 (MT03) Chinese-English

---

[1] The corpora include LDC2000T50, LDC2002T01, LDC2002E18, LDC2003E07, LDC2003E14, LDC2003T17 and LDC2004T07.

dataset as the validation set, NIST 2004 (MT04), NIST 2005 (MT05), NIST 2006 (MT06) datasets as our test sets. Besides, 10M Xinhua portion of Gigaword corpus is used in training language model for SMT.

For English-German, to compare with the results reported by previous work [16,25,34], we used the same subset of the WMT 2014 training corpus[2] that contains 4.5M sentence pairs with 116M English words and 110M German words. The concatenation of news-test 2012 and news-test 2013 is used as the validation set and news-test 2014 as the test set.

4.2 Training Details

We build the described models modified from the Zoph_RNN[3] toolkit which is written in C++/CUDA and provides efficient training across multiple GPUs. Our training procedure and hyper parameter choices are similar to those used by Luong et al. [16]. In the NMT architecture as illustrated in Fig. 2, the encoder has three stacked LSTM layers including a bidirectional layer, followed by a global attention layer, and the decoder contains two stacked LSTM layers followed by the softmax layer.

In more details, we limit the source and target vocabularies to the most frequent 30K words for Chinese-English and 50K words for English-German. The word embedding dimension and the size of hidden layers are all set to 1000. Parameter optimization is performed using stochastic gradient descent(SGD), and we set learning rate to 0.1 at the beginning and halve the threshold while the perplexity go up on the development set. Each SGD is a mini-batch of 128 examples. Dropout was also applied on each layer to avoid over-fitting, and the dropout rate is set to 0.2. At test time, we employ beam search with beam size b = 12.

4.3 Results on Chinese-English Translation

We list the BLEU scores of our proposed model in Table 1. Moses-1 [11] is the state-of-the-art phrase-based SMT system with the default configuration and a 4-gram language model trained on the target portion of training data. Moses-2 is the same as Moses-1 except that the language model is trained using the target data plus 10M Xinhua portion of Gigaword corpus. The BLEU score of our NMT baseline, which is an attention-based NMT as introduced in Sect. 2, is about 4.5 higher than the state-of-the-art SMT system Moses-2.

For the last three lines in Table 1, Enc-Dec pattern outperforms concatenation pattern and even Dec-Enc pattern, which shows Enc-Dec pattern is best approach to take advantage of look-ahead attention. Moreover, our Enc-Dec pattern gets an improvement of +0.93 BLEU points over the state-of-the-art NMT baseline, which demonstrates that the look-ahead attention mechanism is effective for generation in conventional attention-based NMT.

---

[2] http://www.statmt.org/wmt14/translation-task.html.
[3] https://github.com/isi-nlp/Zoph_RNN.

Table 1. Translation results (BLEU score) for Chinese-to-English translation. "†": significantly better than NMT baseline ($p < 0.05$). "‡": significantly better than NMT baseline ($p < 0.01$).

System	MT04	MT05	MT06	Ave
Moses-1	31.08	28.37	30.04	29.83
Moses-2	33.13	31.38	32.63	32.38
NMT baseline	38.96	34.95	36.65	36.85
Concatenation pattern	39.43†	35.40†	36.93	37.25†
Enc-Dec pattern	**39.61**†	**36.50**‡	**37.23**†	**37.78**‡
Dec-Enc pattern	39.00	36.36‡	37.01†	37.46‡

Effects of Translating Long Sentences. A well-known flaw of NMT model is the inability to properly translate long sentences. One of the goals that we integrate the look-ahead attention into the generation of NMT decoder is boosting the performance in translating long sentence. We follow Bahdanau et al. [1] to group sentences of similar lengths together and compute a BLEU score per group, as demonstrated in Fig. 4.

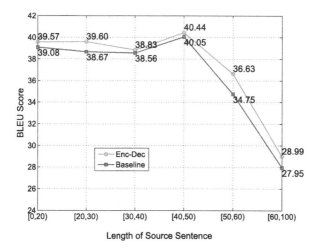

Fig. 4. Length Analysis - translation qualities (BLEU score) of our proposed model and the NMT baseline as sentences become longer.

Although the performance of both the NMT baseline and our proposed model drops rapidly when the length of source sentence increases, our Enc-Dec model is more effective than the NMT Baseline in handling long sentences. Specifically, our proposed model gets an improvement of 1.88 BLEU points over the baseline from 50 to 60 words in source language. Furthermore, when the length of input sentence is greater than 60, our model still outperforms the baseline by 1.04 BLEU points. Experiments show that the look-ahead attention can relieve the burden of LSTM to carry on the target-side long-distance dependencies.

Target Alignment of Look-Ahead Attention. The conventional attention models always refer to some source words when generating a target word. We propose a look-ahead attention for generation in NMT, which also focuses on previous generated words in order to predict the next target word.

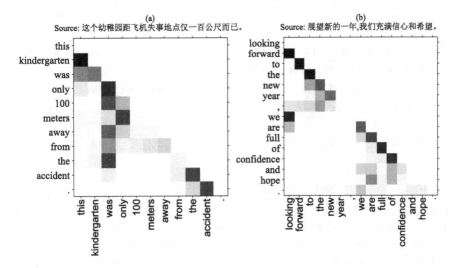

Fig. 5. Target alignment of look-ahead attention.

We provide two real translation examples to show the target alignment of look-ahead attention in Fig. 5. The first line is blank because it does not have look-ahead attention when generating the first word. Every line represents the weight distribution for previous generated words when predicting current target word. More specifically, we find some interesting phenomena. First, target words often refer to verb or predicate which has been generated previously, such as the word "was" in Fig. 5(a).

Second, the heat map shows that the word "we" and the word "looking" have a stronger correlation when translating the Chinese sentence as demonstrated in Fig. 5(b). Intuitively, the look-ahead attention mechanism establishes a bridge to capture the dependency relationship between target words. Third, most target words mainly focus on the word immediately before the current target word, which may be due to the fact that the last generated word contains more information in recurrent neural networks. We can control the influence of the look-ahead attention like Tu et al. [27] to improve translation quality and instead we remain it as our future work.

4.4   Results on English-German Translation

We evaluate our model on the WMT14 translation tasks for English to German, whose results are presented in Table 2. We find that our proposed look-ahead attention NMT model also obtains significant accuracy improvements on large-scale English-German translation.

Table 2. Translation results (BLEU score) for English-to-German translation. "‡": significantly better than baseline($p < 0.01$).

System	Architecture	Voc.	BLEU
Existing systems			
Loung et al. [16]	LSTM with 4 layers+dropout+local att	50K	19.00
Shen et al. [25]	Gated RNN with search + MRT	50K	18.02
Zhou et al. [34]	LSTM with 16 layers + F-F connections	160K	20.60
Our NMT systems			
This work	Baseline	50K	19.84
This work	Enc-Dec pattern	50K	20.36‡

In addition, we compare our NMT systems with various other systems including Zhou et al. [34] which use a much deeper neural network. Luong et al. [16] achieves BLEU score of 19.00 with 4 layers deep Encoder-Decoder model. Shen et al. [25] obtained the BLEU score of 18.02 with MRT techniques. For this work, our Enc-Dec look-ahead attention NMT model with two layers achieves 20.36 BLEU scores, which is on par with Zhou et al. [34] in term of BLEU. Note that Zhou et al. [34] employ a much larger depth as well as vocabulary size to obtain their best results.

5   Related Work

The recently proposed neural machine translation has drawn more and more attention. Most of the existing approaches and models mainly focus on designing better attention models [16,18–20,28], better strategies for handling rare and unknown words [14,17,24], exploiting large-scale monolingual data [3,23,33], and integrating SMT techniques [7,25,30,35].

Our goal in this work is to design a smart attention mechanism to model the dependency relationship between target words. Tu et al. [28] and Mi et al. [19] proposed to extend attention models with a coverage vector in order to attack the problem of repeating and dropping translations. Cohn et al. [6] augmented the attention model with well-known features in traditional SMT. Unlike previous works that attention models are mainly designed to predict the alignment of a target word with respect to source words, we focus on establishing a direct bridge to capture the long-distance dependency relationship between target words. In addition, Wu et al. [31] lately proposed a sequence-to-dependency NMT method, in which the target word sequence and its corresponding dependency structure are jointly constructed and modeled. However, the target dependency tree references are needed for training in this model and our proposed model does not need extra resources.

Very Recently, Vaswani et al. [29] proposed a new simple network architecture, Transformer, based solely on attention mechanisms with multi-headed self attention. Besides, Lin et al. [15] presented a self-attention mechanism which extracts different aspects of the sentence into multiple vector representations. And the self-attention model has been used successfully in some tasks including abstractive summarization and reading comprehension [2,22]. Here, in order to alleviate the burden of LSTM to carry on the target-side long-distance dependencies of NMT, we propose to integrate the look-ahead attention mechanism into the conventional attention-based NMT which is used in conjunction with a recurrent network.

6   Conclusion

In this work, we propose a novel look-ahead attention mechanism for generation in NMT, which aims at directly capturing the long-distance dependency relationship between target words. The look-ahead attention model not only aligns to source words, but also refers to the previous generated words when generating the next target word. Furthermore, we present and investigate three patterns to integrate our proposed look-ahead attention into the conventional attention model. Experiments on Chinese-to-English and English-to-German translation tasks show that our proposed model obtains significant BLEU score gains over strong SMT baselines and a state-of-the-art NMT baseline.

Acknowledgments. The research work has been funded by the Natural Science Foundation of China under Grant No. 61673380, No. 61402478 and No. 61403379.

References

1. Bahdanau, D., Cho, K., Bengio, Y.: Neural machine translation by jointly learning to align and translate. In: Proceedings of ICLR 2015 (2015)
2. Cheng, J., Dong, L., Lapata, M.: Long short-term memory-networks for machine reading. arXiv preprint arXiv:1601.06733 (2016)
3. Cheng, Y., Xu, W., He, Z., He, W., Wu, H., Sun, M., Liu, Y.: Semi-supervised learning for neural machine translation. In: Proceedings of ACL 2016 (2016)
4. Chiang, D.: A hierarchical phrase-based model for statistical machine translation. In: Proceedings of ACL 2005 (2005)
5. Cho, K., van Merrienboer, B., Gulcehre, C., Bahdanau, D., Bougares, F., Schwenk, H., Bengio, Y.: Learning phrase representations using RNN encoder-decoder for statistical machine translation. In: Proceedings of EMNLP 2014 (2014)
6. Cohn, T., Hoang, C.D.V., Vymolova, E., Yao, K., Dyer, C., Haffari, G.: Incorporating structural alignment biases into an attentional neural translation model. arXiv preprint arXiv:1601.01085 (2016)

7. He, W., He, Z., Wu, H., Wang, H.: Improved neural machine translation with SMT features. In: Proceedings of AAAI 2016 (2016)
8. Hochreiter, S., Schmidhuber, J.: Long Short-Term Memory, vol. 9. MIT Press, Cambridge (1997)
9. Junczys-Dowmunt, M., Dwojak, T., Hoang, H.: Is neural machine translation ready for deployment? A case study on 30 translation directions. In: Proceedings of IWSLT 2016 (2016)
10. Kalchbrenner, N., Blunsom, P.: Recurrent continuous translation models. In: Proceedings of EMNLP 2013 (2013)
11. Koehn, P., Hoang, H., Birch, A., Callison-Burch, C., Federico, M., Bertoldi, N., Cowan, B., Shen, W., Moran, C., Zens, R., et al.: Moses: open source toolkit for statistical machine translation. Association for Computational Linguistics (2007)
12. Koehn, P., Knowles, R.: Six challanges for neural machine translation. arXiv preprint arXiv:1706.03872 (2017)
13. Koehn, P., Och, F.J., Marcu, D.: Statistical phrase-based translation. In: Proceedings of ACL-NAACL 2013 (2003)
14. Li, X., Zhang, J., Zong, C.: Towards zero unknown word in neural machine translation. In: Proceedings of IJCAI 2016 (2016)
15. Lin, Z., Feng, M., Santos, C.N.d., Yu, M., Xiang, B., Zhou, B., Bengio, Y.: A structured self-attentive sentence embedding. arXiv preprint arXiv:1703.03130 (2017)
16. Luong, M.T., Pham, H., Manning, C.D.: Effective approaches to attention-based neural machine translation. In: Proceedings of EMNLP 2015 (2015)
17. Luong, M.T., Sutskever, I., Le, Q.V., Vinyals, O., Zaremba, W.: Addressing the rare word problem in neural machine translation. In: Proceedings of ACL 2015 (2015)
18. Meng, F., Lu, Z., Li, H., Liu, Q.: Interactive attention for neural machine translation. In: Proceedings of COLING 2016 (2016)
19. Mi, H., Sankaran, B., Wang, Z., Ge, N., Ittycheriah, A.: A coverage embedding model for neural machine translation. In: Proceedings of EMNLP 2016 (2016)
20. Mi, H., Wang, Z., Ge, N., Ittycheriah, A.: Supervised attentions for neural machine translation. In: Proceedings of EMNLP 2016 (2016)
21. Papineni, K., Roukos, S., Ward, T., Zhu, W.: BLEU: a method for automatic evaluation of machine translation. In: Proceedings of ACL 2002 (2002)
22. Paulus, R., Xiong, C., Socher, R.: A deep reinforced model for abstractive summarization. arXiv preprint arXiv:1705.04304 (2017)
23. Sennrich, R., Haddow, B., Birch, A.: Improving neural machine translation models with monolingual data. In: Proceedings of ACL 2016 (2016)
24. Sennrich, R., Haddow, B., Birch, A.: Neural machine translation of rare words with subword units. In: Proceedings of ACL 2016 (2016)
25. Shen, S., Cheng, Y., He, Z., He, W., Wu, H., Sun, M., Liu, Y.: Minimum risk training for neural machine translation. In: Proceedings of ACL 2016 (2016)
26. Sutskever, I., Vinyals, O., Le, Q.V.: Sequence to sequence learning with neural networks. In: Proceedings of NIPS 2014 (2014)
27. Tu, Z., Liu, Y., Lu, Z., Liu, X., Li, H.: Context gates for neural machine translation. arXiv preprint arXiv:1608.06043 (2016)
28. Tu, Z., Lu, Z., Liu, Y., Liu, X., Li, H.: Modeling coverage for neural machine translation. In: Proceedings of ACL 2016 (2016)
29. Vawani, A., Shazeer, N., Parmar, N., Uszkoreit, J., Jones, L., Gomez, A.N., Kaiser, L., Polosukhin, I.: Attention is all you need. arXiv preprint arXiv:1706.03762 (2016)
30. Wang, X., Lu, Z., Tu, Z., Li, H., Xiong, D., Zhang, M.: Neural machine translation advised by statistical machine translation. In: Proceedings of AAAI 2017 (2017)

31. Wu, S., Zhang, D., Yang, N., Li, M., Zhou, M.: Sequence-to-dependency neural machine translation. In: Proceedings of ACL 2017 (2017)
32. Zhai, F., Zhang, J., Zhou, Y., Zong, C., et al.: Tree-based translation without using parse trees. In: Proceedings of COLING 2012 (2012)
33. Zhang, J., Zong, C.: Exploiting source-side monolingual data in neural machine translation. In: Proceedings of EMNLP 2016 (2016)
34. Zhou, J., Cao, Y., Wang, X., Li, P., Xu, W.: Deep recurrent models with fast-forward connections for neural machine translation. arXiv preprint arXiv: 1606.04199 (2016)
35. Zhou, L., Hu, W., Zhang, J., Zong, C.: Neural system combination for machine translation. In: Proceedings of ACL 2017 (2017)

Modeling Indicative Context for Statistical Machine Translation

Shuangzhi Wu[1(✉)], Dongdong Zhang[2], Shujie Liu[2], and Ming Zhou[2]

[1] Harbin Institute of Technology, Harbin, China
v-shuawu@microsoft.com
[2] Microsoft Research Asia, Bejing, China
{dozhang,shujliu,mingzhou}@microsoft.com

Abstract. Contextual information is very important to select the appropriate phrases in statistical machine translation (SMT). The selection of different target phrases is sensitive to different parts of source contexts. Previous approaches based on either local contexts or global contexts neglect impacts of different contexts and are not always effective to disambiguate translation candidates. As a matter of fact, the indicative contexts are expected to play more important roles for disambiguation. In this paper, we propose to leverage the indicative contexts for translation disambiguation. Our model assigns phrase pairs confidence scores based on different source contexts which are then intergraded into the SMT log-linear model to help select translation candidates. Experimental results show that our proposed method significantly improves translation performance on the NIST Chinese-to-English translation tasks compared with the state-of-the-art SMT baseline.

1 Introduction

In statistical machine translation (SMT) [3,5,12,14] the probabilities of target translation candidates are estimated based on the co-occurrence frequencies with source phrases. Meanwhile the selection of target candidates is affected by limited target contexts computed based on a variant of language models. In practice, source contexts of source phrases are proven helpful in making disambiguation of target translation candidates. Much work has been done to incorporate source context information to improve the translation performance [2,6,13,16,20]. However, these methods just leverage limited local contexts for translation disambiguation, which are often insufficient to model the disambiguation of translation candidates that may have long distance dependencies with the source phrases. Taking the sentence pairs of Chinese and English in Fig. 1 as an example, the source phrase 东西 in bold occurs in the same sub-sentences in both Figs. 1(a) and (b), but it is translated into different target phrases denoted by the solid lines. It is impossible to distinguish these two target translations during SMT decoding merely using the local context with the distance less than 3 words. So it needs longer distance dependencies beyond local contexts to help make disambiguation.

© Springer International Publishing AG 2018
X. Huang et al. (Eds.): NLPCC 2017, LNAI 10619, pp. 224–232, 2018.
https://doi.org/10.1007/978-3-319-73618-1_19

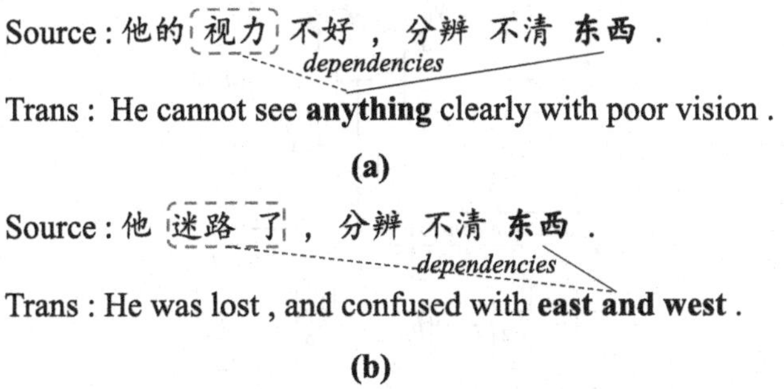

Source : 他的 视力 不好 ， 分辨 不清 **东西** ．
dependencies

Trans : He cannot see **anything** clearly with poor vision .

(a)

Source : 他 迷路 了 ， 分辨 不清 **东西** ．
dependencies

Trans : He was lost , and confused with **east and west** .

(b)

Fig. 1. Two examples of Chinese-English sentence pairs. The phrases in bold are translation pairs connected with solid lines. The indicative context for translation disambiguation are marked in dashed boxes.

Recently, with the success of distributed representation modeling by neural networks, source- and target-side local contexts are fully used to better generate the target translation [4], where global sentence-level information is not adequately concerned. Additionally, global contexts over source sentences have been modeled to help with local translation prediction [7,22]. In these models, the contexts are generated over the entire source sentence for each local translation disambiguation, where they do not pay much attention to the effects of the critical context information named as indicative context which is expected to play more important roles for disambiguation than other contexts. For example in Fig. 1, the translation disambiguation of the same source phrase 东西 should be mainly dominated by its indicative contexts marked in dashed boxes, which are more useful than other context words in these sentences.

In this paper, we propose an indicative context based translation disambiguation model (ICDM) to identify the indicative source context for disambiguating translation candidates for SMT. Our method models both the intertranslation quality of translation pairs and whether the target candidate is suitable for the specific source context. Then a confidence score is calculated for each phrase pair and integrated into SMT decoder as an extra feature. Experimental results demonstrate that our model significantly improves translation accuracy over a state-of-the-art SMT baseline on Chinese-English task.

2   Indicative Context Based Translation Disambiguation

We present an indicative context based translation disambiguation model (ICDM) to help with translation disambiguation for phrase pairs. Our model consists of three parts, a Context-RNN used to map source context into vector space, a Phrase-RNN used to map source phrase into vector space, and a RNNLM which is used to calculate the confidence score for a target phrase given the source context and phrase. Figure 2 gives a graphical overview of our model. Due to space limitation, we only detail the connections at time step t. In

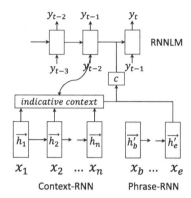

Fig. 2. Overview of ICDM. Only the details at time step t are listed.

this section we will explain ICDM and how to incorporate ICDM into the SMT decoding in detail.

2.1   Model Structure

Given the source sentence $X_1^n := x_1, x_2, x_3, ..., x_n$, source phrase $P_b^e := x_b, x_{b+1}, ..., x_e$, and the target phrase $T_1^m := y_1, y_2, ..., y_m$, where n, m is the length of source sentence and target phrase, x_i, y_i represent the source word and target word, $1 \leq b \leq e \leq n$. The translation disambiguation task is to estimate confidence scores for phrase pairs conditioned on the source sentence X_1^n and phrase P_b^e, which is denoted by $\mathrm{Conf}(P_b^e, T_1^m)$. Thus the task can be modeled as,

$$\mathrm{Conf}(X_1^n, P_b^e, T_1^m) = p(T_1^m | X_1^n, P_b^e) \tag{1}$$

We use two recurrent neural network (RNN) named context-RNN and phrase-RNN to map X_1^n and P_b^e into context vectors denoted by $H_1^n := h_1, h_2, h_3...h_n$ and $H'^e_b := h'_b, h'_{b+1}...h'_e$ respectively. Both RNNs are bidirectional. Empirically, the final hidden vectors h_n and h'_e can be used to represent the source sentence and source phrase. For the target phrase, we use a recurrent neural network language model (RNNLM) to score the target phrase. When integrating h_n and h'_e into the RNNLM, Eq. 1 can be rewritten as Eq. 2

$$\mathrm{Conf}(X_1^n, P_b^e, T_1^m) = \prod_{t=1}^{m} p(y_t | y_{<t-1}, h_n, h'_e) \tag{2}$$

In Eq. 2, the whole source sentence is utilized to provide global source context and the source phrase is used to measure the intertranslation of the phrase pair. For different phrase pairs of one source sentence, this model uses the same source context h_n for translation selection, thus we call this model Single Context-based Disambiguation Model (SCDM). However, different phrase pairs of one source sentence usually depends on different parts of source contexts, the single context is insufficient to distinguish different contexts.

Identifying Indicative Context. To better leverage source contexts to facilitate translation disambiguation, we propose to highlight the indicative context which is dynamically constructed for different phrase pairs of one source sentence. We use the hidden vectors H_1^n of context-RNN to represent the local context of each source word in the source sentence. Our goal is to identify which local context plays a more important role in selecting targets for a certain source phrase. We assign different weights for each local context aiming at highlighting the indicative context. When calculating the RNNLM score of a target phrase, at each time step t, we use a single bilinear [15] transformation to compute a score between the RNNLM hidden state and each source context vector h_i, which is similar with the attention mechanism in [1].

$$e_{it} = h_i W_a s_t \tag{3}$$

where W_a is the weight matrix, s_t is the state of RNNLM at time step t. Then the weight of each context is modeled by,

$$a_{it} = \frac{\exp(e_{it})}{\sum_k \exp(e_{kt})} \tag{4}$$

We expect that the indicative context could have a higher weight than others and dominate the translation disambiguation. However, sometimes there is no explicit indicative context in selecting target phrase, and sometimes the model would make wrong decisions. Thus we define the final source context as the weighted sum of each local context to fully use the source contexts.

$$c_t = \sum_{i=1}^n a_{it} h_i \tag{5}$$

We use c_t to replace h_n as

$$\text{Conf}(X_1^n, P_b^e, T_1^m) = \prod_{t=1}^m p(y_t | y_{<t-1}, c_t, h_e') \tag{6}$$

We named Eq. 6 as the indicative context based translation disambiguation model (ICDM). In Eq. 6, the source context c_t and the source phrase representation h_e' are first combined by

$$c = \tanh(W c_t + U h_e') \tag{7}$$

where U and W are weight matrices. Then c is integrated into RNNLM as context as shown in Fig. 2. Though there are several kinds of combinations for the two context vectors, such as concatenating, accumulating, etc., this kind of combination achieves better results in our work.

2.2   Model Training

To train the model, we collect the training instances from the bilingual corpus according to the word alignment results. Each training instance consists of three parts, source context (i.e. **source sentence excluding the source phrase**, otherwise the target phrase always aligns to its source phrase.), source phrase, and the target phrase which is extracted according to the method in [11]. We use the the cross entropy loss function to train the target phrase RNNLM as Eq. (7):

$$J = \sum_{(X,P,T) \in D} - \log p(T|X, P) \tag{8}$$

where D is the training corpus, T, X, P are the target phrase, source sentence and source phrase. In the update procedure, we leverage the stochastic gradient descent (SGD) algorithm, and Adadelta [21] is used to automatically adapt the learning rate. To speedup decoding when adding ICDM as extra feature to SMT, we use the self-normalize technique [4] for the softmax layer and a shortlist [9] of 10K is used to reduce the output dimension. In addition, we precompute the source context H for all phrase pairs.

2.3 Integration into SMT Decoding

We incorporate the confidence scores into the standard log-linear framework for SMT. Given the context of source sentence, the higher the confidence score is, the better the translation quality of phrase pairs is expected to be. For SMT system, the best translation candidate $\hat{e}$ is calculated by:

$$\hat{e} = \mathrm{argmax}_e P(e|f) \tag{9}$$

where the translation score is given by

$$P(e|f) \propto \sum_i w_i \cdot \log \phi_i(f, e)$$

$$= \underbrace{\sum_k w_k \cdot \log \phi_k(f, e)}_{\text{Standard feature scores}} + \underbrace{w_p \cdot \log \mathrm{Conf}_p(f, e)}_{\text{Confidence scores}} \tag{10}$$

where $\phi_k(f, e)$ denotes the standard feature function and $\mathrm{Conf}_p(f, e)$, w_p are our confidence feature functions and its weights. The detailed feature description is as follows:

Features: Translation model, including translation probabilities and lexical weights for both directions (4 features), 5-gram language model (1 feature), word count (1 feature), phrase count (1 feature), NULL penalty (1 feature), number of hierarchical rules used (1 feature), phrase confidence score (1 feature).

3   Experiments

In this section, we evaluate the performance of our disambiguation model on NIST Chinese-English tasks. The evaluation metric is the case-insensitive IBM BLEU-4 [19].

Table 1. Evaluation results of different methods in BLEU% on four NIST test sets. The "Average" setting is the averaged result of the four test sets.

Settings	NIST 2005	NIST 2006	NIST 2008	NIST 2012	Average
HIERO	37.44	34.81	26.80	27.88	31.73
+NNJM	38.17	35.95	28.04	28.88	32.76
+SCDM	38.28	36.19	28.29	29.02	32.95
+ICDM	38.57	36.65	28.61	29.34	33.29

3.1 Setup

The bilingual data we use is a set of LDC[1] corpus, which consists of around 1M sentence pairs. A 4-gram language model is trained over the English Gigaword corpus (LDC2009T13) and the target monolingual data of the bilingual corpus. The development data is the NIST 2003 dataset, and the test data contains NIST 2005, 2006, 2008 and 2012 datasets. For the disambiguation model training, in order to limit the number of training instances, we limit the frequency of phrase pairs to 3, and only keep top 10 target phrases for each source phrase. Besides, the maximum length of phrase is limited up to 5 The total number of training instance is about 10.3 million. In addition, we use the 30K most frequent words for both Chinese and English. All the remaining words are replaced by a special token "UNK". The hidden dimensions of all RNNs are set to 500.

3.2 Baselines

We have two baselines for comparison. The first is an in-house re-implementation of the hierarchical phrase-based SMT system (HIERO) [3]. The CKY decoding algorithm is used and cube pruning is applied [3,8]. Translation models are trained over the parallel corpus that is automatically aligned using GIZA++ [18] in both directions, and the grow-diag-final heuristic is used to refine symmetric word alignment. For language model, we use an in-house toolkit with modified Kneser-Ney smoothing [10]. The feature weights are tuned by MERT [17].

The second baseline is the HIERO system which incorporates the feedforward neural network joint model [4] named as +NNJM. The target window is set to 3 and the source-side context is set to 11.

3.3 Evaluation on NIST Task

The evaluation results are shown in Table 1. According to the Table 1, +NNJM can improve HIERO by 1.03 points in average, which shows that source context significantly contributes to improving translation performance. Compared with +NNJM, +SCDM performs better on all the test sets, gaining about 0.2 BLEU

---

[1] LDC2003E14, LDC2005T10, LDC2005E83, LDC2006E26, LDC2006E34, LDC2006 E85, LDC2006E92, LDC2003E07, LDC2005T06, LDC2004T08, LDC2005T06.

point improvements in average, which shows global source contexts are more helpful for translation candidate prediction in SMT decoding. Meanwhile, the ICDM outperforms all the others on the whole test sets, where the average improvement is 1.56 compared with HIERO and 0.53 compared with +NNJM. The biggest improvement can be up to 1.86 BLEU points on NIST 2012. The main reason is that ICDM can capture long distance source dependencies and enhance the effect of indicative contexts in predicting translation candidates.

3.4   Analyses of Translation Disambiguation

In this section, we give a case study to explain how our method works. Examples of translation disambiguation are shown in Table 2. We investigate the phrase 有 as an example. Two source sentences with different contexts are selected. Top five target translation candidates are selected from the translation table.

In Table 2, all the phrase pairs are ranked in terms of log confidence scores which vary with different source contexts. We can see that ⟨ 有, have⟩ gets the best confidence score for S1, and ⟨ 有, is there⟩ ranks first for S2, though the log translation probability for the same phrase pair is constant as shown in the $\log P$ column. This result significantly caters to the reference. This shows that our method can leverage source contexts to make a better translation selection.

Table 2. Translation example. log Conf denotes the log confidence score and $\log P$ denotes the log translation probability in the translation table. All the characters are lowercased, and phrases in bold is the phrase pairs.

	S1: 您好我想订个房间. 您有 空房吗?			S2: 请问这附近有 车站吗?		
Reference	hello , i 'd like to make a reservation . do you **have** any rooms ?			excuse me , **is there** a station near here ?		
	Phrase pairs	$\log P$	log Conf	Phrase pairs	$\log P$	log Conf
Conf. Ranking	⟨有, have⟩	-2.19	-1.83	⟨有, is there⟩	-2.89	-1.39
	⟨有, there is⟩	-3.37	-3.00	⟨有, there is⟩	-3.37	-2.82
	⟨有, is there⟩	-2.89	-3.22	⟨有, NULL⟩	-2.51	-4.35
	⟨有, do you have⟩	-2.73	-3.51	⟨有, do you have⟩	-2.73	-5.50
	⟨有, NULL⟩	-2.51	-3.82	⟨有, have⟩	-2.19	-5.53

4   Conclusion and Future Work

In this paper, we propose a translation disambiguation model for SMT. Our model can leverage indicative source contexts for target translation disambiguation. In SMT decoding, appropriate target phrases are selected to best match the source sentence according to the confidence scores. Experimental results show that our method can significantly improvements the state-of-the-art hierarchical phrase-based system.

In the future, we will perform forced decoding for bilingual training sentences and collect the phrase pairs used in order to obtain high-quality pairs to train our model.

References

1. Bahdanau, D., Cho, K., Bengio, Y.: Neural machine translation by jointly learning to align and translate. In: ICLR 2015 (2015)
2. Carpuat, M., Wu, D.: Word sense disambiguation vs. statistical machine translation. In: Proceedings of the 43rd Annual Meeting on Association for Computational Linguistics, pp. 387–394. Association for Computational Linguistics (2005)
3. Chiang, D.: A hierarchical phrase-based model for statistical machine translation. In: Proceedings of the 43rd Annual Meeting on Association for Computational Linguistics, pp. 263–270. Association for Computational Linguistics (2005)
4. Devlin, J., Zbib, R., Huang, Z., Lamar, T., Schwartz, R.M., Makhoul, J.: Fast and robust neural network joint models for statistical machine translation. In: ACL, vol. 1, pp. 1370–1380. Citeseer (2014)
5. Galley, M., Graehl, J., Knight, K., Marcu, D., DeNeefe, S., Wang, W., Thayer, I.: Scalable inference and training of context-rich syntactic translation models. In: Proceedings of the 21st International Conference on Computational Linguistics and the 44th annual meeting of the Association for Computational Linguistics, pp. 961–968. Association for Computational Linguistics (2006)
6. He, Z., Liu, Q., Lin, S.: Improving statistical machine translation using lexicalized rule selection. In: Proceedings of the 22nd International Conference on Computational Linguistics-Volume 1, pp. 321–328. Association for Computational Linguistics (2008)
7. Hu, B., Tu, Z., Lu, Z., Li, H., Chen, Q.: Context-dependent translation selection using convolutional neural network. In: Proceedings of the 53rd Annual Meeting of the Association for Computational Linguistics and the 7th International Joint Conference on Natural Language Processing (Volume 2: Short Papers), pp. 536–541. Association for Computational Linguistics, Beijing, July 2015. http://www.aclweb.org/anthology/P15-2088
8. Huang, L., Chiang, D.: Better k-best parsing. In: Proceedings of the Ninth International Workshop on Parsing Technology, pp. 53–64. Association for Computational Linguistics (2005)
9. Jean, S., Cho, K., Memisevic, R., Bengio, Y.: On using very large target vocabulary for neural machine translation. In: Proceedings of the 53rd Annual Meeting of the Association for Computational Linguistics and the 7th International Joint Conference on Natural Language Processing (Volume 1: Long Papers), pp. 1–10. Association for Computational Linguistics, Beijing, July 2015. http://www.aclweb.org/anthology/P15-1001
10. Kneser, R., Ney, H.: Improved backing-off for m-gram language modeling. In: 1995 International Conference on Acoustics, Speech, and Signal Processing. ICASSP-1995, vol. 1, pp. 181–184. IEEE (1995)
11. Koehn, P.: Statistical significance tests for machine translation evaluation. In: EMNLP, pp. 388–395. Citeseer (2004)
12. Koehn, P., Och, F.J., Marcu, D.: Statistical phrase-based translation. In: Proceedings of the 2003 Conference of the North American Chapter of the Association for Computational Linguistics on Human Language Technology-Volume 1, pp. 48–54. Association for Computational Linguistics (2003)

13. Liu, Q., He, Z., Liu, Y., Lin, S.: Maximum entropy based rule selection model for syntax-based statistical machine translation. In: Proceedings of the Conference on Empirical Methods in Natural Language Processing, pp. 89–97. Association for Computational Linguistics (2008)

14. Liu, Y., Liu, Q., Lin, S.: Tree-to-string alignment template for statistical machine translation. In: Proceedings of the 21st International Conference on Computational Linguistics and the 44th Annual Meeting of the Association for Computational Linguistics, pp. 609–616. Association for Computational Linguistics (2006)

15. Luong, M.T., Pham, H., Manning, C.D.: Effective approaches to attention-based neural machine translation. arXiv preprint arXiv:1508.04025 (2015)

16. Marton, Y., Resnik, P.: Soft syntactic constraints for hierarchical phrased-based translation. In: ACL, pp. 1003–1011 (2008)

17. Och, F.J.: Minimum error rate training in statistical machine translation. In: Proceedings of the 41st Annual Meeting on Association for Computational Linguistics-Volume 1, pp. 160–167. Association for Computational Linguistics (2003)

18. Och, F.J., Ney, H.: Improved statistical alignment models. In: Proceedings of the 38th Annual Meeting on Association for Computational Linguistics, pp. 440–447. Association for Computational Linguistics (2000)

19. Papineni, K., Roukos, S., Ward, T., Zhu, W.J.: BLEU: a method for automatic evaluation of machine translation. In: Proceedings of the 40th Annual Meeting on Association for Computational Linguistics, pp. 311–318. Association for Computational Linguistics (2002)

20. Xiong, D., Zhang, M., Aw, A., Li, H.: A syntax-driven bracketing model for phrase-based translation. In: Proceedings of the Joint Conference of the 47th Annual Meeting of the ACL and the 4th International Joint Conference on Natural Language Processing of the AFNLP: Volume 1-Volume 1, pp. 315–323. Association for Computational Linguistics (2009)

21. Zeiler, M.D.: Adadelta: an adaptive learning rate method. arXiv preprint arXiv:1212.5701 (2012)

22. Zhang, J.: Local translation prediction with global sentence representation. arXiv preprint arXiv:1502.07920 (2015)

A Semantic Concept Based Unknown Words Processing Method in Neural Machine Translation

Shaotong Li[✉], Jinan Xu, Guoyi Miao, Yujie Zhang,
and Yufeng Chen

School of Computer and Information Technology,
Beijing Jiaotong University, Beijing, China
{shaotongli,jaxu,gymiao,yjzhang,chenyf}@bjtu.edu.cn

Abstract. The problem of unknown words in neural machine translation (NMT), which not only affects the semantic integrity of the source sentences but also adversely affects the generating of the target sentences. The traditional methods usually replace the unknown words according to the similarity of word vectors, these approaches are difficult to deal with rare words and polysemous words. Therefore, this paper proposes a new method of unknown words processing in NMT based on the semantic concept of the source language. Firstly, we use the semantic concept of source language semantic dictionary to find the candidate in-vocabulary words. Secondly, we propose a method to calculate the semantic similarity by integrating the source language model and the semantic concept network, to obtain the best replacement word. Experiments on English to Chinese translation task demonstrate that our proposed method can achieve more than 2.6 BLEU points over the conventional NMT method. Compared with the traditional method based on word vector similarity, our method can also obtain an improvement by nearly 0.8 BLEU points.

Keywords: NMT · Unknown words · Semantic dictionary · Semantic concept

End-to-end NMT is a kind of machine translation method proposed in recent years [1–3]. Most of the NMT systems are based on the encoder-decoder framework, the encoder encodes the source sentence into a vector, and the decoder decodes the vector into the target sentence. Compared with the traditional statistical machine translation (SMT), NMT has many advantages. Firstly, NMT automatically models the sentences and learns the features. The problems of feature selection in SMT are very well solved. Secondly, NMT almost does not require any knowledge of the language field. Thirdly, NMT does not rely on large-scale phrase tables, rule tables and language models, so the space occupied by parameters will be greatly reduced.

Despite the above advantages, NMT still has the problem of unknown words which is caused by the limited vocabulary scale. In order to control the temporal and spatial expenses of the model, NMT usually uses small vocabularies in the source side and the target side [4]. The words that are not in the vocabulary are unknown words, which will be replaced by an UNK symbol. A feasible method to solve this problem is to find out the substitutes in-vocabulary words of the unknown words. Li et al. proposed a replacement method based on word vector similarity [4], the unknown words are

© Springer International Publishing AG 2018
X. Huang et al. (Eds.): NLPCC 2017, LNAI 10619, pp. 233–242, 2018.
https://doi.org/10.1007/978-3-319-73618-1_20

replaced by the synonyms in the vocabulary through the cosine distance of the word vector and the language model. However, there are some unavoidable problems with this approach. Firstly, the vectors of rare words are difficult to train; Secondly, the trained word vectors cannot express various semantics of the polysemous words and cannot adapt to the replacement of the polysemous words in different contexts.

To solve these problems, this paper proposes an unknown words processing method which combines the semantic concept of the source language. This method uses WordNet's semantic concept network to seek the near-synonyms of the unknown words as candidate replacement words, and calculate the semantic similarity by integrating the source language model and the semantic concept network to select the best alternative words to replace the unknown words.

Experiments on Chinese to English translation tasks demonstrate that our proposed method can achieve more than 2.6 BLEU points over the baseline system, and also outperform the traditional method based on word vector similarity by nearly 0.8 BLEU points.

The main contributions of this paper are shown as follows:

- An external semantic dictionary is integrated to solve the problem of unknown words in NMT.
- The semantic concept in WordNet is used to obtain the replacement word, which can solve the problem of rare words and polysemous words better.
- A semantic similarity calculation method by integrating the source language models and semantic concept network is proposed. It ensures that the replacement words are close to the unknown words in semantic level, and the purpose of keeping the semantics of the source sentence can be achieved as much as possible.

1 NMT and the Problem of Unknown Words

This section will introduce NMT and the impact of the unknown words on NMT.

1.1 Neural Machine Translation

Most of the proposed NMT systems are based on the encoder-decoder framework and attention mechanism.

The encoder consists of a bidirectional recurrent neural network (Bi-RNN), which can read a sequence $X(x_1, \ldots, x_t)$ and generate a sequence of forward hidden states $\left(\vec{h}_1, \cdots, \vec{h}_\tau\right)$ and a sequence of backward hidden states $\left(\overleftarrow{h}_t, \cdots, \overleftarrow{h}_1\right)$. We obtain the annotation h_i for each source word x_i by concatenating the forward hidden state $\vec{h}_i$ and the backward hidden state $\overleftarrow{h}_i$.

The decoder consists of a recurrent neural network (RNN), an attention network and a logical regression network. At each time step i, the RNN generates the hidden state s_i based on the previous hidden state s_{i-1}, the previous predicted word y_{i-1}, and the context vector c_i which is calculated as a weighted sum of the source annotations by the attention network. Then the logical regression network predicts the target word y_i.

1.2 The Problem of Unknown Words

When predicting the target word at each time step, it is necessary to generate the probability of all the words in the target vocabulary. Therefore, the output dimension of the logical regression network is equal to the target vocabulary size, the total computational complexity will grow almost proportional to the vocabulary size. So train the model with the whole vocabulary is infeasible, which leads to the problem of unknown words caused by the limitation of the vocabulary size.

In NMT system, the unknown words mainly lead to two problems: Firstly, the NMT model is difficult to learn the representation and the appropriate translation of the unknown words, the parameter quality of the neural network is poor. Secondly, the existence of the unknown words increases the ambiguity of the source sentence, affects the alignment accuracy of attention network and the quality of translation result.

2 Framework of Our Method

This paper proposes an approach of unknown words processing with WordNet. In translating process, we firstly mark the input sentence with the part of speech tag (POS-tag), then get the candidate in-vocabulary words set of the unknown words in WordNet. Then, we calculate the semantic similarity between the unknown words and the words in the candidate in-vocabulary words set by integrating the language model and the semantic concept network of WordNet to attain the word with highest similarity as a replacement word. After replacement, we use the trained NMT model to translate the replaced input sentences. During translating, the alignment probabilities of each target words are obtained by the attention network. Finally, the translation of replaced words will be restored by the alignment probabilities and a bilingual dictionary.

The framework of our method is shown in Fig. 1.

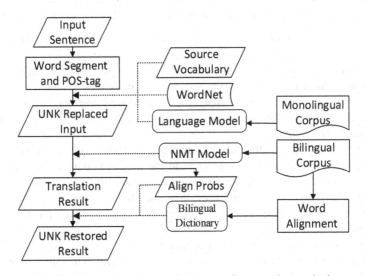

Fig. 1. Framework of our unknown words processing method

2.1   WordNet

WordNet [5] is an English semantic dictionary. WordNet3.0 contains 117659 concept nodes, with 82115 noun nodes, 13767 verb nodes, 18156 adjective nodes and 3621 adverb nodes. These concepts are separately organized into four networks, each semantic concept corresponds to a synonym set. The semantic concepts are connected by various relationships. The most commonly used relationships are Synonymy and Hypernymy/Hyponymy, which are the semantic relations used in this paper.

Synonymy: Synonymous relationship is the most basic semantic relation in Word-Net. The synonym set of a semantic concept is derived from the synonymy relationship.

Hypernymy/Hyponymy: Hypernymy/Hyponymy relationships are the most important semantic relations in WordNet, there is an "*is a*" relationship between the hypo-concept and the hyper-concept, which is transitive.

In this paper, WordNet is adopted to obtain the candidate in-vocabulary words of unknown words. Compared with the corpus-based word vector similarity approach, it has the following advantages: Firstly, it is feasible to find various concepts of polysemy in WordNet, and ensure that the candidate in-vocabulary words set contains replacement words of various semantics. Secondly, as long as the corresponding semantic concept of the unknown word can be found in WordNet, the difference between rare words and common words can be eliminated effectively.

2.2   Replacement of Unknown Words

This paper proposes a set of near-synonym which contains all the similar in-vocabulary words of an unknown word based on semantic concepts. The near-synonym set includes the synonyms of all concepts of the unknown word, the synonyms of the hyper-concepts, and the synonyms of the hypo-concepts. The maximum depth of the semantic concept of the hyper-concept is defined as m. The maximum depth of the hypo-concepts is defined as n. And m and n are adjusted by the preliminary experiment. The strategies for selecting the near-synonyms of the unknown words are as follows:

1. Give the unknown word w and its POS-tag w_{pos}, we find all the semantic concepts of w whose POS-tag is w_{pos}, as a semantic concept set *Synsets_w*.
2. Get the synonyms of all semantic concepts in *Synsets_w*, add all the in-vocabulary words in them to the near-synonym set of w and mark their distance to w as 0.
3. If the near-synonym set of w is empty, then find all the hyper-concepts of concepts in *Synsets_w* whose POS-tag is w_{pos}, within the depth of m, denoted as a semantic concept set *Hyper_synsets_w*.
4. Get the synonyms of all semantic concepts in *Hyper_synsets_w*, add all the in-vocabulary words in these synonyms to the near-synonym set of w and mark their distance to w as the depth of their corresponding hyper-concepts.
5. If the near-synonym set of w is empty, then find all the hypo-concepts of concepts in *Synsets_w* whose POS-tag is w_{pos}, within the depth of n, and form a semantic concept set *Hypo_synsets_w*.
6. Find the synonyms of all semantic concepts in *Hypo_synsets_w*, add all the in-vocabulary words in these synonyms to the near-synonym set of w and mark their distance to w as the depth of their corresponding hypo-concepts.

According to the priority order of the same semantic concept, the hyper-concepts and the hypo-concepts, we generate the candidate in-vocabulary words set of w.

The replacement words should not only be close to the unknown words in semantics, but also should keep the semantics of the original sentence as much as possible. Therefore, this paper defines a semantic similarity calculation approach by integrating the source language model and the semantic concept network, to calculate the semantic similarity between the words in the candidate in-vocabulary words set and the target unknown words, and then selects the best replacement words.

Firstly, a n-gram language model is trained on a source language monolingual corpus. And scores all the candidate words in the context of source sentence. We trained the 3-gram language model in our experiment, so for an unknown word w_i and its candidate replacement word w_i', where i refers the position of w in source sentence, the score on the 3-gram language model is defined as formula 1:

$$Score_{3-gram}(w_i', w_i) = \frac{p(w_i'|w_{i-1}, w_{i-2}) + p(w_{i+1}|w_i', w_{i-1}) + p(w_{i+2}|w_{i+1}, w_i')}{3} \quad (1)$$

The similarity of word pair (w_i', w_i) in WordNet is defined as formula 2:

$$Sim_{WordNet}(w_i', w_i) = \frac{1}{path(w_i', w_i) + 1} \quad (2)$$

where path (w_i', w_i) means the distance between the corresponding concepts of w_i' and w_i in WordNet, which is obtained in the selection strategies mentioned before.

The semantic similarity of the word pair (w_i', w_i) is finally defined as the formula 3:

$$Sim(w_i', w_i) = \sqrt{Score_{3-gram}(w_i', w_i) \cdot Sim_{WordNet}(w_i', w_i)} \quad (3)$$

Finally, the word in the candidate in-vocabulary words with highest similarity is chosen as the final replacement word W_{best}, as shown in formula 4:

$$W_{best} = \arg\max_{w' \in S} Sim(w', w) \quad (4)$$

2.3 Restore Translation for Unknown Words

NMT model is a sequence to the sequence model, we can only find the most likely alignment through the align probability of attention network. However, the performance of the attention network in NMT model is very unstable. In order to reduce the effect of alignment errors, a judged operation is added to the alignment: We align the words in the training corpus with GIZA ++[1] to get a bilingual dictionary, which will contain all words in training corpus and their translations. For the word t_i in the output sentence, if t_i aligns to a replaced word s_j, the previously obtained bilingual dictionary

---

[1] http://code.google.com/p/giza-pp/downloads/list.

will be used to determine the correctness of the alignment: If word pair(s_i, t_i) is in the bilingual dictionary, then the alignment is correct, then replace t_i with the translation of original source word. Otherwise t_i will be kept in the output sentence.

3 Experiments

Since WordNet is an English semantic dictionary, we verify our approach on the English to Chinese translation task.

3.1 Settings

The bilingual data used to train NMT model is selected from the CWMT2015 English-Chinese news corpus, including 1.6 million sentence pairs. The development set and test set are officially provided by CWMT2015, each with 1000 sentences. The word alignment is also carried out on the training set. The language model and the word vectors will be trained on the monolingual data, which contains 1.6 million source sentences in the training set and other 5 million source sentences selected from the CWMT2015 English-Chinese news corpus.

Use the BLEU score [6] to evaluate the translation results.

3.2 Training Details

The hyperparameters of our NMT system are described as follows: the vocabulary size of the source side is limited to 20k, and the target side, 30k. The number of hidden units is 512 for both encoder and decoder. The word embedding dimension of the source and target words is 512. The parameters are updated with Adadelt algorithm [7]. The Dropout method [8] is used at the readout layer, and the dropout rate is set as 0.5.

3.3 Preliminary Experiments

A preliminary experiment is required to determine the maximum depth of the hyper-concept (m) and that of the hypo-concept (n) in the replacement strategy mentioned in Sect. 2.2. Here the unknown words coverage rate of replacement strategy on the development set and the translation quality after replacement on the development set are the basis of determining the maximum depth. Experiments show that when m is greater than 5 or n is greater than 1, the size of the near-synonym set is no longer increased. Therefore, the variation range of m is limited from 0 to 5, and the variation range of n is limited from 0 to 1. The experimental results are as Tables 1 and 2:

Table 1. Unknown words coverage rate (%) of different maximum depth

n	m					
	0	1	2	3	4	5
0	45.9	66.6	71.7	73.1	73.8	73.7
1	46.3	67.5	72.2	74	74.3	74.6

Table 2. BLEU scores (%) of different maximum depth

n	m					
	0	1	2	3	4	5
0	26.02	26.44	26.74	26.81	26.79	26.78
1	26.04	26.46	26.77	**26.82**	26.8	26.79

It can be seen from Table 1 that when m is greater than 3 and n is greater than 1, the changes of coverage rate with depth is not obvious. Table 2 shows that when m equals 3 and n equals 1, the BLEU score is the highest. When m is greater than 3, the BLEU score appears to decrease. With the expansion of the search depth, some candidate words that differ greatly in semantics with target unknown words appear in the near-synonym set resulting in a decline in translation quality.

Based on the results of Tables 1 and 2, in our comparative experiments, the maximum depth of the hyper-concept in the replacement strategy is set to 3, and the maximum depth of the hypo-concept is set to 1.

3.4 Comparative Experiments and Main Results

There are 7 different systems in our comparative experiments:

1. Moses [9]: An open-source phrase-based SMT system with default configuration.
2. RNNSearch: Our baseline NMT system with improved attention mechanism [10].
3. PosUnk: Add an approach proposed by Luong et al. [11] to the baseline NMT system in order to process unknown word problem.
4. w2v&lm: Based on our baseline NMT system, use the approach proposed by Li et al. [4] to replace the unknown words in source language based on source language word vector and the source language model. The word vector is trained by word2vec [12] toolkit, and the 3-gram language model with modified Kneser-Ney smoothing is trained by SRILM [13].
5. w2v&lm_restore&PosUnk: Based on system 4, the restore approach proposed in Sect. 2.3 is used to translate the replaced words, and the remaining unknown words are processed by the method that was used in system 3.
6. wn&lm:Based on the baseline NMT system, our method will use WordNet and the source language model to replace the unknown words in source language. The language model used is the same as the language model used in system 4.
7. wn&lm_restore&PosUnk: Based on the system 6, the replacing approach proposed in Sect. 2.3 is used to translate the replaced words, and the remaining unknown words are processed by the method that was used in system 3.

System 6 and 7 our approaches. System 6 is an NMT system that only adds the unknown words replacing module of source side, and besides that, system 7 also adds a replaced word restoring module of target side as well as the remaining unknown word processing module of target side, so it is our best system. The main experimental results are shown in Table 3.

Table 3. BLEU scores (%) of different systems

System	Development set	Test set	Average
Moses	28.42	25.48	26.95
RNNSearch	25.71	23.22	24.47
PosUnk	27.58	24.89	26.24
w2v&lm	26.26	23.73	25
wn&lm	**26.82**	**24.91**	**25.87**
w2v&lm_restore&PosUnk	27.66	25.02	26.34
wn&lm_restore&PosUnk	**28.33**	**25.86**	**27.1**

The pre-processing NMT system based on our approach (wn&lm) outperforms the baseline system (RNNSearch) by 1.4 BLEU points on average; It also surpasses the pre-process NMT system based on traditional method (w2v&lm) by 0.87 BLEU points in the development set and 1.18 BLEU points in the test set. Our best system (wn&lm_restore&PosUnk) outperforms the baseline system (RNNSearch) by 2.63 BLEU on average; In addition, it surpasses the NMT system which add a simple unknown word processing module (PosUnk) by 0.86 BLEU points, it significantly improves the best NMT system of traditional approach (w2v&lm_restore& PosUnk) by 0.76 BLEU points.

3.5 Comparison of Translating Details

Here we compare the translating details of our system with other systems, we mainly analyze the translating process of unknown words. The main advantage of our approach is that the replacement words selected by our system are more appropriate (Table 4) .

On the one hand, our proposed method keeps the original meaning of source sentences better and provides less impact on subsequent translations. For example, in Example 1, the source word "*restores*" is an unknown word; An "*UNK*" symbol appears, and there is no proper translation of "*restores*"; even after post-processing, "*restores*" is translated to "恢复", other parts of the translation still need improving; The approach based on word vector and language model replaces "*restores*" with an in-vocabulary word "*impair*", but the semantic changes have occurred. It affects the subsequent of translation result; Our system replaces "*restores*" with an in-vocabulary word "*repair*", basically keeping the original meaning. The translation result and the reference are basically the same, and a post-processing module is followed to correct the translation of "*restores*", and ultimately get a better translation results.

On the other hand, appropriate replacement words make the attention better and solve the problem of over-translating and under-translating to some extent. As in Example 2, the source word "*ignifying*", "*divisor*" are unknown words; An "*UNK*" symbol appears, there is no proper translations of "*divisor*" and "*factor*", and the translation of unknown word "*signifying*" is not correct; Because it only generates one "UNK", post-processing only get back the correct translation of "*divisor*" and lose others; The approach based on word vector and language model replaces "*signifying*"

Table 4. Translation instances table

Source	*This paragraph* **restores (unk)** *the old text to preserve a delicate balance.*
Reference	这个 段落 恢复 旧 的 案文 以 保持 一 种 微妙 的 平衡 。
RNNSearch result	这 一 段 是 为了 保存 一 个 微妙 的 平衡 而 UNK 的 。
PosUnk result	这 一 段 是 为了 保存 一 个 微妙 的 平衡 而 恢复 的 。
Replaced source (with w2v&lm)	*This paragraph* **impair** *the old text to preserve a delicate balance.*
w2v&lm result	该 段 损害 了 保持 微妙 平衡 的 旧 案文 。
w2v&lm_restore&PosUnk result	该 段 恢复 了 保持 微妙 平衡 的 旧 案文 。
Replaced source (with wn&lm)	*This paragraph* **repair** *the old text to preserve a delicate balance.*
wn&lm result	该 段 修复 了 旧 的 案文 以 保持 微妙 的 平衡 。
wn&lm_restore&PosUnk result	该 段 恢复 了 旧 的 案文 以 保持 微妙 的 平衡 。
Source	**Signifying (unk)** *an exact* **divisor (unk)** *or factor of a quantity.*
Reference	表示 某 数量 的 准确 除数 或者 因数 。
RNNSearch result	控制 数量 的 一 个 精确 的 UNK 。
PosUnk result	控制 数量 的 一 个 精确 的 除数 。
Replaced source (with w2v&lm)	**Name** *an exact* **divisor (unk)** *or factor of a quantity.*
w2v&lm result	名称 一 个 数量 的 UNK 或 UNK 。
w2v&lm_restore&PosUnk result	名称 一 个 数量 的 确切 或 因素 。
Replaced source (with wn&lm)	**Mean** *an exact* **factor** *or factor of a quantity.*
wn&lm result	指 数量 的 一 个 确切 因素 或 因素 。
wn&lm_restore&PosUnk result	表示 数量 的 一 个 确切 除数 或 因素 。

with an in-vocabulary word "*name*", but the meaning has been changed. In addition, it fails to replace the unknown word "*divisor*". The translation result contains two "*UNK*", affects the alignment of attention network, and post-processing fails to get the correct translation of "*signifying*", parts of the translation are then retrieved, but the translation of "*divisor*" are still missed; Our system replaces "*signifying*" with an in-vocabulary word "*mean*", and replaces "*divisor*" with an in-vocabulary word "*factor*". There is no "*UNK*" in translation, and the alignment is quite good. Therefore, we successfully correct the translation of "*signifying*" and "*divisor*" by post-processing.

4   Conclusion and Future Work

This paper proposes an unknown words processing approach in NMT by integrating semantic concepts of the source language and source language model. This method not only improves the translation of the unknown words but also ensures that the semantics of the source language sentence is complete, and enhances the quality of the entire translation. Moreover, this approach provides a new idea for NMT to integrate external knowledge base. Experiments on English to Chinese translation show that our method not only achieves a significant improvement over the baseline, but also provides some advantages compared with the traditional unknown words processing methods.

Our future work mainly contains three aspects. Firstly, the replacement method proposed in this paper is limited to the replacement of word level. We are going to challenge the phrase level method; Secondly, our proposed method is difficult to deal with some items, for instance, named entities. These entities can be classified and marked as the corresponding symbols; Thirdly, in this paper, the external semantic dictionary is only used in the decoding part. We will focus on integrating the external semantic dictionary into the training process of NMT model.

Acknowledgments. The authors are supported by the National Nature Science Foundation of China (Contract 61370130 and 61473294), and the Fundamental Research Funds for the Central Universities (2015JBM033), and the International Science and Technology Cooperation Program of China under grant No. 2014DFA11350.

References

1. Kalchbrenner, N., Blunsom, P.: Recurrent continuous translation models (2013)
2. Sutskever, I., Vinyals, O., Le, Q.V.: Sequence to sequence learning with neural networks. Adv. Neural. Inf. Process. Syst. **4**, 3104–3112 (2014)
3. Bahdanau, D., Cho, K., Bengio, Y.: Neural machine translation by jointly learning to align and translate. Comput. Sci. (2014)
4. Li, X., Zhang, J., Zong, C.: Towards zero unknown word in neural machine translation. In: International Joint Conference on Artificial Intelligence. AAAI Press, pp. 2852–2858 (2016)
5. Miller, G.A.: WordNet: a lexical database for English. Commun. ACM **38**(11), 39–41 (1995)
6. Papineni, K., Roukos, S., Ward, T., Zhu, W.-J.: BLEU: a method for automatic valuation of machine translation. In: Proceedings of 40th Annual Meeting of the Association for Computational Linguistics, Philadelphia, Pennsylvania, USA, pp. 311–318, July 2002
7. Zeiler, M.D.: ADADELTA: an adaptive learning rate method. Comput. Sci. (2012)
8. Srivastava, N., Hinton, G., Krizhevsky, A., et al.: Dropout: a simple way to prevent neural networks from overfitting. J. Mach. Learn. Res. **15**(1), 1929–1958 (2014)
9. Collins, M., Koehn, P.: Clause restructuring for statistical machine translation. In: Meeting on Association for Computational Linguistics. Association for Computational Linguistics, pp. 531–540 (2005)
10. Meng, F., Lu, Z., Li, H., et al.: Interactive attention for neural machine translation (2016)
11. Luong, M.T., Sutskever, I., Le, Q.V., et al.: Addressing the rare word problem in neural machine translation. Vet. Med. **27**(2), 82–86 (2014). Bulletin of University of Agricultural Sciences and Veterinary Medicine Cluj-Napoca
12. Mikolov, T., Sutskever, I., Chen, K., et al.: Distributed representations of words and phrases and their compositionality. Adv. Neural. Inf. Process. Syst. **26**, 3111–3119 (2013)
13. Stolcke, A.: SRILM—an extensible language modeling toolkit. In: International Conference on Spoken Language Processing. pp. 901–904 (2002)

Research on Mongolian Speech Recognition Based on FSMN

Yonghe Wang, Feilong Bao[✉], Hongwei Zhang, and Guanglai Gao

College of Computer Science, Inner Mongolia University,
Huhhot 010021, China
cswyh92@163.com, ndzhhw@163.com,
{csfeilong, csggl}@imu.edu.cn

Abstract. Deep Neural Network (DNN) model has been achieved a significant result over the Mongolian speech recognition task, however, compared to Chinese, English or the others, there are still opportunities for further enhancements. This paper presents the first application of Feed-forward Sequential Memory Network (FSMN) for Mongolian speech recognition tasks to model long-term dependency in time series without using recurrent feedback. Furthermore, by modeling the speaker in the feature space, we extract the i-vector features and combine them with the Fbank features as the input to validate their effectiveness in Mongolian ASR tasks. Finally, discriminative training was firstly conducted over the FSMN by using maximum mutual information (MMI) and state-level minimum Bayes risk (sMBR), respectively. The experimental results show that: FSMN possesses better performance than DNN in the Mongolian ASR, and by using i-vector features combined with Fbank features as FSMN input and discriminative training, the word error rate (WER) is relatively reduced by 17.9% compared with the DNN baseline.

Keywords: Mongolian · Speech recognition · DNN · FSMN · i-vector
Sequence-criterion training

1 Introduction

Mongolian language has a wide influence in the world, it is the first or the second official language, about 6 millions persons who can speak that language in the Mongolia, Inner Mongolia of China and other districts. However, Mongolian speech recognition is still at its initial research stage. Deep learning methods have been widely used in the field of speech recognition, such as Deep Neural Network (DNN), recurrent neural networks (RNNs) or LSTM-based models [1–3]. But the research of Mongolian speech recognition tasks based on the depth learning method is relatively rare.

Recently, the approaches investigated in [4] proposed a simpler structure for memory neural networks, namely feedforward sequential memory networks (FSMN), which has been proven to have advanced performance on the LVCSR task than DNN and LSTM [4, 5]. FSMN extends the standard feedforward neural networks with some learnable memory blocks in hidden layers. The memory blocks are used to store a fixed-size long context information temporarily as short-term memory mechanism,

© Springer International Publishing AG 2018
X. Huang et al. (Eds.): NLPCC 2017, LNAI 10619, pp. 243–254, 2018.
https://doi.org/10.1007/978-3-319-73618-1_21

which can learn long-term dependencies in sequence data. In this paper, we will introduce FSMN into acoustic modeling in Mongolian speech recognition.

The speech recognition research for Mongolian starts at 2003 in China. The first Mongolian speech recognition system is established by Gao [6]. Then some researches on the design and optimization of the Mongolian acoustic model are undertaken by [7, 8]. The approaches investigated in [9] solve the large vocabulary problem in Mongolian, where segmentation-based approach is applied to the system. More recently, in [10] DNN-based acoustic model was first applied to the Mongolian ASR research, it reduces the Word Error Rate (WER) over 50% against the GMM-HMM. However, compared with other languages such as Chinese and English, there is still a lot of room for optimization in Mongolian speech recognition acoustic model.

In order to improve the performance of the Mongolian language recognition acoustic model, firstly this paper applies the FSMN structure to the acoustic model of the Mongolian speech recognition system and we investigate the FSMN architectures using of different hidden layers (including memory blocks). Further, i-vector based adaptation has been shown to be effective in reverberant environments and can be used for rapid adaptation of the neural network [11], in this paper we use i-vector based neural network adaptation. And lastly, discriminative training was conducted over the FSMN by using maximum mutual information (MMI) and state-level minimum Bayes risk (sMBR), respectively [12].

The rest of the paper is organized as follows: Sect. 2 describes the structure of FSMN. Section 3 draws the i vector extraction method. Section 4 shows MMI and sMBR sequence discriminative training, Sect. 5 details the experimental setup and Sect. 6 reports the experiments. The conclusions are presented in Sect. 7.

2 Acoustic Modeling Based on FSMN

Feedforward sequential memory network is a multi-layer (normally more than three) feed-forward neural network model with single or multiple memory blocks in the hidden layer, which can learn long-term dependencies in sequence data. Figure 1 shows an FSMN structure diagram with two memory block added into hidden layer. These memory blocks are used to encode the information from the preceding and the subsequent frames. And these information make it possible to model long term dependency in the speech sequence.

Given a sequence $X = \{x_1; x_2; ...; x_t\}$, each $x_t \in X$ represents an input data at time instance t. The corresponding hidden layer outputs are denoted as $H = \{h_1; h2; ...; h_t\}$. The structure of a memory block is illustrated in Fig. 2, it uses a tapped-delay structure to encode h_t and its previous N_1 histories activities and N_2 posterior activities into a fixed-sized representation, which is fed into the next hidden layer along with the current hidden activity.

As the Fig. 2 shows, in which the preceding N_1 frames' hidden layer output $h_{t-1}^l, ..., h_{t-N_1}^l$, the current frames' hidden layer output h_t^l and the posterior N_2 frames' hidden layer output $h_{t+1}^l, ..., h_{t+N_2}^l$ are summed up by the trained weight parameters ∂

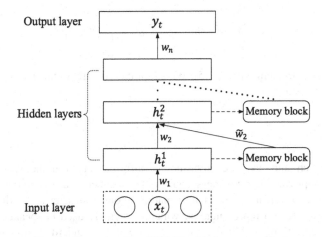

Fig. 1. The structure of FSMN with 2 memory block.

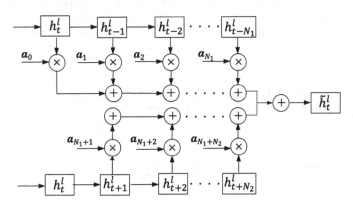

Fig. 2. The structure of memory block in FSMN.

into a context code $\tilde{h}_t^l$. Depending on the encoding method to be used, the weight parameters ∂ can be a scalar or a vector.

If the weight coefficient ∂ is set to a scalar, then FSMN is called scalar FSMN (sFSMN). The formula is defined as:

$$\tilde{h}_t^l = \sum_{i=0}^{N1} a_{t,i}^l \cdot h_{t-i}^l + \sum_{j=1}^{N2} a_{t,M_1-1+j}^l \cdot h_{t+j}^l \tag{1}$$

If the weight coefficient ∂ is set to a vector, then FSMN is called vector FSMN (vFSMN), and the formula is defined as:

$$\tilde{h}_t^l = \sum_{i=0}^{N1} a_{t,i}^l \odot h_{t-i}^l + \sum_{j=1}^{N2} a_{t,M_1-1+j}^l \odot h_{t+j}^l \qquad (2)$$

vFSMN has better modeling power [5]. We adopt the vFSMN in this study, and refer it as the FSMN for short.

3 i-Vector

Separating speech and acoustic environment information from the speech data is important to improve the robustness against the speaker and environment various. i-vector encapsulate all the relevant information about a speaker's identity in a low dimensional fixed-length representation, which are widely used in speaker adaptation of speech recognition. In this paper, we use the standard Gaussian Mixture Model-Universal Background Model (GMM-UBM) to extract the i-vector. Assuming that the speaker and acoustic environment information is mapped to a GMM super vector space, total variability space between the speaker and acoustic environment information is trained by super vector space. The i-vector extraction process is shown in Fig. 3.

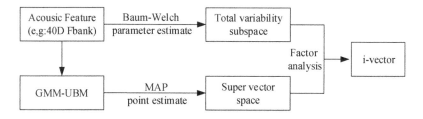

Fig. 3. The structure of i-vector feature extraction

The high-dimensional mean super-vector of a period of speech h with the speaker and acoustic environment information is expressed as:

$$M(h) = m + Tw(h) \qquad (3)$$

where m represents the UBM super vector that is not related to the speaker and the environment. T is a total variability subspace matrix and w is termed as i-vector. The M and m are obtained from the GMM-UBM.

We train GMM-UBM on top of features processed with applying cepstral mean and variance normalization (CMVN) and then transforming with an LDA+MLLT matrix. The GMM parameters are initialized by setting the variance to the global variance of the features, the means to distinct randomly chosen frames and using a part of features to do multiple iterations of training by using expectation maximization (EM) algorithm. For the total variability subspace matrix T, the features used to obtain the Gaussian posteriors are based on sliding-window Cepstral Mean Normalization (CMN), but the actual i-vector extractor sees the original features without CMN. The purpose is that we hope that the appropriate offset can be learned by the i-vector extractor itself.

In this study, we use the i-vector as an additional input feature of neural networks that was proposed by [13]. We illustrate the used FSMN structure and the i-vector feature inputs in Fig. 4. We use Fourier-transform-based log filter-bank (Fbank) coefficients as the input feature. Consequently, a context window of d-dimensional frames of m dimensional acoustic features is augmented with k-dimensional i-vector resulting in a $dm + k$ dimensional as input to the neural network.

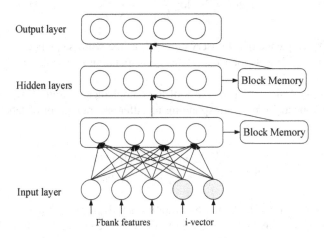

Fig. 4. Diagram of a 2-hidden layer neural network with inputs augmented with i-vectors

4 MMI and sMBR

In the speech recognition system, neural networks are trained to estimate the HMM states posteriors of each frame. To train the neural networks, the cost function is important. Cost function guides the training procedure by setting an optimization direction, and leads the model to a certain optimum. Traditional cost function used in the neural network training only consider the current input. Because they treat every frame as an independent observation, but do not care about the relationship among frames, we called this type of cost functions as frame-level training cost function. Cross-Entropy (CE) is one of the most common choice of frame-level training cost function for the speech recognition system. The CE cost function is defined as:

$$F_{CE} = -\sum_{u=1}^{U} \sum_{t-1}^{T_u} \log p_\theta(s_{ut}/x_{ut}) \tag{4}$$

where T_u represents the total time of utterance u. S_u is the reference state label at time t for utterance u. And X_u is given input at time t for utterance u.

Speech is sequence data, where the every frame has strong relationships with each other. Therefore the frame-level training cost function is not enough for the speech recognition system. Different from the frame-level training cost function, Sequence-discriminative training cost function base on the whole sequences rather than frames. In recent years, a variety of sequence-level cost functions have been proposed. Among them, MMI and sMBR are the most common choice.

The MMI criterion is the mutual information between the distributions of the observation and word sequences. The MMI criterion is:

$$F_{MMI} = \sum_{u=1}^{U} \log \frac{p(X_u/S_u)^k P(W_u)}{\Sigma_w p(X_u/S)^k P(W)} \qquad (5)$$

where X_u as the sequence of all observation; W_u as the word-sequence in the reference for utterance u; S_u is the sequence of states corresponding to W_u; and k is the acoustic scaling factor.

The sMBR is designed on the basis of the compliance with the Bayes risk rule to minimize the expected error corresponding to different granularity of labels, which is defined as:

$$F_{sMBR} = \sum_{u=1}^{U} \frac{\Sigma_w p(X_u/S)^k P(W) A(W, W_u)}{\Sigma_{w'} p(X_u/S)^k P(W')} \qquad (6)$$

where X_u as the sequence of all observation; $A(W, W_u)$ is the raw accuracy of the number of state labels that corresponding to the word sequence W with respect to that corresponding to the reference W_u.

In this study, we use a modified sMBR cost functions that was proposed by [14]. In this modified sMBR cost function, silence, vocalized noise and non-spoken noise are treated as silence. And the silence is treated as any other phone, except that all pdfs of silence phones are collapsed into a single class for the frame-error computation. Therefore, it is not to be penalized to replace one silence phone with another silence phone, but it will be penalized to insert a non-silent phone into a silent area.

5 Experiments Setup

5.1 Dataset

We use a Mongolian speech corpus for acoustic model training, this dataset contains 78 h of speech sampled at 16 kHz and the corpus involves 193 speakers. We divided the corpus into two parts randomly which include a training set and a test set. The training set is about 88% of the whole corpus and each test set is about 12% of the whole corpus. The dataset pronunciation dictionary uses an alphabet of 63 phonemes which include 37 vowels and 26 consonants. For the language model training, a 3-gram language model with about 85 million tokens of Mongolian training text from Mongolian web sites was used.

5.2 ASR System

We implement the Mongolian LVCSR system based on the Kaldi speech recognition toolkit [15]. The base acoustic features are 40-dimensional Fbank feature vector, these features are then processed using utterance level cepstral mean and variance normalization (CMVN) and features in time taking a context size of 7 frames (i.e., ±3) were spliced and projected to 40 dimensions with linear discriminant analysis (LDA). A maximum likelihood linear transform (MLLT) was estimated on the LDA features to train the LDA+MLLT model and speaker adaptive training was performed with FMLLR transform. FMLLR features were then used for training DNN, FSMN and i-vector.

Traditional neural networks usually employ a non-linear operation such as Sigmoid, Tanh function as an activation function; however, it has been shown that rectifier linear unit (ReLU) can improve the performance of NNs [16]. In this paper, all the NNs were trained using a ReLU nonlinearity activation function. In our experiment, parallel training of the NNs using up to 4 GPUs was done, while uses greedy layer-wise supervised training, preconditioned stochastic gradient descent (SGD) technique updates.

6 Experiments

6.1 Baseline Experiments

In our DNN-HMM acoustic model, we used context dependent tri-phones as the units of acoustic modeling. They share a total of 3762 unique context dependent states, which corresponds to the output dimension of the DNN acoustic model. This model uses 40-dimensional Fbank feature, where each feature vector is concatenated with a context window of 15 frames (7 + 1 + 7) to yield an input feature vector size of 600 as DNN input. The labels for training data are created by forced alignment with a classic GMM-HMM acoustic model trained on that data. Neural networks denote the standard 6 layers of fully connected neural networks using ReLU activation functions, each of layers has 1024 nodes or 2048 nodes were used, respectively. We use RBM-based pre-training to initialize DNN layer by layer. The mini-batch size is fixed to 256, and the initial learning rate parameter was set to 0.05 and 0.008 in the pre-training and fine-tuning, separately.

We used a FSMN with 6 hidden layers, each hidden layer has 1024 neurons, in which the former three hidden layers have block memories and the latter three layers are normal hidden layer. We also extract 40-dimensional Fbank feature, because of the inherent memory mechanism of FSMN, it does not need to concatenate too many consecutive frames, therefore these features are augmented with the neighboring frames in 3 context window (i.e., ±1) as input features to FSMN [5]. For each block memory, we set the memory range from the preceding 5 frames to the subsequent 5 frames. The neural network is randomly initialized during training, without using any pre-training method. We use SGD with a mini-batch size of 256 for training task. The initial and final learning rates were specified by hand and equal to 0.05 and 0.008 respectively.

Table 1 shows the results of DNNs and FSMN based acoustic modeling trained on the Mongolian dataset. We can see that the FSMN based acoustic modeling can significantly outperform the DNNs. The hidden layer of DNN contains 2048 nodes showed great improvement of word accuracy compared with 1024 nodes. While the hidden unit of FSMN is 1024, but the performance is still better than the DNN contains 2048 nodes, WER is brought down to 12.90% from 11.94% (relative 7.4%), demonstrating its advantage in Mongolian acoustic modeling.

Table 1. The results (% WER) of DNNs and FSMN, "1024L6" is to be interpreted as 6 hidden layers of 1024 hidden units.

Model	Scale	WER (%)
DNN	1024L6	14.56
DNN	2048L6	12.90
FSMN	1024L6	**11.94**

6.2   Experiments on Different Structure for FSMN

In this section, we investigate the effect of the number of hidden layers of FSMN containing memory blocks on the final Mongolian speech recognition performance. Every FSMN architecture with 6 hidden layers, each of which has 1024 nodes. And all hidden units adopt the rectified linear activation function. In the experiment, instead of adding block memory to each hidden layer, we start adding memory blocks from the hidden layer containing 3 block memories. We use FSMN_3 denotes the former three hidden layers have block memories and the latter three layers are normal hidden layer, FSMN_4 denotes the former four hidden layers have block memories and the latter two layers are normal hidden layer, and so on. The configuration of the neural network in training is the same as that of the baseline FSMN training.

From the experimental results in Table 2, we can see that with the increase of block memory in the hidden layer, the WER is decreased significantly. This is because the increase of the block memory would entitle FSMN to acquire more fixed-size long term temporal contexts relationships information. However, when the number of the block memory in the hidden layer is increasing to 6, the accuracy of speech recognition decreases. The reason is that due to the small amount of the Mongolian training data, the data sparseness would be triggered when the number over block memory of hidden layers reaches 6, which would cause that the neural network cannot learn enough information and the performance of the acoustic model would be compromised.

Table 2. The results (% WER) of FSMN for various structure

Model	WER (%)
FSMN_3	11.94
FSMN_4	11.56
FSMN_5	**11.50**
FSMN_6	12.28

Eventually, using FSMN network architecture achieved 4.8%-10.8% relative WER reduction over the baseline DNN model. The best performance is obtained using the FSMN_5, the WER is reduced from 12.90% to 11.50%. Overall, experimental results indicate that the effectiveness of FSMN in Mongolian speech recognition, being able to model long term temporal contexts in short-term Mongolian speech features.

6.3   Experiments with i-Vector Features

To obtain the i-vector estimation, the GMM-UBM was trained with 512 mixtures computed from 40 perceptual linear prediction coefficients with delta and delta-delta features appended. The LDA and MLLT transforms obtained from GMM-HMM system were used to GMM-UBM. The matrix T was randomly initialized using LDA and updated using the EM algorithm with 10 iterations.

In this experiment, we trained DNNs and FSMNs using the baseline experiment configuration. All neural networks use the ReLU activation function, and we extract k-dimensional i-vector append to the context window of d frames of 40-dimensional Fbank acoustic features resulting in a $40d + k$ dimensional at each time step and the network is fed with these features with no stacking of acoustic frames. In this experiment, we do not apply the cepstral mean normalization to the Fbank features, because i-vector can supply the information about any mean offset of the speakers data, then the network itself is able to do any feature normalization that is needed. To explore the influences of the i-vecotr size, we trained different neural networks with different i-vecotr size. The experimental results are listed in Table 3.

Table 3. The results (% WER) of different dimension i-Vector features using in DNN and FSMN.

Model	i-vector dimensions (k)				
	0	50	100	150	200
DNN	12.90	12.32	**12.24**	12.48	12.54
FSMN	11.94	**11.38**	11.48	11.66	11.97

The eventual experimental results showed that: Compared with the baseline (in first column), by combining the i-vector feature with the Fbank feature as the input, both of the DNNs and FSMNs obtain a considerable improvement. Meanwhile, we observe that different i-vector size will lead to different performance of the neural networks models. For the DNN, the best experimental result is that with a 100-dimensional i-vector led to a WER of 12.24%. For the FSMN, with a 50-dimensional i-vector can obtain the best experimental results, the WER is reduced from 11.94% to 11.38%. However, as the i-vector dimension increases, the accuracy of speech recognition is reduced. Because the increasing amount of information content of the i-vectors presented to the network would lead to the overfitting. On the whole, the experiment shows that using the i-vector as input features provides the neural networks with valuable information in Mongolian speech recognition.

6.4 Sequence-Discriminative Training

In this set of experiments, sequence-discriminative training is investigated on Mongolian large vocabulary continuous speech recognition tasks. Different sequence discriminative criteria MMI and sMBR are compared. The initial models used for sequence-discriminative training are trained from baseline experiments using the Maximum likelihood estimation (MLE) as training criteria. The training start from a set of alignments and lattices that are generated by decoding the training data with a unigram language model. The experimental results in Table 4 indicate that the effectiveness of sequence-discriminative training in Mongolian speech recognition, Different training criteria have little effect on the experimental results. For the DNN, the WER is reduced from 12.90% to 12.06% (relative 6.5%).For the FSMN, the WER is reduced from 11.94% to 11.28% (relative 5.5%).

Table 4. The results (% WER) of DNN and FSMN trained using different criteria

Model	Training criteria		
	MLE	MMI	sMBR
DNN	12.90	12.12	**12.06**
FSMN	11.94	**11.28**	11.34

Finally, we investigated experiments with FSMN system which is trained using i-vector features and sequence-discriminative criteria on the Mongolian large vocabulary continuous speech recognition task. We select the FSMN model in the baseline experiments as the starting point. As shown in Table 5, we can see that for each auxiliary vector, the finally results consistently are better than the baseline FSMN model. And using the sequence-discriminative training can obtain better results than the i-vector features. Moreover these auxiliary vectors are complementary. The best performance is obtained using the i-vector + sequence training setup. The WER is reduced from 11.94% to 10.59% (relative 11.3%).

Table 5. The results (% WER) of different auxiliary information for FSMN

Model	WER (%)
FSMN	11.94
FSMN + sequence training	11.28
FSMN + iVectors	11.38
FSMN + iVectors + sequence training	**10.59**

7 Conclusions

In this paper, we presents the first application of FSMN networks for Mongolian large vocabulary continuous speech recognition tasks, the experimental results show that the FSMN can obtain better performance than the DNN. Compared among different FSMN model architectures, the former three hidden layers with block memory and the latter three layers being normal hidden layer was found to be optimal, WER was relatively reduced by 10.8%. Further, we show the i-vector features and the sequence discriminative training are both effective in the Mongolian speech recognition system. And these auxiliary vectors are complementary, by combining these two method, we can get a relative improvement of 11.3%. Finally, by using the FSMN, i-vector features and the sequence discriminative training, comparing with the DNN baseline, we obtain a WER relative reduction of 17.9%. And the WER score of the best system is 10.59% which is a very good performance record of the Mongolian speech recognition system.

Acknowledgements. This research was supports in part by the China national natural science foundation (No. 61563040, No. 61773224) and Inner Mongolian nature science foundation (No. 2016ZD06).

References

1. Hinton, G., Deng, L., Dong, Y., et al.: Deep neural networks for acoustic modeling in speech recognition: the shared views of four research groups. IEEE Sig. Process. Mag. **29**(6), 82–97 (2012)
2. Graves, A., Mohamed, A., Hinton, G.: Speech recognition with deep recurrent neural networks. In: 38th ICASSP, pp. 6645–6649. IEEE Press, Vancouver (2013)
3. Sak, H., Senior, A.W., Beaufays, F.: Long short-term memory recurrent neural network architectures for large scale acoustic modeling. In: 15th INTERSPEECH, Singapore, pp. 338–342 (2014)
4. Zhang, S.L., Jiang, H., Wei, S., et al.: Feedforward sequential memory neural networks without recurrent feedback. Comput. Sci. arXiv:1510.02693 (2015)
5. Zhang, S., Liu, C., Jiang, H., et al.: Feedforward sequential memory networks: a new structure to learn long-term dependency. Comput. Sci. arXiv:1512.08301 (2015)
6. Gao, G., Biligetu, Nabuqing, Zhang, S.: A Mongolian speech recognition system based on HMM. In: Huang, D.S., Li, K., Irwin, G.W. (eds.) ICIC 2006. LNCS, vol. 4114, pp. 667–676. Springer, Heidelberg (2015). https://doi.org/10.1007/11816171_84
7. Qilao, H., Gao, G.L.: Researching of speech recognition oriented mongolian acoustic model. In: Chinese Conference on 2nd Pattern Recognition, CCPR 2008, pp. 1–6. IEEE Press, Beijing (2008)
8. Bao, F., Gao, G.: Improving of acoustic model for the mongolian speech recognition system. In: Chinese Conference on 2nd Pattern Recognition, CCPR 2009, pp. 1–5. IEEE Press, Nanjing (2009)
9. Bao, F., Gao, G., Yan, X., Wang, W.: Segmentation-based Mongolian LVCSR approach. In: 38th ICASSP 2013, pp. 1–5. IEEE Press, Vancouver (2013)
10. Zhang, H., Bao, F., Gao, G.: Mongolian speech recognition based on deep neural networks. In: Sun, M., Liu, Z., Zhang, M., Liu, Y. (eds.) CCL 2015. LNCS (LNAI), vol. 9427, pp. 180–188. Springer, Cham (2015). https://doi.org/10.1007/978-3-319-25816-4_15
11. Alam, M.J., Gupta, V., Kenny, P., Dumouchel, P.: Use of multiple front-ends and I-vector-based speaker adaptation for robust speech recognition. In: REVERB Workshop. (2014)
12. Xue, S., Abdel-Hamid, O., Jiang, H., Dai, L.: Fast adaptation of deep neural network based on discriminant codes for speech recognition. IEEE/ACM Trans. Audio Speech Lang. Process. **22**(12), 1713–1725 (2014)

13. Senior, A., Lopez-Moreno, I.: Improving DNN speaker independence with I-vector inputs. In: 39th ICASSP, pp. 225–229. IEEE Press, Florence (2014)
14. Peddinti, V., Chen, G., Povey, D., Khudanpur, S.: Reverberation robust acoustic modeling using i-vectors with time delay neural networks. In: 16th INTERSPEECH, Dresden, pp. 2440–2444 (2015)
15. Povey, D., Ghoshal, A., Boulianne, G., Burget, L., Glembek, O., Goel, N., Silovsky, J.: The Kaldi speech recognition toolkit. In: Workshop on Automatic Speech Recognition and Understanding (No. EPFL-CONF-192584). IEEE Signal Processing Society (2011)
16. Maas, A.L., Hannun, A.Y., Ng, A.Y.: Rectifier nonlinearities improve neural network acoustic models. In: 30th ICML Workshop on Deep Learning for Audio, Speech and Language Processing (2013)

Using Bilingual Segments to Improve Interactive Machine Translation

Na Ye[(⊠)], Ping Xu, Chuang Wu, and Guiping Zhang

Human-Computer Intelligence Research Center,
Shenyang Aerospace University, Shenyang 110136, China
yn.yena@hotmail.com, 451908817@qq.com,
{wuchuang, zgp}@ge-soft.com

Abstract. Recent research on machine translation has achieved substantial progress. However, the machine translation results are still not error-free, and need to be post-edited by a human translator (user) to produce correct translations. Interactive machine translation enhanced the human-computer collaboration through having human validate the longest correct prefix in the suggested translation. In this paper, we refine the interactivity protocol to provide more natural collaboration. Users are allowed to validate bilingual segments, which give more direct guidance to the decoder and more hints to the users. Besides, validating bilingual segments is easier than identifying correct segments from the incorrect translations. Experimental results with real users show that the new protocol improved the translation efficiency and translation quality on three Chinese-English translation tasks.

Keywords: Interactive machine translation · Bilingual segment
Translating option · Option diversity

1 Introduction

The performance of machine translation (MT) systems has been greatly improved by the statistical machine translation (SMT) and the neural machine translation (NMT) technology. However, in many tasks which have high quality requirements, the MT output is still not good enough and must be corrected by human translators in a post-editing (PE) stage.

To enhance the human-computer collaboration, Foster [1] introduced the interactive machine translation (IMT) technology. In an IMT system, a correction-prediction process works iteratively. First, the IMT system provides a raw translation. Second, the user validates the longest correct prefix in it and corrects the next word. Third, the system predicts a new suffix which is expected to be better than the previous one. This process is repeated until the correct translation is acquired.

During these years, the IMT technology was developed along with the evolution of the underlying MT models from SMT [2–6] to NMT [7, 8]. Advances also include making better use of the prefix to improve the prediction accuracy [9–14], applying confidence measures to reduce human effort [15, 16], adopting active learning [17] and online learning [18, 19] to learn from user feedback, and integrating automatic speech

© Springer International Publishing AG 2018
X. Huang et al. (Eds.): NLPCC 2017, LNAI 10619, pp. 255–266, 2018.
https://doi.org/10.1007/978-3-319-73618-1_22

recognition [20] and handwritten recognition [21] to multi-modal interaction tasks. Evaluation results show that compared to PE, the prefix-based IMT protocol can increase the human translation quality and reduce the number of key strokes while keeping the translation speed [22–24].

Recently, this left-to-right protocol was extended to make the human-computer interaction more flexible [7, 25]. In the extended protocol, users can validate the segments that should be kept in the translation. However, this protocol also suffers from three issues. First, the positions of the validated segments are not known, so the search process can only be constrained on a soft way [7]. Second, the user validations are restricted to the proposed translation, and no hints of other translating options are available. Third, identifying correct segments from incorrect translations often requires considerable cognitive effort, especially when the translation quality is low.

In this paper we refined the interactivity protocol to validating bilingual segments. During interaction, users are provided with both the source segments and their corresponding translating options. They can select the correct one from these options. In the new protocol, the target-side segments are aligned with their source-side counterparts, so they can be introduced to the decoder on a more direct way. This protocol also provides more hints to the users and requires less cognitive burden. We conducted experimentation with real users on three Chinese-English LDC corpora featuring different domains. Results show significant improvements over the prefix-based system.

2   Interactive Machine Translation

2.1   Prefix-Based IMT

In the traditional prefix-based IMT protocol [2], the system predicts the best suffix under the condition of the given source text s and the user-validated prefix t_p as follows:

$$\hat{t}_s = \underset{t_s}{\operatorname{argmax}} P(t_s \mid s, t_p) = \underset{t_s}{\operatorname{argmax}} P(t_p, t_s \mid s) \tag{1}$$

where $(t_p, t_s) = t$, indicating that the prefix t_p and the predicted suffix t_s concatenate to form a complete translation t. To model $P(t_p, t_s \mid s)$, current approaches filter the translation hypotheses according to their matching results with the prefix.

Although the suffix is probably not quite right, there are some correct segments which should be kept. However, in the prefix-based IMT systems, these segments may lose in the next iteration. The segment-based IMT approaches were proposed to solve this problem.

2.2   Segment-Based IMT

In this protocol [7], users can validate the segments $f_1^N = f_1, \ldots, f_N$ that should be retained in the future interactions. The search process can be modelled by predicting the other segments as follows:

$$\hat{g}_1^N = \underset{g_1^N}{\mathrm{argmax}}\, P(g_1, \ldots, g_N \mid s, f_1, \ldots, f_N)$$

$$= \underset{g_1^N}{\mathrm{argmax}}\, P(f_1, g_1, \ldots, f_N, g_N \mid s) \tag{2}$$

where $g_1^N = g_1, \ldots, g_N$ is the *non-validated* segment sequence that fills f_1^N to form a new translation. The prefix t_p is a particular case of the validated segments. In Eq. (2) the search space is all possible hypotheses containing the segment set $\{f_1, f_2, \ldots, f_N\}$. Figure 1 shows an example of the segment-based IMT protocol.

Source	根据 本条 规则 发出 的 原诉 传票 须 采用 附录 A 表格 10 的 格式 。
MT	The originating summons under section shall be in Form No. 10 in Appendix A.
Reference	An originating summons under this rule shall be in Form No. 10 in Appendix A.

Fig. 1. Example of the segment-based IMT protocol.

In the above figure, framed texts indicate the validated segments. These segments are monolingual and lack the alignment information with the source sentence. The decoder can only predict the next words according to the previously generated words and the immediate next segment, and no source-target alignment information can be used. Thus the guidance of segments in decoding is limited. Another problem is the wrong word "*section*" and the missing word "*this*". Although the user found these mistakes, he/she have no other options to choose from. It is also difficult for users to identify the correct segments from the MT output mixed with wrong words and wrong orders. These problems are intended to be solved in the bilingual segment based IMT protocol.

2.3   Bilingual Segment Based IMT

In this protocol, the source segments are aligned with their target counterparts. For each source segment, multiple translating options are provided. The user can validate bilingual segment pairs in the form of $<f_i, e_i>$. The best translation is acquired as follows:

$$\hat{t} = \underset{t}{\mathrm{argmax}}\, P(t \mid s, f_1, e_1, \ldots, f_N, e_N)$$

$$= \underset{t}{\mathrm{argmax}}\, P(f_1, e_1, \ldots, f_N, e_N, t \mid s) \tag{3}$$

where e_i is the correct translation of f_i validated by the user. The prefix t_p is a particular case of segment pair which has no source counterpart. In Eq. (3) the search space is the hypotheses compatible with these bilingual segments. Figure 2 shows an example of the new protocol.

IT-1	Source	根据	本条	规则	发出 的	原诉 传票		须 采用 附录 A 表格 10 的 格式 。
	User		this	rule		an originating summons		
	MT	Under this rule of an originating summons shall be in Form No. 10 in Appendix A.						
IT-2	User	4						
	Accept	An originating summons under this rule shall be in Form No. 10 in Appendix A.						

Fig. 2. Example of the bilingual segment based IMT protocol.

The user validated three bilingual segments (e.g. the framed parts in the figure). And the MT decoder proposed a translation better than that in Fig. 1. Then the user inputs a prefix "*A*" and decodes again. This time the correct translation is acquired (IT-2).

3   User Interface

3.1   Overview

This paper adopts a user interface illustrated in Fig. 3. The interface consists of two zones. One is the interacting zone which presents the segmented source sentence and the translating options. The segments and the options are aligned vertically by the left. When the mouse hangs over a source segment, a menu with its highest ranked options is displayed and the users can click the best option for validation. The other is the editing zone which presents the MT output when the users finish validation and press the "*translate*" button. Here the users can make corrections as they want, until the translation is accepted. The interacting and the editing process can alternate.

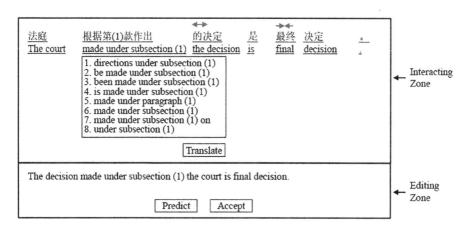

Fig. 3. User interface of the bilingual segment based IMT system.

One prominent advantage of phrase-based SMT is the extraction for long phrases translation. Taking long phrases as the basic translating units can effectively alleviate the word disambiguation problem, thus achieving good results. Therefore, longer segments and their translations are displayed with priority in the interface, and the initial segmentation of the source sentence is performed by forward maximum matching algorithm with the phrase table. The displayed translating options are the highest K options in the phrase table.

The interface also provides three auxiliary functions, namely segment split-merging, translating option re-ranking and suffix predicting.

3.2   Segment Split-Merging

Above each segment, there are two kinds of two-head arrows. One is the splitting arrow (↔), it can split the segment into two smaller segments. The other is the merging arrow (→◄-), it can merge the segment and its next segment into one larger segment.

The arrows appear when the mouse hangs over the segment. If no smaller or no larger segment exists in the phrase table, then the arrow will not show. Once new segments are formed, their translating options will change accordingly.

3.3   Translating Option Re-ranking

By default, the options of a segment are ranked and displayed with their order in the phrase table. However, the highest scoring options are sometimes quite similar. So we offer an alternative mode that increases the diversity of options. The user can choose the default mode or the re-ranking mode before they start translation.

In this mode, the top N translating options in the phrase table are re-ranked to generate a new option list. For each source phrase p, set a new option list $T(T = \varnothing)$. First add the option with highest score in the original phrase table to T. Then traverse the remaining $N-1$ options and find the one with highest diversity with the options in T and insert it to T. Repeat this process until all the N options are re-ranked. The diversity between two options t_i and t_j is measured as follows:

$$D(t_i, t_j) = 1 - \frac{c(t_i, t_j)}{\max\{|t_i|, |t_j|\}} \tag{4}$$

where $c(t_i, t_j)$ is the number of overlapped words (lemmatized) between t_i and t_j.

3.4   Suffix Predicting

In the editing zone, the users can press the "*Prediction*" button to get the predicted suffix from the system. When the button is pressed, the current position of the cursor is recorded, and the characters before the cursor are taken as the prefix. The validated bilingual segments and the prefix are all considered to find the best suffix. Once a new suffix is generated, it will replace the current suffix. If the decoder fails to find any compatible hypothesis, then the suffix will not be changed.

4 Decoding

After the user finishes the validation of bilingual segments in the interacting zone, the system catches the user's choice of translating option for each segment f_i and the current segmentation S of the source sentence. A set is constructed as the constraints for decoding:

$$C = \{S, <p_1, f_1, e_1>, <p_2, f_2, e_2>, \ldots, <p_N, f_N, e_N>\} \tag{5}$$

where p_i is the position of segment f_i in the source sentence. Recording p_i is for avoiding the ambiguity when a segment appears more than once. Note that the user must click on the option before the segment and the option can be considered a validated bilingual segment. If a segment has never been clicked on any of its options, then the segment and its option cannot be used as a constraint.

We use the multi-stack-decoding algorithm for the phrase-based SMT decoder. Two improvements are proposed to meet the constraints. First, in order to make the generation of translation hypotheses compatible with the constraints, S is used as the only segmentation of the source sentence during decoding. Second, the translating options of each source phrase (segment) are constrained by $<p_i, f_i, e_i>$, and only the options containing e_i will be kept and participate in the subsequent decoding process.

As for the auxiliary function of suffix predicting, one more constraint is added to the decoder. The translation hypotheses must match the given prefix t_p.

5 Experiments

5.1 Data Setup

We tested the proposed approach on three different Chinese-English translation tasks with real users. *Laws* consists in laws texts from LDC2000T47 corpus. *Hansards* consists in Hansards texts from LDC2000T50 corpus. *News* consists in news texts from LDC2000T46 corpus. Table 1 gives the main figures of these corpora (S, T and V

Table 1. Main figures of the evaluation corpora.

		Training			Development			Test		
		S	T	V	S	T	V	S	T	V
Laws	Zh	103k	2.0M	29k	2070	49k	5.3k	75	1.4k	533
	En		2.1M	29k		51k	5.2k		1.2k	570
Hansards	Zh	351k	7.8M	75k	2497	64k	8.1k	75	1.2k	592
	En		9.2M	91k		78k	11.3k		1.3k	573
News	Zh	190k	4.8M	64k	2512	72k	10k	75	1.2k	667
	En		5.4M	69k		86k	14k		1.3k	623

account for number of sentences, number of tokens and vocabulary size, respectively. k and M stand for thousands and millions).

The Chinese portions of these data were pre-processed by the ICTCLAS word segmenter[1], and the English portions were tokenized and lowercased. GIZA++ was used for training word alignment models. IRSTLM [26] was used for training 5-gram language models. Moses [27] was used for building phrase-based SMT models, which include 14 default features. MERT [28] was used for adjusting feature weights.

Three IMT systems were evaluated in our experiments. *Baseline* refers to the prefix-based system [2] using PBMT model. *BiSeg* refers to the proposed system without option re-ranking. *BiSeg+D* refers to the proposed system with option re-ranking. In the user interface, the number of displayed translating options is set to 10, and the number of top translating options for re-ranking is set to 20.

5.2 Evaluation Metrics

In the literature of IMT, automatic evaluation metrics are mostly used for assessing prototypes [2, 4, 7] because experiments with real users are quite costly and slow. In these metrics user behaviors are simulated, rather than real user behaviors during interaction. A direct evaluation of an IMT system would require conducting experiments with human users [7], which is done in this paper.

We evaluate the performance of an IMT system from two aspects of efficiency and quality. Translation efficiency is evaluated with three metrics:

1. *Translating Time*: is the most direct metric for measuring human effort during the IMT process. It is defined as the average time spent in translating each sentence.
2. *Key Stroke and Mouse-action Ratio* (KSMR) [2]: measures the user's keyboard and mouse effort during the IMT process.
3. *Decoding Times*: measures the number of decoding times during the IMT process. It is defined as the average decoding times for each sentence.

Translation Quality is evaluated with the *BLEU* score [29]. We take the English portions of the original parallel corpus as the reference and evaluate the users' translation quality. Note that the final translations accepted by the users are all correct, although not exactly the same as the references.

5.3 Participants and Procedures

A group of 9 postgraduates (6 females) from our research group volunteered to perform the evaluation as non-professional translators. All of them are native speakers of Chinese, and proficient in English.

In order to make the participants familiar with the systems, we selected 30 sentences in the *Laws* corpus as warm-up corpus, and let the participants translate with four IMT systems (10 sentences per system). Formal tests began on the second day after the warm-up.

---

[1] http://ictclas.nlpir.org/.

We randomly divided the participants into 3 groups, 3 in each group. The testing set of each corpus was randomly divided into 3 parts, each with 25 sentences. The evaluation is carried out in a counterbalanced fashion.

5.4   Results and Analysis

In order to give an intuitive understanding of the performance of the SMT models, we evaluated the BLEU scores of the underlying SMT engine. Results are 0.3411, 0.1971 and 0.1901 on *Laws*, *Hansards* and *News*, respectively. This indicates that the quality of the translation provided by the SMT engine is readable with some effort.

Table 2 gives the average time of the three user groups on the evaluation corpora. The figures in the brackets are the relative differences between our systems and the Baseline system.

Table 2. Results of translating time with different IMT systems.

	Baseline	BiSeg	BiSeg+D
Laws	101.7 s (−)	83.1 s (−18.3%)	82.7 s (−18.7%)
Hansards	103.0 s (−)	79.5 s (−22.8%)	78.6 s (−23.7%)
News	91.5 s (−)	86.1 s (−5.9%)	84.2 s (−8.0%)

It can be seen that the translating time with our systems is significantly lower than that with the Baseline system. This indicates a significant reduction in human effort. Through observing the IMT process of participants, we have the following findings:

1. The decoding times are less (see Table 4). Since there are many possibilities in segment translation and source sentence segmentation, it is difficult for the decoder of the prefix-based protocol to make the right choice. In the new protocol, the users not only validate the translation of segments, but also determined the segmentation of the source sentence. Thus the search space is greatly reduced.
2. The displayed option list provided by the new protocol is very helpful to the users, especially for long segments and in specialized domain. The segment-based protocol also does not provide this kind of help.
3. Under the new protocol, the users' IMT process can be divided into two stages, in which they focus on validating the segment translation and the segment order respectively. This two-stage translation process with clear task helps users to concentrate and improve their efficiency.

The option diversity can further reduce human effort. In most cases, the correct translating option is contained in the K displayed options. And the users don't always scan the options from top to bottom. In fact, as long as the correct option exists in the list, the users can easily pick it out. Especially for long segments, they usually have only a few options. However, there are also some cases (usually short segments) in which the correct option is not in the list. At this time, re-ranking the options increases the possibility of adding the correct option into the displayed list.

Table 3 gives the KSMR values on three corpora.

Table 3. Results of KSMR with different IMT systems.

	Baseline	BiSeg	BiSeg+D
Laws	0.94 (−)	1.14 (+21.3%)	0.99 (+5.3%)
Hansards	0.55 (−)	0.69 (+25.5%)	0.66 (+20.0%)
News	0.48 (−)	0.71 (+47.9%)	0.68 (+41.7%)

We can see that the KSMR values of our systems are much higher than that of the Baseline system. The increased actions mainly come from four kinds of mouse actions, namely translating option clicking, segment splitting/merging, extra button clicking (such as the button "*translate*") and cursor switching between zones. But these mouse actions don't cost much thinking and action time, so they have little effect on translation efficiency.

Table 4 gives the average decoding times on three corpora.

Table 4. Results of decoding times with different IMT systems.

	Baseline	BiSeg	BiSeg+D
Laws	5.90 (−)	4.52 (−23.4%)	4.07 (−31.0%)
Hansards	3.70 (−)	1.89 (−48.9%)	1.73 (−53.2%)
News	2.80 (−)	2.00 (−28.6%)	1.97 (−29.6%)

Table 4 shows that the decoding times reduce significantly in the new protocol. As mentioned above, the search space is greatly reduced. Through discussions with the participants, they report that it is better to validate the translation of content words and long segments and not to validate the function words and symbols. This avoids unnecessary constraints on decoding and reduces decoding failures.

Table 5 gives the translation quality (BLEU score) on three corpora.

Table 5. Results of translation quality with different IMT systems.

	Baseline	BiSeg	BiSeg + D
Laws	0.3811 (−)	0.3846 (+0.9%)	0.3834 (+0.6%)
Hansards	0.2723 (−)	0.2781 (+2.1%)	0.2775 (+1.9%)
News	0.2418 (−)	0.2673 (+10.5%)	0.2686 (+11.1%)

Results show that the translation quality with our systems is slightly better than that with the Baseline system. This is because the new protocol provides a large number of options, giving users more hints and inspiration to enable them to produce better translations. While in the prefix-based protocol, the users will stop once they get an acceptable translation. However, the improvement is not obvious. The reason is that the users also work on good hypotheses under the prefix-based protocol. And the wrong translations are manually corrected before they can be submitted. So the users will spent more time but the translation quality can still be guaranteed.

Our protocol also has some disadvantages. For some sentences which the decoder can easily find the correct translation after a few word corrections, the prefix-based protocol is more convenient. While in our protocol the users still have to validate the translating options and then perform correction. We can use confidence scores to help users identify these cases and assign suitable protocol for each sentence.

5.5 Comparison with Related Work

Ananthakrishnan [30] proposed an interactive translation system which engages the user in a clarification dialogue to recover from the potential word-sense translation errors. This approach focuses on conversational spoken language translation and aims at solving the semantic class selection errors for certain ambiguous words. The users cannot perform additional interactive clarification operations.

Huang [31] proposed an input method for human translators. The MT technology is deeply integrated into the computer-aided translation system (CAT) to enable human translators to focus on choosing better translation results with less time. Experiments with real users show satisfactory results in accelerating the translation process. This work can be integrated into our protocol and further improve the IMT efficiency.

The work most similar to ours is that of Cheng [32] in which a pick-revise framework for IMT was proposed. This approach identifies the wrongly-translated phrase and selects the correct translation from the translation table. Then the sentence is re-translated with these constraints. In comparison, we extended the mathematical framework of the prefix-based protocol and the segment-based protocol through refining the constraints to bilingual segments. We also designed an interface for real users, which allows the users to split and merge the segmented phrases and provided the translating option re-ranking method that increases the option diversity. These help to improve the human efficiency in a real scenario. Besides, we conducted real-user experiments rather than simulated experiments.

6   Conclusion and Future Work

In this paper, we present a new IMT protocol. We provide users with translating options for each segment in the source sentence, and allow the users to validate bilingual segments in the user interface. In this way, more hints are given to the user and more direct guidance to the decoder. The protocol also helps users to concentrate in a two-stage translating process. We carried out real-user experiments on three corpora from different domains and obtained satisfactory results. Compared with the prefix-based IMT protocol, the new protocol made significant improvements in reducing human effort.

In the future, we will continue to optimize the user interface according to the users' suggestions. We will also consider applying the new input method to help users type faster and applying the confidence measures to determine the suitable protocol for the sentences. Integrating bilingual segments with the NMT framework is another problem worthy of study.

Acknowledgements. This work is supported by the National Natural Science Foundation of China (No. 61402299).

References

1. Foster, G., Isabelle, P., Plamondon, P.: Target-text mediated interactive machine translation. Mach. Transl. **12**(1), 175–194 (1997)
2. Barrachina, S., Bender, O., Casacuberta, F., Civera, J., Cubel, E., Khadivi, S., Lagarda, A., Ney, H., Tomás, J., Vidal, E., Vilar, J.M.: Statistical approaches to computer-assisted translation. Comput. Linguist. **35**(1), 3–28 (2009)
3. Civera, J., Cubel, E., Lagarda, A.L., Picó, D., González, J., Vidal, E., Casacuberta, F., Vilar, J.M., Barrachina, S.: From machine translation to computer assisted translation using finite-state models. In: Proceedings of EMNLP, pp. 349–356 (2004)
4. González-Rubio, J., Ortiz-Martínez, D., Benedí, J.M., Casacuberta, F.: Interactive machine translation using hierarchical translation models. In: Proceedings of EMNLP, pp. 244–254 (2013)
5. Och, F.J., Zens, R., Ney, H.: Efficient search for interactive statistical machine translation. In: Proceedings of EACL, pp. 287–293 (2003)
6. Tomás, J., Casacuberta, F.: statistical phrase-based models for interactive computer-assisted translation. In: Proceedings of COLING/ACL, pp. 835–841 (2006)
7. Peris, Á., Domingo, M., Casacuberta, F.: Interactive neural machine translation. Comput. Speech Lang. **45**, 201–220 (2017)
8. Wuebker, J., Green, S., DeNero, J., Hasan, S., Luong, M.T.: Models and inference for prefix-constrained machine translation. In: Proceedings of ACL, pp. 66–75 (2016)
9. Azadi, F., Khadivi, S.: Improved search strategy for interactive predictions in computer-assisted translation. In: Proceedings of MT Summit, pp. 319–332 (2015)
10. Green, S., Wang, S., Chuang, J., Heer, J., Schuster, S., Manning, C.D.: Human effort and machine learnability in computer aided translation. In: Proceedings of EMNLP, pp. 1225–1236 (2014)
11. Koehn, P., Tsoukala, C., Saint-Amand, H.: Refinements to interactive translation prediction based on search graphs. In: Proceedings of ACL, pp. 574–578 (2014)
12. Ortiz-Martínez, D., García-Varea, I., Casacuberta, F.: Interactive machine translation based on partial statistical phrase-based alignments. In: Proceedings of RANLP, pp. 330–336 (2009)
13. Ye, N., Zhang, G., Cai, D.: Interactive-predictive machine translation based on syntactic constraints of prefix. In: Proceedings of COLING, pp. 1797–1806 (2016)
14. Sanchis-Trilles, G., Ortiz-Martínez, D., Civera, J.: Improving interactive machine translation via mouse actions. In: Proceedings of EMNLP, pp. 485–494 (2008)
15. González-Rubio, J., Ortiz-Martínez, D., Casacuberta, F.: Balancing user effort and translation error in interactive machine translation via confidence measures. In: Proceedings of ACL, pp. 173–177 (2010)
16. Ueffing, N., Ney, H.: Application of word-level confidence measures in interactive statistical machine translation. In: Proceedings of EAMT, pp. 262–270 (2005)
17. González-Rubio, J., Ortiz-Martínez, D., Casacuberta, F.: Active learning for interactive machine translation. In: Proceedings of EACL, pp. 245–254 (2012)
18. Ortiz-Martínez, D., García-Varea, I., Casacuberta, F.: Online learning for interactive statistical machine translation. In: Proceedings of NAACL, pp. 546–554 (2010)

19. Ortiz-Martínez, D.: Online learning for statistical machine translation. Comput. Linguist. **42** (1), 121–161 (2016)
20. Alabau, V., Rodríguez-Ruiz, L., Sanchis, A., Martínez-Gómez, P., Casacuberta, F.: On multimodal interactive machine translation using speech recognition. In: Proceedings of International Conference on Multimodal Interfaces, pp. 129–136 (2011)
21. Alabau, V., Sanchis, A., Casacuberta, F.: Improving on-line handwritten recognition in interactive machine translation. Pattern Recogn. **47**(3), 1217–1228 (2014)
22. Alabau, V., Leiva, L.A., Ortiz-Martínez, D., Casacuberta, F.: User evaluation of interactive machine translation systems. In: Proceedings of EACL, pp. 20–23 (2012)
23. Green, S., Chuang, J., Heer, J., Manning, C.D.: Predictive translation memory: a mixed-initiative system for human language translation. In: Proceedings of Annual Association for Computing Machinery Symposium on User Interface Software and Technology, pp. 177–187 (2014)
24. Sanchis-Trilles, G., Alabau, V., Buck, C., Carl, M., Casacuberta, F., García-Martínez, M., Germann, U., González-Rubio, J., Hill, R.L., Koehn, P., Leiva, L.A., Mesa-Lao, B., Ortiz-Martínez, D., Saint-Amand, H., Tsoukala, C., Vidal, E.: Interactive translation prediction versus conventional post-editing in practice: a study with the CasMaCat workbench. Mach. Transl. **28**(3), 217–235 (2014)
25. González-Rubio, J., Ortiz-Martínez, D., Benedí, J.M., Casacuberta, F.: Beyond prefix-based interactive translation prediction. In: Proceedings of SIGNLL Conference on Computational Natural Language Learning, pp. 198–207 (2016)
26. Federico, M., Bertoldi, N., Cettolo, M.: IRSTLM: an open source toolkit for handling large scale language models. In: Proceedings of Interspeech, pp. 1618–1621 (2008)
27. Koehn, P., Hoang, H., Birch, A., Callison-Burch, C., Federico, M., Bertoldi, N., Cowan, B., Shen, W., Moran, C., Zens, R., Dyer, C., Bojar, O., Constantin, A., Herbst, E.: Moses: open source toolkit for statistical machine translation. In: Proceedings of ACL, pp. 177–180 (2007)
28. Och, F.J.: Minimum error rate training in statistical machine translation. In: Proceedings of ACL, pp. 160–167 (2003)
29. Papineni, K., Roukos, S., Ward, T., Zhu, W.J.: BLEU: a method for automatic evaluation of machine translation. In: Proceedings of ACL, pp. 311–318 (2002)
30. Ananthakrishnan, S., Mehay, D.N., Hewavitharana, S., Kumar, R., Roy, M., Kan, E.: Lightly supervised word-sense translation-error detection and resolution in an interactive conversational spoken language translation system. Mach. Transl. **29**(1), 25–47 (2015)
31. Huang, G., Zhang, J., Zhou, Y., Zong, C.: A new input method for human translators: integrating machine translation. In: Proceedings of IJCAI, pp. 1163–1169 (2015)
32. Cheng, S., Huang, S., Chen, H., Dai, X., Chen, J.: PRIMT: a pick-revise framework for interactive machine translation. In: Proceedings of NAACL, pp. 1240–1249 (2016)

Vietnamese Part of Speech Tagging Based on Multi-category Words Disambiguation Model

Zhao Chen[1], Liu Yanchao[1], Guo Jianyi[1,2(✉)], Chen Wei[1,2],
Yan Xin[1,2], Yu Zhengtao[1,2], and Chen Xiuqin[3]

[1] The School of Information Engineering and Automation,
Kunming University of Science and Technology,
Kunming 650500, Yunnan, China
gjade86@hotmail.com
[2] The Key Laboratory of Intelligent Information Processing,
Kunming University of Science and Technology,
Kunming 650500, Yunnan, China
[3] Kunming University of Science and Technology of International Education,
Kunming, China

Abstract. POS tagging is a fundamental work in Natural Language Processing, which determines the subsequent processing quality, and the ambiguity of multi-category words directly affects the accuracy of Vietnamese POS tagging. At present, the POS tagging of English and Chinese has achieved better results, but the accuracy of Vietnamese POS tagging is still to be improved. For address this problem, this paper proposes a novel method of Vietnamese POS tagging based on multi-category words disambiguation model and Part of Speech dictionary, the multi-category words dictionary and the non-multi-category words dictionary are generated from the Vietnamese dictionary, which are used to build POS tagging corpus. 396,946 multi-category words have been extracted from the corpus, by using statistical method, the maximum entropy disambiguation model of Vietnamese part of speech is constructed, based on it, the multi-category words and the non-multi-category words are tagged. Experimental results show that the method proposed in the paper is higher than the existing model, which is proved that the method is feasible and effective.

Keywords: Multi-category words disambiguation · Vietnamese
Part of Speech dictionary · POS tagging

1 Introduction

Part of speech tagging (POS tagging) is a typical sequence annotation task in natural language processing, which is to give a correct lexical mark for each word in the sentence. It plays a very important role and is widely used in many aspects of natural language processing, such as chunk parsing, syntactic parsing, named entity recognition, noun phrase recognition, semantic analysis and machine translation etc. The study of the POS tagging in Vietnamese can effectively support the research work of

© Springer International Publishing AG 2018
X. Huang et al. (Eds.): NLPCC 2017, LNAI 10619, pp. 267–277, 2018.
https://doi.org/10.1007/978-3-319-73618-1_23

language information processing in Vietnamese, which can be applied to Vietnamese machine translation, information retrieval and speech recognition, which is also the indispensable basis of block recognizer and syntactic analysis of Vietnamese. Therefore, the POS tagging in Vietnamese is one of the key problems and a difficult point in the field of Vietnamese information processing.

The study of the POS tagging had been studied earlier in English and Chinese and has achieved good results. There are three main methods for POS tagging: (1) Rule-based method. Unsupervised learning methods for disambiguation rules are proposed by Brill to solve English POS tagging [1]; Hu proposed an improved conversion method applied to the Latin Mongolian tagging task, and achieved good results [2]; Wang proposed a priority rule-based POS tagging method, which is applied to the Chinese, the tagging accuracy rate can reach 96.4% [3]; The rule-based method is difficult to count all the rules of language completely, and the complexity of the language phenomenon also led to its rules difficult to develop; (2) Statistics-based method. Bernard proposed the use of probability model in English POS tagging [4]; Wang put forward the method for Chinese POS tagging based on SVMTool [5]; Binulal proposed the method for Telugu POS tagging based on SVM [6]; Nongmeikapam used SVM model to do the Manipuri POS tagging [7]; Generally speaking, statistics-based method of POS tagging needs a large scale of training corpus to support machine learning, moreover, if there are fewer frequent part of speech in the training corpus, the marking effect is poor. (3) Hybrid method. Jiang put forward the method of combining rules with statistics to do POS tagging in Japanese [8]. For the POS tagging in Vietnamese, there are already some related work, but the correct rate still needs to be improved, such as, Nghiem-Dinh integrated the common features (lexical features, word context features, POS features and spelling features) and special features (repeat feature, prefix and suffix features) into SVM model for POS tagging, the correct rate is 93.51% [9]; Oanh proposed a new feature based syllable, combining the features based word, and integrated them respectively into the model of MEM (maximum entropy), SVM and CRF (conditional random field), modeling and segmentation, comparing the results of the three models [10]; Phuong proposed the method of maximum entropy incorporated with two kinds of characteristics, one kind is the basic characteristic, which including the relation between the current word and the front and back word, and the relation between the part of speech of the current word and the part of speech of the front and back words, the other is syllable feature. The correct rate of the method is 93.40% [11]. In addition, the above studies ignored the influence of multi-category words on the quality of POS tagging. Vietnamese is the same as English and Chinese, the phenomenon of multi-category words are common/ubiquitous and occupy a large proportion, which brings great difficulties to the lexical analysis and syntactic parsing. Multi-category words processing is very important in POS tagging in lexical analysis

This paper especially studies the influence of multi-category words in the POS tagging in Vietnamese, the Vietnamese dictionary is used to get multi-category words dictionary and non-multi-category words dictionary, then the corpus is divided into multi-category words and non-multi-category words, and then they are marked separately. The benefit of doing so is, for non-multi-category words, that the POS tagging based on the Part of Speech dictionary can achieved good experimental results of near 100% accuracy, which is much better than the experimental results based on statistical algorithms and can avoid the possibility of tagging errors in the manual tagging of corpus, thus reducing the workload of tagging the corpus; For multi-category words, we learned from the existing research, combined with the characteristics of the Vietnamese language, constructed the category words corpus, specially selected multi-category words characteristic, which is not considered in the above study. And the method of Vietnamese POS tagging based on multi-category words disambiguation model and Part of Speech dictionary was proposed, which can effectively solve the problem of fewer parts of speech type tagging effect in training corpus and improve the accuracy of POS tagging in Vietnamese.

2 Linguistic Features of Vietnamese and Construction of Part of Speech Set

Vietnamese has its own unique language features, not only in the POS tagging, but also in different tasks. Up till now there has been no standardized POS tagging corpus in Vietnamese language, therefore, a POS tagging set has been built firstly to construct POS tagging corpus in order to verify the effectiveness of the proposed method.

2.1 Linguistic Features of Vietnamese

Vietnamese are the mother tongue of the Vietnamese state and belong to the South Asian language. It has the following characteristics [12]:

(1) It is a language with a fairly fixed word order, in which consists of subject + predicate + object constitutes subject-verb-object (SVO).
(2) The Vietnamese language is written in a variant of the Latin alphabet, a kind of isolated language, which lack of morphological changes; every morpheme is a simple, isolated syllable;
(3) Vietnamese is a tortuous form of language, its syllable morphology does not produce any change;
(4) The greatest impact on Vietnamese is the phenomenon of linguistics: mutation type, that is, some words have multiple parts of speech, but itself has not changed; Leading to Vietnamese language contains ambiguous part of speech. For example: words: "yêu" as a noun when the "devil", when the verb is "love";
(5) Each word is composed of one or more syllables (morphemes), and the spaces between syllables and syllables are separated by spaces, for example "cơm" (cook) is composed of one syllable of the word; "dưa chuột" (cucumber) is composed of two syllables; "vội vội vàng vàng" (quickly) is composed of four syllable words. Vietnamese does not have a word delimiter, spaces are generally used to distinguish syllables, and no special markings to distinguish words.

3   Construction of Vietnamese Part of Speech Tagging Set

The effective POS tagging set plays an extremely important role in the work of POS tagging. Firstly, a large POS tagging set will increase the markup difficulties, not only in the notes on the corpus, but also on the final training of the POS tagging model; Secondly, a small POS tagging set can't provide enough text information. Therefore, we consider the above two factors and select the appropriate annotation set, which can express the information in the sentence decently, this is extremely important. For Vietnamese, it is difficult to design a good POS tagging set, because the classification of words is highly controversial [13, 14]. Ban and Ban [14] found in their research that the classification of words usually requires three conditions: meaning, group word ability and syntactic function. By analyzing and examining the linguistic features of these three aspects, we designed a POS tagging sets with nineteen tags in this paper, as shown in Table 1.

Table 1. POS tagging sets

POS	The meaning of POS	Examples
N	Common noun	Hiện nay, trung_ương, pháp_chế
E	Preposition	Ở, của, tại
CH	Punctuation	, ! ?
L	Numeral	Những, mọi, các
A	Adjective	Hươu, khoẻ_mạnh, phì
V	Verb	Bầu, được, uỷ_nhiệm
Ny	Proper noun abbreviation	GDP, USA, CHN
Cc	Alternative conjunction and Coordinate conjunction	Và, hay, hoặc
M	Number	Trăm, 4, 2008
R	Adverb	Lại, cũng, ngay
C	Conjunction	Nếu, mà, là
Nc	Unit noun	Ngôi, mảnh, thửa
Np	Proper noun	Hưng_Yên, Bắc_Bộ, Đức
Nu	Metric unit word	USD, ha, kg
X	Idioms, sayings, foreign languages	tại_sao, đến_nỗi, nhất_là
P	Pronoun	chúng_ta, tôi, gì
T	Adverb of degree and modal adverbs	Chính, thôi, đi
I	Interjections and modal words	ạ, ơi, hả
Z	Sino-Vietnamese words	Phó, nguyên, tái

4 Construction of Vietnamese POS Tagging Model

4.1 Dictionary of Multi-category Words and Non-multi-category Words

In this paper, we base on the Vietnamese dictionary and get multi-category words dictionary and non-multi-category words dictionary, in which the multi-category dictionary is 1659 words. The Vietnamese dictionary is from 131071 entries in the dictionary made and checked by our laboratory and 30565 entries crawled from the website (http://vdict.com/).

4.2 Multi-categories Words Corpus

In this paper, we collected a lot of news, entertainment, economy and other types of articles from the Vietnamese news website. The corpus should be treated as follows: first, after sorting, to noise and other operations, a text sentence level corpus was formed; secondly, the Vietnamese word segmentation tool was used to segment the text sentence, and manual proofreading by the Vietnamese language expert, thus forming a sentence-level word segmentation corpus; then making the POS tagging and chunking analysis; finally, using the Vietnamese dictionary, by selecting and extracting, to get multi-category words dictionary, in which 1659 words are included. Based on this dictionary, we program and extract 396946 Vietnamese multi-category words from the POS corpus constructed in advance, which will be used to construct the part of speech disambiguation model.

4.3 Building POS Tagging Model

The method of Vietnamese POS tagging based on multi-category words disambiguation model and Part of Speech dictionary was proposed in this paper, by dividing corpus into multi-category words and non-multi-category words, marking them respectively and to construct a Vietnamese Disambiguation Model, with a view to improving the correct rate of Vietnamese POS tagging. The system block diagram is shown in Fig. 1.

The principle of the proposed system is shown as in Fig. 2.

(1) Preparation of corpus and dictionary. We based on the Vietnamese dictionary and get multi-category words dictionary and non-multi-category words dictionary; and collected a lot of data from the Vietnamese website. By sorting, de-noising, and other operations, we got the sentences to be marked with parts of speech.

(2) Construction of the POS disambiguation model. Combined with Vietnamese characteristics, main Vietnamese POS tagging feature are selected, and the ME model is used to build the part of speech disambiguation model.

(3) Extraction of the multi-category words and non-multi-category words. We extract multi-category words and non-multi-category words from the test corpus for POS tagging based on the Vietnamese multi-category words dictionary;

(4) Automatic part of speech tagging. We match the non-multi-category words based on the Vietnamese non-multi-category words dictionary, match the multi-category words based on the disambiguation model, and then get the part of speech tagging result; finally, we combine the two results together to get the final result.

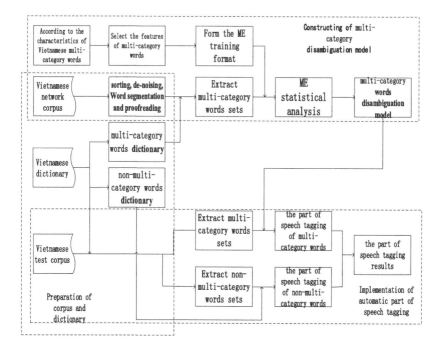

Fig. 1. POS tagging model building system diagram

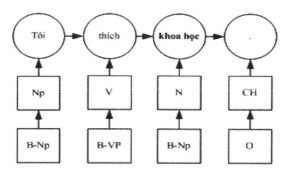

Fig. 2. Example of feature selection

5   Construction of the Part of Speech Disambiguation Model

Multi-functional words are prevalent in various languages, for the Vietnamese language, which also occupy a large proportion; whether or not the part of speech tag is correct directly affect the sentence POS tagging results, but also affect the surrounding POS tagging; In addition, multi-category word has great influence on text segmentation and Machine Translation. Therefore, to build the disambiguation model for multi-functional words is very important. The existing method to solve the problem is as follows: Zhi [15] put forward a POS tagging method in Chinese multi-category words based on Rough Sets a nd fuzzy neural network; Li [16] proposed a rules-based method for Chinese words Tagging, combined with Chinese language characteristics. Although above methods have achieved very good results, no research has been found in the Vietnamese language. In this paper, we trying to use the maximum entropy (http:// homepages.inf.ed.ac.uk/lzhang10/maxent_toolkit.html) model to solve the problem, this is because that, when modeling, you only need to focus on selecting features without having to spend much time considering how to use these features. This method has a flexible selection of features, no additional independent assumptions, strong portability, and a combination of rich information. It can make the unknown part of the amount of information to maximize (entropy to maximize) in the case of ensuring that the existing knowledge is not violated, and thus more suitable for the construction of the disambiguation model.

5.1   Selecting the Features for Multi-category Words

The model effect depends mainly on the quality of features, so it is very important to select good features. The main features in this paper are as follows: (1) Context information features of word or between words (word type contains rich form of information); (2) Contextual information features of Part of Speech (the part of speech can represent the decorate relationship between the part of speech); (3) Context information features of chunk or between chunks, which indicates the role of the word in the sentence, modify the relationship and other information; (4) Sentence component features (subject, predicate, adverbial, etc.). As shown in Fig. 3.

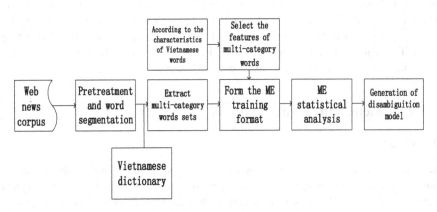

Fig. 3. Multi-category words disambiguation model

5.2   Constructing of Disambiguation Model

The construction of Disambiguation Model is a key part of POS tagging model, which can improve the accuracy of POS tagging and provide basic support for follow-up work. The construction principle of the model is shown in Fig. 4.

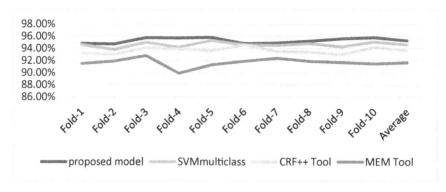

Fig. 4. Ten-fold cross experiment and model comparison

Firstly, using the web crawler program designed by us, we get the news and other different types of corpus, and made a pretreatment to them, such as: de-noising, word segmentation and other operations; secondly, based on the Vietnamese dictionary, the obtained corpus is matched to identify the multi-category word in the corpus set. Then, selecting the characteristics of the Vietnamese multi-category words and then integrating them into the training corpus. Finally, uses the maximum entropy model for statistical analysis, and generates the Vietnamese multi-category words disambiguation model.

5.3 Realizing of Part of Speech Tagging in Vietnamese

The detailed process of Vietnamese POS tagging is as follows: (1) Based on the Vietnamese words dictionary, extracting multi-category words and non-multi-category. (2) Using the disambiguation model get POS tagging result. (3) Extracting non-multi-category results from the non-multi-category words dictionary. (4) Combining the two results together, so as to get POS tagging result.

6 Experiment and Result Analysis

6.1 Data Sets

The data sets used in this paper are some Vietnamese sentence which was token up from the Vietnam News website, they are used as the training corpus and the test corpus. These crawled pages form a text corpus through rules extraction, duplicate removal, manual annotation, etc. The total size is the 27878 sentences and 396946 multi-category words field library, and they are encoded by UTF-8.

6.2 Experimental Evaluation

Precision is a field metric widely used in information retrieval and statistical classification to evaluate the quality of results. Similarly, we can use this evaluation method to use the word tagging task. With the help of the Vietnamese linguists, 27878 Vietnamese sentences were marked and 396,946 multi-category word fields were extracted by program, they are all for experimentation. The results of the word attribute is evaluated using the precision (P), as shown in formula (1).

$$P = \frac{\text{The number of correct parts of speech tagging}}{\text{The number of parts of speech tagging}} \tag{1}$$

The precision is between 0 and 1, and the closer the value is to 1, the higher the precision, the better the effect.

6.3   Experimental Design

In order to verify the performance of proposed system, we designed two sets of experiments to test it. Experiment 1 is mainly using MEM, CRF++, SVM-multiclass model and the proposed method (dictionary + disambiguation model) for comparative experiments; Experiment 2 is mainly used VietTagger developed by Hanoi University (http://vlsp.vietlp.org:8080/demo/?page=resources) and the proposed method in this paper for comparative experiments.

Experiment 1: the 27878 POS tagging of the corpus were divided into ten copies, and then tenfold the cross-validation test was made, i.e., using the popular model of MEM, CRF, SVM as well as the proposed model (dictionary + disambiguation model) for the experiments, comparing the average accuracy rate. The experimental results are shown in Fig. 5.

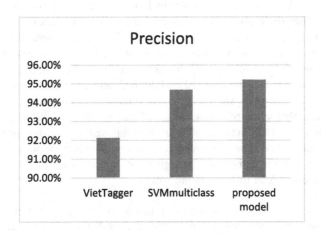

Fig. 5. POS tagging experimental results comparison

As can be seen from Fig. 5, the average accuracy rate of MEM, CRF++, SVM-multiclass, the proposed model is respectively 91.62%, 93.71%, 94.67% and 95.22%; in detail, the accuracy rate of SVM-multiclass model is 0.96% higher than that of

CRF++, and CRF++ is 2.09% higher than that of MEM. It is worth noting the accuracy rate of the proposed model is higher than SVM-multiclass model 0.55%. The experimental results shown that multi-category words disambiguation model can effectively improve the segmentation accuracy of Vietnamese.

Experiment 2: in order to verify the validity of the proposed system, the proposed model with existing POS tagging tools VietTagger and SVM-multiclass model were compared, the experimental results are shown in Table 2 and Fig. 5.

Table 2. POS tagging experimental results

System	Precision
VietTagger	92.13%
SVM-multiclass	94.67%
Proposed method	95.22%

As we can be seen from Fig. 5, the proposed method has achieved good results, 3.09% higher than that of the VietTagger, and 0.55% higher than that of the SVM multiclass, which proves that our method is effective and feasible.

7 Summary

In this paper, we propose a new method for Vietnamese part of speech tagging based on multi-category words disambiguation model. We first used the crawler program to get corpus on the Vietnam news website, including economic, political, cultural and military fields. Then these obtained corpus are processed to form a text corpus. In order to make better use of the corpus, these texts are divided into sentences as training corpus and test corpus, whose total size is the 27878 sentences and 396946 multi-category words field library, and they are encoded by UTF-8. At the same time, 19 kinds of annotation sets are collated and defined, and 27878 sentences were manually annotated; Furthermore, we select the characteristics of common features, special features and disambiguation of chunks as an effective feature of the proposed model. Finally, we prove the POS tagging effect of the proposed method by comparing with the existing main method. The experimental results show that the proposed method can effectively make the Vietnamese POS tagging with an accuracy rate of 95.22%. We hope our study could lead to more future works.

Acknowledgment. This work was supported in part by the key project of National Natural Science Foundation of China (Grant No. 61732005) and the National Natural Science Foundation of China (Grant Nos. 61262041, 61562052 and 61472168).

References

1. Brill, E., Pop, M.: Unsupervised learning of disambiguation rules for part-of-speech tagging. In: Armstrong, S., Church, K., Isabelle, P., Manzi, S., Tzoukermann, E., Yarowsky, D. (eds.) Natural Language Processing Using Very Large Corpora, vol. 11, pp. 27–42. Springer, Dordrecht (1999). https://doi.org/10.1007/978-94-017-2390-9_3
2. Hu, G., Zhang, J., Li, M.: Improved transformation based POS tagging of Latin Mongolian. Comput. Appl. **27**(4), 963–965 (2007). (in Chinese)
3. Wang, G., Wang, X.: POS tagging method based on rule priority. J. Anhui Univ. Technol. Nat. Sci. **25**(4), 426–429 (2008). (in Chinese)
4. Bernard, M.: Tagging English text with a probabilistic model. Comput. Linguist. **20**(2), 1–29 (1994)
5. Wang, L., Che, W., Liu, T.: Chinese POS tagging based on SVMTool. J. Chin. Inf. Process. **23**(4), 16–21 (2009). (in Chinese)
6. Binulal, G.S., Goud, P.A., Soman, K.P.: A SVM based approach to Telugu parts of speech tagging using SVMTool. Int. J. Recent Trends Eng. **1**(2), 183–185 (2009)
7. Nongmeikapam, K., Nonglenjaoba, L., Roshan, A., Singh, T.S., Singh, T.N., Bandyopadhyay, S.: Transliterated SVM based Manipuri POS tagging. In: Wyld, D., Zizka, J., Nagamalai, D. (eds.) ECCV 2012. AISC, vol. 166, pp. 989–999. Springer, Heidelberg (2012). https://doi.org/10.1007/978-3-642-30157-5_98
8. Jiang, S., Chen, Q.: Research on Japanese word segmentation and POS tagging based on rules and statistics. J. Chin. Inf. Process. **24**(1), 117–122 (2010). (in Chinese)
9. Nghiem, M., Dinh, D., Nguyen, M.: Improving Vietnamese POS tagging by integrating a rich feature set and support vector machines. In Proceedings of Research, Innovation and, Vision for the Future, RIVF, pp. 128–133 (2008)
10. Oanh, T.T., Cuong, A.L., Thuy, Q.H., Quynh, H.L.: An experimental study on Vietnamese POS tagging. In: Proceedings of International Conference on Asian Language Processing, IALP, Singapore (2009)
11. Phuong, L.-H., Azim, R.: An empirical study of maximum entropy approach for part-of-speech tagging of Vietnamese texts. In: Proceedings of TALN 2010, Montreal, Canada (2010)
12. Xiong, M.: Research on Vietnamese lexical analysis method. Kunming University of Science and Technology (2016)
13. Ban, D.Q., Ban, H.: Vietnamese Grammar. Education Publisher, Hanoi (2004)
14. Hoa, N.C.: Practical Vietnamese Grammar. Vietnam National University Publisher, Hanoi (2001)
15. Zhi, T., Zhang, Y.: The acquiring method of chinese ambiguity word POS tagging rules based on rough sets and fuzzy neural network. Comput. Eng. Appl. **38**(12), 89–91 (2002). (in Chinese)
16. Li, H., Jia, Z., Yin, H., et al.: Chinese ambiguity word's annotation based on rules. Comput. Appl. **34**(8), 2197–2201 (2014). (in Chinese)

NLP Applications

Unsupervised Automatic Text Style Transfer Using LSTM

Mengqiao Han[1], Ou Wu[2($\boxtimes$)], and Zhendong Niu[1($\boxtimes$)]

[1] School of Computer Science and Technology, Beijing Institute of Technology,
Beijing, China
{michellehan,zniu}@bit.edu.cn
[2] Center for Applied Mathematics, Tianjin University, Tianjin, China
wuou@tju.edu.cn

Abstract. In this paper, we focus on the problem of text style transfer which is considered as a subtask of paraphrasing. Most previous paraphrasing studies have focused on the replacements of words and phrases, which depend exclusively on the availability of parallel or pseudo-parallel corpora. However, existing methods can not transfer the style of text completely or be independent from pair-wise corpora. This paper presents a novel sequence-to-sequence (Seq2Seq) based deep neural network model, using two switches with tensor product to control the style transfer in the encoding and decoding processes. Since massive parallel corpora are usually unavailable, the switches enable the model to conduct unsupervised learning, which is an initial investigation into the task of text style transfer to the best of our knowledge. The results are analyzed quantitatively and qualitatively, showing that the model can deal with paraphrasing at different text style transfer levels.

Keywords: Style transfer · Unsupervised learning · Seq2Seq models

1 Introduction

Recently, style transfer has received increasing and tremendous attention among researchers from various disciplines. This technique has been successfully applied in artistic style transfer of pictures. For example, Gatys [10] used deep neural networks to capture the style of a source picture and the semantic content of a target picture independently, and then transferred the style of the target image by combining the target picture's semantic content with the source picture's style. However, the method proposed in image style transfer cannot be readily applied to the domain of natural language processing. Research on text style transfer is still in an early stage with a wealth of topics remains to be explored.

In natural language processing, style transfer is a part of paraphrasing. Paraphrasing is to express same ideas or present same information [2] in alternative ways, which is an evident subtask in many natural language processing applications, such as Information Retrieval (IR), Question Answering (QA), Information Extraction (IE), Summarization and Natural Language Generation [23].

© Springer International Publishing AG 2018
X. Huang et al. (Eds.): NLPCC 2017, LNAI 10619, pp. 281–292, 2018.
https://doi.org/10.1007/978-3-319-73618-1_24

Several studies have been dealing with paraphrase expression such as a word (lexical paraphrase) or a short phrase (phrasal paraphrase). Such paraphrasing is also called synonymizing, retaining same or similar lexical meaning of the word or the short phrase. The emergence of lexical databases such as WordNet was a significant milestone in this area.

When paraphrase expression becomes longer and more complicated, such as when a different sets of phrases are used to convey the same meaning, it is called syntactic paraphrase. For example, PPDB, a paraphrase database [9], provides an enormous collection of lexical, phrasal, and syntactic paraphrases. PPDB is released in six sizes (S to XXXL), ranging from highest precision/lowest recall to lowest average precision/highest recall. Many researchers have utilized this database to facilitate their research and have generated satisfactory results. Based on PPDB, Beltagy et al. [3] used Markov Logic Networks, and Bjerva et al. [4] adopted a system with formal semantics to recognize textual entailment (RTE). Ji and Eisenstein [14] combined latent features with fine-grained n-gram overlap features. Han et al. [11] used a lexical similarity feature that combined POS tagging, LSA word similarity and WordNet knowledge. Sultan et al. [29] considered the proportions of aligned content words in the two input sentences as semantic textual similarity scores to determine semantic text similarity. Post et al. [22] used a semi-Markov CRF for phrase-based monolingual alignment. Ganitkevitch et al. [8] introduced a method to learn syntactically-informed paraphrases for natural language generation. Yu and Dredze [33] and Rastogi et al. [24] made contributions to improve lexical embeddings. Most studies above applied supervised methods and relied heavily on parallel or pseudo-parallel corpora.

However, existing paraphrasing studies listed above have not focused on systematically transferring the style or register of a text. Systematic transformation is still a relatively unexplored field. Text style transfer focuses on generation, which is one of three related problems [23]: recognition (i.e. identifying whether two textual units are paraphrases of each other), extraction (i.e. extracting paraphrase instances from a thesaurus or a corpus) and generation (i.e. generating a reference paraphrase given a source text) [20]. Text style transfer can be ideally described as follows: given two sets of texts T_1 and T_2 with different styles S_1 and S_2 respectively, the model takes a sample $t_1 \in T_1$ in style S_1 as input and changes the text style from S_1 to S_2. The output $t_{n}ew$ is expected to be in style S_2 but carries the same meaning as t_1. The task is useful because it has many potential applications, such as mimicking celebrities' special speaking or writing styles (i.e. Trump twitter generator), publishing different versions of the same passage or information to reach diverse target audiences (i.e. versions of Bibles), and transforming a genre to make it fit on different platforms (i.e. twitter is shorter and much more casual than news).

To the best of our knowledge, existing studies on style transfer are either under supervised approach [31] or based on matching phrases extracted from corpora [19]. However, in most cases, parallel corpora between two styles are usually hard to find and it is difficult to collect enough parallel or pair-wise data for supervised training. We attempt to resolve such problems by introducing a novel sequence-to-sequence (Seq2Seq) based deep neural network model.

In this paper, we propose an unsupervised method to automatically transfer the style of a text (from early modern English employed by William Shakespeare to modern English) while at the same time retain the text's original semantic content.

The contributions of our works are as follows:

(1) We adopt an auto-encoder deep neural network model with long short-term memory (LSTM) [12] units to enable the encoder to learn a context vector and to decode the vector to words with a specific style;
(2) We introduce two switches with tensor product to control the source and the target styles, which enable unsupervised learning to be implemented in style transfer task;
(3) Unlike previous studies that failed to completely transform the text style, the style transfer method proposed in this paper transforms text's style not only on the lexical, phrasal, or syntactic levels, but also on higher levels including individuality and genre. The transformation is considered as a whole.

The rest of the paper is organized as follows. Section 2 briefly introduces the Seq2Seq deep neural network model and existing studies related to text style transfer. Section 3 describes our proposed Seq2Seq deep neural model for text style transfer (TSTSeq2Seq) that includes four important parts, i.e. switch, encoder, decoder and learning. Section 4 illustrates the details of the experiment, and analyzes the results quantitatively and qualitatively. The conclusions are given in Sect. 5.

2 Seq2Seq Model

The Seq2Seq model has become increasingly popular with its applications to various NLP tasks, such as machine translation [1], speech recognition [18], and dialogue systems [27] producing promising results.

A Seq2Seq model is a recurrent neural network (RNN) [21], which can take a sequence as input and generate a desired sequence. Two most widely used RNN are long short-term memory (LSTM) [12] and gated recurrent unit (GRU) [7].

The Seq2Seq model was first proposed by Sutskever et al. [30] for machine translation. In the model as shown in the Fig. 1, two LSTMs are concatenated

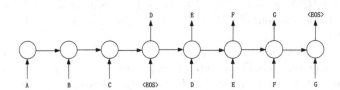

Fig. 1. A basic sequence-to-sequence model consists of two recurrent neural networks: an encoder and a decoder.

as an encoder and a decoder respectively, as LSTM can successfully deal with data with long range temporal dependencies. The target input information (i.e., A B C) will be encoded into an condensed context vector, then the decoder decodes the vector into a sequence of target information as output (i.e., D E F G). The whole process under the Seq2Seq model requires much less human efforts and hand-crafted feature engineering, than the state-of-the art statistical machine translation system Moses, proposed by Koehn et al. [17]. Attention mechanism was later introduced by Bahandatta et al. [1], promoting the model's effectiveness. Seq2Seq model has achieve promising performance in many other tasks besides machine translation.

While paraphrase recognition [16, 28, 32] employing classification techniques such as RAEs, CNNs or RNNs has achieved competitive performance, generating paraphrases is left out of the picture. The generation of paraphrases can be divided into a sequence to sequence learning problem. Nevertheless, generating paraphrases requires far more efforts than operating deep neural networks applications such as image artistic style transformation. Studies such as [13, 25] were among the first to introduce the Seq2Seq model [1] directly to the task of paraphrasing. Cao et al. [6] proposed a Seq2Seq model combined with a copying decoder and a restricted generative decoder to locate the position needed to be copied and to limit the output in the source-specific vocabulary respectively. Prakash et al. [23] initially explored deep learning models for paraphrase generation, proposing multiple stacked LSTM networks by introducing a residual connection between layers. Their proposed models help retain important words in the generated paraphrases.

Similar to the task of style transfer in paraphrasing, Liu et al. [19] proposed an approach to use anchoring-based paraphrase extraction and recurrent neural networks. However, paraphrase replacement in this model partly depends on PPDB paraphrases and can only replace words in a relatively stable position without high-level style transfer on syntactical structure level.

3   The Proposed Model

The Text Style Transfer Seq2Seq model (TSTSeq2Seq) we proposed introduces two switches and some improvements into the general Seq2Seq (encoder-decoder) structure, as illustrated in Fig. 2.

According to Fig. 2, the source text sequence first goes through a switch that embeds the style of the input text. A RNN encoder transforms the information accessed by the switch into a context vector. The context representation is then processed by a RNN decoder and by the second switch that determines the style of the output information. Finally, the target sequence is generated. The details are as follows.

We denote s as a sequence of inputs $s = \{w^1, w^2, \ldots, w^N\}$, where N denotes the length of the sentence. Each sentence ends with a token "$ends$" . The word w is associated with a M-dimensional embedding e_w where $e_w = \{e_w^1, e_w^2, \ldots, e_w^M\}$. Let V denote the vocabulary size. Each sentence s is associated with a M-dimensional representation e_s, $e_s = \{e_{w^1}, e_{w^2}, \ldots, e_{w^N}\}$.

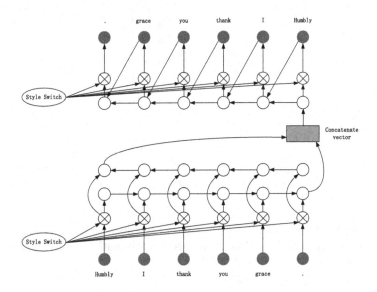

Fig. 2. The architecture of TSTSeq2Seq model

An autoencoder is a neural model where the output units are identical to or directly connected with the input units. Inputs are accessed into a compressed representation by encoding, which is then used to reconstruct it back by decoding. For a sentence autoencoder, both the input X and the output Y are the same sentence s. Four important parts to the proposed model are as follows.

Switch. We introduce a style switch that consists of a tensor product to enable the model to conduct unsupervised learning. The style switch is necessary in our model because pair-wise data is insufficient to conduct supervised learning and unsupervised learning requires a switch to enable the separately training of the autoencoder for two different style of text. Since we seek to transfer a text from one style (a) to another (b), the tensor is set at two values s_i, with i being either a or b. The switch is $s_a = (0, 1)$, when the input sequence is in stye a. The switch will turn into $s_b = (1, 0)$, when the input sequence is in style b. We take an example to explain how tensor product works specifically, which is illustrated in Fig. 3.

s_i decides the input information to be either on the left or the right during a tensor product function, and the weight between the switch and the input of LSTM will be trained accordingly. Therefore, the output of the switch is as follows:

$$x_t^{wi} = W_{se}(s_i \otimes e_t^{wi}), i \in [a, b] . \tag{1}$$

where e_t^{wi} and x_t^{wi} denotes embedding for word and input for LSTM at position t respectively. The subscripts in Eq. (1) indicate time step t, and the superscripts indicate operations of word in style wi. As a result of the operation of tensor

$$x_i \otimes s_a = \begin{bmatrix} x_1 \\ x_2 \\ x_3 \\ x_4 \end{bmatrix} \begin{bmatrix} 0 & 1 \end{bmatrix} = \begin{bmatrix} 0 & x_1 \\ 0 & x_2 \\ 0 & x_3 \\ 0 & x_4 \end{bmatrix}$$

$$y_i \otimes s_b = \begin{bmatrix} y_1 \\ y_2 \\ y_3 \\ y_4 \end{bmatrix} \begin{bmatrix} 1 & 0 \end{bmatrix} = \begin{bmatrix} y_1 & 0 \\ y_2 & 0 \\ y_3 & 0 \\ y_4 & 0 \end{bmatrix}$$

Fig. 3. An example of tensor product

product of style switch s_i and word in style i, weight matrices W_{se} between the switch and the input of LSTM is trained separately without overlapping along the changes in the switch.

Encoder. We build the encoder based on Sutskever's work [30]. Specifically, we use LSTM as the recurrent unit, which often gains a better performance compared to the vanilla RNN. The Bi-directional Recurrent Neural Network (BRNN) [26] is introduced to ensure that the output layer is aware of the contextual information from both of the future and the past states. Then, we concatenate the last states of both forward direction and backward directions together as concatenate vector, which conveys the compressed context information. The encoder is built as follows:

$$\begin{bmatrix} i_t \\ f_t \\ o_t \\ \overline{c_t} \end{bmatrix} = \begin{bmatrix} \sigma \\ \sigma \\ \sigma \\ \tanh \end{bmatrix} W \cdot \begin{bmatrix} \overrightarrow{h_{t-1}} \\ x_t^{wi} \end{bmatrix} . \tag{2}$$

$$c_t = f_t \cdot c_{t-1} + i_t \cdot \overline{c_t} . \tag{3}$$

$$\overrightarrow{h_t^{wi}}(enc) = o_t \cdot c_t . \tag{4}$$

For simplicity, we define $LSTM(x_t^{wi}, \overrightarrow{h_{t-1}}(enc))$ to be the $LSTM$ operation on vectors x_t^{wi} and $\overrightarrow{h_{t-1}}(enc)$ to achieve $\overrightarrow{h_t^{wi}}(enc)$ as in Eqs. (2), (3) and (4). Then we obtain:

$$\overrightarrow{h_t^{wi}}(enc) = LSTM(x_t^{wi}, \overrightarrow{h_{t-1}^{wi}}(enc)) . \tag{5}$$

$$h_s = [\overrightarrow{h_N^{wi}}(enc); \overleftarrow{h_1^{wi}}(enc)] . \tag{6}$$

In Eq. (6), h_s is a concatenate vector of the last states of BRNN in two directions and is regarded as the input to the decoder.

Decoder. As with encoding, the decoding operates on a unidirectional RNN with LSTMs. LSTM outputs at word level for time step t after the control of the switch are obtained by:

$$h_t^{wi}(dec) = LSTM(x_t^{wi}, h_{t-1}^{wi}) . \tag{7}$$

$$y_{t-1}^{wi} = W_{sd}(s_i \otimes h_{t-1}^{wi}(dec)), i \in [a, b] . \tag{8}$$

$$p(w|\cdot) = soft\max(e_w, y_{t-1}^{wi}) . \tag{9}$$

During decoding, the initial time step for Eq. (7) is $h_0^{wi}(d) = h_s$. $LSTM$ word-decoding generates a word token $h_t^{wi}(dec)$ along every time step sequentially. The embedding is then combined with earlier hidden vectors after the switch for the next time step prediction until the ends token is predicted.

Learning. The maximization likelihood estimation (MLE) is used to infer model parameters. Similar to most existing Seq2Seq models, we use cross entropy (CE) to measure the difference of probability distributions. The error of which is back propagated through LSTM. We then apply Adam optimizer [15] with mini-batches to fine tune the weights of the model, as Adam is a popular optimizer to train RNN.

During the training stage, we simultaneously set switches both in encoding and decoding layers to $S_a = [0, 1]$ when the style of the input text is a, and set both switches to $S_b = [1, 0]$ when the style of the input text is b. The switches are simultaneously assigned according to the style of the input.

4 Experiments

We use Shakespeare's plays as training and testing data for the task of paraphrasing owing a specific writing style. These plays are regarded as the most highly-regarded pieces of old English literature and which were written by a famous writer dated from 400 years ago. There are many linguistic resources available online to facilitate our research. We collected 17 Shakespeare plays from Sparknotes website, which is a corpus with corresponding relationship between early modern English employed by William Shakespeare and modern English.

The task is to transfer the style of Shakespeare's text into the style of modern English, while keeping the overall semantic content. In deep learning, a massive data set is usually required to feed into the neural network to get a well-trained model compared with the statistical machine translation (SMT) [5] method. Even though the corpus on Sparknotes is pair-wise, it is still too small to conduct supervised training for the utilized deep model. As a result, we separately train early modern English by Shakespeare and modern English by the autoencoder model with two different switches to control the learning of the styles.

The plays were sentence aligned after tokenizing and lowercasing, producing a total of 42,158 sentence pairs in the Sparknotes data. To utilize the dataset more sufficiently, we perform cross-validation. Specifically, we randomly shuffled and divided the data set into three parts with 33,726 sentences in both styles for training, 4,216 for validation, and 4,216 for testing.

Due to the insufficient data for deep LSTMs, we adopted a two-layer autoencoder and made some improvements upon it. Each LSTM layer consists of 512 hidden neurons and the dimensionality of word embeddings is set to 512.

At the testing stage, the test data in Shakespeare style was fed into the trained model. We set the encoding switch from S_a to S_b to encode and to transfer the style at the same time. The concatenate vector we got at the last time step of encoding was a style-transferred but context-unchanged unit. And then the vector was read by the decoder and the switch was changed into S_b as well, in order to get the modern English paraphrase.

As for evaluation, traditional evaluation metrics such as BLEU score are often considered useful in evaluating the quality of automatic paraphrasing. We computed the BLEU scores of the two models, and the results are shown in Table 1. Our model TSTSeq2Seq with two switches, turned out to achieve a score of **47.47**, higher than the score achieved by the TSTSeq2Seq model with one switch in decoding turned on during testing. Even though the score we achieved is lower than the 66.28 score achieved by the supervised model with default Moses parameters, our model provides a reasonable intuition to conduct text style transfer with non-parallel data. According to the table, it suggests that the switch in the encoding phrase can help change the style of a text and still convey the semantic content of the text to the decoder.

Table 1. BLEU scores of different methods for Shakespearean paraphrase.

Method	Description	BLEU
TSTSeq2Seq_1Switch	Improved Seq2Seq model with only the switch on decoding level turned on during testing using shuffled training set, validation set and testing set mentioned in the experiment part	46.26
TSTSeq2Seq	Improved Seq2Seq model with two switches both on encoding and decoding levels turned on during testing using shuffled training set, validation set and testing set mentioned in the experiment part	47.47

However, we did not use parallel texts for training, and the traditional evaluation metrics such as BLEU scores are therefore meaningless and unconvincing to us [19]. Thus, we evaluated the result of text style transfer intuitively. Examples of style-transferred output sentences as outputs are listed in Table 2.

The paraphrases sampled from the test set can be sorted into different levels of style transfer. Replacements includes changing the word from "ouse" into "revive", the phrase from "come to" into "arrived in", the syntactic from "where was this?" to "where did this happen?". Changes even happen at the general style

Table 2. Examples of style-transferred paraphrases from early modern English by Shakespeare to modern English

Input	Output
but where was this?	but where did this happen?
and wherefore doth lysander deny your love, so rich within his soul, and tender me, forsooth, affection, but by your setting on, by your consent?	and why does lysander deny that he loves you, when he loves you so deeply?
his son was but a ward two years ago	his son was a minor only two years ago.
sir, octavius is already come to rome	sir, octavius has already arrived in rome.
i see him rouse himself to praise my noble act	i see him revive himself to praise my noble act.
where is montjoy the herald?	where is montjoy, the herald?
for, you know, pyramus and thisbe meet by moonlight	because, you know, pyramus and thisbe meet by moonlight.
there was more foolery yet, if i could remember it	there was even more foolishness, if i could only remember it.
o you gods!	oh, you gods!
is that his answer?	is that his answer?
good words are better than bad strokes, octavius	good words are better than bad strokes, octavius.
where is montjoy the herald?	where is montjoy, the herald?

level such as from "wherefore doth lysander deny your love, so rich within his soul, and tender me, forsooth, affection, but by your setting on, by your consent?" to "and why does lysander deny that he loves you, when he loves you so deeply?". In some circumstances, a transferred text in modern English remains the same as the text in the style of Shakespeare's old English. For example, the sentence "good words are better than bad strokes, octavius". remains unchanged. These results can partially verify the effectiveness of the introduction of the switch and style transfer mechanism with autoencoder model in capturing contextual and structural information.

5 Conclusions

In this paper, we have explored automatic text style transfer task by targeting a specific writing style based on our proposed sequence-to-sequence LSTM model. Given that it is impractical to collect sufficient labeled data for the training of a standard deep neural network, we adopted a novel approach in using Shakespeare's plays and their translation in modern English to separately implement unsupervised learning.

In the TSTSeq2Seq model proposed by us, two switches are introduced to control the style of the encoding and the decoding phrases. The two switches allow the model to capture the input's semantic content in a style and to decode the content into another specific output style. Our study suggests that style transfer can be conducted not only at the lexical, phrasal or syntactic levels, but also on a higher level, such as author's individualized writing style and genre preference. The proposed model in this paper can substitute the overall style of a text at the consideration of the whole sentence while preserving the semantic meaning of the original text.

While our work on autoencoder for a sentence with a specific style is only a preliminary effort toward allowing neural models to automatically deal with text style transfer, it nonetheless suggests that neural models are capable of extracting the context information from a stylized text and applying style transfer on it.

References

1. Bahdanau, D., Cho, K., Bengio, Y.: Neural machine translation by jointly learning to align and translate. arXiv preprint arXiv:1409.0473 (2014)
2. Barzilay, R.: Information fusion for multidocument summarization: paraphrasing and generation. Ph.D. thesis, Columbia University (2003)
3. Beltagy, I., Roller, S., Boleda, G., Erk, K., Mooney, R.J.: Utexas: natural language semantics using distributional semantics and probabilistic logic. In: SemEval 2014, p. 796 (2014)
4. Bjerva, J., Bos, J., Van der Goot, R., Nissim, M.: The meaning factory: formal semantics for recognizing textual entailment and determining semantic similarity. In: Proceedings of SemEval (2014)
5. Brown, P.F., Cocke, J., Pietra, S.A.D., Pietra, V.J.D., Jelinek, F., Lafferty, J.D., Mercer, R.L., Roossin, P.S.: A statistical approach to machine translation. Comput. Linguist. **16**(2), 79–85 (1990)
6. Cao, Z., Luo, C., Li, W., Li, S.: Joint copying and restricted generation for paraphrase. arXiv preprint arXiv:1611.09235 (2016)
7. Chung, J., Gulcehre, C., Cho, K., Bengio, Y.: Empirical evaluation of gated recurrent neural networks on sequence modeling. arXiv preprint arXiv:1412.3555 (2014)
8. Ganitkevitch, J., Callison-Burch, C., Napoles, C., Van Durme, B.: Learning sentential paraphrases from bilingual parallel corpora for text-to-text generation. In: Proceedings of the Conference on Empirical Methods in Natural Language Processing, pp. 1168–1179. Association for Computational Linguistics (2011)
9. Ganitkevitch, J., Van Durme, B., Callison-Burch, C.: PPDB: the paraphrase database. In: HLT-NAACL, pp. 758–764 (2013)
10. Gatys, L.A., Ecker, A.S., Bethge, M.: Image transfer using convolutional neural networks. In: Proceedings of the IEEE Conference on Computer Vision and Pattern Recognition, pp. 2414–2423 (2016)
11. Han, L., Kashyap, A., Finin, T., Mayfield, J., Weese, J.: UMBC EBIQUITY-CORE: semantic textual similarity systems. In: Proceedings of the Second Joint Conference on Lexical and Computational Semantics. vol. 1, pp. 44–52 (2013)
12. Hochreiter, S., Schmidhuber, J.: Long short-term memory. Neural Comput. **9**(8), 1735–1780 (1997)

13. Hu, B., Chen, Q., Zhu, F.: LCSTS: a large scale Chinese short text summarization dataset. arXiv preprint arXiv:1506.05865 (2015)
14. Ji, Y., Eisenstein, J.: Discriminative improvements to distributional sentence similarity. In: EMNLP, pp. 891–896 (2013)
15. Kingma, D., Ba, J.: Adam: a method for stochastic optimization. arXiv preprint arXiv:1412.6980 (2014)
16. Kiros, R., Zhu, Y., Salakhutdinov, R.R., Zemel, R., Urtasun, R., Torralba, A., Fidler, S.: Skip-thought vectors. In: Advances in Neural Information Processing Systems, pp. 3294–3302 (2015)
17. Koehn, P., Hoang, H., Birch, A., Callison-Burch, C., Federico, M., Bertoldi, N., Cowan, B., Shen, W., Moran, C., Zens, R., et al.: Moses: open source toolkit for statistical machine translation. In: Proceedings of the 45th Annual Meeting of the ACL on Interactive Poster and Demonstration Sessions, pp. 177–180. Association for Computational Linguistics (2007)
18. Li, X., Wu, X.: Constructing long short-term memory based deep recurrent neural networks for large vocabulary speech recognition. In: 2015 IEEE International Conference on Acoustics, Speech and Signal Processing (ICASSP), pp. 4520–4524. IEEE (2015)
19. Liu, G., Rosello, P., Sebastian, E.: Style transfer with non-parallel corpora. http://prosello.com/papers/style-transfer-s16.pdf
20. Madnani, N., Dorr, B.J.: Generating phrasal and sentential paraphrases: a survey of data-driven methods. Comput. Linguist. **36**(3), 341–387 (2010)
21. Mikolov, T., Karafiát, M., Burget, L., Cernocký, J., Khudanpur, S.: Recurrent neural network based language model. In: Interspeech, vol. 2, p. 3 (2010)
22. Post, M., Ganitkevitch, J., Orland, L., Weese, J., Cao, Y., Callison-Burch, C., Irvine, A., Zaidan, O.F., et al.: Semi-Markov phrase-based monolingual alignment. In: Proceedings of EMNLP, vol. 1, pp. 166–177. Association for Computational Linguistics (2013)
23. Prakash, A., Hasan, S.A., Lee, K., Datla, V., Qadir, A., Liu, J., Farri, O.: Neural paraphrase generation with stacked residual LSTM networks. arXiv preprint arXiv:1610.03098 (2016)
24. Rastogi, P., Van Durme, B., Arora, R.: Multiview LSA: representation learning via generalized CCA. In: HLT-NAACL, pp. 556–566 (2015)
25. Rush, A.M., Chopra, S., Weston, J.: A neural attention model for abstractive sentence summarization. arXiv preprint arXiv:1509.00685 (2015)
26. Schuster, M., Paliwal, K.K.: Bidirectional recurrent neural networks. IEEE Trans. Signal Process. **45**(11), 2673–2681 (1997)
27. Serban, I.V., Klinger, T., Tesauro, G., Talamadupula, K., Zhou, B., Bengio, Y., Courville, A.: Multiresolution recurrent neural networks: an application to dialogue response generation. arXiv preprint arXiv:1606.00776 (2016)
28. Socher, R., Huang, E.H., Pennington, J., Ng, A.Y., Manning, C.D.: Dynamic pooling and unfolding recursive autoencoders for paraphrase detection. In: NIPS, vol. 24, pp. 801–809 (2011)
29. Sultan, M.A., Bethard, S., Sumner, T.: DLS@CU: sentence similarity from word alignment. In: Proceedings of the 8th International Workshop on Semantic Evaluation (SemEval 2014), pp. 241–246 (2014)
30. Sutskever, I., Vinyals, O., Le, Q.V.: Sequence to sequence learning with neural networks. In: Advances in Neural Information Processing Systems. pp. 3104–3112 (2014)

31. Xu, W., Ritter, A., Dolan, W.B., Grishman, R., Cherry, C.: Paraphrasing for style. In: 24th International Conference on Computational Linguistics, COLING 2012 (2012)
32. Yin, W., Schütze, H.: Convolutional neural network for paraphrase identification. In: Proceedings of the 2015 Conference of the North American Chapter of the Association for Computational Linguistics: Human Language Technologies, pp. 901–911 (2015)
33. Yu, M., Dredze, M.: Improving lexical embeddings with semantic knowledge. In: ACL (2), pp. 545–550 (2014)

Optimizing Topic Distributions of Descriptions for Image Description Translation

Jian Tang, Yu Hong$^{(\boxtimes)}$, Mengyi Liu, Jiashuo Zhang, and Jianmin Yao

Soochow University, Suzhou, Jiangsu, China
johnnytang1120@gmail.com, tianxianer@gmail.com, mengyiliu22@gmail.com,
jiasurezhang@gmail.com, jyao@suda.edu.cn

Abstract. Image Description Translation (IDT) is a task to automatically translate the image captions (i.e., image descriptions) into the target language. Current statistical machine translation (SMT) cannot perform as well as usual in this task because there is lack of topic information provided for translation model generation. In this paper, we focus on acquiring the possible contexts of the captions so as to generate topic models with rich and reliable information. The image matching technique is utilized in acquiring the relevant Wikipedia texts to the captions, including the captions of similar Wikipedia images, the full articles that involve the images and the paragraphs that semantically correspond to the images. On the basis, we go further to approach topic modelling using the obtained contexts. Our experimental results show that the obtained topic information enhances the SMT of image caption, yielding a performance gain of no less than 1% BLUE score.

1 Introduction

The caption is defined as a short text which specially describes the image it attached with. Caption translation [6] is admittedly very practical for many current industrial applications, such as e-commerce, social media and computational advertising. By the rapid and effective caption translation (of course in a fashion of automatic processing), users can easily understand the meanings, intentions and subjects of the images posted (or released) in the foreign websites, medium or literatures.

For example, the image in Fig. 1 shows different types of *"Bacalhau"* (in spanish *Bacalhau* means Gadus, a kind of fish living in Atlantic), and the inner captions in the photo detail the difference, including special long-island Gadus, pubertal island Gadus, etc. It is very difficult for a Chinese customer rapidly get deep insight into the difference among the piles of fishes, no matter from the perspective of the objects or the languages in the captions. In this case, theoretically speaking, caption translation can help the user figure out the difference and make a correct decision during the purchase process.

The closely related study to the caption translation is IDT [11], which is newly proposed in the inter-discipline of image processing and language processing. It follows a strict task definition, where the translator is required to translate

© Springer International Publishing AG 2018
X. Huang et al. (Eds.): NLPCC 2017, LNAI 10619, pp. 293–304, 2018.
https://doi.org/10.1007/978-3-319-73618-1_25

Fig. 1. An image and its corresponding captions

a short caption into the target language, under the condition that there isn't any available reference data (contexts, topics and articles) except the corresponding image. In this paper, we limit our research to the IDT schema, including the task definition, corpus and evaluation metric.

Topic information [14,25,27] is admittedly very important for SMT. The topics of a text span (clause or sentence) and the ones of its contexts are constructive to speculating about the correct translations of words, phrases or even the whole text span. For example, the English word "*mouse*" may mean a "*rat*" or a "*cursor controller*", and if provided with the topic about "*wild kingdom*", the translator could correctly translates it as a word of the meaning "*rat*" in the target language.

However, in IDT, there is absence of available contexts for detecting the related topics, and more seriously the caption is generally short and therefore involves fewer informative words for topic modelling, such as the caption "*white mouse, gray mouse and yellow mouse*". Thus when we directly employ an existing SMT system, the commonly-used linguistic knowledge and translation knowledge are actually task-independent. This will unavoidably reduce the translation quality.

In order to overcome the problem, we propose to use the image as a query to retrieve the related contexts to the captions [7]. And then, we use the contexts to reinforce topic modelling in the process of learning language and translation. In practice, we employ a deep convolutional neural network based image processing techniques to implement image-image matching, and further collect wikipedia web pages that contain the similar images. By using the articles in the web pages as the contexts, we re-build the topic model of the target caption and further re-train the language and translation models. In our experiments, our method improves the traditional SMT system [26] with a performance gain of no less than 1% BLUE score.

The rest of the paper is organized as below. In Sect. 2, we detail our approach. Section 3 shows the experimental settings, results and analysis. In Sect. 4, we briefly overview the related work. We draw our conclusion in Sect. 5.

2   Methodology

In order to overcome the shortcomings of translating ambiguous words in captions, we acquire informative and related contexts of the captions from Wikipedia webpages. On the basis, we leverage the contexts to topic modelling for the captions. As what we will show in the upcoming sections, the key issue is to precisely extract the related contexts from the webpages. In this section, we first present the methodological framework and then detail the components respectively.

2.1   Framework

Our approach consists of four primary components, including (1) image search based relevant document acquisition, (2) related context extraction, (3) topic re-modelling and (4) SMT using informative topic models.

We build an image search engine to acquire the Wikipedia webpages which contain similar images to the image of the target caption. The so-called target caption is specified as the caption in the test data, i.e., the one we aim to translate into the target language. In this phase, we employ the dump file of Wikipedia to build a local multimodal database. The database regards the images as indexes. It also preserves the correspondence between the images and their captions and the documents where they occur. In Sect. 2.2, we focus on the deep CNN based image-image matching, which is the most crucial step for acquiring the relevant documents.

When using the image of a target caption as the query to perform information retrieval, we obtain the most relevant document (webpage) to the caption in the database. Such a document is recalled because it contains an image which is visually-similar to the image of the target caption. In order to facilitate the reading of this paper, we simply name the visually-similar image as the mirror image (Mir) in Wikipedia webpage, and the document which holds the Mir as the container (Cnt).

The (Cnt) additionally contains a article and the caption of the Mir. This caption (Mir's caption) can be jointly used with the target caption to provide richer information for topic modelling. But in this paper, we focus on the utilization of the article. Simply, the full text of the article can be directly used as the related context to the target caption. It is because the text is closely related to the Mir. But we argue that there are also many unrelated information in the text, which probably mislead the topic modelling of the target caption. For example, in a Wikipedia webpage about Gadus, there are many blocks corresponding to other name entities and images, such as Department of Fisheries, policies, persons, events and even a book titled with "*The Old Man and the Sea*". Therefore, we come up with the extraction of closely-related contexts from the article. In Sect. 2.3, we will detail the context extraction approach, and in our experiments (Sect. 3), we compare the effects of the caption of the Mir, full text of the article and the extracted contexts on the topic remodelling based caption translation.

Using the contexts extracted from the relevant articles, we remodel the topic of the target caption and put it into use for enhancing the translation model (Sect. 2.4).

2.2   Image Search

We regard the image of the target caption as a query, and search the relevant document (Cnt) in the multimodal database by image-image matching.

We encode the images as image embeddings and use Euclidean distance between embeddings to measure visual similarity. Each image embedding is consisted of a series of image block embeddings. An image block serves as the elementary visual semantics, as usual, occupying a region of 3×3 pixels (see Fig. 2.). To some extent, it plays a role of basic semantic unit just like that of word in linguistics. The block embedding is specified as a vector of real numbers. Each number corresponds to the color value of a pixel. When generating the whole embedding of the image, we first collect all possible blocks by successively moving a sliding window in the size of 3×3 pixels with a margin of 1 pixel, and then concatenate all the block embeddings to compose a uniform vector representation (see Fig. 2.).

Features of images in all datasets were extracted using the 16-layer version of VGGNet (VGG-16)[1] [23], which is a Deep Convolutional Neural Network (CNN) pre-trained on 1,000 object categories of the classification/localization task of the ImageNet Large Scale Visual Recognition Challenge (ILSVRC) [20]. We used Caffe to extract the fully-connected layer (FC7) of VGG-16 before applying the softmax function. The 4096 dimensional vectors from this layer provide the content of images.

2.3   Context Extraction

We select sentences from the article Cnt to form the contexts of the target caption. The sentences are constrained to be relevant to the caption of the mirror image (Mir). Different from the traditional bag-of-word based approach, we introduce sentence-level embeddings into the solution.

By tokenization, we transform a candidate sentence into a series of words. We follow [12] to represent a word with an embedding. Word embedding is a vector of real numbers [16] which is trained to be meaningful using massive semantic contexts. It is capable of representing an unique word sense and the local semantics of the surroundings. We generate the word embedding for each word in the candidate sentence, and concatenate all the embeddings to form a simple sentence-level embedding. Further, an average operation based convolution computing is used to generate a fixed-size sentence embedding.

In practice, we compute embeddings directly by word2vec[2] [11], which is pre-trained over the English articles in the latest 2015 wikipedia dump. We follow [4]

---

[1] https://github.com/ry/tensorflow-vgg16.
[2] https://github.com/jhlau/doc2vec.

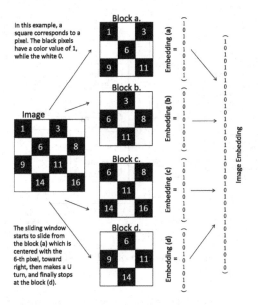

Fig. 2. Image embedding generation

to preprocess the articles, and perform pre-training using the skip-gram architecture [16]. We use a 100 dimensional vector as the word embedding. Euclidean distance is used to measure the similarity between the candidate sentences and the *Mir*'s caption. The candidates which have a similarity no less than the threshold 0.35 will be eventually selected as the relevant contexts.

The semantics based similarity computing generally causes the selection of the over-similar sentences from the *Cnt*. In our case, the contexts are expected to entail more different but related information. In order to meet this requirement, we expand the contexts by involving the sentences around the semantically-similar sentences. We set a sliding window to control the range of expansion. The maximum margins is set as the head and the tail of the paragraph which contains the sentences. In our experiments, we evaluate the effect of different sizes of contexts on the caption translation.

2.4   Topic Remodelling Based Translation Model Reinforcement

The purpose of this part is to integrate the topic distributions into the phrase table in the form of features, which aims at optimizing the translation model. Figure 3 depicts the basic structure of SMT system. The SMT system consists of three modules: translation model, language model and reordering model. We train translation model and reordering model by parrallel training corpus, but just use monolingual corpus of target language to train language model.

Euclidean distance between source image and images in multimodal database will be sorted from small to large, and we select Top10 images as similar images.

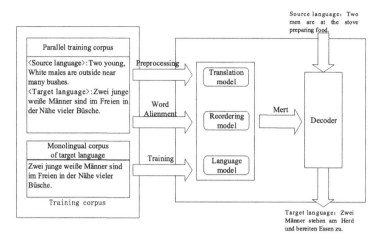

Fig. 3. Structure of SMT system

The average vector of topic distributions of pseudo-documents is used to infer topic distribution of source caption. We use Latent Dirichlet Allocation (LDA)[3] [1] to learn topic distributions of these pseudo-documents and set the dimension of topic vectors to 100. The formula for acquiring the topic distribution is shown as follows:

$$P(T) = \frac{\sum\limits_{i=1}^{10} P_i(T)}{10} \tag{1}$$

$P_i(T)$ denotes the probability that document of i-th similar images belongs to topic T.

We use features extracted from topic distributions to optimize translation model. Features contain positive translation probability, negative translation probability and the topic sensitivity of the phrase pair.

In the training corpus, N denotes the set of sentence pairs which contain phrase pairs (s,t). M denotes the set of sentence pairs which contain source phrase s. K denotes the set of sentence pairs which contains target phrase t. The formulas of positive translation probability are drawn as follows:

$$P(t|s,T) = \frac{\sum\limits_{i=1}^{n} Count_i(s,t)P_i(T)}{\sum\limits_{j=1}^{m} (\sum_{t'} Count_j(s,t'))P_j(T)} \tag{2}$$

$$P(t|s) = \sum\limits_{i=1}^{100} P(t|s,T_i)P(T_i) \tag{3}$$

---

[3] https://github.com/mrquincle/gibbs-lda.

The formulas of negative translation probability are shown as follows:

$$P(s|t,T) = \frac{\sum_{i=1}^{n} Count_i(s,t)P_i(T)}{\sum_{j=1}^{k} (\sum_{s}' Count_j(s',t))P_j(T)} \tag{4}$$

$$P(s|t) = \sum_{i=1}^{100} P(s|t,T_i)P(T_i) \tag{5}$$

The sensitivity of phrase pairs is expressed in terms of cross-entropy and the formulas are constructed as follows:

$$C(T_j) = \sum_{i=1}^{n} Count_i(s,t)P_i(T_j) \tag{6}$$

$$Entropy(s,t) = -\sum_{i=1}^{100} C_i log(C_i) \tag{7}$$

where s denotes source phrase and t denotes target phrase. $P(t|s,T)$ denotes the probability of translating s to t in topic T. $Count_i(s,t)$ denotes the number of phrase pair (s,t) contained in the i-th sentence.

3   Experiments

3.1   Corpus

The data of local multimodal database is from Wikipedia. Training, Development and Test sets are from Multi30k dataset [5] which is an extension of the Flickr30k dataset [19]. The datasets of classification task in this paper are from MS COCO 2014 [15] which contains about 80,000 images with 5 English captions per image. Table 1 shows the distribution of experimental data:

Table 1. Experimental corpus

Data	Source	Scale
Multimodal database	Wikipedia	About 300K
Training set	Multi30k	29K
Development set	Multi30k	1,014
Test set	Multi30k	1,000
Classification images	MS COCO	About 80K
Classification captions	MS COCO	About 400K

3.2   Settings

Our submissions are based on the NiuTrans SMT toolkit [26] to build phrase-based SMT models. They are constructed as follows: First, word alignments in both directions are calculated using GIZA++ [18]. The phrases and reordering tables are extracted using the default settings of the NiuTrans toolkit. The parameters of NiuTrans were tuned on the provided development set, using the MERT [17] algorithm. 3-gram back-off language were built using SRILM [24] and the target side of the parallel corpus. Training was performed using only the data provided by the task organizers, and so systems were built in the constrained setting. The results are evaluated by BLEU-4 value which is case-insensitive. In order to train the translation model incorporating topic information, this paper uses Gibbs sampling method to infer the parameters of LDA model, and uses GibbsLDA++ open source tool to infer the topic distributions. The topic model tool used in this paper uses the following parameters: the number of topics is 100, the super parameters are set to 0.05, and the number of iterations is set to 1000. The image feature is extracted by VGG-16.

In this paper, we conduct nine experiments based on the viewpoint that accurate topic distribution is good for the task of IDT. For Baseline, we conduct a phrase-based translation system that includes translation model, language model and reordering model. Other experiments contain different ways to acquire topic distributions of captions. We acquire topic distributions of source captions from three respects.

Captions from different sources are used to extract topic distribution of captions attached to source images by GPUDMM [13]. Experiments in Table 2 show different sources of captions.

Table 2. Acquiring topic distributions from captions

Methods	Source of caption
DES_GDMM	Captions attached to source images
DES_GDMM_LIB	Captions attached to images in multimodal database

We use different matching methods to acquire articles. These articles are applied to extract topic distributions of captions attached to source images by LDA. Experiments in Table 3 show different matching methods.

Table 3. Different retrieval methods for topic distribution

Methods	Matching methods
IR_ALLTEXT	Image retrieval
TR_ALLTEXT	Text retrieval

Related sentences are selected using different approaches. Pseudo-documents consisting of relevant sentences are applied to extract topic distributions of captions attached to source images by LDA. We use D2V to indicate extracting text features by Doc2vec. In contrast, SKIPS means extracting text features by Skip-Thoughts[4]. RF means using RandomForest to perform classification task. T-CNN[5] is a CNN model for text classification [10]. Experiments in Table 4 show different approaches for selecting relevant sentences.

Table 4. Related sentences for Topic Distribution

Methods	Approaches
DES_D2V	Selecting sentences whose value of similarity to caption below 0.35
DES_SKIPS	This method is different from DES_W2V in that text features are extracted by Skip-Thoughts
RF_ITC	Using RF to Perform binary classification on text and image
T-CNN_ITC_SKIPS	Using softmax to Perform binary classification on text and image

3.3   Results and Analysis

TSR-TXT, TSR-CNN and TSR-HCA are three approaches presented in [6]. The key idea is to perform image retrieval over database of images that are captioned

Table 5. BLEU results of experiments

Method	BLEU(%)
Baseline	32.45
DES_GDMM	31.17
DES_GDMM_LIB	33.09
TR_ALLTEXT	32.65
IR_ALLTEXT	32.9
DES_D2V	33.45
DES_SKIP	33.13
RF_ITC	31.8
T-CNN_ITC_SKIPS	33.01
TSR-TXT	29.7
TSR-CNN	30.6
TSR-HCA	30.3

---

[4] https://github.com/tensorflow/models/tree/master/skip_thoughts.
[5] https://github.com/dennybritz/cnn-text-classification-tf.

in the target language, and use the captions of the most similar images for crosslingual reranking of translation outputs.

Table 5 show that the experiment DES_D2V achieves the best performance. For Baseline, TR_ALLTEXT achieves improvement of 0.25 BLEU point owing to introducing topic information into translation model. IR_ALLTEXT shows improvement of 0.2 BLEU point over TR_ALLTEXT due to rich information of images. The performance of DES_GDMM is poorer than Baseline lying in inaccurate topic information from short texts. DES_D2V improves 0.55 BLEU point and 1 BLEU point over IR_ALLTEXT and Baseline respectively. One explanation can clarify this behavior, sentences selected by text match are not only closely related to images, but also reduce interference information in whole document.

4   Related Work

In the previous year's competition [2], most of the systems were based on the phrase-base SMT in a monolingual setting [22]. [21] learned images information to rerank the results of translation system. [6] presents an approach to improve SMT of image captions by multimodal pivots defined in visual space. The key idea is to perform image retrieval over a database of images that are captioned in the target language, and use the captions of the most similar images for crosslingual reranking of translation outputs.

As the advances of deep learning, Neural Machine Translation (NMT) [8,9] attracts research attention. [3] present a double-attentive multimodal machine translation model which learns to attend to source language and visual features as separate attention mechanisms.

Our work departs from the previous work based on SMT lying in incorporating images information into translation model.

5   Conclusion and Future Work

This paper presents an approach to effectively infer the topic distributions of source captions. By integrating the topic distributions into phrase table, it is proved that topic distribution is beneficial to improve the performance of IDT. The method in this paper selects some sentences from documents to form pseudo-documents, which not only guarantees the richness and diversity of text information, but also ensures text information is similar to captions of source images as far as possible.

From the perspective that the quality of topic distribution influences the performance of IDT. In the future work, we will try from the following two respects: First, extracting part of images associated with captions by neural networks to assist IDT; Second, extracting some sentences closely related to images to learn precise topic distributions.

Acknowledgement. This research work is supported by National Natural Science Foundation of China (Grants No. 61373097, No. 61672367, No. 61672368, No. 61331011, No. 61773276), the Research Foundation of the Ministry of Education and China Mobile, MCM20150602 and the Science and Technology Plan of Jiangsu, SBK2015022101 and BK20151222. The authors would like to thank the anonymous reviewers for their insightful comments and suggestions. Yu Hong, Professor Associate in Soochow University, is the corresponding author of the paper, whose email address is tianxianer@gmail.com.

References

1. Blei, D.M., Ng, A.Y., Jordan, M.I.: Latent Dirichlet allocation. J. Mach. Learn. Res. **3**(Jan), 993–1022 (2003)
2. Bojar, O., Buck, C., Federmann, C., Haddow, B., Koehn, P., Leveling, J., Monz, C., Pecina, P., Post, M., Saint-Amand, H., et al.: Findings of the 2014 workshop on statistical machine translation. In: WMT@ ACL, pp. 12–58 (2014)
3. Calixto, I., Elliott, D., Frank, S.: DCU-UvA multimodal MT system report. In: WMT, pp. 634–638 (2016)
4. Dos Santos, C.N., Gatti, M.: Deep convolutional neural networks for sentiment analysis of short texts. In: COLING, pp. 69–78 (2014)
5. Elliott, D., Frank, S., Sima'an, K., Specia, L.: Multi30k: multilingual English-German image descriptions. arXiv preprint arXiv:1605.00459 (2016)
6. Hitschler, J., Schamoni, S., Riezler, S.: Multimodal pivots for image caption translation. arXiv preprint arXiv:1601.03916 (2016)
7. Hong, Y., Yao, L., Liu, M., Zhang, T., Zhou, W., Yao, J., Ji, H.: Image-image search for comparable corpora construction. In: The 26th International Conference on Computational Linguistics (COLING 2016), p. 16 (2016)
8. Jean, S., Cho, K., Memisevic, R., Bengio, Y.: On using very large target vocabulary for neural machine translation. arXiv preprint arXiv:1412.2007 (2014)
9. Kalchbrenner, N., Blunsom, P.: Recurrent continuous translation models. In: EMNLP, vol. 3, p. 413 (2013)
10. Kim, Y.: Convolutional neural networks for sentence classification. arXiv preprint arXiv:1408.5882 (2014)
11. Le, Q., Mikolov, T.: Distributed representations of sentences and documents. In: Proceedings of the 31st International Conference on Machine Learning (ICML 2014), pp. 1188–1196 (2014)
12. Levy, O., Goldberg, Y.: Dependency-based word embeddings. In: ACL (2), pp. 302–308. Citeseer (2014)
13. Li, C., Wang, H., Zhang, Z., Sun, A., Ma, Z.: Topic modeling for short texts with auxiliary word embeddings. In: Proceedings of the 39th International ACM SIGIR Conference on Research and Development in Information Retrieval, pp. 165–174. ACM (2016)
14. Li, S., Chua, T.S., Zhu, J., Miao, C.: Generative topic embedding: a continuous representation of documents. In: ACL (1) (2016)
15. Lin, T.Y., Maire, M., Belongie, S., Bourdev, L., Girshick, R., Hays, J., Perona, P., Ramanan, D., Zitnick, C.L., Dollar, P.: Microsoft coco: common objects in context. arXiv preprint arXiv:1405.0312 (2014)
16. Mikolov, T., Sutskever, I., Chen, K., Corrado, G.S., Dean, J.: Distributed representations of words and phrases and their compositionality. In: Advances in Neural Information Processing Systems, pp. 3111–3119 (2013)

17. Och, F.J.: Minimum error rate training in statistical machine translation. In: Proceedings of the 41st Annual Meeting on Association for Computational Linguistics, vol. 1, pp. 160–167. Association for Computational Linguistics (2003)
18. Och, F.J., Ney, H.: Improved statistical alignment models. In: Proceedings of the 38th Annual Meeting on Association for Computational Linguistics, pp. 440–447. Association for Computational Linguistics (2000)
19. Plummer, B.A., Wang, L., Cervantes, C.M., Caicedo, J.C., Hockenmaier, J., Lazebnik, S.: Flickr30k entities: collecting region-to-phrase correspondences for richer image-to-sentence models. In: Proceedings of the IEEE International Conference on Computer Vision, pp. 2641–2649 (2015)
20. Russakovsky, O., Deng, J., Su, H., Krause, J., Satheesh, S., Ma, S., Huang, Z., Karpathy, A., Khosla, A., Bernstein, M., et al.: Imagenet large scale visual recognition challenge. arXiv preprint arXiv:1409.0575 (2014)
21. Shah, K., Wang, J., Specia, L.: Shef-multimodal: grounding machine translation on images. In: Proceedings of the First Conference on Machine Translation, vol. 2, pp. 660–665. ACL (2016)
22. Simard, M., Ueffing, N., Isabelle, P., Kuhn, R.: Rule-based translation with statistical phrase-based post-editing. In: Proceedings of the Second Workshop on Statistical Machine Translation, pp. 203–206. Association for Computational Linguistics (2007)
23. Simonyan, K., Zisserman, A.: Very deep convolutional networks for large-scale image recognition. arXiv preprint arXiv:1409.1556 (2014)
24. Stolcke, A., et al.: Srilm-an extensible language modeling toolkit. In: Interspeech. vol. 2002, p. 2002 (2002)
25. Su, J., Wu, H., Wang, H., Chen, Y., Shi, X., Dong, H., Liu, Q.: Translation model adaptation for statistical machine translation with monolingual topic information. In: Proceedings of the 50th Annual Meeting of the Association for Computational Linguistics: Long Papers, vol. 1, pp. 459–468. Association for Computational Linguistics (2012)
26. Xiao, T., Zhu, J., Zhang, H., Li, Q.: NiuTrans: an open source toolkit for phrase-based and syntax-based machine translation. In: Proceedings of the ACL 2012 System Demonstrations, pp. 19–24. Association for Computational Linguistics (2012)
27. Yang, W., Boyd-Graber, J.L., Resnik, P.: A discriminative topic model using document network structure. In: ACL (1) (2016)

Automatic Document Metadata Extraction Based on Deep Networks

Runtao Liu, Liangcai Gao$^{(\boxtimes)}$, Dong An, Zhuoren Jiang, and Zhi Tang

Institute of Computer Science & Technology, Peking University, Beijing, China
{liuruntao,glc,andong,jiangzr,tangzhi}@pku.edu.cn

Abstract. Metadata information extraction from academic papers is of great value to many applications such as scholar search, digital library, and so on. This task has attracted much attention from researchers in the past decades, and many templates-based or statistical machine learning (e.g. SVM, CRF, etc.)-based extraction methods have been proposed, while this task is still a challenge because of the variety and complexity of page layout. To address this challenge, we try introducing the deep learning networks to this task in this paper, since deep learning has shown great power in many areas like computer vision (CV) and natural language processing (NLP). Firstly, we employ the deep learning networks to model the image information and the text information of paper headers respectively, which allow our approach to perform metadata extraction with little information loss. Then we formulate the problem, metadata extraction from a paper header, as two typical tasks of different areas: object detection in the area of CV, and sequence labeling in the area of NLP. Finally, the two deep networks generated from the above two tasks are combined together to give extraction results. The primary experiments show that our approach achieves state-of-the-art performance on several open datasets. At the same time, this approach can process both image data and text data, and does not need to design any classification feature.

Keywords: Information extraction · Ensemble modeling
Convolutional Neural Networks · Sequence labeling
Recurrent Neural Networks

1 Introduction

Automatic metadata extraction from scientific articles is a significant prerequisite for many tasks such as scholar search, information retrieval and digital library. Manual extraction of these metadata is very time-consuming and laborious. Therefore, automatic extraction of scholar document metadata becomes an urgent problem. However, the efficient implementation of metadata extraction is not simple due to different style and scope of metadata provided by authors or publishers.

© Springer International Publishing AG 2018
X. Huang et al. (Eds.): NLPCC 2017, LNAI 10619, pp. 305–317, 2018.
https://doi.org/10.1007/978-3-319-73618-1_26

Recently deep learning has shown great power in computer vision, speech recognition, natural language processing and other fields. Therefore, in this paper we introduce deep learning into the task, document metadata extraction. In detail, our approach contains two types of networks including Convolutional Neural Networks (CNNs) and Recurrent Neural Networks (RNNs) to handle image information and text information of paper headers. Finally, we combine those networks handling image and text respectively into a following Long-Short Term Memory (LSTM) to get the classifications of each line in paper headers.

Comparing to the previous work, the main contribution of our work is: (i) Besides the text information, we also utilize the vision information (e.g., layout, position, font, etc.) of the header of scientific articles. (ii) Our system achieves the best results on several public datasets, compared to other metadata extraction tools. (iii) As far as we know, this paper employs deep learning in the task of document metadata extraction at the first time.

In the following sections, we will introduce our approach and system in details. Section 2 describes the related work about metadata extraction, CNN and RNN. Sections 3, 4 and 5 write about our definition of this extraction task, corresponding model design and our system. Section 6 presents the experimental results on several datasets. Section 7 draws the conclusions and discusses future work.

2   Related Work

2.1   Document Metadata Extraction

Accurate metadata information extraction is of significant importance for digital library and scholar information retrieval system. Since it's too pricey for manual extraction, building a robust and universal extraction tool can remarkably improve the efficiency and quality of the metadata extraction process.

The most widely used approach to this problem is mainly based on three kinds of methods: rules, retrieval and statical machine learning. Rule-based methods utilize a group of rules to extract the document metadata information. Day et al. [4] constructed a hierarchical knowledge representation framework (INFOMAP) to extract citation metadata based on six major citation templates. This kind of methods need a lot of domain knowledges to write these rules, which cause it is not flexible enough in practical scenarios. Another metadata extraction method is based on Information Retrieval related techniques. Cortez et al. [2] construct a knowledge-base from a dataset and then they tag the blocks of splitted reference strings by searching in the knowledge-base. Compared to the previous two methods, machine learning methods don't need expert knowledges and databases. Han et al. [5] utilize SVM classifier to classify every line to different tags. This task can be also regarded as a sequence labeling task. Peng and McCallum [12] use Conditional Random Field (CRF) method on this task and acquire good result.

2.2   Deep Neural Networks

Deep neural networks have shown fantastic performance in many research areas such as CV and NLP. In this section, we briefly review some deep learning approaches which would be utilized in this paper.

Convolutional Neural Network in Image Classification. Krizhevsky et al. [10] proposed an architecture known as AlexNet which got the champion in 2012 ILSVRC (ImageNet Large-Scale Visual Recognition Challenge) achieving a top 5 test error rate of 15.4%. It shows that CNNs are expert in image modeling and extraction of features. [8] proposed their CNN model applied on document image classifications and achieved the state-of-the-art performance, which shows that CNN is also applicable to document images. Besides, CNNs have been applied in sentence modeling tasks. Kim [9] applied the CNNs on the matrix of word vectors, which achieved pretty improvements on several public benchmarks. The above studies show that CNN has a good ability to learn the local and global features separately. It could be used in not only CV tasks but also NLP tasks.

Recurrent Neural Network in Sequence Labeling. Recurrent Neural Network could process tasks with arbitrary sequences of inputs. LSTM which is a kind of RNN and its variants has shown great ability on sequence labeling. Huang et al. [6] proposed a variety of LSTM model named BI-LSTM-CRF to address the sequence tagging task which could utilize probability distribution of tag sequence through the top CRF layer. The above studies show that RNN is an ideal solution for sequence tasks.

3   Problem Definition

As Fig. 1 shows, it's an example of paper header with some metadata highlighted. Seymore et al. [13] defined 15 different tags for the scholar document header in 1999 including Title, Author, Affiliation, Address, Note, Email, Date, Abstract, Introduction, Phone, Keyword, Web, Degree, Pubnum, Page. In addition, they provided a dataset containing 935 headers of computer science research papers. The dataset had become one of the important benchmarks of the header information extraction area from then on. However, as time goes on, more and more evidences show that the 15 different classifications aren't totally suitable for being regarded as the metadata information types nowadays. Classes such as Web, Degree and Pubnum aren't the common content in the header of scholarly document now. Thus, in this paper, we only select the most common eight classes as the metadata tags, including Title, Author, Affiliation, Address, Email, Date, Abstract and Other.

Here we formulate the header metadata information extraction task as follows. Given a sequence of lines of the paper header $\boldsymbol{h} = (h_1, \ldots, h_n)$ and the m

Fig. 1. Paper header example

classifications (tags) $\boldsymbol{tag} = (tag_1, \ldots, tag_m)$, the problem is to match each line h_i of the header $\boldsymbol{h}$ to a specific classification $r_i \in \boldsymbol{tag}$ through a function F:

$$r_i = F(i, \boldsymbol{h})$$

Note that h_i may contain much information of the i-th line. Besides the text content information, the image, layout style, font style, character position or combination and other information may be also included. While the previous work only depends on text information of paper headers to extract their metadata, our approach tries to make full use of the multiple kinds of information from paper headers to make the extraction performance much better. Sometimes a text line contains multiple types of metadata, which are separated by whitespace. Thus, we first segment such lines into fragments according to the whitespace before tagging them. For convenient description, we also call the fragments as lines in this paper.

4   Deep Learning Model Design

This section will describe our deep learning model for extracting metadata from the header of scientific articles. With obtaining the text content and the image information of each line of the paper header, our approach can either solve it as a CV task or as a NLP task and even try to combine these methods or models.

We first explain the sentence model we adopt to map every line of the paper header to its intermediate representations. Then we describe the deep neural network architecture we use for image information and text information respectively. Finally we explain how to ensemble these two networks.

4.1 Sentence Modeling

We first map the text of header lines to corresponding intermediate representation. Inspired by Kim's [9] work, we proposed our model shown in Fig. 2 to learn the representation of the text contents.

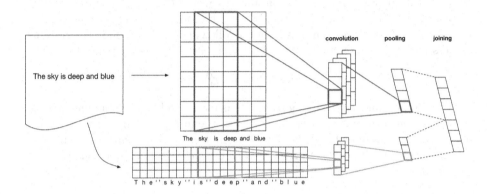

Fig. 2. Sentence model

Formally, given a line of paper header $(w_1, w_2, \ldots, w_t)$, where w_i stands for the k-dimensional word vector or the character vector in this line, and by concatenating these vectors it can be represented as a $t \times k$ matrix. A convolution operation is applied to this matrix with a filter $s \in \mathbb{R}^{l \times k}$ whose stride is l then a feature map could be obtained $c = (c_1, \ldots, c_{t-l+1})$ using following formula, where b is the bias term and the α is a non-linear activation function:

$$c_i = \alpha(s \cdot w_{[i:i+l-1]} + b)$$

Sigmoid, hyberbolic tangent (Tanh) and rectified linear unit (ReLU) are common non-linear activation functions. We choose ReLU as it could let the networks converge faster than standard sigmoid units [3].

We use m' different filters with multiple strides to obtain multiple features $(c_1, \ldots, c_{m'})$. These operations are done in convolutional layers and then these results are put into pooling layers. Pooling operations is a non-linear downsampling operation that could decrease the number of features. There we adopt the common max pooling.

Following their study, we adopt the max pooling strategy and could get the representation of the text information of i_{th} line in paper header.

$$Ptext_i = (max(c_1), \ldots, max(c_m))$$

This section introduces how to obtain the presentation of the text content of scholarly document header lines. The following section will depict the deep networks to get the representation vector of the images of header lines.

4.2 Image Modeling

Here we need to generate fixed-length vectors $I \in \mathbb{R}^{n \times d}$ from the images that effectively represent the corresponding image information. Formally, for an image $I_i \in \mathbb{R}^{height, width}$ which stands the information of i_{th} line, our image model $G(I_i, \theta)$ will output a representation $I_i \subset h_i$ where θ is the set of parameters of this model. Here we adopt the CNN as the model that it could learn the parameters θ itself through minimizing the following loss function in the training process where r_i' stands for the tag of i_{th} line and h stands for paper header.

$$Loss(F(i, h), r_i')$$

We use a minor variant of VggNet [14] as our model. As the number of classification defined in this study is far less than the number of image classification defined in original model and the document images are much simpler than natural images, we modified the VggNet to a more shallow and simpler one to make it more adaptable for this problem.

4.3 Sequence Modeling

Cho et al. [1] proposed a framework called RNN Encoder-Decoder for language translation. As shown in the right part of Fig. 3, the framework consists of two components, the first one encodes a sentence to an intermediate representation and the second decodes it to a target sentence. In our model, the Bi-RNN encoder reads an element x_t in a sequence $(x_1, \ldots, x_n)$ at time t, and generates two hidden states:

$$h_t = f(x_t, h_{t-1}) \quad h_t' = f'(x_t, h_{t+1}')$$

where the h_t, h_t' stand for the two hidden states in two opposite directions and f, f' represent the RNN unit function. Then the decoder will generate the probability distribution on the possible tags following $p(y_i \mid h_t, h_t')$. And the $\overline{y} = max\{p(y_i \mid h_t, h_t')\}$ can be regarded as the most feasible tag for the element x_t. Though this approach has efficiently considered the past and the future information, it doesn't consider the transaction regulation between y_i. [11] indicates that for sequence labeling tasks considering the correlations between neighboring labels could get better result. Formally, $\beta(y)$ denotes the whole tags space for the x and the decoding task is to find the $\overline{y}$ that meets:

$$\overline{y} = argmax\ p(y \mid x)$$

we define score and probability function of a candidate sequence y as:

$$S(x, y) = \prod_{i=1}^{n} \psi(y_i, x)\psi(y_i, y_{i-1})$$

$$p(\boldsymbol{y} \mid \boldsymbol{x}) = \frac{S(\boldsymbol{x}, \boldsymbol{y})}{Z}$$

and the partition function is determined as:

$$Z = \sum_{\boldsymbol{y} \in \beta(\boldsymbol{y})} S(\boldsymbol{x}, \boldsymbol{y})$$

We regard $\psi(y_i, \boldsymbol{x})$ to be the matrix $M_1 \in \mathbb{R}^{n \times m}$, the scores between the i_{th} element and the j_{th} tag output by the bidirectional RNN network and the $\psi(y_i, y_{i-1})$ to be the transaction matrix $M_2 \in \mathbb{R}^{m \times m}$ denoting the score between i_{th} tag and j_{th} tag. As above, our sequence model considers not only the past and future information but also the joint distribution of target label sequence.

5 Information Extraction System Based on Deep Learning

The framework of our metadata extraction system is shown in Fig. 3. The input of this system are PDF files. The image and text of a paper head is obtained with the help of PDFBox[1]. Based on the image model and the sentence model, the output representation vectors will be concatenated together in one representation vector. Finally, our system processes each line in the header and output the most possible tag sequence.

5.1 System Overview

As shown in Fig. 3, our system has following components: image model, sentence model, joint layer and Bi-LSTM-CRF layer.

First, a document whose header contains N lines is put into our system. Then the sentence model get sentence matrices $s_i \in \mathbb{R}^{n \times k}$ for each line l_i by concatenation of the vectors output from the embedding layer. The sentence model will output a fixed length feature vector $Ptext_i \in \mathbb{R}^{len_1}$ The images of this line will be put into the image model, and the model will output a fixed length representation vector $p \in \mathbb{R}^{len_2}$. Then v_i, p_i will be concatenated together in a single representation as $rp_i = [Ptext_i, p_i]$. This vector is then put into the sequence model, Bi-LSTM-CRF network, from whose outputs we could get the final results.

5.2 Word and Char Embedding

We use the public pre-trained word vectors named Global Vectors for Word Representation (GloVe) and there are about 400,000 words which has 200 dimensions in it. We use GloVe to initiate the word embedding layer, while the character embedding will be initialized randomly. In the training process, both the two embedding layers will be fine-tuned to promote the entire network performance.

---

[1] http://pdfbox.apache.org.

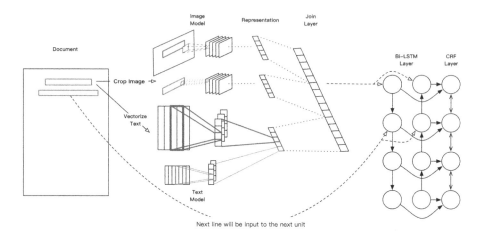

Fig. 3. The overview of our system

5.3   Training and Parameters

In our system, the weights to be trained include the following parts: (i) In the sequence model, the scores matrix $M_1 = \psi(y_i, \boldsymbol{x})$ and the transition matrix $M_2 = \psi(y_i, y_{i-1})$. (ii) In the image model, the parameters $\boldsymbol{\theta}$ of the image deep ConvNet. (iii) In the sentence model, the word and character embedding matrices and the parameters $\boldsymbol{\gamma}$ of the sentence deep ConvNet. The purpose of training process is to maximize the log probability of the correct labeling sequence:

$$log(p(\boldsymbol{y}^* \mid \boldsymbol{x}, f)) = log(Score(\boldsymbol{y}^*, \boldsymbol{x})) - log(Z)$$

Standard back-propagation is used to learn these above parameters of this end-to-end system. In our experiments, after initiating training using Adam for some iterations, we use Stochastic gradient descent (SGD) to continue fine-tuning the model. We adopt early stopping by checking the recorded loss values on validation set for every iteration and select the lowest one as the result model.

On system configure, we retain the first 10 words and 100 characters and truncate the leftover parts for each line. We resize the height of the image of each line to 40 and the width to 200. The dimensions of the word and character embeddings is 200 and 40 respectively. The networks could learn the representations from the input. The lengths of the images representation vector, the characters representation vector and the words representation vector are 2048, 1024 and 1024 respectively. These representations will be joined and put into the two stacked Bi-LSTM networks whose hidden state dimensions are set to 512.

6   Experiment and Evaluation

We evaluate our metadata extraction system on three tasks: (i) metadata extraction only based on image information (ii) metadata extraction only based on text information (iii) metadata extraction based on both image and text information. F-measure is used for performance evaluation. Finally, we compare our system to the existing and available extraction tools and methods like, Parscit [7], SVM [5] and CRF [12]. The results show that our method has achieved much improvement in the extraction performance.

6.1   Datasets

In this section we evaluate our deep networks model on these following datasets. The proportion of each classification is shown in Table 1.

Table 1. The ratio of each class in SEYMORE and OURS

Class	Ratio (SEYMORE)	Ratio (OURS)
Title	8.3%	9.8%
Author	7.2%	10.5%
Affiliation	10.6%	16.8%
Email	3.4%	8.8%
Abstract	50.0%	36.5%
Phone	0.6%	1.4%
Address	6.3%	9.5%
Other	13.6%	6.8%

SEYMORE. This dataset provided by Seymore et al. contains 935 headers with 15 classifications including Title, Author, Affiliation, Address, Note, Email, Date, Abstract, Introduction, Phone, Keyword, Web, Degree, Pubnum and Page. For each line, there is a corresponding tag at its end.

OURS. The dataset contains 75,000 headers and each header contains both image and text data. It's consist of 70,000 noisy items and 5,000 correct items. It will be open and available on the web (http://www.icst.pku.edu.cn/cpdp/header/header_open.rar). The corresponding PDF format papers are crawled from the Internet. Our dataset contains only the following categories: Title, Author, Affiliation, Address, Email, Abstract, Phone, Keyword, and Other.

6.2   Fine-Tuning

Fine-tuning is using another dataset to train the trained networks to let back-propagation process continue to decrease the loss at this dataset. Training deep networks needs tremendous data while it's unrealistic to label hundreds of thousands of data, so we will use tools based on CRF to tag 75,000 paper headers. Even though these data contain noisy information and incorrect labels, we could first use them to train the deep networks for pre-training. Afterwards, we manually label 5,000 instances of header. Then we use 3,000 of them for fine-tuning after training with noisy data and the left 2,000 for testing.

6.3   Experiments on Image

Since the previous public dataset contained only textual information and did not have corresponding image information, the image experiments were performed on OURS dataset as shown in Table 3.

Table 3 shows the performance of the image model for each classification. The image model exhibits a good result on "Title" class because the image instances in "Title" class have significant location information and font features that they are generally located at uppermost with bold font. "Email" and "Phone" classes is also fine because "Email" instances are generally letters with "@"(at) and "Phone" instances are generally numbers with "-"(dash) that they all could be learned by image model. Owing to lack of semantic information, "Author", "Affiliation" and "Address" are not so satisfactory even though they have their respective features; semantic information is more crucial for these classes.

6.4   Experiments on Text

We adopt both word embedding and character embedding in order to catch the semantic features and the characters arrangement features simultaneously. "Title", "Author", "Affiliation" and "Address" have richer semantic features while "Email", "Phone", "Pubnum" and "Web" have more obvious character arrangements features. We test our text model on two datasets, SEYMORE and OURS. The experimental results on SEYMORE and OURS are presented in Tables 2 and 3 respectively.

Table 2. Result on SEYMORE dataset of text model

Class	Parscit (CRF) [7]	Han [5]	Peng [12]	Text model
Title	0.968	0.945	0.971	**0.981**
Author	0.952	0.942	0.975	**0.977**
Affiliation	0.914	0.933	**0.970**	0.963
Address	0.899	0.900	0.958	**0.960**
Email	0.952	0.964	0.953	**0.969**
Abstract	0.988	0.988	**0.997**	0.995
Phone	0.913	0.762	0.979	**0.982**
Average F1	0.941	0.919	0.972	**0.975**

Experimental results show that the performance of our metadata extraction system is much better than the other systems. Existing approaches utilize semantics in the header by means of dictionaries such as name dictionary and country dictionary etc., which results in that they can only obtain very limited semantic content as the dictionaries generally didn't contain many words. Since the word embeddings could utilize the semantic information efficiently, our system shows better performance on "Title", "Author", and "Address". On the other side, char embeddings could find the pattern in the spelling of "Email" and "Phone", thus these classes perform better as well.

6.5 Experiments on Information Union

This section will attempt to evaluate the performance of converging image network and text network. As other datasets didn't contain image information of paper headers, we show the experiment results on our dataset. Our system will utilize both images and texts in our dataset while Parscit only uses the texts.

Table 3. Result on OURS dataset of other tools and our system

Class	SVM	Parscit (CRF) [7]	Image	Text	Image and text
Title	0.891	0.944	0.950	0.969	**0.985**
Author	0.703	0.938	0.905	0.96	**0.966**
Affiliation	0.877	0.934	0.903	0.953	**0.964**
Email	0.971	0.976	0.979	0.965	**0.985**
Abstract	0.970	0.981	0.963	0.983	**0.997**
Phone	0.936	0.961	0.959	0.968	**0.974**
Address	0.745	0.923	0.895	0.947	**0.964**
Average F1	0.870	0.951	0.936	0.963	**0.976**

Table 3 shows the performance of our system which combines the image model and text model. The results show that the overall system performance has been greatly improved after combining these two models. The images carry features such as location, font and layout information, while the texts carry semantic and character arrangements information and the model integration reduces the information loss in the metadata extraction process. As [12] doesn't release corresponding implementations, here we show the results of Parscit, which is based on CRF like [12]. The competitor tool SVM is implemented employing the features referred in [5] as [5] doesn't release corresponding implementations either. The results show that our system does better in all classes than Parscit and the tool based on SVM and has achieved the state-of-art performance.

7 Conclusions

In this paper, we introduce deep learning technology to the problem, metadata extraction, at the first time. This deep networks based extraction approach can automatically learn the feature representation of metadata during the training process, which significantly reduces manual work for feature engineering compared to previous works. Furthermore, our extraction approach utilize two sources of information in paper headers: image content and text content. As a result, the deep learning model utilizing both image and text information shows the better performance on several datasets.

Compared to natural images, document images are much simpler. Thus, it is a valuable question to explore what kind of network structure is suitable for information retrieval from document images in the future. Furthermore, we plan to explore universal architectures based on deep networks that could extract the metadata or structure information from the whole document.

Acknowledgement. This work is supported by the Beijing Nova Program (Z1511 00000315042) and the China Postdoctoral Science Foundation (No. 2016M590019), which is also a research achievement of Key Laboratory of Science, Technology and Standard in Press Industry (Key Laboratory of Intelligent Press Media Technology). We also thank the anonymous reviewers for their valuable comments.

References

1. Cho, K., Van Merriënboer, B., Gulcehre, C., Bahdanau, D., Bougares, F., Schwenk, H., Bengio, Y.: Learning phrase representations using RNN encoder-decoder for statistical machine translation. arXiv preprint arXiv:1406.1078 (2014)
2. Cortez, E., da Silva, A.S., Gonçalves, M.A., Mesquita, F., de Moura, E.S.: A flexible approach for extracting metadata from bibliographic citations. J. Am. Soc. Inf. Sci. Technol. **60**(6), 1144–1158 (2009)
3. Dahl, G.E., Sainath, T.N., Hinton, G.E.: Improving deep neural networks for LVCSR using rectified linear units and dropout. In: 2013 IEEE International Conference on Acoustics, Speech and Signal Processing, pp. 8609–8613. IEEE (2013)
4. Day, M.Y., Tsai, R.T.H., Sung, C.L., Hsieh, C.C., Lee, C.W., Wu, S.H., Wu, K.P., Ong, C.S., Hsu, W.L.: Reference metadata extraction using a hierarchical knowledge representation framework. Decis. Support Syst. **43**(1), 152–167 (2007)
5. Han, H., Giles, C.L., Manavoglu, E., Zha, H., Zhang, Z., Fox, E.A.: Automatic document metadata extraction using support vector machines. In: Proceedings of 2003 Joint Conference on Digital Libraries, pp. 37–48. IEEE (2003)
6. Huang, Z., Xu, W., Yu, K.: Bidirectional LSTM-CRF models for sequence tagging. arXiv preprint arXiv:1508.01991 (2015)
7. Isaac G. Councill, C. Lee Giles, M.Y.K.: ParsCit tool. http://www.comp.nus.edu.sg/entrepreneurship/innovation/osr/parscit/ (2008)
8. Kang, L., Kumar, J., Ye, P., Li, Y., Doermann, D.: Convolutional neural networks for document image classification. In: 2014 22nd International Conference on Pattern Recognition (ICPR), pp. 3168–3172. IEEE (2014)
9. Kim, Y.: Convolutional neural networks for sentence classification. arXiv preprint arXiv:1408.5882 (2014)
10. Krizhevsky, A., Sutskever, I., Hinton, G.E.: ImageNet classification with deep convolutional neural networks. In: Advances in Neural Information Processing Systems, pp. 1097–1105 (2012)
11. Ma, X., Hovy, E.: End-to-end sequence labeling via bi-directional LSTM-CNNs-CRF. arXiv preprint arXiv:1603.01354 (2016)
12. Peng, F., McCallum, A.: Information extraction from research papers using conditional random fields. Inf. Process. Manag. **42**(4), 963–979 (2006)

13. Seymore, K., McCallum, A., Rosenfeld, R.: Learning hidden Markov model structure for information extraction. In: AAAI-1999 Workshop on Machine Learning for Information Extraction, pp. 37–42 (1999)
14. Simonyan, K., Zisserman, A.: Very deep convolutional networks for large-scale image recognition. CoRR abs/1409.1556 (2014)

A Semantic Representation Enhancement Method for Chinese News Headline Classification

Zhongbo Yin[1], Jintao Tang[2], Chengsen Ru[2], Wei Luo[1(✉)], Zhunchen Luo[1],
and Xiaolei Ma[2]

[1] China Defense Science and Technology Information Center, Beijing 100142, China
lwowen79@gmail.com
[2] National University of Defense Technology, Changsha 410073, China

Abstract. Recently there has been an increasing research interest in short text such as news headline. Due to the inherent sparsity of short text, the current text classification methods perform badly when applied to the classification of news headlines. To overcome this problem, a novel method which enhances the semantic representation of headlines is proposed in this paper. Firstly, we add some keywords extracted from the most similar news to expand the word features. Secondly, we use the corpus in news domain to pre-train the word embedding so as to enhance the word representation. Moreover, Fasttext classifier, which uses a liner method to classify text with fast speed and high accuracy, is adopted for news headline classification. On the task for Chinese news headline categorization in NLPCC2017, the proposed method achieved 83.1% of the F-measure, which got the first rank in 33 teams.

Keywords: Semantic representation enhancement
Short text classification · News headline · Word embedding

1 Introduction

With the development of mobile Internet, there are lots of short text such as news headline, microblog and WeChat sent to our mobile everyday. In order to cope with the information exploitation, it is necessary to further process the short texts such as classification. Different from general text classification, short text classification face the problem so-called semantic representation bias because of the lacking of semantic features.

Normally, we use the Vector Space Model (VSM) such as bag of words (BOW) to represent the text semantic. The main idea of VSM is to map text to a vector space which can be used to calculate the semantic similarity between the two text snippets [1]. A simple VSM method is one hot vector, but its vectors usually are too sparse and the vector dimension is too large. In recent years, the more popular method is using neural networks such as word2vec [2] to train a word embedding model, which can map a text to a more dense and continuous vector.

© Springer International Publishing AG 2018
X. Huang et al. (Eds.): NLPCC 2017, LNAI 10619, pp. 318–328, 2018.
https://doi.org/10.1007/978-3-319-73618-1_27

Based on the word2vec's skip-gram representation method, Bojanowski et al. proposed a N-gram approach to add the subword information to the embedding [3] which considers morphological information additionally.

As for the text classification method, the most classic one is Naive Bayesian (Naïve Bayes, NB) algorithm, which is based on Bayesian theorem and feature independent hypothesis [4]. Simultaneously, SVM (support vector machine) and KNN (K-nearest neighbor) also have good performance on Chinese text classification. Compared with these traditional classification methods, the deep learning methods (e.g. CNN and RNN) usually have a better performance but much higher complexity in recent many researches [5,6]. However, Mikolov et al. proves that text classification task is so simple that it does not need the complicated network structure of deep learning methods. Moreover, they put forward a more applicable to large-scale Internet text classification model named Fasttext which is much faster than deep learning approaches [7].

Both text representation and classification methods mentioned above are applied to general texts. However, short texts have the characteristics of sparseness and low-frequency of words. The sparse of words will make it is difficult to count the co-occurrence of features. The low keywords' frequency means that the co-occurrence calculation maybe inaccurate. As a consequence, it would lead to the semantic bias whether using the simplest BOW or the complex embedding. To overcome this problem, this paper focuses on short text semantic representation enhancement.

This paper proposed a novel method for Chinese news headline classification by enhancing semantic representation (CNHCESR), which focuses on the key issues on sparseness and low frequency in short texts. For the sparseness problem, we expand some keywords from the title and snippet parts of the first retrieval result from the search engine. For the bias semantics representation problem caused by low keyword frequency, we build a specific embedding by using the high quality corpus in news domain. Moreover, the Fasttext classification architecture has been used to train a news headline classifier. We do not extend the short texts to general long texts because just several keywords are added to the original texts. Thus, the speed advantage of the short text classification is maintained. Experimental result shows that both the proposed methods to enhance short text representation have a significant improvement in news headline classification.

2 Related Work

In recent years, there are lots of researches in the field of text classification, which is one key task in natural language processing. News headline categorization is one kind of the short text classification, which focuses on short text such as dialog, comment and microblog. As the characteristics of short content, the short text classification is more challenging than traditional long text classification. In order to solve the problem, many researchers have used some external knowledge resources like corpus and thesaurus to improve the existing long text classification methods and make them suitable for short text classification. The existing short text expansion methods can be divided into two categories: one is using network resources [8] and the other is using domain vocabulary. The network resources (e.g., Wikipedia) is easy to get, but the key point is how to gets high quality resource from lots of network resources. The domain vocabulary is used to build knowledge base or LDA (Latent Dirichlet Allocation) model which is a theme model with probability. LDA model can extract related entities or the theme content to achieve the purpose of expanding corpus [9].

Compared with the English text classification, the first step of Chinese text classification is word segmentation which affects the final classification performance. To improve the segmentation quality, Zhou et al. constructed a RNN language model with LSTM, which re-integrated neighboring char into the word form in the process of word segmentation [10]. A better semantic representation and classification performance has been obtained while the text is divided into words' form but not chars.

In order to further excavate the semantic information from the short text, Wang et al. put forward a method to represent the text's apparent semantics and latent aspects [11]. The apparent semantics is caught from Baidubaike by matching vocabulary entry information of the short text; while the latent semantics information is gathered by pLSA method [12]. Finally, the categorization is determined by comparing the specific class' correlation coefficient with the computed coefficient based on the apparent semantic information and latent aspect. Wang and Zhou used the hierarchical relationship provided by Baidubaike to identify the semantic topic for the short text [13]. Though this method, they established a convex optimization model to facilitate the short text classification.

In order to represent the semantic links between the few features of the short text more accurately, many researchers used embedding trained under the existing information to improve the classifier's performance [14]. Yao et al. got a 3% accuracy's promotion by only using the short text training set to train embedding and added them into the classifier as a preprocessing vector [15]. Furthermore, Ma et al. built some richer embeddings trained under the large sample set and got a more pronounced classification performance [16].

In recent years, some machine learning and neural network models have been developed for short text classification and have been proved effective. For example, Yin et al. used the most basic machine learning algorithm SVM in short text classification [17]. Xu et al. developed a CNN model for short text classification, which could develop more semantic information from short text information [18]. Similarly, the short text classification model based on recursive neural network (RNN) and convolution neural network (CNN) designed by Young et al. achieved a pleasurable result in dialog records classification [19].

Although the deep learning methods have achieved a good performance in text classification, they are still facing the problems of huge resource requirement and training time cost. In contrast, Fasttext [7] used a liner approach in text classification and achieved a similar performance as deep learning methods in terms of a relatively small resource and time. Since the Fasttext architecture is used for general long text classification, we expand the short text representation by Internet resources.

3   Fasttext

Fasttext is a new text classification tool developed by Facebook. It provides a simple but efficient method for text representation [3] and text classification [2,7]. For the text representation part, this algorithm train a word embedding, which is similar to the word2vec method. What's different from the word2vec is that the Fasttext representation approach considers additional N-gram in the process of computing embedding. For the text classification part, it only has one hidden layer in the architecture so that the classification process is relatively fast.

Fasttext classification function is similar to word2vec's continue bag of words (CBOW) algorithm [2]. Firstly, the feature vector combined with word sequence is linearly projected to middle hidden layer. Secondly, there is a non-linear activation function which projects middle hidden layer to the categorization label. The difference between Fasttext and CBOW is that Fasttext predicts labels while CBOW predicts middle terms.

Fasttext's official website currently provides the word vector representation of 294 languages. The advantage of Fasttext for text categorization is efficient and fast. Mikolov et al. proved that its performance is on par with deep learning (DL) algorithm, and many orders of magnitude faster than DL algorithm (Fig. 1).

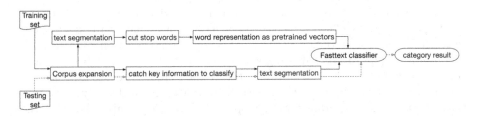

Fig. 1. It is a flow chart of the headline's semantic representation enhancing procedure, where the black solid arrows represent the training process, while the red dotted lines indicate the testing part. (Color figure online)

4   Semantic Representation Enhancement

4.1   Feature Expansion

Compared with the general long text classification, news headline classification is characterized by sparse features and low keyword frequency. Based on this aspect, we need to expand the news headlines' features before classification. In contrast with the LDA based expanding method [20], we use a more simple but reliable approach. With the help of the search engine, the first retrieval's snippet information is gathered for expanding corpus and its keywords are gathered as an additional input corpus to train the classifier.

4.2 Pretreatment

Before classification, the text should be preprocessed such as word segmentation and cutting stop words. In this paper, Jieba is used to segment words for the expanded corpus [21]. As the expanded corpus has a large number of functional words, prepositions, punctuation and other noise which are useless for classification. Therefore, we use the stop word list [22] to filter out the stop words in the expanded corpus.

4.3 Pre-train

The semantic distribution is domain related. The same word may have different meaning in different domains. For instance, the word band means a small group of musicians who play popular music or musical instrument in the domain of entertainment, while it means frequency range in the communication domain. Thus, we crawl the corpus in the news domain to enhance the semantic representation by using the headlines in training dataset as the input of search engine. The expanded corpus, which contains the most similar headlines, descriptions, and snippets, is gathered from the first retrieved result. Then we use the expanded corpus to train a word embedding.

Word embedding is a text representation method that maps text semantics to vector spaces [23]. Previous studies have shown that the text classifier with pre-trained word vector pattern has a better classification performance. The literature [2] proved that using skip-gram method to train embedding and negative-sampling method to optimize the trained embedding would obtain a better vocabulary similarity performance. Simultaneously, the literature [24] proposed that adjusting parameters appropriately was beneficial to improve the performance of word embedding representation. In our experiment, we use the skip-gram + negative-sampling method to train a word embedding and optimize the parameters later.

4.4 Keyword Expansion

Short text are characterized by the feature sparseness problem which makes the calculation of feature co-occurrence difficult and inaccurate. Inaccurate co-occurrence represents inaccurate semantic similarity which is the key point to classify. Therefore, it is beneficial to add some keywords for expanding features.

In this paper, we use TF-IDF algorithm to extract keywords from the search snippets. The experiment shows that the best representation performance is gained by adding 13 keywords into original news headlines.

5 Experiments and Results Analysis

5.1 Dataset Sources

The experimental corpus comes from the NLPCC2017 public evaluation: Chinese news headline categorization. This corpus includes 18 news categories. The categorization of discovery, story, regimen and essay has 4000 headlines in each training set. Other 14 categorizations have 10000 headlines. Each categorization of developing set and testing set contains 2000 news headlines.

The specific headline sample are enumerated in Table 1, where the first column is category and the second displays some specific headline samples. As the headline samples, these news headlines are typical short text, which has a small amount of vocabulary and few features related to categorization. Therefore, it is necessary to enhance the semantic before classification.

Table 1. Samples for dataset.

Category	Title sentence
entertainment	台媒预测周冬雨金马奖封后，大气的倪妮却佳作难出
food	农村就是好，能吃到纯天然无添加的野生蜂蜜，营养又健康
fashion	14 款知性美装，时尚惊艳搁浅的阳光轻熟的优雅
society	新京报动新闻：高铁断电千人"汗蒸"为啥不能开门窗？
history	红军长征在中国革命史上的地位
story	奇闻录：苗族蛊毒到底是真的么？一则真实的中蛊故事
car	轿车型皮卡在中国会有市场么？

5.2 Performance Evaluation Indicators

The classification performance is evaluated by the following indicators: Macro P, Macro R and Macro F1.

$$\text{Marco P} = \frac{1}{m} \sum_{i=1}^{m} \frac{\text{number of true results to } i \text{ category}}{\text{number of result to } i \text{ category}} \tag{1}$$

$$\text{Marco R} = \frac{1}{m} \sum_{i=1}^{m} \frac{\text{number of true results to } i \text{ category}}{\text{number of } i \text{ category in testing set}} \tag{2}$$

$$\text{Marco F1} = \frac{2 \times \text{Marco P} \times \text{Marco R}}{\text{Marco P} + \text{Marco R}} \tag{3}$$

5.3 Baseline

In this paper, we compared our CNHCESR method with three basic deep learning algorithms which were offered by NLPCC2017 [25]: long short-term network (LSTM) [26], neural bag-of-words (NBOW) and convolutional neural networks (CNN) [27].

5.4   Results

Experiment 1: Before Expansion. Table 2 lists the performance of the three DL algorithms and Fasttext approach without expansion. Among the four algorithms, Fasttext achieved the best performance with the least training time. In details, the DL algorithms ran on a server node with eight 3.7 GHz Intel (R) Xeon (R) E5-1620 v2 CPUs and Fasttext approach ran on a 2.4 GHz Intel Core i7 CPU with 2 cores. Although the DL algorithms were trained on a more powerful computing server, the training time was still much more than Fasttext.

Table 2. Performance of classification with original dataset.

Model	Macro P %	Macro R %	Macro F %	Accuracy %	Training time
LSTM	70.2	69.1	69.2	69.1	201 min 12 s
CNN	76.2	75.5	75.8	75.5	32 min 46 s
NBOW	77.8	77.1	77.4	77.1	41 min 03 s
Fasttext	78.0	77.3	77.7	77.3	9 s

Experiment 2: Enhancing Representation with Embedding. Table 3 lists the classification performance of Fasttext and DL algorithms while the 100-dimensional embedding (from baseline or our enhancing method) added into the original short text. Our enhancing embedding was obtained by using the full-scale expanded corpus to train a more elaborate embedding by Fasttext's word representation function. From the Tables 2 and 3, it can be concluded that each classification accuracy will rise at least 1% after adding an pre-train embedding. As a result, it is reasonable to believe that adding the embedding is helpful to improve the classification performance.

Table 3. Performance of classification with original dataset and embedding.

Model	Macro P %	Macro R %	Macro F %	Accuracy %	Training time	Embedding source
LSTM	77.5	76.8	77.1	76.8	97 min 36 s	Baseline
CNN	79.0	78.4	78.7	78.4	30 min 23 s	Baseline
NBOW	79.7	79.0	79.3	79.0	37 min 13 s	Baseline
Fasttext	79.0	78.3	78.7	78.4	49 s	Baseline
LSTM	79.6	79.2	79.4	79.2	99 min 56 s	Enhancing
CNN	79.9	79.3	79.6	79.3	32 min 54 s	Enhancing
NBOW	81.0	80.5	80.8	80.5	30 min 47 s	Enhancing
Fasttext	81.0	80.5	80.8	80.5	23 s	Enhancing

Table 3 shows the performance over a period between the baseline embedding and enhancing embedding. As can be seen in Table 3, each approach had a 2%

promotion after replacing baseline embedding with our enhancing embedding, which indicated that using domain specific resource to train embedding could more accurately represent the semantics of words in this domain.

According to Tables 2 and 3, though the classification performance of Fasttext was almost the same as NBOW which had the best performance in the baselines, Fasttext had a significantly advantage over NBOW in efficiency. Therefore, this paper selected Fasttext method with comprehensive consideration below.

Experiment 3: Enhancing Representation with Keywords. This experiment was based on Experiment 2 with a softmax loss function. This experiment's expanded the original news headline with 13 keywords from the first search snippet. Simultaneously, we used different loss function to promote the performance. As can be seen from Table 4, the classification accuracy was promoted by 1% after changing the loss function from softmax to negative sampling. And it can be promoted at least 2.4% by using the expanded keywords.

Table 4. Performance of classification with keywords expansion.

Corpus	Loss function	Macro P %	Macro R %	Macro F %	Accuracy %
Original	Softmax	79.0	78.3	78.7	78.4
	Negative sampling	79.9	79.4	79.6	79.4
	Hierarchical softmax	76.2	75.5	75.8	75.5
Expand	Softmax	81.2	80.8	81.0	80.8
	Negative sampling	82.2	82.0	82.1	82.0
	Hierarchical softmax	79.2	78.7	79.0	78.7

Experiment 4: Enhancing Representation with Keywords and Embedding. Based on the excellent performance of Fasttext in the experiment 2 and 3, we combined the enhanced embedding and keywords in this experiment. Additionally, we set the n-grams to 2 and negative samples to 10 in this experiment. The fourth experiment results list in the Table 5.

Table 5. Performance of classification with keywords expansion and embedding.

Corpus	Loss function	Embedding	Macro P %	Macro R %	Macro F %	Accuracy %	Training time
Expand	Negative-sampling	Baseline	82.7	82.6	82.6	82.6	57 s
		Enhancing	83.2	83.1	83.1	83.1	26 s

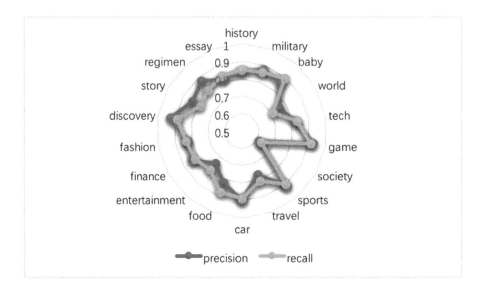

Fig. 2. Performance for specific categorization.

5.5   Results Analysis

Figure 2 shows the specific category accuracy and recall. It can be seen from the classification precision and recall index of world, society, travel, entertainment and story is less than 80%. The main reason is that the above five categories' news covers a widely range and are easy to be confused with other categories. For example, society and world have a high feature coincidence degree which results in the confusion in the classification process.

6   Conclusions

In this paper, we enhanced short text's semantic representation by adding additional keywords of the search snippet and using a more accurate embedding trained with domain-related corpus. Since we just added several keywords to enhance semantic representation, the expanded input is still a short text which is faster in classification. The experiment results proved that, our Chinese news headline enhancing semantic representation method outperform the art-of-states both on performance and efficiency.

Acknowledgements. Firstly, we would like to thank Jintao Tang and Ting Wang for their valuable suggestions on the initial version of this paper, which have helped a lot to improve the paper. Secondly, we also want to express gratitudes to the anonymous reviewers for their hard work and kind comments, which will further improve our work in the future. This work was supported by the National Natural Science Foundation of China (No. 61602490).

References

1. Tang, Q., Guo, Q.-L., Li, Y.-M.: Similarity computing of documents based on VSMJ. Appl. Res. Comput. **25**(11), 3256–3258 (2008)
2. Corrado, G., Mikolov, T., Chen, K., Dean, J.: Efficient estimation of word representations in vector space. arXiv preprint arXiv:1301.3781 (2013)
3. Bojanowski, P., Grave, E., Joulin, A., Mikolov, T.: Enriching word vectors with subword information. arXiv: 1607.04606 (2016)
4. Lachiche, N., Flach, P.A.: Naive Bayesian classification of structured data. Mach. Learn. **57**(3), 233–269 (2004)
5. Sontag, D., Rush, A.M., Kim, Y., Jernite, Y.: Character-aware neural language models. Comput. Sci. 2741–2749 (2015)
6. LeCun, Y., Zhang, X., Zhao, J.: Character-level convolutional networks for text classification. arXiv:1509.01626 (2015)
7. Bojanowski, P., Mikolov, T., Joulin, A., Grave, E.: Bag of tricks for efficient text classification. arXiv:1607.04606 (2016)
8. Horiguchi, S., Phan, X.H., Nguyen, L.M.: Learning to classify short and sparse text and web with hidden topics from large-scale data collections. In: WWW 2008 Refereed Track: Data Mining - Learning, pp. 91–100 (2008)
9. Hu, H., Fan, X.: A new model for Chinese short-text classification considering feature expansion. In: International Conference on Artificial Intelligence and Computational Intelligence, vol. 2, pp. 7–11 (2010)
10. Xu, J., Yang, L., Li., C., Zhou, Y., Xu, B.: Compositional recurrent neural networks for Chinese short text classification. In: IEEE/WIC/ACM International Conference on Web Intelligence, pp. 137–144 (2016)
11. Cai, Y.Q., Chen, Y.W., Wang, J.L., et al.: A method for Chinese text classification based on apparent semantics and latent aspects. J. Ambient Intell. Human. Comput. **6**(4), 473–480 (2015)
12. Probabilistic latent semantic analysis. Proceedings of 15th Conference on Uncertainty in Artificial Intelligence, Stockholm, Sweden, pp. 289–296 (1999)
13. Luo, W., Du, J.X., Chen, Y.W., Zhou, Q.: Classification of Chinese text based on recognition of semantic topics. Cogn. Comput. **8**(1), 114–124 (2016)
14. Liu, X., Wu, X., Sang, L., Xie, F.: Wefest: word embedding feature expansion for short text classification. In: IEEE International Conference on Data Mining Workshops (2017)
15. Huang, J., Zhu, J., Yao, D., Bi, J.: A word distributed representation based framework for large-scale short text classification. In: International Joint Conference on Neural Networks, pp. 1–7 (2015)
16. Zhang, Z., Li, T., Zhang., Y., Ma, C., Wan, X.: Short text classification based on semantics. In: International Conference on Intelligent Computing, vol. 9227, pp. 463–470 (2015)
17. Zhang, H., Yin, C., Xiang, J., A new SVM method for short text classification based on semi-supervised learning. In: Advanced Information Technology and Sensor Application (AITS), pp. 100–103 (2016)
18. Xu, J., Wang, P., Xua, B., et al.: Semantic expansion using word embedding clustering and convolutional neural network for improving short text classification. Neurocomputing **174**(PB), 806–814 (2016)
19. Sequential short-text classification with recurrent and convolutional neural networks. Proceedings of NAACL-HLT 2016, pp. 515–520 (2016)

20. Huiyou, C., Yongjun, H., Jiaxin, J.: A new method of keywords extraction for Chinese short - text classification. New Technol. Libr. Inf. Serv. **234**(6), 42–48 (2013)
21. Jieba Chinese text segmentation, June 2017
22. Stop word list, June 2017
23. Senécal, J.S., Morin, F., Gauvain, J.L., Bengio, Y., Schwenk, H.: Neural probabilistic language models. J. Mach. Learn. Res. **3**(6), 1137–1155 (2006). Springer, Heidelberg
24. Dagan, I., Levy, O., Goldberg, Y.: Improving distributional similarity with lessons learned from word embeddings. Bulletin De La Société Botanique De France **75**(3), 552–555 (2015)
25. Corpus for Chinese news headline categorization, June 2017
26. Schmidhuber, J., Hochreiter, S.: Long short-term memory. Neural Comput. **9**(8), 1735–1780 (1997)
27. Kim, Y.: Convolutional neural networks for sentence classfication. arXiv:1408.5882 (2014)

Abstractive Document Summarization via Neural Model with Joint Attention

Liwei Hou[1], Po Hu[1(✉)], and Chao Bei[2]

[1] School of Computer Science, Central China Normal University,
Wuhan 430079, China
houliwei@mails.ccnu.edu.cn, phu@mail.ccnu.edu.cn
[2] Global Tone Communication Technology Co., Ltd., Beijing 100043, China
beichao202@163.com

Abstract. Due to the difficulty of abstractive summarization, the great majority of past work on document summarization has been extractive, while the recent success of sequence-to-sequence framework has made abstractive summarization viable, in which a set of recurrent neural networks models based on attention encoder-decoder have achieved promising performance on short-text summarization tasks. Unfortunately, these attention encoder-decoder models often suffer from the undesirable shortcomings of generating repeated words or phrases and inability to deal with out-of-vocabulary words appropriately. To address these issues, in this work we propose to add an attention mechanism on output sequence to avoid repetitive contents and use the subword method to deal with the rare and unknown words. We applied our model to the public dataset provided by NLPCC 2017 shared task3. The evaluation results show that our system achieved the best ROUGE performance among all the participating teams and is also competitive with some state-of-the-art methods.

Keywords: Abstractive summarization · Attentional mechanism
Encoder-decoder framework · Neural network

1 Introduction

Document summarization is a task of automatically generating a fluent and condensed summary for a document, while keeping the most important information of it as possible.

Efforts on document summarization can be roughly classified into two categories: extractive and abstractive method. Extractive methods usually generate a summary by simply selecting the most salient sentences from the original document and then directly concatenate them to compose the summary. This kind of summarization approach may produce a summary with good effectiveness and efficiency. However, the summary generated by them have some obvious drawbacks such as inevitable information redundancy within each summary sentence and higher incoherence across summary sentences. Furthermore, pure extractive way is also far from the method that human experts write summaries.

© Springer International Publishing AG 2018
X. Huang et al. (Eds.): NLPCC 2017, LNAI 10619, pp. 329–338, 2018.
https://doi.org/10.1007/978-3-319-73618-1_28

On the contrary, abstractive methods are expected to have more chance to generate better summaries by using more flexible expressions such as paraphrasing, compression or fusion with different words which do not belong to the original document. However, generating a high-quality abstractive summary is much more difficult in practice. Fortunately, the development of neural sequence-to-sequence techniques has made abstractive summarization approaches viable, and a set of recurrent neural network models based on attention encoder-decoder framework are becoming increasingly popular. It is worth noting that most of these models typically focus on summarizing documents with short input sequences and generate shorter summaries like news headlines or one-sentence summaries. When generating a summary for a longer document, they usually suffer from the problems that we mentioned earlier such as the appearance of rare words and repeated phrases in the final summary.

In this paper, we present an encoder-decoder based neural abstractive model with joint attention for single document summarization task. And our contributions are as follows:

- We adopt the subword model to deal with the issue of rare and OOV words via segmenting Chinese words into subword units (more in Sect. 3.1), which has the advantage of simplifying the summarization process and reducing the training efforts at the same time with its accuracy as good as those using a large-vocabulary.
- We also add the attentional mechanism on the output sequence (more in Sect. 3.3) to address the issue of repeated phrases in the summary. By looking back at the previous decoding steps, this mechanism helps our model to make more structured prediction and avoid repeating the same contents significantly.

2   Related Work

Document summarization has drawn much attention for a long time and has seen considerable progress over the years. Existing summarization systems are largely extractive by extracting a certain number of salient sentences from original document in verbatim to form the summary. They have traditionally employed linguistic and statistical features to rank sentences via the combination of unsupervised models (e.g. centroid-based method [1], graph-based method [2, 3], LDA-based method [4]) or supervised models (e.g. SVR-based method [5], CRF-based method [6]) and diverse optimization strategies (e.g. integer linear programming [7], submodular function maximization [8, 9]).

Various extractive summarization methods have been proposed and achieved the state-of-the-art performance. However, people tend to write a summary using their own words based on their understanding of the content and discourse-level semantics of the article, and abstractive summarization is closer to the way yet more challenging. The recent success of sequence-to-sequence frameworks has made abstractive summarization viable, in which a set of recurrent neural network models based on attention encoder-decoder have achieved promising performance on short-text summarization tasks (Chopra et al. [10]; Wang and Ling [11]). To apply these models to more natural language processing tasks including summarization, machine translation and so on, word embedding (Pennington et al. [12]) is first used to convert each word to a fixed vector which can be considered as the inputs of these models. To make these models more scalable, attention mechanism (Bahdanau et al. [13]) is also applied into RNN encoder-decoder architecture to focus on different input information in different timesteps. However, these models often prevent themselves from learning good representations for those new words because of a fixed input and output vocabulary. In order to solve this problem, copy mechanism (Gu et al. [14]) and pointer (Gulcehre et al. [15]) are designed to reduce the rare and unknown words by locating a certain segment of input sequence and putting them into the output sequence appropriately. Although these mechanisms are good ways to solve this problem at a certain degree, they inevitably increase the complexity in both structure and time space, which will to be addressed in our current model.

Additionally, due to the challenges of compressing an original document in a lossy manner and preserving the key concepts of it in the summary, Nallapati et al. [16] proposes to use a hierarchical attention in the encoder model to consider key sentences as well as keywords at the same time. To produce higher quality summary via reducing repeated phrases of it, Paulus et al. [17] presents a deep reinforced model which combines intra-decoder attention and a reinforcement learning-based algorithm.

3   Our Method

Existing abstractive summarization approaches often suffer from the disadvantages of generating repeated words and inability to deal with out-of-vocabulary words appropriately. To address these, in this work we propose to add an attention mechanism on output sequence to avoid repetitive contents and use the subword method to deal with the rare and unknown words. We develop an abstractive neural summarization system with joint attention which consists of several important parts as shown in Fig. 1: subword part, RNN encoder-decoder, joint attention. Next we will illustrate each part of our system in detail.

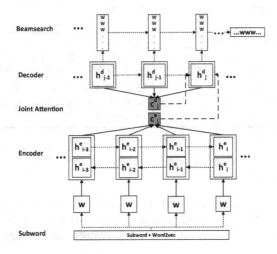

Fig. 1. System architecture

3.1   Subword Part

The main motivation is that some words of document can be recognized by a competent writer even if they are novel to him or her, based on subword units such as morphemes or phonemes. So we propose a hypothesis that a segmentation of rare words into appropriate subword units is sufficient to allow for the RNN encoder-decoder model to generate unknown words in abstractive summarization. And the evaluation results have shown that this hypothesis is feasible (more details will be explained in Sect. 4).

The subword method is initially proposed by Byte Pair Encoding (BPE) which is an effective data compression technique. Sennrich et al. [18] then adopted BPE for word segmentation in neural machine translation (NMT) task which they called subword translation and solved the problem of rare and unknown words. So in this paper, for the similar problem like rare and unknown words in the summary generation, we choose to apply this algorithm to our task.

Firstly, we preprocess all the documents with python word segmentation tool (i.e. jieba toolkit) and then segment each Chinese words into corresponding Chinese characters with symbol '**' in the end, such as '意想不到' to ('意**', '想**', '不**', '到'). Next, we iteratively count all the symbol pairs and replace each occurrence of the most frequent pair ('A','B') with a new symbol 'AB', and for efficiency, we do not consider those pairs that cross Chinese words boundaries. So each merge operation will produce a new symbol which represents a character n-gram. In this way, it reduces a lot of redundant Chinese words. Before the subword method is used, the vocabulary size is 200,004 and after that it becomes 28,193. Actually, it not only can reduce the size of vocabulary, but also can enhance the ability of vocabulary to express some new words. Since it is used in our data preprocessing step, the complexities of the following model construction and training time will not increase. The results of the two segmentation methods are showed in Table 1.

Table 1. Examples of two word segmentation methods

The result of jieba tool	The result of subword method
广 受 关注 的 " 瑞安 孕妇 重度 烧伤 " 一事 有 了 新进展 ： 家属 称 ， 王 芙蓉 现阶段 治疗 急需 型 血小板	广** 受 关注 的 " 瑞安 孕妇 重度 烧伤 " 一事 有 了 新** 进展 ： 家属 称 ， 王 芙** 蓉 现** 阶段 治疗 急需 型 血 ** 小** 板

3.2   RNN Encoder-Decoder

The RNN encoder-decoder framework is the fundamental for many current NLP models and is widely used in machine translation, dialog systems and automatic document summarization. The goal of this framework is to estimate the conditional probability $p(y_1, y_2, \ldots, y_{t'} | x_1, x_2, \ldots, x_t)$, where $\{x_1, x_2, \ldots, x_t\}$ is an input sequence and $\{y_1, y_2, \ldots, y_{t'}\}$, is the corresponding output sequence.

In practice, it is found that a gated RNN such as LSTM or GRU generally performs better than a basic RNN, and bidirectional gated RNN also perform better than uni-directional one. In our model, we adopt a bidirectional neural network with LSTM in encoder and a unidirectional neural network with LSTM in decoder.

Encoder. The LSTM-based encoder maps a set of input sequence vectors $X = \{x_1, x_2, \ldots, x_t\}$ to a set of LSTM state vectors $H^e = \{h_1^e, h_2^e, \ldots, h_t^e\}$:

$$h_t^e = f\left(x_t, h_{t-1}^e\right) \tag{1}$$

where f is the dynamic function of bidirectional LSTM. x_t is a 256 dimension vector training by word2vec. h_{t-1}^e is a 256 dimension vector produced by the bidirectional LSTM states.

The basic RNN encoder-decoder framework just uses a fixed size vector C called context vector to represent the input information:

$$C = \emptyset\left(\{h_1^e, h_2^e, \ldots, h_t^e\}\right) \tag{2}$$

where $\emptyset$ integrates the bidirectional LSTM states H^e into a context vector C.

Decoder. The decoder LSTM is used to predict a target sequence $Y = (y_1, y_2, \ldots, y_{t'})$ by unfolding the context vector C into a set of decoder state vectors $H^d = \{h_1^d, h_2^d, \ldots, h_{t'}^d\}\}$ through the following dynamic function and prediction model:

$$h_{t'}^d = f\left(y_{t'-1}, h_{t'-1}^d, C\right) \tag{3}$$

$$p(y_{t'} | y_{<t'}, X) = g(y_{t'-1}, h_{t'}^d, C) \tag{4}$$

where $h_{t'}^d$ is the decoder LSTM state at t'-timestep, $y_{t'}$ is the predicted target symbol at t'-timestep and $y_{<t'}$ donates the history output $\{y_1, y_2, \ldots, y_{t'-1}\}$. The prediction model is a typical classifier over a very large vocabulary with a softmax layer after the decoder LSTM. In our current model, the softmax layer produces beamsize words on each decoder timestep.

However, basic RNN encoder-decoder framework still has limitations, even if it is classic. Firstly, it requires a fixed length context vector C to act as the representation for the whole input sequence, which may make the information of C insufficient or make the dimension of C higher. Secondly, the semantic vector C might lose the information of the whole sequence and the former information of inputs may be diluted or covered by the latter since all decoder timesteps share one common context vector C. In order to solve these problems, Bahdanau et al. [13] proposes an attention mechanism.

3.3   Joint Attention

The joint attention is a composed attention on both input sequence and output sequence. The attention on input sequence is used to store and deliver more complete information of input on each decoder timestep [13]. And the attention on output sequence is used to avoid repeated phrases by reviewing previous output information. Next, we will introduce these two mechanisms separately, and then the integration of them. The structure of joint attention in our system is showed in Fig. 2.

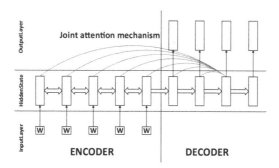

Fig. 2. Neural model of joint attention

Attention on input sequence. The attention mechanism is introduced here to solve the problems of basic RNN encoder-decoder framework mentioned in Sect. 3.2. Instead of one vector C, our attention uses a set of dynamical changing context vectors $\{c_i, c_i, \ldots, c_{t'}\}$ in the decoding process. i.e.

$$e_{ij} = \eta(h_i^d, h_j^e) \tag{5}$$

$$\alpha_{ij} = \frac{\exp(e_{ij})}{\sum_{k=1}^{t'} \exp(e_{ik})} \tag{6}$$

$$c_i = \sum_{j=1}^{t'} \alpha_{ij} h_j^e \tag{7}$$

where η is the function that models the relationship between h_i^d and h_j^e, and it can be defined as a non-linear function. In our model, we first use 2-D convolution layers to extract features from all encoder states and then use a tanh function to get e_{ij}. The α_{ij} is an attention coefficient which indicates the contribution rate of the i-th original Chinese words to the generation of the j-th Chinese words.

Attention on output sequence. Although the attention on input sequence has solved the problems of information loss and insufficient of C which is common used in all decoder timesteps, these attention RNN encoder-decoder models still generate repeated words and phrases, because the output only depends on the latest decoder hidden states. In order to solve this problem, inspired by Paulus et al. [17] that considering the information of all inputs and previous outputs jointly may improve the performance, we combine the information about previously decoded outputs with the latest decoder state to generate a set of context vectors $\{c_1^d, c_2^d, \ldots, c_{t'}^d\}$.

Like above method, our model computes a new decoder context vector $c_{t'}^d$ on each decoding timestep. On the first timestep, we set the initial c_1^d to a vector of zeros. Then for $t' > 1$, we continue the method according to the following equations:

$$e_{t'j}^d = V^d * \tanh\left(h_{t'}^d W^d h_j^d\right) \tag{8}$$

$$\alpha_{t'j}^d = \frac{\exp\left(e_{t'j}^d\right)}{\sum_{k=1}^{t'-1} \exp\left(e_{t'k}^d\right)} \tag{9}$$

$$c_{t'}^d = \sum_{j=1}^{t'-1} \alpha_{t'j}^d h_j^d \tag{10}$$

First, we use tanh function to combine the previous decoder states $\{h_1^d, h_2^d, \ldots, h_{t'-1}^d\}$ with the t'-timestep decoder state $h_{t'}^d$. Then we use a softmax layer to get the attention coefficients $\{\alpha_{t'1}^d, \alpha_{t'2}^d, \ldots, \alpha_{t't'-1}^d\}$. Last, we take these attention coefficients and previous decoder states to obtain the output context vector $c_{t'}^d$.

Two attentions' combination. In order to get the probability of each output word, we first use a linear combination function to embed the two attentions into the t'-timestep decoder state and then use a softmax layer on it:

$$p\left(y_{t'}|y_{<t'}, X\right) = \text{softmax}\left(\text{linear}(h_{t'}^d, c_{t'}^d, c_{t'})\right) \tag{11}$$

4 Experiments

4.1 Dataset

We conduct experiments on a public dataset provided by NLPCC2017 shared task3, which is a Chinese single document summarization task. The dataset includes 50,000 document-summary pairs for training and another 2,000 documents without corresponding summaries for testing. All data is provided by Toutiao.com. The length of the documents is between tens and tens of thousands Chinese characters and the length of the summaries is less than 60 Chinese characters.

4.2   Implementation

We convert the dataset into plain texts and save the news articles and summaries separately. First, we use subword model to process the data after conducting word segmentation by jieba[1] toolkit. Then, we retain 28,193 words in vocabulary and discard the words which are quite rare in nature. Next, we use pre-trained gensim[2] toolkit for the initialization of word vectors which will be further trained in our model. The dimension of all word vectors is 256 in this work.

We use tensorflow for implementation with one layer of bidirectional LSTM for the encoder and one layer of unidirectional LSTM for the decoder. The dimension of all hidden vectors are 128 and the batch size is set to 64 documents. Cross entropy is adopted to calculate the loss and Adam optimizer is used to optimize the loss. In the testing step, the beam sizes for word decoder are 4.

4.3   Evaluation

We adopt the widely used ROUGE-1.5.5 toolkit (Lin [19]) for evaluation. We first compare our model with various state-of-the-art extractive summarization methods provided by the PKUSUMSUM open source toolkit (Zhang et al. [20]) and UniAttention model which is a simple RNN seq2seq baseline model on 500 document-summary pairs of NLPCC2017 shared task3 dataset. The comparison results are shown in Table 2. In Table 3, we compare UniAttention model and our model on 2000 document-summary pairs. The results are the average scores of ROUGE-1, ROUGE-2, ROUGE-3, ROUGE-4, ROUGE-L, ROUGE-SU4, ROUGE-W1.2, which are directly evaluated and provided by NLPCC2017 shared task3 organizers.

Table 2. Comparison results on 500 document-summary pairs using F-measure of ROUGE

Method	Rouge-1	Rouge-2	Rouge-3	Rouge-4	Rouge-L
LexPageRank	0.23634	0.10884	0.05892	0.03880	0.17578
MEAD	0.28674	0.14872	0.08761	0.06124	0.22365
Submodular	0.29704	0.15283	0.08917	0.06254	0.21668
UniAttention	0.33727	0.20032	0.13176	0.10142	0.29440
Our Model	**0.34949**	**0.21172**	**0.14497**	**0.11282**	**0.30662**

The results in Table 2 show that our proposed abstractive method outperforms traditional extractive methods considerably. It also shows superiority over some extractive methods in short summary generating task. The results in Tables 2 and 3 show that our method has improvement over the neural abstractive baseline. And the problem of repeated phrases has a significant improvement.

---

[1] https://pypi.python.org/pypi/jieba/.

[2] http://radimrehurek.com/gensim/.

Table 3. Comparison results on more than 500 document-summary pairs: the score is provided by the track organizers of NLPCC2017 shared task3

Method	Average of ROUGE-1, 2, 3, 4, L, SU4, W-1.2
UniAttention	0.20072
Our Model	**0.22703**

Furthermore, the evaluation results of NLPCC2017 shared task3 are shown in Table 4. The test data have 2000 document-summary pairs, and the scores are also the average scores of ROUGE-1, ROUGE-2, ROUGE-3, ROUGE-4, ROUGE-L, ROUGE-SU4, ROUGE-W1.2. Each team is permitted to submit two version per day between June 5 and June 7, 2017. Table 4 shows the official evaluation results of our model and the peers and shows that our approach achieved the best performance in all participating teams. In summary, our model has a good effectiveness and performance in abstractive single document summarization.

Table 4. Official ROUGE evaluation results for the formal runs of all participating teams

Method	Average of ROUGE-1, 2, 3, 4, L, SU4, W-1.2
Our Model (NLP_ONE)	**0.22102**
ICDD_Mango	0.22093
NLP@WUST	0.21648
CQUT_AC326	0.19138
HIT_ITNLP_TS	0.19133
DLUT_NLPer	0.17537
AC_Team	0.17090
ECNU_BUAA	0.15988
ccnuSYS	0.15790

5   Conclusion

In this paper we tackle the challenging task of abstractive document summarization, which is still less investigated to date and very challenging. We study the difficulty of the existing attention RNN encoder-decoder summarizers, and address the need of producing rare or new words and reduce repeated phrases in the final summary. We adopt subword units and joint attention mechanism to improve the performance of traditional models. Extensive experiments have verified the effectiveness of our proposed approach. Our method also achieved the best performance in the competition of single document summarization track held by NLPCC2017. There is still lots of future work to do. An appealing direction is to combine keywords and key sentences in this neural abstractive model or investigate the neural abstractive method on the multi-document summarization task.

Acknowledgments. This work was supported by the National Natural Science Foundation of China (No. 61402191), the Specific Funding for Education Science Research by Self-determined Research Funds of CCNU from the Colleges' Basic Research and Operation of MOE (No. CCNU16JYKX15), and the Thirteen Five-year Research Planning Project of National Language Committee (No. WT135-11). We also thank Zhiwen Xie for helpful discussion.

References

1. Radev, D.R., Jing, H., Stys, M., Tam, D.: Centroid-based summarization of multiple documents. Inf. Process. Manage. **40**(6), 919–938 (2004)
2. Erkan, G., Radev, D.R.: LexPageRank: prestige in multi-document text summarization. In: EMNLP (2004)
3. Wan, X., Yang, J., Xiao, J.: Manifold-ranking based topic-focused multi-document summarization. In: IJCAI (2007)
4. Titov, I., McDonald, R.: A joint model of text and aspect ratings for sentiment summarization. In: ACL (2008)
5. Li, S., Ouyang, Y., Wang, W., Sun, B.: Multi-document summarization using support vector regression. In: DUC (2007)
6. Nishikawa, H., Arita, K., Tanaka, K., Hirao, T., Makino, T., Matsuo, Y.: Learning to generate coherent summary with discriminative hidden semi-Markov model. In: COLING (2014)
7. Gillick, D., Favre, B.: A scalable global model for summarization. In: ACL (2009)
8. Li, J., Li, L., Li, T.: Multi-document summarization via submodularity. Appl. Intell. **37**(3), 420–430 (2012)
9. Lin, H., Bilmes, J.: Multi-document summarization via budgeted maximization of submodular functions. In: NAACL (2010)
10. Chopra, S., Auli, M., Rush, A.M.: Abstractive sentence summarization with attentive recurrent neural networks. In: NAACL (2016)
11. Wang, L., Ling, W.: Neural network-based abstract generation for opinions and arguments. In: NAACL (2016)
12. Pennington, J., Socher, R., Manning, C.D.: Glove: global vectors for word representation. In: EMNLP (2014)
13. Bahdanau, D., Cho, K., Bengio, Y.: Neural Machine Translation by Jointly Learning to Align and Translate. arXiv preprint arXiv:1409.0473 (2014)
14. Gu, J., Lu, Z., Li, H., Li, V.O.K.: Incorporating copying mechanism in sequence-to-sequence learning. In: ACL (2016)
15. Gulcehre, C., Ahn, S., Nallapati, R., Zhou, B., Bengio, Y.: Pointing the Unknown Words. arXiv preprint arXiv:1603.08148 (2016)
16. Nallapati, R., Zhou, B., dos Santos, C., Gulcehre, C., Xiang, B.: Abstractive text summarization using sequence-to-sequence RNNs and Beyond. In: CoNLL (2016)
17. Paulus, R., Xiong, C., Socher, R.: A Deep Reinforced Model for Abstractive Summarization. arXiv preprint arXiv:1705.04304 (2017)
18. Sennrich, R., Haddow, B., Birch, A.: Neural machine translation of rare words with subword units. In: ACL (2016)
19. Lin, C.-Y.: Rouge: a package for automatic evaluation of summaries. In: ACL (2004)
20. Zhang, J., Wang, T., Wan, X.: PKUSUMSUM: a Java platform for multilingual document summarization. In: COLING (2016)

An Effective Approach for Chinese News Headline Classification Based on Multi-representation Mixed Model with Attention and Ensemble Learning

Zhonglei Lu[1], Wenfen Liu[2(✉)], Yanfang Zhou[1], Xuexian Hu[1], and Binyu Wang[1]

[1] State Key Laboratory of Mathematical Engineering and Advanced Computer, Zhengzhou, Henan, China
lzl_xd6j@163.com, zyf_xd6j@163.com, hxx_xd6j@163.com, wby_xd6j@163.com
[2] Guangxi Key Laboratory of Cryptogpraphy and Information Security, School of Computer Science and Information Security, Guilin University of Electronic Technology, Guilin, Guangxi, China
liuwenfen@guet.edu.cn

Abstract. In NLPCC 2017 shared task two, we propose an efficient approach for Chinese news headline classification based on multi-representation mixed model with attention and ensemble learning. Firstly, we model the headline semantic both on character and word level via Bi-directional Long Short-Term Memory (BiLSTM), with the concatenation of output states from hidden layer as the semantic representation. Meanwhile, we adopt attention mechanism to highlight the key characters or words related to the classification decision, and we get a preliminary test result. Then, for samples with lower confidence level in the preliminary test result, we utilizing ensemble learning to determine the final category of the whole test samples by sub-models voting. Testing on the NLPCC 2017 official test set, the overall F1 score of our model eventually reached 0.8176, which can be ranked No. 3.

Keywords: News headline · Short text · Classification · Multi-representation Ensemble learning

1 Introduction

Chinese news headlines classification faces great challenges for short length, less information, weak information description, scattered themes and big noise, which cause much difficulty in characteristic extraction. With the strong capability of automatic feature extraction, deep learning has become the dominant means of short or very short text classification in recent years. Kim [1] introduced a simple Convolutional Neural Network (CNN) with single convolution layer, which achieved state-of-the-art performance in several NLP tasks, such as sentiment analysis, question classification etc. Lai et al. [2] proposed Recurrent Convolutional Neural Network (RCNN) to model text

© Springer International Publishing AG 2018
X. Huang et al. (Eds.): NLPCC 2017, LNAI 10619, pp. 339–350, 2018.
https://doi.org/10.1007/978-3-319-73618-1_29

classification task on Fudan set, which achieved better performance than CNN. Then character-level convolutional networks (ConvNets) [3] was proposed to classify Chinese news corpus, and obtained better result. Recently, Zhou et al. [4] presented Compositional Recurrent Neural Networks for Chinese short text classification, and got state-of-the-art results.

Under the current deep learning paradigm, there are still two problems in related work. On the one hand, errors in word segmentation easily lead to incorrect or incomplete semantic representation [4], and the Out-Of-Vocabulary (OOV) problem seriously affects the performance of classifiers[1]. On the other hand, there are less targeted means for the weak feature samples, resulting in poor performance.

To solve the above problems, we propose a multi-representation mixed model with attention and a targeted ensemble learning strategy. For problem (1), we integrate character-level feature into word-level feature to obtain headlines representation. The missing semantic information by the error of word segmentation will be constructed; meanwhile, the wrong semantic relevance will be reduced. Considering the strong correlation between certain keywords and classification results, this paper introduces attention mechanism on the basis of multi-representation mixed model. For problem (2), we present two strategies for different testing samples, with multi-representation mixed model attached attention for all testing samples first. For samples with lower prediction confidence, we combine votes from multiple complementary sub-models. Experiments on the NLPCC 2017 Task two datasets show that, the proposed method puts up a good performance, effectively alleviating the influences brought by errors in word segmentation and managing weak feature samples.

The paper is organized as follows. Section 2 describes our multi-representation mixed model with attention. Section 3 introduces the targeted ensemble learning strategy. Experimental results and discussion are reported in Sect. 4. Finally, we draw some conclusions and give the future works.

2   Multi-representation Mixed Model Based on Attention Mechanism

Word segmentation is the first step in Chinese natural language processing, and errors caused by word segmentation can be transmitted to the whole deep neural networks. In order to reduce the impact of word segmentation and improve the overall performance of Chinese news headline classification system, we propose a mixed model of character-level and word-level features based on BiLSTM. By integrating character-level feature into word-level feature, the missing semantic information by the error of word segmentation will be constructed; meanwhile the wrong semantic relevance will be reduced. At the same time, analysis shows that factors determining category of headlines only relate to certain key words or characters, rather than the all. Therefore, this paper introduces attention mechanism to allocate weights to each word

---

[1] According to the SIGHAN (http://www.sighan.org/) Bakeoff data evaluation results, the loss of word segmentation caused by OOV is at least 5 times greater than word sense ambiguation.

or character in the headline, highlighting the key ones. In summary, we propose a word-level and character-level representation mixed model based on attention mechanism which consists of look-up layer, mixed encoding layer, attention layer and softmax classifier. The structure is shown in Fig. 1.

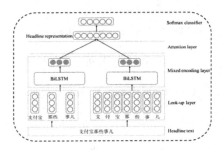

Fig. 1. The structure of multi-representation mixed model based on attention mechanism

2.1 Look-up Layer

Look-up table, a huge word embedding matrix, is the first layer of our model. Each column, which is N-dimensional, corresponds to a word. Given a dictionary D, that is extracted from the training corpus, we can construct a $N \times |D|$-dimensional matrix as the look-up table M. E_{w_i}, the column vector of M in the index of i, is the word embedding for word w_i. As a result, this component maps an input word sequences $\{w_1, w_2, \ldots, w_n\}$ into a series of word embeddings $\{E_{w_1}, E_{w_2}, \ldots, E_{w_n}\}$. This layer contains two look-up tables for characters and words. If pre-trained, we can obtain M from large unlabeled corpus by word2vec[2]. Otherwise, we randomly initialize it.

2.2 Mixed Encoding Layer

This part is based on Recurrent Neural Network (RNN) [5], which is an extension of Feedforward Neural Network (FNN) in time series. It is widely used in machine translation [6], automatic text summarization [7] etc. Unfortunately, the traditional RNN is still hard to apply in practice due to the vanishing and exploding gradient problems [8] during the back propagation training stage. Long Short-Term Memory (LSTM) [9] solves this problem by a more complex internal structure which allows it to remember information for either long or short terms. The structure is shown in Fig. 2.

Given the input sequence $(x_1, x_2, \ldots, x_T)$, we can get the hidden layer states $(h_1, h_2, \ldots, h_T)$ and the memory states $(C_1, C_2, \ldots, C_T)$ as follows.

$$i_t = \sigma(W_i x_t + W_i h_{t-1} + b_i) \tag{1}$$

$$f_t = \sigma\big(W_f x_t + W_f h_{t-1} + b_f\big) \tag{2}$$

---

[2] http://code.google.com/p/word2vec/.

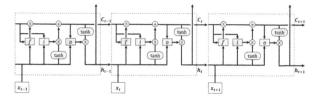

Fig. 2. The structure of LSTM

$$o_t = \sigma(W_o x_t + W_o h_{t-1} + b_o) \tag{3}$$

$$\tilde{C}_t = \tanh(W_c x_t + W_c h_{t-1} + b_c) \tag{4}$$

$$C_t = f_t \odot C_{t-1} + i_t \odot \tilde{C}_t \tag{5}$$

$$h_t = o_t \odot \tanh(C_t) \tag{6}$$

where i, f and o are input, forget and output gate, respectively. x, h and C represent input layer, hidden layer and memory cell, respectively. W and b are weight matrix and bias, namely network's parameters. σ is a sigmoid function, and $\odot$ is element-wise multiplication.

LSTM only encodes the above information, while the following information is equally important to the characterization of the whole semantics. In order to better represent headlines, we propose to use BiLSTM, which reads the headline in both directions with 2 separate hidden layers: the forward and the backward. Thus it can be trained with all the information from history or future for richer semantic representation.

$$\vec{h}_t = LSTM\left(x_t, \vec{h}_{t-1}\right) \tag{7}$$

$$\overleftarrow{h}_t = LSTM\left(x_t, \overleftarrow{h}_{t+1}\right) \tag{8}$$

We summarize the information from the forward and the backward hidden states by concatenating them, i.e.

$$h_t = \left[\vec{h}_t, \overleftarrow{h}_t\right] \tag{9}$$

By this way, the hidden state h_t contains the information of headlines not only in the original order but also in the reverse one. This improves the model's performance in memory. We encode the headlines on character-level and word-level, obtaining semantic vector h_c, h_w, respectively. Thus, the preliminary mixed representation h of headline can be expressed as follows.

$$h = [h_c, h_w] \tag{10}$$

2.3   Attention Layer

Attention mechanism was first used in Neural Machine Translation (NMT). As generating a target language word, not all words contribute equally to the representation of the sentence meaning. Thus, Bahadanau et al. [10] introduced attention mechanism to extract such words which are important to the meaning of the sentence and aggregate the representation of those informative words to form a sentence vector dynamically.

The same is true for Chinese news headline classification. We adopt the attention mechanism to focus on some key words that are strongly correlated to the decision of classification. We can see the attention mechanism in Fig. 3.

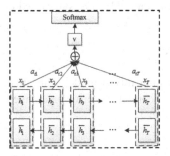

Fig. 3. The structure of attention mechanism

$$u_t = tanh(W_w h_t + b_w) \tag{11}$$

$$a_t = \frac{exp(u_t u_w)}{\sum_{s=1}^{T} exp(u_s u_w)} \tag{12}$$

$$v_w = \sum_{t=1}^{T} a_t h_t \tag{13}$$

We get u_t as a nonlinear representation of h_t for each word through one-layer Multilayer Perception (MLP). Then we measure the importance of the word as similarity of u_t with a word level context vector u_w, and get a normalized importance weight a_t through a softmax layer. Finally, we compute the word-level headline vector v_w that summarizes all the information of words in a headline. We can obtain the character-level headline vector v_c in a similar way. Consequently, we update headline representation in Eq. (10) to h in Eq. (14).

$$h = [v_c, v_w] \tag{14}$$

2.4   Softmax Classifier

Based on the above work, we can obtain the headline representation vector for classification. To be specific, given class number C, the headline representation vector h is mapped to a real-valued vector $\{e_1, e_2, \ldots, e_C\}$ by a linear layer. Then we add a softmax layer to map each real value to conditional probability, which is computed in Eq. (15).

$$P_i = \frac{exp(e_i)}{\sum_{j=1}^{C} exp(e_j)} \tag{15}$$

where $\sum_{i=1}^{C} P_i = 1$.

We use the cross entropy as the loss function, calculating it through back propagation and update parameters with Stochastic Gradient Descent (SGD). The whole model is finally trained end-to-end [11] with supervised classification task.

3   Combination Model

Base on the multi-representation mixed model with attention, we analyze the confidence level distribution of the correct and error predictive samples in development set. The results are shown in Table 1.

Table 1. The confidence level distribution of samples in development set

Total number of error samples	6847			
Confidence of error samples	>0.8	>0.85	>0.9	>0.95
	1051	821	589	218
Total number of correct samples	29153			
Confidence of correct samples	<0.95	<0.9	<0.85	<0.80
	10053	7383	4739	2612

Notes: The accuracy of our multi-representation mixed model with attention is about 0.8098, and there are 36,000 samples in development set.

Statistical results show that, only 15.34% error samples have predictive confidence above 0.80, while only 8.96% correct samples below 0.80. In other words, the rate of error prediction in samples with confidence above 0.80 is very low, and in samples with confidence below 0.80 is relatively high. Furthermore, the proportion of samples with confidence below 0.80 is 23.36, which seems a big scale. So, we propose to construct combination model to vote for the samples with low confidence.

3.1   Model Selection

Besides our multi-representation mixed model with attention, we select N-BoW and CNN [1] as sub-models according to the principle of "difference meets complementation" in feature extraction. Table 2 lists the differences of the N-BoW, CNN and RNN models in text modeling.

Table 2. Comparison of models in text modeling

Model	Advantages	Disadvantages
N-BoW	It trains very fast and is very suitable for online tasks which are strict on the response time. Its effect is acceptable	It seriously relies on word segmentation. It is easy to introduce noise; meanwhile its robustness is weak. Lost sequence order, and no use of context information. More network parameters
CNN	It can model local feature information, and pooling operation can achieve greater span information modeling, extracting the most significant features. It has high efficiency in long text modeling. It trains fast due to parallel computing	Due to the size of windows and other issues, it has higher requirements on parameters tune. It cannot capture the long range dependency of words in a text, and can only process the context in a local window (i.e. the window size of convolution filter), losing some semantic information
RNN	It models the whole sequence order. It can use history and future information to fully model context information and discover long-distance semantic dependencies. It has less network parameters	It trains slowly

3.2 Strategy in Use

The N-BoW and CNN models are trained using the same training data. After obtaining three trained sub-models, we first predict on the whole testing set (TestData) using the single multi-representation mixed model with attention(we just call it CA-BiLSTM). Samples with lower confidence are screened as TestData-2. Then we test our three sub-models on TestData-2, getting three results Result-1, Result-2, Result-3. Finally, we use a simple voting mechanism to determine the category. Specially, for a sample $x \in$ TestData-2, we have three predictive results $R_1(x), R_2(x), R_3(x) \in \{c_1, c_2, \ldots, c_{18}\}$, c_i denotes the category. We take the more one as the category of x. When $R_1(x), R_2(x)$ and $R_3(x)$ are different from each other, the result from our multi-representation mixed model with attention is prevailing. Figure 4 shows the strategy in use.

4   Experiments

4.1   Datasets

The shared task data[3] is collected from several Chinese news websites, such as toutiao, sina etc. There are 18 categories in total. All the headlines are segmented by jieba[4]. Most

---

[3] https://github.com/FudanNLP/nlpcc2017_news_headline_categorization.

[4] https://github.com/fxsjy/jieba.

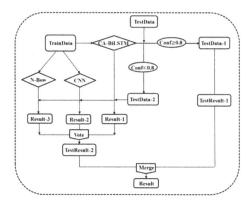

Fig. 4. The structure of our combination model

of title sentence character number is less than 40, with a mean of 21.05. Title sentence word length is even shorter, most of which is less than 20 with a mean of 12.07.

4.2 Experiment Settings

In our experiments, each hidden layer has 400 units. The input is a 200-dimensional vector denotes word embedding or character embedding. We use the longest character-level (40) and word-level (20) length of headlines in the data to unfold all the BiLSTM networks. According to Greff et al. [12] on the experience of parameters setting research, the learning rate is initialized to 0.001, and decay rate [13] per 500 training steps is 0.9. Instead of using a fixed number of epochs, we apply an early stop technique [14] in which the system stops training whenever the F1 score of the development set does not increase after 5 epochs. The specific model parameters are set as shown in Table 3.

Table 3. Parameter configurations of our model

Parameters	Configurations
Maximum length of text (Character)	40
Maximum length of text (Word)	20
Vocabulary size(Character)	6,000
Vocabulary size(Word)	100,000
Embedding dimension(Character)	200
Embedding dimension(Word)	200
Hidden layer size	400
Max epoch	50
Mini-batch size	32
Probability of dropout	0.7
Early stop epoch	5
Learning rate	0.001
Decay rate	0.9

4.3 Results

According to official evaluation requirements, we use the macro-averaged precision, recall and F1 to evaluate the performance. They are defined as:

$$Micro\_avg = \frac{1}{N} \sum_{i=1}^{m} w_i \rho_i \tag{16}$$

where m denotes the number of class, in the case of this dataset is 18. ρ_i denotes the accuracy, recall or F1 score of i-th category, w_i represents how many test examples reside in i-th category, N is total number of examples in the test set.

For ease of description, symbols in each model are specified as follows: "C" means mixed, "A" means attention mechanism, "W" means word-level, "Ch" means character-level, "Ens" means combination model. Thus, CA-BiLSTM is our attention-based multi-representation mixed model.

We first investigate the effect of pre-training, then test the performance of classifiers on single-granularity. After that, the effectiveness of attention mechanism is verified. Finally, we evaluate our combination model (Table 4).

Table 4. The results of each model

Pre-trained or not	Model	Results		
		P	R	F1
No	N-BoW	0.7483	0.7448	0.7465
	CNN	0.7076	0.7021	0.7048
	CA-BiLSTM	0.7438	0.7430	0.7434
Yes	N-BoW	0.7911	0.7835	0.7873
	CNN	0.7692	0.7631	0.7661
	CA-BiLSTM	**0.8098**	**0.8093**	**0.8095**
	WA-BiLSTM	0.7704	0.7702	0.7703
	ChA-BiLSTM	0.7654	0.7650	0.7652
	C-BiLSTM	0.7885	0.7883	0.7884
	Ens-Only	0.8113	0.8108	0.8110
	CA-BiLSTM+Ens	**0.8180**	**0.8172**	**0.8176**

Results show that, each model has a high degree of reliance on pre-training, and the pre-trained look-up table should be large enough to cover all the words. If not, it may result in a certain loss of accuracy. No matter pre-trained or not, our CA-BiLSTM model is better than N-BoW and CNN. Word-level representation of headline is more related to the category decision. When we drop the attention mechanism of CA-BiLSTM, the results will decline. In addition, it can be seen that combination model can predict more accurate than single model, and targeted combination model (CA-BiLSTM+Ens) performs better than the combination model (Ens-Only) directly testing on the whole test set. F1 score of our targeted combination model eventually reaches 0.8176, which can rank No. 3 among the participating teams.

4.4   Discussion

In summary, our CA-BiLSTM model performs better than others under the single-model paradigm. When we adopt combination model, the targeted processing mechanism can fully exploit the complementarity between the sub-models and get the best experimental results. The details of best experimental results are shown in Table 5.

Table 5. The details of best experimental results

Category	P	R	F1
History	0.8146	0.8240	0.8192
Military	0.8330	0.8480	0.8404
Baby	0.8452	0.8815	0.8630
World	0.7081	0.6915	0.6997
Tech	0.7979	0.8330	0.8151
Game	0.8860	0.8820	0.8840
Society	0.5687	0.6270	0.5964
Sports	0.9083	0.8950	0.9016
Travel	0.7385	0.7980	0.7671
Car	0.9061	0.8780	0.8918
Food	0.8284	0.8670	0.8473
Entertainment	0.7514	0.7615	0.7564
Finance	0.8214	0.8120	0.8167
Fashion	0.7998	0.8210	0.8103
Discovery	0.9201	0.8460	0.8815
Story	0.8502	0.7350	0.7884
Regimen	0.8754	0.7590	0.8131
Essay	0.8175	0.8175	0.8175
Overall	0.8180	0.8172	0.8176

As can be seen from Table 5, the accuracy of "society", "world" and "travel" are low. Analysis shows that the "world" and "travel" are highly correlated and prone to significant feature confusion such as country names or district names, resulting in weak identification and prediction. The lack of significant features brings about the lowest indicators to "society" among 18 categories. For "discovery", "car", "sports" and "game", classifier performs very well owing to their obvious and distinguished characteristics.

Further, we visualize the distribution of attention information, as shown in Fig. 5. Only a small part of the headline is strongly related to its category, so our attention mechanism is necessary.

What's more, we get a relatively poor result when removing the stopwords. It means that, there is no need to remove stopwords when modeling very short text because the stopwords contain certain syntax and semantic information. If we remove them, it may destroy the original syntactic structure, even damage the semantics representation.

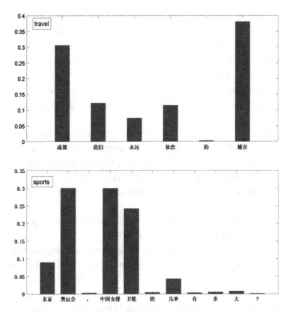

Fig. 5. Visualization of attention

5 Conclusion

This paper presents an effective approach for Chinese news headline classification based on multi-representation mixed model with attention and ensemble learning. We model and integrate the character-level feature into word-level feature of headlines via BiLSTM, alleviating the influence of word segmentation and strengthening the semantic representation. Meanwhile we adopt the attention mechanism to highlight the key characters or words related to the classification decision, with a preliminary test result. Finally, for samples with lower confidence in preliminary test result, we introduce ensemble learning to determine the final category of the whole test samples by sub-models voting. When testing on the NLPCC 2017 official test dataset, we obtain a competitive result. Next, we will integrate part of speech and named entities into our model, because we believe they stress certain potential impact on Chinese news headline classification.

References

1. Kim, Y.: Convolutional neural networks for sentence classification. Eprint Arxiv (2014)
2. Lai, S., Xu, L., Liu, K., et al.: Recurrent convolutional neural networks for text classification. In: AAAI, vol. 333, pp. 2267–2273 (2015)
3. Zhang, X., Zhao, J., LeCun, Y.: Character-level convolutional networks for text classification. In: Advances in Neural Information Processing Systems, pp. 649–657 (2015)

4. Zhou, Y., Xu, B., Xu, J., et al.: Compositional recurrent neural networks for Chinese short text classification. In: 2016 IEEE/WIC/ACM International Conference on Web Intelligence (WI). IEEE, pp. 137–144 (2016)
5. Mikolov, T., Karafiát, M., Burget, L., et al.: Recurrent neural network based language model. In: Interspeech, vol. 2, p. 3 (2010)
6. Cho, K., Van Merriënboer, B., Gulcehre, C., et al.: Learning phrase representations using RNN encoder-decoder for statistical machine translation. arXiv preprint arXiv:1406.1078 (2014)
7. Nallapati, R., Zhou, B., Gulcehre, C., et al.: Abstractive text summarization using sequence-to-sequence RNNS and beyond. arXiv preprint arXiv:1602.06023 (2016)
8. Bengio, Y., Simard, P., Frasconi, P.: Learning long-term dependencies with gradient descent is difficult. IEEE Trans. Neural Netw. **5**(2), 157–166 (1994)
9. Hochreiter, S., Schmidhuber, J.: Long short-term memory. Neural Comput. **9**(8), 1735–1780 (1997)
10. Bahdanau, D., Cho, K., Bengio, Y.: Neural machine translation by jointly learning to align and translate. arXiv preprint arXiv:1409.0473 (2014)
11. Sutskever, I., Vinyals, O., Le, Q.V.: Sequence to sequence learning with neural networks. In: Advances in Neural Information Processing Systems, pp. 3104–3112 (2014)
12. Greff, K., Srivastava, R.K., Koutník, J., et al.: LSTM: a search space odyssey. IEEE Trans. Neural Netw. Learn. Syst. (2016)
13. Srivastava, N., Hinton, G., Krizhevsky, A., et al.: Dropout: a simple way to prevent neural networks from overfitting. J. Mach. Learn. Res. **15**(1), 1929–1958 (2014)
14. Raskutti, G., Wainwright, M.J., Yu, B.: Early stopping and non-parametric regression: an optimal data-dependent stopping rule. J. Mach. Learn. Res. **15**(1), 335–366 (2014)

NLP Fundamentals

Domain-Specific Chinese Word Segmentation with Document-Level Optimization

Qian Yan[1], Chenlin Shen[1], Shoushan Li[1(✉)], Fen Xia[2], and Zekai Du[2]

[1] Natural Language Processing Lab,
School of Computer Science and Technology,
Soochow University, Suzhou, China
{qyan,clshen}@stu.suda.edu.cn, lishoushan@suda.edu.cn
[2] Beijing Wisdom Uranium Technology Co., Ltd., Beijing, China
xiafen@ebrain.ai, 2656460787@qq.com

Abstract. Previous studies normally formulate Chinese word segmentation as a character sequence labeling task and optimize the solution in sentence-level. In this paper, we address Chinese word segmentation as a document-level optimization problem. First, we apply a state-of-the-art approach, i.e., long short-term memory (LSTM), to perform character classification; Then, we propose a global objective function on the basis of character classification and achieve global optimization via Integer Linear Programming (ILP). Specifically, we propose several kinds of global constrains in ILP to capture various segmentation knowledge, such as segmentation consistency and domain-specific regulations, to achieve document-level optimization, besides label transition knowledge to achieve sentence-level optimization. Empirical studies demonstrate the effectiveness of the proposed approach to domain-specific Chinese word segmentation.

Keywords: Chinese word segmentation · Document-level · LSTM · ILP

1 Introduction

The task of word segmentation is to segment the continuous text into isolated words. As a fundamental task in Natural Language Processing (NLP) for those languages without word delimiters, e.g., Chinese [1], word segmentation has been applied as an essential pre-processing step for many NLP tasks, such as named entity recognition [2], event extraction [3], and machine translation [4].

In the literature, most of popular approaches to Chinese word segmentation (CWS) are machine learning-based. In the early years, CWS is treated as a character classification problem, i.e., classifying each Chinese character into a tag according to its position in a word. For instance, position tag B stands for the beginning of a word and E stands for the end of a word. For convenience, we refer to this approach as character-level word segmentation. As a representative, Xue [1] employs a maximum entropy model to CWS.

In recent years, CWS is modeled as a sequence labeling problem where not only the characters are classified to different position tags but also the transition probability

© Springer International Publishing AG 2018
X. Huang et al. (Eds.): NLPCC 2017, LNAI 10619, pp. 353–365, 2018.
https://doi.org/10.1007/978-3-319-73618-1_30

between two nearby position tags are employed to achieve the optimization in the sentence. For example, a segmentation containing the "*EE*" subsequence will be considered impossible in the sentence-level optimization because transition probability from one E to another E is zero due to the fact that a character with tag E always follows a character with tag B or S. For convenience, we refer to this approach as sentence-level word segmentation. As a representative, Tseng et al. [5] employs the well-known conditional random fields (CRF) model to CWS.

However, although character-level and sentence-level word segmentation have achieved much success, they are incapable of handling challenges in domain-specific document-level CWS. Document-level segmentation approaches are especially necessary for domain-specific CWS, since domain-specific texts are often organized in document styles, such as judgments, patents, and scientific papers.

In this paper, we address document-level challenges in domain-specific CWS. First, we apply a long short-term memory (LSTM) classification model to perform character classification and obtain the posterior probabilities belonging to all position tags. Then, we propose a global objective function on the basis on character classification and achieve global optimization via a joint inference approach, named Integer Linear Programming (ILP). Besides various constrains on the label transition to achieve sentence-level optimization, various kinds of constrains on segmentation consistency and domain-specific textual regulation are proposed to achieve document-level optimization. Empirical studies demonstrate the effectiveness of these constraints in document-level word segmentation.

The remainder of this paper is organized as follows. Section 2 overviews related work on the Chinese word segmentation. Section 3 proposes the character-level and sentence-level approaches to CWS. Section 4 proposes our ILP-based approach to document-level CWS. Section 5 presents the experimental results. Finally, Sect. 6 gives the conclusion and future work.

2 Related Work

There has been an enormous amount of work in the research fields of Chinese word segmentation. Existing word segmentation approaches can be mainly categorized into three groups: character-based [5], word-based [6], and both word-and-character-based approaches [7]. This paper mainly focuses on the character-based approaches to CWS.

The pioneer work by Xue [1] first models CWS as a character classification problem and subsequent studies further improve the tagging model into a character sequence labeling problem [5]. In the research line, many studies aim to improve the performance by various manners, such as feature expanding [8], active learning [9], and using different tag sets [10], with shallow learning models like CRF.

More recently, neural network approaches with deep learning models have attracted a great deal of attention. Some novel deep learning models have been adopted in CWS, such as, convolution neural network [11], tensor neural network [12], recursive neural network [13], long short-term memory (LSTM) [14], and gated recursive neural net-work [15]. All these studies demonstrate that the deep learning models have achieved better segmentation results than the shallow learning models.

Different from all above studies, this study performs CWS in a document level. In the first step, our approach applies the label classification approach by LSTM model proposed by previous studies [14] which represents the state-of-the-art performing approach. However, in the following step, our approach aims to obtain a global optimization in the whole document, which has not been researched by any previous studies.

The closest work to ours is a recent work by Li and Xue [16] which deals Chinese patent word segmentation. However, their approach solves the problem by exploiting some document-level features and still applies sentence-level optimization learning model, i.e., CRF. In contrast, our approach optimizes the results with a document-level optimization learning model, i.e., ILP. Furthermore, their approach needs extra document-level labeled data in the specific domain to train the learning model while our approach does not need any labeled data.

3   Character-Level and Sentence-Level CWS

Our approach to sentence-level CWS mainly consists of two steps. In the first step, we apply the LSTM neural network to perform character classification, classifying each character to a position tag, i.e., {B, M, E, S}. Specifically, B, M, and E represent the *Begin*, *Middle*, and *End* of a multi-character segmentation and S represents a *Single* character segmentation. In the second step, we define a global objective function with the character classification results and achieve global optimization via Integer Linear Programming.

3.1   Character-Level CWS with LSTM

In this subsection, we propose the LSTM classification model. Figure 1 shows the framework overview of the LSTM model for character classification. Formally, the input of the LSTM classification model consists of character unigram and bigram embeddings for representing the current character x_i, i.e.,

$$x_i = v_{c_i} \oplus v_{c_{i+1}} \oplus \ldots \oplus v_{c_{i+1},c_{i+2}} \tag{1}$$

where $v_{c_i} \in \mathbf{R}^d$ is a d-dimensional real-valued vector for representing the character unigram c_i and $v_{c_i.c_{i+1}} \in \mathbf{R}^d$ is a d-dimensional real-valued vector for representing the character bigram c_i, c_{i+1}.

Through the LSTM unit, the input of a character is converted into a new representation h_i, i.e.,

$$h_i = LSTM(x_i) \tag{2}$$

Subsequently, the fully-connected layer accepts the output from the previous layer, weighting them and passing through a normally activation function as follows:

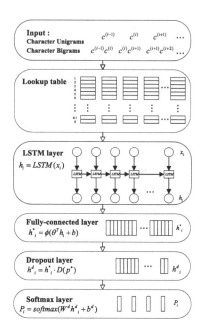

Fig. 1. The framework overview of the LSTM model for character-level CWS

$$h_i^* = dense(h_i) = \phi(\theta^T h_i + b) \tag{3}$$

where ϕ is the non-linear activation function, employed "relu" in our model. h_i^* is the output from the fully-connected layer.

The dropout layer is applied to randomly omit feature detectors from network during training. It is used as hidden layer in our framework, i.e.,

$$h_i^d = h_i^* \cdot D(p^*) \tag{4}$$

where D denotes the dropout operator, p^* denotes a tunable hyper parameter, and h_i^d denotes the output from the dropout layer.

The softmax output layer is used to get the prediction probabilities, i.e.,

$$P_i = softmax(W^d h_i^d + b^d) \tag{5}$$

where P_i is the set of predicted probabilities of the character classification, W^d is the weight vector to be learned, and the b^d is the bias term. Specifically, P_i consist of the posterior probabilities of the current character belonging to each position tag $\{B, M, E, S\}$, i.e.,

$$P_i = <p_{i,B}, p_{i,M}, p_{i,E}, p_{i,S}> \tag{6}$$

3.2   Sentence-Level CWS with ILP

In this subsection, we optimize the obtained results from character classification with Integer Linear Programming (ILP). In the literature, ILP has been widely used in many NLP applications [17].

Specifically, the objective function in ILP is defined as follows:

$$\min \sum_{i=1}^{N} \begin{Bmatrix} y_{i,B} \cdot (-\log p_{i,B}) + y_{i,M} \cdot (-\log p_{i,M}) \\ + y_{i,E} \cdot (-\log p_{i,E}) + y_{i,S} \cdot (-\log p_{i,S}) \end{Bmatrix} \tag{7}$$

Subject to:

$$y_{i,B} \in \{0, 1\} \tag{8}$$

$$y_{i,M} \in \{0, 1\} \tag{9}$$

$$y_{i,E} \in \{0, 1\} \tag{10}$$

$$y_{i,S} \in \{0, 1\} \tag{11}$$

$$y_{i,B} + y_{i,M} + y_{i,E} + y_{i,S} = 1 \tag{12}$$

where N is total number of all characters in the sentence (or the document if applied in document-level word segmentation). $y_{i,B}$ is a Boolean label, denoting whether the final result of current character is B ($y_{i,B} = 1$) or not ($y_{i,B} = 0$). $y_{i,M}, y_{i,E}, y_{i,S}$ denote the same meaning as $y_{i,B}$.

For sentence-level CWS, the constraints implied in the label transition is proposed as following:

(C1): Label transition constraints

This type of constraints limits the position tags of two nearby characters. 4 cases are discussed according to the position tag of the current character.

- **Case (1.1):**

When the position tag of the current character is B, i.e., $y_{i,B} = 1$, the position tag of the next character could only be M or E, i.e., $y_{i+1,M} + y_{i+1,E} = 1$. Otherwise, when $y_{i,B} = 0$, the position tag of the next character could be anyone, i.e., $y_{i+1,M} + y_{i+1,E} = 0$ or 1. Therefore, we obtain the following constraint:

$$y_{i,B} - (y_{i+1,M} + y_{i+1,E}) \leq 0 \tag{13}$$

- **Case (1.2):**

When the position tag of the character is M, we obtain the following constraint:

$$y_{i,M} - (y_{i+1,M} + y_{i+1,E}) \leq 0 \qquad (14)$$

- **Case (1.3):**

When the position tag of the character is E, we obtain the following constraint:

$$y_{i,E} - (y_{i+1,B} + y_{i+1,S}) \leq 0 \qquad (15)$$

- **Case (1.4):**

When the position tag of the character is S, we obtain the following constraint:

$$y_{i,S} - (y_{i+1,B} + y_{i+1,S}) \leq 0 \qquad (16)$$

4   Document-Level CWS

As mentioned in Introduction, although character-level and sentence-level word segmentation have achieved much success, they are incapable of handling challenges in document-level CWS.

One challenge in document-level is how to achieve segmentation consistency in document-level. That is, two text fragments with the same Chinese character sequence should have the same segmentation result as much as possible. Figure 2 shows an instance frequently occurs in the character-level or sentence-level word segmentation where "黄和昌"(*Hechang Huang*) is recognized as a word in the first sentence but segmented into two words, i.e., "黄"(*Huang*) and "和昌"(*Hechang*) in the second sentence. Such segmentation inconsistency should and only can be avoided in document-level. To tackle this challenge, we propose some constrains as follows:

E1:
Segmentation result:
黄和昌 与 被告 签订 协议 。 约定 被告 所借 黄 和昌 500万 元 借款 分 三次 还 清 。
Gold-standard segmentation:
黄和昌 与 被告 签订 协议 。 约定 被告 所借 黄和昌 500 万 元 借款 分 三次 还 清 。

(**English Translation**:
Hechang Huang signed an agreement with the defendant. They were agreed that 500 million Yuan that borrowed from Hechang Huang to the defendant would be paid back in three times.)

Fig. 2. An example with inconsistent segmentation frequently occurred in character-level or sentence-level segmentation

(C2): Segmentation consistency constraints

If two nearby Chinese characters c_i, c_{i+1} are the same as another two nearby Chinese characters c_j, c_{j+1} in a document, we constraint their position labels to be the same, i.e., When $c_i, c_{i+1} = c_j, c_{j+1}$, we have

$$y_{i,B} = y_{j,B}, \, y_{i+1,B} = y_{j+1,B} \tag{17}$$

$$y_{i,M} = y_{j,M}, \, y_{i+1,M} = y_{j+1,M} \tag{18}$$

$$y_{i,E} = y_{j,E}, \, y_{i+1,E} = y_{j+1,E} \tag{19}$$

$$y_{i,S} = y_{j,S}, \, y_{i+1,S} = y_{j+1,S} \tag{20}$$

Another challenge is the consideration of domain-specific textual regulations that are popular in document-level. Figure 3 shows an instance from a judgment (a decision law document of a court). In such text, plaintiffs and defendants are explicitly described in two lines in the front part. It is easy to capture such segmentation regulation from two textual patterns, i.e., "原告 NAME1, (Plaintiff NAME1,)" and "被告 NAME2, (Defendant NAME2,)" where "NAME1" or "NAME2" denotes a person or an organization name. To tackle this challenge, we propose some constrains as follows:

E2:
民事裁定书
（2016）川1425民初404号
原告吕某某，男。委托代理人王刚，某律师事务所律师
被告黄某某，女。委托代理人张可，某律师事务所律师
本院……
(English Translation:
Civil Judgment
(2016) Chuan Civil Trial Num. 1425
    Plaintiff Moumou Lv, Male. Attorney Gang Wang, lawyer of Some Lawyer Office.
    Defendant Moumou Huang, Female. Attorney Ke Zhang, lawyer of Some Lawyer Office.
    This Court……)

Fig. 3. An example from a judgment text

(C3): Textual regulation constraints

In this study, a textual pattern is defined as following:

$$Pattern = \text{``}Tri1 + NAME + Tri2\text{''}$$

where *Tri1* and *Tri2* are two trigger character sequences and *NAME* is a character sequence with variable length. We define that, in this pattern, *Tri1*, *Tri2*, and *NAME* are segmented to be three words.

This type of constrains is domain-specific and document-level. In judgments, we first use some rules to segment the whole document into several parts. Then, we focus on some popular textual patterns in the front part of a judgment. Specifically, we adopt some textual patterns as shown in Table 1.

Table 1. Some textual patterns in the front part of a judgment

Tri1	NAME	Tri2
被告 (Defendant)	NAME1	,
原告 (Plaintiff)	NAME2	,
代理人 (Attorney)	NAME3	,
代表人 (Attorney)	NAME4	,

These patterns are recognized with some regular expressions. Then, we obtain the begin index and end index of the character sequence of *Tri1*, *NAME*, or *Tri2*, which are denoted as q and r. The constraint to segment this character sequence to be word is given as following:

$$y_{q,B} = 1 \tag{21}$$

$$y_{r,E} = 1 \tag{22}$$

$$y_{k,M} = 1 \text{ where } q < k < r \tag{23}$$

5   Experimentation

In this section, extensive experiments are carried out to evaluate the proposed ILP-based approach to domain-specific CWS.

5.1   Experimental Settings

Data Sets: We use two data sets for evaluation. One is from OntoNotes 5.0 which contains six domains: *BN*, *BC*, *NW*, *MZ*, *TC*, and *WB* [18]. The data has been split into three data sets: training, development and test data. The other one is a domain-specific data set which is collected from (http://wenshu.court.gov.cn/) and annotated by ourselves according to the OntoNotes [18] word segmentation guideline. It contains two domains: *Contract* and *Marriage* and each domain contains 100 documents.

Embeddings: We use word2vec (http://word2vec.googlecode.com/) to pre-train character unigram and bigram embeddings using the two data sets.

Hyper-parameters: The hyper-parameter values in the LSTM model are tuned according to performances in the development data.

Evaluation Measurement: The performance is evaluated using the standard precision (P), recall (R) and F score.

Significance test: T-test is used to evaluate the significance of the performance difference between two approaches.

5.2   Experimental Results on Character-Level and Sentence-Level CWS

In this subsection, we test our LSTM with ILP-based approach to character-level and sentence-level CWS. The training and test data are both from OntoNotes5.0 [18].

For comparison, we implement following approaches to CWS:

- **CRF-Char (Character-level):** This is a shallow learning approach which employs conditional random fields (CRF) as the classification algorithm. In the implementation, we apply the tool of CRF++ (http://crfpp.sourceforge.net) and both character unigrams and bigrams are used. The length of the character context window is 2. Note that both the training and development are merged as training data for CRF learning.
- **CRF-Sen (Sentence-level):** This is similar to CRF-Char except adding a label transition feature which is employed to optimize the segmentation results of each sentence. In the implementation, a special feature named "B" is added in the feature template. It is exactly the approach by Tseng [5] which represents the most popular one to CWS before the deep learning approaches appear.
- **LSTM-Char (Character-level):** This is a deep learning approach which employs LSTM as the classification algorithm. This approach is illustrated in Sect. 4 and it is similar to the state-of-the-art approach to CWS, namely LSTM-1, by Chen [14] but missing the sentence inference step.
- **LSTM-Sen (Sentence-level):** This is exactly the state-of-the-art approach to CWS, namely LSTM-1, by Chen [14].
- **LSTM-ILP (C1) (Sentence-level):** This is our approach to CWS which employs ILP to optimize the results of each sentence. Since the optimization is performed in a sentence rather than a document, only the first type of constrains, namely C1, is leveraged.

Due to the space limitation, we report the results of three domains including *BN*, *BC*, and *NW*. Table 2(a)–(c) show the performances of different approaches to CWS in these three domains. From these tables, we can see that the OOV rates in the three domains are in the range of 0.065–0.084, which are all less than 0.1. The low OOV rate in these three domains. In all domains, the segmentation performances are more than 90% in terms of F score.

In character-level CWS, LSTM-Char generally performs better than CRF-Char in terms of F score and OOV Recall.

In sentence-level CWS, LSTM-Sen performs better than CRF-Sen in three domains in terms of F score and in two domains in terms of OOV Recall. Averagely, LSTM-Sen outperforms CRF-Sen in terms of F score, although the improvement is slight. Our

Table 2. Performances of different approaches to CWS (Tested on OntoNotes 5.0)

	P	R	F	R_{OOV}
(a) Performances of different approaches to CWS (Test domain: *BN*, OOV rate: 0.065)				
CRF-Char	0.934	0.934	0.934	0.669
CRF-Sen	0.950	0.948	0.949	0.755
LSTM-Char	0.939	0.940	0.939	0.682
LSTM-Sen	**0.952**	**0.955**	**0.953**	**0.757**
LSTM-ILP (C1)	**0.952**	**0.955**	**0.953**	**0.757**
(b) Performances of different approaches to CWS (Test domain: *BC*, OOV rate: 0.075)				
CRF-Char	0.928	0.936	0.932	0.674
CRF-Sen	0.944	0.949	0.946	0.750
LSTM-Char	0.935	0.942	0.938	0.707
LSTM-Sen	**0.949**	**0.951**	**0.950**	**0.773**
LSTM-ILP (C1)	0.948	0.948	0.948	0.768
(c) Performances of different approaches to CWS (Test domain: *NW*, OOV rate: 0.084)				
CRF-Char	0.928	0.925	0.927	0.677
CRF-Sen	0.952	0.947	0.949	**0.799**
LSTM-Char	0.934	0.939	0.936	0.682
LSTM-Sen	**0.956**	**0.956**	**0.956**	0.791
LSTM-ILP (C1)	0.955	0.954	0.954	0.785

approach LSTM-ILP (C1) performs comparable to LSTM-Sen. This result confirms that, in sentence-level CWS, our approach achieves the state-of-the-art performances.

5.3   Experimental Results on Domain-Specific Document-Level CWS

In this subsection, we test our LSTM with ILP approach to CWS in document-level CWS. The training data is from OntoNotes 5.0 while the test data is from the judgments.

For comparison, besides the approaches in the above subsection, we implement following approaches to CWS:

- **LSTM-Sen + Regulation-Rule**: A straight-forward approach to incorporating domain-specific regulation knowledge for CWS. In this approach, we first perform LSTM-Sen to CWS and then we apply simple rules to recognize words with all textual patterns to refine the results from LSTM-Sen.
- **LSTM-ILP (C2) (Document-level)**: This is our approach to CWS which employs ILP to optimize the results in the whole document. Only the second type of constrains, i.e., segmentation consistency constraints, is used.
- **LSTM-ILP (C3) (Document-level)**: In the same spirit to LSTM-ILP (C2), only the third type of constrains, i.e., textual regulation constraints, is used.

- **LSTM-ILP (Ci + Cj) (Sentence-level and Document-level):** This is our approach to CWS which employs ILP to optimize the results in the whole document. Both the i-th and the j-th types of constrains are used.
- **LSTM-ILP (C1 + C2 + C3) (Sentence-level and Document-level):** This is our approach to CWS which employs ILP to optimize the results in both the sentence-level and document-level. That is to say, all types of constrains are used.

Tables 3 and 4 show the performances of different approaches to CWS tested on the second data set. From these two tables, we can see that the OOV rates in the two domains are in the range of 0.165–0.186, which is much higher than those in the last experiment. The high OOV rate is due to the fact that the training and test data are from different domains.

Table 3. Performances of different approaches to CWS (Test domain: *Contract*, OOV rate: 0.186)

	P	R	F	R_{OOV}
LSTM-Char	0.816	0.837	0.826	0.735
LSTM-Sen	0.816	0.867	0.841	0.777
LSTM-Sen+Regulation-Rule	0.856	0.887	0.871	0.804
LSTM-ILP (C1)	0.837	0.874	0.855	0.795
LSTM-ILP (C2)	0.828	0.843	0.835	0.747
LSTM-ILP (C3)	0.845	0.860	0.853	0.756
LSTM-ILP (C1+C2)	0.845	0.880	0.862	0.809
LSTM-ILP (C1+C3)	0.867	0.896	0.881	0.814
LSTM-ILP (C2+C3)	0.888	0.891	0.889	0.820
LSTM-ILP (C1+C2+C3)	**0.909**	**0.922**	**0.915**	**0.866**

Table 4. Performances of different approaches to CWS (Test domain: *Marriage*, OOV rate: 0.165)

	P	R	F	R_{OOV}
LSTM-Char	0.879	0.875	0.877	0.804
LSTM-Sen	0.896	0.898	0.897	0.866
LSTM-Sen+Regulation-Rule	0.909	0.900	0.905	**0.894**
LSTM-ILP (C1)	0.891	0.887	0.889	0.847
LSTM-ILP (C2)	0.883	0.874	0.878	0.806
LSTM-ILP (C3)	0.884	0.878	0.881	0.816
LSTM-ILP (C1+C2)	0.910	0.903	0.906	0.873
LSTM-ILP (C1+C3)	0.903	0.894	0.898	0.868
LSTM-ILP (C2+C3)	0.894	0.882	0.888	0.834
LSTM-ILP (C1+C2+C3)	**0.919**	**0.908**	**0.913**	**0.894**

When only one type of document-level constrains is employed, the LSTM model with ILP, i.e., LSTM-ILP (C2) or LSTM-ILP (C3), performs significantly better than LSTM-Char in terms of F score (p-value < 0.001), which verifies the effectiveness of using the document-level constrains, i.e., C2 or C3.

When two types of document-level constrains are employed, the LSTM model with ILP, i.e., LSTM-ILP (C1 + C2), LSTM-ILP (C1 + C3) and LSTM-ILP (C2 + C3), perform significantly better than that of using only one (p-value < 0.001).

When both the sentence-level and document-level constrains are employed, our app- roach, i.e., LSTM (C1 + C2 + C3), performs best. Especially, in the *Contract* domain, our approach achieves a gain of 8.9% over LSTM-Char in terms of F score, which is rather impressive. Even compared to the state-of-the-art approach LSTM-Sen, our approach significantly improves the F score from 0.841 to 0.915 (with a gain of 7.4%, p-value < 0.001). Moreover, our approach outperforms LSTM-Char or LSTM-Sen in terms of OOV Recall by a wide margin.

It is worthy to note that LSTM-Sen + Regulation-Rule is a very strong baseline, which implies that regulation rules are very effective for segmenting judgment text. Nevertheless, our approach based on ILP with all constrains significantly outperforms LSTM- Sen + Regulation-Rule in both domains in terms of F score (p-value < 0.001). Especially, in the *Contract* domain, the improvement of our approach over LSTM-Sen + Regulation-Rule is rather impressive, reaching 4.4% in terms of F score.

6   Conclusion

This paper proposes a novel approach to domain-specific CWS which adopts Integer Linear Programming to optimize the character-classification results from the LSTM model. One major advantage of our approach is its convenience to incorporate various kinds of sentence-level and document-level segmentation knowledge, such as label transition, segmentation consistency, and domain-specific textual regulations, by for-mulating them as mathematical constrains in ILP. Empirical studies show that our ILP-based approach with each kind of constrains consistently improves the segmen-tation performance. Moreover, when two or three kinds of constrains are leveraged, the segmentation performance could be further apparently improved.

In our future work, we would like to improve our approach by trying some other kinds of constrains to leverage more kinds of segmentation knowledge to correct the segmentation errors. Furthermore, we would like to test our approach in much more other specific domains, such as scientific and patent documents.

Acknowledgments. This research work has been partially supported by three NSFC grants, No. 61375073, No. 61672366 and No. 61331011.

References

1. Xue, N.W.: Chinese word segmentation as character tagging. Comput. Linguist. Chin. Lang. Process. **8**(1), 29–48 (2003)
2. Gao, J.F., Li, M., Wu, A., Huang, C.N.: Chinese word segmentation and named entity recognition: a pragmatic approach. Comput. Linguist. **31**(4), 531–574 (2005)
3. Chen, C., Ng, V.I.: Joint modeling for Chinese event extraction with rich linguistic features. In: Proceedings of COLING, pp. 529–544 (2012)
4. Zhang, R.Q., Yasuda, K., Sumita, E.: Improved statistical machine translation by multiple Chinese word segmentation. In: Proceedings of the Third Workshop on Statistical Machine Translation, pp. 216–223 (2008)
5. Tseng, H., Chang, P., Andrew, G., Jurafsky, D., Manning, C.: A conditional random field word segmenter for Sighan bakeoff 2005. In: Proceedings of the Fourth SIGHAN Workshop on Chinese Language Processing, pp. 168–171 (2005)
6. Andrew, G.: A hybrid Markov/semi-Markov conditional random field for sequence segmentation. In: Proceedings of EMNLP, pp. 465–472 (2006)
7. Zhang, M., Zhang, Y., Fu, G.: Transition-based neural word segmentation. In: Proceedings of ACL, pp. 421–431 (2016)
8. Shi, Y.X., Wang, M.Q.: A dual-layer CRFs based joint decoding method for cascaded segmentation and labeling tasks. In: Proceedings of IJCAI, pp. 1707–1712 (2007)
9. Li, S.S., Zhou, G.G., Huang, C.R.: Active learning for Chinese word segmentation. In: Proceedings of COLING, pp. 683–692 (2012)
10. Zhao, H., Huang, C.N., Li, M., Lu, B.L.: Effective tag set selection in Chinese word segmentation via conditional random field modeling. In: Proceedings of PACLIC, pp. 87–94 (2006)
11. Zheng, X.Q., Chen, H.Y., Xu, T.Y.: Deep learning for Chinese word segmentation and POS tagging. In: Proceedings of EMNLP, pp. 647–657 (2013)
12. Pei, W., Ge, T., Chang, B.: Max-margin tensor neural network for Chinese word segmentation. In: Proceedings of ACL, pp. 293–303 (2014)
13. Chen, X.C., Qiu, X.P., Zhu, C.X., Huang, X.J.: Gated recursive neural network for Chinese word segmentation. In: Proceedings of ACL, pp. 1744–1753 (2015)
14. Chen, X.C., Qiu, X.P., Zhu, C.X., Liu, P.F., Huang, X.J.: Long short-term memory neural networks for Chinese word segmentation. In: Proceedings of EMNLP, pp. 1197–1206 (2015)
15. Xu, J., Sun, X.: Dependency-based gated recursive neural network for Chinese word segmentation. In: Proceedings of ACL, pp. 567–572 (2016)
16. Li, S., Xue, N.: Effective document-level features for Chinese patent word segmentation. In: Proceedings of ACL, pp. 199–205 (2013)
17. Barzilay, R., Lapata, M.: Aggregation via set partitioning for natural language generation. In: Proceedings of ACL, pp. 359–366 (2006)
18. Hovy, E., Marcus, M., Palmer, M., Ramshaw, L., Weischedel, R.: OntoNotes: the 90% Solution. In: Proceedings of NAACL, pp. 57–60 (2006)

Will Repeated Reading Benefit Natural Language Understanding?

Lei Sha[1(✉)], Feng Qian[2], and Zhifang Sui[1(✉)]

[1] Key Laboratory of Computational Linguistics, School of Electronics Engineering
and Computer Science, Ministry of Education, Peking University, Beijing, China
{shalei,szf}@pku.edu.cn
[2] Institute of Network Computing and Information Systems,
Peking University, Beijing, China
nickqian@pku.edu.cn

Abstract. Repeated Reading (re-read), which means to read a sentence twice to get a better understanding, has been applied to machine reading tasks. But there have not been rigorous evaluations showing its exact contribution to natural language processing. In this paper, we design four tasks, each representing a different class of NLP tasks: (1) part-of-speech tagging, (2) sentiment analysis, (3) semantic relation classification, (4) event extraction. We take a bidirectional LSTM-RNN architecture as standard model for these tasks. Based on the standard model, we add repeated reading mechanism to make the model better "understand" the current sentence by reading itself twice. We compare three different repeated reading architectures: (1) Multi-level attention (2) Deep BiL-STM (3) Multi-pass BiLSTM, enforcing apples-to-apples comparison as much as possible. Our goal is to understand better in what situation repeated reading mechanism can help NLP task, and which of the three repeated reading architectures is more appropriate to repeated reading. We find that repeated reading mechanism do improve performance on some tasks (sentiment analysis, semantic relation classification, event extraction) but not on others (POS tagging). We discuss how these differences may be caused in each of the tasks. Then we give some suggestions for researchers to follow when choosing whether to use repeated model and which repeated model to use when faced with a new task. Our results thus shed light on the usage of repeated reading in NLP tasks.

1 Introduction

Bidirectional LSTM-RNN (BiLSTM) architecture has been successfully applied to sentiment classification [9], question answering [23], Sequence Tagging [6], by capturing syntactic and semantic aspects of text.

Repeated reading, first proposed to alleviate the lack of large scale training and test datasets [4,14]. The motivation is: if we read a sentence again (re-read), we may get a better understanding of the sentence. There are three alternative repeated reading architectures: (1) Multi-level attention (2) Deep BiLSTM (3) Multi-pass BiLSTM.

© Springer International Publishing AG 2018
X. Huang et al. (Eds.): NLPCC 2017, LNAI 10619, pp. 366–379, 2018.
https://doi.org/10.1007/978-3-319-73618-1_31

Multi-level attention is mentioned as impatient reader in [4], which takes first-level attention as weight and take the weighted sum of the BiLSTM outputs as first-level memory, then use first-level memory to generate the second-level attention and the second-level memory and so on. The attention on each word are updated in each level, which lead to the update of memory. The extra information brought by re-read is contained in the second-level attention/memory.

Deep BiLSTM is an alternative repeated reading architecture. After the current sentence is read by an BiLSTM, the outputs of which are taken as the input of the second BiLSTM with different parameters. By reading again, the model can observe the sentence from a more integrated level, which is the effect of repeated reading.

Multi-pass BiLSTM is the third architecture. In this architecture, after the current sentence is read by an BiLSTM, A second BiLSTM with different parameters reads a delimiter and the current sentence again, but its memory state is initialized with the last cell state of the previous BiLSTM. Then the information brought by the second BiLSTM would contribute to the NLP task as extra information.

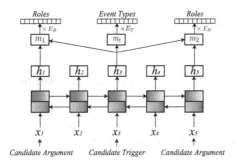

Fig. 1. The standard BiLSTM model.

Our goal in this paper is thus to investigate a number of NLP tasks with the goal of understanding if repeated reading models is useful to natural language understanding, and which kind of repeated reading model would offer specific advantages. We investigate four tasks to show the effect of repeated reading (re-read): (1) part-of-speech tagging: check the effect of re-read on word-level semantic classification, (2) sentiment analysis: check the effect of re-read on phrase-level and sentence-level sentiment classification, (3) semantic relation classification: check the effect of re-read on learning long-distance relationships between two words that may be far apart sequentially, (4) event extraction: check the effect of re-read on extracting hierarchical structure from text.

The principal motivation for this paper is to understand better when repeated reading models are needed to outperform simpler models by enforcing apples-to-apples comparison as much as possible. This paper applies existing models to existing tasks, barely offering novel algorithms or tasks. Our goal is rather

Table 1. The output layer function and objective function of the four task. 1: Part-of-speech tagging; 2: Sentiment Analysis; 3: Semantic relation classification; 4: Event Extraction

Task ID	Output	Objective
1	$O_{pos,t} = E\tanh(Wh_t + b_1) + b_2$	$J_{\text{pos}}(\theta) = \sum_i \sum_j \log p(y^{(i)}[j]|x^{(i)}, \theta)$
2,3	$O_{\text{sa}} = W\left(\frac{1}{N_S}\sum_t^{N_S} h_t\right) + b$	$J_{\text{sa}}(\theta) = \sum_i \log p(y^{(i)}|x^{(i)}, \theta)$
4	$O_{R,t} = E_R\tanh(W_R[h_t, h_{trig}] + b_{wr}) + b_{er}$	$J_{EE}(\theta) = \sum_i \left(\sum_j \log p(y_R^{(i)}[j]|x^{(i)}, \theta)\right.$
	$O_T = E_T\tanh(W_T h_{trig} + b_{wt}) + b_{et}$	$\left. +\lambda \log p(y_T^{(i)}|x^{(i)}, \theta)\right)$

an analytic one, to investigate different versions of repeated reading models. This work helps understand the pros and cons of different repeated reading architectures.

2 Models

2.1 Notations

We denote the text unit S (a phrase or a sentence) as a sequence of tokens/words: $S = \{w_1, w_2, \cdots, w_{N_S}\}$. Each word has a K-dim embedding e_w.

2.2 Standard BiLSTM Model and Application on Different Tasks

Long Short Term Memory (LSTM). LSTM [5] is defined as follows: given a sequence of inputs $X = \{x_1, x_2, \cdots, x_{n_X}\}$, an LSTM associates each timestep with an input, memory and output gate, respectively denoted as i_t, f_t and o_t. We notationally disambiguate e and h: e_t denotes the vector for individual text units (e.g., word or sentence) at time step t, while h_t denotes the vector computed by the LSTM model at time t by combining e_t and h_{t-1}. σ denotes the sigmoid function. The vector representation h_t for each time-step t is given by:

$$\begin{bmatrix} i_t \\ f_t \\ o_t \\ l_t \end{bmatrix} = \begin{bmatrix} \sigma \\ \sigma \\ \sigma \\ \tanh \end{bmatrix} (W \cdot \begin{bmatrix} h_{t-1} \\ e_t \end{bmatrix} + b) \tag{1}$$

where $W \in \mathbb{R}^{4K \times 2K}$, $b \in \mathbb{R}^{4K \times 1}$.

Bidirectional Models. [13] add bidirectionality to the recurrent framework where embeddings are calculated both forwardly and backwardly in each time step:

$$\begin{aligned} \overrightarrow{h_t} &= f(W^{\rightarrow} \cdot [\overrightarrow{h_{t-1}}, e_t] + b^{\rightarrow}) \\ \overleftarrow{h_t} &= f(W^{\leftarrow} \cdot [\overleftarrow{h_{t+1}}, e_t] + b^{\leftarrow}) \end{aligned} \tag{2}$$

Then, the output of time t is $h_t = [\overrightarrow{h_t}, \overleftarrow{h_t}]$.

Baseline Model. The baseline model in this paper is shown in Fig. 1, which is a standard bidirectional LSTM. Since event extraction is the most complicated task among the five, which needs to identify and classify the trigger as well as arguments, we take event extraction as an example in Fig. 1. In event extraction task, the event type and the roles are to be decided by the candidate trigger and candidate arguments. Therefore, each of the output vectors $h_1, h_2, \cdots, h_{N_S}$, after concatenated with the trigger's corresponding output vector h_{trig}, can be taken as the feature vector for role classification. Also, h_{trig} is the feature for event type classification. Then the role output of the t-th word and the event type output can be calculated by Eq. 3.

$$O_{R,t} = E_R \tanh(W_R[h_t, h_{trig}] + b_{wr}) + b_{er}$$
$$O_T = E_T \tanh(W_T h_{trig} + b_{wt}) + b_{et} \qquad (3)$$

where W_R, E_R, W_T, E_T are weight matrices, each dimension of $O_{R,t}$ represents the score of a role and each dimension of O_T represents the score of an event type.

In the event extraction case, given all of our training examples $(x^{(i)}; y_T^{(i)}, y_R^{(i)})$ ($y_T^{(i)}$ is the event type label, $y_R^{(i)}[j]$ is the role label of j-th candidate argument), we can then define the objective function as follows:

$$J_{EE}(\theta) = \sum_i \left(\sum_j \log p(y_R^{(i)}[j]|x^{(i)}, \theta) + \lambda \log p(y_T^{(i)}|x^{(i)}, \theta) \right) \qquad (4)$$

where λ is a hyperparameter to balance the effect of trigger and argument. The conditional probability for event type and role is obtained in Eq. 5:

$$p(r_i|x_t, \theta) = \frac{\exp(O_{R,t}[i])}{\sum_k \exp(O_{R,t}[k])}, p(t_i|x, \theta) = \frac{\exp(O_T[i])}{\sum_k \exp(O_T[k])} \qquad (5)$$

The neural network architectures of other tasks have some minor differences from Fig. 1. For sequence labeling tasks like POS tagging, we only need to classify each token to a certain type, so after denoting $y^{(i)}[j]$ as the POS tag of j-th token in the i-th case, the output layer and objective function is shown in Table 1. For the sequence classification tasks like task 2, we apply average pooling to the output of the BiLSTM, and send the pooling result to the logistic regression classifier.

For the relation classification task, the model needs to know the position of the two entities, so we assign an entity tag to each word using a commonly used encoding scheme BILOU (Begin, Inside, Last, Outside, Unit) [12]. Each entity tag corresponds to an one-hot vector with only the entity tag's corresponding entry is 1. We concatenate each word's embedding with the corresponding tag's vector, and take them as the input of BiLSTM. Then the relation classification can be transferred into sequence classification problem. The output layer and objective function is shown in Table 1.

2.3   Repeated Reading Models

The three possible repeated reading architecture are shown in Fig. 2. All of them are based on the standard bidirectional LSTM architecture.

Multi-level Attention (MLA). In Fig. 2a, the MLA model computes a memory vector by attention mechanism using the BiLSTM output as in Eq. 6.

$$\alpha_1 = \tanh(W_{b1}H + W_{t1}h_{trig}), \ \alpha_1 \in \mathbb{R}^{K \times N_S}$$
$$s_1 = \text{softmax}(w_1\alpha_1), \ s_1 \in \mathbb{R}^{N_S} \tag{6}$$
$$M_1 = s_1H^T, \ M_1 \in \mathbb{R}^K$$

where $H = [h_1, h_2 \cdots h_{N_S}]$, $W_b, W_t \in \mathbb{R}^{K \times K}$, $w_1 \in \mathbb{R}^K$, s_1 is the attention weight. M_1 is the memory vector. To make the model understand the text better, we equip the model with re-read ability by the second attention level as follows [4]:

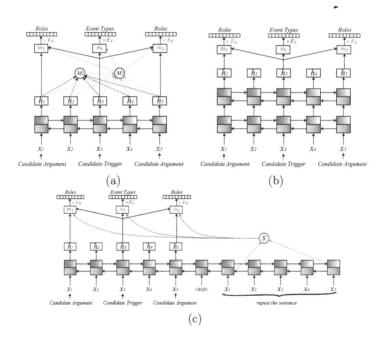

Fig. 2. Three re-read architectures: (a) Multi-level attention (b) Deep BiLSTM (c) Multi-pass BiLSTM

$$\alpha_2 = \tanh(W_{b2}H + W_{t2}h_{trig} + W_m M_1)$$
$$s_2 = \text{softmax}(w_2\alpha_2), \ s_2 \in \mathbb{R}^{N_S} \tag{7}$$
$$M_2 = s_2H^T, \ M_2 \in \mathbb{R}^K$$

Then the output layer is shown as Eq. 8.

$$O_{R,t} = E_R \tanh(W_R[h_t, h_{trig}, M_2] + b_{wr}) + b_{er}$$
$$O_T = E_T \tanh(W_T[h_{trig}, M_2] + b_{wt}) + b_{et} \tag{8}$$

For the other 3 tasks, the attention only depends on the BiLSTM's output and the memory:

$$\alpha_1 = \tanh(W_{b1}H)$$
$$\alpha_2 = \tanh(W_{b2}H + W_m M_1) \tag{9}$$

Deep BiLSTM(DB). In Fig. 2b, we take the output of the BiLSTM as the input of the second BiLSTM [18]. Then the second BiLSTM is the re-read mechanism here. The output layer and objective function are the same as the standard BiLSTM (Table 1).

Multi-pass BiLSTM(MPB). The architecture in Fig. 2c is the third possible architecture of repeated reading. After the current sentence is read by a BiLSTM, a second BiLSTM with different parameters is reading a delimiter and the current sentence again (the second pass). We denote the outputs of the forward and backward LSTMs of the second pass as $H_s^{\rightarrow}$ and $H_s^{\leftarrow}$ respectively. The encoding of the second pass is formed by the concatenation of the final forward and backward outputs $S' = [H_s^{\rightarrow}(N_S), H_s^{\leftarrow}(1)]$.

Then the output layer of event extraction (Task 4) is shown as Eq. 10.

$$O_{R,t} = E_R \tanh(W_R[h_t, h_{trig}, S'] + b_{wr}) + b_{er}$$
$$O_T = E_T \tanh(W_T[h_{trig}, S'] + b_{wt}) + b_{et} \tag{10}$$

The output layer of other tasks are simply replace the "h_t" in Table 1 with "$[h_t, S']$".

3 Experiments

We detail the experiment settings and results in this section. In each case we employed standard training frameworks for the three architectures: for each task, we used stochastic gradient decent using AdaDelta [24] with minibatches. Derivatives are calculated from standard back-propagation [1]. Hyper-parameters are tuned using the development dataset. The hyper-parameters include the size of each hidden layer, learning rate, λ in event extraction and parameters for L_2 penalizations. The model achieving best performance on the development set is used as the final model to be evaluated.

We trained word embeddings on the Wikipedia+Gigaword dataset using the WORD2VEC package[1].

---

[1] https://code.google.com/p/word2vec/.

The number of running iterations is also treated as a hyper-parameter to tune. we repeated the training procedure for each algorithm 20 times and report the average accuracies as well as the statistical significance testing result (we use Wilcoxon signed-rank test). Test scores that achieve significance level of 0.05 are marked by an asterisk (∗).

3.1   Part-of-Speech Tagging

Task Description. We use Wall Street Journal (WSJ) data as our testbed. We use Sections 0–18 of the Wall Street Journal (WSJ) data for training, sections 19–21 for validation and sections 22–24 for testing. For the five architectures (standard BiLSTM, 1-level MLA, 2-level MLA, deep BiLSTM, multi-pass BiLSTM), we take the 50 dimensional word vectors as input. The test accuracy and p value are shown in Table 2.

Table 2. Accuracy for different models on part of speech tagging. The p values are calculated between repeated reading models and the standard model.

	Accuracy	p value
Standard	**91.30**	-
MLA(1-level)	91.09	0.10960
MLA(2-level)	90.92	0.39532
DB	81.31	0.00096∗
MPB	90.74	0.07346

Discussion. According to the result in Table 2, we find that the standard BiL-STM model slightly outperforms most of the repeated reading architectures (1-level MLA, 2-level MLA and MPB), and significantly outperforms the DB model. This result implies that the repeated reading mechanism is not able to provide improvement to word-level POS tag classification, sometimes it can even make the performance worse (DB).

We suggest a few reasons to explain this phenomena. POS tagging is a very simple task, the model can receive enough information after read the sentence once. The MLA keeps a memory which records the understanding of the whole sentences. However, intuitively, in most cases, to decide whether a word is a noun, a verb or an adjective, the context information is enough [22]. The general comprehension of the sentence not only is not necessary, it may sometimes do harm to the understanding of each word. For example, the attention mechanism in MLA will bring semantic information of many other words, which may mislead the model to wrong POS tags.

3.2 Sentiment Analysis

Task Description. For sentiment analysis, we experiment on the Stanford Sentiment TreeBank [20]. We intend to find the effect of repeated reading mechanism on short sequence classification and long sequence classification in this experiment.

Table 3. The average sentence length (word number) of Stanford Sentiment Treebank

	Phrase-level	Root-level	Total
Train	3.71	19.14	4.12
Dev	3.67	19.32	4.08
Test	3.67	19.19	4.08

Stanford Sentiment TreeBank contains gold-standard labels for every parse tree constituent, from the sentence to phrases to individual words. We transformed the dataset as illustrated in Fig. 3. Each phrase is reconstructed from parse tree nodes and treated as a separate data point. Since the original treebank contains 11,855 sentences with 215,154 phrases, the reconstructed dataset contains 215,154 examples. All models (standard model & repeated reading models) are evaluated at both the phrase level (82,600 instances) and the sentence root level (2,210 instances). The average sentence length of this dataset is shown in Table 3. The evaluation result is shown in Table 4(a) and (b) .

Discussion. According to Table 4(a), in the phrase-level sentiment classification, repeated reading models have shown its effective. 1-level MLA, 2-level MLA and

Table 4. (a) Fine-grained classification result (very negative, negative, neutral, positive, very positive). Test set accuracies on the Stanford Sentiment Treebank at phrase-level, root-level and total. The number in brackets are the different from the standard model's result at the corresponding level. The p values are calculated between repeated reading models and the standard model. (b) Coarse-grained classification result (negative, positive). Test set accuracies on the Stanford Sentiment Treebank at phrase-level, root-level and total.

Fine-grained	Phrase-level	Root-level	Total
Standard	80.72	**42.25**	79.91
MLA(1-level)	81.25(+0.53)	40.68(-1.57)	80.06(+0.15)
p value	0.0002*	0.00578*	0.0008*
MLA(2-level)	**81.61(+0.89)**	39.58(-2.67)	**80.15(+0.24)**
p value	0.008*	0.006*	0.0007*
DB	79.61(-1.11)	41.63(-0.62)	78.26(-1.63)
p value	0.0003*	0.03156*	0.03156*
MPB	81.11(+0.39)	42.08(-0.17)	79.88(-0.08)
p value	0.0003*	0.10524	0.87288

(a)

Coarse-grained	Phrase-level	Root-level	Total
Standard	80.79	72.57	79.89
MLA(1-level)	81.47(+0.68)	73.04(+0.47)	80.95(+1.06)
p value	0.0022*	0.0028*	0.0129*
MLA(2-level)	**81.65(+0.86)**	**73.64(+1.07)**	**81.31(+1.42)**
p value	0.0008*	0.0006*	0.0033*
DB	75.99(-4.80)	69.10(-3.47)	75.51(-4.38)
p value	0.0004*	0.0001*	0.0002*
MPB	80.71(-0.08)	72.60(+0.03)	79.78(-0.11)
p value	0.0600	0.158	0.0238

(b)

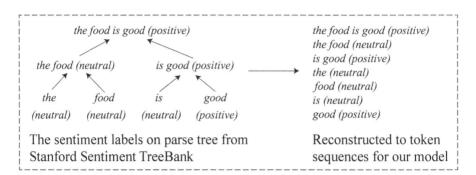

Fig. 3. Transforming Stanford Sentiment Treebank to sequences for sequence models.

MPB model are significantly higher than the standard model. However, in the root-level sentiment classification, the repeated reading models are defeated by the standard model. Since the amount of phrase-level cases is much larger than the root-level cases, the performance of repeated reading models are still higher than the standard model in the total dataset.

We found that in this experiment, repeated reading models perform better at phrase-level sentiment classification but worse at sentence-level sentiment classification in fine-grained classification. But in coarse-grained classification, repeated reading models achieves better performance at both level sentiment classification. As is known to all, much of the sentiment label only depends on single sentiment words like "good" or "bad" instead of the whole phrase or sentence. In the Stanford sentiment Treebank, long sequences contain so much information that it is hard for even the attention mechanism to focus on the sentiment words. Too much redundant information brought by re-reading will mislead the model to judge the sentences as "neutral" instead of their original sentiment class "positive" or "negative". Therefore, repeated reading models were beaten by standard model in root-level fine-grained classification. After we delete the neutral cases (coarse-grained), we can see that repeated reading models can still achieve good results in Table 4(b). On the contrary, short sequences only contain limited information, so it is easier for repeated models to focus on the sentiment words. As a result, repeated reading models achieve better phrase-level result in both fine-grained and coarse-grained classification.

3.3   Semantic Relation Classification

Task Description. We use the SemEval-2010 Task 8 dataset [3] to evaluate the performance of repeated reading models on finding semantic relationships between pairs of nominal. The dataset includes 8,000 training instances and 2,717 test instances. There are 9 relationships (with two directions) and an undirected "Other" class, so the task is formalized as a 19-class classification problem. For example, in "This [machine]$_{e_1}$ has two [units]$_{e_2}$." classifying the relation between [machine] and [units] as Component-Whole(e_2, e_1). The evaluation result is shown in Table 5.

Table 5. Test set accuracies on the SemEval-2010 semantic relationship classification task.

	Accuracy	p value
Standard	75.54	-
MLA(1-level)	75.83 (+0.29)	0.06010
MLA(2-level)	**76.24** (+0.70)	0.01552*
DB	66.23 (−9.31)	0*
MPB	75.43 (−0.11)	0.81034

Discussion. Unlike the earlier tasks, here MLA models (1-level MLA, 2-level MLA) yield much better performance than standard model, MPB model did not achieve significant result, and DB model still cannot beat the standard model. These results suggest that for semantic relation classification task, read for once is not enough. Intuitively, to find semantic relationships, for human beings, they first need to understand the whole sentence, then pay attention to the two nominal, finally consider what kind of relation they have. Just read the sentence for once is not likely to complete such complex process. Since the BiLSTM is a sequential model, it has to remember one nominal until the other one appears. So the attention mechanism may help highlight the important nominal to the model, which may lead to the success of MLA models.

3.4 Event Extraction

Task Description. Event Extraction on the ACE 2005 dataset aims to discover event triggers with specific types and their arguments. ACE 2005 defines the event extraction task as three sub-tasks: identifying the trigger of an event, identifying the arguments of the event and distinguishing their corresponding roles. The newswire texts in ACE2005 dataset are divided into training(529 documents)/dev(10 documents)/testing(40 documents).

ACE2005 defines event as a structure composed of a trigger (a word which can best express the event) and several arguments (each plays a role in the event, 35 roles in total). The events can be classified into 8 types (33 subtypes).

We follow the previous works [7,10,11,15–17] to evaluate the results.

- A trigger is considered to be correct if and only if its event type and offsets can match the reference trigger;
- An argument is correctly identified if and only if its event type and offsets can match any of the reference arguments;
- An argument is correctly identified and classified if and only if its event type, offsets and role can match any of the reference arguments.

The evaluation result is shown in Table 6.

Table 6. Overall Performance of event extraction on ACE2005, The p values are calculated between repeated reading models and the standard model.

	Trigger Cl	Argument Id	Argument Cl
	$F_1(\%)$	$F_1(\%)$	$F_1(\%)$
Standard	51.68	57.44	42.09
MLA(1-level)	53.77(+2.09)	59.34(+1.90)	41.43(−0.66)
p value	0.0022∗	0.0003∗	0.8891
MLA(2-level)	54.68(+3.00)	60.64(+3.20)	42.87(+0.78)
p value	0.0043∗	0.0001∗	0.0124∗
DB	**57.22(+5.54)**	**60.75(+3.31)**	**43.65(+1.56)**
p value	0.0003∗	0.0001∗	0.0002∗
MPB	55.21(+3.53)	59.03(+1.59)	41.32(−0.77)
p value	0.0015∗	0.0102∗	0.0230∗

Discussion. Different from the previous experiment, DB model achieves the best performance in event extraction task. This result can be explained by the property of deep BiLSTM architecture, which can build up progressively higher level representations [2]. Since the event is a hierarchical structure (a trigger with multiple arguments), it requires a higher perspective to better understand the sentence, which can be provided by the deep BiLSTM architecture. At the same time, MLA model also outperforms the standard model. Possible explanation is that the multi-level attention mechanism brings the ability to notice important information in the sentence, which also contributes to the extraction of event's hierarchical structure. However, MPB model didn't achieve significant improvement due to the fact that it is a sequential model, which is difficult to capture the hierarchical information.

4   Discussion

We have compared repeated reading models and standard model for representation learning on 4 distinct NLP tasks. For the best of our knowledge, no one has tried repeated reading mechanism on these tasks. For the comparisons between models, our results come with some caveats: First, we just apply the most basic form of repeated reading mechanism instead of various sophisticated algorithm variant. With the addition of hidden layers and advanced architectures (tensor layer [19], convolution layer [8], highway network [21], etc.) to sophisticated models, it becomes harder and harder to compare models "apple-to-apple". Second, in order to keep fairness when comparing models, we force every model to be trained exactly in the same way: AdaDelta with minibatches, same set of initializations, etc. Therefore, the architecture may not necessarily be the state-of-the-art for the task, and the training method may also not necessarily be the optimal way to train every model. Our conclusions might thus be limited to the algorithms employed in this paper, and it is possible that they can be extended to state-of-the-art models.

Our conclusions can be summarized as follows:

- For tasks like semantic relation extraction and event extraction, they have some relation to structured information. These tasks require several steps for even human beings to analyze. From the experiment, we see that the model need to re-read the sentence to achieve significantly better results. Therefore, re-read process can make the model better understanding a sentence.
- By contrast, in simple tasks like POS tagging, repeated reading mechanism did not bring any improvement. It made the performance worse instead. Since word senses have long been known to be related to POS tags, the word embedding itself is enough for the task. Therefore, repeated reading instead brings redundant information which worsen the performance. We can analogy this to a human psychological phenomena: semantic saturation.
- In phrase-level and sentence-level fine-grained sentiment analysis, we see different effects of repeated reading. In coarse-grained sentiment analysis, we see repeated reading achieves better result than standard model in both phrase-level and sentence-level. Since the neutral sentiment class is easy to be mistakenly classified to when there is redundant information, it would make repeated reading mechanism inefficient. When we cast the neutral class, repeated reading can still show its effectiveness.
- In most tasks, multi-level attention model wins good performance. This suggests that attention mechanism is good at noticing important information in a sentence. For example, it can notice the two nominals in sentiment relation classification task when single nominals need to be associated across a long distance. Also, it can pay attention to the event trigger and arguments when extracting events.
- Deep BiLSTM fails most of the tasks but it achieves the best performance in event extraction. This suggests that if hierarchical structure is not required by the task, the complexity brought by the deep architecture will definitely worsen the performance. The deep architecture is very powerful when dealing with high-level representation.
- Multi-pass BiLSTM seems cannot bring any outstanding benefits for the four tasks. Maybe it is the very reason why it never appears in any previous work.

5 Guidelines for NLPers

After the above discussion, we would like to propose some guidelines for researchers to follow.

When to use? If the task requires to understand the meaning of the whole sentence instead of single words, we suggest to use repeated reading mechanism.

Which to use? If the task requires several specific words (like in sentiment analysis, only several single semantic words can decide the sentiment label of the whole sentence. In relation classification, the relation is between two isolated entities), we suggest to use multi-level attention model.

If the task requires hierarchical structure (like event), we suggest to use deep BiLSTM model.

We do not suggest to use multi-pass BiLSTM model.

6   Conclusion

In this paper, we did an empirical study of repeated reading's effect on natural language understanding. We consider four tasks which represents the word-level semantic classification, phrase-level and sentence-level sentiment classification, long-distance relationship classification, and hierarchical structure extraction. Based on the standard BiLSTM architecture, we propose three possible repeated reading architecture (multi-level attention, deep BiLSTM, multi-pass BiLSTM). Then we analyzed on which kind of task and in which situation would each repeated reading model bring significant improvement. The result would shed light on the usage of repeated reading in NLP tasks.

Acknowledgements. We would like to thank our three anonymous reviewers for their helpful advice on various aspects of this work. This research was supported by the National Key Basic Research Program of China (No. 2014CB340504) and the National Natural Science Foundation of China (No. 61375074, 61273318).

References

1. Goller, C., Kuchler, A.: Learning task-dependent distributed representations by backpropagation through structure. In: 1996 IEEE International Conference on Neural Networks, vol. 1, pp. 347–352. IEEE (1996)
2. Graves, A., Jaitly, N., Mohamed, A.R.: Hybrid speech recognition with deep bidirectional LSTM. In: 2013 IEEE Workshop on Automatic Speech Recognition and Understanding (ASRU), pp. 273–278. IEEE (2013)
3. Hendrickx, I., Kim, S.N., Kozareva, Z., Nakov, P., Ó Séaghdha, D., Padó, S., Pennacchiotti, M., Romano, L., Szpakowicz, S.: Semeval-2010 task 8: multi-way classification of semantic relations between pairs of nominals. In: Proceedings of the Workshop on Semantic Evaluations: Recent Achievements and Future Directions, pp. 94–99. Association for Computational Linguistics (2009)
4. Hermann, K.M., Kociský, T., Grefenstette, E., Espeholt, L., Kay, W., Suleyman, M., Blunsom, P.: Teaching machines to read and comprehend. CoRR abs/1506.03340 (2015)
5. Hochreiter, S., Schmidhuber, J.: Long short-term memory. Neural Comput. **9**(8), 1735–1780 (1997)
6. Huang, Z., Xu, W., Yu, K.: Bidirectional LSTM-CRF models for sequence tagging. CoRR abs/1508.01991 (2015)

7. Ji, H., Grishman, R.: Refining event extraction through cross-document inference. In: Proceedings of the 46th Annual Meeting of the Association for Computational Linguistics, Long Papers, vol. 1, pp. 254–262 (2008)
8. LeCun, Y., Bottou, L., Bengio, Y., Haffner, P.: Gradient-based learning applied to document recognition. Proc. IEEE **86**(11), 2278–2324 (1998)
9. Li, J., Luong, T., Jurafsky, D., Hovy, E.H.: When are tree structures necessary for deep learning of representations? In: EMNLP (2015)
10. Li, Q., Ji, H., Huang, L.: Joint event extraction via structured prediction with global features. In: Proceedings of the 51st Annual Meeting of the Association for Computational Linguistics, Long Papers, vol. 1, pp. 73–82. Association for Computational Linguistics, Sofia, August 2013. http://www.aclweb.org/anthology/P13-1008
11. Liao, S., Grishman, R.: Using document level cross-event inference to improve event extraction. In: Proceedings of the 48th Annual Meeting of the Association for Computational Linguistics, pp. 789–797. Association for Computational Linguistics (2010)
12. Ratinov, L.A., Roth, D.: Design challenges and misconceptions in named entity recognition. In: CONLL (2009)
13. Schuster, M., Paliwal, K.K.: Bidirectional recurrent neural networks. IEEE Trans. Sig. Process. **45**(11), 2673–2681 (1997)
14. Sha, L., Chang, B., Sui, Z., Li, S.: Reading and thinking: re-read LSTM unit for textual entailment recognition. In: COLING, pp. 2870–2879 (2016)
15. Sha, L., Li, S., Chang, B., Sui, Z.: Joint learning templates and slots for event schema induction. In: Proceedings of NAACL-HLT, pp. 428–434 (2016)
16. Sha, L., Li, S., Chang, B., Sui, Z., Jiang, T.: Capturing argument relationship for Chinese semantic role labeling. In: EMNLP, pp. 2011–2016 (2016)
17. Sha, L., Liu, J., Lin, C.Y., Li, S., Chang, B., Sui, Z.: RBPB: regularization-based pattern balancing method for event extraction. In: ACL, vol. 1 (2016)
18. Shi, Y., Yao, K., Tian, L., Jiang, D.: Deep LSTM based feature mapping for query classification. In: Proceedings of the 2016 Conference of the North American Chapter of the Association for Computational Linguistics: Human Language Technologies, pp. 1501–1511. Association for Computational Linguistics, San Diego, June 2016. http://www.aclweb.org/anthology/N16-1176
19. Socher, R., Chen, D., Manning, C.D., Ng, A.Y.: Reasoning with neural tensor networks for knowledge base completion. In: Advances in Neural Information Processing Systems, vol. 26 (2013)
20. Socher, R., Perelygin, A., Wu, J.Y., Chuang, J., Manning, C.D., Ng, A.Y., Potts, C.: Recursive deep models for semantic compositionality over a sentiment treebank. In: Proceedings of the Conference on Empirical Methods in Natural Language Processing (EMNLP), vol. 1631, p. 1642. Citeseer (2013)
21. Srivastava, R.K., Greff, K., Schmidhuber, J.: Highway networks. CoRR abs/1505.00387 (2015)
22. Toutanova, K., Klein, D., Manning, C.D., Singer, Y.: Feature-rich part-of-speech tagging with a cyclic dependency network. In: Proceedings of the 2003 Conference of the North American Chapter of the Association for Computational Linguistics on Human Language Technology-Volume 1, pp. 173–180. Association for Computational Linguistics (2003)
23. Wang, D., Nyberg, E.: A long short-term memory model for answer sentence selection in question answering. In: ACL (2015)
24. Zeiler, M.D.: Adadelta: An adaptive learning rate method. arXiv preprint arXiv:1212.5701 (2012)

A Deep Convolutional Neural Model for Character-Based Chinese Word Segmentation

Zhipeng Xie[✉] and Junfeng Hu

Shanghai Key Laboratory of Data Science, School of Computer Science,
Fudan University, Shanghai, China
{xiezp,15210240075}@fudan.edu.cn

Abstract. This paper proposes a deep convolutional neural model for character-based Chinese word segmentation. It first constructs position embeddings to encode unigram and bigram features that are directly related to single positions in input sentence, and then adaptively builds up hierarchical position representations with a deep convolutional net. In addition, a multi-task learning strategy is used to further enhance this deep neural model by treating multiple supervised CWS datasets as different tasks. Experimental results have shown that our neural model outperforms the existing neural ones, and the model equipped with multi-task learning has successfully achieved state-of-the-art F-score performance for standard benchmarks: 0.964 on PKU dataset and 0.978 on MSR dataset.

1 Introduction

Chinese, as well as most east Asian languages, is written without explicit word delimiters. Therefore, *word segmentation* becomes a preliminary but fundamental procedure that has to be executed before miscellaneous downstream syntactic and semantic analysis. In the past two decades, many statistical methods have been proposed to solve the problem of Chinese word segmentation (or CWS in short), which can be categorized roughly into character-based and word-based approaches.

The character-based models [17] treat word segmentation as a sequence labeling problem, where tags are used to indicate the relative position of characters inside the words that they belong to. Tag prediction is usually made on the basis of extracted features from local windows, inclusive of character identity features, reduplication features [16], and history predictions of previous characters. One disadvantage of character-based models exists in that they can only use limited contextual information, and other valuable contextual information such as surrounding words is hard to get included. To allow word information to be used as features, word-based approaches [1,21] were proposed to rank candidate segmented outputs directly, with the aid of semi-CRF or transition-based methods where word-level features can be easily integrated.

These conventional statistical CWS methods, no matter character-based or word-based, rely heavily to a large extent on the hand-crafted features. Recently,

© Springer International Publishing AG 2018
X. Huang et al. (Eds.): NLPCC 2017, LNAI 10619, pp. 380–392, 2018.
https://doi.org/10.1007/978-3-319-73618-1_32

with the upsurge of deep learning, there is a trend of applying neural network models to NLP tasks, which adaptively learn important features from word/character embeddings [2,12] trained on large quantities of unlabelled text, and thus greatly reduce efforts of hand-crafted feature engineering [5]. Following the trend, several neural models for word segmentation have been developed, among which some are character-based [4,10,11,13,22], and others are word-based [3,9,20]. These neural models have achieved competitive performance.

This paper follows the character-based approach, which has a simpler algorithmic framework and prevails in the task of CWS. The contribution of this paper is three-fold: (1) *Deep* convolutional network is applied to CWS, where position embeddings are automatically constructed from the unigram and bigram features directly related to positions (Sect. 2.1), and hierarchical position representations are built up adaptively from position embeddings such that the representation of each position has a large receptive field (Sect. 2.2). (2) To utilize the large-scale unsupervised text corpus, character bigram embeddings that are pretrained on unsupervised corpus play an important role in the construction of position embeddings (Sect. 2.1). The pretrained bigram embeddings can be thought of features at the midpoint from characters to words; (3) We designed a homogeneous multitask learning framework for Chinese word segmentation (Sect. 3), which treats each supervised dataset a different separate task. It is shown that the segmentation model built for one domain can benefit from the dataset from other domain.

2   The Deep Convolutional Neural Model for CWS

The deep convolutional neural model (or **DCN** model in short) can be thought of as an instantiation of a simple and straightforward deep neural architecture as shown in Fig. 1. The overall architecture takes a modular structure consisting of three main modules, one stacked over another. **Position Embedding Module** constructs a vector representation for each position in input sentence, called *position embedding*, which is expected to encode the information that are directly related to the position. **Deep Representation Module** adaptively constructs hierarchical *position representations* to combine the lower-level representations of each position and its surrounding positions into a higher-level representation of the position. **Tag Scoring Module** assigns tag scores to each position based on the top-level position representation from the deep representation module.

The DCN model proposed in this paper is different from the existing neural ones in several aspects:

– *Deep* convolutional network is used for CWS, which is able to automatically construct best hierarchical representations for positions in sentence. By convolution, the information at a position can flow to its adjacent positions bidirectionally. Deep convolutional network can provide sufficiently large receptive fields. In contrast, most previous methods rely on shallow networks that have only limited receptive field and work on the basis of traditional window-based segmentation [10,13,22]

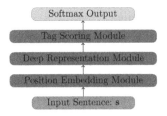

Fig. 1. Deep neural network architecture for CWS

- Recent approaches make use of recurrent neural networks (typically, LSTM), which have potentially infinite receptive field, to build the feature representation for positions in an input sentence. However, the sequential processing mechanism of recurrent neural networks makes it too costly to build hierarchical representations. On the contrary, the deep convolutional network is suitable for the exploitation of modern multi-core computation ability such as GPU.
- To model the tag-tag or tag-character interactions, some models explicitly designed tag-related features, while others explicitly used tag-tag transition probabilities in a viterbi-like decoder. In our model, it is assumed that the induced position representations have naturally contains information about the tags for positions, and therefore, the tag-related information can easily flow implicitly between adjacent positions during their hierarchical representation learning process.

2.1   Position Embeddings

For each position j $(1 \leq j \leq n)$ in a given input sentence $\mathbf{s} = c_1 \cdots c_n$ of length n, we would like to first represent it as a vector $\mathbf{x}_j^{(0)}$ of fixed size, called *position embedding*. To distinguish it from *position representation* in Sect. 2.2, it is required that a position embedding is constructed from features that are *directly* related to the position, while a position representation is obtained by aggregating features from the position and its surroundings.

As shown in Fig. 2, the position embedding $\mathbf{x}_j^{(0)}$ at position j is the concatenation of its unigram embedding $\mathbf{e}_j^{(u)}$ and its bigram embedding $\mathbf{e}_j^{(b)}$.

Unigram Embeddings. Let $\Sigma^{(u)}$ denote the character unigram dictionary of size $|\Sigma^{(u)}|$, and $\mathbf{M}^{(u)}$ denote the (character) unigram embedding matrix of size $d^{(u)} \times |\Sigma^{(u)}|$, where $d^{(u)} = 300$ by default. Each character $c \in \Sigma^{(u)}$ has an associated index $ind(c)$ into the column of the embedding matrix.

Given a sentence of n characters, $\mathbf{s} = c_1 c_2 \ldots c_n$, where c_j is the character unigram at position j $(1 \leq j \leq n)$. The unigram embedding $\mathbf{e}_j^{(u)} \in \mathbb{R}^{d^{(u)} \times 1}$ at position j can be obtained by applying a lookup-table operation on the unigram embedding matrix:

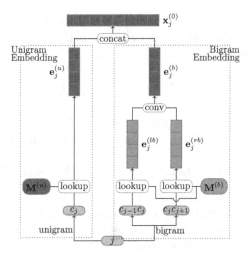

Fig. 2. Module for position embedding.

$$\mathbf{e}_j^{(u)} = \text{lookup}(\mathbf{M}^{(u)}, c_j) = \mathbf{M}^{(u)} \cdot e_{ind(c_j)}$$

where $e_{ind(c_j)}$ is the one-hot representation of the character c_j, i.e. a $|\Sigma^{(u)}|$-dimensional binary column vector that is zero for all elements except for the element at the index $ind(c_j)$.

In our model, the character embedding matrix $\mathbf{M}^{(u)}$ is randomly initialized, and it will get trained via back propagation.

Bigram Embeddings. Besides the unigram dictionary, we also have a character bigram dictionary (denoted by $\Sigma^{(b)}$) of size $|\Sigma^{(b)}|$, and a character bigram embedding matrix (denoted by $\mathbf{M}^{(b)}$) of size $d^{(b)} \times |\Sigma^{(b)}|$. In our model, the character bigram embeddings are pretrained on unsupervised corpus, and the dimensionality of these embeddings is set to 300 as default. Each bigram $cc' \in \Sigma^{(b)}$ has an associated index $ind(cc')$ into the column of the bigram embedding matrix.

Each position j in the input sentence $\mathbf{s}$ is directly related to two character bigrams: the adjacent left character bigram $c_{j-1}c_j$ and the adjacent right character bigram $c_j c_{j+1}$, which can be transformed into the left character bigram embedding $\mathbf{e}_j^{(lb)}$ and the right character bigram embedding $\mathbf{e}_j^{(rb)}$ by looking-up the bigram embedding matrix:

$$\mathbf{e}_j^{(lb)} = \mathbf{M}^{(b)} \cdot e_{ind(c_{j-1}c_j)}$$

$$\mathbf{e}_j^{(rb)} = \mathbf{M}^{(b)} \cdot e_{ind(c_j c_{j+1})}$$

where $e_{ind(cc')}$ is a $|\Sigma^{(b)}|$-dimensional binary column vector that is zero for all elements except for the element at the index $ind(cc')$.

A convolutional layer with filter size 2, stride 1 and zero-padding is then used to get the *position bigram embedding* $\mathbf{e}_j^{(b)}$ for each position j from its left and right character bigram embeddings. Formally,

$$\mathbf{e}_j^{(b)} = \mathbf{W}^{(0)} \left[\mathbf{e}_j^{(lb)} \ \mathbf{e}_j^{(rb)} \right] + \mathbf{b}^{(0)}$$

where $\mathbf{W}^{(0)} \in \mathbb{R}^{d^{(0)} \times d^{(b)} \times 2}$ is a 3-way tensor, $\mathbf{b}^{(0)} \in \mathbb{R}^{d^{(0)}}$ is the bias vector, and $d^{(0)}$ is the dimension of the position bigram embedding space (with 300 as default value).

The use of pretrained bigram embeddings in CWS is based on the following consideration:

- If position j is in the middle of a multi-character word, it is likely that $c_{j-1}c_j$ and $c_j c_{j+1}$ share similar contexts in the unsupervised corpus, and thus have similar embeddings to some degree.
- If position j is at the begin (or end) of a multi-character word, it is unlikely that $c_{j-1}c_j$ and $c_j c_{j+1}$ share similar contexts and thus their embeddings are dissimilar to each other.

2.2   Deep Representation Module

To build up the hierarchical feature representation for character-based CWS, we adopt a deep convolutional representation module which consists of multiple stacked convolutional blocks.

Each convolutional block is a weighted layer followed by a ReLU nonlinearity activation, as shown in Fig. 3.

Fig. 3. Structure of a convolutional block

Because the task at present is to perform character-based CWS, we have to preserve the temporal resolution throughout the module. Therefore, we make the following design choices:

- The filter size in each convolutional block is set to a fixed integer S (by default, $S = 3$), with padding such that the temporal resolution is preserved;
- The stride is set to 1 in each convolutional block (otherwise, the temporal resolution would be reduced);

- We do not use any down sampling (pooling layer) between adjacent convolutional blocks, because the functionality of pooling is to reduce the temporal dimensions.

Let L denote the number of convolutional blocks in the module. The working mechanism of the l-th convolutional block ($1 \leq l \leq L$) is described below:

- A convolutional layer with F filters is performed by taking the dot-product between each filter (or kernel) matrix and each window of size S in the input sequence $\mathbf{x}^{(l-1)}$, resulting in F scalar values for each position j in input sentence. By default, the value of F is set to 600 for all convolutional layers in this module.
- Next, a batch normalization layer goes immediately after the convolutional layer. It normalizes the output of the convolutional layer to zero mean and unit variance, and then transforms it linearly.
- Finally, a element-wise ReLU activation function is applied, so negative activations are discarded.

Stacking L layers of such convolution blocks together results in a receptive field of $((S - 1) \times L + 1)$ positions of the original input sentence. The receptive field of the units in the deeper layers of a convolutional network is larger than the receptive field of the units in the shallow layers. Deep neural networks can adaptively learn how to best combine the lower-level representations of S positions into a higher-level representation in a hierarchically layer-by-layer manner.

2.3   Tag Scoring Module

After processed by the deep convolutional network, each position j is represented by a vector $\mathbf{x}_j^{(L)}$ of size F. The tag scoring module transforms each position representation from a F-dimensional vector $\mathbf{x}_j^{(L)}$ into a K-dimension vector of tag scores $\mathbf{y}_j$. The tag set used is {'B', 'M', 'E', 'S'}, and hence $K = 4$, where 'S' denotes a single character word, while 'B', 'M' and 'E' denotes the begin, middle and end of a multi-character word respectively.

A two-layer feed-forward neural network implements the module:

$$\mathbf{y}_j = f_2\left(g\left(f_1\left(\mathbf{x}_j^{(L)}\right)\right)\right)$$

where f_2 and f_1 are two affine transformations, and g is a element-wise ReLU activation.

Specifically, we have:

$$\mathbf{h}_j = \text{ReLU}\left(\mathbf{W}^{(s,1)} \cdot \mathbf{x}_j^{(L)} + \mathbf{b}^{(s,1)}\right)$$

and

$$\mathbf{y}_j = \mathbf{W}^{(s,2)} \cdot \mathbf{h}_j + \mathbf{b}^{(s,2)}$$

where $\mathbf{W}^{(s,1)}$ is a matrix of size $F \times F$, $\mathbf{b}^{(s,1)}$ is a vector of size F, $\mathbf{W}^{(s,2)}$ is a $F \times K$ matrix, and $\mathbf{b}^{(s,2)}$ is a vector of size K.

2.4   Dropout

Dropout is an effective technique to regularize neural networks by randomly drop units during training. It has achieved a great success when working with feed-forward networks [14], convolutional networks, or even recurrent neural networks [18]. In the DCN model, dropout is applied to both the output of point embedding module and the input of the final layer in the deep representation module, with the same dropout rate.

Furthermore, in order to make the model robust to unknown character unigrams or bigrams, it also drops a position randomly 20% of the time during training.

2.5   Tag Prediction and Word Segmentation

Given the tag scores for a position j, the prediction $\hat{t}_j$ is the tag with the highest predicted tag score:

$$\hat{t}_j = \arg\max_k y_{j,k}$$

where $y_{j,k}$ is the predicted score of tag k at position j.

After all positions have their tags predicted, the sentence is segmented in a simple heuristic way: A character with tag 'B' or 'S' will start a new word, while a character with tag 'M' or 'E' will append itself to the previous word. As a result, the potential inconsistencies in predicted tags are resolved in a near-random manner. For example, the inconsistent adjacent predictions "BMB" will be implicitly changed to "BEB", "BBS" to "BES", etc.

2.6   Model Training

Given the training sentences and ground truth $\{\mathbf{s}_i, \mathbf{t}_i\}_{i=1}^N$, our goal is to learn the parameters that minimize the cross-entropy loss function:

$$\mathbf{L}(\Theta) = \frac{1}{\sum_{i=1}^N |\mathbf{s}_i|} \sum_{i=1}^N \sum_{j=1}^{|\mathbf{s}_i|} t_{i,j} \log \frac{\exp y_{i,j,t_{i,j}}}{\sum_k \exp y_{i,j,k}}$$

where Θ is the set of all parameters, $t_{i,j}$ denotes the gold tag for the position j in sentence $\mathbf{s}_i$, $y_{i,j,k}$ denotes the score of tag k for the position j in $\mathbf{s}_i$.

Here, as a rule of thumb, we do not include a L2-regularization term in the loss function because both dropout and batch normalization have been used to regularize our model.

We used Adam [7] to train our models with a learning rate of 0.001, a first momentum coefficient $\beta_1 = 0.9$, and a second momentum coefficient $\beta_2 = 0.999$. Each model was trained for 50 epochs with minibatch size of 16 sentences.

3   Multi-task Learning

Multi-task learning usually can obtain better generalization ability by making part of a model be shared across tasks. Previous related work mainly focused on jointly modeling heterogeneous multi-tasks such as word segmentation, POS tagging or dependency parsing [8].

Here, we are concerned about homogeneous multi-tasks, all for word segmentation. Suppose that there are multiple supervised datasets for CWS, it is not a good idea to merge them into a single large one, because of the following reasons:

- Different datasets may be used for different NLP tasks, while different NLP tasks may require different segmentation criteria.
- Different datasets may be annotated according to different segmentation standards. For example, the PKU dataset used a standard derived from the Chinese government standard for text segmentation in computer application, while the MSR dataset was segmented according to Microsoft's internal standard.

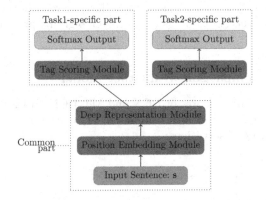

Fig. 4. MT-DCN: a multi-task model for CWS.

Instead, we treat each dataset as a separate task and propose a multi-task model for CWS (called **MT-DCN**) in Fig. 4. For illustration, only two CWS datasets are used here. The common part at the bottom of the model is shared by the two CWS tasks, and as a result, the unigram and bigram embedding matrices and the deep convolutional network for build up hierarchical position representations (together with the corresponding parameter) are all shared by the two tasks. Besides this shared common part, the two tasks have their own specific parts at the top of the model, which are different from each other. The task-specific part is expected to encode the special factors of the corresponding task.

At training time, we divide the two training datasets into a same number of minibatches (1500 minibatches by default), and alternately update one task-specific part with a minibatch from the corresponding dataset. Note that the common part is always updated for each minibatch, no matter which dataset it comes from. At prediction time, which task-specific part to use depends on where the data comes from.

4   Experiments

To evaluate our models, we used two widely used benchmark datasets, PKU and MSR, provided by the Second SIGHAN International Chinese Word Segmentation Bakeoff [6]. The segmentation results are evaluated by the *F-scores*.

To make the comparison fair, we converted the Arabic numbers and English characters in the testing set of PKU corpus from half-width form to full-width form, because they are in full-width form in the training set. This conversion is commonly performed before segmentation in related research work. Except this conversion, we did not make any preprocessing on the datasets.

We implemented the models in Python with Theano (http://deeplearning. net/software/theano/) and Lasagne (http://lasagne.readthedocs.io). We used *word2vec* to derive the embeddings of character bigrams pretained on Chinese Wikipedia corpus[1].

4.1   Empirical Comparison with Other Models

Table 1 summarizes the F-scores of DCN and MT-DCN on the testing datasets of PKU and MSR. Compared with state-of-the-art neural or non-neural models, we have the following observations:

Table 1. Comparison of F-scores with other state-of-the-art CWS systems.

Neural Models	PKU	MSR	Non-neural Model	PKU	MSR
Zheng et al. [22]	92.8	93.9	Zhang and Clark [21]	95.1	97.2
Pei et al. [13]	95.2	97.2	Sun et al. [15]	95.4	97.4
Ma and Hinrichs [10]	95.1	96.6	Zhang et al. [19]	96.1	97.4
Cai and Zhao [3]	95.5	96.5			
Zhang et al. [20]	95.7	97.7			
Liu et al. [9]	95.7	97.6			
Our models					
DCN	95.9	97.7	MT-DCN	**96.4**	**97.8**

---

[1] https://dumps.wikimedia.org/zhwiki/20161120/zhwiki-20161120-pages-articles. xml.bz2.

- The DCN model substantially outperforms the other existing character-based neural models inclusive of [10,13,22]. It also obtains observable higher F-score than the word-based neural models inclusive of [3,9,20]. In addition, it outperforms two cutting-edge non-neural models of [15,21], and is competitive to the model of [19];
- The MT-DCN model achieves the best performance on both datasets among all the compared models, neural or non-neural. With multi-task strategy, the F-score improvement on PKU is more than that on MSR. Possible reason is that the MSR dataset is much larger.

4.2 Learning Curves of DCN Model

Figure 5 shows that the training precedure converges quickly. After the first epoch, the F-score is 94.2 on PKU testing set, and 94.8 on MSR testing set. Just after 10 epoches, the F-scores have been very near to their best.

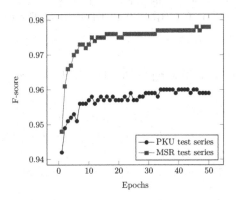

Fig. 5. The learning curve of our DCN model

4.3 Contributions of Techniques

In MT-DCN model, there are three main working techniques: multi-task, pre-trained bigram embeddings, and dropout. To investigate their contributions, we removed each of them from the model, the results are shown in Table 2. The dropout is relatively weak, and multitask and pretrained bigram are comparable in effect. Conclusion can be drawn that data and features are most crucial to CWS.

4.4 Shallow versus Deep Representations

To investigate the effect of the deep convolutional network used in the deep representation module, we replaced it with a shallow one with only a single convolutional layer. With the filter size varying (or equivalently, the size of receptive

Table 2. Technique contributions in MT-DCN

Model	Precision	Recall	F-measure
MT-DCN model	96.7	96.1	96.4
- Mulitask (MSR)	96.3	95.6	95.9
- Bigrams	96.5	95.6	96.0
- Dropout	96.5	95.9	96.2

field), the F-scores on PKU testing data are shown in the "**Shallow**" row. It can be observed that the best performance occurs when the filter size is set to 5, which coincides with the fact that most previous neural models claimed the best context window size to be 5. The "**Deep**" row lists the results of our DCN model with varying number of convolutional layers in $\{1, 2, 4, 6, 8\}$, with corresponding receptive field size in $\{3, 5, 9, 13, 17\}$. Observable improvement is still made when the model is going deeper from 6 to 8. Therefore, the use of deep network has gained about 0.4 (from 95.5 to 95.9) of F-score over the shallow network (Table 3).

Table 3. Comparison of shallow representations and deep representations on PKU dataset.

	Size of receptive field				
	3	5	9	13	17
Shallow	95.3	**95.5**	95.3	95.1	95.2
Deep	95.3	95.7	95.8	95.8	**95.9**

5   Conclusion

In this paper, we propose a deep convolutional neural model for Chinese word segmentation. It uses position embeddings to encode the information directly related to single positions, and then builds up hierarchical position representations adaptively with a deep convolutional network. The model outperforms the other state-of-the-art neural models. In addition, a multi-task strategy is used to enhance the neural model, which improves the performance furtherly.

Acknowledgments. This work is supported by National High-Tech R&D Program of China (863 Program) (No. 2015AA015404). We are grateful to the anonymous reviewers for their valuable comments.

References

1. Andrew, G.: A hybrid Markov/semi-Markov conditional random field for sequence segmentation. In: Proceedings of the 2006 Conference on Empirical Methods in Natural Language Processing, pp. 465–472 (2006)
2. Bengio, Y., Ducharme, R., Vincent, P., Jauvin, C.: A neural probabilistic language model. J. Mach. Learn. Res. **3**, 1137–1155 (2003)
3. Cai, D., Zhao, H.: Neural word segmentation learning for Chinese. In: Proceedings of the 54th Annual Meeting of the Association for Computational Linguistics, vol. 1: Long Papers, pp. 409–420 (2016)
4. Chen, X., Qiu, X., Zhu, C., Liu, P., Huang, X.: Long short-term memory neural networks for Chinese word segmentation. In: Proceedings of the 2015 Conference on Empirical Methods in Natural Language Processing, pp. 1197–1206 (2015)
5. Collobert, R., Weston, J., Bottou, L., Karlen, M., Kavukcuoglu, K., Kuksa, P.: Natural language processing (almost) from scratch. J. Mach. Learn. Res. **12**, 2493–2537 (2011)
6. Emerson, T.: The second international Chinese word segmentation bakeoff. In: Proceedings of the Fourth SIGHAN Workshop on Chinese Language Processing, pp. 123–133 (2005)
7. Kingma, D., Ba, J.: Adam: a method for stochastic optimization. arXiv preprint arXiv:1412.6980 (2014)
8. Kruengkrai, C., Uchimoto, K., Kazama, J., Wang, Y., Torisawa, K., Isahara, H.: An error-driven word-character hybrid model for joint Chinese word segmentation and POS tagging. In: Proceedings of the Joint Conference of the 47th Annual Meeting of the ACL and the 4th International Joint Conference on Natural Language Processing, pp. 513–521 (2009)
9. Liu, Y., Che, W., Guo, J., Qin, B., Liu, T.: Exploring segment representations for neural segmentation models. In: Proceedings of the Twenty-Fifth International Joint Conference on Artificial Intelligence, pp. 2880–2886 (2016)
10. Ma, J., Hinrichs, E.: Accurate linear-time Chinese word segmentation via embedding matching. In: Proceedings of the 53rd Annual Meeting of the Association for Computational Linguistics, pp. 1733–1743 (2015)
11. Mansur, M., Pei, W., Chang, B.: Feature-based neural language model and Chinese word segmentation. In: Proceedings of IJCNLP, pp. 1271–1277 (2013)
12. Mikolov, T., Sutskever, I., Chen, K., Corrado, G.S., Dean, J.: Distributed representations of words and phrases and their compositionality. In: Advances in Neural Information Processing Systems (NIPS), pp. 3111–3119 (2013)
13. Pei, W., Ge, T., Chang, B.: Max-margin tensor neural network for Chinese word segmentation. In: ACL, vol. 1, pp. 293–303 (2014)
14. Srivastava, N.: Improving neural networks with dropout. Ph.D. thesis, University of Toronto (2013)
15. Sun, X., Wang, H., Li, W.: Fast online training with frequency-adaptive learning rates for Chinese word segmentation and new word detection. In: Proceedings of the 50th Annual Meeting of the Association for Computational Linguistics, vol. 1: Long Papers, pp. 253–262 (2012)
16. Tseng, H., Chang, P., Andrew, G., Jurafsky, D., Manning, C.: A conditional random field word segmenter for SIGHAN bakeoff 2005. In: Proceedings of the fourth SIGHAN workshop on Chinese language Processing, pp. 168–171 (2005)
17. Xue, N., Shen, L.: Chinese word segmentation as LMR tagging. In: Proceedings of the Second SIGHAN Workshop on Chinese Language Processing, vol. 17, pp. 176–179 (2003)

18. Zaremba, W., Sutskever, I., Vinyals, O.: Recurrent neural network regularization. arXiv preprint arXiv:1409.2329 (2014)
19. Zhang, L., Wang, H., Sun, X., Mansur, M.: Exploring representations from unlabeled data with co-training for Chinese word segmentation. In: Proceedings of the 2013 Conference on Empirical Methods in Natural Language Processing, pp. 311–321 (2013)
20. Zhang, M., Zhang, Y., Fu, G.: Transition-based neural word segmentation. In: Proceedings of the 54th Annual Meeting of the Association for Computational Linguistics, vol. 1: Long Papers, pp. 421–431 (2016)
21. Zhang, Y., Clark, S.: Chinese segmentation with a word-based perceptron algorithm. In: Proceedings of the 45th Annual Meeting of the Association of Computational Linguistics, pp. 840–847 (2007)
22. Zheng, X., Chen, H., Xu, T.: Deep learning for Chinese word segmentation and POS tagging. In: Proceedings of the 2013 Conference on Empirical Methods in Natural Language Processing, pp. 647–657 (2013)

Chinese Zero Pronoun Resolution: A Chain to Chain Approach

Kong Fang and Zhou Guodong[(⊠)]

School of Computer Science and Technology, Soochow University, Suzhou, China
{kongfang,gdzhou}@suda.edu.cn

Abstract. Chinese zero pronoun (ZP) resolution plays a critical role in discourse analysis. Different from traditional mention to mention approaches, this paper proposes a chain to chain approach to improve the performance of ZP resolution from three aspects. Firstly, consecutive ZPs are clustered into coreferential chains, each working as one independent anaphor as a whole. In this way, those ZPs far away from their overt antecedents can be bridged via other consecutive ZPs in the same coreferential chains and thus better resolved. Secondly, common noun phrases (NPs) are automatically grouped into coreferential chains using traditional approaches, each working as one independent antecedent candidate as a whole. Then, ZP resolution is made between ZP coreferential chains and common NP coreferential chains. In this way, the performance can be much improved due to the effective reduction of search space by pruning singletons and negative instances. Finally, additional features from ZP and common NP coreferential chains are employed to better represent anaphors and their antecedent candidates, respectively. Comprehensive experiments on the OntoNotes corpus show that our chain to chain approach significantly outperforms the state-of-the-art mention to mention approaches. To our knowledge, this is the first work to resolve zero pronouns in a chain to chain way.

Keywords: Chinese zero pronoun resolution
Chain to chain approach · Zero pronoun coreferential chains
Chain-level features

1 Introduction

As a gap in a sentence, a ZP exists when a phonetically null form is used to refer to a real world entity, and an anaphoric ZP (AZP) corefers with a preceding NP. In comparison with overt pronouns, it is more challenging to resolve ZPs due to the lack of syntactic variations and grammatical attributes such as number and gender. Unlike English, Chinese is a pro-drop language. According to our statistics on the Ontonotes corpus, while only 4% of subjects are ZPs in English, this percentage soars to 36% in Chinese. This indicates the necessity of ZP resolution in Chinese understanding. During the past few years, Chinese ZP

© Springer International Publishing AG 2018
X. Huang et al. (Eds.): NLPCC 2017, LNAI 10619, pp. 393–405, 2018.
https://doi.org/10.1007/978-3-319-73618-1_33

resolution has been drawing more and more attention due to its importance to various natural language processing (NLP) applications.

In the literature, most studies on Chinese ZP resolution employ mention to mention approaches [1,3,4,8,13], which resolve each detected ZP and its single candidate independently and thus can only rely on local information. Although various kinds of lexical and syntactic features have been employed in ZP resolution to a certain extent, the performance of Chinese ZP resolution is still far from satisfactory. In this paper, we propose a chain to chain approach to Chinese ZP resolution. In particular, all possible ZPs are first identified and then clustered into coreferential chains in a consecutive way. Then common NPs are automatically grouped into coreferential chains using traditional approaches. Finally, ZP resolution is made between ZP coreferential chains and common NP coreferential chains.

In comparison with traditional mention to mention approaches, our chain to chain approach improves the performance of ZP resolution from three aspects.

- Cluster consecutive ZPs into coreferential chains, each working as one independent anaphor as a whole. In this way, those ZPs far away from their overt antecedents can be better resolved by bridging the coreferential relations via other consecutive ZPs.
- Only consider those mentions in the coreferential chains of common NPs as antecedent candidates and resolve them on a chain to chain basis. That is, those NPs occurring in the same coreferential chain are viewed as one antecedent candidate as a whole. In this way, the search space can be much reduced by pruning singletons and negative instances.
- Employ additional features from ZP and common NP coreferential chains.

2   Background Knowledge

In this section, we introduce the ZP resolution and overview some related work.

2.1   ZP Resolution

Example (1) shows an excerpt from article chtb_0001 in the Chinese part of the OntoNotes corpus. In this example, two ZPs are denoted by "Φ" and the mention "一系列规范建设市场的文件/a series of documents for standardizing the construction market" in the same coreferential chain with the given ZPs is shown in bold. Besides, the corresponding mentions in translated English provided by the corpus are shown in font style.

(1) 为规范建筑行为，防止出现无序现象，新区管委会根据国家和上海市的有关规定，结合浦东开发实际，及时出台了**一系列规范建设市场的文件**，其中 Φ 包括工程施工招投标管理办法、拆迁工作若干规定、整治违章建筑实施办法、通信设施及管线配套建设意见、建设工地施工环境管理暂行办法等，Φ 基本做到了每个环节都有明确而又具体的规定。

("In order to standardize construction procedures and to guard against the emergence of disorderly phenomena, the new region's management committee promptly announced *a series of documents for standardizing the construction market* in accordance with the relevant national regulations and the regulations of Shanghai Municipality, while accommodating the realities of Pudong 's development.

The documents include: management methods for bidding on construction projects; a certain number of regulations for demolition and removal work; implementation methods for fixing construction that violated regulations; construction suggestions for communications installations and cable setups; provisional methods for environmental management at construction work sites; etc.

Essentially *they* are worked out to the point where every single link has clearly defined and specific regulations.")

Just as illustrated in Example (1), in comparison with its English translation, Chinese has much more ZPs and these ZPs can be translated into English common NPs, demonstrative NPs or pronouns. In the literature, ZP resolution contains three subtasks, i.e., **ZP detection**, which extracts all possible ZPs, e.g., the two ZPs in Example (1). **Anaphoricity determination**, for detected ZP, which determines its anaphoricity, i.e., whether the given ZP corefers with a preceding NP. In Example (1), both detected ZPs are anaphoric. In fact, just as noted in Kong and Zhou [8], about 15% of Chinese ZPs on the OntoNotes corpus are non-anaphoric. **Antecedent identification**, which finds the antecedent for every AZP. In Example (1), the same mention "一系列规范建设市场的文件" should be identified as the antecedent of both the first and the second ZP.

2.2 Related Work

Although ZPs are prevalent in Chinese, there is only a few studies, which can be classified into two categories: supervised learning (Zhao and Ng [13], Kong and Zhou [8], Chen and Ng [3–5]) and unsupervised learning (Chen and Ng [1,2]).

For supervised learning, Zhao and Ng [13] proposed a feature-based method to ZP resolution. However, they only focused on the sub-task of antecedent identification. For ZP detection, a simple heuristic rule was employed, suffering from very low precision by introducing too many false ZPs. Kong and Zhou [8] proposed a unified framework for ZP resolution and extracted different kinds of syntactic parse tree structures for three sub-tasks. However, only the performance on gold parse trees was reported. Chen and Ng [4] built the first end-to-end ZP resolver. In particular, they proposed various kinds of syntactic and contextual features and allowed coreference links between multiple zero pronouns. Chen and Ng [5] further proposed an approach to AZP resolution based on deep neural networks to reduce feature engineering efforts involved in exploiting lexical features. In order to eliminate the reliance on annotated data, Chen and Ng [2,3] presented a generative model for unsupervised Chinese ZP resolution. Chen and Ng [1] further proposed an probabilistic model for this task, which tried to jointly identify and resolve zero pronouns. However, both supervised and unsupervised learning strategies described above employ mention to mention approaches to Chinese ZP resolution, which resolve each detected ZP independently and thus can only rely on local information. This is contrary to the basic fact that ZP is a discourse phenomenon. That is ZPs normally don't exist independently.

Besides, for common NP coreference resolution, although mention-pair models have been successfully employed, their weaknesses have drawn much greater attention in recent research. Some improvements are proposed from different perspectives. Mention-ranking models attempt to rank preceding candidates for a given anaphor (Yang et al. [12], Denis and Baldridge [6]), and entity-mention models attempt to determine whether a preceding cluster is coreferent with a given mention (Yang et al. [11], Lee et al. [9]).

Inspired by the above research for common NP coreference resolution, in this paper, we improve the performance of ZP resolution in a chain to chain way. Different from their work, we focus on ZP resolution. There are two obvious differences.

First, in our chain to chain approach, each achieved ZP cluster works as one independent anaphor as a whole. While in mention-ranking and entity-mention models, the anaphor is a mention. Second, for ZP resolution, all complete common NP coreferential chains can be achieved in advance. Only the mentions (NPs) in common NP coreferential chains need be considered as the antecedent candidates. Even after linking some ZP coreferential chains to the specific common NP coreference chains, we only need to consider the NPs in common NP coreferential chains. That is to say, the search space of antecedent is static. While in mention-ranking and entity-mention models, all the partial coreference chains, some singletons and other non-anaphoric mentions preceding the given anaphor should be considered. So the search space of antecedent is dynamic. To some extent, our chain to chain approach is much simpler.

3   Motivation

In this section, we motivate our chain to chain approach by analyzing the problems of traditional mention to mention approaches to ZP resolution.

Just as described above, after extracting possible ZPs, traditional mention to mention approaches view each ZP as an independent anaphor and identify its overt antecedent independently. There are three issues in such a way.

- In Chinese, a long sentence can contain multiple ZPs (e.g., Example (1) has two ZPs). While these consecutive ZPs may have coreferential relations (e.g., the given two ZPs in Example (1)), those ZPs far away from their overt antecedents need to bridge their coreferential relations via other consecutive ZPs. For example, the second ZP in Example (1) refers to the overt antecedent "一系列规范建设市场的文件/a series of documents for standardizing the construction market" of the first ZP by treating the first ZP in Example (1) as bridge. In fact, just as noted in Chen and Ng [4], 22.7% of

ZPs in the OntoNotes corpus appear two or more sentences away from their closest overt antecedents. Moreover, similar to common NP resolution, it is much more difficult to resolve ZPs over longer distances. It is not appropriate to view every ZP as an independent anaphor. Instead, those relevant coreferential relations among multiple ZPs should be exploited to improve ZP resolution.

- Similar to common NP resolution, the search space much influences the resolution performance. Previous research on common NP resolution shows that there is a significant performance gap between gold mentions and automatic mentions due to a large portion of mentions are non-coreferent. Just as noted in Moosavi and Strube [10], more than 80% of mentions are singletons in the OntoNotes English development set. This proportion on Chinese part climbs up to 89.7%. On the one hand, traditional mention to mention approaches normally extract all NPs preceding the given ZP in current and previous two sentences to form the search space for the given ZP. This introduces many non-coreferent mentions. On the other hand, there exist various relations among these mentions, e.g., coreferential relation. Since common NP resolution is much easier than ZP resolution, it is expected that these achieved coreferential relations among common NPs can effectively prune the search space and thus much improve the performance of ZP resolution.
- Traditional mention to mention approaches only consider a pair of mentions and the local information between them. Due to its limitation to the discourse of ZPs, local information is always not enough for correct decision. This motivates the incorporation of chain-level information, i.e. various features defined over clusters of mentions to improve the performance of ZP resolution.

Motivated by above observations, we propose a chain to chain approach to ZP resolution. After detecting all possible ZPs, we firstly cluster consecutive ZPs into coreferential chains and view each ZP coreferential chain as an unified anaphor. In this way, those ZPs far away from their overt antecedents can be bridged via other consecutive ZPs in the same coreferential chains. Then, we only consider those mentions in common NP coreferential chains as the antecedent candidates and resolve them on a chain to chain basis. In this way, singletons and negative instances (i.e., non-coreferent mentions) can be better pruned to reduce the search space and thus improve the performance effectively. Finally, we introduce a set of additional features from common NP and ZP coreferential chains to better represent ZPs and their antecedent candidates.

4   ZP Resolution: Chain to Chain Approach

Similar to previous studies on ZP resolution, our chain to chain approach contains two components, i.e., ZP detection and AZP resolution which combines anaphoricity determination and antecedent identification. For ZP detection, a clause-based approach is employed to generate ZP candidates [7]. Firstly, a simplified semantic role labeling (SRL) framework is adopted to determine clauses from a parse tree. ZP candidates are then generated for each clause in a bottom-up way. Particularly, for upper clauses, all the resolved sub-clauses are viewed as an inseparable "constituent". After generating the ZP candidates, a learning-based classifier is adopted to identify whether a given candidate is a true ZP, with the help of following features.

- Lexical: two words and their POSs before or after the given candidate, and their various combinations.
- Syntactic: whether the lowest clause covering the given candidate has a subject; whether the given candidate is the first gap of the clause; whether the clause is a terminal clause or non-terminal clause; whether the clause has a sibling immediately to its left; whether the left siblings of the clause contain an NP; whether the clause has a sibling immediately to its right; whether the right siblings of the clause contain a VP; whether the syntactic category of the immediate parent of the clause is an IP or VP; whether the path from the clause to the root of the parse tree contains an NP or VP or CP; whether the clause is a matrix clause, an independent clause, a subordinate clause, or others.
- Semantic: whether the clause has an agent or patient argument.

For AZP resolution, our chain to chain approach consists of three steps, i.e., ZP coreferential chain generation, ZP coreferential chain linking, and additional chain-level features incorporation.

4.1   ZP Coreferential Chains Generation

In ZP coreferential chain generation stage, we only consider consecutive ZPs in current and previous two sentences. For multiple consecutive ZPs, we first establish coreferent links between two consecutive ZPs, and then build the coreferential chain by merging the coreferent links using the transitivity principle. Obviously, if only having two consecutive ZPs, just as shown in Example (1), the achieved coreferent link is also the final ZP coreferential chain. For the case containing more than two consecutive ZPs[1], e.g., three ZPs denoted as $ZP1$, $ZP2$ and $ZP3$ respectively, we first pair two consecutive ZPs to generate two instances $(ZP1, ZP2)$, $(ZP2, ZP3)$, then determine the coreferential relation of every instance, and finally merge the two links to achieve the coreferential chain $ZP3 - ZP2 - ZP1$.

Here, establishing coreferent links between two consecutive ZPs is the key point. Fortunately, the involved two ZPs are always close to each other with similar context. In particular, we extract following contextual features to compute the contextual similarity of the two ZPs.

---

[1] A corpus study of the OntoNotes corpus reveals that the case containing more than three consecutive ZPs occupies less than 1%. The proportion of three consecutive ZPs is about 5.8%. The case of two consecutive ZPs occupies about 14.3%. The case of just one ZP occupies the most.

- The pair of grammatical roles of the two given ZPs. We only consider three grammatical roles, i.e., subject, object and other.
- The pair of clause categories of the clauses governing the two given ZPs. Clause category can be independent, subordinate or none.
- The pair of root nodes of the clauses comprising the two ZPs.
- Whether the clauses governing the two ZPs are siblings.
- The path from the root of one clause to the root of the other clause.
- Punctuation list between the two clauses governing the ZPs.

4.2   ZP Coreferential Chains Linking

After achieving ZP coreferential chains, we try to link every ZP coreferential chain to the common NP coreferential chains. Since ZP coreferential chains are always short and the ZPs in the same coreferential chain tend to have similar context, we only consider linking the first ZP of a ZP coreferential chain to a common NP coreferential chain.

Different from the mention to mention approaches, our chain to chain approach retrieves a complete common NP coreferential chain as the antecedent of a given ZP, or none which means the given ZP is non-anaphoric. Therefore, there exist three obvious differences between our chain to chain approach and traditional mention to mention approaches in instance generation.

- Elementary processing unit. Traditional mention to mention approaches conduct instance generation for every ZP. That is, traditional approaches first extract antecedent candidates for every ZP, and then pair the achieved candidates with the given ZP to generate the learning instances. In comparison, our chain to chain approach extracts antecedent candidates for every ZP coreferential chain (i.e., every ZP coreferential chain is viewed as an anaphor as a whole), and pair the achieved candidates with the first ZP of the ZP coreferential chain (i.e., using the first ZP to represent the whole ZP coreferential chain) to generate instances.
- Antecedent candidate extraction. Traditional mention to mention approaches extract the NPs in a search space with some heuristic rules as antecedent candidates. While our chain to chain approach only considers the mentions in coreferential chains. In this way, those non-anaphoric NPs and singletons can be well ignored.
- Pairing strategy. From chain to chain perspective, we do not need to pair every antecedent candidate with the anaphor. For the antecedent candidates in the same coreference chain, only the nearest one need to be considered. That is, we only pair the first ZP of one ZP coreferential chain with the nearest mentions (NPs) in different coreferential chains to generate the instances.

4.3   Incorporating Additional Chain-Level Features

For every instance, we extract various kinds of lexical and syntactic features which have been proven useful in previous work.

- Features on ZP: whether the path of nodes from the ZP to the root of the parse tree contains NP, IP, CP, or VP; whether the ZP is the first or last ZP of the sentence; whether the ZP is in the headline of the text.
- Features on antecedent candidate (CA): whether the CA is a first person, second person, third person, neutral pronoun, or others; whether the CA is a subject, object, or others; whether the CA is in a matrix clause, an independent clause, a subordinate clause, or none of the above; whether the path of nodes from the CA to the root of the parse tree contains NP, IP, CP, or VP.
- Features between ZP and CA: their distance in sentence[2]; whether the CA is the closest preceding NP; whether the CA and the ZP are siblings in the parse tree.

Table 1. Additional chain-level features employed in our chain to chain approach

Feature	Description	Value
ZPNum	The number of ZP occurring in the given ZP coreferential chain. Intuitively, the given ZP coreferential chain having multiple ZPs more likely to be anaphoric	2
ZPRSft	If the given ZP coreferential chain has multiple ZPs, whether all the ZPs have the same grammar role	True
ZPRPt	The grammar roles of every ZP in the given ZP coreferential chain	Sub-Sub
SemClass	The semantic class of the coreferential chain containing the antecedent candidate	Object
Number	Singular or plural of the coreferential chain containing the antecedent candidate	Pluar
Gender	Male, female or unknown, determined by the coreferential chain containing the antecedent candidate	Unknown
ZPCDst	The number of other ZP coreferential chains between the anaphor and current candidate	0
NPCDst	The number of other coreferential chains of common NPs between the anaphor and current candidate	0

Besides, although we only pair the first ZP of a ZP coreferential chain with its antecedent candidates occurring in different coreferential chains of common NPs to generate the learning instances, additional features describing the ZP coreferential chain and the NPs coreferential chain containing the antecedent candidate are introduced to better represent the ZP and the antecedent candidate.

Table 1 shows additional chain-level features introduced in our chain to chain approach. In Example (1), there is a ZP coreferential chain having two ZPs.

---

[2] If the CA and the ZP are in the same sentence, the value is 0; if they are one sentence apart, the value is 1; and so on.

The third column in Table 1 lists the feature values viewing the ZP coreferential chain as the anaphor, and the mention "一系列规范建设市场的文件/a series of documents for standardizing the construction market" as the candidate.

5 Experimentation and Discussion

We evaluate our proposed approach in this section.

5.1 Experimental Setup

Following Chen and Ng [1,5], we employ the Chinese portion of the OntoNotes 5.0 corpus, which was used in the official CoNLL-2012 shared task, in all our experiments. Since only the training and development sets in the CoNLL-2012 data contain ZP coreference annotations, we train our models on the training set and perform evaluation on the development set. Besides, we employ the automatic parse trees provided by the CoNLL-2012 shared task as the default one and report our performance using traditional precision, recall and F1-score. In addition, maximum entropy is employed as our learning-based algorithm. All maximum entropy classifiers are trained using the OpenNLP maximum entropy package[3] with the default parameters (i.e. without smoothing and with 100 iterations). For end-to-end performance, automatic common NP coreference chains are achieved using the Stanford Deterministic Coreference Resolution System[4] with the default Chinese models (i.e. without additional training). Its performance of Chinese common NP resolution can be learned from Lee etc. [9]. To see whether an improvement is significant, we conduct significance testing using paired t-test.

Table 2. Performance of three end-to-end Chinese ZP resolution approaches.

Source	Chen and Ng [1]			Chen and Ng [5]			Our system		
	R(%)	P(%)	F	R(%)	P(%)	F	R(%)	P(%)	F
NW	11.9	14.3	13.0	11.9	12.8	12.3	17.2	24.1	20.1
MZ	4.9	4.7	4.8	9.3	7.3	8.2	10.3	18.4	13.2
WB	20.1	14.3	16.7	23.9	16.1	19.2	21.2	27.4	23.9
BN	18.2	22.3	20.0	22.1	23.2	22.6	19.4	29.1	23.3
BC	19.4	14.6	16.7	21.2	14.6	17.3	25.3	21.2	23.1
TC	31.8	17.0	22.2	31.4	15.9	21.1	35.7	29.4	32.2
Overall	19.6	15.5	17.3	21.9	15.8	18.4	25.8	26.9	26.3

---

[3] http://maxent.sourceforge.net/.
[4] http://stanfordnlp.github.io/CoreNLP/.

5.2   Experimental Results

Table 2 shows the performance of our chain to chain approach. For comparison, Table 2 also includes two state-of-the-art mention to mention approaches, where Chen and Ng [1] is the representative of unsupervised mention to mention approach, and Chen and Ng [5] is the representative of supervised mention to mention approach. These two approaches achieved by far the best performance. We can find that,

- For overall performance, our approach beats the state-of-the-art unsupervised approach, i.e., Chen and Ng [1] by 9.0% in F1-score. In comparison with the state-of-the-art supervised approach, i.e. Chen and Ng [5], our chain to chain approach still outperforms it significantly by 7.9% in F1-score.
- Over different sources, our approach significantly outperforms Chen and Ng [1,5] on all 6 sources by 7.1%/7.8% (NW), 8.4%/5.0% (MZ), 7.2%/4.7% (WB), 3.3%/0.7% (BN), 6.4%/5.8% (BC), and 10.0%/11.1% (TC) in F1-score, respectively. This suggests that our approach works well across different sources.

Similar to traditional ZP resolution, our approach contains two components, ZP detection and AZP resolution. With traditional ZP detection adopted, our chain to chain approach focuses on improving the performance of the second stage. For ZP detection, our ZP detector achieves 59.4%, 70.1% and 64.3% in precision, recall and F1-score respectively when gold parse trees are employed, and the performance drops to 40.2% (P), 60.2% (R) and 48.2% (F) using automatic parse trees.

Just as described above, after identifying all possible ZPs, our chain-to-chain approach divides AZP resolution into three steps, i.e., ZP coreferential chain generation, ZP coreferential chain linking and additional chain-level feature incorporation. In the following, we evaluate these three steps one by one.

Table 3. Performance of ZP coreferential chain generation (GS - using gold standard parse trees, Auto - using automatic parse trees)

	Gold ZPs			Auto ZPs		
	R	P	F	R	P	F
GS	92.4	92.4	92.4	53.7	64.7	58.7
Auto	89.7	89.7	89.7	36.2	56.4	44.1

Table 3 shows the performance of ZP coreferential chain generation. In our evaluation, we say that a ZP coreferential chain is correct only when all the ZPs in the chain are same as the annotated ZP coreferential chain. We can find that,

- Under gold ZPs, ZP coreferential chain generation achieves the performance of 92.4% and 89.7% in F1-score using both gold and automatic parse trees.

In comparison with using gold parse trees, the performance of ZP coreferential chain generation reduces 2.7% in F1-score using automatic parse trees.
- Under auto ZPs, ZP coreferential chain generation achieves 58.7% and 44.1% in F1-score using gold and automatic parse trees, respectively. In comparison with the performance under gold ZPs, we can see the significant performance drop of 14.6% in F1-score in ZP coreferential chain generation due to the errors introduced in ZP detection.

Table 4. Performance of Chinese AZP resolution with gold coreference chains of common NPs

	Gold ZPs			Auto ZPs		
	R	P	F	R	P	F
GS	90.4	90.4	90.4	50.2	61.7	55.4
Auto	86.7	86.7	86.7	33.9	55.1	42.0

After achieving the ZP coreferential chains, we link each ZP coreferential chain into common NP coreferential chains. Table 4 lists the results under gold common NP coreferential chains. We can find that, under gold ZPs, our chain-to-chain approach to AZP resolution can achieve 90.4% and 86.7% in F1-score using gold and automatic parse trees, respectively. And under auto ZPs, our approach also achieves 55.4% and 42.0% in F1-score using gold and automatic parse trees, respectively.

Table 5. Performance of AZP resolution with automatic common NP coreference chains

	Gold ZPs			Auto ZPs		
	R	P	F	R	P	F
GS	60.8	62.9	61.8	37.9	46.8	41.9
Auto	51.9	52.1	52.0	25.4	23.2	24.3

While knowing the standard common NP coreferential chains is an ideal case, evaluating AZP resolution using auto coreferential chains of common NPs is more practical and thus meaningful. Table 5 shows the performance of our chain to chain approach to AZP resolution when automatic coreferential chains of common NPs are considered. We can find that,

- Under gold ZPs, our chain-to-chain approach achieves 61.8% and 52.0% in F1-score using gold standard and automatic parse trees, respectively. In comparison with the results using gold coreferential chains of common NPs shown in Table 4, the F1-score drops by 28.6% and 34.7%, respectively. This suggests the performance of common NP resolution significantly influences ZP resolution.

– Under auto ZPs, our approach achieves 41.9% and 24.3% in F1-score using gold and automatic parse trees, respectively. In comparison with the results using gold common NP coreferential chains, the performance of our chain-to-chain approach drops 13.5% and 17.7% using gold and automatic parse trees, respectively, due to the performance of common NP coreference resolution. In comparison with the results under gold ZPs, the performance drops by 19.9% and 27.7% using gold standard and automatic parse trees, respectively. This suggests the significant influence of ZP detection. Ignoring the influence of ZP detection and other factors, we further compare our results with Chen and Ng [5] under both gold ZPs and gold parse trees. In this setting, our approach achieves 61.8% in F1-score, while their approach achieved 52.2%.

Table 6 shows the performance after additional chain-level features as shown in Table 1 are incorporated when automatic coreference chains of common NPs are adopted. In comparison with Table 5, we can find that, under both gold and auto ZPs, additional chain-level features can improve the performance using both gold standard and automatic parse trees by about 2–3% in F1-score. This suggest the effectiveness of the incorporated chain-level features.

Table 6. Performance of Chinese ZP resolution after additional chain-level features are incorporated under automatic coreference chains of common NPs

	Gold ZPs			Auto ZPs		
	R	P	F	R	P	F
GS	64.5	63.5	64.0	39.7	48.3	43.6
Auto	54.4	57.2	55.8	25.8	26.9	26.3

6 Conclusion and Future Work

In this paper, we improve Chinese zero pronoun resolution from chain-to-chain perspective, i.e., from ZP coreferential chains to common NP coreferential chains. The experimental results on the OntoNotes corpus show that our approach significantly outperforms the state-of-the-art mention to mention approaches.

Although our chain-to-chain approach much improves the performance of AZP resolution, the evaluation suggests that both ZP detection and common NP resolution have heavy impact on the final ZP resolution performance. In future work, we will focus on ZP detection and jointly resolving common NPs and ZPs as a whole.

Acknowledgements. This work is supported by Key Project 61333018 under the National Natural Science Foundation of China, Project 61472264 and 61673290 under the National Natural Science Foundation of China.

References

1. Chen, C., Ng, V.: Chinese zero pronoun resolution: a joint unsupervised discourse-aware model rivaling state-of-the-art resolvers. In: Proceedings of ACL 2015, pp. 320–326. Association for Computational Linguistics (2005)
2. Chen, C., Ng, V.: Chinese zero pronoun resolution: a unsupervised approach combining ranking and integer linear programming. In: Proceedings of AAAI 2014, pp. 1622–1628 (2014)
3. Chen, C., Ng, V.: Chinese zero pronoun resolution: an unsupervised probabilistic model rivaling supervised resolvers. In: Proceedings of EMNLP 2014, pp. 763–774. Association for Computational Linguistics (2014)
4. Chen, C., Ng, V.: Chinese zero pronoun resolution: some recent advances. In: Proceedings of EMNLP 2010, pp. 1360–1365. Association for Computational Linguistics (2010)
5. Chen, C., Ng, V.: Chinese zero pronoun resolution with deep neural networks. In: Proceedings of ACL 2016, pp. 778–788. Association for Computational Linguistics (2016)
6. Denis, P., Baldridge, J.: Specialized models and ranking for coreference resolution. In: Proceedings of EMNLP 2008, pp. 660–669. Association for Computational Linguistics (2008)
7. Kong, F., Zhou, G.: A clause-level hybrid approach to Chinese empty element recovery. In: Proceedings of IJCAI 2013, pp. 2113–2119 (2013)
8. Kong, F., Zhou, G.: A tree kernel-based unified framework for Chinese zero anaphora resolution. In: Proceedings of EMNLP 2010, pp. 882–891. Association for Computational Linguistics (2010)
9. Lee, H., Chang, A., Peirsman, Y., Chambers, N., Surdeanu, M., Jurafsky, D.: Deterministic coreference resolution based on entiy-centric, precision-ranked rules. Comput. Linguist. **39**, 885–916 (2013)
10. Moosavi, N.S., Strube, M.: Search space pruning: a simple solution for better coreference resolvers. In: Proceedings of NAACL 2016, pp. 1005–1011. Association for Computational Linguistics (2016)
11. Yang, X., Su, J., Lang, J., Tan, C.L., Liu, T., Li, S.: An entity-mention model for coreference resolution with inductive logic programming. In: Proceedings of ACL 2008, pp. 843–851. Association for Computational Linguistics (2008)
12. Yang, X., Zhou, G., Su, J., Tan, C.L.: Coreference resolution using competition learning approach. In: Proceedings of ACL 2013, pp. 176–183. Association for Computational Linguistics (2013)
13. Zhao, S., Ng, H.T.: Identification and resolution of Chinese zero pronouns: a machine learning approach. In: Proceedings of EMNLP-CoNLL 2007, pp. 541–550. Association for Computational Linguistics (2007)

Towards Better Chinese Zero Pronoun Resolution from Discourse Perspective

Sheng Cheng, Kong Fang$^{(\boxtimes)}$, and Zhou Guodong

School of Computer Science and Technology, Soochow University, Suzhou, China
20154227040@stu.suda.edu.cn, {kongfang,gdzhou}@suda.edu.cn

Abstract. Chinese zero pronoun (ZP) resolution plays an important role in natural language understanding. This paper focuses on improving Chinese ZP resolution from discourse perspective. In particular, various kinds of discourse information are employed in both stages of ZP resolution. During the ZP detection stage, we first propose an elementary discourse unit (EDU) based method to generate ZP candidates from discourse perspective and then exploit relevant discourse context to help better identify ZPs. During the ZP resolution stage, we employ a tree-style discourse rhetorical structure to improve the resolution. Evaluation on OntoNotes shows the significant importance of discourse information to the performance of ZP resolution. To the best of our knowledge, this is the first work to improve Chinese ZP resolution from discourse perspective.

Keywords: Chinese zero pronoun resolution
Zero pronoun detection · Elementary discourse unit
Tree-style discourse rhetorical structure

1 Introduction

As a gap in a sentence, a ZP exists when a phonetically null form is used to refer to a real world entity. It is well-known that correctly recovering ZP is important to many natural language processing (NLP) tasks. Although Chinese ZP resolution has been much studied in the linguistics literature [16,17], it was not until recently that it became a hot topic in computational linguistics. Although various kinds of lexical and syntactic features have been successfully employed in ZP resolution to a certain extent [2–4,14,23], the contribution of discourse information has been largely ignored. In this paper, we aim to improve the performance of Chinese ZP resolution from discourse perspective, with various kinds of discourse information considered. During the ZP detection stage, elementary discourse units (EDUs) are detected and used to constrain the generation of ZP candidates. During the ZP resolution stage, a tree-style discourse rhetorical structure is employed to limit the search space of the ZP antecedent by filtering out unlikely antecedent candidates. To our knowledge, this is the first work to improve Chinese ZP resolution from discourse perspective.

© Springer International Publishing AG 2018
X. Huang et al. (Eds.): NLPCC 2017, LNAI 10619, pp. 406–418, 2018.
https://doi.org/10.1007/978-3-319-73618-1_34

2 Background Knowledge

In this section, we introduce two related background knowledge, i.e. Chinese ZP and discourse parsing.

2.1 Chinese Zero Pronoun

It is well-known that Chinese is a pro-drop language. Due to the lack of hints (e.g. number or gender) about their possible antecedents, the ZP resolution is much more challenging than traditional coreference resolution. Even worse, as noted in Kong and Ng [11], the statistics on OntoNotes v5.0 show that non-anaphoric ZPs account for more than 10% of the mentions in coreference chains.

Example (1) shows an excerpt of coreference annotation from article chtb_0009 in the Chinese part of the OntoNotes corpus with its translated English counterpart provided in the English part of the OntoNotes corpus as shown in Example (2). In this paper, ZPs are denoted by "Φ" and the mentions in the same coreference chain are shown in same font style (i.e., italic or underline style).

(1) 针对*甘肃*旅游业的发展需求，<u>人保公司</u> 积极推出海外游客保险，还在国内首家推出海外散客保险办法，使 " 八五"期间到*甘肃*观光游览的海外游客全部得到保险保障。
*甘肃省*还积极探索高风险业务，" 八五"期间，Φ 参与卫星发射的共保，Φ 分担的风险金额达一千万元，Φ 支付赔款五百万元，成为西北首家参与航天业务的公司。

(2) Aiming at the development requirements of the *Gansu* tourism industry, *People's Insurance Co.* actively promotes travel insurance for overseas tourists, and took the lead at home in providing insurance for individual overseas tourists, which made sure that all those who came sightseeing in *Gansu Province* during the "eighth five-year plan" period had insurance. *Gansu Province* also actively explored high risk business.
During the "eighth five-year plan" period, *it* participated in the co-insurance of satellite launching, with a shared risk amount reaching 10 million yuan, and paying 5 million yuan in indemnity, became the northwest's first company to participate in the aerospace industry.

From above bilingual example we can find that,

- In Chinese text, one sentence can have multiple ZPs located in different coreference chains (e.g., just as illustrated in Example (1), there are three ZPs in two coreference chains). This accounts for about 6.7% of instances in the Chinese part of the OntoNotes v5.0 corpus.
- The distance between a ZP and its antecedent can be far away (as illustrated in Example (1), the second ZP and its antecedent "人保公司/People's Insurance Co.").

- ZPs can be translated into many different forms, e.g. common NP, demonstrative NP, pronoun or even clause in English (e.g., as illustrated in Example (1), the first ZP is translated into pronoun "it", while the second and the third ZPs are formulated into clauses).
- The resolution of ZPs is difficult, even for a human annotator. In Example (1) the subject of "sharing the risk and paying the indemnity" should be "People's Insurance Co." instead of "Gansu Province" which becomes the subject in its corresponding English annotation due to the wrong resolution of the second ZP.

2.2   Discourse Parsing

Since the release of the Rhetorical Structure Theory Discourse Treebank (RST-DT) [1] and the Penn Discourse Treebank (PDTB) [19], English discourse parsing has attracted increasing attention in recent years [9,10,12]. Meanwhile, the discourse-level annotation for other languages, such as Chinese, has been carried out and achieved considerable success [7,18,24]. With the availability of these discourse corpora, some preliminary research on discourse parsing of other languages has been conducted [8,15,22].

In this paper, we employ the Connective-driven Dependency Treebank (CDTB) corpus [18] and the corresponding end-to-end discourse parser [15] to extract gold and automatic discourse information, respectively. The CDTB corpus is constructed using the Connective-driven Dependency Tree (CDT) scheme [18], which attempts to benefit from both the tree structure adopted by RST and connective driven principle adopted by PDTB, and to address special characteristics of Chinese discourse structure. In the CDT scheme, EDUs are regarded as leaf nodes and connectives are viewed as non-leaf nodes. In particular, connectives are employed to directly represent the hierarchy of the tree structure and the rhetorical relationship of a discourse. Guided by the CDT scheme, the CDTB corpus contains 500 Xinhua newswire articles[1] from the Chinese Treebank (CTB) [21] and is built by adding additional one more layer of discourse annotations. A three-level set of discourse relations are recommended by the CDTB corpus. Among them, first level contains four relations: causality, coordination, transition and explanation, which are further clustered into 17 sub-relations in the second level. For example, relation causality contains 6 sub-relations, i.e. cause-result, inference, hypothetical, purpose, condition and background. In the third level, the connectives are under each sub-relation. In this paper, the 17 sub-relations in the second-level are considered.

For more detail about the CDT scheme and the CDTB corpus, please refer to Li et al. [18]. Figure 1 shows the gold-standard discourse tree corresponding to Example (1). From Fig. 1, we can find that, although Example (1) consists of 2 sentences, this paragraph contains 8 EDUs from the discourse perspective. The CDT-styled discourse parser can provide three kinds of discourse information,

---

[1] Among them, 325 articles overlap with the "NW" section of the OntoNotes corpus. The following oracle experiments are conducted in this part.

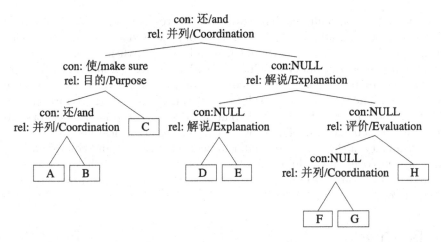

Fig. 1. The gold-standard discourse tree corresponding to Example (1) (There are eight terminal nodes corresponding to EDUs, denoted as A to H. Meanwhile each non-terminal node contains a connective and its corresponding discourse relation category. A. 针对甘肃旅游业的发展需求，人保公司积极推出海外游客保险/Aiming at the development requirements of the Gansu tourism industry, People's Insurance Co. actively promotes travel insurance for overseas tourists B. 还在国内首家推出海外散客保险办法/and took the lead at home in providing insurance for individual overseas tourists C. 使"八五"期间到甘肃观光游览的海外游 客全部得到保险保障/which made sure that all those who came sightseeing in Gansu Province during the "eighth five-year plan" period had insurance D. 甘肃省还积极探索高风险业务/Gansu Province also actively explored high risk business E. "八五"期间，Φ 参与卫星发射的共保/During the "eighth five-year plan" period, it participated in the co-insurance of satellite launching F. Φ 分担的风险金额达一千万元/with a shared risk amount reaching 10 million yuan G. Φ 支付赔款五百万元/paying 5 million yuan in indemnity H. 成为西北首家参与航天业务的公司/became the northwest's first company to participate in the aerospace industry)

i.e., EDUs, discourse relations with connectives and sense categories, and the discourse rhetorical tree structure.

3   Related Work

Although ZPs are prevalent in Chinese, there is only a few works in Chinese ZP resolution. Representative works include Converse [6], Zhao and Ng [23], Kong and Zhou [14], Chen and Ng [2–4].

Converse [6] developed a Chinese ZP corpus, which only deals with dropped subjects/objects and ignores other categories. Zhao and Ng [23] proposed a feature-based method to ZP resolution on the same corpus. Kong and Zhou [14] proposed a unified framework for ZP resolution. In particular, appropriate syntactic parse tree structures are designed to better represent the feature space using tree kernel-based methods.

Chen and Ng [4] built the first end-to-end ZP resolver. In order to eliminate the reliance on annotated data, Chen and Ng [3] presented a generative model for unsupervised Chinese ZP resolution. Chen and Ng [2] further proposed an unsupervised probabilistic model for this task, which tried to jointly identify and resolve ZPs. In particular, some discourse information provided by a salience model is combined in their ZP resolution system. Chen and Ng [5] further proposed an approach to Chinese ZP resolution based on deep neural networks to reduce feature engineering efforts involved in exploiting lexical features.

In summary, although various kinds of lexical, syntactic and contextual features are employed in the literature, the discourse information has been largely ignored. In this paper, we attempt to improve the performance from discourse perspective.

4 Baseline

Our baseline approach is similar to the state-of-the-art as described in Chen and Ng [2], which consists of two components, a ZP detector and a ZP resolver, and works as follows: after generating ZP candidates according to some heuristic rules, the ZP detector is first employed to identify the true ones from the candidates and the ZP resolver is then used to determine the referential chain for each ZP.

4.1 ZP Detection

In our baseline, the ZP detector contains two steps, i.e., ZP candidate generation and ZP identification.

In order to further improve the performance of our baseline, a clause-based approach is employed to generate ZP candidates similar to Kong and Zhou [13]. First, a simplified semantic role labeling (SRL) framework (only including predicate recognition, argument pruning, and argument identification) is adopted to determine clauses from a parse tree. Here, clauses are classified into terminal or non-terminal clauses according to whether covering sub-clauses. Then, ZP candidates are generated for each clause in a bottom-up way. Particularly, for non-terminal clauses, all the sub-clauses having been resolved are viewed as an inseparable "constituent".

After generating the ZP candidates, a learning-based classifier is adopted to identify whether a given candidate is a true ZP, with the help of following features.

- Lexical: two words and their POSs before or after the candidate, and their various combinations.
- Syntactic: whether the lowest clause covering the given candidate has a subject; whether the given candidate is the first gap of the clause; whether the clause is a terminal clause or non-terminal clause; whether the clause has a sibling immediately to its left; whether the left siblings of the clause contain

an NP; whether the clause has a sibling immediately to its right; whether the right siblings of the clause contain a VP; whether the syntactic category of the immediate parent of the clause is an IP or VP; whether the path from the clause to the root of the parse tree contains an NP or VP or CP; whether the clause is a matrix, an independent, a subordinate clause, or others.
- Semantic: whether the clause has an agent or patient argument.

4.2 ZP Resolution

After ZP detection, a mention-pair model is employed to determine whether the given ZP and a candidate antecedent are coreferent. Obviously, the keys to the success of the ZP resolver are the generation of antecedent candidates and the features employed in this resolver. In this paper, we consider all NPs preceding the given ZP as the antecedent candidates only excluding those having the same head as its parent NP in current and previous two sentences. Besides, we create training instances in the typical way as illustrated in Soon et al. [20], which adopts the closest-first resolution strategy, and adopt following features.

- Features on ZP: whether the path of nodes from the ZP to the root of the parse tree contains NP, IP, CP, or VP; whether the ZP is the first or last ZP of the sentence; whether the ZP is in the headline.
- Features on antecedent candidate (CA): whether the CA is a first person, second person, third person, neutral pronoun, or others; whether the CA is a subject, object, or others; whether the CA is in a matrix clause, an independent clause, a subordinate clause, or none of the above; whether the path of nodes from the CA to the root of the parse tree contains NP, IP, CP, or VP.
- Features between ZP and CA: their distance in sentence[2]; whether the CA is the closest preceding NP of the ZP; whether the CA and the ZP are siblings.

5   Discourse-Based Approach

Although various kinds of lexical and syntactic features have been employed in the literature to capture the context of a ZP and achieved some success in Chinese ZP resolution, the performance of the state-of-the-art ZP resolution is still far from satisfaction. In this section, we introduce the motivation of this study and propose a new approach towards better Chinese ZP resolution from discourse perspective.

5.1   Motivation

From a corpus study, we make a statistic analysis on the overlap part of the OntoNotes and the CDTB corpus. The statistics shows that this part contains 7455 EDUs, and among them, 1639 discourse trees are built covering 1310

---

[2] If the CA and the ZP are in the same sentence, the value is 0; if they are one sentence apart, the value is 1; and so on.

explicit discourse relations and 3807 implicit discourse relations. We can have following observations:

- M1: One EDU has at most one ZP. There is only one case that one EDU has multiple ZPs. This indicates the appropriateness of generating ZP candidates on EDU-level.
- M2: There exists close relationship between discourse relation categories and zero anaphora. For example, in the case of two EDUs with the coordination discourse relation, although they always have similar grammar pattern and share the subject, such subject sharing is not considered as ZP phenomenon according to the annotation guideline (e.g., in Example (1), EDU A and B, F and G).
- M3: Due to the hierarchical nature of the discourse rhetorical structure, it is more appropriate to employ the number of discourse relations extracted from a discourse parse tree instead of the linear number of sentences, clauses or EDUs.

Above observations suggest we can move towards better ZP resolution from discourse perspective.

5.2   A EDU-Level Approach to Chinese ZP Detection

In our baseline system, a simplified SRL framework is employed to detect the clauses from syntactic parse trees. Since the achieved clauses can be nested, we generate ZP candidates in a bottom-up way. During subsequent processing, all the resolved clauses are viewed as an inseparable "constituent". It is interesting to notice that none of "constituent" clauses have ZPs. Therefore, our baseline may introduce much more negative instances. This largely harms the performance of our baseline system.

Motivated by the observations in Sect. 5.1 (M1), we skip the clause detection and generate at most one ZP candidate for each EDU. Besides those traditional features capture the context of the EDU from syntactic perspective, additional discourse features as shown in Table 1 are employed in ZP detection from discourse perspective. The third column lists the feature values viewing EDU F in Example (1) as current EDU.

Table 1. Discourse features employed in our ZP detector

Feature	Description	Value
PreEduZP	Whether previous EDU has a ZP	True
PreEduRel	The discourse relation category between previous and current EDUs	None
NxtEduRel	The discourse relation type between next and current EDUs	Coordination
FstCoorRel	Whether current EDU is the first EDU of a coordinating discourse relation	True

5.3 A Discourse Rhetorical Structure-Based Approach to Chinese ZP Resolution

In accordance with ZP detection, a discourse rhetorical structure-based approach is employed to address ZP resolution, extending our baseline system in three aspects:

Extension 1: One more constraints are deployed during the generation of antecedent candidates. The EDUs having the direct coordination discourse relation with the ZP's EDU are not considered. (M2)

Extension 2: The distance between a ZP and its antecedent candidate is redefined. Since the comma in Chinese can function as the English period due to frequent occurrence of long sentences in Chinese, it is not appropriate to employ the number of sentences to measure the distance. Instead, we redefine the distance as the height of the minimal subtree in the discourse rhetorical tree from discourse perspective. Here, the subtree is governed by the EDU containing the given ZP and the EDU containing the antecedent candidate. In Example (1), we can calculate the distance between the second ZP and its antecedent (" 人保公司/People's Insurance Co.") using the discourse rhetorical tree as shown in Fig. 1. First, we find the two EDUs, i.e., A and F. Then, we extract the minimal subtree covering these two EDUs, i.e., the complete discourse tree. Finally, we can have the height of the minimal subtree 4. In this way, we can get the distance between the second ZP and its antecedent as 4. (M3)

Extension 3: Discourse features as shown in Table 2 are introduced in ZP resolution. The third column in Table 2 lists the feature values viewing the ZP in EDU F in Example (1) as the anaphor and the mention "甘肃省" in EDU D as the antecedent candidate.

Table 2. Discourse features employed in our ZP resolver

Feature	Description	Value
MdZP	The number of other ZPs between the given ZP and current candidate	1
MdZERel	If MidZP is larger than 0, the direct discourse relation category between the EDU containing the nearest other ZP and current EDU	None
NtERel	The direct discourse relation category between next EDU (skipping all the direct coordinating EDUs) and current EDU	Evaluation
DscType	The direct discourse relation category between the EDU containing the given ZP and the EDU containing current candidate	None
DscPath	The list of discourse relations between the EDU containing the given ZP and the EDU containing current candidate	*Coordinate* ↑ *Evaluation* ↑ *Explanation* ↓ *Explanation*

6 Experiments and Discussion

In this section, we evaluate the contribution of discourse information comprehensively.

6.1 Experimental Setup

Following Chen and Ng [5], we employ the Chinese portion of the OntoNotes 5.0 corpus, which was used in the official CoNLL-2012 shared task. Since only the training set and development set in the CoNLL-2012 data contain ZP coreference annotations, we train our models on the training set and perform evaluation on the development set. We report our performance using traditional precision, recall and F1-measure. In addition, maximum entropy is employed as our learning-based algorithm. All our maximum entropy classifiers are trained using the OpenNLP maximum entropy package[3] with the default parameters (i.e. without smoothing and with 100 iterations). To see whether an improvement is significant, we conduct significance testing using paired t-test.

6.2 Experimental Results and Discussion

We first compare our discourse-based system with our baseline system to show the contribution of the discourse information. Then we compare our discourse-based system with the state-of-the-art system as described in Chen and Ng's [5].

Contribution of Discourse Information

In order to better understand the contribution of the discourse information to ZP resolution, we conduct a set of experiments on the overlap portion of the OntoNotes and the CDTB corpora (i.e., 325 texts). Considering the limited number of the available texts, we conduct these experiments using 10-fold cross-validation. Compared to our baseline system, all the following improvements are statistically significant ($p < 0.005$).

It should be noted that the performance of the discourse parser depends on that of the syntactic parser. This paper employs the automatic parse trees provided by the CoNLL-2012 shared task as the default one. Besides, we train and evaluate the discourse parser [15] under the default automatic parse trees. As a result, we achieve the performance of 93.8% in F-measure for EDU detection, 52.3% for discourse tree generation, and 53.6% for discourse relation classification. For details, please refer to Kong and Zhou [15].

In order to evaluate the contribution of the introduced discourse information to ZP detection. Table 3 shows the performance of our ZP detector under gold standard and automatic parse trees respectively. From the results we can find that,

- In comparison with using gold standard parse trees, the performance of ZP detection using automatic parse trees drops significantly. This indicates the dependency of our ZP detector on the quality of syntactic parsing.

---

[3] http://maxent.sourceforge.net/.

Table 3. Performance of Chinese ZP detection

	On gold parse trees			On auto parse trees		
	R(%)	P(%)	F	R(%)	P(%)	F
Baseline	58.2	72.9	64.7	39.4	62.7	48.4
+gold dp	78.4	72.6	75.4	68.1	64.4	66.2
+auto dp	71.4	70.5	70.9	50.2	59.4	54.4

- In comparison with our baseline system, incorporating gold discourse information can improve our ZP detector about 10.7% and 17.8% in F-measure under gold and automatic parse trees, respectively.
- In comparison with using gold discourse information, the performance of ZP detection using automatic discourse information drops about 4.5% and 11.8% in F-measure under gold and automatic parse trees respectively. Just as reported in Kong and Zhou [15], the performance of discourse parser much depends on the results of syntactic parser. In spite of this, in comparison with the baseline system, the introduced discourse information also improve the performance of ZP detection about 6.0% in F-measure under automatic setting.

Table 4. Performance of Chinese ZP resolution using gold standard parse trees

	Gold ZPs			Auto ZPs		
	R(%)	P(%)	F	R(%)	P(%)	F
Baseline	50.4	50.4	50.4	30.2	31.4	30.8
+gold dp	62.3	62.3	62.3	44.8	45.6	45.2
+auto dp	54.8	54.8	54.8	37.8	35.6	36.7

In order to evaluate the contribution of the introduced discourse information to ZP resolution, Table 4 shows the performance of our Chinese ZP resolution under gold parse trees. We can find that,

- Using gold standard ZPs, the gold standard discourse information can outperform the baseline system by about 12% in F-measure. This shows the effectiveness of our three extensions during ZP resolution. When the automatic discourse information is employed, the performance improvement drops to about 4.4% in F-measure.
- Using automatic ZPs, the gold standard discourse information can outperform the baseline system by about 14.5% in F-measure, more significant than using gold standard ZPs. When the automatic discourse information is employed, the performance improvement drops to about 6% in F-measure.

Table 5. Performance of end-to-end Chinese ZP resolution

	R(%)	P(%)	F
Baseline	18.2	20.1	19.1
Discourse-based system	20.4	25.6	22.7

Table 5 shows the performance of our end-to-end Chinese ZP resolution system. That is for the given text, our system first conducts syntactic parsing, then employs our ZP detector to identify the ZPs using automatic parse trees, and finally, employs our ZP resolver to determine the antecedents of ZPs. From Table 5, we can find that, the automatic discourse information can improve the performance of the end-to-end ZP resolution system by about 3.6% in F-measure. In comparison with the gold standard parse trees, the improvement decreases by about 14.0% in F-measure. Although as reported in Kong and Zhou [15], the performance of discourse parser much depends on that of syntactic parser, the improvement achieved by the discourse information is still significant.

Comparison with the State-of-the-Art
In order to fairly compare our ZP resolution system with the state-of-the-art system, as described in Chen and Ng [5], we conduct following experiments with the same setting as theirs. Table 6 compares the performance on the OntoNotes corpus. From the results we can find,

- In comparison with Chen and Ng [5], which adopts deep learning approach and achieves the best performance on Chinese ZP resolution up to now, our baseline performs slightly inferior by about 0.6% in overall F1-measure. With the discourse information, our discourse-based system outperforms the state-of-the-art by about 4.5% in overall F-measure.
- Over different sources, our baseline system performs better than Chen and Ng [5] on NW, almost same on MZ and BC, only much worse than Chen and

Table 6. Performance of three end-to-end Chinese ZP resolution systems over different sections of the OntoNotes corpus.

Source	Chen and Ng [5]			Baseline			Discourse-based system		
	R(%)	P(%)	F	R(%)	P(%)	F	R(%)	P(%)	F
NW	11.9	12.8	12.3	13.4	15.7	14.5	19.7	24.1	21.7
MZ	9.3	7.3	8.2	8.9	7.8	8.3	9.3	12.4	10.6
WB	23.9	16.1	19.2	14.2	11.4	12.6	19.2	15.4	17.1
BN	22.1	23.2	22.6	18.5	24.1	20.9	19.4	22.9	21.0
BC	21.2	14.6	17.3	21.6	14.3	17.2	24.3	20.6	22.3
TC	31.4	15.9	21.1	30.1	15.6	20.5	30.7	16.4	21.4
Overall	21.9	15.8	18.4	20.3	15.8	17.8	26.1	20.4	22.9

Ng [5] on WB, BN and TC. With the discourse information, our discourse-based system significantly outperforms Chen and Ng [5] on 3 sources (i.e., NW, MZ and BC) by about 9.4%, 2.4% and 5.0% in F-measure, respectively, only slightly inferior by about 0.3% on TC, and much worse than the-state-of-the-art on WB and BN by about 2.1% and 1.6% in F-measure.

7   Conclusion

In this paper, we focus on improving Chinese ZP resolution from discourse perspective. During ZP detection, we first generate ZP candidates based on EDU, and then extract various kinds of features to model the context of the EDU from both syntactic and discourse perspective. During ZP resolution, the discourse tree structure is employed to improve the resolution performance. Evaluation on OntoNotes shows that the discourse information can significantly improve Chinese ZP resolution. To our best knowledge, this is the first work to improve Chinese ZP resolution from discourse perspective.

Acknowledgements. This work is supported by Project 61472264, 61673290 and 61502149 under the National Natural Science Foundation of China, Key Project 61333018 under the National Natural Science Foundation of China.

References

1. Carlson, L., Marcu, D., Okurowski, M.E.: Building a discourse-tagged corpus in the framework of rhetorical structure theory (2001)
2. Chen, C., Ng, V.: Chinese zero pronoun resolution: a joint unsupervised discourse-aware model rivaling state-of-the-art resolvers. In: Proceedings of ACL 2015, pp. 320–326 (2015)
3. Chen, C., Ng, V.: Chinese zero pronoun resolution: a unsupervised approach combining ranking and integer linear programming. In: Proceedings of AAAI 2014, pp. 1622–1628 (2014)
4. Chen, C., Ng, V.: Chinese zero pronoun resolution: some recent advances. In: Proceedings of EMNLP 2013, pp. 1360–1365 (2013)
5. Chen, C., Ng, V.: Chinese zero pronoun resolution with deep neural networks. In: Proceedings of ACL 2016, pp. 778–788 (2016)
6. Converse, S.: Pronominal anaphora resolution in Chinese. Ph.D., University of Pennsylvania (2006)
7. Huang, H.H., Chen, H.H.: An annotation system for development of Chinese discourse corpus. In: Proceedings of COLING 2012, pp. 223–230 (2012)
8. Huang, H.H., Chen, H.H.: Contingency and comparison relation labeling and structure prediction in Chinese sentences. In: Proceedings of the 13th Annual Meeting of the Special Interest Group on Discourse and Dialogue, pp. 261–269 (2012)
9. Ji, Y., Eisenstein, J.: Representation learning for text-level discourse parsing. In: Proceedings of ACL 2014, pp. 13–24 (2014)
10. Joty, S., Carenini, G., Ng, R., Mehdad, Y.: Combining intra- and multi-sentential rhetorical parsing for document-level discourse analysis. In: Proceedings of ACL 2013, pp. 486–496 (2013)

11. Kong, F., Ng, H.T.: Exploiting zero pronouns to improve Chinese coreference resolution. In: Proceedings of EMNLP 2013, pp. 278–288 (2013)
12. Kong, F., Ng, H.T., Zhou, G.: A constituent-based approach to argument labeling with joint inference in discourse parsing. In: Proceedings of EMNLP 2014, pp. 68–77 (2014)
13. Kong, F., Zhou, G.: A clause-level hybrid approach to Chinese empty element recovery. In: Proceedings of IJCAI 2013, pp. 2113–2119 (2013)
14. Kong, F., Zhou, G.: A tree kernel-based unified framework for Chinese zero anaphora resolution. In: Proceedings of EMNLP 2010, pp. 882–891 (2010)
15. Kong, F., Zhou, G.: A CDT-styled end-to-end Chinese discourse parser. ACM Trans. Asian Low-Resour. Lang. Inf. Process **16**(4), 26:1–26:17 (2017). http://doi.acm.org/10.1145/3099557
16. Li, C.N., Thompson, S.A.: Third-person pronouns and zero-anaphora in Chinese discourse. Syntax Semant. **12**, 311–335 (1979)
17. Li, W.: Topic chains in Chinese discourse. Discourse Process. **37**, 25–45 (2004)
18. Li, Y., Feng, W., Sun, J., Kong, F., Zhou, G.: Building Chinese discourse corpus with connective-driven dependency tree structure. In: Proceedings of EMNLP 2014, pp. 2105–2114 (2014)
19. Prasad, R., Dinesh, N., Lee, A., Miltsakaki, E., Robaldo, L., Joshi, A., Webber, B.: The Penn Discourse TreeBank 2.0. In: Proceedings of LREC 2008, pp. 2961–2968 (2008)
20. Soon, W.M., Ng, H.T., Lim, D.C.Y.: A machine learning approach to coreference resolution of noun phrases. Comput. Linguist. **27**(4), 521–544 (2001)
21. Xue, N., Xia, F., Chiou, F.D., Palmer, M.: The Penn Chinese TreeBank: phrase structure annotation of a large corpus. Nat. Lang. Eng. **11**, 207–238 (2005)
22. Yang, Y., Xue, N.: Chinese comma disambiguation for discourse analysis. In: Proceedings of ACL 2012, pp. 786–794 (2012)
23. Zhao, S., Ng, H.T.: Identification and resolution of Chinese zero pronouns: a machine learning approach. In: Proceedings of EMNLP-CoNLL 2007, pp. 541–550 (2007)
24. Zhou, Y., Xue, N.: The Chinese Discourse TreeBank: a Chinese corpus annotated with discourse relations. Lang. Resour. Eval. **49**(2), 397–431 (2015)

Neural Domain Adaptation with Contextualized Character Embedding for Chinese Word Segmentation

Zuyi Bao, Si Li$^{(\boxtimes)}$, Sheng Gao, and Weiran Xu

Beijing University of Posts and Telecommunications, Beijing, China
{baozuyi,lisi,gaosheng,xuweiran}@bupt.edu.cn

Abstract. There has a large scale annotated newswire data for Chinese word segmentation. However, some research proves that the performance of the segmenter has significant decrease when applying the model trained on the newswire to other domain, such as patent and literature. The same character appeared in different words may be in different position and with different meaning. In this paper, we introduce contextualized character embedding to neural domain adaptation for Chinese word segmentation. The contextualized character embedding aims to capture the useful dimension in embedding for target domain. The experiment results show that the proposed method achieves competitive performance with previous Chinese word segmentation domain adaptation methods.

Keywords: Chinese word segmentation
Contextualized character embedding · Domain adaptation
Neural network

1 Introduction

Chinese word segmentation is a necessary step for Chinese syntactic analysis due to Chinese text comes without word delimiters. Some state-of-the-art Chinese word segmentation systems with statistical techniques [14–16,24,26,28,34,37,38] reported high accuracy with large-scale annotated dataset, such as the Chinese TreeBank (CTB) [31], Peking University and Microsoft Research [12]. However, in actual use, the performance of the segmenter is not satisfying. As large-scale human annotated corpora mainly focus on domains like newswire, word segmentation systems trained on these corpora often suffer a rapid decrease in performance when they are used in other domains such as patents and literature [18,20,25]. In this paper, we consider such problem as *domain adaptation* [11] task.

Until now, two kinds of domain adaptation tasks are studied for Chinese word segmentation. One is annotation standard adaptation [7,15], the other is document type adaptation [19–21,25,35]. The annotation standard adaptation

© Springer International Publishing AG 2018
X. Huang et al. (Eds.): NLPCC 2017, LNAI 10619, pp. 419–430, 2018.
https://doi.org/10.1007/978-3-319-73618-1_35

aims to explore the common underlying knowledge from the corpora with different annotation standards. The document type adaptation is to use one domain document data to label the other domain document, such as using newswire document to label novel document. In this paper, we focus on the document type adaptation. Most previous research [19,20] is based on the hand-crafted model which is difficult and time-consuming. In this paper, we adopt neural domain adaptation method for Chinese word segmentation.

In domain adaptation, the training data domain is often called *source* domain, and the testing data domain is often called *target* domain. Domain adaptation tries to resolve the problem that the training data and testing data are sampled from different distributions. The aim of domain adaptation is to learn a classifier which is trained on data mainly or all from *source* domain but generalizes well on *target* domain. In this paper, we focus on the semi-supervised domain adaptation [10] where annotated data is only available in *source* domain.

During Chinese word segmentation, the same character appeared in different words may be in different position and with different meaning. This observation is caused by the ambiguity of the character. The paper [29] indicates that much of ambiguity in word meaning can be resolved by considering surrounding words. This clue is also suitable for the character. The neural segmenter is usually based on character embeddings. In this paper, we follow this hypothesis that only a few dimensions in the source domain character embeddings are relevant to the target domain and we can turn off most of irrelevant dimensions. We introduce a mask network to turn off some dimensions of character embeddings by contextualizing a character embedding vector. Then the contextualized character embeddings are used in the neural segmenter. Our contributions are as follows:

(1) We introduce a mask model to adaptively mask out each dimension of the source and target embedding vectors to build the contextualized character embedding.
(2) We propose a neural domain adaptation segmenter with contextualized character embedding and show the effectiveness in the experiments.

2   Method

2.1   Contextualized Character Embedding

The amount of commonly used Chinese characters are limited, the meaning of each Chinese character is quite ambiguous. The same character appeared in different words may be in different position and with different meaning. Commonly used character embeddings do not distinguish each meaning of the character and are a mixture of every meaning. In this section, we introduce a contextualized character embedding for Chinese word segmentation.

Embedding is usually a n-dimension vector for each character. The n-dimension can be viewed as n hidden semantics dimensions. We assume that one meaning of the character may be represented by some of n hidden semantics dimensions. According to this assumption, the semantic mask is generated by the contextual information to specify the meaning of each character. Let x_i refers to the embedding of i-th character, a sentence of n characters can be represented as $x_1, x_2, \cdots, x_n$. As it is believed that the contextual information from a window size of 5 characters may be sufficient for Chinese word segmentation [38], we employ a window size of 5 characters to generate the semantic mask. Let $w_i = [x_{i-2}, x_{i-1}, x_i, x_{i+1}, x_{i+2}]$ refers to a concatenate of 5 character embeddings around i-th character. The semantic mask $mask_i$ is generated as:

$$mask_i = \sigma(W w_i + b), \tag{1}$$

where σ is the sigmoid function, W and b are weight matrix and bias term. Then the contextualized character embedding c_i is generated by masking the character embedding x_i as:

$$c_i = mask_i \odot x_i, \tag{2}$$

where $\odot$ is element-wise product.

2.2   Character Sequence Auto-Encoder

In order to train the contextualized character embedding c_i, we propose a unsupervised character sequence to sequence auto-encoder in this section. The architecture of our character sequence to sequence auto-encoder is similar to [27], but our auto-encoder is trained by rebuilding its input sequence. Let c_i refers to the contextualized embedding of i-th character, a sentence of n characters $y_1, y_2, \cdots, y_n$ can be represented as $c_1, c_2, \cdots, c_n$. An encoder is employed to map the sentence into a fix sized vector h_n. Then an decoder is employed to map the fix-sized vector h_n to the original sentence again. Following the implement of [27], we use Long Short-Term Memory (LSTM) network to model the encoder and decoder. The description of a LSTM unit at time step t is defined as follows:

$$i_t, f_t, o_t = \sigma(W_g c_t + U_g h_{t-1} + b_g), \tag{3}$$

$$\tilde{C}_t = \tanh(W_c c_t + U_c h_{t-1} + b_c), \tag{4}$$

$$C_t = i_t \odot \tilde{C}_t + f_t \odot C_{t-1}, \tag{5}$$

$$h_t = o_t \odot \tanh(C_t), \tag{6}$$

where c_t is the input embeddings, σ, tanh are the sigmoid and hyperbolic tangent function, $\odot$ is element-wise product, W and U are weight matrices, b is bias term. The n-th $h^{encoder}$ of encoder is used as fix-sized vector $h_n^{encoder}$. Then the initial hidden state $h_0^{decoder}$ is initialized as $h_n^{encoder}$. During the decoding, a special symbol GO is used as input and a hidden state $h^{decoder}$ is generated at every timestep. Then a softmax layer is appended for predicting the characters of the original sentence. The network is optimized by maximizing the likelihood:

$$\arg\max_\theta p(y_1^n | h_n^{encoder}) = \arg\max_\theta \prod_{t=1}^{n} p(y_t | h_{t-1}^{decoder}), \tag{7}$$

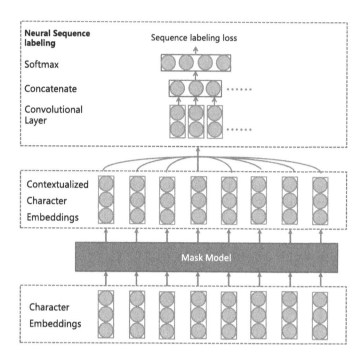

Fig. 1. The proposed MaskCNN.

where θ is the weight arguments in the contextualized character embedding and character sequence to sequence auto-encoder, y_t is the t-th character, the subsequence $y_1^n = (y_1, y_2, \cdots, y_{n-1}, y_n)$, the $h_0^{decoder}$ is initialized by the $h_n^{encoder}$.

2.3 Neural Segmenter

The neural segmenter is built above the contextualized character embedding. In this paper, we take convolutional neural segmenter as an example, but our method is not limited by the architecture of neural networks. The segmenter is simplified from [4], we only reserve the convolutional layer. And the convolutional neural segmenter is equivalent to a feed-forward neural network [9] with multiple window sizes. We decide to take convolutional neural segmenter as our baseline model, due to that (1) convolutional neural segmenters follow most of the word segmentation systems working by sequence labelling [32]; and (2) previous baseline segmenters [19,20,35] are limited with local features. Therefore, it may be unfair to take recurrent networks with context information as rival; (3) the performance of convolutional neural segmenter is comparable with previous baseline segmenters.

The basic unit of convolutional neural networks (CNN) is filters [17]. Take contextualized embedding c as the input. Then features c_i' from a filter i is generated by:

$$c_i' = f(m \otimes c + b), \tag{8}$$

where $\otimes$ is convolution operator, m and b are the weight matrix and bias, f is ReLU in our network. And for each window size, we apply multiple filters to generate multiple feature maps. Features from different feature maps are concatenated. Then a softmax layer is appended for predicting the label of each character. Our neural word segmenter regards Chinese word segmentation as a sequence labelling task. The segmenter adopts BIES (Begin, Inside, End, Single) four labels scheme which represents the position of character inside a word. During the training phase, the cross-entropy cost function is used. And during the testing phase, the label sequences are constructed through beam search.

2.4   Train Strategy

In this section, we propose our neural domain adaptation method based on the contextualized character embedding and name it as MaskCNN. As shown in Fig. 1, the character sequence auto-encoder and the neural segmenter share the same contextualized character embedding layer.

In our method, first, unlabelled data from both *source* and *target* domains are employed to train the contextualized character embedding layer and character sequence auto-encoder through auto-encoder rebuilding loss.[1] During this step, the characteristics of both domains are stored in the contextualized character embedding layer and the contextualized character embedding layer is learned to resolve the character ambiguous by considering surrounding characters.

Then the contextualized character embedding is kept fixed to avoid domain-specific training, and the neural segmenter is trained by *source* domain annotated data. In this step, the segmenter is trained to do word segmentation based on the contextualized character embedding.

3   Experiments

3.1   Dataset

In this paper, the Chinese Treebank (CTB) [31] is selected as the *source* domain data. We train our model by using the annotated data from CTB. The Patent [18] and Zhuxian [35] are used as the *target* domain data. A patent is often a description of a system or solution to a specific technology problem. Patents often contain a high concentration of technical terms which are rare in daily newswire. Zhuxian is a Internet novel which is written in a different style from newswire and contains many novel specific named entity. Some unlabeled target data is used to generate the contextualized character embeddings with the source data. We use the trained model to segment patent and novel data. The statistics of the data is shown in Table 1. We compare our proposed model with methods

---

[1] We try to weight the *target* domains data more, but no significant improvement is observed.

mentioned in [19,35] which are feature-based and lexicon-based methods. We use same amount of unlabelled *target* domain data as previous methods [19,35] to make a fair comparison.

Table 1. Statistics of source and target datasets

Type	Sec.	Source		Sec.	Target	
		CTB5	CTB7		Patent	Zhuxian
sent.	train	18k	36k	unlabel	11k	16k
words.		641k	839k		-	-
sent.	dev.	0.35k	4.8k	dev.	1.5k	0.79k
words.		6.8k	120k		46.2k	20.4k
sent.	test	0.35k	11k	test	1.5k	1.4k
words.		8.0k	241k		48.4k	34.4k

3.2 Hyper-parameter Settings

In the experiments, the hyper parameters are chosen according to the balance of development data performance and training time. For the segmenter, the window size of filters is set as $2, 3, 4, 5$ and feature maps of each window size are 300 with 50% dropout. For mask network, the window size is 5 and the hidden units have the same size as embeddings with no dropout. The size of character and bigram embeddings is 200 with 20% dropout. The bigram embedding is used following the implements of [36]. The hidden unit of LSTM sequence to sequence auto-encoder is 1000 with 50% dropout. The training is done through stochastic gradient descent with a batch size of 16 and Adadelta update rule [33]. The beam size of beam search is 10. We per-train the embeddings using the publicly available Chinese Wikipedia corpus which is 822 MB and contains about 11 million sentences[2]. The embedding vectors are pre-trained using *word2vec* with the continuous skip-gram architecture.

3.3 Differences Between Different Domain

In order to explore the differences between different domains of Chinese word segmentation, we count up the unigrams and bigrams in different domains and the statistics of different domains are listed in Table 2. From the table, we find that almost all of the unigrams in *target* domain are already available in *source* domain, but more than 30% of the bigrams only appear in *target* domain. It is obvious that the main difference between different domains is bigrams or the contextual characters. This inspires us to model the contextualization of characters in different domains through a mask model.

---

[2] http://download.wikipedia.com/zhwiki/latest/.

Table 2. Statistics of different domains. *num* is the amount of unique uni/bigrams. *diff* is the number of *target* domain specific unique uni/bigrams. *cover* is the percentage of uni/bigrams in *target* domain that can be covered by *source* domain.

	CTB5 → Zhuxian		CTB7 → Patent	
Unigrams				
num	4.3k	2.1k	4.5k	1.6k
diff	106 (4.9%)		69 (4.4%)	
cover	99.36%		99.45%	
Bigrams				
num	175k	25k	240k	29k
diff	13k (51.7%)		14k (47.9%)	
cover	67.61%		68.88%	

3.4 Main Results

From CTB5 to Zhuxian. We first compare our methods with the methods from [35] for the adaptation from CTB5 to Zhuxian. The baseline model of [35] is a discriminative joint segmentation and tagging model. Our baseline model is the convolutional neural segmenter. A self-training method is adopted to extend training data by automatically labelling target sentences with the *source* domain training data. The other methods mentioned in [35] used a domain-specific lexicon. As our proposed method do not use the lexicon in this paper, we do not list the results of the other methods mentioned in [35] for comparison.

The results are shown in Table 3. The MaskCNN model achieves an improvement over the baseline by 2.32 absolute percentage. With the bigram embeddings, the result of our proposed method is better than the result of the self-training method.

From CTB7 to Patent. We also examine the performance of our method for the adaptation from CTB7 to Patent. We compare our method with the

Table 3. The results between CTB5 and Zhuxian

Methods	P	R	F1
Zhang et al. [35]			
Baseline	-	-	87.71
+Self-Training	-	-	88.62
Ours			
Baseline	85.91	85.05	85.48
MaskCNN	87.76	87.83	87.80
MaskCNN+bigram	89.75	88.95	89.35

method from [19]. Li and Xue [19] proposed in-domain features and out-of-domain features, which are manual-crafted features, to improve the performance of Chinese patent word segmentation. As mentioned in their paper, the out-of-domain features are extracted to share common characteristics across *source* and *target* domains. The *Out-of-domain features* includes *character POS feature* (C_POS), *word dictionary feature* (Dict) and *character similarity feature* (Sim).

The results are shown in Table 4. In paper [19], the baseline model uses a CRFs model with basic features. From the results, we can see that the performance of our baseline model is comparable to the performance of their baseline model. Our proposed MaskCNN model achieves an improvement over the baseline by 1.12 absolute percentage. Then the MsakCNN model obtains the advanced improvement with the help of bigram embeddings. Although our proposed model does not outperform the best model from the paper [19], the result is very close. As our neural domain adaptation method does not depend on the lexicon, it is much easier for applying without any restriction.

Table 4. The results between CTB7 and patent

Methods	P	R	F1
Li and Xue [19]			
Baseline	86.10	86.30	86.20
Baseline+Features	89.17	88.59	88.88
Ours			
Baseline	86.31	86.30	86.31
MaskCNN	87.98	86.89	87.43
MaskCNN+bigram	88.40	87.87	88.14

4   Related Work

Domain adaptation can be roughly divided into two scenarios, the fully supervised domain adaptation and the semi-supervised domain adaptation [10]. The *easy domain adaptation* is well known for fully supervised scenario. The feature space is first augmented of both *source* and *target* data and then the combined feature space is used to train cross-domain model [10]. But obtaining annotated data could be expensive, and it would be a huge cost to annotate data for every domain. Many semi-supervised domain adaptation methods are proposed in tasks such as the sentiment classification. The main idea is the unsupervised learning of a general representation that works in both domains. Both feature-based [1,22] and neural-based [2,13] semi-supervised domain adaptation methods were explored. There are other divisions for domain adaptation, for example, this problem can be divided into token-supervised and type-supervised methods [35].

Recently, neural network models had been increasingly investigated in Chinese word segmentation for their ability of automatic feature representation [3,5,6,9,23,30,36,38]. These neural models alleviated the burden of manual feature engineering and achieved competitive performance with the hand-crafted models.

In the domain adaptation of Chinese word segmentation, previous works mainly focused on feature-based and lexicon-based methods. Unsupervised character clustering and self-training method were applied [20]. Manually annotated lexicons and sentences achieved significant improvement [35] while partially-annotated data was proved to be more effective [21]. Li and Xue [18,19] annotated a significant amount of Chinese patent data and designed features to capture the distributional characteristics in patents. Qiu and Zhang [25] mined entities in Chinese novel with information extraction techniques.

Choi et al. [8] use the context-dependent word representation to improve the performance of machine translation. In their work, the contextualization disambiguates the meaning of the word by masking out some dimensions of the word embedding vectors based on the context.

5   Conclusion

In this paper, we focus on the semi-supervised scenario of domain adaptation and explore method to adapt the information cross different domains with different document types for neural Chinese word segmentation. We first introduce a mask model to obtain the contextualized character embedding. Then the neural segmenter works above the contextualized character embedding.

In the experiments, we explore the differences between different domains. Experiments show that although previous feature-based and lexicon-based methods are strong domain adaptation methods, our neural domain adaptation method achieves competitive performance without additional lexicons.

Acknowledgement. This work was supported by Beijing Natural Science Foundation (4174098), National Natural Science Foundation of China (61702047) and the Fundamental Research Funds for the Central Universities (2017RC02).

References

1. Blitzer, J., McDonald, R., Pereira, F.: Domain adaptation with structural correspondence learning. In: Proceedings of the 2006 Conference on Empirical Methods in Natural Language Processing, pp. 120–128. Association for Computational Linguistics (2006). http://aclweb.org/anthology/W06-1615
2. Bollegala, D., Maehara, T., Kawarabayashi, K.I.: Unsupervised cross-domain word representation learning. In: Proceedings of the 53rd Annual Meeting of the Association for Computational Linguistics and the 7th International Joint Conference on Natural Language Processing, Long Papers, vol. 1, pp. 730–740. Association for Computational Linguistics (2015). http://aclweb.org/anthology/P15-1071

3. Cai, D., Zhao, H.: Neural word segmentation learning for Chinese. In: Proceedings of the 54th Annual Meeting of the Association for Computational Linguistics, Long Papers, vol. 1, pp. 409–420. Association for Computational Linguistics (2016). http://aclweb.org/anthology/P16-1039

4. Chen, X., Qiu, X., Huang, X.: A long dependency aware deep architecture for joint Chinese word segmentation and POS tagging. arXiv preprint arXiv:1611.05384 (2016)

5. Chen, X., Qiu, X., Zhu, C., Huang, X.: Gated recursive neural network for Chinese word segmentation. In: Proceedings of the 53rd Annual Meeting of the Association for Computational Linguistics and the 7th International Joint Conference on Natural Language Processing, Long Papers, vol. 1, pp. 1744–1753. Association for Computational Linguistics (2015). http://aclweb.org/anthology/P15-1168

6. Chen, X., Qiu, X., Zhu, C., Liu, P., Huang, X.: Long short-term memory neural networks for Chinese word segmentation. In: Proceedings of the 2015 Conference on Empirical Methods in Natural Language Processing, pp. 1197–1206. Association for Computational Linguistics (2015). http://aclweb.org/anthology/D15-1141

7. Chen, X., Shi, Z., Qiu, X., Huang, X.: Adversarial multi-criteria learning for Chinese word segmentation. arXiv preprint arXiv:1704.07556 (2017)

8. Choi, H., Cho, K., Bengio, Y.: Context-dependent word representation for neural machine translation. Comput. Speech Lang. (2016)

9. Collobert, R., Weston, J., Bottou, L., Karlen, M., Kavukcuoglu, K., Kuksa, P.: Natural language processing (almost) from scratch. J. Mach. Learn. Res. **12**, 2493–2537 (2011)

10. Daume III, H.: Frustratingly easy domain adaptation. In: Proceedings of the 45th Annual Meeting of the Association of Computational Linguistics, pp. 256–263. Association for Computational Linguistics (2007). http://aclweb.org/anthology/P07-1033

11. Daume III, H., Marcu, D.: Domain adaptation for statistical classifiers. J. Artif. Intell. Res. **26**, 101–126 (2006)

12. Emerson, T.: The second international Chinese word segmentation bakeoff. In: Proceedings of the Fourth SIGHAN Workshop on Chinese Language Processing (2005). http://aclweb.org/anthology/I05-3017

13. Glorot, X., Bordes, A., Bengio, Y.: Domain adaptation for large-scale sentiment classification: a deep learning approach. In: Proceedings of the 28th International Conference on Machine Learning (ICML 2011), pp. 513–520 (2011)

14. Hatori, J., Matsuzaki, T., Miyao, Y., Tsujii, J.: Incremental joint approach to word segmentation, POS tagging, and dependency parsing in Chinese. In: Proceedings of the 50th Annual Meeting of the Association for Computational Linguistics, Long Papers, vol. 1, pp. 1045–1053. Association for Computational Linguistics (2012). http://aclweb.org/anthology/P12-1110

15. Jiang, W., Huang, L., Liu, Q.: Automatic adaptation of annotation standards: Chinese word segmentation and POS tagging - a case study. In: Proceedings of the Joint Conference of the 47th Annual Meeting of the ACL and the 4th International Joint Conference on Natural Language Processing of the AFNLP, pp. 522–530. Association for Computational Linguistics (2009). http://aclweb.org/anthology/P09-1059

16. Kiat Low, J., Tou Ng, H., Guo, W.: A maximum entropy approach to Chinese word segmentation. In: Proceedings of the Fourth SIGHAN Workshop on Chinese Language Processing (2005), http://aclweb.org/anthology/I05-3025

17. Kim, Y.: Convolutional neural networks for sentence classification. In: Proceedings of the 2014 Conference on Empirical Methods in Natural Language Processing (EMNLP), pp. 1746–1751. Association for Computational Linguistics (2014)
18. Li, S., Xue, N.: Effective document-level features for Chinese patent word segmentation. In: Proceedings of the 52nd Annual Meeting of the Association for Computational Linguistics, Short Papers, vol. 2, pp. 199–205. Association for Computational Linguistics (2014). http://aclweb.org/anthology/P14-2033
19. Li, S., Xue, N.: Towards accurate word segmentation for Chinese patents. arXiv preprint arXiv:1611.10038 (2016)
20. Liu, Y., Zhang, Y.: Unsupervised domain adaptation for joint segmentation and POS-tagging. In: Proceedings of COLING 2012: Posters, pp. 745–754. The COLING 2012 Organizing Committee (2012). http://aclweb.org/anthology/C12-2073
21. Liu, Y., Zhang, Y., Che, W., Liu, T., Wu, F.: Domain adaptation for CRF-based Chinese word segmentation using free annotations. In: Proceedings of the 2014 Conference on Empirical Methods in Natural Language Processing (EMNLP), pp. 864–874. Association for Computational Linguistics (2014). http://aclweb.org/anthology/D14-1093
22. Pan, S.J., Ni, X., Sun, J.T., Yang, Q., Chen, Z.: Cross-domain sentiment classification via spectral feature alignment. In: International Conference on World Wide Web, WWW 2010, Raleigh, North Carolina, USA, April, pp. 751–760 (2010)
23. Pei, W., Ge, T., Chang, B.: Max-margin tensor neural network for Chinese word segmentation. In: Proceedings of the 52nd Annual Meeting of the Association for Computational Linguistics, Long Papers, vol. 1, pp. 293–303. Association for Computational Linguistics (2014). http://aclweb.org/anthology/P14-1028
24. Peng, F., Feng, F., McCallum, A.: Chinese segmentation and new word detection using conditional random fields. In: COLING 2004: Proceedings of the 20th International Conference on Computational Linguistics (2004). http://aclweb.org/anthology/C04-1081
25. Qiu, L., Zhang, Y.: Word segmentation for Chinese novels. In: AAAI, pp. 2440–2446 (2015)
26. Sun, W.: A stacked sub-word model for joint Chinese word segmentation and part-of-speech tagging. In: Proceedings of the 49th Annual Meeting of the Association for Computational Linguistics: Human Language Technologies, pp. 1385–1394. Association for Computational Linguistics (2011). http://aclweb.org/anthology/P11-1139
27. Sutskever, I., Vinyals, O., Le, Q.V.: Sequence to sequence learning with neural networks. In: International Conference on Neural Information Processing Systems, pp. 3104–3112 (2014)
28. Tseng, H., Chang, P., Andrew, G., Jurafsky, D., Manning, C.: A conditional random field word segmenter for SIGHAN bakeoff 2005. In: Proceedings of the Fourth SIGHAN Workshop on Chinese Language Processing (2005). http://aclweb.org/anthology/I05-3027
29. Weaver, W.: Translation. Wiley, Hoboken (1949)
30. Xu, J., Sun, X.: Dependency-based gated recursive neural network for Chinese word segmentation. In: Proceedings of the 54th Annual Meeting of the Association for Computational Linguistics, Short Papers, vol. 2, pp. 567–572. Association for Computational Linguistics (2016). http://aclweb.org/anthology/P16-2092
31. Xue, N., Xia, F., Chiou, F.D., Palmer, M.: The Penn Chinese TreeBank: phrase structure annotation of a large corpus. Nat. Lang. Eng. 11(02), 207–238 (2005)

32. Xue, N.: Chinese word segmentation as character tagging. In: International Journal of Computational Linguistics and Chinese Language Processing, vol. 8, no. 1, February 2003: Special Issue on Word Formation and Chinese Language Processing, pp. 29–48 (2003). http://aclweb.org/anthology/O03-4002
33. Zeiler, M.D.: ADADELTA: an adaptive learning rate method. arXiv preprint arXiv:1212.5701 (2012)
34. Zeng, X., Wong, F.D., Chao, S.L., Trancoso, I.: Co-regularizing character-based and word-based models for semi-supervised Chinese word segmentation. In: Proceedings of the 51st Annual Meeting of the Association for Computational Linguistics, Short Papers, vol. 2, pp. 171–176. Association for Computational Linguistics (2013). http://aclweb.org/anthology/P13-2031
35. Zhang, M., Zhang, Y., Che, W., Liu, T.: Type-supervised domain adaptation for joint segmentation and POS-tagging. In: Proceedings of the 14th Conference of the European Chapter of the Association for Computational Linguistics, pp. 588–597. Association for Computational Linguistics (2014). http://aclweb.org/anthology/E14-1062
36. Zhang, M., Zhang, Y., Fu, G.: Transition-based neural word segmentation. In: Proceedings of the 54th Annual Meeting of the Association for Computational Linguistics, Long Papers, vol. 1, pp. 421–431. Association for Computational Linguistics (2016). http://aclweb.org/anthology/P16-1040
37. Zhang, Y., Clark, S.: Joint word segmentation and POS tagging using a single perceptron. In: Proceedings of ACL 2008: HLT, pp. 888–896. Association for Computational Linguistics (2008). http://aclweb.org/anthology/P08-1101
38. Zheng, X., Chen, H., Xu, T.: Deep learning for Chinese word segmentation and POS tagging. In: Proceedings of the 2013 Conference on Empirical Methods in Natural Language Processing, pp. 647–657. Association for Computational Linguistics (2013). http://aclweb.org/anthology/D13-1061

BiLSTM-Based Models for Metaphor Detection

Shichao Sun and Zhipeng Xie[✉]

Shanghai Key Laboratory of Data Science, School of Computer Science,
Fudan University, Shanghai, China
xiezp@fudan.edu.cn

Abstract. Metaphor is a pervasive phenomenon in our daily use of natural language. Metaphor detection has been playing an important role in a variety of NLP tasks. Most existing approaches to this task rely heavily on the use of human-crafted features built from linguistic knowledge resource, which greatly limits their applicability. This paper presents four BiLSTM-based models for metaphor detection. The first three models use a sub-sequence as the input to BiLSTM network, each with a special kind of sub-sequence extracted from the input sentence. The last model is an ensemble model which aggregate the outputs from the first three models to get the final output. Experimental results have shown the effectiveness of our models.

Keywords: Metaphor detection · BiLSTM
Sub-sequence

1 Introduction

Metaphor is a form of figurative language, where sentences consist of words or phrases deviating from their proper definitions in ways that do not permit a literal interpretation. From a cognitive point of view, metaphor can be thought of as a type of conceptual mappings [10] where abstract concepts are mapped to concrete concepts in order to make the readers understand some characteristics of abstract concepts more easily. For example, the utterance *"Time is money"* [10] emphasizes that the abstract *"time"* is valuable just like the concrete *"money"*. Metaphors are pervasive in natural language. Corpus studies reveal that metaphors appear averagely in every third sentence of general-domain text. In order to interpret the meanings of sentences containing metaphorical expressions, it is necessary to discriminate the metaphorical and the literal use of languages. Due to the prevalence and importance of metaphorical language, effective detection of metaphors is of great value in a variety of practical NLP applications, such as machine translation, information retrieval, opinion mining and so on.

Previous approaches to metaphor detection can be broadly classified into two categories. The one is to detect metaphor in a single sentence that contains a metaphor [16,17], and the other is in the discourse [7,9,12]. Our approach belongs to the first category. Particularly, given an input sentence, the

© Springer International Publishing AG 2018
X. Huang et al. (Eds.): NLPCC 2017, LNAI 10619, pp. 431–442, 2018.
https://doi.org/10.1007/978-3-319-73618-1_36

task is to judge whether a target verb in the sentence is in its metaphorical or literal use. Such kind of metaphors accounts for a substantial proportion of all metaphorical expressions, approximately 60% [13]. As for this task, most of the previous approaches have used a variety of semantic and syntactic features (such as abstractness, imageability, supersenses and so on), which are normally extracted from some external linguistic knowledge resources. We shall introduce some representative approaches in the Sect. 2.

Although these existing approaches have been proved to be able to achieve good performance, their reliance on external linguistic resources has greatly limited their applicability, especially to those languages that are lack of linguistic resources.

To mitigate this shortcoming, we propose to use deep neural networks to train an end-to-end model for metaphor detection. In our approach, BiLSTM network is used to build up the feature vector representations of sentences automatically, without any use of linguistic knowledge resources, except an unsupervised text corpus that are commonly available for most languages. The BiLSTM network is chosen because it is a kind of recurrent neural network with the ability to deal with variable length sequence data, and it has been proved to be effective in a lot of NLP tasks [2,3].

For a given input sentence with a target verb, there are multiple ways to extract a sub-sequence from the sentence, with respect to the target verb. Using different sub-sequences of the sentence as input may affect the performance of BiLSTM model. In other words, different sub-sequences could lead to different feature representation of the sentence via the BiLSTM model. Therefore, we present to extract three kinds of sub-sequences for a given sentence with a target verb. Each kind of sub-sequences corresponds to a single sub-sequence model. In addition, we also propose an ensemble model in order to integrate all these three kinds of sub-sequences together, with the expectation that they can be complementary to each other.

To demonstrate the efficacy of our approaches, we evaluate our model on the metaphor test dataset which was made available by Tsvekov et al. [17]. The dataset is a multilingual test set but we only use the English section. This section contains 111 metaphorical sentences and 111 literal sentences, so it is a balanced dataset.

Our work makes the following contributions: (1) it is the first time that an end-to-end neural model gets proposed to metaphor detection; (2) Our approach is independent of any external linguistic knowledge resources, except pretrained word embeddings on unsupervised text corpus; (3) Three kinds of sub-sequences are presented to be extracted from an input sentence with a target verb, and BiLSTM network is proposed to model these sub-sequences.

2   Related Work

Research in automatic metaphor detection has a very long history, ranging from ruled-based methods by using lexical resources to statistical machine learning models. If you want a more thorough review of metaphor processing systems, we refer the readers to the reviews by Shutova [14]. Here we focus only on the recent approaches using the statistical learning method which often treat metaphor detection as a binary classification problem. For a complete survey, please refer to Shutova [14].

Turney et al. [16] viewed metaphor as a method for transferring knowledge from a familiar, well-understood, or concrete domain to an unfamiliar, less understood, or more abstract domain. They hypothesized that metaphorical word usage is correlated with the degree of abstractness of the word's context. Based on this hypothesis, they used logistic regression algorithm on a feature vector constructed from the abstractness of context words, to classify a word sense in a given context as either literal or metaphorical. In their work, the abstractness ratings for words were calculated automatically by a supervised learning model trained on the MRC database[1].

Heintz et al. [6] applied Latent Dirichlet Allocation (LDA) topic modeling [1] to the problem of automatic extraction of linguistic metaphor and achieved good performance. The hypothesis behind their approach is that a sentence which contains both source and target domain vocabulary could use metaphor, so a sentence which contains different topic may use metaphor. Their result of LDA is 100 topics, where each topic is a probability distribution over the training corpus vocabulary.

Tsvetkov et al. [17] constructed a English metaphor detection system that uses a random forest classifier with conceptual semantic features such as abstractness, imageability, and semantic supersenses. They also supported the hypothesis that metaphors are conceptual, rather than lexical, in nature by showing that their Englished-trained model can detect metaphors in Spanish, Farsi, and Russian.

Klebanov et al. [9] tried to classify each content-word token in a text as a metaphor or non-metaphor. They used various features such as unigrams, part-of-speech, concreteness and topic models to train logistic regression classifier for metaphor detection in running text. The experimental results showed that these features are useful for metaphor detection respectively. It was also shown that the unibram features contribute the most, and the second most effective feature set are the topic models.

Jang et al. [7] hypothesized that topic transition patterns between sentences containing metaphors and their contexts are different from that of literal sentences. They also observed that metaphor is often used to express speaker's emotional experiences and cognitive processes. Therefore, they built up a set of features from the information of sentence-level topic transitions, emotional and cognitive words in metaphorical and literal sentence and their contexts, and used these features to train a support vector machine classifier for metaphor detection.

Most of the existing approaches make use of a variety of features to train classification models for metaphor detection. Most of the features rely on external

---

[1] http://websites.psychology.uwa.edu.au/school/MRCDatabase/uwa_mrc.htm.

lexical, syntactic, or semantic linguistic resources that are not always available (or are expensive to obtain) in all languages, which seriously limits their applicability.

Different from these previous work, this paper presents several metaphor detection models based on BiLSTM neural networks, which are able to build up feature representations of sentences from pretrained word embeddings and do not use any human-crafted features.

3   Our Approach

In this paper, we limit our task to determining whether a sentence contains a metaphoric subject-verb-object relation. Different from existing approaches, we propose to use Long-Short Term Memory (LSTM) model that can automatically construct feature representations of sentences for metaphor detection, instead of human-crafted features created from linguistic resources.

Since LSTM is a recurrent neural network model for sequential data, a straightforward solution is to apply LSTM on the original word sequence of the target sentence. Besides this simple solution, we also explore other two possibilities, i.e., applying LSTM on two different sub-sequences extracted from the target sentence (Sect. 3.1). Correspondingly, three single sub-sequence models based on BiLSTM networks can be constructed, one for each possible kind of sub-sequences, and a fourth model is also proposed as an ensemble model to merge the three single sub-sequence models (Sect. 3.2). Lastly, we introduce train objective for model (Sect. 3.3).

3.1   Three Kinds of Sub-sequences

Because LSTM is the recurrent neural network model based on time sequence, different sequences could affect the performance of LSTM model. We want to know how different sub-sequence of the same sentence affect the result of metaphor detection, and find the best sub-sequence to input LSTM model. We propose three sub-sequences of the sentence to input model and then, we will introduce them, respectively.

The original sequence is the original form of the sentence in the corpus, and it contains all the information that we need to judge whether the sentence contains the metaphorical use of the target verb or not. This is the longest sub-sequence of the sentence, which will slower the training process of the model. In addition, there may exists some noisy information that possibly affect our judgement.

The dependency sub-sequence consists of the target verb, its head word, and all its dependents in the corresponding dependency tree, arranged in their relative positions in the original sentence. In other words, the dependency sub-sequence contains the words that have direct dependency relationship with the target verb, which is expected to provide most information about whether the target verb is in metaphorical or literal use. Other syntactic parts, such as the adjective part of the subject or the object, are excluded from the dependency sub-sequence, which are believed to contain little information about our task.

The SVO sub-sequence is the sub-sequence consisting of the target verb, its subject, and its object in the sentence, which is a most-common form of syntactic constructions. Compared with the dependency sub-sequence, the SVO sub-sequence is more concise, and excludes adverbial information for metaphor detection. On one hand, shorter SVO sub-sequences can speed up the training process. On the other hand, the adverbial information is discarded, which may be indicative of metaphorical use of the target verb to some degree.

An illustrative example. We use a simple example to illustrate the three kinds of sub-sequences. For the original sentence "I have given up smoking for two years.", the dependency tree is shown in Fig. 1, which is generated automatically by a dependency parser. From the dependency tree, we can easily learn that the dependency sub-sequence is "I have given up smoking for", which consists of all the words that are directly connected to the target verb "given". Then according to the dependency relationship in the dependency tree, we can get the subject "I" and the object "smoking" of the target verb "given", and thus the SVO sub-sequence is "I given smoking". It can be easily seen that all the three kinds of sub-sequences contain the information about the use of the target verb, but with different completeness.

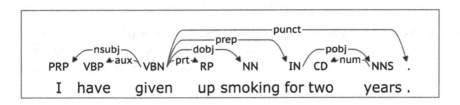

Fig. 1. An illustrative dependency tree

In addition, we think three sub-sequences could better adapt to different sentences. As for the original sentence, it may adapt to the sentence that doesn't have any clause, because the sentence is not too long to increase the burden of model training. The dependency sub-sequence may better adapt to the sentence which the predicate is verb phrase, that is the collocation of verb and preposition. Lastly, the SVO could adapt to the sentence which has too many modifiers, because the SVO can use the most concise sub-sequence to detect metaphor. So we merge three different sequences in order to adapt to all kinds of sentences.

3.2 BiLSTM-Based Models for Metaphor Detection

Recurrent neural networks (RNNs) are powerful models for variable-length sequence data, and are inherently deep in temporal dimension. Long-short term memory (LSTM) is a popular architecture of RNN, which can mitigate the explosive and vanishing gradient problem.

One shortcoming of LSTM is that it only makes use of its left (or previous) context, and does not utilize its right (or future) context. Bidirectional LSTM (BiLSTM) uses two independent LSTMs to process the sequence on two directions separately, and then concatenate the two final output vectors from both directions.

This section will firstly introduce the basics of LSTM and BiLSTM models, and then propose our BiLSTM-based models for metaphor detection.

LSTM is a recurrent neural network with gating mechanism. Here, we adopt the LSTM variant that was introduced by Graves [4]. It comprises four components: an input gate $\mathbf{i}_t$, a forget gate $\mathbf{f}_t$, an output gate $\mathbf{o}_t$, and a memory cell $\mathbf{c}_t$. The formulas for calculating these gate and the memory cell unit are listed as follows:

$$i_t = \sigma_i(x_t W_{xi} + h_{t-1} W_{hi} + w_{ci} \odot c_{t-1} + b_i) \tag{1}$$

$$f_t = \sigma_f(x_t W_{xf} + h_{t-1} W_{hf} + w_{cf} \odot c_{t-1} + b_f) \tag{2}$$

$$c_t = f_t \odot c_{t-1} + i_t \odot \sigma_c(x_t W_{xc} + h_{t-1} W_{hc} + b_c) \tag{3}$$

$$o_t = \sigma_o(x_t W_{xo} + h_{t-1} W_{ho} + w_{co} \odot c_t + b_o) \tag{4}$$

The output of LSTM units is the recurrent network's hidden state, which is computed as follows:

$$h_t = o_t \odot \sigma_h(c_t) \tag{5}$$

BiLSTM has been proved empirically to be effective in performance improvement over LSTM because it can make use of context in both directions and is thus better in making prediction [2,3]. Figure 2 shows the architecture of BiLSTM network.

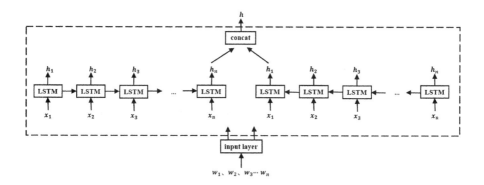

Fig. 2. The architecture of BiLSTM

In our implementation, we process the sequence in two directions, in other words, we process two sequences that the one is the normal sequence, but the other is the reverse sequence. In each direction, all the words x of the sequence will sequentially pass through the LSTM and will get a vector as h which is the feature vector of the sequence which contains the current word and the words before the current word in the sequence, so the last h will become the feature vector of the entire sequence. From two directions, we will get the vector from the normal sequence represented as $\overleftarrow{\mathbf{h}_n}$ and the vector from the reverse sequence represented as $\overrightarrow{\mathbf{h}_n}$. Lastly, we concatenate two vectors of two sequences to form the output of the BiLSTM network represented as $\mathbf{h}$ which could become the feature of the sentence, following the formula:

$$\mathbf{X} = [\mathbf{y}] \tag{6}$$

$$\mathbf{h} = [\overrightarrow{\mathbf{h}_n}, \overleftarrow{\mathbf{h}_n}] \tag{7}$$

The single sub-sequence models are the models with each kind of sub-sequences as the input to the BiLSTM network. The model consists of three layers: input layer, BiLSTM layer, and softmax layer, as shown in Fig. 3. In the input layer (also called the embedding layer), each word in the sub-sequence will be converted to an embedding vector by looking up a pretrained word embedding matrix, and then be fed to the BiLSTM layer. After processed by the BiLSTM layer, the information flows to the softmax layer which transforms the output vector from the BiLSTM layer into a probability distribution over the two class labels: *metaphorical* and *literal*.

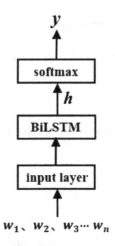

Fig. 3. The single sub-sequence model

The multiple sub-sequences model can be thought of as an ensemble model, which merges three outputs from the BiLSTM layers in the three single sub-sequence models described above, by using the concatenation layer. where three values of h will be connected to become the feature of the sentence as follows:

$$\mathbf{h} = [\mathbf{h_{sen}}, \mathbf{h_{dep}}, \mathbf{h_{svo}}] \qquad (8)$$

then input the result of the concat layer to softmax layer to classify sentence as literal or metaphorical as shown in Fig. 4. Every value of h is get through the method of the single input model's BiLSTM layer. The value of h_1 represents the feature of the original sentence, and the h_2 represents the feature of the dependency sub-sequence, lastly, the h_3 represents the feature of the SVO sequence.

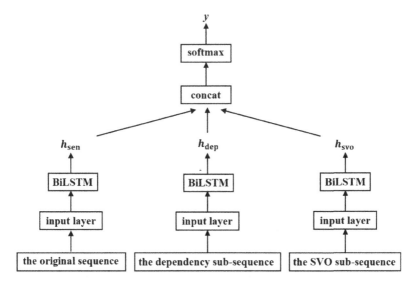

Fig. 4. The multiple sub-sequences model

3.3   Training Objective

We model the metaphor detection task as a binary classification problem, and use the cross entropy loss function:

$$J = -\frac{1}{N} \sum_{i=1}^{N} (y_i' \log(y_i) + (1 - y_i') \log(1 - y_i)) \qquad (9)$$

where N denotes the number of training examples; y_i' is the ground truth label of the i-th training example, and y_i is the models' probability output for the i-th training example.

4   Experimental Results

In this section, we would like to evaluate the proposed models. Firstly, we will introduce the dataset containing the training dataset and test dataset and the data pre-processing (Sect. 4.1), then we will introduce the experiment particulars containing deep learning tools that we use to implement our model, tricks and the hyper-parameters setting in the model (Sect. 4.2). Lastly, we will introduce the results in test set (Sect. 4.3).

4.1   Dataset and Data Pre-processing

Training set is from TroFi[2] corpus that consists of 3737 manually annotated English sentences from the Wall Street Journal. Each sentence in TroFi contains either a literal use or a metaphorical use for one of 50 English verbs.

We firstly used Turbo Parser[3] to parse all the sentences into dependency trees, and then extracted the SVO triples and the dependency sub-sequences from the dependency trees according to the dependency relationships. During the parsing process, we filtered the dependency trees and the SVO triples to eliminate parsing-related errors by a blacklist[4] which was provided by Tsvetkov [17] in 2014 and those with verbs which are not in the TroFi verb list.

The final training dataset consists of only the sentences which can be successfully converted into all the three sub-sequence forms without no error. As a result of the pre-processing, there are 1474 metaphorical sentences and 1046 literal sentences left, among which we randomly select 90% as the training set and the remaining 10% as the validation set.

Test set is the English section of multilingual test sets[5] which is open by Tsvetkov et al. [17] in 2014. The set contains original sentences forms and their SVO forms for 111 metaphorical sentences and 111 literal sentences. So we only need to get dependency sub-sequence by the same method which we use to process the training set. The F1-score of the state-of-the-art system on the test set is 0.79.

4.2   Model Implementation

To implement our model, we use the lasagne[6] which is a lightweight library to build and train neural networks in Theano. It makes common use cases easy, and does not overrate uncommon cases. Besides, it contains the all code implements which we use in our experiment such as LSTM recurrent network, dropout, softmax and so on.

When we train the models, we use the dropout [15] which is a regularization technique for alleviate overfitting in neural networks by preventing complex co-adaptations on training data. We use dropout in input layer and LSTM layer. Besides, we use mini-batch stochastic gradient descent (SGD) with momentum for optimization.

---

[2] http://www.cs.sfu.ca/~anoop/students/jbirke/.

[3] http://www.cs.cmu.edu/~ark/TurboParser/.

[4] https://github.com/ytsvetko/metaphor/blob/master/resources/TroFi/.

[5] https://github.com/ytsvetko/metaphor/blob/master/input/.

[6] https://github.com/Lasagne/Lasagne.

4.3   Hyperparameter Settings

In our models, the dropout rate is set to 0.6 that is a better value found after repeated attempts. And, the learning rate is set to 0.002, because it can avoid that the optimal solution may be missed in the gradient descent process as a result of big learning rate.

In addition, the number of hidden units in LSTM layer is different in different input sub-sequences, because the different sub-sequence contains different granularity information, more specifically, the feature vector of the sub-sequences is different. The number of hidden units in the original sentence, dependency sub-sequence and SVO is set to 150, 60, 40, respectively when we train the single input model. Correspondingly, the number of hidden units in every LSTM layer of the multiple input model is set to 150, 60, 40.

Lastly but not least, we will introduce how to convert the word in sub-sequence to the word embedding. We do it by using the open pre-trained word embedding library[7] which is used just like a dictionary. The library is made by training the word2vec[8] [14] model on Google News corpus (3 billion running words). And the dimensions of the word embedding is 300. Althrough the library contains the most words, very few words can't be found in library. For these words, we will pass them, more unfortunately, if the word is just the verb, we will pass the instance directly.

4.4   Results

We train the four proposed models on the training data, respectively. Three single sub-sequence models are for three different kinds of sub-sequences, the other is multiple sub-sequences model. We test the models on the test set and the experiment results are shown in Table 1. Tsvetkov et al. [17] which is described in detail in relation to prior work.

Table 1. Experimental comparsion of our proposed metaphor detection models.

Sub-sequence	Precision of test set	F_1-score
Original sentence	75.83%	0.77
Dependency sub-sequence	72.71%	0.76
SVO sub-sequence	68.33%	0.74
Multiple sub-sequences model	76.67%	0.78

[7] https://github.com/mmihaltz/word2vec-GoogleNews-vectors.
[8] https://code.google.com/archive/p/word2vec/.

It can be observed from Table 1 that:

- The single sub-sequence model on original sentences has achieved the highest F1-score among all the three single sub-sequence models; while the single sub-sequence model on SVO sub-sequences has got the lowest F1-score. Such observations coincide with our expectation that the adverbial information about the target verb may be helpful to metaphor detection.
- The multiple sub-sequences model outperforms the three single sub-sequence models, which indicates that the three single sub-sequence models are complementary to each other in some degree.
- The multiple sub-sequence model is competitive to the state-of-the-art. However, Tsvetkov et al. [17] achieved the F1-score 0.79 with the help of several conceptual features such as abstractness, imageability, and supersenses, and our approach only uses word embeddings pretrained on an unsupervised text corpus.

5   Conclusions

In this paper, we first propose an end-to-end neural approach for metaphor detection, which does not rely on any external linguistic knowledge resources, except pretrained word embeddings on unsupervised text corpus. We present three kinds of sub-sequences to be extracted from an input sentence with a target verb, and propose to use BiLSTM network to model these sub-sequences. Experimental results have shown the effectiveness of our approach.

Acknowledgments. This work is partially supported by National High-Tech R&D Program of China (863 Program) (No. 2015AA015404), the 2016 Civil Aviation Safety Capacity Development Funding Project, and the project "Aircraft Operation Resource Data Exchange and Integration". We are grateful to the anonymous reviewers for their valuable comments.

References

1. Blei, D.M., Ng, A.Y., Jordan, M.I.: Latent Dirichlet allocation. In: Advances in Neural Information Processing Systems, pp. 601–608 (2002)
2. Graves, A., Schmidhuber, J.: Framewise phoneme classification with bidirectional LSTM and other neural network architectures. Neural Netw. **18**(5), 602–610 (2005)
3. Graves, A., Mohamed, A., Hinton, G.: Speech recognition with deep recurrent neural networks. In: The Proceedings of the 2013 IEEE International Conference on Acoustics, Speech and Signal Processing, pp. 6645–6649 (2013)
4. Graves, A.: Generating sequences with recurrent neural networks. arXiv preprint arXiv:1308.0850 (2013)
5. Hochreiter, S., Schmidhuber, J.: Long short-term memory. Neural Comput. **9**(8), 1735–1780 (1997)
6. Heintz, I., Gabbard, R., Srinivasan, M., Barner, D., Black, D.S., Freedman, M., Weischedel, R.: Automatic extraction of linguistic metaphor with LDA topic modeling. In: Proceedings of the First Workshop on Metaphor in NLP, pp. 58–66 (2013)

7. Jang, H., Jo, Y., Shen, Q., Miller, M., Moon, S., Rosé, C.P.: Metaphor detection with topic transition, emotion and cognition in context. In: Proceedings of the 54th Annual Meeting of the Association for Computational Linguistics, pp. 216–225 (2016)

8. Klebanov, B.B., Leong, C.W., Heilman, M., Flor, M.: Different texts, same metaphor: unigrams and beyond. In: Proceedings of the Second Workshop on Metaphor in NLP, pp. 11–17 (2014)

9. Klebanov, B.B., Leong, C.W., Flor, M.: Supervised word-level metaphor detection: experiments with concreteness and reweighting of examples. In: Proceedings of the Third Workshop on Metaphor in NLP, pp. 11–20 (2015)

10. Lakoff, G., Johnson, M.: Metaphors We Live By. University of Chicago press, Chicago (2008)

11. Mikolov, T., Sutskever, I., Chen, K., Corrado, G.S., Dean, J.: Distributed representations of words and phrases and their compositionality. In: Advances in Neural Information Processing Systems, pp. 3111–3119 (2013)

12. Schulder, M., Hovy, E.: Metaphor detection through term relevance. In: Proceedings of the Second Workshop on Metaphor in NLP, pp. 18–26 (2014)

13. Shutova, E., Teufel, S.: Metaphor corpus annotated for source-target domain mappings. In: Proceedings of LREC, pp. 3255–3261 (2010)

14. Shutova, E.: Design and evaluation of metaphor processing systems. Comput. Linguist. **41**(4), 579–623 (2015)

15. Srivastava, N., Hinton, G.E., Krizhevsky, A., Sutskever, I., Salakhutdinov, R.: Dropout: a simple way to prevent neural networks from overfitting. J. Mach. Learn. Res. **15**(1), 1929–1958 (2014)

16. Turney, P.D., Neuman, Y., Assaf, D., Cohen, Y.: Literal and metaphorical sense identification through concrete and abstract context. In: Proceedings of the 2011 Conference on the Empirical Methods in Natural Language Processing, pp. 680–690 (2011)

17. Tsvetkov, Y., Boytsov, L., Gershman, A., Nyberg, E., Dyer, C.: Metaphor detection with cross-lingual model transfer. In: Proceedings of the Annual Meeting of the Association for Computational Linguistics, pp. 248–258 (2014)

Hyper-Gated Recurrent Neural Networks for Chinese Word Segmentation

Zhan Shi[1,2(✉)], Xinchi Chen[1,2], Xipeng Qiu[1,2], and Xuanjing Huang[1,2]

[1] Shanghai Key Laboratory of Intelligent Information Processing, Fudan University,
825 Zhangheng Road, Shanghai, China
{zshi16,xinchichen13,xpqiu,xjhuang}@fudan.edu.cn
[2] School of Computer Science, Fudan University,
825 Zhangheng Road, Shanghai, China

Abstract. Recently, recurrent neural networks (RNNs) have been increasingly used for Chinese word segmentation to model the contextual information without the limit of context window. In practice, two kinds of gated RNNs, long short-term memory (LSTM) and gated recurrent unit (GRU), are often used to alleviate the long dependency problem. In this paper, we propose the hyper-gated recurrent neural networks for Chinese word segmentation, which enhance the gates to incorporate the historical information of gates. Experiments on the benchmark datasets show that our model outperforms the baseline models as well as the state-of-the-art methods.

1 Introduction

Unlike English and other western languages, Chinese do not delimit words by white-space. Therefore, Chinese word segmentation (CWS) is a preliminary and important pre-process for Chinese language processing. The popular method is to regard word segmentation task as a sequence labeling problem [15,17] and has achieved great success. Due to the nature of supervised learning, the performance of these models is greatly affected by the design of features. These features are explicitly represented by the different combinations of context characters, which are based on linguistic intuition and statistical information. However, the number of features could be so large that the result models are too large to use in practice and prone to overfit on training corpus.

Recently, neural network models have been increasingly focused on for their ability to minimize the effort in feature engineering. [20] firstly applied the general neural framework proposed by [5] to Chinese word segmentation. Following this work, many neural models for word segmentation are proposed and achieved a comparable performance to the traditional state-of-the-art methods, such as neural tensor network [14], gated recursive neural network [3]. However, these neural models just concatenate the embeddings of the context characters, and feed them into neural network. Despite of their success, a limitation of them is that their performances are easily affected by the size of the context window. Intuitively, many words are difficult to segment based on the local information only.

© Springer International Publishing AG 2018
X. Huang et al. (Eds.): NLPCC 2017, LNAI 10619, pp. 443–455, 2018.
https://doi.org/10.1007/978-3-319-73618-1_37

To alleviate these problem, [4] used an LSTM architecture to capture potential long-distance dependencies. After that, LSTM (or alternative GRU) became the popular model for CWS.

In this paper, we propose the hyper-gated recurrent neural networks to model the complicated combinations of characters, and apply it to Chinese word segmentation task. Specifically, we improve the gated RNNs by enhancing their gates. Since the gates play important roles in gated RNNs to control the information flow. To better model the combinations of context characters, we add recurrent connections between the gates.

The contributions of this paper can be summarized as follows:

– We conduct extensive experiments on eight CWS corpora, which is by far the largest number of datasets used simultaneously. The experimental results show that our models outperform the baseline methods.

2   Recurrent Neural Networks for Chinese Word Segmentation

Recently, neural networks are widely applied to Chinese word segmentation (CWS) task [2,12,14,16,18–20]. In this paper, we focus on character based CWS using recurrent neural networks. Usually, character based Chinese word segmentation task is regarded as a sequence labeling problem. Specifically, each character in a sentence is labeled as one of $\mathcal{L} = \{B, M, E, S\}$, indicating the begin, middle, end of a word, or a word with single character.

Generally, the neural architecture of character based CWS could be characterized by three components: (1) a character embedding layer; (2) Recurrent neural network layer for feature extraction and (3) a CRF layer. Figure 1 illustrates the general architecture of CWS.

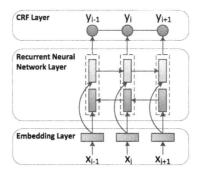

Fig. 1. General neural architecture for Chinese word segmentation.

2.1   Embedding Layer

Regularly, in neural models, the first step is to map discrete language symbols to distributed embedding vectors. Specifically, given a sequence with n characters

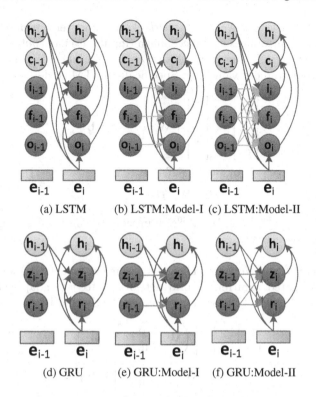

(a) LSTM   (b) LSTM:Model-I (c) LSTM:Model-II

(d) GRU   (e) GRU:Model-I   (f) GRU:Model-II

Fig. 2. Hyper-gated recurrent neural networks. Red lines shows the difference in information flow. (Color figure online)

$X = \{x_1, \ldots, x_n\}$, we should firstly lookup embedding vector for each character x_i from embedding matrix as $\mathbf{e}_{x_i} \in \mathbb{R}^{d_e}$, where d_e is a hyper-parameter indicating the dimensionality of character embedding.

2.2 Recurrent Neural Network Layer

The role of recurrent neural network layer is to extract features by modeling sequential information of a given unsegmented sentences [4]. In this paper, we employ the bi-direction long short-term memory network and the bi-direction gated recurrent neural network for feature extraction.

Simple Recurrent Neural Network. Specifically, simple recurrent neural network (SRNN) could be formalized as:

$$\mathbf{h}_i = \phi\left(\mathbf{W}\begin{bmatrix}\mathbf{e}_{x_i}\\\mathbf{h}_{i-1}\end{bmatrix} + \mathbf{b}\right), \tag{1}$$

where $\mathbf{W} \in \mathbb{R}^{d_h \times (d_e + d_h)}$ and $\mathbf{b} \in \mathbb{R}^{d_h}$. d_h is the dimensionality of hidden state of SRNN.

Long Short-Term Memory Neural Network. Long short-term memory (LSTM) neural network [7] introduces gate mechanism (input gate **i**, output gate **o**, forget gate **f**) and memory cell (memory cell **c**) to maintain longer dependency information and avoid gradient vanishing. Specifically, LSTM could be expressed as:

$$
\begin{bmatrix} \mathbf{i}_i \\ \mathbf{o}_i \\ \mathbf{f}_i \\ \tilde{\mathbf{c}}_i \end{bmatrix} = \begin{bmatrix} \sigma \\ \sigma \\ \sigma \\ \phi \end{bmatrix} \left(\mathbf{W} \begin{bmatrix} \mathbf{e}_{x_i} \\ \mathbf{h}_{i-1} \end{bmatrix} + \mathbf{b} \right), \tag{2}
$$

$$
\mathbf{c}_i = \mathbf{c}_{i-1} \odot \mathbf{f}_i + \tilde{\mathbf{c}}_i \odot \mathbf{i}_i, \tag{3}
$$

$$
\mathbf{h}_i = \mathbf{o}_i \odot \phi(\mathbf{c}_i), \tag{4}
$$

where $\mathbf{W} \in \mathbb{R}^{4d_h \times (d_e + d_h)}$ and $\mathbf{b} \in \mathbb{R}^{4d_h}$. Function $\sigma(\cdot)$ and $\phi(\cdot)$ are sigmoid and tanh functions respectively.

Gated Recurrent Neural Network. The gated recurrent unit (GRU) was proposed by [1] to make gated recurrent neural network (GRU) to adaptively capture dependencies of different time scales. Formally, GRU could be expressed as:

$$
\begin{bmatrix} \mathbf{z}_i \\ \mathbf{r}_i \end{bmatrix} = \begin{bmatrix} \sigma \\ \sigma \end{bmatrix} \left(\mathbf{W}_g \begin{bmatrix} \mathbf{e}_{x_i} \\ \mathbf{h}_{i-1} \end{bmatrix} + \mathbf{b}_g \right), \tag{5}
$$

$$
\tilde{\mathbf{h}}_i = \phi \left(\mathbf{W} \begin{bmatrix} \mathbf{e}_{x_i} \\ \mathbf{r}_i \odot \mathbf{h}_{i-1} \end{bmatrix} + \mathbf{b} \right), \tag{6}
$$

$$
\mathbf{h}_i = \tilde{\mathbf{h}}_i \odot \mathbf{z}_i + \mathbf{h}_{i-1} \odot (1 - \mathbf{z}_i), \tag{7}
$$

where $\mathbf{z}_i$ and $\mathbf{r}_i$ are update gate and reset gate respectively.

Bidirectional Recurrent Neural Network. In order to incorporate information from both sides of sequence, it is common to employ bi-directional recurrent neural network with forward and backward directions. The corresponding Bi-SRNN, Bi-LSTM and Bi-GRU could be derived as:

$$
\mathbf{h}_i = \overrightarrow{\mathbf{h}}_i \oplus \overleftarrow{\mathbf{h}}_i, \tag{8}
$$

where $\overrightarrow{\mathbf{h}}_i$ and $\overleftarrow{\mathbf{h}}_i$ are the forward and backward hidden states at position i respectively. $\oplus$ is a concatenation operation.

2.3 Inference Layer

The objective of inference layer is to figure out the ground truth of labels $Y^* = \{y_1^*, \ldots, y_n^*\}$:

$$
Y^* = \arg\max_{Y \in \mathcal{L}^n} p(Y|X), \tag{9}
$$

where $\mathcal{L} = \{B, M, E, S\}$.

In this paper, we employ conditional random fields (CRF) [10] layer for tag inference. In CRF layer, $p(Y|X)$ in Eq. (9) could be formalized as:

$$p(Y|X) = \frac{\Psi(Y|X)}{\sum_{Y' \in \mathcal{L}^n} \Psi(Y'|X)}. \tag{10}$$

Here, $\Psi(Y|X)$ is the potential function, and we only consider interactions between two successive labels (first order linear chain CRFs):

$$\Psi(Y|X) = \prod_{i=2}^{n} \psi(X, i, y_{i-1}, y_i), \tag{11}$$

$$\psi(\mathbf{x}, i, y', y) = \exp(s(X, i)_y + \mathbf{b}_{y'y}), \tag{12}$$

where $\mathbf{b}_{y'y} \in \mathbf{R}$ is trainable parameters respective to label pair (y', y). Score function $s(X, i) \in \mathbb{R}^{|\mathcal{L}|}$ assigns score for each label on tagging the i-th character:

$$s(X, i) = \mathbf{W}_s^\top \mathbf{h}_i + \mathbf{b}_s, \tag{13}$$

where $\mathbf{h}_i$ is the hidden state of recurrent neural network layer at position i; $\mathbf{W}_s \in \mathbb{R}^{d_h \times |\mathcal{L}|}$ and $\mathbf{b}_s \in \mathbb{R}^{|\mathcal{L}|}$ are trainable parameters.

3 Hyper-Gated Recurrent Neural Networks for Chinese Word Segmentation

Hyper-gated recurrent neural networks enhance the gate mechanism by introducing the sequential information on gates. In this paper, we proposed two types of hyper-gated models for both LSTM and GRU: the gate independent model (Sect. 3.1) and the gate fusing model (Sect. 3.2).

3.1 Model-I: Gate Independent Model

In model-I, the gate independent model, we regard the gates independently. Each of them are only related to the current input embedding $\mathbf{e}_{x_i}$, previous hidden state of $\mathbf{h}_{i-1}$, and corresponding previous gate states.

Hyper-Gated LSTMs. Hyper-gated long short-term memory (HG-LSTM) neural networks build the input gate, forget gate and output gate via another independent recurrent neural network respectively. Specifically, the gate independent HG-LSTM model could be formalized as:

$$\mathbf{i}_i = \mathrm{SRNN}_\sigma(\mathbf{e}_{x_i}, \mathbf{i}_{i-1}, \mathbf{h}_{i-1}), \tag{14}$$

$$\mathbf{o}_i = \mathrm{SRNN}_\sigma(\mathbf{e}_{x_i}, \mathbf{o}_{i-1}, \mathbf{h}_{i-1}), \tag{15}$$

$$\mathbf{f}_i = \mathrm{SRNN}_\sigma(\mathbf{e}_{x_i}, \mathbf{f}_{i-1}, \mathbf{h}_{i-1}), \tag{16}$$

$$\tilde{\mathbf{c}}_i = \mathrm{SRNN}_\phi(\mathbf{e}_{x_i}, \mathbf{h}_{i-1}), \tag{17}$$

$$\mathbf{c}_i = \mathbf{c}_{i-1} \odot \mathbf{f}_i + \tilde{\mathbf{c}}_i \odot \mathbf{i}_i, \tag{18}$$

$$\mathbf{h}_i = \mathbf{o}_i \odot \phi(\mathbf{c}_i), \tag{19}$$

where $\mathrm{SRNN}_\sigma(\cdot)$ and $\mathrm{SRNN}_\phi(\cdot)$ are regular recurrent networks with sigmoid activation $\sigma(\cdot)$ and tanh activation $\phi(\cdot)$ respectively as Eq. (1).

Hyper-Gated GRUs. Hyper-gated GRUs build the update gate and reset gate and output gate via another independent recurrent neural network respectively as well. Specifically, the gate independent HG-GRU model could be formalized as:

$$\mathbf{z}_i = \mathrm{SRNN}_\sigma(\mathbf{e}_{x_i}, \mathbf{z}_{i-1}, \mathbf{h}_{i-1}), \tag{20}$$

$$\mathbf{r}_i = \mathrm{SRNN}_\sigma(\mathbf{e}_{x_i}, \mathbf{r}_{i-1}, \mathbf{h}_{i-1}), \tag{21}$$

$$\tilde{\mathbf{h}}_i = \mathrm{SRNN}_\phi(\mathbf{e}_{x_i}, \mathbf{r}_i \odot \mathbf{h}_{i-1}), \tag{22}$$

$$\mathbf{h}_i = \tilde{\mathbf{h}}_i \odot \mathbf{z}_i + \mathbf{h}_{i-1} \odot (1 - \mathbf{z}_i), \tag{23}$$

where $\mathrm{SRNN}_\sigma(\cdot)$ and $\mathrm{SRNN}_\phi(\cdot)$ are regular recurrent networks with sigmoid activation $\sigma(\cdot)$ and tanh activation $\phi(\cdot)$ respectively as Eq. (1).

3.2   Model-II: Gate Fusing Model

In model-II, the gate fusing model, we additionally take the information interactions of different types of gates into account. Specifically, each type of gate is related to all of other types of gates. Thus, we could derive gate fusing HG-LSTM and gate fusing HG-GRU models as follows.

Hyper-Gated LSTMs. Formally, we could formalize the gate fusing HG-LSTM model by only modifying the Eqs. (14), (15) and (16) as:

$$\mathbf{i}_i = \mathrm{RNN}_\sigma(\mathbf{e}_{x_i}, \mathbf{g}_{i-1}, \mathbf{h}_{i-1}), \tag{24}$$

$$\mathbf{o}_i = \mathrm{RNN}_\sigma(\mathbf{e}_{x_i}, \mathbf{g}_{i-1}, \mathbf{h}_{i-1}), \tag{25}$$

$$\mathbf{f}_i = \mathrm{RNN}_\sigma(\mathbf{e}_{x_i}, \mathbf{g}_{i-1}, \mathbf{h}_{i-1}), \tag{26}$$

where $\mathbf{g}_i$ is the gate fusing state on i-th step, which could be derived by an concatenation operation over gate states (input, output and forget gates) on i-th step:

$$\mathbf{g}_i = \begin{bmatrix} \mathbf{i}_i \\ \mathbf{o}_i \\ \mathbf{f}_i \end{bmatrix} \tag{27}$$

Hyper-Gated GRUs. Similarly, we could formalize the gate fusing HG-GRU model by only modifying the Eqs. (20) and (21) as:

$$\mathbf{z}_i = \mathrm{SRNN}_\sigma(\mathbf{e}_{x_i}, \mathbf{g}_{i-1}, \mathbf{h}_{i-1}), \tag{28}$$

$$\mathbf{r}_i = \mathrm{SRNN}_\sigma(\mathbf{e}_{x_i}, \mathbf{g}_{i-1}, \mathbf{h}_{i-1}), \tag{29}$$

where $\mathbf{g}_i$ is the gate fusing state on i-th step, which could be derived by an concatenation operation over gate states (update and reset gates) on i-th step (Table 2):

$$\mathbf{g}_i = \begin{bmatrix} \mathbf{z}_i \\ \mathbf{r}_i \end{bmatrix} \tag{30}$$

Table 1. Details of eight datasets. N_w and N_c indicate numbers of tokens and characters respectively. $\mathcal{D}_w$ and $\mathcal{D}_c$ are the dictionaries of distinguished words and characters respectively. N_s indicates the number of sentences.

Datasets			N_w	N_c	$|\mathcal{D}_w|$	$|\mathcal{D}_c|$	N_s
Sighan05	MSRA	Train	2.4M	4.1M	88.1K	5.2K	86.9K
		Test	0.1M	0.2M	12.9K	2.8K	4.0K
	AS	Train	5.4M	8.4M	141.3K	6.1K	709.0K
		Test	0.1M	0.2M	18.8K	3.7K	14.4K
Sighan08	PKU	Train	1.1M	1.8M	55.2K	4.7K	47.3K
		Test	0.2M	0.3M	17.6K	3.4K	6.4K
	CTB	Train	0.6M	1.1M	42.2K	4.2K	23.4K
		Test	0.1M	0.1M	9.8K	2.6K	2.1K
	CKIP	Train	0.7M	1.1M	48.1K	4.7K	94.2K
		Test	0.1M	0.1M	15.3K	3.5K	10.9K
	CITYU	Train	1.1M	1.8M	43.6K	4.4K	36.2K
		Test	0.2M	0.3M	17.8K	3.4K	6.7K
	NCC	Train	0.5M	0.8M	45.2K	5.0K	18.9K
		Test	0.1M	0.2M	17.5K	3.6K	3.6K
	SXU	Train	0.5M	0.9M	32.5K	4.2K	17.1K
		Test	0.1M	0.2M	12.4K	2.8K	3.7K

Table 2. Effects of using hyper gates on the test set of PKU dataset. The maximum F value is highlighted for each main block.

Models	P	R	F	OOV
Baselines				
Bi-LSTM	93.67	92.93	93.3	66.09
HG-LSTM (Model-I) with LSTM gates				
+ LSTM gate o	94.04	93.5	93.77	67.76
+ LSTM gates o & i	94.26	93.44	93.85	68.91
+ LSTM gates o & i & f	94.16	93.75	**93.95**	67.45
Baselines				
Bi-GRU	93.65	92.58	93.11	65.65
HG-GRU (Model-I) with GRU gates				
+ GRU gate z	94.13	92.91	93.52	66.12
+ GRU gates z & r	94.05	93.45	**93.75**	67.51

3.3 Hyper-Gated Recurrent Neural Networks with Enhanced Gates

To better integrating the longer dependency information, we further adopt LSTM and GRU to model all types of hyper gates instead of using simple

Table 3. Results of the proposed models on test sets of eight CWS datasets. P, R, F and OOV indicate precision, recall, F value and out-of-vocabulary recall rate respectively.

Models		MSRA	AS	PKU	CTB	CKIP	CITYU	NCC	SXU	Avg.
Hyper-gated LSTM										
Baselines										
Bi-LSTM	P	95.70	93.64	93.67	95.19	92.44	94.00	91.34	94.91	93.86
	R	95.99	94.77	92.93	95.42	93.69	94.15	92.12	95.03	94.26
	F	**95.84**	94.20	93.30	**95.30**	**93.06**	**94.07**	91.73	94.97	**94.06**
	OOV	66.28	70.07	66.09	76.47	72.12	65.79	57.31	71.17	68.16
Stacked Bi-LSTM	P	95.69	93.89	94.10	95.20	92.40	94.13	91.78	94.79	94.00
	R	95.81	94.54	92.66	95.40	93.39	93.99	91.94	95.17	94.11
	F	95.75	**94.22**	**93.37**	**95.30**	92.89	94.06	**91.86**	**94.98**	94.05
	OOV	65.55	71.50	67.92	75.44	70.50	66.35	59.88	69.69	68.35
Hyper-gated LSTM with RNN gates										
Model-I	P	95.81	94.19	94.11	95.39	92.34	93.87	91.47	95.06	94.03
	R	96.21	95.16	93.19	95.24	93.72	94.28	92.27	95.24	94.41
	F	**96.01**	94.67	**93.65**	95.32	93.02	**94.07**	91.87	**95.15**	94.22
	OOV	68.52	72.68	68.44	76.21	71.49	66.50	58.10	70.49	69.05
Model-II	P	95.76	94.34	94.05	95.08	92.90	94.01	91.73	95.28	94.14
	R	95.99	95.13	93.24	95.69	93.68	94.12	92.41	95.01	94.41
	F	95.88	**94.74**	93.64	**95.38**	**93.29**	**94.07**	**92.07**	95.14	**94.28**
	OOV	65.85	71.29	67.39	75.83	73.35	65.88	59.41	71.71	68.84
Hyper-gated LSTM with LSTM gates										
Model-I	P	96.04	94.41	94.02	95.46	92.35	94.24	91.23	95.08	94.10
	R	96.09	95.33	93.20	95.46	93.73	94.15	92.78	95.29	94.50
	F	96.07	**94.87**	93.61	**95.46**	93.04	**94.20**	**92.00**	**95.19**	94.31
	OOV	68.69	70.48	66.57	77.24	70.39	66.59	57.64	70.84	68.56
Model-II	P	96.17	94.29	94.16	95.35	92.64	93.91	91.62	95.13	94.16
	R	96.34	95.23	93.75	95.45	93.78	94.11	92.32	95.14	94.52
	F	**96.26**	94.76	**93.95**	95.40	**93.20**	94.01	91.97	95.14	**94.34**
	OOV	69.20	71.40	67.45	77.21	71.25	65.40	57.96	70.65	68.82
Hyper-gated GRU										
Baselines										
Bi-GRU	P	94.90	93.10	93.65	95.13	91.73	93.66	91.30	94.74	93.53
	R	95.44	93.99	92.58	95.16	93.24	93.90	91.85	95.04	93.90
	F	95.17	**93.54**	93.11	95.15	92.48	**93.78**	**91.57**	**94.89**	93.71
	OOV	63.82	68.38	65.65	75.91	69.46	65.17	55.67	68.77	66.60
Stacked Bi-GRU	P	95.46	92.86	93.65	95.26	92.07	93.59	90.40	94.54	93.48
	R	95.58	94.17	92.84	95.27	93.15	93.68	92.40	94.99	94.01
	F	**95.52**	93.51	**93.25**	**95.26**	**92.60**	93.63	91.39	94.76	**93.74**
	OOV	65.33	69.68	65.81	77.00	70.98	64.68	54.34	69.41	67.15
Hyper-gated GRU with RNN gates										
Model-I	P	95.72	93.92	94.15	95.41	92.62	93.84	91.10	94.81	93.95
	R	96.04	94.97	93.03	95.30	93.65	94.22	92.47	95.15	94.35
	F	95.88	94.45	**93.58**	**95.35**	93.13	94.03	91.78	94.98	94.15
	OOV	67.09	70.85	68.99	77.33	71.09	65.64	57.05	69.64	68.46
Model-II	P	95.85	94.19	94.08	94.84	92.69	93.86	91.45	94.71	93.96
	R	96.05	95.11	92.70	95.75	93.64	94.39	92.33	95.47	94.43
	F	**95.95**	**94.65**	93.38	95.29	**93.16**	**94.12**	**91.89**	**95.09**	**94.19**
	OOV	68.29	71.50	67.80	75.01	71.37	66.73	58.36	69.06	68.52
Hyper-gated GRU with GRU gates										
Model-I	P	95.78	94.32	94.05	95.56	92.67	94.15	91.31	95.00	94.11
	R	95.86	95.00	93.45	95.45	93.50	94.19	92.58	95.25	94.41
	F	95.82	94.66	**93.75**	**95.50**	93.08	**94.17**	91.94	**95.13**	**94.26**
	OOV	67.65	71.31	67.51	78.93	70.60	67.31	57.58	69.71	68.83
Model-II	P	96.00	94.24	94.10	95.20	92.45	93.88	91.19	94.69	93.97
	R	95.97	95.10	93.27	95.25	93.87	94.29	92.77	95.49	94.50
	F	**95.98**	**94.67**	93.68	95.23	**93.15**	94.09	**91.97**	95.09	94.23
	OOV	69.79	72.09	68.49	76.57	71.10	66.18	57.66	69.03	68.86

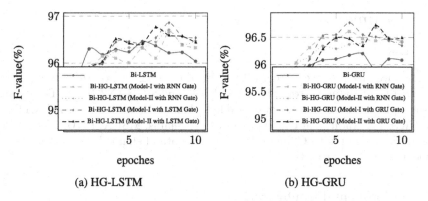

(a) HG-LSTM   (b) HG-GRU

Fig. 3. Convergence speed of the proposed HG-LSTM and HG-GRU models on the development set of PKU dataset.

recurrent neural networks (SRNN). Specifically, we could replace all the hyper gates in Eqs. (14–16), (20–21), (24–26) and (28–29) by $LSTM_\sigma$ or GRU_σ. $LSTM_\sigma(\cdot)$ is a variation of regular LSTM by using sigmoid activation instead of tanh activation. Similarly, $GRU_\sigma(\cdot)$ is a variation of regular GRU by using sigmoid activation instead of tanh activation.

Table 4. Configurations of hyper-parameters.

Character embedding size	$d_e = 50$
Initial learning rate	$\alpha = 0.2$
Loss weight coefficient	$\lambda = 0.05$
LSTM dimensionality	$d_h = 100$
Dropout rate on input layer	$p = 20\%$

4 Training

The training object is to maximize the log conditional likelihood of the true labels. The objective function $\mathcal{J}_{seg}(\Theta)$ can be computed as:

$$\mathcal{J}_{seg}(\Theta) = \frac{1}{2m} \sum_{i=1}^{m} \log p(Y_i|X_i; \Theta) + \lambda||\Theta||_2^2, \tag{31}$$

where Θ denotes all the trainable parameters of the proposed model. m denotes the number of training examples. λ is the coefficient of the regularization term.

We use Adam [9] with minibatches to maximize the objective.

5   Experiments

5.1   Datasets

To evaluate the proposed architecture, we do extensive experiments on eight prevalent CWS datasets from SIGHAN2005 [6] and SIGHAN2008 [8]. The details of the eight datasets are shown in Table 1. Among these datasets, AS, CITYU and CKIP are traditional Chinese, while the remains, MSRA, PKU, CTB, NCC and SXU, are simplified Chinese. We use 10% data of shuffled train set as development set for all datasets.

5.2   Experimental Configurations

Table 4 gives the configurations of the hyper-parameters. Since the scale of each datasets varies, we use different training batch sizes for each corpus. Besides, the batch sizes of AS and MSRA datasets is 512 and 256 respectively, and the batch sizes of the other datasets are 128. To prevent our model from overfitting, we employ dropout strategy after embedding layer with 20% dropout rate (keeping 80% inputs).

For initialization, all parameters is drawn from a uniform distribution $(-0.05, 0.05)$ and the character embedding matrix is pre-trained on Chinese Wikipedia corpus, using word2vec toolkit [13]. Following previous work [4,14], all experiments including baseline results are using bigram feature, with pre-trained character embeddings as initialization.

5.3   Overall Results

Table 3 shows the experimental results of the proposed models on test sets of eight CWS datasets, which has two main blocks. Each main block contains three sub-blocks. These two main blocks show the experimental results on LSTM and GRU respectively.

(1) In the first sub-blocks, we could observe that the performance of Bi-LSTM and Bi-GRU cannot be improved by merely increasing the depth of networks. Besides, averagely speaking, Bi-LSTM outperforms Bi-GRU model (the average F value of Bi-LSTM is 94.06, while the average F value of Bi-GRU is only 93.74).

(2) In the second blocks, the performance of proposed hyper-gated LSTM and hyper-gated GRU using RNN gates is boosted significantly. For HG-LSTM with RNN gates, Model-I and Model-II gain 0.16 and 0.22 improvements on averaging F-measure score respectively compared with Bi-LSTM result (94.06%). For HG-GRU with RNN gates, Model-I and Model-II gain 0.41 and 0.45 improvements on averaging F-measure score respectively compared with stacked Bi-GRU result (93.74%). Compared to the baseline results, the proposed models boost the performance with the help of exploiting sequential information of gates.

(3) In the third blocks, we experiment on more sophisticated hyper gates. By introducing LSTM gates and GRU gates, the performances are further boosted. For HG-LSTM with LSTM gates, Model-I and Model-II obtain 94.31 and 94.34

on averaging F-measure score respectively, with 0.06 improvement compared to HG-LSTM with simple RNN gates. For HG-GRU with GRU gates, Model-I and Model-II obtain 94.26 and 94.23 on averaging F-measure score respectively, with 0.07 improvement compared to HG-GRU with simple RNN gates.

In summary, we could observe that (a) Bi-LSTM outperforms Bi-GRU. (b) The performance of Model-I and Model-II is comparable. No significant boost is observed by using gate fusion, which shows that the information interactions between different types of gates have little contribution to the finial performance. (c) By using more sophisticated hyper gates, the performance is further boosted, which shows that sequential information of gates really contribute to the performance much.

5.4 Effects of Hyper Gates

We also investigates the effects of the proposed hyper gates. Figure 2 gives the results of two models, HG-LSTM (Model-I) with LSTM gates and HG-GRU (Model-I) with GRU gates, on the test set of PKU dataset. There are two main block. As we can see, the performance is boosted gradually when we replace more regular gates by the hyper gates in both blocks. It shows that the proposed hyper gate mechanism could better control the information flow by exploiting the sequential information over gates.

5.5 Convergency

Figure 3 shows the learning curve of the proposed HG-LSTM and HG-GRU on the development set of PKU. As we can see, the proposed models convergence as fast as previous plain LSTM and GRU. With the help of hyper gate mechanism, the HG-LSTM and HG-GRU could be convergent to a better results fast.

6   Related Work

Chinese word segmentation has been studied with considerable efforts in the NLP community. The most popular word segmentation method is based on sequence labeling [17]. Recently, researchers have tended to explore neural network based approaches to reduce efforts of the feature engineering. Among these methods, more and more methods adopts RNN-based architecture to model the contextual information [2, 4, 11, 16, 18, 19].

The gates play important roles in gated RNNs to control the information flow. To better model the combinations of context characters, we enhance the gates by adding recurrent connections between the gates.

7   Conclusion

In this paper, we propose hyper-gated recurrent neural networks to enhance the recurrent connections between the gates for Chinese word segmentation task.

Experiments show that our proposed model performances well on eight benchmark datasets.

Despite Chinese word segmentation being a specific case, our model can be easily generalized and applied to other sequence labeling tasks. In future work, we would like to investigate our proposed models on other sequence labeling tasks.

References

1. Bahdanau, D., Cho, K., Bengio, Y.: Neural machine translation by jointly learning to align and translate. ArXiv e-prints, September 2014
2. Cai, D., Zhao, H.: Neural word segmentation learning for Chinese. arXiv preprint arXiv:1606.04300 (2016)
3. Chen, X., Qiu, X., Zhu, C., Huang, X.: Gated recursive neural network for Chinese word segmentation. In: Proceedings of Annual Meeting of the Association for Computational Linguistics. Pendency Parsing Using Two Heterogeneous Gated Recursive Neural Networks. Proceedings of the Conference on Empirical Methods in Natural Language Processing (2015)
4. Chen, X., Qiu, X., Zhu, C., Liu, P., Huang, X.: Long short-term memory neural networks for Chinese word segmentation. In: EMNLP, pp. 1197–1206 (2015)
5. Collobert, R., Weston, J., Bottou, L., Karlen, M., Kavukcuoglu, K., Kuksa, P.: Natural language processing (almost) from scratch. J. Mach. Learn. Res. **12**, 2493–2537 (2011)
6. Emerson, T.: The second international Chinese word segmentation bakeoff. In: Proceedings of the Fourth SIGHAN Workshop on Chinese Language Processing, vol. 133 (2005)
7. Hochreiter, S., Schmidhuber, J.: Long short-term memory. Neural Comput. **9**(8), 1735–1780 (1997)
8. Jin, G., Chen, X.: The fourth international Chinese language processing bakeoff: Chinese word segmentation, named entity recognition and Chinese POS tagging. In: Sixth SIGHAN Workshop on Chinese Language Processing, p. 69 (2008)
9. Kingma, D., Ba, J.: Adam: a method for stochastic optimization. arXiv preprint arXiv:1412.6980 (2014)
10. Lafferty, J.D., McCallum, A., Pereira, F.C.N.: Conditional random fields: probabilistic models for segmenting and labeling sequence data. In: Proceedings of the Eighteenth International Conference on Machine Learning (2001)
11. Liu, Y., Che, W., Guo, J., Qin, B., Liu, T.: Exploring segment representations for neural segmentation models. arXiv preprint arXiv:1604.05499 (2016)
12. Ma, J., Hinrichs, E.W.: Accurate linear-time Chinese word segmentation via embedding matching. In: ACL (1), pp. 1733–1743 (2015)
13. Mikolov, T., Chen, K., Corrado, G., Dean, J.: Efficient estimation of word representations in vector space. arXiv preprint arXiv:1301.3781 (2013)
14. Pei, W., Ge, T., Baobao, C.: Maxmargin tensor neural network for Chinese word segmentation. In: Proceedings of ACL (2014)
15. Peng, F., Feng, F., McCallum, A.: Chinese segmentation and new word detection using conditional random fields. In: Proceedings of the 20th International Conference on Computational Linguistics (2004)
16. Xu, J., Sun, X.: Dependency-based gated recursive neural network for Chinese word segmentation. In: The 54th Annual Meeting of the Association for Computational Linguistics, p. 567 (2016)

17. Xue, N.: Chinese word segmentation as character tagging. Comput. Linguisti. Chin. Lang. Process. **8**(1), 29–48 (2003)
18. Yao, Y., Huang, Z.: Bi-directional LSTM recurrent neural network for Chinese word segmentation. In: Hirose, A., Ozawa, S., Doya, K., Ikeda, K., Lee, M., Liu, D. (eds.) ICONIP 2016. LNCS, vol. 9950, pp. 345–353. Springer, Cham (2016). https://doi.org/10.1007/978-3-319-46681-1_42
19. Zhang, M., Zhang, Y., Fu, G.: Transition-based neural word segmentation. In: Proceedings of the 54th ACL (2016)
20. Zheng, X., Chen, H., Xu, T.: Deep learning for Chinese word segmentation and POS tagging. In: EMNLP, pp. 647–657 (2013)

Effective Semantic Relationship Classification of Context-Free Chinese Words with Simple Surface and Embedding Features

Yunxiao Zhou[1], Man Lan[1,2(✉)], and Yuanbin Wu[1,2(✉)]

[1] School of Computer Science and Software Engineering,
East China Normal University, Shanghai 200062, People's Republic of China
51164500061@stu.ecnu.edu.cn, {mlan,ybwu}@cs.ecnu.edu.cn
[2] Shanghai Key Laboratory of Multidimensional Information Processing,
Shanghai, China

Abstract. This paper describes the system we submitted to Task 1, i.e., Chinese Word Semantic Relation Classification, in NLPCC 2017. Given a pair of context-free Chinese words, this task is to predict the semantic relationships of them among four categories: Synonym, Antonym, Hyponym and Meronym. We design and investigate several surface features and embedding features containing word level and character level embeddings together with supervised machine learning methods to address this task. Officially released results show that our system ranks above average.

Keywords: Semantic relation classification
Context-free Chinese words · Surface and embedding features
Supervised machine learning

1 Introduction

The Chinese Word Semantic Relation Classification task [1] in NLPCC 2017 is to provide a standard testbed for automatic classification of word semantic relations, which benefits many downstream applications in Natural Language Processing (NLP), such as the construction of semantic networks and recognizing textual entailment [2,3]. Specifically, this task provides pairs of *context-free* Chinese words with different length, and participants are required to classify the semantic relationships of them into four categories: *Synonym*, *Antonym*, *Hyponym* and *Meronym*. These four categories of semantic relations are defined according to quite general ones in lexical semantics, and given two words A and B, their definitions and corresponding examples are shown in Table 1.

Clearly, the purpose of this shared task is to automatically identify semantic relationships of *context-free* Chinese word pairs, which is a bit different from previous studies which identified semantic relations between terms in given texts [3–5]. In many cases, the semantics of a word depends on its context in text.

© Springer International Publishing AG 2018
X. Huang et al. (Eds.): NLPCC 2017, LNAI 10619, pp. 456–464, 2018.
https://doi.org/10.1007/978-3-319-73618-1_38

Table 1. Definitions of semantic relations and corresponding examples.

Relation	Definition	A	B
Synonym	*A* is similar to *B*	消费	花
Hyponym	*A* is a kind of *B*	钢笔	笔
Meronym	*A* is a part of *B*	笔帽	钢笔
Antonym	*A* is contrast to *B*	骄傲	谦虚

Without context between words, the identification of semantic relationships is more challenging. To address this task, we explore a supervised machine learning method which uses several surface features, e.g., character overlaps, length, positional overlaps, etc. In recent years, more and more studies have focused on word or character embeddings as an alternative to traditional hand-crafted features [6–10]. Therefore we examine several types of word level and character level embeddings. Besides, we perform a series of experiments to explore the effectiveness of feature types and supervised machine learning algorithms.

The rest of this paper is organized as follows. Section 2 describes our system framework including feature engineering and learning algorithms. The experiments on training and test data are reported in Sect. 3. Finally, this work is concluded in Sect. 4.

2 System Description

To perform semantic relationship classification of context-free Chinese words, we adopt supervised learning algorithm with surface features extracted from given words and various embedding features. In next, we will introduce feature engineering and learning algorithms.

2.1 Surface Features

Without context, given a pair of Chinese words, we explore four types of surface features, i.e., length features, character overlaps, positional overlaps and sequential overlaps.

2.1.1 Length Features

Given two Chinese words A and B, they may contain different length of characters. Generally, the longer words contain more specific information than the shorter ones, which may imply a kind of *hyponym* relationship, for example, "花" and "菊花". Therefore we design six features to capture this length information using the following six measure functions: $|A|$, $|B|$, $|A| - |B|$, $|B| - |A|$, $|A \cup B|$, $|A \cap B|$, where $|A|$ stands for the number of characters in word A, $|A \cup B|$ denotes the set size of non-repeated words found in either A or B and $|A \cap B|$ stands for the set size of shared characters found in both A and B.

2.1.2 Character Overlaps

Except for antonym relationship, the remaining three semantic relationships more or less indicate a certain degree of semantic similarity or relatedness between two words. Therefore, in light of our previous work addressing semantic relatedness and textual entailment [11], we adopt commonly used functions to calculate the similarity between word A and word B based on their character overlaps. Table 2 shows these three functions used in this work. As a result, we get four character overlap features.

Table 2. Character overlaps similarity measures and their definitions used in our experiments.

Measure	Definition
Jaccard	$S_{jace} = |A \cap B|/|A \cup B|$
Dice	$S_{dice} = 2 * |A \cap B|/(|A| + |B|)$
Overlap	$S_{over} = |A \cap B|/|A|$ and $|A \cap B|/|B|$

2.1.3 Positional Overlaps

The above character overlap feature only records the degree of overlap between two words. In fact, the position of character overlap is crucial for hyponym and meronym relationships. Generally, the character overlaps between two words exist mostly on the head or tail of words. For example, hyponym relation may share the same last character, e.g., "植物油" and "花生油", "房间" and "卫生间". While meronym relation may share the same first character, e.g., "鞋子" and "鞋跟". Therefore, we design the following features to record the positional information of overlaps. Given two words A and B, we implement four types of binary features: (1) whether the prefix of A is the same as B, (2) whether the suffix of A is the same as B, (3) whether the prefix of A is the same as the suffix of B and (4) whether the suffix of A is the same as the prefix of B. Considering these Chinese words with variant length, we set the length of prefix or suffix as 1 and 2, respectively. Totally, we collect eight positional overlap features.

2.1.4 Sequential Overlaps

Previous three features do not take the sequential information into account, while sequential overlaps are quite important for measuring the matching degree between two Chinese words. For example, synonym relationship may contain some instances that one word is sequentially contained in another word, e.g., "宁波" and "宁波市", "法国" and "法兰西共和国". So we design the following features to record the sequential information of overlaps. First, we implement two types of binary features: given two words A and B, we record whether the word A is sequentially included in the word B and vice versa. What's more, we compute the *longest common prefix* and *longest common suffix* for each word pair. As a result, we get four sequential overlap features.

2.2 Embedding Features

The above surface features only capture semantic information between two words based on their surface forms, while word embedding is a continuous-valued vector representation for each word, which usually carries syntactic and semantic information. Therefore, the embedding features are designed to utilize embeddings to obtain the semantic relation between two words. In this work, we train word vectors by using Google *word2vec*[1] [6] with different dimensions, i.e., 50, 100, 200 and 300. The corpus that we used for training word vectors is Wikimedia dumps which will be described in Sect. 3.1. Moreover, as the most fine-grained representation of Chinese, character is the smallest meaningful form in Chinese language, i.e., morpheme. Since different combinations of characters may represent different meanings, we also adopt the fine-grained character level embeddings for this task.

2.2.1 Word Embedding Features

After acquiring the vectors of two words in the word pair, we explore five different ways of interaction in order to capture the semantic relation of the two words as much as possible. The operations between two vectors include *concatenation, multiplication, summation, subtraction* and the *min-max-mean pooling* operations. In our preliminary experiments, word vectors with dimensionality of 100 achieves the best performance, thus in the following experiments, we adopt 100 dimensional word vectors. Besides, preliminary experiments also show that the first two interactive operations have better performance, so we only adopt the *concatenation* and *multiplication* operations between two word vectors as word embedding features.

2.2.2 Character Embedding Features

Considering that character is the smallest meaningful form in Chinese language, we extract features from the character embeddings[2] which are provided by NLPCC 2017 Task 2 [12] with dimensions of 50, 100, 200 and 300. We simply adopt the *min, max* and *mean* pooling operations on all characters in a word to obtain word vectors. Similar to word embedding features, we also use *summation, subtraction, concatenation, multiplication,* and the *min-max-mean pooling* operations to get the interaction information of two words. In our preliminary experiments, the *summation* and *subtraction* operations with 300 dimensional character embeddings achieve the best performance, so we adopt these two operations and obtain 1, 800 dimensional vectors as character embedding features.

2.3 Learning Algorithm

We grant this task as a four-way classification task and explore six supervised machine learning algorithms: Logistic Regression (LR) implemented in *Liblin-*

---

[1] https://code.google.com/archive/p/word2vec.
[2] https://pan.baidu.com/s/1mhPddpu.

ear^3, Support Vector Machine (SVM), Stochastic Gradient Descent (SGD), RandomForest and AdaBoost all implemented in *scikit-learn tools*[4], and XGBoost implemented in *xgboost*[5].

3   Experiments

3.1   Datasets

There are 200 training word pairs and 2000 test word pairs provided by task organizers. Table 3 shows the statistics and distribution of all these word pairs. We perform 3-fold cross-validation on training data set to build classification models.

Table 3. The statistics and distribution of training and test data sets.

Dataset	Synonym	Antonym	Hyponym	Meronym	Total
Train	50	50	50	50	200
Test	500	500	500	500	2,000

The Chinese corpus we used to train word and character vectors is Wikimedia dumps[6], which contains approximate $876, 239$ Web pages. These Web page contents are extracted by Wikipedia Extractor[7] and a total of $3, 736, 800$ sentences are collected after preprocessing. In order to train simplified Chinese word vectors, we first convert traditional Chinese texts into simplified Chinese texts using OpenCC[8] and then tokenize them with jieba tokenizer[9].

3.2   Evaluation Metrics

The official performance evaluation criterion is *macro-averaged F1-score*, which is calculated among four classes (i.e., synonym, antonym, hyponym and meronym) as follows:

$$F_{macro} = \frac{F_{Syn} + F_{Ant} + F_{Hyp} + F_{Mer}}{4} \tag{1}$$

---

[3] https://www.csie.ntu.edu.tw/~cjlin/liblinear/.
[4] http://scikit-learn.org/stable/.
[5] https://github.com/dmlc/xgboost.
[6] https://archive.org/details/zhwiki-20160501.
[7] https://github.com/bwbaugh/wikipedia-extractor.
[8] https://pypi.python.org/pypi/OpenCC.
[9] https://github.com/fxsjy/jieba.

3.3   Experiments on Training Data

Firstly, in order to explore the effectiveness of each feature type, we perform a series of experiments. Table 4 lists the comparison of different contributions made by different features on training set using 3-fold cross-validation with *Logistic Regression* algorithm. We observe the following findings.

(1) All feature types make contributions to semantic relation classification. And the combination of all types of features not only achieves the best performance for the overall classification but also for each semantic category.

(2) The first four surface features act as baseline and they perform better results on synonym and antonym relationships than on the other two semantic relationships. The possible reason is that hyponym and meronym are relatively abstract and surface features cannot adequately capture the semantic information between words.

(3) Word embedding features make a great contribution to semantic relation classification of four classes, especially for meronym and hyponym relationships. It maybe because the pre-trained word embedding usually carries syntactic and semantic information which is benefit for word pair semantic relation prediction.

Table 4. Performance of different features on training data in terms of F1-score (%). ".+" means to add current features to the previous feature set. The numbers in the brackets are the performance increments compared with the previous results.

Features	F_{Syn}	F_{Ant}	F_{Hyp}	F_{Mer}	F_{macro}
Length	51.4	59.1	16.2	0.0	31.7
.+Character overlaps	52.9	57.9	20.2	6.4	34.3 (+2.6)
.+Positional overlaps	63.0	56.8	34.4	49.9	51.0 (+16.7)
.+Sequential overlaps	64.7	56.0	38.2	49.9	52.2 (+1.2)
.+Word embedding	76.0	83.8	75.3	90.2	81.3 (+29.1)
.+Character embedding	**80.0**	**86.6**	**82.5**	**92.5**	**85.4** (+4.1)

Secondly, we also explore the performance of different supervised learning algorithms. Table 5 lists the comparison of different learning algorithms with all above features. Clearly, Logistic Regression algorithm outperforms other algorithms.

Therefore, the system configuration for our final submission is all features and LR algorithm.

3.4   Results on Test Data

Table 6 shows the results of our system and the top-ranked systems provided by organizers for this semantic relation classification task. Compared with the top ranked systems, there is much room for improvement in our work, especially

Table 5. Performance of different learning algorithms on training data in terms of F1-score (%).

Algorithms	F_{Syn}	F_{Ant}	F_{Hyp}	F_{Mer}	F_{macro}
LR	**80.0**	**86.6**	**82.5**	**92.5**	**85.4**
SVM	80.0	85.4	80.0	92.3	84.4
SGD	70.5	85.7	72.7	88.9	79.5
XGBoost	61.1	68.6	52.9	75.7	64.6
AdaBoost	50.4	42.0	52.7	38.1	45.8
RandomForest	78.4	80.4	73.3	88.9	80.2

for the classification performance of synonym relationship. There are several possible reasons for this performance lag. First, the training set is too small to train a robust classification model with strong generalization. Building a large training data set with external resources is necessary. Second, we have not used extra semantic dictionary or coupus such as Tongyici Cilin [13] and Hownet [14] which may be effective for word pair semantic relation classification. Third, we only extract features from two words that need to be classified and have not used some extended resources like the sentences returned from search engines when retrieving the two words. Besides, compared with the results on training data, we see the performance on test data is much lower than that on training set. We observe and find that the Chinese words in the training data are formal, while some informal words exist in the test data, for example, "傻不拉几" and "SIM 卡", which may be the possible reason. Besides, the word pairs in test data are more diverse and are more difficult to identify. Moreover, although most of the word vectors can be trained from large corpora, almost 12% of the words in test data are missed in the word embedding dictionary, so word embedding features may not be as effective as in training data.

Table 6. Performance of our system and the top-ranked systems in terms of F1-score (%). The numbers in the brackets are the official rankings.

Team ID	F_{Syn}	F_{Ant}	F_{Hyp}	F_{Mer}	F_{macro}
Ours	51.9	65.1	68.6	73.3	64.7 (3)
CASIA	90.3	88.3	81.7	83.1	85.9 (1)
Tongji_CU-KG	73.2	78.1	78.8	77.1	76.8 (2)

4   Conclusion

In this paper, we extract several surface features, word embedding and character embedding features from word pairs and adopt supervised machine learning algorithms to perform context-free Chinese word semantic relation classification.

The system performance ranks above average. In future work, we consider to collect more external semantic dictionary and web resources to expand the training set as well as capture semantic information between two Chinese words.

Acknowledgements. This research is supported by grants from NSFC (61402175), Science and Technology Commission of Shanghai Municipality (14DZ2260800 and 15ZR1410700), Shanghai Collaborative Innovation Center of Trustworthy Software for Internet of Things (ZF1213) and Duty Collection Center (Shanghai) of the General Administration of Customs.

References

1. Wu, Y., Zhang, M.: Overview of the NLPCC 2017 shared task: Chinese word semantic relation classification. In: The 6th Conference on Natural Language Processing and Chinese Computing, Dalian, China, 8–12 November 2017
2. Hendrickx, I., Kim, S.N., Kozareva, Z., Nakov, P., Ó Séaghdha, D., Padó, S., Pennacchiotti, M., Romano, L., Szpakowicz, S.: Semeval-2010 task 8: multi-way classification of semantic relations between pairs of nominals. In: Proceedings of the Workshop on Semantic Evaluations: Recent Achievements and Future Directions, pp. 94–99. Association for Computational Linguistics (2009)
3. Hashimoto, K., Stenetorp, P., Miwa, M., Tsuruoka, Y.: Task-oriented learning of word embeddings for semantic relation classification. arXiv preprint arXiv:1503.00095 (2015)
4. dos Santos, C.N., Xiang, B., Zhou, B.: Classifying relations by ranking with convolutional neural networks. arXiv preprint arXiv:1504.06580 (2015)
5. Silva, V.S., Hürliman, M., Davis, B., Handschuh, S., Freitas, A.: Semantic relation classification: task formalisation and refinement. In: COLING 2016, p. 30 (2016)
6. Mikolov, T., Sutskever, I., Chen, K., Corrado, G.S., Dean, J.: Distributed representations of words and phrases and their compositionality. In: Burges, C.J.C., Bottou, L., Welling, M., Ghahramani, Z., Weinberger, K.Q. (eds.) Advances in Neural Information Processing Systems 26, pp. 3111–3119. Curran Associates Inc., Red Hook (2013)
7. Pennington, J., Socher, R., Manning, C.D.: Glove: Global vectors for word representation. In: EMNLP, vol. 14, pp. 1532–1543 (2014)
8. Tang, D., Wei, F., Yang, N., Zhou, M., Liu, T., Qin, B.: Learning sentiment-specific word embedding for twitter sentiment classification. In: ACL, vol. 1, pp. 1555–1565 (2014)
9. Guo, S., Guan, Y., Li, R., Zhang, Q.: Chinese word similarity computing based on combination strategy. In: Lin, C.-Y., Xue, N., Zhao, D., Huang, X., Feng, Y. (eds.) ICCPOL/NLPCC-2016. LNCS (LNAI), vol. 10102, pp. 744–752. Springer, Cham (2016). https://doi.org/10.1007/978-3-319-50496-4_67
10. Pei, J., Zhang, C., Huang, D., Ma, J.: Combining word embedding and semantic lexicon for chinese word similarity computation. In: Lin, C.-Y., Xue, N., Zhao, D., Huang, X., Feng, Y. (eds.) ICCPOL/NLPCC-2016. LNCS (LNAI), vol. 10102, pp. 766–777. Springer, Cham (2016). https://doi.org/10.1007/978-3-319-50496-4_69
11. Zhao, J., Zhu, T., Lan, M.: ECNU: one stone two birds: ensemble of heterogenous measures for semantic relatedness and textual entailment. In: SemEval@ COLING, pp. 271–277 (2014)

12. Qiu, X., Gong, J., Huang, X.: Overview of the NLPCC 2017 shared task: Chinese news headline categorization. arXiv:1706.02883v1 (2017)
13. Jiaju, M., Yiming, Z., Yunqi, G., Hong-Xiang, Y.: Tongyici Cilin. ShangHai Dictionary Publication (1983)
14. Dong, Z., Dong, Q., Hao, C.: Hownet and the Computation of Meaning. World Scientific, Singapore (2006)

Classification of Chinese Word Semantic Relations

Changliang Li[1(✉)] and Teng Ma[1,2]

[1] Institute of Automation, Chinese Academy of Sciences,
Beijing, People's Republic of China
changliang.li@ia.ac.cn, mteng@whu.edu.cn
[2] School of Mathematics and Statistics, Wuhan University, Wuhan 430072,
Hubei, China

Abstract. Classification of word semantic relation is a challenging task in natural language processing (NLP) field. In many practical applications, we need to distinguish words with different semantic relations. Much work relies on semantic resources such as Tongyici Cilin and HowNet, which are limited by the quality and size. Recently, methods based on word embedding have received increasing attention for their flexibility and effectiveness in many NLP tasks. Furthermore, word vector offset implies words semantic relation to some extent. This paper proposes a novel framework for identifying the Chinese word semantic relation. We combine semantic dictionary, word vector and linguistic knowledge into a classification system. We conduct experiments on the Chinese Word Semantic Relation Classification shared task of NLPCC 2017. We rank No.1 with the result of F1 value 0.859. The results demonstrate that our method is very scientific and effective.

Keywords: Word relation classification · Word vector · Semantic lexicons
Linguistic knowledge

1 Introduction

The classification of word semantic relation focuses on lexical level, which purpose is to predict the categorization of semantic relation between two Chinese words. Specifically, given a pair of Chinese words, it is required to recognize this pair of words into one of the following semantic relations: synonym, antonym, hyponym and meronym. In many applications, we need to distinguish words with different semantic meanings, such as information extraction and the construction of semantic networks [1, 2]. This task is a challenging work in natural language processing field.

Some attempts focus on dealing with this problem. One way is to rely on manual semantic resources, such as Tongyici Cilin [3] and HowNet [4]. The semantic relation of some words has been labelled in these resources. It is effective and simple to find the semantic relation by matching dictionaries. However, the drawback is also obvious that we can only recognize the pairs when both of members are presented in the lexicons.

The traditional classification methods utilize various features to train a classifier in a supervised manner. And these features can include lexical bag-of-words features and

© Springer International Publishing AG 2018
X. Huang et al. (Eds.): NLPCC 2017, LNAI 10619, pp. 465–473, 2018.
https://doi.org/10.1007/978-3-319-73618-1_39

other features based on syntactic parse trees. For grammar parsing trees, the path of dependencies between the constituency and the target entity has proven to be useful [5, 6].

In recent years, researchers pay attention to word embedding methods, such as skip-gram model [7–9] and Glove model [10]. This kind of methods has demonstrated outstanding performance in various tasks. Word embeddings are supposed to capture useful syntactic and semantic properties [11]. However, basic embedding methods have drawbacks in nature. One of the limitations is that word embeddings are usually learned by predicting a target word with its local context, leading to only limit information being captured. Therefore, researchers raise interest in integrating lexicons into word embeddings to capture multiple semantics [12–16].

The introduction of the word embeddings provides a new point for our task. Word embeddings are trained by predicting words between noun pairs using lexical relation-specific features on a large unlabeled corpus, which absorbed incorporate relation-specific information into the word embeddings [17]. [18] founded that the learned word representations capture meaningful syntactic and semantic regularities in a very simple way: vector offset.

In this paper, we propose a novel framework that combines word vectors, semantic lexicon and linguistic knowledge for Chinese word semantic relation classification. We firstly match a pair of words with semantic dictionary, and then our system will output the label of these words if matched successful. Otherwise, we will automatically recognize the semantic relationship of these words with supervised model. In this model, we extract three features and combine them as our model input. Besides, we also introduce linguistic knowledge to our model. We conduct experiment on Chinese Word Semantic Classification shared task [19], which provides a benchmark dataset for evaluating the study on word relation classification for Chinese language. And we rank No.1 with the result of 0.859 of F1 value and outperform other methods by a very large margin.

The remainder of this paper is arranged as follows. In Sect. 2, we introduce our method. Section 3 introduces our dataset and experiment settings. Section 4 presents the experiments. Some conclusions are summarized in Sect. 5.

2 Methodology

In this section, we introduce our classification system firstly and then explain each part of the system.

2.1 Classification System

The method consists of three aspects, semantic dictionaries, supervised model and linguistic knowledge. We match a pair of words with a semantic dictionary. If the match is successful, we will output the label of the words in the dictionary. Otherwise, we will utilize supervised model to classify the words semantic relation automatically. Figure 1 gives the overall illustration of our method.

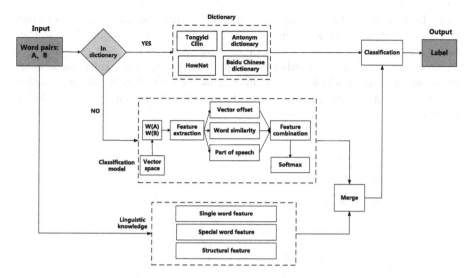

Fig. 1. The overall illustration of our method

2.2 Semantic Relation Classification Based on Dictionary

Tongyici Cilin [3]. This dictionary has a lot of applications. One of which is used to find synonyms of words. So we can use the dictionary to recognize the semantic relationship of a pair of words, and the relationship will be labelled synonyms if these words both involved in the dictionary.

The Cilin dictionary is organized by a 5-layer hierarchical structure. Correspondingly, it supplies 5-layer patterns to generate code for a group of words. And there are three ways to end the code items in the dictionary: "=", "#", "@". "=" stands for synonyms, "#" stands for related words, but not synonymous, "@" represents isolated words, neither synonyms nor related words. For instance, the pair of words (水平/level, 程度/degree) are coded as "Dd12A02=", words (男队/male team, 女队/female team) are coded as "Dd07B09#", and the word (高地/highland) is coded as "Dd09A05@". So we only need those words which code items ended by "=".

HowNet [4]. HowNet is a common knowledge base, which is based on the concepts represented by Chinese and English terms as a description object to reveal the relationship between concepts and concepts and attributes possessed by concepts. HowNet also reflects the semantic relations among words, including hyponyms, synonyms, antonyms and meronyms and so on. So we can use HowNet to find the semantic relationship of two words.

Antonym Dictionary. There are many antonym phrases on the Internet, so we can construct an antonym dictionary which contains high-frequency antonyms. We match a pair of words with the antonyms dictionary, and if the match is successful, then the semantic relationship will be labelled antonyms.

Other Dictionary. We also use the Internet to recognize the semantic relation of a pair of words. Synonyms and antonyms of a word are listed in the Baidu Chinese Dictionary. Through this resource, we can automatically match a pair of words. For example, there is a pair of words (高兴/happy, 难过/sad), if we enter the website: http://hanyu.baidu.com/s?wd=高兴&from=zici, then we will find that the relationship of two words is antonyms. Figure 2 shows the example, and both words are labelled in red blocks.

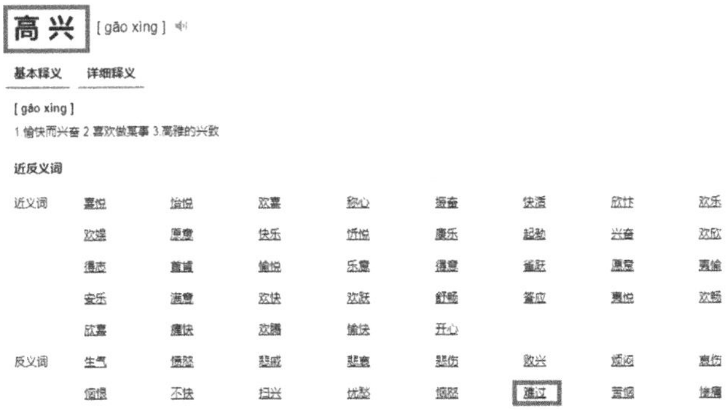

Fig. 2. The example of Baidu Chinese dictionary (Color figure online)

2.3   Semantic Relation Classification Based on Various Features

In this section, we explain the classification model based on various features: vector offset, word similarity and part of speech. This method mainly uses the word embedding to extract the features, and recognize the semantic relation of two words. We will extract features from different angles.

Vector Offset. Vector offset technique is employed in this step, which is a simple algebraic operation performed on the word vectors. For example, vector (King) – vector (Man) + vector (Woman) produces a vector that is closest to the vector representation of the word Queen [18]. As a result, the male/female relationship is learned automatically.

We approximate the above example as a mathematical expression: vector (King) – vector (Queen) ≈ vector (Man) – vector (Woman). We can get some information from this formula. We know that King and Queen are very similar words. This pair of words has many same attributes, such as noble identity, style of the palace, luxury and so on. A significant difference between these two words is that the gender is different, King is male, and Queen is female. Similarly, the main difference between Man and Woman is the gender either. From this point of view, the above formula can depict different semantic parts of two words.

In this way, the model can capture the semantic regularities between a pair of words easily. So we get the first feature of the model.

Given a pair of words (v_{s_1}, v_{s_2}), the feature defines v_{info} as follows:

$$v_{info} = v_{s\_1} - v_{s\_2} \qquad (1)$$

where v_{s_1} and v_{s_2} are vector representations of word w_{s_1} and w_{s_2}.

Cosine Similarity. We extract new feature to characterize semantic similarity between two words. In the field of machine learning, especially in the field of NLP, cosine similarity is often used to calculate the text similarity. So here we depict the semantic similarity by calculating the cosine value of two words vectors. Given a word pair v_{s_1}, v_{s_2}, we use c^* to represent cosine similarity.

Part of Speech. In Chinese words, the words' part of speech can give us a lot of information. If two words are both nouns, their semantic relationship is probably not antonymous, because antonyms are often adjectives or verbs. Under this assumption, we extract part of speech as a feature, and for simplicity, we divide the feature into four parts: nouns, verbs, adjectives, and others, and then encode them. Given a word w_{s_1}, the feature defines p_{s_1} as follows:

$$p_{s\_1} = \begin{cases} 1, & if\ w_{s\_1}\ is\ adjective. \\ 2, & if\ w_{s\_1}\ is\ verb. \\ 3, & if\ w_{s\_1}\ is\ noun. \\ 4, & otherwise. \end{cases} \qquad (2)$$

Classification Model. Now we have obtained three features of depicting semantic relations: v_{info}, c^*, p_{s_i}. p_{s_i} stands for the part of speech of the word w_{s_i}. We combine these features and feed it as our model input.

Given a word pair v_{s_1}, v_{s_2}, we combine these features into a vector defines X:

$$X = (v_{info}, c^*, p_{s\_1}, p_{s\_2}) \qquad (3)$$

Softmax classifier is a supervised model for multi-classification problems, which is very simple but effective. Here, we use the softmax classifier to recognize our data.

2.4 Semantic Relation Classification Based on Linguistic Knowledge

Chinese words have many linguistic features. We can apply these characteristics to our task so as to improve the accuracy of our model. In the previous section, we use the softmax classification model to recognize the semantic relation of words. In this section, we will introduce the characteristics of Chinese word to update the output of the model.

Structural Feature. In Chinese vocabulary, some words have special word structure, and we can use the structure to update the results of our model. For instance, the semantic relation of "树" (tree) and "树枝" (branch), "花" (flower) and "花蕾" (bud), "龟" (turtle) and "龟壳" (turtle shell) are all meronyms. More importantly, these words have the same structure. Their structure is "A and AB". That phenomenon is very common to Chinese vocabulary, so we can use this structural feature into our system. Here is one more example, the semantic relation of "花" (flower) and "玫瑰花" (rose), "蛇" (snake) and "海蛇" (sea snake), "水" (water) and "海水" (sea water) are all hyponyms. And their word structure is "A (蛇) and BA (海蛇)" or "A (花) and BCA (玫瑰花)", anyway, "A" is in the end. In addition, there are many other structural features can be for our reference, and we can make use of the structural features to improve the accuracy of our system.

Special Word Feature. In Chinese vocabulary, some words have no practical meaning, but they are part of a word, such as "子" in the word "椅子". This type of word structure can also help our task. For example, the semantic relationship of "桌子" and "桌腿" is meronyms, and if we remove the "子" from the "桌子", then we will find we can use the word structural feature to update the results of our model.

Single Word Feature. There are many words in the Chinese vocabulary with single word, such as "大" (big) and "小" (small), "胖" (fat) and "瘦" (thin). And normally, these words are antonyms. This is not an accidental phenomenon. In Chinese vocabulary, few synonyms, hyponyms, or meronyms are composed of single word, they are often composed of two words or more words, such as "开心" (happy) and "高兴" (happy), "车票" (ticket) and "火车票" (train ticket), "钢笔" (pen) and "笔帽" (pen cap). So if both words are composed a single word, then we can make sure that the semantic relationship of the pair of words is antonyms.

3   Experiment Settings

3.1   Data Set and Evaluation

The proposed approach is evaluated on the dataset released by NLPCC2017 shared task 1 [19]. The dataset contains 200 sample data and 2000 test word pairs with their semantic category. Our training set contains 913-word pairs, which come from web search and manual annotation, which consist of synonyms, antonyms, hyponyms and meronyms. We trained supervised model with training dataset and used the 200 sample data as validation set.

The performance of our experiments is evaluated by the macro-averaged precision (P), recall (R) and F1-score. So we compute P, R, and F1-score for each relation, and then compute the macro-averaged P, R and F1-score.

4   Results and Analysis

In this section, we show the results of our experiments and analyze the results.

Table 1 shows the results of our entire classification system, including the synonym class, the antonym class, the hyponym class, the meronym class and the macro-averaged score. In Table 1, P represents the precision, R stands for the recall. Our scoring metric is macro-averaged F1-score for four-way classification.

Table 1. Result of our classification system

Category	P	R	F1
Synonym	0.859	0.952	0.903
Antonym	0.945	0.828	0.883
Hyponym	0.770	0.870	0.817
Meronym	0.885	0.784	0.831
Macro-average	**0.865**	**0.859**	**0.859**

As is shown in Table 1, four categories of F1 value have exceeded 0.8, and F1 value of synonym reached 0.903. Specifically, the score of synonym and antonym is significantly better than hyponym and meronym, and their F1-score are both higher than 0.85, indicating that our method is very effective for synonym and antonym. As for the hyponym and meronym, the hyponym P value and the meronym R value are slightly lower. It is due to that in Chinese vocabulary, the semantic relationship of some words is difficult to recognize in these two categories. For example, the semantic relationship of "四大名著" (Four famous novels) and "红楼梦" (Story Stone) is not only hyponyms but also meronyms. In addition, our training data set is relatively small, which will restrict the result of our classification system.

Table 2 shows the comparison of the supervised model and the merging method. In Table 2, SMX means softmax method; DC means dictionary method; LK means linguistic knowledge method. We can see that the result of ID.1 reaches 0.527, which is acceptable given the small training dataset. Besides, the result ID.3 achieves 0.859 of F1 value, which performs 0.332 (63%) higher than ID.1. It illustrates the effectiveness of the merging approach.

Table 2. Results of classification by various models or methods

ID.	Method	P	R	F1
1	SMX	0.576	0.526	0.527
2	SMX + DC	0.761	0.736	0.729
3	SMX + DC + LK	**0.865**	**0.859**	**0.859**

Table 3 shows the results of the classification system by selecting different features. It can be seen that F1 value of ID.1 reaches 0.790, and the result of all features is 0.859, indicating that the feature v_{info} is critical to the whole classification system. Besides, the F1 value of ID.2 performs 0.036 (4.6%) higher than ID.1 duo to the use of feature c^*. The result of ID.3 reaches 0.859 by introducing feature p_{s_i}, and ID.3 is submitted as our final result.

Table 3. Comparison between single and merging features

ID.	Strategy	P	R	F1
1	v_{info}	0.825	0.789	0.790
2	$v_{info} + c^*$	0.843	0.827	0.826
3	$v_{info} + c^* + p_{s\_1} + p_{s\_1}$	**0.865**	**0.859**	**0.859**

5 Conclusion

In this work, we introduce a novel framework for the Chinese word semantic relation classification. This framework utilizes the semantic dictionary, linguistic knowledge and word embedding. The results on NLPCC-2017 shared task 1 have demonstrated the efficiency of our approach. We rank No.1 with the result of F1 score 0.859. Our method can be a new clue to other NLP tasks. A promising future work for us is to extend our model to larger training dataset. And another interesting research point is to find a reasonable combination way of features, which maybe bring more excellent performance.

References

1. Girju, R., Nakov, P., Nastase, V., et al.: Classification of semantic relations between nominals. Lang. Resour. Eval. **43**(2), 105–121 (2009)
2. Hendrickx, I., Su, N.K., Kozareva, Z., et al.: SemEval-2010 task 8: multi-way classification of semantic relations between pairs of nominal. In: The Workshop on Semantic Evaluations: Recent Achievements and Future Directions, pp. 94–99. Association for Computational Linguistics (2009)
3. Mei, J.J., Zhu, Y.M., et al.: Tongyici Cilin. Shanghai Lexicon Publishing Company, Shanghai (1983)
4. Dong, Z., Dong, Q.: HowNet and the Computation of Meaning, pp. 85–95. World Scientific, Singapore (2006)
5. Bunescu, R.C., Mooney, R.J.: A shortest path dependency kernel for relation extraction. In: Conference on Human Language Technology and Empirical Methods in Natural Language Processing. Association for Computational Linguistics, pp. 724–731 (2005)
6. Zhang, M., Zhang, J., Su, J., et al.: A composite kernel to extract relations between entities with both flat and structured features. In: International Conference on Computational Linguistics and, Meeting of the Association for Computational Linguistics, Proceedings of the Conference, Sydney, Australia, 17–21 July. DBLP (2006)
7. Mikolov, T., Chen, K., Corrado, G., Dean, J.: Efficient estimation of word representations in vector space. In: Proceedings of Workshop at ICLR (2013a)
8. Mikolov, T., Sutskever, I., et al.: Distributed representations of words and phrases and their compositionality. In: Proceedings of NIPS, pp. 3111–3119 (2013b)
9. Levy, O., Goldberg, Y.: Neural word embedding as implicit matrix factorization. In: Advances in neural information processing systems, pp. 2177–2185 (2014)
10. Pennington, J., Socher, R., Manning, C.D.: Glove: Global vectors for word representation. In: Proceedings of EMNLP, vol. 14, pp. 1532–1543 (2014)
11. Turian, J., Ratinov, L., Bengio, Y.: Word representations: a simple and general method for semi-supervised learning. In: ACL 2010 Proceedings of the 48th Annual Meeting of the Association for Computational Linguistics, pp. 384–394 (2010)
12. Mrkšić, N., Séaghdha, D.O., et al.: Counter-fitting word vectors to linguistic constraints. arXiv preprint arXiv:1603.00892 (2016)
13. Nguyen, K.A., Walde, S.S.I., Vu, N.T.: Integrating distributional lexical contrast into world embeddings for antonym-synonym distinction. arXiv preprint arXiv:1605.07766 (2016)
14. Chen, Z., Lin, W., et al.: Revisiting word embedding for contrasting meaning. In: Proceeding of ACL, pp. 106–115 (2015)

15. Rothe, S., Schütze, H.: AutoExtend: extending word embeddings to embeddings for synsets and lexemes. In: Proceedings of the ACL-IJNLP, pp. 1793–1803 (2015)
16. Faruqui, M., Dodge, J., et al.: Retrofitting word vectors to semantic lexicons. In: Proceedings of NAACL (2015)
17. Hashimoto, K., Stenetorp, P., Miwa, M., et al.: Task-oriented learning of word embeddings for semantic relation classification. Comput. Sci. (2015)
18. Mikolov, T., Yih, W.T., Zweig, G.: Linguistic regularities in continuous space word representations. In: NAACL HLT (2013)
19. Wu, Y., Zhang, M.: Overview of the NLPCC 2017 shared task: Chinese word semantic relation classification. In: The 6th Conference on Natural Language Processing and Chinese Computing, Dalian, China (2017)

Social Network

Identification of Influential Users Based on Topic-Behavior Influence Tree in Social Networks

Jianjun Wu[1,2], Ying Sha[1,2(✉)], Rui Li[1,2], Qi Liang[1,2], Bo Jiang[1,2], Jianlong Tan[1,2], and Bin Wang[1,2]

[1] Institute of Information Engineering, Chinese Academy of Sciences,
Beijing 100093, China
{wujianjun,shaying,lirui,liangqi,jiangbo,tanjianlong,wangbin}@iie.ac.cn
[2] School of Cyber Security, University of Chinese Academy of Sciences,
Beijing 100029, China

Abstract. Identifying influential users in social networks is of significant interest, as it can help improve the propagation of ideas or innovations. Various factors can affect the relationships and the formulation of influence between users. Although many studies have researched this domain, the effect of the correlation between messages and behaviors in measuring users' influence in social networks has not been adequately focused on. As a result, influential users can not be accurately evaluated. Thus, we propose a topic-behavior influence tree algorithm that identifies influential users using six types of relationships in the following factors: message content, hashtag titles, retweets, replies, and mentions. By maximizing the number of affected users and minimizing the propagation path, we can improve the accuracy of identifying influential users. The experimental results compared with state-of-the-art algorithms on various datasets and visualization on TUAW dataset validate the effectiveness of the proposed algorithm.

Keywords: Influence tree · Influential users · Topic-behavior network

1 Introduction

Social networks are important real-time information media that have hooked users who want to express their opinions, follow hot topics, and stage protests. Influence is usually defined as "the ability to change the mind and behaviors of others [9]". But there is no comprehensive definition for user influence currently. Social influence is described as the ability of users to influence the emotions, opinions, or behaviors of other users. Merton [12] divides opinion leaders into two classes: single opinion leaders, who only have significant influence in a particular area; and polymorphic opinion leaders, who have significant influence in several areas.

© Springer International Publishing AG 2018
X. Huang et al. (Eds.): NLPCC 2017, LNAI 10619, pp. 477–489, 2018.
https://doi.org/10.1007/978-3-319-73618-1_40

The influential users discussed in this paper comprise both single and polymorphic opinion leaders. They are defined as users of higher rank who possess either single-topic or multi-topic influence, measured by specific algorithms, and who trigger social behaviors of other users via their messages.

Identifying influential users needs to measure users' influence firstly. Three important factors should be considered when measuring users' influence: network structure, message content, and users' behaviors. State-of-the-art techniques used to identify influential users in social networks do not comprehensively cover all potentially affected users and propagation paths of minimum time. To address this problem, we propose an algorithm that identifies influential users based on the correlation between topics and behaviors from two aspects: "messages→topics" and "topics→social behaviors". This method provides a unified overview of the network structure, message content, and users' behaviors. More specifically, topic-behavior heterogeneous networks are constructed across three types of relationships between users and user influence trees are constructed by using the minimum total propagation time in the networks. Next, we measure each user's influence by leveraging topic-behavior influence tree model.

The main contributions of this paper are as follows: (1) An influential user identification algorithm that covers the maximum number of affected users as well as the minimum propagation path time is designed based on the topic-behavior influence trees. (2) The influence of a topic is determined by topic-explicit influence relationships between the users which is based on a combination of rules of links and behaviors with topic decay factor. (3) Both the design of topic-behavior heterogeneous networks and the generation of users influence trees based on the optimization of minimum propagation time path are demonstrated.

The remainder of this paper is organized as follows. Section 2 reviews related work. Section 3 outlines the influential user determination problem. Section 4 explains the construction of the topic-behavior network and learning parameters of users relationships in the network. Section 5 proposes an influence tree model based on the topic-behavior network. Section 6 presents and discusses the experimental results. Finally the paper concludes in Sect. 7.

2   Related Work

Existing research on influential users in social networks can be divided into four categories primarily based on the area of focus: network structure, message content, both network structure and message content, and behavior.

The methods based on network structure typically assume that there is a positive proportional relationship between the distance between users and size of influence. Examples of typical algorithms are PageRank, HITS, Degree Centrality, Closeness Centrality, Betweenness Centrality, IARank, KHYRank, etc. In addition, because of the existence of zombie fans, lack of interest, and other factors, users have varying amounts of influence in different communities, and on different topics.

The methods based on the message content are typically developed by considering both message propagation behavior [4] and the message content itself.

They overcome the disadvantage of the influence calculation method, which relies on the topics.

The methods based on both message content and network structure include LDA and associated topic models, such as Twitter Rank and TunkRank. While TunkRank [3] algorithm is based on each user's influence on their fans, Twitter Rank considers only the network link between fans and friends. Katsimpars et al. [8] proposed a supervised random walk algorithm in this category, which employs a user's historical information to calculate his/her influence using the supervised random walk method, which is sensitive to variations in topic.

With regard to the behavioral aspects, Goyal et al. [5] proposed a method in which user influence is calculated by using the ratio of the number of acts producing an effect to the number of acts performed by all users. Iwata [7] utilized the idea that user-event triggered behavior is influenced by previous events. They designed a function that modeled the influence of different entries adopted by users. Methods such as Independent Cascade (IC) and Susceptible-infected (SI) are simplifications of reality that have an inherent weakness as they neglected the actual propagation path of messages.

To overcome these shortcomings, we use an influence tree approach that considers the network structure, message, and behavior. The proposed algorithm analyzes and measures user influence at the topic-behavior level to determine influential users effectively.

3 Problem Formulation

One of the important tasks underpinning this study is the identification of influential users (i.e., computation and measurement of user influence).

The value of the influence, such as u, is expressed using an influence tree with u as the root. In contrast to other algorithms, the value of the influence comprehensively considers two parameters simultaneously-all the users, potentially those users affected by u, and the minimum propagation time to each target user. The impact of homophily between users is eliminated from this computation.

The function probability of the influence of user u is defined as

$$I_u = f_Q(u, S, \Theta) \quad u \subseteq S \tag{1}$$

where $f(\cdot)$ is the influence calculation function of user u, S is the set of target users affected by u, and Θ represents relationship parameters between u and elements in S, $\Theta = (P_{u \to v}, t_{u \to v})_{v \in S}$. $P_{u \to v}$ represents the probability of the source user's impact on the target user, $t_{u \to v}$ describes the message propagation time. I_u represents the value of the influence of user u in the social network. The influence calculation function has both monotonous and sub-model attributes.

4 Topic-Behavior Network Reconstruction

This section explains the construction of the topic-behavior network. Section 4.1 describes the representation of relationships between users. Section 4.2 elaborates on topic relationships and parameter learning. Section 4.3 denotes the behavioral relationship and parameter learning, and Sect. 4.4 discusses the reconstruction of the topic-behavior relationship network and formulation of parameters.

4.1 Relationships Between Users

In this paper, the relationship between users in social networks is expressed by $G = (V, E)$. The nodes $V = (v_i)_{i=1}^n$ represents the set of users. E denotes the set of directed edges, $e_{ij}^{\Psi} \in E$ specifies the directed link between node v_i and node v_j for relationship type Ψ. The relationship type $\Psi \in \{d, h, r, p, m, f\}$ are classified into three groups: topic-based (d, h), behaviors of topic-based (r, p, m), and follower/followee relationships f. A topic relationship comprises both relationship d, formed from the similarity of the messages, and relationship h, formed from the hashtag title similarity. A behavioral relationship comprises retweet r, reply p, and mention m. In the later sections, the topic-based relationships are briefly described as topic relationships, and relationships of behaviors of topic-based are described as behavioral relationships.

The edges of topic-behavior network that are generated by merging the topic relationships with the behavioral relationships. Then, the user influence tree is generated from this network, and user influence is calculated to identify influential users; the associated framework is shown in Fig. 1.

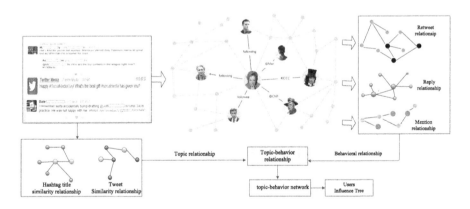

Fig. 1. Architecture used to identify influential users

4.2 Topic Relationship

Topic Relationship. The topic relationship between two users consists of the relationship d, as well as the relationship h. Its parameter describes the size of the influence of a user with respect to both the topic and propagation time. Before the merger, there should exist at least of one of d and h between users.

Relationship d **and** h. The messages of the node are first parsed to form a set with the node as the element. These sets consist of two types: messages sets and hashtag title sets. Then, the word2vec model is employed to train the word vector. In the node messages set, The distance $dist\,(i,j)^1$ is used to calculate the topic similarity between node v_i and node v_j, which leads to the generation of node set S_z^d with relationship d. Similarly, in the hashtag title set, node set S_z^h is generated for relationship h, and the union of these sets is given by S_z^T, $S_z^T = S_z^d \cup S_z^h$.

Parameter Learning for Topic Relationship

Definition 1. The parameters of the topic relationship are expressed in terms of a pair array. The former represents the influence probability $P\left(S_{u \to v,z}\right)$ of user u on user v for topic z. Denoting that the psychological impact of v received from u for z is generated with the influence probability of d and h [14]. The latter is the minimum time interval among all messages pairs $\{m_i, m_j\}$ from user u to user v. m_i is posted by user u for topic z, and m_j is the subsequent message by user v that has the highest similarity to m_i. The probability can be expressed using the following formula.

$$P\left(S_{u \to v,z}\right) = kx_{u \to v,z}^b \tag{2}$$

where b denotes the number of constituent elements in the topic relationship, k is a constant, and $x_{u \to v,z}$ denotes the psychological influence of v when messages from u for topic z are accepted, $v \in S_z^T$, which is expressed as follows:

$$x_{u \to v,z} = \frac{P\left(d\right) + P\left(h\right)}{\sqrt{\left(P\left(d\right)\right)^2 + \left(P\left(h\right)\right)^2}} \tag{3}$$

Parameter Learning of Relationship d **and** h. This paper focuses on both the direct influence and the effect of multiple repetitions of the topic. The homophily-driven influence is excluded by using the rules method. The scope of the influence of the node v_i for topic z, $v_i \in S_z^T$, is limited within S_z^T. The nodes that do not discuss the topic z outside S_z^T do not need to be considered, thereby reducing the number of the nodes to be analyzed.

Definition 2. If the time of message m_i of v_i is prior to the time of the message m_j of v_j, and both v_i and v_j satisfy a relationship from the relationship rules stated in the appendix (not shown here), then we say that message m_i has a direct influence on message m_j with probability P_{ij}. P_{ij} represents the probability of influence of the message, $P_{ij} = \frac{1}{k}$, where k is the total number of a topic for the remaining nodes satisfying any of the previously mentioned relationships rules after the time of m_i.

---

[1] $dist\,(i,j)$ is the Cosine Similarity between vector i and vector j.

Definition 3. If a message m_i of v_i influences message m_j of v_j with probability P_{ij}, then all the messages of v_i that influence v_j will eventually result in a cumulative influence of v_i on v_j (a multiple-times influence), which represents the topic influence of v_i on v_j. Its probability is expressed as $P_{i,j}$, $P_{i,j} = e^{-\eta w_{i,j}}$, where $w_{i,j} = \prod P_{ij}$ and η is the topic decay factor. The value of η is the reciprocal of the similarity of the topic. Moreover, $\eta \in [1, \infty]$; the greater the similarity, the smaller is the value of η, and the slower is the topic decay.

Definition 4. The propagation of the topic from v_i to v_j is the smallest of the time intervals between the message tuple $\{m_i, m_j\}$, where m_j is the message of v_j that has the largest similarity to m_i of v_i, m_i is posted before m_j.

4.3   Behavioral Relationship

Behavioral Relationship. The behavioral relationship edges between users is formed from retweet r, reply p, and mention m, As stated above, the behavioral relationship parameters also describe the size of the influence and propagation time between the users for one topic.

Definition 5. The behavioral relationship between users is defined by merging the relationship between retweet r, reply p, and mention m, At least one behavior should exist between the users prior to the merger. Otherwise, no behavioral relationship will exist between them.

Relationship Retweet r, Replies p, and Mentions m. In contrast to [1], the three behavioral relationships discussed in this paper are subdivided by topic. The degree of the influence of the behavioral relationships can be expressed by Θ, such as node v_i for topic z, it is only necessary to define the degree of influence between nodes (i.e., the magnitude of the influence of node v_i for topic z on the remaining nodes in S_z^A, $v_i \in S_z^A$).

Parameters Learning for Behavioral Relationship

Definition 6. For the parameters Θ of the behavioral relationship, the former represents the probability of the behavioral influence of user u on the user v for topic z, where it is expressed as $P(A_{u \to v, z})$, the latter represents the time interval of the pair $\{m_i, m_j\}$. For the retweet and reply behavior, m_i is a message of user u being retweeted or replied to by v, m_j is the message after being retweeted or replied to by v. For the mention behavior, m_i is a message of user u that mentions v. m_j is the message or reply sent by v. It is the message of user v with the highest similarity. Considering $P(A_{u \to v, z})$, it can be represented as follows:

$$P(A_{u \to v, z}) = k x_{u \to v, z}^b \tag{4}$$

where b, k, and $x_{u \to v, z}$ are as described above, The $x_{u \to v, z}$ is given as follows:

$$x_{u \to v, z} = \frac{P(r) + P(p) + P(m)}{\sqrt{(P(r))^2 + (P(p))^2 + (P(m))^2}} \tag{5}$$

Parameters Learning of Retweets r**, Replies** p **and Mentions** m

Definition 7. The influence probability of any message m_i of u that trigger a behavior of user v is expressed as q_i, which is given by $q_i = \frac{x_{m_i}}{\sum_{i=1}^{n} x_{m_i}}$, where n is the number of messages of u associate with a certain topic that can trigger the behaviors of other users, and x_{m_i} is the total number of behavioral users caused by m_i.

Definition 8. The probability that v_i will extend a behavioral influence on v_j is given by $\left(\frac{1}{e}\right)^{w_{i,j}}$, where $w_{i,j} = \prod q_k$, and k denotes the number of messages in v_i that triggered a behavior from v_j.

4.4 Topic-Behavior Network Reconstruction

Topic-Behavior Edge Relationship

Definition 9. Topic-behavior relationship edges are constructed by merging the topic and behavioral relationships. Before the merger occurs, at least one topic or behavioral relationship should exist between the users; otherwise, no topic-behavior relationship edge will exist between the users.

Parameter Learning. The topic-behavior relationship edge parameter is represented by a binary array. The former denotes the influence probability $P\left(I_{u \to v, z}\right)$ of user u on user v. The latter represents the shorter time interval of the two relationships between u and v. $P\left(I_{u \to v, z}\right)$ is expressed as follows:

$$P\left(I_{u \to v, z}\right) = k x_{u \to v, z}^{b} \tag{6}$$

where b is the number of constructing the topic-behavior relationship between users, k is a constant, and $I_{u \to v, z}$ represents the psychological influence of v received from u for topic z, $v \in V$, which is expressed as follows:

$$x_{u \to v, z} = \frac{P\left(S_{u \to v, z}\right) + P\left(A_{u \to v, z}\right)}{\sqrt{\left(P\left(S_{u \to v, z}\right)\right)^2 + \left(P\left(A_{u \to v, z}\right)\right)^2}} \tag{7}$$

Reconstruction Procedure. In this paper, we use the direct connection method to construct the network structure. The topic-behavior network is constructed using the users of the topic-behavior relationship edges as the nodes, and edges as the network paths. The network structure generated is a Bayesian network structure, designed such that the amount of stimulus received by each node is related to all of its parent nodes. Multiple source paths exist, but there is only one source path from the parent node.

5 Influence Tree Model

In this section, we present the generation algorithm for the topic-behavior influence tree (TBIT), which covers all users that are potentially affected by each user and the path with the minimum propagation time. The algorithm is divided into two parts: (1) influence tree generation based on the topic-behavior relationship network, and (2) influential user identification.

5.1 Influence Tree Generation

Consider u as an instance in Fig. 2. The topic influence tree of u is formed by using u as a starting point for the root in the topic-behavior network by employing the highest probability adjacent edges (P_{ud}, P_{uw}) of u as the starting edges. Then, breadth-first search is used to determine the path of u to each affected node. In this manner, the influence tree of u is constructed.

The foundation of the influence tree formation for user u involves selecting the minimum propagation time path of u to each affected user. we used a heuristic search method to accomplish this. As shown in Fig. 2, the user set influenced by u is $\{d, w\}$, and the possible propagation paths of the influence of u to w are $u \rightarrow w$, $u \rightarrow d \rightarrow w$. The process of selecting the most likely propagation path is as follows.

if $\Delta t_{ud} > \Delta t_{uw}$, $d \nrightarrow w$
else if $\Delta t_{ud} + \Delta t_{dw} < \Delta t_{uw}$, $u \rightarrow d \rightarrow w$
else if $\Delta t_{ud} < \Delta t_{uw}$ and $\Delta t_{ud} + \Delta t_{dw} < \Delta t_{uw}$, $u \rightarrow w$
else
$\qquad u \rightarrow w$

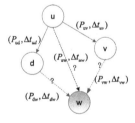

Fig. 2. Illustration of influence path from u to w

5.2 Identifying Influential Users

The influence of a user in social network is expressed by the user influence tree. As described above, this tree is generated using a heuristic search method in the topic-behavior network, where the influence probability is expressed as follows:

$$P(Q_{uz}) = P(Q_{uz}|z) P(z|u) \tag{8}$$

where $P(z|u)$ represents the probability that user u is interested in topic z. This probability is calculated based on the ratio of the number of messages of user u for topic z to the total number of messages of user u. $P(Q_{uz})$ represents the probability that other users are influenced by user u for topic z, which is equal to the cumulative sum of the product of the influence received by all of the nodes in the tree Q_{uz} with u representing both the root and the influence weight. $P(Q_{uz}|z)$ is expressed as

$$P(Q_{uz}|z) = \sum_{(u,v)\in E} \left(w(u,v) \sum_{i=1}^{k} P(S_{x_i \to v,z}) \right)_{x_i,v\in V} \tag{9}$$

where $P(S_{x_i \to v,z})_{x_i,v\in V}$ represents the probability of the influence of parent node x_i that is accepted by v in Q_{uz}. k represents the number of parent nodes of v, and $\sum_{i=1}^{k} P(S_{x_i \to v,z})_{x_i,v\in V}$ represents the total amount of influence from all of the parent nodes accepted by v. $w(u,v)$ is the influence weight, which is expressed as follows:

$$w(u,v) = \frac{P(S_{u \to v,z})_{v\in V}}{\sum_{i=1}^{k} P(S_{x_i \to v,z})_{x_i,v\in V}} \tag{10}$$

According to both Stevens theorem [14] and the PageRank algorithm, $w(u,v)$ represents the influence of u on v, which is closely related to the number of parent nodes (receiving size) of v in the topic-behavior network. When the number of parent nodes of v is larger (a larger receiving size), the influence of u on v is relatively small and vice versa. The influence tree probability Q_u of the user u for all topics can be expressed as

$$P(Q_u) = \sum_{z=1}^{n} P(Q_{uz}|z) P(z|u)$$

$$= \sum_{z=1}^{n} \left\{ \left(\left(w(u,v) \sum_{i=1}^{k} P(S_{x_i \to v,z}) \right)_{x_i,v\in V} \right) P(z|u) \right\} \tag{11}$$

In this study, the problem of determining the maximum influence tree of a user is transformed into an optimization problem for the maximum influence subtree with u as the root. Given the set of all users potentially influenced by a user, the search for the minimum time tree is expressed as

$$\underset{\forall u\in V, S\subseteq V-\{u\}}{\arg\min} \quad C(Q_u) \quad s\cdot t\cdot \quad f_Q(u,S) \tag{12}$$

where $C(Q_u)$ represents the total propagation time of influence tree Q_u of u.

6   Experimental Results

6.1   Experimental Setup

Data Preparation. The experimental data used to evaluate and validate the proposed TBIT algorithm proposed in this paper is derived from two actual datasets: The Unofficial Apple Weblog(TUAW)[10] dataset and the Twitter dataset.

TUAW dataset is a blog dataset that contains 17,831 posts and 6,655 users, with data spanning from 2004 to 2008; the Twitter dataset was obtained using a network spider designed by us in 2016. Data in the latter set were collected from May 28 to June 7, and consisted of 1,075,447 tweet, 376,000 follower/followee relationships. From this, 5,714 users and 279,371 tweets were filtered out before the experiment was performed.

Comparison Methods and Evaluation Metrics. The TBIT algorithm was compared with other social network user influence ranking algorithms, such as MIIB [10], TwitterRank (TR) [15], PageRank (PgR) [11], ProfileRank (ProR) [13] and several single feature-based algorithms.

The effectiveness and stability of the TBIT algorithm was evaluated using the Top 10%, Top 20%, and Top 40% user sequences through correlation experiments. We compared our method with a baseline algorithm by using performance evaluation measures such as the Kendall coefficients, length of influence tree, stability of users' influence, and the OSim [6] in social network.

6.2   Performance Analysis

It can be seen from Fig. 3 that, based on the TUAW dataset, the higher the participation of the bloggers, the more active the blogger is and the stronger the influence that the multi-topic discussing user has on others users. However, the topic also becomes more likely to drift, causing the users' influence formed from a single topic to deviate. The title and content of blogger posts are strongly correlated. Similarly, Fig. 4 shows that the content and title of users' posts demonstrate almost the same trend. Specifically, the title represents a topic indicator that is strongly associated with the content itself, which indicates that the influence of some users is not particularly correlated to the lengths of their messages in social networks.

For the TUAW dataset, the TBIT algorithm was experimentally compared with various single feature-based algorithm, including MIIB, MIBI, and MIBIX algorithms for the Top 10% user sequence [10]. The results demonstrate similar correlations with the Kendall coefficients. In particular, there is a large overlap for the Top 10 users, such as Scott McNulty (Top1), and Dave Caolo (Top2), where the value of OSim is 0.7 between TBIT and MIIB (not shown here), which denotes higher generalization ability and stability than other algorithms.

As observed from Table 1(a), TBIT demonstrates stronger correlation with the other algorithms with respect to both the Top 20% and Top 40% [2]. In addition, its correlation with ProR with respect to the Top 20% is 1.0, which

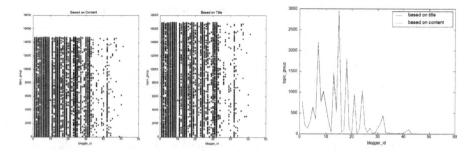

Fig. 3. Topics for users' influence tweet   **Fig. 4.** Trend similarity between topics

Table 1. Correlation with different algorithms by Kendall

(a) Comparing by Twitter Dataset

	Top10	Top20	Top40
TBIT vs. TR	0.422	0.804	0.629
TBIT vs. ProR	0	1	0.951
TBIT vs. PgR	0	0.894	0.488
TR vs. ProR	0.644	0.427	0.461
TR vs. PgR	0.6	0.734	0.572
ProR vs. PgR	0	0.778	0.446

(b) Comparing by TUAW Dataset

	Top10
TBIT vs. MIIB	0.244
TBIT vs. MIBIX	0.200
TBIT vs. MIBI	0.244
MIIB vs. MIIBX	-0.067
M_comments vs. Topic_multiply	0.511
M_comments vs. M_link	-0.422

is an isolated case. OSim provides a correlation value of 0.25 between TBIT and PgR, and a value of 0.175 between TR and PgR (not shown here). This is because TBIT considers the long-distance influence between users, whereas TR does not consider indirect interaction. Overall, based on the Twitter dataset, the stability of the correlation between TBIT and TR is stronger than that between TBIT and ProR. This is probably because neither of them consider the user's behaviors, and TR considers the follower/followee behavior. Table 2 shows that among the most influential users on each topic, identified by the TR algorithm based on the ten topics generated by the LDA model, three of the top ten percent users are generated by TBIT algorithm, and two among the ten percent users are generated by the TR algorithm. SCMex is the most influential user for Topic 2 and is well represented among the top 10% ranked by the two algorithms. The calculated stability of TBIT is better than that of the others with respect to multiple-topic users.

Other experimental results (not shown here) illustrate the lengths of the retweets influence tree of the top four users ranked by different algorithms. The messages of the influential users extracted by TBIT exhibit strong user retweeted capabilities, and the number of affected users for each of the top four users is, respectively, 132, 131, 122, and 131, respectively. These values are not observed for ProR because this algorithm only deals with the content of the tweet and

Table 2. Most influential users discovered from single topic

Topic no.	2	4	6	0
Influentials	SCMex	heyheykylie	HighVoltageTat	sfzoo
Topic words	Awesome great tonight check today open shop making store tomorrow	Reno airport international people health car food service digital summit	Posted photo city trump philippines gop 2015 play university church	Great zoo favorite coming photo part time twitter talks creative

not the behavior, whereas the behavioral participation of other users leads to the spread of influence. Figure 5 shows the relationships between influential users and other users in the topic community. Influential users have different influences in different communities, i.e., different topic communities have different topic organizers and influential users. If a user has strong influences in a few communities or topics, they can be defined as an influential user.

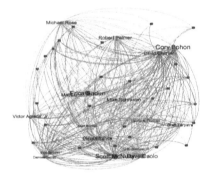

Fig. 5. Relation between the influential and other users in the topic community

7   Conclusions

This research analyzed the influence of users by employing two perspectives: "messages→topics" and "topics→social behaviors". Further, a method for identifying influential users based on the topic-behavior joint relationship network was proposed. In the proposed method, user influence trees were generated based on the topic-behavior joint network by mining relationships between users and the messages propagation time. Experimental results validated the efficiency of the proposed method.

Acknowledgments. This work is supported by National Science and Technology Major Project under Grant No. 2017YFB0803003, The National Key Research and Development Program of China (grant No. 2016YFB0801003), Natural Science Foundation of China (No. 61702508).

References

1. Bizid, I., Nayef, N., Boursier, P., Faiz, S., Morcos, J.: Prominent users detection during specific events by learning on and off-topic features of user activities. In: 2015 IEEE/ACM International Conference on Advances in Social Networks Analysis and Mining, pp. 500–503. ACM, New York (2015)
2. Cha, M., Haddadi, H., Gummadi, P.K., et al.: Measuring user influence in Twitter: the million follower fallacy. Association for the Advancement of Artificial Intelligence (2010)
3. Tunkelang, D.: A twitter analog to pagerank (2009). http://thenoisychannel.com/2009/01/13/a-twitter-analog-to-pagerank/
4. Gomez-Rodriguez, M., Leskovec, J., Krause, A.: Inferring networks of diffusion and influence. In: 16th ACM SIGKDD International Conference on Knowledge Discovery and Data Mining, pp. 1019–1028. ACM, New York (2010)
5. Goyal, A., Bonchi, F., Lakshmanan, L.V.S.: Learning influence probabilities in social networks. In: Proceedings of the 3rd ACM International Conference on Web Search and Data Mining, New York (2010)
6. Haveliwala, T.H.: Topic-sensitive PageRank. In: World Wide Web conference (2002)
7. Iwata, T., Shah, A., Ghahramani, Z.: Discovery latent influence in online social activities via shared cascade poisson processes. In: Proceedings of the 19th ACM SIGKDD International Conference on Knowledge Discovery and Data Mining, pp. 266–274. ACM, New York (2013)
8. Katsimpars, G., Vogiatzis, D., et al.: Determining influential users with supervised random walks. In: The 24th International Conference on World Wide Web, New York (2015)
9. Katz, E., Lazarsfeld, P.F.: Personal Influence: The Part Played by People in the Flow of Mass Communications. The Free Press, New York (1955)
10. Khan, H.U., Daud, A., Malik, T.A.: MIIB: a metric to identify top influential bloggers in a community. J. Plos One 10(9), e0138359 (2015)
11. Page, L., Brin, S., et al.: The PageRank citation ranking: bringing order to the Web. Stanford InfoLab (1999)
12. Merton, R.K.: Social Theory and Social Structure. Free Press, Glencoe (1957)
13. Silva, A., Guimaraes, S., Meira, W., et al.: ProfileRank: finding relevant content and influential users based on information diffusion. In: 7th Workshop on Social Network Mining and Analysis. ACM, New York (2013)
14. Stevens, S.S.: On the psychophysical law. Psychol. Rev. 64(3), 153–181 (1957)
15. Weng J., Lim, E.-P., et al.: TwitterRank: finding topic-sensitive influential Twitterers. In: 3rd ACM International Conference on Web Search and Data Mining, New York, pp. 216–231 (2010)

Hierarchical Dirichlet Processes with Social Influence

Jin Qian, Yeyun Gong, Qi Zhang$^{(\boxtimes)}$, and Xuanjing Huang

Fudan University, Shanghai, China
{12110240030,yygong12,qz,xjhuang}@fudan.edu.cn

Abstract. The hierarchical Dirichlet process model has been successfully used for extracting the topical or semantic content of documents and other kinds of sparse count data. Along with the growth of social media, there have been simultaneous increases in the amounts of textual information and social structural information. To incorporate the information contained in these structures, in this paper, we propose a novel non-parametric model, social hierarchical Dirichlet process (sHDP), to solve the problem. We assume that the topic distributions of documents are similar to each other if their authors have relations in social networks. The proposed method is extended from the hierarchical Dirichlet process model. We evaluate the utility of our method by applying it to three data sets: papers from NIPS proceedings, a subset of articles from Cora, and microblogs with social network. Experimental results demonstrate that the proposed method can achieve better performance than state-of-the-art methods in all three data sets.

1 Introduction

Probabilistic topic models have demonstrated their effectiveness in analyzing sparse high-dimensional count data, including recent innovations such as probabilistic latent semantic analysis (PLSA) [8], latent Dirichlet allocation (LDA) [4], hierarchical Dirichlet processes (HDP) [17], and so on. Because of the ability of nonparametric Bayesian methods to handle an unbounded number of topics, among existing techniques, these nonparametric Bayesian methods have received more and more attention and have found broad applications, such as retrieval [6], image processing [15], topic detection and traction [11,18], and so on.

With the dramatic increase in Web 2.0 applications, the textual information and social structural information have simultaneously grown. For example, from conference proceedings or online journal articles, we can obtain not only the content of articles, but also co-authorship networks of authors and citation networks. In Twitter-like services, except for the microblogs published by the users, the following and retweet relations also evolve social networks among users. In addition to these examples, we can easily find many other data collections with network structures attached, including emails, blogs, and forums. However, most of the current nonparametric Bayesian models usually take only the textual information into consideration. Hence, much more attention should

© Springer International Publishing AG 2018
X. Huang et al. (Eds.): NLPCC 2017, LNAI 10619, pp. 490–502, 2018.
https://doi.org/10.1007/978-3-319-73618-1_41

be given to the development of methods to take advantage of network structures to advance the effectiveness in analyzing sparse count data.

Several works have studied the problem from different aspects. Mei et al. [13] proposed the use of a discrete regularization framework to extend the PLSA and LDA to achieve the task. Topic-link LDA model [10] tries to simultaneously perform topic modeling and community detection in a framework extended from LDA. Jie et al. [16] transferred the social influence problem into a topical factor graph model and proposed a topical affinity propagation on the factor graph to identify the topic-specific social influence. A relational topic model [5] was developed based on LDA and incorporated the links between documents as binary random variables. However, due to the unbounded number of topics, nonparametric Bayesian methods cannot be directly incorporated into these frameworks. There are a number of extensions of nonparametric Bayesian methods from different aspects, including temporal information [7,14,19], shared characteristics [9], and time or space distance dependent Chinese restaurant process (ddCRP) [3].

The ddCRP clusters data in a biased way: each data point is more likely to be clustered with other data that are near it in an external sense. For example we can use ddCRP to model the topics distribution of the documents. In the ddCRP, the topics distribution of document is sampled from the connected documents depend on the distance. However, our work reconstructed the topics distribution integrated other documents depend on the social structural information of authors.

In this paper, we propose a novel non-parametric model, social hierarchical Dirichlet process (sHDP), to take both textual and the social structural information of authors into consideration for modeling topics distribution. The topics distribution of document in sHDP is reconstructed based on the social structural information of authors. The work is motivated by the observation that if two authors have close relation in social networks, they may have similar interests and would talk about similar topics. Hence, the topic distributions of documents posted by them should have a high chance to be similar. Based on the assumption, we extend HDP model by incorporating the influence of social structure. Different from HDP, which models the dependence among groups through sharing the same set of discrete parameters, the proposed method sHDP is built on top of the social Chinese restaurant franchise (sCRF) process, which has the feature that mixture weights associated with parameters are different and influenced by social structure for different groups. To demonstrate the effectiveness of the proposed method, we use three data sets to evaluate the proposed method and compare the results with those of state-of-the-art methods. The experimental results demonstrate that the proposed method can achieve significantly better performance than previous methods with or without taking the structure information into consideration.

To summarize, the contributions of this paper are:

– We propose a novel non-parametric model, which involves both textual and structural information.

– We detail the method through the social Chinese restaurant franchise process and describe a Gibbs sampling algorithm for posterior inference.
– Experimental results show that the proposed method achieves better performance in three different kinds of data sets.

2   Social Hierarchical Dirichlet Processes

In this work, we aim to model the topic distributions for the data sets consist of both text documents (S) and associated network structure $(\mathfrak{G})$. Text documents can be web pages, microblogs, papers, and so on. The network structure can be social network, linking graph, co-author/citation graph, and so on. Let d_i and d_j to represent the ith and jth document in S respectively. $f_{d_i d_j}$ denotes the social influence between the two documents and can be calculated based on the network structure $\mathfrak{G}$. It measures the degree of how these two documents have the same topic.

2.1   The Preliminaries

A Dirichlet process is a random process, that is a probability distribution over distributions, parameterized by a scaling parameter γ and a base probability measure H. We denote it by $G_0 \sim DP(H, \gamma)$.

A perspective on the Dirichlet process is provided by the *Pólya urn scheme* [2]. A sequence of variables $\theta_1, \theta_2, \ldots$ are independent and identically distributed according to G_0. The Pólya urn representation of θ results from integrating out G_0 is as follows:

$$\theta_i | \theta_1, \ldots, \theta_{i-1}, \gamma, H \sim$$
$$\sum_{l=1}^{i-1} \frac{i}{i-1+\gamma} \delta_{\theta_l} + \frac{\gamma}{i-1+\gamma} H. \tag{1}$$

Let $\phi_1, \ldots, \phi_K$ be the distinct values taken on by $\theta_1, \ldots, \theta_{i-1}$, and m_k be the number of values $\theta_{i'} = \phi_k$ for $1 \le i' < i$. Then, the Eq. (1) can be re-expressed as:

$$\theta_i | \theta_1, \ldots, \theta_{i-1}, \gamma, H \sim$$
$$\sum_{k=1}^{K} \frac{m_k}{i-1+\gamma} \delta_{\theta_{\phi_k}} + \frac{\gamma}{i-1+\gamma} H.$$

The Pólya urn scheme is closely related to the Chinese restaurant process (CRP) [1]. In this metaphor, take θ_i to be a customer entering a restaurant with infinitely many tables, each serving a unique dish ϕ_k. Each arriving customer chooses a table, in proportion to how many customers are currently sitting at that table. With some positive probability proportional to γ, the customer starts a new, previously unoccupied table.

For each value θ_i, let z_i be an indicator random variable that picks out the unique value ϕ_k, such that $\theta_i = \phi_{z_i}$. We can get:

$$z_i | z_1, \ldots, z_{i-1}, \gamma, H \sim$$

$$\sum_{k=1}^{K} \frac{m_k}{i-1+\gamma} \delta(z_i, k) + \frac{\gamma}{i-1+\gamma} \delta(z_i, k^{new}),$$

where K is the number of unique value. m_k is the number of indicator random variables taking the value k. k^{new} is a previously unseen value.

A second perspective on the Dirichlet process is stick-breaking construction. The stick-breaking construction considers a probability mass function $\{\beta_k\}_{k=1}^{\infty}$ on a countably infinite set, where the discrete probabilities are defined as follows:

$$\pi_k | \gamma \sim Beta(1, \gamma) \quad \beta_k = \pi_k \prod_{l=1}^{k-1} (1 - \pi_l), \tag{2}$$

A random draw $G_0 \sim DP(\gamma, H)$ can be expressed as:

$$G_0 = \sum_{k=1}^{\infty} \beta_k \delta_{\theta_k} \quad \theta_k | H \sim H, \quad k = 1, 2 \ldots \tag{3}$$

Dirichlet process can be used to model for a group data, while in many domains there are several groups of data produced by related, but distinct, generative processes. For this data, Teh et al. [17] proposed a hierarchical Dirichlet process (HDP) to link the group-specific Dirichlet processes. A HDP is a distribution over a set of random probability measures over probability space $(\Theta, \mathcal{B})$. Assume we have D groups of data and the dth group is denoted as $\{w_{dn}\}_{n=1,\ldots,N_d}$. It defines a set of random probability measures $(G_d)_{d \in D}$. For the D data sets different group-specific G_d are drawn from $DP(\alpha_{d0}, G_0)$, in which G_0 is drawn from another DP with concentration parameter γ and base probability measure H. For each of these groups, w_{dn} is drawn from the model $w_{dn} \sim F(\theta_{dn})$ with parameters $\theta_{dn} \sim G_d$. Putting everything together, the generative model for HDP is represented as:

$$G_0 | \gamma, H \sim DP(\gamma, H)$$
$$G_d \sim DP(\alpha_{d0}, G_0)$$
$$\theta_{dn} \sim G_d$$
$$w_{dn} \sim F(\theta_{dn}),$$

where $d \in D$ and $n = 1, \ldots, N_d$. In the hierarchical structure, different observations w_{dn} and $w_{dn'}$ in the same group share the same parameters θ^* based on the probability measure G_d. Moreover, since all G_d are composed of the same set of atoms $\{\theta_k^*\}_{k=1}^{\infty}$, the observations across different groups share parameters as a consequence of the discrete form of G_0. The clusters in each group d, assumed by the set $\{\theta_{dn}\}_{n=1,\ldots,N_d}$, are inferred via the posterior density function on the

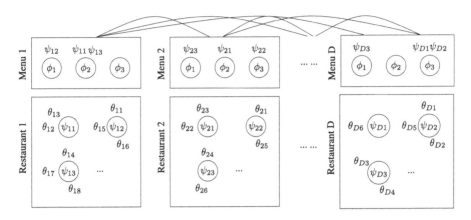

Fig. 1. A depiction of the social Chinese restaurant franchise (sCRF) process. Each restaurant is represented by a rectangle and has its own menu. The menus between different restaurants will influence each other. Customer θ_{dn} in restaurant d is seated at a table. Tables are represented by circles. A dish on a table is served from its menu ϕ_k. ψ_{dt} is an indicator to index items on the menu for a specific table.

parameters, with the likelihood function selecting the set of discrete parameters $\{\theta_k^*\}_{k=1}^\infty$ most consistent with the data $\{w_{dn}\}_{n=1,\dots,N_d}$. Meanwhile, clusters (and, hence, associated cluster parameters $\{\theta_k^*\}_{k=1}^\infty$ are shared across multiple data sets, as appropriate.

Since in the HDP different groups share the same parameters θ^*, the social relationship between groups has not been consider. The purpose of this paper is to extend the HDP to incorporate the structural information.

2.2 The Proposed Method

The proposed social hierarchical Dirichlet process extends from HDP, where documents share the same global measure G_0. In sHDP, each document has its own specific high-level random measure G_0^d. It is distributed as a Dirichlet process with concentration parameter γ and base probability measure H.

$$G_0^d|\gamma, H \sim DP(\gamma, H), \tag{4}$$

$G_0^d(d \in D)$ are tied together by the social influence. The random measures G_d are conditionally independent given G_0^d, with distributions given by a Dirichlet process with base probability measure G_0^d.

$$G_d|\alpha, G_0^d \sim DP(\alpha, G_0^d), \tag{5}$$

$$G_0^d|\psi_{1:k}, H, \gamma \sim$$
$$DP(\alpha + m_{d\cdot}^*, \sum_k \frac{m_{dk}^*}{m_{d\cdot}^* + \alpha}\delta(\psi_k) + \frac{\alpha}{m_{d\cdot}^* + \alpha}H). \tag{6}$$

Integrating out the random measure G_d and G_0^d through the Chinese restaurant process, we can get a social Chinese restaurant franchise process (sCRF). In this metaphor (see Fig. 1), we have a restaurant franchise and each restaurant has a menu for itself. For each table of each restaurant, the first customer sits on will order a dish, and all customers sit on the same table will share the dish. In different restaurants and different tables, the dish can be same, which is controlled by the social influence. In this setup, the restaurants correspond to documents, and the customers correspond to the parameters θ. Let $\phi_1, \phi_2, \ldots, \phi_K$ denote K random variables distributed according to H. We use the variable ψ_{dt} to represent the dish served at table t in the restaurant d. Each θ_{dn} is related to one ψ_{dt}, we use t_{dn} as the index of them. Each ψ_{dt} is related to one ϕ_k, we use k_{dt} as the index. We use n_{dtk} to represent the number of customers in restaurant d at table t with dish k. And we use $n_{d.k}$ to represent the number of customers in restaurant d on the tables which serve the dish k. The notation m_{dk}^*, which equals to $\sum_{q \in D_d} f_{dq} m_{qk}$, represents the influenced number of dish k for restaurant d. D_d is the restaurant set which are connected with the restaurant d. m_{qk} denotes the number of tables in restaurant q with dish k. f_{dq} is the social influence between document d and q, we can calculate it based on the network structure. $m_{d.}^*$ represents the influenced number of tables for restaurant d. In summary, we can get the conditional distribution of θ_{dn}:

$$\theta_{dn} | \theta_{d1}, \ldots, \theta_{d,n-1}, \alpha, G_0^d \sim$$

$$\sum_{t=1}^{T_d} \frac{n_{dtk_{dt}}}{n-1+\alpha} \delta_{\psi_{dt}} + \frac{\alpha}{n-1+\alpha} G_0^d,$$

where T_d is a count of tables in restaurant d. And we can obtain the conditional distribution of ψ_{dt}:

$$\psi_{dt} | \psi_{11}, \psi_{12}, \ldots, \psi_{21}, \ldots, \psi_{dt-1}, \gamma, H \sim$$

$$\sum_{k=1}^{K} \frac{m_{dk}^*}{m_{d.}^* + \gamma} \delta_{\phi_k} + \frac{\gamma}{m_{d.}^* + \gamma} H.$$

The generative process of sCRF is shown in Algorithm 1.

From Algorithm 1, we can get the generation process of document d. Each word w_{dn} in document d is drawn from $F(\theta_{dn})$, the parameter θ_{dn} can select a cluster(table) t with probability $\frac{n_{dtk_{dt}}}{n-1+\alpha}$. Also θ_{dn} has probability $\frac{\alpha}{n-1+\alpha}$ to choose a new cluster(table) t^{new}, then it can choose a new topic k^{new} with probability $\frac{\gamma}{m_{d.}^* + \gamma}$ and increment K or choose an existing topic k with probability $\frac{m_{dk}^*}{m_{d.}^* + \gamma}$. In social hierarchical Dirichlet process, the topic distributions of different documents connected with social influence.

Algorithm 1. The generation process of sCRF

---

for each restaurant $d \in D$ **do**

   for each customer θ in restaurant d **do**

      Choose table $t \propto \frac{n_{dtk_{dt}}}{n-1+\alpha}$

      Choose a new table $t^{new} \propto \frac{\alpha}{n-1+\alpha}$

      if Choose a new table t^{new} **then**

         Sample a new dish for this table.

         Choose an existing dish $k \propto \frac{m_{dk}^*}{m_{d.}^* + \gamma}$

         Choose a new dish $k^{new} \propto \frac{\gamma}{m_{d.}^* + \gamma}$

      end if

   end for

end for

2.3 Inference

We use Gibbs sampling method to obtain samples of hidden variable assignment. In this model, we need to sample table **t** for each customer and dish **k** for each table.

The sampling probability of table t_{dn} is as follows:

$$p(t_{dn} = t | \mathbf{t}_{\neg dn}, \mathbf{k}) \propto$$

$$\begin{cases} n_{dt}^{\neg dn} f_{\neg w_{dn}}^{k_{dt}}(w_{dn}), & t \text{ is an existing table} \\ \alpha p(w_{dn} | \mathbf{t}_{\neg dn}, t_{dn} = t^{new}, \mathbf{k}), & t \text{ is a new table} \end{cases},$$

where $n_{dt}^{\neg dn}$ is a count of customers at table t in restaurant d; $\neg dn$ denotes the counter calculated without considering the customer n in restaurant d; $f_{\neg w_{dn}}^{k_{dt}}(w_{dn})$ is the likelihood of generating w_{dn} for existing table t, which can be calculated by:

$$f_{\neg w_{dn}}^{k_{dt}}(w_{dn}) =$$
$$\frac{\int f(w_{dn}|\phi_k) \prod\limits_{d'n' \neq dn, z_{d'n'} = k} f(w_{d'n'}|\phi_k) h(\phi_k) d(\phi_k)}{\int \prod\limits_{d'n' \neq dn, z_{d'n'} = k} f(w_{d'n'}|\phi_k) h(\phi_k) d(\phi_k)},$$

where $k = k_{dt}$ is the dish served at table t in restaurant d. And $p(w_{dn}|\mathbf{t}_{\neg dn}, t_{dn} = t^{new}, \mathbf{k})$ is the conditional distribution of w_{dn} for $t_{dn} = t^{new}$, which can be calculated by integrating out the possible values of $k_{dt^{new}}$ as follows:

$$p(w_{dn}|\mathbf{t}_{\neg dn}, t_{dn} = t^{new}, \mathbf{k}) =$$

$$\sum_{k=1}^{K} \frac{m_{dk}^*}{m_{d.}^* + \gamma} f_{\neg w_{dn}}^k(w_{dn}) + \frac{\gamma}{m_{d.}^* + \gamma} f_{\neg w_{dn}}^{k^{new}}(w_{dn}),$$

where m_{dk}^* is the influenced number of tables which assigned to dish k for restaurant d. $m_{d.}^*$ is the total influenced number of tables for restaurant d;

$f_{\neg w_{dn}}^{k^{new}}(w_{dn}) = \int f(w_{dn}|\phi)h(\phi)d\phi$ is the prior density of w_{dn}; the prior probability that the new table t^{new} served a new dish k^{new} is proportional to γ.

If the sampled value of t_{dn} is equal to t^{new}, we can obtain a sample of $k_{dt^{new}}$
by sampling from:

$$p(k_{dt^{new}} = k|\mathbf{t}, \mathbf{k}_{\neg dt}) \propto$$

$$\begin{cases} m_{dk}^* f_{\neg w_{dn}}^k(w_{dn}), & k \text{ is an existing dish} \\ \gamma f_{\neg w_{dn}}^{k^{new}}(w_{dn}), & k \text{ is a new dish} \end{cases}.$$

The probability that t_{dn} takes on a particular previously used value t is
proportional to n_{dt}. So if some table t becomes unoccupied after updating t_{dn},
the probability that this table can be reoccupied will be zero. As a result, we may
delete the corresponding k_{dt} from the data structure. If as a result of deleting
k_{dt}, some dish k becomes unused for any table, we delete this kind of dish as
well.

The sampling probability of dish k_{dt} for the table t is as follows:

$$p(k_{dt} = k|\mathbf{t}, \mathbf{k}_{\neg dt}) \propto$$

$$\begin{cases} m_{dk}^{*\neg dt} f_{\neg \mathbf{w}_{dt}}^k(\mathbf{w}_{dt}), & k \text{ is an existing dish} \\ \gamma f_{\neg \mathbf{w}_{dt}}^{k^{new}}(\mathbf{w}_{dt}), & k = k^{new} \text{ is a new dish} \end{cases},$$

where $\mathbf{w}_{dt}$ is the customers at table t in restaurant d. When we change k_{dt},
actually, the dish for all the customers at this table have changed, $f_{\neg \mathbf{w}_{dt}}^k(\mathbf{w}_{dt})$ is
the likelihood for the customers on this table.

2.4 Social Influence

As described in the previous section, network structures can be transferred into
social influence and incorporated into sHDP. In this work, we propose a simple
method to compute the influence between documents based on structural information. Each document has some specific authors. Firstly, we calculate the number of links between two authors. Then, based on the number of links between
authors, we can inference the affect parameter f_{dq} between document d and
document q as follows:

$$f_{dq} = \exp \left(\sum_{a_d \in A_d} \sum_{a_q \in A_q} \eta_{a_d, a_q} \frac{N_{a_d, a_q}}{0.5 N_{a_d} + 0.5 N_{a_q}} \right),$$

where A_d is the set of authors of document d, A_q is the set of authors of doc-
ument q; $\eta_{a_d, a_q} = \frac{1}{Z} \frac{1}{I_{a_d} * I_{a_q}}$, Z is the normalization term; I_{a_d} and I_{a_q} are the
rank number of author a_d in the document d and author a_q in the document q
respectively; N_{a_d, a_q} is the count of links between author a_d and author a_q; N_{a_d}
is the total number of links connect to author a_d; N_{a_q} is the number of links
connect to author a_q.

Table 1. Statistics of the three data sets

Data Set	Doc.	Words	Vocabulary size	Links	Author
NIPS	5,179	1,607,205	11,890	15,404	13,784
CORA	9,842	358,824	2,620	78,721	21,101
SINA	468,177	1,358,010	11,596	12,329	1,318

Except the influence from the neighbours, we assume that it may also be influenced from other documents. This ensures sharing of global topic. Hence, we calculate the influence number of topic k for document d by the following equation:

$$m_{dk}^* = \sum_{q_o \in D^o} \lambda m_{q_o,k} + \sum_{q_r \in D^d} f_{d,q_r} m_{q_r,k},$$

where D^o is the document set which is not neighbours of document d; λ is the influence parameter from document set D^o.

3   Experiments

3.1   Data Sets and Settings

To examine the effectiveness of the proposed sHDP model, we constructed three datasets: the papers from NIPS proceedings, articles published in CORA, and microblogs from Sina Weibo[1]. The **NIPS** dataset contains full papers from NIPS proceedings between 1987 and 2013 and was obtained by crawling the documents and authors from the official NIPS website. The dataset contains 5,179 papers and 13,784 authors. The **CORA** dataset, which was constructed by McCallum et al. [12], contains abstracts from the CORA[2] computer science research paper archive. The title and abstract of each research paper is treated as the content. In total, there are 9,842 papers and 21,101 authors represented in the CORA dataset.

The **SINA** dataset contains microblogs crawled in the following manner. Firstly, we randomly selected 10 users as the central users. Then we collected the 1-*ego* network for all the central users based on their "following" relationships. All of the microblogs posted by these users from Jul. 1, 2013 to Sep. 30, 2013 were collected to construct the dataset. Using these steps, we gathered 468,177 microblogs belonging to 1,318 users in total. Each individual microblog posted by a user is treated as a separate document. Since there are no spaces between words in Chinese sentences, we used Stanford Word Segmenter[3] to split each microblog into a sequence of words.

---

[1] Sina Weibo is one of the most popular websites providing microblogging services in China. http://www.weibo.com.

[2] http://www.cora.justresearch.com.

[3] http://nlp.stanford.edu/software/segmenter.shtml.

The NIPS and CORA social networks are constructed based on co-author relationships, however the SINA dataset uses the *following* relationships between users for this purpose. For all of the documents, we removed the words whose frequency is more than 2000 or less than 50. For the NIPS and CORA datasets, we randomly selected 1,000 documents for testing and used the others as training data. For the SINA dataset, we randomly selected 100 documents for testing and 1,218 documents for training. The detailed statistics of the three datasets are given in Table 1.

For comparison with the proposed method, we also evaluated LDA, HDP, and the relational topic model (RTM) [5] using the same three datasets. LDA and HDP have been widely used for modeling topics. In this project, we evaluated them on the constructed datasets. However, as we mentioned in the previous sections, they do not take structural information into consideration. To compare the proposed method with the methods incorporating structural information, we evaluated RTM[4], which extends LDA and incorporates link information in the constructed datasets. To quantitatively evaluate the proposed method against the baselines, we used perplexity as the evaluation metric.

We ran sHDP and HDP with 1000 iterations of Gibbs sampling. Both of them use a symmetric Dirichlet distribution with parameters of 0.5 as the prior of base measure H over topic distributions. In sHDP and HDP, the concentration parameters are were given vague gamma priors, $\gamma \sim Gamma(5, 0.1)$ and $\alpha_0 \sim Gamma(5, 1)$. Posterior samples are were obtained with the Chinese restaurant franchise sampling scheme. The distributions over topics in LDA and RTM are were assumed to be symmetric Dirichlet with parameters $\alpha = 50.0/L$, with L being the number of topics, $\beta = 0.1$. γ is not used in LDA and RTM. These parameters are determined by 5-folds cross-validation on training data.

3.2 Evaluation Results

Table 2 shows the comparison of the proposed method, sHDP, with the state-of-the-art methods on the three evaluation datasets. From the results, we see that sHDP achieves much better performance than the other methods in all three datasets. sHDP achieved percentage decreases in perplexity over HDP of 8.8%, 7.8%, and 6.6% when run on the NIPS, CORA, and SINA datasets, respectively. The relative improvements achieved by sHDP on the NIPS and CORA datasets are better than the improvements observed on the SINA dataset. One of the main reasons for this performance difference may be the method of constructing the social network since co-authors are more likely to have similar interests and may publish papers with similar topics. From the table, we also observe that RTM achieves better performance than HDP and LDA on all three datasets. This demonstrates that the availability of structural information can create a performance advantage for the task of topic modeling.

---

[4] The toolkit was downloaded from the website of the authors. https://www.cs.princeton.edu/~blei/topicmodeling.html.

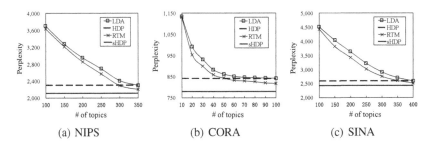

(a) NIPS   (b) CORA   (c) SINA

Fig. 2. Perplexity results on the NIPS, CORA and SINA for LDA, HDP, RTM, and sHDP.

Table 2. Perplexity of different methods in all three data sets.

Methods	NIPS	CORA	SINA
LDA	2297	843	2595
HDP	2298	841	2591
RTM	2203	818	2519
sHDP	**2111**	**780**	**2431**

Consistent with the results reported by previous research, HDP achieves performance similar to that of LDA for all three datasets. Since the number of topics is one of the most sensitive hyperparameters for LDA and RTM, we evaluated it for all three datasets and show the results in Fig. 2. From the results, we observe that the values which are used to achieve the best performance are different for different datasets. These results also demonstrate the advantages of non-parametric methods. This advantage is one of the key reasons why we tried to extend HDP to incorporate social influence in this project.

Table 3 shows the topics extracted from the CORA dataset using HDP and sHDP. For each topic, we list the top five words with the highest probabilities. From the table, we observe that although HDP extracts reasonable topics, all five topics extracted by it have their limitations. For example, the word "method", which is a commonly used word in the computer science domain, is in the top list of Topic 1. Comparing this result with the topics extracted by sHDP, we see that the five topics identified by sHDP are much better. Topic 1 covers papers about neural networks, Topic 2 is related to the domain of the graph, Topic 3 corresponds to programming, Topic 4 includes statistics, and Topic 5 is closely related to experimental procedures.

Table 3. An illustration of five topics for CORA data set. Five words with the highest conditional probability for each topic are given. We use the oval box to highlight the inappropriate words in the topics extracted by HDP.

	No	Words
HDP	1	Learning neural network training [method]
	2	Tree graph [minimum] [test] [cost]
	3	Language program object type [implementation]
	4	Distribution [model] probability [test] random
	5	Debug [single] process program proof
sHDP	1	Neural network learning training hidden
	2	Graph tree node path edge
	3	Code program parallel language java
	4	Distribution markov probability Bayesian statistical
	5	Debug experiment error program analysis

4 Conclusions

In this paper we introduced a novel social hierarchical Dirichlet process model, sHDP, to incorporate structural information for modeling topics. In sHDP, the social network structure will transfer into the levels of influence between documents. We detailed sHDP through the social Chinese restaurant franchise process and described a Gibbs sampling algorithm for posterior inference. For evaluating the proposed method, we constructed three datasets. Experimental results demonstrated that structural information can significantly benefit topical modeling, and the proposed method achieved better performance than the state-of-the-art methods for all three datasets.

References

1. Aldous, D.J.: Exchangeability and related topics. In: Hennequin, P.L. (ed.) École d'Été de Probabilités de Saint-Flour XIII—983. LNM, vol. 1117, pp. 1–198. Springer, Heidelberg (1985). https://doi.org/10.1007/BFb0099421
2. Blackwell, D., MacQueen, J.B.: Ferguson distributions via pólya urn schemes. Ann. Stat. **1**, 353–355 (1973)
3. Blei, D.M., Frazier, P.I.: Distance dependent Chinese restaurant processes. J. Mach. Learn. Res. **12**, 2461–2488 (2011)
4. Blei, D.M., Ng, A.Y., Jordan, M.I.: Latent Dirichlet allocation. J. Mach. Learn. Res. **3**, 993–1022 (2003)
5. Chang, J., Blei, D.M.: Relational topic models for document networks. In: International Conference on Artificial Intelligence and Statistics, pp. 81–88 (2009)
6. Cowans, P.J.: Information retrieval using hierarchical Dirichlet processes. In: Proceedings of the 27th Annual International ACM SIGIR Conference on Research and Development in Information Retrieval, pp. 564–565. ACM (2004)

7. Fox, E.B., Sudderth, E.B., Jordan, M.I., Willsky, A.S.: An HDP-HMM for systems with state persistence. In: Proceedings of the 25th International Conference on Machine Learning, ICML 2008, pp. 312–319. ACM, New York (2008). http://doi.acm.org/10.1145/1390156.1390196

8. Hofmann, T.: Probabilistic latent semantic indexing. In: Proceedings of the 22nd Annual International ACM SIGIR Conference on Research and Development in Information Retrieval, pp. 50–57. ACM (1999)

9. Kim, S., Smyth, P.: Hierarchical Dirichlet processes with random effects. In: NIPS, pp. 697–704 (2006)

10. Liu, Y., Niculescu-Mizil, A., Gryc, W.: Topic-link LDA: joint models of topic and author community. In: Proceedings of the 26th Annual International Conference on Machine Learning, ICML 2009, pp. 665–672. ACM, New York (2009). http://doi.acm.org/10.1145/1553374.1553460

11. McCallum, A., Corrada-Emmanuel, A., Wang, X.: Topic and role discovery in social networks. Computer Science Department Faculty Publication Series, p. 3 (2005)

12. McCallum, A., Nigam, K., Rennie, J., Seymore, K.: Automating the construction of internet portals with machine learning. Inf. Retr. J. **3**, 127–163 (2000). www.research.whizbang.com/data

13. Mei, Q., Cai, D., Zhang, D., Zhai, C.: Topic modeling with network regularization. In: Proceedings of the 17th International Conference on World Wide Web, pp. 101–110. ACM (2008)

14. Ren, L., Dunson, D.B., Carin, L.: The dynamic hierarchical Dirichlet process. In: Proceedings of the 25th International Conference on Machine Learning, ICML 2008, pp. 824–831. ACM, New York (2008). http://doi.acm.org/10.1145/1390156.1390260

15. Sivic, J., Russell, B.C., Efros, A.A., Zisserman, A., Freeman, W.T.: Discovering objects and their location in images. In: Tenth IEEE International Conference on Computer Vision, ICCV 2005, vol. 1, pp. 370–377. IEEE (2005)

16. Tang, J., Sun, J., Wang, C., Yang, Z.: Social influence analysis in large-scale networks. In: Proceedings of the 15th ACM SIGKDD International Conference on Knowledge Discovery and Data Mining, KDD 2009, pp. 807–816. ACM, New York (2009). http://doi.acm.org/10.1145/1557019.1557108

17. Teh, Y.W., Jordan, M.I., Beal, M.J., Blei, D.M.: Hierarchical Dirichlet processes. J. Am. Stat. Assoc. **101**(476), 1566–1581 (2006)

18. Wang, X., McCallum, A.: Topics over time: a non-Markov continuous-time model of topical trends. In: Proceedings of the 12th ACM SIGKDD International Conference on Knowledge Discovery and Data Mining, pp. 424–433. ACM (2006)

19. Zhang, J., Song, Y., Zhang, C., Liu, S.: Evolutionary hierarchical Dirichlet processes for multiple correlated time-varying corpora. In: Proceedings of the 16th ACM SIGKDD International Conference on Knowledge Discovery and Data Mining, KDD 2010, pp. 1079–1088. ACM, New York (2010). http://doi.acm.org/10.1145/1835804.1835940

A Personality-Aware Followee Recommendation Model Based on Text Semantics and Sentiment Analysis

Pan Xiao$^{(\boxtimes)}$, YongQuan Fan, and YaJun Du

School of Computer and Software Engineering, Xihua University,
Chengdu 610039, China
1049434055@qq.com

Abstract. As the popularity of micro-blogging sites, followee recommendation plays an important role in information sharing over
microblogging platforms. But as the popularity of microblogging sites
increases, the difficulty of deciding who to follow also increases. The
interests and emotions of users are often varied in their real lives. On
the contrary, some other features of micro-blog are always unchangeable
and they cannot describe the users characteristics very well. To solve this
problem, we propose a personality-aware followee recommendation model
(PSER) based on text semantics and sentiment analysis, a novel personality followee recommendation scheme over microblogging systems based
on user attributes and the big-five personality model. It quantitatively
analyses the effects of user personality in followee selection by combining
personality traits with text semantics of micro-blogging and sentiment
analysis of users. We conduct comprehensive experiments on a large-scale
dataset collected from Sina Weibo, the most popular mircoblogging system in China. The results show that our scheme greatly outperforms
existing schemes in terms of precision and an accurate appreciation of
this model tied to a quantitative analysis of personality is crucial for
potential followees selection, and thus, enhance recommendation.

Keywords: Followee recommendation · Personality traits
Semantic analysis · Sentiment analysis

1 Introduction

Since the emergence of social networks and microblogging sites, such as Twitter and Sina Weibo, hundreds of millions of users have become to use the
microblogging service. In the context, finding high quality social ties becomes
a difficult task due to the continuous expansion of microblogging communities.

Y. Fan—This work is supported by the National Nature Science Foundation (Grant
No. 61472329 and 61532009), the Key Natural Science Foundation of Xihua University (Z1412620) and the Innovation Fund of Postgraduate, Xihua University.

© Springer International Publishing AG 2018
X. Huang et al. (Eds.): NLPCC 2017, LNAI 10619, pp. 503–514, 2018.
https://doi.org/10.1007/978-3-319-73618-1_42

In microblogging systems, user follow or are followed by each other. In this regard, if user x follows user y, we can refer to x as y's follower, and y as x's followee [1]. There are many reasons for a user to follow some users because they publish interesting information, others because they have the same interests.

The so-called personality is not only the impact of each person's thinking, behavior and decision-making, and maintain its long-term stability, but also affect its social relations. Scientific research shows that there is a significant relationship between human personality and behavior in the real world [2]. Over the years, psychological researchers have been able to understand the personality traits and are committed to find a system.

Through the analysis of the personality of the social network users, we can achieve large-scale access to the user's personality data, which is conducive to the personality of the information in-depth research and extensive application. However, there are few researches on personality theory in the previous studies, but the research on the social network which is related to the social psychological characteristics is actually related to personality. There are many problems in the field of social computing, which are more or less related to personality theory. The potential value of personality prediction will be very helpful in solving these problems.

On the other hand, the user is susceptible to the outside world, this is because the user's needs are more extensive, the human emotional perception is relatively rich. Therefore, the user's textual and emotional expression largely reflects their personality traits, Particularly, text information and emotional information are also important factors to reflect user behavior.

The rest of this paper is organised as follows. In Sect. 2, we discuss related work. Section 3 presents the followee recommendation method we propose. In Sect. 4, We propose PSER model. In Sect. 5, we evaluate the performance of our design experiment and summarise the conclusions obtained from the performed experiment evaluation.

2   Related Work

Personalized recommendation technology is the core and critical technology of E-commerce recommendation system. The recommendation technology based on the fusion link topology is to abstract the social information into a meaningful social network [3]. However, these traditional methods only focus on how to improve the accuracy of recommendation, while ignoring the inherent characteristics of the user behavior is determined by their personality characteristics [4].

With the rapid development of the Internet and the convenience of user network data acquisition, the researchers began to try to use the user's online behavior to predict the user's personality. In recent years, with the rapid growth of Internet users and the increasing coverage of users, real-time network data provides a new research perspective for the research of network users' personality. Hamburger and Benartzi [5] analyzes the network behavior and the relationship between them and obtains the user's network behavior data by questionnaire.

In order to study the personality traits of users on the social networking platform, Quercia et al. [6] conducted a large five personality test for some popular users on Facebook and anlalyzed the association between the number of interactions and personality traits. The study by Mairesse et al. [7] Shows that linguistic features can be used for personality analysis. Hu and Pu [8] and Tkalcic et al. [3] presented approaches to include personality scores as complementary information in traditional rating-based collaborative recommendation systems. Both relied on the explicit assessment of personality through the Big Five test and the IPIP questionnaire respectively. Wu et al. [9] aimed at adding personality scores to a content-based movie recommendation system in order to generate more personalised and diverse recommendations.

In the past, the recommended algorithm is often based on the user's registration information, labels. These factors which are not easily changed can calculate the user's similarity. The user's interests and emotions in the daily life will be subtle changes, and user needs have gradually become very wide, which makes the recommended algorithm cannot be guaranteed the effect. The literature [10] uses social networks that mark spanning trees and relational graphs to discover followee. However, the range of recommendations for this approach cannot be extended. The literature [11] translates the recommendation into the link forecasting problem. The social label of this method is more fixed. Therefore, the user is usually chosen so freely that the user's features are not accurately expressed and the user's emotional uncertainty in the face of different events is not taken into account.

In real life, the user is vulnerable to the outside world. The reason is that the various needs of a wide range of human, emotional perception is relatively rich, which led to the common recommendation model can not meet the needs of users in a timely manner. In the online social network, the information that appears in a posting, forwarding, or commenting not only contains the user's interest, but also implied the user's emotional characteristics, which can be recommended as a very important reference data.

All of the presented approaches share the same drawbacks. First, they included a relatively small number of users. Second, personality was self-assessed through questionnaires. The own view of themselves reported by users could not reflect their actual behaviour and, in turn, their real personality [12]. Finally, the approaches were tested in the context of item recommendation using collaborative filtering techniques, none of the works include personality in the context of user recommendation in social networks. In consequence, the impact of personality in social recommendation systems is yet to be proven.

3   Our Method

In social networks, users generally have few changes to the registration information. As time goes on, the user's interest in labels and hobbies change a bit, so we focus on the user's recent behavior best reflects the user's interest. The literature [13] shows that different users in the online social network interact with each other through microblogging to influence emotions. Usually micro-blog information will contain two types of information, that is, text information and user emotional information. We mark it as TE = {Text, Emotion}. Also, we also consider personality traits. The recommendation algorithm presented in this paper can be combined with the user's interests and emotions, as well as personality traits. The experimental results show that the proposed algorithm is more effective than the traditional recommendation algorithm in generating the followee who are interested in the user.

3.1   User Micgroblogging Text Analysis

In this section, we discuss the importance of micro-blog text in recommendation. Microblogging text content is basically more compact and important vocabulary and contains a lot of information. In the use of text similarity calculation method, it is necessary to extract the keywords from the text, which is used as a user's personalized label, and then the similarity of the user is calculated for recommendation. But in Chinese words, there are many synonyms, antonyms and similar words which are easy to be confused. Therefore, in view of the characteristics of short microblogging, the semantic analysis of the text which user published is based on the existing "synonym forest" in this paper. This method first calculates the text similarity, and then calculates the emotion similarity. Because the extracted user's text content contains a variety of different subject information, we compare the threshold after calculating the similarity of text content and filtering out the theme of the text to find the similar user, which can improve the computational efficiency of the recommendation and improve the accuracy of recommendation.

Text Similarity Analysis. When calculating the user's text similarity, we first need to use vectorization to describe the Microblogging of the user U_i and U_j.

$$te_i = (te_{i1} = (T_{i1}, E_{i1}), \ldots, te_{in} = (T_{in}, E_{in})) \tag{1}$$

$$te_j = (te_{j1} = (T_{j1}, E_{j1}), \ldots, te_{jn} = (T_{jn}, E_{jn})) \tag{2}$$

The intersection of text similarity between user U_i and U_j is denoted as T_{com}.

$$T_{com} = T_{U_i} \cap T_{U_j} = \{t_{com1}, t_{com2}, \ldots, t_{comn}\} \tag{3}$$

The text contents which users published are successively in time. Therefore if the content of the text is closer to the current time, the ability to represent the user is stronger. In order to reduce the deviation caused by the time variation, this paper adds the corresponding weight value to reflect the influence of time change when calculating the similarity of microblogging text content. When T_{com} is empty, it means that there is no similarity between the two users' text, that is, the text similarity is 0, the formula is as follows:

$$Sim(te_i, te_j) = \begin{cases} \sum_{k=1}^{m}(wf_k \times Sim(T_{ik}, T_{jk})) & \text{if } T_{com} \neq \emptyset \\ 0 & \text{if } T_{com} = \emptyset \end{cases} \quad (4)$$

where T_{ik} and T_{jk} represent the textual content of U_i and U_j in kth days respectively. wf_k is the weight assigned to the user's kth text information, and m represents the number of selected texts. Specially, we define $\sum_{k=1}^{m} wf_k = 1$. Also, with the increase of k, the value of wf_k becomes larger, which means that the textual content published time closer to the current time and the stronger the characterization of the user. In this paper, we use Jaccard distance to compute text similarity [14], as follows:

$$Sim(T_{ik}, T_{jk}) = \frac{N(T_{ik}) \bigcap N(T_{jk})}{\sqrt{|N(T_{ik})||N(T_{jk})|}} \quad (5)$$

where $N(T_{ik})$ and $N(T_{jk})$ represent the collection of keywords in the user U_i and U_j in kth day microblogging. In order to guarantee the efficiency of recommendation, we select the threshold $\delta = 0.4$ for this step to be recommended list and to be filtered.

3.2   User Sentiment Analysis

In this section, we discuss the role of user sentiment in the followee recommendation. In the "psychology dictionary", the emotion is described as a kind of attitude experience whether which meet their own needs. Therefore, whether to meet the needs of users, in essence, is the user's emotional analysis at the recommended.

In the social media, the user's character determines that he will have different emotional responses to different things and problems, which have a certain impact on their behavior. Microblogging information not only express the user's views on different issues, but also contains their emotional information, which are helpful to analyze the user's emotions. People with similar emotions have a certain cohesive force, and the emotion analysis of users has been used in product recommendation [15], which has remarkable effect.

Emotional Similarity Analysis. The main task of calculating the similarity of emotion is to extract the emotional vocabulary generated by the user in the text. In particular, the extraction of emotional words is mainly based on corpus and dictionary [16]. In this paper, because the object of study is Chinese vocabulary, the dictionary based method is adopted. We have defined a dictionary, which is used to count and mark the common degree emotion words, including 19 adverbs of degree and set subscript according to the importance of degree's order. We compute the similarity of two emotional words by subscript distance. If the microblogging contains multiple emotional words, we choose the subscript of the largest keywords in the extraction, which can better reflect the user's emotions. Similar to the calculation of text similarity, the sentiment similarity calculation takes into account the temporal factors, in which the vector of the emotional word dictionary is defined as follows:

$$Emotion_{dict} = \{em_1, em_2, \ldots, em_i\} \tag{6}$$

Then, the method for calculating the emotional similarity of two users is as follows:

$$Sim(U, U_i) = \sum_{k=1}^{m} (wf_k \times \frac{1}{1 + \alpha |E - E_i|}) \tag{7}$$

where α is the distance decay parameter, The distance between the two emotional degree words shows that the similarity between the two is smaller, and vice versa. If the emotion words of two users are in the same location, the similarity is 1. If the distance is far, you need to refer to the value of α, and then calculate. When we get the final list of followees recommended, we need to filter the list to ensure the recommended quality, which is similar to the threshold of the text similarity, and the threshold ε is 0.4 we experimentally obtained.

3.3 Personality-Based Factors

The Big-Five Personality Model. The "Big Five" model of personality dimensions has emerged as one of the most well-researched and well-regarded measures of personality structure in recent years. The model's five domains of personality, Openness, Conscientiousness, Extroversion, Agreeableness, and Neuroticism, were conceived by Tupes and Christal as the fundamental traits that emerged from analyses of previous personality across age, gender, and cultral lines.

The Matching Calculation of the Personality Traits. TextMind is a Chinese language psychological analysis system developed by Computational Cyber-Psychology Lab, Institute of Psychology, Chinese Academy of Sciences. TextMind provides easy access to analysis the preferences and degrees of different categories in text, which provides an all-in-one solution from automatic Chinese words segmentation to psychological analysis. The processing to dictionary, text and punctuation is optimized to simplified Chinese, and the categories is compatible to LIWC [7]. The TextMind is the same as the SC-LIWC dictionary. Through the relationship between the function of these words and the text, in this paper, we can obtain the relationship between each word in TextMind Chinese psychological analysis system dictionary and each specific factor in the big five personality. Because many words have multiple functions, in this content, we match these functional words with the big five personality, and then, the value of the comprehensive calculation and the average calculation is taken as the relationship between the term and each factor in the big five personality. The character factor values for the ith dimension in word w are defined as follows:

$$BFM(\omega_i) = \frac{\sum_{j=1}^{n} P_{ij}}{n} \tag{8}$$

In Eq. (8), ω_i denotes the ith personality factor in word w. n indicates that word w has n functional nouns. P_{ij} represents the relationship between the jth word function and the ith personality factor. The functional word of TextMind and BFM corresponding a correspondence table can be divided into five groups.

First of all, we filter the number of micro-blogging published more than 10, and then the user all the microblogging text is assembled into a large text. We put each user's micro-blogging text information into the TextMind and statistical processing in frequency. In this paper, we calculate the personality score vector of each dimension of the big five personality according to the BFM correspondence table [7]. The user u's personality score in the ith dimension is calculated as follows:

$$Score(u)_i = \frac{\sum_{j=1}^{N_i} k_{\omega_j} \cdot BFM(\omega_{ji})}{N_i} \tag{9}$$

where $BFM(\omega_{ji})$ denotes the personality factor value of the jth-class word in the ith dimension in the micro-blogging text published by the user u. k_{ω_j} represents the word frequency of the jth-class word ω of the microblogging text published by the user u. N_i is the total number of functional words that are statistically relevant under the ith personality dimension. We use the Eq. (9) to calculate the average score between five dimensions in the table, which were μ_E, μ_A, μ_C, μ_N, μ_O, and then we put the user scores compared with the average correlation score. If it is higher than the average, it shows that the user has the personality characteristics of the dimension.

Matching the Personality Traits Between Users. The purpose of this study is to recommend followee, so the personality matching score between a user u and the potential blogger pf is expressed as follows:

$$TPM(u, pf) = \mu(\sum MS(u, pf, dim)) \tag{10}$$

In Eq. (10), $TPM(u, pf)$ is the total personality matching (TPM) score between user u and potential followee pf. μ is the average value of each dimension. $MS(u, pf, dim)$ indicates the personality matching score of the user u and the potential recommendation followee pf in a certain dimension.

Next, the matching score calculation formula for each dimension is defined as follows [1]:

$$scoreAgreement(u, pf, dim) = \begin{cases} 0.5 & \text{both u and pf are dimension} \\ 0.25 & \text{either u or pf are dimension} \\ 0 & \text{None is dimension} \end{cases} \tag{11}$$

4 Personality-Aware Followee Recommendation Model Based on Text Semantics and Sentiment Analysis

Personality-aware followee recommendation model (PSER) based on text semantics and sentiment analysis proposed in this paper is shown in Fig. 1.

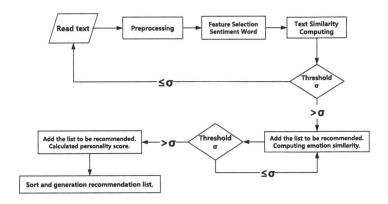

Fig. 1. PSER model

In this paper, the text similarity of two users can be calculated by formula (5) get the first recommended list. Because different users in the expression of things will produce different emotional differences, so we need to continue to analyze the user's emotions. Microblogging text often contains some emotional vocabulary. According to the custom emotional dictionary, we extract the user's emotional word, and then calculate the emotional similarity, in order to filter the first recommendation list.

The PSER algorithm steps are in Algorithm 1:

Algorithm 1. The PSER algorithm

Input: The ID of user U
Output: Recommended list RFL
1: initial $R_m List = \emptyset, R_m = \emptyset$
2: **for** $U_i \in U_{list}$ **do**
3:     $Sim(U, U_i) = \sum_{k=1}^{m}(wf_k \times Sim(T_k, T_{ik}))$
4:     **if** $Sim(U, U_i) > \sigma$ **then**
5:         Add U_i to $R_m List$
6:     **end if**
7: **end for**
8: **for** $U_i \in R_m List$ **do**
9:     $Sim(U, U_i) = \sum_{k=1}^{m}(wf_k \times \frac{1}{1+\alpha|E-E_i|})$
10:     **if** $Sim(U, U_i) > \varepsilon$ **then**
11:         Add U_i to RL
12:     **end if**
13: **end for**
14: **for** $U_i \in RL$ **do**
15:     $TPM(U, U_i) = \mu(\sum MS(U, U_i, dim))$
16: **end for**
17: Add to RFL in descending order
18: return RFL

---

5   Experiment

In this section, we evaluate our design using experiment. We use the large-scale dataset crawled from Sina Weibo, the most popular microblogging system in China. The dataset contains 256.7 million users' social link information and 550 million tweets. The dataset include tweets, user relations and user background information.

5.1   Experimental Evaluation Criteria

In the recommender system, the most commonly used criteria is the precision and recall rate of Top-K recommendation. At the same time, we have added the evaluation criteria P@N because we need to consider the order of users in the recommendation results.

The precision can be expressed as the ratio of the number of followees to the total number of followees recommended, the formula is as follows:

$$Precision = \frac{N_{hit}}{N_r} \tag{12}$$

where N_{hit} indicates the number of followees recommended correctly. N_r is the total number of recommended followees.

The recall rate can be expressed as the correct recommendation of the number of followees and the total number of followees. The formula is as follows:

$$Recall = \frac{N_{hit}}{N_A} \tag{13}$$

where N_{hit} indicates the number of followees recommended correctly. N_A is the total number of followees of the user.

5.2   Experimental Design

In experiment, We designed two sets of experiments to show our results.

Exp 1. In the analysis of the user's emotional information, the formula (7) is used to calculate. This experiment selects the best value of α through the change of F-measure.

Exp 2. Generally, the traditional recommendation algorithm of followee and friend are the same. Therefore, the contrast methods used in the experiment are as follows:

FOF+: Calculating followee's recommendation based on users' common followees [17].

FOF+Tag: This method performs tag similarity matching according to the user's common followees [18].

UMFR (Unified Micro-blog Followees Recommendation): This method combines information about labels, location, attendance, and hot topics [19].

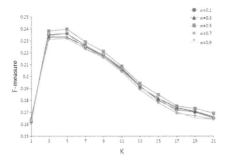

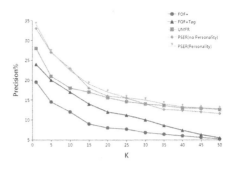

Fig. 2. Comparison of F-measure values at different values

Fig. 3. Comparison of precision values at different values

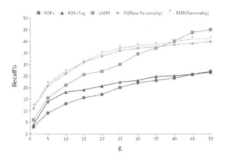

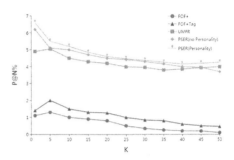

Fig. 4. Comparison of F-measure values at different values

Fig. 5. Comparison of P@N values at different values

5.3   Results

We compare our design with several existing schemes including FOF+, FOF+Tag, UMFR. In the experiment, the value of α is calculated by formula (7) and the experimental results show that the Fig. 2. Figure 2 shows that the recommended effect can be the best when $\alpha = 0.5$. Therefore, in the user's emotional word similarity calculation, we take $\alpha = 0.5$ into Eq. (3).

Firstly, we use the randomly stratified sampling strategy to sample in the raw data. According to the number of users followees for the division, we randomly sampled in each layer of the user. Our experiments were conducted on sampled users, and the result can be calculated for the final precision, recall rate, and P@N value. The experimental results of the precision rate, recall rate and P@N value of the experimental data are shown in Figs. 3, 4 and 5.

Figure 3 shows the precision rate contrast diagram under different algorithms. As can be seen from the Fig. 3, the algorithm we proposed has higher recommendation effect when the number of recommendation is less than 35 in this paper. Moreover, after adding personality traits, the precision rate has obviously improved.

Figure 4 shows the recall rate contrast diagram under different algorithms. It can be seen from the Fig. 4 that the algorithm proposed in this paper can maintain good results when the recommended number is less than 40, and the addition of personality traits can also improve the recall rate.

Figure 5 shows the P@N contrast diagram under different algorithms. As can be seen from the Fig. 5, the algorithm proposed in this paper is that the effect of the other algorithm is better in P@N. After adding personality traits, the algorithm slightly improved the P@N without considering the personality traits, and P@N tended to be steady as the number of recommended followees increased.

Through these experiments, we can see that the user's emotional analysis and personality traits can improve the recommended precision rate and recall rate to a certain extent. However, in the experiment without personality, the recommendation model proposed in this paper will decline with the increase of the recommended users.

6   Conclusions

In this paper, we propose a personality-aware followee recommendation model based on text Semantics and sentiment analysis (PSER), a novel personality followee recommendation scheme over microblogging systems based on text Semantics and sentiment analysis and the big-five personality model. This paper analysed how user personality conditions the followee selection process by combining a quantitative analysis of personality traits with the most commonly used predictive factors for followee recommendation.

Experiments show that the combination of the text semantics, emotional analysis and personality traits of followees recommended algorithm precision is higher than the traditional recommended algorithm. Also, this model can improve the recommendation quality and improve the novelty of the recommendation.

The combined attributes were insert into a recommendation algorithm that computed the similarity among target users and potential followees. We conduct experiments using large-scale traces form Sina Weibo to evaluate our design. Results show that PSER model greatly outperforms existing recommendation schemes.

References

1. Tommasel, A., Corbellini, A., Godoy, D., et al.: Personality-aware followee recommendation algorithms: an empirical analysis. Eng. Appl. Artif. Intell. **51**(C), 24–36 (2016)
2. Selfhout, M., Burk, W., Branje, S., et al.: Emerging late adolescent friendship networks and Big Five personality traits: a social network approach. J. Pers. **78**(2), 509–538 (2010)
3. Tkalcic, M., Kunaver, M., Tasic, J., et al.: Personality based user similarity measure for a collaborative recommender system. In: Proceedings of the 5th Workshop on Emotion in Human-Computer Interaction-Real world challenges, pp. 30–37 (2009)

4. Gao, R., Hao, B., Bai, S., et al. Improving user profile with personality traits predicted from social media content. In: ACM Conference on Recommender Systems, pp. 355–358. ACM (2013)

5. Hamburger, Y.A., Benartzi, E.: The relationship between extraversion and neuroticism and the different uses of the Internet. Comput. Hum. Behav. **16**(4), 441–449 (2000)

6. Quercia, D., Lambiotte, R., Stillwell, D., et al.: The personality of popular Facebook users. In: ACM Conference on Computer Supported Cooperative Work, pp. 955–964. DBLP (2012)

7. Mairesse, F., Walker, M.A., Mehl, M.R., et al.: Using linguistic cues for the automatic recognition of personality in conversation and text. J. Artif. Intell. Res. **30**(1), 457–500 (2007)

8. Hu, R., Pu, P.: Enhancing collaborative filtering systems with personality information. In: Proceedings of the Fifth ACM Conference on Recommender Systems, pp. 197–204. ACM (2011)

9. Wu, W., Chen, L., He, L.: Using personality to adjust diversity in recommender systems. In: ACM Conference on Hypertext and Social Media, 225–229. ACM (2013)

10. Gou, L., You, F., Guo, J., et al.: SFViz: interest-based friends exploration and recommendation in social networks. In: Visual Information Communication - International Symposium. ACM (2011). Article no. 15

11. Yang, T., Cui, Y.D., Jin, Y.H.: BPR-UserRec: a personalized user recommendation method in social tagging systems. J. China Univ. Posts Telecommun. **20**(1), 122–128 (2013)

12. Godin, F., Slavkovikj, V., Neve, W.D., et al. Using topic models for Twitter hashtag recommendation, pp. 593–596 (2013)

13. Xiong, X.B., Zhou, G., Huang, Y.Z., et al.: Dynamic evolution of collective emotions in social networks: a case study of Sina weibo. Sci. China Inf. Sci. **56**(7), 1–18 (2013)

14. Sui, X., Lee, T.-H., Whang, J.J., Savas, B., Jain, S., Pingali, K., Dhillon, I.: Parallel clustered low-rank approximation of graphs and its application to link prediction. In: Kasahara, H., Kimura, K. (eds.) LCPC 2012. LNCS, vol. 7760, pp. 76–95. Springer, Heidelberg (2013). https://doi.org/10.1007/978-3-642-37658-0_6

15. Bao, S., Xu, S., Zhang, L., et al. Joint emotion-topic modeling for social affective text mining. In: IEEE International Conference on Data Mining, pp. 699–704. IEEE (2009)

16. de Silva, N.F.F., Hruschka, E.R., Hruschka Jr., E.R.: Tweet sentiment analysis with classifier ensembles. Decis. Support Syst. **66**, 170–179 (2014)

17. Hsu, W.H., King, A.L., Paradesi, M.S.R., et al.: Collaborative and structural recommendation of friends using weblog-based social network analysis. In: AAAI Spring Symposium: Computational Approaches to Analyzing Weblogs, USA, pp. 55–60. AAAI (2006)

18. Chu, C.H., Wu, W.C., Wang, C.C., et al.: Friend Recommendation for location-based mobile social networks. In: Seventh International Conference on Innovative Mobile and Internet Services in Ubiquitous Computing. IEEE Computer Society, pp. 365–370 (2013)

19. Feng, S., Zhang, L., Wang, D., et al.: A unified microblog user similarity model for online friend recommendation. Commu. Comput. Inf. Sci. **496**, 286–298 (2014)

A Novel Community Detection Method Based on Cluster Density Peaks

Donglei Liu, Yipeng Su, Xudong Li, and Zhendong Niu$^{(\boxtimes)}$

School of Comupter Science, Beijing Institute of Technology,
5 South Zhongguancun Street, Haidian District, Beijing, China
{liudonglei,su_yipeng,lixudong,zniu}@bit.edu.cn

Abstract. Community structure is the basic structure of a social network. Nodes of a social network can naturally form communities. More specifically, nodes are densely connected with each other within the same community while sparsely between different communities. Community detection is an important task in understanding the features of networks and graph analysis. At present there exist many community detection methods which aim to reveal the latent community structure of a social network, such as graph-based methods and heuristic-information-based methods. However, the approaches based on graph theory are complex and with high computing expensive. In this paper, we extend the density concept and propose a density peaks based community detection method. This method firstly computes two metrics-the local density ρ and minimum climb distance δ -for each node in a network, then identify the nodes with both higher ρ and δ in local fields as each community center. Finally, rest nodes are assigned with corresponding community labels. The complete process of this method is simple but efficient. We test our approach on four classic baseline datasets. Experimental results demonstrate that the proposed method based on density peaks is more accurate and with low computational complexity.

Keywords: Social network · Community detection · Density peak

1 Introduction

Social activities and social relations of people in real life constitute a network of relationships which is called social network. Each node in the network represents a person, and the edges represent some kinds of social relations between nodes, such as friendship, family relations. With the development of Internet technology and web services application, more and more people migrate their real social relationships to the online social network sites (OSN), such as the famous Facebook, Twitter, WeChat and Sina weibo site.

Online social network sites could map and extend the social network of people. On OSN sites people can easily post their daily activities, pictures, comments, repost their friends' posts, follow new friends, and manage their friends

© Springer International Publishing AG 2018
X. Huang et al. (Eds.): NLPCC 2017, LNAI 10619, pp. 515–525, 2018.
https://doi.org/10.1007/978-3-319-73618-1_43

groups. Online social network sites greatly facilitate people's social activities, and makes it easier to build new friendships and to manage their existing relationships between friends.

Community structure is the basic structure of a social network, that is to say, nodes of a social network will spontaneously form groups of nodes, which are called communities. There exist many community detection methods based on graph theory and heuristic information, such as Infomap [17,18], Fastgreedy [5] and Louvain [2], the state-of-the-art greedy method.

However, the graph-based methods are complex and have high computational complexity. In this paper, we extend the density concept and propose a density peaks based community detetion method. This method firstly computes two metrics: the local density ρ and minimum climb distance δ for each node in a network, then treats the nodes with both higher ρ and δ as a local extreme point and a community center. Finally, Each node is assigned to the community label which the closest community center belongs to. The complete process of method is simple but efficient. We tested our method on four classic baseline datasets and a large dataset. Experimental results demonstrate that the proposed method based on density peaks is relatively accurate and with low computational complexity.

To address the above challenges, we propose a density-peaks based community detection approach, and summarize our technical contributions as follows:

- We extend the original density peak based cluster method to find the communities in social network.

The rest of this paper is organized as follows. Section 2 reviews the current community detection work. Section 3 presents our proposed algorithm based on density peaks. Section 4 presents the experiments and results analysis. Finally we conclude in Sect. 5.

2   Related Work

2.1   Social Network Definition

In order to describe the community detection problem accurately, we first introduce notations used in this paper. A social network, in mathematical context, can be formulated as a graph $G = (V, E)$ consisting of a set of nodes V representing the users, and a set of edges E denoting the relationships between users (e.g. followees or followers). $|V| = N$ denotes the number of nodes, and $(i, j) \in E$ denotes the edge from node i to node j $(i, j \in V)$, where A is the adjacency matrix of the network and $A_{ij} = 1$ represents the existence of edge (i, j) and $A_{ij} = 0$, otherwise.

2.2   Classical Community Detection Methods

Community detection methods aim to reveal the latent community structure in the social network. There exist a wide range of different community detection algorithms which follow different strategies in the literature [9].

Girvan-Newman method. The Girvan-Newman method is a seminal method used to detect communities in complex systems [11]. This method is based on edge's betweenness which identifies number of shortest-path passing this edge. The idea is that the betweenness of the edges connecting two communities is typically high, as many of the shortest paths between nodes in separate communities go through them. By removing edges owning maximum betweenness iteratively, the complex network is divided into many reasonable communities, and the result is a dendrogram. The computational complexity of GN method is $O(m^2n)$, where m is the number of edges and n is the number of nodes.

Modularity-based methods. The family of methods based on maximizing modularity is the biggest one in community detection algorithms. Modularity scores high those partitions containing communities with an internal edge density larger than that expected in a given graph model, which is almost always an ER model [14,15].

Several strategies have been proposed for modularity optimization, such as agglomerative greedy [5], Fast Newman [13], CNM method [4]. A multilevel approach Louvain has been proposed which scales to graphs with hundreds of millions of objects [2]. However, it has been reported that modularity has resolution limits [10]. Modularity is unable to detect small and well defined communities when the graph is large, and its maximization delivers sets with a tree-like structure, which cannot be considered communities.

2.3 Density Cluster-Based Method

There are several density cluster-based methods, such as SCAN (A Structural Clustering Algorithm for Networks, SCAN) [20] and DENGRAPH-ho (Density-based hierarchical community detection for explorative visual network analysis) [19].

The SCAN algorithm, derived from DBSCAN (Density-based Spatial Clustering of Applications with Noise, DBSCAN) [7], is capable of discovering communities, hubs, and outliers in a network. A community is grown from a group of centralized nodes which all satisfy a given neighborhood size. A user-defined threshold ε is introduced to define the neighborhood of a node. SCAN uses the ε-neighborhood of a node and groups it with those who share a common set of neighbors. A structural similarity measure is used to calculate the similarity between two nodes.

DENGRAPH-ho algorithm uses its own DENGRAPH (DENGRAPH: A Density-based Community Detection Algorithm) [8] density cluster method which derived from DBSCAN to update the current community structure of a network from a previously detected structure and its changes over time. This method can discover overlapping communities, by allowing each node to inherit multiple community labels instead of one. Also, to define a density-based neighborhood of a node, DENGRAPH uses the distance between two nodes, while SCAN uses neighborhood similarity.

3   Community Detection by Cluster Density Peaks

DensityPeak [16] is a new density based method proposed by Rodriguez and Laio. The basic idea of this method is that cluster centers are characterized by a higher density than their neighbors' and by a relatively large distance from points with higher densities. This method is simple and can recognize clusters regardless of their shape and the dimensionality of the space in which they are embedded. However, this method is developed for data in Euclidean space, and not fit for network data. Based on the similar idea, we propose a novel community detection method based on density peaks. We firstly check whether the social network addresses density peak phenomenon–the density peaks which with both higher ρ and δ will be a community center, then explore which definition of the metric ρ and δ can better reflect this phenomenon.

3.1   Definitions of Local Density ρ and Minimum Climb Distance δ

Rodriguez's new density peaks-based clustering method defines two metrics for each node. Because the definitons of the two metrics are about vector space, and cannot be adapted to network data straightforwardly, we extend the two metrics. We call the two metrics as the local density ρ and minimum climb distance δ separately according to their semantic meanings.

$$\rho_i = \frac{1}{2} \sum_{k,j \in \{i\} \cup F_i} A_{kj}. \tag{1}$$

where A is the adjacency matrix of the network defined in Sect. 2.1, and F_i is the set of nodes which directly connect with node i. So the ρ_i means the number of edge of the subgraph formed by node i and its neighbors.

$$\delta_i = \min_{j:\rho_j > \rho_i} (d_{ij}). \tag{2}$$

where d_{ij} denotes the length of shortest path between node i and j. For the node with highest density $\delta_i = \max_j (d_{ij})$.

For each node i, local density ρ_i is the number of edge of the subgraph formed by node i and its neighbors, and minimum climb distance δ_i is the minimum distance to nodes whose local density is higher than the node i. We meaningfully call this distance as climb distance, because this distance δ_i is the minimum distance from the node i up to any node with higher density than node i.

Rodriguez found the phenomenon that each cluster center point has higher local density and longer minimum distance, like peaks of the mountain, and other nodes have lower local density.

In our approach, we use the length of shortest path between nodes as the distance between every two nodes, which satisfies the triangle inequality condition required by Rodriguez's method. For the local density metric, we examine two different measurements, such as the node degree and the number of edges of the subgraph formed by node and its neighbors, and we find that the latter definition is better.

3.2   Procedure of the Community Detection by Cluster Density Peaks

We propose the community detection method by Density Peaks (DP-D). We firstly computes two metrics-the local density ρ and minimum climb distance δ for each node in a network, then treats the nodes with both higher ρ and δ as a local extreme point and a community center. Finally, each node is assigned with the label found by the density weighted major voting label propagation process.

Thus the general form of our community structure finding algorithm is as follows:

1. For each node i, computing the number of edges of the subgraph formed by node i and its neighbors as the local density ρ_i for node i.
2. For each node i, computing the minimum distance to nodes whose local density is higher than the node i as the minimum climb distance δ_i for node i. To decrease the computing time, we can search the k-hop neighbors of node i and get the first node j with higher ρ_j than node i, then $\delta_i = k$.
3. Ploting the 2-D decision graph by using the ρ as the x-axis and δ as y-axis. For example, Fig. 2 shows the decision graph for the Zarchary's Karate Club network whose network structure is plotted as Fig. 1. The nodes in the upper right region of Fig. 2(a) have higher local density ρ and longer minimum distance δ, such as the two nodes in Fig. 2. Using these nodes as community centers. To easily select the centers, we also plot the γ-rank figure as Fig. 2(b) where $\gamma_i = \rho_i * \delta_i$.
4. Every rest node is assigned to the label found by the density weighted major voting label propagation process. That is to say, we firstly count the sum of density of each community label of the labeled neighbors of node i, and then assign the community label with maximum sum of density to node i.

Complexity. The time complexity of step 1 described above is $O(m + n)$, where n is the number of nodes and m is the number of edges. The time complexity of step 2 is $O(n)$. The time complexity of step 4 is $O(n)$. The total time complexity of our methods is $O(m + n)$.

4   Experiments

In this section we provide an overview of the datasets and methods which we will use in our experiments.

4.1   Datasets

An overview of the networks we consider in our experimetns is given in Table 1.

Zarchary's Karate Club Network [21]. The well-known Zarchary's karate network is a classic society network. This network contains 34 nodes and 78 edges which represent members in a karate network and connections between them. In real world, members of the club are separated into two communities because

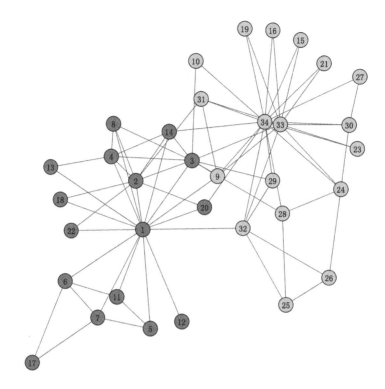

Fig. 1. Zarchary's Karate Club Network. The two communities are denoted by different colors (Color figure online)

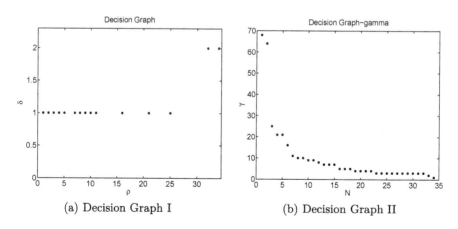

Fig. 2. Decision Graph for the Zarchary's Karate Club Network. (a) $\delta - \rho$ (b) $\gamma - rank$ the top two nodes are community centers

Table 1. Classic social networks

Datasets	Nodes	Edges	Communities	Q-value
Karate	34	78	2	0.3715
Dolphins	62	159	2	0.3787
Polbooks	105	441	3	0.4149
Polblogs	1222	19089	2	0.4052

of the dispute between club administrator (node 1) and principal karate teacher (node 33). Figure 1 shows the whole network.

Dolphin Social Network [12]. The Dolphins network is an undirected social network of frequent associations between 62 bottlenose dolphins in a community living in Doubtful Sound, New Zealand. The network was compiled from seven years of field studies of the dolphins, with ties between dolphin pairs being established by observation of statistically significant frequent association. The network splits naturally into two groups. The split into two groups appears to correspond to a known division of the dolphin community [12].

Books about US politics. A network of books about US politics published around the time of the 2004 presidential election and sold by the online bookseller Amazon.com. Edges between books represent frequent copurchasing of books by the same buyers. The network was compiled by V. Krebs and can be found in this websit[1].

Political Blogs [1]. Those blogs form two communities according to their political attitude. Links between blogs were automatically extracted from a crawl of the front page of the blog. In addition, the authors drew on various sources (blog directories, and incoming and outgoing links and posts around the time of the 2004 presidential election) and classified the first 758 blogs as left-leaning and the remaining 732 as right-leaning. In our experiments, we remove the isolated nodes and just focus on the maximum component which has 1222 nodes and 19089 edges.

4.2 Evaluation Metrics

Modularity. We use the classic modularity measure as the metric for our experiments. Modularity is the most used measure in evaluating the quality of communities found by community detection algorithms. The modularity of a partition is a scalar value between -1 and 1 that measures the density of links inside communities compared to links between communities. Modularity [14,15] is simply defined as:

$$Q = \frac{1}{2m} \sum_{i,j} [A_{ij} - \frac{k_i k_j}{2m}] \phi(c_i, c_j) \qquad (3)$$

where A is the adjacency matrix of the network, k_i is the degree of node i, and $\phi(c_i, c_j)$ is 1 if nodes i and j have the same community membership, and 0

---

[1] http://www-personal.umich.edu/~mejn/netdata/.

otherwise, and $m = \frac{1}{2}\sum_{i,j} A_{ij}$. This definition indicates that for each node pair (i, j) which shares communities, its contribution to modularity is positive if i, j are linked and is negative otherwise. It matches our intuition that nodes inside one community tends to build links with each other.

Modularity has been used to compare the quality of the partitions obtained by different community detection methods, but also as an objective function to optimize [13]. Unfortunately, it is computationally expensive to search all such partitions for finding the optimal value of modularity since modularity optimization is NP-hard problem [3]. However, many approximation methods were introduced to find high-modularity partitions to deal with large network in a reasonable time, such as the Louvain method [2].

NMI. The normalized mutual information (NMI) [6] is an information-theoretic-based measurement. It is currently widely used in measuring the performance of clustering algorithms. Formally, the measurement metric NMI can be defined as

$$NMI(A, B) = \frac{-2\sum_{i=1}^{C_A}\sum_{j=1}^{C_B} N_{ij}log(\frac{N_{ij}N}{N_{i.}N_{.j}})}{\sum_{i=1}^{C_A} N_{i.}log(\frac{N_{i.}}{N}) + \sum_{j=1}^{C_B} N_{.j}log(\frac{N_{.j}}{N})} \tag{4}$$

where N is the confusion matrix, where the rows correspond to the real communities, and the columns correspond to the found communities. N_{ij} is the number of nodes in the real community i that appear in the found community j. The number of real communities is denoted C_A and the number of found communities is denoted C_B, the sum over row i of matrix N_{ij} is denoted $N_{i.}$ and the sum over column j is denoted $N_{.j}$. If the found partitions are identical to the real communities, then NMI takes its maximum value of 1. If the partition found by the algorithm is totally independent of the real partition, for example when the entire network is found to be one community, NMI $= 0$. In our experiments, we use the NMI metric to measure the difference between the communities found by methods and the ground-truth.

4.3 Comparison Methods

We select three methods to compare with our method:

1. Fastgreedy method [5]: The Fastgreedy community detection algorithm is an algorithm based on the greedy optimization of modularity. This algorithm merges individual nodes into communities in a way that greedily maximizes the modularity score of the graph. It can be proven that if no merge can increase the current modularity score, the algorithm can be stopped since no further increase can be achieved.

2. Louvain method [2]: The Louvain community detection algorithm is an algorithm for performing community detection in networks by maximizing a modularity function which uses local moving strategy to greedily maximize the modularity of the structure after processed by the Louvain method. It starts with all vertices in clusters by themselves. Then, for each vertex, it tries to

reassign the vertex to the cluster of its neighbor which increases the modularity value the most. If reassigning to a neighbor's cluster does not increase the modularity value, it stays with its current cluster. This process repeats until no vertices can find a better cluster to be reassigned to. The algorithm then contracts each cluster into a supervertex, keeping track of the number of multiple edges between the clusters as the edge weight. The self loops are also kept. The whole process is then repeated on this new graph until the contraction does not reduce the number of nodes. The Louvain algorithm is fast and produces good solutions in practice. In this paper, we use the freely available C++ implementation of the method written by E. Lefebvre[2] to conduct the comparision experiments.

3. Infomap method [17,18]: The Infomap algorithm is based on the principles of information theory. Infomap characterizes the problem of finding the optimal clustering of a graph as the problem of finding a description of minimum information of a random walk on the graph. The algorithm maximizes an objective function called the Minimum Description Length, and in practice an acceptable approximation to the optimal solution can be found quickly. In this paper, we use the freely available Python implementation of the Python-igraph package[3] to conduct the comparision experiments.

4.4 Experiment Results and Analysis

Tables 2 and 3 show the Q and NMI values of communities found by our method and baseline methods on four datasets.

From Table 2, we can see that communities found by our proposed method is identical to the real communities on karate and dolphins datasets (NMI = 1.0). For the two large datasets polbooks and polblogs, our method also get higher NMI than other methods. The modularity values of our method are lower than those found by other methods, because those method are specifically designed to maximize the modularity value but our method is not. Our method mainly reveals the real community structure whose modularity value maybe not high.

Furthermore, our experiments show that the social network also have the phenomenon that each cluster center points have higher local density and longer minimum distance, like peaks of the mountain, and other nodes have lower local density. If we treat the local density of one node as the personal influence in his social network, this phenomenon may mean that the person prefers to attach connection with whom with higher influence.

---

[2] http://perso.uclouvain.be/vincent.blondel/research/louvain.html.
[3] Python-igraph package.

Table 2. Experiment results NMI-value

Datasets	Fastgreedy	Infomap	Louvain	DP-D
Karate	0.6925	0.6995	0.5866	**1.0**
Dolphins	0.5727	0.5662	0.6647	**1.0**
Polbooks	0.5308	0.4935	0.5125	**0.6012**
Polblogs	0.6461	0.4872	0.6440	**0.6633**

Table 3. Experiment results Q-value

Datasets	Groundtruth	Fastgreedy	Infomap	Louvain	DP-D
Karate	0.3715	0.3807	0.4020	**0.4188**	0.3715
Dolphins	0.3787	0.4955	**0.5277**	0.5185	0.3787
Polbooks	0.4149	0.5019	**0.5228**	0.5205	0.4495
Polblogs	0.4052	0.4269	0.4227	**0.4270**	0.4200

5   Conclusions

In this paper, We proposed a simple but efficient community detection method based on cluster density peaks. Our method can mainly reveal the real community structure with high NMI. For the future work, we can extend this method to find overlapping communities where nodes may belong to many different communities.

References

1. Adamic, L.A., Glance, N.: The political blogosphere and the 2004 U.S. election: divided they blog. In: Proceedings of the 3rd International Workshop on Link Discovery, LinkKDD 2005, pp. 36–43. ACM, New York (2005). http://doi.acm.org/10.1145/1134271.1134277
2. Blondel, V.D., Guillaume, J.L., Lambiotte, R., Lefebvre, E.: Fast unfolding of communities in large networks. J. Stat. Mech.: Theory Exp. **2008**(10), P10008 (2008)
3. Brandes, U., Delling, D., Gaertler, M., Gorke, R., Hoefer, M., Nikoloski, Z., Wagner, D.: On modularity clustering. IEEE Trans. Knowl. Data Eng. **20**(2), 172–188 (2008). http://dx.doi.org/10.1109/TKDE.2007.190689
4. Clauset, A.: Finding local community structure in networks. Phys. Rev. E **72**, 026132 (2005). http://link.aps.org/doi/10.1103/PhysRevE.72.026132
5. Clauset, A., Newman, M.E.J., Moore, C.: Finding community structure in very large networks. Phys. Rev. E **70**, 066111 (2004). http://link.aps.org/doi/10.1103/PhysRevE.70.066111

6. Danon, L., Díaz-Guilera, A., Duch, J., Arenas, A.: Comparing community structure identification. J. Stat. Mech.: Theory Exp. **2005**(09), P09008 (2005). http://stacks.iop.org/1742-5468/2005/i=09/a=P09008
7. Ester, M., Kriegel, H.P., Sander, J., Xu, X.: A density-based algorithm for discovering clusters a density-based algorithm for discovering clusters in large spatial databases with noise. In: Proceedings of the Second International Conference on Knowledge Discovery and Data Mining, KDD 1996, pp. 226–231. AAAI Press (1996). http://dl.acm.org/citation.cfm?id=3001460.3001507
8. Falkowski, T., Barth, A., Spiliopoulou, M.: DENGRAPH: a density-based community detection algorithm. In: Proceedings of the IEEE/WIC/ACM International Conference on Web Intelligence, WI 2007, pp. 112–115. IEEE Computer Society, Washington, DC (2007). http://dx.doi.org/10.1109/WI.2007.43
9. Fortunato, S.: Community detection in graphs. Phys. Rep. **486**(3–5), 75–174 (2010). http://www.sciencedirect.com/science/article/pii/S0370157309002841
10. Fortunato, S., Barthélemy, M.: Resolution limit in community detection. Proc. Natl. Acad. Sci. **104**(1), 36–41 (2007)
11. Girvan, M., Newman, M.E.J.: Community structure in social and biological networks. Proc. Natl. Acad. Sci. **99**(12), 7821–7826 (2002). http://www.pnas.org/content/99/12/7821.abstract
12. Lusseau, D., Schneider, K., Boisseau, O., Haase, P., Slooten, E., Dawson, S.: The bottlenose dolphin community of doubtful sound features a large proportion of long-lasting associations. Behav. Ecol. Sociobiol. **54**(4), 396–405 (2003). http://dx.doi.org/10.1007/s00265-003-0651-y
13. Newman, M.E.J.: Fast algorithm for detecting community structure in networks. Phys. Rev. E **69**, 066133 (2004). http://link.aps.org/doi/10.1103/PhysRev E.69.066133
14. Newman, M.E.J., Girvan, M.: Finding and evaluating community structure in networks. Phys. Rev. E **69**, 026113 (2004). http://link.aps.org/doi/10.1103/PhysRev E.69.026113
15. Newman, M.E.: Modularity and community structure in networks. Proc. Natl. Acad. Sci. **103**(23), 8577–8582 (2006)
16. Rodriguez, A., Laio, A.: Clustering by fast search and find of density peaks. Science **344**(6191), 1492–1496 (2014). http://www.sciencemag.org/content/344/6191/1492.abstract
17. Rosvall, M., Axelsson, D., Bergstrom, C.T.: The map equation. Eur. Phys. J. Spec. Topics **178**(1), 13–23 (2009). http://dx.doi.org/10.1140/epjst/e2010-01179-1
18. Rosvall, M., Bergstrom, C.T.: Maps of random walks on complex networks reveal community structure. Proc. Natl. Acad. Sci. U.S.A. **105**(4), 1118–1123 (2008)
19. Schlitter, N., Falkowski, T., et al.: DenGraph-HO: density-based hierarchical community detection for explorative visual network analysis. In: Bramer, M., Petridis, M., Nolle, L. (eds.) Research and Development in Intelligent Systems XXVIII, pp. 283–296. Springer, Londonpp (2011). https://doi.org/10.1007/978-1-4471-2318-7_22
20. Xu, X., Yuruk, N., Feng, Z., Schweiger, T.A.J.: SCAN: a structural clustering algorithm for networks. In: Proceedings of the 13th ACM SIGKDD International Conference on Knowledge Discovery and Data Mining, KDD 2007, pp. 824–833. ACM, New York (2007). http://doi.acm.org/10.1145/1281192.1281280
21. Zachary, W.W.: An information flow model for conflict and fission in small groups. J. Anthropol. Res. **33**, 452–473 (1977)

Text Mining

Review Rating with Joint Classification and Regression Model

Jian Xu, Hao Yin, Lu Zhang, Shoushan Li[(✉)], and Guodong Zhou

Natural Language Processing Lab, School of Computer Science and Technology,
Soochow University, Suzhou, China
{jxu1017,hyin,lzhang0107}@stu.suda.edu.cn,
{lishoushan,gdzhou}@suda.edu.cn

Abstract. Review rating is a sentiment analysis task which aims to predict a recommendation score for a review. Basically, classification and regression models are two major approaches to review rating, and these two approaches have their own characteristics and strength. For instance, the classification model can flexibly utilize distinguished models in machine learning, while the regression model can capture the connections between different rating scores. In this study, we propose a novel approach to review rating, namely joint LSTM, by exploiting the advantages of both review classification and regression models. Specifically, our approach employs an auxiliary Long-Short Term Memory (LSTM) layer to learn the auxiliary representation from the classification setting, and simultaneously join the auxiliary representation into the main LSTM layer for the review regression setting. In the learning process, the auxiliary classification LSTM model and the main regression LSTM model are jointly learned. Empirical studies demonstrate that our joint learning approach performs significantly better than using either individual classification or regression model on review rating.

Keywords: Sentiment analysis · Review rating · LSTM

1 Introduction

Sentiment analysis has attracted increasing attention along with the recent boom of e-commerce and social network systems [1]. In sentiment analysis, review rating is a foundational task which aims to automatically assign a score to a review where the score often has a fixed range, such as 1–5 and 1–10. Review rating plays a key role in many real applications, such as recommendation system [2], online advertising [3] and information retrieval [4]. For instance, in a recommendation system, one popular way to recommend a product is to sort all products according to their rating scores which are obtained from the review rating component.

Recently, the leading approaches to review rating deem it as a standard classification problem and have achieved respectable performances in many review rating tasks. For instance, review rating tasks with "5-star" or "10-star" rating systems are considered as a 5-class or 10-class classification problems and we can apply one-vs-all method to return it to several binary classification problems [5]. However, the main

X. Huang et al. (Eds.): NLPCC 2017, LNAI 10619, pp. 529–540, 2018.
https://doi.org/10.1007/978-3-319-73618-1_44

criticism of the classification approaches to review rating is that classification approaches do not consider the similarity between class labels. For example, "1-star" is intuitively closer to "2-star" than to "4-star".

Another kind of optional approaches to review rating deem the review rating task as a regression problem which has a natural advantage over the similarity between class labels because of the consideration of different loss between different class labels in the loss function. However, previous studies find that the regression models do not always perform better than classification models. For instance, Pang and Lee [6] empirically show that regression models perform better than classification models in the review rating tasks involving 4 stars but they perform worse than classification models in the review rating tasks involving 3 stars.

Although both the classification and regression models have achieved some success in the study of review rating, most of these methods are built with shallow learning architectures. In recent years, learning methods with deep architectures have achieved significant success in many natural language processing (NLP) tasks, such as machine translation [7], question answering [8] and text categorization [9]. It is a pressing need to extensively exploit the effectiveness of the deep learning methods on the task of review rating.

In this paper, we employ a popular deep learning method, named Long Short-Term Memory (LSTM) network, to perform review rating in terms of both classification and regression models. The main merit of the LSTM method lies in that it equips with a special gating mechanism that controls access to memory cells and it is powerful and effective at capturing long-term dependencies [10].

Furthermore, in order to exploit advantages of both the classification and regression models, we propose a novel approach, namely joint classification and regression model, to review rating. Specifically, we separate the review rating task into a main task (review regression) and an auxiliary task (review classification). An auxiliary representation learned from the auxiliary task with an auxiliary Long Short-Term Memory (LSTM) layer is integrated into the main task for joint learning. With the help of the auxiliary task, our approach boosts the performance of the main task. The experimental result demonstrates that our approach performs better than either the classification LSTM model or the regression LSTM model.

The remainder of this paper is organized as follows. Section 2 overviews related work on review rating. Section 3 presents some basic LSTM approaches to review rating. Section 4 presents our joint classification and regression approach to review rating. Section 5 evaluates the proposed approach. Finally, Sect. 6 gives the conclusion and future work.

2   Related Work

In the last decade, sentiment analysis has become a hot research area in natural language processing [1]. In this area, review rating is an important task and has attracted more and more attention since the pioneer work by Pang and Lee [6].

One major research line on review rating is to design effective features. Following Pang and Lee [6]'s work, most studies focus on designing effective textural features of reviews, since the performance of a rating predictor is heavily dependent on the choice of feature representation of data. For instance, Qu et al. [11] introduce the bag-of-opinion representation, which consists of a root word, a set of modifier words from the same sentence, and one or more negation words. Beyond textural features, user information is also investigated in the literature of review rating. For instance, Gao et al. [12] use user leniency and product polarity for review rating; Li et al. [13] utilize the textual topic and user-word factors for sentiment analysis. Moreover, polarity shifting is also useful to review rating. For instance, Li et al. [14] propose a machine learning approach to incorporate polarity shifting information into a document-level sentiment classification system. Features learned from other domains can also be useful. For instance, Li and Zong [15] propose a multi-domain sentiment classification approach that aims to improve performance through fusing training data from multiple domains.

Another major research line on review rating is to propose novel learning models. Pang and Lee [6] pioneer this field by regarding review rating prediction as a classification/regression problem. They build the rating predictor with machine learning method under a supervised metric labeling framework. Socher et al. [16] introduce a family of recursive neural networks for sentence-level semantic composition. Convolutional neural networks are widely used for semantic composition [17] by automatically capturing local and global semantics. Sequential models like Gated Recurrent Neural Network are also verified as strong approaches for semantic composition [18]. However, it is worthy to note that although these deep learning approaches have been well applied in review rating, they all focus on classification models rather than regression models.

Our work follows the second research line, which aims to propose stronger learning models for review rating. Unlike all above studies, our work is the first to integrate both classification and regression models for review rating and demonstrates that the proposed joint model is a better choice for review rating than using either a classification or a regression learning model.

3 Basic LSTM Models for Review Rating

In this section, we describe some basic LSTM approaches to review rating. The first subsection introduces basic LSTM network. The second subsection delineates the LSTM approach to review classification. The third subsection delineates the LSTM approach to review regression.

3.1 Basic LSTM Network

Long short-term memory network (LSTM) is proposed by Hochreiter and Schmidhuber [10] and it is designed to specifically address this issue of learning long-term dependencies. The LSTM maintains a separate memory cell inside it that updates and exposes its content only when deemed necessary. A number of minor modifications to the standard LSTM unit have been made. In this study, we apply the implementation used by Graves [19] to map the input sequence to a fixed-sized vector.

The architecture of a LSTM unit consists of an input gate i, an output gate o, a forget gate f, a hidden state h, and a memory cell c. At each time step t, the LSTM unit is updated as follows:

$$i_t = \sigma(W_i x_t + U_i h_{t-1} + V_i c_{t-1}) \tag{1}$$

$$f_t = \sigma\left(W_f x_t + U_f h_{t-1} + V_f c_{t-1}\right) \tag{2}$$

$$o_t = \sigma(W_o x_t + U_o h_{t-1} + V_o c_{t-1}) \tag{3}$$

$$\widetilde{c}_t = \tanh(W_c x_t + U_c h_{t-1}) \tag{4}$$

$$c_t = f_t \odot c_{t-1} + i_t \odot \widetilde{c}_t \tag{5}$$

$$h_t = o_t \odot \tanh(c_t) \tag{6}$$

where x_t denotes the input at time step t, σ denotes the logistic sigmoid function, $\odot$ denotes elementwise point multiplication. W, U and V represent the corresponding weight matrices connecting them to the gates. Intuitively, the forget gate controls how much the information is discarded in each memory unit, the input gate controls the amount of updated information in each memory unit, and the output gate controls the exposure of the internal memory state.

3.2   Review Rating with LSTM Classification Model

Figure 1 illustrates the classification model architecture for review rating with a LSTM layer. We utilize T^{input} to represent the input, and the input propagates through the LSTM layer, yielding the high-dimensional vector, i.e.,

$$h = LSTM(T^{input}) \tag{7}$$

where h is the output from the LSTM layer.

Subsequently, the fully-connected layer is applied. The fully-connected layer accepts the output from the previous layer, weighting them and passing through a normally activation function as follows:

$$h^* = dense(h) = \phi(\theta^T h + b) \tag{8}$$

where ϕ is the non-linear activation function, employed "ReLU" in our model. h^* is the output from the fully-connected layer.

The dropout layer has been very successful on feed-forward networks [20]. By randomly omitting feature detectors from the network during training, it can obtain less interdependent network units and achieve better performance, which is used as a hidden layer in our framework, i.e.,

$$h^d = h^* \cdot D(p^*) \tag{9}$$

where D denotes the dropout operator, p^* denotes a tuneable hyper parameter (the probability of retaining a hidden unit in the network), and h^d denotes the output from the dropout layer.

The softmax output layer is used for a classification task. The output from the previous layer is then fed into the output layer to get the prediction probabilities, i.e.,

$$p = softmax(W^d h^d + b^d) \tag{10}$$

where p is the set of predicted probabilities of the review classification, W^d is the weight vector to be learned, and b^d is the bias term.

Our classification model for review rating is trained to minimize a categorical cross-entropy loss function. Specially, the loss function is defined as follows:

$$loss_C = -\frac{1}{m} \sum_{i=1}^{m} \sum_{j=1}^{l} y_{ij} \log p_{ij} \tag{11}$$

where $loss_C$ is the loss function of the classification model for review rating, m is the total number of samples, l is the number of review categories, y_{ij} indicates whether the i-th sample truly belongs to the j-th category, and p_{ij} refers to the predicted probability.

3.3   Review Rating with LSTM Regression Model

Figure 2 illustrates the regression model architecture for review rating with a LSTM layer. From Figs. 1 and 2, we can see that most layers, such as the LSTM layer, the fully-connected layer, and the dropout layer, are the same as those in the classification model, which has been described in the last subsection.

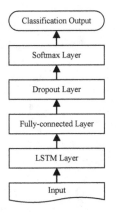

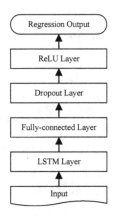

Fig. 1. LSTM classification model   **Fig. 2.** LSTM regression model

Different from the classification model, our regression model utilizes a rectified linear unit output layer instead of a softmax layer, i.e.,

$$f = \text{ReLU}(W^d h^d + b^d) \tag{12}$$

where W^d and b^d take the same meaning to the classification model above. f is the predicted value, which is a discrete variable.

For the regression model, we employ "mean squared error" for loss function. Specially, the loss function is defined as follows:

$$loss_R = \frac{1}{2m} \sum_{i=1}^{m} ||f_i - y_i||^2 \tag{13}$$

where $loss_R$ is the loss function of review regression, y_i is real value and f_i is the predicted value of i-th sample, and m is the total number of the training samples.

4 Review Rating with Joint Classification and Regression Model

Figure 3 gives the overall architecture of joint classification and regression model which contains a main LSTM layer and an auxiliary LSTM layer. In our study, we consider the review regression task as the main task and the review classification task as the auxiliary task. The goal of the approach is to employ the auxiliary representation to assist the regression performance of the main task. The main idea of our joint classification and regression approach lies in that the auxiliary LSTM layer is shared by both the main and auxiliary tasks so as to leverage the learning knowledge from both the classification and regression models.

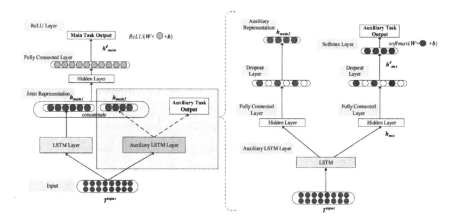

Fig. 3. Overall architecture of the proposed joint-LSTM model for review rating

4.1 The Main Task

Formally, the main regression representation of the main task is generated from both the main LSTM layer and the auxiliary LSTM layer respectively:

$$h_{main1} = LSTM_{main}(T^{input}) \tag{14}$$

$$h_{main2} = LSTM_{aux}(T^{input}) \tag{15}$$

The output h_{main1} represents the representation for the regression model via the main LSTM layer and the output h_{main2} represents the representation for the regression model via the auxiliary LSTM layer.

Then we concatenate the two regression representations as the input of the hidden layer in the main task

$$h_{main}^d = dense_{main}(h_{main1} \oplus h_{main2}) \tag{16}$$

where h_{main}^d denotes the outputs of fully-connected layer (dense layer) in the main task, and $\oplus$ denotes the concatenate operator.

4.2 The Auxiliary Task

The auxiliary representation is also generated by the auxiliary LSTM layer, which is a reused LSTM layer and is employed to bridge across the classification and regression models. The reused LSTM layer encodes both the same input sequence with the same weights:

$$h_{aux} = LSTM_{aux}(T^{input}) \tag{17}$$

where h_{aux} represents the representation for the classification model via the reused LSTM layer.

Then a fully-connected layer is utilized to obtain a feature vector for classification, which is the same as the hidden layer in the main task:

$$h_{aux}^d = dense_{aux}(h_{aux}) \tag{18}$$

where h_{aux}^d denotes the output of fully-connected layer (dense layer) in the auxiliary task. Other layers including a dropout layer and a softmax layer, as shown in Fig. 3, are the same as those which have been described in Sect. 3.2.

4.3 Joint Learning

Finally, we define our joint cost function for joint classification and regression model as a linear combination of the cost functions of both the main task (i.e., the regression task) and auxiliary task (i.e., the classification task) as follows:

$$loss_{joint-LSTM} = loss_R + loss_C \qquad (19)$$

We take RMSprop as the optimizing algorithm. All the matrix and vector parameters in neural network are initialized with uniform samples in $[-\sqrt{6/(r+c)}, \sqrt{6/(r+c)}]$, where r and c are the numbers of rows and columns in the matrices. In order to avoid over-fitting, the dropout strategy is used to both the main LSTM layer and auxiliary LSTM layer.

5 Experimentation

In this section, we systematically evaluate the performance of our joint classification and regression model for review rating.

5.1 Experimental Settings

Data Settings: Our data are from Mcauley [21] which are collected from Amazon[1]. The data contain 10 domains, i.e., Books, CDs, Phones, Clothing, Electronics, Health, Kitchen, Movies, Sports and Toys. Each domain's ratings range from 1 star to 5 stars. In each domain, we extract a balanced data set from the collected data, i.e., 1000 samples from each star. We use 80% of the data in each review category as the training data and the remaining 20% data as the test data. We also set aside 10% from the training data as the validation data which are used to tune learning algorithm parameters.

Representation: For word representation, we employ skip-gram algorithm (gensim[2] implementation) by word2vec to pre-trained word embedding on the whole data. The length of each text is set to a fixed size.

Basic Prediction Algorithms: (1) Support vector machine (SVM), a popular shallow-learning algorithm, is implemented with the libSVM[3] toolkit. Moreover, we implement SVM regression algorithm with the linear kernel, namely SVR for review rating. (2) LSTM, as the basic prediction algorithm in our approach, is implemented with the tool Keras[4]. It is used in both the classifier and regressor for review rating.

Parameters Setting: (1) The parameters of SVM and SVR are set as defaults. (2) The hyper parameters of LSTM are well tuned on the validation data by the grid search method, and most important hyper parameters are shown in Table 1.

Evaluation Metric: We employ the coefficient of determination R^2 to measure the performance on review rating. Coefficient of determination R^2 is used in the context of

---

[1] http://Amazon.com/.

[2] http://radimrehurek.com/gensim/.

[3] http://www.csie.ntu.edu.tw/~cjlin/libsvm/.

[4] https://github.com/fchollet/keras.

Table 1. Parameter setting in learning LSTM

Parameter description	Value
Dimension of the LSTM layer output	128
Dimension of the full-connected layer output	64
Learning rate	0.01
Dropout probability for regression	0.5
Dropout probability for classification	0.5
Epochs of iteration	30

statistical models with the main purpose to predict the future outcomes on the basis of other related information. R^2 is a number between 0 and 1. R^2 nearing 1.0 indicates that a regression line fits the data well. Formally, the coefficient of determination R^2 is defined as follows:

$$R^2 = 1 - \frac{SS_{err}}{SS_{tot}} \tag{20}$$

$$SS_{tot} = \sum_i \left(y_i - \bar{y} \right)^2 \tag{21}$$

$$SS_{err} = \sum_i (y_i - f_i)^2 \tag{22}$$

$$\bar{y} = \frac{1}{n} \sum_{i=1}^{n} y_i \tag{23}$$

where y_i is the real value and f_i is the predicted value of each sample.

Significance Test: We randomly split the whole data into training and test data 10 times and employ two different learning approaches, namely A1 and A2, to perform review rating. Then, we employ t-test to perform the significance test to test whether the learning approach A1 performs better than A2 (or otherwise).

5.2   Experimental Results

For a thorough comparison, we implement several approaches to review rating. These approaches are introduced as follows.

- **SVM:** The support vector machine classifier with all the parameters default.
- **C_LSTM:** The LSTM classification model which is described is Sect. 3.2.
- **SVR:** The support vector machine regressor with all the parameters default.
- **R_LSTM:** The LSTM regression model which is described in Sect. 3.3.
- **AVG_LSTM:** A straightforward approach to integrate the LSTM classification and regression models. Specifically, this approach consists of two main stages. In the

first stage, we train a LSTM classifier and regressor respectively. In the second stage, we simply combine the results from the classifier and regressor by averaging them. For instance, if the result of the LSTM classifier is 1 star and the result of the LSTM regressor is 3 star, the combining result is the average of them, i.e., $(1 + 3)/2 = 2$star.

- **JOINT_LSTM:** This is our approach to integrate the LSTM classification and regression models by learning an auxiliary representation for joint learning, which is described in Sect. 4 in detail.

Table 2 shows the performances of different approaches to review rating. From this table, we obtain following findings.

Table 2. Performances of different approaches to review rating

		Books	CDs	Phones	Clothing	Electronics
Classification	SVM	0.115	0.144	0.082	0.087	0.003
	C_LSTM	0.341	0.350	0.235	0.305	0.224
Regression	SVR	0.352	0.411	0.342	0.390	0.333
	R_LSTM	0.502	0.522	0.437	0.500	0.442
Joint	AVG_LSTM	0.506	0.508	0.425	0.488	0.422
	JOINT_LSTM	**0.540**	**0.557**	**0.455**	**0.520**	**0.466**
		Health	Kitchen	Movies	Sports	Toys
Classification	SVM	0.077	0.278	0.200	0.269	0.307
	C_LSTM	0.306	0.377	0.347	0.372	0.440
Regression	SVR	0.346	0.458	0.399	0.437	0.460
	R_LSTM	0.444	0.554	0.481	0.529	0.559
Joint	AVG_LSTM	0.465	0.540	0.495	0.524	0.557
	JOINT_LSTM	**0.472**	**0.565**	**0.520**	**0.542**	**0.572**

Regression models perform much better than classification models. Specifically, SVR outperforms SVM with a wide margin and R_LSTM consistently outperforms C_LSTM with a wide margin. This is mainly due to the fact that the regression models are more suitable for the evaluation metric R^2. Significance test shows that SVR significantly outperforms SVM (p-value < 0.001) and R_LSTM significantly outperforms C_LSTM (p-value < 0.001).

In regression models, R_LSTM performs much better than SVR in all 10 domains. This result encourages to apply deep learning approaches to the task of review rating. Significance test shows that R_LSTM significantly outperforms SVR (p-value < 0.001).

When combining the LSTM classification and LSTM regression models, AVG_LSTM performs well in some domains, such as Books, Health, and Movies, achieving better R^2 than R_LSTM. However, in some other domains, such as CDs, Phones, and Clothing, it performs worse than R_LSTM. These results demonstrate th at simply averaging the results of C_LSTM and R_LSTM would not always improve the performances of R_LSTM.

When combining the LSTM classification and LSTM regression models, JOINT_LSTM outperforms R_LSTM in all 10 domains. Averagely, JOINT_LSTM improves R_LSTM with about 0.024 in R^2. This result verifies the effectiveness of the proposed joint model to review rating. Significance test shows that our approach, i.e., JOINT_LSTM, significantly outperforms both R_LSTM and AVG_LSTM (p-value < 0.01).

6 Conclusion

In this paper, we propose a novel approach, namely joint classification and regression model, to review rating, by exploiting advantages of both the review classification and regression models. In our approach, we employ an auxiliary LSTM layer to learn the auxiliary representation in the review classification task (as the auxiliary task) and employ it in the regression task (as the main task). To achieve this, a neural network based model, namely joint LSTM, is employed to bridge across the classification and regression models via a shared LSTM layer. Empirical studies demonstrate that the LSTM model is appropriate for both the review classification and regression task. Moreover, the results show that our joint learning approach significantly boosts the performance of the main regression task in all 10 domains.

In our future work, we would like to improve joint LSTM by looking for better classification models for review rating. Furthermore, we would like to apply our proposed joint LSTM model in other NLP applications which involve both the classification and regression implementations.

Acknowledgments. This research work has been partially supported by three NSFC grants, No. 61375073, No. 61672366 and No. 61331011.

References

1. Pang, B., Lee, L.: Opinion mining and sentiment analysis. Found. Trends® Inf. Retr. **2**(1–2), 1–135 (2008)
2. Yang, D., Zhang, D., Yu, Z., et al.: A sentiment-enhanced personalized location recommendation system. In: Proceedings of the 24th ACM Conference on Hypertext and Social Media, pp. 119–128. ACM (2013)
3. Fan, T.-K., Chang, C.-H.: Sentiment-oriented contextual advertising. In: Boughanem, M., Berrut, C., Mothe, J., Soule-Dupuy, C. (eds.) ECIR 2009. LNCS, vol. 5478, pp. 202–215. Springer, Heidelberg (2009). https://doi.org/10.1007/978-3-642-00958-7_20
4. Zhang, M., Ye, X.: A generation model to unify topic relevance and lexicon-based sentiment for opinion retrieval. In: Proceedings of the 31st Annual International ACM SIGIR Conference on Research and Development in Information Retrieval, pp. 411–418. ACM (2008)
5. Rifkin, R., Klautau, A.: In defense of one-vs-all classification. J. Mach. Learn. Res **5**(Jan), 101–141 (2004)

6. Pang, B., Lee, L.: Seeing stars: exploiting class relationships for sentiment categorization with respect to rating scales. In: Proceedings of the 43rd Annual Meeting on Association for Computational Linguistics, pp. 115–124. Association for Computational Linguistics (2005)

7. Bahdanau, D., Cho, K., Bengio, Y.: Neural machine translation by jointly learning to align and translate. arXiv preprint arXiv:1409.0473 (2014)

8. Iyyer, M., Boyd-Graber, J.L., Claudino, L.M.B., et al.: A neural network for factoid question answering over paragraphs. In: EMNLP, pp. 633–644 (2014)

9. Zhang, M.L., Zhou, Z.H.: Multilabel neural networks with applications to functional genomics and text categorization. IEEE Trans. Knowl. Data Eng. **18**(10), 1338–1351 (2006)

10. Hochreiter, S., Schmidhuber, J.: Long short-term memory. Neural Comput. **9**(8), 1735–1780 (1997)

11. Qu, L., Ifrim, G., Weikum, G.: The bag-of-opinions method for review rating prediction from sparse text patterns. In: Proceedings of the 23rd International Conference on Computational Linguistics, pp. 913–921. Association for Computational Linguistics (2010)

12. Gao, W., Yoshinaga, N., Kaji, N., et al.: Modeling user leniency and product popularity for sentiment classification. In: IJCNLP, pp. 1107–1111 (2013)

13. Li, F., Wang, S., Liu, S., et al.: SUIT: a supervised user-item based topic model for sentiment analysis. In: AAAI, vol. 14, pp. 1636–1642 (2014)

14. Li, S., Lee, S.Y.M., Chen, Y., et al.: Sentiment classification and polarity shifting. In: Proceedings of the 23rd International Conference on Computational Linguistics, pp. 635–643. Association for Computational Linguistics (2010)

15. Li, S., Zong, C.: Multi-domain sentiment classification. In: Proceedings of the 46th Annual Meeting of the Association for Computational Linguistics on Human Language Technologies: Short Papers, pp. 257–260. Association for Computational Linguistics (2008)

16. Socher, R., Perelygin, A., Wu, J.Y., et al.: Recursive deep models for semantic compositionality over a sentiment treebank. In: Proceedings of the Conference on Empirical Methods in Natural Language Processing (EMNLP), pp. 1631–1642 (2013)

17. Johnson, R., Zhang, T.: Effective use of word order for text categorization with convolutional neural networks. arXiv preprint arXiv:1412.1058 (2014)

18. Tang, D., Qin, B., Liu, T.: Document modeling with gated recurrent neural network for sentiment classification. In: EMNLP, pp. 1422–1432 (2015)

19. Graves, A.: Generating sequences with recurrent neural networks. arXiv preprint arXiv: 1308.0850 (2013)

20. Hinton, G.E., Srivastava, N., Krizhevsky, A., et al.: Improving neural networks by preventing co-adaptation of feature detectors. arXiv preprint arXiv:1207.0580 (2012)

21. McAuley, J., Pandey, R., Leskovec, J.: Inferring networks of substitutable and complementary products. In: Proceedings of the 21th ACM SIGKDD International Conference on Knowledge Discovery and Data Mining, pp. 785–794. ACM (2015)

Boosting Collective Entity Linking via Type-Guided Semantic Embedding

Weiming Lu$^{(\boxtimes)}$, Yangfan Zhou, Haijiao Lu, Pengkun Ma, Zhenyu Zhang, and Baogang Wei

College of Computer Science and Technology,
Zhejiang University, Hangzhou, China
luwm@zju.edu.cn

Abstract. Entity Linking (EL) is the task of mapping mentions in natural-language text to their corresponding entities in a knowledge base (KB). Type modeling for mention and entity could be beneficial for entity linking. In this paper, we propose a type-guided semantic embedding approach to boost collective entity linking. We use Bidirectional Long Short-Term Memory (BiLSTM) and dynamic convolutional neural network (DCNN) to model the mention and the entity respectively. Then, we build a graph with the semantic relatedness of mentions and entities for the collective entity linking. Finally, we evaluate our approach by comparing the state-of-the-art entity linking approaches over a wide range of very different data sets, such as TAC-KBP from 2009 to 2013, AIDA, DBPediaSpotlight, N3-Reuters-128, and N3-RSS-500. Besides, we also evaluate our approach with a Chinese Corpora. The experiments reveal that the modeling for entity type can be very beneficial to the entity linking.

1 Introduction

Entity Linking (EL) is the task of mapping mentions in natural-language text to their corresponding entities in a knowledge base (KB). One of the major challenges for EL is that mentions are often ambiguous, which can only be resolved with an appropriate context. For example, *Washington* in sentence *"In 1775, the Second Continental Congress commissioned **Washington** as commander-in-chief of the Continental Army in the American Revolution"* refers to *George Washington*, while *Washington* in sentence *"As of 2010, there were an estimated 81,734 immigrants living in **Washington**."* refers to *Washington, D.C.*

Several approaches have been proposed to improve the performance of EL, such as collective entity linking approaches [5,7,10–13,30], entity relatedness learning [2,13,21], and neural network approaches [9,23,27].

Obviously, the essential step of EL is to define a similarity measure between mention and entity. However, previous approaches usually used handcrafted features to measure the similarity, such as surface features, context features and special features [29]. Afterwards, generative models such as entity-mention

X. Huang et al. (Eds.): NLPCC 2017, LNAI 10619, pp. 541–553, 2018.
https://doi.org/10.1007/978-3-319-73618-1_45

model [6] and selective context model [15] were proposed for similarity measurement. Recently, deep learning approaches are becoming increasingly popular for the EL task. For example, a neural network was proposed to model context, mention and entity for entity disambiguation [23]. Words and entities are mapped into the same continuous vector space for named entity disambiguation by extending the skip-gram model [27].

However, there are still some places to boost entity linking. First, the context of mention should be modeled as a sequence to capture the semantics, while the context were both modeled as a bag of words in [23,27]. Second, the types of mention and entity would be the hints for entity linking. In the above examples, the mention following the verb *commission* may be a person, while the mention following *living in* may be a location. In addition, we found that the words in categories or tags indicate both the semantic and type of entity. For example, entity *George Washington* has categories such as *American surveyors*, *commanders in chief*, and *Presidents of the United States*. While, entity *Washington, D.C.* has categories such as *Capital districts and territories*, *Washington metropolitan area*, *Planned cities in the United States*. Obviously, the categories are exactly consistent with the semantic and type of mentions in context.

Based on the above observations, we propose a type-guided semantic embedding approach to boost collective entity linking. We use bidirectional Long Short-Term Memory (BiLSTM) to model the context, and use dynamic convolutional neural network (DCNN) [14] to model the categories. Then, we build a graph with the semantic relatedness of mentions and entities based on the semantic embedding for collective entity linking. We evaluate our approach by comparing the state-of-the-art entity linking approaches over a wide range of very different data sets, such as TAC-KBP from 2009 to 2013, AIDA, DBPediaSpotlight, N3-Reuters-128, and N3-RSS-500. Besides, we also evaluate our approach with a Chinese Corpora.

The rest of the paper is structured as follows: We describe the type-guided semantic embedding for entity linking in Sect. 2, and present our experimental results in Sect. 3. Section 4 reviews the related works and Sect. 5 gives the conclusion.

2   Model

In this section, we first describe our type-guided semantic embedding, and then we boost the collective entity linking through the embedding.

2.1   Type-Guided Semantic Embedding

The typed-guided semantic embedding for mention and entity is illustrated as Fig. 1.

As mentioned above, we use BiLSTM and DCNN to learn the representations of mention and entity respectively. Their resulting vector representations x_m and

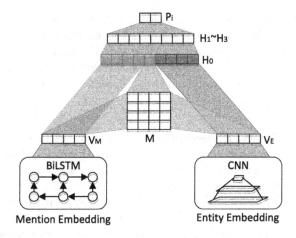

Fig. 1. Typed-guided semantic embedding

x_e can be used to compute a mention-entity similarity score through a similarity matrix M. Then, the join layer concatenates x_m, x_e and the similarity score into a single vector, which is then passed through three fully connected hidden layers. Finally, the output of the hidden layers is further fed to the softmax classification layer, which will generate a initial mention-entity linking probability. The details will be elaborated in the following sections.

BiLSTM Based Mention Embedding. In order to capture the type and semantic of a mention, we apply BiLSTM to model the context $c_m = [..., x_{m-2}, x_{m-1}, x_m, x_{m+1}, x_{m+2}, ...]$ of the mention x_m, as shown in Fig. 2.

Since the word itself and its POS type are both important for mention embedding, so the vector of each context word x_m is made up of two parts: a word

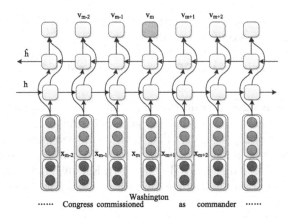

Fig. 2. Mention embedding by BiLSTM

embedding and a type embedding. The word embedding is represented by a W_x-dimensional vector, and initialized by word2vec with the skip-gram model, while the type embedding is represented by a W_t-dimensional vector, and initialized by a one-hot vector. Finally, the outputs of the forward and backward of BiLSTM are concatenated as the mention embedding v_m for x_m. The window size of the context is S.

DCNN Based Entity Embedding. Since the words in categories or tags indicate both the semantic and type of entity, and they are orderless, so we use DCNN [14], which is a convolution neural network with dynamic k-max pooling, to model the category of entity.

The DCNN network has three convolutional layers with four feature maps each, and same padding is used in each layer. There is a k-max pooling layer after each convolutional layer, and a folding layer is applied between the last convolutional layer and the k-max pooling layer. Finally, the output of the last k-max pooling layer is flattened as a vector v_e to be the entity embedding. The detailed DCNN network is shown in Fig. 3, where each solid circle represents one feature map of the CNN network, and the input of the DCNN network is the category of each entity, which contains a bag of words $x_1, x_2, ..., x_L$.

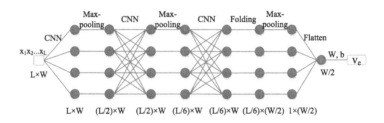

Fig. 3. Category embedding by DCNN

In the figure, each word in the category is represented by a W_x-dimensional word embedding from word2vec, so the input of the DCNN network is a $L \times W_x$ vector. The pooling parameter k of three k-max pooling layers is 2, 3 and $max(L/6, 1)$. The details of the DCNN can be referred to [14].

Embedding Training. To train the embedding, we concatenate the mention embedding v_m, the entity embedding v_{e_i} and their similarity score $s(v_m, v_{e_i}) = v_m^T \cdot M \cdot v_{e_i}$ as a vector $H_0 = [v_m^T, s(v_m, v_{e_i}), v_{e_i}^T]$, and then pass H_0 through three hidden fully connected layers as shown in Fig. 1. That is, $H_1 = \sigma(W_0 \cdot H_0 + b_0)$, $H_2 = \sigma(W_1 \cdot H_1 + b_1)$, and $H_3 = \sigma(W_2 \cdot H_2 + b_2)$. Finally, H_3 is further passed to a softmax layer to obtain a initial mention-entity linking probability p_i between mention m and entity e_i.

Given a training set $\mathcal{T} = \{t_i = \{(m_i, c_i, E_i, e_{i_j}) | e_{i_j} \in E_i\}, i = 1, 2, ..., |\mathcal{T}|\}$, for each training sample t_i, m_i is the mention, c_i is the context of m_i, E_i

is the entity candidate set for m_i, and e_{i_j} is the target entity. So the vector $y_i = [y_{i_1}, y_{i_2}, ..., y_{i_{|E_i|}}]$ can be represented the linking information for the entity candidate set for mention m_i, where $y_{i_j} = 1$ and $y_{i_k} = 0$ for $k \neq j$.

Finally, the embeddings are learned by minimizing the cross-entropy cost function: $J(\theta) = -\sum_{t_i \in T} \sum_{j=1}^{|E_i|} y_{i_j} \log p_{i_j} + \lambda ||\theta||$, where θ are all parameters needed in the type-guided semantic embedding network. Here, we use RMSprop to optimize the parameters θ by using TensorFlow.

2.2   Collective Entity Linking

Since all mentions in the same sentence or paragraph are encouraged to resolve to entities that are related to each other, so we integrate the type-guided semantic embedding into the collective entity linking framework for the better linking performance.

We first construct a mention-entity graph $\mathcal{G} = \langle \mathcal{V}, \mathcal{E} \rangle$, where $\mathcal{V}$ is a set of nodes and $\mathcal{E}$ is a set of edges. $\mathcal{V}$ includes three types of nodes: mentions $M = \{m_1, m_2, ..., m_N\}$, their candidate entities $E = \{E_1, E_2, ..., E_N\}$ and some unambiguous entities $E' = \{e'_1, e'_2, ..., e'_{|E'|}\}$. Taking Fig. 4 as an example, there are two mentions m_1 and m_2, and each of them has several candidate entities. For instance, m_1 has its candidate entities e_{1_1} and e_{1_2}, and m_2 has its candidate entities e_{2_1} and e_{2_2}. In addition, there are two unambiguous entities e'_1 and e'_2.

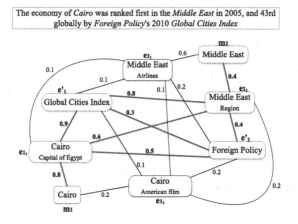

Fig. 4. Collective entity linking

There are two types of weighted edges in $\mathcal{G}$: entity-entity edge and mention-entity edge. Let W be the weight matrix of the graph $\mathcal{G}$. Then the weight of edge between mention m_i and its candidate entity e_{i_j} is computed as $W_{ij} = p_{i_j}$, which is calculated through the type-guided semantic embedding network. In order to compute the weight of an entity-entity edge, we learn the *Paragraph Vector* [16] for each entity from its content of the corresponding wikipedia article, and then compute the weight of edge between two entities e_i and e_j as $W_{ij} = \cos(v_{e_i}, v_{e_j})$, where v_{e_i} is the paragraph vector for entity e_i. The weight matrix W could be normalized for each row.

After the construction of the mention-entity graph, we utilize Random Walk with Restart [24] to calculate the score of each candidate entity $e_{i_j} \in E_i$ for mention m_i. Then, mention m_i could be linked to the entity with the highest score.

Formally, we initialize a $|\mathcal{V}|$-dimensional vector s by $s[i] = 1/|M|$ when $\mathcal{V}_i$ is a mention node. Then the formula $r = (1 - \lambda) \cdot W \cdot r + \lambda \cdot s$ is computed iteratively until convergence, where $r \in R^{|\mathcal{V}| \times 1}$ and can be initialized as s. Here, $r[i_j]$ can be considered as the score of its corresponding entity e_{i_j}. Finally, the entity linked to mention m_i should be $e(m_i) = \arg\max_{e_{i_j} \in E_i} r[i_j]$.

3 Experiments

3.1 Experimental Settings

Since our approach is language independent, we conduct the experiments on both Chinese corpora and English corpora.

For Chinese corpora, we collected articles in Baidu Baike[1], which is a large-scale collaborative Chinese encyclopedias like Wikipedia, and built a Chinese knowledge base (CKB) like DBPedia. Each entity in the CKB has its properties, categories, description and so on. Similarly, we used Wikipedia as the knowledge base for entity linking on English corpora.

For the English corpora, we evaluated our approach over a wide range of different data sets, such as TAC-KBP, AIDA/CoNLL-Complete, DBpediaSpotlight, N3-Reuters-128, and N3-RSS-500.

In order to train the type-guided semantic embedding network, a large training set should be provided, so we created the training set automatically based on the inner-links in each article. Specifically, we assume that the inner-links in Wikipedia and Baidu Baike are all correct at first, therefore an sample (m_i, c_i, E_i, e_{i_j}) can be added to the training set if and only if (i) the anchor text of the inner-link is m_i, and it links to an entity e_{i_j}. (ii) more than two entities can be found according to the surface form or the synonyms of m_i, then these entities can be served as the entity candidate set E_i. The testing set for Chinese corpora is also generated similarly. Both the training set and testing set are generated randomly. Finally, we generated 743,978 samples for training and 55,716 samples for testing on Chinese corpora.

In the evaluation, we computed both micro (aggregates over all mentions) and macro (aggregates over all documents) precision scores for the entity linking.

3.2 Results on Chinese Corpora

When evaluating our approach on Chinese corpora, we set $W_x = 400$, $W_t = 148$, $S = 40$ in the semantic embedding and $\lambda = 0.5$ in the collective entity linking framework through cross validation.

---

[1] http://baike.baidu.com/.

In addition to baseline *PriorProb* which links to surface forms to the entities with the highest prior probability, we also compared our approach with some state-of-the-art entity disambiguation approaches such as DSRM [13] and LIEL [22]. In *PriorProb+CEL*, we assigned the weight of the edge between entity and mention with the prior probability during collective entity linking. The experimental results are shown in Table 1.

Table 1. Results on Chinese corpora

Method	Micro Prec.	Marco Prec.
PriorProb	0.6983	0.6844
LIEL	0.7063	0.7189
DSRM	0.7434	0.7296
PriorProb+CEL	0.7191	0.7123
Our approach	**0.8107**	**0.8211**

From the table, we can see that our approach can obtain the best performance. Besides, in order to prove the effectiveness of the type-guided semantic embedding, we replaced the prior popularity $p(e_i|m)$ with our learned similarity score $s(v_m, v_{e_i})$ in DSRM, and improved DSRM by 3.42 and 5.25 % points on micro and macro precisions.

3.3   Results on English Corpora

In order to compare our approach with other entity disambiguation frameworks on publicly available data sets on English corpora, we used GERBIL (General Entity Annotation Benchmark Framework)[2] to evaluate the approaches on the D2KB task, whose goal is to map a set of given entities mentions to entities from a given knowledge base or to NIL. GERBIL is an evaluation framework for semantic entity annotation, and has provided several annotators (i.e. Babelfy [18] and DBPedia Spotlight [17]) and datasets (i.e. DBpediaSpotlight, N3-Reuters-128, N3-RSS-500).

The first step of EL is to generate the possible entity candidates for each mention m. We resorted to the Wikipedia search engine to retrieve all related entities as the candidates. However, the target entities are NIL in some cases in the TAC-KBP datasets, but we can still find the target entity for the mention according to the search results. For example, in a document fragment from TAC-KBP 2009 dataset: *"two years later when the Canton Bulldogs beat the Chicago Cardinals"*. The mention *"Canton Bulldogs"* is linked to NIL according to the dataset, but the Wikipedia entry for *"Canton Bulldogs"* (American football team) is available at present which is created in 2015. The reason is

---

[2] http://aksw.org/Projects/GERBIL.html.

that some Wikipedia pages are created after the dataset construction, so our approach would return wrong entity according to the ground truth. Thus, we removed those cases from the TAC-KBP datasets, and only retained English cases. Finally, we formed two types of datasets for each TAC-KBP dataset from 2009 to 2013:

1. TAC-KBP(sub): the target entity is among the candidates, whose size is at least 2.
2. TAC-KBP(full): TAC-KBP(sub) + the cases with its' target may be NIL.

We carried out the experiments with the TAC-KBP (2009–2013) datasets on the GERBIL framework, and the results are shown in Table 2.

From the table, we find that our approach significantly outperforms the other approaches on the TAC-KBP datasets except TAC-KBP 2012. The main reason

Table 2. Results on TAC-KBP datasets

Annotator	micro F1	macro F1	micro F1	macro F1
	TAC-KBP 2009(sub)		TAC-KBP 2009(full)	
WAT	0.717	0.681	0.5849	0.5134
DBPedia Spotlight	0.6063	0.5878	0.5449	0.4906
AIDA	0.5644	0.4552	0.531	0.4318
Babelfy	0.5606	0.5556	0.4919	0.4078
Kea	0.4782	0.3728	0.3416	0.236
FREME_NER	0.445	0.3262	0.3148	0.3148
Our approach	**0.8467**	**0.8315**	**0.7061**	**0.6985**
	TAC-KBP 2010(sub)		TAC-KBP 2010(full)	
WAT	0.745	0.7333	0.5624	0.449
DBPedia Spotlight	0.588	0.5765	0.5007	0.4034
AIDA	0.5501	0.5059	0.4166	0.4166
Babelfy	0.6267	0.6157	0.5332	0.4382
Kea	0.5726	0.549	0.4868	0.3866
FREME_NER	0.4835	0.3451	0.3476	0.2437
Our approach	**0.8634**	**0.8549**	**0.7948**	**0.7743**
	TAC-KBP 2011(sub)		TAC-KBP 2011(full)	
WAT	0.6998	0.6777	0.4635	0.4
DBPedia Spotlight	0.6542	0.6379	0.4633	0.3727
AIDA	0.4335	0.3953	0.3406	0.2739
Babelfy	0.5896	0.5847	0.4228	0.325
Kea	0.4179	0.3887	0.3179	0.2693
FREME_NER	0.358	0.2492	0.317	0.317
Our approach	**0.7483**	**0.7309**	**0.6632**	**0.6568**

(*continued*)

Table 2. (*continued*)

	TAC-KBP 2012(sub)		TAC-KBP 2012(full)	
WAT	0.3382	0.3257	0.2955	0.2469
DBPedia Spotlight	**0.513**	**0.5038**	**0.5239**	**0.5051**
AIDA	0.2692	0.2545	0.245	0.1773
Babelfy	0.4849	0.4707	0.3193	0.2884
Kea	0.2721	0.2697	0.2803	0.2738
FREME_NER	0.1845	0.1272	0.1181	0.0797
Our approach	0.3732	0.369	0.3043	0.284
	TAC-KBP 2013(sub)		TAC-KBP 2013(full)	
WAT	0.6598	0.6531	0.5784	0.461
DBPedia Spotlight	0.6875	0.6735	0.5794	0.5032
AIDA	0.6108	0.5204	0.5286	0.4269
Babelfy	0.7158	0.6939	0.6249	0.5341
Kea	0.6108	0.5204	0.5286	0.4269
FREME_NER	0.2923	0.1939	0.2739	0.1769
Our approach	**0.7755**	**0.7755**	**0.7126**	**0.6964**

for the degradation in TAC-KBP 2012 is: many mentions in TAC-KBP 2012 refer to locations and places, such as *Bristol, Porto* and *Lyon*. However, the corresponding candidate entities for these mentions all have the same type (eg. *Location* and *Place*), which makes our approach unsuitable a little.

We also carried out the experiments on the GERBIL framework with its provided annotators and datasets, including AIDA [11], Babelfy [18], FREME NER[3], Kea [26], WAT [19], DBPedia Spotlight [17], Dexter [1], euNER [4], xLisa [28], and NERD-ML [25]. The results are shown in Table 3.

Overall, our approach reaches the best averaged F1 of all approaches. In detail, our approach significantly outperforms all other approaches on the N3-Reuters-128 and N3-RSS-500 data sets, but performs comparatively poor on the AIDA/CoNLL-Complete and DBpediaSpotlight data sets. There are two reasons for the performance degradation. Firstly, As in TAC-KBP 2012 dataset, many mentions in AIDA/CoNLL-Complete and DBpediaSpotlight also refer to the candidate entities with the same type (eg. Location, Place and Person). Secondly, the datasets contain some structured data such as tables and lists in Web pages, which can reduce the performance of BiLSTM for mention embedding, since they are not in sequence, and then further reduce the performance of our approach.

---

[3] https://github.com/freme-project/freme-ner.

Table 3. The comparison of macro-averaged F1 for different approaches through GERBIL

Annotator	AIDA/CoNLL-Complete	DBpediaSpotlight	N3-Reuters-128	N3-RSS-500	Average
WAT	**0.6708**	0.6778	0.4286	0.364	0.5353
DBPedia Spotlight	0.4897	0.6863	0.265	0.161	0.4005
AIDA	0.4942	0.1648	0.317	0.374	0.3375
Babelfy	0.5993	0.5115	0.3877	0.381	0.4699
Kea	0.5834	0.7247	0.4502	0.389	0.5368
FREME_NER	0.5901	**0.8202**	0.4709	0.379	0.5651
Dexter	0.4704	0.2506	0.3037	0.293	0.3294
euNER	0.4735	0.1938	0.3394	0.32	0.3317
xLisa	0.3616	0.5724	0.2879	0.368	0.3975
NERD-ML	0.1164	0.5282	0.3418	0.3013	0.3219
Our approach	0.61	0.6131	**0.5538**	**0.621**	**0.5995**

4 Related Work

Entity linking is beneficial to annotate text by linking mentions appearing in text with their corresponding entities in the knowledge bases, so it has been widely studied in the last decade, and there is a comprehensive survey [20] for entity linking recently.

Traditional approaches [3,8] addressed the entity linking problem by comparing the similarity between context information of a mention and the corresponding candidate entities in KB. Nowadays, several approaches have been proposed to improve the performance of EL, such as collective entity linking approaches [5,7,10–13,30], entity relatedness learning [2,13,21], and neural network approaches [9,23,27].

Collective entity linking approaches assume that entities occurred in the same document would have a high global coherence. [7] proposed a graph-based collective entity linking method, which can jointly infer the referent entities of all mentions in document by exploiting both the global interdependence between different EL decisions and the local mention-to-entity compatibility. [10] proposed a stacking based collective entity linking method, which stacks a global predictor on top of a local predictor to collect coherence information from neighboring decisions. [12] proposed a semi-supervised graph regularization model for entity linking in tweets by incorporating both local and global evidences from multiple tweets. [5] proposed a coherence model with an attention mechanism, where the score for each candidate only depends on a small subset of mentions, since an entity may only have relations to a small subset of other entities.

In addition, entity relatedness learning, which learns the semantic similarity between entities for coherence modeling, can also boost collective entity linking approaches. For example, [21] measured the semantic similarity between Wikipedia concepts based on the taxonomy of the knowledge base. [2] discovered suitable entity relatedness functions that can better support the entity linking task. [13] presented a semantic relatedness model (DSRM) based on deep neural networks (DNN) and semantic knowledge graphs (KGs) to measure entity semantic relatedness. [30] also measured the relatedness between entities based on semantic embeddings that capture entity and document contexts.

More recently, neural networks are widely used to address the EL task. For example, [9] proposed a deep learning approach with stacked denoising auto-encoders and supervised fine-tuning to learn context-entity similarity measure for entity disambiguation. [23] encoded mention, context and entity with a tensor neural networks for entity linking. [27] proposed a joint learning method to map words and entities into the same continuous vector space for entity linking.

5   Conclusion

In this paper, we propose a type-guided semantic embedding approach to boost collective entity linking. We used the Bidirectional Long Short-Term Memory (BiLSTM) to model the context of a mention, and dynamic convolutional neural network (DCNN) to model the type of an entity. Then, we built a graph with the semantic relatedness of mentions and entities for the collective entity linking. Finally, we evaluated our approach by comparing the state-of-the-art entity linking approaches over a wide range of very different data sets, such as TAC-KBP from 2009 to 2013, AIDA, DBPediaSpotlight, N3-Reuters-128, and N3-RSS-500. Besides, we also evaluated our approach with a Chinese Corpora. The experiments reveal that the modeling for entity type can be very beneficial to the entity linking.

Acknowledgements. This work is supported by the Zhejiang Provincial Natural Science Foundation of China (No. LY17F020015), the Chinese Knowledge Center of Engineering Science and Technology (CKCEST), and the Fundamental Research Funds for the Central Universities (No. 2017FZA5016).

References

1. Ceccarelli, D., Lucchese, C., Orlando, S., Perego, R., Trani, S.: Dexter: an open source framework for entity linking. In: Proceedings of the Sixth International Workshop on Exploiting Semantic Annotations in Information Retrieval, ESAIR 2013, pp. 17–20. ACM, New York (2013). http://doi.acm.org/10.1145/2513204.2513212
2. Ceccarelli, D., Lucchese, C., Orlando, S., Perego, R., Trani, S.: Learning relatedness measures for entity linking. In: Proceedings of the 22nd ACM International Conference on Information & Knowledge Management, pp. 139–148. ACM (2013)
3. Cucerzan, S.: Large-scale named entity disambiguation based on Wikipedia data. In: EMNLP-CoNLL (2007)
4. Dojchinovski, M., Kliegr, T.: Entityclassifier.eu: real-time classification of entities in text with Wikipedia. In: Blockeel, H., Kersting, K., Nijssen, S., Železný, F. (eds.) ECML PKDD 2013. LNCS (LNAI), vol. 8190, pp. 654–658. Springer, Heidelberg (2013). https://doi.org/10.1007/978-3-642-40994-3_48

5. Globerson, A., Lazic, N., Chakrabarti, S., Subramanya, A., Ringaard, M., Pereira, F.: Collective entity resolution with multi-focal attention. In: ACL (2016)
6. Han, X., Sun, L.: A generative entity-mention model for linking entities with knowledge base. In: ACL (2011)
7. Han, X., Sun, L., Zhao, J.: Collective entity linking in web text: a graph-based method. In: Proceedings of the 34th International ACM SIGIR Conference on Research and Development in Information Retrieval, SIGIR 2011, pp. 765–774. ACM, New York (2011). http://doi.acm.org/10.1145/2009916.2010019
8. Han, X., Zhao, J.: NLPR_KBP in TAC 2009 KBP track: a two-stage method to entity linking. In: TAC (2009)
9. He, Z., Liu, S., Li, M., Zhou, M., Zhang, L., Wang, H.: Learning entity representation for entity disambiguation. In: ACL (2013)
10. He, Z., Liu, S., Song, Y., Li, M., Zhou, M., Wang, H.: Efficient collective entity linking with stacking. In: EMNLP, pp. 426–435 (2013)
11. Hoffart, J., Yosef, M.A., Bordino, I., Fürstenau, H., Pinkal, M., Spaniol, M., Taneva, B., Thater, S., Weikum, G.: Robust disambiguation of named entities in text. In: Proceedings of the Conference on Empirical Methods in Natural Language Processing, pp. 782–792. Association for Computational Linguistics (2011)
12. Huang, H., Cao, Y., Huang, X., Ji, H., Lin, C.Y.: Collective tweet wikification based on semi-supervised graph regularization. In: ACL (2014)
13. Huang, H., Heck, L., Ji, H.: Leveraging deep neural networks and knowledge graphs for entity disambiguation. CoRR abs/1504.07678 (2015)
14. Kalchbrenner, N., Grefenstette, E., Blunsom, P.: A convolutional neural network for modelling sentences. arXiv preprint arXiv:1404.2188 (2014)
15. Lazic, N., Subramanya, A., Ringgaard, M., Pereira, F.: Plato: a selective context model for entity resolution. TACL **3**, 503–515 (2015)
16. Le, Q.V., Mikolov, T.: Distributed representations of sentences and documents. In: ICML, vol. 14, pp. 1188–1196 (2014)
17. Mendes, P.N., Jakob, M., García-silva, A., Bizer, C.: DBpedia spotlight: shedding light on the web of documents. In: Proceedings of the 7th International Conference on Semantic Systems (I-Semantics) (2011)
18. Moro, A., Raganato, A., Navigli, R.: Entity linking meets word sense disambiguation: a unified approach. Trans. Assoc. Comput. Linguist. **2**, 231–244 (2014)
19. Piccinno, F., Ferragina, P.: From TagME to WAT: a new entity annotator. In: Proceedings of the First International Workshop on Entity Recognition & Disambiguation, pp. 55–62. ACM (2014)
20. Shen, W., Wang, J., Han, J.: Entity linking with a knowledge base: issues, techniques, and solutions. IEEE Trans. Knowl. Data Eng. **27**, 443–460 (2015)
21. Shen, W., Wang, J., Luo, P., Wang, M.: LINDEN: linking named entities with knowledge base via semantic knowledge. In: WWW (2012)
22. Sil, A., Florian, R.: One for all: towards language independent named entity linking. In: ACL (2016)
23. Sun, Y., Lin, L., Tang, D., Yang, N., Ji, Z., Wang, X.: Modeling mention, context and entity with neural networks for entity disambiguation. In: Proceedings of the International Joint Conference on Artificial Intelligence (IJCAI), pp. 1333–1339 (2015)
24. Tong, H., Faloutsos, C., Pan, J.Y.: Random walk with restart: fast solutions and applications. Knowl. Inf. Syst. **14**, 327–346 (2008)
25. Van Erp, M., Rizzo, G., Troncy, R.: Learning with the web: Spotting named entities on the intersection of NERD and machine learning. In: # MSM, pp. 27–30 (2013)

26. Waitelonis, J., Sack, H.: Named Entity Linking in# Tweets with KEA (2016)
27. Yamada, I., Shindo, H., Takeda, H., Takefuji, Y.: Joint learning of the embedding of words and entities for named entity disambiguation. In: CoNLL (2016)
28. Zhang, L., Rettinger, A.: X-LiSA: cross-lingual semantic annotation. Proc. VLDB Endow. **7**(13), 1693–1696 (2014). https://doi.org/10.14778/2733004.2733063
29. Zheng, Z., Li, F., Huang, M., Zhu, X.: Learning to link entities with knowledge base. In: HLT-NAACL (2010)
30. Zwicklbauer, S., Seifert, C., Granitzer, M.: Robust and collective entity disambiguation through semantic embeddings. In: SIGIR (2016)

Biomedical Domain-Oriented Word Embeddings via Small Background Texts for Biomedical Text Mining Tasks

Lishuang Li[(⊠)], Jia Wan, and Degen Huang

School of Computer Science and Technology, Dalian University of Technology, Dalian, China
lilishuang314@163.com

Abstract. Most word embedding methods are proposed with general purpose which take a word as a basic unit and learn embeddings by words' external contexts. However, in the field of biomedical text mining, there are many biomedical entities and syntactic chunks which can enrich the semantic meaning of word embeddings. Furthermore, large scale background texts for training word embeddings are not available in some scenarios. Therefore, we propose a novel biomedical domain-specific word embeddings model based on maximum-margin (BEMM) to train word embeddings using small set of background texts, which incorporates biomedical domain information. Experimental results show that our word embeddings overall outperform other general-purpose word embeddings on some biomedical text mining tasks.

Keywords: Word embeddings · Biomedical domain-oriented word embeddings
Small background texts

1 Introduction

One of the most important tasks of the bioinformatics is to help biologists extract the useful data from the biomedical literature published in geometric progression. The current mainstream methods for Biomedical Information Extraction (BIE) have fully utilized word embeddings [1, 2], which are usually used as extra features or inputs. Recent years have witnessed the success of word embeddings, which have been widely used in many common NLP tasks and biomedical text mining tasks, including language modeling [3], word sense disambiguation [4], semantic composition [5], entity recognition [6], syntactic parsing [7, 8], biomedical named entity recognition [9] and biomedical event extraction [10]. Word embeddings have demonstrated the ability of well representing linguistic and semantic information of a text unit [11–13] and high quality embeddings can improve the performance of models. However, the word embeddings which these methods used are designed with general purpose. Experimental evidence showed that domain irrelevant word embeddings trained on large collections of texts were not good enough for biomedical domain Natural Language processing (NLP) [14]. Biomedical-oriented word embeddings can outperform general-purposed ones, and further improve the performance of biomedical NLP

© Springer International Publishing AG 2018
X. Huang et al. (Eds.): NLPCC 2017, LNAI 10619, pp. 554–564, 2018.
https://doi.org/10.1007/978-3-319-73618-1_46

systems. Therefore, we consider several kinds of domain-specific functional units in biomedical text, such as widely existed biomedical entities, which are incorporated in our model.

Word embeddings in previous works were often trained on large scale unlabeled texts. For example, Pennington et al. used Wikipedia, Giga word 5 and Common Crawl to learn word embeddings, each of which contained billions of tokens [15]. However, there is not always a monotonic increase in performance as the amount of background texts increase. In addition, background texts in some biomedical domain are still comparatively scarce resource such as electronic medical records, which makes it difficult to obtain large scale background texts. Thus the existing word embeddings models cannot give play to its advantages and a biomedical domain-specific word embeddings training model using small background texts is motivated. Inspired by the advantages of Support Vector Machine (SVM) in solving the small data set, we utilize maximum-margin theory and Li et al.'s method [16] to train word embeddings, which can efficiently learn high quality vector representation of words from small set of unlabeled texts.

According to the analysis above, we propose a novel biomedical domain-oriented word embeddings method based on maximum-margin, named as BEMM, which utilizes small background texts and integrates biomedical domain information. Firstly, we consider biomedical text as a sequence of words, syntactic chunks, part-of-speech (POS) tags and biomedical entities, and present a new model for the learning of word, chunk, POS and entity embeddings. Secondly, we take the advantages of SVM in solving the small data set and propose the hierarchical maximum-margin to train word embeddings on the small background texts.

The goal of the proposed word embeddings method is to improve the performance of biomedical information extraction systems such as event extraction. We compare our BEMM and the other model architectures using two different systems for biomedical text mining, i.e., the LSTM based Bacteria Biotope event extraction and Passive-aggressive (PA) [17] Online Algorithm based Biomedical Event Extraction. The experimental results show that our model has many advantages and outperforms other models on these tasks.

2 Related Work

Biomedical text mining tasks are important for the biologists. Potential information can be extracted from biomedical literatures. Utilizing the information in biomedical research contributes to the understanding of the disease mechanism and development of disease diagnosis. Word embeddings have been used in the field of the biomedical text mining tasks. Mehryary et al. [18] used a combination of several Long Short-Term Memory (LSTM) networks over syntactic dependency graphs for biomedical event extraction, which also added embeddings to enrich the input information. Li et al. [19] utilized a hybrid method that combined both a rule-based method and a machine learning-based method to extract biomedical semantic relations from texts, which used word embeddings as features.

Representation of words as continuous vectors has a long history [20, 21]. There are two ways to learn the word embeddings.

Matrix factorization methods for generating low-dimensional word representations have roots stretching as far back as LSA. These methods utilize low-rank approximations to decompose large matrices that capture statistical information about a corpus. The latest efficient word representation model based on matrix factorization is GloVe, by which Pennington et al. [15] leveraged statistical information by training only on the nonzero elements in a word-word co-occurrence matrix, rather than on the entire sparse matrix or on individual context windows in a large corpus.

Another approach is to learn word representations that aid in making predictions within local context windows. Neural network structure as a popular model architecture has also played an important role in learning useful word embeddings. For example, Bengio et al. [3] proposed neural network language model (NNLM), where a feed-forward neural network with a linear projection layer and a non-linear hidden layer was used to learn the word vector representation and a statistical language model. Recently, Mikolov et al. [11] proposed two efficient models, continuous bag-of-words model (CBOW) and skip-gram model, to learn word embeddings from large-scale text corpora. The training objective of CBOW is to combine the embeddings of context words to predict the target word, while skip-gram is to use the embedding of each target word to predict its context words. These two architectures both greatly reduce the computational complexity. In this work, we directly extend these architectures, and focus on the training of word embeddings suitable for the field of biomedical words.

3   Method

In this section, we explore a biomedical domain-specific word embeddings model based on maximum-margin to train word embeddings using small set of background texts, which incorporates domain information such as biomedical entities. Figure 1 shows the overall framework of our method, which consists of two components, extracting functional units (Sect. 3.1) and training of embeddings based on maximum-margin integrating functional units (Sect. 3.2). In the following sections we will illustrate our method in detail.

3.1   Extracting Functional Units

In the stage of extracting functional units, our main work is to obtain the background texts and process it. Firstly, we download abstract texts from the PubMed to get the background texts. Then the texts are split into sentences, and we tokenize the sentence into atomic units. Finally, we use GENIA Dependency parser (GDep) [22] to extract functional units containing biomedical information. GDep is often used to parse the sentences in the biomedical domain, so we utilize it to process our background texts. The functional units we extract include stem, chunk, entity and POS tags, which are described in detail below. Our model contains biomedical domain information compared to the skip-gram model only using the information of the words itself. And we take the input sentence "contains pathogenic bacteria in red blood cells" as an example.

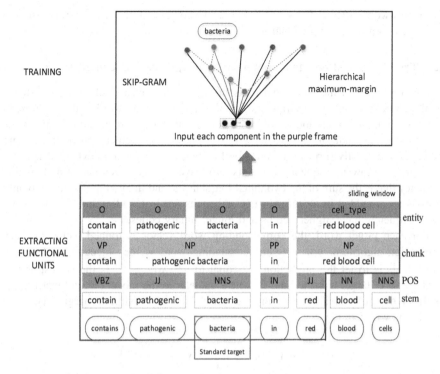

Fig. 1. The overall framework of our method. (Color figure online)

Stem. Although we all know that "contains" is the third person singular form of "contain", the machines do not realize it. Instead, the machines regard "contain" and "contains" as two totally different tokens. Considering the stem can solve the problem.

POS tags. POS reflects the role of words in a sentence, which is important for the analysis of a sentence structure. So we use the POS to train embeddings to gain more information.

Chunk. Only considering words and stems may be not enough, because in this case the model trains "pathogenic" using "bacteria", ignoring the truth that "pathogenic" is the modifiers of "bacteria". However, "pathogenic bacteria" should be considered as a whole. Therefore, in our method, we consider syntactic chunks as a parallel layer of word sequences.

Entity. While the chunk helps understanding the meaning of words, biomedical entities can improve the word embeddings from another perspective. Entity layer provides fine-grained understanding of biomedical text.

After getting all functional units from the texts, we utilize sliding window to obtain the context information of the target word, including the words and functional units, by which the target word would be trained. Many neural embeddings use a sliding window of size k around the target word w, so $2k$ contexts are produced: the k words before

w and the k words after w. For $k = 2$ in Fig. 1, the contexts of the target word w are w_{-2}, w_{-1}, w_{+1}, w_{+2} and their functional units.

3.2   Training Based on Maximum-Margin Integrating Functional Units

As Fig. 1 shows, all the functional units in the purple box, including words, stems, chunks, POS and entities, are trained using the standard target word in the red box. In order to minimize the computational complexity, our model architecture removes the hidden layer. In addition, the training model uses a hierarchical maximum-margin strategy, which firstly sorts all the units by frequency of words in the vocabulary, then makes the two lowest frequency elements into leaves and creates a parent node with a frequency that is the sum of the two units' frequencies, and finally repeats this step until all units are included in a Huffman tree. All units are leaf nodes, and the units with lower frequency have higher depths and longer binary codes.

For each target word, the corresponding word vector is trained using the back propagation algorithm. For a given surrounding word y, the objective of the word embeddings is to let the prediction $\hat{y}^{(i)}$ equal to $y^{(i)}$, where $x^{(i)}$ is the corresponding word vector of target word w_i, and θ is the parameter of the model (weight matrix). t is the label of each category. We introduce the idea of maximum-margin. The cost function is with Eq. (1).

$$J(\theta) = \max\left(0, 1 + \max_{t \neq y^{(i)}} \theta_t^T x^{(i)} - \theta_{y^{(i)}}^T x^{(i)}\right). \tag{1}$$

On each iteration if the Eq. (2) is satisfied:

$$1 + \max_{t \neq y^{(i)}} \theta_t^T x^{(i)} - \theta_{y^{(i)}}^T x^{(i)} > 0, \tag{2}$$

We perform with Eq. (3) where α is the learning rate:

$$\theta_t := \theta_t - \alpha x^{(i)}, \tag{3}$$

and Eq. (4):

$$\theta_{y^{(i)}} := \theta_{y^{(i)}} + \alpha x^{(i)}, \tag{4}$$

and Eq. (5):

$$x^{(i)} := x^{(i)} - \alpha\left(\theta_t - \theta_{y^{(i)}}\right). \tag{5}$$

3.3   Complexity of the Model

Our proposed model architecture is similar to the skip-gram model. We use each target word as an input to a log-linear classifier with continuous projection layer, and predict functional units within a certain window before and after the target word. In our model architecture, the non-linear hidden layer is removed and a log-linear classifier is built. For the model, the training complexity is proportional to the Eq. (6):

$$O = E \times T \times Q, \tag{6}$$

where E is the number of the training epochs and T is the number of the words in the background texts. Q can be represented as the Eq. (7):

$$Q = C \times (D + D \times \log_2 V), \tag{7}$$

where C is the functional units before and after the target words, D is the dimension of the input layer and V is size of the vocabulary.

4 Experiments

The objective of this study is to train word embeddings which represent biomedical semantic regularities and further improve the performance of BIE systems. To evaluate the performance of the word embeddings, we download background documents from PubMed to train word embeddings, and then apply them into two different BIE systems, respectively for Bacteria Biotope (BB) event extraction [1] and Biomedical Event Extraction (BEE). To make a careful comparison between the widely used other model architectures and our model, we design two different experiments. One is that both models utilize the same small background texts to train word embeddings for BB event extraction. The other is that the other model architectures employ the large scale background texts and our model applies the small scale background texts for BEE.

Note that (1) the two biomedical text mining tasks are only used for evaluating the word embeddings, so we just explain the tasks briefly in the following sections, and (2) since the two systems are not the main focus of this paper, we only introduce the general schemes of them, and (3) we train word embeddings using skip-gram and our BEMM with same parameters, e.g., same size of sliding window 5, same starting learning rate 0.025, and same word vector dimension 50, and (4) we aim to obtain state-of-the-art word embeddings, not biomedical text mining systems, therefore, we focus on the comparison of word embeddings rather than biomedical systems.

4.1 Bacteria Biotope Event Extraction

The purpose of the BB task is to study the interaction mechanisms of the bacteria with their environment from genetic, phylogenetic and ecology perspectives. The BB event extraction task has been put forward in the BioNLP-ST[1].

The BB event extraction can be treated as a classification problem. We use LSTM with a top layer of softmax to classify each BB instance and word embeddings are used as inputs in the LSTM model. In this paper, we evaluate six word embeddings models

---

[1] http://2016.bionlp-st.org/tasks/bb2.

respectively on different scale corpora leveraging BB event extraction task. These six models are presented below: the skip-gram model and the cbow model in the Word2Vec tool; the model of glove; the model based on functional units not using maximum-margin theory, named as BE; the model based on maximum-margin theory not using functional units, named as MM; the model integrating functional units and maximum-margin theory, i.e. BEMM.

The corpora are the abstracts downloaded from PubMed, which use "bacteria" as the key word. The sizes of the corpora after the GDep parser are 50M, 100M, 150M, and 200M. We use a window size of 5 and the threshold for sub-sampling is set to 0; the initial learning rate is set to 0.025; and we keep all words that occur in the background text. We train word embeddings with 50 dimensions and also try different dimensions such as 100 dimensions, 200 dimensions and 400 dimensions whose F-score is 56.89%, 56.25% and 56.77% respectively. So we only show the result of 50 dimensions.

The results are shown in Fig. 2. We could observe when we use the small background texts to train word embeddings, our BEMM, BE models significantly outperform other models. The rationality is analyzed as follows: (1) The word embeddings trained by BE contain more domain information, so the LSTM can learn more from the inputs when the word embeddings are used as inputs. (2) Maximum-margin theory has a relatively good performance in the small background texts, which has been verified on the SVM. Therefore, the word embeddings trained by MM could perform well. (3) The model BEMM combining functional units and the maximum-margin has gained both strengths. It can not only get more semantic information, but also be able to be competent in small background texts.

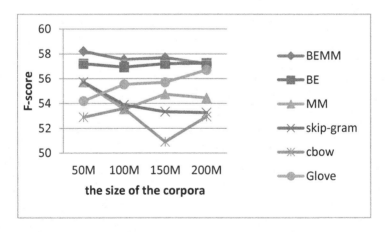

Fig. 2. The results of six models for the BB event task.

We also compare the performance between the system using BEMM and the currently first-rate system [23] for the BB event task. The results are shown in Table 1.

Both methods apply LSTM to conduct the BB event task using word embeddings. From the Table 1, we can see that the F-score of system using BEMM is 1.07

Table 1. Comparison with existing system

Methods	F-score	Recall	Precision
System using BEMM	**58.21%**	**66.96%**	51.47%
Li's method	57.14%	57.99%	**56.32%**

percentage points higher than the currently best system, which proves that our BEMM has a positive effect on the results.

4.2 Biomedical Event Extraction

To further evaluate the generalization ability of our model, we have also experimented with another BIE task, namely biomedical event extraction. Biomedical event extraction focuses on the detailed behavior of bio-molecules, which refers to the state change of one or more biomedical entities and includes expression, transcription, etc. Our experiments are conducted on the commonly used dataset MLEE [24].

We compare two word embeddings based on the same PA model. One is the word embeddings trained by our model BEMM on small background texts, and the other is the word embeddings trained by the skip-gram model on large background texts. Parameter settings are described below.

- *Word Embeddings on Small Background Texts.* The background texts are abstracts downloaded from PubMed with different key word "protein". The dimensions of word embeddings are set to 400; the size of the background text after the GDep parser is 50M. And the rest parameters are set the same as the previous experiment.
- *Word Embeddings on Large Background Texts.* The way we train word embeddings is as follows: First, abstract texts are downloaded from the public database, PubMed, with the size of about 5.6G. Then, all abstracts are split into sentences and tokenized into tokens. Finally, all tokenized sentences are sent into the skip-gram model. The parameters, window sizes and dimensions, are set 7 and 400 respectively.

Li et al.'s [25] have demonstrated the effectiveness of the word embeddings of 400 dimensions on BEE task. Therefore, we use the embeddings of 400 dimensions. To verify the effect of word embeddings on the performance of the task, we set all the parameters to the same in the PA model except for the word embeddings and the results are shown in Table 2.

From Table 2, we can observe that the F-score of our method is 2.83 percentage points higher than the other, because our model makes full use of the biomedical semantic information, although it only uses small scale background texts. The experimental results prove that our approach is effective on small background texts.

Table 2. Comparison between BEMM and the skip-gram for BEE task.

Word embeddings	F-score	Recall	Precision
BEMM	**79.37%**	**78.01%**	**80.77%**
Skip-gram	76.54%	73.29%	80.09%

5   Discussion

From the above experimental results, we can conclude that our model outperforms well on the biomedical text mining tasks and mainly includes the following important advantages:

Integrating Functional Units. We do not just use the word itself to obtain the word embeddings, but also fully exploit linguistic and biomedical functional units such as entities, which are integrated into word embeddings. Therefore, our model can achieve the vector representation of each word and functional units, and we apply these word embeddings with rich semantic information to the biomedical text mining tasks, so that the model can learn more and the results are more accurate.

Utilizing Maximum-margin Theory. The maximum-margin theory can well handle small training samples. Therefore, the maximum-margin classification is used to train our model in order to solve the problem of insufficient corpus, which makes the word embeddings trained by small corpus still has a good performance. In our framework, at the output layer, we use the hierarchical structure which is implemented by the Huffman tree. Then, we take advantage of the maximum-margin classification to make predictions in each branch of the tree.

Temperate Computational Complexity. Our framework structure is similar to the skip-gram model, so our model also has a low computational complexity. Under the same corpus and the number of the iterations, the computational complexity of our model and the skip-gram model are of an order of magnitude. Overall, the computational complexity of our model is moderate.

6   Conclusion

This paper proposes a novel biomedical domain-oriented word embeddings model using small background texts which integrates the biomedical semantic information. There are three major contributions of this work:

Firstly, we incorporate functional units including stem, POS tags, chunk and entities into the word embeddings to enrich semantic expression.

Secondly, we utilize the maximum-margin theory to deal with the problem of insufficient background texts.

Thirdly, the experimental results show that our word embeddings are effective on BIE applications.

In the future works, we plan to consider more biomedical domain knowledge to train better word embeddings for biomedical text mining applications, for example, deep syntactic information, external knowledge bases such as Gene Ontology, Drug Bank, etc.

Acknowledgment. The authors gratefully acknowledge the financial support provided by the National Natural Science Foundation of China under No. 61672126.

References

1. Deléger, L., Bossy, R., Chaix, E., Ba, M., Ferré, A., Bessières, P.: Overview of the bacteria biotope task at BioNLP shared task 2016. In: Bionlp Shared Task Workshop - Association for Computational Linguistics, pp. 12–22 (2016)
2. Chaix, E., Dubreucq, B., Fatihi, A., Valsamou, D., Bossy, R., Ba, M.: Overview of the regulatory network of plant seed development (SeeDev) task at the BioNLP shared task 2016. In: Bionlp Shared Task Workshop - Association for Computational Linguistics, pp. 1–11 (2017)
3. Bengio, Y., Vincent, P., Janvin, C.: A neural probabilistic language model. J. Mach. Learn. Res. 3(6), 1137–1155 (2003)
4. Chen, X., Liu, Z., Sun, M.: A unified model for word sense representation and disambiguation. In: Conference on Empirical Methods in Natural Language Processing, pp. 1025–1035 (2014)
5. Zhao, Y., Liu, Z., Sun, M.: Phrase type sensitive tensor indexing model for semantic composition. In: Twenty-Ninth AAAI Conference on Artificial Intelligence, pp. 2195–2201 (2015)
6. Collobert, R., Weston, J., Karlen, M., Kavukcuoglu, K., Kuksa, P.: Natural language processing (almost) from scratch. J. Mach. Learn. Res. 12(1), 2493–2537 (2011)
7. Socher, R., Lin, C.Y., Ng, A.Y., Manning, C.D.: Parsing natural scenes and natural language with recursive neural networks. In: International Conference on Machine Learning, ICML 2011, pp. 129–136 (2011)
8. Socher, R., Bauer, J., Manning, C.D., Ng, A.Y.: Parsing with compositional vector grammars. In: Meeting of the Association for Computational Linguistics, pp. 455–465 (2013)
9. Tang, B., Cao, H., Wang, X., Chen, Q., Xu, H.: Evaluating word representation features in biomedical named entity recognition tasks. Biomed. Res. Int. 2014(2), 1–6 (2014)
10. Li, C., Rao, Z., Zhang, X.: LitWay, discriminative extraction for different bio-events. In: Bionlp Shared Task Workshop, pp. 32–41 (2016)
11. Mikolov, T., Chen, K., Corrado, G., Dean, J.: Efficient estimation of word representations in vector space. arXiv preprint arXiv:1301.3781 (2013a)
12. Mikolov, T., Yih, W.T., Zweig, G.: Linguistic regularities in continuous space word representations. In: Proceedings of the Conference of the North American Chapter of the Association for Computational Linguistics: Human Language Technologies, pp. 746–751 (2013)
13. Tang, D., Wei, F., Yang, N., Zhou, M., Liu, T., Qin, B.: Learning sentiment-specific word embedding for twitter sentiment classification. In: Meeting of the Association for Computational Linguistics, pp. 1555–1565 (2014)
14. Jiang, Z., Li, L., Huang, D., Jin, L.: Training word embeddings for deep learning in biomedical text mining tasks. In: IEEE International Conference on Bioinformatics and Biomedicine, pp. 625–628 (2015)
15. Pennington, J., Socher, R., Manning, C.: Glove: global vectors for word representation. In: Conference on Empirical Methods in Natural Language Processing, pp. 1532–1543 (2014)
16. Li, L., Jiang, Z., Liu, Y., Huang, D.: Word representation on small background texts. In: Li, Y., Xiang, G., Lin, H., Wang, M. (eds.) SMP 2016. CCIS, vol. 669, pp. 143–150. Springer, Singapore (2016). https://doi.org/10.1007/978-981-10-2993-6_12
17. Crammer, K., Dekel, O., Keshet, J., Shalev-Shwartz, S., Singer, Y.: Online passive-aggressive algorithms. J. Mach. Learn. Res. 7(3), 551–585 (2006)

18. Mehryary, F., Björne, J., Pyysalo, S., Salakoski, T., Ginter, F.: Deep learning with minimal training data: TurkuNLP entry in the BioNLP shared task 2016. In: Bionlp Shared Task Workshop, pp. 73–81 (2016)

19. Li, L., Qin, M., Huang, D.: Biomedical event trigger detection based on hybrid methods integrating word embeddings. In: Chen, H., Ji, H., Sun, L., Wang, H., Qian, T., Ruan, T. (eds.) CCKS 2016. CCIS, vol. 650, pp. 67–79. Springer, Singapore (2016). https://doi.org/10.1007/978-981-10-3168-7_7

20. Hinton, G.E., McClelland, J., Rumelhart, D.E.: Distributed representations. Parallel Distrib. Process.: Explor. Microstruct. Cogn. 1, 77–109 (1986)

21. Rumelhart, D.E., Hinton, G.E., Williams, R.J.: Learning representations by back-propagating errors. Parallel Distrib. Process.: Explor. Microstruct. Cogn. 323(6088), 533–536 (1986)

22. Sagae, K., Tsujii, J.I.: Dependency parsing and domain adaptation with LR models and parser ensembles. In: Proceedings of the CoNLL Shared Task Session of EMNLP-CoNLL 2007, pp. 1044–1050 (2007)

23. Li, L., Zheng, J., Wan, J., Huang, D., Lin, X.: Biomedical event extraction via long short term memory networks along dynamic extended tree. In: IEEE International Conference on Bioinformatics and Biomedicine, pp. 739–742 (2016)

24. Pyysalo, S., Ohta, T., Miwa, M., Cho, H.C., Tsujii, J., Ananiadou, S.: Event extraction across multiple levels of biological organization. Bioinformatics 28(18), 575–581 (2012)

25. Li, L., Liu, S., Qin, M., Wang, Y., Huang, D.: Extracting biomedical event with dual decomposition integrating word embeddings. Trans. Comput. Biol. Bioinform. 13, 669–677 (2015)

Homographic Puns Recognition Based on Latent Semantic Structures

Yufeng Diao[1,2], Liang Yang[1], Dongyu Zhang[1], Linhong Xu[3],
Xiaochao Fan[1], Di Wu[1], and Hongfei Lin[1(✉)]

[1] Dalian University of Technology, Dalian 116024, People's Republic of China
hflin@dlut.edu.cn
[2] Inner Mongolia University for Nationalities,
Tongliao 028043, People's Republic of China
[3] Dalian University of Foreign Languages,
Dalian 116044, People's Republic of China

Abstract. Homographic puns have a long history in human writing, being a common source of humor in jokes and other comedic works. It remains a difficult challenge to construct computational models to discover the latent semantic structures behind homographic puns so as to recognize puns. In this work, we design several latent semantic structures of homographic puns based on relevant theory and design sets of effective features of each structure, and then we apply an effective computational approach to identify homographic puns. Results on the SemEval2017 Task7 and Pun of the Day datasets indicate that our proposed latent semantic structures and features have sufficient effectiveness to distinguish between homographic pun and non-homographic pun texts. We believe that our novel findings will facilitate and stimulate the booming field of computational pun research in the future.

Keywords: Homographic · Puns · Latent semantic structures

1 Introduction

A pun is a form of wordplay in which one signifier suggests two or more meanings by exploiting polysemy, or phonological similarity to another signifier, for an intended humorous or rhetorical effect. Meantime, puns are a common source of humor in jokes and other comedic works. In literature, speeches and slogans, puns are also standard rhetorical ploys, where they can also be used non-humorously. For example, Sumerian cuneiform and Egyptian hieroglyphs were originally based on punning systems [1], and Shakespeare is famous for his puns [2] even in his non-comedic works. As we known, both humorous and non-humorous puns offer an interesting subject for extensive study, which leads to insights into the nature of wordplay and double-meaning.

The task of pun classification is significant in NLP and a number of relevant studies have focused on this. Such as Redfern divides puns into homophonic puns and homographic puns, which uses homonyms and the polysemy of the word respectively [3]. Delabastita [4] also classifies puns into four types: homonyny, homophony,

X. Huang et al. (Eds.): NLPCC 2017, LNAI 10619, pp. 565–576, 2018.
https://doi.org/10.1007/978-3-319-73618-1_47

honography, and paronyny. Most work is referenced with the classification system of Redfern, our work is also based on their analysis.

Homographic puns and homophonic puns have their own characteristics. One is to solve the problem about synonyms and the other is to solve the problem about homonyms. It cannot use the same model to distinguish the two types of puns. In our research, we mainly focus on homographic puns because they are most commonly used and easily accessible in existing text corpora. However, the homographic puns of the current works are not systematically deduced and interpreted from the features dimension.

To tackle the problem, we propose a computational semantic model to recognize homographic puns according to the related theory. This work is not the first to deal with puns recognition, but it is the first of its kind to recognize homographic puns with the four latent semantic structures on theory motivated feature design and analysis. Our contributions are listed in the following.

- The paper systematically derives the latent semantic structures behind homographic puns from puns theories, covering the four structures to affect factors.
- The paper identities sets of optimized and induced characteristics of each structure that distinguish homographic puns from non-homographic puns.
- Results on the datasets of SemEval Task7 and Pun of the Day show that our method is effective to recognize homographic puns.

2   Related Work

Puns have been discussed in rhetorical and literary criticism since ancient times, and in recent years have increasingly become a respectable research topic. Therefore, it is surprising that they have attracted little attention in the fields of computational linguistics and natural language processing [5]. In this section, we mainly review some previous work that is relevant to ours.

Some researchers studying puns tend to have a phonological or syntactic puns rather than semantic puns. Kao et al. [6] proposed a computational model of linguistic humor in Puns, which enable powerful explanatory measures from the dimensions of ambiguity and distinctiveness. Jaech et al. [7] considered that puns create humor through the relationship between a pun and its phonologically similar target. All of these are analyzed as phonological puns from ambiguity and so on.

Recently, Miller and Gurevych [8] proposed methods for homographic puns to identify the double meanings from word sense disambiguation. Huang et al. [9] introduced a novel framework which considered positions as the important indicators for homographic pun location identification. However, the homographic puns in most of those works are not systematically deduced and interpreted from the features dimension.

Compared with puns recognition, puns generation has received quite a lot attention in the past decades [10, 11]. Hempelmann [10] created a theory to model the factors to imperfect punning and outline the implementation of this measure for the evaluation of possible puns. Hong and Ong [11] presented T-PEG, a system that utilized phonetic and semantic linguistic resources to automatically extract word relationships in puns automatically and store the knowledge in template form.

The application of puns in humor is also one of the focuses of this study. Taylor and Mazlack [12] proposed an N-gram approach based on the fixed syntactic context for identifying when puns are utilized for humorous effect in English jokes. Similar work can also be found in Taylor [13], which described humor recognition relying on Ontological Semantics by transforming content. Yang et al. [14] treated humor detection as a classification task, which identifies several semantic structures and applies a useful approach to recognizing humor.

It is an important research question with several real-world applications. For example, puns are particularly common in the advertising, where used not only to create humor but also to induce in the audience a valenced attitude toward the target [15, 16]. It has often been argued that humor can enhance human-computer interaction [17] and appending the canned humor into a user interface can increase user satisfaction [18]. Puns are often used in a second language classroom. Mormot et al. [19] thought puns are useful teaching tools to improve the level of English for students. Although puns are often used in many discourse types, the applications cannot deal with them very well because of the ambiguity.

3 Features of Latent Structures Behind Puns

In this section, we formulate homographic puns as a traditional classification problem. We propose the latent structures behind homographic puns in four aspects to compute and detect homographic puns: (a) Inconsistency; (b) Ambiguity; (c) Emotion and (d) Linguistic. For each latent structure, there is a list of features to capture the latent accessible indicators of homographic pun recognizing.

3.1 Inconsistency Structure

In Wales' point of view [20], the starting point of puns is that the speaker tries to use different meanings to produce something. According to philosopher Grice [21], he found that people in actual verbal communication do not always strictly abide by this principle and sometimes violates it either naturally or half unconsciously. So that this inconsistency is an important cause of the phenomenon of puns. A pun arises from the view of two or more incongruous and inapposite circumstances, considered as united in a complex object or assemblage.

For example, "Money doesn't grow on trees. But it blossoms at our branches." The following "Money doesn't grow on trees" and "blossoms at our branches" example presents an inconsistency structure, which analyzed the effect of a pun.

We design two types of features, Separation and Repetition, to measure the semantic distance between word pairs in a sentence. The inconsistency of the pun can be seen as semantic incoherence, analyzed by semantic distance differences in puns, which can be calculated by Word Embedding and N-gram Language Model.

Word Embedding represents semantic information in lower dimensional dense space. The paper used Word2Vec[1] for Word Embedding. Meantime, training Language Model (LM) is a way to collect rules by utilizing the fact that words do not appear in an arbitrary order. We used the KenLM Toolkit [22] to train the N-gram LMs built from the external corpus, newswire sections of Brown corpus [23].

- Separation/Repetition: we compute the maximum/minimum semantic distance of word pairs in a sentence. This way we gain the Separation/Repetition feature by utilizing Word2Vec to compute the cosine similarity. The formula is as follows.

$$\text{similarity}(A, B) = \frac{A \cdot B}{\|A\|_2 \cdot \|B\|_2} \tag{1}$$

- Semantic Coherence: we compute the score to measure the semantic coherence in a sentence by utilizing LM according to KenLM Toolkit.

3.2   Ambiguity Structure

Ambiguity means that a word may have multiple meanings [24], which represents the presence of incongruous sentence meanings is a critical component of many puns [8]. The pun is a clever intention to let one word relate to two aspects. For ambiguity of puns, the main reason is that the word has the meaning of the surface but is forced to produce another deeper and obscurer meaning structures because of the constraints of the pun context as shown in the example below. "Before he sold Christmas trees, he got himself spruced up." In this sentence, we find that the word spruced not only has the meaning of the spruce tree but also has the meaning of making yourself or something look neater and tidier.

The multiple possible meanings of words supply people with different comprehensions. We apply the lexical resource WordNet[2] to obtain the ambiguity of the sentence. Firstly, we use an NLTK POS tagger to distinguish noun, verb, adjective, and adverb which mainly representing the ambiguity of the pun [5]. We calculate the semantic dispersion of a word combined with POS information as

$$\text{PSD} = \frac{1}{P(|S_{pos}|, 2)} \sum_{s_i, s_j \in S_{pos}} d(S_i, S_j) \tag{2}$$

where S_{pos} is the specific POS set of synsets (s_0, ..., s_n) for a word which POS information is the same in a sentence; $P(|S_{pos}|, 2)$ means the collection of two words from the synonym each time, and $d(s_i, s_j)$ is the length of the hypernym path between synsets (s_i, s_j) by WordNet. Then sum the semantic dispersion of the words in a sentence and divide by the sentence length. The features are as follows.

---

[1] https://code.google.com/p/word2vec/.

[2] http://www.nltk.org/howto/wordnet.html.

- Sense Farmost/Average/Closest: we also use an NLTK POS tagger to identify noun, verb, adjective, and adverb words. Then, we compute the largest/average/smallest Path Similarity of any of the above word senses according to the corresponding POS in a sentence [25].

3.3   Emotion Structure

Puns can produce euphemistic, subtle, and humorous effects. For example, Van Mulken [26] found that a pun in an advertisement is a way of humor so that the utterances can give listeners a pleasant experience. The friendly feeling may increase the audience's positive feelings and recognition of the advertised product. It is a fact that a pun is essentially associated with sentiment and subjectivity. For instance, a sentence is to be identified as a pun if it contains some words with a strong sentiment, such as "charged" as follows.

"The two guys caught drinking battery acid will soon be charged."

Each word relating with positive or negative sentiments is the emotional reflection of the writer. To identify the word-level sentiment and affect, we utilize the open resource SenticNet [27], which provides annotations and rich effective information with measuring the subjectivity and sentiment of words. This resource enables us to design features of two types: polarity and sentics.

- Polarity: we compute sum of polarity scores, average of polarity scores, total absolute polarity scores, and average absolute polarity scores for all the words.
- Sentics: we respectively calculate the total score, average score, total absolute score, and average absolute score of all the words for the above four dimensions.

3.4   Linguistics Structure

Because our target texts are very short consisting of one or two sentences, we adopt the word-level syntax such as POS tagger, location, sentence length, and semantic information. For each aspect, we design useful features to capture the latent semantic information.

POS Feature. Each pun contains exactly one single content word (noun, verb, adjective, adverb) behind the sentence [5], which we named the candidate pun words. For example, "Boyle said he was under too much pressure." Here, the pun word is "pressure" which is a noun. According to this, we use the POS tagger of NLTK to analyze the text. They also affect the semantic match information which we will introduce as below. POS features are as follows.

- Candidate pun word numbers: we compute the candidate pun word numbers of noun, verb, adjective, and adverb.
- Ratios of POS words: we compute the ratios of noun, verb, adjective, and adverb in a sentence.

Position Feature. In accordance with Miller and Turković [5], most puns are located towards the end of the context. Therefore, the position of the candidate pun words can affect the judgment of Puns. For example, "Here is how the track meet is going to run." The word "run" is the pun word whose location is at the end of the sentence. The features are as below.

- Position largest/smallest/average: we compute the largest/smallest/average position of the candidate pun words in a sentence.

Sentence Length. Barbieri and Saggion [28] proposed that the structural information is useful to measure the difference between instances. Sentences with different lengths will have a certain influence on whether or not they are puns.

- Sentence length: we calculate the length of any sentence.
- Sentence difference: we calculate the length difference from the previous sentence and average word length.

Semantic Information. We utilize the WordNet to analyze the ambiguity of the puns in Sect. 4.2. In addition, we also capture the matching relationship and antonymy relationship between words in a sentence.

First, we consider the matching relation between noun and noun, verb and verb, adjective and adjective, adverb and adverb. Because the candidate pun words are from them, they have a latent semantic relation with the same type words. The semantic similarity can be computed by WordNet. For example, "I used to be a banker but I lost interest." The word "interest" is pun word. This word has two meanings: benefit and savor. Here "interest" is the meaning of benefit. We could compute the semantic similarity between (used, lost) and (banker, interest).

Then, we also measure the antonyms relation among the candidate pun words. The antonyms of the word "fall" are "ascent," "rise," "ascend," and "increase" according to WordNet. The detailed features are shown as follows.

- Largest similarity: we compute largest Path Similarity by matching relation between noun and noun, verb and verb, adjective and adjective, adverb and adverb.
- Antonym existence: we compute the existence of antonyms among the candidate pun words in a sentence.
- Antonyms largest/average: we compute the largest/average antonyms number of the candidate pun words in a sentence.

4 Experiments

We consider homographic puns recognition as a traditional text classification problem. In this section, we verify the performance of the disparate latent semantic structures we extracted on homographic puns recognition.

4.1   Experimental Setting

In this section, we first analyze the datasets used in our experiments, then introduce the evaluation metrics and baseline methods, and finally present the details of the training process of our proposed model.

Datasets. To validate the effectiveness of the proposed model, we conduct experiments on two datasets: SemEval Task7[3] and Pun of the Day[4].

SemEval-2017 Task7 Data. This task is to detect and interpret English puns, containing homographic and heterographic puns. As our research interests are in lexical semantics rather than phonology, we focus on homographic puns, which are those described by Mill and Turković [5]. It contains punning and non-punning texts. Each text contains a maximum of one pun. Table 1 provides a detailed statistical description to our datasets.

Table 1. Statistics on SemEval Task7 and pun of the day datasets

Dataset	#Positive	#Negative	Average length	Average length of positive puns	Average length of negative puns
Task7	1607	643	13.1	13.9	10.8
Pun of the day	2423	2403	13.5	12.2	13.8

Pun of the Day. The Pun of the Day dataset only includes pun text. To obtain negative samples for the pun classification task, this dataset collected the negative samples from four resources, namely AP News[5], New York Times, Yahoo! Answer[6], and Proverb. Table 1 provides a detailed statistical description to our datasets.

Metrics. The standard precision, recall, accuracy, and F1 measures which is utilized in Semeval2017 task7 evaluation is adopted as the metrics.

Baselines. We compare the following baseline methods.

- Bag of Words (**BOW**): The BOW is used to capture a series of words in a sentence which should distinguish pun and non-pun of homographic puns.
- Language Model (**LM**): The LM allocates a pun/non-pun probability based on a statistical method to the words of a sentence through probability distributions. It does not need a classifier to train the corpus.
- AVGWord2Vec: It presents the average word embedding of a sentence according to the distributional latent semantic meaning representation [29].

---

[3] SemEval2017 Task7: http://alt.qcri.org/semeval2017/task7/.

[4] Pun of the Day: http://www.punoftheday.com/.

[5] http://hosted.ap.org/dynamic/fronts/HOME?SITE=AP.

[6] https://answers.yahoo.com/.

- HPCF: Here, we denote the combination of the four latent structures as Homographic Puns Core Features (**HPCF**).
- AVGWord2Vec_ HPCF: Here, we combine HPCF with AVGWord2Vec which having a well performance of this task.

Training Details. The paper conducts 5 fold cross-validation experiments, each using 60% of the samples for training a detecting model, 20% for estimating the parameters, and 20% for predicting new samples. The training corpus of word embedding is from Wiki. The dimension of word embeddings is 300.

We choose Gradient Boosted Decision Tree (GBDT), a powerful boosting method based on decision trees as our classification algorithm. This is consistent with Zhang and Liu's [30].

4.2   Homographic Puns Recognition

We investigate how the combination of the latent semantic structures performs compared with our suggested baselines and the results are presented in Table 2.

Table 2. Comparison of different methods of homographic puns recognition

	SemEval2017 task7				Pun of the day			
	Accuracy	Recall	Precision	F1	Accuracy	Recall	Precision	F1
HPCF	0.796	0.938	0.808	0.861	0.730	0.807	0.702	0.767
Bag of Words (BOW)	0.768	0.847	0.832	0.806	0.709	0.663	0.732	0.685
Language Model (LM)	0.588	0.774	0.688	0.668	0.510	0.764	0.508	0.612
AVGWord2Vec	0.716	0.800	0.803	0.756	0.901	0.899	0.903	0.900
BOW_HPCF	0.802	**0.954**	0.805	0.871	0.907	0.905	0.908	0.906
AVGWord2Vec_HPCF	**0.836**	0.944	**0.845**	**0.887**	**0.914**	**0.906**	**0.920**	**0.910**

First, HPCF contains Inconsistency, Ambiguity, Emotion, and Linguistic structures has a better performance for homographic puns recognition compared with BOW and LM. This proves that the latent semantic structure derived from the theory has enough rationality. The inappropriate LM also demonstrates, which we relieve the specific domain differences and capture the real puns. The inadequacy of BOW also indicates that we can understand the order in which words appear in the original sentence.

Second, BOW_HPCF, which is the combination of BOW and HPCF, is superior to BOW and HPCF in the two datasets. The reason is that it contains sufficient latent semantics information and the order of words in a sentence. But BOW_HPCF is inferior to AVGWord2Vec_HPCF. Because it involves enough latent structures such as Ambiguity structure but not enough distributional semantics.

Last, AVGWord2Vec_HPCF, which achieved 0.91 F-score, has the best classification performance in Pun of the Day. The reason is that this combination takes into consideration the latent semantic structures and semantic word meanings. In SemEval2017 task7, this conclusion is almost coincident besides that BOW_HPCF has the best recall. From the results, it finally indicates that our proposed latent semantic structures are efficient in interpreting homographic puns in depth.

The best performing system in the Semeval2017 Task7 is Fermi [31]. It also casts this problem as a supervised learning classification problem. This model uses a recurrent neural network to train the classifier. The result achieves 0.899 by F1-score. So in the future, we will try deep learning methods to settle this problem.

4.3 The Effect of Latent Semantic Structures

We examine the performance of above different structures by the same classifier GBDT on two datasets. To ensure fairness, we do not adjust any parameters here. We explore that how the different latent semantic structures affect homographic puns recognition performance and display the results in Fig. 1. We have the following observations:

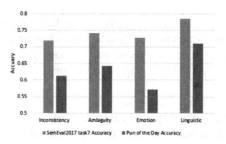

Fig. 1. Different latent structures' contribution to homographic puns recognition

First, according to the results, we can see that all the latent structures in the two datasets have a consistent performance. It is obvious that Linguistic structure performs the best among all the latent semantic structures in the two datasets. The reason is that puns are closely related to the location, part of speech, and collocation of ambiguous words.

Second, the performance of Ambiguity structure in the two datasets ranks second, which showed most puns are well structured and handled with multiple meanings or aspects. It is evident Emotion Structure performs the worst in Pun of the Day because the emotion of homographic puns is harder to mine and analyze.

Last, different from the Pun of the Day dataset, the worst performance of the structures in the SemEval task7 is the Inconsistency structure. The reason is the contrasting or incongruous meaning of the Inconsistency structure which played is puzzled to find abundant and useful information. This demonstrates that homographic puns latent structures are not expressed similarly in different datasets.

Then, it also examines the relevance among the four latent structures and conduct ablation experiments to examine the recognition. Each time, we remove one or two structures and observe how the performance changes. It summarizes the results in Table 3 and have the following observations.

Table 3. The relevance of latent structures to effect homographic puns recognition.

	SemEval2017 task7				Pun of the day			
	Accuracy	Recall	Precision	F1	Accuracy	Recall	Precision	F1
All	**0.796**	**0.938**	**0.808**	**0.861**	**0.730**	**0.807**	**0.702**	**0.767**
All-Inconsistency	0.783	0.928	0.800	0.849	0.718	0.791	0.692	0.753
All-Ambiguity	0.771	0.924	0.790	0.841	0.713	0.783	0.689	0.746
All-Emotion	0.789	0.934	0.803	0.855	0.730	0.803	0.702	0.765
All-Linguistic	0.759	0.931	0.776	0.836	0.659	0.733	0.641	0.694
Emotion+Linguistic	0.770	0.923	0.790	0.840	0.704	0.783	0.679	0.741
Ambiguity+Linguistic	0.780	0.929	0.797	0.848	0.725	0.809	0.697	0.765
Ambiguity+Emotion	0.751	0.927	0.770	0.830	0.656	0.729	0.638	0.691
Inconsistency+Linguistic	0.785	0.921	0.806	0.848	0.723	0.784	0.700	0.752
Inconsistency+Emotion	0.738	0.909	0.767	0.815	0.610	0.682	0.598	0.644
Inconsistency+Ambiguity	0.756	0.914	0.781	0.828	0.667	0.739	0.647	0.701

First, all the latent structures used together outperforms the other combinations in the two datasets. It demonstrates that the mutual interaction and influence of the whole latent structures can more effectively recognize the homographic puns. It also proves that our structures based on the homographic pun theory, which systematically derived and explained, are valid.

Second, for three structures working together to effect the recognition, All–Emotion (contains Inconsistency, Ambiguity, and Linguistic structure) performs the best in the two datasets, which means that Emotion offers little effective information to help the detection of puns, and meanwhile Emotion could be related loosely with other structures. In contrast with All–Emotion, the performance of All–Linguistic (contains Inconsistency, Ambiguity, and Emotion structure) in the two datasets performs worst. It is consistent with the above part that Linguistic knowledge is very important to identify puns and could be effectively matched with other latent structures.

Last, we validate how well two structures effect the detection of homographic puns between the latent structures. The results demonstrate that different collocation structures are represented differently in various contexts. In the SemEval2017 task7, Ambiguity + Linguistic and Inconsistency + Linguistic have the best performance meanwhile. That means Linguistic is related with Inconsistency or Ambiguity more than Emotion. In the Pun of the Day, Ambiguity + Linguistic also has the strongest performance and Inconsistency + Linguistic comes second. As shown in Table 3, the rest of the distributions of puns recognition are generally consistent. In the two datasets, Inconsistency + Emotion has the worst performance, so we conjecture that Inconsistency and Emotion put together may hurt the performance.

5   Conclusion and Future Work

In this work, we focus on understanding homographic pun language through homographic puns recognition. For this purpose, we presented a computational and effective approach to identify puns. We proposed four latent semantic structures behind the homographic puns based on relevant theory. In view of the designed sets of effective features related with each structure, we established different computational classifiers considering the association among the four structures to identify puns. The experimental results conducted on the two datasets show that our proposed latent semantic structures have sufficient effectiveness. The performances on homographic puns recognition are superior compared with several baselines.

As future work, we would like to find the characteristics of homographic and homophonic puns, employ the deep learning methods to recognize the puns, and then apply our discoveries to the procedure of automatic generation of puns. Those are all promising jobs we can pursue in the future.

Acknowledgments. This work is partially supported by grant from the Natural Science Foundation of China (No. 61632011, 61702080, 61602079), the Fundamental Research Funds for the Central Universities (No. DUT16ZD216, DUT17RC(3)016).

References

1. Pollack, J.: The Pun Also Rises. Penguin Publishing Group (2011)
2. Tanaka, K.: The pun in advertising: a pragmatic approach. Lingua **87**(1), 91–102 (1992)
3. Redfern, W.: Puns. Scriblerian Kit-Cats **19**(2), 204 (1987)
4. Delabastita, D.: Focus on the pun: wordlplay as a special problem in translation studies. Target **6**(2), 223–243 (1994)
5. Miller, T., Turković, M.: Towards the automatic detection and identification of English puns. Eur. J. Humour Res. **4**(1), 59–75 (2016)
6. Kao, J.T., Levy, R., Goodman, N.D.: A computational model of linguistic humor in puns. Cogn. Sci. **40**(5), 1270–1285 (2015)
7. Jaech, A., Koncel-Kedziorski, R., Ostendorf, M.: Phonological pun-derstanding. In: Proceedings of NAACL-HLT, pp. 654–663 (2016)
8. Miller, T., Gurevych, I.: Automatic disambiguation of English puns. In: ACL, vol. 1, pp. 719–729 (2015)
9. Huang, Y.H., Huang, H.H., Chen, H.H.: Identification of homographic pun location for pun understanding. In: Proceedings of the 26th International Conference on World Wide Web Companion. International World Wide Web Conferences Steering Committee, pp. 797–798 (2017)
10. Hempelmann, C.F.: Paronomasic puns: target recoverability towards automatic generation. Diss. Abs. Int. **64**(11), 4029 (2003)
11. Hong, B.A., Ong, E.: Automatically extracting word relationships as templates for pun generation. In: The Workshop on Computational Approaches to Linguistic Creativity. Association for Computational Linguistics, pp. 24–31 (2010)
12. Taylor, J.M., Mazlack, L.J.: Computationally recognizing wordplay in jokes. In: Proceedings of the 26th Annual Conference of the Cognitive Science Society (CogSci 2004), pp. 1315–1320 (2004)
13. Taylor, J.M.: Computational detection of humor: a dream or a nightmare? The ontological semantics approach. In: Proceedings of the 2009 ACM International Joint Conference on Web Intelligence and Intelligent Agent Technology, vol. 3, pp. 429–432 (2009)
14. Yang, D., Lavie, A., Dyer, C., et al.: Humor recognition and humor anchor extraction. In: EMNLP, pp. 2367–2376 (2015)

15. Valitutti, A., Strapparava, C., Stock, O.: Textual affect sensing for computational advertising. In: Proceedings of the AAAI Spring Symposium on Creative Intelligent Systems, pp. 117–122, March 2008
16. Monnot, M.: Puns in advertising: ambiguity as verbal aggression. Maledicta **6**, 7–20 (1982)
17. Hempelmann, C.F.: Computational humor: beyond the pun? In: Raskin, V. (ed.) The Primer of Humor Research. Humor Research, vol. 8, pp. 333–360. Mouton de Gruyter, Berlin (2008)
18. Morkes, J., Kernal, H.K., Nass, C.: Effects of humor in task-oriented human–computer interaction and computer-mediated communication: a direct test of SRCT theory. Hum.-Comput. Interact. **14**(4), 395–435 (1999)
19. Mormot, M., Adelstein, A., Bulusu, L.: Immigrant mortality in England and Wales 1970–1978. Popul. Trends **20**
20. Lems, K.: Laughing all the way: teaching English using puns. In: English Teaching Forum. US Department of State. Bureau of Educational and Cultural Affairs, Office of English Language Programs, SA-5, 2200 C Street NW 4th Floor, Washington, DC 20037, vol. 51, no. 1, pp. 26–33 (2013)
21. Wales, K.: A Dictionary of Stylistics. Routledge, Abingdon (2014)
22. Heafield, K., Pouzyrevsky, I., Clark, J.H., Koehn, P.: Scalable modified Kneser-Ney language model estimation. In: Proceedings of the 51st Annual Meeting of the Association for Computational Linguistics, Sofia, Bulgaria, pp. 690–696 (2013)
23. Kucera, H., Francis, W.N.: Computational Analysis of Present-Day American English. Brown University Press, Providence (1967)
24. Bekinschtein, T.A., Davis, M.H., Rodd, J.M., et al.: Why clowns taste funny: the relationship between humor and semantic ambiguity. J. Neurosci. **31**(26), 9665–9671 (2011)
25. Reyes, A., Rosso, P., Buscaldi, D.: From humor recognition to irony detection: the figurative language of social media. Data Knowl. Eng. **74**, 1–12 (2012)
26. Van Mulken, M., Van Enschot-van, D.R., Hoeken, H.: Puns, relevance and appreciation in advertisements. J. Pragmat. **37**(5), 707–721 (2005)
27. Cambria, E., Hussain, A.: Sentic Computing: Techniques, Tools, and Applications. Springer Science & Business Media, Dordrecht (2012). https://doi.org/10.1007/978-94-007-5070-8
28. Barbieri, F., Saggion, H.: Modelling irony in Twitter: feature analysis and evaluation. In: LREC, pp. 4258–4264 (2014)
29. Mikolov, T., Sutskever, I., Chen, K., et al.: Distributed representations of words and phrases and their compositionality. In: Advances in Neural Information Processing Systems, pp. 3111–3119 (2013)
30. Zhang, R., Liu, N.: Recognizing humor on Twitter. In: ACM International Conference on Conference on Information and Knowledge Management, pp. 889–898. ACM (2014)
31. Miller, T., Hempelmann, C.F., Gurevych, I.: SemEval-2017 task 7: detection and interpretation of English puns. In: Proceedings of the 11th International Workshop on Semantic Evaluation (SemEval-2017), Vancouver, BC (2017)

Short Papers

Constructing a Chinese Conversation Corpus for Sentiment Analysis

Yujun Zhou[1,2,3], Changliang Li[1(✉)], Bo Xu[1], Jiaming Xu[1], Lei Yang[1,2,3], and Bo Xu[1]

[1] Institute of Automation, Chinese Academy of Sciences,
Beijing, People's Republic of China
{zhouyujun2014,changliang.li,boxu,jiaming.xu,
yanglei2014,xubo}@ia.ac.cn
[2] University of Chinese Academy of Sciences,
Beijing, People's Republic of China
[3] Jiangsu Jinling Science and Technology Group Co., Ltd.,
Nanjing, People's Republic of China

Abstract. Sentiment analysis plays an important role in many applications. This paper introduces our ongoing work related to the sentiment analysis on Chinese conversation. The main purpose is to construct a Chinese conversation corpus for sentiment analysis and provide a benchmark result on this corpus. To explore the effectiveness of machine learning based approaches for sentiment analysis on Chinese conversation, we firstly collected conversational data from some online English learning websites and our instant messages, and manually annotated it with three sentiment polarities and 22 fine-grained emotion classes. Then we applied multiple representative classification methods to evaluate the corpus. The evaluation results provide good suggestions for the future research. And we will release the corpus with gold standards publicly for research purposes.

Keywords: Chinese conversation · Short text · Sentiment analysis
Machine learning · Deep neural networks

1 Introduction

The rapid development of information technology and the explosive growth of social media produce massive conversation texts. There have a variety of sources, such as Instant Message (IM, e.g. WeChat) and Social Networking Site (SNS, e.g. Weibo). By above tools, communication between people become more conveniently and efficiently. Through communication, people can express their views, attitudes and emotions about some items or events, which play a critical role in many applications. For example, chat conversations from SNS can be used for cyber-crime investigation [1]. However, with the huge amount of information available online, collecting and analyzing these conversation texts is a challenging task. Therefore, machines have to be applied to help people to collect and

© Springer International Publishing AG 2018
X. Huang et al. (Eds.): NLPCC 2017, LNAI 10619, pp. 579–590, 2018.
https://doi.org/10.1007/978-3-319-73618-1_48

process data. Sentiment analysis or opinion mining is such an approach, which has been popular over the years.

Sentiment analysis not only can detect opinion text, but also can analyze its polarity (i.e. positive, negative and neutral) and intensity (i.e. weak, medium, strong and extreme), and identify the associated source or opinion holder, topic, target entity or aspect of the opinion [2]. Many works have been done on sentiment analysis, which can be summarized as two types of approaches, i.e. sentiment knowledge-based approach and machine learning based approach [3]. The machine learning based approach is usually a supervised method that can be transformed to be a text classification problem, which builds classifier from a dataset with manually annotated sentiment classes. The traditional machine learning approaches heavily count on hand-crafted features, including lexical, syntactic and semantic features. However, it is time consuming and becomes more harder with the massive growth of the amount of data. Fortunately, inspired by the successful applications of deep neural networks (DNNs) in computer vision, image analysis and speech recognition, many researchers have started to conduct sentiment analysis with neural networks and achieved competitive results compared with traditional models recently [4-7].

For sentiment analysis based on machine learning, the corpus is fundamental to the training of the emotional classifier because it contains much emotion information in the form of words, phrases, sentences, paragraphs and documents. In Chinese sentiment analysis, the researchers have developed a few datasets. For example, Quan and Ren [8] constructed a blog corpus containing 1,487 documents with the manual annotation of eight emotion classes, and annotated emotion in text at three levels, i.e. document, paragraph and sentence. Li et al. [9] crawled 2,270 movie reviews from social websites and created a Chinese sentiment treebank with labeled parse trees. Zhao et al. [2] firstly collected online customer reviews from several famous Chinese forum sites, then created a fine-grained corpus for Chinese sentiment analysis including polarity, target entity and aspect etc. Additionally, the 8th SIGHAN Workshop on Chinese Language Processing (SIGHAN-8) provided a dataset for the task of topic-based Chinese message polarity classification [10]. After studying the sources of many Chinese sentiment datasets in the literatures, Peng et al. [11] concluded that majority of their domains were reviews and blogs in hotels, products and movies. To our best knowledge, there have many Chinese sentiment datasets without the consideration of sentiment classification for the whole conversation.

A conversation is a sequence of many utterances (i.e. sentences), which usually comprises two utterances at least. In general, not all sentences in a conversation express the sentiment category of the whole conversation. Without considering the speakers, a conversation is similar to a long document that is a sequence of many sentences. Consequently, one of the interesting questions is that how well the approaches (e.g. Recurrent Convolutional Neural Networks [12] and FastText [13]) of sentiment analysis used in the documents can be applied to conversational data. And, wether there are some improved methods, which can be closely integrated with conversational features. It is worth noting that each sentence in a conversation is a short text, which may be informal and sparse. Motivated by above questions, we firstly collected conversational data from some online English learning websites and our instant messages, then annotated 22 emotion classes, and evaluated multiple popular machine learning based methods on this dataset for sentiment polarity classification.

2 Construction of Corpus

In this section, we will describe our works on data collection and annotation.

2.1 Data Collection

For Chinese conversation corpus, each conversation is a multi-round dialogue, which contains two or more utterances. And each utterance is produced by a participant (i.e. the speaker). We mainly collected the conversational data from two online English learning websites[1,2] which providing oral dialogues in actual situations, and some selected instant messages (i.e. Tencent QQ and WeChat) of ourselves. The corpus ranges from many different topics, such as sports, shopping, diet and health. Hence, we manually selected the texts expressing the speakers emotion and removed the conversations that were incomprehensible or ambiguous. Table 1 shows an example of the Chinese conversation corpus.

Table 1. A typical example of the Chinese conversation corpus. A and B denote the two speakers respectively.

A：大卫，我要去中国。 David, I' m going to China.
B：真的吗？你是怎么得到这个机会的？ Really? How did you get the chance?
A：你知道的。我参加了中文竞赛。 You know. I took part in the Chinese contest. 我获得了第一名，他们给了我这个奖励。 I was the best and they gave me this reward. 我不必为我这次旅行掏钱。 I don' t have to pay for my trip.
B：恭喜。你真是幸运啊！ Congratulations. How lucky you are!

2.2 Annotation

The raw data had no emotional category. For each conversation, our annotators determined its emotion by understanding its meaning. Two annotators were trained to annotate the corpus independently. Each annotator tagged the half of

---

[1] http://talk.oralpractice.com/.
[2] http://talk.tingvoa.com/.

the raw data, and carried out cross-checking for each other. When disagreement arised, they discussed and negotiated with each other until reached the consensus. The final determination should be made by a third party, if they cannot reach a consensus.

The whole annotation work was divided into two stages as follows. In the first stage, we selected eight emotion classes (expect, joy, love, surprise, anxiety, sorrow, angry and disgust) as the initial set of the emotional categories, which was introduced by Quan and Ren [8]. If meeting a new emotional category, we added it to the set. Given a Chinese conversation, we only assigned an emotional category for it, and removed the conversations that were incomprehensible or ambiguous. In the second stage, we assigned an emotional polarity (i.e. positive, negative or neutral) for each conversation by its emotional category.

After the tagging finished, the total number of common emotional categories corresponding to the effective conversations is 22, i.e. appreciate, congratulation, encourage, joy, love, optimistic, praise, angry, apology, complaint, criticism, disappointment, disgust, fear, oppose, pessimism, refuse, regret, sorrow, agreement, hesitate and surprise. However, with the continuous collecting of corpus, the emotional categories will gradually increase. Actually, we also tagged other emotions, but the number of conversations in each category was less than 5, so we did not choose them. Given a collection of conversational data, the annotators labeled each conversation as one of the emotion classes with respect to the meaning of it. Table 2 shows the Chinese conversation corpus statistics. Finally, we categorized 1,757 conversations into the 22 emotion classes. Additionally, 405 non-sentiment conversation texts were categorized into the twenty-third class "other". Each conversation is stored in a different file named after the emotion class, such as "joy001.txt". Table 3 shows the common emotion classes statistics of the corpus.

In order to discover the sentiment polarity on a whole conversation, we further annotated the corpus. Polarity refers to the sentiment orientation of a given target entity, aspect or implicit aspect. In this paper, we consider only three polarity tags, i.e. positive, negative and neutral. By the emotion classes of the conversations, the annotators categorized them into three classes. Table 4 shows the polarities statistics of the corpus.

Table 2. The statistics of the Chinese conversation corpus.

Corpus statistics	Num.
The number of conversations	2,162
The number of total sentences	12,663
Max sentences per conversation	34
Avg. sentences per conversation	6
Max length per sentence	277
Avg. length per sentence	17

Table 3. The statistics of the emotion classes.

No.	Class	Num.	No.	Class	Num.
1	appreciate	60	12	disappointment	26
2	congratulation	65	13	disgust	115
3	encourage	22	14	fear	51
4	joy	107	15	oppose	28
5	love	142	16	pessimism	21
6	optimistic	26	17	refuse	65
7	praise	280	18	regret	6
8	angry	122	19	sorrow	85
9	apology	83	20	agreement	130
10	complaint	291	21	hesitate	14
11	criticism	10	22	surprise	8

Table 4. The statistics of the sentiment polarities.

Polarity	Emotion class	Num.
positive	appreciate, congratulation, encourage, joy love, optimistic, praise	702
negative	angry, apology, complaint, criticism disappointment, disgust, fear, oppose pessimism, refuse, regret, sorrow	903
neutral	agreement, hesitate, surprise, other	557

We will release the corpus[3] publicly for research purposes. Now the corpus is not very large because the annotation procedure is manual and time-consuming. In the future, to enlarge the corpus, we will apply semi-automatic annotation method.

3 Automatic Polarity Classification

One of the most obvious applications of our corpus is to utilize the machine learning based approaches for automatic polarity classification. This task is actually a text categorization problem. Many methods have been developed for text classification. In this work, we apply multiple approaches to categorize the polarity of the whole Chinese conversation, including linear methods, support vector machines (SVMs) and neural network methods.

---

[3] https://github.com/njoe9/ccsa.

3.1   Classification Methods

Linear Methods. Zhang et al. [14] used bag-of-words (BoW) and bag-of-ngrams (ngrams) as features to represent the documents, and applied a linear classifier based on multinomial logistic regression (LR) to classify the document-level sentiments. We adopted the same way to represent and classify the Chinese conversation.

BoW and its TFIDF are the two representation methods for each conversation. For the BoW, we use the counts of each word as features. For the TFIDF, we use the TFIDF value of each word as features.

Ngrams and its TFIDF are the same as BoW. We use all the bigrams of the text as features.

SVMs. We take unigrams (i.e. bag of words) and bigrams (i.e. bag of bigrams) as features to represent each conversation respectively. Following Tang et al. [6], we use the LibLinear[4] to train SVM classifier.

Neural Network Methods. Most neural methods for text classification are variants of convolutional or recurrent networks. We select the representative neural networks methods as follows.

CNN: Since convolutional neural networks (CNNs) have achieved the state-of-the-art results on many text classification datasets, we implemented the model [15] and conducted experiments with word embedding.

RNN: We implemented a single layer recurrent neural network with LSTM (Long Short-Term Memory) and bidirectional LSTM (BLSTM), and conducted experiments with word embedding respectively.

RCNN: Lai et al. [12] proposed a two-layer neural model, the first layer applied a bi-directional recurrent structure to represent texts with word embedding, and the second layer selected the salient features in the texts using a max-pooling mechanism. We implemented the RCNN model with word embedding and LSTM-RNNs instead of vanilla RNNs.

FastText: Joulin et al. [13] introduced a fast text classification method, which averaged all of the word representations in each text into a text representation that was fed to a hierarchical softmax layer to classify the documents. We implemented the method to categorize Chinese conversations.

HAN: Yang et al. [16] proposed the HAN model based on attention mechasim for document classification. We implemented the model with LSTM and BLSTM respectively, i.e. HAN-LSTM and HAN-BLSTM.

HANs: Zhou et al. [17] developed the HANs model for Chinese short text classification, which combined the word- and character-level attention mechanism to represent short text. We explored the effectiveness of the model on the task of polarity classification for Chinese conversation.

H-HANs: Considering the structural characteristics of the Chinese conversation, we developed a hierarchical neural network based on the HANs model,

---

[4] http://www.csie.ntu.edu.tw/~cjlin/liblinear/.

i.e. H-HANs. The model first incorporated the speaker with each utterance and fed the sentence sequence into the HANs model to get the attentive representation. Then the model used a attention-based BLSTM to produce the conversational representation with the sequence of sentence vectors. Finally, the conversation-level attentive vector was fed into a softmax layer to categorize the sentiments.

3.2   Evaluation Metrics

In this work, we categorize the Chinese conversations into three classes, i.e. positive, negative and neutral. we assume that each conversation only can be categorized into one sentiment polarity class. We evaluate the classification methods in terms of precision, recall and F_1-score for predicting positive, negative and neutral conversations respectively. Then we use weight-averaged F_1-score (including Precision and Recall) for methods comparison in the evaluation. We describe the equations as follows.

$$Precision = \frac{Correct.Number}{Category.Number} \tag{1}$$

$$Recall = \frac{Correct.Number}{Golden.Number} \tag{2}$$

$$F_1 = \frac{2 \times (Precision \times Recall)}{Precision + Recall} \tag{3}$$

$$Weight - averaged \quad F_1 = \frac{(P_n \times P_{F_1} + N_n \times N_{F_1} + O_n \times O_{F_1})}{Dataset.Number} \tag{4}$$

In above equations, the *Correct.Number* and *Category.Number* denote the numbers of correct and all results categorized by the method in each emotion polarity class respectively, and the *Golden.Number* denotes the testing set size of each class. P_n, N_n, and O_n denote the numbers of the positive (P), negative (N) and neutral (O) conversations in the testing set, P_{F_1}, N_{F_1}, and O_{F_1} denote the F_1-scores of three polarities respectively.

4   Evaluation

In this section, we first describe the experimental dataset and setup. Then, we present the empirical results and compare various models.

4.1   Datasets

For experimental dataset, we choose 80 percent of the corpus for training and 20 percent for testing. Hence, we obtain 1,729 training examples and 433 testing examples respectively. In the testing set, 137 conversations are positive accounting for 31.6%, 191 conversations are negative accounting for 44.1% and 105 conversations are neutral accounting for 24.3%.

4.2   Experimental Setup

For the methods except the HAN and H-HANs models, their inputs are the fixed length texts. The HAN and H-HANs models are all hierarchical architecture, whose input are a sequence of the utterances in a conversation. Hence, we concatenate all utterances without the speakers in each conversation to form a long text which is the input for other methods (we assume that max length of each text is 300).

We use Jieba[5] to conduct Chinese word segmentation for each utterance text, and initialize the lookup tables of input texts with the 100-dimensional word and character embeddings respectively. Note that we directly apply the word and character embeddings from [18]. The hyperparameters of our neural models are tuned on the validation set and early stopping is utilized within 20 epoches. Dropout rate of 0.4 is set to obtain better performance. We use stochastic gradient descent to train all models with learning rate of 0.01 and momentum of 0.9. Table 5 shows the hyper parameter settings. For the H-HANs model, the choices of max sentences per conversation and max length per sentence are 20 and 50 respectively.

Table 5. The experimental parameter settings in our models.

Parameter	Choice	Experiment range
Max sentences per conversation	15/20	10, 15, 20
Max length per sentence	80/50	80, 100, 200, 600
Word/Character embedding dimension	100	50, 100, 300
LSTM/CNN hidden layer size	100	64, 100, 128, 256
Dropout rate	0.4	0.4, 0.5
Epoch size	20	10, 15, 20
Mini-batch size	8	8, 16, 32, 64

4.3   Results and Discussion

Table 6 shows a detailed comparison of the methods. Experimental results show that traditional text classifier such as LR (Row 1) and SVMs (Row 6) models obtained better performance relatively. However, the CNN, LSTM and BLSTM models (Rows 9 to 11) only using word embedding do not perform well. Based on these basic neural networks models, several improved models proposed. Rows 12 and 14 indicate that the compositional models achieve significant improvements. The HANs model (Row 17) outperforms all other methods (Rows 1 to 16). It is worth noting that the FastText classifier is the fastest method and its performance is also close to the HANs. Based on the HANs model, the H-HANs model achieves the state-of-the-art performance, resulting in an weight-averaged F_1-score of 80.3%.

---

[5] https://github.com/fxsjy/jieba.

Table 6. The experimental results of polarity classification in weight-averaged percent for Chinese conversation.

Methods	F_1 (Precision, Recall)
BoW [14]	73.3 (73.4, 73.7)
BoW TFIDF [14]	72.6 (74.4, 73.7)
Ngrams [14]	55.1 (62.7, 59.4)
Ngrams TFIDF [14]	51.2 (68.1, 57.0)
SVM + Unigrams [6]	67.4 (67.3, 67.7)
SVM + Unigrams TFIDF [6]	73.6 (73.6, 74.1)
SVM + Bigrams [6]	56.7 (59.3, 58.9)
SVM + Bigrams TFIDF [6]	56.1 (61.1, 59.1)
CNN [15]	67.8 (68.8, 68.1)
LSTM	65.5 (70.6, 67.9)
BLSTM	62.3 (64.9, 62.8)
RCNN [12]	76.9 (78.2, 76.7)
FastText [13]	75.9 (76.5, 76.2)
HAN-LSTM [16]	73.8 (75.8, 73.7)
HAN-BLSTM [16]	64.2 (75.0, 64.2)
HANs-BLSTM [17]	66.3 (74.1, 66.7)
HANs-BLSTM+CNN [17]	78.1 (78.9, 77.8)
H-HANs (ours)	**80.3** (82.3, 80.4)

From Table 6, we observe that the approaches of H-HANs, HANs-BLSTM+CNN and RCNN get top three performance rankings. Table 7 shows the F_1-score (Precision, Recall) in percent of above three methods on each individual emotion polarity class. Evaluation results indicate that the H-HANs model obtains the best results on "negative" and "other" classes respectively, however the HANs-BLSTM+CNN method achieves the best performance on "positive" class. The three approaches all achieve better performance on "negative" class than on the other two classes. It may be the reason that the corpus size of the "negative" class is larger than the other two classes.

Table 7. F_1-score (Precision, Recall) in percent of each individual emotion polarity class by three methods.

No.	Class	Training	Test	RCNN	HANs-BLSTM+CNN	H-HANs
1	positive	565	137	77.7 (89.5, 68.6)	**80.5** (88.6, 73.7)	79.5 (69.2, 93.4)
2	negative	712	191	81.7 (79.3, 84.3)	82.0 (80.7, 83.2)	**86.9** (92.9, 81.7)
3	neural	452	105	67.0 (61.6, 73.3)	67.8 (63.1, 73.3)	**69.2** (80.0, 61.0)

Table 8. The conversation examples of multi-polarity and implicit polarity.

Case	Conversation Example	Emotion Class	Polarity
multi-polarity	A：你有什么体育爱好？ What sports interests do you have? B：我不喜欢踢足球。 I don't like playing football. 但我爱看足球比赛。 But I love watching football matches. A：酷！ Cool!	love	positive
implicit polarity	A：这件衣服怎么样？ How about this dress? B：符合我的口味！ Match my taste!	love	positive

It must be noticed that the sentiment analysis on Chinese conversation we describe in this paper is not to be mixed with sentiment analysis of the speakers. This work applies the text classification methods to categorize sentiment polarities (i.e. positive, negative and neutral attitudes) that may be mapped onto the speakers experience of the conversation as a whole. When a conversation only contains one emotion class, this emotion class is an independent emotion and easy to be categorized relatively. However, all conversations in our corpus are from real-world scenes. There are two cases that may affect the whole classification performance, namely multi-polarity and implicit polarity. The first line in Table 8 indicates that the intuition is love which can be the only emotion in the conversation, but disgust emotion combines with it. Meanwhile, among the sentiment utterances, not all aspects are modified by polarity words. The second line in Table 8 shows that the sentence of speaker B does not contain the obvious sentiment words, but actually expresses the opinion as "positive" for the aspect "dress".

Evaluation results point out that the selected classification approaches can be used to categorize sentiment polarity on Chinese conversation, while performance has yet to be further improved. The H-HANs model achieves the best result, however there are some information in Chinese conversation to be taken into account and to be studied further. As mentioned above, conversations are joint efforts by two or more different speakers. The speakers may influence each other and their utterances are dependent on the previous utterances. Thus, we should explore the different speakers and their interaction context, and develop a more appropriate classification model to improve performance further. Meanwhile, we also should further improve the detecting accuracy of the multi-polarity and implicit polarity in a conversation.

5 Conclusion and Future Work

We introduced a new Chinese conversation corpus for sentiment analysis, which were collected from some online English learning websites and our instant messages. The corpus contains three sentiment polarities (positive, negative and neutral) and comprises 22 fine-grained emotion classes currently, where the none-sentiment conversations are categorized into the "other" class. To evaluation, we selected multiple representative classification approaches to categorize sentiment polarities on the corpus, and reported the benchmark result. Experimental results show that performance should be improved further. Our corpus also can be used for many applications, such as fine-grained sentiment classification, and aspect-oriented sentiment analysis. The corpus with gold standards will be released publicly for research purposes.

In the future, we will collect and annotate more Chinese conversations to extend our corpus. We will also explore methods for other sentiment analysis tasks and improve the existing algorithms with inspiration from the corpus.

Acknowledgments. This work is supported by the National Natural Science Foundation (No. 61602479), National High Technology Research and Development Program of China (No. 2015AA015402) and National Key Technology R&D Program of China under No. 2015BAH53F02.

References

1. Husin, N., Abdullah, M.T., Mahmod, R.: A systematic literature review for topic detection in chat conversation for cyber-crime investigation. Int. J. Digit. Content Technol. Appl. **8**(3), 22 (2014)
2. Zhao, Y., Qin, B., Liu, T.: Creating a fine-grained corpus for chinese sentiment analysis. IEEE Intell. Syst. **30**(1), 36–43 (2015)
3. Zhang, L., Chen, C.: Sentiment classification with convolutional neural networks: an experimental study on a large-scale Chinese conversation corpus. In: 12th International Conference on Computational Intelligence and Security (CIS 2016), pp. 165–169 (2016)
4. Socher, R., Perelygin, A., Wu, J.Y., Chuang, J., Manning, C.D., Ng, A.Y., Potts, C., et al.: Recursive deep models for semantic compositionality over a sentiment treebank. In: EMNLP 2013, vol. 1631, p. 1642 (2013)
5. Kalchbrenner, N., Grefenstette, E., Blunsom, P.: A convolutional neural network for modelling sentences. In: Proceedings of the 52nd ACL, pp. 655–665 (2014)
6. Tang, D., Qin, B., Liu, T.: Document modeling with gated recurrent neural network for sentiment classification. In: EMNLP 2015, pp. 1422–1432 (2015)
7. Chen, H., Sun, M., Tu, C., Lin, Y., Liu, Z.: Neural sentiment classification with user and product attention. In: EMNLP 2016, pp. 1650–1659 (2016)
8. Quan, C., Ren, F.: Construction of a blog emotion corpus for Chinese emotional expression analysis. In: EMNLP 2009, pp. 1446–1454 (2009)
9. Li, C., Xu, B., Wu, G., He, S., Tian, G., Hao, H.: Recursive deep learning for sentiment analysis over social data. In: 2014 IEEE/WIC/ACM International Joint Conferences on Web Intelligence (WI) and Intelligent Agent Technologies (IAT), vol. 1, pp. 180–185 (2014)

10. Liao, X., Li, B., Xu, L.: Overview of topic-based Chinese message polarity classification in SIGHAN 2015. In: ACL-IJCNLP 2015, p. 56 (2015)
11. Peng, H., Cambria, E., Hussain, A.: A review of sentiment analysis research in Chinese language. Cogn. Comput. **9**(4), 1–13 (2017)
12. Lai, S., Xu, L., Liu, K., Zhao, J.: Recurrent convolutional neural networks for text classification. In: AAAI 2015, pp. 2267–2273 (2015)
13. Joulin, A., Grave, E., Bojanowski, P., Mikolov, T.: Bag of tricks for efficient text classification. CoRR abs/1607.01759 (2016)
14. Zhang, X., Zhao, J., LeCun, Y.: Character-level convolutional networks for text classification. In: NIPS 2015, pp. 649–657 (2015)
15. Kim, Y.: Convolutional neural networks for sentence classification. In: EMNLP 2014, pp. 1746–1751 (2014)
16. Yang, Z., Yang, D., Dyer, C., He, X., Smola, A., Hovy, E.: Hierarchical attention networks for document classification. In: NAACL HLT 2016 (2016)
17. Zhou, Y., Xu, J., Cao, J., Xu, B., Li, C., Xu, B.: Hybrid attention networks for Chinese short text classification. In: CICLing 2017 (2017)
18. Zhou, Y., Xu, B., Xu, J., Yang, L., Li, C., Xu, B.: Compositional recurrent neural networks for Chinese short text classification. In: 2016 IEEE/WIC/ACM International Conference on Web Intelligence, pp. 137–144 (2016)

Improving Retrieval Quality Using PRF Mechanism from Event Perspective

Pengming Wang[1,2(✉)], Peng Li[1,2], Rui Li[1,2], and Bin Wang[1,2]

[1] Institute of Information Engineering, Chinese Academy of Sciences,
Beijing 100093, China
{wangpengming,lipeng,lirui,wangbin}@iie.ac.cn
[2] School of Cyber Security, University of Chinese Academy of Sciences,
Beijing 100029, China

Abstract. Pseudo-relevance feedback (PRF) has proven to be an effective mechanism for improving retrieval quality. However, using general PRF mechanism would usually be demonstrated with poor performance when the retrieval objective is an event. Intuitively, event-oriented query often involves special properties of event object, which cannot easily be expressed with keyword-based event query, and might cause the deviation from target event to feedback documents. In this paper, an original, simple yet effective event-oriented PRF mechanism (EO-PRF) that takes into account the drawbacks of PRF mechanism from an event perspective to improve retrieval quality is proposed. This EO-PRF mechanism innovates by making use of some extra event knowledge to improve retrieval quality by integrating target event information with the initial query. Empirical evaluations based on TREC-TS 2015 dataset and standard benchmarks, namely mainstream non-feedback retrieval method, and state-of-the-art pseudo feedback methods, demonstrate the effectiveness of the proposed EO-PRF mechanism in event-oriented retrieval.

Keywords: Event-oriented retrieval · Pseudo relevance feedback
Event mixture model · Language model

1 Introduction

In ad-hoc retrieval, as the expressibility of initial query q is limited, it is difficult to acquire expected result that ranking documents only based on $sim(q, d)$. In several technologies which turn to improve the precision of retrieval results, pseudo-relevance feedback (PRF) might be the most effective one, and has been validated in almost all retrieval models. The basic idea of PRF is to assume that top-ranked documents in ad-hoc retrieval result are relevant, so the updated query expression q' can be obtained by learning from these documents and consequently retrieval quality can be improved through ranking documents based on $sim(q', d)$. However, if the retrieval objective is an event, using general PRF mechanism would usually be demonstrated with poor performance.

© Springer International Publishing AG 2018
X. Huang et al. (Eds.): NLPCC 2017, LNAI 10619, pp. 591–600, 2018.
https://doi.org/10.1007/978-3-319-73618-1_49

From an event perspective, event-oriented retrieval could be considered as a special task of IR, as shown in Fig. 1. Intuitively, there is a target event hidden behind the initial query, and it might cause the deviation from target event to feedback documents event when using general PRF mechanism. For instance, given an event query "iraq bombing" by a user who takes an interest in the developments of bomb event in Iraq, it's clear that we should not only think about the query keyword "iraq" and "bombing" during the retrieval process, the time and place where the event is taking place, including each stage of the evolution on subordinate states of iraq, should also be considered. Therefore, we should find ways to make use of the information of target event to improve retrieval quality.

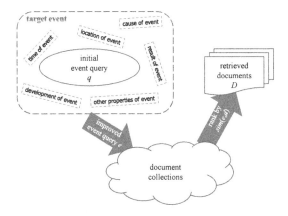

Fig. 1. Event-oriented retrieval. The main difference against conventional IR is that the result of event-oriented retrieval should be the documents with high $sim(e, d)$ instead of documents with high $sim(q, d)$, that is, the retrieved documents should describe the relevant content of the target event.

With the development of knowledge base, there is a negative trend in static information need, instead, the retrieval aims for events (event-oriented retrieval) is playing an increasingly important role. While how to identify the target event exactly, and use the event information with initial query, is a fundamental issue in event-oriented retrieval task that needs to be addressed as a matter of urgency, which is also the starting point of this paper.

2   Related Work

In our understanding, there are two lines of research associated with the work in this paper, which will be briefly reviewed below:

The first line is improving the effectiveness and robustness of pseudo-relevance feedback through a variety of ways. The simplest method is directly building language model on pseudo feedback set, but it does not account for the noise in feedback set. Zhai and Lafferty [1] proposed using a two-component mixture model to fit the feedback documents, where one component is a fixed background language model $p(w|C)$ estimated using the collection and the other is an unknown, to-be-discovered topic model $p(w|\theta_F)$. This technique has been proved to effectively distinguish noise from real feedback, so it has become a mainstream method. Furthermore, based on KL-divergence retrieval model, representative methods for estimating query models are Relevance Model [2], Divergence Minimization Model [1], etc. However, these works do not make the special consideration from event perspective during the retrieval process, as the analysis stated above, ER task shows its own particular characteristics, so the same method which can obtain improvement in general retrieval task, might not get the same effect in event-oriented retrieval task.

The second line of research related to our work is improving retrieval performance with the consideration of event characteristics during the retrieval process. [3] novelly proposes a bipartite graph to exclusively describe an event, and in [4], authors proposed a graph-based model for event-centered information retrieval. They structure both queries and documents as graphs of event mentions and employ graph kernels to measure the query-document similarity. However, these two methods are both sophisticated and time-consuming. Aiming at the demand for event information by users, [5] propose a method: local analysis-based event-oriented (LA-EO) query expansion, which divides query terms into two categories: event terms and qualifying terms. [6] propose a method of query expansion based on event ontology (denoted by EO-QE). The paper emphatically discusses the concept of event four-tuple and the different query expansion strategies based on different event elements. There exists a common problem in these methods that most of them are heuristics, which can not be explained in a principled framework.

The research mentality of this paper is to find an efficient approach to integrate as much target event information as possible into initial query through a principled manner, and then improve retrieval performance.

3 Proposed EO-PRF Mechanism

The EO-PRF mechanism presented in this paper is based on Kullback-Leibler (KL) divergence retrieval model. In KL-divergence model, the retrieval task is reduced to two subtasks, i.e., estimating θ_Q and θ_D respectively. The estimation of document model θ_D is similar to that in the query likelihood retrieval model, but the estimation of query model θ_Q offers interesting opportunities of leveraging some extra information to improve retrieval accuracy. Specifically, some pre-built event language models can be exploited to improve our estimate of θ_Q.

3.1 Pre-building Event Language Model

In order to identify the target event hidden behind the initial query accurately, we should build some language models for known events beforehand. An event language model[1] refers to a multinomial distribution of all terms in a event, in other words, if we have to describe a event, the terms we used should follow the term distribution of corresponding event language model. It is clearly that there are tremendous differences between different event language models.

Formally, given a event e and the vocabulary of that event $V = \{w_1, w_2, \ldots\}$, the unigram language model of that event is: $\theta_e = \{p(w_i|\theta_e)\}_{i=1}^{|V|}$, where $\sum_{i=1}^{|V|} p(w_i|\theta_e) = 1$.

There are many options for building event language model, the approach used in this paper is following: Pulling out a fixed number of documents (for instance, 100) for each event from event-annotated corpus, and establishing the language model of that event through counting terms' frenquency in corresponding documents.

It is important to note that new event would emerge continuously, so we can not build language model for all events. Consequently, we assume there also exist an unknown event e_u and corresponding language model θ_u. In this paper, the term distribution in θ_u is supposed to be consistent with the term distribution in whole document set[2]. The language model of unknown event would not established until whole document set has been acquired, so in the following sections, the known event set E_k would not contain unknown event e_u.

3.2   The Generation of Pseudo-Feedback Set from Event Perspective

With known event set E_k, we can build a complete event set: $E = E_k \cup \{e_u\}$. The target event $e_{estimate}$ hidden behind initial query should be a element of E, but due to its unknown nature, we have to identify $e_{estimate}$ based on the term distribution in feedback document set.

Then, we can simulate the generation process of pseudo-feedback set according to the probability of $e_{estimate}$ in E, as shown in Fig. 2.

As we can see in this figure, when we generate a term in feedback document, we would sample a term using $\theta_{combined}$, in other words, we would first decide which model to use based on the corresponding event probability. Thus, the log-likelihood function for the entire set of feedback documents is:

$$
\begin{aligned}
\log p(F|\theta_{combined}) &= \sum_{w \in V} c(w, F) \log(p(w)) \\
&= \sum_{w \in V} c(w, F) \log(\sum_{i=1}^{k} \lambda_i p(w|\theta_{e_i}) + (1 - \sum_{i=1}^{k} \lambda_i) p(w|\theta_{e_u})).
\end{aligned}
\tag{1}
$$

where $c(w, F)$ is the count of term w in the set of feedback documents F.

---

[1] For the sake of efficiency, the language model presented in this paper is always a unigram language model.

[2] This is reasonable as, in general, we only need to confirm $\theta_{e_{estimate}} \notin \{\theta_{e_i}\}_{i=1}^{k}$ if $e_{estimate} = e_u$, however, the term distribution in whole document set can be seen as a mixture of multiple events, so it would not be consistent with any known event language model.

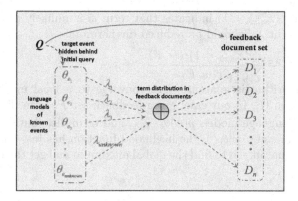

Fig. 2. Event mixture model for pseudo-feedback set. From an event perspective, we can use a mixture model of all events in E, $\theta_{combined}$, to simulate the generation process of pseudo-feedback set.

Next we have to adjust the probability in each event to maximize that log-likelihood function, and then identify the target event hidden behind.

3.3 Fitting the Feedback Documents Using Event Mixture Model

Intuitively, λ_i indicates how much faith should we put in $e_{estimate} = e_i$, so we can finally determine what event $e_{estimate}$ is by that weight. To do that we have to fit the mixture model $\theta_{combined}$ into pseudo-feedback set, that is, we have to adjust the event weights $\{\lambda_i\}_{i=1}^k$ to best reflecting the term distribution in feedback document set. Quite evidently, there exist a group of latent variables between events and terms which can represent the probability of a term generated by some event language model, so it is naturally think that we can realize the log-likelihood function's maximization through expectation-maximization (EM) algorithm. Specifically, the EM algorithm would improve $\theta_{combined}$ by iteratively alternating between an E-step and an M-step.

In the E-step, we would use the following equation to compute the posterior probability of a term w being generated using $p(\cdot|\{\theta_{e_i}\}_{i=1}^k)$ (or $p(\cdot|\theta_{e_{unknown}})$) based on the current estimate of $\theta_{combined}$:

$$\textbf{E-step: } p(z_{w,e_i} = 1) = \frac{\lambda_i^{(n)} p(w|\theta_{e_i})}{\sum_{i=1}^k \lambda_i^{(n)} p(w|\theta_{e_i}) + (1 - \sum_{i=1}^k \lambda_i^{(n)}) p(w|\theta_{e_u})}$$

where $z_{w,e_i} \in [0,1]$ is a hidden variable indicating whether term w is generated using some known event language model θ_{e_i} ($z_{w,e_i} = 1$) or the unknown event language model θ_{e_u} ($z_{w,e_u} = 1$).

Intuitively, we try to guess which model has been used to generate term w. However, $p(z_{w,e_i} = 1)$ does not tell us for sure whether term w is generated using θ_{e_i}, it's only a expectation probability. Thus, in the M-step of the EM algorithm, we would use a discounted term count (i.e., $c(w, F)p(z_{w,e_i} = 1)$) for estimating λ_{e_i}. A term count is discounted more if $p(z_{w,e_i} = 1)$ is small, which makes sense because a small $p(z_{w,e_i} = 1)$ indicates that term w is unlikely generated using θ_{e_i}, thus the weight λ_{e_i} should be reduced furthermore.

M-step: $\lambda_i = \dfrac{\sum_{w \in V} p(z_{w,e_i} = 1)c(w, F)}{\sum_{w \in V} c(w, F)}$

The EM algorithm is guaranteed to converge to a local maximum of the likelihood function [7]. In our case, given feedback set F, term distributions in pre-built event language models $p(w|\theta_{e_i})_{i=1}^{k}$, and term distribution in unknown event language model $p(w|\theta_{e_u})$, the likelihood function has just one local maximum, so we are guaranteed to find the global maximum and get the most optimal weight set $\{\lambda_i\}_{i=1}^{k}$.

3.4 Identifying the Target Event

Intuitively, we need a weight threshold μ with which we can do that, if there exists an event weight λ_i in the most optimal event weight set $\{\lambda_i\}_{i=1}^{k}$ and it meets the condition $\lambda_i \geq \mu$, and then we can believe for any $e_j \in \{E - e_i\}$, we have $\lambda_i \gg \lambda_j$, consequently, e_i can be identified as the target event hidden behind initial query. Otherwise, if no such $e_i \in E$ exists, e_u would be identified as the target event. In evaluation section, we will discuss the optimal setting of μ.

4 Improving Retrieval Quality with EO-PRF

At present, an interpolation method is widely adopted to improve initial query in pseudo-relevance feedback. Specifically, let θ_Q be the current query model and θ_e be the language model of target event. The updated new query model θ_Q' is given by

$$p(w|\theta_Q') = (1 - \alpha)p(w|\theta_Q) + \alpha p(w|\theta_e). \qquad (2)$$

where $\alpha \in [0, 1]$ is an interpolation parameter to control the amount of feedback.

In addition, an improved estimate of θ_Q' may give nonzero probabilities to potentially many other non-query terms. This clearly would cause a concern of scoring efficiency. A common solution to this problem is that we truncate the query language model θ_Q' so that we only keep the highest probability words according to $p(w|\theta_Q')$.

Note that the setting of interpolation parameter α and truncation number would has significant impact on the retrieval performance, we will set multiple groups of these super-parameters to verify the validity of EO-PRF in validation section.

5 Evaluation

5.1 Experimental Set

As the relatively few event-annotated corpus, we use a dataset for TREC Temporal Summarization task[3], which called TREC-TS 2015. The corpus consist

---

[3] http://www.trec-ts.org/.

of 350,223 event-annotated documents, which respectively belong to 6 coarse classes and 20 fine classes. The detailed distribution is presented in Table 1.

Table 1. The event distribution in TREC-TS 2015 corpus

Corpus	Coarse event	Fine classes	Document number
TREC-TS 2015	Accident	India power blackouts	15384
		Vauxhall helicopter crash	33514
		Uss guardian grounding	12516
		Brazzaville explosion	2754
		Thane building collapsed	4580
		Savar building collapse	26845
		Carnival triumph fire	8542
		Total	104135
	Protest	Innocence of muslims protests	43316
		Catalan protest	17178
		Total	60494
	Earthquack	Aceh earthquake	5089
		Haida gwaii earthquake	3156
		Total	8245
	Conflict	Konna battle	34879
	Storm	Cyclone nilam	15525
	Bombing	Quetta bombing	6068
		Iraq bombing	50614
		Suicide bomber ankara	8419
		Los angeles arson	28785
		Baghdad bomb	5700
		Aleppo university explosion	6746
		Hyderabad explosion	20613
		Total	126945
	Overall tally		350223

In order to identify the target event accurately, we treat the 20 fine classes in TREC-TS 2015 corpus as known events. To avoid over-fitting and obtain accurate results, we randomly generate 10 subset from the whole dataset, each of which contains 20,000 documents and 500 documents for each event individually. The experimental results given below are all based on an average of 10-fold cross-validation method on the 10 subsets.

We implemented our document pre-processing on the top of Lucene toolkit[4]. Following the TREC standard, we retrieve 1,000 documents for each query, and

---

[4] Available at http://lucene.apache.org/.

use mean average precision (MAP) as the primary performance measure. In all the experiments, we first use the basic KL-divergence method without feedback to retrieve a ranked list of documents for each query as our feedback documents. Dirichlet Prior smoothing is used and the smoothing parameter is set to 2000 as recommended in [8]. We then perform pseudo-relevance feedback with a certain number of top-ranked documents from the initial retrieval results (100 in this paper). We truncate the updated query language model to keep some highest probability terms and use the KL-divergence method again to perform a second round retrieval.

5.2   The Effectiveness of EO-PRF to Identify the Target Event

Intuitively, the effectiveness of EO-PRF greatly depends on whether identify the target event accurately. As stated above, EO-PRF uses EM algorithm to identify target event through fitting event language models to the feedback documents. In EO-PRF, the optimal weight set greatly depends on the convergence threshold of EM algorithm and the weight threshold to determine the convergence of EM algorithm. We assume that EM algorithm would be converged if the difference between likelihood function values is less than pre-set convergence threshold (10^{-13} in this paper) for ten times.

We have calculated the correct-identified events under different weight threshold μ, as shown in Table 2 (As there would be more than one event be identified if $\mu \leq 0.23$ and no event would be identified if $\mu \geq 0.9$, the range of threshold is set to $\mu \in [0.3, 0.8]$).

Table 2. The correct-identified events under different weight threshold μ

Weight threshold μ	0.3	0.4	0.5	0.6	0.7	0.8
Total event No.	20					
Correct-identified events (*count1*)	15	13	8	6	1	1
Incorrect-identified events (*count2*)	3	1	1	0	0	0
Unknown events	2	6	11	14	19	19
Intuitive gain	0.9	1.1	0.6	0.6	0.1	0.1

Intuitively, identifying correct event would achieve benefits for retrieval result, identifying incorrect event would damage retrieval performance more serious, while none of known event be identified would be no impact on retrieval performance, thus "intuitive gain" can be set to "$0.1 \times count1 - 0.2 \times count2$".

As we can see, setting event weight threshold μ to 0.4 would gain the most benefit, in further experiment we will adopt that weight threshold.

5.3   The Analysis of Retrieval Quality

According to the discussion above, the interpolation parameter α and truncation term number would has significant impact on the retrieval quality in pseudo-relevance feedback. Therefore, we use 6 different setting of these two parameters to evaluate the effectiveness of EO-PRF compared with some other methods. The MAP results of 20 event queries are shown in Table 3, where we compare EO-PRF with (1) the baseline no-feedback run (KL), (2) pseudo-relevance feedback directely used the language model of feedback set(FM), and (3) two-component mixture feedback model which is considered to be the-start-of-date in PRF framework(SMM) [8,9].

Table 3. The retrieval quality comparison of EO-PRF and other methods (MAP)

Parm. α	Truncation No.	KL	FM	SMM	EO-PRF	Impr: (over KL)	Impr: (FM)	Impr: (SMM)
0.8	10	0.5907	0.6304	0.6476	0.6873	16.35%*	9.03%*	6.13%*
	20	0.5907	0.6424	0.6542	0.6885	16.56%*	7.18%*	5.24%*
	40	0.5907	0.6240	0.6365	0.6905	16.90%*	10.66%*	8.48%*
0.6	10	0.5907	0.6266	0.6365	0.6832	15.66%*	9.03%*	7.34%*
	20	0.5907	0.6529	0.6676	0.6970	18.00%*	6.75%*	4.40%*
	40	0.5907	0.6109	0.6325	0.7059	19.50%*	15.55%*	11.60%*

*The improvement is statistically significant at the level of 0.05 according to the Wilcoxon signed rank test.

Overall, pseudo-relevance feedback methods have obvious advantage in performance over KL method in almost all parameter settings, in the meanwhile, we notice that EO-PRF method is always better than other comparative approaches, and the improvement is statistically significant in almost all cases, indicating that as a pseudo feedback method, EO-PRF is effective and robust w.r.t. using different setting of parameters for feedback, and be able to provide considerable benefits for retrieval performance.

In addition to this, we should also take note that in contrast to other methods, EO-PRF has good stability. Specifically, from Table 3 we can notice whether FM or SMM, their MAP value is unstable when truncation number changes. When truncation number increases from 10 to 20, their MAP value increases, while truncation number increases from 20 to 40, their MAP value reduces considerably. One possible explanation is that as we use more terms truncated from pseudo feedback set (FM) or fitted topic model (SMM), the more noise integrated into the initial query, so that the affect becomes more harmful for retrieval performance. In the meanwhile, we can see that when truncation number increases from 10 to 40, MAP value of EO-PRF is monotonically increased, and the growth rates remain stable. The possible explanation is that the terms of EO-PRF are extracted from the language model of target event, so we can assume that there has hardly any noise in truncated terms.

6   Conclusions and Future Work

In this paper, we propose an event-oriented pseudo-relevance feedback mechanism (EO-PRF). The experimental results in TREC-TS 2015 corpus show that comparing with other methods, the retrieval method with EO-PRF can not only acquire better retrieval performance, but also better stability for different settings of pseudo feedback parameters.

Nevertheless, the experimental results of FM and SMM shown above are all based on 100 feedback documents, consequently, it still needs to be demonstrated that when feedback document number increases, whether the feedback terms extracted in the two methods would be more accurate, and then whether the retrieval performance of them would be very close or may even surpass that of EO-PRF.

Acknowledgment. This work was supported by the National Natural Science Foundation of China (61572494), the National Key Research and Development Program of China (grant No. 2016YFB0801003), the National Natural Science Foundation of China (61462027) and the fund project of Jiangxi Province Education Office (GJJ160529).

References

1. Lv, Y., Zhai, C.: Revisiting the divergence minimization feedback model. In: Proceedings of the 23rd ACM International Conference on Conference on Information and Knowledge Management, pp. 1863–1866. ACM (2014)
2. Duan, H., Zhai, C., Cheng, J., Gattani, A.: A probabilistic mixture model for mining and analyzing product search log. In: Proceedings of the 22nd ACM International Conference on Information & Knowledge Management, pp. 2179–2188. ACM (2013)
3. Yang, W., Li, R., Li, P., Zhou, M., Wang, B.: Event related document retrieval based on bipartite graph. In: Cui, B., Zhang, N., Xu, J., Lian, X., Liu, D. (eds.) WAIM 2016. LNCS, vol. 9658, pp. 467–478. Springer, Cham (2016). https://doi.org/10.1007/978-3-319-39937-9_36
4. Glavaš, G., Šnajder, J.: Event-centered information retrieval using kernels on event graphs. In: TextGraphs-8 at Empirical Methods in Natural Language Processing (EMNLP 2013) (2013)
5. Zhong, Z., Zhu, P., Li, C., Guan, Y., Liu, Z.: Research on event-oriented query expansion based on local analysis. J. China Soc. Sci. Tech. Inf. **31**(2), 151–159 (2012)
6. Zhong, Z., Li, C., Guan, Y., Liu, Z.: A method of query expansion based on event ontology. J. Converg. Inf. Technol. **7**(9), 364–371 (2012)
7. Dempster, A.P., Laird, N.M., Rubin, D.B.: Maximum likelihood from incomplete data via the EM algorithm. J. R. Stat. Soc. Ser. B (Methodol.) **39**, 1–38 (1977)
8. Zhai, C., Lafferty, J.: A study of smoothing methods for language models applied to ad hoc information retrieval. In: Proceedings of the 24th Annual International ACM SIGIR Conference on Research and Development in Information Retrieval, pp. 334–342. ACM (2001)
9. Tao, T., Zhai, C.: A mixture clustering model for pseudo feedback in information retrieval. In: Banks, D., McMorris, F.R., Arabie, P., Gaul, W. (eds.) Classification, Clustering, and Data Mining Applications, pp. 541–551. Springer, Heidelberg (2004). https://doi.org/10.1007/978-3-642-17103-1_51

An Information Retrieval-Based Approach to Table-Based Question Answering

Junwei Bao[1(✉)], Nan Duan[2], Ming Zhou[2], and Tiejun Zhao[1]

[1] Harbin Institute of Technology, Harbin, China
baojunwei001@gmail.com, tjzhao@hit.edu.cn
[2] Microsoft Research Asia, Bejing, China
nanduan@microsoft.com, mingzhou@microsoft.com

Abstract. We propose a simple yet effective information retrieval based approach to answer complex questions with open domain web tables. Specifically, given a question and a table, we rank all table cells based on their representations, and select the cells of the highest ranking score as the answer. To represent a cell, we design rich features which leverage both the semantic information of the question and the structure information of the table. The experiments are conducted on WIKITABLE-QUESTIONS dataset in which the questions have complex semantics. Compared to a semantic parsing based method, our approach improves the accuracy score by 6.03 points.

1 Introduction

Knowledge-based question answering approaches [1,3,5,6,10,13–15] which rely on curated knowledge bases (CKB), e.g., Freebase [2], face some problems. First of all, the CKBs cover general domain knowledge very well, but still suffer from incompleteness on specific domains, such as e-commerce. Furthermore, these approaches usually have large search spaces, since the CKBs include abundant entities and predicates. Last but not the least, the manually defined predicates are limited in fixed schema which is hard to be extended.

In contrast, web tables[1] are a kind of real open domain data which contain valuable information. In addition, web tables also have formal structures and the attributes of web tables are not limited to fixed schema. Therefore, table-based question answering (TBQA) has been paid much attention to [7–9,12,17]. [17] present a neural enquirer to query a single synthetic table but not real web tables. [8,9] propose to use semantic parsing based (SP-based) approaches which require expert knowledge to design deduction rules. [7,12] focus on information retrieval based (IR-based) approaches where the features are mainly designed for *simple* single-relation questions [16].

In this paper, we follow the line of the IR-based approaches, and propose a simple yet effective method to answer *complex* questions based on web tables.

---

[1] https://en.wikipedia.org/wiki/Table_(information).

© Springer International Publishing AG 2018
X. Huang et al. (Eds.): NLPCC 2017, LNAI 10619, pp. 601–611, 2018.
https://doi.org/10.1007/978-3-319-73618-1_50

Specifically, given a question and a table, we rank all table cells based on their representations, and select the cells of the highest ranking score as the answer. To represent a cell, we design rich features which leverage both the semantic information of the question and the structure information of the table. We conduct experiments on a subset of WIKITABLEQUESTIONS dataset, in which the questions are *complex* and the tables are real web tables. We filter some instances to make sure that the golden answers are contained by the table cells. Our approach outperforms a SP-based method by 6.03 points in terms of accuracy score.

Compared to previous TBQA approaches, our method has two advantages. First, our IR-based approach does not require to explicitly parse a question to a logic form. It directly represents a question with a compact real-valued vector composed of a set of feature values. This dramatically reduces the search space of the candidates. Second, our approach can handle not only the single-relation questions which require the answer cell and the detected anchor cell in the same row, but also questions which contain complex semantics.

2   Related Work

Previous works on table-based question answering mainly have two genres: semantic parsing based (SP-based) approaches and information retrieval based (IR-based) methods. We compare our work with these two kinds of research lines.

The first line is SP-based methods on TBQA such as [8]. In their work, a question is firstly parsed into a logical form, namely lambda-DCS, which is a semantic tree explicitly representing the meaning of the question in a compositional manner, and then the logical form is executed based on the structured knowledge to get the answer. The logical form in this method can help to understand the semantic structure of a question, which also increase the difficulty of question answering itself. To generate a logical form, chart parsing are usually adopted to generate a large search space although some pruning technics are used. Besides, lexicalized sparse features are used which require large scale training data.

The second genre is IR-based approach. [12] propose a table cell search method which firstly searches topic cells among all the tables, and then ranks the cells in the same row with the topic cells based on some features mainly for anchoring the answer type. This method considers table selection procedure which is a practical component that can select one or more from a lot of tables. While the assumption that the topic cell and the answer cell in the same row limits it to answer simple single relation questions but not more complex ones. [7] use IR-based approach to rank table cells for multiple-choice questions and provides a data set of multiple-choice questions.

In this work, we follow the line of IR-based approach. Compared to SP-based approaches, we don't need to explicitly parse a question to a logic form but directly represents a question with a compact real-value vector composed of a set of feature values. This dramatically reduces the search space of the candidates and make the QA procedure high-efficiency. Compared to IR-based approaches, our proposed method can handle not only the simple single relation questions which require the answer cell and the detected anchor cell in the same row, but also complex questions with multiple constraints on the answer or other complicated semantics.

3   Task Overview

3.1   Table

A table T is composed of $M * N$ cells, where M denotes the row size and N denotes the column size. Each cell $C \in T$ can be represented as a triple $\langle r, a, v \rangle$, where $C.r$ is the index of the row that C is in, $C.a$ is the attribute of the cell, and $C.v$ is the value of the cell. Given a row $\tilde{r}$ and an attribute $\tilde{a}$, we can pinpoint the cell $C = T_{\langle \tilde{r}, \tilde{a} \rangle}$.

3.2   IR-Based TBQA

Formally, given a question Q and a table T, table-based QA (or TBQA) is defined as a task that aims to find one or multiple cells from T as answers to Q. Each cell $C \in T$ is represented by a vector composed of a set of feature values, and then scored and ranked by the distribution $p(C|Q,T)$ defined as follows:

$$p(C|Q,T) = \frac{\max_{A \in E} \exp\{\sum_{i=1}^{K} \lambda_i \cdot h_i(C, A, Q, T)\}}{\sum_{C' \in T} \max_{A' \in E} \exp\{\sum_{i=1}^{K} \lambda_i \cdot h_i(C', A', Q, T)\}} \tag{1}$$

– $A \in E$ represents an anchor cell which is detected in Q based on T.
– $h_i(\cdot)$ denotes the ith feature function.

Figure 1 shows an example. T is a table which contains m rows, and 4 columns including attributes Year, City, Country, and Nations. Q is a question based on T. "2008" is an anchor cell detected in Q based on T. "UK" is an answer candidate which is represented by a real-valued vector.

According to the above description, our IR-based TBQA approach is decomposed into three steps: anchor cell detection, answer cell representation, and answer cell ranking as follows:

1. **Anchor Cell Detection.** This step finds a cell from T as the anchor cell, whose value should be contained by Q. Detecting such anchor cells from tables is important to TBQA, as for a portion of table-based questions, we need to use the anchor cell information to pinpoint the answer cell;

2. **Answer Cell Representation.** This step generates a representation $\mathcal{R}_C(Q, T, C_A) = [h_1, ..., h_K]$ for each cell $C \in T$ based on Q, T, and an anchor cell C_A. Each h_k is a feature used in answer cell ranking, which measures how possible C can be considered as the answer cell of Q;

Q: Which country hosted the Olympic Games after 2008?

$$h_{row} = p(+|P_A)$$

$h_{ansType} = \cos(E_{Country}, E_{P_A})$
$h_{ancType} = \cos(E_{Year}, E_{P_A})$
$h_{attrOverlap} = |Set_{Country} \wedge Set_{P_A}|$

$h_{first} = p(-|P_A)$ $h_{larger} = p(+|P_A)$
$h_{last} = p(-|P_A)$ $h_{smaller} = p(-|P_A)$
$h_{above} = p(-|P_A)$ $h_{equal} = p(-|P_A)$
$h_{below} = p(+|P_A)$

T:

	Year	City	Country	Nations
0	1896	Athens	Greece	14
1	1900	Pairs	France	24
...	...	...	...	...
m-3	2004	Athens	Greece	201
m-2	2008	Beijing	China	204
m-1	2012	London	UK	204

Fig. 1. An example of the table-based QA task.

3. **Answer Cell Ranking.** This step ranks all cells in the table based on their representations.

Comparing to the traditional knowledge-based QA task, TBQA has the following two characteristics:

- *open domain and freshness.* Traditional curated knowledge bases (e.g., Freebase) can cover general domain knowledge very well, but lack of contents for specific domains, such as sales or medical domains. On the other hand, there are large scale domain-specific knowledge stored as tables for such domains, and they are often updated in a timely manner.
- *simple schema and limited search space.* Compared to traditional knowledge bases, the schema of a table is simple, and the number of cells contained is usually limited as well. This brings convenience for developing effective QA methods based on tables.

Based on the above two characteristics, we can see that TBQA is a good complementary to knowledge-based QA, and has values to many practical applications. In this paper, we assume that the table $\mathcal{T}$ is given for each question, and the answers of a question are always contained by the table. We leave table selection part and answering questions whose answers are not contained by tables as our future work.

4 Approach

4.1 Anchor Cell Detection

As the first step, we select a cell from the table as the anchor cell. Detecting anchor cells from tables is important to TBQA, as for a portion of questions, we need to use the anchor cell information to pinpoint the answer cells. Specifically, we use a simple trie-tree which stores all cell values of a table T to detect the anchor cells $\{A\}$ from a question Q. Each anchor cell A corresponds to a question pattern P_A. We obtain P_A by replacing $A.v$ in Q with a placeholder #.

4.2   Answer Cell Representation

We represent each table cell $C \in T$ with a real-valued vector, which is computed based on a set of well-designed features. As multiple anchor cells could be detected for a question, the same cell in a table may have multiple answer cell representations. We select the one with the maximum score based on Eq. 1. In this section, we will introduce the construction of an answer cell representation including four types of features.

Row-wise Feature. A row-wise feature h_{row} is designed to measure the probability that a cell $C \in T$ can be considered as the answer in terms of the relative row position between C and a detected anchor cell A.

$$h_{row} = p(tag(C, A, T)|P_A)$$

where $tag(C, A, T)$ is "+" if C and A are in the same row, and "−" otherwise. The estimation for $p(tag(C, A, T)|P_A)$ can be considered as a binary classification task. To train the classifier, we acquire training data by: (1) collecting ⟨question pattern, tag⟩ pairs from labeled ⟨question, table, answer⟩ triples; (2) training the binary classifier based on the collected pairs by a CNN model.

Table 1. Constraint functions and the definition.

Index	Function	Description
1	$first(\cdot)$	It returns "+" if $C.r$ is the first row where $A.v$ exists, and "−" otherwise
2	$last(\cdot)$	It returns "+" if $C.r$ is the last row where $A.v$ exists, and "−" otherwise
3	$above(\cdot)$	It returns "+" if $C.r$ is above $A.r$, i.e., $C.r = A.r - 1$, and "−" otherwise
4	$below(\cdot)$	It returns "+" if $C.r$ is below $A.r$, i.e., $C.r = A.r + 1$, and "−" otherwise
5	$larger(\cdot)$	It returns "+" if numerical values $T_{\langle C.r, A.a\rangle}.v > A.v$, and "−" otherwise
6	$smaller(\cdot)$	It returns "+" if numerical values $T_{\langle C.r, A.a\rangle}.v < A.v$, and "−" otherwise
7	$equal(\cdot)$	It returns "+" if numerical values $T_{\langle C.r, A.a\rangle}.v = A.v$, and "−" otherwise

Column-wise Feature. We observe that the attribute of the answer cell usually denotes the answer type of a question, and the question pattern typically includes the information of the answer type. Motivated by this observation, we design a feature $h_{ansType}$ which measures the relatedness of an attribute $C.a$ and a question pattern P_A to help locate the answer column.

$$h_{ansType} = \cos(E_{C.a}, E_{P_A})$$

where $E_{C.a}$ denotes the embedding vector of $C.a$, and E_{P_A} denotes the embedding vector of P_A.

Similarly, the relatedness of the attribute $A.a$ and the question pattern P_A is helpful for anchor cell disambiguation. Therefore, we design the second column-wise feature $h_{ancType}$ as follows:

$$h_{ancType} = \cos(E_{A.a}, E_{P_A})$$

where $E_{A.a}$ is the embedding vector of $A.a$.

As the training data is limited, some attributes are unseen in the test phase. To address this problem, we design the third column-wise feature

$$h_{attrOverlap} = |Set_{C.a} \wedge Set_{P_A}|$$

where $Set_{C.a}$ and Set_{P_A} denotes the words in $C.a$ and P_A, respectively. Each word is stemmed and is not a stop-word. The advantage of $h_{attrOverlap}$ is that it does not depend on the training data.

We leverage the architecture of CDSSM [11] to learn the embeddings of question patterns and attributes for $h_{ansType}$ and $h_{ancType}$.

Constraint-wise Features. Some questions have constraints on choosing the answers. For example, *"after 2008"* in the question in Fig. 1 is a constraint. Therefore, we design constraint-wise features to measure the probability that a cell $C \in T$ satisfies a constraint.

$$h_{cons} = p(tag(C, A, T)|P_A)$$

where $tag(C, A, T))$ represents a kind of constraint function which returns "+" or "−". Based on the observation on a development set, we define 7 constraint functions in Fig. 1, each of which corresponds to a constraint-wise feature.

The estimation of $p(tag(C, A, T)|P_A)$ can be considered as a binary classification task. We acquire the training data of the classification models by the following two steps: (1) Collect ⟨question pattern, tag⟩ pairs from labeled ⟨question, table, answer⟩ triples for each kind of constraint; (2) Train the classifiers for constraints 1 to 4 using a logistic regression model with lexicalized features, and for constraints 5 to 7 using a CNN model.

Selection and Exception Features. Through observing the development set, we find that there are two kinds of notable questions, i.e., selection and exception questions.

A selection question is defined as a binary-choice question with the right answer and a wrong answer mentioned by the question. Answering a selection question usually requires to determine the **relation**[2] r of the two choices on some **attribute**[3] a. For example, the question in Fig. 2 is a selection question

---

[2] A relation can be $>$, $<$, $=$ or $\neq$.

[3] An attribute can be an attribute in the table, or Count which counts the number of rows that a cell value appears in, or Index which returns the row index of a cell.

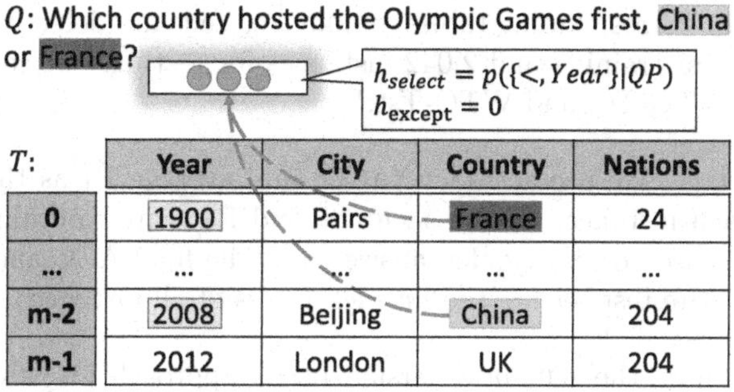

Fig. 2. An example for selection and exception features.

with two choices, "*China*" and "*France*". Answering this question requires to determine which Year of the two choices is earlier. We design a feature h_{select} to estimate the probability that a cell C can be considered as the right answer among the two choices C and A.

$$h_{select} = \max_{\langle r,a \rangle \in compare(C,A,T)} p(\langle r,a \rangle | QP)$$

where QP is obtained by replacing the two choices in the question with "#1" and "#2". Function $compare(C, A, T)$ enumerates all possible relation-attribute pairs based on C, A, and T. The estimation of $p(\langle r,a \rangle | QP)$ can be viewed as a classification task. We extract the training data from labeled ⟨question, table, answer⟩ triples and train the classifier with a CNN model.

We design an exception feature h_{except} to prune answer candidates. h_{except} indicates that whether a candidate should be excluded from the candidates. Specifically, $h_{except} = 1$ if the candidate cell C is mentioned after some key phrases in the question, such as "besides" and "except", and $h_{except} = 0$ otherwise.

4.3 Answer Cell Ranking

Formally, given a question Q and a table T, a candidate cell C is scored and ranked by the probability $p(C|Q,T)$ defined by Eq. 1. We rank each answer cell based on a learned ranker. To obtain the training data for the ranker, we extract features for each instance in the training set. Each positive instance is assigned with a score of 1. Each randomly selected negative instance is assigned with a score of 0. There are a variety of methods can be used to train the ranker. In this work, we adopt the lambda-rank [4] to train the ranker.

5 Experiment

5.1 Experiment Setting

Dataset. WIKITABLEQUESTIONS [8] contains 22,033 question-answer pairs on 2,108 tables. In this paper, we select a sub-set to ensure that the answers are contained by the corresponding tables and anchor cells are detected. We obtain 3,794 instances for training and 2,042 instances for testing. For convenient, we name them as WTQ-Trn and WTQ-Tst.

Evaluation Metric. We use accuracy (ACC) and average F1 as the evaluation metrics. For each instance, we use accuracy and F1 score to evaluate the predicted answers based on the golden answer set. The final ACC and average F1 scores on the entire test set are the *average* scores of all instances.

Baseline. We chose the semantic parsing based approach [8] as our baseline. [9] also conduct experiments on WIKITABLEQUESTIONS, but they do not evaluate the accuracy of their results. We use SEMPRE[4] to train the model of the baseline on WTQ-Trn and test the model on WTQ-Tst.

5.2 Experiment Result

We first compare the search space of the two systems. The baseline system generates **1,011.7** logical forms for a question on average, while our system directly ranks **361.2** cells on average.

Table 2. Experiment results of the baseline and our **IR-TBQA** approach on WTQ-Tst.

Setting	F1	ACC
[8]	47.21	47.01
IR-TBQA	**54.50**	**53.04**
IR-TBQA w/o row-wise	39.10	36.04
IR-TBQA w/o column-wise	26.70	19.49
IR-TBQA w/o constraint-wise	38.49	35.11
IR-TBQA w/o selection and exception	46.81	44.96

Table 2 shows the experiment results of the baseline and our IRTBQA approach with different settings. The results indicate that our IRTBQA approach outperforms the baseline by an ACC score of 6.03 (47.01 to 53.04) and an average F1 score of 7.29 (47.21 to 54.50). We remove each type of features at one time to show their impacts on the results. Removing row-wise features, column-wise features, constraint-wise features and selection and exception features, the results decrease 17.00, 33.55, 17.93 and 8.08 points on ACC, respectively. The results indicate that each type of features help improve the performance of our approach. The four types of features are designed from different perspectives, including question understanding and answer locating. We also find that the performance decrease a lot by removing the column-wise feature. This is because the

---

[4] https://github.com/percyliang/sempre.

column-wise features are the only ones that focus on locating column positions, while the others mainly focus on locating row positions (Fig. 3).

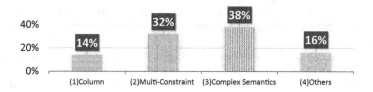

Fig. 3. The distribution of error types.

5.3   Error Analysis and Discussion

We randomly sample 100 instances with wrongly predicted answers for error analysis. We classify the errors in to four types. (1) 14% of the errors are caused by predicting the wrong columns. Obtaining more <question pattern, attribute> training data to pinpoint the columns is very important for TBQA. (2) 32% of the errors are caused because these questions contain multiple constrains. For example, in question *"what was the first year he scored more than 4 touchdowns"*, both *"first"* and *"more than 4 touchdowns"* are constraints. We leave designing multi-constraint features to future work. (3) 38% of the questions have complex semantics. For example, the question *"which team did lau nim yat play for after he was transferred?"* has a clause *"after he was transferred"* to limit the answers. Features for other complex semantics are put to future work. (4) 16% of the questions are not correctly answered due to the ranking and labelling problem. For instance, *"which opponent is listed after cleveland freeze in the table?"* should have multiple answers, but the labeled golden standard only contains one answer.

6   Conclusion and Future Work

We propose a simple yet effective information retrieval (IR) based approach to answer complex questions with web tables. Our IR-based approach directly ranks table cells based on dense feature values, which reduces the search space. Furthermore, we design rich features which leverage both the semantic information of the question and the structure information of the table. We conduct experiments on standard dataset and prove the effectiveness of our approach. Since we assume that the input is a question-table pair, we leave the table selection to our future work. Besides, we will consider to give a solution to the questions that have no anchor cells detected or without its answers appearing in the tables.

References

1. Berant, J., Chou, A., Frostig, R., Liang, P.: Semantic parsing on Freebase from question-answer pairs. In: Proceedings of the 2013 Conference on Empirical Methods in Natural Language Processing, Seattle, Washington, USA, pp. 1533–1544. Association for Computational Linguistics, October 2013. http://www.aclweb.org/anthology/D13-1160

2. Bollacker, K., Evans, C., Paritosh, P., Sturge, T., Taylor, J.: Freebase: a collaboratively created graph database for structuring human knowledge. In: Proceedings of the 2008 ACM SIGMOD International Conference on Management of Data, pp. 1247–1250. ACM (2008)

3. Bordes, A., Chopra, S., Weston, J.: Question answering with subgraph embeddings. In: Proceedings of the 2014 Conference on Empirical Methods in Natural Language Processing, EMNLP 2014, Doha, Qatar, 25–29 October 2014, A Meeting of SIGDAT, a Special Interest Group of the ACL, pp. 615–620 (2014). http://aclweb.org/anthology/D/D14/D14-1067.pdf

4. Burges, C.J.: From ranknet to lambdarank to lambdamart: an overview. Learning **11**, 23–581 (2010)

5. Dong, L., Wei, F., Zhou, M., Xu, K.: Question answering over freebase with multi-column convolutional neural networks. In: Proceedings of the 53rd Annual Meeting of the Association for Computational Linguistics and the 7th International Joint Conference on Natural Language Processing (vol. 1: Long Papers), Beijing, China, pp. 260–269. Association for Computational Linguistics, July 2015. http://www.aclweb.org/anthology/P15-1026

6. Fader, A., Zettlemoyer, L., Etzioni, O.: Open question answering over curated and extracted knowledge bases. In: Proceedings of the 20th ACM SIGKDD International Conference on Knowledge Discovery and Data Mining, pp. 1156–1165. ACM (2014)

7. Jauhar, S.K., Turney, P.D., Hovy, E.: Tables as Semi-structured Knowledge for Question Answering (2016)

8. Pasupat, P., Liang, P.: Compositional semantic parsing on semi-structured tables. arXiv preprint arXiv:1508.00305 (2015)

9. Pasupat, P., Liang, P.: Inferring logical forms from denotations. arXiv preprint arXiv:1606.06900 (2016)

10. Reddy, S., Täckström, O., Collins, M., Kwiatkowski, T., Das, D., Steedman, M., Lapata, M.: Transforming dependency structures to logical forms for semantic parsing. Trans. Assoc. Comput. Linguist. **4**, 127–140 (2016)

11. Shen, Y., He, X., Gao, J., Deng, L., Mesnil, G.: Learning semantic representations using convolutional neural networks for web search. In: Proceedings of the Companion Publication of the 23rd International Conference on World Wide Web Companion, pp. 373–374. International World Wide Web Conferences Steering Committee (2014)

12. Sun, H., Ma, H., He, X., Yih, W.T., Su, Y., Yan, X.: Table cell search for question answering. In: Proceedings of the 25th International Conference on World Wide Web, pp. 771–782. International World Wide Web Conferences Steering Committee (2016)

13. Xu, K., Reddy, S., Feng, Y., Huang, S., Zhao, D.: Question answering on freebase via relation extraction and textual evidence. In: Proceedings of the 54th Annual Meeting of the Association for Computational Linguistics (vol. 1: Long Papers), Berlin, Germany, pp. 2326–2336. Association for Computational Linguistics, August 2016. http://www.aclweb.org/anthology/P16-1220

14. Yao, X.: Lean question answering over freebase from scratch. In: Proceedings of NAACL-HLT, pp. 66–70 (2015)

15. Yih, W.T., Chang, M.W., He, X., Gao, J.: Semantic parsing via staged query graph generation: question answering with knowledge base. In: Proceedings of the 53rd Annual Meeting of the Association for Computational Linguistics and the 7th International Joint Conference on Natural Language Processing (vol. 1: Long Papers), Beijing, China, pp. 1321–1331. Association for Computational Linguistics, July 2015. http://www.aclweb.org/anthology/P15-1128

16. Yih, W.T., He, X., Meek, C.: Semantic parsing for single-relation question answering. In: ACL, vol. 2, pp. 643–648. Citeseer (2014)

17. Yin, P., Lu, Z., Li, H., Kao, B.: Neural Enquirer: Learning to Query Tables with Natural Language (2015)

Building Emotional Conversation Systems Using Multi-task Seq2Seq Learning

Rui Zhang, Zhenyu Wang$^{(\boxtimes)}$, and Dongcheng Mai

Department of Software Engineering, South China University of Technology,
Guangzhou, People's Republic of China
z.rui16@mail.scut.edu.cn, wangzy@scut.edu.cn, dongchengmai@gmail.com

Abstract. This paper describes our system designed for the NLPCC 2017 shared task on emotional conversation generation. Our model adopts a multi-task Seq2Seq learning framework to capture the textual information of post sequence and generate responses for each type of emotions simultaneously. Evaluation results suggest that our model is competitive on emotional generation, which achieves 0.9658 on average emotion accuracy. We also observe the emotional interaction in human conversation, and try to explain it as empathy at the psychological level. Finally, our model achieves 325 on total score, 0.545 on average score and won the fourth place on total score.

Keywords: Conversation generation · Emotions · Multi-task Seq2Seq

1 Introduction

The NLPCC 2017 emotional conversation generation shared task focuses on generating emotional coherent responses in Chinese. This task is challenging due to the difficulty of capturing emotional factors and the complex mechanism of human emotions. There have been prior works [1,11,14,15] on emotional conversation, however, most of them are either rule-based or limited to small-scale data, not extensible to large-scale data.

Recently, large-scale conversation generation approaches [12,13,16] have been investigated, thanks to the advance of deep learning. Inspired by these end-to-end approaches, Zhou et al. proposed Emotional Chatting Machine (ECM) [20], a model in the encoder-decoder framework of large-scale sequence-to-sequence generation that can respond to users emotionally. However, ECM had to specify an emotion category to be generated, which need an external decision maker.

In this paper, we propose a multi-emotional conversation system (MECS) to generate emotional coherent responses. The model consists of two main components: (1) a multi-emotion response generator to generate responses for each type of emotions simultaneously, and (2) an output selector to choose the most appropriate response using intra-ranking and inter-ranking policies.

We evaluate our model at both context level and emotion level. The experimental results show that our model is competitive in emotional conversation

© Springer International Publishing AG 2018
X. Huang et al. (Eds.): NLPCC 2017, LNAI 10619, pp. 612–621, 2018.
https://doi.org/10.1007/978-3-319-73618-1_51

generation task, which achieves 0.9658 on average emotion accuracy. We report on a detailed analysis of the evaluation results in the NLPCC 2017 shared task. The evaluation results indicate that the multi-task framework performs well on emotional conversation generation, although the single-layer GRU architecture is too simple to capture complex textual information.

In emotion interaction analysis, we also find that people tend to achieve the same emotional state in conversation. We try to explain this phenomenon as empathy at the psychological level.

The rest of the paper is arranged as follows. In Sect. 2 we discuss the detail of data preprocessing. In Sect. 3 we present MECS, our approach for emotional conversation generation task. In Sect. 4 we outline the experiments. We close with our conclusions in Sect. 5, and a discussion of future work.

2   Preprocessing

2.1   Data Cleaning

There are some specific symbols, excess punctuations and Cantonese text in raw text. We clean the text by removing the specific symbols and excess punctuations. In order to remove Cantonese text from the raw data, we crawl some Cantonese text and Chinese text as training data from Weibo, and construct a classify model using convolutional neural network introduced by Kim [8]. After data preprocessing, about 85.9% of post-response pairs have been retained, as shown in Table 1.

Table 1. Data distribution of clean data.

Categories of responses	Original data	Clean data
Other	198,069	172,197
Like	200,001	169,371
Sadness	181,252	158,657
Disgust	200,001	176,207
Anger	139,883	115,740
Happiness	200,001	168,821
Total	1,119,207	960,993

2.2   Response Expansion

We expand the data for training a multi-task emotional conversation model, since the format of the raw data is one-to-one: each pair contains one post and only one response, together with their emotional information.

The training data are firstly grouped according to the emotion categories of responses. Each post-response pair is expanded to a tuple with one post and six emotional responses, corresponding to different emotion types respectively. The original emotional response is retained, while the missing responses are filled by searching the most appropriate responses from the corresponding emotional groups using a retrieve-based method. The retrieve-based approach is introduced as follows:

We train a LDA topic model using gensim[1], and calculate text similarity using both topic similarity and cosine similarity:

$$F_{sim}(p_1, p_2) = \lambda S_{topic}(p_1, p_2) + (1 - \lambda)S_{cosine}(p_1, p_2) \tag{1}$$

where λ is set to 0.5. S_{topic} is topic similarity calculated by the LDA model and S_{cosine} is cosine similarity defined as:

$$S_{cosine}(p_1, p_2) = \frac{\overrightarrow{v_1} \cdot \overrightarrow{v_2}}{\|\overrightarrow{v_1}\| \|\overrightarrow{v_2}\|} \tag{2}$$

where p_1 and p_2 are post text, corresponding to word vectors $\overrightarrow{v_1}$ and $\overrightarrow{v_2}$ respectively.

Formula (1) calculates the similarity between two posts at both text-level and topic-level. Yet the retrieve-based model picks out the most similar pair evaluated by Formula (1), and returns the respective response as result.

To measure the appropriateness of expanded training pairs, we employ human judgements to evaluate a random sample of 500 items. Each item is assigned to 3 judges, who are asked to decide whether the responses are topic coherent. Results for human evaluation show that about 40.93% of expanded responses is acceptable.

3   System Description

3.1   Multi-emotional Conversation Generation

Inspired by Luong et al. [10], we propose a multi-emotional conversation system. Given a new post, our model is to generate six responses simultaneously, corresponding to each kind of emotions respectively, which are {other, like, sadness, disgust, anger, happiness}, as shown in Fig. 1. The encoder and decoders of the multi-task Seq2Seq model are implemented with GRU [4], since GRU performs comparable to LSTM [5] but has less parameters and easier to train.

One-to-Many Architecture. In order to generate responses that are coherent with the target emotion categories, we adopt a one-to-many Seq2Seq architecture. Each decoder is independent of others, but shares the same encoder.

Given a post sequence $\mathbf{X} = (x_1, x_2, \cdots, x_n)$, the encoder converts $\mathbf{X}$ to its hidden representations $\mathbf{h} = (h_1, h_2, \cdots, h_n)$ using GRU, briefly defined as:

$$h_t = \mathbf{GRU}(h_{t-1}, x_t) \tag{3}$$

Details of GRU is introduced by Cho et al. [4].

---

[1] https://radimrehurek.com/gensim/.

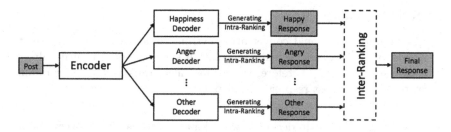

Fig. 1. The general framework and dataflow of MECS.

Each decoder takes the embedding of a previously decoded word y_{t-1}^i and a context vector c_t^i, and updates its state s_t^i using another GRU:

$$s_t^i = \mathbf{GRU}(s_{t-1}^i, [c_t^i; e(y_{t-1}^i)]) \tag{4}$$

where i is the emotional decoder index, $e(y_{t-1}^i)$ is the corresponding word vector of y_{t-1}^i, and $[c_t^i; e(y_{t-1}^i)]$ is the concatenation of the two vectors. The attention mechanism [2] is applied to learn context vector c_t^i, which depends on the previous state s_{t-1}^i of the decoder:

$$c_t^i = \sum_{t=1}^{T} \alpha_{kt}^i h_t \tag{5}$$

$$\alpha_{kt}^i = \frac{exp(e_{kt}^i)}{\sum_{j=1}^{T} exp(e_{kj}^i)} \tag{6}$$

$$e_{kt}^i = (v_a^i)^{\top} tanh(W_a^i s_{k-1}^i + U_a^i h_k) \tag{7}$$

where α_{kt}^i is the weight of hidden layer representation h_t of the post sequence for the ith decoder. It is noteworthy that the hidden representations $\mathbf{h}$ of post sequence are shared between each emotional decoder.

Finally, the output probability distribution o_t^i of the next token y_t^i is computed as:

$$y_t^i \sim o_t^i = P(y_t^i | y_{t-1}^i, \cdots, y_1^i, c_t^i) \tag{8}$$

$$= softmax(W_o^i s_t^i) \tag{9}$$

and the next token y_t^i is generated by sampling from the distribution o_t^i.

Training. The objective function is based on the cross entropy error between the predicted token distribution o_t^i and the gold distribution p_t^i in the training corpus, defined as:

$$L(\theta) = -\sum_{t} p_t^{i^{\top}} log(o_t^i) \tag{10}$$

Since each task in MECS is similar, we adopt an alternating training approach as introduced by Dong et al. [6].

3.2 Ranking Policy

Though the multi-emotional conversation system could generate responses for all emotion types, however, a real conversation system should return only one response, instead of six. Therefore, we propose intra-ranking and inter-ranking policies to select the best response as output.

Intra-ranking. For each decoder, we adopt beam-search to over-generate responses. These responses are ranked using:

$$p(\mathbf{Y}|\mathbf{X}) = \prod_{t=1}^{N_y} p(y_t|x_1, x_2, \cdots, x_T, y_1, y_2, \cdots, y_{t-1}) \tag{11}$$

$$= \prod_{t=1}^{N_y} \frac{exp(f(s_t, e_{y_t}))}{\sum_{y'} exp(f(s_t, e_{y'}))} \tag{12}$$

where $f(s_t, e_{y_t})$ denotes the corresponding output on the last projection layer for word y_t, and N_y denotes the length of response sequence $\mathbf{Y}$. Ultimately, we select the sentence with highest score as the output of this decoder.

Inter-ranking. After responses for different emotion types have been generated, an inter-ranking policy is adopted to select the most appropriate response as the final output. In MECS, however, we rank the results among emotional decoders directly based on the score calculated by Formula (11). This naive policy tends to choose a fluent expression without considering the emotion type of input text. Therefore, it is not capable to simulate the emotion interaction in human conversation, as discussed in Sect. 4.2.

4 Experiments

4.1 Model Details

We adopt single-layer GRU for encoding and decoding, each of which consists of a different set of parameters. Each GRU layer consists of 128 hidden neurons, and the dimensionality of word embedding is also set to 128. The model is trained on a single GTX1060 GPU for less than 3 days. Other training details are given as below.

- GRU parameters and embeddings are initialized from a uniform distribution in [0,1).
- Stochastic gradient decent is implemented and learning rate is set to 0.5, with a decay rate of 0.99.
- Batch size is set to 128. Epoch size is set to 20.
- Beam-search is adopted with beam size of 5, and buckets are applied to generate response with appropriate length. Buckets are set to [(5,10), (10, 15), (20, 25), (40, 50)].

4.2   Experimental Results and Analysis

Evaluating a response generation model is still an open problem. Following [17] we employ perplexity as an evaluation metric at the context level, since BLEU is not suitable for measuring conversation generation, as argued in [9]. To evaluate the model at the emotion level, we adopt emotion accuracy as the agreement between the expected emotion category and the predicted emotion category of the response generated by the corresponding emotional decoder, using the same Bi-LSTM emotion classifier mentioned in the homepage[2] of the shared task. The results are shown in Table 2.

Table 2. Quantitative evaluation in terms of perplexity and emotion accuracy.

Categories of responses	Perplexity	Emotion accuracy
Other	383.86	0.9467
Like	79.14	0.9895
Sadness	77.26	0.9886
Disgust	318.73	0.9171
Anger	103.33	0.9533
Happiness	54.36	0.9996
Average	169.45	0.9658

As can be seen, our model performs well in emotion accuracy, but the perplexity of the decoders varies widely, since each decoder is trained on definitely different pairs. Thanks to the multi-task framework, each decoder is trained to respond in a specific emotional state, tends not to generate response with ambiguous emotion. Furthermore, tokens that express other emotions might not appear in the training pairs for the specific decoder. For example, the words "resentful" tends not to appear in a happy response. Hence, we can even customize the dictionary for each decoder separately, to reduce model parameters and improve emotion accuracy.

However, it is worth noting that the accuracy rate here is falsely high more or less. Since we use only single-layer GRU for encoding and decoding, the model tends to generate dull responses. For example, the word "haha", which is also a significant identifier token for the emotion classifier, appears almost in every result in "happiness" category.

4.3   Emotion Interaction Analysis

Moreover, we evaluate the inter-ranking mechanism by visualizing the emotion interaction. Emotion interaction pattern (EIP) is defined as $<e_p, e_r>$, as introduced in [20], is the pair of emotion categories of a post and its response. The value of an EIP is the conditional probability $P(e_r|e_p) = P(e_r, e_p)/P(e_p)$. We visualize the emotion interaction pattern as Fig. 2.

---

[2] http://www.aihuang.org/p/challenge.html.

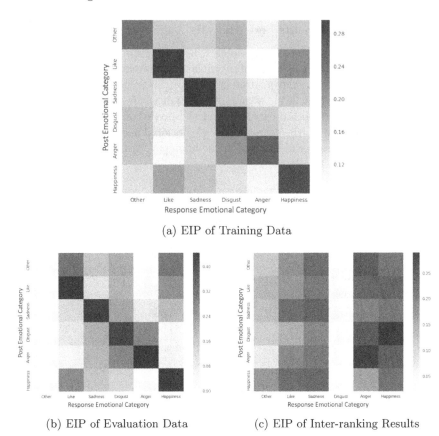

(a) EIP of Training Data

(b) EIP of Evaluation Data   (c) EIP of Inter-ranking Results

Fig. 2. Visualization of emotion interaction.

Unlike the analysis of [20], we observed some interesting features in training data, as shown in Fig. 2(a). Obviously, the color of the blocks on the diagonal is much darker, which means that people tend to response in the same emotional state in a conversation. We believe that this phenomenon can be explained by empathy. Empathy is the capacity to understand what another person is experiencing from within the other person's frame of reference, as defined in [3]. The same phenomenon is also observed in the evaluation data, as shown in Fig. 2(b), although the evaluation data does not contain responses in "other" category.

Unfortunately, as shown in Fig. 2(c), the inter-ranking policy is not capable to simulate the empathy phenomenon. As discussed in Sect. 3.2, the inter-ranking mechanism tends to select sentences generated by the decoder which has lower perplexity, for example, the decoder of "happiness" category. On the other hand, responses generated by a decoder with higher perplexity, such as the decoder of "other" or "disgust" category, are difficult to be selected. Therefore, the results of this ranking mechanism might be focused, although it can guarantee the fluency of the response.

4.4 Shared Task Evaluation Results

Results of our model and other top competitors in the shared task are shown in Table 3. Our model achieves 325 on total score and won the fourth place on this indicator. According to the summary report, the number of results submitted by each team is very different, so the total score and the average score can reflect the effect of the model to a certain extent. The table below lists only the top-ranked teams which completely submit the results.

Table 3. Human evaluation results in NLPCC 2017 shared task.

Model	0 points terms	1 point terms	2 points terms	Total terms	Total score	Average score
samsung-1	267	82	247	596	276	0.966443
Babbling-2	305	19	271	595	561	0.942857
samsung-2	272	93	231	596	555	0.931208
Ours	**428**	**11**	**157**	**596**	**325**	**0.545302**
Babbling-1	424	41	131	596	303	0.508389
gry-1	449	31	116	596	263	0.441275

We also conducted a detailed analysis of each emotional decoder. The human evaluation results and analysis are as follows (Table 4):

Table 4. Human evaluation results among emotional categories for MECS.

Emotion categories	0 points terms	1 point terms	2 points terms	Total terms	Total score	Average score
Like	100	0	33	133	66	0.496241
Sadness	82	0	37	119	74	0.621849
Disgust	133	6	5	144	16	**0.111111**
Angry	59	2	10	71	22	0.309859
Happiness	54	3	72	129	147	**1.139535**

As can be seen, our model generates a large amount of 0 points terms, which means the generation result is not coherent or not fluent. Due to the poor capability of single-layer GRU to capture semantics features, our model is not sufficient to produce high-quality responses. The evaluation results are consistent with the analysis in Table 2: the "happiness" decoder with lowest perplexity generates responses with highest quality, and decoders with high perplexity (such as "disgust" decoder) performs poorly.

On the other hand, our model generates few 1 point terms, which means the generation result is coherent and fluent but not emotionally consistent. As discussed in Sect. 4.2, our model achieves a high emotional accuracy. The human evaluation result here is also consistent with our experimental result, which shows that our model performs well in the emotional generation task.

5   Conclusions and Future Works

In this paper, an emotional conversation system based on multi-task Seq2Seq framework is proposed. Although this model behaved moderately in NLPCC 2017 shared task, the evaluation of further experiments shows that multi-task framework could behave competitively on emotional generation.

Our approach leaves a lot of room for extensions. First of all, the single-layer GRU architecture is too simple to capture the complex information of input text, and is not capable enough to generate informative and interesting responses. In addition, with our naive inter-ranking policy, this model cannot simulate the empathy phenomenon in human conversation.

For future work, we plan to enhance the ability of our model to generate topic coherence responses, as discussed in [7,18,19,21]. We also consider designing an appropriate ranking policy to capture the emotion interaction and make the conversation system more human.

Acknowledgements. This work is supported by the Science and Technology Program of Guangdong Province, China (2015B010131003). The authors also thank the editors and reviewers for their constructive editing and reviewing, respectively.

References

1. André, E., Rehm, M., Minker, W., Bühler, D.: Endowing spoken language dialogue systems with emotional intelligence. In: André, E., Dybkjær, L., Minker, W., Heisterkamp, P. (eds.) ADS 2004. LNCS (LNAI), vol. 3068, pp. 178–187. Springer, Heidelberg (2004). https://doi.org/10.1007/978-3-540-24842-2_17
2. Bahdanau, D., Cho, K., Bengio, Y.: Neural machine translation by jointly learning to align and translate. arXiv preprint arXiv:1409.0473 (2014)
3. Bellet, P.S., Maloney, M.J.: The importance of empathy as an interviewing skill in medicine. JAMA **266**(13), 1831–1832 (1991)
4. Cho, K., Van Merriënboer, B., Gulcehre, C., Bahdanau, D., Bougares, F., Schwenk, H., Bengio, Y.: Learning phrase representations using RNN encoder-decoder for statistical machine translation. arXiv preprint arXiv:1406.1078 (2014)
5. Chung, J., Gulcehre, C., Cho, K., Bengio, Y.: Empirical evaluation of gated recurrent neural networks on sequence modeling. arXiv preprint arXiv:1412.3555 (2014)
6. Dong, D., Wu, H., He, W., Yu, D., Wang, H.: Multi-task learning for multiple language translation. In: ACL, pp. 1723–1732 (2015)
7. Gu, J., Lu, Z., Li, H., Li, V.O.: Incorporating copying mechanism in sequence-to-sequence learning. arXiv preprint arXiv:1603.06393 (2016)
8. Kim, Y.: Convolutional neural networks for sentence classification. arXiv preprint arXiv:1408.5882 (2014)

9. Liu, C.W., Lowe, R., Serban, I.V., Noseworthy, M., Charlin, L., Pineau, J.: How not to evaluate your dialogue system: an empirical study of unsupervised evaluation metrics for dialogue response generation. arXiv preprint arXiv:1603.08023 (2016)

10. Luong, M.T., Le, Q.V., Sutskever, I., Vinyals, O., Kaiser, L.: Multi-task sequence to sequence learning. arXiv preprint arXiv:1511.06114 (2015)

11. Michal, P., Pawel, D., Wenhan, S., Rafal, R., Kenji, A.: Towards context aware emotional intelligence in machines: computing contextual appropriateness of affective states. In: Proceedings of the Twenty-First International Joint Conference on Artificial Intelligence (IJCAI 2009), pp. 1469–1474. AAAI (2009)

12. Ritter, A., Cherry, C., Dolan, W.B.: Data-driven response generation in social media. In: Proceedings of the Conference on Empirical Methods in Natural Language Processing, pp. 583–593. Association for Computational Linguistics (2011)

13. Shang, L., Lu, Z., Li, H.: Neural responding machine for short-text conversation. arXiv preprint arXiv:1503.02364 (2015)

14. Skowron, M.: Affect listeners: acquisition of affective states by means of conversational systems. In: Esposito, A., Campbell, N., Vogel, C., Hussain, A., Nijholt, A. (eds.) Development of Multimodal Interfaces: Active Listening and Synchrony. LNCS, vol. 5967, pp. 169–181. Springer, Heidelberg (2010). https://doi.org/10.1007/978-3-642-12397-9_14

15. Skowron, M., Rank, S., Theunis, M., Sienkiewicz, J.: The good, the bad and the neutral: affective profile in dialog system-user communication. In: D'Mello, S., Graesser, A., Schuller, B., Martin, J.-C. (eds.) ACII 2011. LNCS, vol. 6974, pp. 337–346. Springer, Heidelberg (2011). https://doi.org/10.1007/978-3-642-24600-5_37

16. Sutskever, I., Vinyals, O., Le, Q.V.: Sequence to sequence learning with neural networks. In: Advances in Neural Information Processing Systems, pp. 3104–3112 (2014)

17. Vinyals, O., Le, Q.: A neural conversational model. arXiv preprint arXiv:1506.05869 (2015)

18. Wen, T.H., Gasic, M., Mrksic, N., Su, P.H., Vandyke, D., Young, S.: Semantically conditioned LSTM-based natural language generation for spoken dialogue systems. arXiv preprint arXiv:1508.01745 (2015)

19. Xing, C., Wu, W., Wu, Y., Liu, J., Huang, Y., Zhou, M., Ma, W.Y.: Topic aware neural response generation. In: AAAI, pp. 3351–3357 (2017)

20. Zhou, H., Huang, M., Zhang, T., Zhu, X., Liu, B.: Emotional chatting machine: emotional conversation generation with internal and external memory. arXiv preprint arXiv:1704.01074 (2017)

21. Zhou, H., Huang, M., Zhu, X.: Context-aware natural language generation for spoken dialogue systems. In: COLING, pp. 2032–2041 (2016)

NLPCC 2017 Shared Task Social Media User Modeling Method Summary by DUTIR_923

Dongzhen Wen, Liang Yang, HengChao Li, Kai Guo, Peng Fei,
and HongFei Lin[(⊠)]

Dalian University of Technology, Dalian 116023, Liaoning, China
hflin@dlut.edu.cn

Abstract. User attribute classification plays an important role in the Internet advertising, public opinion monitoring. While the user points of interest prediction helps the online social media services creating more value. In this paper, aiming at solving the user attributes classification tasks we combine the feature engineering and deep Learning method to reach a higher rank. User attribute classification task is divided into two sub-tasks, in sub-task one, we use the user's POI (point of interest) check-in history and popular POI location information to predict the next POI that user may visit the future. Sub-task 2 needs to predict the gender of the user. We use the Stacking method to carry out the feature fusion method to complete the feature extraction, based on the output of the logistic regression model then features will be sent to XGBoost model to perform the prediction. In addition, we also used the Convolution neural network model to dig out the user tweets information. Here we replace the conventional Max Pooling method with Attention Pooling in order to minimum the information lost in neural network training. Finally, two methods are given to give a more accurate result.

Keywords: Geographic location information · Popular POI prediction
Stacking model · Attention pooling

1 Introduction

The construction of the user image is particularly important in Internet services and many social products. An active Internet user will generate a wide variety of virtual user data at all times in real life.

Through the analysis of these user's online behavioral characteristics, online services provider can provide many services such as advertising recommendations [1, 2], social networking friends recommended [3], music recommended [4] are based on this the user's image to describe the construction.

With the traditional service industry access to the Internet, users can be pre-scheduled service on a real network, and consumer services within a specified time. So the concept of user interest points has appeared in Internet map service. A typical point of interest for users can be popular food and beverage outlets, subway stations and other transportation hubs, banking and other government agencies and other service agencies. At the same time, a business model encourages users to "check in" on

© Springer International Publishing AG 2018
X. Huang et al. (Eds.): NLPCC 2017, LNAI 10619, pp. 622–631, 2018.
https://doi.org/10.1007/978-3-319-73618-1_52

the network in reality service establishments, while advertising for businesses to conduct spontaneous user, giving the user concessions. This makes it possible to predict the user's points of interest [5].

The object of this evaluation is combined with the user's social information, and the user has check-in user interest point for user information and user points of interest gender prediction, evaluation is divided into two sub-tasks, the user gender prediction and forecasting user point of interest.

1.1   POI Recommendation

Subtasks required to predict the POI of a user to be accessed next check-in information according to user's social network information and user POI ever visited.

The user's interest prediction can be transformed into the recommendation system question. According to the user's access characteristics, the most mature recommendation algorithm is the collaborative filtering algorithm [6, 7]. By constructing the user commodity matrix combination matrix decomposition and matrix multiplication method to calculate the degree of correlation between users and goods, then the best matched goods will be recommended to the user.

In this task, our approach is slightly different from the traditional method. Through the analysis of the POI prediction problem, we can find that there are two kinds of problems to be solved for the point of interest that the user is about to visit. First, the location of the user's location and the prediction of the geographical location of the user's visit are the other. Determination of user interest.

Then in Jeffrey McGee's work they propose a location estimator Friendly Location that leverages the relationship between the strength of the tie between a pair of users, and the distance between the pair. They combine the graph analysis with decision tree model, then use the results as the input to a maximum likelihood estimator to predict a user's location [8].

Finally we got inspiration from the work of Liu. First they perform a preference transition (over location categories) prediction. And then perform the category-aware POI recommendation. They employ Matrix factorization to predict a user's preference transitions over categories and then her preference on locations in the corresponding categories [9].

1.2   Gender Prediction

After reviewing the relevant literature at home and abroad, we find that the gender prediction is more mature and the most basic method is to classify the user attributes by mining the implicit information in the user's tweet [10]. The user's online relationship information, the user's interest label information and the check-in information in the social network can be used as the characteristic to predict the user's attribute. Combined with the characteristics of the means of feature engineering and traditional machine learning methods to predict the gender of the user has been able to achieve a good results [11].

Some neural networks have been used to carry out user gender classification after the rise of NN (neural network) in recent years. In the field of image recognition, CNN is used to carry out gender prediction under face recognition. David Bamman and Antipov et al. [12]. Used CNN and improved CNN to achieve gender prediction by recognizing face images [13]. In the field of text classification Kim using CNN for text classification research, making CNN to achieve gender classification possible. With the development of NN to the present, the performance of CNN in various tasks makes it possible for many researchers to carry out research on its application in specific fields [14]. In 2014 the google DL team put forward the Attention mechanism to improve the accuracy of image recognition, so far attention mechanism in many tasks on the outstanding performance, the use of similar to the human eye to observe the attention of the image of the mechanism, some key information elements are captured during the training process [15, 16]. Enhance its weight in the training process to better tap the hidden features. While using Max-Pooling in CNN will sometimes losing information when perform NN training, this paper proposes an Attention-Pooling method to improve the performance of CNN. In our paper, we will combine the traditional machine learning method and the depth learning method under the characteristic engineering to complete Subtask Two.

2 Methods

This part mainly introduces the method we used in two subtask. Subtask one we use the method of geostatistical forecasting. Through the determination of the position of the user, the user points out all the user's points of interest in the data set, and finally selects 10 optimal results are recommended. Sub-task 2 uses two methods to compare the results of the fusion, the first method using feature engineering combined with the traditional classifier classification, first of all three characteristics of the user using the stacking method for feature fusion, and then input to the XGBoost model Boost model training, and ultimately the results. The second method uses the CNN after the Attention-Pooling mechanism to improve the user's gender prediction by digging the information of the user's tweet data. Finally, the results obtained by the two models are weighted by voting and the final result is obtained.

2.1 Subtask One

For POI forecasting, we use the POI forecasting method based on user location information. The method mainly includes the following two aspects.

First of all, through the user's check-in information for statistical analysis, because the normal geographical location information is stable, so by the user check-in information analysis can be obtained by the user's basic activity range. It is possible to recommend the point of interest for the user's position after determining the scope of the user's activity.

Our user location analysis model is shown as Fig. 1, where circles represent a certain user's activities range. Red crosses represent the POI which user had checked-in, then the cross in blue means those which had not been this user checked-in. Our location-based POI prediction method based on these user-POI-location model.

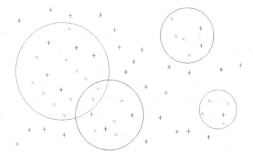

Fig. 1. User's range of activities with check-in POI (Color figure online)

The second point is based on the heat points of interest statistics, we take into account when a point of interest for the hot points of interest, the probability of being accessed compared to the attendance of popular points of interest, is to be greater. The training set of data given in this task is large, so there is reason to believe that the data points in the statistics of the popular points of interest in the actual situation is indeed people willing to visit the location.

The method of user point of interest prediction shown in Fig. 2. Our core prediction algorithm is based on the location information of the points of interest visited by the user, combined with the location information of the points of interest that have been calculated to the point of interest that the user may visit next To predict. The algorithm first counts all the points of interest and their geographical location in the training data set as the basis for the prediction.

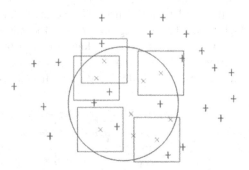

Fig. 2. User POI prediction model

After that, the user id in the predicted task is analyzed to calculate the point of interest that the user has visited. Here, a parameter dst = 0.01 is set, which represent an POI searching range. Then the POI within the range of 1 km near the location of the POI that the user has visited to will be add into the candidate set using for the user POI prediction. Subsequent to the candidate sets are sorted by the heat of the points of interest after the predicted points of interest for all the users have been predicted. Finally, take out the top 10 hot points of interest as the user's final prediction results to output, thus complete a user's point of interest prediction.

2.2   Subtask Two

Through the analysis of the data set can be found in this task in the data set is not balanced. The vast majority of users have a focus on the relationship with the attention, the user interested in the label information and the user has visited the POI information. A few users have tweet information. Therefore, it is difficult to construct the characteristics of the user simply by means of text-based feature extraction. We propose an XGBoost training model for stacking fusion using logistic regression features and a volume and neural network model combined with Attention mechanism. The following two models will be described separately.

Feature Fusion Method Based on Stacking Model

After the training set data analysis can be drawn, the user's attention, check-in data and user tag information for the current user coverage is more comprehensive, so the use of these three types of data for logical regression. We first through the data preprocessing operation, the same user all the check-in location information and tag information and attention to the relationship between the information aggregation, easy to follow-up processing. For label data in the training set, the tags are encoded by binarization to facilitate the training of subsequent models.

In the training data set, we used the 5-fold cross validation to model the training. The training data is divided into five parts, four of which are used for model training, and as a standard data set for offline test. Then we use Logistic regression, the feature fusion of the Stacking method is carried out for the three types of features.

Here in order to avoid confusion, we will train the set of data as TrainReal, test set data recorded as TestReal.

The concrete structure is shown in Fig. 3. In the process of feature fusion, 50% is still used for stacking. It should be noted here that we divide the training set data TrainReal, four of which are used as training sets and one for training and verification of logical regression as a validation set. After the logical regression results of the five verification sets are concatenated, the results are combined with the predictive results of the test regression data TestReal, and finally the stacking fusion result is formed.

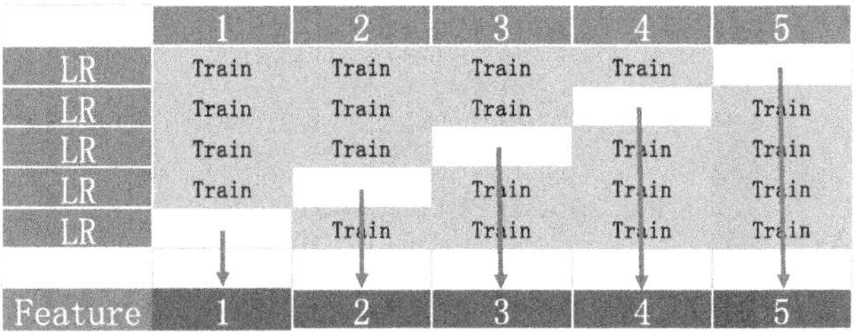

	1	2	3	4	5
LR	Train	Train	Train	Train	
LR	Train	Train	Train		Train
LR	Train	Train		Train	Train
LR	Train		Train	Train	Train
LR		Train	Train	Train	Train
Feature	1	2	3	4	5

Fig. 3. Stacking model based on logistic regression result

We use the Stacking feature fusion model on uid, tag, poi these three feature domains to get more advanced features. Finally, we use these features as input to train the XGBoost model, test the model on the test data set TestReal, and then use the model to predict the final results.

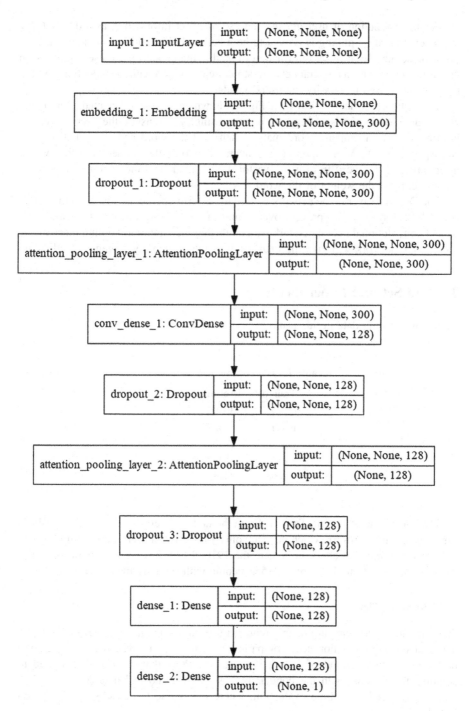

Fig. 4.

For the prediction of user gender, the use of tweet information as a data set, the characteristics of its mining is proved to be a better choice, so in this evaluation task, we also use the use of tweet information to predict the gender of the user Methods. In this task, a convolutional neural network structure combined with the Attention Pooling mechanism is used to classify the users' gender.

The network structure shown in Fig. 4, drawn by a method named plot_modle which included in Keras. After data preprocessing, we translate the user's tweeting information into a sentence-word matrix, then treat the word and convert it into the corresponding ID. After inputting the neural network, the model take the weight information of the word from word2vector model, then send these to the Embedding layer to express the weight of the word.

The Dropout layer in the network is used to perform operations similar to the neural network "cut synapse" to prevent overturning in the training process. Followed by a typical convolutional neural network structure using the Attention Pooling mechanism. Finally, the network will give the final result of the probability of gender prediction.

3 Data Set and Experiments

Here's the training data in this task:

Table 1. Train dataset user numbers

Train data	User number
check-in	301958
tweet	74377
tag	197088
social	6302377
profile	241553

Data details are shown in Table 1. From the table we can see that there are 301958 users' check-in records, of which there are only 74,377 tweet users, accounting for only 24% of the number of check-in. Where the 197088 user has tag information for user attribute classification. There are 241553 people with sexually marked users.

3.1 Subtask One

Subtask one experiments are mainly required to evaluate the three values of PRF, and the results of the prediction need comparing with the standard data set. Here we got a problem that this method of forecasting uses the POIs that the user has visited to combine the forecast with the popular POI, so there is no real data set on the line without the need for offline evaluation, where the online test results are 1.66% on F1@10.

3.2   Subtask Two

The parameters used in the Xgboost model are shown in Table 2. The loss function uses logical regression, which are highly compatible with this task, and the booster parameter is chosen using gbtree. Since the amount of data is large, the maximum depth of the selected tree is 8. Subsample, colsample_bytree and other parameters using the typical value as the training parameters. After experimenting with the parameters of the XGBoost model, the model did not show better results, so it would be appropriate to use typical values for training.

Table 2. XGBoost training parameters

Name	Value
objective	binary:logistic
booster	gbtree
max_depth	8
min_child_weight	2
subsample	0.9
colsample_bytree	0.8
eta	0.01
lambda	0
alpha	0
silent	1

When using the Stacking model for feature fusion, the average accuracy of the results of the logistic regression model output is shown in Table 3, where we divide the training data (TrainReal) by 5 fold, each of which uses one of them as each Verification set, the remaining four as a training set to verify the accuracy of the verification set to obtain the average rate of the data shown in the table. Finally, the prediction probability of the sexes obtained from the three feature fields is averaged, and the accuracy rate of 79.82% can be obtained. The above steps are used to complete the feature extraction step. Then we introduce the feature quantity obtained from the three fields into the XGBoost model. The training results are shown in Table 4.

Table 3. Features fusion

Feature	LR
poi	74.00%
uid	75.32%
tag	77.62%
average	79.82%

Table 4. XGBoost accuracy

XGBoost	Accuracy
no poi	81.53%
no tag	79.67%
no uid	80.70%
all	83.76%
only tweet	91.23%
total	84.15%

Where no poi, no tag, no uid indicates the accuracy of the final result under the condition that the feature is missing. All represents the final prediction accuracy of the XGBoost model under the presence of three features. Through the comparison, all these three features have a positive contribution to the results.

On line five we can see on CNN which modified by Attention Pooling mechanism have a high accuracy on tweets data. While from Table 1 we can see there's only 25% user have tweets, this method can't be used as the primary forecast method. After combining the XGBoost model with the results of the gender prediction, we calculate the probability of the gender prediction of the two models, we got 83.76% on offline accuracy, and the online accuracy is 82.85%.

4   Conclusion and Future Work

In this paper, a POI prediction method based on user POI access history is used to analyze the POIs in the vicinity of the locations visited by analyzing the POIs visited by users, combining their geographical location information and existing POI data. Task one of the questions raised. For the sub-task two we use the feature fusion model under the machine learning methods and depth learning methods, and the two predictions of the results of integration. But the final results of the performance is not too high to enhance, through the analysis, we determined that because of the use of a simple average number of ways to model integration, the method is too simple.

In the future work, consider adding the tweet feature to the feature fusion model to calculate. While trying to better integrate the two models. In this paper, the fusion of the two methods is only a simple two of the results of gender prediction of the results of the average, follow-up can try to more depth of the model fusion experiment. Therefore, the subsequent stacking model can be derived from the fusion features into CNN with attention to learn.

Acknowledgments. This work is partially supported by grant from the Natural Science Foundation of China (Nos. 61632011, 61562080, 61602079), the Fundamental Research Funds for the Central Universities (DUT16ZD216, DUT17RC(3)016).

References

1. Chan, C.C., Lin, Y.C., Chen, M.S.: Recommendation for advertising messages on mobile devices. In: International Conference on World Wide Web, pp. 235–236. ACM (2014)
2. Yang, X., Deng, T., Guo, Z., et al.: Advertising keyword recommendation based on supervised link prediction in multi-relational network. In: Proceedings of the 26th International Conference on World Wide Web Companion. International World Wide Web Conferences Steering Committee, pp. 863–864 (2017)
3. Wang, J., Wang, B., Duan, L., et al.: Interactive ads recommendation with contextual search on product topic space. Multimedia Tools Appl. **70**(2), 799–820 (2014)
4. Gong, J., Gao, X., Song, Y., Cheng, H., Xu, J.: Individual friends recommendation based on random walk with restart in social networks. In: Li, Y., Xiang, G., Lin, H., Wang, M. (eds.) SMP 2016. CCIS, vol. 669, pp. 123–133. Springer, Singapore (2016). https://doi.org/10. 1007/978-981-10-2993-6_10
5. Wang, X., Wang, Y.: Improving content-based and hybrid music recommendation using deep learning. In: Proceedings of the 22nd ACM International Conference on Multimedia, pp. 627–636. ACM (2014)
6. Shi, Y., Larson, M., Hanjalic, A.: Collaborative filtering beyond the user-item matrix: a survey of the state of the art and future challenges. ACM Comput. Surv. (CSUR) **47**(1), 3 (2014)
7. Liu, H., Hu, Z., Mian, A., et al.: A new user similarity model to improve the accuracy of collaborative filtering. Knowl.-Based Syst. **56**, 156–166 (2014)
8. McGee, J., Caverlee, J., Cheng, Z.: Location prediction in social media based on tie strength. In: Proceedings of the 22nd ACM International Conference on Information & Knowledge Management, pp. 459–468. ACM (2013)
9. Liu, X., Liu, Y., Aberer, K., et al.: Personalized point-of-interest recommendation by mining users' preference transition. In: Proceedings of the 22nd ACM International Conference on Information & Knowledge Management, pp. 733–738. ACM (2013)
10. van de Loo, J., De Pauw, G., Daelemans, W.: Text-based age and gender prediction for online safety monitoring. Int. J. Cyber-Secur. Digit. Forensics (IJCSDF) **5**(1), 46–60 (2016)
11. Bamman, D., Eisenstein, J., Schnoebelen, T.: Gender identity and lexical variation in social media. J. Socioling. **18**(2), 135–160 (2014)
12. Antipov, G., Berrani, S.A., Dugelay, J.L.: Minimalistic CNN-based ensemble model for gender prediction from face images. Pattern Recogn. Lett. **70**, 59–65 (2016)
13. Levi, G., Hassner, T.: Age and gender classification using convolutional neural networks. In: Proceedings of the IEEE Conference on Computer Vision and Pattern Recognition Workshops, pp. 34–42 (2015)
14. Kim, Y.: Convolutional neural networks for sentence classification. arXiv preprint arXiv: 1408.5882 (2014)
15. Mnih, V., Heess, N., Graves, A.: Recurrent models of visual attention. In: Advances in Neural Information Processing Systems, pp. 2204–2212 (2014)
16. Er, M.J., Zhang, Y., Wang, N., et al.: Attention pooling-based convolutional neural network for sentence modelling. Inf. Sci. **373**, 388–403 (2016)

Babbling - The HIT-SCIR System for Emotional Conversation Generation

Jianhua Yuan, Huaipeng Zhao, Yanyan Zhao,
Dawei Cong, Bing Qin[✉], and Ting Liu

Harbin Institute of Technology, Harbin, China
{jhyuan,hpzhao,yyzhao,dwcong,qinb,tliu}@ir.hit.edu.cn

Abstract. This paper describes the HIT-SCIR emotional response agent "Babbling" to the NLPCC 2017 Shared Task 4 on emotional conversation generation. Babbling consists of two parts, one is a rule based model for picking generic responses and the other is a neural work based model. For the latter part, we apply the encoder-decoder [1] framework to generate emotional response given the post and assigned emotion label. To improve the content coherency, we use LTS [2] for acquiring a better first word. To generate responses with consistent emotions, we employ the emotion embeddings to guide emotionalizing process. To produce more content coherent and emotion consistent responses, we include the attention mechanism [3] and its extension, multi-hop attention (MTA) [4]. The rule based part and neural network based part are ranked the second and fifth place respectively according to the total score.

Keywords: Seq2Seq model · Emotion embeddings
Multi-hop attention

1 Introduction

As a vital part of human intelligence, emotional intelligence includes the ability to perceive, understand, express and control emotions. Although there exist a great deal of models tackling conversation generation problems on large-scale social network data, it remains a huge challenge to generate text with controllable emotions. Driven by this challenge, NLPCC 2017 organizes a shared task to propel the research progress in emotional text generation. In the NLPCC 2017 shared task 4 on Emotional Conversation Generation (ecg), given a Chinese weibo post $X = (x_1, x_2, ..., x_n)$ and a user-specified emotion emo, ecg aims at generating a response $Y = (y_1, y_2, ..., y_m)$ which is not only fluent and coherent with the post but also expresses the same emotion as the specified one. The emotion categories are {anger, disgust, happiness, like, sadness} [5]. For example, given a post "I lost my job yesterday" and a user-specific emotion "sadness", it is appropriate to say "I'm sorry to hear that" to express sadness.

In this paper, we present HIT-SCIR's approach "Babbling" to tackling the task of generating emotional responses. "Babbling" system has two subsystems,

© Springer International Publishing AG 2018
X. Huang et al. (Eds.): NLPCC 2017, LNAI 10619, pp. 632–641, 2018.
https://doi.org/10.1007/978-3-319-73618-1_53

a rule based model that is ranked the second place and a neural network based model which is ranked the fifth place in terms of total score. For the rule based system, we make a candidate response set for each emotion. These five sets consist of responses taken from training responses that are fluent in content but don't contain any specific topics. Moreover, each sentence has a distinct emotional tendency consistent with the emotion of its corresponding candidate set. Since sequence to sequence (Seq2Seq) based models have achieved excellent performance in neural machine translating [1], text generation [6], human-robot conversation [7], etc., we adopt the Seq2Seq model for our neural network based part. In addition to the basic Seq2Seq model, we incorporate LTS mechanism to get more content aware and more meaningful first word of the response. Attention mechanism is also employed in order to generate more topic-coherent words in the response sequences. To produce responses with controllable emotions, we add the emotion embeddings [8] to attend the source post, which performs the emotion transition of the response. Furthermore, we extend the previous single hop attention process to a multi-hop one, which is expected to get more abstract and coherent representation of source post.

In the following section, we first describe the rule based response generation model in Sect. 2. Then, in Sect. 3 we present the details of the Seq2Seq structure, MTA for more abstract content and emotion representations, LTS for a better first word and Emotion Embeddings for emotion transition from post to response. Sect. 4 gives the data statistics, implementation details and experimental results. We also discuss the effectiveness of each mechanism in Seq2Seq model in Sect. 4. Finally, we draw conclusions in Sect. 5 and include the future work.

2   Rule Based Model

In this section, we present the rule based model in Babbling, showing how to get more generic, less topic-specific and apparently emotional responses. Since Seq2Seq models are not yet mature enough for general purpose conversation generation, it is helpful to respond to the post with generic sentences showing obvious emotion, which also serves as a strong baseline for the neural network based model.

First, we use a Bi-LSTM to classify the responses in the training data into five emotion categories and get five sets of responses corresponding to each emotion. Then, to get more robust and less topic-specific responses, we conduct name entity recognition on five sets in order to removing those sentences with name entities. After that, we leave out sentences which have pronouns referring to organizations, names representing geographical places, person, morpheme, direction, or other nouns using LTP [9] POS tagging feature. Furthermore, we discard sentences containing low frequency words and non-relevant high frequency words iteratively. Finally we get the top-100 sentences for each set manually. When given a post and a emotion category, the rule-based model randomly fetch one sentence from the set corresponding to assigned emotion and output that sentence as the final response directly.

3   Seq2Seq Model

First, We present an overview of our Seq2Seq model for emotional conversation generation.

From a perspective of probability, the Seq2Seq model is equivalent to find a target response $Y = (y_1, y_2, ..., y_m)$ that maximize the conditional probability of Y given the source post $X = (x_1, x_2, ..., x_n)$, i.e., $argmax_Y p(Y|X)$. In the context of neural conversation generation, we fit the Seq2Seq model to maximize the conditional probability of $p(response|post)$. After learning the conditional distribution, the Seq2Seq model can generate a proper response by searching for the sentence that maximizes the conditional probability when given a source post.

A typical Seq2Seq model consists of an encoder and a decoder, both of which are often implemented with RNN or its variations like LSTM, GRU [10], etc. We adopt a unidirectional, two layers GRU for both the encoder and decoder in this case.

In this framework, an encoder reads from a source post, a sequence of word vectors $X = (x_1, x_2, ..., x_n)$ into a context vector c. The most common way to compute c is:

$$h_t = GRU_{encoder}(x_t, h_{t-1}) \qquad (1)$$

and

$$c = f(h_1, h_2, ..., h_n) \qquad (2)$$

where h_t is the hidden state at time t, and c is a context vector calculated by the hidden states. And it is more common to use the attention mechanism to make use of all the hidden states when calculating c.

For the decoder part, another GRU is trained to predict the next word y_t given all the previous words $\{y_1, y_2, ..., y_{t-1}\}$ and context vector c. Then, the hidden state representation at time step t in the decoder can be described as:

$$s_t = GRU_{decoder}(s_{t-1}, y_{t-1}) \qquad (3)$$

Furthermore, the conditional probability in the decoder can be defined as:

$$p(y_t|\{y_1, y_2, ..., y_{t-1}; X\}) = Softmax(s_t, c_t) \qquad (4)$$

where c_t is context vector at time step t for predicting the current word and can be calculated using all hidden states or simplified as the last hidden state of encoder.

Finally, the word at time step t can be predicted by mapping the probability over the whole vocabulary.

While it still remains a big challenge for a vanilla Seq2Seq model to generate both fluent and topic coherent responses, we integrate several techniques into the basic Seq2Seq model to improve the content quality as well as the emotion consistency. An illustration of our approach is given in Fig. 1, which has LTS, MTA and Emotion Embeddings based on the Seq2Seq model.

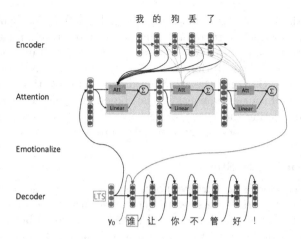

Fig. 1. An illustration of our Seq2Seq model with multi-hop attention (3 hops), LTS and emotion embeddings.

3.1 Multi-hop Attention

Ideally, the encoder can encode all the information in the source sequence into a dense, fixed-length context vector c. However, Bahdanau et al. [3] find that a fixed-length vector c (1) may not be able to preserve all the useful information of source sequence for losing the information of words at the beginning of sequences (2) can not model the different contributions of different words in the source sequence when making predictions at a decoding step. To solve these problems in the basic Seq2Seq model, they propose the attention mechanism, where all the hidden outputs of source sequence are used instead of only the last hidden output and a weighted sum of these hidden outputs is calculated as the new context vector. In this way, the context vector c_i is distinct for every time step in the decoder, which is denoted as:

$$c_i = \sum_{j=1}^{N} \alpha_{ij} h_j \qquad (5)$$

Here, the weight α_{ij} for i-th hidden outputs of encoder is computed by:

$$\alpha_{ij} = \frac{exp(o_{ij})}{\sum_{k=1}^{N} exp(o_{ik})} \qquad (6)$$

$$o_{ij} = a(s_{i-1}^{T} h_j) \qquad (7)$$

where a is a non-linear activation function like *sigmoid* or *tanh* and can be considered as the similarity measurement between the hidden state in decoder and hidden outputs in encoder, which is taken as a weight in this case.

Computational models which are composed of multiple processing layers have shown the ability to learn high level representations of data by multiple levels of abstraction [4,11]. Motivated by these works, we extend the attention process which is essentially a weighted sum compositional function, to a multiple layers variation. More abstractive representations are acquired through multiple computational layers where each layer/hop selects more important context words and transforms the representations from the previous layer to higher and more abstract level ones. By doing the attention process multiple times, more important information of source sequence will be chosen and generate a better representation for predicting the target sequence, which we hope could help handle both semantic and emotional compositionality problems.

3.2   LTS Learning to Start

In most Seq2Seq models, a start symbol is usually manually set to serve as the previous generated word for first word generation in the decoder. Though the initialization of the first word is so small a detail that could be ignored easily, we believe it is a vital part of the Seq2Seq model, just as the saying goes that "Well begun is half done". However, a start symbol fails to distinguish between different source input and may lead to the model preferring to predicting some high frequency words [6,12].

To tackle the above drawbacks of the start symbol, we employ Learning To Start (LTS) in decoder for generating the first word of the predicted sequence. In LTS, the first word is predicted independently from the decoder. The probability of the first word can be formulated as:

$$y_0 = \sigma(\sigma(W_i c + b_i)E + b_e) \tag{8}$$

where c is the context vector and here is the last hidden state of the encoder, W_i is a weight matrix to be learned in the model, b_i, b_e are bias vectors, E is the embedding matrix of the decoder, σ is a non-linear activation function.

Intuitively, the above formula builds a tie between the context vector and embedding space of decoder, which connect the information from the source sequence and the information from all the candidate words to be predicted. Note that, the generation of first word is only decided by the encoder's state which differs among source sentences and gets rid of influence of start symbol, which together reduce the loss of information from encoder.

3.3   Emotion Embeddings

To enable the model generating responses with user-specific emotion categories, We introduce the emotion embeddings. We attach the emotion category embeddings to the attention process, which can directly guide the choice of context information and shift the emotion tendency from source sequence to the user-specific one. Each of the five emotion embedding is represented by a low dimensional, dense, real-valued vectors. We randomly initialize the emotion embeddings and jointly train them with other parts of the model. And the conditional probability in the decoder can be updated as:

$$p(y_t | \{y_1, y_2, ..., y_{t-1}; X\}) = Softmax(s_t, e_t, c_t) \tag{9}$$

where e_t is the emotion embedding of user-specific category.

4   Experiments

We describe experimental settings, detail model implementation and report the empirical results in this section.

4.1   Dataset

We train our model on a large datasets (Zhou et al. [8]) extracted from Weibo, which has 1,119,207 pairs of (post, response). Statistics of the datasets are given in Table 1. We use the provided emotion label given by a Bi-LSTM and visualize the distribution of emotion transition information in Fig. 2.

Table 1. Statistics of the datasets.

Dataset	Post	Response
Weibo-train	1,119,207	1,119,207
Weibo-test	5,418	5,418
Weibo-evaluation	200	200

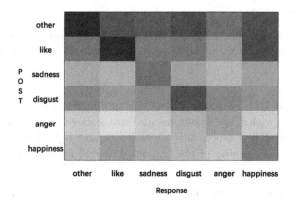

Fig. 2. Visualization of emotion transition from post to response in Weibo training data, where the color darkness indicates the percentage of each kind of transition.

Since there isn't any standard metric to evaluate the generation results, the NLPCC 2017 Shared Task adopts a manual evaluation. A response will get one point if its content is both fluent and appropriate. An additional point will be awarded if the response express the correct emotion category consistent with the user-specific one. For it being too costly to manually label all the submitted posts, 200 posts are chosen as the final evaluation set. The statistics of the evaluation set is shown in Table 2.

Table 2. Statistics of the final evaluation set.

Emotion category	Like	Sad	Disgust	Angry	Happy	Total
Number of post	57	30	40	21	52	200
Percent of post	29%	15%	20%	11%	52%	100%
Responses to be generated	133	119	144	71	129	596

4.2 Model Implementations

We use a two layer GRU as the post encoder with hidden layer of size 200 and apply the same setting to the decoder. The encoder and decoder use different vocabularies where words occur no more than five times are removed from post and response respectively. Those rare words are replaced with UNK. And an additional end symbol is added to both the post and response sentences. We set both the word embedding size and emotion size to 100. According to the analysis of sentence length of post and responses, we set the maximum time step in encoder and decoder to 10 and adopt batch training whose batch size is set to 64. We initialize the parameters by sampling from a uniform distribution $(-0.1, 0.1)$. We use sampled softmax [13] to speed up the prediction process. Our models are implemented using Tensorflow 0.12 [14].

4.3 Results

In this section, we first give the qualitative analysis of the our model based on the generation results. Then we present the human evaluation results from NLPCC Shared Task.

Effectiveness of LTS. We compare the results between basic Seq2Seq model and its extension with LTS. Examples in Table 3 shows that, model using LTS can generate better first words and more fluent and topic coherent responses. LTS can improve the quality of the first word as well as the whole sentence.

Table 3. Comparison of generation results between basic Seq2Seq model and LTS extension

Model	Post	Response
Seq2Seq	"梦寐以求的垃圾食品，耶！好吃好吃。"	"抄送你一天不可不可虐待火腿肠"
Seq2Seq + LTS	"梦寐以求的垃圾食品，耶！好吃好吃。"	"好开心啊"
Seq2Seq	"训练结束，冬至啦！回家吃老妈给包的饺子去喽?????"	"我妈说我妈说我去吃榨菜"
Seq2Seq + LTS	"训练结束，冬至啦！回家吃老妈给包的饺子去喽?????"	"冬至，吃饺子，吃饺子 。"

Emotion Transition with Emotion Embeddings. Figure 2 shows the distribution of emotion transition of training data. We can see that the response usually carry the same emotion label as the post. For example, it's rare for a post with a "like" label to have a "anger" response and vice versa. The portion of transition from "like" to "happiness" and from "happiness" to "like" are similar, which shows the closeness of two emotions as well as implies the difficult for the emotion classifier to distinguish between "like" and "happiness". In other words, the performance of emotion classifier has great impact on emotional response generation. After applying the emotion embedding during the attention process, the Seq2Seq model can generate response with user-specific emotions, as shown in Table 4. In our model, the emotion embeddings in the attention process play the key role in emotional conversation generation.

Table 4. Example responses with user-specific emotions generated by Seq2Seq model with emotion embeddings

Post	Post Emotion	User-specific emotion	Response
"生活就是要这种态度，牙再大，也要笑！哈哈。"	like	like	"恩，很有哲理!"
"生活就是要这种态度，牙再大，也要笑！哈哈。"	like	anger	"我是被逼的！！!"
"上帝啊，终于放暑假啦！"	happy	happy	"好期待啊！"
"上帝啊，终于放暑假啦！"	happy	disgust	"你就不能别说点别的么"

Human Evaluations. We present the human evaluation results of NLPCC 2017 Shared Task 4 Emotional Conversation Generation in Table 5. Our rule based submission Babbling_2 and Seq2Seq model Babbling_1 with LTS, MTA and Emotion Embeddings are ranked the second place and the fifth place respectively. The rule based system outperforms the neural network based model with a large margin, which means neural conversation are still far from satisfactory and it is more plausible to combine both of systems. What's more, our Babbling_1 only goes through preliminary processing of responses by truncating sentences until end symbol and removing duplications at the end of sentences. And we observe that when the Seq2Seq model need to reply "sad" responses when given the "sad" post, it tends to generate "哈哈，我也是！" ("Haha, me too!"), which hurts the performance and can be further improved by simple post processing.

Table 5. Final evaluation results of NLPCC 2017 Shared Task. 0 point, 1 point and 2 pionts represent number of responses which get 0, 1 and 2 points respectively.

Team_id	0 ponit	1 point	2 points	Total number	Total score
samsung_1	267	82	247	596	576
Babbling_2	305	19	271	595	561
samsung_2	272	93	231	596	555
SMIPG_1	428	11	157	596	325
Babbling_1	424	41	131	596	303
gry_1	449	31	116	596	263
shield_1	76	26	93	195	212
ECNU_1	44	10	89	143	188
NUSTM_2	102	9	84	195	177
ECNU_2	56	9	83	148	175
SMIPG_2	505	12	79	596	170
NUSTM_1	117	8	70	195	148
NLP-More_1	122	7	66	195	139
NLP-More_2	122	7	66	195	139
Personalized emotional chatting system based on deep learning_1	50	9	23	82	55
NEUDM_1	101	1	5	107	11

5   Conclusions and Future Work

In this work, we present the emotion conversation system Babbling of HIT-SCIR, which comprised of a rule base system and a neural network base system. We employ LTS, MTA and Emotion Embeddings into our Sequence-to-Sequence architecture and demonstrate their effectiveness through generated examples. Though our model is superior to the basic Seq2Seq model, the rule based system still serves as a strong baseline for all the neural network model.

In the future work, for emotionalization part, we would like to apply better emotion classifier to help improve the accuracy of emotion transition. and explore other novel ways of emotion transition; for the Seq2Seq model, we would like to try memory network [4, 15] as the sequence encoder, which will drastically speed up the MTA process while not hurting the performance.

Acknowledgement. This work was supported by the National High Technology Development 863 Program of China (No. 2015AA015407) and National Natural Science Foundation of China (No. 61632011 and No. 61370164).

References

1. Sutskever, I., Vinyals, O., Le, Q.V.: Sequence to sequence learning with neural networks. In: Advances in Neural Information Processing Systems, pp. 3104–3112 (2014)

2. Zhu, Q., Zhang, W., Zhou, L., et al.: Learning to start for sequence to sequence architecture. arXiv preprint arXiv:1608.05554 (2016)

3. Bahdanau, D., Cho, K., Bengio, Y.: Neural machine translation by jointly learning to align and translate. arXiv preprint arXiv:1409.0473 (2014)

4. Tang, D., Qin, B., Liu, T.: Aspect level sentiment classification with deep memory network. arXiv preprint arXiv:1605.08900 (2016)

5. Xu, L., Lin, H., Pan, Y., et al.: Constructing the affective lexicon ontology. J. Chin. Soc. Sci. Tech. Inf. **27**(2), 180–185 (2008)

6. Serban, I.V., Sordoni, A., Bengio, Y., et al.: Hierarchical neural network generative models for movie dialogues. CoRR, abs/1507.04808 (2015)

7. Shang, L., Lu, Z., Li, H.: Neural responding machine for short-text conversation. arXiv preprint arXiv:1503.02364 (2015)

8. Zhou, H., Huang, M., Zhang, T., et al.: Emotional chatting machine: emotional conversation generation with internal and external memory. arXiv preprint arXiv:1704.01074 (2017)

9. Che, W., Li, Z., Liu, T.: LTP: a Chinese language technology platform. In: Proceedings of the COLING 2010: Demonstrations, Beijing, China, pp. 13–16, August 2010

10. Chung, J., Gulcehre, C., Cho, K., Bengio, Y.: Empirical evaluation of gated recurrent neural networks on sequence modeling. arXiv preprint arXiv:1412.3555 (2014)

11. LeCun, Y., Bengio, Y., Hinton, G.: Deep learning. Nature **521**(7553), 436–444 (2015)

12. Sordoni, A., Galley, M., Auli, M., et al.: A neural network approach to context-sensitive generation of conversational responses. arXiv preprint arXiv:1506.06714 (2015)

13. Jean, S., Cho, K., Memisevic, R., et al.: On using very large target vocabulary for neural machine translation. arXiv preprint arXiv:1412.2007 (2014)

14. Abadi, M., Agarwal, A., Barham, P., et al.: TensorFlow: large-scale machine learning on heterogeneous distributed systems. arXiv preprint arXiv:1603.04467 (2016)

15. Weston, J., Chopra, S., Bordes, A.: Memory networks. arXiv preprint arXiv:1410.3916 (2014)

Unsupervised Slot Filler Refinement via Entity Community Construction

Zengzhuang Xu, Rui Song, Bowei Zou$^{(\boxtimes)}$, and Yu Hong

Soochow University, Suzhou, Jiangsu, China
nedxuwork@gmail.com, cnsr27@gmail.com, zoubowei@suda.edu.cn,
tianxianer@gmail.com

Abstract. Given an entity (query), slot filling aims to find and extract the values (slot fillers) of its specific attributes (slot types) from a large-scale of document collections. Most existing work of slot filling models slot fillers separately and only considers direct relations between slot fillers and query, ignoring other slot fillers in context. In this paper we propose an unsupervised slot filler refinement approach via entity community construction to filter out the incorrect fillers collaboratively. The community-based framework mainly consists of (1) filler community generated by a point-wise mutual information-based hierarchical clustering, and (2) query community constructed by a co-occurrence graph model.

1 Introduction

Slot Filling (SF) is the task of finding and extracting the slot fillers of specified slot types for a given query entity from a large-scale of document collections of natural language texts [1], which plays a vital role in structured Knowledge Base Population (KBP). For instance, given a person query *Donald Trump* and slot type `per:city_of_birth`, a correct slot filler should be *New York City*.

We analyze the results of all submitted systems on KBP 2013 English Slot Filling (ESF) task and find that the incorrect slot fillers are prone to the following two scenarios: (1) the slot filler is wrong but it belongs to another slot type, (e.g., query: *Donald Trump*, filler: *New York City*, type: `per:employee_or_member_of`); (2) The slot filler does not belong to any type in ESF task (e.g., query: *Donald Trump*, filler: *Sao Paulo*). The proportions of these two kinds of cases are 17.62% and 82.38%, respectively. This paper focuses on the latter errors.

Furthermore, we find that the co-occurrence of two slot fillers is high in one document when they are related to the query, while low co-occurrence corresponds to unrelated fillers. For example, as shown in Fig. 1, for query *Merce Cunningham*[1], the related slot fillers (grey color) usually come up with each other, while the unrelated ones (white color) distribute separately. Therefore, the core problem is how to group related fillers for slot filler refinement.

Inspired by [2], an entity community is defined as a group of connected entities that are more connected to each other than to the rest of entities. We propose a novel unsupervised community-based filler refinement framework, which

---

[1] queryID: SF13_ENG_038, in KBP 2013 ESF data set.

© Springer International Publishing AG 2018
X. Huang et al. (Eds.): NLPCC 2017, LNAI 10619, pp. 642–651, 2018.
https://doi.org/10.1007/978-3-319-73618-1_54

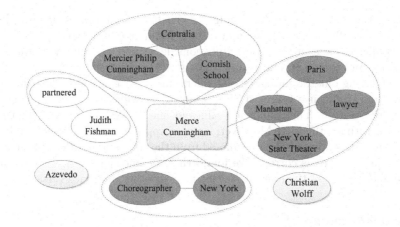

Fig. 1. A portion of the submitted fillers for query *Merce Cunningham*

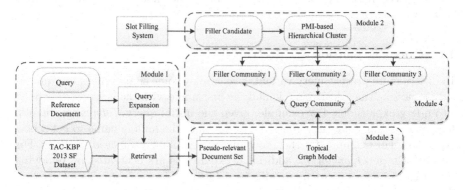

Fig. 2. Entity community-based slot filler refinement framework

consists of four modules: query expansion and retrieval, filler community construction, query community construction, and filler filtering, as shown in Fig. 2. Among them, the filler communities are built by a pointwise mutual information (PMI)-based hierarchical clustering, and the query community is constructed by a co-occurrence graph model.

2 Related Work

Given the responses and confidence values produced by multiple slot filling systems, the SFV task of the TAC-KBP track [3] aims at determining whether each response is true or false. Most existing SFV systems regard this task as an SF response processing problem, which employ only the outputs and confidence values of multiple SF systems, ignoring the semantic correlations between slot fillers and query. Previous SFV studies leverage various techniques, such as weighted voting [4], multi-dimensional truth finding model [5], and stacked ensembles [6].

However, these studies need to obtain the outputs of multiple systems, which may lead to conflicting and redundant results. Compared with the previous work, our slot filler refinement framework fully considers the relation between the filler candidates and the query and is independent of the SF systems.

For filtering out the unrelated slot fillers, most existing methods utilize the outputs and confidence values of SF systems [7,8], which is heavily affected by the algorithm itself. The confidence values in one SF system are difficult to be combined with another one. Moreover, existing approaches which usually rely on the features on sentence level are suffered from the substantial unrelated entities, even if the slot type is correct. We found that if some slot fillers are unrelated to the query, most of them are irrelevant to each other, and vice versa.

3   Methodology

The architecture of our entity community-based slot filler refinement system as illustrated in Fig. 2.

3.1   Query Expansion and Retrieval

To obtain more precise query variants, we employ some simple rules. For queries of type *person*, the token string joined the first name with the last name is added into query expansions. For example, given the initial query *Tahawwur Hussain Rana*, we obtain *Tahawwur Rana*. We abbreviate the middle name to get a new expansion. For example, for the above query, we obtain *Tahawwur H. Rana*. For queries of type *organization*, additional expansions are generated by removing the original name by common suffixes of business forms (e.g., *Inc.*, *Corp.*). If the query is an abbreviation or full name, we obtain its corresponding full or abbreviation form as query expansion (e.g., *International Business Machines* ⇔ *IBM*). We retrieve documents using Lucene package[2] [9] by initial query and its expansions as the pseudo-relevant document set (Abbr. PR-set) to the query.

3.2   Filler Community Construction

Given a query entity, its slot fillers are always inclined to occur in one document. Hence we intend to cluster slot filler candidates by the similarity between them. PMI measures the difference between the probability of the co-occurrence given the joint distribution and the probability of the co-occurrence given the marginal distributions of two random variables [10]. In this paper, within the PR-set, we take advantage of PMI to evaluate the distance between the two slot filler candidates, f_1 and f_2:

$$PMI(f_1, f_2) = p(f_1, f_2) \log \frac{p(f_1, f_2)}{p(f_1)p(f_2)}, \tag{1}$$

---

[2] http://lucene.apache.org.

where $p(f_1, f_2)$ is probability of the co-occurrence of f_1 and f_2; $p(f_1)$ and $p(f_2)$ are the probability of f_1 and f_2 occurred, respectively. Equation (1) can be written as

$$PMI(f_1, f_2) = \log AB - \log A - \log B + \log N, \tag{2}$$

where AB denotes the count of documents where f_1 and f_2 co-occurred; A and B denote the counts of documents where f_1 and f_2 occurred, respectively; N denotes the total number of documents in PR-set. Then normalized by

$$PMI_{norm}(f_1, f_2) = \frac{PMI(f_1, f_2) - PMI_{min}}{PMI_{max} - PMI_{min}}, \tag{3}$$

$$PMI_{min} = \log 0.5 - \log A - \log B + \log N, \tag{4}$$

$$PMI_{max} = \log(0.5 * (A + B)) - \log A - \log B + \log N, \tag{5}$$

and the distance between f_1 and f_2:

$$Dis(f_1, f_2) = 1 - PMI_{norm}(f_1, f_2). \tag{6}$$

For a query entity, we group its entire slot filler candidates by using a hierarchical clustering with the farthest-first traversal algorithm [11]. Intuitively, we should try either to improve compactness of individual clusters, or to increase relative separation between them. We perform the following steps.

Step1: Calculate the minimum spanning tree MST^i of each cluster C_k^i by Prim's algorithm [12].
Step2: Calculate the compact distance values cd^i by the sum of weights of all edges in each minimum spanning tree MST^i; and calculate the separate distance values sd^i by the minimum distance between two clusters.
Step3: Calculate the compact-separate proportion CSP^i [13].
Step4: Calculate the average value of CSP.

Finally, we select the optimal k with the maximum value of CSP as the number of clusters, and obtain the filler candidate cluster set $C_{k(opt)}$ as our filler community. Algorithm 1 summarizes the procedure.

3.3   Query Community Construction

Given a query entity, we first select top-100 related documents from the PR-set by their topical similarity scores to the reference document of query. To calculate the latent topical distributions of documents, Latent Dirichlet Allocation (LDA) [14] is directly employed. Then the similarity between two documents is measured by their corresponding topical distributions. Formally, we denote topic distribution as T, and calculate the similarity by the Hellinger Distance [15]:

$$Hdis(d_i, d_j) = \frac{1}{\sqrt{2}} \sqrt{\sum_{t_k \in T} (\sqrt{P(t_k|d_i)} - \sqrt{P(t_k|d_j)})^2} \tag{7}$$

Algorithm 1. Procedure of hierarchical clustering (HC: Hierarchical Clustering; *MST*: Minimum Spanning Tree; *cd*: compact distance; *sd*: separate distance; *CSP*: Compact-Separate Proportion)

1: **Input:** Filler Candidate Set: S

               PMI matrix:

               $P = \{PMI_{norm}(i,j)|i{\in}S, j{\in}S\}$

2: **Output:** Filler Candidate Clusters: $C_{k(opt)}$

3: **for** $k = 1$ **to** $|S|$ **do** {*iterations*}

4:     $C_k = \text{HC}(S, P, k)$

5:     **for** $i = 1$ **to** k **do** {*iterations*}

6:        $MST^i = \text{Prim}(C_k^i)$ (Step1)

7:        $cd^i = \dfrac{\sum weight(MST^i)}{C_k^i}$ (Step2)

8:        $sd^i = min_{1\leq m\leq k, m\neq n}\{min\{dist(x_m,x_n)|x_m{\in}C^i, x_n{\in}C^j\}\}$

9:        $CSP^i = \dfrac{sd^i - cd^i}{sd^i + cd^i}$ (Step3)

10:     **end for**

11:     $avgCSP_k = \dfrac{1}{k}\sum\limits_{i=0}^{k-1} CSP^i$ (Step4)

12: **end for**

13: $k(opt) = argmax_{1\leq k\leq|S|}\{avgCSP_k\}$

Graph-based approaches often represent co-occurrence as a graph and use the statistical properties to obtain the relationship of entities. We extract entities from the related document set and construct entity graph for each document. Formally, the undirected entities graph is defined as $C_q(V, E)$, where vertex set $V = \{v_i\}$ denotes the set of related entities to the query, and E denotes an edge set, with each edge e_{ij} representing co-occurrence relationship between entity v_i and v_j in the scope of one sentence. Intuitively, when the division of community is a good one, there are many edges within communities but only a few between them. Therefore we employ an edge betweenness algorithm to identify the boundaries of communities [16]. An edge betweenness is the number of the shortest paths between pairs of vertices that run along it. This algorithm removes one edge with the highest edge betweenness at each iteration. [17] provides a check for termination of the division process by maximizing the Modularity of community structure, which is calculated by

$$Q = \frac{s+1}{4m}\sum_{ij}\left(A_{ij} - \frac{k_i k_j}{2m}\right),\qquad(8)$$

where m is the total number of edges in the graph, k_i and k_j are the degrees of the vertices v_i and v_j, respectively, A_{ij} denotes the number of edges between vertices v_i and v_j, and s is 1 if v_i and v_j are in the same sub-graph and -1 otherwise. We regard the entities in all graphs as the query community.

Finally, we apply a simple rule to filter out unrelated slot fillers to the given query (as shown in Fig. 2). Within each filler community, if all of fillers were not found in the query community, we filter out this community. In other words, we only remain the filler community which has partial overlap with query community.

4   Experimental Results

4.1   Settings

Experiments are conducted on all of the submitted results of TAC-KBP 2013 ESF task. Some slot types[3] are not contained in our dataset, since their values are not entities. For further testing whether our approach could improve the performance of SF task, we also select the top-3 best-performing systems in TAC-KBP 2013 ESF task to evaluate our slot filler refinement approach, including **LSV** (1st) [18], **RPI-BLENDER** (2nd) [19], and **Stanford** (4th) [20].

For fair comparison, we use the same ground-truth and adopt the official TAC evaluation tool by precision, recall, and F-measure. Moreover, we adopt other two statistical measures, the sensitivity (True Positive Rate, TPR) and the specificity (True Negative Rate, TNR) [21]. The former relates to the filtering system's ability to detect and retain the correct fillers, while the latter emphasizes on the filtering system's ability to detect and filter the incorrect fillers.

$$Sensitive(TPR) = \frac{TP}{P}, Specificity(TNR) = \frac{TN}{N}, \qquad (9)$$

where TP denotes the number of correct fillers which are not filtered, P denotes the total number of correct fillers, TN denotes the number of incorrect fillers which are filtered, and N denotes the total number of incorrect fillers.

We conduct statistical significance testing using one sample t-test ("***", "**", and "*" denote p-values of an improvement smaller than 0.01, in-between (0.01, 0.05] and bigger than 0.05). We employ GibbsLDA++[4] [22] with parameters $= 50/T$ and $= 0.1$ [23]. Such LDA model is trained on 100,000 documents from TAC-KBP 2013 ESF data set.

4.2   Overall Performance

We run our system on 27,655 of pooling responses which contains all submitted results of TAC-KBP 2013 ESF task. Table 1 shows the overall performance.

---

[3] per:{cause_of_death, date_of_birth, date_of_death, age, charges} and
   org:{date_founded, date_dissolved, number_of_employees_members, website}.
[4] http://gibbslda.sourceforge.net.

We can see that our filler refinement approach improves the performance on all submitted results (pooling response) by about 7% significantly. It also shows that this approach filters out about 27% (5,821 of 21,211 with normal configuration) of incorrect fillers, with a little loss of about 4% (269 of 6,444) of correct fillers.

Table 1. Overall performance on the submitted results and the top-3 systems of TAC-KBP 2013 ESF task. (**Normal**: a slot filler is marked as correct only if it matches a gold filler and its justification are true; **Anydoc**: a slot filler is marked as correct solely based on string matching with gold fillers, but ignoring justifications. FR: Filler Refinement).

Conf.	SF system	P(%)	R(%)	F1	TPR(%)	TNR(%)
Normal	Pooling response + FR(***)	23.30	100.00	37.80	N/A	N/A
		28.63	95.83	**44.09**	95.83 (6,175/6,444)	27.44 (5,821/21,211)
	LSV + FR(**)	39.72	29.09	33.58	N/A	N/A
		43.49	28.88	**34.71**	99.30 (425/427)	14.97 (88/648)
	RPI-BLENDER + FR(***)	40.73	29.02	33.89	N/A	N/A
		48.32	28.41	**35.78**	97.89 (417/426)	28.06 (174/620)
	Stanford + FR(**)	35.89	28.41	31.71	N/A	N/A
		39.09	28.07	**32.67**	98.80 (412/417)	13.83 (103/745)
Anydoc	Pooling response + FR(***)	27.72	100.00	43.40	N/A	N/A
		34.02	95.72	**50.20**	95.72 (7,337/7,665)	28.82 (5,762/19,990)
	LSV + FR(**)	46.70	34.41	39.62	N/A	N/A
		50.97	34.06	**40.83**	99.00 (497/502)	16.58 (95/573)
	RPI-BLENDER + FR(***)	44.46	31.87	37.13	N/A	N/A
		52.72	31.19	**39.19**	97.85 (455/465)	29.78 (173/581)
	Stanford + FR(**)	40.79	32.49	36.17	N/A	N/A
		44.02	31.80	**36.93**	97.89 (464/474)	14.24 (98/688)

It also shows that our slot filler refinement approach consistently promotes the performance of all SF systems (with the maximum gain 2%), especially on precision (with the maximum gain about 8%). Moreover, the overall performance with different configurations (**normal** and **anydoc**) indicates that our approach is independent of the slot filler justification. Additionally, note that such filtering method itself would naturally lead to the decline of recall, since all of the processes are based on the outputs of the SF system.

4.3   Discussion and Analysis

Similarity Measurement. Besides the PMI, we also explore other two co-occurrence measurements to estimate similarity between slot filler candidates.

Entitys TF_IDF: For slot fillers f_a and f_b in one filler community, we modify the TF_IDF score for measuring the co-occurrence similarity of slot fillers:

$$TF\_IDF(f_a, f_b) = tf \times idf = \frac{N(f_a, f_b | D_q)}{N(D_q)} \times \log \frac{N_{total}}{N(f_a, f_b)}, \qquad (10)$$

where $N(D_q)$ denotes the number of documents containing query q, $N(f_a, f_b|D_q)$ denotes the number of documents containing both fillers f_a and f_b in D_q, N_{total} denotes the total number of documents in data set, and $N(f_a, f_b)$ denotes the number of documents containing both fillers f_a and f_b.

Dice Similarity Coefficient (DSC): The DSC measures the fillers that two documents have in common as a proportion of all the fillers in both documents [24].

$$DSC = \frac{2 \times N(f_a, f_b|D_q)}{N(f_a|D_q) + N(f_b|D_q)}, \tag{11}$$

where $N(f_a, f_b|D_q)$ is the same as Eq. (10), $N(f_a|D_q)$ and $N(f_b|D_q)$ are the number of documents containing f_a and f_b in D_q, respectively.

Table 2 lists the performance on the entire submitted results of TAC-KBP 2013 ESF task and RPI-BLENDER system. It shows that the performance of PMI co-occurrence similarity is slightly better than the other two, which may avoid overcompensating common unrelated entities to the query entity. For example, the query *Merce Cunningham* is seen with the incorrect slot filler *Washington* more frequently (442 times) than the correct slot filler *Mayme*

Table 2. Performances by different similarity measurements with **anydoc** configuration.

SF system	OC-Sim	P(%)	R(%)	F1	TPR(%)	TNR(%)
Pooling response	N/A	27.72	100.00	43.40	N/A	N/A
+FR	TF_IDF	33.68	95.86	49.84	95.86(7,348/7,665)	27.60(5,518/19,990)
	DSC	33.85	95.83	50.02	95.83(7,345/7,665)	28.18(5,634/19,990)
	PMI	34.02	95.72	**50.20**	95.72(7,337/7,665)	28.82(5,762/19,990)
RPI-BLENDER	N/A	44.46	31.87	37.13	N/A	N/A
+FR	TF_IDF	52.60	31.12	39.10	97.63(454/465)	29.60(172/581)
	DSC	52.49	31.12	39.07	97.63(454/465)	29.26(170/581)
	PMI	52.72	31.19	**39.19**	97.85(455/465)	29.78(173/581)

Table 3. Distribution of related slot filler cluster and unrelated slot filler cluster. (|cluster| denotes the rank of a cluster; R denotes the clusters that are judged as *Related* to given queries by our approach; UnR denotes the clusters that are judged as *UnRelated* to given queries.)

Query ID	|cluster| = 1		|cluster| > 1	
	R	UnR	R	UnR
SF13_ENG_004	2	9	3	1
SF13_ENG_011	1	19	9	2
SF13_ENG_016	1	8	3	1
SF13_ENG_063	3	8	2	0
SF13_ENG_072	2	18	5	2

Joach[5] (only one time). Here PMI penalizes the incorrect slot filler for its popularity and the correct slot filler is preferred.

Distribution of Related and Unrelated Slot Filler Cluster. According to the analysis of five queries that selected randomly, we demonstrate our prerequisites that: (1) if fillers are related to the query, they are more likely to be clustered (comparing column 2 and 4 in Table 3); (2) conversely (unrelated), they might incline to belong to different clusters (comparing column 3 and 5 in Table 3). Query community and filler community identify groups of contextual cues that constrain each of the entities in a community to a single sense. Thus the slot fillers in a same community can help each other to determine whether they are related to the query entity or not collaboratively.

5   Conclusion

Slot filler refinement work is very important to SF task. In this paper we propose an unsupervised community-based slot filler refinement approach which consists of filler communities constructed by a PMI-based hierarchical clustering algorithm and a query community constructed by a co-occurrence graph model. In the future we will focus on exploring more information, such as the "docid" and "offset" of the filler candidate.

Acknowledgement. This research work is supported by National Natural Science Foundation of China (Grants No. 61672367, No. 61672368, No. 61703293), the Research Foundation of the Ministry of Education and China Mobile, MCM20150602 and the Science and Technology Plan of Jiangsu, SBK2015022101 and BK20151222. The authors would like to thank the anonymous reviewers for their insightful comments and suggestions.

References

1. Surdeanu, M.: Overview of the TAC2013 knowledge base population evaluation: English slot filling and temporal slot filling. In: Proceedings of the Sixth Text Analysis Conference (TAC) (2013)
2. Fortunato, S.: Community detection in graphs. Phys. Rep. **486**(3), 75–174 (2009)
3. Ji, H., Grishman, R., Dang, H.T., Griffitt, K., Ellis, J.: Overview of the TAC 2010 knowledge base population track. In: Proceedings of the Third Text Analysis Conference (TAC) (2010)
4. Sammons, M., Song, Y., Wang, R., Kundu, G., Tsai, C.T., Upadhyay, S., Ancha, S., Mayhew, S., Roth, D.: Overview of UI-CCQ systems for event argument extraction, entity discovery and linking, and slot filler validation. In: Proceedings of the Seventh Text Analysis Conference (TAC) (2014)
5. Yu, D., Huang, H., Cassidy, T., Ji, H., Wang, C., Zhi, S., Han, J., Voss, C.R., Magdon-Ismail, M.: The wisdom of minority: unsupervised slot filling validation based on multi-dimensional truth-finding. In: Proceedings of the 25th International Conference on Computational Linguistics (COLING), pp. 1567–1578 (2014)

---

[5] With slot type `per:parents`.

6. Rajani, N.F., Viswanathan, V., Bentor, Y., Mooney, R.J.: Stacked ensembles of information extractors for knowledge-base population. In: Proceedings of the 53rd Annual Meeting of the Association for Computational Linguistics and the 7th International Joint Conference on Natural Language Processing (ACL), pp. 177–187 (2015)
7. Xu, S., Zhang, C., Niu, Z., Mei, R., Chen, J., Zhang, J., Fu, H.: Bit's slot-filling method for TAC-KBP 2013. In: Proceedings of the Sixth Text Analysis Conference (TAC) (2013)
8. Nguyen, T.H., He, Y., Pershina, M., Li, X., Grishman, R.: New York University 2014 knowledge base population systems. In: Proceedings of the Seventh Text Analysis Conference (TAC) (2014)
9. Białecki, A., Muir, R., Ingersoll, G., Imagination, L.: Apache Lucene 4. In: SIGIR 2012 Workshop on Open Source Information Retrieval (2012)
10. Angeli, G., Premkumar, M.J., Manning, C.D.: Leveraging linguistic structure for open domain information extraction. In: Proceedings of the 53rd Annual Meeting of the Association for Computational Linguistics and the 7th International Joint Conference on Natural Language Processing (ACL), pp. 344–354 (2015)
11. Dasgupta, S., Long, P.M.: Performance guarantees for hierarchical clustering. J. Comput. Syst. Sci. **70**(4), 555–569 (2005)
12. Prim, R.C.: Shortest connection networks and some generalizations. Bell Labs Tech. J. **36**(6), 1389–1401 (1957)
13. Pakhira, M.K.: A fast k-means algorithm using cluster shifting to produce compact and separate clusters (research note). Int. J. Eng.-Trans. A: Basics **28**(1), 35–43 (2015)
14. Blei, D.M., Ng, A.Y., Jordan, M.I.: Latent dirichlet allocation. J. Mach. Learn. Res. **3**(Jan), 993–1022 (2003)
15. Rao, C.R.: A review of canonical coordinates and an alternative to correspondence analysis using Hellinger distance. Qüestiió: quaderns d'estadística i investigació operativa **19**(1), 23–63 (1995)
16. Girvan, M., Newman, M.E.: Community structure in social and biological networks. Proc. Nat. Acad. Sci. **99**(12), 7821–7826 (2002)
17. Clauset, A., Newman, M.E., Moore, C.: Finding community structure in very large networks. Phys. Rev. E **70**(6), 066111 (2004)
18. Roth, B., Barth, T., Wiegand, M., Singh, M., Klakow, D.: Effective slot filling based on shallow distant supervision methods. In: Proceedings of the Sixth Text Analysis Conference (TAC) (2013)
19. Yu, D., Li, H., Cassidy, T., Li, Q., Huang, H., Chen, Z., Ji, H., Zhang, Y., Roth, D.: RPI-BLENDER TAC-KBP2013 knowledge base population system. In: Theory and Applications of Categories (2013)
20. Angeli, G., Chaganty, A.T., Chang, A.X., Reschke, K., Tibshirani, J., Wu, J., Bastani, O., Siilats, K., Manning, C.D.: Stanford's 2013 KBP system. In: Proceedings of the Sixth Text Analysis Conference (TAC) (2013)
21. Powers, D.M.W.: Evaluation: from precision, recall and F-measure to ROC, informedness, markedness and correlation. J. Mach. Learn. Technol. **2**(1), 37–63 (2011)
22. Griffiths, T.: Gibbs Sampling in the Generative Model of Latent Dirichlet Allocation (2002)
23. Griffiths, T.L., Steyvers, M.: Finding scientific topics. Proc. Nat. Acad. Sci. **101**(Suppl. 1), 5228–5235 (2004)
24. Lewis, J., Ossowski, S., Hicks, J., Errami, M., Garner, H.R.: Text similarity: an alternative way to search medline. Bioinformatics **22**(18), 2298–2304 (2006)

Relation Linking for Wikidata Using Bag of Distribution Representation

Xi Yang, Shiya Ren, Yuan Li, Ke Shen, Zhixing Li$^{(\boxtimes)}$, and Guoyin Wang

Chongqing Key Laboratory of Computational Intelligence, Chongqing University of Posts and Telecommunications, Chongqing 400065, People's Republic of China
lizx@cqupt.edu.cn

Abstract. Knowledge graphs (KGs) are essential repositories of structured and semi-structured knowledge which benefit various NLP applications. To utilize the knowledge in KGs to help machines to better understand plain texts, one needs to bridge the gap between knowledge and texts. In this paper, a Relation Linking System for Wikidata (RLSW) is proposed to link the relations in KGs to plain texts. The proposed system uses the knowledge in Wikidata as seeds and clusters relation mentions in text with a novel phrase similarity algorithm. To enhance the system's ability of handling unseen expressions and make use of the location information of words to reduce false positive rate, a *bag of distribution* pattern modeling method is proposed. Experimental results show that the proposed approach improves traditional methods, including word based pattern and syntax feature enriched system such as OLLIE.

Keywords: Relation linking · Knowledge graph · NLP

1 Introduction

Knowledge graph (KG) is able to provide structured and connected information between entities. Before utilizing knowledge graph in natural language understanding applications, one of the main challenge is mapping the knowledge in KGs to plain texts. Entity linking is one attempt towards this challenge. It links the surface names in the texts to corresponding entity objects in KGs. While most research focus on entity linking [2,3], few attention has been paid on mapping relations in KGs to texts which we called *Relation Linking*.

Table 1 shows the number of possible patterns of 9 different relations collected from Wikipedia. The second column is the number of sentences that contains corresponding mentions, namely positive samples. The third column is the number of distinct accurate patterns in these sentences and the last column is the number of distinct patterns extracted by OLLIE [8]. One may use virous relation expressions extracted OLLIE directly to link relations to texts. However, it may suffer from two drawbacks. Firstly, these patterns cannot cover all the possible expressions of the relations so it will inevitably encounter low recall problem when dealing with new texts. Secondly, it is difficult to find if an accurate pattern

© Springer International Publishing AG 2018
X. Huang et al. (Eds.): NLPCC 2017, LNAI 10619, pp. 652–661, 2018.
https://doi.org/10.1007/978-3-319-73618-1_55

Table 1. Statistic of patterns and sentences of 9 relations in Wikidata

Relations	# of sentences	# of Acc. patterns	# of OLLIE patterns
Father	6,630	92	205
Mother	3,324	31	81
Child	4,396	39	185
Spouse	7,586	106	146
Language	3,958	13	85
Country	10,116	76	407
Religion	2,239	30	58
Edu	5,033	81	130
Politic	5,530	85	133

is really a mention of the given relation since there exists a lot of noise in the automatically labelled data.

To address these problems, this paper proposes a Relation Linking System for Wikidata (RLSW) which learns flexible relation patterns from Wikidata and Wikipedia. For each relation defined in Wikidata, one or more patterns that can cover various natural language phrases in Wikipedia articles are learnt. As a result, each pattern can cover a cluster of words sequence. It has to be noticed that although RLSW is designed for Wikidata, the framework proposed in this paper can be immigrated to other KGs easily.

Bridging the gap between KGs and plain texts is one vital step in NLP. The RLSW proposed in this paper focuses on mapping relations to plain texts and its contributions are as follows:

- A framework for relation linking is proposed while much research focus on entity linking. In this framework, word sequences are clustered and then are connected to relations in KGs.
- A new phrase similarity scoring method is proposed for pattern clustering. It combines semantic distance and spacial distance of words and produces better results than *bag of words* settings.
- A new phrase pattern algorithm is proposed. In the proposed algorithm, a pattern is a set of distributions of words. We also give the algorithm to obtain these patterns from phrases and match new phrases with these patterns.

The rest of this paper is organized as follows. Section 2 reviews related work about the topic. The general framework and key part of RLSW are described in Sects. 3 and 4. Section 5 gives results to the examine the proposed RLSW. Finally, in Sect. 6, conclusions are summarized.

2   Related Work

RLSW contains several necessary procedures and each procedure relates to a specific research topic. In this section, we will briefly survey existing related work such as relation extraction, sentence similarity and entity linking.

2.1   Relation Extraction

As a typical subtask of information extraction, relation extraction identifies the relation between entities which is closely related to relation linking. NELL [8] learned many types of knowledge from self-supervised experience with self-reflection. The system classified pairs of phrases by learning boolean-valued relation. The relation is limited by the type that mostly are *is-a* or *class-of.* Wu and Weld [11] presented WOE^{parse} which used features generated from dependency parsing trees to extract *subj-rel-obj* tuples. However, this method relies on the output of dependency parsing and any errors of dependency parsing may cause error propagation. OLLIE overcame WOE's limitations and extracted relations by including contextual information from the sentences. However, OLLIE fails to consider the connection between unstructured text and structured information.

2.2   Sentence Similarity

RLSW adopts sentence similarity to cluster relation mentions. Much research in recent years has been reported in this task. Li et al. [7] utilized information from a structured lexical database and corpus statistics to calculate the semantic similarity of two sentences. He et al. [4] proposed a multiplicity of perspectives by using a convolutional neural network to extract features and then used multiple similarity metrics to compare sentences at different granulates. When faced large amounts of training data, it cannot perform well. The WMD, presented by Kusner et al. [6], learned semantically meaningful representations for words. However, these approaches only consider the semantic similarity between words, while in natural language, the position of words also matters. In this paper, a location-sensitive WMD algorithm is proposed to capture the words location information for the calculation of sentence similarities.

2.3   Entity Linking

Entity linking is another task of mapping knowledge in KGs to texts which determines the identity of entities mentioned in text in a structured KG. There have been a great number of studies in entity linking. Shen et al. [10] used two candidate entity ranking methods such as supervised ranking and unsupervised ranking to get top entity for mapping to KB. Another application is the ZenCrowd [2] which implemented large-scale entity linking using probabilistic reasoning and crowd-sourcing techniques. Han et al. [3] proposed a graph-based collective EL method, which can model and exploit the global interdependence between different EL decisions. These studies on entity linking have not taken the relationship between entities into account to provide the whole picture of information in knowledge graph mapping. As a supplement, RLSW is proposed to build connections between relations in KG and their mentions in texts.

3   Problem Definition

Formally, the relation linking is a mapping from natural language mentions to relations in KGs which can be defined as follows:

$$f : \mathscr{M} \rightarrow \mathscr{R}$$

where $\mathscr{M}$ is the set of possible mentions of relations and $\mathscr{R}$ is the set of relations in KG. In practice, mention $m \in \mathscr{M}$ is a sequence of words.

The task of relation linking is to find the mentions of a relation. E.g., mentions such as *is born in*, *is the hometown of*, *come from* can be linked to Wikidata relation *birthplace*. Since it is impossible to enumerate all possible mentions, one alternative is approximating f with relation classification algorithm $\hat{f}$ which takes word sequence as input and decides if it contains a relation mention.

4   Relation Linking Using Bag of Distribution Representation

The goal of relation linking is to link the mention of relations to KGs. Figure 1 shows the architecture of the proposed framework. First, for a given relation (in Wikidata, *property* is used instead of *relation*), such as *father* (P22), SPARQL API is used to query $\langle subj., obj. \rangle$ pairs from Wikidata and then sentences contains both subject and object from Wikipedia articles are selected as the source sentences of relation mentions. Second, the obtained mentions are clustered using a new similarity scoring method proposed in this paper. Third, each mention cluster is represented as a Bag of Distribution (BoD) and last, a classifier is trained based on the mention vectors which consists of the fitness between the mention and the BoDs. The main contributions of this work focus on the clustering part and the BoD pattern learning part.

4.1   Preprocessor

The main goal of preprocessor is to obtain sufficient data for the learning and training. It consists of two steps. First, obtaining $\langle subj., obj. \rangle$ pairs from Wikidata. Second, finding relation mentions according to $\langle subj., obj. \rangle$ pairs.

As for the first step, Wikidata SPARQL API [5] is used. We first get a list of entities of a selected category (e.g. *HUMAN*), then query the property value (e.g. *father*) of these entities to build $\langle subj., obj. \rangle$ pairs list. At the second step, $\langle subj., obj. \rangle$ pairs are used to find relation mentions from corresponding Wikipedia Articles. Each sentence that matches a $\langle subj., obj. \rangle$ pair be selected and the word sequence between the label of subject and the label of object is annotated as relation mentions.

To get rid of noises, only mentions that contains 4–10 words are reserved for further processing.

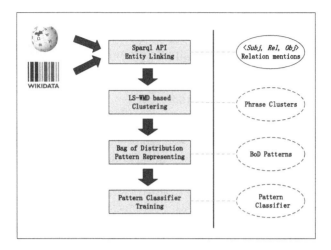

Fig. 1. Architecture of RLSW

4.2 Mention Clustering

Mention Clustering aims at grouping mentions to mining patterns. There are various natural language representations for a given relation and it's better to mine patterns from groups of similar mentions instead from all mentions.

Since mentions are word sequence but not numeric vectors, one needs to give an effective measure for word sequence pairs before clustering. Word Mover's Distance (WMD) [6] leverages word embedding to measure the semantic distances between words and then uses Earth Mover Distance (EMD) to measure the distance between word sequences. However, due to the natural of EMD, WMD does not take into consideration the location and order of words. In fact, apart from semantic similarity between words, syntactic information plays a vital role in sentence understanding. For instance, the meaning of two sentences *John's father is Dan* and *John is the father of Dan* is very close according to WMD and therefor the system would not tell if this is a mention of relation *son* or *father*. To address this problem, the position information of words is imported in this work when calculating the similarity between word sequences.

Location Sensitive Word Mover's Distance: In WMD, words are represented as embedding vectors and the calculation of distance between words is converted to the calculation of distance between vectors. Since location of words also matters, one needs to add location information to the calculation of distances between words. In this work, the location of a word in a sequence is encoded a value between 0 and 1. Given a mention $\{w_1, w_2, ...w_n\}$, the location value of w_i is calculated as:

$$loc(w_i) = \frac{1}{n} * (i - 0.5)$$

E.g., given mention *is the son of*, the location value of *son* $loc(w_3) = \frac{1}{4}(3-0.5) = 0.625$. The bias 0.5 is used to ensure that the location value lies in the center of word's range in the sentence. As a result, the location differences between words can be calculated as the absolute difference between their location values. These location differences are imported to WMD as follows:

$$min_{\mathbf{T} \geq 0} \sum_{i,j=1}^{n} \mathbf{T}_{ij} D_{sem+loc}(s_i, s'_j)$$

$$suject\ to : \sum_{j=1}^{n} \mathbf{T}_{ij} = d_i\ \forall i \in \{1, ..., n\} \tag{1}$$

$$\sum_{i=1}^{n} \mathbf{T}_{ij} = d'_j\ \forall j \in \{1, ..., n\}$$

where s_i is the i_{th} word of s, d_i is the weight of i_{th} word of s, T is the flow matrix which defines the mass from words in s to words in s' and $D_{sem+loc}(s_i, s'_j)$ is the similarity distance between s_i and s'_j. It is composed of the semantic distance and syntactic distance, namely,

$$D_{sem+loc}(s_i, s'_j) = \alpha D_{sem}(s_i, s'_j) + (1 - \alpha)D_{loc}(s_i, s'_j), \alpha \in [0, 1] \tag{2}$$

α is hyperparameter and its value is detailed in Sect. 5.2. Semantic distance is calculated as in WMD, and location distance is calculated as stated in this paper. Since this measurement takes into consideration the location of words, it is named as Location Sensitive Word Mover's Distance (LSWMD).

Density Peaks Based Clustering (DPC): In this paper, Density Peak Based Clustering [9] is chosen as the clustering algorithm for relation mentions because of its efficiency and ability of handling distance matrix. Currently, clustering center are manually selected and the number of clusters is manually set which is controlled within ten.

4.3   Bag of Distribution Pattern Representing

After detailed data observation, we find that for a given relation, the locations of words in mentions are relatively stable. E.g., although relation *father* has many different mentions such as *was son of, was daughter of, is first son of*, the word *was/is* always locates at the front of the mention and *son/daughter* always locates at the second half. If one uses a distribution to describe a word in the mentions, it may provide much more information than frequency based methods.

Since the location of words are encoded as values between 0 to 1, beta distribution is selected to model the location distribution of words. As a result, a mention cluster that contains a list of mentions can be converted to a list of weighted beta distributions of words. The probability density of the beta distribution indicates how likely the word appears in some position and the weight indicates that how frequently the word appears in the mention cluster. A Bag of Distribution Representing of a mention cluster is defined as follows:

$$BoD(c) = \{(p_i, \alpha_i, \beta_i) | w_i \in W_c\} \tag{3}$$

where c is a cluster of mentions, W_c is the vocabulary of c, $p_i = \frac{count(w_i)}{\sum_i count(w_i)}$ is the probability of w_i in W_c. α_i and β_i is the parameter of modeled beta distribution of word w_i.

Mention Scoring: Given a mention $m = \{w_1, w_2, ...w_n\}$, its fitness towards a given BoD pattern c is calculated as follows:

$$fit_{BoD(c)}(m) = \sum_{w_i}^{w_i \in m} p_{w_i} * \int_{range(w_i)} Beta(\alpha_{w_i}, \beta_{w_i}) \qquad (4)$$

where $range(w_i)$ is the normalized location range of word w_i in m. E.g., $r(son)$ in $is\ son\ of$ is $[0.333, 0.667]$. An alterative method is using a vector to describe the fitness between m and $BoD(c)$ where the components of this vector is the fitness of single word in m w.r.t $BoD(c)$.

4.4   Relation Classification

For each mention, a vector which consists of its finesses towards all BoD patters is build. We use a window which is generated by sentence frequency to san the testing sentences and find the most matched word strings as the mention of a relation. The rest sentences are selected as negative samples. The last component of RLSW is a relation classifier trained on such vectors. GBDT is used as the classifier in our experiment. For testing sentences to be linked, we first find the candidate word sequences by window from them and then convert each word sequence to a vector. The trained classifier takes the vector as input to decide if it should be linked to the given relation.

5   Experiments and Evaluations

5.1   Data Sets

The relations used in experiments are manually collected from Wikidata. For convenience, all relations are associated with category $HUMAN$. In total, 20,000 entities are queried from Wikidata and due to the data sparse problem, not all entities have all property values of these selected relations. The Wikipedia page of these 20,000 is crawled as the source plain text and the matching method described in Sect. 4.1 is used to find mentions. At last, about 3,000–10,000 sentences are matched for these relations. The details can be found in Table 1.

5.2   Experiments Setting

Since RLSW is a framework that can collaborate with different kinds of instance based matching method, four series of experiments are conducted, i.e., $Accurate$ $Pattern(Acc.)$, $OLLIEPattern(OLLIE)$, $BoD + AccuratePattern(BoD(Acc))$ and $BoD + OLLIEPattern(BoD(OLLIE))$. $Acc.$ uses the word sequences in training samples directly to match mentions from testing sentences. $OLLIE$ parses all training samples and selects the predicates in tuples contained correct $\langle subj., obj.\rangle$ pairs as templates to match mentions. $BoD(Acc.)$ learns BoD patterns from word sequences used in $Acc.$ and $BoD(OLLIE)$ learns BoD patterns from predicates extracted by *OLLIE*. For all relations, 10-fold cross-validation is used to evaluate all tested methods. *Acc.* and *OLLIE* do not need to be trained and false samples are used to calculate the confidence of patterns.

We find that the selection of cut-off distance d_c in DPC has little effect on the results. So we set the around 1% quantile as the DPC parameter.

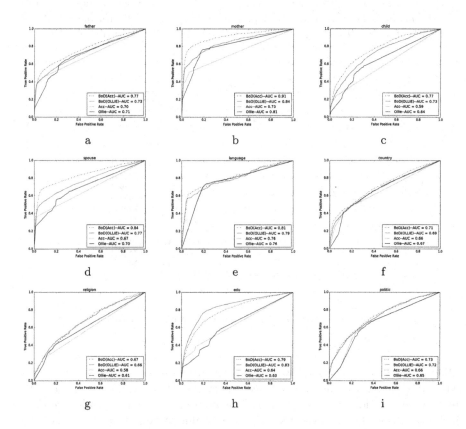

Fig. 2. Experimental results of 4 tested methods

5.3 Performance Analysis

This subsection reports and discusses the experimental results of all four tested methods. The performance is compared using AUC value.

Overall Performance Comparison

From Fig. 2 we can see that:

- BoD Pattern brings improvements to both *Acc.* and *OLLIE* on all relations, especially for the relation *mother*, *spouse* and *edu*. It reserves low FPR at the early stage and produces higher TPR than the baseline as the growth of FPR. It means that BoD Pattern recalls more true positive samples with the

same amount of false positive samples. E.g., for relation *mother*, the TPR of
BoD(Acc) is 0.8 at a FPR 0.1 while the TRP of *Acc* and *OLLIE* are 0.6.

– *OLLIE* outperforms *Acc.* in 6 of 9 relations. One possible reason is that
accurate pattern contains too much noise that leads a high FPR.
– BoD pattern brings more significance improvements to *Acc*. Although *OLLIE*
outperforms *Acc.*, after the denoising of *BoD*, it archives a higher AUC than
OLLIE in most relations. The dependency or syntactical information prevent
OLLIE find word sequence that are not syntactically close to each other.

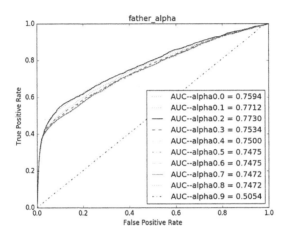

Fig. 3. The AUC of BoD(OLLIE) with different α on relation *father*

Discussion of α: α controls the ratio of semantic distance and location distance
when calculating the distance between mentions. Here we tested how RLSW's
performance varies with the α value of the relation *father*; the results are shown
in Fig. 3. It can be observed that the AUC value is best when the α is 0.2. It
has been empirically proved [1] that a sentence similarity measure performs best
when semantic measure is weighted more than syntactic measure. Therefore, a
small α value is preferred in practice. In experiments of this work, α is set to 0.2
for all relations.

6   Conclusions

In this paper, a new framework of relation linking for knowledge graphs called
RLSW is proposed. The relation mentions are clustered with location sensitive
phase similarity measurements algorithm LSWMD and then each cluster is represented as a Bag of Distributions of words. For each testing word sequence, a
classifier is used to decide if it should be linked to the given relation.

However, there are still a lot work to do in future. First, shallow syntax feature such as PoS tags can be used for similarity calculation. Second, the entities of subject and object can be taken into consideration when building relation patterns. Last, in future, we plan to develop a plain text oriented deduction system based on relation linking and entity linking techniques with the data provided by KGs such as Wikidata.

Acknowledgments. This paper is supported by the national key R&D of China program (No. 2016YFB1000900), NFSC program young scholar project (No. 61502066), scientific and technological research program of Chongqing municipal education commission (No. KJ1500438), basic and frontier research project of Chongqing, China (No. cstc2015jcyjA40018).

References

1. Achananuparp, P., Hu, X., Zhou, X., Zhang, X.: Utilizing Sentence Similarity and Question Type Similarity to Response to Similar Questions in Knowledge-Sharing Community (2008)
2. Demartini, G., Difallah, D.E., Cudré-Mauroux, P.: ZenCrowd: leveraging probabilistic reasoning and crowdsourcing techniques for large-scale entity linking. In: International Conference on World Wide Web, pp. 469–478 (2012)
3. Han, X., Sun, L., Zhao, J.: Collective entity linking in web text: a graph-based method. In: Proceeding of the International ACM SIGIR Conference on Research and Development in Information Retrieval, SIGIR 2011, Beijing, China, pp. 765–774, July 2011
4. He, H., Gimpel, K., Lin, J.: Multi-perspective sentence similarity modeling with convolutional neural networks. In: Conference on Empirical Methods in Natural Language Processing, pp. 1576–1586 (2015)
5. Huang, J., Abadi, D.J., Ren, K.: Scalable SPARQL querying of large RDF graphs. Proc. VLDB Endow. **4**(11), 1123–1134 (2011)
6. Kusner, M.J., Sun, Y., Kolkin, N.I., Weinberger, K.Q.: From Word Embeddings to Document Distances, pp. 957–966 (2015)
7. Li, Y., McLean, D., Bandar, Z.A., O'Shea, J.D., Crockett, K.: Sentence similarity based on semantic nets and corpus statistics. IEEE Trans. Knowl. Data Eng. **18**(8), 1138–1150 (2006)
8. Schmitz, M., Bart, R., Soderland, S., Etzioni, O.: Open language learning for information extraction. In: Joint Conference on Empirical Methods in Natural Language Processing and Computational Natural Language Learning (2012)
9. Rodriguez, A., Laio, A.: Clustering by fast search and find of density peaks. Science **344**(6191), 1492–1496 (2014)
10. Shen, W., Wang, J., Han, J.: Entity linking with a knowledge base: issues, techniques, and solutions. IEEE Trans. Knowl. Data Eng. **27**(2), 443–460 (2015)
11. Wu, F., Weld, D.S.: Open information extraction using Wikipedia. In: Proceedings of the Meeting of the Association for Computational Linguistics, ACL 2010, Uppsala, Sweden, 11–16 July 2010, pp. 118–127 (2010)

Neural Question Generation from Text: A Preliminary Study

Qingyu Zhou[1(✉)], Nan Yang[2], Furu Wei[2], Chuanqi Tan[3], Hangbo Bao[1], and Ming Zhou[2]

[1] Harbin Institute of Technology, Harbin, China
qyzhgm@gmail.com, baohangbo@hit.edu.cn
[2] Microsoft Research, Beijing, China
nanya@microsoft.com, fuwei@microsoft.com, mingzhou@microsoft.com
[3] Beihang University, Beijing, China
tanchuanqi@nlsde.buaa.edu.cn

Abstract. Automatic question generation aims to generate questions from a text passage where the generated questions can be answered by certain sub-spans of the given passage. Traditional methods mainly use rigid heuristic rules to transform a sentence into related questions. In this work, we propose to apply the neural encoder-decoder model to generate meaningful and diverse questions from natural language sentences. The encoder reads the input text and the answer position, to produce an answer-aware input representation, which is fed to the decoder to generate an answer focused question. We conduct a preliminary study on neural question generation from text with the SQuAD dataset, and the experiment results show that our method can produce fluent and diverse questions.

1 Introduction

Automatic question generation from natural language text aims to generate questions taking text as input, which has the potential value of education purpose [9]. As the reverse task of question answering, question generation also has the potential for providing a large scale corpus of question-answer pairs.

Previous works for question generation mainly use rigid heuristic rules to transform a sentence into related questions [2,9]. However, these methods heavily rely on human-designed transformation and generation rules, which cannot be easily adopted to other domains. Instead of generating questions from texts, [19] proposed a neural network method to generate factoid questions from structured data.

In this work we conduct a preliminary study on question generation from text with neural networks, which is denoted as the Neural Question Generation (NQG) framework, to generate natural language questions from text without pre-defined rules. The Neural Question Generation framework extends the sequence-to-sequence models by enriching the encoder with answer and lexical features to

---

Q. Zhou—Contribution during internship at Microsoft Research.

X. Huang et al. (Eds.): NLPCC 2017, LNAI 10619, pp. 662–671, 2018.
https://doi.org/10.1007/978-3-319-73618-1_56

generate answer focused questions. Concretely, the encoder reads not only the input sentence, but also the answer position indicator and lexical features. The answer position feature denotes the answer span in the input sentence, which is essential to generate answer relevant questions. The lexical features include part-of-speech (POS) and named entity (NER) tags to help produce better sentence encoding. Lastly, the decoder with attention mechanism [1] generates an answer specific question of the sentence.

Large-scale manually annotated passage and question pairs play a crucial role in developing question generation systems. We propose to adapt the recently released Stanford Question Answering Dataset (SQuAD) [18] as the training and development datasets for the question generation task. In SQuAD, the answers are labeled as subsequences in the given sentences by crowed sourcing, and it contains more than 100K questions which makes it feasible to train our neural network models. We conduct the experiments on SQuAD, and the experiment results show the neural network models can produce fluent and diverse questions from text.

2   Approach

In this section, we introduce the NQG framework, which consists of a feature-rich encoder and an attention-based decoder. Figure 1 provides an overview of our NQG framework.

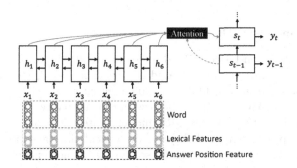

Fig. 1. Overview of the Neural Question Generation (NQG) framework.

2.1   Feature-Rich Encoder

In the NQG framework, we use Gated Recurrent Unit (GRU) [4] to build the encoder. To capture more context information, we use bidirectional GRU (BiGRU) to read the inputs in both forward and backward orders. Inspired by [3,14], the BiGRU encoder not only reads the sentence words, but also hand-crafted features, to produce a sequence of word-and-feature vectors. We concatenate the word vector, lexical feature embedding vectors and answer position indicator embedding vector as the input of BiGRU encoder. Concretely, the BiGRU encoder reads the concatenated sentence word vector, lexical features, and answer position feature, $x = (x_1, x_2, \ldots, x_n)$, to produce two sequences of hidden vectors, i.e., the forward sequence $(\boldsymbol{h}_1, \boldsymbol{h}_2, \ldots, \boldsymbol{h}_n)$ and the backward sequence $(\boldsymbol{h}_1, \boldsymbol{h}_2, \ldots, \boldsymbol{h}_n)$. Lastly, the output sequence of the encoder is the concatenation of the two sequences, i.e., $h_i = [\boldsymbol{h}_i; \boldsymbol{h}_i]$.

Answer Position Feature. To generate a question with respect to a specific answer in a sentence, we propose using answer position feature to locate the target answer. In this work, the BIO tagging scheme is used to label the position of a target answer. In this scheme, tag B denotes the start of an answer, tag I continues the answer and tag O marks words that do not form part of an answer. The BIO tags of answer position are embedded to real-valued vectors throu and fed to the feature-rich encoder. With the BIO tagging feature, the answer position is encoded to the hidden vectors and used to generate answer focused questions.

Lexical Features. Besides the sentence words, we also feed other lexical features to the encoder. To encode more linguistic information, we select word case, POS and NER tags as the lexical features. As an intermediate layer of full parsing, POS tag feature is important in many NLP tasks, such as information extraction and dependency parsing [12]. Considering that SQuAD is constructed using Wikipedia articles, which contain lots of named entities, we add NER feature to help detecting them.

2.2   Attention-Based Decoder

We employ an attention-based GRU decoder to decode the sentence and answer information to generate questions. At decoding time step t, the GRU decoder reads the previous word embedding w_{t-1} and context vector c_{t-1} to compute the new hidden state s_t. We use a linear layer with the last backward encoder hidden state $\boldsymbol{h}_1$ to initialize the decoder GRU hidden state. The context vector c_t for current time step t is computed through the concatenate attention mechanism [11], which matches the current decoder state s_t with each encoder hidden state h_i to get an importance score. The importance scores are then normalized to get the current context vector by weighted sum:

$$s_t = \mathrm{GRU}(w_{t-1}, c_{t-1}, s_{t-1}) \tag{1}$$

$$s_0 = \tanh(\mathbf{W}_d \boldsymbol{h}_1 + b) \tag{2}$$

$$e_{t,i} = v_a^\top \tanh(\mathbf{W}_a s_{t-1} + \mathbf{U}_a h_i) \tag{3}$$

$$\alpha_{t,i} = \frac{\exp(e_{t,i})}{\sum_{i=1}^n \exp(e_{t,i})} \tag{4}$$

$$c_t = \sum_{i=1}^n \alpha_{t,i} h_i \tag{5}$$

We then combine the previous word embedding w_{t-1}, the current context vector c_t, and the decoder state s_t to get the readout state r_t. The readout state is passed through a maxout hidden layer [7] to predict the next word with a softmax layer over the decoder vocabulary:

$$r_t = \mathbf{W}_r w_{t-1} + \mathbf{U}_r c_t + \mathbf{V}_r s_t \tag{6}$$

$$m_t = [\max\{r_{t,2j-1}, r_{t,2j}\}]_{j=1,\ldots,d}^{\top} \tag{7}$$

$$p(y_t|y_1,\ldots,y_{t-1}) = \mathrm{softmax}(\mathbf{W}_o m_t) \tag{8}$$

where r_t is a $2d$-dimensional vector.

2.3   Copy Mechanism

To deal with the rare and unknown words problem, [8] propose using pointing mechanism to copy rare words from source sentence. We apply this pointing method in our NQG system. When decoding word t, the copy switch takes current decoder state s_t and context vector c_t as input and generates the probability p of copying a word from source sentence:

$$p = \sigma(\mathbf{W}s_t + \mathbf{U}c_t + b) \tag{9}$$

where σ is sigmoid function. We reuse the attention probability in Eq. 4 to decide which word to copy.

3   Experiments and Results

We use the SQuAD dataset as our training data. SQuAD is composed of more than 100K questions posed by crowd workers on 536 Wikipedia articles. We extract sentence-answer-question triples to build the training, development and test sets[1]. Since the test set is not publicly available, we randomly halve the development set to construct the new development and test sets. The extracted training, development and test sets contain 86,635, 8,965 and 8,964 triples respectively. We introduce the implementation details in the appendix.

We conduct several experiments and ablation tests as follows:

PCFG-Trans. The rule-based system (see footnote 1) modified on the code released by [9]. We modified the code so that it can generate question based on a given word span.

s2s+att. We implement a seq2seq with attention as the baseline method.

NQG. We extend the s2s+att with our feature-rich encoder to build the NQG system.

NQG+. Based on NQG, we incorporate copy mechanism to deal with rare words problem.

---

[1] We re-distribute the processed data split and PCFG-Trans baseline code at http://res.qyzhou.me.

NQG+Pretrain. Based on NQG+, we initialize the word embedding matrix with pre-trained GloVe [17] vectors.

NQG+STshare. Based on NQG+, we make the encoder and decoder share the same embedding matrix.

NQG++. Based on NQG+, we use both pre-train word embedding and STshare methods, to further improve the performance.

NQG - Answer. Ablation test, the answer position indicator is removed from NQG model.

NQG - POS. Ablation test, the POS tag feature is removed from NQG model.

NQG - NER. Ablation test, the NER feature is removed from NQG model.

NQG - Case. Ablation test, the word case feature is removed from NQG model.

3.1   Implementation Details

Model Parameters. We use the same vocabulary for both encoder and decoder. The vocabulary is collected from the training data and we keep the top 20,000 frequent words. We set the word embedding size to 300 and all GRU hidden state sizes to 512. The lexical and answer position features are embedded to 32-dimensional vectors. We use dropout [20] with probability $p = 0.5$. During testing, we use beam search with beam size 12.

Lexical Feature Annotation. We use Stanford CoreNLP v3.7.0[2] [13] to annotate POS and NER tags in sentences with its default configuration and pre-trained models.

Model Training. We initialize model parameters randomly using a Gaussian distribution with Xavier scheme [6]. We use a combination of Adam [10] and simple SGD as our the optimizing algorithms. The training is separated into two phases, the first phase is optimizing the loss function with Adam and the second is with simple SGD. For the Adam optimizer, we set the learning rate $\alpha = 0.001$, two momentum parameters $\beta_1 = 0.9$ and $\beta_2 = 0.999$ respectively, and $\epsilon = 10^{-8}$. We use Adam optimizer until the BLEU score on the development set drops for six consecutive tests (we test the BLEU score on the development set for every 1,000 batches). Then we switch to a simple SGD optimizer with initial learning rate $\alpha = 0.5$ and halve it if the BLEU score on the development set drops for twelve consecutive tests. We also apply gradient clipping [16] with range $[-5, 5]$ for both Adam and SGD phases. To both speed up the training and converge quickly, we use mini-batch size 64 by grid search.

3.2   Human Evaluation

We evaluate the PCFG-Trans baseline and NQG++ with human judges. The rating scheme is provided in Table 1.

---

[2] https://stanfordnlp.github.io/CoreNLP/.

Table 1. Human rating scheme.

Score	Rating scheme
3-good	The question is meaningful and matches the sentence and answer very well
2-borderline	The question matches the sentence and answer, more or less
1-bad	The question either does not make sense or matches the sentence and answer

The human judges are asked to label the generated questions if they match the given sentence and answer span according to the rating scheme and examples. We provide some example questions with different scores in Table 2. For the first score 3 example, the question makes sense and the target answer "reason" can be used to answer it given the input sentence. For the second score 2 example, the question is inadequate for answering the sentence since the answer is about prime number. However, given the sentence, a reasonable person will give the targeted answer of the question. For the third score 1 example, the question is totally wrong given the sentence and answer.

Table 2. Human rating scheme examples, **I** is input, **O** is output, the underlined words are target answers.

Score	Sentence and generated question
3	**I:** -lsb- ... -rsb- for <u>reason</u> is the greatest enemy that faith has; it never comes to the aid of spiritual things"
	O: what is the biggest enemy that faith has have?
2	**I:** in all other rows -lrb- a = 1, 2, 4, 5, 7, and 8 -rrb- there are <u>infinitely many prime numbers</u>
	O: how many numbers are in all other rows?
1	**I:** while genghis khan never conquered all of china, his <u>grandson</u> kublai khan completed that conquest and established the yuan dynasty that is often credited with re-uniting china
	O: who did kublai khan defeat that conquered all of china?

3.3 Results and Analysis

We report BLEU-4 score [15] as the evaluation metric of our NQG system.

Table 3 shows the BLEU-4 scores of different settings. We report the beam search results on both development and test sets. Our NQG framework outperforms the PCFG-Trans and s2s+att baselines by a large margin. This shows that the lexical features and answer position indicator can benefit the question generation. With the help of copy mechanism, NQG+ has a 2.05 BLEU improvement

Table 3. BLEU evaluation scores of baseline methods, different NQG framework configurations and some ablation tests.

Model	Dev set	Test set
PCFG-Trans	9.28	9.31
s2s+att	3.01	3.06
NQG	10.06	10.13
NQG+	12.30	12.18
NQG+Pretrain	12.80	12.69
NQG+STshare	12.92	12.80
NQG++	**13.27**	**13.29**
NQG−Answer	2.79	2.98
NQG−POS	9.83	9.87
NQG−NER	9.50	9.29
NQG−Case	9.91	9.89

since it solves the rare words problem. The extended version, NQG++, has 1.11 BLEU score gain over NQG+, which shows that initializing with pre-trained word vectors and sharing them between encoder and decoder help learn better word representation.

Human Evaluation. We evaluate the PCFG-Trans baseline and NQG++ with human judges. The rating scheme is, Good (3) - The question is meaningful and matches the sentence and answer very well; Borderline (2) - The question matches the sentence and answer, more or less; Bad (1) - The question either does not make sense or matches the sentence and answer. We provide more detailed rating examples in Table 2. Three human raters labeled 200 questions sampled from the test set to judge if the generated question matches the given sentence and answer span. The inter-rater aggreement is measured with Fleiss' kappa [5].

Table 4 reports the human judge results. The kappa scores show a moderate agreement between the human raters. Our NQG++ outperforms the PCFG-Trans baseline by 0.76 score, which shows that the questions generated by NQG++ are more related to the given sentence and answer span.

Table 4. Human evaluation results.

Model	AvgScore	Fleiss' kappa
PCFG-Trans	1.42	0.50
NQG++	2.18	0.46

Ablation Test. The answer position indicator, as expected, plays a crucial role in answer focused question generation as shown in the NQG−Answer ablation test. Without it, the performance drops terribly since the decoder has no information about the answer subsequence.

Ablation tests, NQG−Case, NQG−POS and NQG−NER, show that word case, POS and NER tag features contributes to question generation.

Case Study. Table 5 provides three examples generated by NQG++. The words with underline are the target answers. These three examples are with different question types, namely WHEN, WHAT and WHO respectively. It can be observed that the decoder can 'copy' spans from input sentences to generate the questions. Besides the underlined words, other meaningful spans can also be used as answer to generate correct answer focused questions.

Table 5. Examples of generated questions, I is the input sentence, G is the gold question and O is the NQG++ generated question. The underlined words are the target answers.

I:	in 1226, immediately after returning from the west, genghis khan began a retaliatory attack on the tanguts
G:	in which year did genghis khan strike against the tanguts?
O:	in what year did genghis khan begin a retaliatory attack on the tanguts?
I:	in week 10, manning suffered a partial tear of the plantar fasciitis in his left foot
G:	in the 10th week of the 2015 season, what injury was peyton manning dealing with?
O:	what did manning suffer in his left foot?
I:	like the lombardi trophy, the "50" will be designed by tiffany & co.
G:	who designed the vince lombardi trophy?
O:	who designed the lombardi trophy?

Type of Generated Questions. Following [21], we classify the questions into different types, i.e., WHAT, HOW, WHO, WHEN, WHICH, WHERE, WHY and OTHER.[3] We evaluate the precision and recall of each question types. Figure 2 provides the precision and recall metrics of different question types. The precision and recall of a question type T are defined as:

$$\text{precision}(T) = \frac{\#(\text{true T-type questions})}{\#(\text{generated T-type questions})} \tag{10}$$

$$\text{recall}(T) = \frac{\#(\text{true T-type questions})}{\#(\text{all gold T-type questions})} \tag{11}$$

---

[3] We treat questions 'what country', 'what place' and so on as WHERE type questions. Similarly, questions containing 'what time', 'what year' and so forth are counted as WHEN type questions.

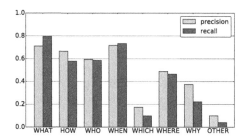

Fig. 2. Precision and recall of question types.

For the majority question types, WHAT, HOW, WHO and WHEN types, our NQG++ model performs well for both precision and recall. For type WHICH, it can be observed that neither precision nor recall are acceptable. Two reasons may cause this: (a) some WHICH-type questions can be asked in other manners, e.g., 'which team' can be replaced with 'who'; (b) WHICH-type questions account for about 7.2% in training data, which may not be sufficient to learn to generate this type of questions. The same reason can also affect the precision and recall of WHY-type questions.

4   Conclusion and Future Work

In this paper we conduct a preliminary study of natural language question generation with neural network models. We propose to apply neural encoder-decoder model to generate answer focused questions based on natural language sentences. The proposed approach uses a feature-rich encoder to encode answer position, POS and NER tag information. Experiments show the effectiveness of our NQG method. In future work, we would like to investigate whether the automatically generated questions can help to improve question answering systems.

References

1. Bahdanau, D., Cho, K., Bengio, Y.: Neural machine translation by jointly learning to align and translate. In: Proceedings of 3rd International Conference for Learning Representations, San Diego (2015)
2. Chali, Y., Hasan, S.A.: Towards topic-to-question generation. Comput. Linguist. **41**(1), 1–20 (2015)
3. Chen, D., Manning, C.: A fast and accurate dependency parser using neural networks. In: Proceedings of the 2014 Conference on Empirical Methods in Natural Language Processing (EMNLP), Doha, Qatar, pp. 740–750. Association for Computational Linguistics, October 2014
4. Cho, K., van Merrienboer, B., Gulcehre, C., Bahdanau, D., Bougares, F., Schwenk, H., Bengio, Y.: Learning phrase representations using RNN encoder-decoder for statistical machine translation. In: Proceedings of the 2014 Conference on Empirical Methods in Natural Language Processing (EMNLP), Doha, Qatar, pp. 1724–1734. Association for Computational Linguistics, October 2014

5. Fleiss, J.L.: Measuring nominal scale agreement among many raters. Psychol. Bull. **76**(5), 378 (1971)
6. Glorot, X., Bengio, Y.: Understanding the difficulty of training deep feedforward neural networks. In: AISTATS, vol. 9, pp. 249–256 (2010)
7. Goodfellow, I.J., Warde-Farley, D., Mirza, M., Courville, A.C., Bengio, Y.: Maxout networks. In: ICML, vol. 3, no. 28, pp. 1319–1327 (2013)
8. Gulcehre, C., Ahn, S., Nallapati, R., Zhou, B., Bengio, Y.: Pointing the unknown words. In: Proceedings of the 54th Annual Meeting of the Association for Computational Linguistics, Berlin, Germany, Long Papers, vol. 1, pp. 140–149. Association for Computational Linguistics, August 2016
9. Heilman, M.: Automatic factual question generation from text. Ph.D. thesis, Carnegie Mellon University (2011)
10. Kingma, D., Ba, J.: Adam: a method for stochastic optimization. In: Proceedings of 3rd International Conference for Learning Representations, San Diego (2015)
11. Luong, T., Pham, H., Manning, C.D.: Effective approaches to attention-based neural machine translation. In: Proceedings of the 2015 Conference on Empirical Methods in Natural Language Processing, Lisbon, Portugal, pp. 1412–1421. Association for Computational Linguistics, September 2015
12. Manning, C.D., Schütze, H., et al.: Foundations of Statistical Natural Language Processing, vol. 999. MIT Press, Cambridge (1999)
13. Manning, C.D., Surdeanu, M., Bauer, J., Finkel, J., Bethard, S.J., McClosky, D.: The stanford CoreNLP natural language processing toolkit. In: Association for Computational Linguistics (ACL) System Demonstrations, pp. 55–60 (2014)
14. Nallapati, R., Zhou, B., glar Gulçehre, Ç., Xiang, B.: Abstractive text summarization using sequence-to-sequence RNNs and beyond. In: Proceedings of the 20th SIGNLL Conference on Computational Natural Language Learning (2016)
15. Papineni, K., Roukos, S., Ward, T., Zhu, W.J.: BLEU: a method for automatic evaluation of machine translation. In: Proceedings of the 40th Annual Meeting on Association for Computational Linguistics, pp. 311–318. Association for Computational Linguistics (2002)
16. Pascanu, R., Mikolov, T., Bengio, Y.: On the difficulty of training recurrent neural networks. In: ICML, vol. 3, no. 28, pp. 1310–1318 (2013)
17. Pennington, J., Socher, R., Manning, C.D.: Glove: global vectors for word representation. In: Empirical Methods in Natural Language Processing (EMNLP), pp. 1532–1543 (2014)
18. Rajpurkar, P., Zhang, J., Lopyrev, K., Liang, P.: SQuAD: 100,000+ questions for machine comprehension of text. arXiv preprint arXiv:1606.05250 (2016)
19. Serban, I.V., García-Durán, A., Gulcehre, C., Ahn, S., Chandar, S., Courville, A., Bengio, Y.: Generating factoid questions with recurrent neural networks: the 30M factoid question-answer corpus. In: Proceedings of ACL 2016, Berlin, Germany, pp. 588–598. Association for Computational Linguistics, August 2016
20. Srivastava, N., Hinton, G.E., Krizhevsky, A., Sutskever, I., Salakhutdinov, R.: Dropout: a simple way to prevent neural networks from overfitting. J. Mach. Learn. Res. **15**(1), 1929–1958 (2014)
21. Wang, S., Jiang, J.: Machine comprehension using match-LSTM and answer pointer. arXiv preprint arXiv:1608.07905 (2016)

Answer Selection in Community Question Answering by Normalizing Support Answers

Zhihui Zheng[1], Daohe Lu[2], Qingcai Chen[1($\boxtimes$)], Haijun Yang[2], Yang Xiang[1], Youcheng Pan[1], and Wei Zhong[2]

[1] Intelligent Computation Research Center, Harbin Institute of Technology Shenzhen Graduate School, Shenzhen, China
zhihui.zchina@gmail.com, qingcai.chen@gmail.com,
xiangyang.hitsz@gmail.com, youch.pan@gmail.com
[2] WeBank Co., Ltd., Qianhai, China
{leslielu,navyyang,wesleyzhong}@webank.com

Abstract. Answer selection in community question answering (cQA) is a common task in natural language processing. Recent progress focuses on not only pure question-answer (QA) match but also support answers [4]. In this paper, we argue that the performance can drop dramatically if noisy support answers are selected. To tackle the above issue, we propose a novel way to leverage the contributions of support answers: the match scores which are firstly normalized by the correlations between the question and the corresponding similar questions, such that the negative effect from the noisy answers can be reduced. The model applies word-to-word attention to improve QA match and employs cosine similarity as the normalization factor for support answers. Compared with previous work, experiments on the Yahoo! Answers L4 dataset show that our model achieves superior P@1 and MRR results.

Keywords: Answer selection · Support answer · Normalization Attention

1 Introduction

Answer selection in community question answering (cQA) provides abundant high-quality human-to-human question answer (QA) pairs, and is greatly valuable for information retrieval systems. The task can be defined as follows: Given a question and a pool of candidate answers, select the best answer. In this paper, we focus on the non-factoid questions, each of which is expected to be answered with a sequence of descriptive text.

Recently, many deep learning methods are applied to this task. Most of them [1–3] merely use similarities between questions and candidate answers to measure the match degree of the pairs. However, semantic gap still exists due to the insufficient understanding towards the semantic match of the cQA thread itself. [4] introduced support answers (the best answers of similar questions) to help

© Springer International Publishing AG 2018
X. Huang et al. (Eds.): NLPCC 2017, LNAI 10619, pp. 672–682, 2018.
https://doi.org/10.1007/978-3-319-73618-1_57

bridge the gap. The main idea is that similar questions have similar answers which can somehow improve the information capacity carried by the QA pairs. However, retrieval system may offer noisy similar questions, which bring negative contributions to the original understanding. A typical example is shown below.

Question: How do male penguins survive without eating for four months?
Best answer: Male penguins don't eat for 60 days. The female comes back after 2 months, and the male goes to feed again...

Similar question: How do you lose a lot of weight in 3 months (20 pounds) without taking pills and eating right?
Best answer for similar question: You need to get your body into a calorie deficit situation when you are burning more calories...

Here, the topic of the given question is about *How penguins survive*, but the retrieved similar question is about *How a person loses weight*. Exactly the questions are not similar at all. To address this issue, we reweight the contributions of each support answer through normalizing the match scores by the correlations between the original question and the corresponding similar questions.

In our model, we firstly compute a basic match score between the question and the candidate answer. Then for each support question-answer pair, we compute the similarity (denoted as support score) between the candidate answer and the support answer normalized by the correlation between the question and the corresponding similar question. The match score and the support scores make up the similarity between the question and the candidate answer. To effectively model the match degree of a question and the candidate answer, we propose a novel deep neural network model with different combinations of Long Short Term Memory (LSTM), attention mechanism (ATT) and Convolutional Neural Networks (CNN). LSTM is applied to generate hidden states of the sequences (question or answer text), then we apply attention mechanism to capture how much the current answer word affects the match of the QA pair, finally we use CNN to generate representations of the sequences. We conducted experiments on 123,116 questions extracted from Yahoo! Answers L4 dataset[1], and the results show that our model performs better than the baseline methods both on P@1 and MRR values.

The contribution of this paper is mainly two folds: (1) We normalize the contributions of support answers in a novel way so that more informative related answers can be selected. (2) We achieve the start-of-the-art results on the Yahoo! Answers L4 dataset.

The rest of the paper is organized as following: Sect. 2 describes the related work for answer selection; Sect. 3 introduces our proposed model in detail; Experiments and results are discussed in Sect. 4; We draw our conclusions in Sect. 5.

2   Related Work

In the literature, methods for answer selection in cQA can be roughly divided into three groups: feature-based methods, parsing trees and deep neural networks.

---

[1] http://webscope.sandbox.yahoo.com.

Linguistic tools and external resources are widely utilized by feature-based methods to capture shallow semantic relations between questions and answers. For example, [5] used WordNet to construct semantic features. [6] employed bag-of-words features, lexical features and non-textual features, which achieved not bad results using simple classifiers. Some works transformed answer selection problem to syntactic match, where the similarity of question and answer is computed from parsing trees. [7,8] used minimal tree edit distance to match two parsing trees. Discriminate tree kernel features were automatic extracted from parsing trees in [9]. But parsing tree-based methods perform badly in low-quality sentences (i.e. spoken language in cQA).

Some recent works used deep learning methods for answer selection task. Many applied convolutional neural networks to capture semantics, in which sentences are encoded to dense vectors [10,11]. Combining convolutional and recurrent structures have been investigated in prior work other than question answering [12–14]. With deep learning methods, answer selection problem is usually approached in two ways. First, through question-answer pairwise learning, a joint feature vector is constructed and the task can be converted into a classification or ranking problem [15,16]. Second, the match similarity can be computed by question and answer representations [1,3,17,18]. [4] regarded the best answers of the similar questions as support answers, and reinforce the match degree through correlations between candidate answers and support answers. However, (Pang et al. [4]) doesn't consider the similarities between the original questions and the corresponding similar questions, our proposed model is inspired from this and explores the correlations between the candidate answers and the support answers sufficiently.

Additionally, attention-based methods have been proposed and get promising results on many NLP tasks, such as machine translation [19], machine reading comprehension [20] and textual entailment [21]. Attention mechanisms learn to focus on word-to-word correlations, in which different parts of encoded units input have different weights over decoding units. Basically, one-way attention is being widely used, but [21] developed a two-way attention mechanism, which runs through one sentence over the other and in turn. [22] developed an hierarchical attention through pairwise match matrix of a document and a query, which indicating the match degree of each word in document and query.

3   Approach

3.1   Overview

The overview of the architecture is shown in Fig. 1. The similarities of a question and the candidate answer includes: the match score of the question and the candidate answer, and the multiple support scores from the support answers which are normalized by similar questions. First, the similarity between the question and the candidate answer is generated as a basic match score. For each support QA pair, the similarity between the candidate answer and the support

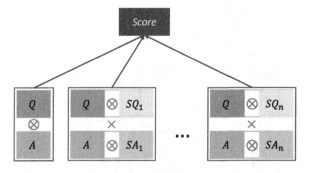

Fig. 1. The overview of the architecture. SQ_i means the i-th similar question, while SA_i means the corresponding best answer.

answer is calculated and then normalized by similarity between the original question and the corresponding similar question.

In more detail, a match model to calculate the similarity between a question and an answer is shown in Fig. 2. The question embeddings and the answer embeddings are input to the LSTM layer, respectively. Then an attention mechanism is followed to capture the contribution of each answer word over the question. CNN layers are followed to generate the representations of the question and the answer, respectively. Finally, the model calculates the cosine value of the question and the answer.

3.2 LSTM

LSTM is proposed to tackle the gradient vanishing problem, which can learn long distance dependable language structure information [23]. In our approach, we adopted a slightly modified implementation of LSTM in [24]. In the LSTM architecture, there are three gates (input i, forget f and output o) and a cell memory activation vector c. The vector formulas for recurrent hidden layer function in this version of LSTM network are implemented as following:

$$i_t = \sigma(W_{xi}x_t + W_{hi}h_{t-1} + b_i), \tag{1}$$

$$f_t = \sigma(W_{xf}x_t + W_{hf}h_{t-1} + b_f), \tag{2}$$

$$c_t = f_t c_{t-1} + i_t \tau(W_{xc}x_t + W_{hc}h_{t-1} + b_c), \tag{3}$$

$$o_t = \sigma(W_{xo}x_t + W_{ho}h_{t-1} + b_o), \tag{4}$$

$$h_t = o_t \theta(c_t), \tag{5}$$

where τ and θ are usually set as the tanh function. W_s and b_s are weights and biases for each gate. The gate functions can decide what should be passed or retained, thus control whether certain information can be propagated or overwritten across the recurrent network. In our model, LSTM is applied over each question and answer sequences to generate hidden output.

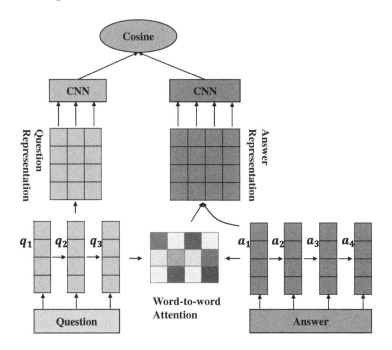

Fig. 2. LSTM-ATT-CNN match model

3.3   Attention

Attention mechanism was first introduced to natural language processing by [19]. By applying attention in an encoder-decoder framework, the model can figure out the contributions of the encoded units to the generation of current unit using an automatic alignment.

In our model, we adopt the attention mechanism proposed in [22]. Assume a question and a candidate answer sequence embeddings, denoted as $h_q \in \mathbb{R}^{|\mathcal{Q}|*d}$ and $h_a \in \mathbb{R}^{|\mathcal{A}|*d}$, where d is the dimension of LSTMs, the pair-wise match matrix between question and answer is computed by their dot product.

$$M(i,j) = h_q(i) \cdot h_a(j), \tag{6}$$

After getting the pair-wise match matrix M, we apply a row-wise softmax function to get probability distributions in each row, where each row is an individual answer-level attention to a single question word. We denote $q(t) \in \mathbb{R}^{|\mathcal{Q}|}$ as the answer-level attention regarding question word at time t, which can be seen as a question-to-answer attention.

$$q(t) = softmax(M(t,1), ..., M(t,|\mathcal{A}|)), \tag{7}$$

Then we average all the $q(t)$ to get an averaged question-level attention q.

$$q = \frac{1}{|\mathcal{Q}|} \sum_{t=1}^{|\mathcal{Q}|} q(t), \tag{8}$$

Then we apply a column-wise softmax function to the match matrix M to get question-level attentions. We denote $a(t) \in \mathbb{R}^{|\mathcal{A}|}$ as the question-level attention regarding answer word at time t, which can be seen as a answer-to-question attention.

$$a(t) = softmax(M(1, t), ..., M(|\mathcal{Q}|, t)), \tag{9}$$

$$a = [a(1), a(2), ..., a(|\mathcal{A}|)], \tag{10}$$

Finally, we calculate dot product of a and q to get the "attended answer-level attention" $s \in \mathbb{R}^{|\mathcal{A}|}$.

$$s = a \odot q, \tag{11}$$

With the attended answer-level attention, we construct a new answer embeddings by

$$\hat{h_a} = h_a \odot s, \tag{12}$$

to get attended answer embeddings, which in our model is then input to CNN layer.

3.4 CNN

Different from [4], we use the CNN architecture proposed in [11], since we found it performed better than CSM [10]. The input of CNN is the distributed representation of a sentence, which is produced through mapping each word index into the pre-trained word embeddings. Let $z_i \in \mathbb{R}^k$ be the k-dimensional word vector corresponding to the i-th word in the sentence. A sentence of length n (padded to the length n) is represented as

$$z_{1:n} = z_1 \oplus z_2 \oplus ... \oplus z_n, \tag{13}$$

where $\oplus$ is the concatenation operator and $z_{1:n}$ refers to the concatenation of the words $z_i, z_{i+1}, ..., z_{i+j}$. A convolution operation involves a filter $w \in \mathbb{R}^{hk}$, which is applied to a window of h words to produce a new feature. For example, a feature c_i is generated from a window of words z_{i+h-1} by

$$c_i = f(w \cdot z_{i:i+h-1} + b), \tag{14}$$

where $b \in \mathbb{R}$ is a bias term and f is a non-linear function such as the hyperbolic *tanh*. This filter is applied to each possible window of words in the sentence $z_{1:h}, z_{2:h+1}, ..., z_{n-h+1:n}$ to produce a feature map

$$c = [c_1, c_2, ..., c_{n-h+1}], \tag{15}$$

with $c \in \mathbb{R}^{n-h+1}$. Max-pooling operation is applied over the feature map and the maximum value $\hat{c} = max\{c\}$ is taken as the feature corresponding to this particular filter. In the experiments, we adopted four convolution filters with lengths 3, 4 and 5, each of which is followed by a max pooling to select the most effective feature. The flattened output vectors for each filter are concatenated as the output of the CNN layer.

3.5   Support Answers

[4] used support answers to reinforce the match degree between a question and its candidate answers. However, some support answers may be noisy, just like the example shown below.

Question: How can I make my living room look bigger?
Best answer: You can make your living room look bigger by using light colours. Light colors reflect light, while dark colors...

Similar question 1: How can i get my room look bigger?
Best answer for similar question 1: Use light colours when you decorate and put some mirrors in.

Similar question 2: How can I make my eyes look bigger?
Best answer for similar question 2: I'm part korean and sometimes i like to make my eyes look a little bigger. Here's what i do...

The similar question 1 is about *room*, which is the same as the original question, while the similar question 2 is about *eye*, which is totally different. The method in [4] will introduces noises to the model. To address the problem, we first normalize the support answers by the correlations between the question and its similar questions in our model. Following [4], we use BM25 [25] to obtain the similar questions for the original questions. With the similar questions and their best answers, we can obtain two kinds of similarities, one from the question and candidate answer directly, the other from the candidate answer and the normalized support answer. The similarity we adopted is cosine, and the match score is produced by combining the two kinds of similarities, which is described as follows.

$$S(Q, A) = \lambda_1 v_Q \otimes v_A + \sum_{i=1}^{m} \lambda_{2i} v_Q \otimes v_{SQ}^i \times v_A \otimes v_{SA}^i, \qquad (16)$$

where λ_1 and λ_{2i} are combining parameters, which are tuned by hand on validation set.

Similar to [3,15,17], we define the training objective as a hinge loss.

$$L = max\{0, M - sim(q, a^+) + sim(q, a^-)\}, \qquad (17)$$

where a^+ is the best answer for question, a^- is randomly a non-best answer chosen from the same question, and M is a margin.

4   Experiments

We conducted experiments on the Yahoo! Answers L4 dataset to evaluate our model. The data set contains 142,627 questions and their candidate answers. After filtering out the questions which only contain one candidate answer, it remains 123,116 questions, which are split into train, validation, and test set, which contains 98,492, 12,312, and 12,312 questions, respectively. The statistics of the dataset are listed in Table 1. The average length of questions in tokens is approximately 6, while the average length of answer is approximately 12. Averagely, each question has roughly 55 candidate answers.

Table 1. Statistics of Yahoo! Answers L4 dataset.

	Train	Dev	Test
No. of questions	98,492	12,312	12,312
No. of answers	640,422	79,686	79,878
Avg. candidate answers	6.5	6.5	6.5
Avg. length of questions	12.5	12.5	12.5
Avg. length of answers	55.6	55.5	54.8

The evaluation metrics include P@1 and MRR, which are measured in the following forms.

$$P@1 = \frac{1}{|\mathbb{Q}|} \sum_{Q \in \mathbb{Q}} \mathbb{I}(r_Q = 1), \tag{18}$$

$$MRR = \frac{1}{|\mathbb{Q}|} \sum_{Q \in \mathbb{Q}} \frac{1}{r_Q}, \tag{19}$$

where r_Q denotes the rank of the best answer.

4.1   Setup

The proposed models are implemented with Tensorflow [26]. And we use the 300-dimensional word embeddings that were trained and provided by Glove [27]. We set the word embeddings static during the training. Adam [28] is the optimization strategy and the learning rate is set to be 1e-2. We trained our model in mini-batches (with batch size as 64). The dimension of LSTM output vectors is 300. For CNN, we used four convolutional filters with lengths 3, 4 and 5, with the number of filters is 200. Finally, λ_1 and λ_{2i} are all set to be 1.0, and we set $M = 1.0$ for the hinge loss function.

4.2   Results and Discussions

In this section, we provide detailed analysis on the experimental results. Figure 3 shows that as m (when $m > 1$) increases, CNN-SQA outperforms CNN-SA more and more obviously both in P@1 and MRR. We don't consider the cases of $m > 5$, since it introduces too many noises for the match of the QA system.

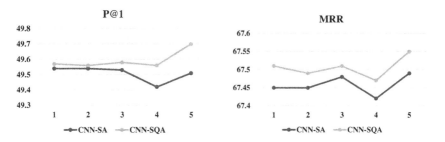

Fig. 3. The P@1 and MRR of Yahoo! Answers L4 dataset using varying number (denoted as m) of similar question-answer pairs. SA means using support answers following [4], while SQA means using normalized support answers.

Table 2 summarizes the results of our own models. From row (B) and (C), we see that using LSTM gains more improvement than using SQA, which is perhaps because LSTM captures long range information effectively. Row (E) corresponds to the result with word-to-word attention, in which the P@1 score improves about 1.7% compared to row (C). One possible explanation is that word-to-word attention is effective to find out the contributions of a sequence to the corresponding sequence. The last row show the best result of our model, in which the P@1 score gains an improvement of 4.5% than the baselines.

Table 2. Results on Yahoo! Answers L4 dataset (P@1/MRR). SQA means using normalized support answers, ATT means using word-to-word attention after LSTM.

Model	P@1	MRR
BM25	39.4	59.9
CSM [10]	47.6	66.6
SPAN [4]	48.5	67.2
A. CNN	48.02	66.24
B. CNN-SQA ($m=3$)	49.58	67.51
C. LSTM-CNN	50.57	68.66
D. LSTM-CNN-SQA	52.56	69.80
E. LSTM-ATT-CNN	52.29	69.65
F. LSTM-ATT-CNN-SQA	**53.14**	**70.14**

5   Conclusion

In this paper, we address the following problem: how can we normalize the noisy support answers to better understand the match similarities between a question and its candidate answers. We propose a deep learning model, in which the match degree of a question and answer is described by not only their similarity, but also support answers normalized by the corresponding similar questions. We use a hybrid model which combine the strength of both recurrent and convolutional neural networks. Additionally, we apply a simple sequence over sequence attention mechanism, in order to reweight the answer embeddings. We conduct experiments on Yahoo! Answers L4 dataset and the results demonstrate that our model outperforms the baselines. Future work may be evaluating the proposed methods for different tasks, such as textual entailment and text generation.

Acknowledgments. This paper is supported by the National High Technology Development 863 Program of China (No. 2015AA015405) and the Maker Special Fund of Shenzhen (No. GRCK20160 82611002620). We thank the reviewers for their constructive suggestions on this paper.

References

1. Qiu, X., Huang, X.: Convolutional neural tensor network architecture for community-based question answering. In: IJCAI, pp. 1305–1311 (2015)
2. Lu, Z., Li, H.: A deep architecture for match short texts. In: Advances in Neural Information Processing Systems, pp. 1367–1375 (2013)
3. Tan, M., dos Santos, C., Xiang, B., Zhou, B.: Improved representation learning for question answer match. In: Proceedings of the 54th Annual Meeting of the Association for Computational Linguistics (2016)
4. Pang, L., Lan, Y., Guo, J., Xu, J., Cheng, X.: SPAN: understanding a question with its support answers. In: AAAI, pp. 4250–4251 (2016)
5. Yih, W.T., Chang, M.W., Meek, C., Pastusiak, A.: Question Answering Using Enhanced Lexical Semantic Models (2013)
6. Hou, Y., Tan, C., Wang, X., Zhang, Y., Xu, J., Chen, Q.: HITSZICRC: exploiting classification approach for answer selection in community question answering. In: Proceedings of the 9th International Workshop on Semantic Evaluation, SemEval, vol. 15, pp. 196–202 (2015)
7. Wang, M., Manning, C.D.: Probabilistic tree-edit models with structured latent variables for textual entailment and question answering. In: Proceedings of the 23rd International Conference on Computational Linguistics, pp. 1164–1172. Association for Computational Linguistics (2010)
8. Yao, X., Van Durme, B., Callison-Burch, C., Clark, P.: Answer extraction as sequence tagging with tree edit distance. In: HLT-NAACL, pp. 858–867. Citeseer (2013)
9. Severyn, A., Moschitti, A.: Automatic feature engineering for answer selection and extraction. In: EMNLP, vol. 13, pp. 458–467 (2013)
10. Kalchbrenner, N., Grefenstette, E., Blunsom, P.: A convolutional neural network for modelling sentences. In: Proceedings of the 52nd Annual Meeting of the Association for Computational Linguistics (2014)

11. Kim, Y.: Convolutional neural networks for sentence classification. In: Proceedings of the 2014 Conference on Empirical Methods in Natural Language Processing (EMNLP), pp. 1746–1751. Association for Computational Linguistics (2014)
12. Donahue, J., Anne Hendricks, L., Guadarrama, S., Rohrbach, M., Venugopalan, S., Saenko, K., Darrell, T.: Long-term recurrent convolutional networks for visual recognition and description. In: Proceedings of the IEEE Conference on Computer Vision and Pattern Recognition, pp. 2625–2634 (2015)
13. Sainath, T.N., Vinyals, O., Senior, A., Sak, H.: Convolutional, long short-term memory, fully connected deep neural networks. In: 2015 IEEE International Conference on Acoustics, Speech and Signal Processing (ICASSP), pp. 4580–4584. IEEE (2015)
14. Xiang, Y., Zhou, X., Chen, Q., Zheng, Z., Wang, X., Qin, Y.: Incorporating label dependency for answer quality tagging in community question answering via CNN-LSTM-CRF. In: COLING (2016)
15. Hu, B., Lu, Z., Li, H., Chen, Q.: Convolutional neural network architectures for match natural language sentences. In: Advances in Neural Information Processing Systems, pp. 2042–2050 (2014)
16. Wang, D., Nyberg, E.: A long short-term memory model for answer sentence selection in question answering. In: Meeting of the Association for Computational Linguistics and the International Joint Conference on Natural Language Processing, pp. 707–712 (2015)
17. Feng, M., Xiang, B., Glass, M.R., Wang, L., Zhou, B.: Applying deep learning to answer selection: a study and an open task. In: 2015 IEEE Workshop on Automatic Speech Recognition and Understanding (ASRU), pp. 813–820. IEEE (2015)
18. Yu, L., Hermann, K.M., Blunsom, P., Pulman, S.: Deep learning for answer sentence selection. arXiv preprint arXiv:1412.1632 (2014)
19. Bahdanau, D., Cho, K., Bengio, Y.: Neural machine translation by jointly learning to align and translate. arXiv preprint arXiv:1409.0473 (2014)
20. Hermann, K.M., Kocisky, T., Grefenstette, E., Espeholt, L., Kay, W., Suleyman, M., Blunsom, P.: Teaching machines to read and comprehend. In: Advances in Neural Information Processing Systems, pp. 1693–1701 (2015)
21. Rocktäschel, T., Grefenstette, E., Hermann, K.M., Kociský, T., Blunsom, P.: Reasoning about entailment with neural attention. arXiv preprint arXiv:1509.06664 (2015)
22. Cui, Y., Chen, Z., Wei, S., Wang, S., Liu, T., Hu, G.: Attention-over-attention neural networks for reading comprehension. arXiv preprint arXiv:1607.04423 (2016)
23. Hochreiter, S., Schmidhuber, J.: Long short-term memory. Neural Comput. 9(8), 1735–1780 (1997)
24. Graves, A., Jaitly, N., Mohamed, A.R.: Hybrid speech recognition with deep bidirectional LSTM. In: 2013 IEEE Workshop on Automatic Speech Recognition and Understanding (ASRU), pp. 273–278. IEEE (2013)
25. Robertson, S., Zaragoza, H.: The probabilistic relevance framework: BM25 and beyond. Found. Trends Inf. Retrieval 3(4), 333–389 (2009)
26. Abadi, M., Agarwal, A., Barham, P., Brevdo, E., Chen, Z., Citro, C., Corrado, G.S., Davis, A., Dean, J., Devin, M., et al.: TensorFlow: large-scale machine learning on heterogeneous distributed systems. arXiv preprint arXiv:1603.04467 (2016)
27. Pennington, J., Socher, R., Manning, C.D.: Glove: global vectors for word representation. In: EMNLP, vol. 14, pp. 1532–1543 (2014)
28. Kingma, D., Ba, J.: Adam: a method for stochastic optimization. arXiv preprint arXiv:1412.6980 (2014)

An Empirical Study on Incorporating Prior Knowledge into BLSTM Framework in Answer Selection

Yahui Li[✉], Muyun Yang, Tiejun Zhao, Dequan Zheng, and Sheng Li

Harbin Institute of Technology, Harbin, China
yhli@mtlab.hit.edu.cn

Abstract. Deep learning has become the state-of the art solution to answer selection. One distinguishing advantage of deep learning is that it avoids manual engineering via its end-to-end structure. But in the literature, substantial practices of introducing prior knowledge into the deep learning process are still observed with positive effect. Following this thread, this paper investigates the contribution of incorporating different prior knowledge into deep learning via an empirical study. Under a typical BLSTM framework, 3 levels, totaling 27 features are jointly integrated into the answer selection task. Experiment result confirms that incorporating prior knowledge can enhances the model, and different levels of linguistic features can improve the performance consistently.

Keywords: Deep learning · BLSTM · Prior knowledge
Incorporating · Answer selection

1 Introduction

Deep learning has become an important research issue for various tasks of NLP. Its end-to-end modeling avoids the cumulative error resulted from previous pipelined model framework. Thus deep learning makes researchers free from such cumbersome tasks as feature designing, selection and annotation and so on. And large amounts of research results have shown the effectiveness of deep learning, such as machine translation (Bahdanau et al. 2014), opinion mining (Poria et al. 2016) and document classification (Yang et al. 2016).

In recent years, the progress of deep learning in NLP is focus on improving model performance. On the one hand, deep learning in NLP has constantly improved its models to better capture information. For example, the utlization of RNN (Recurrent Neural Network (Elman 1990)) or Bidirectional RNN can capture the context information of a sequence. Furthermore, LSTM (Long Short-Term Memory Neural Network (Hochreiter and Schmidhuber 1997)), which is a variant of RNN, has further augmented the network's memory capacity. And the attention mechanism in neural machine translation (Bahdanau et al. 2014), is actually modeling the word alignment information between two sequences.

© Springer International Publishing AG 2018
X. Huang et al. (Eds.): NLPCC 2017, LNAI 10619, pp. 683–692, 2018.
https://doi.org/10.1007/978-3-319-73618-1_58

On the other hand, we also observe some researchers have tried to incorporate existing knowledge into the deep learning models, with positive gain in performance for most cases (if not all). Considering traditional NLP works have accumulated large amounts well designed linguistic knowledge, well-known feature engineering skills, available resources, it is really natural to preserve the existing knowledge still in the deep learning process. In fact, how to incorporate these prior knowledge effectively is an issue worth exploring.

In NLP area, two approaches of deep learning are well addressed: CNN and RNN. CNN achieved good performance in sentence classification (Kim 2014) etc., while the later RNN especially LSTM has gradually attracted researchers' attention. Due to its high ability of modeling context information, LSTM has shown better results in such tasks as machine translation (Bahdanau et al. 2014) etc. And especially in the classical task of answer selection (Tan et al. 2015), BLSTM has become the de facto solution (Tan et al. 2015; Wang and Nyberg 2015).

In this paper, we focus on answer selection task, considering the knowledge obtained in previous works of this task, conduct an empirical study on incorporating word level, sentence level and QA pair level knowledge into BLSTM framework in answer selection. Based on the classical BLSTM framework, we incorporated 3 levels of knowledge, which make a difference on the performance, at last we obtain a total promotion of 26.9% in MAP.

The rest of the paper is organized as follows: Sect. 2 gives a brief review of the previous works of incorporating prior knowledge into deep learning frameworks in NLP; Sect. 3 describes the basic framework of BLSTM for answer selection; Sect. 4 gives the exploration of ways to incorporate prior knowledge into BLSTM in answer selection; The experiment results will be discussed in detail in Sect. 5; And we will draw a conclusion in the last section.

2   Related Work

Answer selection is a sub-task of QA (Question Answering), which has become a hot topic. It can be formulated as follows: Given a question q and it's corresponding answer pool $\{a_1, a_2, \ldots, a_n\}$, n is the number of candidate answers, our target is to find the best k answers, where $1 \leqslant k \leqslant n$. A question or answer is a token sequence of arbitrary length, and one question may correspond to more than one ground-truth answers.

In recent work of answer selection, the main stream is deep learning based approach, and the best performing model is most frequently observed on BLSTM. The key advantage to deep learning is its end-to-end modeling avoids the cumulative error resulted from pipeline framework, and makes researchers free from cumbersome feature engineering. Nevertheless, substantial practices of introducing prior knowledge into the deep learning process are still observed with positive effect. Here we start from the task of answer selection, trying to briefly survey on existing practices of incorporating prior knowledge into deep learning.

In the task of answer selection, researchers have tried to incorporate different prior knowledge into different deep learning models. Severyn and Moschitti (2016) use CNN for learning an optimal representation of question and answer sentences, and use a joint layer concatenated all intermediate vectors into a single vector: the relevance score calculated by the optimal sentence representations and any additional features. They include the word level features of overlapping words in two modes: (i) feature vector mode - plugged overlapping word counts replicating (Yu et al. 2014) into the final representation; and (ii) embeddings mode - augment the representation of input words with additional binary-like word overlap indicator features. The results are significantly better than no overlap information using. Adding word overlap information in mode (i) results in a considerable generalization improvement. In contrast, encoding the relational information about overlapping words in a pair directly into word embeddings shows even larger improvement on TRAIN, the promotions on MAP and MRR are 0.0945 and 0.0906 respectively.

Apart from answer selection, we also observe that in other tasks of NLP such as sentiment analysis and short text classification, researchers also have tried to incorporate domain knowledge into deep learning framework, and bring an enhance to the model.

For the task of sentiment analysis, Huang et al. (2016) used a hierarchical LSTM model to model the retweeting/replying process. They incorporate additional contexts in Tweets as information, such as social context, conversation-based context and topic-based context, and take each type of context as a binary-value feature and encode it into a 0 or 1. Then the additional context feature vector as an extension of the input vector is fed into every gate in tweet-level LSTM network. The experiment shows that the additional contexts contribute superior performance with a promotion of 0.004 on Accuracy and 0.015 on Macro-F1.

Apart from the above ideas, another paper (Wang et al. 2016) conduct short text classification base on CNN, and expand the short text with synonym as information. They use CNN to extract high level features, and incorporate related word embeddings pre-trained over large-scale external corpus to introduce semantic knowledge and expand the short text. Specifically, they compute the representations of semantic units appearing in short texts, then find their nearest word embeddings (NWEs), then these restricted NEWs form expanded matrices which act as supervision information to detect precise semantics. Finally, the projected matrix and the expanded matrices are simply combined in input layer and fed into a CNN in parallel. Experimental results showed the effectiveness of this method on two benchmarks compared with 8 popular methods. It should be noted that this approach requires the prior knowledge to be formulated via word embedding at the input layer, which is not readily available for most of cases, and, therefore, is not the focus of this paper.

3   BLSTM Based Answer Selection Framework

In this section, we describe a classical BLSTM based framework for answer selection, which use BLSTM to obtain the question and answer sentences' distributed semantic representations, and then use the relevance metric to measure the relevance score of QA pairs.

According to Yu et al. (2014), the answer selection task can be regraded as a binary classification task, for each answer a_k in answer pool if it is a ground truth, then it's label lbl_k is 1, 0 otherwise. Due to the final target is sorting, so the Softmax method is employed to get the probability of $lbl_k = 1$, and then sort by the probability. That is, after the semantic representation of QA pair is obtained, the following formula is used to calculate the probability of $lbl_k = 1$:

$$P(lbl_k = 1|q, a_k) = Softmax(q^T M a_k + b) \qquad (1)$$

q and a_k is the semantic representation of question and answer, b is the bias, and M is a converting matrix, which can also be treated as a relevance matrix to get the relevance score of the QA pair, The relevance score is converted to a probability through the Softmax layer.

The model is trained to minimise the negative log-likelihood of the training set, and in order to prevent overfitting, 2-norm is added as a penalty term, the loss function is calculated as below:

$$L = -\log \prod_n p(y_n|q_n, a_n) + \lambda \|\theta\|_F^2 \qquad (2)$$

λ is the coefficient for the penalty term, θ represents parameter set, containing M and b.

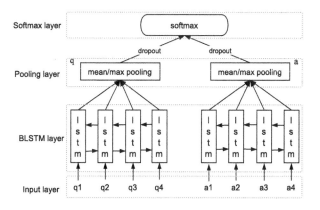

Fig. 1. BLSTM framework for answer selection

The framework of BLSTM for answer selection is illustrated in Fig. 1. In the input layer, question and answer's word embedding as input, and each sentence is modeled by a BLSTM, the BLSTM implementation is as Wang and Nyberg (2015). There are three ways to generate question or answer's semantic representation: (1) mean pooling; (2) max pooling; (3) just concatenate the last time stamp's vectors in both directions. After pooling the sentence's semantic representation is generated, and in order to prevent overfitting, we use dropout mechanism before generating the semantic representation. The final step is to calculate the relevance score by a relevance matrix, then the score is sent to Softmax layer.

4   Incorporating Prior Knowledge into BLSTM Framework in Answer Selection

In this section, we firstly introduce the different levels of prior knowledge we can utilize for answer selection. And then in experiment, we choose some specific features for each level, and illustrate how to incorporate these prior knowledge into the BLSTM framework.

4.1   Prior Knowledge in Different Levels

Word level. The input unit of deep learning model is word embedding, beyond that, we can also utilize the POS (Part of Speech) information, named entity information, etc.

Sentence level. In addition to the distributed representation of question or answer sentences generated by the BLSTM, we can also incorporate additional sentence level features. Topic model based sentence representation is a good choice. BTM (Biterm Topic Model (Yan et al. 2013)), a topic model for short texts has become a hot in recent. And in contrast to word embedding, which includes the local word co-occurance information, topic feature of a sentence can be viewed as including the global semantic information.

QA pair level. QA pair's surface string similarity is useful for measuring the QA pair's matching degree. N-gram matting related or LCS (longest common sub-sequence) etc. is commonly used to measure the matching degree. Beside these, from the view of MT (Machine Translation), we can also obtain useful features. That is, treating the question as reference, and answer as candidate, using MT evaluation metrics such as BLEU and NIST (Papineni et al. 2002; Doddington 2002), we can obtain the relevance between QA pair. In our experiment, we extract the following pair relevance features (25 in total, (Wu et al. 2016)) and divide them into four groups:

- group1: n-gram and word matching related
  - Overlap count and precision on n-gram: overlap count and precision on n-gram for QA pair;
  - Overlap count on word: total count of same words in QA pair and total count of same nouns/verbs in QA pair;
- group2: string difference related

- LCS: sum of all the same sub-sequence length in QA pair;
- Edit distance: the minimum steps to transform the answer to question under the insertion, deletion and substitution operations;
- group3: information retrieval related
  - TF-ISF sum: each intersected word in QA is weighted by TF*ISF, then sum them up (ISF is in the same calculation as IDF);
  - Cosine similarity: question or answer is represented by VSM, and each word is weighted by TF*ISF, then calculate the cosine similarity between two vectors;
- group4: MT evaluation metrics related
  - BLEU and NIST scores.

4.2   Strategies to Incorporate Prior Knowledge into BLSTM

As the prior knowledge we can utilize is of different levels, so we use different strategies to incorporate.

Firstly, for word level, POS for example, as the input of BLSTM is word embedding, a straight forward idea is to encode each kind of POS as a embedding, just like word embedding, and concatenate each word's POS embedding with its word embedding in input layer as the input of BLSTM. And by adding POS information, the polysemy in language may be relieved to some extend.

Secondly, considering the sentence level prior knowledge, that is, topic vector, an intuitive idea is to concatenate the topic vector with the distributed representation generated by BLSTM in pooling layer, and through this, the sentence's representation is augmented.

Lastly, for QA pair level, each pair relevance feature has the same meaning with semantic relevance generated by BLSTM, so we can calculate their weighted sum to get the final relevance, the formula updated as follow:

$$P(lbl_k = 1|q, a_k) = Softmax(q^T M a_k + M_s s + b) \tag{3}$$

q, a, M and b is same as above, s indicates the surface similarity feature vector, M_s is the coefficient matrix to s.

Another idea of incorporating these pair relevance features is to firstly pad the feature vector with zero to the same length with word embedding, which act as a pseudo-embedding, and after the word embeddings of question or answer are input into BLSTM entirely, the padded feature vector can be input after the last time stump. Although we don't know the physical meaning to this, but as a way to incorporate additional features to BLSTM, it is worth a try.

5   Experiment

We evaluated the different prior knowledge incorporating strategies described in this paper on a standard answer selection dataset. We briefly introduce the dataset before describing our experimental setup. Finally, we report our results.

5.1 NLPCC DBQA Dataset

We conducted our experiment on the dataset of NLPCC-ICCPOL 2016 shared task open domain Chinese question answering DBQA dataset. Which includes a training set and a testing set, they assign a set of documents to human annotators. For each document, a human annotator will (1) first, select a sentence from the document, and (2) then, write down a natural language question, whose answer should be the selected sentence (Duan 2016). The statistic of labeled QA pairs are given in Table 1.

5.2 Experimental Setup

The word embeddings (dim = 50) are pretrained using GloVe on gigaWods corpus, we use the AdaDelta algorithm for training, and all hyperparameters are optimized with the MAP score on the development data. The parameters of two BLSTMs are set share (coz its better performance), and pooling strategy is max-pooling (coz its better performance).

Table 1. Statistics of the DBQA datasets

# of labeled Q-A pairs (training set)	14,609
# of labeled Q-A pairs (testing set)	9,870
# of average candidate answers per question	21

To illustrate the empirical study on incorporating different knowledge into BLSTM framework, we extract different kinds of features belonging to different levels. POS feature embedding is in 20-dim, and is initialized using formula (4) as Glorot and Bengio (2010). As the average sentence lengths of the NLPCC DBQA corpus is 21 (for question) and 26 (for answer), which indicates that the dataset belongs to short text, so we use BTM to extract the topic feature, and the dimension of topic feature is 50, the iteration num is 500, and α, β is set default. As for the pair relevance features, we tried two incorporating strategies, and when they were incorporated into the layer before Softmax, we incorporated them group by group, so as to analysis the effectiveness of each group.

$$W \sim U(-\frac{\sqrt{6}}{\sqrt{Dim}}, \frac{\sqrt{6}}{\sqrt{Dim}}) \tag{4}$$

5.3 Results and Analysis

The evaluation metric is MAP (Voorhees et al. 1999) and MRR (Robertson et al. 2000). Table 2 summarises the results of our models. BLSTM indicates the basic BLSTM framework for answer selection; +POS indicates we try to incorporate POS information into it; +topic is the model which incorporates topic feature; then we tried two strategies to incorporate pair relevance features into the basic BLSTM model, that is, importing to the input layer (noted as +pair_{group1+2+3+4}_I) or the layer before Softmax (noted begin with +pair and end with _BS). Instead of incorporating all the pair relevance features into the layer before Softmax at the same time, we incorporate them group by group, and the group information is described as Sect. 4.1. After all the above exploration, we also try to integrate different features, trying to find the best feature combination.

Table 2. Experiment results of incorporating different prior knowledge

Model		MAP	MRR
Baseline	BLSTM	0.457	0.458
Word level	+POS	0.472	0.473
Sentence level	+topic	0.531	0.533
QA pair level	+pair_{group1}_BS	0.634	0.634
	+pair_{group1+2}_BS	0.635	0.635
	+pair_{group1+2+3}_BS	0.645	0.645
	+pair_{group1+2+3+4}_BS	0.646	0.647
	+pair_{group1+2+3+4}_I	0.436	0.464
Combination	+POS+topic	0.641	0.642
	+POS+topic+pair_{group1+2+3+4}_BS	0.726	0.727

Experiment shows that among different levels of prior knowledge, the pair relevance features incorporated into the layer before Softmax contribute most, it seems group1 (n-gram and word matching related) is of most importance, and when incorporating the remaining features (group2, group3 and group4), the performance gets more better. Considering the strategy of incorporating pair relevance features into the input layer, it performs worse than the former obviously, we guess that it may because this strategy violated the original aim of through the BLSTM to model the word co-occurrence information to generate the distributed representation of sentence. The topic feature seems a good feature to utilize. The combination of POS and topic knowledge performs a big performance improvement, and finally when we integate POS, topic, and all pair relevance features (to the layer before Softmax), the model performs best.

6   Conclusion

This paper examines the effectiveness of incorporating prior knowledge into deep learning models in answer selection. We collect word level, sentence level and QA pair level features with obvious linguistic interpretations. Experiments indicate that the incremental combination of the above knowledge consistently improves the BLSTM performance, at last we obtain a total promotion of 26.9% in MAP.

Nevertheless, this is a confined observation from answer selection task only. A comprehensive view demands further examination of this issue in other NLP tasks such as MT, dialogue system etc. In addition, the best way of incorporating prior knowledge into deep learning in NLP is a non-negligible issue, lying also in our schedule for future study.

Acknowledgement. This study was partially funded by National High-tech R&D Program of China (863 Program, No. 2015AA015405), and National Natural Science Foundation of China (Nos. 61370170 and 61402134). Besides, we would like to give many thanks to Shanshan Zhao (HIT) for helping with her BLSTM framework tool, Fangying Wu (HIT) for offering suggestions in extracting those QA-pair level features.

References

Bahdanau, D., Cho, K., Bengio, Y.: Neural machine translation by jointly learning to align and translate. arXiv preprint arXiv:1409.0473 (2014)

Doddington, G.: Automatic evaluation of machine translation quality using n-gram co-occurrence statistics. In: Proceedings of the Second International Conference on Human Language Technology Research, pp. 138–145. Morgan Kaufmann Publishers Inc. (2002)

Elman, J.L.: Finding structure in time. Cogn. Sci. **14**(2), 179–211 (1990)

Glorot, X., Bengio, Y.: Understanding the difficulty of training deep feedforward neural networks. In: Proceedings of the Thirteenth International Conference on Artificial Intelligence and Statistics, pp. 249–256 (2010)

Hochreiter, S., Schmidhuber, J.: Long short-term memory. Neural Comput. **9**(8), 1735–1780 (1997)

Huang, M., Cao, Y., Dong, C.: Modeling rich contexts for sentiment classification with LSTM. arXiv preprint arXiv:1605.01478 (2016)

Kim, Y.: Convolutional neural networks for sentence classification. arXiv preprint arXiv:1408.5882 (2014)

Duan, N.: Overview of the NLPCC-ICCPOL 2016 shared task: open domain Chinese question answering. In: Lin, C.-Y., Xue, N., Zhao, D., Huang, X., Feng, Y. (eds.) ICCPOL/NLPCC -2016. LNCS (LNAI), vol. 10102, pp. 942–948. Springer, Cham (2016). https://doi.org/10.1007/978-3-319-50496-4_89

Papineni, K., Roukos, S., Ward, T., Zhu, W.-J.: BLEU: a method for automatic evaluation of machine translation. In: Proceedings of the 40th Annual Meeting on Association for Computational Linguistics, pp. 311–318. Association for Computational Linguistics (2002)

Poria, S., Cambria, E., Gelbukh, A.: Aspect extraction for opinion mining with a deep convolutional neural network. Knowl.-Based Syst. **108**, 42–49 (2016)

Robertson, S.E., Walker, S., Beaulieu, M.: Proceedings of the 8th Text Retrieval Conference (TREC-8), pp. 77–82 (2000)

Severyn, A., Moschitti, A.: Modeling relational information in question-answer pairs with convolutional neural networks. arXiv preprint arXiv:1604.01178 (2016)

Tan, M., dos Santos, C., Xiang, B., Zhou, B.: LSTM-based deep learning models for non-factoid answer selection. arXiv preprint arXiv:1511.04108 (2015)

Voorhees, E.M., et al.: The TREC-8 question answering track report. In: TREC 1999, pp. 77–82 (1999)

Wang, D., Nyberg, E.: A long short-term memory model for answer sentence selection in question answering. In: ACL, vol. 2, pp. 707–712 (2015)

Wang, P., Xu, B., Xu, J., Tian, G., Liu, C.-L., Hao, H.: Semantic expansion using word embedding clustering and convolutional neural network for improving short text classification. Neurocomputing **174**, 806–814 (2016)

Wu, F., Yang, M., Zhao, T., Han, Z., Zheng, D., Zhao, S.: A hybrid approach to DBQA. In: Lin, C.-Y., Xue, N., Zhao, D., Huang, X., Feng, Y. (eds.) ICCPOL/NLPCC - 2016. LNCS (LNAI), vol. 10102, pp. 926–933. Springer, Cham (2016). https://doi.org/10.1007/978-3-319-50496-4_87

Yan, X., Guo, J., Lan, Y., Cheng, X.: A biterm topic model for short texts. In: Proceedings of the 22nd International Conference on World Wide Web, pp. 1445–1456. ACM (2013)

Yang, Z., Yang, D., Dyer, C., He, X., Smola, A., Hovy, E.: Hierarchical attention networks for document classification. In: Proceedings of NAACL-HLT, pp. 1480–1489 (2016)

Yu, L., Hermann, K.M., Blunsom, P., Pulman, S.: Deep learning for answer sentence selection. arXiv preprint arXiv:1412.1632 (2014)

Enhanced Embedding Based Attentive Pooling Network for Answer Selection

Zhan Su[1], Benyou Wang[1,3], Jiabin Niu[1], Shuchang Tao[1],
Peng Zhang[1(✉)], and Dawei Song[1,2]

[1] Tianjin Key Laboratory of Cognitive Computing and Application,
School of Computer Science and Technology, Tianjin University,
Tianjin, People's Republic of China
shuishen112@gmail.com, wabywang@tencent.com,
{niujiabin,taoshuchang,pzhang}@tju.edu.cn, dawei.song2010@gmail.com
[2] Department of Computing and Communications,
The Open University, Milton Keynes, UK
[3] Tencent, Shenzhen, China

Abstract. Document-based Question Answering tries to rank the candidate answers for given questions, which needs to evaluate matching score between the question sentence and answer sentence. Existing works usually utilize convolution neural network (CNN) to adaptively learn the latent matching pattern between the question/answer pair. However, CNN can only perceive the order of a word in a local windows, while the global order of the windows is ignored due to the window-sliding operation. In this report, we design an enhanced CNN (https://github.com/shuishen112/pairwise-deep-qa) with extended order information (e.g. overlapping position and global order) into inputting embedding, such rich representation makes it possible to learn an order-aware matching in CNN. Combining with standard convolutional paradigm like attentive pooling, pair-wise training and dynamic negative sample, this end-to-end CNN achieve a good performance on the DBQA task of NLPCC 2017 without any other extra features.

1 Introduction

Recently, deep learning approaches have been successfully applied to a variety of Natural Language Processing (NLP) tasks, such as Sentiment Analysis [1], Automatic Conversation [2] and Paraphrase Identification [3]. Compared with traditional approaches [4,5], which require manual features and rely on domain experience, deep learning approaches have ability to automatically learn optimal feature representation. For Question Answering, deep learning approaches have also achieved good performance [6–8] in both English and Chinese datasets.

In this paper, our focus is Document-based Question Answering (DBQA), also known as Answer Selection (AS), which is a typical subtask of Question Answering. Given a question, DBQA task is to find accurate answers from a pool of pre-selected answer candidates [9] and the selection process is based on

© Springer International Publishing AG 2018
X. Huang et al. (Eds.): NLPCC 2017, LNAI 10619, pp. 693–700, 2018.
https://doi.org/10.1007/978-3-319-73618-1_59

the similarity matching between question and answers. Due to the sentences of DBQA are short texts, we utilize Convolutional Neural Network (CNN) architecture to model the sentences.

Although CNN has a strong ability to extract robust features, CNN is still unable to find out all the useful information, such as overlap which has been proved efficient for our QA task [7]. In addition, different words contribute different weights to the sentence. Despite of the meaning of words, the position of tokens in the sentence is also important. In our previous work, we have given a detailed explanation about the importance of the position information [10]. In order to tackle the above problems, we enchance the CNN by encoding position information and word overlap into word representation by additional dimensions [11]. For a typical text matching task, the representation not only contain the information of the text itself, but also the interdependence between the question/answer. The comparative effective method to model the relation of question/answer is attention mechanism at present [3,12]. In this paper, we also investigate this mechanism to our architecture.

In addition to the sentence representation, the ranking approach is also a key. The common used ranking approaches are pointwise and pairwise strategies. Compared with the pointwise approach, the pairwise approach take advantage of more information about the ground truth [7]. For the sampling strategy in pairwise, Dynamic Negative Sampling (DNS) will largely improve the effect of the models.

Thus, the main characteristics of our model are as follow: First, we take position information and word overlap into consideration to obtain rich representation. Second, we utilize attention mechanism to exploit the interdependence between question/answer. Third, we employ pairwise ranking approach and DNS to improve the performance of our model.

2   Model Architecture

2.1   Convolution Neural Network

In this work, we apply two kinds of CNN architectures into QA task. One is a simple QA-CNN, and the other is the attentive pooling network which has attract great attention in QA task. Both architectures can not capture the position information when the convolution filter slide through the sentence matrices. Convolutions and pooling operations will lose information about the local order of words. To tackle this deficiency, we extend word embedding with additional dimensions, such as overlap and position information. The approach can make the model more suitable for the Chinese DBQA task.

As is shown in the Fig. 1. Given a QA pair(q, a), we truncate or pad the text sentence to a fixed length so that the sentence matrices have the same dimension as shown in the Fig. 1. The first layer of our model contains two sequences of word embeddings, $q^{emb} = r^{w_1}, ..., r^{w_M}$ and $a^{emb} = r^{w_1}, ..., r^{w_L}$, where the length of question is M and the length of answer is L. Then we equip our model with an overlap embedding and a sense of order by embedding

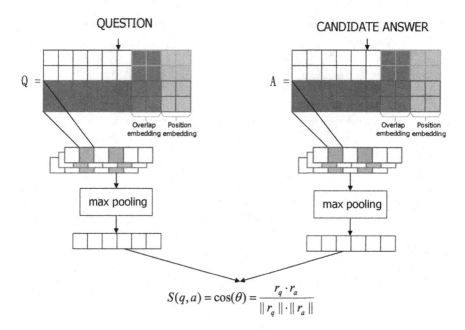

Fig. 1. Basic architecture of CNN

the position of input tokens. Then we obtain the input element representations $e = (w_1 + o_1 + p_1, ..., w_m + o_m + p_m)$ where the o is the overlap embedding and the p is the position embedding.

In the second layer, we typically use convolution filters, whose width is the same as the width of the input matrix, to slide over the sentence matrix. The height may vary, but sliding windows over 2–5 words at a time is typical. Then we apply a max-pooling to the output of convolution filters, which convert the matrix to vector representations r^q, r^a. In the last layer we compute the cosine similarity between these two representations.

2.2 Attentive Pooling Neural Network

The simple QA-CNN learn representation of input individually. Instead of using max pooling, we use the attentive pooling networks so that the representation of the question and answer can be learned by the QA pairs. As shown in Fig. 2, the output of convolution are matrices $Q \in R^{c \times M}$ and $A \in R^{c \times L}$. The matrix $G \in R^{M \times L}$ can be computed as follows:

$$G = tanh(Q^T U A) \tag{1}$$

$U \in R^{c \times c}$ are parameters and can be learned by our model. G is soft alignment between the k-size context windows of Q and A, We can obtain important-score vectors $g^q \in R^M$ and $g^a \in R^L$ after applying column-wise and row-wise

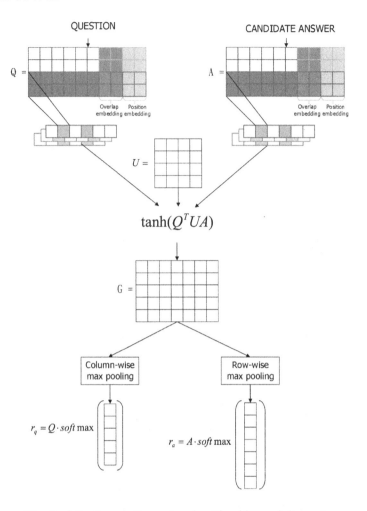

Fig. 2. Attentive pooling network with additional dimension

max-pooling over G. Then the attention vectors δ^q and δ^a can be computed by applying softmax function over importan-score vectors. The final representation of q and a are as follows:

$$r^q = Q\delta^q \tag{2}$$

$$r^a = A\delta^a \tag{3}$$

We will compute the cosine similarity between the r^q and r^a like in the simple QA-CNN.

2.3   Triplet Ranking Loss Function

Instead of treating the task as a pointwise classification problem, our input pairs are triplet items *(question,positive answer,negative answer)*. Given a question

q,we can sample positive pairs (q, a^+) and negative pairs (q, a^-) where a^+, a^- donate the positive and negative answer, respectively. Our goal is to learn a representation function $f(.)$ which can make the score of positive pairs is larger than the negative pairs.

$$f(q, a^+) > f(q, a^-), \forall q, a^+, a^- \qquad (4)$$

we use triplet ranking hing loss

$$L = max(0, m - f(q, a^+) + f(q, a^-)) + \lambda \parallel W \parallel^2 \qquad (5)$$

where λ is a regularization parameter, and W is the parameters of CNN model.

2.4 Sampling Strategy

In our DBQA task,we use two sampling strategies which has proven to be effective in QA task [13].

Random Sampling: Given a question, we randomly select one negative answer for each positive answer.

Dynamic Negative Sampling: In general, what confuse our model are some of the confusing negative cases rather than those obvious wrong answers. Thus, instead of using random strategy, we can use the most competitive negative answer. In each epoch, we compute the similarity between the question and negative answers. We pick the highest score negative answer as the most competitive sample.

3 Experimental Evaluation

3.1 Dataset

The DBQA task in nlpcc 2017 provides three datasets. The number of QA pairs in training data is 181882, the number in test1 and test2 data is 122531 and 47372, respectively. The unique questions in training, test1, test2 datasets is 8772, 5997, 2550. We utilize the pynlpir tool to segment the sentences. The max length of question tokens is 40, while the max length of answer tokens is 1076. The length is shown in the Fig. 3. Since the length of most of the answers is less than 75, we truncate the answer length to 75.

3.2 Embedding

The embedding in this task is very important. We train our own 300 dimension embedding by word2vec tool [14]. The raw corpus is Chinese Wikipedia. After putting all the tokens in the dataset into a dictionary, we can find 50% tokens in our pretrained embedding. There are a large number of places, names, numbers which we can't obtained by the raw corpus. So We assign a random vector between -0.5 and 0.5 for these tokens which means we will lose some important information.

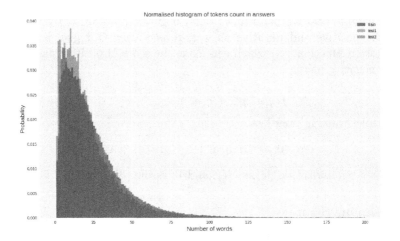

Fig. 3. The length of answer tokens in datasets

3.3 Result

We implement our model using the open source tools tensorflow[1] and train the model in 50 epochs. The performance of our model is shown in Table 1:

Table 1. Result

Method	Pooling	Loss	MAP(test1)	MAP(test2)
CNN-base	Max	Pointwise	0.408	0.371
CNN-base	Max	Pairwise	0.782	0.657
CNN-base	Max	Pairwise	0.784	0.661
CNN-base	Attentive	Pairwise	0.772	0.646
+overlap	Max	Pointwise	0.820	0.553
+overlap	Max	Pairwise	0.828	0.674
+overlap	Attentive	Pairwise	0.811	0.672
+positon, overlap	Max	Pointwise	0.815	0.554
+positon, overlap	Attentive	Pairwise	0.819	**0.675**
+positon, overlap	Max	Pairwise	**0.834**	**0.679**

CNN-base means that we do not use any additional feature embedding. Compared with pointwise *CNN-base*, we can see that pairwise *CNN-base* has a better result. The dynamic negative sampling and random sampling both contribute to our model. We regard the *CNN-base* model as a baseline. The *+overlap* is our enhanced model with extended overlap embedding, The *+position* is our model

---

[1] https://www.tensorflow.org/.

with extended position information. The result indicate that the enhanced model is much better than the *CNN-base* model especially for test1. All the work we did depends on test1 which result in ranking 5th among the 21 submissions.

Table 2. Sensitivity analysis

Loss	Em-dim	Extend-dim	Region-size	MAP(test1)	MAP(test2)
Pointwise	50	2	1, 2, 3, 5	0.801	0.513
Pointwise	50	5	1, 2, 3, 5	0.814	0.540
Pointwise	50	1	1, 2, 3, 5	0.827	0.563
Pointwise	300	10	1, 2, 3, 5	0.820	0.553
Pointwise	50	20	1, 2, 3, 5	0.824	0.530
Pairwise	50	2	1, 2, 3, 5	0.795	0.639
Pairwise	50	5	1, 2, 3, 5	0.795	0.620
Pairwise	50	10	1, 2, 3, 5	0.807	0.629
Pairwise	50	20	1, 2, 3, 5	0.800	0.624
Pairwise	300	2	1, 2, 3, 5	0.822	0.6560
Pairwise	300	5	1, 2, 3, 5	0.826	0.654
Pairwise	300	10	1, 2, 3, 5	0.834	0.679
Pairwise	300	20	1, 2, 3, 5	0.831	0.653
Pairwise	300	10	1, 2	0.813	0.653
Pairwise	300	10	2, 3	0.817	0.657
Pairwise	300	10	3, 4	0.816	0.655
Pairwise	300	10	4, 5	0.816	0.647
Pairwise	300	10	9, 10	0.812	0.627
Pairwise	300	50	1, 2 ,3, 5	0.820	0.629

To improve the performance, We tune some hyperparameters and present the result in Table 2. The *Em-dim* is dimension of our pretrained embedding. The *extend-dim* is dimension of our additional feature embedding. The *region-size* is a hyperparameter of convolution filter shape.

4   Conclusion

In this paper, we implement an enhanced convolution neural network by extending our word embedding with additional feature, such as overlap and position information. Instead of treating the task as pointwise classfication, we use a pairwise ranking approach with a triplet ranking loss function. The results demonstrate pairwise ranking approach is more suitable for NLPCC DBQA task than pointwise. We utilize the max pooling and attentive pooling network with dynamic negative sample strategy. In the future, we will add more features to our convolution neural network to improve the performance on DBQA task.

References

1. Kim, Y.: Convolutional neural networks for sentence classification. arXiv preprint arXiv:1408.5882 (2014)
2. Hu, B., Lu, Z., Li, H., Chen, Q.: Convolutional neural network architectures for matching natural language sentences. In: Advances in Neural Information Processing Systems, pp. 2042–2050 (2014)
3. Yin, W., Schütze, H., Xiang, B., Zhou, B.: ABCNN: attention-based convolutional neural network for modeling sentence pairs. arXiv preprint arXiv:1512.05193 (2015)
4. Severyn, A.: Automatic feature engineering for answer selection and extraction. In: EMNLP (2013)
5. Yih, W.T., Chang, M.W., Meek, C., Pastusiak, A.: Question answering using enhanced lexical semantic models. In: Meeting of the Association for Computational Linguistics, pp. 1744–1753 (2013)
6. Yu, L., Hermann, K.M., Blunsom, P., Pulman, S.: Deep learning for answer sentence selection. arXiv preprint arXiv:1412.1632 (2014)
7. Severyn, A., Moschitti, A.: Learning to rank short text pairs with convolutional deep neural networks. In: SIGIR, pp. 373–382. ACM (2015)
8. Fu, J., Qiu, X., Huang, X.: Convolutional deep neural networks for document-based question answering. In: Lin, C.-Y., Xue, N., Zhao, D., Huang, X., Feng, Y. (eds.) ICCPOL/NLPCC -2016. LNCS (LNAI), vol. 10102, pp. 790–797. Springer, Cham (2016). https://doi.org/10.1007/978-3-319-50496-4_71
9. Yang, Y., Yih, W.-T., Meek, C.: WikiQA: a challenge dataset for open-domain question answering. In: EMNLP, pp. 2013–2018 (2015)
10. Wang, B., Niu, J., Ma, L., Zhang, Y., Zhang, L., Li, J., Zhang, P., Song, D.: A Chinese question answering approach integrating count-based and embedding-based features. In: Lin, C.-Y., Xue, N., Zhao, D., Huang, X., Feng, Y. (eds.) ICCPOL/NLPCC -2016. LNCS (LNAI), vol. 10102, pp. 934–941. Springer, Cham (2016). https://doi.org/10.1007/978-3-319-50496-4_88
11. Severyn, A., Moschitti, A.: Modeling Relational Information in Question-Answer Pairs with Convolutional Neural Networks (2016)
12. Santos, C.D., Tan, M., Xiang, B., Zhou, B.: Attentive Pooling Networks (2016)
13. Lin, J., Rao, J., He, H.: Noise-contrastive estimation for answer selection with deep neural networks. In: CIKM (2016)
14. Mikolov, T., Sutskever, I., Chen, K., Corrado, G.S., Dean, J.: Distributed representations of words and phrases and their compositionality. In: Advances in Neural Information Processing Systems, pp. 3111–3119 (2013)

A Retrieval-Based Matching Approach to Open Domain Knowledge-Based Question Answering

Han Zhang[1(✉)], Muhua Zhu[2], and Huizhen Wang[1]

[1] Natural Language Processing Laboratory at Northeast University,
Shenyang, China
kobe1992724@outlook.com, wanghuizhen@mail.neu.edu.cn
[2] Tencent AI Lab, Shenzhen, China
muhuazhu@tencent.com

Abstract. In this paper, we propose a retrieval and knowledge-based question answering system for the competition task in NLPCC 2017. Regarding the question side, our system uses a ranking model to score candidate entities to detect a topic entity from questions. Then similarities between the question and candidate relation chains are computed, based on which candidate answer entities are ranked. By returning the highest scored answer entity, our system finally achieves the F1-score of 41.96% on test set of NLPCC 2017. Our current system focuses on solving single-relation questions, but it can be extended to answering multiple-relation questions.

Keywords: Question answering · Knowledge base · Entity linking
Relation chain inference

1 Introduction

Automatic open-domain question answering is a challenging problem in the fields of information retrieval and natural language processing. In the direction of question answering, recent years have seen a surge of research interests in knowledge-based question answering (KBQA) in both academia and industry, which is defined to be retrieving a specific entity from knowledge base as the answer to a given question. In this paper, we introduce our system which is designed specifically for the KBQA competition in NLPCC 2017.

The challenge of retrieval-based KBQA is how to match unstructured natural language questions with structured data in knowledge base. To understand a question, it is necessary to figure out the topic entity and relation chain inside the question. Thus, **topic entity linking** and **relation chain inference** are the most important modules in our system.

To detect the topic entity in a question, n-gram words that appear both in the question and mention list of knowledge base are selected as candidate mentions. Then we extract their lexical features, syntactic features and features building on a sequence labeling model. These features are used as inputs to a ranking model: RankNet [1]. The

© Springer International Publishing AG 2018
X. Huang et al. (Eds.): NLPCC 2017, LNAI 10619, pp. 701–711, 2018.
https://doi.org/10.1007/978-3-319-73618-1_60

RankNet model outputs the scores of candidate mentions. At last, candidate mentions are linked to candidate entities.

In the relation chain inference module, we use as features the similarity scores computed at character-level, word-level and semantic-level respectively. BLEU is an evaluation method proposed for machine translation. We reform it into character-based F1 BLEU which acts as a character-level similarity feature. Word-based cosine similarity is used as a word-level similarity feature. Regarding semantic-level features, we use convolution neural network (CNN) [2] to represent both questions and corresponding relation chains as semantic vectors. The cosine similarity between semantic vectors of questions and relation chains is used as a semantic-level feature. We also use RankNet to score candidate relation chains in this module.

Our system finally achieve the F1-score of 41.96% on the test set of NLPCC 2017 and ranks 2nd among all the participants. The rest of this paper is structured as follows: we review related work in Sect. 2, describe the system architecture and detailed modules of our system in Sect. 3, and present the experimental results in Sect. 4. Finally, Sect. 5 presents our conclusion and future work.

2 Related Work

Knowledge-based question answering is a challenging task in the field of NLP. The mainstream approaches can be divided into three categories: semantic parsing based [3–7], information extraction based [8–10] and retrieval based [11–13].

The semantic parsing based approaches translate natural language questions into a series of semantic representations in logic forms. They query the answer in knowledge base through the corresponding query statement. Yih et al. [14] present a semantic parsing method via staged query graph generation. Convolution neural network is used to calculate the similarities between question and relation chains.

The information extraction based approaches extract topic entities from questions and generate a knowledge base subgraph with the topic entity node as the center. Each node in the subgraph can be used as a candidate answer. By examining the questions and extracted information according to some rules or templates, they obtain the feature vectors of the questions. A classifier is then constructed to filter candidate answers based on input feature vectors. Yao and Van Durme [15] associate question features with answer patterns described by Freebase. They also exploit ClueWeb, mined mappings between knowledge base relations and natural language text, and show that it helps both relation prediction and answer extraction.

The idea of retrieval-based method is similar to that of information extraction based methods. The question and candidate answers are mapped to distributed representation. The distributed representations are trained on labeled data, aiming to optimize the matching function between the question and the correct answer. Zhang et al. [16] combine bi-directional LSTM with an attention mechanism to represent the questions dynamically according to diverse focuses of various candidate answers.

These approaches work well on the English open dataset **WebQuestion**. However, their performances on a Chinese KBQA dataset have not been presented before.

3 Our Approach

Figure 1 illustrates the system architecture of our approach. The first step of our system is to conduct word segmentation, POS tagging, named entity recognition and dependency parsing on an input question. On the base of the preprocessing results, the entity linking module is used to detect a topic mention in the question. Mentions appearing in a question are selected as candidates. We use a pairwise ranking model, RankNet to score candidate mentions. In the relation chain inference module, features designed at three different levels are used to measure the similarity between a question and candidate relation chains. Finally, we rank candidate answer entities by calculating the weighted sum of scores in the entity linking module and relation chain inference module. The candidate answer entity with the highest score is outputted as the final answer.

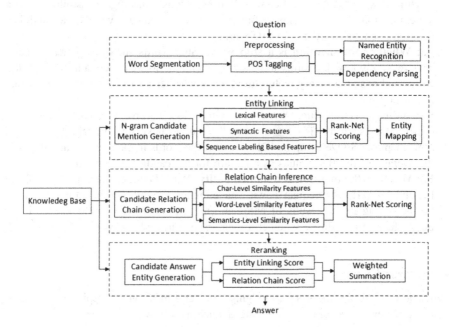

Fig. 1. System architecture of our approach

3.1 Entity Linking

Our entity linking module is used to detect a topic mention in the question. We first combine N-gram words to generate candidate phrases by ranging N from 1 till to the length of the input question.[1] Then we check the mention list of our knowledge base to retain candidate phrases that appear in the mention list. Such candidate phrases are used as **candidate mentions**. Because of the enormous amount of mentions in the knowledge base, a question generally has more than one candidate mention. In order to rank

---

[1] The length of a sentence refers to the number of word counts.

these candidate mentions, we extract their lexical features, syntactic features and features that build on a sequence labeling model.

- **Lexical Features**

Mentions in the knowledge base have different probabilities of being a topic mention from the perspective of lexicology. The lexical features used in our system are defined as follows:

> **F1: String length of the mention.** A mention with a bigger string length (such as "海带/炒/猪肝 ‖ stir fried liver with kelp") is more likely to be a topic mention than shorter ones (such as "海带 ‖ kelp"). So we use the number of word tokens in a candidate mention as a feature.
>
> **F2: Whether enclosed in a book title mark.** The mention in a book title mark (such as " 《红楼梦》 ‖ A dream of Red Mansions") has high possibility to be a topic mention. So we design a binary feature to indicate whether a candidate mention is enclosed by a boot title mark.
>
> **F3: Whether the mention is a stop word.** Stop words such as ("什么 ‖ what") have relatively low possibility to be a topic mention. So we collect a list of 800 stop words and design a binary feature to indicate whether a candidate mention appears in the stop-word list.
>
> **F4: Average IDF value.** A mention with a low Inverse Document Frequency (IDF) value (such as "在/哪里 ‖ where") tends to have low probabilities to be a topic mention. So we compute IDF values of the words in the mention and then use the average of the IDF values as a feature for the candidate mention.
>
> **F5: Whether the mention is a named entity.** Named entities (such as "李军 ‖ Jun Li" and "龙泉镇 ‖ Longquan Town") have higher possibility to be a topic mention. So, according to the results of automatic named entity recognition, we design a binary feature to indicate whether a mention is a named entity.

- **Syntactic Features**

Syntactic features are important to judging whether a mention is a topic mention. The syntactic features used in our system are defined as follows:

> **F6: Whether the mention is a noun or noun phrase.** We design the binary feature to indicate whether a mention is a noun phrase. A mention is regarded as a noun phrase if (1) the words in the mention have the "ATT" dependency relations only, and (2) the mention ends with a noun. Figure 2 shows an example for this feature where "国际/贸易/实务 ‖ practice of international trade" is recognized as a noun phrase.

Fig. 2. An illustrating example for F6.

F7: Whether the mention is the subject (object) when the object (subject) is a pronoun. This feature encodes the syntactic relation between the subject and object in the dependency tree of a question. As the example in Fig. 3 shows, the object "谁 || who" is a pronoun and the corresponding subject "李军 || Jun Li" tends to be a topic mention.

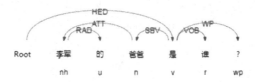

Fig. 3. An illustrating example for F7.

F8: Whether the mention precedes the POS pattern "r + q + n". We find that topic entities tend to appear before the POS pattern "r + q + n", as the example in Fig. 4 shows, where the topic mention "红楼梦 || A dream of Red Mansions" is followed by the pattern "r + q + n".

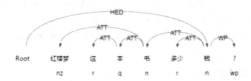

Fig. 4. An illustrating example of F8.

- **Sequence Labeling Model-Based Feature**

F9: Sequence Labeling Score. We utilize a neural sequence labeling model to assign scores to candidate mentions, which is demonstrated in Fig. 5. We use Bi-LSTM [17] to encode words in a question, which is capable of learning long-term dependencies between words and taking into consideration both the previous and future context. Candidate mentions are represented with the tags of **BEG** and **END**, which are output of the softmax layer.

Specifically, the output of softmax layer is $S_i(tag)$, where i is the position in the question. c refers to a candidate mention. b and e are the first position and last position of c in the question. The probabilistic score of c is calculated as:

$$P(c) = S_{b-1}("BEG") * S_{e+1}("END") \tag{1}$$

To train the sequence labeling model, we use the cross entropy loss function:

$$loss = -\sum y_c * \log(P(c)) + (1 - y_c) * log(1 - P(c)) \tag{2}$$

where $y_c = 1$ if c is a positive candidate, and otherwise $y_c = 0$.

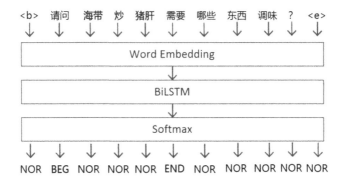

Fig. 5. The sequence labeling model for scoring candidate mentions

The above features are fed to RankNet, a single hidden layer neural network with a pairwise loss function. RankNet is in charge of ranking candidate mentions.

Finally, candidate mentions are linked to candidate entities. Due to the limited size of training data, our system does not perform entity disambiguation.

3.2 Relation Chain Inference

Relation chain is defined to be the path from a topic entity to its corresponding answer entity in the knowledge base. We can generate candidate relation chains according to candidate entities from the question. Because all the questions in NLPCC 2017 dataset are single-relation ones, we take the relation chains of length 1 as candidates. The resulting candidate relation chains are in a large number, so selection of relation chains cannot be formalized as a multi-class classification problem. In this work, we generalize questions into question patterns by replacing the candidate mention with the tag "<entity>". Then we use character-level, word-level and semantic-level features to measure the similarities between the question pattern and candidate relation chains.

- **Character-Level F1 BLEU as Similarity**

BiLingual Evaluation Understudy (BLEU) [18] is an evaluation metric proposed for the task of machine translation to measure the quality of a machine generated translation against translation references. The basic BLEU (without Brevity Penalty) formula is defined as follows when there is only one reference translation:

$$P_n = \frac{\sum_{w_n \in c} Min(Count_c(w_n), Count_r(w_n))}{\sum_{w_n \in c} Count_c(w_n)} \tag{3}$$

$$BLEU_N = \sqrt[N]{\prod_{n=1}^{N} P_n} \tag{4}$$

where c is a candidate translation, r is a reference translation, w_n is an n-gram that appears in candidate translation and $Count_c(w_n)$ is the counts of w_n appearing in c. As shown in the formula, basic BLEU only measures the accuracy of a candidate translation, the recall, however, is not considered.

We adapt the basic BLEU measure to compute character-level similarity. We first change the word-based n-grams into character-based n-grams. Second, in order to consider both accuracy and recall, we change the formula into an F1 measure. To this end, we use the mean value instead of square root of the product, which aims to get a smooth value when one of the F_n is equal to 0. The improved character-based F1 BLEU is defined as follows:

$$overlap_n = \sum_{w_n \in c} Min(Count_c(w_n), Count_r(w_n)) \tag{5}$$

$$P_n = \frac{overlap_n}{\sum_{w_n \in c} Count_c(w_n)} \tag{6}$$

$$R_n = \frac{overlap_n}{\sum_{w_n \in r} Count_r(w_n)} \tag{7}$$

$$F_n = \frac{P_n * R_n}{2 * (P_n + R_n)} \tag{8}$$

$$Char\ Based\ F1\ BLEU_N = \frac{1}{N} \sum_{n=1}^{N} F_n \tag{9}$$

where c is a candidate relation chain and r is a question pattern. By contrast to character-based and word-based cosine similarities, this F1 BLEU metric manages to combine both fine-grained and coarse-grained n-grams and can reduce the negative impact caused by word segmentation errors.

- **Word-Based Cosine Similarity**

This is a traditional method to calculate the similarity between two texts. We remove stop-words in a question pattern and corresponding candidate relation chains. Then we represent them as vectors using the approach of bag-of-words, based on which similarity is calculated with the cosine function.

- **CNN-Based Semantics Similarity**

As shown in Fig. 6, we utilize CNN models to represent a question pattern and its candidate relation chains as semantic vectors respectively, one model for the question pattern and the other model for relation chains. The first layer of the networks is an

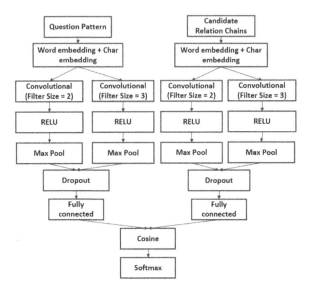

Fig. 6. CNN-based similarity module in our system

embedding layer. We use word2vec toolkit to train word and character embeddings.[2] The final representation of a word is the concatenation of its word embedding and the embeddings of its characters inside. The second layer is convolution layer. We use 200 filters with context windows of 2 words, and 200 filters with context windows of 3 words. A max-pooling operation is applied for feature mapping. Finally, a fully-connected layer outputs semantic vectors of the question pattern and candidate relation chains.

Based on the semantic vectors outputted by CNN, we compute the cosine similarity between a question pattern and candidate relations. The final layer is a softmax layer. The output of softmax is defined as follows:

$$P(r|q) = \frac{e^{Cosine(q,r)}}{\sum_{r' \in C} e^{Cosine(q,r')}} \tag{10}$$

where q is a question pattern, r is a candidate relation chain, and C is the set of candidate relation chains. The cross entropy loss function, as the objective of optimization, is defined as follows:

$$loss = - \sum_{q} log(P(r_q^+|q)) \tag{11}$$

where r_q^+ is the positive candidate relation chain of q.

---

[2] https://code.google.com/archive/p/word2vec/.

3.3 Ranking Answer Entities

Candidate topic entities and candidate relation chains are obtained in aforementioned two modules. Then we generate the candidate answer entities. The scores returned by entity linking and relation chain inference are used together to rank candidate answer entities. The scoring function for ranking answer entities is defined as follows:

$$score_{answer\_entity} = \gamma * score_{topic\_entity} + (1 - \gamma) * score_{relation\_chain} \qquad (12)$$

The entity which ranks highest is returned as the final answer to an input question.

4 Experiments

4.1 Dataset

In this paper, we used the dataset provided by the NLPCC 2017 open domain KBQA competition. The dataset includes 24,479 single-relation question-answer pairs for training, a Chinese knowledge base with 43M SPO triples, and 7M mapping data from mentions to entities. The test set contains 48,850 questions. Most of questions are noise data that are excluded for system performance evaluation. After removing the noise data, there are 7,631 questions remaining to be answered.

Because the questions in the dataset are all single-relation questions, what we really need for building the system are question-triple pairs rather than question-answers pairs. To this end, we used gold-standard answers to extract answer triples backward from the knowledge base. We randomly sampled 200 automatically generated question-triple pairs and manually evaluated the accuracy. The accuracy of the sample data is 96%. We use 20,479 of question-triple pairs as training data and 4,000 for system development.

4.2 Setup

The word embeddings used in our sequence labeling model and CNN models are pre-trained by using word2vec. We used the skip-gram model [19] and the dimension was set to 256. In order to prevent overfitting, we utilized both dropout and batch normalization techniques. SGD was adopted as the optimization method. Regarding the two DNN models, the initial learning rate and decay rate were set to 0.05 and 0.7 respectively. Learning rate decay comes to play after 20 epochs for sequence labeling model training and 30 epochs for CNN model training. Mini-batching is also used and the batch sizes were set to 10 and 20 respectively.

Our KBQA system is multitasking. As shown in Eq. (12), we use linear combination to add the scores returned by entity linking and relation chain inference. We tuned the combination parameter γ on the validation set and finally set it to 0.76.

4.3   Results

The organizer of NLPCC 2017 provided a CNN-based KBQA system. We used it as our baseline system and compared the results of the baseline system and our system on the NLPCC 2017 KBQA test set. We also evaluated the accuracy of our system when using character-based F1 BLEU, word-based cosine similarity and CNN-based similarity separately in the relation chain inference module. The results are presented in Table 1. From the results we can see that the performance of our system is superior to the performance of the baseline system.

Table 1. The results of the baseline and our system

	Accuracy	Recall	F1 score
Baseline system	16.4	16.4	16.4
Char-based F1 BLEU	36.7	48.4	38.5
Word-based cosine similarity	28.8	52.7	31.2
CNN-based similarity	38.5	41.2	38.7
All features	41.3	43.6	42.0

Table 1 shows that character-based F1 BLEU outperforms word-based cosine similarity because it considers both coarse-grained and fine-grained literal similarities between the question and relation chains. The CNN-based similarity method captures semantic information, thus it is better than other two similarity measures. We get the best results when combining all the three similarity-based features. Our system achieves the F1-score of 41.96% on the test set and obtains the 2nd place in the final leaderboard.

4.4   Error Analysis

We randomly sampled 200 error cases and analyzed the causes of these errors. We find that 69.5% of errors are attributed to annotation errors occurring in the dataset. Such annotation errors include "annotated answer entity not in knowledge base" (32.5%), "wrong answer entity" (13%), "no relation chain connected to topic entity can match with the question" (9%), "topic entity not in knowledge base (8.5%)" and "no enough information exits in the question for entity disambiguation" (6.5%). 23% of them are caused by relation chain errors and the other 7.5% are caused by entity linking. Our system still have room for further improvement.

5   Conclusion

In this paper, we described our KBQA system for NLPCC 2017 KBQA competition. Our system adopts a multitask framework, which uses an entity linking model to detect topic entities and a model combining three similarity methods to find out the relation chain that is asked in a question. Our system performs well on test set, though there is room left for our system to improve. Due to the limited size of training data, we do not process multi-relation questions and entity disambiguation. It will be what we plan to work on in the future.

References

1. Burges, C., Shaked, T., Renshaw, E., Lazier, A., Deeds, M., Hamilton, N., Hullender, G.: Learning to rank using gradient descent. In: ICML (2005)
2. Szegedy, C., Liu, W., Jia, Y., Sermanet, P., Reed, S., Anguelov, D., Erhan, D., Vanhoucke, V., Rabinovich, A.: IEEE (2015)
3. Zettlemoyer, L.S., Collins, M.: Learning to map sentences to logical form: structured classification with probabilistic categorial grammars. In: UAI (2005)
4. Kwiatkowski, T., Zettlemoyer, L., Goldwater, S., Steedman, M.: Inducing probabilistic CCG grammars from logical form with higher-order unification. In: EMNLP (2010)
5. Liang, P., Jordan, M.I., Klein, D.: Learning dependency-based compositional semantics. In: ACL (2011)
6. Berant, J., Chou, A., Frostig, R., Liang, P.: Semantic parsing on freebase from question-answer pairs. In: EMNLP (2013)
7. Berant, J., Liang, P.: Semantic parsing via paraphrasing. In: ACL (2014)
8. Bast, H., Haussmann E.: More accurate question answering on freebase. In: Information and Knowledge Management (2015)
9. Fader, A., Zettlemoyer, L., Etzioni, O.: Open question answering over curated and extracted knowledge bases. In: Knowledge Discovery and Data Mining (2014)
10. Yao, X.: Lean question answering over freebase from scratch. In: ACL (2015)
11. Bordes, A., Chopra, S., Weston, J.: Question answering with subgraph embeddings. In: EMNLP (2014)
12. Bordes, A., Weston, J., Usunier, N.: Open question answering with weakly supervised embedding models. In: ECML (2014)
13. Dong, L., Wei, F., Zhou, M., Xu, K.: Question answering over freebase with multi-column convolutional neural networks. In: ACL (2015)
14. Yih, W., Chang, M.-W., He, X., Gao, J.: Semantic parsing via staged query graph generation: question answering with knowledge base. In: ACL (2015)
15. Yao, X., Van Durme, B.: Information extraction over structured data: question answering with freebase. In: ACL (2014)
16. Zhang, Y., Liu, K., He, S., Ji, G., Liu, Z., Wu, H., Zhao, J.: Question answering over knowledge base with neural attention combining global knowledge information. arXiv:1606.00979 (2016)
17. Ma, X., Hovy, E.: End-to-end sequence labeling via bi-directional LSTM-CNNs-CRF. arXiv:1603.01354 (2016)
18. Papineni, K., Roukos, S., Ward, T., Zhu, W.-J.: BLEU: a method for automatic evaluation of machine translation. In: ACL (2002)
19. Mikolov, T., Chen, K., Corrado, G., Dean, J.: Efficient estimation of word representations in vector space. Comput. Sci. (2013)

Improved Compare-Aggregate Model for Chinese Document-Based Question Answering

Ziliang Wang[✉], Weijie Bian, Si Li, Guang Chen, and Zhiqing Lin

Pattern Recognition and Intelligent System, Beijing University of Posts
and Telecommunications, Xitucheng Road 10, Beijing 100876, China
ziliang23@163.com

Abstract. Document-based question answering (DBQA) is a sub-task in question answering. It aims to measure the matching relation between questions and answers, which can be regarded as sentence matching problem. In this paper, we introduce a Compare-Aggregate architecture to handle the word-level comparison and aggregation. To deal with the noisy information in traditional attention mechanism, the k-top attention mechanism is proposed to filter out irrelevant words. Subsequently, we propose a combined model to merge matching relation learned by Compare-Aggregate model with shallow features to generate the final matching score. We evaluate our model on Chinese Document-based Question Answering (DBQA) task. The experimental results show the effectiveness of our proposed improved methods. And our final combined model achieves second place result on the DBQA task of NLPCC-ICCPOL 2017 Shared Task. The paper provides the technical details of the proposed algorithm.

Keywords: Question answering · Compare-Aggregate architecture
Deep learning · Hybrid features · Sentence matching

1 Introduction

Document-based question answering (DBQA) aims to find one or more sentences from document to answer the given question. Document-based question answering can be regarded as sentence matching problem which is to calculate the matching relation between questions and answers. Sentence matching problem is a common and critical issue in many natural language processing tasks, for example, paraphrase identification (PI) [14], textual entailment (TE) [1], answer selection (AS) [2]. These tasks have similar targets to calculate the matching relation between two sentences, and the only difference lies in the final prediction layers which depend on the tasks, such as predicting their relation, calculating the match score of two given sentences.

In previous works, there are two main kinds of deep learning frameworks to deal with sentence matching problem. The first one is Siamese architecture [2,4,13,15], and the other one is Compare-Aggregate architecture [10–12]. The

© Springer International Publishing AG 2018
X. Huang et al. (Eds.): NLPCC 2017, LNAI 10619, pp. 712–720, 2018.
https://doi.org/10.1007/978-3-319-73618-1_61

Siamese architecture applies the same neural network encoder to two sentences individually and calculates the matching score between these two outputs of encoder. Essentially, it focuses on sentence-level information. As for Compare-Aggregate architecture, it first compares two sentences on a lower level by attention mechanism, like words or phrases level, and gets the comparison vectors. Finally, it uses recurrent neural network or convolutional neural network to aggregate these comparison vectors into an aggregated vector as the input of feed-forward network to make the final prediction. In answer selection task, the Compare-Aggregate architecture [12] achieves excellent performances on several answer selection dataset.

To better deal with DBQA task, we design our model based on the Compare-Aggregate architecture [12], because it can capture more interactive features between two sentences which is important for the sentence matching task. However, the conventional Compare-Aggregate architecture has its own limitation. The model in [12] uses traditional attention method to get attention-weighted word vectors, and uses the sum of all attention-weighted word vectors to get the attention-weighted representations. In fact, there are several irrelevant words in answer sentences when we deal with answer selection task. If we use the sum of all attention-weighted word vectors, the noisy information will also be introduced. Because the number of irrelevant words may be large. In this paper, we propose a k-top attention mechanism to reduce the influence of noise information produced by irrelevant words. Besides, we investigate some shallow features, such as length of sentences and the number of common words in two sentences, and combine these features with the output matching score of our Compare-Aggregate model as the input of logistic regression model to make the final prediction.

Our contributions can be summarized as follows. First, we introduce basic Compare-Aggregate model. Then we propose k-top attention mechanism to emphasize more attention on relevant parts of sentences and filter out noise information. Second, we introduce some shallow features to train the final matching model, which makes contributions to the performance of our improved model in NLPCC-ICCPOL 2017 Shared Task on DBQA.

The remaining of this paper is organized as follows. Section 2 describes related work of DBQA. Section 3 provides the details of our proposed model. Extensive experimental results are shown in Sect. 4. And we conclude this paper in Sect. 5.

2   Related Work

Sentence matching problem has been studied for several years. The approach with hand-craft features is a traditional way to measure the similarity between two sentences. However, this kind of features only capture the shallow semantic meaning of sentences, and it can not deal with inherent ambiguities in natural languages. To better learn the meaning of sentences, neural network method has been introduced in sentence matching problem. There are two main kinds of neural network methods in this field. The first one is Siamese architecture. It applies same neural network encoder to two sentences respectively and gets their sentence-level embedding vectors. With these sentence-level embedding vectors, Siamese architecture can do the matching decision using matching measures, such as cosine similarity and euclidean distance [2,5,9,13,15]. The other one is Compare-Aggregate architecture. This model firstly compare two sentences in smaller units like words and phrases, then the comparison results are aggregated by convolutional neural network (CNN) and recurrent neural network (RNN) into a vector to make the final prediction [3,10,12].

3   Model

3.1   Compare-Aggregate Matching Model

In this part, we introduce our Compare-Aggregate matching model which is to predict the matching relation between questions and answers. Our Compare-Aggregate architecture is based on the model in [12]. The first step of the model is to calculate the soft attention weights of each word in answer to express the relevance of this word to the question. After that, model applies this soft-attention weights to the answer via compare operation so that it can produce an attention-weighted answer vector. Then we apply convolutional neural network on it to aggregate the information of this attention-weighted answer vector and it generates a final vector. We use this vector to predict the matching score between question and answer. The main improvement to original Compare-Aggregate model [12] in this paper lies in attention mechanism. As we mentioned before, previous attention mechanism introduces some noise information. To tackle this problem, we propose a k-top mechanism to control the use of attention information.

The framework of our model is presented in Fig. 1. As shown in Fig. 1, our model has five layers: word embedding layer, soft-attention layer, comparison layer, aggregation layer, prediction layer.

Word Embedding Layer. We use $Q = (q_1, q_2, ..., q_{l_q})$ and $A = (a_1, a_2, ..., a_{l_a})$ to represent question and answer as the input of our model. In a sentence, each word is represented as d_0-dimensional pre-trained word embedding [8].

Soft-Attention Layer. In this layer, we apply attention mechanism to measure the interaction between question and answer. First, we compute the attention matrix $S \in \mathbb{R}^{l_q \times l_a}$. The element s_{ij} in attention matrix S denotes the similarity between ith word in q and jth word in a. Here we simply use dot operation to calculate the similarity,

$$s_{ij} = sim(q_i \cdot a_j). \tag{1}$$

Then we normalize the attention weights by column,

$$e_{ij} = \frac{exp(s_{ij})}{\sum_{x=1}^{l_q} exp(s_{xj})}, \tag{2}$$

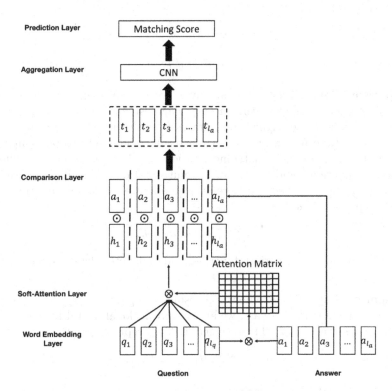

Fig. 1. Architecture of improved Compare-Aggregate model.

These weights e_{ij} are applied to each word in q and the soft aligned sub-phrases h_j are the sum of the product of corresponding e_{ij} and q_i. The formula is as follows:

$$h_j = \sum_{i=1}^{l_q} e_{ij} q_i, \tag{3}$$

where h_j stands for the relevant vector from the entire question aligned to the jth word in answer A.

From the Eq. (3), we can see that each aligned sub-phrases h_j contains all fragments in Q. However, not every fragment reflects the relevance information between Q and A. Actually, only a small part of fragments are meaningful in a sentence. As a result, this method of combination involves irrelevant fragments which act as noise information for the following layers. Here we propose k-top attention mechanism to only combine the meaningful fragments to capture the aligned sub-phrases h_j. So that the k-top attention mechanism can filter noise information. We use $e = e_{1j}, e_{2j}, ..., e_{ij}$ to denote the attention weight e_{ij} between ith word in question and jth word in answer. Then we only maintain the top k attention weight e_{ij}, and the others are set to zero. Here we use G to represent the set of top k attention weights.

$$e_{ij} = \frac{e_{ij}}{\sum_i^G e_{ij}} \quad i \in G, \tag{4}$$

$$e_{ij} = 0 \quad i \notin G. \tag{5}$$

Comparison Layer. From previous layer, we get an aligned sub-phrases h_j which represents a weighted version of q that best matches a_j. In comparison layer, we compare these aligned sub-phrases h_j with the jth word a_j in answer. We use vector t_j to represent comparison result. There are several comparison functions to measure their matching relation. In [12], they compare different comparison functions, and element-wise multiplication is a simple but effective way for comparing two vectors. Here we also adopt element-wise multiplication as our comparison function,

$$t_j^{'} = f(a_j, h_j) = a_j \otimes h_j, \tag{6}$$

where $f()$ represents comparison function, and $\otimes$ denotes element-wise multiplication.

Aggregation Layer. The comparison results $t = \{t_1, t_2, ..., t_{l_a}\}$ have the same length with answer. In this part, we apply convolutional neural network to t to aggregate these vectors [7]. Then we get the final representation vectors,

$$R = CNN\left([t_1, t_2, ..., t_{l_a}]\right), \tag{7}$$

Prediction Layer. For each training sample, we use one question Q and its candidate answer set $A = A_1, A_2, ..., A_N$ as input, and the target label set is $Y = Y_1, Y_2, ..., Y_N$. Then model outputs a score vector S,

$$Score_j = R_j^T W. \tag{8}$$

W is the parameter of prediction layer and it converts the R_j into the matching score of question Q and jth answer A_j. We apply softmax operation over all matching score of candidate answers,

$$S_j = \frac{exp(Score_j)}{\sum_{i=1}^N exp(Score_i)}, \tag{9}$$

S_j stands for the matching score between question and jth candidate answer. We also normalize the target labels Y. And we use KL-divergence as the training loss function of our model.

3.2   Combined Matching Model

Shallow Features. Previous works [6,15] show the effectiveness of shallow features in sentence matching problem as a supplement to neural network model. Therefore, we design some shallow features as a supplement to our Compare-Aggregate model, including length of question, length of answer, Inverse Document Frequency (IDF) counts and the number of words which appear in both post and response except stopwords. Each word has its IDF value which is calculated based on post sentences and IDF counts is the sum of IDF values of common words in post and response.

Hybrid LR Model. In previous section, we introduce two kinds of matching features: matching score from Compare-Aggregate model and shallow features. In order to combine advantages of them, we introduce logistic regression model to learn the combined matching score model. The score function is defined as follows,

$$P\left(y = 1|x; \theta\right) = g\left(\theta^T x\right) = \frac{1}{1 + e^{-\theta^T x}} \tag{10}$$

where $\theta \in \mathbb{R}^n$ is the model parameter to be learned, n stands for the number of features, $x \in \mathbb{R}^n$ denotes the input features. Here we use the matching score from Compare-Aggregate model as a feature. We regard it as a binary classification problem, and the training objective function is shown as follows,

$$L\left(\theta\right) = \log \prod P\left(y|x; \theta\right) = \sum \left(y \log g\left(\theta^T x\right) + (1 - y) \log \left(1 - g\left(\theta^T x\right)\right)\right) \tag{11}$$

where $y \in \{0, 1\}$ represents whether the response is correct or not, and $g\left(x\right)$ is defined in (10). Finally, we use $P\left(y = 1|x; \theta\right)$ as the matching score between question and answer.

4   Experiment

4.1   Dataset and Evaluation Metric

Dataset. We evaluate our model on Chinese Document-based QA (DBQA) task which is a sub-task of Open Domain Question Answering shared task. The dataset consists of two parts: dbqa-train and dbqa-test. We split dbqa-train into training set and validation set in ratios of 3:2. Some statistical information is shown in Table 1,

Table 1. Statistics of dataset.

Dataset	The size of QA-pairs
Training set	181882
Validation set	122531
Test set	47372

Evaluation Metric. The DBQA task aims to select sentences from the given document to answer the question, so each question may have several correct answers. Here we use Mean Reciprocal Rank (MRR) and Mean Average Precision (MAP) as the evaluation metrics.

$$MRR = \frac{1}{|Q|} \sum_{i=1}^{|Q|} \frac{1}{rank_i} \tag{12}$$

$$MAP = \frac{1}{|Q|} \sum_{i=1}^{|Q|} AveP\left(C_i, A_i\right) \tag{13}$$

where $|Q|$ represents question set, $rank_i$ denotes the rank of the first correct answer for question Q_i. $AveP\left(C, A\right) = \frac{\sum_{k=1}^{n}(P(k) \cdot rel(k))}{min(m,n)}$ stands for the average precision.

4.2 Experiment Setup

We employ chinese word segmentation tools named Jieba[1] to segment sentences into words. Word embedding is chosen to represent the words in sentences as the input of our Compare-Aggregate model. Specially, word2vec [8] is applied to train the chinese word embeddings based on 1G Wikipedia dataset. The dimension of chinese word embedding is set to 200.

4.3 Results and Analysis

To exhibit the promotion of our proposed approaches, the experiments can be divided into three parts. The base model is our Compare-Aggregate model (Compare-Aggregate). After which we apply our k-top attention mechanism to filter noise information (Compare-Aggregate with k-top). Finally, we combine the matching score from Compare-Aggregate model with shallow features using logistic regression (LR) model (Hybrid-LR). We use training set to train our Compare-Aggregate model and the final LR model, then choose the model which achieves the best MAP performance on the validation set as our final model. The model performances are shown in Table 2.

Table 2. Model performances on DBQA dataset.

Model	MRR	MAP
Compare-Aggregate	0.6246	0.6218
Compare-Aggregate with k-top	0.6785	0.6736
Hybrid-LR	0.6896	0.6858

From the model performances, we can see that our basic Compare-Aggregate model already achieves a very high performance without any hand-craft features.

---

[1] https://github.com/fxsjy/jieba.

With the k-top attention mechanism, model performance has been improved by 5.4% in MRR and 5.2% in MAP, which confirms our hypothesis about the noisy information in traditional attention mechanism. Additionally, shallow features improve the model performance by 1.1% in MRR and 1.2% in MAP, we explain this phenomena with reason that these shallow features measure the matching relation from different perspectives. For example, when a new word appears which is not seen before in training or embedding vector is not available, it is regarded as unknown. Actually the new word may be a new entity like a name of person or restaurant which is full of information. If the new word appears in both two sentences, it may be important. That is why the feature of common words count works.

5   Conclusion

In this paper, we propose a Compare-Aggregate model with k-top attention mechanism. Compared with previous Compare-Aggregate model, our proposed model can emphasize more attention on relevant segments of sentences. After combining the matching score from Compare-Aggregate model with shallow features, the performance of our hybrid LR model is further improved. And it achieves superior performance on the DBQA task of NLPCC-ICCPOL 2017 Shared Task.

Acknowledgments. This work is supported by Beijing Natural Science Foundation (4174098), the Fundamental Research Funds for the Central Universities (2017RC02) and the Natural Science Foundation of China under Grant No. 61671078 and 61471058. The authors are partially supported by CAS-NDST Lab under Grant No. CAS-NDST201701.

References

1. Bowman, S.R., Angeli, G., Potts, C., et al.: A large annotated corpus for learning natural language inference. In: Proceedings of the Conference on Empirical Methods in Natural Language Processing (2015)
2. Feng, M., Xiang, B., Glass, M.R., Wang, L., Zhou, B.: Applying deep learning to answer selection: a study and an open task. In: IEEE Workshop on Automatic Speech Recognition and Understanding (ASRU), pp. 813–820. IEEE (2015)
3. He, H., Lin, J.: Pairwise word interaction modeling with deep neural networks for semantic similarity measurement. In: Proceedings of NAACL-HLT, pp. 937–948 (2016)
4. Bromley, J., Guyon, I., LeCun, Y., et al.: Signature verification using a "Siamese" time delay neural network. In: Advances in Neural Information Processing Systems, pp. 737–744 (1994)
5. Rao, J., He, H., Lin, J.: Noise-contrastive estimation for answer selection with deep neural networks. In: Proceedings of the CIKM, pp. 1913–1916 (2016)
6. Kang, L., Hu, B., Wu, X., Chen, Q., He, Y.: A short texts matching method using shallow features and deep features. In: Zong, C., Nie, J.Y., Zhao, D., Feng, Y. (eds.) NLPCC 2014. CCIS, vol. 496, pp. 150–159. Springer, Heidelberg (2014). https://doi.org/10.1007/978-3-662-45924-9_14

7. Kim, Y.: Convolutional neural networks for sentence classification. In: EMNLP (2014)
8. Mikolov, T., Sutskever, I., Chen, K., Corrado, G.S., Dean, J.: Distributed representations of words and phrases and their compositionality. In: Advances in Neural Information Processing Systems, pp. 3111–3119 (2013)
9. Tan, M., dos Santos, C.N., Xiang, B., Zhou, B.: Improved representation learning for question answer matching. In: Meeting of the Association for Computational Linguistics, pp. 464–473 (2016)
10. Parikh, A.P., Täckström, O., Das, D., Uszkoreit, J.: A decomposable attention model for natural language inference. In: EMNLP (2016)
11. Wang, S., Jiang, J.: Learning natural language inference with LSTM (2015)
12. Wang, S., Jiang, J.: A compare-aggregate model for matching text sequences. arXiv preprint arXiv:1611.01747 (2016)
13. Yang, Y., Yih, W.T., Meek, C.: WikiQA: a challenge dataset for open-domain question answering. In: EMNLP, pp. 2013–2018 (2015)
14. Yin, W., Schütze, H.: Convolutional neural network for paraphrase identification. In: HLT-NAACL, pp. 901–911 (2015)
15. Yin, W., Schütze, H., Xiang, B., Zhou, B.: ABCNN: attention-based convolutional neural network for modeling sentence pairs. arXiv preprint arXiv:1512.05193 (2015)

Transfer Deep Learning for Low-Resource Chinese Word Segmentation with a Novel Neural Network

Jingjing Xu[1,2(✉)], Shuming Ma[1,2], Yi Zhang[1,2],
Bingzhen Wei[1,2], Xiaoyan Cai[3], and Xu Sun[1,2]

[1] MOE Key Laboratory of Computational Linguistics,
Peking University, Beijing, China
[2] School of Electronics Engineering and Computer Science,
Peking University, Beijing, China
jingjingxu@pku.edu.cn
[3] School of Automation, Northwestern Polytechnical University, Xi'an, China

Abstract. Recent studies have shown effectiveness in using neural networks for Chinese word segmentation. However, these models rely on large-scale data and are less effective for low-resource datasets because of insufficient training data. We propose a transfer learning method to improve low-resource word segmentation by leveraging high-resource corpora. First, we train a teacher model on high-resource corpora and then use the learned knowledge to initialize a student model. Second, a weighted data similarity method is proposed to train the student model on low-resource data. Experiment results show that our work significantly improves the performance on low-resource datasets: 2.3% and 1.5% F-score on PKU and CTB datasets. Furthermore, this paper achieves state-of-the-art results: 96.1%, and 96.2% F-score on PKU and CTB datasets.

Keywords: Chinese word segmentation · Transfer learning

1 Introduction

Chinese word segmentation (CWS) is an important step in Chinese natural language processing. The most widely used approaches [11,19] treat CWS as a sequence labelling problem in which each character is assigned with a tag. Formally, given an input sequence $\mathbf{x} = x_1x_2...x_n$, it produces a tag sequence $\mathbf{y} = y_1y_2...y_n$. Many exsiting techniques, such as conditional random fields, have been successfully applied to CWS [7,13,16,18,24]. However, these approaches incorporate many handcrafted features. Therefore, the generalization ability is restricted.

In recent years, neural networks have become increasingly popular in CWS, which focused more on the ability of automated feature extraction. Collobert et al. [4] developed a general neural architecture for sequence labelling tasks. Pei et al. [10] used convolutioanl neural networks to capture local features within a

© Springer International Publishing AG 2018
X. Huang et al. (Eds.): NLPCC 2017, LNAI 10619, pp. 721–730, 2018.
https://doi.org/10.1007/978-3-319-73618-1_62

fixed size window. Chen et al. [2] proposed gated recursive neural networks to model feature combinations. The gating mechanism was also used by Cai and Zhao [1].

However, this success relies on massive labelled data and are less effective on low-resource datasets. The major problem is that a small amount of labelled data leads to inadequate training and negatively impacts the ability of generalization. However, there are enough corpora which consist of massive annotated texts. All can be used to improve the task. Thus, we propose a transfer learning method to address the problem by leveraging high-resource datasets.

First, we train a teacher model on high-resource datasets and then use the learned knowledge to initialize a student model. Previous neural network models usually use random initialization which relies on massive labelled data. It is hard for a randomly initialized model to achieve the expected results on low-resource datasets. Motivated by that, we propose a teacher-student framework to initialize the student model. However, it is hard to directly make use of high-resource datasets to train the student model because different corpora have different data distributions. The shift of data distributions is a major problem. To address the problem, we propose a weighted data similarity method which computes a similarity of each high-resource sample with a low-resource dataset. Experiment results show that using our transfer learning method, we substantially improve the performance on low-resource datasets.

With the increasing of layers which are designed to improve the ability of feature extraction, the training speed is becoming limit. To speed up training, we explore mini-batch asynchronous parallel (MAP) learning on neural segmentation in this paper. Existing asynchronous parallel learning methods are mainly for sparse models [12]. For dense models, like neural networks, asynchronous parallel methods bring inevitable gradient noises. However, the theoretical analysis by Sun [15] showed that the learning process with gradient errors can still be convergent on neural models. Motivated by that, we explore the MAP approach on neural segmentation in this paper. The parallel method accelerates training substantially and the training speed is almost five times faster than a serial mode.

The main contributions of the paper are listed as follows:

- A transfer learning method is proposed to improve low-resource word segmentation by leveraging high-resource corpora.
- To speed up training, mini-batch asynchronous parallel learning on neural word segmentation is explored.

2   Transfer Learning by Leveraging High-Resource Datasets

Previous neural word segmentation models are less effective on low-resource datasets since these models only focus on in-domain supervised learning. Furthermore, there are enough corpora which consist of massive annotated texts.

For scenarios where we have insufficient labelled data, transfer learning is an effective way to improve the task. Motivated by that, we propose a transfer learning method to leverage high-resource corpora.

First, we propose a teacher-student framework to initialize a model with the learned knowledge. We train a teacher model on a dataset where there is a large amount of training data (e.g., MSR). The learned parameters are used to initialize a student model. Therefore, the student model is trained from the learned parameters, rather than randomly initialization.

Second, the student model is trained by the weighted data similarity method. However, since different corpora have different data distributions, it is hard to directly make use of high-resource datasets to train the student model. Thus, to avoid the shift of data distributions, high-resource corpora are used to train the student model based on the weighted data similarity method. This method identifies the similarity of each high-resource sample with a low-resource dataset. We use different learning rates for different samples. A learning rate is adjusted by the weighted data similarity automatically. The weighted data similarity w_i^t is updated as follows.

First, calculate the update rate a^t:

$$e^t = (1 - \frac{2 * p^t * r^t}{p^t + r^t}) \tag{1}$$

$$a^t = \frac{1}{2}log\frac{1 - e^t}{e^t} \tag{2}$$

where p^t and r^t are precision and recall of the student model on high-resource data. The update rate a^t is determined by the error rate e^t. The error rate is a simple and effective way to evaluate the data similarity.

Next, update the data similarity after t iterations:

$$S^{t+1} = (w_1^{t+1}, ..., w_i^{t+1}, ..., w_N^{t+1}) \tag{3}$$

$$w_i^{t+1} = \frac{w_i^t}{Z^t * m} \sum_{j=1}^{m} exp(a^t I(y_{i,j} = p_{i,j})) \tag{4}$$

where m is the length of sample i, $I()$ is the indicator function which evaluates whether the prediction $p_{i,j}$ is equal with the gold label $y_{i,j}$ or not and Z^t is the regularization factor which is computed as:

$$Z^t = \sum_{i} \frac{w_i^t}{m} \sum_{j=1}^{m} exp(a^t I(y_{i,j} = p_{i,j})) \tag{5}$$

Finally, the weighted data similarity is used to compute the learning rate α_i^t:

$$\alpha_i^t = \alpha^t * w_i^t \tag{6}$$

where α^t is the fixed learning rate for a low-resource dataset, w_i^t indicates the similarity between sentence i and a low-resource corpus, which ranges from 0 to 1.

3   Unified Global-Local Neural Networks

Insufficient data puts forward higher requirements for feature extraction. Our key idea is to combine several kinds of weak features to achieve the better performance. Unlike previous networks which focus on a single kind of feature: either complicated local features or global dependencies, our network has an advantage of combining complicated local features with long dependencies together. Both of them are necessary for CWS and should not be neglected. Our network is built on a simple encoder-decoder structure. A encoder is designed to model local combinations and a decoder is used to capture long distance dependencies.

First, words are represented by embeddings stored in a lookup table $D^{|v|*d}$ where v is the number of words in the vocabulary and d is the embedding size. The lookup table is pre-trained on giga-word corpus where unknown words are mapped to a special symbol. The inputs to our model are $x_1, x_2, ..., x_n$ which are represented by $D = D_{x_1}, D_{x_2,...,D_{x_n}}$.

We first extract a window context $H^0 \in R^{n,k,d}$ from an input sequence which is padded with special symbols according to the window size:

$$H^0_{i,j} = D[i + j] \tag{7}$$

where n is the sentence length, k is the window size and d is the embedding length. H^0 will be input to the encoder to produce complicated local feature representations.

Encoder. The encoder is composed of filter recursive networks. According to the filter size, we first choose every patch and input it to gate function to get next layer $H^1 \in R^{n,k-f_1+1,d}$ where f_1 is the filter size of 1th hidden layer.

In a gate cell of filter recursive networks, output H^1 of the ith, j^{th} hidden node is computed as:

$$H^1_{i,j} = z_h \odot h' + \sum_{d_i=0}^{f_1-1} (z_{d_i} \odot H^0_{i,j+d_i}) \tag{8}$$

where z_h and z_{d_i} are update gates for new activation h' and inputs, while $\odot$ means element-wise multiplication. To simplify the cell, z_h, z_{d_i} are computed as:

$$\begin{bmatrix} z_h \\ z_0 \\ ... \\ z_{d_i} \\ ... \\ z_{f_1-1} \end{bmatrix} = sigmoid(U \begin{bmatrix} h' \\ H^0_{i,j} \\ ... \\ H^0_{i,j+d_i} \\ ... \\ H^0_{i,j+f_1-1} \end{bmatrix}) \tag{9}$$

where $U \in R_{(f_1+1)d*(f_1+1)d}$ and the new activation h' is computed as:

$$h^{'} = tanh(W \begin{bmatrix} r_0 \odot H_{i,j}^0 \\ ... \\ r_{d_i} \odot H_{i,j+d_i}^0 \\ ... \\ r_{f_1-1} \odot H_{i,j+f_1-1}^0 \end{bmatrix}) \tag{10}$$

where $W \in R_{d*f_1d}$ and $r_0, ..., r_{f_1-1}$ are reset gates for inputs, which can be formalized as:

$$\begin{bmatrix} r_0 \\ ... \\ r_{d_i} \\ ... \\ r_{f_1-1} \end{bmatrix} = sigmoid(G \begin{bmatrix} H_{i,j}^0 \\ ... \\ H_{i,j+d_i}^0 \\ ... \\ H_{i,j+f_1-1}^0 \end{bmatrix}) \tag{11}$$

These operations will repeat until we get $H^l \in R^{n,1,d}$ which is reduced dimension to $H^l \in R^{n,d}$.

Decoder. The decoder is composed of bi-directional long short-term memory network (Bi-LSTM). The local features encoded by filter recursive neural networks are refined into global dependencies and then decoded to tag sequences in this stage.

4   Mini-Batch Asynchronous Parallel Learning

With the development of multicore computers, there is a growing interest in parallel techniques. Researchers have proposed several schemes [25], but most of them require locking so the speedup is limited. Asynchronous parallel learning methods without locking can maximize the speedup ratio. However, existing asynchronous parallel learning methods are mainly for sparse models. For dense models, like neural networks, asynchronous parallel learning brings gradient noises which are very common and inevitable. Read-read conflicts break the sequentiality of training procedure, read-write and write-write conflicts lead to incorrect gradients. Nevertheless, Sun [15] proved that the learning process with gradient errors can still be convergent. Motivated by that, we train our model in the asynchronous parallel way.

We find that Adam [6] is a practical method to train large neural networks. Therefore, we run the asynchronous parallel method based on Adam training algorithm.

The training algorithm is realized without any locking. For each mini-batch, we uniformly distribute it into different processors. Processors compute the increment of gradient Δw_t in parallel, where w_t is stored in a shared memory and each processor can read and update it.

Table 1. Comparisons between UGL and baselines on low-resource datasets: PKU and CTB.

Models	PKU			CTB		
	P	R	F	P	R	F
Bi-LSTM	94.1	92.6	93.3	94.2	94.5	94.3
GRNN	94.5	93.6	94.0	94.8	94.9	94.8
UGL	95.2	94.1	**94.6**	95.4	95.2	**95.3**

5   Experiments

The proposed model is evaluated on three datasets: MSR, PKU and CTB. We treat MSR as a high-resource dataset, PKU and CTB as low-resource datasets. MSR and PKU are provided by the second International Chinese Word Segmentation Bakeoff [5]. CTB is from Chinese TreeBank 8.0 and split to training and testing sets in this paper. We randomly split 10% of the training sets to development sets which are used to choose the suitable hyper-parameters. All idioms, numbers and continuous English characters are replaced to special flags. The improvements achieved by an idiom dictionary are very limited, less than 0.1% F-score on all datasets. The character embeddings are pretrained on Chinese gigaword by word2vec. All results are evaluated by F_1-score which is computed by the standard Bakeoff scoring program.

Table 2. Improvements of our proposal on low-resource datasets: PKU and CTB.

Models	PKU	CTB
Bi-LSTM	93.3	94.3
UGL	94.6	95.3
+Transfer learning	**95.6**	**95.8**
Improvement	**2.3**	**1.5**
Error rate reduction	**34.3**	**26.3**

5.1   Setup

Hyper-parameters are set according to the performance on development sets. We evaluate the mini-batch size m in a serial mode and choose $m = 16$. Similarly, the window size w is set as 5, the fixed learning rate α is set as 0.01, the dimension of character embeddings and hidden layers d is set as 100. $d = 100$ is a good balance between model speed and performance.

Inspired by Pei et al. [10], bigram features are applied to our model as well. Specifically, each bigram embedding is represented as a single vector. Bigram embeddings are initialized randomly. We ignore lots of bigram features which

Table 3. Comparisons with state-of-the-art neural networks on lower-resource datasets: PKU and CTB.

	Models	PKU			CTB		
		P	R	F	P	R	F
Unigram	Zheng et al. [26]	92.8	92.0	92.4	*	*	*
	Pei et al. [10]	94.4	93.6	94.0	*	*	*
	Cai and Zhao [1]	95.8	95.2	95.5	*	*	*
	Our work	96.0	95.1	**95.6**	95.9	95.8	**95.8**
Bigram	Pei et al. [10]	*	*	95.2	*	*	*
	Ma and Hinrichs [9]	*	*	95.1	*	*	*
	Zhang et al. [21]	*	*	95.7	*	*	*
	Our work	96.3	95.9	**96.1**	96.2	96.1	**96.2**

Table 4. Comparisons with previous traditional models on lower-resource datasets: PKU and CTB.

Models	PKU			CTB		
	P	R	F	P	R	F
Tseng [18]	*	*	95.0	*	*	*
Zhang et al. [22]	*	*	95.1	*	*	*
Zhang and Clark [23]	*	*	94.5	*	*	*
Sun et al. [17]	*	*	95.4	*	*	*
Our work	96.3	95.9	**96.1**	96.2	96.1	**96.2**

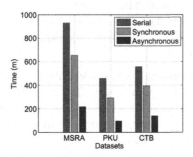

Fig. 1. Comparisons of training time among serial, synchronous and asynchronous algorithms on three datasets.

only appear once or twice since these bigram features not only are useless, but also make a bigram lookup table huge.

All experiments are performed on a commodity 64-bit Dell Precision T5810 workstation with one 3.0 GHz 16-core CPU and 64 GB RAM. The C# multiprocessing module is used in this paper.

5.2   Results and Discussions

Table 2 shows the improvement of our proposed approach. The proposed approach is compared with Bi-LSTM which is a competitive and widely used model
for neural word segmentation. Experiment results show that our proposed approach achieves substantial improvement on low-resource datasets: 2.3% and 1.5%
F-score on PKU and CTB datasets. Besides, the error rate is decreased by 34.3%
and 26.3%.

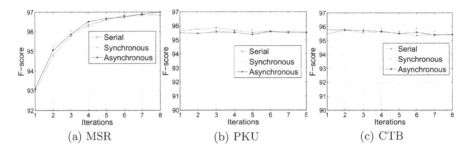

Fig. 2. Comparisons of F-score performance among serial, synchronous and asynchronous algorithms on three datasets.

Transfer Learning. The improvement of transfer learning is shown in Table 2.
We choose MSR as a high-resource dataset. Results on PKU and CTB datasets
all show improvement: 1.0% F-score on PKU dataset and 0.5% on CTB dataset.
A high-resource dataset not only decreases the number of out-of-vocabulary
words, but also improves results of in-vocabulary words. The size of PKU dataset
is far less than that of CTB dataset and we achieve the better improvement on
PKU dataset. It shows that our transfer learning method is more efficient on
datasets with lower resource.

Unified Global-Local Neural Networks. We reconstruct some of state-of-
the-art neural models in this paper: Bi-LSTM and GRNN. Table 1 shows that
our model outperforms baselines on low-resource datasets: PKU and CTB. It
proves that combining several weak features is an effective way to improve the
performance on low-resource datasets.

Comparisons with State-of-the-art Models. Table 3 shows comparisons
between our work and latest neural models on low-resource datasets: PKU and
CTB. Experiment results show that our work largely outperforms state-of-the-
art models which are very competitive. Since the dictionary used in Chen et al. [2]
is not publicly released, our work is not comparable with Chen et al. [2].

   We also compare our work with traditional models on low-resource datasets:
PKU and CTB, several of which take advantage of a variety of feature templates and dictionaries. As shown in Table 4, our work achieves state-of-the-art
results. Although our model only uses simple bigram features, it outperforms
the previous state-of-the-art methods which use more complex features.

Mini-Batch Asynchronous Parallel Learning. We run the proposed model in asynchronous, synchronous and serial modes to analyze the parallel efficiency. The number of threads used in asynchronous and synchronous modes is 15. The comparisons are shown in Figs. 1 and 2. It can be clearly seen that the asynchronous algorithm achieves the best speedup ratio without decreasing F-score compared with synchronous and serial algorithms. The asynchronous parallel algorithm is almost 5x faster than the serial algorithm.

6 Conclusions

The major problem of low-resource word segmentation is insufficient training data. Thus, we propose a transfer learning method to improve the task by leveraging high-resource datasets. Experiment results show that our work largely improves the performance on low-resource datasets compared with state-of-the-art models. Finally, our parallel training method brings substantial speedup and the training speed is almost 5x faster than a serial mode.

Acknowledgments. We thank the anonymous reviewers for their valuable comments. This work was supported in part by National High Technology Research and Development Program of China (863 Program, No. 2015AA015404), National Natural Science Foundation of China (No. 61673028).

References

1. Cai, D., Zhao, H.: Neural word segmentation learning for Chinese. In: Meeting of the Association for Computational Linguistics (2016)
2. Chen, X., Qiu, X., Zhu, C., Huang, X.: Gated recursive neural network for Chinese word segmentation. In: ACL (1), pp. 1744–1753. The Association for Computer Linguistics (2015)
3. Chen, X., Qiu, X., Zhu, C., Liu, P., Huang, X.: Long short-term memory neural networks for Chinese word segmentation. In: EMNLP, pp. 1197–1206. The Association for Computational Linguistics (2015)
4. Collobert, R., Weston, J., Bottou, L., Karlen, M., Kavukcuoglu, K., Kuksa, P.: Natural language processing (almost) from scratch. J. Mach. Learn. Res. **12**, 2493–2537 (2011)
5. Emerson, T.: The second international Chinese word segmentation bakeoff. In: Proceedings of the Fourth SIGHAN Workshop on Chinese Language Processing, pp. 123–133 (2005)
6. Kingma, D., Ba, J.: Adam: a method for stochastic optimization. Comput. Sci. (2014)
7. Lafferty, J.D., McCallum, A., Pereira, F.C.N.: Conditional random fields: probabilistic models for segmenting and labeling sequence data. In: Proceedings of the Eighteenth International Conference on Machine Learning, Number 8 in ICML 2001, pp. 282–289 (2001)
8. Liu, Y., Zhang, Y., Che, W., Liu, T., Wu, F.: Domain adaptation for CRF-based Chinese word segmentation using free annotations. In: Moschitti, A., Pang, B., Daelemans, W. (eds.) EMNLP, pp. 864–874. ACL (2014)
9. Ma, J., Hinrichs, E.W.: Accurate linear-time Chinese word segmentation via embedding matching. In: ACL (1), pp. 1733–1743 (2015)

10. Pei, W., Ge, T., Chang, B.: Max-margin tensor neural network for Chinese word segmentation. In: Proceedings of the 52nd Annual Meeting of the Association for Computational Linguistics, Baltimore, Maryland, Long Papers, vol. 1, pp. 293–303. Association for Computational Linguistics (2014)
11. Peng, F., Feng, F., McCallum, A.: Chinese segmentation and new word detection using conditional random fields. In: Proceedings of the 20th International Conference on Computational Linguistics, Stroudsburg, PA, USA, COLING 2004. Association for Computational Linguistics (2004)
12. Recht, B., Ré, C., Wright, S.J., Niu, F.: HOGWILD: a lock-free approach to parallelizing stochastic gradient descent. In: NIPS, pp. 693–701 (2011)
13. Sun, W., Xu, J.: Enhancing Chinese word segmentation using unlabeled data. In: Conference on Empirical Methods in Natural Language Processing, EMNLP 2011, 27–31 July 2011, John Mcintyre Conference Centre, Edinburgh, UK, A Meeting of SIGDAT, A Special Interest Group of the ACL, pp. 970–979 (2011)
14. Sun, X.: Structure regularization for structured prediction. In: Advances in Neural Information Processing Systems 27, pp. 2402–2410 (2014)
15. Sun, X.: Asynchronous parallel learning for neural networks and structured models with dense features. In: COLING (2016)
16. Sun, X., Li, W., Wang, H., Qin, L.: Feature-frequency-adaptive on-line training for fast and accurate natural language processing. Comput. Linguist. **40**(3), 563–586 (2014)
17. Sun, X., Wang, H., Li, W.: Fast online training with frequency-adaptive learning rates for Chinese word segmentation and new word detection. In: Proceedings of the 50th Annual Meeting of the Association for Computational Linguistics, Jeju Island, Korea, Long Papers, vol. 1, pp. 253–262. Association for Computational Linguistics (2012)
18. Tseng, H.: A conditional random field word segmenter. In: Fourth SIGHAN Workshop on Chinese Language Processing (2005)
19. Xue, N., Shen, L.: Chinese word segmentation as LMR tagging. In: Proceedings of the 2nd SIGHAN Workshop on Chinese Language Processing (2003)
20. Zhang, M., Zhang, Y., Che, W., Liu, T.: Type-supervised domain adaptation for joint segmentation and POS-tagging. In: EACL, pp. 588–597 (2014)
21. Zhang, M., Zhang, Y., Fu, G.: Transition-based neural word segmentation. In: Meeting of the Association for Computational Linguistics, pp. 421–431 (2016)
22. Zhang, R., Kikui, G., Sumita, E.: Subword-based tagging by conditional random fields for Chinese word segmentation. In: Proceedings of the Human Language Technology Conference of the NAACL, Stroudsburg, PA, USA, NAACL-Short 2006, Companion Volume, Short Papers, pp. 193–196. Association for Computational Linguistics (2006)
23. Zhang, Y., Clark, S.: Chinese segmentation with a word-based perceptron algorithm. In: Proceedings of the 45th Annual Meeting of the Association of Computational Linguistics, Prague, Czech Republic, pp. 840–847. Association for Computational Linguistics (2007)
24. Zhao, H., Huang, C., Li, M., Lu, B.-L.: A unified character-based tagging framework for Chinese word segmentation. ACM Trans. Asian Lang. Inf. Process. **9**(2), 5 (2010)
25. Zhao, K., Huang, L.: Minibatch and parallelization for online large margin structured learning. In: HLT-NAACL, pp. 370–379. The Association for Computational Linguistics (2013)
26. Zheng, X., Chen, H., Xu, T.: Deep learning for Chinese word segmentation and POS tagging. In: EMNLP, pp. 647–657. ACL (2013)

AHNN: An Attention-Based Hybrid Neural Network for Sentence Modeling

Xiaomin Zhang, Li Huang, and Hong Qu$^{(\boxtimes)}$

School of Computer Science and Engineering, University of Electronic Science
and Technology of China, Chengdu 610054, People's Republic of China
`hongqu@uestc.edu.cn`

Abstract. Deep neural networks (DNNs) are powerful models that
achieved excellent performance on many fields, especially in Nature
Language Processing (NLP). Convolutional neural networks (CNN) and
Recurrent neural networks (RNN) are two mainstream architectures of
DNNs, are wildly explored to handle NLP tasks. However, those two
type models adopt totally different ways to work. CNN is supposed to
be good at capturing local features while RNN is considered to be able to
summarize global information. In this paper, we combine the strengths
of both architectures and propose a hybird model AHNN: Attention-
based hybrid Neural Network, and use it in sentence modeling study.
The AHNN utilizes attention based bidirectional dynamic lstm to obtain
a better representation of global sentence information, then uses a parallel convolutional layer which has three different size filters and a max
pooling layer to obtain significant local information. Finally, the two
results are used together to feed into an expert layer to obtain results.
Experiments show that the proposed architecture AHNN is able to summarize the context of the sentence and capture significant local features
of sentence which is important for sentence modeling. We evaluate the
proposed architecture AHNN on NLPCC News Headline Categorization
test set and achieve 0.8098 test accuracy, it is a competitive performance
compare with other teams in this task.

Keywords: Nature Language Processing (NLP) · Sentence modeling
News Headline Categorization · Convolutional neural networks
Recurrent neural networks

1 Introduction

Sentence modeling is a fundamental task in the field of Natural Language Processing, which aims to learn low-dimensional and meaningful semantic of sentences for tasks such as news headline categorization, sentiment analysis, document summarization and so on [1]. Traditional approaches usually rely on artificial designed features or consider sentences as unordered word set [2], such as the
bag-of-words model, which leads to fail to obtain word order then fail to extract

© Springer International Publishing AG 2018
X. Huang et al. (Eds.): NLPCC 2017, LNAI 10619, pp. 731–740, 2018.
https://doi.org/10.1007/978-3-319-73618-1_63

semantic information [3,4]. Deep neural networks (DNNs) are extremely power-ful machine learning models and achieved more excellent performance on many aspects such as speech recognition [5], visual object recognition [6] and NLP tasks [7]. Convolutional neural networks (CNN) and Recurrent neural networks (RNN) are two mainstream models for NLP problem. Generally, we think CNNs are hierarchical and RNNs are sequential architectures. CNNs obtain features by stacking multiple layers which include convolution layers and pooling layers. A convolution layer consist K linear filters to extract local features then immedi-ately after a pooling layer to reduce the number of dimensions and keep features shift, rotation invariant property. However, CNN architecture has a significant limitation, since many NLP problems are expressed with sequences that lengths are unknown in advance. RNNs are able to handle sequential problems which propagate historical information via a chain-like neural network architecture, it can obtain better semantic information than CNNs. Usually, RNNs are more efficient in traditional NLP task, like Neural Machine translate (NMT) [7,9,10] and text summarization [11], etc. Recent, CNN model has great progress in NMT task, Gehring *et al.* [12] proposed a CNN-based model to acquire the state of the art BLEU (a metric of machine translation) score on a standard data.

Much prior work has exploited Deep Neural Networks in NLP tasks. Owing to the ability to capture local significant semantic features, CNN has been suc-cessfully applied on it, Kim [13] proposed a CNN architecture with multiple filters and two channels of word vectors for sentence classification. To capture word relations of varying sizes, Kalchbrenner *et al.* [14] proposed a dynamic k-max pooling mechanism. RNNs are good at handle sequence question [7] because they have a ability of explicitly modeling time-series data and deal with variable-length data. Recent years, RNNs have been used successful for image captioning [8,15] and speech recognition [16], it reveal that RNNs have strong ability to capture global information of inputs. To benefit from the advantages of both RNN and CNN, much work has been down to hybrid those two structures. zhou *et al.* [17] proposed C-LSTM which apply CNN to text data and feed consecu-tive window features directly to LSTM, this architecture enables LSTM to learn long-range dependencies from higher-order sequential features. Er *et al.* [18] pro-posed APCNN which introduced an attention pooling-based convolutional neural network for sentence modelling.

So far, we learned that CNN is able to learn local representations from tem-poral or spatial data but lacks the ability of learning sequential correlations [17] while RNN is specialized for sequential modelling but unable to extract features in a parallel way. To benefit from the advantages of both RNN and CNN, we propose a hybrid architecture neural network: Attention-based Hybrid Neural Network model (AHNN) by combining RNN and CNN to model sen-tences. We first utilize a multiple filters convolutional layer to extract significant semantic features, simultaneity, we utilize attention based bidirectional dynamic long short-term memory network to learn the primary semantic features form sentences. Then we feed these two outputs to an expert layer to get the final sentence representation. Experimental results show our model acquired 0.8098 test accuracy on NLPCC News Headline Categorization test set, indicate that our approach is effective and has a competitive performance comparable other teams in this task.

2 Background

Our work is built on CNN and attention-based RNN, they are simultaneously generate target representation in different views.

2.1 Word Representation

Word representation has been widely used in NLP task because it can map words into vectors convenient for mathematical operation, like Euclidian distance. But traditional one hot representation just a symbol and not only lose the connection between words but also too sparse. Until Bengio *et al.* propose a neural network language model [19] that could project words to a lower dimensional vector space, word representation technique has drawn a lot of attention of researchers [20–25], the most popular is Mikolov *et al.* [24] and Pennington *et al.* [25] proposed model. Those approaches can generate vector of words with similar semantic close to each other (in Euclidian distance). Like this:

$$Vec(Man) + Vec(King) - Vec(Queen) = Vec(Woman)$$

This suggest that those approach capture the both semantic and syntactic information.

To distinguish those non-semantic representation methods, technique that can generate representation vectors and keep semantic information be called word embedding. Now, word embeeding has been applied to most NLP tasks. In this paper, we used the pre-trained 200-dimensional word embedding provided by the NLPCC official.

2.2 Convolutional Neural Networks

Convolutional Neural Networks (CNN) was proposed for computer vision task initially [26] and have good performance, recently a CNN-based model has been proven to effective for sequence to sequence tasks [12]. Common CNN architecture is very simple with one convolution layer follow by one pooling layer.

Convolution layer include K filters to extract variety features. The input to a convolutional layer is a feature map $Z_i(u, v)$ where $Z_i \in R^c$, C is the number of channels. The output of convolution layer is a new feature map Z_{i+1}, obviously, $Z_{i+1} = \sigma_i(w_i z_i + b_i)$, where w_i and b_i denote the i-th filter kernel and bias respectively, σ is a activation function.

Pooling layer through feature dimensionality reduction to enhance model's robustness. There are two kinds of pooling method, one is max pooling, another is average pooling. The input of pooling layer is the feature map of convolution layer generated, max pooling operation is $h = max(z)$ and average pooling operation is $h = average(z)$.

2.3   Recurrent Neural Networks

Another underlying framework in our work is Recurrent Neural Networks (RNN). Because RNN is good at capture contextual information and handle sequence task, most NLP tasks adopt this model.

RNN reads the input sentence representation $x = (x_1, ..., x_n)$ at each time step i and generate a hidden state h_i which updates as $h_i = f(x_i, h_{i-1})$, f is a non-linear activation function may be as simple as an element-wise logistic sigmoid function and as complex as a long short-term memory (LSTM) or gated recurrent unit (GRU) [27]. To avoid the problem of gradient exploding or vanishing, most of researchers chosen the latter two.

Due to obtain better contexture information, an improvement RNN architecture proposed, which has two layers of hidden nodes named Bi-RNN [28]. As the name suggests, the Bi-RNN has two RNN stacked, one RNN gather information from first input to the last one while another gather information in reverse order.

3   The Model

Our model is a hybrid neural network architecture that has three components: parallel CNN, attention-based RNN, and an expert layer, the architecture described in Fig. 1. The parallel CNN and attention-based RNN transformed a source sentence into a list of vector, expert layer used to make a decision.

Let (X, Y) be a source sentence and label data pair, $X = (x_1, ..., x_n)$ be the sequence of n words in the source sentence would be feed into parallel CNN and attention-based RNN. Where $(c_1, ..., c_n)$ is the parallel CNN result that is the local representation in Fig. 1, and $(r_1, ..., r_n)$ is the output of attention-based RNN layer which is the intermediate representation in Fig. 2. We adopt wide

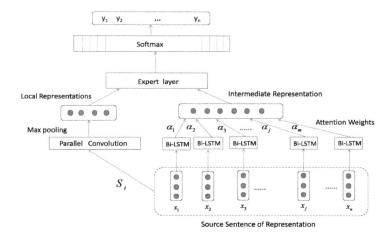

Fig. 1. Our model architecture.

convolution so that the input and output size of convolution are the same, and the hidden size of bi-LSTM is calculate as follow:

$$h = \frac{d \times p}{2} \tag{1}$$

where d is the dimension of x_i and p is the number of parallel CNN. Using those two outputs into expert layer:

$$e = W(r_1, ..., r_n) + V(c_1, ..., c_n) \tag{2}$$

where W and V are weight matrices. According the chain rule the conditional probability of the sequence $P(Y|X)$ can be decomposed as:

$$P(Y|X) = P(Y|e) = \prod_i P(Y|r_1, ..., r_n; c_1, ..., c_n) \tag{3}$$

3.1 Parallel CNN

We have described CNN with the simplest architecture that has one pooling layer after one convolution layer. Actually there have been many improvements, such as add one more convolutional layer before pooling layer to extract more abstract features or use top-K values of pooling layer to enhance robustness of model.

Our model adopted parallel CNN produces local representation, which has three convolution layers in parallel and each convolution layer has different size of filter windows, it is widely used in NLP tasks [13]. This model aims to use multi-view to learn multi types of embedding of local regions so that they can complement each other to improve model accuracy and experiments show it works well. The convolution operation is governed by:

$$C_i = g(w_i^T x_{i:i+m-1} + b_i) \tag{4}$$

where i denote number of different size of flitter windows and m denote the widows size, in our experiment $i = 3$, $m = 3,4,5$. Then we concatenated C_i as $C' = [C_1; C_2; C_3]$. After that, we conduct a max-pooling layer: $C = max(C')$ to obtain features. Experimental result shows that parallel CNN with different filter window size improves the model's learning capacity. The architecture shows in Fig. 1.

3.2 Attention-Based RNN

The first proposed attention-based neural network model is a neural machine translation model [9], it can (soft-)searched for a set of positions in source sentences when model generates a word in a translation, like people's attention. It inspired us to create an attention-based RNN layer to focus on word which has most relevant information of the class.

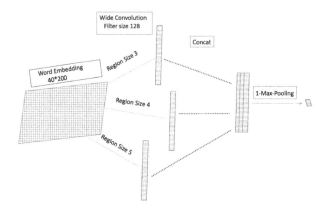

Fig. 2. Details of parallel CNN.

In our experiment, attention-based RNN layer produces intermediate representation at every time step i to obtain the global information of a source sequence that related to the class informations. The intermediate representation r depends on a sequence of annotations $h = (h_1, h_2, ..., h_n)$ which the RNN maps the input setence x and weights α_i: $r = \sum_i \alpha_i h_i$, where $h_i = [\overrightarrow{h_i^T}; \overleftarrow{h_i^T}]$ is the annotation of x_i from a bi-directional RNN to extract more complete semantic features. Thus, the intermediate representation r contains information of whole input sequence with a focus on the category information.

It should be noted that unlike the existing attention-based encoder-decoder approach in [9], here the weights α_i is computed by:

$$\alpha_i = \frac{\exp(f(w_i))}{\sum_i \exp(f(w_i))} \tag{5}$$

where w_i is common parameters which would be learned in training phrase. This mechanism can scores how well the input around time step i and the sentence label match.

3.3 Expert Layer

For news headline classification, sometimes a few words can determine its category, and sometimes must integrate the entire sentence to classify correct. Also, CNN is able to capture local significant features but lacks the ability of learning sequential correlations, and attention based Bi-LSTM can provide a better summary of the sentence information but unable to extract features in a parallel way. Ultimately, we adopt an expert layer to combine the advantages of these two models. Expert layer is efficient for systems composed of more than one separate networks and used for a long time [29]. In our experiment, the CNN layer and attention-based Bi-LSTM layer are regard as an expert respectively and we blend those results with a linear combination layer to decide how much weight to assign to each expert. To do this, the size of the Bi-LSTM hidden layer should be determined by the number of convolution filters and the number of parallel CNNs. The final error is defined as follow:

$$E = ||t - \sum_i p_i o_i||^2 \tag{6}$$

where o_i is the output vector of expert i, p_i is the contribution weight of expert i to the combined output vector, and t is the target output vector.

4 Experiment

4.1 NLPCC News Headline Categorization Task

We evaluate our AHNN model on NLPCC News Headline Categorization task. This task aims to evaluate the automatic classification techniques for very short text, i.e., Chinese news headlines. Each news headline (i.e., news title) is required to be classified into one or more predefined categories.

The official announced standards dataset to participants are three parts: train dataset (15600 sentences), develop dataset (3600 sentences) and test dataset (3600 sentences). Each data set have 18 classes. We also used the official announced three models as baseline where NBow is the best model achieved 0.783 accuracy.

4.2 Training Details

We used three pairs of CNN as parallel CNN layer, each of them has three filter windows size and all of them have 128 filters, we should note that the filter windows size and the number of feature maps may have large effects on the performance. The RNN layer has 192 cells which is decided by the filter number of CNN layer: $(3 * 128)/2$, as we note in 3.3. All the two layers used 200-dimensional word embeddings and other details are listed in Table 1. Hpyer-parameters setting inspired by [30]. Beside this, We also utilized some tricks which do help to improve accuracy in our experiment:

- **Label-Smoothing regularization** [31]: Label-smoothing technique is a useful method to handle over-fitting problems which is computed by $(1 - \varepsilon_{ls}) \times inputs + \frac{\varepsilon_{ls}}{K}$, where k is number of class, ε_{ls} is hyper-parameters we used 0.1.
- **Orthogonal initialization for recurrent neural networks:** We employed orthogonal initialization to combat exploding and vanishing gradients in RNNs, this initialization method allows gradients for backpropagate more effectively.
- **Clipping Gradients:** We applied clipping gradients by value to eliminate the effect of exploding gradient.
- **Xavier initializer for linear activations** [32]: We adopt tanh activation and initialize it with Xavier initializer which apply a properly scaled uniform distribution for initialization and more suitable for linear activations.

Table 1. Hyper-parameters adopted

Embedding size	CNN filter size	Batch size	Dropout rate	Learning rate	Decay rate
200	3,4,5	64	0.5	0.0002	0.9

4.3   Experimental Results and Discussions

We compare our approach against baseline of NLPCC and two another hybrid model CLSTM [17] and APCNN [18] on NLPCC official test set of News Headline Categorization (Table 2).

Table 2. The performance of each model on the NLPCC official test set.

Model	Micro P	Micro R	Micro F	Accuracy
LSTM	0.760	0.747	0.7497	0.747
CNN	0.769	0.763	0.764	0.763
NBOW	0.791	0.783	0.784	0.783
CLSTM	0.7767	0.7717	0.7742	0.77166
APCNN	0.7853	0.7763	0.7808	0.77633
AHNN(Ours)	**0.8102**	**0.8098**	**0.8099**	**0.80983**

We used four metrics to evaluate the quality of each model, our model performs very well, it demonstrate that our model is highly effective in improving learning capability. This is because we adopt word-level attention mechanism to improve the weights of meaningful words in sentence and introduce an expert layer to comprehensive consider the local information and summary information.

5   Conclusion

Sentence Modeling is a practical problem, also is a hot issue in NLP. Traditionally, researchers used CNN, RNN or improved architecture to model this problem. In this paper, we propose a hybrid neural network model AHNN for this task. We use parallel CNN to obtain better local information and attention-based LSTM to let the model focus on information relevant to the categorization, which is encouraged by attention-based neural machine translate model to pay attention on words that around the one is about to translate. Then, an expert layer is utilized to combine the outputs of parallel CNN and attention-based RNN to obtain better result. We test our model AHNN on the News Headline Categorization task of NLPCC and achieve 0.8098 test accuracy, that reveal the AHNN is efficient and has a competitive performance compare with other teams in this task.

Acknowledgment. This work was supported in part by the National Science Foundation of China under Grants 61573081 and the Fundamental Research Funds for Central Universities under Grant ZYGX2015J062.

References

1. He, D., Zhang, H., Hao, W., et al.: An attention-based hybrid neural network for document modeling. IEICE Trans. Inf. Syst. **100**(6), 1372–1375 (2017)
2. Bingham, E., Kabn, A., Girolami, M.: Topic identification in dynamical text by complexity pursuit. Neural Process. Lett. **17**(1), 69–83 (2003)
3. LeCun, Y., Bengio, Y., Hinton, G.: Deep learning. Nature **521**(7553), 436–444 (2015)
4. Wang, S., Manning, C.D.: Baselines and bigrams: simple, good sentiment and topic classification. In: Proceedings of the 50th Annual Meeting of the Association for Computational Linguistics: Short Papers-Volume 2. Association for Computational Linguistics, pp. 90–94 (2012)
5. Hinton, G., Deng, L., Yu, D., et al.: Deep neural networks for acoustic modeling in speech recognition: the shared views of four research groups. IEEE Sig. Process. Mag. **29**(6), 82–97 (2012)
6. Krizhevsky, A., Sutskever, I., Hinton, G.E.: ImageNet classification with deep convolutional neural networks. In: Advances in Neural Information Processing Systems, pp. 1097–1105 (2012)
7. Sutskever, I., Vinyals, O., Le, Q.V.: Sequence to sequence learning with neural networks. In: Advances in Neural Information Processing Systems, pp. 3104–3112 (2014)
8. Mao, J., Xu, W., Yang, Y., et al.: Deep captioning with multimodal recurrent neural networks (m-RNN). arXiv preprint arXiv:1412.6632 (2014)
9. Bahdanau, D., Cho, K., Bengio, Y.: Neural machine translation by jointly learning to align and translate. arXiv preprint arXiv:1409.0473 (2014)
10. Wu, Y., Schuster, M., Chen, Z., et al.: Google's neural machine translation system: bridging the gap between human and machine translation. arXiv preprint arXiv:1609.08144 (2016)
11. Zhang, Y., Er, M.J., Zhao, R., et al.: Multiview convolutional neural networks for multidocument extractive summarization. IEEE Trans. Cybern. (2016)
12. Gehring, J., Auli, M., Grangier, D., et al.: Convolutional sequence to sequence learning. arXiv preprint arXiv:1705.03122 (2017)
13. Kim, Y.: Convolutional neural networks for sentence classification. In: EMNLP (2014)
14. Kalchbrenner, N., Grefenstette, E., Blunsom, P., et al.: A convolutional neural network for modelling sentences. In: Proceedings of the 52nd Annual Meeting of the Association for Computational Linguistics. Association for Computational Linguistics, pp. 212–217 (2014)
15. Vinyals, O., Toshev, A., Bengio, S., et al.: Show and tell: a neural image caption generator. In: Proceedings of the IEEE Conference on Computer Vision and Pattern Recognition, pp. 3156–3164 (2015)
16. Graves, A., Jaitly, N.: Towards end-to-end speech recognition with recurrent neural networks. In: Proceedings of the 31st International Conference on Machine Learning (ICML2014), pp. 1764–1772 (2014)
17. Zhou, C., Sun, C., Liu, Z., et al.: A C-LSTM neural network for text classification. arXiv preprint arXiv:1511.08630 (2015)

18. Er, M.J., Zhang, Y., Wang, N., et al.: Attention pooling-based convolutional neural network for sentence modelling. Inf. Sci. **373**, 388–403 (2016)
19. Bengio, Y., Ducharme, R., Vincent, P., et al.: A neural probabilistic language model. J. Mach. Learn. Res. **3**(Feb), 1137–1155 (2003)
20. Mikolov, T., Sutskever, I., Chen, K., et al.: Distributed representations of words and phrases and their compositionality. In: Advances in neural information processing systems, pp. 3111–3119 (2013)
21. Collobert, R., Weston, J.: A unified architecture for natural language processing: deep neural networks with multitask learning. In: Proceedings of the 25th International Conference on Machine Learning. ACM, pp. 160–167 (2008)
22. Mnih, A., Hinton, G.E.: A scalable hierarchical distributed language model. In: Advances in neural information processing systems, pp. 1081–1088 (2009)
23. Turian, J., Ratinov, L., Bengio, Y.: Word representations: a simple and general method for semi-supervised learning. In: Proceedings of the 48th Annual Meeting of the Association for Computational Linguistics. Association for Computational Linguistics, pp. 384–394 (2010)
24. Mikolov, T., Chen, K., Corrado, G., Dean, J.: Efficient estimation of word representations in vector space. In: Proceedings of International Conference on Learning Representation (ICLR), Scottsdale, AZ, USA (2013)
25. Pennington, J., Socher, R., Manning, C.D.: Glove: global vectors for word representation. In: EMNLP, vol. 14, pp. 1532–1543 (2014)
26. LeCun, Y., Bottou, L., Bengio, Y., et al.: Gradient-based learning applied to document recognition. Proc. IEEE **86**(11), 2278–2324 (1998)
27. Cho, K., Van Merriënboer, B., Gulcehre, C., et al.: Learning phrase representations using RNN encoder-decoder for statistical machine translation. arXiv preprint arXiv:1406.1078 (2014)
28. Schuster, M., Paliwal, K.K.: Bidirectional recurrent neural networks. IEEE Trans. Sig. Process. **45**(11), 2673–2681 (1997)
29. Jacobs, R.A., Jordan, M.I., Nowlan, S.J., et al.: Adaptive mixtures of local experts. Neural Comput. **3**(1), 79–87 (1991)
30. Zhang, Y., Wallace, B.: A sensitivity analysis of (and practitioners' guide to) convolutional neural networks for sentence classification. arXiv preprint arXiv:1510.03820 (2015)
31. Szegedy, C., Vanhoucke, V., Ioffe, S., et al.: Rethinking the inception architecture for computer vision. In: Proceedings of the IEEE Conference on Computer Vision and Pattern Recognition, pp. 2818–2826 (2016)
32. Glorot, X., Bengio, Y.: Understanding the difficulty of training deep feedforward neural networks. In: Proceedings of the Thirteenth International Conference on Artificial Intelligence and Statistics, pp. 249–256 (2010)

Improving Chinese-English Neural Machine Translation with Detected Usages of Function Words

Kunli Zhang[1], Hongfei Xu[1], Deyi Xiong[2], Qiuhui Liu[1], and Hongying Zan[1(✉)]

[1] School of Information Engineering, Zhengzhou University,
Zhengzhou 450001, Henan, China
{ieklzhang,iehyzan}@zzu.edu.cn, hfxunlp@foxmail.com,
liuqhano@foxmail.com
[2] School of Computer Science and Technology, Soochow University,
Soochow 215006, Jiangsu, China
dyxiong@suda.edu.cn

Abstract. One of difficulties in Chinese-English machine translation is that the grammatical meaning expressed by morphology or syntax in target translations is usually determined by Chinese function words or word order. In order to address this issue, we develop classifiers to automatically detect usages of common Chinese function words based on Chinese Function usage Knowledge Base (CFKB) and initially propose a function word usage embedding model to incorporate detection results into neural machine translation (NMT). Experiments on the NIST Chinese-English translation task demonstrate that the proposed method can obtain significant improvements on the quality of both translation and word alignment over the NMT baseline.

1 Introduction

End-to-end neural machine translation has got rapid progress in recent years. Sutskever et al. (2014) used deep Long Short-Term Memory (LSTM) proposed by Hochreiter and Schmidhuber (1997) as encoder and decoder to build an NMT model. Bahdanau et al. (2014) introduced attention to NMT by jointly learning to align and translate, which improves the translation of long sentences. Luong et al. (2015) proposed a more efficient and simple attention model with input-feeding which achieves the state-of-the-art result on English-German translation. Unlike conventional SMT, NMT uses a deep neural network to model the translation procedure.

This work is partially supported by National Basic Research Program of China (2014CB340504), National Natural Science Foundation of China (No. 61402419, No. 60970083), National Social Science Foundation (No. 14BYY096), Basic research project of Science and Technology Department of Henan Province (No. 142300410231, No. 142300410308) and science and technology project of Science and Technology Department of Henan Province (No. 172102210478).

© Springer International Publishing AG 2018
X. Huang et al. (Eds.): NLPCC 2017, LNAI 10619, pp. 741–749, 2018.
https://doi.org/10.1007/978-3-319-73618-1_64

NMT has achieved better results than SMT in many language pairs, but both NMT and SMT have shown a significant gap in Chinese related translation tasks compared to other language translation. The wrong understanding of a content word may just relate to the local information around the word in the sentence, but the wrong understanding of a function word may lead to the wrong understanding of the word phrase or even the whole sentence (Lu and Ma 1999). For example:

Zài HuìJiàn JiéShù Hòu JiēShòu JìZhě CǎiFǎng Shí, BùShí MéiYǒu ZhíJiē Tán Dào YīLāKè. (*when interviewed by reporters after the meeting, bush did not mention iraq directly.*) The baseline NMT system produces the following translation:

when the meeting ended , bush did not directly discuss iraq.

Without the information of the particular usage of "**Zài**", the model does not realize that the meeting event has already happened, but after being provided with the "**Zài**"'s usage, it can generate this translation correctly:

when meeting with reporters after the meeting , bush did not directly discuss iraq.

Thus it can be seen that function words in Chinese often express and contain the syntax and semantic information of a sentence which have a crucial impact on the correct understanding of the whole sentence. Therefore, NMT may get a better result combined with common Chinese function word usages. In this paper, we select the function words in Chinese Function Usage Knowledge Base (CFKB) which are frequently used and have complex usages, including adverbs, auxiliary words, prepositions, conjunctions and modal particles, and then propose a variety of methods to incorporate their usages into NMT to improve translation quality.

2 Chinese Function Word Usages and Automatic Recognition

2.1 Chinese Function Word Usages

Chinese function words are closed. Chinese function words are far fewer but more frequently used than content words (Lv and Zhu 2002). The different usages of the same function word have a great influence on the understanding and processing of the semantic meaning of a sentence. Linguistics have researched on function words from different angles, but NLP systems need a powerful knowledge base to support it. To meet this requirement, under the guidance of Shiwen et al. (2003)'s trinity design concept, Zhang et al. (2015) constructed computational linguistics oriented Chinese Function Word usage Knowledge Base (CFKB), which contains three parts: Chinese function word dictionary which explains the details of function word usage, Chinese function word usage rule base which formalizes the function word usage, and Chinese function word usage annotated corpus which manually tags and proofreads the function word usages of 7 months' *People's Daily*. In CFKB, the semantics and usages of function word are described in detail, and the usages have been tagged in corpus, which can provide the effective basis for the usages recognition and the semantics understanding of function words.

2.2   Automatic Recognition of Chinese Function Word Usages

In this paper, we deploy a GRU (Cho et al. 2014) based model and a CRF model to automatically recognize the usages of the auxiliary word "De", adverbs "Cái", "Jiù" and "Dōu", preposition "Zài" and auxiliary word and modal particle "Le" to improve the performance of NMT. In the experiments, we select the model which has better performance from the two models for the specific function word to tag the function word usages of the NMT corpus.

We use word unigrams, bigrams and trigrams within a five-word window, combined with POS-tag and a bigram tag window as features for the CRF recognizer of usages of function words.

Compare with CRF, GRU can capture long-distance features effectively with its reset gate and update gate. We deploy a GRU model to capture features and feed the features into a linear classifier in order to achieve better performance. We concatenate the word embedding v_{d1} and its POS-tag embedding v_{d2} as the input embedding of the model to get better performance:

$$v_t = v_{d1} \oplus v_{d2}$$

Inspired by Chen et al. (2015), we use a lookahead window which contains the following two time-steps of the input sequence as the input to the model to capture bi-directional features more effectively. The input to GRU at time-step t can be formulized as:

$$\mathbf{x}_t = v_t \oplus v_{t+1} \oplus v_{t+2}$$

For example, while tagging auxiliary "De" in sequence "JǐTǐ/n De/u_de5_t2_1a LìLiàng/n./wj", the usage of "De" (noun+De+noun) can be more easily handled by foreseeing the next time-step's input. Sometimes there maybe another word like an adjective word to modify the noun. Therefore combining current time-step's input with a lookahead window with size 2 can be very helpful.

We use multi-margin criterion to train the model. It optimizes a multi-class classification hinge loss (margin-based loss) between the output of the model and the correct answer. There are only several function words in a sentence, which makes the content words give much more loss to the model than function words. To solve this problem, we reset the loss of the other words except the target function word to zero, so that the model can pay all attention to correctly recognize the usage of the function words.

The automatic recognition of function word usages experiments based on CFKB corpus. The corpus is randomly divided into training set, validation set and test set with the ratio of 9:0.5:0.5. Adam proposed by Kingma and Ba (2014) is used to train the neural models. We measure the performance of recognizing function word usages by Precision. The results are shown in Table 1. "#Usages"

Table 1. Precision of GRU and CRF

Words	GRU	CRF	#Usages
De_ud	**80.60**	74.92	37
Zài_p	68.38	**74.88**	9
Le_ul	**94.16**	91.81	7
Le_y	**95.84**	95.43	7
Jiù_d	79.15	**80.65**	20
Cái_d	**86.05**	84.79	9
Dōu_d	**90.15**	87.45	11

means the number of usages of the corresponding function word. Experiments conducted in this paper only cover a small part of Chinese function words in CFKB, because we suspect that some infrequent words are unable to receive sufficient training due to the lack of data.

3 NMT with Chinese Function Word Usages

3.1 NMT Model

Let $s = [s_1, ..., s_I]$ and $t = [t_1, ..., t_J]$ be the source and the target sentence in question, where I and J are the length of s and t. NMT will generate the most probable target sequence given the source sequence:

$$\arg\max_{t \in \mathrm{T}} p(t|s)$$

NMT model consists of an encoder neural network which reads the source language sequence and a decoder neural network that generates the target language sequence. We model the source language sequence and its function word usage sequence as well as the target language sequence at the same time. The model is trained to find the target language sequence with highest probability given the source language sequence and its function word usages sequence. Let $u = [u_1, ..., u_I]$ be the function word usage sequence of the source language sentence. The model can be formulized as:

$$\arg\max_{t \in \mathrm{T}} p(t|s; u)$$

3.2 NMT with Function Word Usages

Three embedding representation methods are proposed to add the function word usages into NMT. The first method uses the function word usages as features and gives an unique tag to the other words that are either content words or function words which are not considered in this study. The input embedding

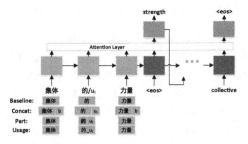

Fig. 1. Illustration of embedding representation methods

is the concatenation of the word embedding and feature embedding. We refer to this method as "concat". The second method does not give an unique tag to the other words besides the function words in our interest, but splits the embedding of a function word to two parts. The first part is its word embedding and the second part is its feature embedding. The sum of the dimension of the two parts of the function word is equal to the dimension of the other words. We call this method "part". The last method distinguishes the function words by their usages. It considers the function words with different usages as different words and trains independent word embedding for each usage. We call the third method "usage". These three representation methods are shown in Fig. 1.

4 Experiments

4.1 Settings

In this paper, both encoder and decoder are two-layers LSTM with 500 hidden units with dropout rate 0.3 between the layers. The dimension of word embedding is 500. The model is trained by Stochastic Gradient Descent (SGD) with a simple learning rate decay method. The learning rate starts with 1 and halves for every epoch. When the average loss on validation set does not change in 5 continuous epoches, we think that the model has already been sufficiently trained and stop the training scripts. It takes about 25 epoches to train a model.

4.2 Data and Results

Experiments are based on OpenNMT by Klein et al. (2017). We use 1.25M sentence pairs[1] as training set. We keep 50,000 words with higher frequency in the corpus and replace the other words with a unique "unk" tag in the experiments. We choose NIST 2006 test set as our validation set, and report the case-insensitive 4-gram NIST BLEU scores on NIST 2002 to 2006 and 2008 test

---

[1] Extracted from LDC2002E18, LDC2003E07, LDC2003E14, Hansards portion of LDC2004T07, LDC2004T08 and LDC2005T06.

Table 2. Scores for different function words

Word	Method	05	06	08	Avg.
Baseline		31.61	31.74	24.38	29.24
De_ud	Concat	**32.48**	**32.86**	24.46	**29.93**
	Usage	32.34	32.24	24.54	29.71
	Part	31.97	32.61	24.48	29.69
Zài_p	Concat	32.19	32.75	**24.85**	**29.93**
	Usage	31.92	32.30	24.18	29.47
Le_ul	concat	32.08	32.80	24.59	29.82
	Usage	31.99	32.85	24.56	29.80
Le_y	Concat	31.65	32.66	24.44	29.58
	Usage	31.96	32.23	23.79	29.33
Jiù_d	Concat	31.56	31.78	24.32	29.22
	Usage	31.45	32.44	23.84	29.24
Cái_d	Concat	32.11	32.68	24.33	29.71
	Usage	31.68	32.24	24.30	29.41
Dōu_d	Concat	31.91	32.22	24.42	29.52
	Usage	31.99	32.27	24.02	29.43

sets for the translation task. Due to the space limit, only 05, 06 and 08 results are shown in Table 2[2].

Soft Alignment Error Rate (SAER, Tu et al. 2016) is used to evaluate the alignment quality of the translation. 900 manually aligned Chinese-English sentence pairs from Liu and Sun (2015) are used as the test corpus. The results are shown in Table 3.

Chinese function word usages play a guide role for the correct understanding of the Chinese sentences and there are some examples[3] retrieved from the test sets:

1: MùQián, MǒuXiē XīFāng GuóJiā YǐJīng XuānBù ZhōngZhǐ Duì JīnBāBùWéi **De/u_de5_t2_1e** JīngJì YuánZhù. (*at present, some western nations have already announced their termination of economic aid to zimbabwe.*)

BASE: *at present, some western countries have announced their economic aid to zimbabwe.*

---

[2] We observe that the "concat" and "usage" method perform better than the "part" method in terms of both translation and alignment quality in "DE"'s experiment. Therefore we don't have the experiments of "part" method with the other function words.

[3] After the Chinese sentence is its reference translation, "BASE" means baseline model, "FNMT" means model with function word usages, text after "/" is the usage of Chinese function words.

Table 3. AER and SAER

Words	Methods	AER	SAER
Baseline		46.80	68.19
De_ud	Concat	45.58	67.17
	usage	**44.92**	**66.77**
	Part	45.97	67.09
Zài_p	Concat	45.93	67.27
	Usage	45.82	67.77
Le_ul	Concat	45.76	67.22
	Usage	45.96	67.93
Le_y	Concat	45.95	67.54
	Usage	46.79	67.63
Jiù_d	Concat	46.50	68.16
	Usage	46.61	68.26
Cái_d	Concat	45.70	67.86
	Usage	45.85	67.36
Dōu_d	Concat	46.64	68.16
	Usage	46.02	67.87

FNMT: *at present, some western countries have announced* the termination of *economic aid to zimbabwe.*

2: **Zài/p_zai4_4** ZhèGè YuánZé ZhǐDǎo Xià, Bā Yǐ ShuāngFāng 1993Nián **Zài/p_zai4_4** HuáShèngDùn QiānShǔ Le GuānYú BāJīSīTǎn LínShí ZìZhì De YuánZé XuānYán. (*under the guidance of this principle, palestine and israel have already signed a declaration in principle of palestine self-rule in washington in 1993.*)

BASE: *under this principle, the two sides signed a declaration on the principle of palestinian interim autonomy in 1993.*

FNMT: *under* the guidance of *this principle, palestine and israel signed a declaration on the* palestinian interim autonomy in washington *in 1993.*

3: DàSài Jiāng TūChū XiāngGǎng HuíGuī 5 ZhōuNián **De/u_de5_t2_1a** XǐQìng QìFēn , ChōngFèn ZhǎnShì ZhōngGuó ShūHuà **De/u_de5_t2_1a** YìShù MěiLì. (*the competition will highlight the festival atmosphere of the fifth anniversary of hongkong 's return, and fully demonstrate the charm of art of chinese traditional painting and calligraphy.*)

BASE: *the competition will highlight the celebration of the five th anniversary of hong kong 's return to the motherland and fully display the artistic charm of chinese paintings.*

FNMT: *the competition will highlight the* festive atmosphere *of hong kong 's return to the five th anniversary of the reunification of the motherland and fully demonstrate the artistic charm of chinese paintings.*

We have run the baseline experiments 10 times and report the best result in this paper to prove that the improvements are not noise. There are 7,688 sentence pairs in test sets, 5,279 sentences of which contain the auxiliary word "De", while the adverb "Dōu' only appears in 316 sentences of the whole test sets. The frequency of words may explain why the usages of some low-frequency function words fail to show an obvious effect.

5   Related Work

Chang et al. (2009) divide "De" into 4 classes by how the word "De" will be translated to and use the classes to replace "De" for SMT. Sennrich and Haddow (2016) add linguistic features to NMT by concatenating the embeddings. Tu et al. (2016) model coverage for NMT and get a significant enhancement of the translation and alignment quality. Zan and Zhu (2011) study on Chinese function word usages and construct CFKB. Zan and Zhang (2009) investigate the automatic recognition of "Cái"'s usages. Zhang and Zan (2013) research on the automatic recognition of adverb "Dōu". Zhang et al. (2012) study on the recognition of common preposition usage. Liu et al. (2017) investigate auxiliary word "De" and propose a general CRF template and a deep neural network model for the recognition of its usages.

6   Conclusion

In this paper, we have studied on how to use Chinese function word usages in NMT by various embedding representation methods. Experiment results show that Chinese function word usages can attribute to improve the quality of Chinese-English translation. Future work includes finding a better method to automatically recognize the usages of Chinese function words and adjusting CFKB for NMT task. We would also like to explore how to effectively integrate the usages of multiple function words into NMT at the same time.

Acknowledgement. We thank the anonymous reviewers for their insightful comments and suggestions.

References

Bahdanau, D., Cho, K., Bengio, Y.: Neural machine translation by jointly learning to align and translate. Comput. Sci. (2014)

Chang, P.C., Jurafsky, D., Manning, C.D.: Disambiguating "DE" for Chinese-English machine translation. In: The Workshop on Statistical Machine Translation, pp. 215–223 (2009)

Chen, X., Qiu, X., Zhu, C., Liu, P., Huang, X.: Long short-term memory neural networks for Chinese word segmentation. In: Conference on Empirical Methods in Natural Language Processing, pp. 1197–1206 (2015)

Cho, K., Van Merrienboer, B., Gulcehre, C., Bahdanau, D., Bougares, F., Schwenk, H., Bengio, Y.: Learning phrase representations using RNN encoder-decoder for statistical machine translation. Comput. Sci. (2014)

Hochreiter, S., Schmidhuber, J.: Long short-term memory. Neural Comput. 9(8), 1735–1780 (1997)

Kingma, D.P., Ba, J.: Adam: a method for stochastic optimization. Comput. Sci. (2014)

Klein, G., Kim, Y., Deng, Y., Senellart, J., Rush, A.M.: OpenNMT: open-source toolkit for neural machine translation (2017)

Liu, Q., Zhang, K., Xu, H., Zan, H., Yu, S.: Research on automatic recognition of auxiliary de. In: Proceedings of CLSW2017 (2017). (in Chinese)

Liu, Y., Sun, M.,: Contrastive unsupervised word alignment with non-local features. In: Twenty-Ninth AAAI Conference on Artificial Intelligence, pp. 2295–2301 (2015)

Lu, J.M., Ma, Z.: Scattered Essays of Modern Chinese Function Words. Language and Culture Press, Beijing (1999). (in Chinese)

Luong, M.T., Pham, H., Manning, C.D.: Effective approaches to attention-based neural machine translation. Comput. Sci. (2015)

Lv, S.X., Zhu, D.X.: Grammatical Rhetoric. Liaoning Education Press, Beijing (2002). (in Chinese)

Sennrich R., Haddow, B.: Linguistic input features improve neural machine translation, pp. 83–91 (2016)

Sutskever, I., Vinyals, O., Le, Q.V.: Sequence to sequence learning with neural networks. In: Advances in Neural Information Processing Systems, vol. 4, pp. 3104–3112 (2014)

Tu, Z., Lu, Z., Liu, Y., Liu, X., Li, H.: Modeling coverage for neural machine translation. In: Proceedings of the 54th Annual Meeting of the Association for Computational Linguistics, pp. 76–85 (2016)

Shiwen, Y., Zhu, X., Liu, Y.: Knowledge-base of generalized functional words of contemporary chinese. J. Chin. Lang. Comput. 13, 89–98 (2003)

Zan, H., Zhang, J.: Studies on automatic recognition of chinese adverb CAI's usages based on statistics. In: 2009 International Conference on Natural Language Processing and Knowledge Engineering, NLP-KE, pp. 1–5 (2009). (in Chinese)

Zan, H., Zhu, X.: Research on the chinese function word usage knowledge base. Int. J. Asian Lang. Process. 21(4), 185–198 (2011). (in Chinese)

Zhang, J., Zan, H.: Automatic recognition research on chinese adverb DOU's usages. Acta Scientiarum Naturalium Universitatis Pekinensis 49(1), 165–169 (2013). (in Chinese)

Zhang, K., Zan, H., Chai, Y., Han, Y., Zhao, D.: Survey of the Chinese function word usage knowledge base. J. Chin. Inf. Process. 29(3), 1–8 (2015). (in Chinese)

Zhang, K., Zan, H., Han, Y., Zhang, T.: Studies on automatic recognition of contemporary chinese common preposition usage. In: Ji, D., Xiao, G. (eds.) CLSW 2012. LNCS (LNAI), vol. 7717, pp. 219–229. Springer, Heidelberg (2013). https://doi.org/10.1007/978-3-642-36337-5_23

Using NMT with Grammar Information and Self-taught Mechanism in Translating Chinese Symptom and Disease Terminologies

Lu Zeng, Qi Wang$^{(\boxtimes)}$, and Lingfei Zhang

East China University of Science and Technology, Shanghai 200237, China
dsx4602@163.com

Abstract. Neural Machine Translation (NMT) based on the encoder-decoder architecture is a proposed approach to machine translation, and has achieved promising results comparable to those of traditional approaches such as statistical machine translation. However, a NMT system usually needs a large number of parallel corpora to train the model, which is difficult to get in some specific areas, e.g. symptom and disease terminologies. In this paper, we propose two approaches to make full use of the source-side monolingual data to make up the lack of parallel corpora. The first approach uses part-of-speech of source-side symptom and disease terminologies to get their grammar information. The second approach employs a self-taught learning algorithm to get more synthetic parallel data. The proposed NMT model obtains significant improvements in translating symptom and disease terminologies from Chinese into English. Improvements up to 2.13 BLEU points are gained, compared with the NMT baseline system.

Keywords: Neural Machine Translation · Seq2Seq model
Source-side monolingual data · Symptom and Disease terminologies

1 Introduction

With the rapid development of medical informatization, in order to promote international medical communication, there is an urgent need to translate Chinese symptoms and diseases into English. In addition, symptom and disease translation plays an important role in cross-lingual entity linking. As for symptom and disease terminologies, they have some characteristics which cause the difficulties of translation: (a) A symptom or a disease can be expressed by diverse textual expressions. For example, *headache* is equivalent to "头疼", "头痛" and "头部疼痛" in Chinese. More commonly, a symptom has multiple modifiers to express slightly different semantic meanings. For example, "疼痛" (pain) with different modifiers can be written as "放射性疼痛" (radiative pain) and "游走性疼痛" (wandering pain). (b) Symptoms are composable and some symptoms can be constructed as sentences instead of phrases,

© Springer International Publishing AG 2018
X. Huang et al. (Eds.): NLPCC 2017, LNAI 10619, pp. 750–759, 2018.
https://doi.org/10.1007/978-3-319-73618-1_65

such as "晚餐后饱胀感明显加重" (Abdominal floating becomes more serious after dinner).

Recently, a newly emerging approach to machine translation is proposed by Kalchbrenner and Blunsom [1], Sutskever et al. [2] and Cho et al. [3], which is called Neural Machine Translation (NMT). Most previous work on neural networks for machine translation is in the general field, which usually has a large number of parallel corpus to train NMT models. However, as for symptom and disease terminologies, it is difficult to get lots of parallel data. Thus, finding a way of using a certain number of corpora to improve the quality of machine translation becomes important. Recently, there are lots of successful cases [4–6] that adds extra information, such as monolingual target sentences or SMT features, to the model of NMT. Inspired by that, we exploit source-side monolingual data, i.e. adding part-of-speech (POS) features and synthesizing parallel corpus, to the NMT model, so as to improve the translation quality.

In this paper, we design, with simplicity and effectiveness in mind, two novel approaches added to attention-based models in translating symptom and disease terminologies from Chinese into English: One is a *feature-added* approach in which uses part-of-speech of source-side terminologies. The other one is a *scale-added* approach in which obtains more synthetic high-quality parallel data by self-taught learning algorithm. The former approach takes into account the feature of part-of-speech, which is often used in natural language processing. The latter approach first builds an attention-based NMT system as the baseline system with the available parallel corpora, then obtain more synthetic parallel data by translating the source-side monolingual symptom and disease terminologies with the baseline system and retain high-quality parallel data through obtaining the verification of a general translation software, i.e. Baidu API[1].

Experimentally, we demonstrate that both of our approaches are effective on Chinese-to-English translation in symptom and disease terminologies. Compared to the baseline model of NMT, the attention-based model with the *feature-added* approach has got 0.73 BLEU promotion, the attention-based model with the *scale-added* approach has got 2.02 BLEU promotion, and the attention-based model with both of the two approaches has got 2.13 BLEU promotion.

2   Related Work

Attention-based encoder-decoder models for machine translation have been actively investigated in recent years. Some researchers have studied how to improve attention mechanisms [7,8] and how to train attention-based models to translate between many languages [9,10].

There has been some previous work on adding useful information into the NMT model. Sennrich et al. [4] explored strategies by mixing monolingual target sentences into the training set without changing the neural network architecture to improve the translation quality of NMT systems. Gulcehre et al. [11] presented

---

[1] https://fanyi.baidu.com/translate.

a way to effectively integrate a language model (target language) into a NMT system. Zhang and Zong [5] investigated the usage of the source-side large-scale monolingual data in NMT and aim at enhancing its encoder network so that they can obtain quality context vector representations. Sennrich and Haddow [6] investigate some linguistic features that are attached to each individual words, including lemmas, subword tags, POS tags, dependency labels, etc. Note that different from Rico Sennrich et al., our method is based on characters rather than words. What's more, in addition to the POS tags, we also consider relative positions of Chinese characters in words.

For an overview of self-taught learning, there have been several uses of self-taught learning in machine translation before. Ueffing et al. [12] repeatedly translated sentences from the development set or test set and used the generated translations to improve the performance of the SMT system with a self-taught learning. Luong et al. [13] investigated multi-task learning framework, in which a simple skip-thought vectors were employed to model the monolingual data. Zhang and Zong [5] proposed a self-learning algorithm by which they can take full advantage of the source-side monolingual data. Sennrich et al. [14] use automatic back-translations of target-side monolingual corpus as synthetic training data, while in our paper, we use source-side monolingual corpus, rather than target-side monolingual corpus. We also try to select high quality synthetic parallel data to improve translation.

3   Attention-Based NMT

Given the source sentence, $x_1,...,x_n$, NMT uses a neural network approach to compute the conditional probability p(Y|X) of the target sentence, $y_1,...,y_m$. The attention-based approach proposed in [15] belongs to the encoder-decoder architecture. The whole model, including both the encoder and decoder, is jointly trained to maximize the log-likelihood of the bilingual training corpus.

The encoder of the NMT uses a pair of recurrent neural networks (RNN), which consists of forward and backward RNNs [16]. The forward RNN reads input sequence X = $(x_1,...,x_n)$ in a direction from left to right, and obtain a sequence of forward hidden states $(\overrightarrow{h_1},...,\overrightarrow{h_n})$, in which $\overrightarrow{h_j} = RNN(\overrightarrow{h_{j-1}}, x_j)$. The backward RNN reads input sequence X in an opposite direction from right to left, resulting in a sequence of backward hidden states $(\overleftarrow{h_1},...,\overleftarrow{h_n})$. Then the model concatenates forward hidden state and backward one at each time step to build a sequence of annotation vectors C = $(h_1,...,h_n)$, where $h_j = [\overrightarrow{h_j}; \overleftarrow{h_j}]$.

The decoder of the NMT uses a single layer RNN. At each time step t, the decoder using soft-alignment mechanism decides on which annotation vectors are most relevant, and the context vector c_t is obtained from the weighted sum of the annotation vectors h_j, which in turn, is computed by a feedforward neural network f, which takes h_j, the previous decoder's hidden state s_{t-1} and the previous output y_{t-1} as input: $e_{tj} = f(s_{t-1}, h_j, y_{t-1})$. The outputs e_{tj} are then normalized by softmax, and used as the alignment weight to get the context vector c_t of the t_{th} word in the translation. And the s_t is the t_{th} hidden state of the decoder and is calculated by the previous hidden state s_{t-1}, the previous output y_{t-1} and the context vector c_t. The formula is that: $s_t = RNN(s_{t-1}, y_{t-1}, c_t)$.

4   Adding POS Features of Source-Side Terminologies

In this section, we use part-of-speech to get more grammar information in symptoms and diseases, which is called *feature-added* approach. We combine Chinese character embedding and POS features together to train the model. Usually, word embedding is used as the input of NMT models. However, in this paper, we use Chinese character embedding as the input, in order to achieve better performance. As for the POS features, we propose two cases to represent. One is using One-hot Encoding for the different part-of-speech. The other is to train embedding of each part-of-speech, which we call POS-Embedding. Like training word embedding, we replace Chinese characters with the POS of the word which the character belongs to, and employ word2vec [17] to get POS-Embedding. Specifically, in addition to considering the part-of-speech, we also consider the position of POS: For the first character of a word, we add the flag "B" after its part of speech, otherwise, add the flag "I". Take "恒牙萌出明显延迟" (Marked delay in eruption of permanent teeth) as an example, which is shown in Fig. 1. After segmenting, the POS of "恒牙" (permanent teeth) is "N". For the first character "恒", its POS feature becomes "N_B", and the POS feature of the other character (i.e. "牙") becomes "N_I".

Fig. 1. Example of NMT translation using POS features

5   Adding Synthetic High-Quality Parallel Data by Self-taught Learning Algorithm

As mentioned in the previous section, the whole model, including both the encoder and decoder, is jointly trained to maximize the log-likelihood of the bilingual training corpus. If the training data is ampler, the NMT model will get a better performance. In other words, more bilingual parallel data can generate better and more robust models. However, bilingual data of symptom and disease terminologies are scarce. Hence, we want to generate more high-quality bilingual data by using the source-side terminologies which we don't have their target translation together with the parallel terminologies which we can easily obtain. After getting the synthetic high-quality bilingual data, we use the parallel data and the synthetic data to train a new model for a better translation.

A self-taught learning algorithm, which we call *scale-added* approach, is proposed to tackle the issue that the scale of parallel corpus is too small. The algorithm consists of three steps. First, we train an attention-based NMT model as the baseline system with all the available bilingual parallel data. Second, we choose source-side terminologies in some specific methods which will be introduced below, and then the baseline system automatically translates the source-side terminologies into the target language. Third, we select some high-quality target translations of source-side terminologies. After that, we regard the source-side data along with the corresponding target translation as new parallel data, which combine with the original parallel data together to train a new NMT model.

It is quite obvious that the quality of synthetic parallel data has a great impact on the NMT model, so we propose two steps to guarantee the quality of synthetic parallel data. In the first step, we only retain the synthetic source-side terminologies in which each character should appear in the original source-side parallel data. The second step stands on the view of selecting target translation: Given a source-side terminology S_s, we adopts the baseline system to generate its target translations T_p, and then use Baidu API to translate T_p into S_p, whose language is the same as S_s. We define a indicator Overlap Ratio (OLR) which is calculated by Jaccard similarity: $OLR(S_s, S_p) = \frac{|S_s \cap S_p|}{|S_s \cup S_p|}$. The selection of high-quality synthetic parallel data must satisfy the condition that the OLR is not less than the threshold θ.

6   Experimental Settings

6.1   Dataset

In this paper, we focus on the Chinese-to-English translation in symptom and disease terminologies. Some medical knowledge bases and websites can provide terminology data for us. We obtain parallel data from CHPO[2] and SNOMED CT, as well as the category of symptoms and diseases in Baidu Baike[3]. Besides, we also obtain source-side terminology data from a knowledge base of symptoms in Chinese [18]. We get 30 K unrepeated bilingual terminology pairs and 80 K unrepeated Chinese terminologies which don't have corresponding English translation. To speed up the training procedure, we remove all the terminologies whose length is over 15 words. In term of monolingual Chinese terminologies, we only retain the terminologies in which each character should appear in the source-side of the bilingual parallel data.

Preprocessing: We consider each Chinese character as a symbol, rather than segment the Chinese terminologies. It is different from other approaches which use words [5,11], and we only choose the Chinese characters which occur at least 5 times. As for the English side of the parallel terminologies, we use the tokenizer

---

[2] http://wiki.chinahpo.org/.

[3] http://baike.baidu.com/wikitag/taglist?tagId=75953/.

script from Moses decoder[4] tokenizing the terminologies and choose the English word which occurs at least 5 time. The sizes of the vocabularies for Chinese and English are 2.6 K and 3.7 K, respectively.

6.2   Train and Evaluation Details

The input and output of the model are sequences of one-hot vector whose dimensionality correspond to the size of the source and target vocabularies, respectively. Each Chinese character is projected into the continuous space of 100-dimensional Euclidean space first using word2vec [17] to reduce the dimensionality. As for the *feature-added* approach, we use Ansj[5] to segment Chinese terminologies in order to get POS features, and the sequences of characters and POS features are concatenated together as a whole sequence which is used to train the NMT model. Each model is trained using stochastic gradient decent algorithm AdaGrad [19]. The dimension of hidden layers is 1024, and the batch size of the models is 128.

In order to explore the impact of different embedding (i.e. our character embedding and others' word embedding [5,11]) trained with different corpus on translation quality, we design a contrast test with two cases using different embeddings. For Case 1, we only use the source-side terminology of parallel data to train character embedding and word embedding. For Case 2, in addition to the source-side terminology of parallel data, we also use the monolingual terminology to train embeddings. Note that the dimension of word embedding is the same as that of character embedding.

In order to explore the impact of different representations of POS features and different concat ways on translation quality, we design a contrast test with two representations of POS features using two different concat ways. For POS features, we use One-hot Encoding or POS-Embedding. The dimension of POS-Embedding is 100 which is pre-trained through word2vec. As for the concat ways, we concatenate the POS feature at the front or back of the Chinese character embedding.

In order to explore the impact of OLR, we firstly set the threshold θ to 0.75 based on experience. When finding out which corpus is better for character embedding, we secondly search for the best θ using different percentages of synthetic parallel data descending ordered by OLR.

The training set consists of 24 K bilingual terminology pairs along with 80 K Chinese terminologies which don't have corresponding English translation, and the test set consists of 6 K bilingual terminology pairs. We use case-insensitive 4-gram BLEU score as the evaluation metric [20].

6.3   Models to be Compared

In this paper, we compare four models of NMT, in which one is the baseline and the others are proposed in this paper. We list the models as follows:

---

[4] http://www.statmt.org/moses/.
[5] https://github.com/NLPchina/ansj_seg.

RNNSearch: This is the baseline of the experiment. It is an attention-based model of NMT which is proposed by Bahdanau [15].

RNNSearch-POS: This NMT model employs *feature-added* approach. It makes use of part-of-speech features besides Chinese character embedding.

RNNSearch-Scale: This NMT model employs *scale-added* approach, which makes use of the source monolingual data by applying the self-taught learning algorithm.

RNNSearch-POS-Scale: This NMT model employs both the *feature-added* approach and the *scale-added* approach.

7 Experimental Results

In this section, we will present experimental results of different models for the translation of symptom and disease terminologies.

Table 1 shows the results of the baseline model with different corpus for word embedding and character embedding. Firstly, comparing the two columns, we can observe that Case 2 has improved 2.54 BLEU in average, which means a larger corpus can obtain a better embedding. That is to say, if we use more corpus, we can get better quality of translation. Secondly, comparing the two rows, it obviously shows that character embedding has greater BLEU than word embedding, with the promotion of 7.21 BLEU in average. This is because the Chinese words are too sparse to train word embedding, and the word-level approaches may have segmentation error, which shows the necessity of our character embedding.

Table 1. Translation results (BLEU scores) of the baseline model with different corpus for word embedding and character embedding

	Case 1	Case 2
Word embedding	21.31	22.63
Character embedding	27.30	**31.06**

As for the different concat ways of the RNNSearch-POS model with character embedding, the results are presented in Table 2. Comparing the two rows, we find that concatenating the POS feature at the back of character embedding is better than those in which the POS feature is at the front of character embedding. Comparing the two columns both in Case 1 and Case 2, we find that using POS-Embedding achieves better performance than One-hot Encoding. In the following experiments, we take the setting of the best result as the default setting, i.e. set the POS-Embedding at the back of the character embedding.

Then, we provide the results of our proposed models with different corpus in Table 3. Firstly, it obviously shows that the approaches we proposed have greatly improved the quality of translation, compared with the baseline model.

Table 2. Translation results (BLEU scores) of the RNNSearch-POS model in different concat ways with different corpus using character embedding

	Case 1		Case 2	
	One-hot	POS-Embedding	One-hot	POS-Embedding
POS at the front	27.65	28.04	31.42	31.68
POS at the back	27.92	28.49	31.64	**31.79**

Particularly, the BLEU in Case 1 has greater promotion than that in Case 2, so we can conclude that the less training data for character embedding we *can* exploit, the more contribution our models have made. Secondly, comparing the four rows of Case 2, the model which employs both *feature-added* approach and *scale-added* approach performs the best among the four models. Specifically, the NMT model adopting POS features can improve 0.73 BLEU points, compared with the baseline. In addition, the NMT model using synthetic high-quality parallel data also outperform the baseline by 1.34 BLEU points. Furthermore, the RNNSearch-POS-Scale makes the most progress, with an improvement up to 1.99 BLEU points.

Table 3. Translation results (BLEU scores) of different models with different corpus

	Case 1	Case 2
RNNSearch	27.30	31.06
RNNSearch-POS	28.49 (+1.19)	31.79 (+0.73)
RNNSearch-Scale	29.64 (+2.34)	32.40 (+1.34)
RNNSearch-POS-Scale	30.47 **(+3.17)**	**33.05**(+1.99)

*The improvements brought by our models compared to the baseline score is highlighted in parentheses.

Finally, Fig. 2 shows the translation results of the four models with different percentages (descending ordered by OLR) of the synthetic parallel data whose OLR is over 0.75 (we set the threshold θ to 0.75) in Case 2. It is obvious that the RNNSearch-POS-Scale model still performs the best among the four models. In addition, when the quality of synthetic parallel data is high enough, i.e. the percentage is not too high, the more synthetic parallel data is used, the more improvements of translation can get. However, when the quality of the synthetic parallel data turns worse, the performance of translation will also get worse. For the RNNSearch-POS-Scale model, when the percentage is greater than 60%, BLEU is reduced sightly due to addition of much noisy synthetic parallel data. When the percentage is lower than 60%, we again observe a drop in BLEU, because the synthetic parallel data added becomes too less. Thus, we can conclude that the model employing both *feature-added* approach and *scale-added* approach with the top 60% (the percentage corresponds to the thresh-

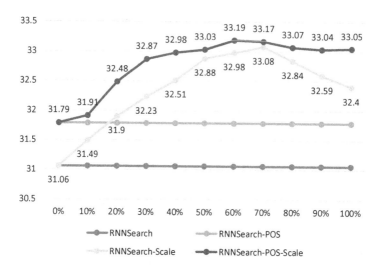

Fig. 2. Translation results (BLEU scores) of the four models with different percentages

old θ=0.87) synthetic parallel data is able to achieve the best result, with an improvement up to 2.13 BLEU points, compared to the baseline model. Besides, the RNNSearch-Scale model reaches its highest point when the percentage is 70%, whose corresponding threshold θ is 0.85, and improve the translation quality by 2.02 BLEU points, compared with the baseline model.

8   Conclusion and Future Work

In this paper, we propose two approaches to make full use of the monolingual data for NMT. The first approach is called *feature-added* approach, which uses part-of-speech of source-side terminologies of parallel data. The second approach is called *scale-added* approach. It employs the self-taught learning algorithm to get more high-quality synthetic parallel data. We empirically evaluate these approaches in translating symptom and disease terminologies from Chinese into English. The experiments show improvements in BLEU when using our approaches on small parallel data. Comparing our approaches with the baseline NMT model, the RNNSearch-POS-Scale model with the threshold θ=0.87 of the synthetic parallel data is able to achieve the best result (up to +2.13 BLEU points). In future, we attempt to apply our methods in translating symptom and disease terminologies from English into Chinese. Besides, we plan to further investigate the possibility to extend our method to other domains.

Acknowledgements. This research has been supported by the National High Technology Research and Development Program (863 Program) funded by China Ministry of Science and Technology (Program No. 2015AA020107) and the National Science Foundation of China (No. 61402173).

References

1. Kalchbrenner, N., Blunsom, P.: Recurrent continuous translation models. In: EMNLP, vol. 3, p. 413 (2013)
2. Sutskever, I., Vinyals, O., Le, Q.V.: Sequence to sequence learning with neural networks. In: Advances in Neural Information Processing Systems, pp. 3104–3112 (2014)
3. Cho, K., Van Merriënboer, B., Bahdanau, D., Bengio, Y.: On the properties of neural machine translation: encoder-decoder approaches. arXiv preprint arXiv:1409.1259 (2014)
4. Sennrich, R., Haddow, B., Birch, A.: Improving neural machine translation models with monolingual data. arXiv preprint arXiv:1511.06709 (2015)
5. Zhang, J., Zong, C.: Exploiting source-side monolingual data in neural machine translation. In: Proceedings of EMNLP (2016)
6. Sennrich, R., Haddow, B.: Linguistic input features improve neural machine translation. arXiv preprint arXiv:1606.02892 (2016)
7. Luong, M.T., Pham, H., Manning, C.D.: Effective approaches to attention-based neural machine translation. arXiv preprint arXiv:1508.04025 (2015)
8. Tu, Z., Lu, Z., Liu, Y., Liu, X., Li, H.: Modeling coverage for neural machine translation. arXiv preprint arXiv:1601.04811 (2016)
9. Dong, D., Wu, H., He, W., Yu, D., Wang, H.: Multi-task learning for multiple language translation. In: ACL (1), pp. 1723–1732 (2015)
10. Firat, O., Cho, K., Bengio, Y.: Multi-way, multilingual neural machine translation with a shared attention mechanism. arXiv preprint arXiv:1601.01073 (2016)
11. Gulcehre, C., Firat, O., Xu, K., Cho, K., Barrault, L., Lin, H.C., Bougares, F., Schwenk, H., Bengio, Y.: On using monolingual corpora in neural machine translation. arXiv preprint arXiv:1503.03535 (2015)
12. Ueffing, N., Haffari, G., Sarkar, A., et al.: Transductive learning for statistical machine translation. In: Annual Meeting-Association for Computational Linguistics, vol. 45, p. 25 (2007)
13. Luong, M.T., Le, Q.V., Sutskever, I., Vinyals, O., Kaiser, L.: Multi-task sequence to sequence learning. arXiv preprint arXiv:1511.06114 (2015)
14. Sennrich, R., Haddow, B., Birch, A.: Edinburgh neural machine translation systems for WMT 16. arXiv preprint arXiv:1606.02891 (2016)
15. Bahdanau, D., Cho, K., Bengio, Y.: Neural machine translation by jointly learning to align and translate. arXiv preprint arXiv:1409.0473 (2014)
16. Schuster, M., Paliwal, K.K.: Bidirectional recurrent neural networks. IEEE Trans. Sig. Process. **45**(11), 2673–2681 (1997)
17. Goldberg, Y., Levy, O.: word2vec explained: Deriving mikolov et al.'s negative-sampling word-embedding method. arXiv preprint arXiv:1402.3722 (2014)
18. Ruan, T., Wang, M., Sun, J., Wang, T., Zeng, L., Yin, Y., Gao, J.: An automatic approach for constructing a knowledge base of symptoms in Chinese. In: IEEE International Conference on Bioinformatics and Biomedicine, BIBM 2016, Shenzhen, China, 15–18 December 2016, pp. 1657–1662 (2016)
19. Duchi, J., Hazan, E., Singer, Y.: Adaptive subgradient methods for online learning and stochastic optimization. J. Mach. Learn. Res. **12**(Jul), 2121–2159 (2011)
20. Papineni, K., Roukos, S., Ward, T., Zhu, W.J.: BLEU: a method for automatic evaluation of machine translation. In: Proceedings of the 40th Annual Meeting on Association for Computational Linguistics, pp. 311–318. Association for Computational Linguistics (2002)

Learning Bilingual Lexicon for Low-Resource Language Pairs

ShaoLin Zhu[1,2,3], Xiao Li[1,2], YaTing Yang[1,2(✉)], Lei Wang[1,2],
and ChengGang Mi[1,2]

[1] The Xinjiang Technical Institute of Physics and Chemistry,
Chinese Academy of Sciences, Urumqi, China
yangyt@ms.xjb.ac.cn
[2] Key Laboratory of Speech Language Information Processing of Xinjiang,
Urumqi, China
[3] University of Chinese Academy of Sciences, Beijing, China

Abstract. Learning bilingual lexicon from monolingual data is a novel idea in natural language process which can benefit many low-resource language pairs. In this paper, we present an approach for obtaining bilingual lexicon from monolingual data. Our method only requires a small seed bilingual lexicon and we use the Canonical Correlation Analysis to construct a shared latent space to explain two monolingual embeddings how to be linked. Experimental results show that a considerable precision and size bilingual lexicon can be learned in Chinese-Uyghur and Chinese-Kazakh monolingual data.

1 Introduction

Bilingual lexicon is one of the most important linguistic resources for cross-lingual natural language processing, including cross-lingual information retrieval, machine translation, and annotation projection for a variety of natural language processing tasks. Naturally, the size and quality of the bilingual lexicon have a pivotal impact on these tasks (Levow et al. 2005).

Most traditional approaches use word alignment in bilingual lexicon induction (BLI), although this method has proven effective for obtaining bilingual lexicon, it relies on parallel data heavily. This method only applies to a limited number of domains between resource-rich languages. Therefore, recent studies have focused their efforts on finding word translation pairs from monolingual data, which is both significant and more challenging (Koehn and Knight 2002; Fung and Cheung 2004; Haghighi et al. 2008; Zhang et al. 2017; Vulić et al. 2016).

The surge of continuous vector representation of words, commonly known as word embeddings, has obtained a big success in many tasks (such as Language Model, Chinese Word Segmentation and Texts Classification et al.). A natural extension of interest from monolingual to multilingual word embeddings has occurred recently (Klementiev et al. 2012; Mikolov et al. 2013a; Hermann and Blunsom 2014a) when operating in multilingual settings. For example, an accurate linear transformation can be established between two monolingual embeddings spaces by using a seed lexicon (Mikolov and Sutskever 2013). Those methods show that word embeddings denoting similar semantics

X. Huang et al. (Eds.): NLPCC 2017, LNAI 10619, pp. 760–770, 2018.
https://doi.org/10.1007/978-3-319-73618-1_66

share the similar bilingual embedding space. However, this hypothesis is not always true in all language pairs. If the two languages are analogous such as English-French, English-Spanish et al. (see Fig. 1), the shared bilingual space is existing. When the two languages have a big difference such as Chinese-Uyghur, Chinese-Kazakh, a considerable bilingual lexicon can't be obtained through the shared bilingual space. In our study, we construct a latent canonical space to link the bilingual translations in order to overcome the drawbacks of existing methods (see Fig. 2 in Sect. 3).

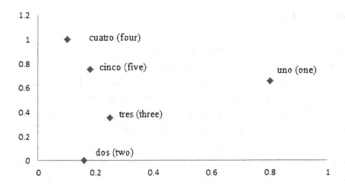

Fig. 1. Different language in a vector space

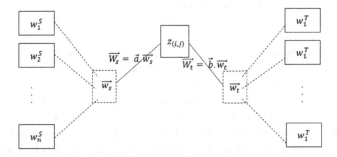

Fig. 2. Illustration of our shared latent space. Each monolingual vector can be transformed into a latent space to explain the source and target spaces how to be linked.

In our method, we only need a small seed bilingual lexicon about a few hundred entries to reveal the latent canonical space by canonical correlation analysis (CCA). Then we can obtain a big bilingual lexicon from two monolingual texts. The similarity of two embeddings in semantics is also closer in distance (Mikolov et al. 2013a). Therefore, we could reveal a few new translation pairs by connecting seeds. We also attempt to utilize them to provide further information about the two monolingual embeddings should be translated. We conduct experiments on two language pairs: Chinese-Uyghur, Chinese-Kazakh. The results show that even only a small seed lexicon and no parallel texts, a sizable set of high-precision translations can be obtained.

The mainly contribution of this paper is as follows: (i) this paper obtain bilingual lexicon from monolingual texts, to deal with the limitation of the scarce resources. (ii) We firstly induce the bilingual lexicon in Chinese-Kazakh. We explore a possible approach for the parallel corpus construction of Chinese-Kazakh for the future. (iii) our method don't need a lot of bilingual resource such as sentence-aligned parallel texts, we only need a small bilingual seed lexicon about hundreds of entries to induce a large scale bilingual lexicon from monolingual data.

2   Related Works

Many previous work attempt to learn bilingual word embeddings (Upadhyay et al. 2016). However, most of them require parallel data as the cross-lingual signal (Zou et al. 2013; Chandar et al. 2014; Hermann and Blunsom 2014; Kočiský et al. 2014; Gouws et al. 2015; Luong et al. 2015; Coulmance et al. 2015), which renders them unattractive for bilingual lexicon induction because word alignment can already find high-quality word translation pairs (Och and Ney 2003).

The current research on inducing BLI critically relies on sentence-aligned parallel data or readily available bilingual lexicons to achieve this task (e.g., to build similar representations for similar concepts in different languages such as January-januari, dog-hund or sky-hemel in English-French). We may classify the current work in four different groups:

(i)   the models that rely on hard word alignments obtained from parallel data to constrain the learning of BWEs (Klementiev et al. 2012; Zou et al. 2013; Wushouer et al. 2014);

(ii)   the models that use the alignment of parallel data at the sentence level (Kočiský et al. 2014; Hermann and Blunsom 2014a, 2014b; Chandar et al. 2014; Shi et al. 2015; Gouws et al. 2015);

(iii) the models that critically require readily available Document-aligned data (Vulić et al. 2016; Liu et al. 2013).

(iiii) the models that typically require readily available and rather large bilingual seed lexicons (Mikolov et al. 2013b; Faruqui and Dyer 2014; Xiao and Guo 2014).

The main disadvantage of previous work is the limited availability of parallel data and bilingual lexicons, resources which are scarce and/or domain-restricted for plenty of language pairs. In this work, we significantly alleviate the requirements: unlike prior work, we show that BLI may be induced solely on a small seed lexicon without any additional need for parallel data. Note that (in theory) the work from Zhang et al. (2017), Haghighi et al. (2008) may also be extended. Unlike these two models, we fully mine the context to strengthen the BLI. Our method based on the hypothesis theory that the cross-lingual semantic similar embeddings have the same context vectors. We will discuss the method in more detail in Sect. 3.

3 Methodology

This section describes our methods and implementation in detail. We firstly introduce our model and how we learn to construct the shared bilingual space. Then we will explain the matching in detail.

3.1 Model

Like most methods that learn bilingual word embeddings, we obtain this from monolingual and cross-lingual data. However, unlike the common used cross-lingual term that draws signals from parallel sentences or comparable data, our method includes a context matching term that attempts to improve bilingual word embeddings. The idea can maximize the following objective function simply:

$$\mathcal{J}(W^s, W^t) = \mathcal{J}_{mono} + \alpha \mathcal{J}_{context} + \delta \mathcal{J}_{match} \tag{1}$$

As input, we set a monolingual corpus as in a source language and a monolingual corpus in a target language. Let $V^s = (s_1, s_2, \ldots, s_n)$ donate n words appearing in the source language, the target language V^t is defined by symmetry. Based on S and T, out goal is to output a matching **m** between S and T. we represent **m** as a set of integer pairs so that (,) $\in$ **m** if the two words are matched. Where $W^s \in R^{D \times V^s}$ is the model parameters, representing D-dimensional word embeddings, while the W^T follows by symmetry. Parameters α and δ control the relative weighting of the terms.

The monolingual term $\mathcal{J}_{mono}$ ensure that similar words in each language are assigned similar embeddings and aim to capture the semantic structure of each language. Since the two corpora are non-parallel, $\mathcal{J}_{mono}$ consists of two monolingual sub-models that are independent of each other:

$$\mathcal{J}_{mono} = \mathcal{J}_{mono}^S(W^s) + \mathcal{J}_{mono}^T(W^T) \tag{2}$$

As a common practice (Gouws et al. 2015), we select the well established open-source tools Word2Vec[1] (Mikolov et al. 2013a) for our monolingual term.

The context term $\mathcal{J}_{context}$ ensures that the similar words across languages are assigned similar context embeddings, and encourages embeddings of word translation pairs. It can be achieved by applying a similarity on their vector representations:

$$\mathcal{J}_{context} = \sum \frac{Con(W^s).Con(W^T)}{|Con(W^s)|.|Con(W^T)|} \tag{3}$$

$$Con(W^s) = W_1^s + W_2^s + \ldots + W_k^s \tag{4}$$

The term $Con(W^s)$ is a context vector of the word W^s. Along with the CBOW model of Mikolov et al., a window of word is set as the context vector.

---

[1] Word2vec: https://code.google.com/p/word2vec/.

Then, we generate the match. For each matched pair of words, we need to generate the latent canonical vector that connect the source to target. The latent vector is computed form the monolingual corpus and the seed lexicon. See Sect. 3.2 for the detail inference. Our matching term is inspired by CCA (Bach and Jordan 2005). We assume that each target word in the target corpus should be matched to a single source word or a special empty word, and multiple occurrences of the same target word should all be matched to the same source word. Then we can write out our matching term:

$$\mathcal{J}_{match} = \log p\left(W_s^S, W_t^T\right) = \log \sum_m p\left(\mathbf{m}, W_s^S, W_t^T, \theta\right) \tag{5}$$

With respect to the model parameters $\theta = (\Psi_s, \Psi_t)$, The arbitrary covariance parameter Ψ_s explains the source specific variations which are not captured by W_s^S. Especially, W_s^S is the result that transformed by the CCA (see Fig. 2). $\mathcal{J}_{match}$ explains the source word and target word how can be tied. We can use the *Pearson* correlation coefficient to explain the match term. Therefore, we have:

$$p\left(\mathbf{m}, W_s^S, W_t^T, \theta\right) = corr\left(W_s^S, W_t^T\right) = \frac{cov\left(W_s^S, W_t^T\right)}{\sigma_s.\sigma_t} \tag{6}$$

where σ_s is standard deviation of W^S and $cov\left(W_s^S, W_t^T\right)$ is the arbitrary covariance. If the two words are truly translations, it will be better to explain their correlation through this.

3.2   Inference

In this section, we explain how to construct the latent space to tie the two monolingual vectors in detail. The transformation of the shared latent space is established by CCA on seed lexicon terms as the follow practice: we use the tools Word2vec and set the dimensional as 100 to train the monolingual vector. For each word vector of source language $\vec{v}_i^s$, $i = \{1, 2, \ldots, N\}$, and N is the source vocabulary size, while the target language v_i^t follows by symmetry. For the one source vector $\vec{v}_i^s = (x_1, x_2, \ldots, x_n)$, where n is the dimensional of vector. Set one target vector $\vec{v}_i^t = (y_1, y_2, \ldots, y_n)$ similarly. In order to analysis the correlation of source and target language, we assume that there are two vectors $\vec{a} = (a_1, a_2, \ldots, a_n)$ and $\vec{b} = (b_1, b_2, \ldots, b_n)$ making:

$$\vec{u} = \vec{a}^T.\vec{v}_i^s \tag{7}$$

$$\vec{v} = \vec{b}^T.\vec{v}_j^t \tag{8}$$

$$\rho_{\vec{u},\vec{v}} = corr(\vec{u}, \vec{v}) = \frac{cov(\vec{u}, \vec{v})}{\sigma_{\vec{u}}.\sigma_{\vec{v}}} \tag{9}$$

Therefore, the problem transform into searching the two vector $\vec{a}$ and $\vec{b}$ to maximize the correlation coefficient $\rho_{\vec{u},\vec{v}}$. $\sigma_{\vec{u}}$ is a standard deviation of $\vec{u}$ and $cov(\vec{u}, \vec{v})$ is the arbitrary covariance of $\vec{u}$ and $\vec{v}$. In order to maximize $\rho_{\vec{u},\vec{v}}$, we should obtain the arbitrary covariance of the source language vector $\vec{v^s}$ and target language $\vec{v^t}$. The arbitrary covariance of source vector Σ_{11}, while the target is Σ_{22}. We use Σ_{12} as arbitrary covariance of source and target vector:

$$cov(\vec{u}, \vec{v}) = \vec{a}^T.\Sigma_{12}.\vec{b} \tag{10}$$

$$corr(\vec{u}, \vec{v}) = \frac{cov(\vec{u}, \vec{v})}{\sigma_{\vec{u}}.\sigma_{\vec{v}}} = \frac{\vec{a}^T.\Sigma_{12}.\vec{b}}{\sqrt{\vec{a}^T.\Sigma_{11}.\vec{a}}.\sqrt{\vec{b}^T.\Sigma_{22}.\vec{b}}} \tag{11}$$

Our objective is maximizing $corr(\vec{u}, \vec{v})$ and the method is constructing a Lagrangian equation:

$$£ = \vec{a}^T\Sigma_{12}\vec{b} - \frac{\lambda}{2}\left(\vec{a}^T\Sigma_{11}\vec{a} - 1\right) - \frac{\theta}{2}\left(\vec{b}^T.\Sigma_{22}.\vec{b} - 1\right) \tag{12}$$

Then, we can induce[2]:

$$\Sigma_{11}^{-1}\Sigma_{12}\Sigma_{22}^{-1}\Sigma_{21}.\vec{a} = \lambda.\vec{a} \tag{13}$$

$$\Sigma_{22}^{-1}\Sigma_{21}\Sigma_{11}^{-1}\Sigma_{12}.\vec{b} = \lambda.\vec{b} \tag{14}$$

The problem can be described as searching eigenvalues and feature vector. The vectors of $\vec{a}$ and $\vec{b}$ can be obtained by steps (13) and (14). Then we can calculate the shared latent space in steps (7) and (8).

4   Experiments

In this section, we describe the dataset and experimental methodology used throughout this work. Then we present the experimental results and discussion.

4.1   Data

In our experiments, each testing system requires a source and target monolingual corpus. We use the crawler Scrapy[3] to obtain monolingual corpus from multilingual websites: Chinese-Kazakh and Chinese-Uyghur. We also retain only words that occur at least 100 times in the monolingual corpus. For the Chinese side, we first implement

---

[2] We omitted the derivation process, if you want to learn more, the work of Bach and Jordan (2005) is good for you.

[3] Scrapy: https://pypi.python.org/pypi/Scrapy/1.4.0.

OpenCC[4] to normalize characters to be simplified, and perform Chinese word segmentation using Jieba[5]. The preprocessing of Uyghur and Kazakh side involves tokenization, POS tagging, lemmatization, which are carried out by a tool developed by our team. Note that even when corpora are derived from parallel sources, no explicit use is ever made of document or sentence-level alignments. In particular, our method is robust to permutations of the sentences in the corpora. The statistics of the preprocessed data is given in Table 1.

Table 1. Statistics of dataset

Corpus	Language	#sentences number	Vocabulary size
Chinese-Uyghur	zh	453,030	161,050
	uy	355,120	117,385
Chinese-Kazakh	zh	453,030	161,050
	ka	211,140	120,600

4.2 Setup and Evaluation

Since we built a one-to-one bilingual lexicon by obtaining one-to-one translation pairs, the lexicon quality is the best reflected in the F_1 measure:

$$F_1 = \frac{Ture\ translation\ pairs}{All\ word\ pairs} \tag{15}$$

In order to carry out an objective evaluation, the best method is constructing a gold standard lexicon for reference. However, the gold standard lexicon can be found. In order to carry out the evaluation, for Chinese-Uyghur, we use a Chinese-Uyghur translation system to translate the source side vocabulary. For Chinese-Kazakh, we use a Chinese-Kazakh bilingual lexicon. Then the translations in the target language (Chinese) are queried again in the reverse direction to translate back to the source language, and those that don't match with the original source words are discarded. In order to ensure the quality of evaluation, we use a Chinese synonym lexicon to treat the synonym words as right translations. Finally, we can calculate the F_1 to measure.

We also compare our method with the existing system. The BilBOWA[6] is a state-of-the-art bilingual distributed representation learner. It was designed to obtain cross-lingual signals from parallel sentences, but this scenario does not fit the bilingual lexicon induction task. In our work, we nonetheless apply this method by treating each seed word translation pair as s parallel sentence pair.

---

[4] OpenCC: https://pypi.python.org/pypi/opencc-python/.

[5] Jieba: https://pypi.python.org/pypi/jieba/.

[6] BilBOWA: https://github.com/gouwsmeister/bilbowa.

4.3 Results and Discussion

In this section we examine how system performance varies when crucial elements are altered. The crucial elements mainly contain seed lexicon size and result size.

4.3.1 Overall Performance

In our work, we use the Chinese-Uyghur and Chinese-Kazakh seed lexicon about 500 entries. The results are given in Table 2 and the performance of our system and the BilBOWA are shown. The BilBOWA attain considerably lower performance for the two language pairs contrasting to our method. We analysis that two reasons make the poor performance:

Table 2. The statistics of two methods about two language pairs

Corpus	Methods	Lexicon size	Precision
zh-Uy	Ours	30,735	43.5%
	BilBOWA	30,735	8.6%
Ch-Ka	Ours	28,630	45.1%
	BilBOWA	28,630	7.5%

(1) The BilBOWA require parallel sentences as the seed to induce bilingual lexicon, while the fact is that the resource is very scarce for some language pairs, such as our situation. The study of Chinese-Uyghur language pair is still in the initial stage, especially the study of Chinese-Kazakh is a blind person. Our method only need a small seed lexicon (about 500 entries) and monolingual corpus, a considerable precision and size bilingual lexicon can be induced. Ours solve the harsh condition that have not parallel corpus.

(2) The harsh condition make the BilBOWA achieve a poor performance, it have to face the fact that only hundreds of translation pairs are provided. The situation result that the seed words are too few to link vocabularies of two distinct languages. However, the success of our approach demonstrates that it is actually possible to obtain a considerable precision and size bilingual lexicon from monolingual corpus.

Chinese-Uyghur and Chinese-Kazakh are low-resource language pairs with limited parallel data. In fact, many language pairs suffer this problem. Our methods don't need parallel data and only the monolingual data can obtain a considerable lexicon. The monolingual data can be attained easily from the multilingual websites.

4.3.2 Effect of Seed Lexicon Variation

All of our experiments so far need a small seed lexicon to induce the bilingual lexicon. In order to explore the affection of size of the seed lexicon, we vary the seed lexicon size to demonstrate this effect. Figure 3 shows the precisions of the tested systems for Chinese-Uyghur and Chinese-Kazakh.

From the Fig. 3, we can observe that our method both achieve a higher performance in Chinese-Uyghur and Chinese-Kazakh than BilBOWA. It appears that new

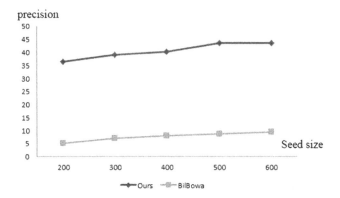

Fig. 3. Precisions of the result for Chinese-Uyghur in different seed lexicon size

word translation pairs exposed by the shared latent space for the small initial bilingual seed lexicon. As for the baseline system BilBOWA, the limited number of seeds lexicon considerably degrades performance. We analysis that BilBOWA don't expose more bilingual information by the limited numbers of seeds lexicon and it need parallel data to induce. Therefore, our method is particularly appealing in realistic resource-scarce scenarios for its limited requirement for a seed lexicon, which can be obtained easily.

4.3.3   Effect of Result Lexicon Size Variation
So far, we should note that due to lack of a gold seed lexicon, we only evaluate results indirectly. Therefore, we cannot calculate the recall rate of the result and analysis the relationship of recall rate and precision. However, we can vary the threshold to select different size of lexicon. The relationship can be present indirectly by varying the size of obtaining results. Figure 4 shows this relationship.

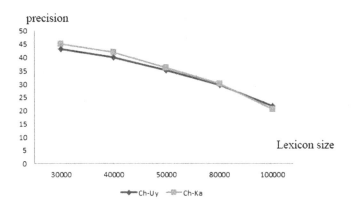

Fig. 4. Precisions in different result lexicon size

From the Fig. 4, we can observe when varying the threshold to obtain different, the precision is different. Note that varying the threshold in order to reduce the similarity to obtain more lexicon entries. It can be interpreted as increasing the size of obtaining result make the at the expense of precision. From the figure we can immediately conclude that we must discard some number of entries in order to attain a considerable precision. In this experiment, the all number of words in experimental corpus is 120,000, but we only select about 30,000 entries. However, we can obtain the precision is 43%.

5 Conclusion and Outlook

In this paper, we explore bilingual lexicon induction from monolingual data with a small seed lexicon in low-resource language pairs (Chinese-Uyghur and Chinese-Kazakh). We use the seed lexicon to construct a shared latent space to link two monolingual embeddings, then, we introduce a matching strategy to implement our learning objective. Although the harsh condition that only monolingual data and a little bilingual knowledge are provided, we show that our method still obtain a considerable bilingual lexicon.

Our current work is only initial preparation for Chinese-Uyghur and Chinese-Kazakh machine translation. We can obtain parallel sentences by constructing bilingual lexicon. In our future work, we will further explore how to train machine translation system only using non-parallel corpus.

Acknowledgments. This work is supported by the Xinjiang Fun under Grant (No. 2015KL031), the West Light Foundation of The Chinese Academy of Sciences (No. 2015-XBQN-B-10), the Xinjiang Science and Technology Major Project (No. 2016A03007-3) and Natural Science Foundation of Xinjiang (No. 2015211B034).

References

Munteanu, D.S., Marcu, D.: Improving machine translation performance by exploiting non-parallel corpora. Comput. Linguist. **31**, 477–504 (2005)

Mikolov, T., Chen, K., Corrado, G., Dean, J.: Efficient estimation of word representations in vector space. In: ICLR Workshop (2013a)

Mikolov, T., Sutskever, I., Chen, K., Corrado, G.S., Dean, J.: Distributed representations of words and phrases and their compositionality. In: NIPS (2013b)

Mikolov, T., Sutskever, I.: Distributed representations of words and phrases and their compositionality. In: Advances in Neural Information Processing Systems (2013)

Cao, H., Zhao, T., Zhang, S.: A distribution-based model to learn bilingualword embeddings. In: Proceedings of COLING (2016)

Bach, F.R., Jordan, M.I.: A probabilistic interpretation of canonical correlation analysis (2005)

Vulić, I., Moens, M.-F.: A study on bootstrapping bilingual vector spaces from non-parallel data (and nothing else). In: Proceedings of the 2013 Conference on Empirical Methods in Natural Language Processing (2013)

Gouws, S., Bengio, Y., Corrado, G.: BilBOWA: fast bilingual distributed representations without word alignments. In: JMLR (2015)

Wushouer, M., Ishida, T., Lin, D.: Bilingual dictionary induction as an optimization problem. In: International Conference on Language Resources & Evaluation (2014)

Zhang, M., Peng, H., Liu, Y.: Bilingual lexicon induction from non-parallel data with minimal supervision. In: AAAI (2017)

Haghighi, A., Liang, P., Berg-Kirkpatrick, T.: Learning bilingual lexicons from monolingual corpora. In: ACL (2008)

Shi, T., Liu, Z., Liu, Y.: Learning cross-lingual word embeddings via matrix co-factorization. In: Proceedings of the 53rd Annual Meeting of the Association for Computational Linguistics (2015)

Vulić, I., Kiela, D., Clark, S.: Multi-modal representations for improved bilingual lexicon learning. In: ACL (2016)

Vulić, I., Korhonen, A.: On the role of seed lexicons in learning bilingual word embeddings. In: ACL (2016)

Vulić, I., Moens, M.-F.: Probabilistic models of cross-lingual semantic similarity in context based on latent cross-lingual concepts induced from comparable data. In: EMNLP (2014)

Gouws, S., Søgaard, A.: Simple task-specific bilingual word embeddings. In: The 2015 Annual Conference of the North American Chapter of the ACL (2015)

Liu, X., Duh, K., Matsumoto, Y.: Topic models + word alignment = a flexible framework for extracting bilingual dictionary from comparable corpus (2013)

Exploring the Impact of Linguistic Features for Chinese Readability Assessment

Xinying Qiu[1], Kebin Deng[2(⊠)], Likun Qiu[3], and Xin Wang[4]

[1] Guangdong University of Foreign Studies, Guangzhou, China
[2] South China University of Technology, Guangzhou, China
ecdengkb@scut.edu.cn
[3] Ludong Univeristy, Yantan, China
[4] Southwestern University of Finance and Economics, Chengdu, China

Abstract. Readability assessment plays an important role in selecting proper reading materials for language learners, and is applicable for many NLP tasks such as text simplification and document summarization. In this study, we designed 100 factors to systematically evaluate the impact of four levels of linguistic features (shallow, POS, syntactic, discourse) on predicting text difficulty for L1 Chinese learners. We further selected 22 significant features with regression. Our experiment results show that the 100-feature model and the 22-feature model both achieve the same predictive accuracies as the BOW baseline for the majority of the text difficulty levels, and significantly better than baseline for the others. Using 18 out of the 22 features, we derived one of the first readability formulas for contemporary simplified Chinese language.

Keywords: Automatic Readability Assessment · Feature selection

1 Introduction

Automatic Readability Assessment (ARA) is a process to evaluate the reading difficulty level of a piece of text. It has been an active area of research in computational linguistics over the past two decades. Readability assessment can support not only the selection of proper reading materials for L1 and L2 language learners, but also the evaluation of the complexity of documents in specialized domains such as news, contracts, and information disclosure. ARA is also an important technology applicable for many NLP tasks such as text simplification, web page classification, and document summarization.

Traditional measures of text readability focus on vocabulary and syntactic aspects of text complexity. More recent research development incorporates other research perspectives including discourse structure [1], and cohesion [2], resulting in a wide range of supervised machine learning models that used both theory driven and data driven features [3, 4]. Computational approaches to readability assessment are generally built and evaluated using gold standard corpora labeled by publishers or teachers. Other research uses eye tracking variables such as fixation count, and second pass reading duration [5].

© Springer International Publishing AG 2018
X. Huang et al. (Eds.): NLPCC 2017, LNAI 10619, pp. 771–783, 2018.
https://doi.org/10.1007/978-3-319-73618-1_67

Most of the existing work on automatic readability assessment is conducted for English, with quite a lot more work on other languages such as Swedish [6], German [7], and Japanese [8]. In contrast, research on Chinese readability assessment is quite limited for both L1 and L2 learning, where a lot more research progress is made for traditional Chinese data rather than for simplified Chinese language [3, 9, 10].

The purpose of this study is to systematically analyze the impact of linguistic features for assessing the reading difficulty level of simplified Chinese reading materials for L1 learners. More specifically, we designed 100 features at four different levels: shallow, POS, syntactic, and discourse, and apply classification models for predicting the reading levels of Chinese textbooks for elementary, junior high, and senior high school students. We further regressed these 100 features for different readability levels and selected 22 significant features. Our experiment results show that the 100 feature model and the 22 feature model both achieve the same predictive accuracies as the BOW baseline for the majority of the text difficulty levels, and significantly better than baseline for the other levels. Using 18 out of these 22 features, we derived one of the first readability formulas for contemporary simplified Chinese language.

The paper is organized as follows. Section 2 introduces related work. Section 3 discusses our research methodology, including design of linguistic features, data statistics, experiment design and evaluation. Section 4 presents the experiment results and analysis. Section 5 gives conclusions and directions for future work.

2   Related Work

The earliest readability study could be dated back to 1921 when Thorndike used the term frequency to evaluate the reading difficulty level of English text book. Since then, many research has been conducted to analyze the linguistic features at different levels for generating readability formula [11–13]. With the development of NLP technologies, more recent studies focus on building predictive models with machine learning algorithms. Tables 1 and 2 summarize these two types of approaches: formula derivation, and predictive models.

In Table 1, the most widely used Chinese readability formula is that of Yang [9]. However, Yang's formulas were based on text books in traditional Chinese. Researchers in China have tackled the problems of deriving readability formulas with simplified Chinese text materials used in mainland China [14–17]. However, many of these studies suffer from problems including extremely small sample size, research tailored for special group of users, and lack of solid experimental validation.

Table 2 presents research with NLP approaches on readability prediction for various languages. Jiang [4] proposed a graph-based classification framework with bag-of-words model and TF-IDF matrix to correlate words based on similarities on sentence-level readability. The model was evaluated on 6 grades of Chinese primary school text book, with the highest F score achieved up to 0.7889. Sung [3] evaluated 30 linguistic features and SVM classification model for predicting the readability levels of primary school text books in traditional Chinese used in Taiwan. They achieved predictive accuracies ranging from 53.62% up to 95.74%.

Table 1. Types of features used in readability formula derivation.

Authors or formula	Character	Syllables	Words	Phrases	Sentence	Text language
Flesch [11]		√			√	English
Fog Index [12]		√			√	
Flesch Index [13]		√	√			
Yang [9]	√		√		√	Traditional Chinese
荆溪昱 [10]		√			√	
孙汉银 [14]	√		√		√	Simplified Chinese
王蕾 [15]			√		√	
杨金余 [16]	√		√	√	√	
左虹等 [17]	√		√			

Table 2. Levels of features used in readability predictive models.

Authors	Shallow	Morphological	POS	Syntactic	Language model	Discourse	Text language
Feng [1]	√		√	√	√	√	English
Hancke [7]	√	√	√	√	√		German
Pilan [6]	√	√	√	√			Swedish
Todirascu [2]			√	√		√	French
Sato [8]	√				√		Japanese
Sung [3]	√		√	√		√	Traditional Chinese
Jiang [4]	√		√	√			Simplified Chinese

3   Research Methodology

Our work contributes to this line of readability prediction research using NLP and computational linguistics approaches. We evaluate our model using 6-grade of primary school text book, 3-grade of Junior High School and 1 set of Senior High School text book, in simplified Chinese. We believe this is one of the first attempts at systematically evaluating readability levels of simplified Chinese covering a wide range of text books. Unlike previous work focusing on designing and experimenting with different classification frameworks, the purpose of this study is to select and analyze the underlying linguistic features that may explain how different levels of readability may be affected, and derive readability formula for simplified Chinese.

We use bag-of-words model and SVM classifiers as our baseline model. We designed 100 features of four linguistic levels to test their contribution to readability prediction. We further filtered out 22 significant features with regression. We tested the impact of these two set of linguistic features using a 10-level and 8-level text difficulty data sets to ensure the robustness of the experiment results. Finally, we derived a formula for readability assessment with 18 significant features at 99% confidence level.

3.1 Features

We designed 100 factors covering four linguistic levels: shallow features, POS features, syntactic features, and discourse features. The definitions and categories of these features are detailed in Table 3.

Table 3. Linguistic features.

Level	Aspect	Feature definition (Bolded features are the 22 significant features)
Shallow features	*Character complexity*	1. Percentage of most-common characters per document
		2. Percentage of second-most-common characters per document
		3. Percentage of all common-characters per document
		4. Percentage of low-stroke-count characters per document
		5. Percentage of medium-stroke-count characters per document
		6. Percentage of high-stroke-count characters per document
		7. Average number of strokes per word per document
	Word complexity	**8. Average number of characters per word per document**
		9. Average number of characters per unique word per document
		10. Number of two-character words per document
		11. Percentage of two-character words per document
		12. Number of three-character words per document
		13. Percentage of three-character words per document
		14. Number of four-character words per document
		15. Percentage of four-character words per document
		16. Number of five-up-character words per document
		17. Percentage of five-up-character words per document
	Sentence complexity	**18. Average number of multi-character words per sentence**
		19. Average number of words per sentence
		20. Average number of characters per sentence
		21. Average number of characters (including punctuations, numerical, and symbols) per sentence
	Document length	**22. Number of characters per document**
		23. Number of characters (including punctuations, numerical, and symbols) per document
POS features	*Adjectives*	**24. Percentage of adjectives per document**
		25. Percentage of unique adjectives per document
		26. Number of unique adjectives per document
		27. Average number of adjectives per sentence
		28. Average number of unique adjectives per sentence

(continued)

Table 3. (*continued*)

Level	Aspect	Feature definition (Bolded features are the 22 significant features)
	Functional words	29. Percentage of functional words per document
		30. Percentage of unique functional words per document
		31. Number of unique functional words per document
		32. Average number of functional words per sentence
		33. Average number of unique functional words per sentence
	Verbs	34. Percentage of verbs per document
		35. Number of unique verbs per document
		36. Percentage of unique verbs per document
		37. Average number of verbs per sentence
		38. Average number of unique verbs per sentence
	Nouns	39. Percentage of nouns per document
		40. Number of unique nouns per document
		41. Percentage of unique nouns per document
		42. Average number of nouns per sentence
		43. Average number of unique nouns per sentence
		44. Percentage of All-Nouns per document
		45. Number of unique All-Nouns per document
		46. Percentage of unique All-Nouns per document
		47. Average number of All-Nouns per sentence
		48. Average number of unique All-Nouns per sentence
	Content words	49. Percentage of content words per document
		50. Number of unique content words per document
		51. Percentage of unique content words per document
		52. Average number of content words per sentence
		53. Average number of unique content words per sentence
	Idioms	54. Percentage of idioms per document
		55. Number of unique idioms per document
		56. Percentage of unique idioms per document
		57. Average number of idioms per sentence
		58. Average number of unique idioms per sentence
	Adverbs	59. Percentage of adverbs per document
		60. Percentage of unique adverbs per document
		61. Number of unique adverbs per document
		62. Average number of adverbs per sentence
		63. Average number of unique adverbs per sentence
Syntactic features	*Phrases*	64. Average number of noun phrases per sentence
		65. Average number of verbal phrases per sentence
		66. Total number of noun phrases per document
		67. Total number of verbal phrases per document

(*continued*)

Table 3. (*continued*)

Level	Aspect	Feature definition (Bolded features are the 22 significant features)
		68. Total number of prepositional phrases per document
		69. Average length of noun phrases per document
		70. Average length of verbal phrases per document
		71. Average length of prepositional phrases per document
	Clauses	72. Average number of sentences with clauses per document
		73. Percentage of sentences without clauses against all sentences per document
		74. Average number of clauses per sentence
	Sentences	75. Average number of sentences per document
		76. Average height of parse tree per document
Discourse features	*Entity density*	77. Total number of entities per document
		78. Total number of unique entities per document
		79. Percentage of entities per document
		80. Percentage of unique entities per document
		81. Average number of entities per sentence
		82. Average number of unique entities per sentence
		83. Percentage of named entities per document
		84. Average number of named entities per sentence
		85. Percentage of named entities against total number of entities per document
		86. Percentage of nouns per document
		87. Percentage of Not-NE nouns per document
		88. Average number of nouns per sentence
		89. Average number of Not-NE nouns per sentence
		90. Average number of Not-Entity nouns per sentence
	Cohesion	91. Percentage of conjunctions per document
		92. Number of unique conjunctions per document
		93. Percentage of unique conjunctions per document
		94. Average number of conjunctions per sentence
		95. Average number of unique conjunctions per sentence
		96. Percentage of pronouns per document
		97. Number of unique pronouns per document
		98. Percentage of unique pronouns per document
		99. Average number of pronouns per sentence
		100. Average number of unique pronouns per sentence

Shallow Features: Shallow features refer to those metrics limited to the superficial text properties, and are used in many traditional readability formulas. We designed 23 features related to character, word, sentence, and document length aspects of the Chinese text as shown in Table 3.

Character complexity: 7 features were designed to capture the character complexity of Chinese language, using the count of strokes, and the distribution of common characters.

Character Categorization by Stroke-Count: In previous research, the categorization of low, medium, and high stroke-count of characters is mainly studied for traditional Chinese [3]. One important contribution of this paper is our proposed character categorization by stroke-count for simplified Chinese. The number of strokes from our data set ranges from 1 up to 25. We calculated the frequency of unique character of the same stroke-count, and performed a histogram analysis as in Fig. 1. (We also performed similar calculation with each character's collection frequency, achieving similar results). We picked count 10 as the medium stroke-count and thus calculated stroke 5 as 25% quantile, and stroke 16 as the 75% quantile. Therefore, we define characters with stroke count between 1 and 5 inclusive as low-stroke-count characters, between 6 and 15 inclusive as medium-stroke-count, and from 16 up as high-stroke-count characters.

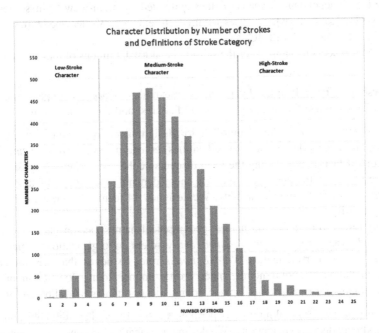

Fig. 1. Character distribution by number of strokes and definition of stroke category.

Difficult characters: We used the two lists of the most common and the second most common characters released by the State Language Commission to design features that reflect the percentage of difficult characters in the text.

The features at the *"word complexity"*, *"sentence complexity"*, and *"document length"* are quite self-explanatory. We refer readers to the definitions in Table 3.

POS Features: Part-of-speech based features have been shown to be useful in readability prediction in many languages. In some research, these features are also labeled as "semantic" or "lexical" category. We focus on 7 categories of tags: *adjectives, nouns, verbs, adverbs, idioms, functional words*, and *content words*. Among them, *content words* include nouns, verbs, numbers, adjectives, adverbs, idioms, abbreviations, quantity, pronoun, other noun-modifier, state words, foreign words, and morphemes. *Functional words* refer to conjunctions, exclamation, prefix, onomatopoeia, suffix, auxiliary, and non-lexeme. We designed a total of 40 POS features.

Syntactic Features: Parse tree features have been studied to show the grammatical complexity of text. We focus on three aspects: *phrases*, which include various factors based on noun phrases, verbal phrases, and prepositional phrases; *clauses*, which capture the complexity of the embedded structure of a sentence; and *sentence* features, which reflects the overall sentence complexity.

Clauses: The presence or absence of compound clauses and the number of clauses in a sentence can be used to reflect the structural complexity of sentences in a document. We use the "independent clause (IC)" tags annotated by multi-view Chinese treebank and parser [18] to identify the clauses within each sentence. We designed three features using clauses annotated with IC tags.

We refer readers to Table 3 for the self-explanatory definitions of these 13 syntactic features.

Discourse Features: Inspired by previous researchers' work, we implemented two types of 24 discourse features: *entity-density* features, and *cohesion* features.

Entity Density Feature: The assumption for designing entity-related feature is that entities such as general nouns and named entities serve as major information carrier and are important factors influencing the local discourse coherence. The hypothesis is that the more entities introduced in a text, the more demands they make of the readers' processing skills and memory capacity. We designed 14 features to measure the effect of entity density.

Entity refers to organization names, geographical names, person names, temporal nouns, and other proper nouns. *Named entity* refers to organization names, geographical names, person names. *Not-NE nouns* refer to nouns that are not named entities, including temporal nouns, other proper nouns, nouns, location noun, and direction noun. *Not-entity nouns* include nouns, location nouns, and direction noun.

Cohesion Feature: Psycholinguistic experiments have shown that high cohesion level within text may decrease readability. We designed 10 features in cohesive dimension to investigate its importance for assessing text readability.

3.2 Data Statistics

We collected Chinese text books from three publishers widely used for native learners covering elementary, junior high, and senior high school education. Texts of grades 1 to 6 are for elementary school education, grades 7 to 9 for Junior High School, and grade 10 for Senior High School. For retaining text of the same genre for better feature calculation and consistency in text difficulty assessment, we omitted playwrights, poetry, and classical literature. The data statistics are given in Table 4.

Table 4. Text books data statistics.

Grade	People's press	Jiangsu education press	Beijing normal univ. press	Total
1	24	35	34	93
2	66	35	46	147
3	73	47	44	164
4	76	38	41	155
5	61	50	37	148
6	60	41	62	163
7	35	37	23	95
8	42	46	48	136
9	23	28	40	91
10	32			32
Total # of Docs	498	357	375	1224

3.3 Experiments and Evaluation

Our baseline is Bag-of-Words (**BOW**) **Model** where each text is represented as a vector of 30,813 terms. We use Lib-SVM with RBF kernel and scaling to better model sparse vectors of high dimensions.

We proposed two linguistic feature models to represent documents. One is to use the 100 linguistic features (**100-Feature-Model**). Second, we performed logistic regression of the 100 features on the 10-level and 8-level data, and selected features that are significant at 99% or 95% for 10-level and/or 8-level categories. We used these 22 features only to represent each text (**22-Feature Model**). We use Lib-SVM linear classifier with no scaling of vectors for classification, LTP[1] platform for word segmentation, POS tagging, and named entity recognition, NiuParser[2] for syntactic parsing and grammatical labeling, and multi-view Chinese treebank and parser [18] for clause annotation.

We evaluate our models with two types of readability level design. One is to use the 10-level text. In a second design for robustness test, we group junior high school texts into level 7, and senior high school data as level 8. We perform 5-fold cross validation for each model. Paired-two-tailed T-test is performed to compare the differences in average predictive accuracies among the three models.

---

[1] http://www.ltp-cloud.com/.

[2] http://www.niuparser.com/.

4 Results and Analysis

In Table 5, T-test p values show that 100-Feature model achieve the same accuracies as BOW model for all levels except for level 4 and 10 where 100-Feature model performs significantly better than BOW at 90% and 99% confidence level respectively. The 22-Feature model performs equally well as the 100-Feature model, except for level 1 where the 22-Feature model performs significantly better at the 90% confidence level.

Table 5. Model average accuracy comparison for 10-level readability prediction.

Level	Average accuracy			Paired two-tailed T-test p value	
	BOW model	100-feature model	22-feature model	BOW vs 100-feature	100-feature vs 22-feature
1	93.95%	94.12%	95.35%	0.83	0.07
2	87.98%	86.86%	86.69%	0.34	0.73
3	87.17%	86.44%	86.52%	0.11	0.37
4	87.17%	87.42%	87.42%	0.07	0.99
5	87.66%	87.91%	87.83%	0.21	0.37
6	86.27%	86.68%	86.60%	0.23	0.37
7	92.88%	91.68%	91.99%	0.13	0.63
8	88.48%	88.89%	88.81%	0.22	0.37
9	92.23%	92.49%	92.48%	0.71	0.98
10	96.16%	97.71%	98.04%	0.01	0.24
Avg.	90.00%	90.02%	90.17%		

Table 6 presents results for our robustness experiment where we test the three models with 8-level text difficulty categories. Again, the 100-Feature model performs better than BOW model at level 4 and 8 (i.e. levels 4 and 10 for 10-level assessment) and the same as BOW model at all other levels. The 22-Feature model performs the same as 100-Feature model, except for level 1 where the 22-Feature models is better at 90% confidence level.

We use the 22 features to perform regression on the 10-level text data. We select 18 of them at 99% confidence level and derive readability formula as follows[3]:

$$y = -7.9291 + 1.2441x_1 + 0.0408x_2 + 1.7763x_3 + 0.7466x_4 - 29.5241x_5$$
$$+ 0.1073x_6 + 3.7729x_7 - 0.5338x_8 - 0.0677x_9 + 36.4785x_{10}$$
$$+ 1.533x_{11} - 7.7032x_{12} + 6.2422x_{13} - 5.9512x_{14} - 0.3011x_{15}$$
$$- 0.3609x_{16} + 0.3473x_{17} + 1.4679x_{18}$$

---

[3] This 18-feature formula and another 22-feature formula not presented in this paper are pending patent application.

Table 6. Model average accuracy comparison for 8-level readability prediction.

Level	Average accuracy			Paired two-tailed T-test p value	
	BOW model	100-feature model	22-feature model	BOW vs 100-feature	100-feature vs 22-feature
1	93.95%	94.12%	95.35%	0.83	0.07
2	87.98%	86.86%	86.69%	0.34	0.73
3	87.17%	86.44%	86.52%	0.11	0.37
4	87.17%	87.42%	87.42%	0.07	0.99
5	87.66%	87.91%	87.83%	0.21	0.37
6	86.27%	86.68%	86.60%	0.23	0.37
7	84.88%	83.59%	80.56%	0.57	0.19
8	96.16%	97.71%	98.04%	0.01	0.24
Avg.	88.91%	88.84%	88.63%		

such that:

x_1 : average number of unique entities per sentence

x_2 : average length of prepositional phrases per document

x_3 : percentage of sentences without clauses against all sentences per document

x_4 : average number of clauses per sentence

x_5 : percentage of unique functional words per document

x_6 : number of unique functional words per document

x_7 : percentage of unique nouns per document

x_8 : average number of unique nouns per sentence

x_9 : number of unique conjunctions per document

x_{10} : percentage of unique conjunctions per document

x_{11} : average number of conjunctions per sentence

x_{12} : average number of characters per word per document

x_{13} : average number of characters per unique word per document

x_{14} : percentage of three-character words per document

x_{15} : average number of multi-character words per sentence

x_{16} : average number of words per sentence

x_{17} : average number of characters per sentence

x_{18} : average number of strokes per word per document.

5 Conclusions

In this study, we systematically evaluate the impact of linguistic features on predicting the text difficulty of simplified Chinese. We use the elementary school, junior high school and senior high school Chinese text book as our data set. We design 100 factors covering four aspects of shallow features, POS features, syntactic features, and discourse features. In preparation for these features, we define three categories of characters by stroke counts. We further select 22 significant features.

Results show that, our 100-feature model and 22-feature model both achieve the same accuracy as the BOW model for the majority of the text difficulty level predictions, and significantly better than baseline for the other levels. The 22-Feature model can achieve an average predictive accuracy of 90.17%. These results indicate that we have captured some of the major factors that influence and explain the reading difficulty level of simplified Chinese text for L1 learners. Using 18 significant features from regression, we derived one of the first readability formulas for contemporary simplified Chinese language. We expect to extend this research for evaluating Chinese documents in other application domains.

Acknowledgements. This work was supported by National Social Science Fund (Grant No. 17BGL068). We thank Taipeng Li, Qiuxia Liu, Nankang Liang, Shuying Liu, Jiahao Wei, and workshop participants at Southwestern University of Finance and Economics for their helpful comments and support.

References

1. Feng, L.: Automatic readability assessment. Ph.D. thesis. The City University of New York (2010)
2. Todirascu, A., et al.: Are cohesive features relevant for text readability evaluation? In: Proceedings of 26th International Conference on Computational Linguistics (COLING 2016), pp. 987–997 (2016)
3. Sung, Y.T., et al.: Leveling L2 texts through readability: combining multilevel linguistic features with the CEFR. Modern Lang. J. **99**(2), 371–391 (2015)
4. Jiang, Z., et al.: A graph-based readability assessment method using word coupling. In: Proceedings of the 2015 Conference on Empirical Methods on Natural Language Processing (EMNLP 2015), pp. 411–420 (2015)
5. van Schijndel, M., Schuler, W.: Addressing surprisal deficiencies in reading time models. In: Proceedings of the Workshop on Computational Linguistics for Linguistic Complexity (CL4LC 2016), pp. 32–37 (2016)
6. Pilán, I., et al.: Predicting proficiency levels in learner writings by transferring a linguistic complexity model from expert-written coursebooks. In: Proceedings of 26th International Conference on Computational Linguistics (COLING 2016), pp. 2101–2111 (2016)
7. Hancke, J., Vajjala, S., Meurers, D.: Readability classification for German using lexical, syntactic, and morphological features. In: Proceedings of 24th International Conference on Computational Linguistics (COLING 2012), pp. 1063–1080 (2012)
8. Sato, S., et al.: Automatic assessment of Japanese text readability based on a textbook corpus. In: Proceedings of the 6th Language Resources and Evaluation Conference (LREC 2008), pp. 654–660 (2008)
9. Yang, S.: A readability formula for Chinese language. Ph.D. thesis. University of Wisconsin–Madison (1970)
10. 荆溪昱.中学国文教材的适读性研究: 适读年级值的推估.教育研究资讯, 第3期 (1995)
11. Flesch, R.: A new readability yardstick. J. Appl. Psychol. **32**(3), 221 (1948)
12. Gunning, R.: The fog index after twenty years. J. Bus. Commun. **6**(2), 3–13 (1969)
13. Kincaid, J.P., et al.: Derivation of new readability formulas for navy enlisted personnel. Naval Technical Training Command Millington TN Research Branch (1975)
14. 孙汉银. 中文易读性公式, 北京师范大学 (1992)

15. 王蕾, 初中级日韩留学生文本可读性公式初探, 北京语言大学 (2005)
16. 杨金余, 高级汉语精读教材语言难度测定研究, 北京大学 (2008)
17. 左虹,朱勇. 中级欧美留学生汉语文本可读性公式研究. 世界汉语教学 2, 263–276 (2014)
18. Qiu, L., et al.: Multi-view Chinese treebanking. In: Proceedings of 25th International Conference on Computational Linguistics (COLING 2014), pp. 257–268 (2014)

A Semantic-Context Ranking Approach for Community-Oriented English Lexical Simplification

Tianyong Hao[1(✉)], Wenxiu Xie[1], and John Lee[2]

[1] School of Information Science and Technology,
Guangdong University of Foreign Studies, Guangzhou, China
haoty@gdufs.edu.cn, vasiliky@outlook.com
[2] Department of Linguistics and Translation, City University of Hong Kong,
Kowloon Tong, Hong Kong
jsylee@cityu.edu.hk

Abstract. Lexical simplification under a given vocabulary scope for specified communities would potentially benefit many applications such as second language learning and cognitive disabilities education. This paper proposes a new concise ranking strategy for incorporating semantic and context for lexical simplification to a restricted scope. Our approach utilizes WordNet-based similarity calculation for semantic expansion and ranking. It then uses Part-of-Speech tagging and Google 1T 5-gram corpus for context-based ranking. Our experiments are based on a publicly available data sets. Through the comparison with baseline methods including Google Word2vec and four-step method, our approach achieves best F1 measure as 0.311 and Oot F1 measure as 0.522, respectively, demonstrating its effectiveness in combining semantic and context for English lexical simplification.

1 Introduction

The lexical substitution task can be used to examine the capabilities of word sense disambiguation built by researchers on a task that has potential for natural language processing applications [9]. As a task of lexical substitution, lexical simplification is used to replace the complex words and expressions of a given sentence with simpler alternatives of equivalent meaning [11], aiming to reduce the reading complexity of a sentence by incorporating a more accessible vocabulary [18]. For example, given the sentence "The Convent has been the official residence of the Governor of Gibraltar since 1728," the system may simplify the target word "residence" into "home".

Lexical simplification would be potentially useful to many applications, such as question answering, summarization, sentence generation, paraphrase acquisition, text simplification and lexical acquisition [5,10,19]. Particularly, it can potentially benefit second language learning. For example, lexical simplification has been proved to have a positive impact on EFL (English as a Foreign Language) listening comprehension at low language proficiency levels [14]. There

© Springer International Publishing AG 2018
X. Huang et al. (Eds.): NLPCC 2017, LNAI 10619, pp. 784–796, 2018.
https://doi.org/10.1007/978-3-319-73618-1_68

is increasing evidence that many secondary school graduates will need a much larger vocabulary than they have already developed if they are to undertake further study [16]. For instance, the Hong Kong Education Bureau made a vocabulary list for Basic Education and Senior Secondary Education in order to promote higher English vocabulary. Lexical simplification for the community is therefore necessary.

Accordingly, the task of lexical simplification designed for specified communities is somewhat different from the original simplification task with candidate substitute generation. Systems may not always be able to return substitution results due to the restricted scope of target restricted vocabulary. Another key problem is candidate scoring and ranking according to a given context [19]. Though existing works have reported ranking algorithms utilizing "context words as bag of words," n-grams, syntactic structures, and classifiers, e.g., [4,6,11], how to utilize semantic and context information together effectively for improving the ranking performance of substitution candidates remains a challenging research topic.

This paper proposes a concise strategy for combining both semantic and context ranking in lexical simplification for a restricted vocabulary scope. It utilizes commonly used WordNet-based semantic similarity measures, Part-of-Speech tag matching, and n-grams while concentrates on the strategies for semantic and context ranking. Our experiments are based on a publicly available dataset containing 500 manually annotated sentences. The results present that our approach outperforms baseline methods, thus demonstrates its effectiveness in community-oriented lexical simplification tasks.

2 Related Work

Lexical simplification is a challenging task as the substitution must preserve both original meaning and grammatically of the sentence being simplified [11]. It generally consists of three steps [12]. In the first step - substitution generation, it generates a list of candidate words, as $c_1, c_2, \cdots, c_n$, for the target word w, while the context of the target word is not taken into consideration. In the second step - substitution selection, it selects the best candidates to replace the target word in the given sentence. In the final step - substitution ranking, it re-ranks the candidates in terms of their simplicity.

There are a number of research and shared tasks on lexical simplification. One of the widely known tasks is SemEval Task 10, which involves a lexical sample of nouns, verbs, adjectives and adverbs. Both annotators and systems select one or more substitutes for a target word in the context of a sentence. The data were selected from the English Internet Corpus of English from the Internet without POS tags. Annotators can provide up to three substitutes, but all should be equally appropriate. They are instructed to provide a phrase if they cannot obtain a good single word substitution. They can also use a slightly more general word if it is semantically close to the target word [9]. [3] also addressed the data available difficulty in lexical simplification and proposed simple English

Wikipedia as a new text simplification task. [2] presented a strategy to learn to simplify sentences using Wikipedia. [8] proposed to improve text simplification language modeling using unsimplified text data. [6] proposed a new lexical simplifier using Wikipedia data. [20] proposed a monolingual tree-based translation model for sentence simplification. [6] included learning from aligned sentences from Wikipedia and simple Wikipedia, while [9] addressed similarity measures based on thesauri or WordNet. [1] proposed to use similarity measures and [6,15] proposed to use feature-based approach in substitution selection. However, the existing methods have two problems: (1) low performance thus are difficult for practical usage; (2) lack of effective integration of semantic and context relevance though both of the strategies have been applied.

Particularly, there is a need of lexical simplification for specified communities. The communities usually have a list of what their members would regard as "simple words." Such a word list is often compiled by the department of education for the purpose of regulating the teaching of English as a second language, or as part of a controlled language for machine translation software [13]. Furthermore, this list can be used in the substitution generation step, to filter out candidate words that are not "simple." There is seldom research about the community-oriented English lexical simplification. [7] performed lexical simplification based on 5,404 words as basic vocabulary to learn that elementary school children are expected to know. However, the work has not been compared with commonly used lexical simplification methods.

It seems that the problem of community-oriented lexical simplification restricts the substitutions into a restricted scope, which may dramatically reduce the problem difficulty. However, according to our experiments, the performance of community-oriented lexical simplification has no obvious advantages than that of common simplification tasks using the same commonly used methods. This is because the communities made simple-word list usually contains most of common easy words already. In addition, some target words are simplified to certain simple words that are not included in the simple-word list, or substitution candidates have to be selected from the list even though the candidates are not good enough. Consequently, the community-oriented lexical simplification is also a difficult task even with a relatively "smaller" vocabulary.

3   The Ranking Approach

We propose a simple approach for combining both semantic similarity and sentence fluency in selecting the best simplified word. This approach takes an English sentence as input, a target word in the sentence to be simplified, and a list of (simple) candidate words that can potentially replace the target word. First, we score the candidates according to their semantic relevance and filter out those that are semantically distant; then, we rank the candidates in terms of how well they fit the original sentence context. This is based on the consideration that lexical substitution needs to ensure the similar semantic meaning and grammatically fit to the original sentence. We mainly focus on the effective combination of the two processes.

Intuitively, semantic-based ranking and context-based ranking can be combined directly to obtain finial ranking. However, the combination strategy may dramatically affect simplification performance and efficiency. For example, the n-gram method can rank a candidate to the top even the semantic meaning of the candidate is largely different from the target word. For example, the target word "remainder" in the sentence "the remainder of the soup list evokes eastern Europe···" was commonly substituted by "end" rather than the gold answer "rest," simply because the frequency of gram "the end of" is higher. Moreover, POS labeling and matching can reduce the grammatical mismatching cases of candidate words and reduce the volume of candidate words.

Therefore, we propose a combination strategy by applying Target Word Part-of-Speech (TWPOS) matching to intentionally reduce candidates from community vocabulary (e.g., EDB list). Afterwards, we apply semantic similarity calculation, in which word Synset Part-of-Speech (SYNPOS) matching is used at the same time. Finally, we employ context relevance calculation for combination ranking. In the strategy, TWPOS and SYNPOS are mainly used for filtering candidates in unmatched POS tags, while the semantic similarity calculation and context relevance calculation are for ranking. The overall strategy is shown as Fig. 1.

TWPOS matches the POS tags of the target words in original sentences with that of candidate words for keeping the same POS tags. This is based on the consideration that any substitution word should grammatically fit the original sentence. However, in the calculation process, experimental data may lack POS tags for target words. We thus apply commonly used POS tagging tools, e.g. NLTK libraries. Though it is arguable that commonly used automated tagging methods may not ensure the annotation quality, our preliminary experiments demonstrated even simple POS tagging can benefit context-based ranking, which is further reported in the experiment section.

For a target word in a sentence, the POS of word synsets as SYNPOS is an independent factor without considering the POS of the target word TWPOS. Conventionally, each of synset pairs is calculated using similarity measures in the semantic computation of two words. However, the synset pair in different POS tags, e.g., verb and noun, can be filtered out to both reduce the occasional cases that synsets in different POS tags have high similarity and to speed up the calculation process.

In the semantic-based ranking, there are widely used open source semantic similarity measures. For example, a list of semantic similarity libraries such as Path and Wup based on WordNet is frequently applied. For a pair of words c_1 and c_2, the Path measure uses the shortest path between c_1 and c_2 while Wup measure uses the shortest path and the depth of their least common subsume in the WordNet taxonomy. The calculations using Path and Wup are shown as Eqs. (1) and (2).

$$Sim_{Path}(c_1, c_2) = \frac{1}{1 + len(c_1, c_2)} \tag{1}$$

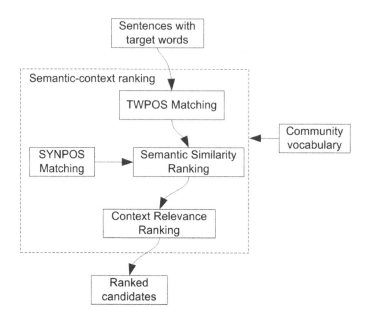

Fig. 1. The framework of our semantic-context combination ranking strategy for community-oriented lexical simplification

$$Sim_{wup}(c_1, c_2) = \frac{2dep(lcs(c_1, c_2))}{len(c_1, c_2) + 2dep(lcs(c_1, c_2))} \tag{2}$$

We thus rank the substitution candidates according to similarity through comparing with a similarity threshold ξ. The candidates with similarity lower than ξ are filtered out considering that semantic meaning equivalence is the base of lexical simplification and efficiency. The parameter tuning is shown in the experiment section.

One conventional way for context relevance ranking is to extract candidate strings as n-grams. Afterwards, the target word in the string is replaced with candidate word to calculate the probability of word in the string. In each round, every combination of string is retrieved from a reference corpus for getting its frequency. For example, for the target word "finally" in the sentence fragment, "where Mr. Larson worked finally closed last year", the extracted strings are "Larson worked finally", "worked finally closed" and "finally closed last" when n is set to 3. Accordingly, a candidate word "eventually" can be used to replace "finally" in these strings to calculate their corresponding context relevance values.

For a candidate word w_i and its target word w_t in the sentence *sen*, the rank of the candidate word is calculated by the Eqs. (3) and (4), where $Match_{tw}(w_i, w_t)$ is the binary value denoting the matching between the POS tags of w_i and w_t. $Sem(w_i, w_t)$ is the semantic similarity between the candidate word and the target word w_t while Sem_{syn} is the similarity with SYNPOS after the filtering with ξ. $Relv_{con}(w_i, sen)$ is the context fitting of the word w_i to the sentence *sen*. The $Relv_{con}$ is defined as the maximum value of the frequency of a candidate word with surrounding context divided by its maximum frequency value. Here, we apply square root to normalize the value range as the relevance value is usually small due to the large of maximum frequency. After that, we use a parameter β to balance the semantic and context relevance, where the parameter is further described in the experiment section. From the equation, the higher relevance of the candidate w_i to the target word and the sentence, the smaller of final rank value for the candidate thus the better choice for simplification.

$$R(w_i) = \frac{Match_{tw}(w_i, w_t)}{Sem_{syn}(w_i, w_t) + \beta\sqrt{Relv_{con}(w_i, sen)}} \tag{3}$$

$$Match_{tw}(w_i, w_t) = \begin{cases} 1 & pos(w_i) = pos(w_t) \\ 0 & pos(w_i) \neq pos(w_t) \end{cases} \tag{4}$$

4 Evaluation

4.1 Dataset

Our dataset is a publicly available Mechanical Turk Lexical Simplification Data Set[1], which contains 500 manually annotated sentences. The target word for every sentence is annotated by 50 independent annotators. We keep only those sentences whose target words are not in the EDB community list and whose gold answers are in the list, and name it as Dataset A. We further identify that some annotations have very small supports from human annotators. Considering the annotations as the gold answer should have more annotators' consent, we empirically set a minimum support as 20% (10 of 50) and remove all the annotations with their supports below the threshold to construct as Dataset B. Eventually, Dataset A has 249 sentences and Dataset B has 119 sentences, with 26.5 words a sentence on average.

4.2 Metrics

We apply widely used evaluation metrics: Accuracy@N, Best, and Oot (out of ten) measures [9]. Accuracy@N validates top N ($N = 1, \cdots 10$) simplification results by system and check if any of them is within gold annotations. If matched, the system results are marked as correct. The final accuracy thus is calculated as the number of correct matches divided by the total number of sentences.

Best measure acquires the credit for each correct guess (annotation) by dividing by the number of guesses. The first guess with the highest count is taken as the best guess. The measure is to evaluate how the system matches the best of human annotations. The metrics including best and Oot are represented as Eqs. (5)–(6).

---

[1] http://www.cs.pomona.edu/~dkauchak/simplification.

$$Precision_{best} = \frac{\sum_{a_i : i \in A} \frac{\sum_{res \in a_i} freqres}{|a_i|}}{|A|}, Recall_{best} = \frac{\sum_{a_i : i \in T} \frac{\sum_{res \in a_i} freqres}{|a_i|}}{|T|} \quad (5)$$

$$Precision_{oot} = \frac{\sum_{a_i : i \in A} \frac{\sum_{res \in a_i} freqres}{|H_i|}}{|A|}, Recall_{oot} = \frac{\sum_{a_i : i \in T} \frac{\sum_{res \in a_i} freqres}{|H_i|}}{|T|} \quad (6)$$

Different from Best measure, Oot measure allows a system to make up to 10 guesses. The credit for each correct guess is not divided by the number of guesses. With 10 guesses there is a better chance that the system find the responses of the gold annotations. In performance comparison, we use F1 score for both Best and Oot measure.

4.3   Baselines

Several baseline methods are implemented for performance comparison. The baselines include the widely used WordNet-based similarity measures such as Eqs. (1) and (2) without context ranking. In addition, the following state-of-the-art methods are also used as baselines.

Four-step method uses WordNet synonym based on four criteria in order, as the same baseline used in [9]. The criteria consists of (1) Synonyms from the first synset of the target word, and ranked with frequency data obtained from the BNC, (2) synonyms from the hypernyms (verbs and nouns) or closely related classes (adjectives) of the first synset, ranked with the frequency data, (3) Synonyms from all synsets of the target word, and ranked using the BNC frequency data, and (4) synonyms from the hypernyms (verbs and nouns) or closely related classes (adjectives) of all synsets of the target, ranked with the BNC frequency data.

Word2vec is a two-layer neural net to group the vectors of similar words together in vector space for calculating similarity mathematically [17]. Its input is a text corpus and its output is a set of vectors: feature vectors for words in that corpus. Word2vec creates vectors that are distributed numerical representations of word features, features such as the context of individual words. It is not a deep neural network but turns text into a numerical form that deep nets can understand.

4.4   Parameter Tuning

To optimize the similarity threshold ξ and the semantic-context ranking parameter β, we use 295 randomly selected sentences from the SemEval-2007 Task 10 dataset[2] rather than the Wikipedia dataset as the training dataset due to the limited size of the testing dataset. For each evaluation metric, we calculate the performance by setting ξ from 0.1 to 0.9 with the interval as 0.1. From the result shown in Table 1, the performance on all the measures changes slightly when ξ is from 0.5 to 0.9. Overall, the system achieves best performance when ξ equals

---

[2] http://nlp.cs.swarthmore.edu/semeval/tasks/.

Table 1. The performance using the evaluation metrics with different similarity thresholds

ξ	Accuracy										Best			Oot		
	@1	@2	@3	@4	@5	@6	@7	@8	@9	@10	P	R	F1	P	R	F1
0.1	0.193	0.322	0.386	0.424	0.495	0.505	0.536	0.536	0.539	0.566	0.103	0.103	0.103	0.370	0.370	0.370
0.2	0.193	0.319	0.380	0.424	0.488	0.512	0.536	0.536	0.536	0.569	0.118	0.118	0.118	0.371	0.371	0.371
0.3	**0.217**	**0.353**	0.383	0.444	0.485	0.502	0.508	0.525	0.556	**0.569**	**0.142**	**0.142**	**0.142**	**0.381**	**0.381**	**0.381**
0.4	0.200	0.339	**0.407**	**0.498**	**0.539**	**0.539**	**0.563**	**0.563**	**0.566**	0.566	0.114	0.114	0.114	0.368	0.368	0.368
0.5	0.203	0.349	0.386	0.431	0.492	0.495	0.505	0.515	0.515	0.515	0.131	0.127	0.129	0.358	0.345	0.351
0.6	0.203	0.349	0.386	0.431	0.492	0.495	0.505	0.515	0.515	0.515	0.131	0.127	0.129	0.358	0.345	0.351
0.7	0.203	0.349	0.386	0.431	0.492	0.495	0.505	0.515	0.515	0.515	0.131	0.127	0.129	0.358	0.345	0.351
0.8	0.203	0.349	0.386	0.431	0.492	0.495	0.505	0.515	0.515	0.515	0.131	0.127	0.129	0.358	0.345	0.351
0.9	0.203	0.349	0.386	0.431	0.492	0.495	0.505	0.515	0.515	0.515	0.131	0.127	0.129	0.358	0.345	0.351

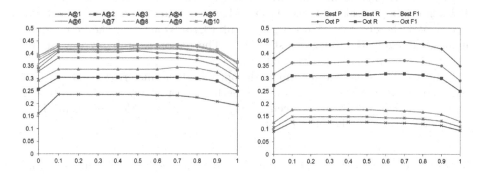

Fig. 2. The performance using the evaluation metrics with different weights β

0.3. We thus select 0.3 as the optimized value for the parameter ξ. After that, we use the same strategy to optimize the weight β by reviewing the performance change on the training dataset. As shown in Fig. 2, our approach achieves the highest performance on Accuracy@N and Best measure when β equals 0.5 but obtains highest performance on Oot measure when β equals 0.7. Considering the Best measure as priority since the correctness of the first answer is more related to user satisfaction, we thus select 0.5 as the optimized value for β.

4.5   Results

We utilize Google 1T n-gram corpus (as Grank), providing the frequencies for 1 to 5-length grams, as reference data in the calculation. Theoretically, the longer gram contains more context information and thus could be better in the representation of sentence context. We try all the gram lengths to view their performance difference on the training dataset so as to find which gram length is more appropriate. We obtain the performance using all the measures and compare their differences by using the strategies, where TWPOS and SYNPOS have not been applied to observe the direct difference compared with the original Path

Table 2. The performance comparison of different strategies using various lengths of grams from Google 1T n-gram corpus

Strategies	Accuracy										Best			Oot		
	@1	@2	@3	@4	@5	@6	@7	@8	@9	@10	P	R	F1	P	R	F1
Path	0.217	0.353	0.383	0.444	0.485	0.502	0.508	0.525	0.556	0.569	0.142	0.142	0.142	0.381	0.381	0.381
Path+Grank(1grams)	0.142	0.332	0.373	0.434	0.461	0.475	0.495	0.522	0.542	0.553	0.081	0.081	0.081	0.368	0.368	0.368
Path+Grank(2grams)	0.197	0.336	0.424	0.458	0.485	0.495	0.505	0.529	0.556	0.563	0.12	0.12	0.120	0.377	0.377	0.377
Path+Grank(3grams)	0.268	**0.393**	**0.447**	**0.471**	0.495	0.505	0.512	**0.549**	0.563	**0.58**	**0.174**	**0.174**	**0.174**	**0.388**	**0.388**	**0.388**
Path+Grank(4grams)	**0.271**	0.383	0.437	0.468	0.498	0.508	**0.532**	0.546	**0.569**	0.58	0.166	0.166	0.166	0.387	0.387	0.387
Path+Grank(5grams)	0.247	0.383	0.42	0.464	**0.502**	**0.512**	0.525	0.539	0.556	0.566	0.152	0.152	0.152	0.381	0.381	0.381

similarity. The result is shown in Table 2. From the result, Path plus Grank (1grams) or Grank (1grams) achieve worse performance compared with original Path similarity. Grank (3grams), Grank (4grams), and Grank (5grams) achieve better performance but, surprisingly, Grank (3grams) achieves the best performance, exceeding the other two strategies. The reason is probably the limited size of 4grams and 5grams in the corpus.

Afterwards, we use 3grams and all the optimized parameters ($\xi = 0.3$, $\beta = 0.5$) to compare our approach with baseline methods on the two testing datasets A and B. The final result using Accuracy@N is shown in Table 3 and using Best and Oot measures is shown in Fig. 3.

Table 3. The performance comparison with baseline methods on Dataset A and Dataset B

Dataset	Methods	Accuracy									
		@1	@2	@3	@4	@5	@6	@7	@8	@9	@10
Dataset A	Four-step method	0.217	0.265	0.321	0.333	0.357	0.369	0.373	0.382	0.382	0.382
	Word2vec	0.12	0.133	0.137	0.137	0.137	0.137	0.137	0.137	0.137	0.137
	Path	0.201	0.281	0.329	0.353	0.365	0.386	0.394	0.402	0.418	0.426
	Path+SYNPOS	0.189	0.277	0.317	0.349	0.365	0.39	0.406	0.414	0.426	0.43
	Path+TWPOS	0.173	0.265	0.305	0.325	0.333	0.357	0.365	0.365	0.382	0.386
	Path+SYNPOS+Grank	0.217	0.305	0.325	0.369	0.39	0.402	0.418	0.426	**0.438**	**0.438**
	Path+TWPOS+Grank	0.197	0.281	0.321	0.353	0.357	0.373	0.382	0.386	0.394	0.398
	Path+SYNPOS+TWPOS+Grank	**0.237**	**0.305**	**0.337**	**0.382**	**0.41**	**0.418**	**0.422**	**0.43**	0.43	0.434
Dataset B	Four-step method	0.218	0.286	0.311	0.345	0.353	0.37	0.37	0.37	0.37	0.378
	Word2vec	0.176	0.176	0.176	0.176	0.176	0.176	0.176	0.176	0.176	0.176
	Path	0.218	0.294	0.328	0.361	0.395	0.412	0.42	0.429	0.437	0.445
	Path+SYNPOS	0.193	0.294	0.328	0.353	0.387	0.412	0.42	0.429	0.445	0.454
	Path+TWPOS	0.21	0.277	0.311	0.336	0.37	0.387	0.395	0.403	0.412	0.42
	Path+SYNPOS+Grank	0.235	**0.319**	**0.37**	**0.403**	0.403	0.412	0.42	0.42	**0.454**	**0.454**
	Path+TWPOS+Grank	0.235	0.294	0.353	0.378	0.378	0.387	0.395	0.403	0.42	0.429
	Path+SYNPOS+TWPOS+Grank	**0.261**	0.311	0.361	**0.403**	**0.429**	**0.437**	**0.437**	**0.437**	0.437	0.437

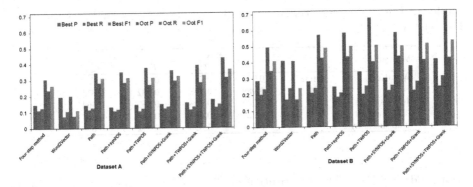

Fig. 3. The overall of our semantic-context combination ranking strategy for community-oriented lexical simplification

In the comparison, we set our ranking approach as Path+SYNPOS+ TWPOS+Grank and compared it with Four-step method, Word2vec, Path, and the strategy combinations of our approach. From the results as shown in Table 3, our approach achieves best performance on all Accuracy@N, Best and Oot measure. Compared with the Four-step method, on the Dataset A, the performance is improved with Best P from 0.145 to 0.176 (21.4%) and Best F1 from 0.126 to 0.148 (17.5%), while Oot P from 0.306 to 0.437 (42.8%) and Oot F1 from 0.266 to 0.365 (37.2%). On the Dataset B, our approach improved Best P from 0.287 to 0.416 (44.9%), Best R from 0.203 to 0.248 (22.2%), best F1 from 0.238 to 0.311(30.7%), while improved Oot P from 0.497 to 0.713 (43.5%), oot R from 0.351 to 0.425 (21.1%), Oot F1 from 0.411 to 0.533 (29.7%). Word2vec has highest Best P as 0.193 on Dataset A and the second high Best P as 0.41 on Dataset B. However, its performances using Best R and Oot measure are low, causing low overall F1 scores. The results also demonstrate that the combination ranking approach achieves much better performance than any of the individual methods.

4.6 Discussions

Word2vec is widely used for context similarity calculation. However, in our evaluation, it does not achieve expected high performance though it is more and more popular in text similarity calculation tasks. This is partially because the constructed vectors for word representation take relevant words as context rather than semantically equivalent words. For example, a candidate word "Secured_Noteholders" has relative high similarity to the target word "informal". In addition, we find some results returned by Word2vec are contradictory to the purpose of lexical simplification. For example, the candidate (checked with EDB list) with highest similarity to target word "reasonable" is "unreasonable", so as "informal" to "formal", "earlier" to "later", and "forth" to "back" in our testing. The vectors using Word2vec also contains typo cases as the typos are frequently used in the same context, e.g., "resonable" (the correct word is "reasonable")

Table 4. The performance comparison with baseline methods on Dataset A and Dataset B

Methods		Dataset A		Dataset B	
		C_{best}	C_{all}	C_{best}	C_{all}
WordNet	norvig	0.934	0.763	0.919	0.724
	LDC	**0.989**	**0.808**	**0.982**	**0.773**
4-step synsets		0.285	0.143	0.353	0.364
Path_similarity		0.727	0.648	0.664	0.667
Wup similarity		0.751	0.696	0.672	0.674

as a candidate word. The substitution of the cases may cause serious learning problem for students as either the original meaning has been changed or the learning words are in incorrectly spelled.

Viewing the coverage of the methods to gold answers can potentially help understand the compatibility of the methods. We therefore conduct a ceiling test on the two datasets. To analyze the effect of the similarity threshold parameter, we computed how often the gold answer is still included among the candidates after performing filtering by the threshold. Alternatively, this can be interpreted as the ceiling of system performance, assuming the context ranking works perfectly. We therefore define the ceiling for the best gold answer only as C_{best} and for all gold answers as C_{all}. For the four-step baseline, we used two frequency corpora: Norvig and LDC. For other baselines, we use optimized parameters in the testing. The result is shown in Table 4.

We also evaluate the efficiency. Our TWPOS and SYNPOS strategies are able to improve running as fewer candidates are generated. According to our experiments on Dataset A testing data, Path measure runs 1185.6 s. TWPOS decrease the time usage to 975.9 s while SYNPOS decrease it to 542.7 s. The combination of TWPOS and SYNPOS further decrease it to 439.7 s (62.9% improvement), dramatically improving the running efficiency.

Our proposing approach is a concise combination strategy and can be utilized to other available similarity calculation methods and context ranking methods. One advantage of it is that our approach is an independent module so that it can be added to commonly used semantic similarity calculation measures (e.g., Path measure in the paper) without the need to change the original program. The experiments also present more than 15% performance improvement. Therefore, this is meaningful as users can utilize the strategy to integrate their familiar or adaptable or accessible tools for simplification performance improvement. It also helps real-time lexical simplification due to the efficiency improvement and this could to be a benefit for real application development and implementation.

5   Conclusions

This paper proposes a semantic-context combination ranking strategy for English lexical simplification to a restricted vocabulary. The strategy elaborately integrates commonly used semantic similarity calculation methods and context-based ranking methods as well as two POS-based matching to improve both performance and efficiency. The comparison results with baseline methods presented that our approach is more effective in community-oriented English lexical simplification.

Acknowledgments. This work was supported by the Innovation and Technology Fund (Ref: ITS/132/15) of the Innovation and Technology Commission, the Government of the Hong Kong Special Administrative Region, National Natural Science Foundation of China (No. 61772146 & No. 61403088), and Innovative School Project in Higher Education of Guangdong Province (No. YQ2015062).

References

1. Biran, O., Brody, S., Elhadad, N.: Putting it simply: a context-aware approach to lexical simplification. In: Proceedings of the 49th Annual Meeting of the Association for Computational Linguistics: Human Language Technologies, HLT 2011, pp. 496–501. Association for Computational Linguistics, Stroudsburg (2011)
2. Coster, W., Kauchak, D.: Learning to simplify sentences using Wikipedia. In: Proceedings of the Workshop on Monolingual Text-to-Text Generation, pp. 1–9. Association for Computational Linguistics (2011)
3. Coster, W., Kauchak, D.: Simple English Wikipedia: a new text simplification task. In: Proceedings of the 49th Annual Meeting of the Association for Computational Linguistics: Human Language Technologies: Short Papers, vol. 2, pp. 665–669. ACL (2011)
4. Dagan, I., Glickman, O., Gliozzo, A., Marmorshtein, E., Strapparava, C.: Direct word sense matching for lexical substitution. In: Proceedings of the 21st International Conference on Computational Linguistics and the 44th Annual Meeting of the ACL, ACL-44, pp. 449–456. ACL, Stroudsburg (2006)
5. Glavaš, G., Štajner, S.: Simplifying lexical simplification: do we need simplified corpora. In: Proceedings of the 53rd Annual Meeting of the Association for Computational Linguistics, vol. 2, pp. 63–68 (2015)
6. Horn, C., Manduca, C., Kauchak, D.: Learning a lexical simplifier using Wikipedia. In: ACL, vol. 2, pp. 458–463 (2014)
7. Kajiwara, T., Matsumoto, H., Yamamoto, K.: Selecting proper lexical paraphrase for children. In: Proceedings of the Twenty-Fifth Conference on Computational Linguistics and Speech Processing (ROCLING 2013) (2013)
8. Kauchak, D.: Improving text simplification language modeling using unsimplified text data. In: ACL, vol. 1, pp. 1537–1546 (2013)
9. McCarthy, D., Navigli, R.: Semeval-2007 task 10: English lexical substitution task. In: Proceedings of the 4th International Workshop on Semantic Evaluations, SemEval 2007, pp. 48–53. Association for Computational Linguistics, Stroudsburg (2007). http://dl.acm.org/citation.cfm?id=1621474.1621483
10. Paetzold, G.H., Specia, L.: Unsupervised lexical simplification for non-native speakers. In: Thirtieth AAAI Conference on Artificial Intelligence (2016)
11. Paetzold, G.H.: Reliable lexical simplification for non-native speakers. In: NAACL-HLT 2015 Student Research Workshop (SRW), p. 9 (2015)
12. Paetzold, G.H., Specia, L.: Lexenstein: a framework for lexical simplification. In: ACL-IJCNLP 2015, vol. 1, no. 1, p. 85 (2015)

13. Saggion, H., Bott, S., Rello, L.: Simplifying words in context. Experiments with two lexical resources in Spanish. Comput. Speech Lang. **35**, 200–218 (2016)

14. Shirzadi, S.: Syntactic and lexical simplification: the impact on EFL listening comprehension at low and high language proficiency levels. J. Lang. Teach. Res. **5**(3), 566–571 (2014)

15. Specia, L., Jauhar, S.K., Mihalcea, R.: Semeval-2012 task 1: English lexical simplification. In: Proceedings of the First Joint Conference on Lexical and Computational Semantics, pp. 347–355. Association for Computational Linguistics (2012)

16. The Education Bureau, Curriculum Development Institute: Enhancing English Vocabulary Learning and Teaching at Primary Level. Technical report, The Hong Kong Special Administrative Region (2016)

17. Wolf, L., Hanani, Y., Bar, K., Dershowitz, N.: Joint word2vec networks for bilingual semantic representations. Int. J. Comput. Linguist. Appl. **5**(1), 27–44 (2014)

18. Yakovets, N., Agrawal, A.: Simple: lexical simplification using word sense disambiguation (2013)

19. Zhao, S., Zhao, L., Zhang, Y., Liu, T., Li, S.: Hit: web based scoring method for English lexical substitution. In: Proceedings of the 4th International Workshop on Semantic Evaluations, SemEval 2007, pp. 173–176. ACL, Stroudsburg (2007)

20. Zhu, Z., Bernhard, D., Gurevych, I.: A monolingual tree-based translation model for sentence simplification. In: Proceedings of the 23rd International Conference on Computational Linguistics, pp. 1353–1361. Association for Computational Linguistics (2010)

A Multiple Learning Model Based Voting System for News Headline Classification

Fenhong Zhu, Xiaozheng Dong, Rui Song, Yu Hong$^{(\boxtimes)}$, and Qiaoming Zhu

Soochow University, Suzhou, Jiangsu, China
{fhzhu,xzdong}@stu.suda.edu.cn, cnsr27@gmail.com,
tianxianer@gmail.com, qmzhu@suda.edu.cn

Abstract. This paper presents the framework and methodologies of Soochow university team's news headline classification system for NLPCC 2017 shared task 2. The submitted systems aim to automatically classify each Chinese news headline into one or more predefined categories. We develop a voting system based on convolutional neural networks (CNN), gated recurrent units (GRU), and support vector machine (SVM). Experimental results show that our method achieves a Macro-F1 score of about 81%, outperforming most strong competitors, and ranking at 6th in the 32 participants.

1 Introduction

Chinese news headline classification can be regarded as a task of short text classification [1]. Therefore, it also encounters similar obstacles to that in the task, including (1) there is absence of informative contexts available for generating reliable topic models, and (2) traditional statistical feature engineering methods cannot take rich information from the short texts to use. Besides, empirical findings also show that some headlines even fail to abide by the standard grammar and pragmatic rules. Listed below are the examples where we can find the problems mentioned above.

(1) "念念不忘，必有回响" (Contexts are required)
    <Translation: *Never forget, but definitely having responses*>

(2) "因为一样东西这个后娘竟给孩子磕头" (Lack of discriminative features)
    <Translation: *The stepmother kowtowed to her child for one thing*>

(3) "贾建军少林三光剑视频" (Irregular grammar)
    <Translation: *Jianjun Jia Shaolin Sanguang sward video*>

Convolutional Neural Networks (CNN) is admittedly effective in text representation and semantic computation. By convolution computation of the word embedding [2], it is capable of capturing local semantic information in sentences and providing an abstract concept-level representation for each. Therefore, CNN enables the recognition of semantically-similar texts even if they are short and lack details. For example, by CNN, a headline classifier may determine the example (1) as homogeneous with

X. Huang et al. (Eds.): NLPCC 2017, LNAI 10619, pp. 797–806, 2018.
https://doi.org/10.1007/978-3-319-73618-1_69

another headline (" 不忘初心，方得始终" Translation: "*Never forget the original will and hence we eventually achieve the goal*"). This is very helpful in the headline classification.

By contrast, Recurrent Neural Networks (RNN) takes into consideration the long-distance semantic relationship between words. Therefore, RNN can still represent the comprehensive semantics even if the sentence constituents are not dependent on each other. Therefore, we argue that the RNN based semantic representation may overcome the problems of irregular grammar and pragmatics. For example, by RNN, a headline classifier may determine the example (3) as homogeneous with the example " 贾建军表演少林三光剑的视频" (Translation: "*Jianjun Jia performs the vedio of Shaolin Sanguang sword*").

In this paper, we attempt to cooperate the CNN with RNN as well as a traditional feature engineering based learning model (Support Vector Machine, SVM for short). We form an intuitive rule based voting algorithm to support the cooperation. By the jointly use of the models and the voting mechanism, we enhance the special effects of the models on the headline classification for different cases.

We put the cooperative method into use for the NLPCC 2017 shared task 2. The test results show that the method outperforms most of the participants' systems, achieving a F1-score of about 81%.

The rest of the paper is organized as follows. We brief the related work in Sect. 2. Section 3 presents the details of our method, including voting rules, CNN, RNN and SVM models. We show the experimental settings and results in Sect. 4. We draw the conclusion in Sect. 5.

2   Related Work

Recently, identifying the topic of a short text has been widely studied. Due to shortness and sparse informative features, short text clustering is very challenging. In this section, we briefly overview the previous work for overcoming the problem.

Some research enriches the contextual information by using large external corpora. Hu et al. [3] improve the performance of clustering short texts by making use of internal and external semantics. Banerjee et al. [4] use external corpora Wikipedia to cluster the short texts. Although these approaches enrich the contextual information, they make the representations of text more complex.

Other researchers mine the topics of texts to cluster the texts. Phan et al. [5] mine a collection of hidden topics based on Latent Dirichlet Allocation [6] from external large-scale corpora, and build a general framework for short and sparse texts classification. Chen et al. [7] propose a method to leverage topics at multiple granularity.

In addition, researchers also put forward other effective approaches. Zelikovitz and Hirsh [8], Yih and Meek [9] improve the performance of classification by computing the semantic similarity of short texts. Wang et al. [10] propose a new method by building a strong feature thesaurus based on LDA and information gain models.

Recently, methodology has been rapidly put forward with the development of neural networks. Word embedding learned by neural language models [11, 12], which is a distributed representation of a word, can express the semantic features of a word in its low dimensions. Combining with word embeddings, some classification methods based on neural networks are proposed. Kim [13] uses convolutional neural networks for sentence classification. Lai et al. [14] cooperate the recurrent structure with max pooling for text classification.

3   Methodology

3.1   Multiple Classification Models Based Voting

In a series of experiments, we analyze the results obtained by using CNN, GRU and SVM respectively. The correct intersection size of the three classifiers is 24383 (account for 67.73% in 36,000 test instances), and the collection size of all mistakenly classified instances is 4,321 (account for 12% of the test data). These show a possibility of using intuitive rule based voting algorithm to cooperate the models. The structure of our voting system is shown in Fig. 1, and the rules of voting are described immediately after the Figure. We will illustrate the Rule 3 by the example (4), and analyze the effectiveness of the voting system.

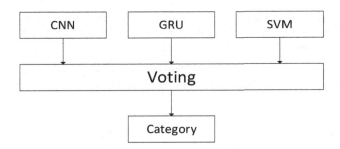

Fig. 1. The structure of voting system.

- Rule 1, when the results of three methods are all inconsistent, we support the result of CNN.
- Rule 2, when the results of CNN and GRU are consistent, we completely ignore the result of traditional method (SVM), and classify the news headline into the result of neural networks.
- Rule 3, when the results of CNN and GRU are inconsistent, then we consider the result of traditional method.

(4) " 菲律宾为了对抗中国连自己的核心利益都不要了！"
    <Translation: *Philippines even gives up its crucial benefit in order to fight against China.*>

See the example (4), the model of CNN based classifies it into the topic of "*world*", while the GRU based classifier throws it into the topic of "*military*". From the per-spective of high-level semantics or concept, it seems the example does relate to the two classes, however it eventually should be classified into the class "*military*". And it can be found that the statistical distributions of the keywords in the headline help the decision-making in a correct way, such as the two organizations and the three words "*fight*", "*crucial*" and "*benefit*". Therefore, we propose to use TFIDF (term frequency, inverse document frequency) based SVM model to make the final decision, just like that of Rule 3.

Some other concerns cause the continuous use of the rule based approach. Considering the voting limitation of the fixed convolution window of CNN, a small size may lose some important information. By contrast, a window in larger size may lead to an enormous parameters space. In other words, it will increase the time-consuming. The size is generally set to be 3 in many recent work. However, we find that such as window may result in the loss of contextual information. By contrast, it has been widely accepted that GRU takes into account the meaning of the entire text. However, GRU doesn't perform better than CNN in our case.

Table 1 shows the performances of CNN-based and GRU-based achieved on the 36,000 news headlines. It can be found that the performance of CNN is slightly better than GRU's.

Table 1. Comparison of voting systems based on CNN and GRU. Original-acc means the accuracy obtained by single model such as the model which merely based on CNN, and Voting-acc means the accuracy after voting mechanism.

Model	Original-acc	Voting-acc
CNN-based	79.19	80.77
GRU-based	78.83	80.47

(5) "美文: 请别再玩**手机**了，好吗？"
    <Translation: *Beautiful essay: please no more play* **mobile phone**>

We analyze the underlying reason which makes it happen. Our survey shows that GRU shows some bias during the headline classification. See the example (5), where the word highlighted with bold-font is dominant than the rest. However, because the key components can appear anywhere in a text rather than at the end, it could reduce the effectiveness when it is used to capture the semantics of the whole short text. Such as that in the example (5), "*mobile phone*" may be considered as a more important feature. However, CNN is an unbiased model. News headlines are always impressive by discriminative words such as "*beautiful essay*" in the above example, CNN makes use of the function of capturing the most important features for classification.

3.2   Model of Convolutional Neural Networks (CNN)

Following Kim [13], we present a variant of the CNN architecture. The structure of CNN is illustrated in Fig. 2 (left). Let $x_i \in \mathcal{R}^k$ be the k-dimensional word vector corresponding to the *i-th* word in the sentence. Then a text of length N is represented as the concatenation of its word vector,

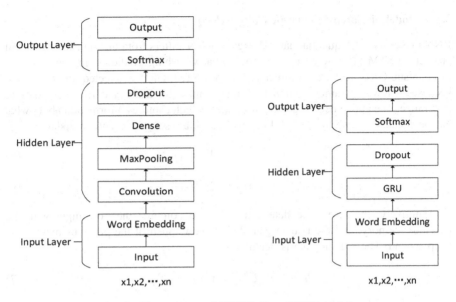

Fig. 2. The structure of CNN (left) and GRU (right).

$$x_{1:n} = x_1 \oplus x_2 \oplus \ldots \oplus x_n, \qquad (1)$$

Let $x_{i:i+j}$ refer to the concatenation of words $x_i, x_{i+1}, \ldots, x_{i+j}$.

In this work, the networks learn a weight vector W_c and a bias term b_c for the filter. We employ the convolution layer over word embeddings to extract local features, there is a window of h words which generates a feature c_i by

$$c_i = f(W_c \cdot x_{i:i+h-1} + b_c), \qquad (2)$$

where f is a non-linear activation function. This filter is applied to each possible window of words in the sentences $\{x_{1:h}, x_{2:h+1}, \ldots, x_{n-h+1:n}\}$ to produce a feature map

$$c = [c_1, c_2, \ldots, c_{n-h+1}]. \qquad (3)$$

In order to capture the most important feature, we apply a max pooling operation over the feature map and take the maximum value $c' = max(c)$.

We employ dropout on the fully connected layer to avoid overfitting. Finally, we use

$$y = softmax(W \cdot x + b) \qquad (4)$$

to classify the short texts.

3.3   Model of Gated Recurrent Units (GRU)

RNN makes use of sequential data. However, RNN suffers from the vanishing gradient problem. LSTM [15] were designed to combat vanishing gradients through a gating mechanism. GRU [16] are a simpler variant of LSTM. GRU is selected for our system because of fewer parameters, and thus may train a bit faster and need less data to generalize. The above networks have a memory which captures information about what has been calculated so far. A GRU has two gates, a reset gate r, and an update gate z,

$$r = \sigma(U^r x_t + W^r s_{t-1}), \tag{5}$$

$$z = \sigma(U^z x_t + W^z s_{t-1}). \tag{6}$$

Intuitively, the reset gate determines how to combine the new input with the previous memory, and the update gate defines how much of the previous memory to keep around. The hidden state is decided by

$$h = tanh\left(U^h x_t + W^h(r * s_{t-1})\right), \tag{7}$$

$$s_t = (1 - z) * h + z * s_{t-1}. \tag{8}$$

By learning the parameters for its gates, the network learn how its memory should behave. The structure of GRU is illustrated in Fig. 2 (right).

4   Experiments

4.1   Datasets

We participate in NLPCC 2017 shared task 2, and the task's goal is to classify Chinese news headline into one or more predefined categories. There are 18 categories such as entertainment, sports, and so on. The detailed information of categories is shown in Table 2.

Table 2. The information of categories.

Category	Train	Dev	Test	Category	Train	Dev	Test
Entertainment	10000	2000	2000	Military	10000	2000	2000
Sports	10000	2000	2000	History	10000	2000	2000
Car	10000	2000	2000	Baby	10000	2000	2000
Society	10000	2000	2000	Fashion	10000	2000	2000
Tech	10000	2000	2000	Food	10000	2000	2000
World	10000	2000	2000	Discovery	4000	2000	2000
Finance	10000	2000	2000	Story	4000	2000	2000
Game	10000	2000	2000	Regimen	4000	2000	2000
Travel	10000	2000	2000	Essay	4000	2000	2000

In this dataset, there are 156,000 posts in the training dataset, 36,000 posts in the development dataset, and 36,000 posts in submission dataset for measuring the performance of our system.

4.2 Experimental Settings

- **Word Embedding Model:** We initialize word vectors obtained from an unsupervised neural language model, which improve the semantic features of words. We utilize the publicly available *Word2Vec*[1] model. The model is trained by *Gensim*[2], the vectors have dimensionality of 256. Words not present in the set of predefined words are initialized into zero vectors of 256 dimensions. In this task, we set a matrix of 30 * 256 for each title through the *Word2Vec* model as the input of CNN and GRU. If the length of the text is shorter than 30 words, zero will be set in the dimensions of absent words. Otherwise, the exceeding part will be ignored.
- **Convolutional Neural Networks:** In the convolution layer, the dimensionality of the output space is 128, the size of convolution window is 3, and *tanh* is used as an activation function. Then we apply a max pooling layer over the feature map, the size of pooling window is 2. The dimensionality of the out space of the fully connected layer is 64. In order to avoid overfitting, we set 0.5 as the rate of dropout. The fully connected layer uses *softmax* for classification. Finally, when compiling the model, the loss function is *categorical_crossentropy*, the optimizer is *Adadelta*, and the number of iterations is 5 times.
- **Gated Recurrent Units:** In the GRU layer, the dimensionality of the output space is 128, the activation function is *tanh*, the rate of dropout is 0.5. We set *softmax* as classification function in the fully connected layer. Finally, when compiling the model, the loss function is *categorical_crossentropy*, the optimizer is *adam*, and the number of iterations is 3 times.
- **Support Vector Machine:** We use the *sklearn*[3] toolkit. The representations of texts are generated by *TfidfVectorizer*. Thus, we obtain a model of TFIDF. We train the model of *LinearSVC* with the input of the representations of texts obtained by TFIDF and the corresponding labels. Finally, we get a model of *LinearSVC*.

4.3 Experimental Results and Discussion

We adopt the macro-averaged precision, recall and F1 score to evaluate the performance of Chinese news headline classification, three kinds of score are computed as the NLPCC 2017 shared task 2 Guidelines described. Table 3 presents the performance of our system compared with the top-ranked, median-ranked and average-ranked system on the submission dataset.

---

[1] http://spaces.ac.cn/archives/4304/comment-page-1.

[2] http://radimrehurek.com/gensim/models/word2vec.html.

[3] http://scikit-learn.org/stable/.

Table 3. The performances of our system and the top-ranked, average-ranked, and median-ranked system for task offered by the organizer.

Compared system	P	R	F1	Acc
Top	83.11	82.97	83.04	82.97
Ours	81.16	80.77	80.96	80.77
Median	78.96	78.53	78.75	78.52
Average	73.31	72.27	72.77	72.27

Our system ranks 6rd in the shared task 2, is just 2.20% lower than the top one, and much higher than the averaged-ranked and median-ranked scores. It indicates that our voting system has achieved good results for this task.

Table 4 presents the results of various methods on testing dataset. We brief these methods as follows. The baseline has implemented some basic deep learning models such as neural bag-of-words (NBoW), CNN, and LSTM. For comparing, we implement some classification methods. For text representation, we use classical TFIDF to represent the statistical distributions of the keywords. Considering disorder of words, we append the order of words at the end of the representation. The two approaches employ SVM classifier. In order to compare the performance of classifiers, we also use the method of TFIDF, and employ K-Nearest Neighbor (KNN) classifier. However, the above feature selection methods do not take semantics of words into account, we try to use the topic model LDA. We also attempt to use *Doc2vec* [17] model to capture the semantic features of texts, however, the result is pretty terrible. In addition, we implement the classification by CNN and GRU. By comparing the above methods, we propose our voting system, and we can obtain the following findings.

Table 4. The results of various methods on the testing dataset. The top, middle, and bottom parts are the results of baseline, some methods we implemented, and the voting system we proposed.

Model	P	R	F1	Acc
CNN-multichannel	76	75	75	75
LSTM	76	76	76	76
NBOW	79	78	78	78
TFIDF+SVM	78	77	77	77
TFIDF & Order of words+SVM	45	44	44	44
TFIDF+KNN	67	57	59	57
LDA+SVM	47	45	43	45
CNN	80	79	79	79
GRU	79	79	79	79
Ours	**81.16**	**80.77**	**80.96**	**80.77**

- When we compare the approaches of neural networks (e.g., CNN) with the widely used traditional methods (e.g., TFIDF+KNN), the experimental results show that the former mostly outperform the latter. It proves that neural networks can capture more semantics of words and contextual information of features compared with traditional methods. For example, TFIDF only considers the statistical distributions of the keywords, which ignores contextual information completely, and it suffers from the sparse data problem. Although we add the order of words in this representation, the result is still pretty bad. We also attempt to employ the topic models such as LDA. However, LDA uses co-occurrence between words and documents, there are few keywords in short texts. Thus it is not suitable for features representation of short texts.

- When comparing the CNN and LSTM of the baseline with the CNN and GRU we implemented, we find that our implementations achieve a better result than the baseline. We analyze it from two aspects, (1) **representations of texts**. We use a large number of external corpora, and it makes features representation of short texts more precise. (2) **Neural networks classifiers**. CNN-multichannel vs CNN, the baseline use a multichannel CNN based on static and non-static word vectors, we only use a single-channel based on static word vectors. We think that the quantity of information of short texts is relatively little, using multichannel to enforce its features, which may be led to superfluous features. So instead of multichannel, using single channel obtains a better result. LSTM vs GRU, the baseline use LSTM, and we use a simpler variant of LSTM named GRU. we think that the training data we have is not enough for deep learning, and parameters of the GRU model are fewer than LSTM's, so it needs less training data, and it can train a bit faster.

5   Conclusion

In this paper, by cooperating the CNN with GRU as well as SVM, we develop a voting system to automatically classify Chinese news headlines into a predefined category. In this system, the CNN selects more discriminative features, the GRU makes up the size of filter window of CNN, and the SVM serves as an auxiliary function. As a result, our submission system gets a good performance. We will do more work to improve the system performance, such as add entity to the features representation.

Acknowledgments. This research work is supported by National Natural Science Foundation of China (Grants No. 61373097, No. 61672367, No. 61672368, No. 61331011, No. 61773276), the Research Foundation of the Ministry of Education and China Mobile, MCM20150602 and the Science and Technology Plan of Jiangsu, SBK2015022101 and BK20151222. The authors would like to thank the anonymous reviewers for their insightful comments and suggestions.

References

1. Song, G., Ye, Y., Du, X., Huang, X., Bie, S.: Short text classification: a survey. J. Multimedia **9**(5), 635–643 (2014)
2. Mikolov, T., Sutskever, I., Chen, K., Corrado, G.S., Dean, J.: Distributed representations of words and phrases and their compositionality. In: Advances in Neural Information Processing Systems, pp. 3111–3119 (2013)
3. Hu, X., Sun, N., Zhang, C., Chua, T.S.: Exploiting internal and external semantics for the clustering of short texts using world knowledge. In: Proceedings of the 18th ACM Conference on Information and Knowledge Management, pp. 919–928. ACM (2009)
4. Banerjee, S., Ramanathan, K., Gupta, A.: Clustering short texts using Wikipedia. In: Proceedings of the 30th Annual International ACM SIGIR Conference on Research and Development in Information Retrieval, pp. 787–788. ACM (2007)
5. Phan, X.H., Nguyen, L.M., Horiguchi, S.: Learning to classify short and sparse text and web with hidden topics from large-scale data collections. In: Proceedings of the 17th International Conference on World Wide Web, pp. 91–100. ACM (2008)
6. Blei, D.M., Ng, A.Y., Jordan, M.I.: Latent Dirichlet allocation. J. Mach. Learn. Res. **3**(Jan), 993–1022 (2003)
7. Chen, M., Jin, X., Shen, D.: Short text classification improved by learning multi-granularity topics. In: IJCAI, pp. 1776–1781 (2011)
8. Zelikovitz, S., Hirsh, H.: Improving short text classification using unlabeled background knowledge to assess document similarity. In: Proceedings of the Seventeenth International Conference on Machine Learning, vol. 2000, pp. 1183–1190 (2000)
9. Yih, W.T., Meek, C.: Improving similarity measures for short segments of text. In: AAAI, vol. 7, no. 7, pp. 1489–1494 (2007)
10. Wang, B.K., Huang, Y.F., Yang, W.X., Li, X.: Short text classification based on strong feature thesaurus. J. Zhejiang Univ.-Sci. C **13**(9), 649–659 (2012)
11. Bengio, Y., Ducharme, R., Vincent, P., Jauvin, C.: A neural probabilistic language model. J. Mach. Learn. Res. **3**(Feb), 1137–1155 (2003)
12. Mikolov, T.: Statistical language models based on neural networks. Presentation at Google, Mountain View, 2nd April (2012)
13. Kim, Y.: Convolutional neural networks for sentence classification. arXiv preprint arXiv:1408.5882 (2014)
14. Lai, S., Xu, L., Liu, K., Zhao, J.: Recurrent convolutional neural networks for text classification. In: AAAI, vol. 333, pp. 2267–2273 (2015)
15. Hochreiter, S., Schmidhuber, J.: Long short-term memory. Neural Comput. **9**(8), 1735–1780 (1997)
16. Cho, K., Van Merriënboer, B., Gulcehre, C., Bahdanau, D., Bougares, F., Schwenk, H., Bengio, Y.: Learning phrase representations using RNN encoder-decoder for statistical machine translation. arXiv preprint arXiv:1406.1078 (2014)
17. Le, Q., Mikolov, T.: Distributed representations of sentences and documents. In: Proceedings of the 31st International Conference on Machine Learning (ICML 2014), pp. 1188–1196 (2014)

Extractive Single Document Summarization via Multi-feature Combination and Sentence Compression

Maofu Liu[1,2], Yan Yu[1,2], Qiaosong Qi[1,2], Huijun Hu[1,2],
and Han Ren[3(✉)]

[1] College of Computer Science and Technology,
Wuhan University of Science and Technology, Wuhan 430065, China
[2] Hubei Province Key Laboratory of Intelligent Information Processing and
Real-Time Industrial System, Wuhan University of Science and Technology,
Wuhan 430065, China
[3] Laboratory of Language Engineering and Computing,
Guangdong University of Foreign Studies, Guangzhou 510006, China
hanren@whu.edu.cn

Abstract. In this paper, we attempt to extract and generate the short summary for the news article with the length limit of 60 Chinese characters. Firstly, we preprocess the news article by segmenting sentences and words, and then extract four kinds of central words to form the keyword dictionary based on parsing tree. After that, the four kinds of features, i.e. the sentence weight, the sentence similarity, the sentence position and the length of sentence, will be employed to measure the significance of each sentence. Finally, we extract two sentences in the descending order of significance score and compress them to get the summary for each news article. This approach can analyze the grammatical elements from original sentences in order to generate compression rules and trim syntactic elements according to their parsing trees. The evaluation results show that our system is efficient in Chinese news summarization.

Keywords: Single document summarization · Multi-feature combination
Sentence extraction · Parsing tree · Sentence compression

1 Introduction

With the rapid growth of social network services and the dramatic increase of social media, the user would like to read the information in summary form without losing his or her favorite contents. Of course, the summary should contain the core content of the original text, and organize it in a semantic coherent template, aiming to improve the user's information efficiency. Nowadays, the news article is the most conventional social media, because there are a lot of events happening every day and the news has been constantly being updated. Therefore, it is meaningful to make an automatic generation of extractive summary from a single news article, which is not only convenient for readers, but also for storage.

© Springer International Publishing AG 2018
X. Huang et al. (Eds.): NLPCC 2017, LNAI 10619, pp. 807–817, 2018.
https://doi.org/10.1007/978-3-319-73618-1_70

Derived from a core task in natural language processing, i.e. automatic summarization, news document summarization techniques have been widely explored on DUC (Document Understanding Conference) and TAC (Text Analysis Conference). Currently, existing datasets for document summarization are mainly English texts, whereas news summarization of Chinese texts has seldom been explored. To this end, a shared task in NLPCC2017, namely Chinese single document summarization, has been defined, and the aim is to automatically generate short summaries for given Chinese news articles. In this task, all data come from Toutiao.com[1], and the length of each short summary is less than 60 Chinese characters.

This paper describes our participating system in such task. Our system automatically extracts the most relevant sentences from Chinese news article according to significance score of each sentence by measuring four kinds of features of such sentence. And then, the extracted sentences are compressed into their condensed forms with preceding defined rules.

2 Related Work

Automatic text summarization is a traditional problem in natural language processing. In 1958, the first automatic abstracting system was put forward by Luhn [1]. Currently, there are two ways in this area, i.e. extraction and generation. The first one is to segment an article into small units, and then extract some of them as the summary of such article, while the second one is to generate a summary for an article without using any existing sentences or phrases in it, which is mainly based on natural language understanding technologies. Based on them, many researchers proposed models to extract or generate summaries from documents. Liu et al. [2] established a model based on feature combination to generate summary for the given news article. John and Wilscy [3] proposed text Summarization based on feature score and random forest classification. Moawad and Aref [4] summarized a single document by creating a rich semantic graph from the original document. Hirao et al. [5] transformed RST trees into dependency trees and used them for single document summarization. Sentence compression is a related task of summary generation [6]. Cohn and Lapata [7] presented a tree-to-tree transduction method for sentence compression. Alias et al. [8] derived some heuristic sentence compression rules in generating compressed sentences to construct a single summary. Filippova and Alfonseca [9] presented a long short-term memory approach to deletion-based sentence compression.

This paper proposes an approach by combining sentence extraction and summary generation, aiming at leveraging the advantages for each of them. Firstly, we select key words based on semantic information, and then choose sentences with high scores based on sentence ranking and ordering. Finally, news summaries are generated according to sentence compression by syntactic pruning. Evaluation results show that our system takes the third place in all the participating systems.

---

[1] http://www.toutiao.com/.

3   Our System

In this section, we will describe the overview of our system, including keyword selection, feature extraction and combination, key sentence selection, and sentence compression.

3.1   System Architecture

Our system consists of four steps, i.e. data preprocessing, keyword selection, multi-feature combination, sentence extraction and compression. Figure 1 can illustrate the architecture of our system in detail.

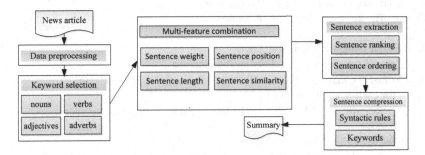

Fig. 1. System architecture

In data preprocessing, the main work is to segment the Chinese words. We choose Stanford Chinese word segmentation tools[2] in our system. To ensure some types of name entities, for example person name and organization, being segmented correctly, we use both forward-matching algorithm and backward-matching algorithm, and the basic idea of forward-matching algorithm is to scan the candidate sequence in turn from the beginning of the starting word. If the repetition is found, the collinear probability is calculated, and if the collinear probability is greater than a certain threshold, the repeated string is considered as a whole. The backward-matching algorithm is the same as the forward-matching one except the scanning direction.

3.2   Keyword Selection

As the basic elements of the sentence, a collection of words can be combined to a sentence. If we complete the selection of words by the statistical methods, it will not contain the semantic information, so the statistical-based methods have some limitations.

According to the preceding analysis, our system uses the keywords, referring to the central words in a sentence, to improve the single document summarization. In fact, the

---

[2] http://www-nlp.stanford.edu/software/segmenter.shtml.

central word is the dominant grammatical element, such as noun, verb, adjective and adverbial phrase. The document by data preprocessing stage will be inputted into the syntax parser in the form of sentences. We choose Stanford Parser software[3] to obtain the parsed sentence in our system. The basic elements are extracted by pruning the results after parsing, and the principle of extraction is carried out according to the definition of the basic elements. In our system, we directly select four types of the central words as keywords, i.e. noun in noun phrase, verb in verb phrase, adjective in adjective phrase, and adverb in adverb phrase, and form a keyword dictionary. The following Algorithm 1 can describe the keyword extraction and selection in our system in detail.

Algorithm 1. The keyword selection

Input: The sentence set *SensSet* of a document
Output: The keyword dictionary *Keysdic*
begin
1. for each sentence *Sen* in *SensSet*
2.   *ParsedSen*=parse(*Sen*); //parsing the sentence
3.   (*NPList, VCList, ADJPList, ADVPList*)=ExtractNVA (*ParsedSen*);
4.   for each *NN∥NR* in *NPList*
5.   *Keysdic*.add(*NN∥NR*); //selecting and adding the noun keyword
6.   end for
7.   for each *VV∥VA∥VC* in *VCList*
8.   *Keysdic*.add(*VV∥VA∥VC*); //selecting and adding the verb keyword
9.   end for
10.   for each *JJ* in *ADJPList*
11.   *Keysdic*.add(*JJ*); //selecting and adding the adjective keyword
12.   end for
13.   for each *AD* in *ADVPList*
14.   *Keysdic*.add(*AD*); //selecting and adding the adverb keyword
15.   end for
16. end for
end

To evaluate the importance of keyword, the term frequency (TF) is used to calculate the word weight. The TF is the most simple and traditional statistical feature to reserve the most significant keywords. The word weight can be obtained by the following formula (1).

$$ww_i = TF(w_i) = \frac{n_i}{\sum_{j=1}^{K} n_j} \ (w_i \in keyword\ dictionary) \tag{1}$$

---

[3] https://nlp.stanford.edu/software/lex-parser.html.

where ww_i is the weight of the word w_i, and K and n_i represent the total occurrence number of keyword dictionary in a document and the occurrence number of the word w_i respectively. The word weights and the words themselves are collected to construct the keyword dictionary.

3.3 Multi-feature Combination

At the sentence level, our work concentrates on calculating the importance for each sentence via four kinds of features, i.e. the sentence weight, the sentence similarity, the sentence position and the length of sentence.

(1) The sentence weight

How many keywords a sentence contains is the most important and it is the direct information to judge whether the sentence is significant or not. In our system, the sentence weight is the sum of weights of all the words in this sentence. The weight of the ith sentence, ws_i, can be calculated by the following formula (2).

$$ws_i = \sum_{j=1}^{N} ww_j \tag{2}$$

where ww_j means the weight of the jth word in the ith sentence, calculated by the preceding formula (1), and N stands for the length of the word set of the ith sentence.

(2) The sentence similarity

The extractive document summarization is to find the salient subset of text spans that contain the main semantic information of the document. Therefore, the sentence similarity can be used to measure the degree of correlation, and the similarity between the sentence and the others in the document can be used to represent the sematic of information carried in this sentence. Our system uses the cosine similarity, to express the ith sentence similarity, which showed in the following formula (3).

$$sim_i = \sum_{j=1, j\neq i}^{N} sim(s_i, s_j) = \sum_{j=1, j\neq i}^{N} \frac{ws_i \cdot ws_j}{\sqrt{ws_i^2 * ws_j^2}} \tag{3}$$

where ws_i and ws_j refer to the weight of the ith and j^{th} sentence separately, and N denotes the length of the sentence set of the document.

(3) The sentence position

When going through the news article, we can usually capture the central topic of the article after reading the several sentences in the first paragraph or the last paragraph. In order to prevent the loss of significant information, the sentences will be given the different weights depending on their locations in the document. The standard calculation is applied for the sentence position feature, pos_i, using the following formula (4).

$$pos_i = \frac{n - p_i + 1}{n} \tag{4}$$

where n is the total number of the sentences in the document, and p_i is the position of the ith sentence in the document.

(4) The length of sentence

If the sentence is too long, it will carry irrelevant information, and in contrast, it may lose the salient information. So if the length of a sentence is close to the average sentence length of the document, it should be assigned the larger significance score. And the normal distribution model can meet our requirement of our system. The length of the ith sentence, len_i, can be computed by the following formula (5).

$$len_i = \frac{1}{\sqrt{2\pi}\sigma} e^{-\frac{(x_i - \mu)^2}{2\sigma^2}} \tag{5}$$

where μ and x_i denote the average sentence length and the length of the ith sentence in the document, and σ is the standard deviation, which can be calculated by the following formula (6).

$$\sigma^2 = \frac{\sum_{i=1}^{n} (x_i - \mu)^2}{n} \tag{6}$$

where n is the total number of the sentences in the document.

3.4 Sentence Extraction and Compression

According to the four kinds of features mentioned above, the significance score of the ith sentence, $SenScore_i$, can be determined by the linear weighting, illustrated by the following formula (7).

$$SenScore_i = (\lambda_1 ws_i + \lambda_2 sim_i + \lambda_3 pos_i + \lambda_4 len_i)/(\lambda_1 + \lambda_2 + \lambda_3 + \lambda_4) \tag{7}$$

where the λ_1, λ_2, λ_3 and λ_4 represent the weights of the four kinds of features respectively.

The score of sentence would be calculated according to the formula (7), and then we will rank the sentences according to their scores. Since the final length of the summary is limited within 60 Chinese characters and the average length of each sentence in the training set is 38.98 Chinese characters, we will extract two sentences with the top-2 highest score, and then the preliminary summary system will be formed according to the order of the original text.

With the length limit of 60 Chinese characters, we aim to develop the sentence compression algorithm that can shorten the length of the extracted sentences without changing their original meanings. Generally speaking, there are two types of sentence compression algorithms, i.e. statistic-based ones and rule-based ones. The statistic-based sentence compression algorithms need a large scale of manually corpus, and therefore, we have selected the syntactic rules based sentence compression algorithm in our system.

The key point of sentence compression based on syntactic rules is to analyze the grammatical elements of the original sentence, and remove constituents to generate the compressed sentence according to syntactic rules derived from the parsing tree of the original sentence. Our system mainly applies the heuristic compression rules to the syntactic analysis of each sentence, and then makes the decision which composition of each node in the parsing tree should be removed. We also choose Stanford Parser software to obtain parsing tree for each sentence in our system. Moreover, we also combine multiple constrains to improve the linguistic quality of the compressed sentences in our system. Under the guidance of linguistic knowledge, we list the following examples according to the compression rules in brief.

Rule 1: If the sentence includes brackets, then the brackets and the contents in the brackets will be removed. The reason is that the brackets in the news article generally act as the role of the explanation, and it will not affect the meaning of the original sentence after removing them.

Rule 2: If the temporal phrase is very long in the sentence, such as "2017-6-5 11:14:00" and "2017 年6月22日星期四 (Thursday, June 22, 2017)"All examples in English version are translated from the Chinese ones., then we will delete it from the sentence, because this type of the long phrase is very common in the news article, and it will not make great change to the sentence meaning with its deletion.

Rule 3: If the sentence contains the adjective or adjective phrase, then the adjective and adjective phrase can be removed. The reason is that the adjective or adjective phrase is mainly used to modify the restricted nouns, belonging to the secondary component in the sentence, and can be removed from the sentence. The Chinese sentence "马儿在绿油油的草地上吃草 (The house is grazing in the green grass)" can be changed to "马儿在草地上吃草 (The horse is grazing in the grass)" after removing the adjective 绿油油的 (green)".

Rule 4: If the sentence holds the positive adverb or adverb phrase, then we can delete the positive adverb or adverb phrase. Generally speaking, the adverb or adverb phrase is be used to express the state in a sentence to modify the verb, adjective, or the whole sentence. And however, for the negative adverb or adverb phrase, such as "不(no)", "没(not)", "不能(cannot)", we cannot remove it directly, and otherwise, the meaning of the sentence will be changed to the opposite one with the deletion of the negative adverb or adverb phrase.

Rule 5: If the sentence includes the prepositional phrase, then the prepositional phrase can be removed from the sentence. The prepositional phrase mainly intends to limit the subject, such as the temporal limit "于今晚(tonight)", the location limit "在我家(in my house)". It will not dramatically affect the meaning of the sentence with the removal of the prepositional phrase.

Rule 6: This one is related to the compression of the clause, and if a clause does not contain any key words, then it can be removed.

With the series of syntactic rules, our system can remove the secondary language information from the sentence, and obtain the more salient compressed form of the sentence. But there will be punctuation or sentence structure errors, and we have the syntax and semantic corrections for the compressed sentences to get our final news summary.

4 Experiments

In this section, we will discuss the evaluation results of our system in NLPCC Chinese single document summarization task.

In this paper, we adopt an approach based on key sentence extraction and sentence compression to generating Chinese news summary. To evaluate the quality of generated summaries for Chinese news articles, the well-known evaluation tool, ROUGE, has been used, and the tool presents five ROUGE scores, i.e. ROUGE-1, ROUGE-2, ROUGE-3, ROUGE-4 and ROUGE-SU4. The ROUGE tool also generates recall, precision and F-measure for each evaluation.

4.1 Multi-feature Combination

In the training phase, our system tries to search the best weights for the feature combination of the four kind of features. The experimental results with the different weights for the feature combination on the training set are showed in Table 1. In Table 1, the values before the four kinds of features represent the weights of $\lambda_1, \lambda_2, \lambda_3$, and λ_4.

Table 1. The experimental results for the weights optimization

Combination and weights	ROUGE-1	ROUGE-2	ROUGE-3	ROUGE-4	ROUGE-SU4
Ws + 2Pos + Sim + Len	0.51609	0.18918	0.09971	0.07281	0.20172
Ws + 2pos + 0.5Sim + 0.5Len	0.53160	0.20657	0.11163	0.08235	0.21344
Ws + 2Pos + 0Sim + 0Len	0.52093	0.19818	0.10072	0.08203	0.21046

According to the Table 1, the different weights for the four kinds of features have the different influence on the experimental results. We try to find out the best weight for each feature, and we select the weights in second line of the above Table 1 on the testing set.

4.2 Sentence Compression

The sentence compression plays an important role in the document summarization task. After simplifying the long sentences into the short ones with preserving important information according to the heuristic linguistic rules, the pre-extracted candidate sentences can be compressed, and the examples for sentence compression results are listed in the following.

Example 1:

一名男子乘电梯下楼，到距离三层三四个台阶处，他的鞋突然被扶梯卡住，
不能动弹。(A man took the elevator down the stairs, but when reaching three or four steps to the third floor, his shoes were suddenly stuck by the escalator and he could not move.)

The preceding example is extracted from the testing set. Firstly, we choose Stanford Parser software to obtain parsing tree for this sentence, and the parsing tree is showed in the following Fig. 2.

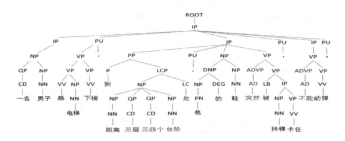

Fig. 2. The parsing tree

According to the Rules 4 and 5 mentioned above, after deleting the adverb phrase "突然 (suddenly)" and the prepositional phrase "到距离三层三四个台阶处 (when reaching three or four steps to the third floor)" in the parsing tree, the system can hold the compressed sentence, i.e. "一名男子乘电梯下楼，他的鞋被扶梯卡住,不能动弹。 (A man took the elevator down the stairs, but his shoes were stuck by the escalator and he could not move.)". From this example, we can also find that the second negative adverb phrase "不能(could not)" cannot be removed from the parsing tree, and otherwise, the meaning of the original sentence will be changed.

Example 2:

发布日期：2016-03-22<Paragraph>19:19:24据澎湃新闻上周五报道,中国最

大的电商公司阿里巴巴正在为员工盖"福利房",对员工按市场价的六折出售。

(Release date: 2016-03-22 <Paragraph> 19:19:24 Alibaba, China's biggest e-commerce company, is building apartments to sell to its employees at a discount of about 40%, the PengPai news reports on last Friday.).

According to the Rule 1, "<Paragraph>" should be removed, and the long temporal phrase "2016-03-22 19:19:24" also should be deleted according to the Rule 2, and meanwhile there are other phrases in this sentence that should be deleted. In the end, the condensed sentence is "中国电商公司阿里巴巴盖"福利房",对员工六折出售。" (Alibaba, China's e-commerce company, is building apartments to sell to its employees at a discount of about 40%.)".

From the preceding examples, we can find that some of the compressed sentences are not smooth, but they can fully represent the central semantic information of the original sentences.

4.3   Official Evaluation Results

In official evaluation, the peer summaries are automatically compared with the reference summaries by using the ROUGE toolkit. The character-based ROUGE-2 and ROUGE-SU4 Recall/F-measure is used as evaluation metrics. The following Fig. 3 is the official evaluation results for all the participants.

Our group has occupied the third position among all the groups. The results show that our system is efficient in Chinese news summarization.

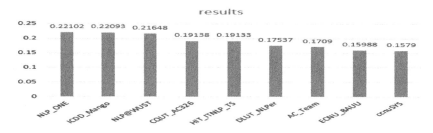

Fig. 3. Evaluation results for all task groups

5   Conclusion

In this paper, we focus on the single document summarization task and adopt the sentence extraction and compression to generate a short text for the Chinese news article. The sentence extraction is achieved by the combination of four kinds of features and the sentence compression is accomplished by parsing tree and syntactic rules. The experimental results show that our system is efficient in generating a single document summarization for news article.

In the future, we will introduce more features into the Chinese single document summarization, such as coherent and semantic features. The other methods, like neural network based on attention model [10], will be also applied to selecting the salient sentences in our future work.

Acknowledgments. The work presented in this paper is partially supported by the Major Projects of National Social Science Foundation of China under No. 11&ZD189, Natural Science Foundation of China under No. 61402341, Planning Foundation of Wuhan Science and Technology Bureau under No. 2016060101010047, and Open Foundation of Hubei Province Key Laboratory under No. 2016znss05A.

References

1. Luhn, H.: The automatic creation of literature abstracts. IBM J. Res. Dev. **2**(2), 159–165 (1958)
2. Liu, M., Wang, L., Nie, L.: Weibo-oriented Chinese news summarization via multi-feature combination. In: Li, J., Ji, H., Zhao, D., Feng, Y. (eds.) NLPCC 2015. LNCS (LNAI), vol. 9362, pp. 581–589. Springer, Cham (2015). https://doi.org/10.1007/978-3-319-25207-0_55
3. John, A., Wilscy, M.: Random forest classifier based multi-document summarization system. In: International Conference on Computer Engineering and Systems, pp. 132–138 (2013)
4. Moawad, I., Aref, M.: Semantic graph reduction approach for abstractive text summarization. In: International Conference on Computer Engineering and Systems, pp. 132–138 (2012)
5. Hirao, T., Yoshida, Y., Nishino, M.: Single-document summarization as a tree knapsack problem. In: Conference on Empirical Methods in Natural Language Processing, pp. 1515–1520 (2013)
6. Napoles, C., Durme, B.: Evaluating sentence compression: pitfalls and suggested remedies. In: Workshop on Monolingual Text-to-text Generation, pp. 91–97 (2011)
7. Cohn, T., Lapata, M.: Sentence compression as tree transduction. J. Artif. Intell. Res. **34**(1), 637–674 (2009)
8. Alias, S., Mohammad, S.K., Hoon, G.K.: A Malay text summarizer using pattern-growth method with sentence compression rules. In: Third International Conference on Information Retrieval and Knowledge Management, pp. 7–12. IEEE (2017)
9. Filippova, K., Alfonseca, E.: Sentence compression by deletion with LSTMs. In: Conference on Empirical Methods in Natural Language Processing, pp. 360–368 (2015)
10. Nallapati, R., Zhou, B.: Abstractive Text Summarization Using Sequence-to-Sequence RNNs and Beyond. IBM Watson (2016)

A News Headlines Classification Method Based on the Fusion of Related Words

Yongguan Wang, Binjie Meng, Pengyuan Liu$^{(\boxtimes)}$, and Erhong Yang

School of Information Science, Beijing Language and Culture University,
Beijing, China
yongguan1992@163.com, mllrose@126.com,
liupengyuan@pku.edu.cn, yerhong@blcu.edu.cn

Abstract. Short text classification is a challenging work as a result of several words, usually fewer than 20 words, in each text which brings about a problem of feature sparsity. In this paper, we propose a method of extending short text to cope with the problem of data sparsity. Additionally, we combine extension of short text, which forms a new representation with the word vector of each word in the short text trained by word2vec model on large-scale corpus. Furthermore, the new representation works as input for neural bag-of-words (NBOW) model. We evaluate this method on NLPCC 2017 Evaluation Task 2. The experimental results show that extension of short text extension with NBOW model outperforms baselines and can achieve excellent performance on the news headline classification task.

Keywords: Short text classification · NBOW · Text extension

1 Introduction

Short text classification is the task of automatically labeling short documents, such as news headlines and weibo blogs, which has numerous applications including topic categorization, sentiment analysis, or question answering. Until now, general machine learning methods, such as support vector machine (SVM), Naive Bayes Classifier (short text) and k-nearest neighbors (KNN), can be applied in text categorization and achieve desired performance. However, these methods based on BOW representation usually get unsatisfactory performance when processing short text features.

Short text, such as Chinese news headlines, usually consists of dozens of words, which provides limited contextual information and thus results in high sparsity in the text presentation. To solve this problem, the researchers put attention to text representation and classifier optimization. The existing methods in this field can be roughly classified into two groups. The first one is to expand short text features by utilizing external repositories (e.g. Wikipedia and web search-engine based). For example, Sahami and Heilman [1] calculated the short text document similarity and incorporated the extended short text, which is based on the web search results. Bollegala et al. [2] also added web search engine information as extended short text. Besides, web page ranking and lexical and syntax analysis was taken into consideration. Phan et al. [3] proposed a classification algorithm to extract useful information from Wikipedia. In his

© Springer International Publishing AG 2018
X. Huang et al. (Eds.): NLPCC 2017, LNAI 10619, pp. 818–827, 2018.
https://doi.org/10.1007/978-3-319-73618-1_71

model, LDA is also used to obtain topic information from short text. Then he merged these feature words and topic information as expanded short text. However, the performance of these methods highly depends on whether the extended knowledge matches the short text.

Another group of methods consist of the deep neural networks based on language model, such as CNNs and RNNs. With the rapid development of deep learning, neural language models and their variations have achieved remarkable results on various classification tasks such as sentiment analysis and question-type classification. Kim [4] applied a simple CNN with a single convolution layer on top of pre-trained word vectors obtained from an unsupervised neural language model for sentence level classification. Despite little tuning of hypermeters, the simple model achieves excellent results on classification tasks. Kalchbrenner et al. [5] introduced a Dynamic Convolution neural networks (DCNN) model, which employed dynamic k-max pooling to keep sequential information. RNN [6] is able to deal with sequences of any length and capture long-term dependencies, and LSTM [7] can avoid the problem of gradient exploding or vanishing that occur in standard RNN. These two models and their variations [8–10] are often applied in classification tasks. In addition, Sentence representation is the basic work of text categorization. Sentence modeling [5, 11–13] is also related to our task.

In this paper, we introduce a model based on related filtering and extension of short text for short text classification. In order to make full use of semantic and syntactic information in the short text, we propose a method of short text extension. First of all, we find related words about each word in short text, which can easily be retrieved from the word vectors trained by word2vec [13] model on large-scale corpus. We treat the related words as an extension of each word, and the vector representation of each word and it's extension are merged into a new representation. The new representation is thought as the sentence feature vector, which is the input of the classification model. In this paper, NBOW model, CNN model and LSTM model are treated as three basic classification models. In addition, there are two different ways to filter the related words. One is to filter with the TFIDF values of the words, and the other is to calculate the word similarity based on word2vec model. These two methods are performed respectively in this paper, and the results manifest that combining TFIDF value with word similarity as a filter of the related words is the best one compared with other filters. And adding NBOW model as the classification model can get the best performance compared with other baseline models, such as CNN, LSTM and NBOW models in the headline classification task. Besides, the word vectors in three baseline models are initialized randomly.

2 NBOW Model of Fusion Related Words

In this section we will describe our model in detail. The model we proposed in this paper consists of two parts. The first part is the baseline model NBOW, whose main function is to learn text representation from input short texts and classify the texts. The other part is short text expansion, which is to obtain extension of the short text. In this part, we firstly train the word vectors by word2vec model, from which we calculate distance (similarity) between each target word and other words. The related words are the nearest several words to the target words, which are then selected by the filter of word TFIDF value and similarity. After this, the related words after being selected form the extension of the short text, which is fused into the NBOW model to make classification. The model structure is shown in Fig. 1.

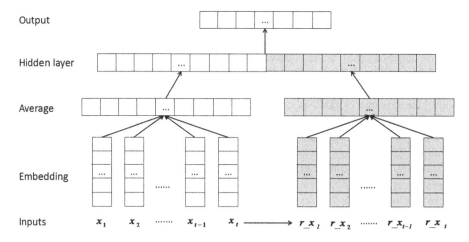

Fig. 1. Model architecture

2.1   Short Text Representation

A news title sentence of length t (padded where necessary) is represented as $x = [x_1, x_2, \ldots, x_t]$, where x_i stands for the d-dimensional word vectors of the i_{th} word in the sentence. In our model, we firstly input the t d-dimensional word vectors for the average operation, and get a d-dimensional word vector z_x, which is the representation of the sentence. Then, the representation z_x of sentence is used as input of hidden layer, and the ReLU (Rectified Linear Units) function is the activation function which is to calculate the hidden layer output h_x.

$$ReLU(x) = \begin{cases} x, x > 0 \\ 0, x \leq 0 \end{cases} \tag{1}$$

$$h_x = ReLU(w \cdot z_x + b) \tag{2}$$

2.2   Short Text Extensions

News headlines are short texts, which contain less semantic information and less features. When using the NBOW model for classification, its' performance is not as good as long text, so extending short text is a method to improve performance.

We propose a method of expanding the short text, which is treated as the input for classification model. In this paper, word2vec model is used to train the distributed vector representation of words, and then the relevant words of the words in sentence are determined by the distance between the word and its target word. Given a news headline sentence x, where x_i represents the i_{th} word. Find the m related words $r\_x_i = \left[r\_x_i^{(1)}, r\_x_i^{(2)}, \ldots, r\_x_i^{(m)} \right]$ of x_i through the pre-trained word2vec model, and calculate the similarity $sim\_x_i = \left[sim\_x_i^{(1)}, sim\_x_i^{(2)}, \ldots, sim\_x_i^{(m)} \right]$ of words pairs, where $sim\_x_i^{(j)}$ stands for the cosine distance between the word x_i and the word $r\_x_i^{(j)}$. Thus, we extend a sentence x whose length is t to obtain $t \times m$ related words $[r\_x_1, r\_x_2, \ldots, r\_x_t]$.

2.3 Related Word Filtering

In order to reduce the noise in the extended text, the relative words of short text will be filtered. Firstly, the corpus data of training set is statistically calculated to calculate the TFIDF value of all words. For each input sample of sentence x, a threshold τ is set for the TFIDF value. If the TFIDF value of some word in the sentence is smaller than τ, all the related words of this word are discarded. Then the word similarity is used to filter all the related words. The first way is to select top m related words by the similarity of word pairs for each word, and the other is to set the similarity threshold φ. If the similarity of one word is less than φ, the word will be filtered out. In our experiments, only the first is used after all these operations, we obtain the final related words r_x of one sentence.

2.4 Fusion Related Words

For an input sentence x, all related words r_x are used as input, where r_x is actually the word vector of all related words, obtained from the pre-trained word2vec model. First, the vector of all the related words are made an average operation. After that, we get a d-dimensional word vector r_z_x which is related information of the sentence x, and then we can get the output r_h_x after going through one hidden layer. Then we connect the sentence representation h_x and r_h_x, and obtain a new sentence representation h_x', which is a 2d-dimensional vector.

$$r\_h_x = Relu(w \cdot r\_z_x + b) \tag{3}$$

$$h_x' = h_x + r\_h_x \tag{4}$$

2.5 Classification

At the output layer, a full connection layer is applied to classify sentences after which output the classification results. The sentence representation vectors h_x' is used as input and calculate the output y. According to the real classification labels of training data, the model parameters are updated by back propagation algorithm.

$$y = \text{softmax}\left(w \cdot h_x' + b\right) \tag{5}$$

3 Experiments

3.1 Dataset

We conduct our experiment with the dataset of NLPCC 2017 Evaluation Task 2–Chinese News Headline Categorization, whose data released by NLPCC 2017 is collected from several Chinese news websites, such as toutiao, sina, and so on. In this task, most title sentence word numbers are less than 20, with a mean of 12.07. All the sentences are segmented by the python Chinese segmentation tool jieba, and the number of all categories in the dataset is 18. The complete dataset consists of training set, validation set and test set. The detailed information of each category and sub dataset is shown in Table 1. (The information of categories and sub datasets).

Table 1. The information of categories

Category	Train	Dev	Test
Entertainment	10000	2000	2000
Sports	10000	2000	2000
Car	10000	2000	2000
Society	10000	2000	2000
Tech	10000	2000	2000
World	10000	2000	2000
Finance	10000	2000	2000
Game	10000	2000	2000
Travel	10000	2000	2000
Military	10000	2000	2000
History	10000	2000	2000
Baby	10000	2000	2000
Fashion	10000	2000	2000
Food	10000	2000	2000
Discovery	4000	2000	2000
Story	4000	2000	2000
Regimen	4000	2000	2000
Essay	4000	2000	2000

3.2 Settings

We implemented our model based on Tensorflow—an open source software library for numerical computation using data flow graph. We initialized the word vectors with the dimension of 200, which was pre-trained by word2vec [11] on several of corpus, such as Wikipedia documents, sougou news corpus and People's Daily corpus. The embedding layers in our model requires fixed-length input, we define 40 to represent the maximum length of sentence in the datasets, and pad zero at the end of the last word in the sentence whose length is shorter than max length. For all neural network models, batch size is initialized to a value of 64. Besides, the number of filter in CNN model, which is also called window, is initialized with 128. And to capture different syntactic and semantic information, the size of filter is 1, 2 and 3. As for LSTM model, we set 300 as hidden size.

3.3   Model Variations

In the experiment, we tested our approach based on the three baseline models, and compared the results of different models. Explanations for different model representations are as follows (The representation of other models is similar to that of CNN).

- CNN-w2v: Using CNN model for classification and using pre-trained vectors from word2vec.
- CNN-w2v-extension: Using CNN model for classification and using pre-trained vectors from word2vec, extending input sentences (News headlines) by related words. For each word, we set the number of extensions m to 10.
- CNN-w2v-extension-filters: Using CNN model for classification and using pre-trained vectors from word2vec, extending input sentences (News headlines) by related words. In addition, using the TFIDF value to filter the related words.

3.4   Results and Discussion

By comparing the baseline model (without pre-trained word vector) and baseline+ word2vec model, we can find that the accuracy of using pre-trained word vector as the original input for news headlines classification is higher than that of the original input using the random initialization of the word vector. The reason is that the word vectors trained by the word2vec tool contain contextual semantic information, so they can get better results in text classification. Then, comparing NBOW-w2v-extension model and NBOW-w2v model, the results show that it is effective to classify short texts after expansion, and can obviously improve classification performance. However, the use of TFIDF filtering related words has a slight increase in NBOW models, but other models do not improve performance. We argue that this is because the expansion scale of news heading sentences in our experiments is not large. Therefore, the noise introduced by this cannot have a strong impact on classification. In addition, most neural network models have the ability to automatically extract features from inputs, which are in fact similar to filter functions. So, in our experiments, adding filters does not significantly improve classification performance (Tables 2 and 3).

Table 4 shows the results of misclassification of the NBOW-w2v-extension-filter model. We can find by analysis that the category information contained in some news headlines is ambiguous. For example, the word "营养价值" in sentence 3 means that the sentence may belong to the category of regimen, and another word "吃" in the same sentence means that it should belong to the category of food. So we infer that without

Table 2. Accuracy of different models

Group	Model	Accuracy%
CNN	CNN	59.54
	CNN-w2v	69.13
	CNN-w2v-extension	80.62
	CNN-w2v-extension-filter	78.46
LSTM	LSTM	74.70
	LSTM-w2v	79.20
	LSTM-w2v-extension	80.13
	LSTM-w2v-extension-filter	80.06
NBOW	NBOW	78.30
	NBOW-w2v	80.09
	NBOW-w2v-extension	81.10
	NBOW-w2v-extension-filter	**81.34**

Table 3. The test result of NBOW-w2v-extension-filter model

Tag	Precision	Recall
<unk>	0.0000	0.0000
History	0.8219	0.8535
Military	0.8377	0.8565
Baby	0.8250	0.8865
World	0.7131	0.7095
Tech	0.8094	0.8240
Game	0.8962	0.8760
Society	0.5727	0.6205
Sports	0.8931	0.8895
Travel	0.7334	0.8170
Car	0.8941	0.8825
Food	0.8200	0.8790
Entertainment	0.7375	0.7825
Finance	0.8090	0.8195
Fashion	0.8037	0.8150
Discovery	0.9372	0.8575
Story	0.8585	0.7435
Regimen	0.8909	0.7515
Essay	0.8553	0.7775
Overall	0.8134	0.8134

news text, a news headline sentence can belong to several categories at once. This led to the difficulty of classifying them correctly. Table 5 shows the extension of a news headlines. For example, in the absence of extensions, the sentence "特朗普上台，美国会减弱针对中俄军事压力？" classification results are world,

This is a wrong result. After the sentence was extended, we got some words, such as "军队","反恐" and so on. These words can be used to expand the features of military categories. However, when extending a sentence, it may extend to some words related to another category. Therefore, when a sentence contains different categories of information, how to choose the right word is a problem to be solved.

Table 4. Examples of misclassification of NBOW-w2v-extension-filter

	News headline	Classification result	Correct result
1	你是我心头的痛——记《安生与七月》	essay	story
2	你本来就拥有的5大奢侈品	fashion	baby
3	它的营养价值很高，但有很多人却不敢吃	food	regimen

Table 5. The comparison of classification results between NBOW models

Input text	Extended words	Classification result (no extension)	Classification result (extension)	Correct result
不只是地球，其他星球也下雪！还有粉红色的雪呢！	...月球 火星 星球 行星 冥王星 宇宙 地球.表面 太阳系 外太空 人类系 国度 银河系 月球 下雨 有雪 大雪 刮风 落雪...	travel	discovery	discovery
特朗普上台，美国会减弱针对中俄军事压力？	罗姆尼 希拉里 麦凯恩 奥巴马 共和党 杜特蒂 萨科齐 美国 共和党 国防 政治 军队 反恐 军事力量 外交 网络战 武装力量 防务 军备...	world	military	military

4 Conclusion

In this paper, we propose a model based on neural bag of words (NBOW) on top of word2vec, which merges with related words and TFIDF filters for news headlines classification. We have described a series of experiments with convolution neural networks (CNN), long-short-term memory network (LSTM) and neural bag of words (NBOW) on top of word2vec. And we have demonstrated that our model performs best among all the other models. In particular, the related words are a good supplement of syntactic and semantic information for classification, which also solve the problem of data sparsity to some degree.

Our model can be applied to sentence modeling as well as other natural language processing tasks. Future works can modify our model to complete long text classification tasks.

Acknowledgment. This research project is supported by Science Foundation of Beijing Language and Culture University (supported by "the Fundamental Research Funds for the Central Universities") (17PT05); Supported by Major Project of the National Language Committee of the 12th Five-Year Research Plan in 2015 (No. ZDI125-55)

References

1. Sahami, M., Heilman, T.D.: A web-based kernel function for measuring the similarity of short text snippets. In: Proceedings of the 15th International Conference on World Wide Web, pp. 377–386. ACM (2006)
2. Bollegala, D., Matsuo, Y., Ishizuka, M.: Measuring semantic similarity between words using web search engines. WWW **7**, 757–766 (2007)
3. Phan, X.H., Nguyen, L.M., Horiguchi, S.: Learning to classify short and sparse text & web with hidden topics from large-scale data collections. In: Proceedings of the 17th International Conference on World Wide Web. ACM, New York, pp. 91–100 (2008)
4. Kim, Y.: Convolutional neural networks for sentence classification. In: EMNLP, pp. 1746–1751 (2014)
5. Kalchbrenner, N., Grefenstette, E., Blunsom, P.A.: Convolutional neural network for modelling sentences. arXiv preprint arXiv:1404.2188 (2014)
6. Tang, D., Qin, B., Liu, T.: Document modeling with gated recurrent neural network for sentiment classification. In: EMNLP, pp. 1422–1432 (2015)
7. Tai, K.S., Socher, R., Manning, C.D.: Improved semantic representations from tree-structured long short-term memory networks, pp. 1556–1566. ACL (2015)
8. Liang, D., Zhang, Y.: AC-BLSTM: asymmetric convolutional bidirectional LSTM networks for text classification (2016)
9. Yogatama, D., Dyer, C., Ling, W., et al.: Generative and discriminative text classification with recurrent neural networks. arXiv preprint arXiv:1703.01898 (2017)
10. Mou, L., Peng, H., Li, G., et al.: Discriminative neural sentence modeling by tree-based convolution. arXiv preprint arXiv:1504.01106 (2015)
11. Chen, X., Qiu, X., Zhu, C., et al.: Sentence modeling with gated recursive neural network. In: EMNLP, pp. 793–798 (2015)

12. Zhang, Y., Wallace, B.: A sensitivity analysis of (and practitioners' guide to) convolutional neural networks for sentence classification. arXiv preprint arXiv:1510.03820 (2015)
13. Mikolov, T., Sutskever, I., Chen, K., Corrado, G.S., Dean, J.: Distributed representations of words and phrases and their compositionality. In Advances in Neural Information Processing Systems 26: 27th Annual Conference on Neural Iformation Processing Systems 2013. Proceedings of a Meeting held 5–8 December, 2013, Lake Tahoe, Nevada, USA, pp. 3111–3119 (2013)

Resolving Chinese Zero Pronoun with Word Embedding

Bingquan Liu[1], Xinkai Du[2], Ming Liu[1]([✉]), Chengjie Sun[1],
Guidong Zheng[1], and Chao Zou[1]

[1] Harbin Institute of Technology, Harbin, Heilongjiang, China
mliu@insun.hit.edu.cn
[2] Huilan Technology, Beijing, China

Abstract. Elliptical sentences are frequently seen in Chinese, especially in some particular situations, such as dialogues, which is challengeable to understand specific semantic. Chinese zero pronoun resolution, which recovers a noun phrase in the elliptical position, is an effective method to help machines understand natural languages. Traditional methods use the features, which are extracted from syntactic parsing trees manually. However, the long running time and the inaccuracy of automatic parsing algorithms have a bad influence on practical applications. In this work, we propose a new method based on long-short-term memory network that calculates dense vector representations for mention pairs without using features from syntactic parsing trees. These representations, which capture significant semantics for zero pronoun resolution, are built on distributed representation of words in surrounding contexts and candidate antecedents. Our method contributes to reducing the manual work of extracting features from parsing tress, which improves the F1-score of Chinese zero pronoun resolution system. Experimental results on OnotoNotes 5.0 Chinese dataset show our method achieves better performance compared with the state-of-the-art method.

Keywords: Chinese zero pronoun resolution · Deep learning
Long-short-term memory network · Distributed representation

1 Introduction

Anaphora, which is a common phenomenon in discourses or dialogues, will bring much ambiguity to understand semantics. There is a special anaphora phenomenon called zero anaphora of which anaphoric pronouns are omitted. In Chinese language, the subject or object can be omitted when it can be recovered from the context or is little interested for the reader/listener to know. In Chinese Treebank, the position where subject or object is elliptical is annotated with small *pro*, and it is called zero pronoun (ZP). Sometimes, we can recover ZP with other mentions (usually overt noun phrase NP, including overt pronoun OP, meanwhile another ZP but little significance) which refer to the same entity or event with ZP, but sometimes cannot. Thus, the ZP which can be recovered is called anaphoric zero pronoun (AZP) and the coreferential mention

© Springer International Publishing AG 2018
X. Huang et al. (Eds.): NLPCC 2017, LNAI 10619, pp. 828–838, 2018.
https://doi.org/10.1007/978-3-319-73618-1_72

of AZP is called antecedent. Most AZPs have antecedents which appear in the front of them. There is a simple example which is selected from OntoNotes 5.0 showing as follow:

已经有*[13名阿拉伯裔民众]*在*[*pro*]*支持巴勒斯坦的示威事件中丧生。

[13 Arabs] have died in *[*pro*]* support-Palestine demonstration.

where *[*pro*]* is used to denote an AZP which refers to antecedent *[13 Arabs]*.

Compared with OP resolution, AZP resolution is a more challenging task. In OP resolution, there are many effective semantic features, such as *NUMBER* and *GENDER*, which make it possibly to judge consistency between the OP and the antecedent and identify if they are coreferential. However, we can see there are no OPs in the example above, just a *pro*.Thus, it is a great challenge to extract features for AZPs and AZP-NP pairs.

In this paper, we propose two methods which calculate dense vector representations to denote the features of AZPs or AZP-NP pairs built from distributed representation of words instead of extracting from syntactic parsing trees which was used in the previous works. The first approach is a sample method, but it needs to select some important words by handicraft, such as verb, object words, and then gets the features of AZP-NP pairs. Another approach uses long-short-term memory (LSTM) network to calculate the features of AZP-NP pairs which can capture deeper semantic knowledge from distributed representation of words in surrounding contexts and candidate antecedents. After getting the features of AZP-NP pairs, both of the methods use three-layer artificial neural network as classifier to predict the probability that if AZP and NP which in the AZP-NP pairs refer to the same entity or event, and then choose the best NP as the antecedent of the AZP to complete resolution according to the probability of AZP-NP pairs.

2 Related Work

Chinese has much more zero anaphora phenomenon than English language owing to the different thinking modes underlying the two languages. Thus, this section briefly overviews the related work on Chinese ZP resolution.

ZP resolution is usually divided into two subtasks, AZP identification which is to recognize the position where AZP appears and AZP resolution which is to choose the antecedent for the AZP. Many related works take more attention to the second subtask so that there are less thorough studies of AZP identification.

In AZP identification subtask, rule-based methods [1, 2] are simple, effective, and robust enough for the next subtask because of the high recall. Meanwhile, machine-learning methods [1, 3] on AZP identification subtask often provides higher precision and F-score.

In AZP resolution subtask, the related works can be split into three main approaches: rule-based method, supervised machine-learning method and unsupervised machine-learning method.

Rule-based method

Rule-based methods for AZP resolution were adopted at the beginning of the studies. Converse [4] may be the earliest researcher who built the Chinese AZP resolution corpus based on the Penn Chinese Treebank (CTB) and started the work on Chinese AZP resolution. His rule-based approach which used the Hobbs' Algorithm [5] was applied to resolve both pronouns and zero pronouns.

The Centering Theory [6] which has been proved to be an extremely useful theory of discourse coherence and salience can discover the important entity which plays a central role in the context. Yeh and Chen [7] employed centering theory and constraint rules to complete a resolution system. In addition, Zhang [8] made a research on ellipsis recovery for Chinese dialogue based on the centering theory which was used in question answering system.

Supervised machine-learning method

Supervised machine-learning methods for AZP resolution are all based on mention pair model [9] which is a machine-learning architecture for coreference resolution. In Chinese ZP resolution, researchers replace mention pairs with AZP-NP pairs and predict whether NP and AZP refer to the identical entity.

The first machine learning approach for identification and resolution of Chinese Zero pronouns was proposed by Zhao and Ng [1]. They made a specific definition of ZP resolution and gave the evaluation in terms of recall, precision and F-measure which was adopted in this paper. They extracted twelve features of AZP, ten features of overt NP and four features of AZP-NP pair from the standard word segmentation, POS tags and syntax parsing trees provided by CTB. Then they trained the AZP resolution classifier using the J48 decision tree learning algorithm. The results showed that their method was better than the heuristic rule-based methods before.

Kong and Zhou [3] employed the syntax parsing tree architecture which was surrounding AZP and overt NP as inputs. Then they applied context-sensitive convolution tree kernels to calculate the similarity between AZP and overt NP by training support vector machine (SVM) classifier.

Song and Wang [10] combined the two subtasks, which were AZP identification and AZP resolution, into a unified machine learning framework with Markov logic to make joint inference and joint learning. In their method, they used shallow parsing information to build local and global rules, and then inferred by the method of integer linear programming. The parameters of model were estimated by Margin Infused Relaxation Algorithm.

Unsupervised machine-learning method

The unsupervised machine-learning methods were proposed in last two years and got better results than machine-learning methods. The first unsupervised approach which was proposed by Chen and Ng [11] employed a rank model trained on Opscoreference annotations to resolve ZPs. In addition, by using integer linear programming, it could enhance the compatibility between the overt pronoun and its governing verb to improve the accuracy of the model. The F-score evaluated on OntoNotes 5.0 was 48.7% with gold AZP and parsing trees.

Chen and Ng [2] also proposed an unsupervised probabilistic generative model based on a novel hypothesis that a probabilistic pronoun resolver trained on overt pronouns in unsupervised manner could be used to resolve ZPs. The model got 47.7% F-score on OntoNotes 5.0. Chen and Ng [12] improved the model in [2] and got the state-of-the-art resolver.

3 Our Methods

In this section, we propose two different methods of AZP resolution. Firstly, we employ the mention pair model of co-reference resolution with using word embedding as features. Secondly, we employ LSTM to calculate deeper semantic representation of the mention pair.

3.1 AZP Resolution

In many previous works, researchers extracted features or rules from parsing tree, but the resolvers did not work well on automatic parsing tree. Therefore, we attempt to use distributed representation of words to generate dense vector representations for AZP-NP pairs instead of extracting features from gold parsing tree.

The distributed representation of words is also called word embedding which came from neural probabilistic language model [13] initially. That Mikolov [14] simplified and improved the model by removing the hidden layer made it be widely used in many natural language tasks and get good results.

In this part, we propose two approaches to solve AZP with using word embedding. One of the two approaches called simple neural network (SNN) method uses the distance features and dense vector representation which is handicrafted. The other one called LSTM method uses LSTM network to capture significant semantics information from words in surrounding contexts and candidate antecedents to denote the features of AZP-NP. In LSTM method, there are no handcrafted features except distance features. Except those, all features are learned by model.

3.2 SNN Method

This method selects distributed representation of important words to extract features for AZP-NP pair. The features of the AZP-NP pairs contains 8 parts which are described as follow:

1. Distance features: the log value of the sentence distance and the word distance between the AZP and the candidate antecedent.
2. Representation of candidate antecedent: the mean value of the distributed representation of words which appear in candidate antecedent.
3. Above context representation of candidate antecedent: the mean value of the distributed representation of words which appear in the front of the candidate antecedent.
4. Follow context representation of candidate antecedent: the mean value of the distributed representation of words which appear behind the candidate antecedent.

5. Context representation of AZP: the mean value of the distributed representation of words which appear surround of the AZP.
6. Embedding of key verb in candidate antecedent's sentence: the candidate antecedent's key verb is the nearest verb to the candidate antecedent in the same sentence.
7. Embedding of key verb in AZP's sentence: the AZP's key verb is the first verb which appears behind the AZP in the same sentence.
8. Embedding of object in AZP's sentence: the object is the first noun behind the key verb of AZP.

Note that we use log values in *feature 1*, because on one hand, that the distance features is much easier to learn using gradient descent compared to the other embedding features, on the other hand, the growth properties of log function reflects the distance the candidate antecedent away from the AZP. Meanwhile in features 2, 3, 6, 7 and 8, if there is no context words, candidate antecedent's key verb, AZP's key verb or AZP's object, the embedding will be set with all zeros and in features 2, 3 and 4, exist a sliding window to extract words in the context. Furthermore, in features 7 and 8, we use the first verb behind AZP as the key verb and use object not subject, because almost AZPs which is about 95% in our corpus play a role of subject in the sentence.

In features 2, 3, 4 and 5, we use mean values to denote the composition distributed representation which can capture the mean semantic feature of every words. Because distributed representation is trained based on language model, we hope to get the similarity between AZP's and candidate antecedent's context by features 3, 4 and 5, and the coherence of the sentence if candidate is recovered in AZP position by features 2 and 5. In addition, distributed representation always works well on relationship mining, and the relation between verb and object or subject is an import relationship in the sentence, thus we hope to get the relation between candidate antecedent and key verb of AZP by features 2 and 7.

We merge these features into one long vector, and then use 3-layer neural network as classifier to learn the semantic information below. When training the parameters, the negative log likelihood loss which was regularized by l2 with a rate of 0.1 was minimized with stochastic gradient descent method of which learning rate is 0.03. We copy positive cases 4 times to balance the dataset. In this method, there are 50 dimensions for our word embeddings, 352 dimensions for the input layer, 50 dimensions for sigmoid hidden layer and 1 dimension for output layer. The final output is taken to be the probability that candidate antecedent is the correct antecedent of AZP.

3.3   LSTM Method

LSTM uses long short term network [15–17] with mean pooling to calculate deeper semantic feature representation of the AZP-NP pair. LSTM network is a special kind of recurrent neural network which is widely used in many natural language tasks. The new structure called memory which LSTM uses to control inputs and outputs, thus LSTM can restore useful information, and drop useless information.

The inputs contain indexes of words in the vocabulary and distance features which is the same with that in SNN method. If the word does not exist in the vocabulary, we use default word index −1 to represent it. The projection layer is to replace index of words with corresponding embedding. The embeddings of word which index is −1 is a vector with all zeros.

The LSTM layer is the key layer which calculates deeper features of AZP-NP pair. In this layer, there two LSTM architectures, one is for context, the other one is for candidate antecedent. Because of the gate structure of LSTM, we believe it can capture useful semantic information. Then the mean pooling layer gets the mean semantic features of LSTM outputs. Our method is just like using LSTM layer and mean pooling layer to calculate the features of AZP-NP pair, and then input them to a neural network, but the parameters are updated together. The final output $p(a, z)$ is taken to be the probability that a is the correct antecedent of z. Thus, we minimize the negative log likelihood of the data to learn the parameters θ of this method:

$$L(\theta) = -\frac{1}{n} \sum_{a,z \in mentions} \log(y_i p(a, z) + (1 - y_i)(1 - p(a, z))) \tag{1}$$

where n is the size of mentions' set and y_i is a boolean variable that takes value 1 if candidate antecedent and AZP are coreferential and 0 if otherwise.

During training our model, we minimize the loss which was regularized by l2 with a rate of 0.1 solved by stochastic gradient descent using 0.3 as its learning rate. We copy positive cases 4 times to balance the dataset. There are 50 dimensions for our word embeddings, 50 dimensions for our LSTM layer, 50 dimensions for our sigmoid hidden layer and 1 dimension for predicting, thus there are about 51 k parameters in our method. We set the max number of iterative steps with 50, evaluate our model on development dataset after each epoch and select the highest scoring parameters as the final model.

4   Experiments

In this section, we realize our method using Theano [18, 19] which is a packet for deep learning and can build network architecture easily. We compare our methods with baselines in many aspects and the results show our methods are competitive.

4.1   Preparation Work

Dataset. For evaluation, we employ the Chinese portion of the OntoNotes 5.0 that was used in the official CoNLL-2012 shared task. We use the train set as our train set and development set as our test set, because of the previous experiments of Chen and Ng [1, 2]. In the dataset, the zero pronoun is marked as *pro* in parser tree, and consider a zero pronoun as anaphoric if it is coreferential with a preceding zero pronoun or overt NP which is antecedent. The documents in corpus come from Broadcast News (BN), Newswire (NW), Broadcast Conversation (BC), Telephone Conversation (TC), Web Blog (WB) and Magazine (MZ).

Evaluation measures. We express the results of ZP resolution in terms of recall (R), precision (P) and F-score (F).

Baseline system. In AZP identification subtasks, we employ two baselines. One is a rule-based method mentioned in Chen and Ng's work [2] (CN14), and the other one is a machine-learning method proposed in Chen and Ng's work [1] (CN13) and compared in Chen and Ng's paper [1, 2]. In AZP resolution subtasks, we employ the resolution system of Chen and Ng [11] (CN15) which has achieved the best result to date.

Evaluation settings. In AZP resolution subtasks, following Chen and Ng [1], we evaluate our model in three settings. In setting 1, we assume the availability of gold syntax parsing trees and gold AZPs both of which can be extracted from annotated corpus. In setting 2, our system uses gold syntax parsing trees and the AZPs which is distinguished by the AZP identification method we proposed in Sect. 3.2. In setting 3, our system employs the automatic syntax parsing trees provided by CoNLL-2012 shared task and automatic AZPs. In addition, we provide the result of our system with gold AZP and automatic syntax parsing trees as setting 4. All of the setting use the same parameters which are trained in setting 1.

4.2   Results and Analysis

AZP identification. Table 1 is the result of AZP identification subtask. As we can see, the method based on heuristic has a higher recall value than machine-learning approach, but lower precision value. Our method which combines GRU with rules balance the GRU method and rule-based method, and gets better result than the two baselines both in gold parser and automatic parser, no matter in recall, precision or F1-score. In addition, our GRU method which does not use features from parsing trees is better than the baseline system with automatic parsing trees, but it also has a far distance to the methods with gold syntax parsing.

Table 1. Result of AZP identification subtask

	Gold parsers			System parsers		
Systems	R	P	F	R	P	F
CN14 (Rule-based)	72.4	42.4	53.4	42.3	26.8	32.8
CN13 (Supervised)	50.6	55.1	52.8	30.8	34.4	32.5
Ours (Rule-based)	93.4	27.0	41.8	57.0	17.7	27.1
Ours (Rule-based + GRU)	73.3	42.8	54.1	46.0	28.6	35.2
Ours (GRU)	–	–	–	31.5	36.9	34.0

AZP resolution with setting 1. The result of AZP resolution with setting 1 is shown in Table 2. As we can see, compared with CN15 baseline system, our SNN method has resulted in a 1.4% increase in overall F-score and 1.8% in our LSTM method. In BN source, SNN method gets a top value 58.0%. What's more, compared with our SNN method, our LSTM method is more balanced in each source.

Table 2. Result of AZP resolution subtask with setting 1

G,G	CN15			Ours (SNN)			Ours (LSTM)		
Source	R	P	F	R	P	F	R	P	F
Overall (1713)	50.0	50.4	50.2	51.6	51.6	51.6	52.0	52.0	52.0
NW (84)	46.4	46.4	46.4	41.7	41.7	41.7	50.0	50.0	50.0
MZ (162)	38.9	39.1	39.0	35.2	35.2	35.2	38.9	38.9	38.9
WB (284)	51.8	51.8	51.8	49.7	49.7	49.7	48.9	48.9	48.9
BN (390)	53.8	53.8	53.8	58.0	58.0	58.0	55.4	55.4	55.4
BC (510)	49.2	49.6	49.4	52.9	52.9	52.9	55.5	55.5	55.5
TC (283)	51.9	53.5	52.7	54.4	54.4	54.4	52.3	52.3	52.3

Compared with traditional method, our method consider more about context. In SNN method, besides distributed representation of words, we also extract features such as key verb of AZP, the key verb of candidate antecedent and the object of AZP. These features have more semantic information, especially containing complex relationship between each features. All of these make our SNN method performance well. In LSTM, we make full use of the attribute which has a memory and can forget the useless information, and the distributed representation of AZP-Pair is learned by itself without manual works. It is a successful deep-learning method for AZP resolution.

AZP resolution with setting 2. Table 3 shows the results of AZP resolution with setting 2. From the results, we can see that our method is weaker than the CN15 baseline system. That CN15 jointly identifies and resolves AZPs and therefore can consider more comprehensive information. Farther more, the parameters of our AZP resolution method are trained on setting 1 which do not consider the condition that ZP is not AZP, but automatic AZP identification provides the ZPs.

AZP resolution with setting 3. Table 4 shows the results of AZP resolution with setting 3. As we can see that our SNN method gets 18.2% F-score and LSTM method gets 17.9% in overall source which are better than CN15 baseline system. In MZ source, our methods are less than baseline in setting 1, but better in setting 3.

Table 3. Result of AZP resolution subtask with setting 2

G,A	CN15			Ours (SNN)			Ours (LSTM)		
Source	R	P	F	R	P	F	R	P	F
Overall (1713)	35.7	26.2	30.3	31.8	26.9	29.1	34.4	24.6	28.7
NW (84)	32.1	28.1	30.0	23.8	23.3	23.5	29.8	24.3	26.7
MZ (162)	29.6	19.6	23.6	20.4	23.1	21.6	22.8	19.8	21.2
WB (284)	39.1	22.9	28.9	27.8	24.0	25.8	29.6	19.9	23.8
BN (390)	30.8	30.7	30.7	31.5	30.0	30.7	33.1	24.8	28.4
BC (510)	35.9	26.6	30.6	32.6	26.3	29.1	37.1	26.6	31.0
TC (283)	43.5	28.7	34.6	43.8	28.9	34.8	44.2	27.7	34.0

In this setting, we use automatic syntax parsing trees which cause the large decrease of baseline system on F-score, because CN15 uses the context features extracted from parsing tree so that it depends so much on parsing tree. Our system generates features from distributed representation of surrounding words. Thus, our systems in setting 3 are better than baseline.

AZP resolution with setting 4. Table 5 shows the result of AZP resolution with setting 4. In this part, we use the method (CN14) proposed by Chen and Ng [2] which just obtains lower performance than the best system CN15 in setting 1. The result of CN14 in Table 5 uses the setting 1 which uses the gold syntax parsing trees and gold AZP, and our system uses setting 4 which uses the automatic syntax parsing trees and gold AZP. For Table 5, we can see that our LSTM method is a little better than CN14, although CN14 uses the gold syntax parser. This results show our methods reduce the dependence of parser greatly.

Table 4. Result of AZP resolution subtask with setting 3

A, A	CN15			Ours (SNN)			Ours (LSTM)		
Source	R	P	F	R	P	F	R	P	F
Overall (1713)	19.6	15.5	17.3	21.7	15.7	18.2	19.4	16.6	17.9
NW (84)	11.9	14.3	13.0	10.7	9.0	9.8	10.7	13.6	12.0
MZ (162)	4.9	4.7	4.8	7.4	8.8	8.1	7.4	10.2	8.6
WB (284)	20.1	14.3	16.7	15.9	12.0	13.7	14.1	13.3	13.7
BN (390)	18.2	22.3	20.0	24.9	20.6	22.6	20.5	21.5	21.0
BC (510)	19.4	14.6	16.7	22.0	12.9	18.4	19.6	16.2	17.8
TC (283)	31.8	17.0	22.2	34.3	16.7	22.5	32.2	17.2	22.4

Table 5. Result of AZP resolution subtask with setting 4

A, G	CN14 (G,G)			Ours (SNN)			Ours (LSTM)		
Source	R	P	F	R	P	F	R	P	F
Overall (1713)	48.4	48.9	48.7	48.4	48.5	48.4	49.0	49.0	49.0
NW (84)	39.1	38.1	38.1	42.9	42.9	42.9	50.0	50.0	50.0
MZ (162)	30.9	31.1	31.0	32.7	32.7	32.7	37.7	37.7	37.7
WB (284)	50.4	50.4	50.4	44.0	44.0	44.0	43.3	43.3	43.3
BN (390)	45.9	45.9	45.9	53.9	54.1	54.0	53.3	53.6	53.5
BC (510)	53.5	54.1	53.8	50.6	50.6	50.6	51.6	51.6	51.6
TC (283)	53.7	56.1	54.9	52.0	52.0	52.0	50.2	50.2	50.2

5 Conclusion and Future Work

We propose a deep learning approach for Chinese zero pronoun resolution. In this paper, we calculate a dense vector to represent the features of mention pair from distributed representation of related word instead of extracting features from syntax parsing trees. Our methods reduce the dependency on the parsing trees and the results on OntoNotes 5.0 show that our methods are competitive to the state-of-the-art resolver.

Obviously, our work just a basic model with deep learning method, and there is much room for improvement. In future work, we plan to add attention model in our system to capture the important words which may be useful in the sentences, try deeper architecture to calculate deeper semantic information, or joint the two subtasks into a deep learning framework to build an end-to-end model for Chinese zero resolution. Meanwhile, we will attempt to find a new method without parser which can get rid of the dependency of parser completely.

References

1. Zhao, S., Ng, H.T.: Identification and resolution of Chinese zero pronouns: a machine learning approach. In: EMNLP-CoNLL 2007, pp. 541–550 (2007)
2. Chen, C., Ng, V.: Chinese zero pronoun resolution: an unsupervised probabilistic model rivaling supervised resolvers. In: EMNLP, pp. 763–774 (2014)
3. Kong, F., Zhou, G.: A tree kernel-based unified framework for Chinese zero anaphora resolution. In: Proceedings of the 2010 Conference on Empirical Methods in Natural Language Processing, pp. 882–891. Association for Computational Linguistics (2010)
4. Converse, S.P.: Pronominal anaphora resolution in Chinese. University of Pennsylvania (2006)
5. Hobbs, J.R.: Resolving pronoun references. Lingua **44**(4), 311–338 (1978)
6. Grosz, B.J., Weinstein, S., Joshi, A.K.: Centering: a framework for modeling the local coherence of discourse. Comput. Linguist. **21**(2), 203–225 (1995)
7. Yeh, C.L., Chen, Y.C.: Zero anaphora resolution in Chinese with shallow parsing. J. Chin. Lang. Comput. **17**(1), 41–56 (2007)
8. 张伟男, 张宇, 刘挺. 基于中心理论的中文对话省略恢复研究. 第六届全国信息检索学术会议论文集, 2010
9. Mccarthy, J.F., Lehnert, W.G.: Using decision trees for coreference resolution. In: Proceedings of the 14th International Joint Conference on Artificial Intelligence, pp. 1050–1055 (2000)
10. Song, Y., Wang, H.F.: Chinese zero anaphora resolution with Markov Logic. J. Comput. Res. Dev. **52**(9), 2114–2122 (2015)
11. Chen, C., Ng, V.: Chinese zero pronoun resolution: an unsupervised approach combining ranking and integer linear programming. In: AAAI, pp. 1622–1628 (2014)
12. Chen, C., Ng, V.: Chinese zero pronoun resolution: a joint unsupervised discourse-aware model rivaling state-of-the-art resolvers. In: Proceedings of the 53rd Annual Meeting of the Association for Computational Linguistics and the 7th International Joint Conference on Natural Language Processing, pp. 320–326 (2015)
13. Bengio, Y., Ducharme, R., Vincent, P., Jauvin, C.: A neural probabilistic language model. J. Mach. Learn. Res. **3**(6), 1137–1155 (2003)
14. Mikolov, T., Chen, K., Corrado, G., Dean, J.: Efficient estimation of word representations in vector space. arXiv preprint arXiv:1301.3781 (2013)
15. Hochreiter, S., Schmidhuber, J.: Long short-term memory. Neural Comput. **9**(8), 1735–1780 (1997)

16. Gers, F.A., Schmidhuber, J., Cummins, F.: Learning to forget: continual prediction with LSTM. Neural Comput. **12**(10), 2451–2471 (2000)
17. Graves, A.: Supervised Sequence Labelling with Recurrent Neural Networks. Studies in Computational Intelligence, vol. 385. Springer, Heidelberg (2012). https://doi.org/10.1007/978-3-642-24797-2
18. Bastien, F., Lamblin, P., Pascanu, R., Bergstra, J., Goodfellow, I., Bergeron, A., Bouchard, N., Warde-Farley, D., Bengio, Y.: Theano: new features and speed improvements. In: NIPS Workshop on Deep Learning and Unsupervised Feature Learning (2012)
19. Bergstra, J., Breuleux, O., Bastien, F., Lamblin, P., Pascanu, R., Desjardins, G., Turian, J., Warde-Farley, D., Bengio, Y.: Theano: a CPU and GPU math expression compiler. In: Proceedings of the Python for Scientific Computing Conference (2010)

Active Learning for Chinese Word Segmentation on Judgements

Qian Yan, Limin Wang, Shoushan Li$^{(\boxtimes)}$, Huan Liu,
and Guodong Zhou

Natural Language Processing Lab, School of Computer Science and Technology,
Soochow University, Suzhou, China
{qyan, lmwang, 20164227044}@stu.suda.edu.cn,
{lishoushan, gdzhou}@suda.edu.cn

Abstract. This paper aims to perform the task of Chinese Word Segmentation on judgements. For this task, the main challenge is the lack of the annotated corpus. To alleviate this challenge, this paper proposes an active learning approach. Specifically, on the basis of a few initial annotated samples, a new active learning approach is proposed to annotate some informative characters, and then select the context around these characters for annotation. In the active learning approach, it not only considers the uncertainty of the sample, but also leverages the redundancy of the sample for the selection of informative characters. Furthermore, this paper adopts the local annotation strategy, which select a substrings around the informative characters rather than the whole sentences and thus could also reduce the annotation. The empirical study demonstrates that the proposed approach effectively reduces the annotation cost and performances better than other baseline sample selection strategies under the same scale of annotation.

Keywords: Chinese word segmentation · Active learning · Judgements

1 Introduction

Recently, with the rapid development of modern social, people's consciousness of their legal rights in China has been being strengthened constantly and they tend to solve problems with legal ways. Under this underground, numerous cases have been appearing, which results in a great deal of judgements. Such a large scale of judgements implies some great potential applications. For instance, the judgements could be used to build an information retrieval system, so that people could find information more exactly and efficiently. Basically, Chinese word segmentation (CWS) is a foundational task for judgement automatic processing, such as information retrieval and translation.

Word segmentation is a fundamental task in Natural Language Processing (NLP) for those languages without word delimiters, e.g., Chinese [1]. Word segmentation has been applied as an essential preprocessing step for many other NLP tasks, such as named entity recognition [2], event extraction [3], and machine translation [4]. In the literature, some popular approaches to CWS systems report a high performance

© Springer International Publishing AG 2018
X. Huang et al. (Eds.): NLPCC 2017, LNAI 10619, pp. 839–848, 2018.
https://doi.org/10.1007/978-3-319-73618-1_73

at the level of 95–97%, and these systems typically require a large scale of pre-segmented corpus for training. However, the collection of the judgements on such a scale is very time-consuming and resource-intensive.

There are two strong challenges for CWS on judgement. First, the judgments are organized in various categories of laws, such as *Contract* law and *Marriage* law. It is very time-consuming to annotate every category. Second, we need to annotate the new words continually when more and more new types of cases arise. This annotation process is rather money-consuming.

In this paper, we aim to apply the active learning approach to reduce the annotation cost and propose a novel active learning approach to CWS on judgements. In our approach, we adopt two kinds of sample selection strategies, i.e., uncertainty, and duplication measurements, to select *informative* characters. Moreover, we adopt the context selection strategy, which selects substrings around each *informative* character to annotate instead of the whole sentence. In the experiment, we perform CWS in the judgments and the empirical studies show that the proposed approach effectively improves the performances of CWS with a small amount of annotated data.

The remainder of this paper is organized as follows. Section 2 overviews related work. Section 3 introduces some background on data collection. Section 4 proposes our active learning approach for CWS on judgements. Section 5 evaluates our approach. Finally, Sect. 6 gives the conclusion and future work.

2 Related Work

In recent years, there has been an enormous amount of work in the research field of Chinese word segmentation. Basically, these methods can be mainly categorized into two groups: supervised and unsupervised approaches.

Unsupervised methods aim to build a segmentation system without any lexicon or labelled data. They often start from an empirical definition of a word and then use some statistical measures, e.g. mutual information [5, 6], to learn words from a large unlabelled data resource. Although these unsupervised methods can capture many strong words, their performance is often not high enough for the practical use.

The supervised methods attempt to acquire a model based on a dictionary or a labelled data set. The pioneer work on machine learning-based approaches to CWS by Xue [1] first models the segmentation task as a character classification problem and subsequent studies further improve the tagging model into a character sequence labeling problem [7]. The goal of sequence labeling is to assign labels to all elements in a sequence, which can be handled with Maximum Entropy (ME) [8] and Conditional Random Fields (CRF) [9]. In the research line, many other studies aim to improve the performance by various manners, such as feature expanding [10], semi-supervised learning [11], and using different tag sets [12], with shallow learning models like conditional random field (CRF). More recently, some deep learning models have been adopted in CWS, such as, convolution neural network [13], recursive neural network [14], and long short-term memory (LSTM) [15, 16].

Although there are various studies CWS individually, there are few studies of active learning on CWS. One related work is about active learning on Japanese word segmentation via Support Vector Machines (SVM) [17]. The study annotates the whole sentence as a basic unit, which needs the collection of the data on such a scale is very time-consuming and resource-intensive. Li [18] propose an active learning approach to CWS and their approach adopts the word boundary detection method for word segmentation and annotates only uncertain boundaries. However, the performance of word boundary detection is worse than character-labeling based methods.

Unlike above studies, our study proposes an active learning approach to CWS on judgements, which greatly improves the adaptation performance with the help of a small amount of labelled data.

3 Data Annotation

In this study, we use the text from the government public website (i.e., http://wenshu.court.gov.cn/). The data set is annotated by ourselves. It contains judgments, a kind of law documents that records the process and result of the people's court. The judgments are organized in many various domains of laws and we pick two popular domains, i.e., *Contract* law and *Marriage* law. In each category, we manually annotate 100 judgment documents.

We annotate Chinese judgments following the CTB word segmentation guidelines by Xia [19]. Some popular applied guidelines, together with some examples in Chinese judgments, are introduced below.

(1) *CD + N*

If a measure word can be inserted between *CD* and *N* without changing the meaning, tag it as *CD + N*; otherwise, tag it as one word (*N*).

Some examples in judgments: 一方 (*one side*), 各方 (*each side*), and 两者 (*both*).

(2) *N1 + N2: N1* modifies *N2*

If it is 1 + 1 or 2 + 1 (i.e., *N1* has one or two hanzi and *N2* has one hanzi), treat *N1 + N2* as one word.

Some examples in judgments: 成都市 (*Chengdu City*), 武侯区 (*Wuhou District*).

(3) *V + N*

In this pattern, we assume *V* is *VV*. If *V* modifies *N*, treat *V + N* as one word and tag it as a noun.

Some examples in judgments: 为证 (*as a proof*), and 为由 (*as a reason*).

Two annotators are asked to annotate the data. Due to the clear annotation guideline, the annotation agreement is very high, reaching 99.2%. The disagreement instances are mainly due to the carelessness of one annotator and are easy to be corrected. Some statics of our annotated data are summarized in Table 1.

Table 1. Statics of the annotated data

Domain	# of words	# of document
Contract	66755	100
Marriage	46425	100

4   Active Learning CWS on Judgement

4.1   Framework Overview

Figure 1 illustrates the framework of our active learning approach to CWS on judgements, where a novel selection strategy to choose *informative* characters in the training set, together with a context selection strategy to obtain the context of the *informative* characters. In the following subsections, we introduce the process of our approach in details.

Input:

Labelled training data L_S ;

Unlabelled training data U_T ;

The character selection strategy $\phi(c_i)$;

The context selection strategy $Context(c_i)$;

Output:

Automatically labelled test data L_T

Procedure:

a) Initialize $L_T = \varnothing$

b) Repeating k times

b1)   Learn a segmenter using current L_S

b2)   Use current segmenter to label all the unlabelled characters

b3)   Use the character selection strategy $\phi(c_i)$ to select top-N *informative* characters from U_T

b4)   For each *informative* character c_i, obtain the context ΔL_T with the context selection strategy $Context(c_i)$.

b5) $L_T = L_T + \Delta L_T$, and $U_T = U_T - \Delta L_T$

Fig. 1. The framework of our active learning approach to CWS

4.2   Sample Selection Strategy

In the literature, uncertainty sampling [20] and Query-By-Committee (QBC) [21] are two popular selection schemes in active learning. Different from all above strategies, this paper adopts the active learning strategy which not only considering the uncertainty of the sample, but also combining the duplication of the sample to select the *informative* characters in the training set. Furthermore, we propose a context selection strategy to select substrings to annotate instead of the whole sentences.

4.2.1 *Informative* Character Selection Strategy

In uncertainty sampling, a learner queries the instance which is most uncertain to label. As a multi classification problem, we calculate the uncertainty with the entropy measurement, i.e.,

$$Uncertaninty(c_i) = - \sum_{y \in \{B,M,E,S\}} p(y \mid c_i) \log p(y \mid c_i) \tag{1}$$

where $p(y \mid c_i)$ denotes the posterior probability that the character c_i is labelled as y. The higher the confidence value is, the more *informative* the character is thought to be. After computing the uncertainty scores, all the characters are ranked according to their uncertainty values.

A major problem with uncertainty sampling is that it may cause duplicate annotation. That is to say, some instances in the "*N*-best" queries may be similar. To minimize the manual annotation effort, we need to present some measurement among the instances which could be used to avoid duplicate annotation. Fortunately, we find that the similarity between two characters is higher related to their surrounding character N-grams and thus we can evaluate the duplication value with the help of the surrounding character bigrams.

In this study, we record the frequencies of all surrounding N-grams ($N = 3$) in a set S_{ccc}, where $f_{c_{i-1}c_ic_{i+1}} \in S_{ccc}$ indicates the frequency of the character N-grams ($N = 3$) $c_{i-1}c_ic_{i+1}$ and is initialized to 0. During training, we go through all the characters in the unlabelled data only once and the frequency of the surrounding bigram is updated serially as:

$$f_{c_{i-1}c_ic_{i+1}} + \, = 1 \tag{2}$$

where $c_{i-1}c_ic_{i+1}$ is the surrounding character N-grams ($N = 3$) of current character c_i. Meanwhile, the duplication of character c_i measured by the frequency of its surrounding N-grams ($N = 3$):

$$repeating(c_i) = \log(f_{c_{i-1}c_ic_{i+1}} + 1) \tag{3}$$

It is worth mentioning that above measure is a dynamic one. It is possible that two characters with the same character N-grams ($N = 3$) context are assigned with different duplicate values during training. Specifically, the character with a first appearing N-grams ($N = 3$) has the lowest duplication value while the characters appearing afterwards will have higher values and thus are not likely to be picked as the top *informative* ones. In this way, the duplicate-annotated words can be avoided to some extent.

In summary, our character selection strategy is defined by employing both the uncertainty and duplication measurements, i.e.,

$$\phi(c_i) = Uncertainty(c_i) / repeating(c_i) \tag{4}$$

The higher the value is, the more *informative* the character is thought to be.

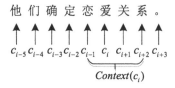

	B	M	E	S
c_{i-1}	0.99	0.008	0.001	0.001
c_i	0.39	0.20	0.40	0.01
c_{i+1}	0.80	0.03	0.02	0.15
c_{i-1}	0.002	0.01	0.98	0.007

Fig. 2. An example of an *informative* character and its selected context

4.2.2 Context Selection Strategy

In active learning for CWS, the context of the character is essential for determining the label of the character. Based on this, we need to annotate not only the N-top *informative* characters but also their context.

In our approach, we select the context with the left and right boundaries of each *informative* character. Specifically, the posterior probability of the left boundary character belongs to the label B or S must be greater than the threshold value. Similarly, the posterior probability of the right boundary character belongs to the label S or E must be greater than the threshold value. Therefore, we can select the context of each *informative* character using the following selection strategy:

If

$$P(B \text{ or } S \,|\, c_{i-m}) > T \text{ and } P(E \text{ or } S \,|\, c_{i+n}) > T \qquad (5)$$

Then, we obtain the context of this *informative* character, i.e.,

$$Context(c_i) = [c_{i-m}, c_{i+n}] \qquad (6)$$

where T is the threshold value, c_{i-m} is the left boundary and c_{i+n} is the right boundary. Figure 2 shows an example of an *informative* character and its selected context.

5 Experimentation

In this section, we have systematically evaluated our approach to active learning to CWS on judgements.

5.1 Experimental Settings

The basic segmenter in the active learning process is implemented with a public tool for CRF implementation, i.e. CRF++ (http://crfpp.sourceforge.net), the feature template are listed in Table 2. In all experiments, we use the standard F1 score as our main performance measurement.

Table 2. The feature template in CRF++

#Unigram	#Bigram
U01:%x[−1,0]	B
U02:%x[0,0]	
U03:%x[1,0]	
U04:%x[−1,0]/%x[0,0]	
U05:%x[0,0]/%x[1,0]	
U06:%x[1,0]/%x[2,0]	

5.2 Experimental Results

5.2.1 The Results of CWS Based on CRF and LSTM

In this experiment, we use the data with two domains, *Contract* law and *Marriage* law, are from the judgments. In each domain, we use 80 judgments as training data and the remaining 20 judgments as test data. For comparison, we implement two approaches, i.e., CRF model and LSTM [15] for CWS. These two approaches are illustrated as follows:

- **CRF:** The CRF tool has been introduced in Sect. 5.1.
- **LSTM:** a state-of-the-art approach to CWS, which is proposed by Chen et al. [15]. The parameters setting in the LSTM model are listed in Table 3.

Table 3. Parameter setting in LSTM

Parameters-description	value
Dimension-of-the-LSTM-layer-output	128
Dimension-of-the-full-connected-layer-output	64
Dropout probability	0.5
Epochs of iteration	30

Table 4 shows the performances of the two approaches to CWS. From this table, we can see that in the *Contract* law and *Marriage* law, the two approaches nearly yield similar performances. Note that in active learning, we need to train the model in many times to select *informative* samples iteratively. Therefore, we pick the CRF model as our training model due to its comparable performance to LSTM but its costing much less training time. In the following experiment on active learning, we use CRF for training and test in our active learning approach.

Table 4. Experimental results of CRF and LSTM in two domains

	Contract	Marriage
CRF	0.952	0.973
LSTM	0.956	0.971

5.2.2   The Results of Active Learning on CWS

In this experiment, in each domain, we randomly pick 5 judgements as initial labelled data, 75 judgements as unlabelled data, and 20 judgements as test data. In active learning, we select top-15 *informative* characters in the unlabelled data and their context substrings for manual annotation. For comparison, we implement following sample selection strategies for active learning-based approaches to CWS on judgements.

- **Random:** which randomly selects the sentence samples from the unlabelled data for manual annotation.
- **Uncertainty:** which selects the sentence samples from the unlabelled data by the uncertainty confidence for manual annotation.
- **Our Approach:** which has been illustrated in Sect. 4.2. The parameter T is set to be 0.9.

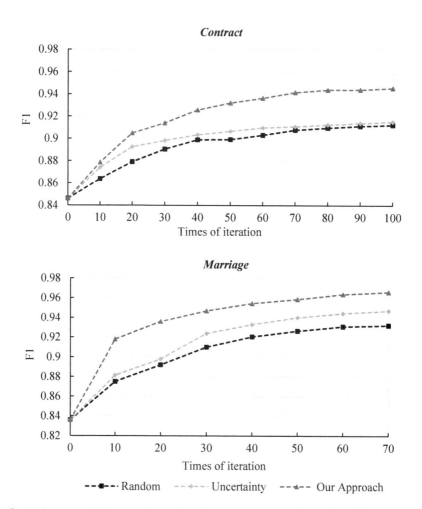

Fig. 3. Performance (F1) comparison of active learning approaches with different sampling strategies

Figure 3 shows the performances of different approaches to CWS with different sample selection strategies. From this figure, we can see that:

(1) Using the uncertainty strategy is effective for sample selection in active-learning-based approach to CWS on judgements. It performs consistenlty better than the random selection strategy. This encourages to employ active learning approach to select samples for annotation than random selection.

(2) Our approach performs much better than the uncertainty strategy. After about 70 iterations, our approach yields excellent performances, 0.941 in the *Contract* domain and 0.967 in the *Marriage* domain. The success of our approach benefits from both considering the duplication measurement and using the context selection strategy.

6 Conclusion

In this paper, we propose an active learning approach to CWS on judgements, which aims to perform Chinese word segmentation on judgements. During the process of active learning, we not only consider the uncertainty of a character, but also introduce the duplication measurement of a character to select the *informative* characters. Furthermore, our approach leverages a context selection strategy to select substrings for annotation instead of the whole sentence. Empirical studies show that our active learning approach performs much better than using the uncertainty-based active learning approach and our approach could quickly obtain comparable performance to using all labelled data from the training set with only a small amount of selected data from the training set.

In our future work, we would like to improve the performance on active learning for CWS on judgements by exploring the better sample selection strategies. Moreover, we would like to apply our approach to active learning on CWS tasks in some other domains.

Acknowledgments. This research work has been partially supported by three NSFC grants, No. 61375073, No. 61672366 and No. 61331011.

References

1. Xue, N.W.: Chinese word segmentation as character tagging. Comput. Linguist. Chin. Lang. Process. **8**(1), 29–48 (2003)
2. Gao, J.F., Li, M., Wu, A., Huang, C.N.: Chinese word segmentation and named entity recognition: a pragmatic approach. Comput. Linguist. **31**(4), 531–574 (2005)
3. Chen, C., Ng, V.I.: Joint modeling for Chinese event extraction with rich linguistic features. In: Proceedings of COLING, pp. 529–544 (2012)
4. Zhang, R.Q., Yasuda, K., Sumita, E.: Improved statistical machine translation by multiple Chinese word segmentation. In: Proceedings of the Third Workshop on Statistical Machine Translation, pp. 216–223 (2008)

5. Sproat, R., Shih, C.A.: Statistical method for finding word boundaries in Chinese text. Comput. Process. Chin. Orient. Lang. **4**(4), 336–351 (1990)
6. Maosong, S., Dayang, S., Tsou. B.K.: Chinese word segmentation without using lexicon and hand-crafted training data. In: Proceedings of ACL, pp. 1265–1271 (2002)
7. Tseng, H., Chang, P., Andrew, G., Jurafsky, D., Manning, C.: A conditional random field word segmenter for sighan bakeoff 2005. In: Proceedings of the Fourth SIGHAN Workshop on Chinese Language Processing, pp. 168–171 (2005)
8. Berger, A.L., Pietra, V.J.D., Pietra, S.A.D.: A maximum entropy approach to natural language processing. Comput. Linguist. **22**(1), 39–71 (1996)
9. Lafferty, J., McCallum, A., Pereira, F.: Conditional random fields: probabilistic models for segmenting and labeling sequence data. In: Proceedings of ICML, pp. 282–289 (2001)
10. Shi, Y.X., Wang, M.Q.: A dual-layer CRFs based joint decoding method for cascaded segmentation and labeling tasks. In: Proceedings of IJCAI, pp. 1707–1712 (2007)
11. Sun, W.W., Xu, J.X.: Enhancing Chinese word segmentation using unlabeled data. In: Proceedings of EMNLP, pp. 970–979 (2011)
12. Zhao, H., Huang, C.N., Li, M., Lu, B.L.: Effective tag set selection in Chinese word segmentation via conditional random field modeling. In: Proceedings of PACLIC, pp. 87–94 (2006)
13. Zheng, X.Q., Chen, H.Y., Xu, T.Y.: Deep learning for Chinese word segmentation and POS tagging. In: Proceedings of EMNLP, pp. 647–657 (2013)
14. Chen, X.C., Qiu, X.P., Zhu, C.X., Huang, X.J.: Gated recursive neural network for Chinese word segmentation. In: Proceedings of ACL, pp. 1744–1753 (2015)
15. Chen, X.C., Qiu, X.P., Zhu, C.X., Liu, P.F., Huang, X.J.: Long short-term memory neural networks for Chinese word segmentation. In: Proceedings of EMNLP, pp. 1197–1206 (2015)
16. Cai, D., Zhao, H.: Neural word segmentation learning for Chinese. In: Proceedings of ACL, pp. 409–420 (2016)
17. Sassano, M.: An empirical study of active learning with support vector machines for Japanese word segmentation. In: Proceedings of EMNLP, Proceedings of ACL, pp. 505–512 (2002)
18. Li, S.S., Zhou, G.G., Huang, C.R.: Active learning for Chinese word segmentation. In: Proceedings of COLING, pp. 683–692 (2012)
19. Xia, F.: The segmentation guidelines for the Penn Chinese Treebank (3.0) (2000)
20. Lewis, D.D., Gale, W.A.: A sequential algorithm for training text classifiers. In: Proceedings of SIGIR, pp. 3–12 (1994)
21. Seung, H.S., Opper, M., Sompolinsky, H.: Query by committee. In: Proceedings of the Fifth Annual Workshop on Computational Learning Theory, pp. 287–294 (1992)

Study on the Chinese Word Semantic Relation Classification with Word Embedding

E. Shijia[(✉)], Shengbin Jia, and Yang Xiang

Tongji University, Shanghai 201804, People's Republic of China
{436_eshijia,shengbinjia,shxiangyang}@tongji.edu.cn

Abstract. This paper describes our solution to the NLPCC 2017 shared task on Chinese word semantic relation classification. Our proposed method won second place for this task. The evaluation result of our method on the test set is 76.8% macro F1 on the four types of semantic relation classification, i.e., synonym, antonym, hyponym, and meronym. In our experiments, we try basic word embedding, linear regression and convolutional neural networks (CNNs) with the pre-trained word embedding. The experimental results show that CNNs have better performance than other methods. Also, we find that the proposed method can achieve competitive results with small training corpus.

Keywords: Relation classification · Word embedding
Convolutional neural network

1 Introduction

The fine-grained recognition of word semantic relations is a challenging task for natural language processing (NLP), especially for the Chinese language. To the best our knowledge, many systems of semantic relation detection have mainly relied on manually constructed ontologies. As the development of representation learning, the deep neural networks and word embedding have been achieved promising results on many NLP tasks. We can attempt to recognize the word semantic relations automatically by calculating the distance between the two words in the vector space, as words that are similar to each other will tend to be distributed in the same region.

In this paper, we describe our system for the NLPCC 2017 shared task on Chinese word semantic relation classification. We evaluated several methods such as word analogy, linear regression, and CNN with the pre-trained word embedding. All of the word vectors we use are trained with the available public corpus.

The rest of this paper is structured as follows. Section 2 contains related work; In Sect. 3, we describe the methods used in this work. Experimental results and discussions are presented in Sect. 4, and finally, we give some concluding remarks in Sect. 5.

© Springer International Publishing AG 2018
X. Huang et al. (Eds.): NLPCC 2017, LNAI 10619, pp. 849–855, 2018.
https://doi.org/10.1007/978-3-319-73618-1_74

2   Related Work

The task word semantic relation classification on English dataset has been evaluated on a few shared tasks before, including relational similarity in SemEval-2012 [1], word to sense matching in SemEval-2014 [2], hyponym-hypernym relations in SemEval-2015 [3] and semantic taxonomy (hypernymy) in SemEval-2016 [4]. Also, in CongAlex-2014 [5], there is a shared task about semantic association. To accomplish these tasks, researchers will first use the trained word embeddings as important features of the words. With the introduction of neural language model [6] and the development of representing words as vectors [7], especially for the log linear word embedding architecture of Mikolov [8] which provides an efficient and simplified training methodology, researchers can obtain their own word embeddings for different purposes. Therefore, the word embedding training programs such as word2vec[1] and GloVe [9] have been widely used. Using word analogy for recognizing word semantic relations has been addressed in [10–12]. The core idea of using word embedding to solve the word semantic relation classification is that pairs of words that share a certain semantic relation will have similar cosine distance. For example, ("queen" - "king") $\approx$ ("woman" - "man"), ("China" - "Beijing") $\approx$ ("Japan" - "Tokyo"), and ("China" - "Chinese") $\approx$ ("America" - "American").

In addition to word embedding, linear regression classifiers, e.g., logistic regression and support vector machine, and models based on CNN have also been applied to this task. [13] uses a logistic regression classifier for hypernym pair identification. [14,15] propose a convolutional deep neural network to extract lexical features and then use a *softmax* classifier to predict the relationship between two words. In this paper, we do not use any syntactic features, other than the word embeddings.

3   Model Description

In this section, we describe the pre-trained word embeddings and the models and that we have tried in this task.

3.1   Pre-Trained Word Embedding

We have two kinds of pre-trained word embeddings. They were trained based on the different corpus.

Baike Embedding. We use a large-scale corpus crawled from Baidu Encyclopedia to learn the pre-trained Chinese word embeddings with word2vec. The text corpus size is about 960 GB, and the embedding size is 300. We train the embedding with negative sampling, using skip-gram and window size of 5.

---

[1] https://code.google.com/archive/p/word2vec.

Sogou News Embedding. This kind of word embedding is built with word2vec from the opening Sogou News corpus with 300 dimensions. The size of the corpus is about 3.6 GB. The other parameters are just same as the training of Baike Embedding.

3.2 Linear Regression

We get the cosine similarity distance between the words in our prepared train set; then we use the simple logistic regression classifier to predict labels based on the numerical value of the similarity distance.

3.3 Convolutional Neural Network with Word Embedding

Due to the linear regression method does not achieve good performance in our experiment, we use a CNN based architecture to model the pair of words. In addition to solve the problem of image classification [16], the capability of capturing local correlations along with extracting higher-level correlations through pooling empowers CNN to model the word sequence naturally from consecutive context windows [17]. Collobert et al. [18] apply convolutional filters to successive windows for a given sequence to extract global features by the max-pooling operation. Kim [19] propose a CNN architecture with multiple filters and varying window sizes to capture word relations of varying sizes. Kalchbrenner et al. [20] propose a dynamic k-max pooling mechanism that is capable of explicitly capturing short and long-range relations. All the examples above prove that the CNN model can model the words or sentences effectively. As shown in Fig. 1, in our proposed model, we first feed the pair of input words to the embedding layer. The embedding layer uses the pre-trained word vectors mentioned above as the initial weights, and that can be updated during the training process. Next in the model is a convolution layer. After the convolution operations, we apply the 1-MaxPooling operation. The last hidden layer is a Dense layer with 128 neurons. Also, we add a dropout layer before the last layer to avoid overfitting. Finally, we use the outputs of *softmax* to select the target label.

3.4 Parameter Tuning

Unlike the tasks of recognition of English word semantic relation, the NLPCC Shared Task 1 does not provide standard train set. Therefore, to tune the parameters of the neural network, we have constructed a train set from HIT-CIR Tongyici Cilin, HowNet, and resource on the Internet. The detailed information is shown in Table 1.

We can find that the classes in the training data are highly imbalanced. Therefore, we use the oversampling method to make the number of samples belonging to different classes as evenly distributed as possible. Then, We use 10% of the training data as validation set and use it to tune various hyperparameters like dropout ranges, the number of filters and filter sizes of the CNN layer.

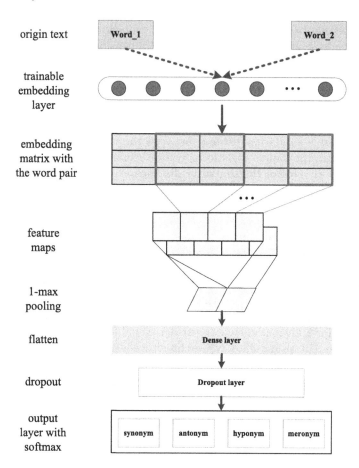

origin text

trainable
embedding
layer

embedding
matrix with
the word pair

feature
maps

1-max
pooling

flatten

dropout

output
layer with
softmax

Fig. 1. The CNN based architecture to model the word pair

Table 1. The statistics of the train set

Relation	#Word pairs
Synonym	39,787
Antonym	1,701
Hyponym	5,830
Meronym	215

4   Experiments

4.1   Implementation

Our proposed model in this task was built from scratch using Keras[2]. The convolution lay was with 250 filters each for filter sizes 1 and 2. The dropout rate is 0.2. We trained the model based on CNN by the *Adam* optimizer [21] with a mini-batch size of 128.

4.2   Evaluation Set

The evaluation set [22] is this task contains 10,000 word pairs where 2,000 word pairs are constructed by the human, and the other word pairs are generated using a large dictionary. Because the Chinese vocabulary size is very large, the test set will have some obscure word. This also adds some difficulty to this task.

4.3   Results

The proposed method with this shared task got the second place in the NLPCC 2017 Shared Task 1. Tables 2 and 3 show the experimental results.

Table 2. The macro-averaged F1-Score for four-way classification

Method	F1-Score	Precision	Recall
Logistic regression	0.359	0.382	0.340
CNN with word embedding	0.767	0.802	0.765

Table 3. The detailed results of the CNN based model in each category

Category	F1-Score	Precision	Recall
Synonym	0.732	0.612	0.91
Antonym	0.781	0.959	0.658
Hyponym	0.788	0.792	0.784
Meronym	0.771	0.847	0.708

4.4   Discussions

As shown in Table 2, the method based on CNN achieves better performance than the simple logistic regression. Because there is no provided train set, we first consider how to construct representative training corpus so that the trained model can have enough generalization ability. However, even if the corpus is

---

[2] https://keras.io.

large enough, in the test set, there are still words that have never been seen before. For this problem, we eventually adopt the character level embedding which can solve the out-of-vocabulary (OOV) problem to a certain extent. The experimental results also prove that the feature modeling of deep neural networks is better than the traditional learning methods.

Furthermore, to validate the performance of our model, we also do some extra experiments on the final evaluation dataset. For all the evaluation data, we use the standard 5-fold cross-validation to test whether our proposed model can perform better results when we have a large number of training data. The experimental results are shown in Table 4.

Table 4. 5-fold cross-validation results for the entire evaluation data

Method	F1-Score	Precision	Recall
Logistic regression	0.420	0.431	0.410
CNN with word embedding	0.827	0.842	0.813

As we expect, the performance of the related methods can be further improved if we adopt large training data. It also reflects the importance of building a high quality corpus from another perspective.

5   Conclusion

In this paper, we have introduced an effective convolutional neural network model with word embedding to solve the Chinese word semantic relation classification task. Also, our experimental results show that although the proposed model is relatively simple, it still has a certain competitiveness in practice. For the future work, we can learn accurate models through available high quality corpus and try to use transfer learning to improve the generalization ability of the models.

Acknowledgments. We would like to thank members in our lab and the anonymous reviewers for their helpful feedback. This work was supported by the National Basic Research Program of China (2014CB340404), the National Natural Science Foundation of China (71571136), and the Project of Science and Technology Commission of Shanghai Municipality (16JC1403000, 14511108002).

References

1. Mohammad, S.M., Holyoak, K.J.: SemEval-2012 task 2: measuring degrees of relational similarity. In: Joint Conference on Lexical and Computational Semantics, pp. 356–364 (2012)
2. Jurgens, D., Pilehvar, M.T., Navigli, R.: SemEval-2014 task 3: cross-level semantic similarity. In: International Workshop on Semantic Evaluation (2014)

3. Bordea, G., Buitelaar, P., Faralli, S., Navigli, R.: SemEval-2015 task 17: taxonomy extraction evaluation (texeval). SemEval-2015, vol. 452, no. 465, p. 902 (2015)
4. Bordea, G., Lefever, E., Buitelaar, P.: SemEval-2016 task 13: taxonomy extraction evaluation (texeval-2). In: SemEval-2016, pp. 1081–1091. Association for Computational Linguistics (2016)
5. Rapp, R., Zock, M.: The cogalex-iv shared task on the lexical access problem. In: The Workshop on Cognitive Aspects of the Lexicon, pp. 1–14 (2014)
6. Bengio, Y., Ducharme, R., Vincent, P., Jauvin, C.: A neural probabilistic language model. J. Mach. Learn. Res. 3(Feb), 1137–1155 (2003)
7. Collobert, R., Weston, J.: A unified architecture for natural language processing: deep neural networks with multitask learning. In: Proceedings of the 25th International Conference on Machine Learning, pp. 160–167 (2008)
8. Mikolov, T., Chen, K., Corrado, G., Dean, J.: Efficient estimation of word representations in vector space. arXiv preprint arXiv:1301.3781 (2013)
9. Pennington, J., Socher, R., Manning, C.D.: Glove: global vectors for word representation. In: EMNLP, vol. 14, pp. 1532–1543 (2014)
10. Levy, O., Goldberg, Y., Dagan, I.: Improving distributional similarity with lessons learned from word embeddings. Trans. Assoc. Comput. Linguist. 3, 211–225 (2015)
11. Gladkova, A., Drozd, A., Matsuoka, S.: Analogy-based detection of morphological and semantic relations with word embeddings: what works and what doesn't. In: SRW@HLT-NAACL, pp. 8–15 (2016)
12. Vylomova, E., Rimell, L., Cohn, T., Baldwin, T.: Take and took, gaggle and goose, book and read: evaluating the utility of vector differences for lexical relation learning. arXiv preprint arXiv:1509.01692 (2015)
13. Snow, R., Jurafsky, D., Ng, A.Y.: Learning syntactic patterns for automatic hypernym discovery. In: Advances in Neural Information Processing Systems, pp. 1297–1304 (2005)
14. Zeng, D., Liu, K., Lai, S., Zhou, G., Zhao, J., et al.: Relation classification via convolutional deep neural network. In: COLING, pp. 2335–2344 (2014)
15. dos Santos, C.N., Xiang, B., Zhou, B.: Classifying relations by ranking with convolutional neural networks. arXiv preprint arXiv:1504.06580 (2015)
16. Krizhevsky, A., Sutskever, I., Hinton, G.E.: Imagenet classification with deep convolutional neural networks. In: Advances in Neural Information Processing Systems, pp. 1097–1105 (2012)
17. Hu, B., Lu, Z., Li, H., Chen, Q.: Convolutional neural network architectures for matching natural language sentences. In: Advances in Neural Information Processing Systems, pp. 2042–2050 (2014)
18. Collobert, R., Weston, J., Karlen, M., Kavukcuoglu, K., Kuksa, P.: Natural language processing (almost) from scratch. J. Mach. Learn. Res. 12(1), 2493–2537 (2011)
19. Kim, Y.: Convolutional neural networks for sentence classification. Eprint arXiv arXiv:1408.5882 (2014)
20. Kalchbrenner, N., Grefenstette, E., Blunsom, P.: A convolutional neural network for modelling sentences. Eprint arXiv arXiv:1404.2188 (2014)
21. Kingma, D., Ba, J.: Adam: a method for stochastic optimization. arXiv preprint arXiv:1412.6980 (2014)
22. Yunfang, W., Minghua, Z.: Overview of the NLPCC 2017 shared task: Chinese word semantic relation classification. In: 6th Conference on Natural Language Processing and Chinese Computing (2017)

HDP-TUB Based Topic Mining Method for Chinese Micro-blogs

Yaorong Zhang[1], Bo Yang[2], Li Yi[2(✉)], Yi Liu[2],
and Yangsen Zhang[1(✉)]

[1] Beijing Information Science and Technology University, Beijing, China
zhangyangsen@163.com
[2] National Computer Network Emergency Response Technical Team
Coordination Center, Beijing, China
Yili@cert.org.cn

Abstract. Topic models are important tools for mining the potential topics of text. However, the existing topic model is mostly derived from latent Dirichlet allocation (LDA), which requires the number of topics to be specified in advance. In order to mine the topic of Chines micro-blogs automatically, we propose a nonparametric Bayesian model, named HDP-TUB model, which is derived from hierarchical Dirichlet Process (HDP). In this model, we assume non-exchangeability of data, and use temporal information, user information and theme tags (TUB) to solve the sparsity problem caused by the short text. In order to construct the HDP-TUB model, the CRF (Chinese Restaurant Franchise) method is extended to integrate the temporal information, user information and topic tag information. Experiments show that the HDP-TUB model outperforms the LDA model and the HDP model in the perplexity and the difference between topics.

Keywords: Topic mining · HDP-TUB model · Hierarchical Dirichlet Process
Chinese Restaurant Franchise

1 Introduction

According to the "38th Statistics Report on China Internet Development" [1], at the end of December 2016, there were 710 million netizens in China, 21.32 million more than in 2015. Of these, 34.0% used Weibo as their main social software. The large number of users and the enormous amount of information they generate make Weibo the main tool for online communication, dissemination of information, and expression of opinions in China. Unlike traditional blogs, the micro-blogs are more concise and informal. Therefore, how to find users' interested content from the massive data quickly and accurately has become more difficult. The current search technology of micro-blogs is mostly relying on keywords, which cannot provide satisfactory results owing to the short text of micro-blogs. An effective way to improve the micro-blogs retrieval is mining the potential topics of micro-blogs and use the topics to reflect the semantic content of micro-blogs.

© Springer International Publishing AG 2018
X. Huang et al. (Eds.): NLPCC 2017, LNAI 10619, pp. 856–865, 2018.
https://doi.org/10.1007/978-3-319-73618-1_75

Topic models are mainly divided into parametric Bayes models and nonparametric Bayes models. Latent Dirichlet allocation (LDA) is a typical parametric Bayes model. It extracts the potential topics of documents by the co-occurrence information of words. However, compared to the traditional text, the short text of micro-blogs leads to the lack of co-occurrence information and a serious sparsity problem. Moreover, LDA model needs to specify the number of topics in advance, and the selection of the number directly affects the performance. Hierarchical Dirichlet Process (HDP) is a typical nonparametric Bayes model, which can automatically determine the number of clusters and estimate the distribution parameters of clustering. Various models derived from HDP have been widely used in text mining, music content recognition, image retrieval, video surveillance data processing and other fields.

2 Related Research

Topic models are a kind of probabilistic generative model, which is often used to mine potential topics from large scale document set. It assumes that topics generate words following certain rules. When the words of documents are known, the topic structure of the documents can be deduced by probability, then the topic distribution of the document set is obtained.

LDA is a typical parametric Bayes model [2], which treats documents as the probability distribution of topics, and the topic as the probability distribution of words. In essence, LDA uses the co-occurrence information of the terms at the document level to reveal the topic structure contained in the document, which has achieved good results in the topic mining of news [3] and scientific literature [4]. However, owing to the shortness of micro-blog text and the lack of co-occurrence information, there will be a serious sparsity problem when apply LDA directly to micro-blog data. To solve this problem, researchers made use of the temporal information and interactive information of micro-blogs and proposed several LDA-derived models to improve the topic mining efficacy of micro-blogs. Zhang and Sun [5] proposed a LDA-derived model, MB-LDA, which takes into account micro-blog's contact relationships and text association relationships in micro-blog topic mining. In the research of Wang et al. [6], a temporal aware topic model called TM-LDA is proposed to learn the transition parameters among topics by minimizing the prediction error on topic distribution in subsequent postings. These models require specified number of topics in the training process. Considering that the volume of micro-blogs is vast and the number of topics is difficult to estimate according to prior knowledge, trying to search the appropriate number of topics is very time-consuming. The nonparametric Bayesian model, by contrast, is more suitable for mining topics from micro-blogs without setting the number of topics in advance.

HDP is a typical nonparametric Bayes model [7] which treat each document as a collection of observable words. The words are clustered according to the topic so the topic distribution of the document is finally determined. The topics of every document follows the same Dirichlet process, thereby ensuring that the document set shares the same topics. Because HDP assumes that the data is exchangeable and ignores the additional information such as the time of the data, the topic mining of HDP is not effective when the topics of the dataset exhibits temporal patterns. In recent years, researchers have proposed several HDP-derived models to improve the effect of topic mining by using the temporal information. Li and Li [8] proposed an evolved HDP model, EHDP, which consists of a series of HDPs with temporal information. Each HDP relies on adjacent HDPs to mine news topics over time. In the work of Ma et al. [9], an online topic evolution model is proposed for topic modeling of new documents without traversing historical information. Kim and Oh [10] proposed an improved model based on HDP, which consists of document level CRP (Chinese Restaurant Process) and document-set level ddCRP (distance depend CRP). The ddCRP calculates the time interval between the document creations, and then solves the dependencies between the documents according to the defined decay function. The model has achieved good results in the topic mining of academic papers. Although these models perform well in topic mining for academic papers and news, but for micro-blogs, considering only the temporal patterns is not enough to solve the sparsity problem.

3   The HDP-TUB Model

The aim of topic mining is to detect the potential topics from the micro-blog text. If micro-blog text is represented as a set $S = \{s_1, s_2, \ldots, s_I\}$, where s_i is one post of the micro-blog text and I is the total number of posts. Every post can be represented as a tuple: $s_i = \{x_i, u_i, t_i, b_i\}$. Here, x_i is a sequence of words: $x_i = \{x_{i1}, x_{i2}, \ldots, x_{ij}\}$, $j \in \{1, 2, \ldots, V\}$ and V is the size of vocabulary, u_i is the poster of this blog, t_i is the timestamp and b_i is the theme tag. Assuming that a micro-blog can be represented as a probability distribution of topics and the topics can be represented as probability distribution of all words in the vocabulary, so the aim of micro-blog topic mining is to find the K potential topics from set S. The topics are represented as $\Phi = \{\Phi_1, \Phi_2, \ldots, \Phi_K\}$.

3.1   HDP Topic Model

HDP is essentially a hierarchical structure of Dirichlet process. HDP assumes that the document set shares the same topics, and the number of topics is not limited. The two-layer HDP model for text mining can be represented as Eq. (1):

$$
\begin{aligned}
G_0 &\sim DP(\gamma, H) \\
G_i | G_0 &\sim DP(\alpha_0, G_0)
\end{aligned}
\tag{1}
$$

Firstly, sampling G_0 from the base distribution H and the Dirichlet process with concentration parameter γ. Then sampling the distribution G_i of each topic from the base distribution G_0 and the Dirichlet process with concentration parameter α_0. In this way, the topic distribution of every document follows the base distribution H, which guarantee that the documents share same topics. Usually, the base distribution H is a Dirichlet distribution with parameter η. Each topic Φ_k is an independent sample of H. The process of sampling each word x_{ij} in document s_i is as Eq. (2):

$$\theta_{ij} \sim G_i$$
$$x_{ij} \mid \theta_{ij} \sim F\left(\theta_{ij}\right) \tag{2}$$

In Eq. (2), θ_{ij} is a series of stochastic variable following the independent identical distribution of G_i, which indicates the topics assigned to x_{ij}. $F\left(\theta_{ij}\right)$ is the distribution of x_{ij} with parameter θ_{ij}. In order to simplify the calculation of HDP sampling process, F is usually chosen as polynomial distribution, which constructs a conjugate distribution with the base distribution H.

In order to sample HDP, the corresponding construction method should be designed to infer the posterior distribution of the parameters. Chinese Restaurant Franchise (CRF) is one of the widely used construction methods. In CRF, I restaurants share the same menu: $\Phi = \{\Phi_1, \Phi_2, \ldots, \Phi_K\}$, K is the number of dishes. The i th restaurant can accommodate L_i tables: $\psi_{il}, l \in (1, 2, \ldots, L_i)$, and each table can accommodate N_{il} customers. Customers are free to choose a table and each table serve only one dish. The first customer at the table order a dish and other customers share the dish. Different tables from same or different restaurants can serve the same dish. In topic mining of text, restaurants, customers and dishes correspond to documents, words and topics. Regard the distribution parameter θ_{ij} of word x_{ij} as customers, it sits at table ψ_{il} with a probability of $\frac{n_{il}}{\alpha_0 + j - 1}$, here n_{il} is the current number of customers at the l th table of i th restaurant, and the dish this table served is Φ_k. Or it sits at a new table with a probability of $\frac{\alpha_0}{\alpha_0 + j - 1}$. If the customer chose a new table, according to the popularity of dishes, the customer specifies dish Φ_k with a probability of $\frac{m_k}{\sum_k m_k + \gamma}$, here m_k is the number of tables that dish Φ_k served, or specifies a new dish with a probability of $\frac{\gamma}{\sum_k m_k + \gamma}$. This process can be represented as Eqs. (3) and (4):

$$\theta_{ij} \mid \theta_{i1:i,j-1}, a_0, G_0 \sim \sum_{l=1}^{L_i} \frac{n_{il}}{\alpha_0 + j - 1} \delta_{\psi_{il}} + \frac{a_0}{\alpha_0 + j - 1} G_0 \tag{3}$$

$$\psi_{il} \mid \psi_{i1:i,l-1}, \gamma, H \sim \sum_{k=1}^{K} \frac{m_k}{\sum_k m_k + \gamma} \delta_{\Phi_k} + \frac{\gamma}{\sum_k m_k + \gamma} H \tag{4}$$

Here, δ_x is a point mass function centered at x. The construction of CRF is the process of distributing tables and dishes for customers, which corresponds to the topic distribution of words and the topic clustering of the document set. Once the CRF is constructed, the posterior inference methods, such as the Markov chain Monte Carlo (MCMC) method, can be used to solve the HDP topic model. Thus the topic distribution of the whole document set can be obtained.

3.2 HDP-TUB Model

To solve the problem of topic mining for Chinese micro-blogs, we propose the HDP-TUB model based on HDP. HDP-TUB integrated the temporal information, user information and theme tags to improve the performance of topic model. The model is based on following assumptions: (1) If the post time of two micro-blogs is similar, they may touch on the same hotspot and share the topic distribution of this hotspot. (2) If two micro-blogs are posted by a same poster or one of them followed the other, they may implicate the user's interests and share the topic distribution of the user's interests. (3) If two micro-blogs contain the same theme tag, they may touch on the abstract concepts or events associated with the theme and share the topic distribution of the theme. According to the above assumptions, the HDP-TUB model aggregates the topic related micro-blogs to enrich the co-occurrence information of word terms and effectively overcome the problem of data sparsity. Compared with existing topic models, the HDP-TUB model has the two main advantages. On one hand, it can automatically search the appropriate number of topics, while parametric Bayes models need to specify the number of topics in advance. On the other hand, it can guarantee the non-exchangeability of data, which is an important characteristic of micro-blog text.

Similar to the CRF construction of HDP, the HDP-TUB model is constructed by a derived CRF method. This construction method is composed of two layers. In document level, the Chinese restaurant process (CRP) method is used to distribute customers to tables. In the level of document set, the distant depend CRP (ddCRP) method is used to distribute dishes to tables. The dish served on a table depends on the other associated tables. To be specific, if the restaurants of two tables located close to each other (which means the post time of two micro-blogs is similar), the owner of the tables are associated (which means the posers of the micro-blogs are associated), or two tables have the same specialty (which means two micro-blogs contain the same theme tag), these tables are regarded as associated.

Firstly, the following variables are defined: l_{ij} denotes the index of tables that word x_{ij} sits at, $l = \{l_{ij} : \forall(i,j)\}$. k_{il} denotes the index of dishes that table ψ_{il} serves, $k = \{k_{il} : \forall(i,l)\}$. z_{ij} denotes the index of word x_{ij}'s topics, $z = \{z_{ij} : \forall(i,j)\}$. n_k denotes the number of words in topic Φ_k and n_k^v denotes the number of words with an index of v in topic Φ_k. If there is a minus in the superscript of a variable, it denotes the count of variables excluding the one specified by the superscript. For example, l^{-ij} denotes the table index excluding l_{ij}, and $n_k^{-x_{ij}}$ denotes the numbers of customers that served dish Φ_k excluding customer x_{ij}.

The HDP-TUB model is constructed by three steps. The first step is to sample the distribution parameter θ_{ij} for each word. We use CRP to model the text, so the sampling process is the same as Eq. (3). The second step is to sample the dishes served for each table ψ_{il}. In this step, ddCRP is used and the topic distribution of micro-blogs is affected by associated micro-blogs. The sampling process is represented as Eq. (5):

$$\psi_{il} \mid \psi_{i1:i,l-1}, \gamma, H \sim \sum_{k=1}^{K} \frac{\sum_{i'l' \neq il, \Phi_{i'l'} = \Phi_k} D_{i'l',il}}{\sum_{i'l' \neq il} D_{i'l',il} + \gamma} \delta_{\Phi_k} + \frac{\gamma}{\sum_{i'l' \neq il} D_{i'l',il} + \gamma} H \qquad (5)$$

In Eq. (5), $D_{i'l',il}$ represents the degree of association between table ψ_{il} and $\psi_{i'l'}$, which is determined by post time t_i, poster u_i and theme tag b_i. It is calculated by Eq. (6), and the value is proportional to the degree of association between the tables.

$$D_{i'l',il} = d(t_i, t_{i'}) + c(u_i, u_{i'}) + sign(b_i, b_{i'}) \tag{6}$$

Here, $d(t_i, t_{i'})$, $c(u_i, u_{i'})$ and $sign(b_i, b_{i'})$ denotes the degree of association between table ψ_{il} and $\psi_{i'l'}$ at time, user and theme tag respectively. They are calculated by Eqs. (7)–(9). Here, the units of time are days. If the two micro-blogs were posted on the same day, $d(t_i, t_{i'}) = 1$. With the increase of time interval, the value of $d(t_i, t_{i'})$ decrease in an exponential form. And when $|t_i - t_{i'}| \geq 7$, $d(t_i, t_{i'})$ close to 0.

$$d(t_i, t_{i'}) = e^{-|t_i - t_{i'}|/3} \tag{7}$$

$$c(u_i, u_{i'}) = \begin{cases} 1, u_i = u_{i'} \\ 0.5, u_i \text{ followed } u_{i'} \text{ or } u_{i'} \text{ followed } u_i \\ 0, \text{ other conditions} \end{cases} \tag{8}$$

$$sign(b_i, b_{i'}) = \begin{cases} 1, b_i = b_{i'} \\ 0, b_i \neq b_{i'} \end{cases} \tag{9}$$

The third step is to sample each observable word x_{ij}. The base distribution H is Dirichlet distribution, the word distribution F of topics is polynomial distribution, and they constructed a conjugate distribution. According to the recursive properties of Γ function, when the topic index of x_{ij} is k, the contingent probability of sampling x_{ij}, denoted as $f_k(x_{ij} : z_{ij} = k)$, can be calculated by Eq. (10).

$$f_k(x_{ij} : z_{ij} = k) = \frac{\Gamma(V\eta)}{\Gamma(n_k + V\eta)} \frac{\prod_v \Gamma(n_k^v + \eta)}{\Gamma^V(\eta)} \tag{10}$$

Once $f_k(x_{ij} : z_{ij} = k)$ is calculated, for certain l and k, the distribution of text set x can be calculated by Eq. (11):

$$P(x \mid l, k) = \prod_k f_k(x_{ij} : z_{ij} = k) \tag{11}$$

When the HDP-TUB model is constructed, we use MCMC method to sample two layers of CRPs respectively.

4 Results and Analysis

In this study, we compared the effect of LDA model, HDP model and HDP-TUB model on real micro-blog data. The experimental setup and the results are as follows.

4.1 Experimental Data

The dataset used in this study are real micro-blog data from Sina Weibo. Preprocessing is needed before we can mine topics from these data, including three steps. Firstly, we need to extract the post time, poster information and theme tags from the original Weibo text. Secondly, some interference information should be filtered from the text, including interactive information, URLs and Weibo emoji. Finally, we need to segment the sentences into word sequences and delete stop words. After preprocessing, we retained the micro-blogs longer than 8 words, and got a dataset containing 6540586 micro-blogs from 26546 different users.

4.2   Evaluation Metric

The quality of the topics was evaluated by Kullback-Leibler divergence (KL divergence), perplexity and scores of the top n words ($S@n$) given manually. The KL divergence is used to measure the difference between topics, which is calculated by Eq. (12). The difference between topics is proportional to the value of the KL divergence. When the value of KL divergence of two topics equals to 0, the two topics are exactly the same.

$$KL(\Phi_1, \Phi_2) = \sum_{x_{ij}} P(x_{ij} \mid \Phi_1) log \frac{\sum_{x_{ij}} P(x_{ij} \mid \Phi_1)}{\sum_{x_{ij}} P(x_{ij} \mid \Phi_2)} \qquad (12)$$

The perplexity can be interpreted as how uncertain is the model on which topic the document belongs to, which is calculated by Eq. (13). The lower the perplexity, the better the effect of the topic model.

$$perplexity(x) = exp\left(-\sum_i \sum_j \frac{log \sum_k P(\Phi_k)P(x_{ij} \mid \Phi_k)}{\sum_i N_i} \right) \qquad (13)$$

The $S@n$ is given by volunteers. For example, if a volunteer thinks that among the top 10 words of a certain topic, 8 of them belongs to the same topic accurately, then the $S@10$ of this topic is 8. We invited 5 volunteers having the background of natural language processing to score the topics.

4.3   Experimental Results

In this study, we compared the performance of LDA, HDP and HDP-TUB model. The topic number K is set to 100 for LDA model, the hyper parameters α and β of Dirichlet distribution is set to 0.5 and 0.02. In the HDP model and the HDP-TUB model, the hyper parameter η of base distribution H is set to 0.5, and the concentration parameters followed the gamma prior distribution: $\gamma \propto \Gamma(1, 0.1)$, $\alpha_0 \propto \Gamma(1, 1)$.

The number of topic of the three models are shown as Fig. 1. According to Fig. 1, the HDP-TUB model has the largest number of topics, followed by the HDP model. For the LDA model, he number of topics was determined in advance, so it does not vary with the number of iterations. Some of the topics mined by the three models are listed in Table 1.

Figures 2, 3 and 4 are the KL divergence of the three models. The horizontal and vertical coordinates are topics, and the depth of the points' color represents the KL

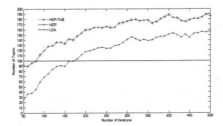

Fig. 1. The number of topics of the three models

Table 1. Instances of topics mined by the three models

LDA			HDP			HDP-TUB		
Topic 1	Topic 2	Topic 3	Topic 1	Topic 2	Topic 3	Topic 1	Topic 2	Topic 3
投资	笑	喜欢	视频	全文	电影	艺术	医生	微博
中国	日常	女生	直播	男子	摄影	展览	医院	红包
公司	狗	关注	秒拍	发生	作品	艺术家	药	手机
美元	搞	男生	决赛	新闻	导演	博物馆	健康	转发
市场	奇葩	恋爱	集锦	人员	拍摄	作品	手术	粉丝
互联网	宝宝	时尚	赛事	女子	来自	美术	病	活动
上市	萌	家居	精彩	头条	年度	创作	患者	会员
大盘	猫	生活	精选	民警	故事	开幕	科普	转发
板块	可爱	设计	解说	安全	剧情	文物	门诊	积分
指数	熊猫	感觉	视频	全文	电影	匠心	治疗	抢

distance of the corresponding two topics. The lighter the color, the larger the KL divergence and the better the performance of the model. As we can see, the color of Fig. 2 is the shallowest. This is because the number of topics mined by the LDA model is relatively small, so the difference between topics are relatively large. The color of Fig. 4 is slightly shallower than Fig. 3, which means that the HDP-TUB model reached a better difference between topics than the HDP model while mined more topics.

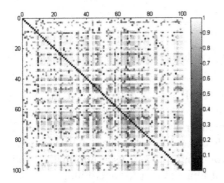

Fig. 2. The KL divergence of LDA model

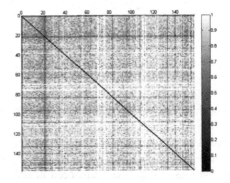

Fig. 3. The KL divergence of HDP model

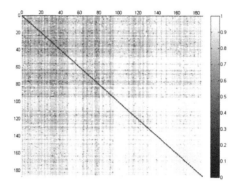

Fig. 4. The KL divergence of HDP-TUB model

Figure 5 shows the perplexity of the three models. In the aspect of perplexity, the HDP-TUB model is superior to the LDA model, which means that the automatic determination of the number of topics is better than setting manually. The HDP-TUB model is slightly better than the HDP model, which proved that temporal information, user information and theme tags improves the effect of topic mining.

Figure 6 shows the $S@10$ score of the three models given by five volunteers. The vertical axis in the figure is the average score of all topics mined by each model. As can be seen from the figure, the score of HDP-TUB model is slightly higher than HDP model, and is significantly higher than LDA model.

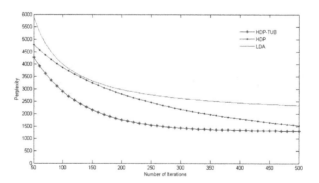

Fig. 5. The Perplexity of the three models

In conclusion, the HDP-TUB model and HDP model outperformed the LDA model, which proved that determining the number of topics automatically can better divide the topics of micro-blogs than set the number manually. The HDP-TUB model mined more topics than the HDP model with better KL divergence and perplexity, which proved that the introduction of temporal information, user information and theme tags in our model enhanced the effect of topic mining for micro-blogs.

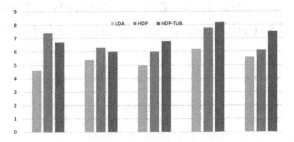

Fig. 6. The $S@10$ score of the three models

5 Summary

Aiming at the automatic topic mining for micro-blogs, we proposed a HDP-TUB model based on the HDP model, and integrated temporal information, user information and theme tags into our model. The model can make good use of the characteristics of micro-blog and achieve good results of topic mining. The future work will consider how to further improve the effect of topic mining by using more characteristics of micro-blog itself. For example, the user community information, micro-blog's propagation patterns, etc.

References

1. Statistical Report on the Internet Development of China. China Internet Network Information Center (2016)
2. Blei, D.M., Ng, A.Y., Jordan, M.I.: Latent Dirichlet Allocation. JMLR.org (2003)
3. Xiangdong, L., Chaozhi, B., Li, H.: Multi granularity sub topic partitioning method based on LDA model and HowNet. Appl. Res. Comput. **32**(6), 1625–1629 (2016)
4. Peng, G., Yuefen, W., Zhu, B.: Analysis of topic extraction in scientific literature based on IDA topic model under different corpus. Libr. Inf. Serv. **60**(2), 1120121 (2016)
5. Zhang, C., Sun, J.: Large scale microblog mining using distributed MB-LDA. In: International Conference on World Wide Web, pp. 1035–1042. ACM (2012)
6. Wang, Y., Agichtein, E., Benzi, M.: TM-LDA: efficient online modeling of latent topic transitions in social media. In: ACM SIGKDD International Conference on Knowledge Discovery and Data Mining, pp. 123–131. ACM (2012)
7. Blei, D.M.: Probabilistic topic models. Commun. ACM **55**(4), 77–84 (2012)
8. Li, J., Li, S.: Evolutionary hierarchical Dirichlet process for timeline summarization meeting of the association for computational linguistics, pp. 556–560. ACL (2013)
9. Ma, T., Qu, D., Ma, R.: Online topic evolution modeling based on hierarchical Dirichlet Process. In: IEEE International Conference on Data Science in Cyberspace, pp. 400–405. IEEE (2016)
10. Kim, D., Oh, A.: Accounting for data dependencies within a hierarchical Dirichlet process mixture model. In: ACM Conference on Information and Knowledge Management, CIKM 2011, pp. 873–878. DBLP, Glasgow (2011)

Detecting Deceptive Review Spam
via Attention-Based Neural Networks

Xuepeng Wang[1,2], Kang Liu[1(✉)], and Jun Zhao[1,2]

[1] National Laboratory of Pattern Recognition, Institute of Automation,
Chinese Academy of Sciences, Beijing 100190, China
{xpwang,kliu,jzhao}@nlpr.ia.ac.cn
[2] University of Chinese Academy of Sciences, Beijing 100049, China

Abstract. In recent years, the influence of deceptive review spam has further strengthened in purchasing decisions, election choices and product design. Detecting deceptive review spam has attracted more and more researchers. Existing work makes utmost efforts to explore effective linguistic and behavioral features, and utilizes the off-the-shelf classification algorithms to detect spam. But the models are usually compromised training results on the whole datasets. They failed to distinguish whether a review is linguistically suspicious or behaviorally suspicious or both. In this paper, we propose an attention-based neural networks to detect deceptive review spam by distinguishingly using linguistic and behavioral features. Experimental results on real commercial public datasets show the effectiveness of our model over the state-of-the-art methods.

1 Introduction

As increasingly used by customs and businesses, online reviews have formed a booming market. There emerge a large number of websites which provide online review services, such as Amazon, Yelp and TripAdvisor. Positive reviews often mean profits and fame for business and individuals [21]. It has been reported that positive rating scores help the restaurants on Yelp to sell out more products and earn revenue increasing [2,22]. As a result, driven by great commercial profit, more and more business owner begin to hire people to write deceptive positive reviews to promote their own products, and/or post fake negative reviews to discredit their competitors. Such individuals are called review spammers, and the fake reviews are defined as deceptive review spam [10,21]. It is urgent to detect deceptive review spam to maintain the trust of the review host websites.

The earliest academic investigations were carried by Jidal and Liu [10]. They studied 5.8 million reviews and 2.14 million reviewers from Amazon. A large number of duplicate reviews were found indicating that review spam was widespread. Several types of features were proposed and logistic regression was used for model building [10]. The majority of followed work takes it as a binary classification task. The researchers have made utmost efforts to explore effective features to indicate the review spam. For example, Unigram, POS and other linguistic features were explored by Ott et al. [28], Li et al. [19] and Hai et al. [8].

X. Huang et al. (Eds.): NLPCC 2017, LNAI 10619, pp. 866–876, 2018.
https://doi.org/10.1007/978-3-319-73618-1_76

Activity window, extremity of rating and other behavioral features were investigated and applied by Mukherjee et al. [27] and Rayana and Akoglu [29].

So far, previous work has proposed lots of effective approaches. However, researchers mainly focus on feature engineering and just apply the off-the-shelf classification algorithms to detect spam. But exploiting more effective algorithms or models is also significant for this task. Most of the review spam detecting models are usually compromised training results on the whole datasets, over the linguistic and behavioral features. But for the real commercial reviews on the Yelp website, some deceptive reviews are linguistically suspicious, some are behaviorally suspicious[1]. For linguistically suspicious review spam, the behavioral features which seem normal are actually noises for the detection models. But the learnt weight matrices of the traditional detection models are fixed for all the reviews in the datasets. They can not make a special identification for each review. So there needs to find a new way to further distinguishingly utilize the linguistic and behavioral features.

In this paper, we propose an attention-based neural networks by dynamically learning weights for linguistic and behavioral features for each training example. It can learn to distinguish whether each of the review spam is linguistically suspicious or behaviorally suspicious or both. More specifically, we take several effective behavioral features, which were exploited in previous work, as the inputs of the MLP hidden layer in our model. Then we get the behavioral feature vectors from the outputs of the MLP. We employ a convolutional neural network (CNN) to exact the linguistic features of a review, and take the outputs of the CNN as the linguistic feature vectors. Next, we take the behavioral feature vectors as the target hidden states and the linguistic feature vectors as source hidden states. Then an attention function is applied to calculate the score, which indicates how behaviorally suspicious a review is in the given linguistic environment. As well when the linguistic feature vectors are the target hidden states and the behavioral feature vectors are source hidden states, the attention function can also calculate how linguistically suspicious a review is in the given behavioral environment. Then the features vectors are tuned by the calculated scores. We concatenate the outputs of attention layer (the tuned feature vectors) with the original feature vectors. At last, the concatenated vectors go through a softmax layer to make predictions.

In summary, the contributions of this work are as follows:

- In stead of focusing on feature engineering as the most previous work did, we turn to find a more effective algorithm to tackle the deceptive review spam detecting task.
- We proposed an attention-based model neural networks by distinguishingly utilizing the linguistic and behavioral features for detecting each review spam. It learns dynamic weights for each training example. Compared with previous models, it can learn that whether a deceptive review is linguistically suspicious or behaviorally suspicious or both.

---

[1] https://www.yelp-support.com/article/What-is-Yelp-s-recommendation-software?.

– The experiments carried on the real commercial public datasets show that, the proposed model preforms more effectively than the state-of-the-art work, in both hotel and restaurant domains.

2   Related Work

Detecting review spam is a more difficult task than detecting other forms of spam, such as email spam [3], web search engine spam [7], blog spam [14] and tagging spam [15]. The deceptive review spam detection problem was firstly explored by Jindal and Liu [10]. They analysed 5.8 million reviews and 2.14 reviewers from the popular Amazon.com. They showed how widespread the problem of fake reviews was. Then they built their own dataset, and simply use near-duplicate reviews as examples of deceptive reviews. Several linguistic and behavioral features were proposed and logistic regression was applied for detection. Most followed work has made major efforts to discover suspicious clues and design effective features.

The Work Exploiting Linguistic Features. The first dataset of gold-standard deceptive review spam was released by Ott et al. [28] with employing crowd-sourcing through the Amazon Mechanical Turk. At the same time, they investigate the effectiveness of psychological and linguistic clues on identifying review spam. Several writing features were explored by Harris [9]. Then they applied several human- and machine-based assessment methods on the features. Feng et al. [5] focused on the syntactic stylometry in the review spam problem. Li et al. [19] was interesting exploring the general difference of language usage between deceptive and truthful reviews. Moreover, Li et al. [18] investigated the positive-unlabeled learning problem with unigrams and bigrams features. Kim et al. [13] analysed the semantic frame features in the deceptive review texts.

The Work Exploiting Behavioral Features. The reviewers' rating behavioral features were investigated by Lim et al. [20]. Jindal et al. [11] found several unusual review patterns which can represent suspicious behaviors of reviews. Li et al. [16] proposed a two-view semi-supervised method based on behavioral features. Feng et al. [6] focused on describing the distributions of reviewer's unusual behaviors. Xie et al. [34] applied the abnormal temporal patterns of reviewers to detect singleton reviews at resellerratings.com. Mukherjee et al. [24] studied a principal method to model the spamicity of reviewers. The behavioral feature of review co-occurrence was found by Fei et al. [4] in review bursts. By analysing the review at Dianping.com, Li et al. [17] found the temporal and spatial patterns in reviewers' footprints. [12] also investigated the temporal features of the reviews at Yelp websites. Moreover, the experiments carried by Mukherjee et al. [27] proved that reviewers' behavioral features are more effective than reviews' linguistic features on the realistic commercial datasets. Wang et al. [31] investigated the reviewers' behaviors in the online store review graph. Akoglu et al. [1]

exploit the network effect among reviewers and products. There is also some work that detected review spam by combining using the linguistic and behavioral features. Mukherjee et al. [26] proved the effectiveness of the combination of linguistic features and behavioral features. Besides, Rayana and Akoglu [29] utilized lots of clues from review text, reviewers' behaviors and the review graph structure to make a collective review spam detection.

The Work Detecting Review Spammers. The previous work referred above are mainly focusing on detecting review spam. There were also some work exploring detecting the review spammers. Wang et al. [32] identified online store review spammers via social graph. Another work [25] researched the group spamming activity. This work was the first attempt to solve the problem of review spammers from a group collaboration between multiple spammers. In this paper, we focus on detecting deceptive review spam by utilizing linguistic and behavioral features.

3 The Proposed Model

In this section, we further explain our attention-based neural networks in detail as shown in Fig. 1. As we referred in Sect. 1, most of the previous work focuses on exploiting effective features and just applies the off-the-shelf classification models to detect spam. Although the model can learn to identify the deceptive reviews, the trained models are usually compromised results over the whole

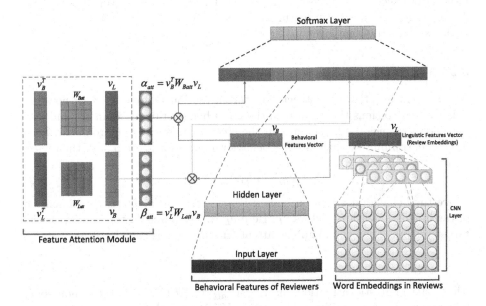

Fig. 1. Illustration of our model.

datasets. It can figure out whether a review is deceptively suspicious, but it can not distinguish whether the review is linguistically suspicious or behaviorally suspicious. We find that some spammers on the website post reviews without any elaborate disguise, we can identify them by linguistic features. For example, there are lots of exclamation sentences contained in the negative spam for defaming [29]. However, some crafty spammers are good at writing plausible reviews with abundant experiences [27]. We have to figure out the suspicious behaviors in their activities. So we propose a novel attention-based neural networks. Compared with the previous work, it can learn dynamic weights for each review in the datasets, and further distinguish the suspiciousness category of the review spam by the feature attention mechanism.

3.1   The Feature Extraction Module

As shown in Fig. 1, we employ a MLP layer to extract behavioral feature vectors v_B from the inputs of effective behavioral features F_B. The output of the MLP layer is calculated as

$$v_B = \tanh\left(W_B F_B + b_B\right), \tag{1}$$

where $W_B \in \mathbb{R}^{D_B \times D_o}$, D_B is the dimension of the behavior feature inputs, D_o is the dimension of the MLP's outputs.

To extract the linguistic feature vectors, we adopt a convolutional neural network with word embeddings $e\left(w_i\right) \in \mathbb{R}^{D_w}$. Compared with the discrete manual features used in previous work and the RNN model, Ren and Zhang [30] have proved that the CNN can capture complex global semantic information and perform more effectivelys. We set n filter weight matrices $\widehat{W} = \{W_1, W_2, \ldots W_n\}$. Then we get the linguistic feature vectors v_L from the outputs of each filter utilizing a max pooling layer.

3.2   The Feature Attention Module

As shown in Fig. 1, we construct a feature attention module to learn how linguistically suspicious the spam is in the given behavioral environment, and how behavioral suspicious the spam is in the given linguistically environment. During model training we calculate the behavioral attention score α_{att} of the review spam by

$$\alpha_{att} = v_B^T W_{Batt} v_L, \tag{2}$$

where the behavioral attention matrix $W_{Batt} \in \mathbb{R}^{D_B \times D_L}$, D_L is the dimension of the linguistic feature vectors v_L. Here v_L is the source vectors and v_B is the target vectors. Then the linguistic attention score β_{att} is calculated as

$$\beta_{att} = v_L^T W_{Latt} v_B, \tag{3}$$

where the linguistic attention matrix $W_{Latt} \in \mathbb{R}^{D_L \times D_B}$. For the non-spam review, we also set two attention matrix W'_{Batt} and W'_{Latt}, and calculate the attention score same as the Eqs. 2 and 3.

Next we calculate the weighted feature vectors as

$$v'_B = \alpha_{att} v_B, \tag{4}$$

$$v'_L = \beta_{att} v_L, \tag{5}$$

Then the concatenation of the weighted feature vectors and the feature vectors is taken as the inputs of the softmax layer.

$$v = [v'_B : v_B : v'_L : v_L] \tag{6}$$

$$o = W_{sft} v + b_{sft}, \tag{7}$$

where $W_{sft} \in \mathbb{R}^{2*(D_B+D_l) \times D_{sft}}$, D_{sft} is the output dimension of the linear layer in softmax layer. The category prediction probability is calculated as

$$p(c_i \mid \theta) = \frac{\exp(o_i)}{\sum_{j=1}^{n_o} \exp(o_j)}, \tag{8}$$

where c_i is the prediction category, n_o is the number of categories, $\theta = [W_B, b_B, \widehat{W}, W_{Batt}, W_{Latt}, W'_{Batt}, W'_{Latt}, W_{sft}, b_{sft}]$. Finally, our training objective is to minimize the cross-entropy loss over plus a l_2-regularization term,

$$\mathcal{L}(\theta) = -\sum_{i=1}^{N} \log(c_i \mid \theta) + \frac{\lambda}{2} \|\theta\|^2 \tag{9}$$

We use Adam algorithm to minimize the loss function in Eq. 9. We initial all the matrix and vector parameters with uniform samples in $(\sqrt{6(r+c)}, \sqrt{6(r+c)})$, where r and c are the numbers of rows and columns of the matrices. For the word embeddings, we initial them with the vectors of 200-dimensions which are trained on Yelp review datasets [27], using the CBOW model proposed by Mikolov et al. [23].

When the model identifies the review spam in the testing datasets, we take the maximum conditional probabilities respectively calculated through W_{Batt}, W_{Latt}, W'_{Batt} and W'_{Latt} as the prediction labels.

4   Experiments

4.1   Datasets and Evaluation Metrics

Datasets: To evaluate the effectiveness of our model, we conduct the publicly released datasets which contain the realistic commercial reviews from the Yelp website. The datasets were widely used in the work of Mukherjee et al. [26], Mukherjee et al. [27], Rayana and Akoglu [29] and Wang et al. [33]. There are also other publicly available datasets for experiments. But some of them [10, 20, 34] are human labelled, and have been proved not to be reliable by Ott et al. [28]. Some of them [28] are generated by crowd sourcing, which have been proved not fully reflecting the realistic characteristics of the commercial review spam by Mukherjee et al. [27]. The statistics of the Yelp datasets used in this paper are listed in Table 1.

Table 1. Yelp labeled dataset statistics.

Domain	Hotel	Restaurant
Fake	802	8368
Non-fake	4876	50149
% fake	14.1%	14.3%
# reviews	5678	58517
# reviewers	5124	35593

Evaluation Metrics: We select precision (P), recall (R), F1-Score (F1) and accuracy (A) as metrics.

4.2   Our Model v.s. The State-of-the-Arts Work

In this paper, we compare our attention-based neural networks with the state-of-the-arts work to test the effectiveness. One of the compared work is presented by Mukherjee et al. [26]. Mukherjee et al. [26] analysed the reviews at the Yelp websites and proposed eight effective statistical behavioral features (e.g., the Activity Window, the Percentage of Positive Reviews). They also proved that the bigram is more effective than other previous linguistic features (e.g., POS, Deep Syntax and Information Gain) in detecting the realistic commercial deceptive review spam. Then they applied SVM and naïve Bayes respectively on the behavioral and linguistic features, and got the best performance with SVM. Another compared work is accomplished by Wang et al. [33]. To collectively utilize the global information in the review system, they proposed eleven asymmetric relations between reviewers and products. Then they learnt the representations of reviews by the tensor decomposition algorithm in a low dimension feature space. They proved that the leant representations are more effective than the traditional statistic features. In fact, their representations (i.e. the concatenation of reviewer embeddings and product embeddings) can be regarded as a kind of behavioral feature vectors. They also took the bigram as the linguistic features. Same with Mukherjee et al. [26], Wang et al. [33] applied the SVM on their learnt behavioral feature vectors and linguistic features to detect deceptive review spam. For fair experimental comparison, we apply our model respectively on the behavioral features proposed by Mukherjee et al. [26], and the behavioral features vectors learnt by Wang et al. [33]. For our model, we set the window size of the CNN filters to 2 for extracting linguistic features from bigram word embeddings. Besides, we set the number of convolution matrices to 30, D_B to 100, λ to $0.1E-6$. All the hyper-parameters are tuned by grid search on the development dataset.

The results of compared experiments are shown in Table 2. We first compare our attention-based neural networks with the work of Mukherjee et al. [26] on the same eight statistical behavioral features and bigrams (Table 2(a,b) rows 1, 3). Our model results in around 2.5% improvement in F1 and 2.1% improvement in A at the hotel domain, and results in around 1.8% improvement in F1 and

Table 2. SVM classification results across behavioral features linguistic features (bigrams here) by Mukherjee et al. [26], the classification results achieved by our model without attention mechanism using the features in Mukherjee et al. [26] (Our_model_noAtt_M), and the results achieved by our model with attention mechanism using the features in Mukherjee et al. [26] (Our_model_withAtt_M); the SVM classification results across bigrams and behavioral feature vectors learnt by Wang et al. [33], the classification results achieved by our model without attention mechanism using the features in Wang et al. [33] (Our_model_noAtt_W), the classification results achieved by our model with attention mechanism using the features in Wang et al. [33] (Our_model_withAtt_W). All the results here are 5-fold CV results. Both the training and testing use balanced data (50:50). Improvements of our model are statistically significant with p < 0.005 based on paired t-test.

Features	P	R	F1	A		P	R	F1	A	
Mukherjee et al. [26]	82.8	86.9	84.8	85.1	1	84.5	87.8	86.1	86.5	1
Our_model_noAtt_M	85.4	86.5	86.0	85.9	2	85.9	87.5	86.7	86.6	2
Our_model_withAtt_M	86.3	88.5	**87.3**	**87.2**	3	87.4	88.4	**87.9**	**87.8**	3
Wang et al. [33]	84.2	89.9	87.0	86.5	4	86.8	91.8	89.2	89.9	4
Our_model_noAtt_W	86.8	88.5	87.6	87.5	5	88.9	91.3	90.1	90.0	5
Our_model_withAtt_W	88.1	89.7	**88.9**	**88.8**	6	89.4	93.0	**91.2**	**91.0**	6

(a) Hotel   (b) Restaurant

1.3% improvement in A at the restaurant domain. These results show that, compared with directly applying the off-the-shelf classification algorithm on the features, our model make a more effective performance with the bi-directional attention mechanism, to distinguish the suspicious type of review spam. Then we compared our model to the work of Wang et al. [33] on their learnt behavioral feature vectors and bigrams (Table 2(a,b) rows 4, 6). Our model results in around 1.9% improvement in F1 and 2.3% improvement in A at the hotel domain, and results in around 2.0% improvement in F1 and 1.1% improvement in A at the restaurant domain. It proves that our model is more effective than the method in Wang et al. [33] as well. This is probably because of that the feature attention module can learn how behavioral suspicious each review spam is, when given the corresponding linguistic features, and vice versa.

4.3   The Effectiveness of the Feature Attention Module

To further evaluate the effectiveness of our feature attention module, we compared our model with attention module to that without attention module (Table 2(a,b) rows 2, 3, 5, 6). When we move out the attention module, our model performs slightly better than Mukherjee et al. [26] and Wang et al. [33] in some domain metrics. Specifically, it performs 0.1% better in A at the restaurant domain (Table 2(b) rows 1, 2). And it performs 0.6% better in F1 at the hotel domain (Table 2(a) rows 4, 5). But some improvements are relatively obvious. For example, it performs 1.2% better in F1 at the hotel domain (Table 2(a) rows 1, 2). This indicates that the model only with the MLP and CNN module can hardly do a robust performance. When we add the attention module in our model, the experimental results show that the attention mechanism help to perform 1.5% better in F1 and 1.2% better in A at both domain in average (Table 2(a,b) rows 2, 3, 5, 6). It proves that the attention module actually helps to identify deceptive review spam by distinguishing the suspicious type of review.

- [**REVIEW EXAMPLE**][2] AMAZING!!!! I've been to quite a few gastronomy driven restaurants...some have been mind blowing...some not. But Alinea was beyond! ...But how can you really give justice t this whole presentation? I CAN'T!!! ...I'd have to say this was the most amazing place I've ever eaten at! Our waiters ranged from normal to pretentious...but whatever...the food was amazing. The presentation..amazing...the decor (especially when you walk into the hallway from the street.... amazing...the attention to detail....amazing! I would definitely be back because this place is freakin AMAZING!!!!!
- Behavioral Attention Score: 0.1537; Behavioral Features: $RL = 0.78$, $RC = 0.35$, $AW = 0.41$, $PR = 0.60$; Linguistic Attention Score: 0.9727.

4.4   The Attention Spam Example in Datasets

To further present the effect of our attention-based neural networks, we list an attention deceptive review spam example during testing our model with bidirectional attention mechanism on the features used by Mukherjee et al. [26] at the restaurant domain. As shown in the above review example, the behavioral features seem very normal, for example the behavioral feature Review Length with the normalization value 0.78 indicates that it is a long review. Mukherjee et al. [27] found that the average number of words per non-spam review is relatively longer than that of spam review. But when we turn to the context of the review, we find that it contains lots of exclamation points and all-capital words. It describes the restaurant in a strongly promoting mood. So the review is very suspicious on linguistic features.

In this review example, the behavioral features are noises for the traditional detection models. Inversely, there are other deceptive reviews which are behaviorally suspicious and seem normal in linguistic features. The linguistic features are noises for them. But the learnt weight matrices of the traditional detection models are fixed for all the reviews in the datasets. The models are actually compromised training results. They fail to make a special identification for each review. So our model adopts the feature attention module to learn dynamic weights (attention score α_{att} and β_{att}) for linguistic and behavioral features for each training example. Indeed, as shown in [**REVIEW EXAMPLE**] the linguistic attention score learnt by our model is larger than the behavioral attention score. It indicates that, for this linguistically suspicious review spam, our model has dynamically paid more attention to the linguistic features than the behavioral features.

---

[2] An attention deceptive review spam example during testing our model with bidirectional attention mechanism on the features used by Mukherjee et al. [26] at the restaurant domain.

5   Conclusion

We introduced a neural network framework with attention mechanism for detecting deceptive review spam. The attention mechanism can learn dynamic weights for linguistic and behavioral features for each training sample. The proposed model not only achieves state-of-the-art performance, but also shows the importance of linguistic and behavioral features according to the weights provided by the attention mechanism. Extensive experiments show that our model outperforms all baseline models and achieves precision, recall, and F-value. In the future, we will explore more effective methods for the task.

Acknowledgments. This work was supported by the Natural Science Foundation of China (No. 61533018), the National Basic Research Program of China (No. 2014CB340503) and the National Natural Science Foundation of China (No. 61502493).

References

1. Akoglu, L., Chandy, R., Faloutsos, C.: Opinion fraud detection in online reviews by network effects. In: ICWSM 2013, vol. 13, pp. 2–11 (2013)
2. Anderson, M., Magruder, J.: Learning from the crowd: regression discontinuity estimates of the effects of an online review database. Econ. J. **122**, 957–989 (2012)
3. Carreras, X., Marquez, L.: Boosting trees for anti-spam email filtering. arXiv preprint cs/0109015 (2001)
4. Fei, G., Mukherjee, A., Liu, B., Hsu, M., Castellanos, M., Ghosh, R.: Exploiting burstiness in reviews for review spammer detection. In: ICWSM 2013. Citeseer (2013)
5. Feng, S., Banerjee, R., Choi, Y.: Syntactic stylometry for deception detection. In: ACL 2012, pp. 171–175. Association for Computational Linguistics (2012)
6. Feng, S., Xing, L., Gogar, A., Choi, Y.: Distributional footprints of deceptive product reviews. In: ICWSM 2012 (2012)
7. Gyongyi, Z., Garcia-Molina, H.: Web spam taxonomy. In: AIRWeb 2005 (2005)
8. Hai, Z., Zhao, P., Cheng, P., Yang, P., Li, X.L., Li, G.: Deceptive review spam detection via exploiting task relatedness and unlabeled data. In: EMNLP 2016, pp. 1817–1826 (2016)
9. Harris, C.: Detecting deceptive opinion spam using human computation. In: AAAI 2012 (2012)
10. Jindal, N., Liu, B.: Opinion spam and analysis. In: WSDM, pp. 219–230. ACM (2008)
11. Jindal, N., Liu, B., Lim, E.P.: Finding unusual review patterns using unexpected rules. In: CIKM 2010, pp. 1549–1552. ACM (2010)
12. Santosh, K.C., Mukherjee, A.: On the temporal dynamics of opinion spamming: case studies on yelp. In: WWW, pp. 369–379 (2016)
13. Kim, S., Chang, H., Lee, S., Yu, M., Kang, J.: Deep semantic frame-based deceptive opinion spam analysis. In: CIKM 2015, pp. 1131–1140. ACM (2015)
14. Kolari, P., Java, A., Finin, T., Oates, T., Joshi, A.: Detecting spam blogs: a machine learning approach. In: AAAI 2006, vol. 21, p. 1351. AAAI Press/MIT Press, Menlo Park/Cambridge (2006)
15. Koutrika, G., Effendi, F.A., Gyöngyi, Z., Heymann, P., Garcia-Molina, H.: Combating spam in tagging systems. In: AIRWeb 2007, pp. 57–64. ACM (2007)

16. Li, F., Huang, M., Yang, Y., Zhu, X.: Learning to identify review spam. In: IJCAI 2011, vol. 22, p. 2488 (2011)
17. Li, H., Chen, Z., Mukherjee, A., Liu, B., Shao, J.: Analyzing and detecting opinion spam on a large-scale dataset via temporal and spatial patterns. In: AAAI (2015)
18. Li, H., Liu, B., Mukherjee, A., Shao, J.: Spotting fake reviews using positive-unlabeled learning. Computación y Sistemas **18**, 467–475 (2014)
19. Li, J., Ott, M., Cardie, C., Hovy, E.: Towards a general rule for identifying deceptive opinion spam. In: ACL 2014, pp. 1566–1576. Association for Computational Linguistics (2014)
20. Lim, E.P., Nguyen, V.A., Jindal, N., Liu, B., Lauw, H.W.: Detecting product review spammers using rating behaviors. In: Proceedings of 19th CIKM, pp. 939–948. ACM (2010)
21. Liu, B.: Sentiment Analysis: Mining Opinions, Sentiments, and Emotions. Cambridge University Press, Cambridge (2015)
22. Luca, M.: Reviews, reputation, and revenue: the case of Yelp.com. In: Harvard Business School NOM Unit Working Paper (12–016) (2011)
23. Mikolov, T., Sutskever, I., Chen, K., Corrado, G.S., Dean, J.: Distributed representations of words and phrases and their compositionality. In: NIPS 2013, pp. 3111–3119 (2013)
24. Mukherjee, A., Kumar, A., Liu, B., Wang, J., Hsu, M., Castellanos, M., Ghosh, R.: Spotting opinion spammers using behavioral footprints. In: SIGKDD. ACM (2013)
25. Mukherjee, A., Liu, B., Glance, N.: Spotting fake reviewer groups in consumer reviews. In: WWW, pp. 191–200. ACM (2012)
26. Mukherjee, A., Venkataraman, V., Liu, B., Glance, N.: Fake review detection: classification and analysis of real and pseudo reviews. Technical report UIC-CS-2013-03 (2013)
27. Mukherjee, A., Venkataraman, V., Liu, B., Glance, N.S.: What yelp fake review filter might be doing? In: ICWSM (2013)
28. Ott, M., Choi, Y., Cardie, C., Hancock, T.J.: Finding deceptive opinion spam by any stretch of the imagination. In: ACL 2011, pp. 309–319 (2011)
29. Rayana, S., Akoglu, L.: Collective opinion spam detection: bridging review networks and metadata. In: SIGKDD 2015, pp. 985–994. ACM (2015)
30. Ren, Y., Zhang, Y.: Deceptive opinion spam detection using neural network. In: COLING 2016, pp. 140–150. The COLING 2016 Organizing Committee (2016)
31. Wang, G., Xie, S., Liu, B., Yu, P.S.: Review graph based online store review spammer detection. In: ICDM, pp. 1242–1247. IEEE (2011)
32. Wang, G., Xie, S., Liu, B., Yu, P.S.: Identify online store review spammers via social review graph. TIST **3**(4), 61 (2012)
33. Wang, X., Liu, K., He, S., Zhao, J.: Learning to represent review with tensor decomposition for spam detection. In: EMNLP 2016. Association for Computational Linguistics (2016)
34. Xie, S., Wang, G., Lin, S., Yu, P.S.: Review spam detection via temporal pattern discovery. In: KDD 2012, pp. 823–831. ACM (2012)

A Tensor Factorization Based User Influence Analysis Method with Clustering and Temporal Constraint

Xiangwen Liao[1,2], Lingying Zhang[1,2], Lin Gui[1,2(✉)], Kam-Fai Wong[3], and Guolong Chen[1,2]

[1] College of Mathematics and Computer Science, Fuzhou University, Fuzhou, China
liaoxw@fzu.edu.cn, fzu_zly@163.com, guilin.nlp@gmail.com, fzucgl@126.com
[2] Fujian Provincial Key Laboratory of Networking Computing and Intelligent Information Processing, Fuzhou University, Fuzhou, China
[3] The Chinese University of Hong Kong, Sha Tin, Hong Kong
kfwong@se.cuhk.edu.hk

Abstract. User influence analysis in social media has attracted tremendous interest from both the sociology and social data mining. It is becoming a hot topic recently. However, most approaches ignore the temporal characteristic that hidden behind the comments and articles of users. In this paper, we introduce a Tensor Factorization based on User Cluster (TFUC) model to predict the ranking of users' influence in micro blogs. Initially, TFUC obtain an influential users cluster by neural network clustering algorithm. Then, TFUC choose influential users to construct tensor model. A time matrix restrain TFUC expect CP decomposition and ranked users by their influence score that obtained from predicted tensor at last. Our experimental results show that the MAP of TFUC is higher than existing influence models with 3.4% at least.

1 Introduction

User influence analysis, which aims to analyze influence among users in social network, has become a hot topic in the research of social media recently. It has been widely applied in many other research fields such as marketing [1], search engine [2] and sentiment analysis [3–6]. In this paper, we focus on the topic level user influence in micro blogs (Chinese tweets).

On the tweets or micro blogs, there exist several pioneer studies. Zamparas et al. [7] identify influential users by calculating similarity coefficient between users and their friends or followers. Mao et al. [8] use a conditional probability model to measure users' social influence. Cai et al. [9] propose an Pagerank based model to measure user opinion influence. For the topic level user influence, Weng et al. [2] propose the TwitterRank to calculate user influence score. Cui et al. [10] apply probabilistic hybrid factor matrix factorization to predict a more elaborate social influence named item level influence. Chen et al. [3] propose a MIRC algorithm to group twitter users into different categories. Wang et al. [11]

© Springer International Publishing AG 2018
X. Huang et al. (Eds.): NLPCC 2017, LNAI 10619, pp. 877–886, 2018.
https://doi.org/10.1007/978-3-319-73618-1_77

calculate user influence and then apply it to group recommendations. Wei et al. [12] take users' opinion and topic relevance into their 3-order tensor to measured user influence.

However, most of topic level user influence analysis on micro blogs above haven't taken a full consideration of the temporal characteristic that behind the interaction between users. Moreover, the tensor factorization based user influence analysis performs well in top 5 or top 10 user ranking but poorly at mean average precision. The main reason is that the factorization aims to compress the tensor into low dimensions by retaining the important factors. In this paper, we propose a Tensor Factorization based on User Cluster (TFUC) model to cluster influential users into a certain groups, measure users' influence score from the influential cluster and rank users by their influence score in the end. The experimental results on user influence ranking precision demonstrate the superiority of TFUC over various existing user influence models such as twitteRank, OOLAM and HF_CP_ALS.

The rest of the paper is organized as follows. Section 2 provides a basic definition of our problem. Section 3 presents our proposed model for user influence analysis. Section 4 discusses evaluation results. Finally, Sect. 5 concludes the work and outlines the future directions.

2   Problem Setup

The user influence analysis aims to rank the user in social media. The goal of our method is to learn a function to map each user into a score for ranking.

Assuming there are numbers of users in the micro blogs, we denote users who post articles as $U_P = \{u_{p1}, u_{p2}, u_{p3}, \cdots, u_{pn}\}$, where n is the number of users. We present articles as $D = \{(d_1, t_1), (d_2, t_2), \cdots, (d_q, t_q)\}$. Each single article d_i is consist of a collection of comment and comment time pair, we formally define d_i as $d_i = \{(c_{i1}, t_{i1}), (c_{i2}, t_{i2}), \cdots, (c_{il}, t_{i1})\}$, where l is the number of comments that article d_i was received. We denote users who posted comments as $U_c = \{u_{c1}, u_{c2}, u_{c3}, \cdots, u_{cm}\}$, where m is the total number of users who has ever posted any comments on any d_i. Every user who posted comment associated with some common characteristics. Therefore, we let $F_c = \{f_{c1}, f_{c2}, \cdots, f_{cm}\}$ represent users' fan characteristic and $P_c = \{sP_{c1}, P_{c2}, \cdots, P_{cm}\}$ represent users' post characteristic.

It is difficult to measure user influence from only one influence aspect according to Embar's [13] theory, thus, we analyze users' global influence from four primary influence characteristics: users' comment accumulation $I_{ca}(u_{pi}, U_c, D)$, users' opinion strength $I_o(u_{pi}, U_c, D)$, users' fans activity $I_l(u_{pi}, U_c, P_c)$ and users' network centrality $I_v(u_{pi}, U_c, F_c)$.

Following the definition above, we can conclude user influence analysis as follows: given a topic a, find a mapping $Inf_a(U_p, U_c, F_c, P_c, D) \rightarrow (I_o, I_l, I_v)$, calculate users influence score by aggregating four users' characteristics I_{ca}, I_o, I_l, I_v and finally rank users base on these influence scores.

3   User Influence Analysis Model

In this section, we will detail the user influence analysis model. First we use a neural network clustering method to identify low influence score cluster. In order to obtain a better result, we use a multi-layer architecture of network to detect all possible linear combination of features in clustering model. Then, we use a tensor factorization method to predict user influence.

3.1   Neural Network Clustering Model

It is easy to know that the user whose influence ranking is higher would have a significant probability of receiving higher comment accumulation, stronger opinion strength, more centrical in the network and his fans may more activity by observing dataset. On this basis, we propose a neural network clustering approach to partition data into clusters by integrating different user characteristics. We aim to filter users with no influence or low influence in U_P. These four user characteristics are obtained as follows:

(1) We denote J as the total number of comment users in user u_{pi}'s whole articles. Given a time window t, we can obtain comment accumulation of u_{pi} by following aggregate function:

$$I_{ca}(u_{pi}) = \sum_{j=1}^{J} 1 - \exp(-\beta_{u_{pi}u_{cj}}(D)t) \tag{1}$$

where β_{uv} is the transmission rate parameter and the computing process of it can be described as follows:

$$\beta_{u_{pi}u_{cj}}(D) = \frac{\rho_{u_{pi}u_{cj}}(D)}{\Delta_{u_{pi}u_{cj}}(D)} \tag{2}$$

$$\rho_{u_{pi}u_{cj}}(D) = \sum_{di \in D} \delta(pu = u_{pi})\delta(cu = u_{cj}) \tag{3}$$

$$\Delta_{u_{pi}u_{cj}}(D) = \sum_{di \in D} \delta(pu = u_{pi})\delta(cu = u_{cj})(t_{u_{cj}} - t_{u_{pi}}) \tag{4}$$

pu is the user who posts articles and cu is the user who posts comments on pu's articles, $\delta(x = y)$ is an indicator function which's result is 1 where $x = y$ and 0 otherwise.

(2) We use following equation to represent u_{pi}'s opinion strength:

$$I_o(u_{pi}) = \sum_{j=1}^{J} O(u_{cj}) \tag{5}$$

where $O(u_{cj})$ is an indicator function, which's result is 1 where u_{cj} has ever posted a positive or non-polarity comment and -1 where u_{cj} posted a negative comment. The opinion polar of each u_{pi}'s comments is calculated by sentiment word dictionary.

(3) u_{pi}'s fans activity is obtained as follow:

$$I_l(u_{pi}) = \sum_{j=1}^{J} p_{u_{cj}} \tag{6}$$

(4) u_{pi}'s network centrality can be obtained as follow:

$$I_c(u_{pi}) = \sum_{j=1}^{J} f_{u_{cj}} \tag{7}$$

We next investigate how to take advantage of those four influence characteristics to partition users in U_P into clusters. Formally, we denote each input samples as $\mathbf{Y} = [y_1, y_2, y_3, y_4]$, where y_{i1}–y_{i4} represent $I_{ca}(u_{pi}), I_o(u_{pi}), I_l(u_{pi}), I_c(u_{pi})$ respectively. The model also specifies multiple clustering centers which are denoted as C_n, where n is the number of clustering centers. Each center C_i also have four elements with the form of $[c_{i1}, c_{i2}, c_{i3}, c_{i4}]$. Then the loss function of the clustering problem can be formulated as follows:

$$L(Y; I_{ca}, I_o, I_l, I_c) = \frac{1}{2} \sum_{i,j} (w_{ij} y_i - c_{ki})^2 \tag{8}$$

where w_{ij} is the weight of each connection between input layer and interlayer, C_k is the clustering center which Y belongs to.

We apply stochastic gradient descent when we update each w_{ij}. Therefore, we have

$$w_{ij}^{(t+1)} = w_{ij}^{(t)} - \eta(w_{ij}^{(t)} y_i^2 - y_i c_{ki}) \tag{9}$$

Considering that the weights require multiple batches of updates, we update clustering centers as following form for each batch:

$$c_{ki} = \frac{\sum_{i,j} w_{ij} \delta_{C_k}(y_i)}{count_{C_k}(Y)} \tag{10}$$

where the result of $\delta_{C_k}(x_i)$ is 1 if sample y_i belongs to the cluster which's center is C_k and 0 otherwise. The denominator in Eq. (12) is the total number of samples in the cluster which's center is C_k.

3.2   Construction of Tensor User Influence Model

After Clustering, we choose the cluster that contained most of latent influential users in U_P to construct the tensor model, we denote users in this cluster as U_P' where $U_P' \subseteq U_P$. We use a 3-order tensor $\mathbf{X} \in R^{I \times J \times K}$ to represent our user influence model, where I is the total number of users in U_P', J is the total number of comment users in U_c and K is the total number of influence characteristics that contained in tensor. Similar to the neural network clustering model we describe in Sect. 3.1, we consider three influence characteristics and take them into each tensor slice respectively.

(1) Users' opinion tensor slice: Each element in this slice is represented as follow:

$$X_{ij1} = O(u_{cj})\delta\,(cu = u_{cj})\,\delta(pu = u_{pi}) \tag{11}$$

where $O(u_{cj})$ is the same indicator function as mentioned in Eq. (5).

(2) Users' fans activity tensor slice: In this slice, every element can be represent as

$$X_{ij2} = p_{u_{cj}}\delta\,(cu = u_{cj})\,\delta(pu = u_{pi}) \tag{12}$$

(3) Users' network centrality tensor slice: We calculate each element of this slice as follow:

$$X_{ij3} = f_{u_{cj}}\delta\,(cu = u_{cj})\,\delta(pu = u_{pi}) \tag{13}$$

3.3   Factorization of Tensor User Influence Model

To increase the users' influence score whose propagation ability is strong and decrease the score of whom post a large number of articles but received few comments, we add a time constraint matrix into tensor latent user factor matrix. The loss function of rank-R CP decomposition is written as

$$L_\rho = \frac{1}{2}\sum_{ijk}\left(\mathbf{X}_{ijk} - \sum_{r=1}^{R}\mathbf{A}_{ir}\mathbf{B}_{jr}\mathbf{C}_{kr}\right)^2 + \frac{1}{2}\rho\sum_{i=1}^{I}\sum_{r=1}^{R}\mathbf{Q}_{ii}|\mathbf{A}_{ir}|^2 + \frac{1}{2}\rho\left(\|\mathbf{B}\|^2 + \|\mathbf{C}\|^2\right) \tag{14}$$

where $\mathbf{Q}$ is a time constraint matrix obtained from Eq. (1). $\mathbf{Q}$ is a diagonal matrix and each element of the main diagonal is obtained as follow:

$$\mathbf{Q}_{ii} = I_{ca}(u_{pi}) \tag{15}$$

The corresponding optimization problem is given by

$$\min_{\lambda, A, B, C} L_\rho(\mathbf{X}; \mathbf{A}, \mathbf{B}, \mathbf{C}) \tag{16}$$

We apply stochastic gradient descent to expect tensor decomposition. According to the theory suggested by Meahara et al. [14], the gradient of the loss function (18) is

$$\frac{\partial L_\rho}{\partial \mathbf{A}}(\mathbf{X}; \mathbf{A}, \mathbf{B}, \mathbf{C}) = -\mathbf{Y}(\cdot, \mathbf{B}, \mathbf{C}) + \mathbf{AT}(\mathbf{B}, \mathbf{C}) + \rho\mathbf{QA} \tag{17}$$

We can derive from the theory of Acar et al. [15] that

$$\mathbf{T}(\mathbf{B}, \mathbf{C}) = \mathbf{B}^T\mathbf{B}\mathbf{C}^T\mathbf{C} \tag{18}$$

$$\mathbf{Y}(\cdot, \mathbf{B}, \mathbf{C}) = \mathbf{X}_{(1)}\mathbf{Z}_1 \tag{19}$$

where $\mathbf{X}_{(1)}$ is the model-1 unfolding of our tensor model, $\mathbf{Z}_1 = \mathbf{C}\odot\mathbf{B}$, symbol $\odot$ denotes the Khatri-Rao products between two matrices. $\mathbf{T}(\mathbf{A}, \mathbf{C})$, $\mathbf{T}(\mathbf{A}, \mathbf{B})$, $\mathbf{Y}(\mathbf{A}, \cdot, \mathbf{C})$, $\mathbf{Y}(\mathbf{A}, \mathbf{B}, \cdot)$ can be obtained in the same way.

By substituting Eq. (21) into stochastic gradient descent method, we can obtain a rule for updating tensor latent matrix $\mathbf{A}$:

$$
\begin{aligned}
\mathbf{A}^{(t+1)} &= \mathbf{A}^{(t)} - \eta^{(t)}\frac{\partial L_\rho}{\partial \mathbf{A}} \\
&= \mathbf{A}^{(t)}[\mathbf{I} - \eta^{(t)}\mathbf{T}^{(t)}(\mathbf{B}^{(t)}, \mathbf{C}^{(t)})] + \eta^{(t)}\mathbf{Y}^{(t)}(\cdot, \mathbf{B}^{(t)}, \mathbf{C}^{(t)}) - \eta^{(t)}\rho\mathbf{Q}\mathbf{A}^{(t)}
\end{aligned}
\tag{20}
$$

where η is the step size. The updating rule of latent matrices $\mathbf{B}$ and $\mathbf{C}$ are much simpler because there are no constraint on them during the whole updating process. Due to space limitations, we just list the updating rule of $\mathbf{B}$ and the rule for $\mathbf{C}$ is similar to $\mathbf{B}$.

$$
\begin{aligned}
\mathbf{B}^{(t+1)} &= \mathbf{B}^{(t)} - \eta^{(t)}\frac{\partial L_\rho}{\partial \mathbf{B}} \\
&= \mathbf{B}^{(t)}[\mathbf{I} - \eta^{(t)}\mathbf{T}_\rho^{(t)}(\mathbf{A}^{(t)}, \mathbf{C}^{(t)})] + \eta^{(t)}\mathbf{Y}^{(t)}(\mathbf{A}^{(t)}, \cdot, \mathbf{C}^{(t)})
\end{aligned}
\tag{21}
$$

3.4   Measurement of Users Influence

We calculate users' influence from three different influence scores which are users' opinion strength $I_o(u_{pi})$, fans activity $I_l(u_{pi})$ and network centrality $I_v(u_{pi})$. Users' opinion strength is obtained as follow:

$$
I_o(u_{pi}) = \sum_{j=1}^{r} \widehat{\mathbf{X}}_{ij1}
\tag{22}
$$

where tensor $\widehat{\mathbf{X}}$ is predicted from tensor $\mathbf{X}$. Fans activity $I_l(u_{pi})$ and network centrality $I_v(u_{pi})$ are obtained from other tensor slices likewise. To unify the scale of measurement, we normalize each influence scores respectively by min-max normalized function. After that, we combine these three normalized scores to receive users' final influence score as follow:

$$
I(u_{pi}) = S_i \times (I_o(u_{pi}) + I_l(u_{pi}) + I_v(u_{pi}))
\tag{23}
$$

where S_i is a topic similarity metric which obtained the same as [12].

4   Experiments

4.1   Datasets

To study user influence in micro blogs, we choose a popular micro blogs platform in China named Sina Weibo. We crawled 2015 seed users in four topics from October 31, 2016 to December 1, 2016. On this basis, we crawled all seed users' articles and all comment users' information. In the end, we crawled 38,674 articles and 235,078 comment information of 134,961 comment users. Due to the lack of annotated data, we choose three people to manually annotate users' influence ranking for our experiments. The method of annotation referred to [12] and the average kappa value of these three people is 0.6660.

4.2   Baseline

We compared our method TFUC with several baselines:

- TwitterRank [2], which calculate user influence with comments relationship among users in a certain topic;
- OOLAM [9], an TwitterRank analogous method. It divides the comment interaction among users into positive and negative parts and calculate users' opinion influence in each polar graph respectively;
- OOLAM_SM, a method based on OOLAM of which the results consider the users' topic similarity;
- HF_CP_ALS [12], a existing tensor user influence model. It combines users' opinion and topic relevance into tensor model and remain nonnegative during CP decomposition.
- CP_SGD on the four influence characteristics which's seed users do not choose from the latent influence users cluster U_P' but choose from all users U_P;

4.3   Precision of User Influence Ranking

Our work is mainly compare the ranking precision of our method with baseline. Therefore, we select 3 precision evaluations as follow:

$$P@k = \frac{|A_k \cap B_k|}{k} \tag{24}$$

where A_k is the real top-k user influence ranking list and B_k is the top-k user influence ranking list predicted by experiments.

$$AP = \frac{\sum_{i=1}^{n} |A_i \cap B_i|/i}{n} \tag{25}$$

where i represents different rank position and n is the total number of users.

$$MAP = \frac{\sum_a AP^a}{ca} \tag{26}$$

where superscript a represents a certain topic and ca is the number of topics. Table 1 gives the comparisons of $P@k$ among our method and baselines. We can see that our method gets optimal value in most of the $P@k$ evaluation except the $P@20$ of topic law. The results in Table 2 clearly show that the precision of our method is better than the baseline TwitterRank obviously. It proved that a user whose opinion strength is stronger, fans is more activity and propagation ability is higher would be a more influential one. The performance of our method improves at least 10% than the method of OOLAM. It reflects to some degree that users with higher propagation ability and higher topic similarity would receive higher influence value. The results of our method are better than the baseline OOLAM_SM, which due to the temporal characteristic that is considered. HF_CP_ALS didn't consider temporal characteristics, therefore, the users who own high propagation ability would not result in good influence score. The

Table 1. Ranking precision comparions.

Method	Law			Method	Basketball		
	$P@5$	$P@10$	$P@20$		$P@5$	$P@10$	$P@20$
TwitterRank	0.20	0.10	0.10	TwitterRank	0.00	0.00	0.00
OOLAM	**0.40**	0.40	0.60	OOLAM	0.40	0.40	0.30
OOLAM_SM	**0.40**	**0.50**	0.60	OOLAM_SM	0.40	**0.50**	0.40
HF_CP_ALS	**0.40**	0.40	**0.65**	HF_CP_ALS	0.40	0.30	0.50
CPSGD	**0.40**	**0.50**	0.55	CPSGD	0.40	0.40	0.60
Our method	**0.40**	**0.50**	0.60	Our method	**0.60**	**0.50**	**0.70**
Method	Economy			Method	Health		
	$P@5$	$P@10$	$P@20$		$P@5$	$P@10$	$P@20$
TwitterRank	0.00	0.00	0.05	TwitterRank	0.00	0.00	0.00
OOLAM	0.20	0.30	0.40	OOLAM	0.40	0.40	0.40
OOLAM_SM	0.20	0.40	**0.50**	OOLAM_SM	0.40	0.40	0.40
HF_CP_ALS	0.20	0.30	0.45	HF_CP_ALS	0.20	0.20	0.50
CPSGD	**0.40**	**0.60**	**0.50**	CPSGD	0.40	0.40	0.45
Our method	**0.40**	**0.60**	**0.50**	Our method	0.40	0.40	**0.65**

Table 2. AP and MAP comparisons.

Method	AP				MAP
	Law	Basketball	Economy	Health	
TwitterRank	0.1160	0.1303	0.0818	0.0633	0.0979
OOLAM	0.6602	**0.6570**	0.5211	0.5730	0.6028
OOLAM_SM	0.6578	0.6027	0.5443	0.4960	0.5752
HF_CP_ALS	0.5577	0.5537	0.4254	0.3695	0.4766
CPSGD	0.6668	0.5640	0.5828	0.5781	0.5979
Our method	**0.7159**	0.6212	**0.5989**	**0.6110**	**0.6368**

precision of our method has improved 10% to 20% than the method CPSGD. It means that we filter some low rank users by clustering is useful.

Experiments above reveal that our method has a better performance. To be more convictively, we calculated the AP and MAP of each method. Figure 1 gives the precision in different value i of each method. The larger the area under the curve is, the higher the AP is. Table 2 shows the AP and MAP of our method and baselines in detail. The AP value of our method didn't reach optimal value only under the topic of basketball. By observing the previous cluster result of our method, we found that some users may obtain quite a lot of comments in a short period but their fans are few. Those users obtained more comments may just because the topic they discussed is a hot topic. Although the AP value of our method didn't reach optimal value in every topic, the MAP value of our method is better than other baselines. It is also proved that the prediction results of our method have a better performance than baselines.

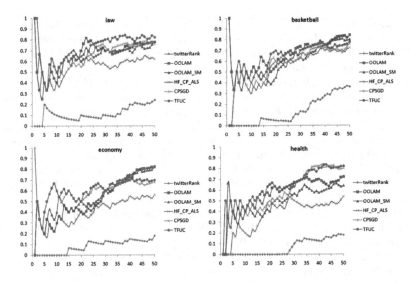

Fig. 1. Precision in different value i of each method

5 Conclusion

In this work, we propose a Tensor Factorization based on User Cluster (TFUC) model to predict the ranking of users' influence in micro blogs. Firstly, TFUC model partitions users into two different parts: influential part and uninfluential part. After clustering, TFUC expected CP decomposition with stochastic gradient descent method to expedite decomposition. TFUC also involves a time constraint matrix into tensor latent user factor matrix during the decomposition to further promote the influential users' score. The experimental results show that the user influence ranking precision of TFUC is better than other baselines with 3.4% at least, such as twitterRank, OOLAM and HF_CP_ALS.

Acknowledgement. This research project was supported by the National Natural Science Foundation of China (No. 61772135 and No. U1605251), the Open Project of Key Laboratory of Network Data Science & Technology of Chinese Academy of Sciences (No. CASNDST201606) and the Director's Project Fund of Key Laboratory of Trustworthy Distributed Computing and Service (BUPT), Ministry of Education (No. 2017KF01).

References

1. Badashian, A.S., Stroulia, E.: Measuring user influence in github: the million follower fallacy. In: Proceedings of 3rd International Workshop on CrowdSourcing in Software Engineering, May 16, 2016, Austin, Texas, USA, pp. 15–21 (2016)
2. Weng, J., Lim, E.-P., Jiang, J., He, Q.: Twitterrank: finding topic-sensitive influential twitterers. In: Proceedings of 3rd International Conference on Web Search and Web Data Mining, 4–6 February 2010, New York, NY, USA, pp. 261–270 (2010)

3. Chen, C., Gao, D., Li, W., Hou, Y.: Inferring topic-dependent influence roles of twitter users. In: 37th International ACM SIGIR Conference on Research and Development in Information Retrieval, 06–11 July 2014, Gold Coast, QLD, Australia, pp. 1203–1206 (2014)

4. Li, D., Tang, J., Ding, Y., Shuai, X., Chambers, T., Sun, G., Luo, Z., Zhang, J.: Topic-level opinion influence model (TOIM): an investigation using tencent microblogging. JASIST **66**(12), 2657–2673 (2015)

5. Gui, L., Xu, R., He, Y., Lu, Q., Wei, Z.: Intersubjectivity and sentiment: from language to knowledge. In: Proceedings of 25th International Joint Conference on Artificial Intelligence, 9–15 July 2016, New York, NY, USA, pp. 2789–2795 (2016)

6. Gui, L., Zhou, Y., Xu, R., He, Y., Qin, L.: Learning representations from heterogeneous network for sentiment classification of product reviews. Knowl.-Based Syst. **124**, 34–45 (2017)

7. Zamparas, V., Kanavos, A., Makris, C.: Real time analytics for measuring user influence on twitter. In: 2015 IEEE 27th International Conference on Tools with Artificial Intelligence, pp. 591–597. IEEE (2015)

8. Mao, J., Liu, Y., Zhang, M., Ma, S.: Social influence analysis for micro-blog user based on user behavior. Chin. J. Comput. **37**(4), 791–800 (2014)

9. Cai, K., Bao, S., Yang, Z., Tang, J., Ma, R., Zhang, L., Su, Z.: OOLAM: an opinion oriented link analysis model for influence persona discovery. In: 4th International Conference on Web Search and Web Data Mining, Hong Kong, China, pp. 645–654, February 2011

10. Cui, P., Wang, F., Yang, S., Sun, L.: Item-level social influence prediction with probabilistic hybrid factor matrix factorization. In: Proceedings of 25th AAAI Conference on Artificial Intelligence, AAAI 2011, 7–11 August 2011, San Francisco, California, USA (2011)

11. Wang, J., Liu, Z., Zhao, H.: Topic oriented user influence analysis in social networks. In: IEEE/WIC/ACM International Conference on Web Intelligence and Intelligent Agent Technology, 6–9 December 2015, Singapore, vol. I, pp. 123–126 (2015)

12. Wei, J., Chen, C., Liao, X., Chen, G., Cheng, X.: User social influence analysis based on constrained nonnegative tensor factorization. J. Commun. **37**(6), 154 (2016)

13. Embar, V.R., Bhattacharya, I., Pandit, V., Vaculín, R.: Online topic-based social influence analysis for the Wimbledon championships. In: Proceedings of 21th ACM SIGKDD International Conference on Knowledge Discovery and Data Mining, 10–13 August 2015, Sydney, NSW, Australia, pp. 1759–1768 (2015)

14. Maehara, T., Hayashi, K., Kawarabayashi, K.-i.: Expected tensor decomposition with stochastic gradient descent. In: Proceedings of 30h AAAI Conference on Artificial Intelligence, Phoenix, Arizona, USA, 12–17 February 2016, pp. 1919–1925 (2016)

15. Acar, E., Dunlavy, D.M., Kolda, T.G.: A scalable optimization approach for fitting canonical tensor decompositions. J. Chemometr. **25**(2), 67–86 (2011)

Cross-Lingual Entity Matching
for Heterogeneous Online Wikis

Weiming Lu[✉], Peng Wang, Huan Wang, Jiahui Liu, Hao Dai,
and Baogang Wei

College of Computer Science and Technology,
Zhejiang University, Zhejiang, China
luwm@zju.edu.cn

Abstract. Knowledge bases play an increasing important role in many applications. However, many knowledge bases mainly focus on English knowledge, and have only a few knowledge for low-resource languages (LLs). If we can map the entities in LLs to these in high-resource languages (HLs), many knowledge such as relation between entities can be transferred from HLs to LLs.

In this paper, we propose an efficient and effective Cross-Lingual Entity Matching approach (CL-EM) to enrich the existing cross-lingual links by learning to rank framework with the learned language-independent features, including cross-lingual topic features and document embedding features. In the experiments, we verified our approach on the existing cross-lingual links between Chinese Wikipedia and English Wikipedia by comparing it with other state-of-art approaches. In addition, we also discovered 141,754 new cross-lingual links between Baidu Baike and English Wikipedia, which almost doubles the number of the existing cross-lingual links.

1 Introduction

Knowledge bases play an increasingly important role in many applications such as information retrieval, machine translation, and question answering. However, many knowledge bases mainly focus on English knowledge, and have only a few knowledge for low-resource languages (LLs). For example, DBPedia [8] contains 4.68 million entities in English, but only contains 0.78 millions entities in Chinese[1]. On the other hand, there are two large-scale Chinese encyclopedias named Baidu Baike[2] and Hudong Baike[3], which both have more than 12 millions articles. But these is no mature Chinese knowledge base. Therefore, if we can map the entities in LLs to the entities in high-resource languages (HLs), many knowledge (i.e. relations between entities) can be transferred from HLs to LLs.

---

[1] http://wiki.dbpedia.org/dbpedia-2016-04-statistics.
[2] http://baike.baidu.com.
[3] http://www.baike.com.

© Springer International Publishing AG 2018
X. Huang et al. (Eds.): NLPCC 2017, LNAI 10619, pp. 887–899, 2018.
https://doi.org/10.1007/978-3-319-73618-1_78

In this paper, we try to address the entity matching problem in the cross-lingual environment, especially for the Chinese and English entities, but the task is not trivial. The main challenges are as follows: (1) Different languages are used to describe cross-lingual entities, so the similarity between them can not be calculated directly since they are in different word space. Can we find some language-independent features for cross-lingual entity matching? (2) Millions of articles exist in both Wikipedia and Baidu Baike. How to develop an efficient and effective approach to deal with such large-scale data sets?

In order to solve the above challenges, we take full advantage of the limited but useful English-Chinese cross-lingual links within Wikipedia. We first use them to generate candidates for reducing the computation, and then train a cross-lingual topic model and a cross-lingual document representation model to extract the language-independent features.

Our contributions are as follows: (1) We propose an efficient and effective Cross-Lingual Entity Matching approach (CL-EM) to enrich the existing cross-lingual links by learning to rank with some language-independent features. (2) We evaluate our approach on the existing cross-lingual links in Wikipedia. In practice, we can find the corresponding cross-lingual entity in Wikipedia or NIL for entities in Baidu Baike.

2   Related Work

2.1   Entity Matching

Currently, most works focus on monolingual entity matching tasks such as SIGMa [6], LINDA [2] and PARIS [14] by utilizing the structural information of RDF triples (subject, predicate, object) in knowledge bases. For example, SIGMa [6] presented a Simple Greedy Matching algorithm for aligning knowledge bases with an iterative propagation procedure. LINDA [2] is also an iterative greedy algorithm for entity matching by using prior similarity and contextual similarity from its neighboring entities. PARIS [14] computed alignments not only for entities, but also for classes and relations based on a probabilistic framework.

However, Chinese encyclopedias such as Baidu Baike only contain raw articles as in Wikipedia. Therefore, the traditional approaches mentioned above are not feasible for the cross-lingual entity matching between Baidu Baike and English Wikipedia, since they use RDF triples or ontologies in matching. While our approach does not rely on RDF triples, and only uses language independent features of articles.

Crowdsourcing also has attracted significant attention in entity resolution (e.g., [15–17]). However, crowdsourcing is not the focus of our paper.

2.2   Cross-Lingual Links Discovery

The most related work is to discover cross-lingual links within Wikipedia. Babel-Net [11] and YAGO3 [10] both aim to build a multilingual knowledge base, but they mainly relied on machine translation to discover cross-lingual links. In addition, [9] also used machine translation to interlink documents described in English and Chinese languages.

Besides machine translation based approaches, [13] tackled the cross-lingual links discovery between German and English Wikipedia using a classification-based approach. They designed several features include chain link count feature, text features and graph features. However, the text features based on text overlap and similarity are strong features with good classification results according to their experiments, so the approach may not be suitable for other language pairs, such as English and Chinese.

The existing cross-lingual links of Wikipedia are also widely used. For example, [18] proposed a factor graph based approach with link-based features to predict new cross-lingual links in Wikipedia. [12] proposed Cross-Language Explicit Semantic Analysis (CL-ESA) by using the existing cross-language links to represent documents in different languages as vectors for cross-lingual information retrieval.

3   Problem Formulation

In this section, we formally define the cross-lingual entity matching problem.

In encyclopedias such as Wikipedia and Baidu Baike, each article can be represented as a seven-tuple $x = \{tl, abs, txt, clg, tags, ilnk, olnk\}$, where tl, abs, clg and txt are title, abstract, catalog and content of the article x, $tags$, $ilnk$ and $olnk$ are the sets of category tags, inlinks and outlinks of x. Therefore, the cross-lingual entity matching problem can be defined as follows:

Problem (Cross-lingual Entity Matching). *Given two encyclopedias* $\mathcal{X}_1 = \{x_i^1 \mid i = 1, 2, \ldots, M\}$ *and* $\mathcal{X}_2 = \{x_i^2 \mid i = 1, 2, \ldots, N\}$ *in different languages (e.g.* $\mathcal{X}_c = \{x_i^c\}$ *and* $\mathcal{X}_e = \{x_i^e\}$ *are encyclopedias in Chinese and English respectively), the goal of the cross-lingual entity matching is to find, for each article* $x_i^1 \in \mathcal{X}_1$, *an equivalent article* $x_i^2 \in \mathcal{X}_2$ *or NIL if there is no equivalent entity in* $\mathcal{X}_2$.

4   Cross-lingual Entity Matching

In this section, we will describe the cross-lingual entity matching approach in detail. We first give an overview of the approach, and then elaborate the candidate selection, feature extraction and candidate ranking respectively.

Figure 1 shows the overview of the approach. When given an query entity $x_i^1 \in \mathcal{X}_1$, we first generate a set of candidate entities $\mathcal{C}(x_i^1) = \{x_j^2 \in \mathcal{X}_2\}_{j=1}^{|C|}$ from $\mathcal{X}_2$ to reduce the complexity of entity matching, and then extract features such as handcrafted feature, topic feature and document embedding for each entity pair $(x_i^1, x_j^2 \in \mathcal{C}(x_i^1))$. Finally, the equivalent entity from $\mathcal{C}$ (or NIL) is selected within the ranking layer.

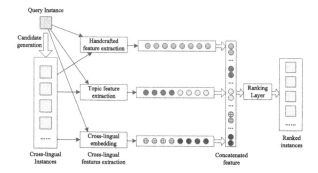

Fig. 1. The overview of the cross-lingual entity matching

4.1   Candidate Selection

It is time consuming to select the equivalent entity from millions of entities when given a query entity, so we use a candidate selection strategy to reduce the complexity.

According to the *chain link hypothesis* [13], given an article $x_i^1 \in \mathcal{X}_1$, if there is a *chain link* between x_i^1 and $x_j^2 \in \mathcal{X}_2$, then x_j^2 could be one of the equivalent entity candidates. Formally, the *chain link* between x_i^1 and x_j^2 is defined as: $x_i^1 \to x_p^1 \equiv x_q^2 \leftarrow x_j^2$, where x_i^1 and x_q^2 are articles in $\mathcal{X}_1$, x_j^2 and x_q^2 are articles in $\mathcal{X}_2$. $x_p^1 \equiv x_q^2$ means there is a cross-lingual link between x_p^1 and x_q^2, and $x_i^1 \to x_p^1$ means there is a inner-link in x_i^1 pointing to x_p^1. We denote the equivalent entity candidate of x_i^1 as $\mathcal{C}_{all}(x_i^1) = \{x_j^2 \mid \exists x_p^1 \in \mathcal{X}_1, \exists x_q^2 \in \mathcal{X}_2, x_i^1 \to x_p^1 \equiv x_q^2 \leftarrow x_j^2\}$.

However, there are still many candidate entities in $\mathcal{C}_{all}(x_i^1)$, so we should reduce the $\mathcal{C}_{all}(x_i^1)$ further. Obviously, if there are more chain links between two entities, these two entities are more likely to be equivalent. In order to verify this assumption, we randomly selected 3000 Chinese articles with the existing cross-lingual links to the English articles from Wikipedia, denoted as $\{(x_i^c, x_i^e) \mid x_i^c \in \mathcal{X}_c, x_i^e \in \mathcal{X}_e, x_i^c \equiv x_i^e, i = 1, 2, \dots, 3000\}$, and generated the candidate entity set $\mathcal{C}_n(x_i^c)$ for each article x_i^c, which has top n candidate entities ranked by the number of *chain links*. Then, we checked whether x_i^e is in the $\mathcal{C}_n(x_i^c)$, and got $Pr(x_i^e \in \mathcal{C}_{1000}(x_i^c)) = 79.67\%$, $Pr(x_i^e \in \mathcal{C}_{5000}(x_i^c)) = 86.03\%$, and $Pr(x_i^e \in \mathcal{C}_{all(57447)}(x_i^c)) = 94.17\%$. We find that most of the equivalent entities are in the candidate set $\mathcal{C}_{all}$, and $n = 1000$ is a good trade-off between the precision and the complexity. Therefore, we selected the equivalent entity for x_i^1 from the candidate set $\mathcal{C}_{1000}(x_i^1)$ in the following sections.

4.2   Feature Extraction

In order to select the equivalent entity for x_i^1 from the candidate set $\mathcal{C}_{1000}(x_i^1)$, we should calculate the equivalence score for each pair $(x_i^1, x_j^2 \in \mathcal{C}_{1000}(x_i^1))$, and then rank them according to the scores. The features used in the ranking procedure include three types: handcraft features, cross-lingual topic feature and document embedding feature.

Handcraft Features. Intuitively, if two articles x_i^1 and x_j^2 have similar titles through translation, and they link to several equivalent entities and categories, then they would likely to be equivalent. Thus, we define eight handcraft features as follows.

FEATURE 1 (TITLE SIMILARITY)
We translate the title of article x_i^c from Chinese to English, and then calculate the edit distance between two titles as the feature: $f_1 = edit\_distance(TransC2E(x_i^c.tl), x_j^e.tl)$.

If two articles have equivalent inlinks, outlinks and categories, they tend to be equivalent, which has been adequately proven in [18], so we design the 2nd to 8th features based on the existing cross-lingual links as follows.

FEATURE 2 (OUTLINK OVERLAP): $f_2 = |\{(a,b) \,|\, a \equiv b, a \in x_i^c.olnk, b \in x_j^e.olnk\}|$

FEATURE 3 (JACCARD COEFFICIENT OF OUTLINK): $f_3 = f_2/(|x_i^c.olnk| + |x_j^e.olnk| - f_2)$

FEATURE 4 (NORMALIZED OUTLINK OVERLAY): $f_4 = f_2/(\max(|\{(a,b) \,|\, a \equiv b, a \in x_i^c.olnk, b \in x_j^e.olnk, x_j^e \in \mathcal{C}(x_i^c)\}|)))$

FEATURE 5 (INLINK OVERLAP): $f_5 = |\{(a,b) \,|\, a \equiv b, a \in x_i^c.ilnk, b \in x_j^e.ilnk\}|$

FEATURE 6 (JACCARD COEFFICIENT OF INLINK): $f_6 = f_3/(|x_i^c.ilnk| + |x_j^e.ilnk| - f_5)$

FEATURE 7 (TAGS OVERLAP): $f_7 = |\{(a,b) \,|\, a \equiv b, a \in x_i^c.tags, b \in x_j^e.tags\}|$

FEATURE 8 (JACCARD COEFFICIENT OF TAGS): $f_8 = f_3/(|x_i^c.tags| + |x_j^e.tags| - f_7)$

Finally, the handcraft features of two articles x_i^1 and x_j^2 can be represented as $v_h(x_i^1, x_j^2) = [f_1, f_2, \ldots, f_8]$.

Cross-lingual Topic Model. If two articles x_i^1 and x_j^2 are equivalent even in different languages, they must have similar topic distribution.

In order to represent the articles in both $\mathcal{X}_1$ and $\mathcal{X}_2$ using the same topic set, we learn a topic model for $\mathcal{X}_1$ and $\mathcal{X}_2$ simultaneously. We first construct the *pseudo document* by concatenating the abstracts and catalogs of two equivalent articles as $d_i = \{x_i^1.abs \cup x_i^1.clg \cup x_i^2.abs \cup x_i^2.clg \,|\, x_i^1 \equiv x_i^2, x_i^1 \in \mathcal{X}_1, x_i^2 \in \mathcal{X}_2\}$. Then, we apply LDA (Latent Dirichlet Allocation) [1] on the *pseudo document* set $D = \{d_i\}$ to learn the cross-lingual topic model. With this model, we can map article x_i in both $\mathcal{X}_1$ and $\mathcal{X}_2$ into a topic distribution vector $v_t(x_i)$ with the same topic set.

In our experiment, we generated the *pseudo document set* from 100,000 article pairs in Wikipedia, and some examples of topics generated by our approach are shown in Table 1, where top 5 terms in two languages ranked by the probability in three topics are listed.

From the table, we find that LDA can conceptually cluster highly similar terms into the same topics, even they are in different languages. Based on the cross-lingual topic model, articles in both $\mathcal{X}_1$ and $\mathcal{X}_2$ can be represented with the same topic sets.

Table 1. Examples of topics generated by cross-lingual topic model

Topic 1		Topic 2		Topic 3	
Chinese	English	Chinese	English	Chinese	English
电影(film)	film	位于(located at)	city	运动员(athlete)	team
美国(American)	series	平方公里(square km)	area	效力(play for)	season
作品(production)	music	人口(population)	river	冠军(champion)	league
日本(Japanese)	new	面积(area)	town	球队(team)	club
导演(director)	release	城市(city)	population	比赛(race)	cup

Cross-lingual Document Embedding. Recently, representation learning methods such as Paragraph Vectors [7] have been proposed to learn continuous distributed vector representations for pieces of texts, and outperform other document modeling algorithms like LDA [3]. However, articles in $\mathcal{X}_1$ and $\mathcal{X}_2$ represented by Paragraph Vectors are in different language spaces, they can not be compared with each other directly. Therefore, we learn the cross-lingual document embedding vector for every article in both $\mathcal{X}_1$ and $\mathcal{X}_2$ with a deep rank model based on the Paragraph Vectors.

Suppose article x_i is represented as $f(x_i)$ in the embedding space, then the similarity between two articles x_i and x_j is measured by: $D(f(x_i), f(x_j)) = ||f(x_i) - f(x_j)||_2^2$. The smaller the distance $D(x_i, x_j)$ is, the more similar between the article x_i and x_j are. For a triplet $t_q = (x_q^1, x_p^2, x_n^2)$, where $x_q^1 \equiv x_p^2$ and $x_n^2 \in \mathcal{C}_{1000}(x_q^1)/x_p^2$, we can define the loss as: $l(x_q^1, x_p^2, x_n^2) = max\{0, g + D(f(x_q^1), f(x_p^2)) - D(f(x_q^1), f(x_n^2))\}$, where g is a margin parameter. Finally, our objective function is:

$$\min \sum_{q \in Q} \xi_q + \lambda ||W||_2^2$$

$$\text{s.t. } max\{0, g + D(f(x_q^1), f(x_p^2)) - D(f(x_q^1), f(x_n^2))\} < \xi_q$$

$$\forall x_q^1, x_p^2, x_n^2 \text{ such that } x_q^1 \equiv x_p^2, x_n^2 \in \mathcal{C}_{1000}(x_q^1)/x_p^2$$

where W is the parameters of $f(\cdot)$, λ is the parameter to improve the generalization, and Q is the training data. The neural network of the deep ranking model is shown in the Fig. 2, which includes three full-connected layers and a local normalized layer, and then a ranking layer on the top evaluates the hinge loss of a triplet.

Training a deep neural network usually needs a large amount of training data, thus we randomly select 100,000 articles $Q = \{x_q^1 | \exists x_p^2 \equiv x_q^1, x_q^1 \in \mathcal{X}_1, x_p^2 \in \mathcal{X}_2\}$, and then form ten triplets $\{x_q^1, x_p^2, x_n^2\}$ for each $x_q^1 \in Q$ as following: At first, we select the equivalent article $x_p^2 \in \mathcal{X}_2$ for x_q^1, and then select five articles from $\mathcal{C}_{1000}(x_q^1)/x_p^2$ and five articles from $\mathcal{X}_2/\mathcal{C}_{1000}(x_q^1)$ respectively as the x_n^2. In our experiment, we used TensorFlow[4] to train our model, and parameters were set with $\lambda = 0.1$, $g = 0.8$, batch size $= 400$ and learning rate $= 0.001$.

---

[4] https://www.tensorflow.org/.

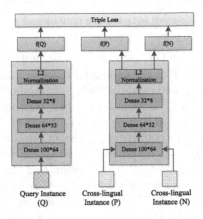

Fig. 2. Cross-lingual documents embedding

4.3 Candidate Ranking

Given an article $x_i^1 \in \mathcal{X}_1$, we want to select the equivalent article (or NIL) from $\mathcal{C}_{1000}(x_i^1)$. In this section, we model the problem as a *learning to rank* problem.

We apply RankSVM [5] as the ranking model, and take the features extracted in the previous sections as the input. Formally, the training data set is denoted as $S = \{(x_i^1, \mathcal{C}_{1000}(x_i^1)), \mathbf{y}_i\}_{i=1}^m$, where a feature vector for an article pair $(x_i^1, x_j^2 \in \mathcal{C}_{1000}(x_i^1))$ is created by concatenating the extracted features $v_{ij} = v_a(x_i^1, x_j^2) = [v_h(x_i^1, x_j^2), v_t(x_i^1), v_t(x_j^2), f(x_i^1), f(x_j^2)]$, $\mathbf{y}_i = [y_{i,1}, y_{i,2}, \ldots, y_{i,|\mathcal{C}_{1000}(x_i^1)|}]$, and $y_{i,j} = 1$ when $x_i^1 \equiv x_j^2$, otherwise $y_{i,j} = 0$.

With the ranking model, we can rank the articles in $\mathcal{C}_{1000}(x_i^1)$ for x_i^1 according to their relevance score $y_{i,j}$. However, there may be no equivalent article in $\mathcal{C}_{1000}(x_i^1)$ to x_i^1 in reality. That is, the article with the highest relevance score may not be the equivalent article to x_i^1, or these is even no equivalent article in the ranking candidates. Therefore, we define two thresholds to disambiguate the *NIL* and the equivalent article, inspired by [19]: $t_1 = h - margin_1 \cdot (h - avg)$ and $t_2 = margin_2 \cdot (h - avg)$, where h, s and avg are the highest, second-highest and average scores in $\mathbf{y}_i$, $margin_1$ and $margin_2$ are two margin parameters, which are determined in the experiments. If $s < t_1$, the article with the highest score can be considered as the equivalent article, and if $s > t_2$, there would be no equivalent article.

5 Experiments

5.1 Datasets

We constructed two datasets from Wikipedia:

DATASET 1: As in [18], we randomly selected 2000 Chinese Wikipedia articles with existing cross-lingual links to English articles, denoted as D, and then picked out the corresponding 2000 English articles to form 2000 cross-lingual article pairs. Here, 2000 English articles are considered as the candidate articles $\mathcal{C}_{2000}(x_i^c)$ for each Chinese article $x_i^c \in \mathcal{X}_c$.

DATASET 2: Similar to the DATASET 1, we randomly selected 3000 Chinese Wikipedia articles with existing cross-lingual links to English articles, denoted as D, but we used the proposed candidate selection method to generate $\mathcal{C}_{1000}(x_i^c)$ for each Chinese article $x_i^c \in \mathcal{X}_c$ from all English Wikipedia articles. Then, we checked whether the equivalent article $x_i^e \in \mathcal{X}_e$ for x_i^c exists in $\mathcal{C}_{1000}(x_i^c)$. Only 2390 Chinese articles have its equivalent articles in the candidate set, so we used this 2390 Chinese articles with its equivalent articles as the DATASET 2.

Obviously, it is more challenging when evaluating the approaches with the DATASET 2, since the articles in the candidate set are very similar.

For each dataset, we used 75% of the data as the training data, and the remaining data as the testing data.

5.2 Comparison Methods

We compared our approach with the following methods:

- **Title Match (TM).** We translate the title of Chinese article into English through Baidu Translate API[5], and then match the title with English articles in the candidate set to check whether they are exactly same.
- **Title Similarity (TS).** Similar to TM, TS considers the article with the minimal edit distance between the translated title and the title of each English article in the candidate set as the equivalent article.
- **Support Vector Machine (SVM).** We used handcrafted feature v_h as the input, and trained SVM classifiers on the DATASET 1 and DATASET 2 respectively.
- **Similarity Aggregation (SA).** Here, we considered the average similarity of some handcrafted features as the article similarity. Thus, for each Chinese article, we select the most similar English article as the equivalent article. In order to evaluate the influence of the *Title Similarity*, we calculated the article similarity in two ways: $SA_1(x_i^c, x_j^e) = (f_1 + f_3 + f_6 + f_8)/4$ and $SA_2(x_i^c, x_j^e) = (f_3 + f_6 + f_8)/3$.
- **Cross-Language Explicit Semantic Analysis (CL-ESA)** [12]. CL-ESA is the cross-lingual extension to the Explicit Semantic Analysis (ESA) approach [4]. Here, we used the terms having existing cross-lingual links to represent articles in both $\mathcal{X}_c$ and $\mathcal{X}_e$.

In the experiments, we used precision, recall and F-score as the evaluation metrics.

5.3 Results

In this section, we only evaluate the performance of the candidate ranking, and don't predict the exactly equivalent article and NIL by comparing the ranking scores to the thresholds t_1 and t_2, which will be evaluated in the next section.

---

[5] http://api.fanyi.baidu.com.

Table 2. Results on DATASET 1

Methods	Prec.	Rec.	F_1
TM	100.00%	24.55%	39.42%
TS	59.30%	59.30%	59.30%
SA_1	85.35%	85.35%	85.35%
SA_2	82.00%	82.00%	82.00%
SVM	75.20%	92.50%	82.80%
CL-EM (v_h)	92.30%	92.30%	92.30%
CL-EM (v_a)	92.50%	92.50%	**92.50%**

Table 3. Results on DATASET 2

Methods	Prec.	Rec.	F_1
TM	97.65%	26.03%	41.10%
TS	56.03%	56.03%	56.03%
SA_1	65.60%	65.60%	65.60%
SA_2	34.73%	34.73%	34.73%
CL-ESA	7.3%	7.3%	7.3%
CL-EM (v_h)	68.75%	68.75%	68.75%
CL-EM ($v_h + v_t$)	69.44%	69.44%	69.44%
CL-EM (v_a)	70.28%	70.28%	**70.28%**

Since TM and SVM try to predict whether x_i^c and $x_j^e \in \mathcal{C}(x_i^c)$ is equivalent, so it is possible that none of the article in $\mathcal{C}(x_i^c)$ is the equivalent article. While for TS, SA, CL-ESA and our approach, they rank the articles in the candidate set, and consider the Top 1 as the equivalent article, so they have the same recall and precision. The comparison results of DATASET 1 are shown in the Table 2.

From the table, we can see that (1) Since TM is based on the exact title matching, so the precision reaches to 100%, but it has a very low recall because of improper translation. (2) TS increases the recall by ranking the candidate articles according to the title similarity, but it decreases the precision. (3) SVM and SA both considered all the handcraft features, so their F_1 scores are larger than 80%. Especially, the F_1 scores of SA and SVM are larger than that of TS, which indicates that the in-links, out-links and tags are very useful in cross-lingual entity matching. In addition, the results between SA_1 and SA_2 indicates the usefulness of title similarity in cross-lingual entity matching. (4) Our approach CL-EM outperforms other methods significantly. When only using the handcraft features, CL-EM can reach the F_1 score 92.3% straightforwardly, but only 0.2% can be improved when adding cross-lingual topic features and document embedding features. This may be because the articles in DATASET 1 are quit different, the handcraft features can be adequate to distinguish them well.

For the more challenging dataset DATASET 2, we obtained a worse performance than that in the DATASET 1. The details are shown in the Table 3.

From the table, we can see that CL-EM still outperforms all other methods significantly. Since many articles have the same title, but refer to different entities in the real world, so the precision of TM doesn't reach to 100%. In addition, cross-lingual topic feature and article embedding feature can indeed improve the cross-lingual entity matching by comparing CL-EM(v_h), CL-EM($v_h + v_t$) and CL-EM(v_a). Surprisingly, we only obtain 7.3% for CL-ESA, because the articles in the candidate set are very similar.

In addition, we also evaluate the performance of CL-EM according to the Top-K precision by: $prec_k = \dfrac{\sum_{x_i^c \in D} |\delta(x_i^e \in TopK(\mathcal{C}_{1000}(x_i^c)) \mid x_i^e \equiv x_i^c)|}{|D|}$, where $TopK(\mathcal{C}_{1000}(x_i^c))$ is the top k articles in the candidate set $\mathcal{C}_{1000}(x_i^c)$ for article

x_i^c according to the ranking score. $\delta(true) = 1$ and $\delta(false) = 0$. Table 4 shows the results. Obviously, the precision increases along with the larger k. Indeed, most of the equivalent articles are ranked in the Top k list. Thus, in our practical system, we show the Top k list to users, and users can select and click the equivalent cross-lingual article. With this user crowdsourcing activities, we can improve the quality of cross-lingual entity matching.

Table 4. Evaluation for the Top K articles in the candidate set

k	1	2	5	10
$prec_k$	70.28%	75.28%	81.81%	86.25%

When training the cross-lingual document embedding model, different margin parameter g would influence the model. Thus, we evaluate the model with different g and the different ways of concatenating two document embedding vectors. The results are shown in Table 5, where v_1v_2, $|v_1 - v_2|$ and $||v_1 - v_2||_2$ are three ways to combine two vector $v_1 = f(x_i^1)$ and $v_2 = f(x_j^2)$. v_1v_2 is to concatenate two vectors, $|v_1 - v_2|$ is a N-dimensional vector $< |v_{1_1} - v_{2_1}|, |v_{1_2} - v_{2_2}|, \ldots, |v_{1_N} - v_{2_N}| >$ and $||v_1 - v_2||_2$ is the Euclidean distance of two vectors. According to the result, we chose $g = 0.8$ and $||v_1 - v_2||_2$ in the experiments since they reach the best performance.

Table 5. The F_1 of CL-EM with different settings in cross-lingual document embedding

g	v_1v_2	$|v_1 - v_2|$	$||v_1 - v_2||_2$
0.1	68.75%	68.47%	68.47%
0.5	68.61%	68.61%	69.86%
0.8	68.33%	69.03%	**70.28%**
1.0	68.61%	69.58%	68.19%

5.4 Equivalence Judgement Evaluation

In this section, we evaluate the performance of equivalence judgement by turning the parameters $margin_1$ and $margin_2$. In the equivalence judgement, we not only need to judge exactly whether the article with the highest relevance score in $\mathcal{C}(x_i^1)$ is equivalent to the article x_i^1 (Task 1), but also need to judge whether there is no equivalent article in $\mathcal{C}(x_i^1)$ for the article x_i^1 (Task 2). Therefore, we constructed two datasets DATASET_TOP1 and DATASET_NIL from Baidu Baike and English Wikipedia.

DATASET_TOP1: This dataset is used for Task 1. We randomly selected 300 positive samples $P = \{x_i^c \,|\, Top(\mathcal{C}(x_i^c)) = x_i^e \,\&\&\, x_i^c \equiv x_i^e, i = 1, 2, \ldots, 300\}$, and then selected 300 negative samples $N = \{x_i^c \,|\, Top(\mathcal{C}(x_i^c)) \neq x_i^e \,\&\&\, x_i^c \equiv x_i^e, i = 1, 2, \ldots, 300\}$. Here, $Top(\mathcal{C}(x_i^c))$ is the article with the highest relevance score in $\mathcal{C}(x_i^c)$ for x_i^c.

DATASET_NIL: This dataset is used for Task 2. We randomly selected 600 positive samples $P = \{x_i^c \mid x_i^e \notin C(x_i^c) \&\& x_i^c \equiv x_i^e, i = 1, 2, \ldots, 600\}$, and then selected 600 negative samples $N = \{x_i^c \mid Top(C(x_i^c)) = x_i^e \&\& x_i^c \equiv x_i^e, i = 1, 2, \ldots, 300\} \cup \{x_i^c \mid x_i^e \in C(x_i^c) \&\& x_i^c \equiv x_i^e, i = 1, 2, \ldots, 300\}$.

We assume Q is the equivalence judgement results. For task 1, $Q = \{x_i^c \mid s < t_1\}$ and $Q = \{x_i^c \mid s > t_2\}$ for Task 2, where s, t_1 and t_2 are defined in Sect. 4.3. Then, the precision and recall are calculated as: $p = |Q \cap P|/|Q|$ and $r = |Q \cap P|/|P|$. Since precision is more important than recall, so we also calculated $F_{0.5}$ as $\frac{1.25 \cdot (p+r)}{0.25 \cdot p + r}$. The results are shown in Figs. 3 and 4.

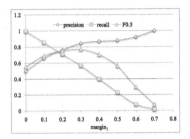

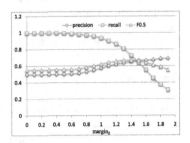

Fig. 3. performance for Top 1 equivalence judgement varies with parameter $margin_1$ in DATASET_TOP1

Fig. 4. performance for NIL detection varies with parameter $margin_2$ in DATASET_NIL

From the figures, we can see that precision increases when $margin_1$ and $margin_2$ get larger, but recall decreases. Therefore, we selected $margin_1 = 0.3$ and $margin_2 = 1.3$ to discover cross-lingual links between Baidu Baike and English Wikipedia.

Finally, we used our approach to discover new cross-lingual links between Baidu Baike and English Wikipedia. We crawled 10,143,321 articles from Baidu Baike, and then extracted 407,092 cross-lingual links of articles and 82,452 cross-lingual links of categories which already exist between Chinese Wikipedia and English Wikipedia. Then we obtained 173,259 equivalent articles in Baidu Baike among these existing cross-lingual links of articles. Therefore, we used these 173,259 links between Baidu Baike and English Wikipedia as the seed and finally found 141,754 new cross-lingual links between Baidu Baike and English Wikipedia. Table 6 shows some examples of the discovered cross-lingual links.

Table 6. The examples of the discovered cross-lingual links

Chinese articles (types are in the bracket)	English articles in ranked lists (bold indicates the correct links)
山濑功治 (Person)	**Koji Yamase**, Yokohama Flügels, 1998 Gamba Osaka season, Shinji Tanaka, 1997 J. League
瀛台泣血 (Movie)	**The Last Tempest**, Empress Dowager Cixi, The Empress Dowager, Hundred Days' Reform, The Last Emperor
维容 (Location)	**Vijon**, Salleron, Réunion, Bouzanne, Besanon
查尔斯·泰勒 (Person)	Liberia, **Charles Taylor (Liberian politician)**, Special Court for Sierra Leone, Sierra Leone, Second Liberian Civil War

6   Conclusion

In this paper, we propose an efficient and effective Cross-Lingual Entity Matching approach (CL-EM) to enrich the existing cross-lingual links by learning to rank framework with some language-independent features. We verified our approach on the existing cross-lingual links between Chinese Wikipedia and English Wikipedia by comparing it with other state-of-art approaches. In addition, we also discovered 141,754 new cross-lingual links between Baidu Baike and English Wikipedia, which almost doubles the number of the existing cross-lingual links.

Acknowledgements. This work is supported by the Zhejiang Provincial Natural Science Foundation of China (No. LY17F020015), the Chinese Knowledge Center of Engineering Science and Technology (CKCEST), and the Fundamental Research Funds for the Central Universities (No. 2017FZA5016).

References

1. Blei, D.M., Ng, A.Y., Jordan, M.I.: Latent Dirichlet allocation. J. Mach. Learn. Res. **3**, 993–1022 (2001)
2. Böhm, C., de Melo, G., Naumann, F., Weikum, G.: Linda: distributed web-of-data-scale entity matching. In: CIKM, pp. 2104–2108. ACM (2012)
3. Dai, A.M., Olah, C., Le, Q.V.: Document embedding with paragraph vectors. CoRR abs/1507.07998 (2015)
4. Gabrilovich, E., Markovitch, S.: Computing semantic relatedness using Wikipedia-based explicit semantic analysis. In: IJCAI (2007)
5. Joachims, T.: Optimizing search engines using clickthrough data. In: KDD (2002)
6. Lacoste-Julien, S., Palla, K., Davies, A., Kasneci, G., Graepel, T., Ghahramani, Z.: SIGMa: simple greedy matching for aligning large knowledge bases. In: KDD, pp. 572–580. ACM (2013)
7. Le, Q.V., Mikolov, T.: Distributed representations of sentences and documents. In: ICML (2014)
8. Lehmann, J., Isele, R., Jakob, M., Jentzsch, A., Kontokostas, D., Mendes, P.N., Hellmann, S., Morsey, M., van Kleef, P., Auer, S., Bizer, C.: DBpedia - a large-scale, multilingual knowledge base extracted from Wikipedia. Semantic Web **6**, 167–195 (2015)
9. Lesnikova, T., David, J., Euzenat, J.: Interlinking English and Chinese RDF data sets using machine translation. In: KNOW@LOD (2014)
10. Mahdisoltani, F., Biega, J., Suchanek, F.M.: Yago3: a knowledge base from multilingual Wikipedias. In: CIDR (2015)
11. Navigli, R., Ponzetto, S.P.: BabelNet: the automatic construction, evaluation and application of a wide-coverage multilingual semantic network. Artif. Intell. **193**, 217–250 (2012)
12. Sorg, P., Cimiano, P.: Cross-language information retrieval with explicit semantic analysis. In: CLEF (2008)
13. Sorg, P., Cimiano, P.: Enriching the crosslingual link structure of Wikipedia - a classification-based approach. In: AAAI Workshop on Wikipedia and Artificial Intelligence (2008)
14. Suchanek, F.M., Abiteboul, S., Senellart, P.: Paris: probabilistic alignment of relations, instances, and schema. Proc. VLDB Endow. **5**(3), 157–168 (2011)

15. Vesdapunt, N., Bellare, K., Dalvi, N.: Crowdsourcing algorithms for entity resolution. Proc. VLDB Endow. **7**(12), 1071–1082 (2014)
16. Wang, J., Kraska, T., Franklin, M.J., Feng, J.: Crowder: crowdsourcing entity resolution. Proc. VLDB Endow. **5**(11), 1483–1494 (2012)
17. Wang, J., Li, G., Kraska, T., Franklin, M.J., Feng, J.: Leveraging transitive relations for crowdsourced joins. In: SIGMOD, pp. 229–240. ACM (2013)
18. Wang, Z., Li, J.Z., Wang, Z., Tang, J.: Cross-lingual knowledge linking across wiki knowledge bases. In: WWW (2012)
19. Zwicklbauer, S., Seifert, C., Granitzer, M.: Robust and collective entity disambiguation through semantic embeddings. In: SIGIR (2016)

A Unified Probabilistic Model for Aspect-Level Sentiment Analysis

Daniel Stantic$^{(\boxtimes)}$ and Fei Song

University of Guelph, Guelph, ON, Canada
daniel.stantic@gmail.com, fsong@uoguelph.ca
http://www.uoguelph.ca

Abstract. Aspect-level sentiment analysis aims to delve deep into opinionated text to discover sentiments expressed about specific aspects of the discussed topics. Aspect detection is often achieved by topic modelling. Probabilistic modelling has been one of the more popular approaches for both topic modelling and sentiment analysis. Incorporating Part-Of-Speech (POS) information and modelling the emphasis placed on each topic have been shown to improve the quality of such models. Previous approaches to aspect-level sentiment analysis typically model only some of these components or rely on external tools or resources to provide some of the information. In this paper, we develop a new, unified probabilistic model that can capture topics, topic weights, syntactic classes, and sentiment levels from unstructured text without relying on any external sources of information. Our solution builds on the ideas of the existing probabilistic models but generalizes them into a unified framework with some novel extensions.

Keywords: Aspect-level sentiment analysis · Topic models
Syntax models · Probabilistic models

1 Introduction

With the increasing amount of opinionated text on the World Wide Web, users are likely to find reviews on almost anything that can be evaluated subjectively. The opinions expressed for such an entity are often detailed, covering not just the overall topic but also the specific aspects of that topic. For example, a user writing a review for a camera may express his overall satisfaction with the camera but also talk specifically about different aspects such as picture quality, battery life, ease of use, etc. Aspect-level sentiment analysis aims to determine the sentiments expressed about the specific aspects as well as the overall topic in opinionated text. It has many useful applications such as online review analysis, opinionated web search and consumer satisfaction analysis [10].

Sentiment analysis is a form of text classification that sorts opinionated text into positive and negative categories. However, in contrast to topic classification, we cannot always rely on the repeated occurrences of certain words to perform

© Springer International Publishing AG 2018
X. Huang et al. (Eds.): NLPCC 2017, LNAI 10619, pp. 900–909, 2018.
https://doi.org/10.1007/978-3-319-73618-1_79

sentiment classification because sentiment words and phrases are more context-dependent. For example, the word "cold" usually expresses positive sentiment when talking about a refreshing beverage but a negative sentiment when talking about the demeanor of a customer service employee. Another challenge is the subtlety in some sentiment expressions. When examining the sentence "How can anyone sit through this movie?" we see no positive or negative words yet the reviewer is clearly (to humans) expressing a negative sentiment.

There have been many methods proposed for aspect-level sentiment analysis [4–6,11,15]. Although recent solutions have focused on utilizing deep learning techniques [12,13], solutions based on probabilistic models such as LDA [1] still have their advantages in terms of reducing dimensionality, extracting aspects and related sentiments, and associating the related words for them [7–9]. Probabilistic models that include Part-Of-Speech (POS) information have been shown to outperform the ones that do not since POS classes can help distinguish words that express sentiment over the ones that do not [8,18]. There has also been research showing that accounting for the emphasis placed on topics results in further improvements [16,17]. Previous probabilistic approaches typically model only some of these components or rely on external sources to provide some of the information. In this paper, we develop a new, unified probabilistic model that can capture topics, topic weights, syntactic classes, and sentiment levels without relying on any external sources of information. Our solution builds on the ideas of the existing probabilistic models but generalizes them into a unified framework with some novel extensions. Our experiments show results comparable or superior to those from the state-of-the-art probabilistic systems.

The rest of this paper is organized as follows. Section 2 briefly describes related work. Section 3 presents our model. Experimental setup and results are outlined in Sect. 4. Finally, Sect. 5 concludes the paper with thoughts on future work.

2   Related Work

Our model builds on and is inspired by several other models. In this section we give a brief overview of each of them.

Joint Sentiment/Topic (JST) [9] model is the first model to our knowledge to extend LDA for the purposes of aspect-level sentiment analysis. In JST, each sentiment label is associated with a topic distribution in contrast to LDA that has a single topic distribution per document. Words are then drawn from a distribution defined by both topic and sentiment. This approach assumes that every word is related to a topic and expresses a sentiment, an assumption that is often incorrect as there are many words that are purely functional and/or do not express any sentiment at all.

Aspect and Sentiment Unification Model (ASUM) [7] is very similar to JST. The authors argued that if the words from a single sentence came from the same model then each model would focus on the regional co-occurrences of the words in a document. Hence, ASUM treats each sentence as a unit of topic and sentiment. Subsequent research, including our own, has found that treating sentences in such a way is too limiting.

Sentiment Topic Model with Decomposed Prior (STDP) [8] is the first model to our knowledge to model the fact that not all words express sentiment. The authors use a POS tagger to tag each word with its POS class before applying their model for aspect-level sentiment analysis. The model includes a distribution over POS classes modeling the probability that a word with a given POS class expresses sentiment. A word is drawn by first drawing an indicator variable from that distribution. If the indicator variable is true, the word is drawn from a joint sentiment-topic distribution just like with JST. If the indicator variable is false, the word is drawn from a topic distribution similar to LDA. This model still assumes that each word is, at least, related to a topic and uses a list of stopwords to filter out some words that are unlikely to identify a topic or express sentiment. It also relies on an external source of information to label each word with a POS class. Our model overcomes both of these deficiencies.

Latent Rating Regression (LRR) [16] model and the subsequent Latent Aspect Rating Analysis Model (LARAM) [17], written by the same authors, were collectively the first to introduce the notion of topic weights - the relative emphasis placed on each topic. In both models the overall rating of a review is assumed to be given and the topics, sentiments and weights are inferred based on that input. That is contrary to our model that derives the overall sentiment from the aspect sentiments. These models also assume that every word is associated to both topic and sentiment, similarly to JST and ASUM.

Part of Speech LDA (POSLDA) [3] combines LDA with a Bayesian Hidden Markov Model (HMM) to model topic and syntax simultaneously. The POS classes modeled by the HMM component are split into semantic and purely functional ones. Topic modeling is only applied to the words associated with a semantic class. As stated in [3], combining both topic and syntax information in one model helps us capture the interactions between the two so that we can produce stronger modeling results. For example, the word "book" can be both a noun and a verb, and if we know that the topic being considered is "airline", it is more likely to be a verb. Similarly, if we know that the word "seal" is a noun, it is more likely to be related to "marine animals" than "construction" as in "seal a crack". Although not a sentiment analysis model, POSLDA was a big influence in our own work as will be seen in the next section.

3   Our Model

3.1   Generative Process

POSLDA [3] can be seen as the starting point for us; therefore we call our model SentPOSLDA. Similarly to POSLDA, our model categorizes words into syntactic categories using a Bayesian HMM. It does not tag words with specific POS classes such as nouns and verbs but rather clusters them into categories based on syntactic similarity. We designate a subset of the syntactic classes as semantic, for words that potentially identify a topic/aspect or express a sentiment, and we designate the other classes as purely functional. We add a component to model the probability of a word being a sentiment word or a non-sentiment word based on its syntactic class, borrowing the ideas from Li et al's STDP [8]. However, instead of using a POS tagger, we take advantage of the syntax modelling component of our model. We restrict this component to operate on semantic classes only. Based on this component, a word in a semantic class is modelled by one of two models depending on whether it is a sentiment word or a non-sentiment word. Non-sentiment words are modelled using a joint Bayesian HMM and LDA [1] model exactly like with POSLDA. To derive a sentiment analysis component for sentiment words, we draw inspiration from JST [9]. However, whereas JST has a topic distribution for each sentiment label, our model has a sentiment distribution for each topic. Intuitively, this is a more appropriate approach for what we are trying to achieve. A topic distribution for each sentiment label answers the question "which topics does the author like/dislike more than others?" whereas our approach answers the question "how much does the author like each topic?". We also do not explicitly model an overall sentiment that influences aspect sentiments but rather derive the overall sentiment from the individual sentiments of the underlying aspects. To get the overall sentiment for a document we make the simplifying assumption that the more a person talks about a topic the more important that topic is to that person. Under this assumption, the topic proportions are equivalent to the topic weights in LRR [16]/LARAM [17] and we can thus derive the overall sentiment in a similar way.

Intuitively, our model simulates the following process a user would follow to write a review:

1. The user decides to write a review describing a set of topics. She also decides how much she likes/dislikes each topic.
2. She first selects a POS group for the next word she will use, following the rules of syntax.
3. Depending on the POS group selected, she makes a choice over expressing something topic related or using a functional word to form a bigger phrase.
   (a) If she decides to use a functional word she picks the word from the selected syntax class and goes back to step 2.
   (b) Otherwise, based on the POS group, she chooses to either identify a topic or express a sentiment about a topic.
       i. If she chooses to identify a topic, she picks the topic to identify. She then picks a word to identify that topic and goes back to step 2.
       ii. Otherwise, she picks a sentiment associated with a topic she mentioned in the current sentence. She then picks a word to express that sentiment and goes back to step 2.

Notice that in step 3.b.ii we further restrict the expression of a sentiment to a topic that was mentioned in the current sentence. Such dependence between a sentiment word and its target is something that is missing in all the models we described so far. ASUM [7] is the only one that can somewhat mimic that as it operates at the level of a sentence.

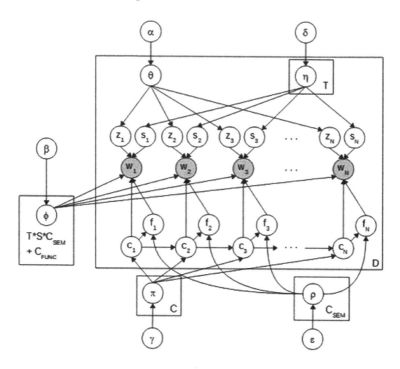

Fig. 1. Graphical representation of SentPOSLDA.

The graphical representation of our model is shown in Fig. 1 and the formal generative process is as follows:

1. For each row π_r in π for the POS classes, draw $\pi_r \sim$ Dirichlet(γ)
2. For each semantic POS class c, draw $\rho_c \sim$ Beta(ϵ)
3. For each word distribution $\phi_i \in \phi$, draw $\phi_i \sim$ Dirichlet(β)
4. For each document d:
   (a) Draw topic distribution $\theta_d \sim$ Dirichlet(α)
   (b) For each topic z, draw sentiment distribution $\eta_{d,z} \sim$ Dirichlet(δ)
   (c) For each word token w_i in document d:
       i. Draw POS class $c_i \sim \pi_{c_{i-1}}$
       ii. If $c_i \in C_{FUNC}$: draw word $w_i \sim \phi_{c_i}^{FUNC}$
       iii. Else:
           A. Draw topic $z_i \sim \theta_d$
           B. Draw sentiment/non-sentiment indicator $f_i \sim \rho_{c_i}$
           C. If $f_i =$ true: Draw sentiment $s_i \sim \eta_{d,z_i}$, then draw word $w_i \sim \phi_{c_i,z_i,s_i}^{SEM}$
           D. Else: Draw word $w_i \sim \phi_{c_i,z_i}^{SEM}$.

3.2 Inference

We use collapsed Gibbs sampling for inference and Minka's fixed-point method for hyperparameter optimization. There are three cases to cover: (1) the word is purely functional (2) the word is semantic but does not express sentiment and (3) the word is semantic and expresses sentiment. The joint posterior of the relevant variables then is as follows:

1. $c_i \in C_{FUNC}$:

$$p(c_i \,|\, c_{-i}, w) \propto p_{c_i} \cdot \frac{n_{w_i}^{(c_i)} + \beta}{n^{(c_i)} + W\beta} \tag{1}$$

2. $c_i \in C_{SEM}$ and $f_i = \text{false}$:

$$p(c_i, z_i, f_i \,|\, c_{-i}, z_{-i}, f_{-i}, w) \propto p_{c_i} \cdot \frac{n_{z_i}^{(d)} + \alpha_{z_i}}{n^{(d)} + \alpha} \cdot \frac{n_{w_i}^{(c_i, z_i)} + \beta}{n^{(c_i, z_i)} + W\beta} \cdot \frac{n_{f_i}^{(c_i)} + \epsilon_{f_i}}{n^{(c_i)} + \epsilon} \tag{2}$$

3. $c_i \in C_{SEM}$ and $f_i = \text{true}$:

$$p(c_i, z_i, s_i, f_i \,|\, c_{-i}, z_{-i}, s_{-i} f_{-i}, w)$$

$$\propto p_{c_i} \cdot \frac{n_{z_i}^{(d)} + \alpha_{z_i}}{n^{(d)} + \alpha} \cdot \frac{n_{w_i}^{(c_i, z_i, s_i)} + \beta}{n^{(c_i, z_i, s_i)} + W\beta} \cdot \frac{n_{s_i}^{(d, z_i)} + \delta_{s_i}}{n^{(d, z_i)} + \delta} \cdot \frac{n_{f_i}^{(c_i)} + \epsilon_{f_i}}{n^{(c_i)} + \epsilon} \tag{3}$$

where p_{c_i} is:

$$p_{c_i} = \frac{n_{(c_{i-2}, c_{i-1}, c_i)} + \gamma_{c_i}}{n_{(c_{i-2}, c_{i-1})} + \gamma} \cdot \frac{n_{(c_{i-1}, c_i, c_{i+1})} + \gamma_{c_i}}{n_{(c_{i-1}, c_i)} + \gamma} \cdot \frac{n_{(c_i, c_{i+1}, c_{i+2})} + \gamma_{c_i}}{n_{(c_i, c_{i+1})} + \gamma} \tag{4}$$

After sufficient burn-in time, all words are assigned to syntactic classes and the relevant ones are also assigned topics and sentiments. We can then estimate several probabilities at the document and word level. Of the most interest to us is the approximate probability of a sentiment expressed for a topic in a document:

$$\eta_{z_i, s_i, d} = \frac{n_{s_i}^{(d, z_i)} + \delta_{s_i}}{n^{(d, z_i)} + \delta} \tag{5}$$

3.3   Seeding

In order to compare the output of our model to the given aspect ratings, we use both sentiment and topic seed words to coerce the model to match the given aspect and rating categories. Although many probabilistic models such as LDA and POSLDA are unsupervised approaches, the resulting word distributions do not normally match the categories interpretable to humans, as observed by Chang et al. [2]. By using seed words for certain categories, we are essentially incorporating the prior information so that the results can be more interpretable. The seeding approach we have chosen is to "pin" the seed words in the desired categories for the duration of the sampling process so that their assignments never change.

3.4   Post-Processing

Overall Sentiment. Under the assumption made in Sect. 3.1, the overall sentiment for a document can be derived as follows:

$$Overall_{d,s} = \frac{\sum_{z=1}^{T} \theta_z \eta_{z,s,d}}{\sum_{i=1}^{S} \sum_{z=1}^{T} \theta_z \eta_{z,i,d}} \tag{6}$$

Undetected Sentiments. It is entirely possible for the author of a review to provide a rating for each aspect but only mention some of the aspects in the review. In our model, we would not detect any sentiments for the aspects that were not mentioned and the counts in Eq. 5 would all equal to 0 for those aspects. Consequently, the equation would be reduced to δ_s/δ, which is roughly the overall sentiment for the entire corpus. Obviously, this is a bad estimate. A more appropriate estimate is the overall sentiment of the review. We therefore calculate the overall sentiment first, ignoring any aspects that were not mentioned, and then use the overall sentiment as an estimate for those missing aspects.

4   Experiments and Results

4.1   Data Set

We use the TripAdvisor data set that Wang et al. used for their experiments with LRR [16] and LARAM [17]. The TripAdvisor web site allows users to rate hotels on up to seven aspects in addition to the overall rating: value, room, location, cleanliness, check in/front desk, service and business service. The users can provide a rating on a scale from 1 to 5 with 1 being the worst rating and 5 being the best. To compare such a rating to the outcome of our solution we collapse the ratings so that a rating of 1 or 2 is treated as negative and a rating of 4 or 5 as positive. We ignore all ratings of 3 since they do not indicate a positive or negative sentiment. Some basic analysis revealed that this dataset is very biased towards the positive. Over all of the aspects and the overall rating, positive reviews accounted for 63% to 75% of the total, negative ones accounted for 6% to 15% and the rest were neutral.

4.2   Results

Since STDP has outperformed other models, and for brevity, we will only show a comparison between our model and STDP. We did not do a comparison with LRR or LARAM since the problem those models tackle is detecting aspect sentiments on a 5-point scale given the overall sentiment, a task quite different from our own. Table 1 shows the accuracy for both STDP and SentPOSLDA for both overall and aspect sentiment. Both models were fairly consistent with their performance, however SentPOSLDA outperformed STDP in every category.

A deeper analysis, taking into account that the data set is biased towards the positive, reveals the strengths and weaknesses of each model as presented in

Table 1. Accuracy comparison between STDP and SentPOSLDA.

Aspect	STDP	SentPOSLDA
Overall	0.749	0.856
Value	0.697	0.836
Rooms	0.712	0.863
Location	0.674	0.864
Cleanliness	0.760	0.894
Front desk	0.750	0.973
Service	0.679	0.846
Business service	0.708	0.809

Table 2. The F-measure scores show that both models performed well on positive reviews but struggled with negative ones. This was not surprising considering that negative reviews are much shorter (typically a few hundred characters) than positive ones (typically several thousand) which implies they cover fewer topics and express fewer sentiments, making it more difficult to infer information.

We also observed that our model performed better than STDP on positive reviews while STDP performed better than SentPOSLDA on negative ones. We suspect that the reason our model struggled with the sentiment category that has fewer reviews is that our hyperparameter optimization might have made the model itself more biased. Finally, looking at the average F-measure score, we see that the overall performance of our model is roughly comparable to STDP. This final result demonstrates that our model, generalized to capture more complex information, can perform just as well as solutions that rely on specialized tools such as POS taggers and stemmers.

Table 2. F-Measure comparison between STDP and SentPOSLDA. Higher scores are bolded.

Aspect	Positive ratings		Negative ratings		Average	
	STDP	SentPOSLDA	STDP	SentPOSLDA	STDP	SentPOSLDA
Overall	0.844	**0.864**	**0.548**	0.410	**0.696**	0.637
Value	0.804	**0.854**	**0.449**	0.353	**0.627**	0.603
Rooms	0.816	**0.881**	0.419	**0.473**	0.618	**0.677**
Location	0.796	**0.905**	**0.255**	0.207	0.526	**0.556**
Cleanliness	0.857	**0.915**	**0.486**	0.407	**0.672**	0.661
Front Desk	0.847	**0.942**	**0.457**	0.415	0.652	**0.678**
Service	0.789	**0.867**	**0.389**	0.312	0.589	0.590
Business Service	0.788	**0.829**	**0.505**	0.257	**0.647**	0.543

5 Conclusions and Future Work

We introduced a new probabilistic model for aspect-level sentiment analysis. Unlike previous models, our model is able to distinguish between purely functional words, topic-identifying words and sentiment expressing words. The distinction is based on an integrated syntax model, removing the need for a POS tagger such as the one used for STDP. The sentiment analysis component of our model provides an output that is more practical than that of JST, ASUM and STDP. Our solution also takes into account the emphasis placed on each aspect without expecting the overall sentiment to be given, in contrast to LRR and LARAM. Finally, we add a few heuristics such as topic filtering and aspect rating approximation to get the best performance out of the resulting model.

Our experiments showed that our generalized model's performance is comparable to the state-of-the-art probabilistic solutions that rely on external tools. One potential area for further improvement would be with the hyperparameter optimization since the experiments have indicated that the model might tend to align with the bias of the dataset. Since we are attempting to capture fine-grained aspect sentiments, another interesting avenue of research would be to incorporate granularity into the model itself by, for example, basing the topic modelling component on MG-LDA [14] rather than LDA.

References

1. Blei, D.M., Ng, A.Y., Jordan, M.I.: Latent Dirichlet allocation. J. Mach. Learn. Res. **3**, 993–1022 (2003)
2. Chang, J., Boyd-Graber, J., Wang, C., Gerrish, S., Blei, D.M.: Reading tea leaves: how humans interpret topic models. In: Neural Information Processing Systems, NIPS 2009, pp. 288–296. Curran Associates Inc., Red Hook (2009)
3. Darling, W.M.: Generalized probabilistic topic and syntax models for natural language processing. Ph.D. thesis, University of Guelph, Guelph, Ontario, Canada (9 2012)
4. Goldberg, A.B., Zhu, X.: Seeing stars when there aren't many stars: graph-based semi-supervised learning for sentiment categorization. In: Proceedings of 1st Workshop on Graph Based Methods for Natural Language Processing, TextGraphs-1, pp. 45–52. Association for Computational Linguistics, Stroudsburg (2006)
5. Hatzivassiloglou, V., McKeown, K.R.: Predicting the semantic orientation of adjectives. In: Proceedings of 8th Conference on European Chapter of the Association for Computational Linguistics, EACL 1997, pp. 174–181. Association for Computational Linguistics, Stroudsburg (1997)
6. Hu, M., Liu, B.: Mining and summarizing customer reviews. In: Proceedings of 10th ACM SIGKDD International Conference on Knowledge Discovery and Data Mining, KDD 2004, pp. 168–177. ACM, New York (2004)
7. Jo, Y., Oh, A.H.: Aspect and sentiment unification model for online review analysis. In: Proceedings of 4th ACM International Conference on Web Search and Data Mining, WSDM 2011, pp. 815–824. ACM, New York (2011)
8. Li, C., Zhang, J., Sun, J.T., Chen, Z.: Sentiment topic model with decomposed prior. In: SDM, pp. 767–775. SIAM (2013)

9. Lin, C., He, Y.: Joint sentiment/topic model for sentiment analysis. In: Proceedings of 18th ACM Conference on Information and Knowledge Management, CIKM 2009, pp. 375–384. ACM, New York (2009)
10. O'Connor, B., Balasubramanyan, R., Routledge, B.R., Smith, N.A.: From tweets to polls: linking text sentiment to public opinion time series. In: Proceedings of International AAAI Conference on Weblogs and Social Media, ICWSM 2010, pp. 122–129. Association for the Advancement of Artificial Intelligence, Palo Alto (2010)
11. Pang, B., Lee, L., Vaithyanathan, S.: Thumbs up?: sentiment classification using machine learning techniques. In: Proceedings of ACL-2002 Conference on Empirical Methods in Natural Language Processing, EMNLP 2002, vol. 10. pp. 79–86. Association for Computational Linguistics, Stroudsburg (2002)
12. Socher, R., Perelygin, A., Wu, J.Y., Chuang, J., Manning, C.D., Ng, A.Y., Potts, C.: Recursive deep models for semantic compositionality over a sentiment Tree-Bank. In: Proceedings of 2013 Conference on Empirical Methods in Natural Language Processing, EMNLP 2013, pp. 1631–1642. Association for Computational Linguistics, Stroudsburg (2013)
13. Tang, D., Qin, B., Liu, T.: Aspect level sentiment classification with deep memory network. In: Proceedings of 2016 Conference on Empirical Methods in Natural Language Processing, EMNLP 2016, pp. 214–224. Association for Computational Linguistics, Stroudsburg (2016)
14. Titov, I., McDonald, R.T.: Modeling online reviews with multi-grain topic models. CoRR abs/0801.1063 (2008)
15. Turney, P.D.: Thumbs up or thumbs down?: semantic orientation applied to unsupervised classification of reviews. In: Proceedings of 40th Annual Meeting on Association for Computational Linguistics, ACL 2002, pp. 417–424. Association for Computational Linguistics, Stroudsburg (2002)
16. Wang, H., Lu, Y., Zhai, C.: Latent aspect rating analysis on review text data: a rating regression approach. In: Proceedings of 16th ACM SIGKDD International Conference on Knowledge Discovery and Data Mining, KDD 2010, pp. 783–792. ACM, New York (2010)
17. Wang, H., Lu, Y., Zhai, C.: Latent aspect rating analysis without aspect keyword supervision. In: Proceedings of 17th ACM SIGKDD International Conference on Knowledge Discovery and Data Mining, KDD 2011, pp. 618–626. ACM, New York (2011)
18. Zhou, H., Song, F.: Aspect-level sentiment analysis based on a generalized probabilistic topic and syntax model. In: Proceedings of FLAIRS-28 Conference, Special Track on Applied Natural Language Processing, pp. 241–244. International Florida Artificial Intelligence Research Society, USA (2015)

An Empirical Study on Learning Based Methods for User Consumption Intention Classification

Mingzhou Yang, Daling Wang$^{(\boxtimes)}$, Shi Feng, and Yifei Zhang

Northeastern University, Shenyang, China
yangmingzhou11@163.com,
{wangdaling,fengshi,zhangyifei}@cse.neu.edu.cn

Abstract. Recently, huge amount of text with user consumption intentions have been published on the social media platform, such as Twitter and Weibo, and classifying the intentions of users has great values for both scientific research and commercial applications. User consumption analysis in social media concerns about the text content representation and intention classification, whose solutions mainly focus on the traditional machine learning and the emerging deep learning techniques. In this paper, we conduct a comprehensive empirical study on the user intension classification problem with learning based techniques using different text representation methods. We compare different machine learning, deep learning methods and various combinations of them in tweet text presentation and users' consumption intention classification. The experimental results show that LSTM models with pre-trained word vector representation can achieve the best classification performance.

Keywords: Consumption intention · Intention classification
Text representation · Machine learning · Deep learning

1 Introduction

With the development of social media, more and more users like to express their views, ideas, and other contents on the platform. There is a large amount of information released by different users to express their needs to some kind of commodity or service, which is the so-called user consumption intention. These online texts with consumption intentions are of great value to both scientific research and commercial application. Therefore, consumption intention analysis in text data has drawn wide attentions in recent years.

One existing solution is regarding user consumption intension analysis as a classification problem [1–4]. Based on this idea, the user generated texts (such as reviews, discussions, and posts published by users in social media) are used to train classifiers using either traditional machine learning techniques [1–3] or the emerging deep learning algorithms [4]. In addition, how to effectively represent the text for modeling user intensions is still a challenging task.

© Springer International Publishing AG 2018
X. Huang et al. (Eds.): NLPCC 2017, LNAI 10619, pp. 910–918, 2018.
https://doi.org/10.1007/978-3-319-73618-1_80

In this paper, we conduct an empirical study for learning based user consumption intention classification in user generated texts. We apply different language models to represent the texts, and use traditional machine learning and emerging deep learning techniques respectively for classifying the consumption intentions embedded in the texts. Our purpose is exploring the characteristics of machine learning and deep learning techniques in classifying users' intentions.

As a whole, our main contributions in this paper are as follows:

(1) We implement the representation of text using traditional language model such as TF-IDF and neural language model such as Word2Vec.

(2) We train different classifiers using traditional machine learning methods such as SVM and Naïve Bayes, and deep learning methods such as RNN and LSTM.

(3) We conduct comprehensive experiments by combining the different text presentation models and different classification methods, and discuss the characteristics of above models according to the experimental results.

The remainder of this paper is structured as follows: Sect. 2 describes the problem of consumption intention classification, and gives our implementation framework. In Sect. 3, we analyze a series of experiments conducted for exploring the characteristics of different text presentation and classification techniques. We introduce the related work in Sect. 4. Finally we conclude the paper and give the future work in Sect. 5.

2 Problem and Approach Description

2.1 Problem Description

In social media, user generated text include two types, i.e. with consumption intention and without consumption. For the former, the intention may be *"I want to buy a new dress"* or *"I'm going to see the sea in Dalian"*. The above two sentences express clear consumption requirement. For the latter ones, such as *"The street is too dirty"* or *"I'm so glad you're all right!"*, the text only express some emotions, but not intentions.

In previous literature, consumption intention is categorized into six classes including "Food & Drink", "Travel", "Career & Education", "Goods & Services", "Event & Activities", and "Trifle" [3]. The detailed explanations are as follows. We give examples of each category in Table 1.

- Food: Want to have some food or drink.
- Travel: Want to visit some specific points of interests or places.
- Career: Want to get a job, get a degree or do something for self-realization.
- Goods: Want to have some non-food/non-drink goods (e.g., car) or services (e.g., haircut).
- Trifle: Want to talks about daily routine, or some mood trifles.
- Event: Want to participate in some activities which do not belong to the aforementioned categories (e.g., concert).

Table 1. Categories of intent tweets

Category	Example
Food	hungry…i need a salad……four more days to the BEYONCE CONCERT…
Travel	I need a vacation really bad. I need a trip to Disneyland!
Career	this makes me want to be a lawyer RT someuser new favorite line from an…
Goods	mhmmm, i wannna a new phone. Services… i have to go to the hospital…
Trifle	on my way to go swimming with the twoon@someuser; i love her so muchhhhh!
Event	I'm so happy that I get to take a shower with myself. :D

Based on the class labels, models can be trained for user consumption intention classification.

2.2 Implementation Framework

In this paper, we also use the six intension classes and "Non-Intention" as labels. For the empirical study, we consider different text presentation and intention classification technique, so our framework is shown as Fig. 1.

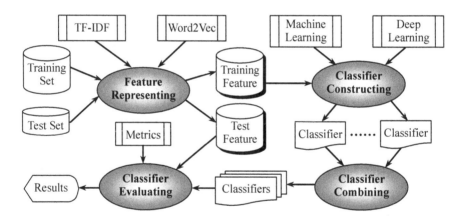

Fig. 1. Framework of machine learning and deep learning for intention classification

The Training and Test Set have been annotated with six consumption intentions and "Non-Intention". There are four operations in the framework.

- Feature Representing: For every text in Training Set and Test Set, TF-IDF or Word2Vec are used to represent it, and the results are Training Feature Set and Test Feature Set.
- Classifier Constructing: For above Training Feature Set, machine learning techniques such as SVM and Naïve Bayes, and deep learning techniques such as RNN and LSTM are applied to construct classifier. The results are some different classifiers.

- Classifier Combining: Based on different feature representing methods, different classifiers, and their different combinations, new classifiers are constructed. The results are some recombination classifiers.
- Classifier Evaluating: For Test Set, based on its feature representation and some evaluation metrics e.g. *F*-score, above new recombination classifiers are evaluated.

2.3   Text Feature Presentation and Classifier Construction

In feature representation, we consider TF-IDF [5] and Word2Vec [6] model respectively. In this paper, the text feature vector represented by TF-IDF is used to construct traditional machine learning classifiers, and the ones by Word2Vec is used to construct traditional machine learning and deep learning classifiers. Figure 2 shows the feature presentation and classifier construction for intention mining detail in Fig. 1.

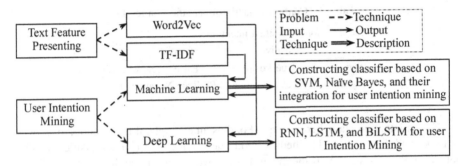

Fig. 2.   Problem, techniques used, and corresponding descriptions

Based on TF-IDF, we utilize traditional machine learning techniques such as SVM and Naïve Bayes to construct different classifiers. The results include SVM classifier, Naïve Bayes classifier, and SVM + Naïve Bayes classifier. In addition, we utilize SMOTE method to balance dataset.

Based on Word2Vec, we utilize traditional machine learning techniques such as SVM and SVM + Naïve Bayes, and further utilize deep learning techniques such as RNN and LSTM to construct different classifiers. The results include SVM classifier, RNN classifier, SVM + Naïve Bayes classifier, LSTM classifier, and BiLSTM (bidirectional LSTM) classifier.

3   Experiments

3.1   Experiment Setup

We evaluate above classifiers by experiments. The dataset is from Twitter. With the process in [3], the resultant statistical information of the dataset is shown as Table 2. In the Table 2, we can see the dataset have the problem of imbalanced data. And the number of tweet in "Non-Intent" and "Trifle" class is nearly twice as much as that of other classes except "Event" class.

Table 2. Statistical information of experiment data

Non-intent	Food	Travel	Career	Goods	Trifle	Event	Total
531	245	187	159	251	436	321	2130

After reprocessing the dataset such as removing stop-words and balancing data classes, we use above classifiers and their combinations to classify consumption intentions. We apply F-score to evaluate the classification results. For a binary classification, the true class labels and the ones obtained by classifiers can constitute True Positive (*TP*), False Positive (*FP*), True Negative (*TN*), and False Negative (*FN*). In this paper, for an intention (e.g. Food), the corresponding confusion matrix is shown as Table 3.

Table 3. Confusion matrix of classification results

True intention	Classified intention	
	Positive	Negative
Positive	True Positive (*TP*)	False Negative (*FN*)
Negative	False Positive (*FP*)	True Negative (*TN*)

For an intention class, here we take Food as an example, if the intention of a tweet is Food, and the tweet is classified as Food, the result is *TP*. If it is classified as other intention, the result is *FN*. If the intention of a tweet is not Food, but it is classified as Food, the result is *FP*. If it is classified as other intention, the result is *TN*. So do other intentions.

According to the confusion in Table 3, precision (*P*), recall (*R*), and F-score are defined as Formula (1).

$$P = \frac{TP}{TP + FP} \quad R = \frac{TP}{TP + FN} \quad F\text{-score} = \frac{2 \times P \times R}{P + R} \tag{1}$$

3.2 Experiment Results and Analysis

Our experiments concern the following classification methods besides SVM^{TI} and NB^{TI} (The superscript TI means TF-IDF feature representation).

- $SVM^{TI} + NB^{TI}$: It is ensemble of SVM and Naïve Bayes classifiers, where TF-IDF is used to represent features.
- SVM^{200}, SVM^{400}: The SVM classifiers utilize 200, 400 dimensional word vectors as features respectively.
- SVM^{SMOTE}: The SVM classifiers use the SMOTE method to balance dataset.
- NB^{SMOTE}: The Naïve Bayes classifiers use the SMOTE method to balance dataset.
- $SVM^{100} + NB^{TI}$: It is the ensemble of SVM and Naïve Bayes classifier, and 100 dimensions word vector is the input of SVM.

- RNN[100], LSTM[100]: The RNN and LSTM are used as classifier respectively, and 100 dimensional word vectors are used as their inputs.
- BiLSTM[100]: It is bidirectional LSTM with 100 dimensional word vectors as its input.

We show the *F*-score results of different feature presentations, classifiers, and their combinations in Figs. 3, 4, 5, 6, and 7.

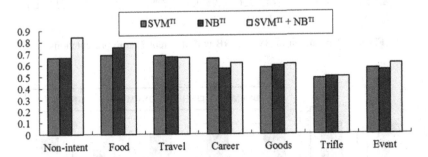

Fig. 3. Comparison of traditional machine learning methods

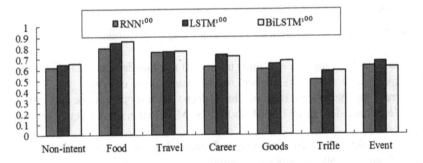

Fig. 4. Comparison of advanced deep learning methods

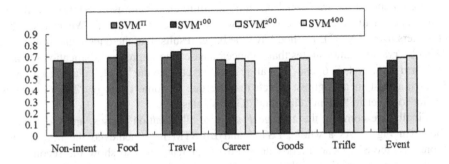

Fig. 5. Comparison of SVM with different feature presentations

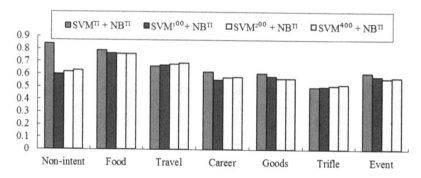

Fig. 6. Comparison of SVM + NB with different feature presentations

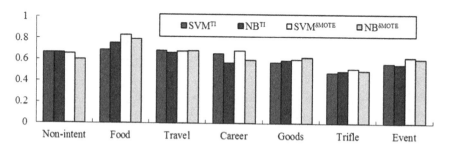

Fig. 7. Comparison of traditional machine learning methods using SMOTE method

Figure 3 is the comparison of three traditional machine learning classifiers. We can see their ensemble model has the best results almost in all classes.

Figure 4 is the comparison of three deep learning classifiers. For the same Word2Vec dimension, both LSTM and BiLSTM classifiers have better results than RNN in most classes.

In Fig. 5, for SVM, the word vector features show better results than traditional TF-IDF features in all the dimension settings.

Moreover, when combining SVM and Naïve Bayes, TF-IDF based classifier seems better than the word vector. The phenomenon is shown in Fig. 6.

We compared the traditional machine learning classifiers using SMOTE with the traditional machine learning classifiers without using it in Fig. 7. We can see the classifiers using SMOTE method have the better results than the ones without using it. This observation demonstrates that balanced dataset can improve classification quality.

Form Figs. 3, 4, 5, 6, and 7, in all results, we can see the "Trifle" class has a lower F-score almost in all figures, which may be due to some tweet in "Trifle" class is similar to tweet in "Event" class and "Goods" class.

Finally, we compare the average F-score of all intention classes, and the result is shown in Fig. 8. As a whole, LSTM and BiLSTM have achieved the best results. Moreover, the SVM classifiers with word vector features also show the second best results. This observation further demonstrates that distributed word embedding can improve classification quality for both traditional classifiers and deep models.

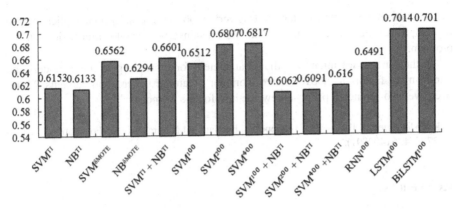

Fig. 8. Comparison of average *F*-score for different classes of intention

In addition, for the same dataset, Wang et al. gave classification results [3] (Non-Intent 35.56%, Food 54.63%, Travel 58.64%, Career 45.73%, Goods 43.25%, Event 27.13%, Trifle 20.04%). Our results outperform Wang's method in all classes.

4 Related Work

Our work focuses on user consumption intention classification in social media text based on shallow and deep learning techniques. We do not consider extracting intention features from the text as [3]. In fact, in consumption intention analysis, there are many researches from different aspects. Besides text, the existing researches also consider other factors such as user behaviors [2, 7], user emotions [8], user interaction and participation [9], product features [10], website characteristics [11], and more factors [12]. Some literatures utilize other techniques such as innovation diffusion theory and the technology acceptance model [13] to detect user intensions.

Our purpose in this paper is exploring the characteristics of traditional machine learning and deep learning techniques in classifying users' intention for user generated text date, not proposing a new theory and technique. So we do not compare our work with above related work. But this work can be as our further research.

5 Conclusion and Future Work

For user generated text data in social media, we apply traditional and advanced language model to represent the text feature, and utilize learning based techniques to classify user consumption intention embedded in the text. We implement different classifiers using different text features, and evaluate their classification performance by experiments. Experiment results show that the LSTM models can achieve the best *F*-Score in model classes.

Obviously, the overall mechanism and detailed techniques used in this paper are not novel. However, how to utilize exist techniques to present tweet text feature, discover and class users' consumption intentions is very important for the special application. So our empirical study is significant, and indeed conveys valuable information on the problem.

In the further, we intend to adjust parameters for more deep learning models and import more factors as above related work for obtaining better improvements. Moreover, we also intend to propose new method for the purpose.

Acknowledgment. This project is supported by National Natural Science Foundation of China (61370074, 61402091).

References

1. Pérez-Vera, S., Alfaro, R., Allende-Cid, H.: Intent classification of social media texts with machine learning for customer service improvement. In: HCI, vol. 13, pp. 258–274 (2017)
2. Shi, F., Ghedira, C.: Intention-based online consumer classification for recommendation and personalization. In: HotWeb 2016, pp. 36–41 (2016)
3. Wang, J., Cong, G., Zhao, W., Li, X.: Mining user intents in Twitter: a semi-supervised approach to inferring intent categories for tweets. In: AAAI 2015, pp. 318–324 (2015)
4. Ding, X., Liu, T., Duan, J., Nie, J.: Mining user consumption intention from social media using domain adaptive convolutional neural network. In: AAAI 2015, pp. 2389–2395 (2015)
5. Hiemstra, D.: A probabilistic justification for using tf $\times$ idf term weighting in information retrieval. Int. J. Digit. Libr. **3**(2), 131–139 (2000)
6. Mikolov, T., Chen, K., Corrado, G., Dean, J.: Efficient estimation of word representations in vector space. CoRR abs/1301.3781 (2013)
7. Fortes, N., Moreira, A., Saraiva, J.: Determinants of consumer intention to use online gambling services: an empirical study of the Portuguese market. IJEBR **12**(4), 23–37 (2016)
8. Akman, I., Mishra, A.: Factors influencing consumer intention in social commerce adoption. IT People **30**(2), 356–370 (2017)
9. Phang, C., Zhang, C., Sutanto, J.: The influence of user interaction and participation in social media on the consumption intention of niche products. Inf. Manag. **50**(8), 661–672 (2013)
10. Chen, C.: Young female consumers' perceptions and purchase intentions towards character economy. In: HCI, vol. 9, pp. 382–392 (2017)
11. Chen, Y., Wu, C.: Influence of website design on consumer emotion and purchase intention in travel websites. IJTHI **12**(4), 15–29 (2016)
12. Shang, S., Wu, Y., Sie, Y.: Generating consumer resonance for purchase intention on social network sites. Comput. Hum. Behav. **69**, 18–28 (2017)
13. Agag, G., El-Masry, A.: Understanding consumer intention to participate in online travel community and effects on consumer intention to purchase travel online and WOM: an integration of innovation diffusion theory and TAM with trust. Comput. Hum. Behav. **60**, 97–111 (2016)

Overview of the NLPCC 2017 Shared Task: Chinese Word Semantic Relation Classification

Yunfang Wu[✉] and Minghua Zhang

Key Laboratory of Computational Linguistics, Ministry of Education,
Peking University, Beijing 100871, China
{wuyf,zhangmh}@pku.edu.cn

Abstract. Word semantic relation classification is a challenging task for natural language processing, so we organize a semantic campaign on this task at NLPCC 2017. The dataset covers four kinds of semantic relations (synonym, antonym, hyponym and meronym), and there are 500 word pairs per category. Together 17 teams submit their results. In this paper, we describe the data construction and experimental setting, make an analysis on the evaluation results, and make a brief introduction to some of the participating systems.

Keywords: Word semantic relation · Synonym · Antonym · Hyponym
Meronym

1 Introduction

The automatic recognition of word semantic relations is a challenging task for natural language processing. Words with different semantic relations are often mixed together when doing lexical sematic computation. For example, according to the "distributional hypotheses", we can automatically get the following "similar words" based on a large corpus (Shi et al. 2013):

水果：蔬菜; 果品; 香蕉; 瓜果; 西红柿; 肉类; 苹果; 干果; 茶叶; 果汁
猛涨：暴涨; 飞涨; 飙升; 上涨; 猛跌; 看涨; 暴跌; 攀升; 上扬; 回落

Among the top 10 similar words with "水果|fruit", "果品-水果", "瓜果-水果" are synonymous, while "香蕉-水果", "苹果-水果" are hyponym words. Among the top 10 similar words with "猛涨|rise)", "暴涨-猛涨", "飞涨-猛涨", "飙升-猛涨" are synonymous, while "猛跌-猛涨", "暴跌-猛涨", "回落-猛涨" are antonymous.

However, we need distinguish different kinds of semantic relations clearly in real-world applications. For example, in query expansion for information retrieval, we should recognize the synonym and hyponym of the target words; in sentiment analysis, we need identify words with contrastive meanings.

In English, there are a few benchmark datasets for classifying semantic relations between nominals. Task 4 at SemEval-1 (Girju et al. 2007) provided a binary-labeled dataset for seven relations. Task 8 at SemEval-2010 (Hendrickx et al. 2009) presented a

X. Huang et al. (Eds.): NLPCC 2017, LNAI 10619, pp. 919–925, 2018.
https://doi.org/10.1007/978-3-319-73618-1_81

multi-way classification task for ten semantic relations. Recently, various neural network models and deep learning methods are used to classify semantic relations on the SemEval-2010 dataset. Zhou et al. (2016) proposed attention based bidirectional Long Short-Term Memory Networks (AttBLSTM) to capture the most important semantic information in a sentence. Wang et al. (2016) employed multi-level attention CNNs for relation classification.

Our goal of this task is to create a testbed for automatic classification of Chinese word semantic relations, to measure different approaches on this task and to check the effectiveness of different knowledge bases on describing semantic relations.

Given some pairs of words, the system is asked to classify them into four semantic categories: synonym, antonym, hyponym and meronym. The dataset provides these four categories of semantic relations, and each category contains 500 instances of word pairs. Different from the English relation classification task, our word pairs are out of context and don't locate in any sentences. Our task is also different from most work in information extraction, which tends to focus on specific classes of named entities and on more fine-grained relations.

Our task has received much attention from researchers. Totally 48 teams registered our task and finally 17 teams submitted their results.

2   Task Setup

2.1   Dataset Construction

We manually created the testbed of word pairs with different semantic relations. The selected words consist of nouns, verbs and adjectives, as well as some functional words like adverbs and conjunctions. The selected words are variable-length, including single-character words, two-character words, three-character words and four-character words (idioms). We also pick up some ambiguous words with multiple senses. Some examples of word pairs in our test data are given in Table 1.

The four categories of semantic relations are the most general ones in lexical semantics, which can be defined as follows. Give two words A and B:

- Synonym: A is similar to B, e.g., 色彩缤纷 vs. 姹紫嫣红
- Antonym: A is contrast to B, e.g., 骄傲 vs. 谦虚
- Hyponym: B is a kind of A, e.g., 菊花 vs. 花.
- Meronym: B is a part of A, e.g., 花蕾 vs. 花.

2.2   Experiment Setting

Our test data totally consists of 2,000 word pairs, and no training data is provided. We first released 200 word pairs as the trial data before the evaluation phrase. All kinds of strategies are welcome, including the traditional corpus-based distributional similarity, dictionary-based semantic computation, as well as the recently developed word

Table 1. Some examples in our test data

Word 1	word 2	relation
花	菊花	hyponym
花	花蕾	meronym
花	消费	synonym
笔	钢笔	hyponym
钢笔	笔帽	meronym
百年不遇	十年九不遇	synonym
蓝瘦香菇	难受	synonym
U盘	闪存盘	synonym
好玩	没意思	antonym
花哨	朴实	antonym
讲究	邋遢	antonym
高产	歉收	antonym
目不转睛	东张西望	antonym
标点	逗号	hyponym
毒药	鹤顶红	hyponym
方言	粤语	hyponym
刀	刀刃	meronym
乐团	指挥	meronym
眼镜	镜片	meronym

embedding methods and deep learning models. Also, the participating systems are encouraged to use external resources.

In order to avoid over-fitting on this small test data, we released a large collection of 10,000 word pairs in the testing phrase. Our 2,000 word pairs were mixed in the large data, and the other word pairs were randomly generated from a large dictionary.

We will compute precision (P), recall (R), and F1-Score for each of four relations, and then compute the macro averaged P, R and F. Our official scoring metric is macro-averaged F1-score for four-way classification:

$$F_{macro} = \frac{F_{syn} + F_{ant} + F_{hyp} + F_{mer}}{4} \tag{1}$$

3 Evaluation Results

Together 17 teams participated in our task and submitted 17 systems. Table 2 reports the overall evaluation results, listing the team name, the macro averaged P, R and F. The winner system of our task is CASIA with an F-value of 0.859, which outperforms the second best system Tongji_CU-KG by 9 points. Relatively far from the first two systems, we find four systems: ECNU, Aicyber, QLUT and DLUT_NLPer, which obtain F-values 0.647, 0.639, 0.634, 0.622 respectively. There are two systems whose performances are below the random guess baseline (0.25). The macro-averaged value of two systems (BLCU! and "Talk is easy") is *none*, because they didn't submit the results of all four categories.

Table 2. The overall evaluation results

System name	Macro-average		
	F	P	R
CASIA	0.859	0.865	0.859
Tongji_CU-KG	0.768	0.803	0.765
ECNU	0.647	0.651	0.648
Aicyber	0.639	0.674	0.633
QLUT	0.634	0.875	0.517
DLUT_NLPer	0.622	0.626	0.623
AISIGHT-D	0.526	0.537	0.533
NJUST-IRTM-UPUP	0.509	0.704	0.401
BISTU-AI-ONE	0.459	0.490	0.475
MuXing Lake Team	0.428	0.533	0.445
CQUT_ACFUN	0.402	0.512	0.394
SWU-1010	0.395	0.422	0.396
hlt@suda	0.390	0.504	0.442
Driving Force	0.245	0.263	0.255
March	0.198	0.342	0.280
BLCU!	*none*	*none*	*none*
Talk is easy	*none*	*none*	*none*

Table 3 reports the evaluation results of synonym, antonym, hyponym and meronym, respectively. The winner system CASIA performs best in all three relations: synonym, antonym and meronym. The system "Talk is easy" only submitted the result of hyponym, and it performs best in this category and is much better than CASIA. The system QLUT obtains the second rank in synonym with an F value of 0.80, which is far better than its overall result 0.63.

Comparing the four sematic relations, the synonym is relatively easy to identify, while hyponym and meronym pose challenging tasks for classification. The lowest score (F value) of synonym is 0.31, while the lowest score of hyponym is only 0.13 and meronym is only 0.11.

Table 3. The evaluation results of four categories

System	Synonym			Antonym			Hyponym			Meronym		
	F	P	R	F	P	R	F	P	R	F	P	R
CASIA	**0.90**	0.86	0.95	**0.88**	0.95	0.83	**0.82**	0.77	0.87	**0.83**	0.88	0.78
Tongji	**0.73**	0.61	0.91	**0.78**	0.96	0.66	**0.79**	0.79	0.78	**0.77**	0.85	0.71
ECNU	0.52	0.55	0.50	0.65	0.62	0.68	0.69	0.65	0.73	**0.73**	0.79	0.68
Aicyber	0.68	0.85	0.57	0.63	0.57	0.71	0.57	0.50	0.67	0.67	0.77	0.58
QLUT	**0.80**	0.86	0.76	**0.70**	0.97	0.55	0.56	0.76	0.44	0.48	0.92	0.32
DLUT	0.67	0.63	0.71	0.62	0.59	0.65	0.62	0.68	0.56	0.58	0.60	0.57
AISIGHT	0.39	0.46	0.33	0.53	0.55	0.51	0.58	0.49	0.71	0.61	0.65	0.57
NJUST	0.60	0.91	0.44	0.75	0.96	0.62	0.37	0.49	0.30	0.31	0.45	0.24
BISTU	0.57	0.45	0.80	0.45	0.49	0.41	0.41	0.46	0.37	0.41	0.56	0.32
MuXing	0.52	0.42	0.69	0.33	0.88	0.21	0.44	0.41	0.49	0.41	0.43	0.40
CQUT	0.54	0.82	0.41	0.41	0.64	0.30	0.39	0.28	0.63	0.27	0.32	0.23
SWU-1010	0.36	0.36	0.37	0.43	0.35	0.53	0.35	0.37	0.34	0.44	0.60	0.34
hlt@suda	0.46	0.34	0.69	0.33	0.63	0.22	0.15	0.52	0.09	0.62	0.52	0.77
Driving	0.31	0.26	0.37	0.27	0.23	0.33	0.21	0.28	0.17	0.19	0.28	0.15
March	0.41	0.26	0.88	0.15	0.35	0.10	0.13	0.33	0.08	0.11	0.42	0.06
BLCU!	0.46	0.78	0.33	0.63	0.58	0.69	0.51	0.36	0.85	none	none	none
Talk is easy	none	none	none	none	none	none	**0.88**	0.92	0.84	none	none	none

4   Participating Systems

This section will make a brief introduction to some of the participating systems, describing the classifying approaches and the used features.

CASIA. This system ranks No.1 in our task, achieving a macro-average F score of 0.859 (Li. et al. 2017), which is highly competitive for future work. The authors propose a framework for Chinese semantic relation classification, by combing semantic dictionaries, a classifier based on word vectors and heuristic rules according to linguistic knowledge. First, they search for a pair of words in a dictionary and output the semantic category defined in the dictionary. The used dictionaries include Tongyici Cilin, HowNet, Antonym Dictionary and Baidu Chinese Dictionary. Then, those word pairs that are out of dictionaries are fed to a softmax classifier, which employs features including word embeddings and parts of speech. Finally, some rules based on Chinese linguistics properties are applied to further improve the performance. The experimental results show that the semantic dictionaries and linguistic rules significantly improve the performance.

Tongji_CU-KG. This system ranks No. 2 in our task with an F score of 0.768 (Shijia et al. 2017). This paper employs a convolutional neural network (CNN) classifier using pre-trained word embeddings. They feed the pair of input words to the embedding layer and apply the 1-maxpooling operation, and use the outputs of softmax to select the target label. In order to tune the parameters of the neural network, they have constructed a training set from Tongyici Cilin, HowNet, and resources on the Internet.

ECNU. This system ranks No. 3 in our task with an F score of 0.647 (Zhou et al. 2017). They adopt a supervised learning algorithm Logistic Regression to do semantic relation classification, by using a verity of features. They explore four types of surface features, i.e., length features, character overlaps, positional overlaps and sequential overlaps. Further, they utilize word embedding features and character embedding features. In order to capture the semantic relation of two words, they explore different ways of interaction on word embeddings, including concatenation, multiplication, summation, subtraction and the min-max-mean pooling. However, the training data only consists of 200 word pairs that the organizer released as a trial data. The training data is too small to train a good model.

QLUT. This system obtains an F score of 0.634. It makes use of various knowledge resources to classify word semantic relations, including TongyiciCilin, HowNet, Bidubaike, Biaduhanyu and the English BableNet. The most interesting part is their experimental results, which demonstrate the effectiveness of different resources in identifying semantic relations. For example, TongyiciCilin obtains an F score of 0.679 in synonym relation recognition; BaiduHanyu obtains an F score of 0.630 in antonym relation recognition; the English BableNet obtains an F score of 0.603 in hyponym relation recognition.

NJUST-IRTM-UPUP. This system performs moderately with an F score of 0.509. The main method is that human manually construct rules or patterns according to some knowledge bases. The rule-based method obtains high precision for synonym and antonym, but gets low performances in hyponym and meronym.

5 Conclusion

This paper gives an overview of the NLPCC 2017 shared task 1 "Chinese word semantic relation classification". We release a benchmark data, which contains 2,000 word pairs and covers four kinds of semantic relations: synonym, antonym, hyponym and meronym. 17 teams participated in our task, and some of them obtained promising results. We hope our dataset can encourage more research on Chinese word semantic relation classification.

Acknowledgement. This work is supported by National High Technology Research and Development Program of China (2015AA015403), National Natural Science Foundation of China (61371129).

References

Shi, J., Wu, Y., Qiu, L., Lv, X.: Chinese lexical semantic similarity computation based on large-scale corpus. J. Chin. Inf. Process. **27**(1), 1–6 (2013)
Girju, R., Nakov, P., Nastase, V., Szpakowicz, S., Turney, P., Yuret, D.: SemEval-2007 task 04: classification of semantic relations between nominals. In: International Workshop on Semantic Evaluations (2007)

Hendrickx, I., Su, N.K., Kozareva, Z., Nakov, P., Pennacchiotti, M., Romano, L., et al.: SemEval-2010 task 8: multi-way classification of semantic relations between pairs of nominals. In: The Workshop on Semantic Evaluations: Recent Achievements & Future Directions (2009)

Zhou, P., Shi, W., Tian, J., Qi, Z., Li, B., Hao, H., et al.: Attention-based bidirectional long short-term memory networks for relation classification. In: Proceedings of ACL-2016 (2016)

Wang, L., Cao, Z., Melo, G.D., Liu, Z.: Relation classification via multi-level attention CNNs. IN: Proceedings of ACL-2016 (2016)

Li, C., Ma, T., Cheng, J., Xu, B.: Classification of word semantic relations via combining vector with linguistic knowledge and resource. IN: Proceedings of NLPCC-2017 (2017)

Shijia, E., Jia, S., Xiang Y.: Study on the Chinese word semantic relation classification with word embedding. IN: Proceedings of NLPCC-2017 (2017)

Zhou, Y., Lan, M., Wu, Y.: Effective semantic relationship classification of context-free Chinese words with simple surface and embedding features. In: Proceedings of NLPCC-2017 (2017)

Overview of the NLPCC 2017 Shared Task: Emotion Generation Challenge

Minlie Huang[✉], Zuoxian Ye, and Hao Zhou

State Key Laboratory of Intelligent Technology and Systems,
Tsinghua National Laboratory for Information Science and Technology,
Department of Computer Science and Technology, Tsinghua University,
Beijing 100084, People's Republic of China
aihuang@tsinghua.edu.cn

Abstract. It has been a long-term goal for AI to perceive and express emotions. Inspired by Emotional Chatting Machine [1], we propose a challenge task to investigate how well a chatting machine can express emotion by generating a textual response to an input post. The task is defined as follows: given a post and a pre-specified emotion class of the generated response, the task is to generate a response that is appropriate in both topic and emotion. This challenge has attracted more 40 teams registered, and finally there are 10 teams who submitted results. In this overview paper, we will report the details of this challenge, including task definition, data preparation, annotation schema, submission statistics, and evaluation results.

1 Introduction

In recent years, there has been a rising tendency in AI research to enhance Human-Computer Interaction by humanizing machines. However, to create a robot capable of acting and talking with a user at the human level requires the robot to understand human cognitive behaviors, while one of the most important human behaviors is expressing and understanding emotions and affects. As a vital part of human intelligence, emotional intelligence is defined as the ability to perceive, integrate, understand, and regulate emotions.

In recent years, deep learning approaches have advanced dialogue/ conversation generation significantly. Thanks to the success of sequence-to-sequence generation models in machine translation [2,3], these models were soon applied to conversation generation [4], including the neural responding machine [5], the hierarchical recurrent encoder-decoder neural network [6], and many others [7]. Existing works mainly focus on improving the content quality of generated responses by employing superior decoding strategies [8–10]. Other attempts to improve content quality include considering additional topic words [11,12], topic categories [13], persona information [14], or other retrieved responses [15].

Though a variety of models have been proposed for large-scale conversation generation, it is still quite challenging (and yet to be addressed) to generate

© Springer International Publishing AG 2018
X. Huang et al. (Eds.): NLPCC 2017, LNAI 10619, pp. 926–936, 2018.
https://doi.org/10.1007/978-3-319-73618-1_82

emotional responses. Very recently, Zhou et al. [1] proposed an emotional chatting machine that is able to generate responses that are appropriate not only in content but also in emotion expression. Inspired by this work, we define the challenge task in this paper accordingly, but we reformulate the task with a new dataset.

In this challenge, participants are expected to generate Chinese responses that are not only appropriate in content but also adequate in emotion, which is quite important for building an empathic chatting machine. For instance, if user says "My cat died yesterday", the most appropriate response may be "It's so sad, so sorry to hear that" to express *sadness*, but also could be "Bad things always happen, I hope you will be happy soon" to express *comfort*.

2   Task Definition

This task is defined as follows: Given a Chinese post $X = (x_1, x_2, \cdots, x_n)$, and a user-specified emotion category of the response to be generated, the goal is to generate a response $Y = (y_1, y_2, \cdots, y_m)$ that is coherent with the emotion category. The emotion categories are in {*Anger, Disgust, Happiness, Like, Sadness, Other*} , the same as defined in the NLPCC Emotion Classification Challenge[1]. Each team can submit at most two runs.

3   Dataset Description

The dataset is constructed from Weibo posts and replies/comments. More than 1 million Weibo post-response pairs are provided to participants for training their models. The test dataset consists of about 5000 posts while 200 of the posts will be manually assessed, and for each post, at most 3 emotion classes will be manually specified to indicate the emotion class of a generated response. Participating systems should generate a response for each emotion class. Note that participants should generate responses for all posts with appropriate emotion classes. Which part of the posts will be manually checked is unknown to participants for fair comparison.

During the construction of the dataset, we trained a bidirectional LSTM model for emotion classification which will be used to classify the emotion of a post/response. The classifier was trained on the data from the NLPCC 2013/2014 Emotion Classification Challenge. The accuracy of our classifier for six-way classification is about 64%, for more details please refer to Zhou et al. [1].

With the help of the emotion classifier, we select those responses that have a small value of *classification entropy*, defined as follows:

$$CE = -\frac{1}{\log K} \sum_{k=1}^{K} p_k \log p_k \tag{1}$$

---

[1] Please refer to http://tcci.ccf.org.cn/conference/2014/dldoc/evataŝk1.pdf.

where p_k is the probability of class k given by the emotion classifier, and K is the total number of classes. Note that $0 \leq CE \leq 1$, and **0** indicates the least uncertainty of the prediction. In this way, we can select those pairs whose responses have obvious emotional expressions.

We provide about 5000 test posts to participants, but we are only able to manually evaluate 200 posts due to the heavy annotation load. The 200 posts are selected by considering the following factors:

- For each emotion class, select the posts that have a small value of classification entropy, as defined by Eq. 1.
- The post should not be context-dependent. In other words, understanding of the post does not require any other context or background knowledge.
- The post should not include rare words or English words.

Finally, we manually decide three emotion classes for each post, and for each emotion class, participants are required to generate a response. The statistics of the test posts are shown in Table 1.

Table 1. The statistics of the test posts.

Emotion category	Like	Sad	Disgust	Angry	Happy	Total
Number of posts	57	30	40	21	52	200
Percentage	29%	15%	20%	11%	26%	100%
Number of responses to be generated	133	119	144	71	129	596

Notably, the emotion label of these data is noisy. Participants are encouraged to implement the emotion classifier by themselves and with their own data, but all details must be reported and all resources should be accessible to the community to let other researchers reproduce their results. Note that no additional data is permitted to train the generation model.

4   Annotation Schema

The submitted post-response pairs are evaluated by the following metrics:

Emotion Consistency: whether the emotion class of a generated response is the same as the pre-specified class.
Coherence: whether the response is appropriate in terms of both logically coherent and topic relevant content.
Fluency: whether the response is fluent in grammar and acceptable as a natural language response.

Our labeling procedure is shown by the following pseudocode [16]:

```
IF (Coherence and Fluency)
    IF (Emotion Consistency)
        LABEL 2 ## Score 2 for perfect responses
    ELSE
        LABEL 1 ## Score 1 for coherent and fluent
ELSE
    LABEL 0 ## Score 0 for others
```

We present some annotation examples in Table 2.

Table 2. Some annotation examples.

Post	爱狗还会做饭的男人，最帅了！	Emotion class	Coherence and Fluency	Emotion Consistency	Label
Response 1	会做饭的男人是很帅的啊	Like	Yes	Yes	2
Response 2	哈哈，我也觉得	Like	Yes	No	1
Response 3	这是哪部电影里的?	Disgust	No	Yes	0
Response 4	哈哈，你也是	Like	No	No	0
Response 5	我爱你会	Disgust	No	Yes	0
Response 6	这是同主义同的道！	Disgust	No	No	0

Particularly, for those repeatedly occurred contents in a response, if a subsequence of content occurs repeatedly no more than 3 times, it will be judge as fluent, otherwise not fluent. Some examples are shown in Table 3.

Table 3. The examples of the fluency judgement on responses with repetitive words.

Response	Fluency
悲哀，悲哀，悲哀。	Yes
飘逸，飘逸，飘逸！	Yes
好可爱，好可爱！	Yes
哈哈哈，当然啦	Yes
疯了。疯了。全疯了	Yes
对的对的对的对的对的对的对的对的对的	No
我骗骗骗骗我骗你信不信不信我反正信了	No
中国的教育教育教育教育教育教育教育教育教育教育教育教育教育教育教育教育教育教育	No
矮贱贱贱贱贱贱贱贱贱，你爱你，我也不爱你了	No
不关我事不关我事不关我事不关我事不关我事！	No

5 Submission Statistics

We received 16 submissions from 10 teams before the deadline of submission. Since we provide about 5000 test posts to participants, we compute the statistics of the submissions, which is shown in Table 4. We can see the number of submission ranges from 32508 to 5417. About half of the submissions generate responses for all emotion categories for each post, but another half of the submissions generate much fewer responses.

Furthermore, we calculate the statistics of the submissions on the 200 posts which will be manually evaluated. The ideal, expected number of responses is 596 (see Table 1), where there are 7 submissions that have 596 responses. However, the other submissions have submitted much less responses due to the fact that the participants did not generate responses for multiple emotion categories. Some teams even submitted results for *Other* (Null) emotion, however, this part of data is not evaluated at all.

Table 4. The statistics of the submission on the 5000 test posts.

Team name	Null	Like	Sad	Disgust	Angry	Happy	Total
Babbling_1	0	5418	5418	5418	5418	5418	27090
Babbling_2	0	5418	5418	5418	5418	5418	27090
ECNU_1	1432	1780	478	654	496	578	5418
ECNU_2	1211	1899	464	404	787	653	5418
gry_1	5418	5418	5418	5418	5418	5418	32508
NEUDM_1	1511	1119	744	754	392	898	5418
NLP-More_1	992	2070	303	1368	408	276	5417
NLP-More_2	992	2070	303	1368	408	276	5417
NUSTM_1	992	2071	303	1368	408	276	5418
NUSTM_2	992	2071	303	1368	408	276	5418
Personalized Emotional Chatting System Based on Deep Learning_1	1666	42	210	18	1365	2116	5417
samsung_1	5417	5417	5417	5417	5417	5417	32502
samsung_2	5417	5417	5417	5417	5417	5417	32502
shield_1	993	2071	303	1367	408	276	5418
SMIPG_1	5418	5418	5418	5418	5418	5418	32508
SMIPG_2	5418	5418	5418	5418	5418	5418	32508

6 Evaluation Results

The submitted results from all teams are aggregated together. After de-duplication, we obtained 5628 post-response pairs. Then, these pairs are randomly shuffled but the submission identifier for each pair is recorded. We resort to Baidu Data Crowdsourcing Service for manual evaluation. Each pair is annotated by three curators which are trained with our annotation schema and illustrating examples. The annotation statistics is shown in Table 5.

We can see that there are 219 pairs to which all annotators have assigned different labels. For these pairs, we asked an additional curator for further annotation. The final label of these pairs is decided by the majority principle. We can see that the annotation has fairly good agreement.

Table 5. The statistics of annotation agreement.

	All three agree	Two agree	All different
Number of pairs	3413	1996	219
Percentage	61%	35%	4%

We compute the overall score and the average score for each submission run, as follows:

$$OverallScore = \sum_{i=0}^{2} i * Num_i \qquad (2)$$

$$AverageScore = \frac{1}{N_t} \sum_{i=0}^{2} i * Num_i \qquad (3)$$

where Num_i is the number of pairs which has a label of i for each submission run, and N_t is the total number of pairs for each run.

Considering that the total number of pairs varies dramatically across different submission runs, we believe that both total score and average score can partially reveal the quality of submission. There are three runs that have remarkably higher total scores while the average score is also high; and there are three runs that have high average score but the total score is remarkably less than the highest total score.

6.1 Overall Results

See Table 6.

Table 6. The result of the overall score and average score.

Team name	Label 0	Label 1	Label 2	Total	Overall score	Average score
samsung_1	267	82	247	596	576	0.966443
Babbling_2	305	19	271	595	561	0.942857
samsung_2	272	93	231	596	555	0.931208
SMIPG_1	428	11	157	596	325	0.545302
Babbling_1	424	41	131	596	303	0.508389
gry_1	449	31	116	596	263	0.441275
shield_1	76	26	93	195	212	1.087179
ECNU_1	44	10	89	143	188	1.314685
NUSTM_2	102	9	84	195	177	0.907692
ECNU_2	56	9	83	148	175	1.182432
SMIPG_2	505	12	79	596	170	0.285235
NUSTM_1	117	8	70	195	148	0.758974
NLP-More_1	122	7	66	195	139	0.712821
NLP-More_2	122	7	66	195	139	0.712821
Personalized Emotional Chatting System Based on Deep Learning_1	50	9	23	82	55	0.670732
NEUDM_1	101	1	5	107	11	0.102804

6.2 Emotion-Specific Results

To investigate how the submitted systems perform on emotion expression with respect to emotion category, we also compute the scores for each emotion category, which is listed in the following Tables 7, 8, 9, 10 and 11.

Table 7. The result on the emotion category of *Like*.

Team name	Label 0	Label 1	Label 2	Specific	Specific score	Specific average score
samsung_1	50	16	67	133	150	1.12782
Babbling_2	55	4	74	133	152	1.142857
samsung_2	49	14	70	133	154	1.157895
SMIPG_1	100	0	33	133	66	0.496241
Babbling_1	92	5	36	133	77	0.578947
gry_1	90	4	39	133	82	0.616541
shield_1	15	3	38	56	79	1.410714
ECNU_1	11	1	26	38	53	1.394737
NUSTM_2	24	2	30	56	62	1.107143
ECNU_2	26	1	23	50	47	0.94
SMIPG_2	105	2	26	133	54	0.406015
NUSTM_1	31	1	24	56	49	0.875
NLP-More_1	32	2	22	56	46	0.821429
NLP-More_2	32	2	22	56	46	0.821429
Personalized Emotional Chatting System Based on Deep Learning_1	0	0	0	0	0	0
NEUDM_1	25	0	1	26	2	0.076923

Table 8. The result on the emotion category of *Happiness*.

Team name	Label 0	Label 1	Label 2	Specific	Specific score	Specific average score
samsung_1	36	22	71	129	164	1.271318
Babbling_2	39	9	80	128	169	1.320313
samsung_2	38	23	68	129	159	1.232558
SMIPG_1	54	3	72	129	147	1.139535
Babbling_1	71	8	50	129	108	0.837209
gry_1	84	6	39	129	84	0.651163
shield_1	21	2	27	50	56	1.12
ECNU_1	10	3	28	41	59	1.439024
NUSTM_2	23	1	26	50	53	1.06
ECNU_2	11	2	22	35	46	1.314286
SMIPG_2	93	3	33	129	69	0.534884
NUSTM_1	21	3	26	50	55	1.1
NLP-More_1	24	2	24	50	50	1
NLP-More_2	24	2	24	50	50	1
Personalized Emotional Chatting System Based on Deep Learning_1	37	4	17	58	38	0.655172
NEUDM_1	18	0	0	18	0	0

Table 9. The result on the emotion category of *Sadness*.

Team name	Label 0	Label 1	Label 2	Specific	Specific score	Specific average score
samsung_1	56	15	48	119	111	0.932773
Babbling_2	77	3	39	119	81	0.680672
samsung_2	54	23	42	119	107	0.89916
SMIPG_1	82	0	37	119	74	0.621849
Babbling_1	82	11	26	119	63	0.529412
gry_1	90	5	24	119	53	0.445378
shield_1	14	2	13	29	28	0.965517
ECNU_1	8	2	21	31	44	1.419355
NUSTM_2	15	0	14	29	28	0.965517
ECNU_2	5	3	25	33	53	1.606061
SMIPG_2	102	4	13	119	30	0.252101
NUSTM_1	15	1	13	29	27	0.931034
NLP-More_1	14	0	15	29	30	1.034483
NLP-More_2	14	0	15	29	30	1.034483
Personalized Emotional Chatting System Based on Deep Learning_1	6	3	2	11	7	0.636364
NEUDM_1	28	1	3	32	7	0.21875

Table 10. The result on the emotion category of *Disgust*.

Team name	Label 0	Label 1	Label 2	Specific	Specific score	Specific average score
samsung_1	88	24	32	144	88	0.611111
Babbling_2	99	1	44	144	89	0.618056
samsung_2	92	26	26	144	78	0.541667
SMIPG_1	133	6	5	144	16	0.111111
Babbling_1	116	13	15	144	43	0.298611
gry_1	127	11	6	144	23	0.159722
shield_1	16	13	11	40	35	0.875
ECNU_1	8	3	9	20	21	1.05
NUSTM_2	25	3	12	40	27	0.675
ECNU_2	6	1	6	13	13	1
SMIPG_2	138	3	3	144	9	0.0625
NUSTM_1	34	1	5	40	11	0.275
NLP-More_1	33	2	5	40	12	0.3
NLP-More_2	33	2	5	40	12	0.3
Personalized Emotional Chatting System Based on Deep Learning_1	0	0	0	0	0	0
NEUDM_1	25	0	1	26	2	0.076923

As can be seen from these results, the average score for *Like and Happiness* is much higher than other emotion categories. This may be due to the fact that the train data for emotion categories *sad, disgust, and sadness* are much less than those for *Like and Happiness*. Therefore, there is no sufficient data to train the generation models. This observation is consistent to [1] which reports worse generation performance on the minor emotion categories.

Table 11. The result on the emotion category of *Angry*.

Team name	Label 0	Label 1	Label 2	Specific	Specific score	Specific average score
samsung_1	37	5	29	71	63	0.887324
Babbling_2	35	2	34	71	70	0.985915
samsung_2	39	7	25	71	57	0.802817
SMIPG_1	59	2	10	71	22	0.309859
Babbling_1	63	4	4	71	12	0.169014
gry_1	58	5	8	71	21	0.295775
shield_1	10	6	4	20	14	0.7
ECNU_1	7	1	5	13	11	0.846154
NUSTM_2	15	3	2	20	7	0.35
ECNU_2	8	2	7	17	16	0.941176
SMIPG_2	67	0	4	71	8	0.112676
NUSTM_1	16	2	2	20	6	0.3
NLP-More_1	19	1	0	20	1	0.05
NLP-More_2	19	1	0	20	1	0.05
Personalized Emotional Chatting System Based on Deep Learning_1	6	2	4	12	10	0.833333
NEUDM_1	5	0	0	5	0	0

7 Models from Submission Teams

In this section, we briefly summarized the models reported by the submission teams. We quickly went through the submitted reports from all participating teams.

First, the top performing systems do not consider much how emotion expression should be addressed in generation models. For *Samsung*, the model retrieves similar responses and then feeds the top ranked response into a Seq2Seq model, and uses a learning-to-rank module to rerank responses from retrieval based models and the generation model. But they do not address emotion particularly. For *Babbling*, the rule-based submission (where they just select from a fixed set of responses) has much stronger performance than their generation-based model.

Second, even though there is no much elaborated consideration to address the emotion factor in generation models, a commonly used strategy is to feed the generation model with an emotion category embedding. However, as reported in [1], this simple strategy did not make much difference in the submission.

Third, there are some other models. For instance, there is a multi-task model which treats the generation for one emotion category as a task. However, the performance seems to not comparable to the top performing systems.

8 Summary

In this paper, we present the task definition, datasets, evaluation metrics, and results for the emotional conversation generation challenge. This is the first attempt of letting a chatting machine to express emotion via textual output in the setting of large-scale conversation generation, however, we find that it is a long way to produce satisfactory results.

- First, almost for all submissions, the proportion of 0-scored pairs is large, demonstrating that many pairs are not appropriate in content nor in emotion.
- Second, the average score is still very low (less than 1.0) showing that the overall performance is still far from satisfactory.
- Third, the training data was crawled from Weibo, but such data is different from real human conversation data. Furthermore, there are much less sad/disgust/angry responses than happy and joyful ones in such data, preventing the models from generating good responses for the minor emotion categories.
- Last, disappointingly, we did not see very sophisticated design to address the emotion factor in generation models. And the top performing systems also adopt retrieved results, showing that generation models still have much room to improve.

Acknowledgments. Dr. Minlie Huang and Mr. Hao Zhou designed the task and Dr. Minlie Huang wrote the manuscript. Mr. Zuoxian Ye processed all the data. We would like to thank Prof. Xiaoyan Zhu for her support to this work.

References

1. Zhou, H., Huang, M., Zhang, T., Zhu, X., Liu, B.: Emotional chatting machine: emotional conversation generation with internal and external memory. arXiv preprint arXiv:1704.01074 (2017)
2. Sutskever, I., Vinyals, O., Le, Q.V.: Sequence to sequence learning with neural networks. In: Advances in Neural Information Processing Systems, pp. 3104–3112 (2014)
3. Bahdanau, D., Cho, K., Bengio, Y.: Neural machine translation by jointly learning to align and translate. arXiv preprint arXiv:1409.0473 (2014)
4. Vinyals, O., Le, Q.V.: A neural conversational model. arXiv preprint arXiv:1506.05869 (2015)
5. Shang, L., Lu, Z., Li, H.: Neural responding machine for short-text conversation. In: Proceedings of 53rd Annual Meeting of the Association for Computational Linguistics and 7th International Joint Conference on Natural Language Processing of the Asian Federation of Natural Language Processing, ACL 2015, 26–31 July 2015, Beijing, China (Long Papers), vol. 1, pp. 1577–1586 (2015)
6. Serban, I.V., Sordoni, A., Bengio, Y., Courville, A.: Pineau, J.: Hierarchical neural network generative models for movie dialogues. arXiv preprint arXiv:1507.04808 (2015)
7. Sordoni, A., Galley, M., Auli, M., Brockett, C., Ji, Y., Mitchell, M., Nie, J.-Y., Gao, J., Dolan, B.: A neural network approach to context-sensitive generation of conversational responses. In: NAACL HLT 2015, 2015 Conference of the North American Chapter of the Association for Computational Linguistics: Human Language Technologies, 31 May - 5 June 2015, Denver, Colorado, USA, pp. 196–205 (2015)

8. Li, J., Galley, M., Brockett, C., Gao, J., Dolan, B.: A diversity-promoting objective function for neural conversation models. In: NAACL HLT 2016, 2016 Conference of the North American Chapter of the Association for Computational Linguistics: Human Language Technologies, 12–17 June 2016, San Diego California, USA, pp. 110–119 (2016)
9. Li, J., Monroe, W., Jurafsky, D.: A simple, fast diverse decoding algorithm for neural generation. CoRR, abs/1611.08562 (2016)
10. Shao, L., Gouws, S., Britz, D., Goldie, A., Strope, B., Kurzweil, R.: Generating long and diverse responses with neural conversation models. CoRR, abs/1701.03185 (2017)
11. Xing, C., Wu, W., Wu, Y., Liu, J., Huang, Y., Zhou, M., Ma, W.-Y.: Topic aware neural response generation. In: Proceedings of 31st AAAI Conference on Artificial Intelligence, 4–9 February 2017, San Francisco, California, USA, pp. 3351–3357 (2017)
12. Mou, L., Song, Y., Yan, R., Li, G., Zhang, L., Jin, Z.: Sequence to backward and forward sequences: a content-introducing approach to generative short-text conversation. In: Proceedings of the Conference on 26th International Conference on Computational Linguistics, pp. 3349–3358 (2016)
13. Xiong, K., Cui, A., Zhang, Z., Li, M.: Neural contextual conversation learning with labeled question-answering pairs. CoRR, abs/1607.05809 (2016)
14. Li, J., Galley, M., Brockett, C., Spithourakis, G., Gao, J., Dolan, W.B.: A persona-based neural conversation model. In: Proceedings of 54th Annual Meeting of the Association for Computational Linguistics, ACL 2016, 7–12 August 2016, Berlin, Germany (Long Papers), vol. 1 (2016)
15. Song, Y., Yan, R., Li, X., Zhao, D., Zhang, M.: Two are better than one: an ensemble of retrieval-and generation-based dialog systems. arXiv preprint arXiv:1610.07149 (2016)
16. Shang, L., Sakai, T., Lu, Z., Li, H., Higashinaka, R., Miyao, Y.: Overview of the NTCIR-12 short text conversation task. In: NTCIR (2016)

Overview of the NLPCC-ICCPOL 2017 Shared Task: Social Media User Modeling

Fuzheng Zhang[✉], Defu Lian, and Xing Xie

Microsoft Research Asia, Beijing, China
{fuzzhang, xingx}@microsoft.com, dove@uestc.edu.cn

Abstract. In this paper, we give the overview of the social media user modeling shared task in the NLPCC-ICCPOL 2017. We first review the background of social media user modeling, and then describe two social media user modeling tasks in this year's NLPCC-ICCPOL, including the construction of the benchmark datasets and the evaluation metrics. The evaluation results of submissions from participating teams are presented in the experimental part.

Keywords: User modeling · Social media · Recommendation

1 Background

With the widespread of social media websites in the internet, and the huge number of users participating and generating infinite number of contents in these websites, the need for personalization increases dramatically to become a necessity. One of the major issues in personalization is building users' profiles, which depend on many elements; such as the used data [1, 2], the application domain they aim to serve [3, 4], the representation method and the construction methodology [5, 6]. Another major issue in personalization is personalized recommendation, which can be divided into different methods including contented based methods [7, 8], collaborative filtering based methods [9, 10], and hybrid methods [11, 12].

In the industry field, many influential user modeling products have been built, such as Netflix movie recommendation system, Amazon item recommendation system, etc. These kinds of systems are immerging into every user's life.

Under such circumstance, in this year's NLPCC-ICCPOL shared task, we call the social media user modeling task that cover both personalized recommendation and user profiling tasks.

The remainder of this paper is organized as follows. Section 2 describes the provided dataset. In Sect. 3, we describe the detail of these two shared tasks. Section 4 describes evaluation metrics, and Sect. 5 presents the evaluation results of different submissions. We conclude the paper in Sect. 6, and point out our plan on future user modeling activities.

© Springer International Publishing AG 2018
X. Huang et al. (Eds.): NLPCC 2017, LNAI 10619, pp. 937–941, 2018.
https://doi.org/10.1007/978-3-319-73618-1_83

2 Data Description

The data, collected from a social media platform, contains the following five aspects:

(1) checkins.txt describes users' location visits. The format is as follows, where POI is the location id user visits, Cate1, Cate2, Cate3 is the category of the POI in a hierarchical level. Lat and Lng is the latitude and longitude information and Name is the location name.

user	POI	Cate1	Cate2	Cate3	Lat	Lng	Name

(2) profile.txt describes users' profiles. Currently only gender is provided.

user	gender

(3) social.txt describes users' social tie, where User1 follows User2 on this social media platform.

user 1	user2

(4) tags.txt describes users' tags. Each line contains a user and related tag.

user	tag

(5) tweets.txt describes what user posted. Each line contains a user and the posted tweet.

tweet	user

All the information is anonymous. All the files are UTF-8 encodes and tab separated.

3 Task Description

Given the social media dataset including the following heterogenous information: users' profiles (gender), social ties (following relationship), users' tags, users' published tweets, and users' location visits, the NLPCC-ICCPOL 2017 social media user modeling shared task includes two shared tasks for social media dataset: Interested Location Prediction task and User Profiling task.

3.1   Interested Location Prediction Task

Given users' some historical location visits and other provided information, predict what locations a user is interested to visit in the future.

3.2   User Profiling Task

Given users' other information expect profiles, predict each user's profile information.

4   Evaluation Metrics

(1) The submit file format of Interested Location Prediction subtask will be like this:

User1,POI1,POI2,....
User2,POI3,POI4...

Where all the users in the test data appeared in training data, and for each user, the predicted POI should be contained in the training data, but not appear in this user's visit history.

The quality of this subtask will be evaluated by $F1@K(K = 10)$, where $|H_i|$ is the correctly predicted locations for user i's top K prediction, $P_i@K$, $R_i@K$ and $F1_i@K$ is the precision, recall and $F1$ for a user i.

$$P_i@K = \frac{|H_i|}{K}, \quad R_i@K = \frac{|H_i|}{|V_i|}, \quad F1_i@K = \frac{P_i@K * R_i@K}{P_i@K + R_i@K}$$

$$F1@K = \frac{1}{N}\sum_{i=1}^{N} F1_i@K$$

(2) User Profiling subtask focus on gender prediction, the submit file format will be like this:

User1,m
User2,f

The quality of this subtask will be evaluated by accuracy, where $Label_i$ is the ground truth gender and $Predict_i$ is the predicted gender, δ is the indicator function where $Label_i$ and $Predict_i$ is the same.

$$Accuracy = \frac{1}{N}\sum_{i=1}^{N} \delta(Label_i, Predict_i)$$

5 Evaluation Results

There are totally 47 teams registered for the above two shared tasks, and 16 teams submitted their results. Tables 1 and 2 lists the evaluation results of Interested Location Prediction subtask and User Profiling subtask respectively.

Table 1. Evaluation results of the interested location prediction subtask.

	F1@10
Team 1	0.0167
Team 2	0.0166
Team 3	0.0116
Team 4	0.0028
Team 5	0.0027
Team 6	0.0017
Team 7	0.0015
Team 8	0.0003

Table 2. Evaluation results of the user profiling subtask.

	Accuracy
Team 1	0.8564
Team 2	0.8285
Team 3	0.7721
Team 4	0.7636
Team 5	0.7549
Team 6	0.7455
Team 7	0.5624
Team 8	0.3410

6 Conclusion

This paper briefly introduces the overview of this year's two social media user modeling shared tasks. We have 47 teams registered and 16 teams submitted final submissions, which has been a great progress for the user modeling community. In the future, we plan to provide more social media datasets and call for new user modeling tasks.

References

1. Zhong, Y., Yuan, N.J., Zhong, W., Zhang, F., Xie, X.: You are where you go: inferring demographic attributes from location check-ins. In: Proceedings of the Eighth ACM International Conference on Web Search and Data Mining, pp. 295–304 (2015)
2. Abel, F., Gao, Q., Houben, G.-J., Tao, K.: Semantic enrichment of Twitter posts for user profile construction on the social web. In: Antoniou, G., Grobelnik, M., Simperl, E., Parsia, B., Plexousakis, D., De Leenheer, P., Pan, J. (eds.) ESWC 2011. LNCS, vol. 6644, pp. 375–389. Springer, Heidelberg (2011). https://doi.org/10.1007/978-3-642-21064-8_26
3. Zhang, F., Zheng, K., Yuan, N.J., Xie, X., Chen, E., Zhou, X.: A novelty-seeking based dining recommender system. In: The International Conference, pp. 1362–1372 (2015)
4. Morita, M., Shinoda, Y.: Information filtering based on user behavior analysis and best match text retrieval. In: Proceedings of the 17th Annual International ACM SIGIR Conference on Research and Development in Information Retrieval, pp. 272–281 (1994)
5. Adomavicius, G., Tuzhilin, A.: User profiling in personalization applications through rule discovery and validation. In: Proceedings of the Fifth ACM SIGKDD International Conference on Knowledge Discovery and Data Mining, pp. 377–381 (1999)
6. Zhang, F., Yuan, N.J., Lian, D., Xie, X.: Mining novelty-seeking trait across heterogeneous domains. In: Proceedings of the 23rd International Conference on World Wide Web, pp. 373–384 (2014)
7. Pazzani, M.J., Billsus, D.: Content-based recommendation systems. In: Brusilovsky, P., Kobsa, A., Nejdl, W. (eds.) The Adaptive Web. LNCS, vol. 4321, pp. 325–341. Springer, Heidelberg (2007). https://doi.org/10.1007/978-3-540-72079-9_10
8. Popescul, A., Pennock, D.M., Lawrence, S.: Probabilistic models for unified collaborative and content-based recommendation in sparse-data environments. In: Proceedings of the Seventeenth Conference on Uncertainty in Artificial Intelligence, pp. 437–444 (2001)
9. Koren, Y., Bell, R., Volinsky, C.: Matrix factorization techniques for recommender systems. Comput. **42**(8) (2009). (Long. Beach. Calif.)
10. Rendle, S., Freudenthaler, C., Gantner, Z., Schmidt-Thieme, L.: BPR: Bayesian personalized ranking from implicit feedback. In: Proceedings of the Twenty-Fifth Conference on Uncertainty in Artificial Intelligence, pp. 452–461 (2009)
11. Zhang, F., Yuan, N.J., Lian, D., Xie, X., Ma, W.-Y.: Collaborative knowledge base embedding for recommender systems. In: Proceedings of the 22nd ACM SIGKDD International Conference on Knowledge Discovery and Data Mining, pp. 353–362 (2016)
12. Zhang, F., Yuan, N.J., Zheng, K., Lian, D., Xie, X., Rui, Y.: Exploiting dining preference for restaurant recommendation. In: Proceedings of the 25th International Conference on World Wide Web, pp. 725–735 (2016)

Overview of the NLPCC 2017 Shared Task: Single Document Summarization

Lifeng Hua[1(✉)], Xiaojun Wan[2(✉)], and Lei Li[1(✉)]

[1] Toutiao AI Lab, Beijing, China
{hualifeng,lileilab}@bytedance.com
[2] Institute of Computer Science and Technology,
Peking University, Beijing, China
wanxiaojun@pku.edu.cn

Abstract. In this paper, we give an overview for the shared task at the 6th CCF Conference on Natural Language Processing & Chinese Computing (NLPCC 2017): single document summarization. Document summarization aims at conveying important information and generating significantly short summaries for original long documents. This task focused on summarizing the news articles and released a large corpus, TTNews corpus (TTNews corpus can be downloaded at https://pan.baidu.com/s/1bppQ4z1), which was collected for single document summarization in Chinese. In this paper, we will introduce the task, the corpus, the participating teams and the evaluation results.

Keywords: Single document summarization · NLPCC 2017
TTNews corpus

1 Introduction

Document summarization has been an important role in today's fast-grow information time. Now, the Internet products tens of millions of documents everyday and it is impossible for human being to manually summarize them, or even though read them. So the technology of automatic document summarization is necessary for us to obtain and reorganize the information from the Internet.

The methods of document summarization can be defined as extractive and abstractive summarization [1]. The extractive summarization attempts to extract key sentences or key phrases from the original document and then reorders these fragments into a summary. Meanwhile the abstractive summarization focused on generating new fragments and new expressions which are based on the understanding of this document.

Additionally, the document summary can be produced from a single document or multiple documents [2]. In this shared task, we just focus on single document summarization.

X. Huang et al. (Eds.): NLPCC 2017, LNAI 10619, pp. 942–947, 2018.
https://doi.org/10.1007/978-3-319-73618-1_84

2   Task

Traditional news article summarization techniques have been widely explored on the DUC and TAC conferences, and existing corpora for document summarization are mainly focused on western languages, while Chinese news summarization has seldom been explored. In this shared task, we aim to investigate single document summarization techniques for Chinese news articles. It is defined as a task of automatically generating a short summary for a given Chinese news article.

We will provide a large corpus for evaluating and comparing different document summarization techniques. This corpus has a test/training set consisting of a large number of Chinese news articles with reference summaries, together with a large number of news articles without reference summaries (perhaps for semi-supervised methods). Almost these news articles and reference summaries are used for news browsing and propagation at Toutiao.com.

3   Data

TTNews corpus contains test set and training set. For the training set, it contains a large set of news articles browsed on Toutiao.com and corresponding human-written summary which was used on news pushing and other tasks on Toutiao.com. Furthermore it contains another large set of news articles without summary (perhaps for semi-supervised methods). For the test set, it just contains the news articles. The news articles are from lots of different sources and meanwhile contain of different topics, such as sports, foods, entertainments, politics, technology, finance and so on.

As far as we know, TTNews corpus is the largest single document summarization corpus in Chinese. There are 50,000 news articles with summary and 50,000 news articles without summary in training set, and 2000 news articles in test set. As shown in Table 1, the mean length of the short summary is 45 Chinese characters.

The example of a news article and its reference summary is shown in Table 2.

Table 1. Statistical information of TTNews corpus

	Number	Mean length of news article	Mean length of news summary
Training (with summary)	50000	1036	45
Training (without summary)	50000	1526	/
Test	2000	1037	45

Table 2. An example of news article and reference summary

News summary:
韩媒称朝鲜外交官在莫桑比克走私犀牛角被抓，将犀牛角放在外交邮袋中运往中国，再在黑市上销售，以赚取外汇
News article:
参考消息网 5 月 30 日报道美国之音广播援引韩国驻南非大使馆相关负责人的话报道称，朝鲜外交官被爆在非洲莫桑比克走私濒临灭种野生动物犀牛角。据韩国《中央日报》5 月 29 日报道，大使馆相关负责人匿名表示，"被曝光的人是朝鲜驻南非大使馆参赞朴哲俊（音）和居住在南非的朝鲜跆拳道教练金钟秀"，"（当地）这是从马普托警察厅的奥兰度·木杜马尼（音）发言人那里确认的事实"。据当地警察厅称，朴参赞和金教练 5 月 3 日在莫桑比克马普托中部的市场上从当地偷猎者那里购买了 4.616 公斤犀牛角，在用车辆运输的过程中被抓获。据悉，当地警察厅接到举报出动，将这些人当场抓获。关于濒临灭绝动植物交易的国际公约禁止进行犀牛角相关商业交易。即使以学术研究目的进行国家间贸易，也要出示两国政府颁发的进出口许可证。美国之音报道称，朝鲜不顾公约，利用外交官特权从事犀牛角走私。外交官在通过国境时免搜查，外交邮袋也未经外交官负责人同意不能检查。韩国驻南非大使馆相关负责人表示，莫桑比克是犀牛栖息地，朝鲜驻莫桑比克保健代表部多次走私犀牛角，交给朝鲜驻南非大使馆，大使馆将其放在外交邮袋中运往中国。驻中国的朝鲜相关负责人收到走私货物后在黑市上作为中药材销售。《国家地理》今年 3 月报道称，犀牛角作为以真犀角为名的中药材在黑市上以每公斤 6.5 万美元左右的价格进行交易。报道称，朝鲜利用外交官特权赚取外汇的现象最近逐渐频繁起来。上个月，在禁止销售酒水的巴基斯坦，朝鲜外交官夫妇在大街上无执照销售芝华士（Chivas Regal）等洋酒被揭发。今年 3 月，在孟加拉国，朝鲜外交官拿着装有 27 公斤金块的行李在入境时被海关查获。报道称，庆南大学教授林乙出（音，朝鲜学系）表示，"因联合国、美国和韩国的对朝制裁，资金来源被切断的朝鲜当局施压要赚取外汇，并指示大使馆运营费也要自行筹措"。报道说，还有分析称，部分外交官尝到了"钱的滋味"，主动犯下这种罪行。东国大学教授（朝鲜学系）金榕炫分析称，"因上级指示而放手赚取外汇的外交官们知道通过交易能够创收的方法，因此表现得更积极" …

4   Participants

Each team was allowed to submit at most 5 runs of results in the period of this shared task. The participants were allowed to use any NLP resources and toolkits, but not allowed to use any other news articles with reference summaries.

There were 9 teams submitting their final results in this shared task. The participating teams are shown in Table 3. And they totally submitted 29 runs of result for validation. Both extractive summarization and abstractive summarization was used by the participating teams.

Table 3. Introduction of participating teams

Team name	Organization name
NLP_ONE	Central China Normal University
ICDD_Mango	Beijing Information Science and Technology University
NLP@WUST	Wuhan University of Science and Technology
CQUT_AC326	Chongqing University of Technology
HIT_ITNLP_TS	Harbin Institute of Technology
DLUT_NLPer	Dalian University of Technology
AC_Team	Chongqing University of Technology
ECNU_BUAA	Beihang University, East China Normal University
ccnuSYS	Central China Normal University

5   Evaluation

The single document summarization was evaluated automatically.

5.1   Evaluation Metric

We used ROUGE [3] for automatic evaluation metric. ROUGE is the short-hand of Recall-Oriented Understudy for Gisting Evaluation, and contains a set of metrics used for automatic document summarization, machine translation evaluation and other tasks in NLP. We defined the mean value of ROUGE-1, ROUGE-2, ROUGE-3, ROUGE-4, ROUGE-L, ROUGE-SU4, ROUGE-W-1.2 scores as the overall evaluation score. And we used ROUGE-1.5.5 toolkit to compute the overall score. Note that the length of each summary was limited to 60 Chinese characters at our shared task, so we used -l 60 for truncating longer news summary.

5.2   Results

There are 9 submitted teams in this shared task, and the results are shown in Table 4. As Table 4 given, NLP_ONE, ICCD_Mango and NLP@WUST have better results than others.

5.3   Some Representative Systems

In this section, some representative systems will be brief introduced.

LEAD system is a extractive summarization baseline system. It tasks the first 60 characters one by one from the document as a summary.

ccnuSYS system uses an LSTM encoder-decoder architecture [4] with attention mechanism [5] to generate abstractive summary [6,7] for this shared task. It uses the article as input sequence and the summary as output sequence.

Table 4. Evaluation results

	ROUGE-2	ROUGE-4	ROUGE-SU4	Overall Score
NLP_ONE	22.89	12.81	21.24	22.10
ICDD_Mango	23.82	12.04	21.19	22.09
NLP@WUST	22.53	10.39	20.81	21.65
CQUT_AC326	19.62	7.83	18.12	19.14
HIT_ITNLP_TS	19.33	8.38	17.86	19.13
DLUT_NLPer	17.64	7.58	16.35	17.54
AC_Team	18.16	7.88	15.92	17.09
ECNU_BUAA	15.73	6.86	14.72	15.99
ccnuSYS	15.58	6.57	14.47	15.79
LEAD	20.91	11.75	19.28	20.31

NLP_ONE system is also focused on abstractive summarization. Due to the shortcoming of traditional attention encoder-decoder models, this work proposes to add an new attention mechanism on output sequence and uses the subword method. And it gets a significant improvement.

NLP@WUST system uses an feature engineering based sentence extraction framework to get extractive summary for this shared task. After the extraction processing, it adds an sentence compression algorithm [8] for compressing shorter summary. And the performance is further improved.

6   Conclusion

This paper briefly introduces the overview of single document summarization shared task at NLPCC 2017. There are 9 participants having submitted final results. And some participants get exciting results in this corpus. Meanwhile, we release a large Chinese news articles and reference summaries corpus (TTNews corpus) for more large-scale research in Chinese document summarization.

Acknowledgement. We are very grateful to the colleagues from our company for their efforts to annotate the data and Knowledge Engineering Group of Tsinghua University for the help of building the submission system. And we also would like to thank the participants for their valuable feedback and results.

References

1. Nenkova, A., McKeown, K.: A survey of text summarization techniques. In: Aggarwal, C., Zhai, C. (eds.) Mining Text Data, pp. 43–76. Springer, Heidelberg (2012). https://doi.org/10.1007/978-1-4614-3223-4_3
2. Das, D., Martins, A.F.T.: A survey on automatic text summarization. Literature Surv. Lang. Stat. II Course CMU **4**, 192–195 (2007)

3. Lin, C.-Y.: Rouge: a package for automatic evaluation of summaries. In: Proceedings of the ACL-04 Workshop Text Summarization Branches Out, Barcelona, Spain, vol. 8 (2004)
4. Sutskever, I., Vinyals, O., Le, Q.V.: Sequence to sequence learning with neural networks. In: Advances in Neural Information Processing Systems, pp. 3104–3112 (2014)
5. Bahdanau, D., Cho, K., Bengio, Y.: Neural machine translation by jointly learning to align and translate. arXiv preprint arXiv:1409.0473 (2014)
6. Nallapati, R., Zhou, B., Gulcehre, C., Xiang, B., et al.: Abstractive text summarization using sequence-to-sequence RNNs and beyond. arXiv preprint arXiv:1602.06023 (2016)
7. Cheng, J., Lapata, M.: Neural summarization by extracting sentences and words. arXiv preprint arXiv:1603.07252 (2016)
8. Cohn, T.A., Lapata, M.: Sentence compression as tree transduction. J. Artif. Intell. Res. **34**, 637–674 (2009)

Overview of the NLPCC 2017 Shared Task: Chinese News Headline Categorization

Xipeng Qiu$^{(\boxtimes)}$, Jingjing Gong, and Xuanjing Huang

School of Computer Science, Fudan University,
825 Zhangheng Road, Shanghai, China
{xpqiu,jjgong15,xjhuang}@fudan.edu.cn

Abstract. In this paper, we give an overview for the shared task at the CCF Conference on Natural Language Processing & Chinese Computing (NLPCC 2017): Chinese News Headline Categorization. The dataset of this shared task consists 18 classes, 12,000 short texts along with corresponded labels for each class. The dataset and example code can be accessed at https://github.com/FudanNLP/nlpcc2017_news_headline_categorization.

1 Task Definition

This task aims to evaluate the automatic classification techniques for very short texts, i.e., Chinese news headlines. Each news headline (i.e., news title) is required to be classified into one or more predefined categories. With the rise of Internet and social media, the text data on the web is growing exponentially. Make a human being to analysis all those data is impractical, while machine learning techniques suits perfectly for this kind of tasks. After all, human brain capacity is too limited and precious for tedious and non-obvious phenomenons.

Formally, the task is defined as follows: given a news headline $x = (x_1, x_2, ..., x_n)$, where x_j represents jth word in x, the object is to find its possible category or label $c \in \mathcal{C}$. More specifically, we need to find a function to predict in which category does x belong to.

$$c^* = \operatorname*{argmax}_{c \in \mathcal{C}} f(x; \theta_c), \tag{1}$$

where θ is the parameter for the function.

2 Data

We collected news headlines (titles) from several Chinese news websites, such as toutiao, sina, and so on.

There are 18 categories in total. The detailed information of each category is shown in Table 1. All the sentences are segmented by using the python Chinese segmentation tool *jieba*.

Some samples from training dataset are shown in Table 2.

© Springer International Publishing AG 2018
X. Huang et al. (Eds.): NLPCC 2017, LNAI 10619, pp. 948–953, 2018.
https://doi.org/10.1007/978-3-319-73618-1_85

Table 1. The information of categories.

Category	Train	Dev	Test
Entertainment	10000	2000	2000
Sports	10000	2000	2000
Car	10000	2000	2000
Society	10000	2000	2000
Tech	10000	2000	2000
World	10000	2000	2000
Finance	10000	2000	2000
Game	10000	2000	2000
Travel	10000	2000	2000
Military	10000	2000	2000
History	10000	2000	2000
Baby	10000	2000	2000
Fashion	10000	2000	2000
Food	10000	2000	2000
Discovery	4000	2000	2000
Story	4000	2000	2000
Regimen	4000	2000	2000
Essay	4000	2000	2000

Table 2. Samples from dataset. The first column is Category and the second column is news headline.

Category	Title Sentence
world	首辩在即希拉里特朗普如何备战
society	山东实现城乡环卫一体化全覆盖
finance	除了稀土股，还有哪个方向好戏即将..
travel	独库公路再次爆发第三次泥石流无法...
finance	主力资金净流入9000 万以上28 股...
sports	高洪波：足协眼中的应急郎中
entertainment	世界级十大喜剧之王排行榜

Table 3. Statistical information of the dataset.

Category	Size	Avg. Chars	Avg. Words
Train	156000	22.06	13.08
Dev.	36000	22.05	13.09
Test	36000	22.05	13.08

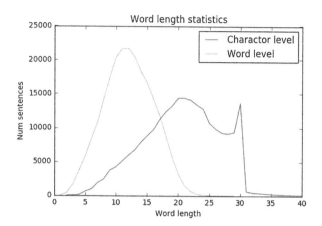

Fig. 1. The blue line is *character length* statistic, and blue line is *word length*. (Color figure online)

Length. Figure 1 shows that most of title sentence character number is less than 40, with a mean of 21.05. Title sentence word length is even shorter, most of which is less than 20 with a mean of 12.07 (Table 3).

The dataset is released on github https://github.com/FudanNLP/nlpcc2017_news_headline_categorization along with code that implement three basic models.

3   Evaluation

We use the macro-averaged precision, recall and F1 to evaluate the performance. The Macro Avg. is defined as follow:

$$Macro\_avg = \frac{1}{m} \sum_{i=1}^{m} \rho_i$$

And Micro Avg. is defined as:

$$Micro\_avg = \frac{1}{N} \sum_{i=1}^{m} w_i \rho_i$$

where m denotes the number of class, in the case of this dataset is 18. ρ_i is the accuracy of ith category, w_i represents how many test examples reside in ith category, N is total number of examples in the test set.

4   Baseline Implementations

As a branch of machine learning, Deep Learning (DL) has gained much attention in recent years due to its prominent achievement in several domains such as Computer vision and Natural Language processing.

Table 4. Results of the baseline models.

Model	Macro P	Macro R	Macro F	Accuracy
LSTM	0.760	0.747	0.7497	0.747
CNN	0.769	0.763	0.764	0.763
NBoW	0.791	0.783	0.784	0.783

We have implemented some basic DL models such as neural bag-of-words (NBoW), convolutional neural networks (CNN) [3] and Long short-term memory network (LSTM) [2].

Empirically, 2 Gigabytes of GPU Memory should be sufficient for most models, set batch to a smaller number if not.

The results generated from baseline models are shown in Table 4.

5   Participants Submitted Results

There are 32 participants actively participate and submit they predictions on the test set. The predictions are evaluated and the results are shown in Table 5.

6   Some Representative Methods

In this section, we gives three representative methods.

[4] proposed a novel method which enhances the semantic representation of headlines. It first adds some keywords extracted from the most similar news to expand the word features. Then, it uses the corpus in news domain to pre-train the word embedding so as to enhance the word representation. At last, it utilizes Fasttext classifier, which uses a liner method to classify texts with fast speed and high accuracy.

[1] developed a voting system based on convolutional neural networks (CNN), gated recurrent units (GRU), and support vector machine (SVM).

[5] proposed an efficient approach for Chinese news headline classification based on multi-representation mixed model with attention and ensemble learning. It first models the headline semantic both on character and word level via Bi-directional Long Short-Term Memory (BiLSTM), with the concatenation of output states from hidden layer as the semantic representation. Meanwhile, it adopts attention mechanism to highlight the key characters or words related to the classification decision. And lastly it utilizes ensemble learning to determine the final category of the whole test samples by sub-models voting.

Table 5. Results submitted by participants.

Participant	Macro P	Macro R	Macro F	Accu.
P1	0.831	0.829	0.830	0.829
P2	0.828	0.825	0.826	0.825
P3	0.818	0.814	0.816	0.814
P4	0.816	0.809	0.813	0.809
P5	0.812	0.809	0.810	0.809
P6	0.811	0.807	0.809	0.807
P7	0.809	0.804	0.806	0.804
P8	0.806	0.802	0.804	0.802
P9	0.803	0.800	0.802	0.800
P10	0.805	0.800	0.802	0.800
P11	0.799	0.798	0.798	0.798
P12	0.797	0.795	0.796	0.795
P13	0.793	0.789	0.791	0.789
P14	0.791	0.789	0.790	0.789
P15	0.792	0.787	0.789	0.786
P16	0.786	0.783	0.785	0.783
P17	0.778	0.775	0.777	0.775
P18	0.785	0.775	0.780	0.775
P19	0.785	0.775	0.780	0.775
P20	0.766	0.765	0.765	0.765
P21	0.768	0.759	0.764	0.759
P22	0.768	0.748	0.758	0.748
P23	0.744	0.729	0.736	0.729
P24	0.729	0.726	0.728	0.726
P25	0.745	0.700	0.722	0.700
P26	0.734	0.688	0.710	0.688
P27	0.698	0.685	0.691	0.685
P28	0.640	0.633	0.637	0.633
P29	0.645	0.629	0.637	0.629
P30	0.437	0.430	0.433	0.430
P31	0.474	0.399	0.433	0.399
P32	0.053	0.056	0.054	0.056

7   Conclusion

Since large amount of data is required for machine learning techniques like deep learning, we have collected considerable amount of news headline data and contributed to the research community. We also found that the performance of news headline classification still need be improved. We hope that our dataset provides a valuable training data and a testbed for text classification task.

References

1. Zhu, F., Dong, X., Song, R., Hong, Y., Zhu, Q.: A multiple learning model based voting system for news headline classification. In: Proceedings of the CCF Conference on Natural Language Processing & Chinese Computing (2017)
2. Hochreiter, S., Schmidhuber, J.: Long short-term memory. Neural Comput. **9**(8), 1735–1780 (1997)
3. Kim, Y.: Convolutional neural networks for sentence classification. arXiv preprint arXiv:1408.5882 (2014)
4. Yin, Z., Tang, J., Chengsen, Luo, W., Luo, Z., Ma, X.: A semantic representation enhancement method for Chinese news headline classification. In: Proceedings of the CCF Conference on Natural Language Processing & Chinese Computing (2017)
5. Lu, Z., Liu, W., Zhou, Y., Hu, X., Wang, B.: An effective approach for Chinese news headline classification base on multi-representation mixed model with attention and ensemble learning. In: Proceedings of the CCF Conference on Natural Language Processing & Chinese Computing (2017)

Overview of the NLPCC 2017 Shared Task: Open Domain Chinese Question Answering

Nan Duan[(⊠)] and Duyu Tang

Microsoft Research Asia, Beijing, China
{nanduan,dutang}@microsoft.com

Abstract. In this paper, we give the overview of the open domain Question Answering (or open domain QA) shared task in the NLPCC 2017. We first review the background of QA, and then describe two open domain Chinese QA tasks in this year's NLPCC, including the construction of the benchmark datasets and the evaluation metrics. The evaluation results of submissions from participating teams are presented in the experimental part.

Keywords: Question answering · Knowledge-based QA
Document-based QA · Table-based QA

1 Background

Question Answering (or QA) is a fundamental task in Artificial Intelligence, whose goal is to build a system that can automatically answer natural language questions. In the last decade, the development of QA techniques has been greatly promoted by both academic field and industry field.

In the academic field, with the rise of large scale curated knowledge bases, like Yago, Satori, Freebase, etc., more and more researchers pay their attentions to the knowledge-based QA (or KBQA) task, such as semantic parsing-based approaches [1–7] and information retrieval-based approaches [8–16]. Besides KBQA, researchers are interested in document-based QA (or DBQA) as well, whose goal is to select answers from a set of given documents and use them as responses to natural language questions. Usually, information retrieval-based approaches [18–22] are used for the DBQA task.

In the industry field, many influential QA-related products have been built, such as IBM Watson, Apple Siri, Google Now, Facebook Graph Search, Microsoft Cortana and XiaoIce etc. These kinds of systems are immerging into every user's life who is using mobile devices.

Under such circumstance, in this year's NLPCC shared task, we call the open domain QA task that cover both KBQA and DBQA tasks. Our motivations are two-folds:

1. We expect this activity can enhance the progress of QA research, esp. for Chinese;
2. We encourage more QA researchers to share their experiences, techniques, and progress.

X. Huang et al. (Eds.): NLPCC 2017, LNAI 10619, pp. 954–961, 2018.
https://doi.org/10.1007/978-3-319-73618-1_86

Besides these two tasks mentioned above, we also prepared a new task: Table-based QA (TBQA). However, there is no final submission for this task, so we skip the description of this task in this paper.

The remainder of this paper is organized as follows. Section 2 describes two open domain Chinese QA tasks. In Sect. 3, we describe the benchmark datasets constructed. Section 3 describes evaluation metrics, and Sect. 4 presents the evaluation results of different submissions. We conclude the paper in Sect. 5, and point out our plan on future QA evaluation activities.

2 Task Description

The NLPCC 2017 open domain QA shared task includes two QA tasks for Chinese language: knowledge-based QA (KBQA) task and document-based QA (DBQA) task.

2.1 KBQA Task

Given a question, a KBQA system built by each participating team should select one or more entities as answers from a given knowledge base (KB). The datasets for this task include:

- **A Chinese KB.** It includes knowledge triples crawled from the web. Each knowledge triple has the form: <Subject, Predicate, Object>, where 'Subject' denotes a subject entity, 'Predicate' denotes a relation, and 'Object' denotes an object entity. A sample of knowledge triples is given in Fig. 1, and the statistics of the Chinese KB is given in Table 1.

```
新还珠格格 ||| entity.primaryName ||| 新还珠格格
新还珠格格 ||| 中文名 ||| 新还珠格格
新还珠格格 ||| 外文名 ||| New my fair Princess
新还珠格格 ||| 出品时间 ||| 2011年和2014年
新还珠格格 ||| 出品公司 ||| 上海创翱文化传播有限公司
新还珠格格 ||| 制片地区 ||| 中国大陆，中国台湾
新还珠格格 ||| 拍摄地点 ||| 横店影视城
新还珠格格 ||| 发行公司 ||| 上海创翱文化传播有限公司
新还珠格格 ||| 首播时间 ||| 2011年7月16日
新还珠格格 ||| 导演 ||| 李平，丁仰国
新还珠格格 ||| 编剧 ||| 琼瑶，黄素媛
新还珠格格 ||| 主演 ||| 李晟，海陆，张睿，李佳航，潘杰明，赵丽颖，邱心志，邓萃雯，刘雪华
新还珠格格 ||| 集数 ||| 总共98集-第一部1至37集-第二部37至74集-第三部74至98集
新还珠格格 ||| 每集长度 ||| 前三部：45分钟 第四部：48分钟
新还珠格格 ||| 类型 ||| 古装，爱情，励志，喜剧
新还珠格格 ||| 上映时间 ||| 前三部：2011年07月16日至2011年9月8日第四部：2016年暑期档
新还珠格格 ||| 在线播放平台 ||| 芒果TV，PPTV,暴风影音，优酷，搜狐。
新还珠格格 ||| 总策划 ||| 杨文红，苏晓
新还珠格格 ||| 出品人 ||| 欧阳常林
新还珠格格 ||| 总监制 ||| 魏文彬
新还珠格格 ||| entity.description ||| 《新还珠格格》翻拍自琼瑶经典之作《还珠格格》，由李晟、海
```

Fig. 1. An example of the Chinese KB.

- **Training set and testing set.** We assign a set of knowledge triples sampled from the Chinese KB to human annotators. For each knowledge triple, a human annotator will write down a natural language question, whose answer should be the object entity of the current knowledge triple. In last year's NLPCC KBQA task, we

Table 1. Statistics of the Chinese KB.

# of Subject Entities	8,721,640
# of Triples	47,943,429
# of Averaged Triples per Subject Entity	5.5

released 14,609 labeled QA pairs as training set, and 9,870 labeled QA pairs as testing set. In this year, we provide a new testing set, which includes 7,631 labeled QA pairs. We follow the same way to annotate this dataset as we did last year. Besides, we also used Automatic Question Generation technique to generate a set faked questions, and mixed them into human labeled questions to form a larger testing set. These generated questions and their corresponding answers will be ignored in the evaluation phase. The statistic of labeled QA pairs and an annotation example are given in Table 2:

Table 2. Statistics of the KBQA datasets.

# of Labeled Q-A Pairs (training set, 2016)		14,609
# of Labeled Q-A Pairs (testing set, 2016)		9,870
# of Labeled Q-A Pairs (testing set, 2017)		7.631
An Example	Triple	<微软，创始人，比尔盖茨>
	Labeled Question	微软公司的创始人是谁?
	Golden Answer	比尔盖茨

In KBQA task, any data resource can be used to train necessary models, such as entity linking, semantic parsing, etc., but answer entities should come from the provided KB only.

2.2 DBQA Task

Given a question and its corresponding document, a DBQA system built by each participating team should select one or more sentences as answers from the document. The datasets for this task include:

- **Training set and testing set.** We assign a set of documents to human annotators. For each document, a human annotator will (1) first, select a sentence from the document, and (2) then, write down a natural language question, whose answer should be the selected sentence. In last year's NLPCC DBQA task, we released 8,772 labeled Q-document pairs as training set, and 5,779 labeled Q-document pairs as testing set. In this year, we provide a new testing set as well, which includes 2,500 labeled QA pairs. Like KBQA, we released a larger testing set by adding some automatically generated questions and ignored them during the evaluation phase. The statistic of labeled QD pairs and an annotation example are given in Table 3:

Table 3. Statistics of the DBQA datasets.

# of Labeled Q-D Pairs (training set, 2016)	8,772
# of Labeled Q-D Pairs (testing set, 2016)	5,779
# of Labeled Q-D Pairs (testing set, 2017)	2,500
A Q-D Pair Example	俄罗斯贝加尔湖的面积有多大？ \t 贝加尔湖 中国古代称为北海 位于俄罗斯西伯利亚的南部 \t 0 俄罗斯贝加尔湖的面积有多大？ \t 贝加尔湖是世界上最深 容量最大的淡水湖 \t 0 俄罗斯贝加尔湖的面积有多大？ \t 贝加尔湖贝加尔湖是世界上最深和蓄水量最大的淡水湖 \t 0 俄罗斯贝加尔湖的面积有多大？ \t 它位于布里亚特共和国(Buryatiya) 和伊尔库茨克州(Irkutsk) 境内 \t 0 俄罗斯贝加尔湖的面积有多大？ \t 湖型狭长弯曲 宛如一弯新月 所以又有"月亮湖"之称 \t 0 俄罗斯贝加尔湖的面积有多大？ \t 湖长636公里平均宽48公里 最宽79.4公里 面积3.15万平方公里 \t 1 俄罗斯贝加尔湖的面积有多大？ \t 贝加尔湖湖水澄澈清冽 且稳定透明(透明度达40.8米) ，为世界第二 \t 0

As shown in the example in Table 3, a question (the 1st column), question's corresponding document sentences (the 2nd column), and their answer annotations (the 3rd column) are provided. If a document sentence is the correct answer of the question, its annotation will be 1, otherwise its annotation will be 0. The three columns will be separated by the symbol '\t'.

In DBQA task, any data resource can be used to train necessary models, such as paraphrasing model, sentence matching model, etc., but answer sentences should come from the provided documents only.

3 Evaluation Metrics

The quality of a KBQA system is evaluated by **Averaged F1**, and the quality of a DBQA system is evaluated by **MRR**, **MAP**, and **ACC@1**.

- **Averaged F1**

$$AveragedF1 = \frac{1}{|Q|} \sum_{i=1}^{|Q|} F_i$$

F_i denotes the F1 score for question Q_i computed based on C_i and A_i. F_i is set to 0 if C_i is empty or doesn't overlap with A_i. Otherwise, F_i is computed as follows:

$$F_i = \frac{2 \cdot \frac{\#(C_i,A_i)}{|C_i|} \cdot \frac{\#(C_i,A_i)}{|A_i|}}{\frac{\#(C_i,A_i)}{|C_i|} + \frac{\#(C_i,A_i)}{|A_i|}}$$

where $\#(C_i, A_i)$ denotes the number of answers occur in both C_i and A_i. $|C_i|$ and $|A_i|$ denote the number of answers in C_i and A_i respectively.

- **MRR**

$$MRR = \frac{1}{|Q|} \sum_{i=1}^{|Q|} \frac{1}{rank_i}$$

$|Q|$ denotes the total number of questions in the evaluation set, $rank_i$ denotes the position of the first correct answer in the generated answer set C_i for the ith question Q_i. If C_i doesn't overlap with the golden answers A_i for Q_i, $\frac{1}{rank_i}$ is set to 0.

- **MAP**

$$MAP = \frac{1}{|Q|} \sum_{i=1}^{|Q|} AveP(C_i, A_i)$$

$AveP(C, A) = \frac{\sum_{k=1}^{n}(P(k) \cdot rel(k))}{min(m,n)}$ denotes the average precision. k is the rank in the sequence of retrieved answer sentences. m is the number of correct answer sentences. n is the number of retrieved answer sentences. If $min(m, n)$ is 0, $AveP(C, A)$ is set to 0. $P(k)$ is the precision at cut-off k in the list. $rel(k)$ is an indicator function equaling 1 if the item at rank k is an answer sentence, and 0 otherwise.

- **ACC@N**

$$Accuracy@N = \frac{1}{|Q|} \sum_{i=1}^{|Q|} \delta(C_i, A_i)$$

$\delta(C_i, A_i)$ equals to 1 when there is at least one answer contained by C_i occurs in A_i, and 0 otherwise.

4   Evaluation Results

There are 35 teams submitted their results. Tables 4 and 5 lists the evaluation results of DBQA and KBQA tasks respectively.

Table 4. Evaluation results of the DBQA task.

	MRR	MAP	ACC@1
Team 1	0.720194	0.716594	0.592
Team 2	0.689619	0.68576	0.5556
Team 3	0.685011	0.680963	0.5512
Team 4	0.683674	0.680067	0.5492
Team 5	0.677203	0.673271	0.54
Team 6	0.675772	0.670828	0.5356
Team 7	0.672872	0.668659	0.5372
Team 8	0.664586	0.660256	0.5244
Team 9	0.660674	0.658893	0.5144
Team 10	0.652062	0.649218	0.5056
Team 11	0.583311	0.580741	0.4284
Team 12	0.557158	0.556341	0.3996
Team 13	0.54846	0.545021	0.372
Team 14	0.533575	0.531831	0.3692
Team 15	0.506718	0.503114	0.3404
Team 16	0.494292	0.491736	0.3288
Team 17	0.436557	0.434162	0.2696
Team 18	0.402115	0.40085	0.2172
Team 19	0.384112	0.382343	0.2016
Team 20	0.384112	0.382343	0.2016
Team 21	0.353259	0.352269	0.1744

Table 5. Evaluation results of the KBQA task.

	Average Precision	Average Recall	Average F1
Team 1	0.472284104	0.472284104	0.472284104
Team 2	0.412615314	0.435984799	0.419647927
Team 3	0.401511483	0.418817979	0.406784423
Team 4	0.395205646	0.41410038	0.400818095
Team 5	0.372886909	0.413052025	0.386275281
Team 6	0.351565082	0.478050059	0.371838481
Team 7	0.357257566	0.381994496	0.36381076
Team 8	0.339840781	0.364696632	0.347019363
Team 9	0.339819304	0.36522081	0.346864086
Team 10	0.329966705	0.360896344	0.338715307
Team 11	0.328349034	0.359061722	0.337029202
Team 12	0.313589307	0.313589307	0.313589307
Team 13	0.269689425	0.269689425	0.269689425
Team 14	0.213995544	0.213995544	0.213995544

5   Conclusion

This paper briefly introduces the overview of this year's two open domain Chinese QA shared tasks. In the future, we plan to provide more QA datasets for Chinese QA field. Besides, we plan to extend the QA tasks from Chinese to English as well, and promote new QA tasks, such as Table-based QA.

References

1. Wang, Y., Berant, J., Liang, P.: Building a semantic parser overnight. In: ACL (2015)
2. Pasupat, P., Liang, P.: Compositional semantic parsing on semi-structured tables. In: ACL (2015)
3. Pasupat, P., Liang, P.: Zero-shot entity extraction from web pages. In: ACL (2014)
4. Bao, J., Duan, N., Zhou, M., Zhao, T.: Knowledge-based question answering as machine translation. In: ACL (2014)
5. Yang, M.-C., Duan, N., Zhou, M., Rim, H.-C.: Joint relational embeddings for knowledge-based question answering. In: EMNLP (2014)
6. Berant, J., Chou, A., Frostig, R., Liang, P.: Semantic parsing on freebase from question-answer pairs. In: EMNLP (2013)
7. Kwiatkowski, T., Choi, E., Artzi, Y., Zettlemoyer, L.: Scaling semantic parsers with on-the-fly ontology matching. In: EMNLP (2013)

8. Bordes, A., Usunier, N., Chopra, S., Weston, J.: Large-scale simple question answering with memory network. In: ICLR (2015)
9. Weston, J., Bordes, A., Chopra, S., Mikolov, T.: Towards AI-complete Question Answering: A Set of Prerequisite Toy Tasks. arXiv (2015)
10. Dong, L., Wei, F., Zhou, M., Xu, K.: Question answering over freebase with multi-column convolutional neural networks. In: ACL (2015)
11. Yih, W., Chang, M.-W., He, X., Gao, J.: Semantic parsing via staged query graph generation: question answering with knowledge base. In: ACL (2015)
12. Yao, X.: Lean question answering over freebase from scratch. In: NAACL (2015)
13. Berant, J., Liang, P.: Semantic parsing via paraphrasing. In: ACL (2014)
14. Yao, X., Van Durme, B.: Information extraction over structured data: question answering with freebase. In: ACL (2014)
15. Bordes, A., Weston, J., Chopra, S.: Question answering with subgraph embeddings. In: EMNLP (2014)
16. Bordes, A., Weston, J., Usunier, N.: Open question answering with weakly supervised embedding models. In: Calders, T., Esposito, F., Hüllermeier, E., Meo, R. (eds.) ECML PKDD 2014. LNCS (LNAI), vol. 8724, pp. 165–180. Springer, Heidelberg (2014). https://doi.org/10.1007/978-3-662-44848-9_11
17. Yang, Y., Yih, W., Meek, C.: WIKIQA: a challenge dataset for open-domain question answering. In: EMNLP (2015)
18. Miao, Y., Yu, L., Blunsom, P.: Neural variational inference for text processing. arXiv (2015)
19. Wang, D., Nyberg, E.: A long short term memory model for answer sentence selection in question answering. In: ACL (2015)
20. Yin, W., Schütze, H., Xiang, B., Zhou, B.: ABCNN: attention-based convolutional neural network for modeling sentence pairs. In: ACL (2016)
21. Yu, L., Hermann, K.M., Blunsom, P., Pullman, S.: Deep learning for answer sentence selection. In: NIPS Workshop (2014)
22. Yan, Z., Duan, N., Bao, J., Chen, P., Zhou, M., Li, Z., Zhou, J.: DocChat: an information retrieval approach for chatbot engines using unstructured documents. In: ACL (2016)

Author Index

Printed in the United States
By Bookmasters